Business Law and the Environment -- BUS 5

Custom Edition for Bristol Community College

David P. Twomey | Marianne Moody Jennings

CENGAGE
Learning

Australia • Brazil • Japan • Korea • Mexico • Singapore • Spain • United Kingdom • United States

CENGAGE
Learning

Business Law and the Legal Environment -- BUS 51: Custom Edition for Bristol Community College

Executive Editors:
 Maureen Staudt
 Michael Stranz

Senior Project Development Manager:
 Linda deStefano

Marketing Specialist:
 Courtney Sheldon

Senior Production/Manufacturing Manager:
 Donna M. Brown

PreMedia Manager:
 Joel Brennecke

Sr. Rights Acquisition Account Manager:
 Todd Osborne

Cover Image:
 Getty Images*

Business Law and the Legal Environment -- BUS 51, Custom Edition for Bristol Community College
Twomey | Jennings

> For product information and technology assistance, contact us at
> **Cengage Learning Customer & Sales Support, 1-800-354-9706**
>
> For permission to use material from this text or product,
> submit all requests online at **cengage.com/permissions**
> Further permissions questions can be emailed to
> **permissionrequest@cengage.com**

This book contains select works from existing Cengage Learning resources and was produced by Cengage Learning Custom Solutions for collegiate use. As such, those adopting and/or contributing to this work are responsible for editorial content accuracy, continuity and completeness.

Compilation © 2010 Cengage Learning

ISBN-13: 978-1-111-63100-0

ISBN-10: 1-111-63100-X

Cengage Learning
5191 Natorp Boulevard
Mason, Ohio 45040
USA

Cengage Learning is a leading provider of customized learning solutions with office locations around the globe, including Singapore, the United Kingdom, Australia, Mexico, Brazil, and Japan. Locate your local office at:
international.cengage.com/region.

Cengage Learning products are represented in Canada by Nelson Education, Ltd.

For your lifelong learning solutions, visit **www.cengage.com/custom.**
Visit our corporate website at **www.cengage.com.**

Printed in the United States of America

Brief Table of Contents |

Chapter 1

THE NATURE AND SOURCES OF LAW

W hy have law? If you have ever been stuck in a traffic jam or jostled in a crowd leaving a stadium, you have observed the need for order to keep those involved moving in an efficient and safe manner. The interruptions and damages from Internet viruses demonstrate the need for rules and order in this era of new technology. When our interactions are not orderly, whether at our concerts or through our e-mail, all of us and our rights are affected. The order or pattern of rules that society uses to govern the conduct of individuals and their relationships is called **law**. Law keeps society running smoothly and efficiently.

law–the order or pattern of rules that society establishes to govern the conduct of individuals and the relationships among them.

A. Nature of Law and Legal Rights

Law consists of the body of principles that govern conduct and that can be enforced in courts or by administrative agencies. The law could also be described as a collection or bundle of rights.

1. Legal Rights

right–legal capacity to require another person to perform or refrain from an action.

duty–an obligation of law imposed on a person to perform or refrain from performing a certain act.

A **right** is a legal capacity to require another person to perform or refrain from performing an act. Our rights flow from the U.S. Constitution, state constitutions, federal and state statutes, and ordinances at the local levels, including cities, counties, and boroughs. Within these sources of rights are also duties. A **duty** is an obligation of law imposed on a person to perform or refrain from performing a certain act.

Duties and rights coexist. No right exists in one person without a corresponding duty resting on some other person or persons. For example, if the terms of a lease provide that the premises will remain in a condition of good repair so that the tenant can live there comfortably, the landlord has a corresponding duty to provide a dwelling that has hot and cold running water.

2. Individual Rights

The U.S. Constitution gives individuals certain rights. Those rights include the right to freedom of speech, the right to due process or the right to have a hearing before any freedom is taken away, and the right to vote. There are also duties that accompany individual rights, such as the duty to speak in a way that does not cause harm to others. For example, individuals are free to express their opinions about the government or its officials, but they would not be permitted to yell "Fire!" in a crowded theater and cause unnecessary harm to others. The rights given in the U.S. Constitution are rights that cannot be taken away or violated by any statutes, ordinances, or court decisions. These rights provide a framework for the structure of government and other laws.

3. The Right of Privacy

One very important individual legal right is the right of privacy, which has two components. The first is the right to be secure against unreasonable searches and seizures by the government. The Fourth Amendment of the U.S. Constitution

right of privacy—the right to be free from unreasonable intrusion by others.

guarantees this portion of the **right of privacy**. A police officer, for example, may not search your home unless the officer has a reasonable suspicion (which is generally established through a warrant) that your home contains evidence of a crime, such as illegal drugs. If your home or business is searched unlawfully, any items obtained during that unlawful search could be excluded as evidence in a criminal trial because of the Fourth Amendment's exclusionary rule. **For Example,** in the murder trial of O.J. Simpson, Judge Lance Ito excluded some of the evidence the police had obtained from inside Mr. Simpson's Ford Bronco, which was parked on the street outside his home. Judge Ito ruled that the officers should have first obtained a warrant for the locked vehicle, which was not going to be taken anywhere because Mr. Simpson was out of town at that time.

CASE SUMMARY

When Warrants Are Involved, No Brief Photographs

FACTS: In the early morning hours of April 16, 1992, a special team of Deputy U.S. Marshals and police officers executed warrants that had been issued against Dominic Wilson, who was wanted for robbery, theft, and assault and who had a "use caution" warning posted on law enforcement files and records. The team was accompanied by a reporter and a photographer from the *Washington Post*, who had been invited by the marshals to accompany them as part of a Marshals Service ride-along policy.

The officers, with media representatives in tow, entered the dwelling noted in the warrant at 6:45 A.M. The home they entered and that was on the arrest warrant actually belonged to Dominic's parents, Charles and Geraldine Wilson. Charles and Geraldine were still in bed. When they heard the officers enter the home, Charles Wilson, dressed only in a pair of briefs, ran into the living room to investigate. He angrily cursed the officers. Geraldine Wilson then entered the living room to investigate, wearing only a nightgown. She observed her husband being restrained by the armed officers. Dominic Wilson was not in the house, and the officers left. However, the *Washington Post* photographer had already taken numerous pictures of the confrontation between the police and Charles Wilson. The *Washington Post* never published its photographs of the incident.

The Wilsons filed suit against the officers for invasion of their privacy and violation of their Fourth Amendment rights. The district court found that the officers could be held liable. The Court of Appeals reversed and found that the officers had immunity. The U.S. Supreme Court granted *certiorari* because of several conflicting circuit decisions on the issue of cameras and reporters being present during arrests and warrant executions.

DECISION: The Court held that although there were reasons for having the reporters and cameras present, such as public relations, safety for officers, and assistance, those reasons were not sufficient enough to disregard the Fourth Amendment rights of the homeowners. Citing "a man's home is his castle," the Court noted the longstanding history of protecting individuals in their homes. The Court held that having reporters and photographers along in the execution of a warrant is a violation of the Fourth Amendment rights of the parties being searched. Officers can be subject to some liability for their failure to honor privacy protections. [**Wilson v Layne, 526 US 603 (1999)**][1]

---

[1] Police officers who record the arrest of a DUI suspect have not violated the suspect's privacy, State v Morris, 214 P 3d 883 (UT App 2009).

A second aspect of the right of privacy protects individuals against intrusions by others. Your private life is not subject to public scrutiny when you are a private citizen. This right is provided in many state constitutions and exists through interpretation at the federal level in the landmark case of *Roe v Wade*,[2] in which the U.S. Supreme Court established a right of privacy that gives women the right to choose whether to have an abortion.

These two components of the right to privacy have many interpretations. These interpretations are often found in statutes that afford privacy rights with respect to certain types of conduct. **For Example,** a federal statute provides a right of privacy to bank customers that prevents their banks from giving out information about their accounts except to law enforcement agencies conducting investigations. Some laws protect the rights of students. **For Example,** the Family Educational Rights and Privacy Act of 1974 (FERPA, also known as the *Buckley Amendment*) prevents colleges and universities from disclosing students' grades to third parties without the students' permission. From your credit information to your Social Security number, you have great privacy protections.

4. Privacy and Technology

Technology creates new situations that may require the application of new rules of law. Technology has changed the way we interact with each other, and new rules of law have developed to protect our rights. Today, business is conducted by computers, wire transfers of funds, e-mail, electronic data interchange (EDI) order

---

ethics&the law

Googling Job Applicants

A recent survey shows a new component in the background searches performed by potential employers of job applicants:

- 61 percent of professional service firms, including accounting, consulting, engineering, and law firms, do Google searches on their job candidates.

- Fifty percent of professional services hired by employers to do background checks use Google.

One employer commented that a Google search is so simple that it would be irresponsible not to conduct such a search. Experts tell college students to remember that what may seem to be something noncontroversial in your youth can later come back to haunt you when you begin your professional career. Their advice is to watch what you put in MySpace, Facebook, and all other Internet sites. Discuss privacy rights and whether there is any legal issue when information is posted voluntarily on the Internet. Is there an ethical issue with these types of searches?

Source: Sandhya Bathija , "Have a Profile on MySpace? Better Keep It Clean," *National Law Journal*, June 4, 2007, 10.

---

[2] 410 US 113 (1973).

placements, and the Internet. We still expect that our communication is private. However, technology also affords others the ability to eavesdrop on conversations and intercept electronic messages. The law has stepped in to reestablish that the right of privacy still exists even in these technologically nonprivate circumstances. Some laws now make it a crime and a breach of privacy to engage in such interceptions of communications.[3] (See Chapter 11)

e-commerce&cyberlaw

Employers, E-mail, and Privacy

Scott Kennedy, a computer system administrator for Qualcomm Corporation in San Diego, California, discovered that somebody had obtained unauthorized access (or "hacked into," in popular parlance) the company's computer network. Kennedy contacted the Federal Bureau of Investigation (FBI). Working together, Kennedy and the FBI were able to trace the intrusion to a computer on the University of Wisconsin at Madison network. They contacted Jeffrey Savoy, the University of Wisconsin computer network investigator, who found evidence that someone using a computer on the university network was in fact hacking into the Qualcomm system and that the user had gained unauthorized access to the university's system as well. Savoy traced the source of intrusion to a computer located in university housing, the room of Jerome Heckenkamp, a computer science graduate student at the university. Savoy knew that Heckenkamp had been terminated from his job at the university computer help desk two years earlier for similar unauthorized activity.

While Heckenkamp was online and logged into the university's system, Savoy, along with detectives, went to Heckenkamp's room. The door was ajar, and nobody was in the room. Savoy entered the room and disconnected the network cord that attached the computer to the network. In order to be sure that the computer he had disconnected from the network was the computer that had gained unauthorized access to the university server, Savoy wanted to run some commands on the computer. Detectives located Heckenkamp, explained the situation, and asked for Heckenkamp's password, which Heckenkamp voluntarily provided. Savoy then ran tests on the computer and copied the hard drive without a warrant. When Heckenkamp was charged with several federal computer crimes, he challenged the university's access to his account and Savoy's steps that night, including the copy of the hard drive, as a breach of his privacy. Was Heckenkamp correct? Was his privacy breached?

[U.S. v Heckenkamp, 482 F3d 1132 (CA 9 2007).]

B. Sources of Law

constitution—a body of principles that establishes the structure of a government and the relationship of the government to the people who are governed.

Several layers of law are enacted at different levels of government to provide the framework for business and personal rights and duties. At the base of this framework of laws is constitutional law. Constitutional law is the branch of law that is based on the constitution for a particular level of government. A **constitution** is a

---

[3] *State v Christensen*, 79 P3d 12 (CA Wash 2003).

body of principles that establishes the structure of a government and the relationship of that government to the people who are governed. A constitution is generally a combination of the written document and the practices and customs that develop with the passage of time and the emergence of new problems. In each state, two constitutions are in force: the state constitution and the federal Constitution.

statutory law–legislative acts declaring, commanding, or prohibiting something.

Statutory law includes legislative acts. Both Congress and the state legislatures enact statutory law. Examples of congressional legislative enactments include the Securities Act of 1933 (Chapter 46), the Sherman Antitrust Act (Chapter 5), the bankruptcy laws (Chapter 35), and consumer credit protection provisions (Chapter 33). At the state level, statutes govern the creation of corporations, probate of wills, and the transfer of title to property. In addition to the state legislatures and the U.S. Congress, all cities, counties, and other governmental subdivisions have some power to adopt ordinances within their sphere of operation. Examples of the types of laws found at this level of government include traffic laws, zoning laws, and pet and bicycle licensing laws.

administrative regulations–rules made by state and federal administrative agencies.

Administrative regulations are rules promulgated by state and federal administrative agencies, such as the Securities and Exchange Commission and the National Labor Relations Board. These regulations generally have the force of statutes.

private law–the rules and regulations parties agree to as part of their contractual relationships.

Even individuals and businesses create their own laws, or **private law**. Private law consists of the rules and regulations parties agree to as part of their contractual relationships. **For Example,** landlords develop rules for tenants on everything from parking to laundry room use. Employers develop rules for employees on everything from proper computer use to posting pictures and information on bulletin boards located within the company walls. Homeowner associations have rules on everything from your landscaping to the color of your house paint.

case law–law that includes principles that are expressed for the first time in court decisions.

Law also includes principles that are expressed for the first time in court decisions. This form of law is called **case law**. When a court decides a new question or problem, its decision becomes a **precedent**, which stands as the law in future cases that involve that particular problem.

precedent–a decision of a court that stands as the law for a particular problem in the future.

Using precedent and following decisions in similar cases is the doctrine of *stare decisis*. However, the rule of *stare decisis* is not cast in stone. Judges have some flexibility. When a court finds an earlier decision to be incorrect, it overrules that decision. **For Example,** in 1954, the U.S. Supreme Court departed from the general rule of *stare decisis* in *Brown v Board of Education*.[4] In that case, the Court decided that its 1896 decision *Plessy v Ferguson*,[5] that held separate facilities for blacks were equal to facilities for whites, was incorrect.

stare decisis–"let the decision stand"; the principle that the decision of a court should serve as a guide or precedent and control the decision of a similar case in the future.

common law–the body of unwritten principles originally based upon the usages and customs of the community that were recognized and enforced by the courts.

Court decisions do not always deal with new problems or make new rules. In many cases, courts apply rules as they have been for many years, even centuries. These time-honored rules of the community are called the **common law**. Statutes sometimes repeal or redeclare the common law rules. Many statutes depend on the common law for definitions of the terms in the statutes.

Law also includes treaties made by the United States and proclamations and executive orders of the president of the United States or of other public officials.

[4] 349 US 294 (1954).
[5] 163 US 537 (1895).

C. Uniform State Laws

To facilitate the national nature of business and transactions, the National Conference of Commissioners on Uniform State Laws (NCCUSL), composed of representatives from every state, has drafted statutes on various subjects for adoption by the states. The best example of such laws is the Uniform Commercial Code (UCC).[6] (See Chapters 23–31, Chapter 34.) The UCC regulates the sale and leasing of goods; commercial paper, such as checks; funds transfers; secured transactions in personal property; banking; and letters of credit. Having the same principles of law on contracts for the sale of goods and other commercial transactions in most of the 50 states makes doing business easier and less expensive. Other examples of uniform laws across the states include the Model Business Corporations Act (Chapter 44), the Uniform Partnership Act (Chapter 42), and the Uniform Residential Landlord Tenant Act (Chapter 51). The Uniform Computer Information Transactions Act (UCITA) as well as the Uniform Electronic Transactions Act (UETA) are new technology statutes that have been adopted or are under consideration for passage by the states. These two uniform laws and versions of them take contract law from the traditional paper era to the paperless computer age.

D. Classifications of Law

substantive law–the law that defines rights and liabilities.

procedural law–the law that must be followed in enforcing rights and liabilities.

equity–the body of principles that originally developed because of the inadequacy of the rules then applied by the common law courts of England.

Law is classified in many ways. **Substantive law** creates, defines, and regulates rights and liabilities. **Procedural law** specifies the steps that must be followed in enforcing those rights and liabilities. For example, the laws that grant employees protection against discrimination are substantive laws. The regulations of the Equal Employment Opportunity Commission (EEOC) for bringing suits against or investigations of employers for discrimination charges are procedural laws. The laws that prohibit computer theft are substantive laws. The prosecution of someone for computer theft follows procedural law. Law may also be classified in terms of its origin from Roman (or civil) law, from English common law based on customs and usages of the community,[7] or from the law merchant. Law may be classified according to subject matter, such as the law of contracts, the law of real estate, or the law of wills.

Law is at times classified in terms of principles of law and principles of equity. The early English courts were very limited as to the kinds of cases they could handle. Persons who could not obtain relief in those courts would petition the king to grant them special relief according to principles of **equity** and justice. In the course of time, these special cases developed certain rules that are called *principles of equity*. In general,

---

[6] The UCC has been adopted in every state, except that Louisiana has not adopted Article 2, Sales. Guam, the Virgin Islands, and the District of Columbia have also adopted the UCC. The NCCUSL has adopted amendments to Article 8, Investment Securities (1977 and 1994), and Article 9, Secured Transactions (1999, and as amended 2001). There have been new articles of the UCC: Article 2A, Leases, and Article 4A, Funds Transfers. The United Nations Convention on Contracts for the International Sale of Goods (CISG) has been adopted as the means for achieving uniformity in sale-of-goods contracts on an international level. Provisions of CISG were strongly influenced by Article 2 of the UCC.

[7] For example, in *Washington State Grange v Washington Republican Party,* 552 US 442 (2008), Justice Antonin Scalia wrote, "Washington's law is like a law that encourages Oscar the Grouch (Sesame Street's famed bad-taste resident of a garbage can) to state a "preference" for Campbell's at every point of sale, while barring the soup company from disavowing his endorsement, or indeed using its name at all, in those same crucial locations." In *BMW of North America, Inc. v Gore,* 517 US 559 (1996), Justice Scalia, in his dissenting opinion, wrote, "One expects the court to conclude, 'To thine own self be true.'"

sports&entertainment law

On March 17, 2005, former and current major league baseball (MLB) players, Commissioner Bud Selig, and the parents of young baseball players who had taken their own lives after taking steroids testified before the U.S. House of Representatives Government Reform Committee. The House held the hearings to determine whether government regulation of baseball is necessary.

Committee Chair Tom Davis made an opening statement with the following excerpts:

> Fourteen years ago, anabolic steroids were added to the Controlled Substance Act as a Schedule III drug, making it illegal to possess or sell them without a valid prescription. Today, however, evidence strongly suggests that steroid use among teenagers—especially aspiring athletes—is a large and growing problem.
>
> Today we take the committee's first steps toward understanding how we got here, and how we begin turning those numbers around. Down the road, we need to look at whether and how Congress should exercise its legislative powers to further restrict the use and distribution of these substances.
>
> Our specific purpose today is to consider MLB's recently negotiated drug policy; how

the testing policy will be implemented; how it will effectively address the use of prohibited drugs by players; and, most importantly, the larger societal and public health ramifications of steroid use.

Mark McGwire, now a retired MLB player and a record holder, stated during the hearings:

> Asking me, or any other player, to answer questions about who took steroids in front of television cameras, will not solve this problem. If a player answers 'no,' he simply will not be believed. If he answers 'yes,' he risks public scorn and endless government investigations. My lawyers have advised me that I cannot answer these questions without jeopardizing my friends, my family, or myself. I intend to follow their advice.[*]

Give a list of all the laws, rights, and duties you can find in this information.

[*] **http://reform.house.gov/GovReform/Hearings/EventSingle.aspx? EventID=1637**. Click on Mark McGwire

the rules of equity apply when the remedies provided at law cannot provide adequate relief in the form of monetary damages. At one time, the United States had separate law courts and equity courts. Except in a few states, these courts have been combined so that one court applies principles of both law and equity. A party may ask for both legal and equitable remedies in a single court.[8] **For Example,** suppose a homeowner contracts to sell his home to a buyer. If the homeowner then refuses to go through with the contract, the buyer has the legal remedy of recovering damages. The rules of equity go further, when appropriate, and could require the owner to actually transfer the ownership of the house to the buyer. Such remedies require a court order for specific conduct, known as *specific performance.* Equitable remedies may also be available in certain contract breaches (see Chapter 2, 12 and 20).

[8] For example, Jennifer Lopez and Marc Anthony filed suit against the manufacturer of a British company that produces baby carriages for using their images on its Web site and in ads without permission; they asked for $5 million in damages as well as an injunction to stop use of their photos and likenesses in the company's ads. *Lopez v Silver Cross,* 2009 WL 481386 (CD Cal).

lawflix

And Justice for All (1979) (R)

An excellent film that gives an overview of the judicial system in Maryland. Rights, precedent, and the role of lawyers are all topics for satire and analysis in the movie.

Check out LawFlix at **www.cengage.com/blaw/dvl** to access movie clips that illustrate business law concepts.

MAKE THE CONNECTION

SUMMARY

Law provides rights and imposes duties. One such right is the right of privacy, which affords protection against unreasonable searches of our property and intrusion into or disclosure of our private affairs.

Law consists of the pattern of rules established by society to govern conduct and relationships. These rules can be expressed as constitutional provisions, statutes, administrative regulations, and case decisions. Law can be classified as substantive or procedural, and it can be described in terms of its historical origins, by the subject to which it relates, or in terms of law or equity.

The sources of law include constitutions, federal and state statutes, administrative regulations, ordinances, and uniform laws generally codified by the states in their statutes. The courts are also a source of law through their adherence to case precedent under the doctrine of *stare decisis* and through their development of time-honored principles called the common law.

LEARNING OUTCOMES

After studying this chapter, you should be able to clearly explain:

A. NATURE OF LAW AND LEGAL RIGHTS

LO.1 Discuss the nature of law and legal rights

> See *Wilson v Layne*, p. 5.
> See E-Commerce and Cyberlaw, p. 7.

B. SOURCES OF LAW

LO.2 List the sources of law

> See the **For Example** discussion of landlords developing rules for tenants on everything from parking to laundry room use on p. 8.

See the Sports & Entertainment Law discussion of steroids in baseball on p. 10.

C. UNIFORM STATE LAWS

LO.3 Explain uniform state laws

See the list and explanation of uniform laws on p. 9.

D. CLASSIFICATIONS OF LAW

LO.4 Describe the classifications of law

See the discussion of law, equity, and substantive law on p. 9.

See footnote 8 with the discussion of the Jennifer Lopez/Marc Anthony suit on p. 10.

KEY TERMS

administrative regulations	equity	right
case law	law	*stare decisis*
common law	precedent	statutory law
constitution	private law	substantive law
duty	procedural law	
	right of privacy	

QUESTIONS AND CASE PROBLEMS

1. Glenda Brunette, a 60-year old widow, operates a pedigreed cat breeding business on her 11-acre ranch and avocado farm in Ojai, California. You can enter Brunette's ranch only by passing through a locked gate that has a "No Trespass" sign. Concerned citizens reported to the Humane Society that Brunette was "selling cats that looked sick, with eyes matted shut and covered in flies and feces." The Humane Society, a quasi-public body in California, can investigate reports of animal cruelty, impound animals, place liens on property, and bring criminal charges against citizens. The Humane Society obtained a warrant to search Brunette's property and invited Tim Dewar of the *Ojai Valley News* to come along and photograph the search of the ranch. Dewar came in his own car and arrived after the Humane Society had severed the lock on the gate. When he arrived, Dewar went in and began photographing the search, the animals, and Brunette. Brunette filed suit against Dewar and the *Ojai Valley News* for invasion of her privacy. Can she recover damages? Be sure to refer to the *Wilson v Layne* case (on p. 5) as you consider your answer. *Brunette v Humane Society of Ventura County,* 294 F3d 1205 (CA 9).

2. The Family Educational Rights and Privacy Act (FERPA) protects students' rights to keep their academic records private. What duties are imposed and upon whom because of this protection of rights? Discuss the relationship between rights and duties.

3. List the sources of law.

4. What is the difference between common law and statutory law?

5. Classify the following laws as substantive or procedural:

   a. A law that requires public schools to hold a hearing before a student is expelled

   b. A law that establishes a maximum interest rate for credit transactions of 24 percent

   c. A law that provides employee leave for the birth or adoption of a child for up to 12 weeks

   d. A law that requires the county assessor to send four notices of taxes due and owing before a lien can be filed (attached) to the property

6. What do uniform laws accomplish? Why do states adopt them? Give an example of a uniform law.

7. Cindy Nathan is a student at West University. While she was at her 9:00 A.M. anthropology class, campus security entered her dorm room and searched all areas, including her closet and drawers. When Cindy returned to her room and discovered what had happened, she complained to the dorm's senior resident. The senior resident said that this was the university's property and that Cindy had no right of privacy. Do you agree with the senior resident's statement? Is there a right of privacy in a dorm room?

8. Professor Lucas Phelps sent the following e-mail to Professor Marlin Jones: "I recently read the opinion piece you wrote for the *Sacramento Bee* on affirmative action. Your opinion is incorrect, your reasoning and analysis are poor, and I am embarrassed that you are a member of the faculty here at Cal State Yolinda." Professor Jones forwarded the note from Professor Phelps to the provost of the university and asked that Professor Phelps be disciplined for using the university e-mail system for harassment purposes. Professor Phelps objected when the provost contacted him: "He had no right to forward that e-mail to you. That was private correspondence. And you have no right of access to my e-mail. I have privacy rights." Do you agree with Professor Phelps? Was there a breach of privacy?

9. Under what circumstances would a court disregard precedent?

10. What is the difference between a statute and an administrative regulation?

11. What is the difference between a remedy in equity and other forms of judicial remedies?

12. Give examples of areas covered by federal laws. Give examples of areas covered by city ordinances. What are the limitations on these two sources of laws? What could the laws at these two levels not do?

13. What is the principle of *stare decisis?*

14. List some purposes of law that you were able to spot in reading this chapter.

15. During the 2001 baseball season, San Francisco Giants player Barry Bonds hit 73 home runs, a new record that broke the one set by Mark McGwire in 2000 (72 home runs). FN Be sure to read the text box on p.9 for more background on McGwire's hitting prowess. When Mr. Bonds hit his record-breaking home run, the ball went into the so-called cheap seats. Alex Popov was sitting in those seats and had brought along his baseball glove for purposes of catching any hits that might come into the stands. Everyone sitting in the area agreed that Mr. Popov's glove touched Bonds's home-run ball. Videotape also shows Mr. Popov's glove on the ball. However, the ball dropped and, following a melee among the cheap-seat fans, Patrick Hayashi ended up with Bonds's home-run ball. Mr. Popov filed suit for the ball, claiming it as his property. Such baseballs can be very valuable. The baseball from Mr. McGwire's record-breaking home run in 2000 sold for $3 million. List those areas of law that will apply as the case is tried and the owner of the baseball is determined.

Chapter 2

THE COURT SYSTEM AND DISPUTE RESOLUTION

Despite carefully negotiated and well-written contracts and high safety standards in the workplace or in product design and production, businesses can still encounter disputes that may result in a lawsuit. **For Example,** you could hire the brightest and most expensive lawyer in town to prepare a contract with another party and believe the final agreement is "bulletproof." However, even a bulletproof contract does not guarantee performance by the other party, and a lawsuit for damages may be necessary.

Business disputes can be resolved in court or through alternative means. This chapter covers the structure of the court system and the litigation process as well as alternative means used outside the court system to resolve disputes.

A. THE COURT SYSTEM

court–a tribunal established by government to hear and decide matters properly brought to it.

A **court** is a tribunal established by government to hear and decide matters brought before it, provide remedies when a wrong has been committed, and prevent possible wrongs from happening. A court could award money damages to a business party for a breach of contract, but it could also issue an injunction to halt patent infringement. **For Example,** in 2006, a court's threat to issue an injunction to shut down operation of the BlackBerry wireless e-mail device system resulted in a settlement of the patent infringement case between Research in Motion, Ltd. (RIM), the BlackBerry service provider, and NTP, Inc., the company that had won its patent infringement case against RIM for the technology used in the BlackBerry device.[1]

1. The Types of Courts

jurisdiction–the power of a court to hear and determine a given class of cases; the power to act over a particular defendant.

subject matter jurisdiction–judicial authority to hear a particular type of case.

original jurisdiction– the authority to hear a controversy when it is first brought to court.

general jurisdiction–the power to hear and decide most controversies involving legal rights and duties.

Every type of court is given the authority to decide certain types or classes of cases. The power to hear cases is called **jurisdiction**. One form of jurisdiction, **subject matter jurisdiction**, covers the type of proceedings that the court holds. A court with **original jurisdiction** is the trial court or the court with the authority to conduct the first proceedings in the case. **For Example,** a court of original jurisdiction would be one where the witnesses actually testify, the documents are admitted into evidence, and the jury, in the case of a jury trial, is present to hear all the evidence and to make a decision.

Other types of subject matter jurisdiction are applicable to courts. A court with **general jurisdiction** has broad authority over different types of cases. The authority of a court with general jurisdiction can extend to both general civil and criminal cases. When a general jurisdiction trial court hears criminal cases, it conducts the trials of those charged with crimes. When a general trial court exercises its civil jurisdiction, it uses its authority to hear civil disputes, such as breach of contract cases and disputes about leases between landlords and tenants.

---

[1] RIM eventually settled the suit with NTP by agreeing to pay $612.5 million.

limited (special) jurisdiction–the authority to hear only particular kinds of cases.

A court with **limited** or **special jurisdiction** has the authority to hear only particular kinds of cases. **For Example,** many states have courts that can hear only disputes in which the damages are $10,000 or less. Many types of courts have special jurisdiction, including juvenile courts, probate courts, and domestic relations courts. States vary in the names they give these courts, but all are courts of special or limited jurisdiction because they have very narrow authority for their subject matter jurisdiction. In the federal system, courts with limited or special jurisdiction include bankruptcy courts and the U.S. Tax Court.

appellate jurisdiction–the power of a court to hear and decide a given class of cases on appeal from another court or administrative agency.

A court with **appellate jurisdiction** reviews the work of a lower court. **For Example,** a trial court may issue a judgment that a defendant in a breach of contract suit should pay $500,000 in damages. That defendant could appeal the decision to an appellate court and seek review of the decision itself or even the amount of the damages.[2] An **appeal** is a review of the trial and decision of the lower court. An appellate court does not hear witnesses or take testimony. An appellate court, usually a panel of three judges, simply reviews the transcript and evidence from the lower court and determines whether there has been **reversible error**. A reversible error is a mistake in applying the law or a mistake in admitting evidence that affected the outcome of the case. An appellate court can **affirm** or **reverse** a lower court decision or **remand** that decision for another trial or additional hearings.

appeal–taking a case to a reviewing court to determine whether the judgment of the lower court or administrative agency was correct. (Parties– appellant, appellee)

reversible error–an error or defect in court proceedings of so serious a nature that on appeal the appellate court will set aside the proceedings of the lower court.

affirm–action taken by an appellate court that approves the decision of the court below.

reverse–the term used when the appellate court sets aside the verdict or judgment of a lower court.

remand–term used when an appellate court sends a case back to trial court for additional hearings or a new trial.

C A S E   S U M M A R Y

Law and Order on TV and in the Court

FACTS: Andrea Yates was charged with capital murder in the drowning deaths of her five young children. Mrs. Yates had been in and out of treatment facilities, had been taking antidepressants, and was under the care of several experts for her depression. She was also experiencing postpartum depression when she drowned each of her five children in the bathtub at their family home. She then called her husband to ask him to come home and also called 9-1-1.

She entered a "not guilty by reason of insanity" plea, and 10 psychiatrists and two psychologists testified at the trial about Mrs. Yates's mental condition before, during, and after the deaths of the children.

Dr. Parke Dietz, the psychiatrist for the prosecution, testified that he believed Mrs. Yates knew right from wrong and that she was not insane at the time of the drownings. Dr. Dietz had also served as a consultant for the television series *Law and Order* and testified as follows about one of the shows in the series:

As a matter of fact, there was a show of a woman with postpartum depression who drowned her children in the bathtub and was found insane and it was aired shortly before the crime occurred.

The prosecution used this information about the television show to cross-examine witnesses for Mrs. Yates and also raised its airing in its closing argument to the jury.

---

[2] A case that is sent back for a redetermination of damages is remanded for what is known as *remittur*.

CASE SUMMARY

Continued

The jury found Mrs. Yates guilty. The defense lawyers later discovered that Dr. Dietz was mistaken and that there had been no such *Law and Order* show on postpartum depression. They appealed on the grounds that the evidence was material, prejudiced the jury, and required a new trial.

DECISION: The court held that because Dr. Dietz had testified about the show, that his testimony and the subject matter of the show were a part of the prosecution's examination of defense witnesses, that the prosecution raised the airing of the show in closing arguments, and that the defense had to respond by talking about it meant that the testimony was material. Inasmuch as it was false, there was a reversible error and a retrial was required without the untrue and highly prejudicial evidence. **[Yates v State, 171 SW 3d 215 (Tex App 2005)]**[3]

2. The Federal Court System

The federal court system consists of three levels of courts. Figure 2.1 illustrates federal court structure.

federal district court—a general trial court of the federal system.

(A) FEDERAL DISTRICT COURTS. The **federal district courts** are the general trial courts of the federal system. They are courts of original jurisdiction that hear both civil and criminal matters. Criminal cases in federal district courts are those in which the defendant is charged with a violation of federal law (the U.S. Code). In addition to the criminal cases, the types of civil cases that can be brought in federal district courts include (1) civil suits in which the United States is a party, (2) cases between citizens of different states that involve damages of $75,000 or more, and (3) cases that arise under the U.S. Constitution or federal laws and treaties.

Federal district courts are organized within each of the states. There are 94 federal districts (each state has at least one federal district and there are 89 federal districts in the United States with the remaining courts found in Puerto Rico, Guam, etc.). Judges and courtrooms are assigned according to the caseload in that geographic area of the state.[4] Some states, such as New York and California, have several federal districts because of the population base and the resulting caseload. Figure 2.2 shows the geographic structure of the federal court system, including the appellate circuits.

The federal system has additional trial courts with limited jurisdiction, differing from the general jurisdiction of the federal district courts. These courts include, for example, the federal bankruptcy courts, Indian tribal courts, Tax Court, Court of Federal Claims, Court of Veterans Appeals, and the Court of International Trade.

(B) U.S. COURTS OF APPEALS. The final decision in a federal district court can be appealed to a court with appellate jurisdiction. In the federal court system, the federal districts are grouped together geographically into 12 judicial circuits, including one for the District of Columbia. Additionally, a thirteenth federal circuit, called the *Federal Circuit,* hears certain types of appeals from all of the circuits,

---

[3] Mrs. Yates was found to be criminally insane in her 2006 retrial and is now institutionalized.
[4] For complete information about the courts and the number of judgeships, go to 28 USC §§ 81-144 and 28 USC §133.

FIGURE 2-1 | *The Federal Court System*

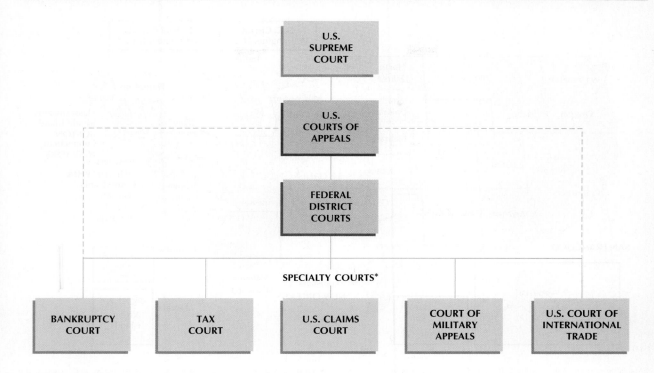

*Appeals often go directly to U.S. Courts of Appeals.

en banc–the term used when the full panel of judges on the appellate court hears a case.

including specialty cases such as patent appeals. Each circuit has an appellate court called the U.S. Court of Appeals, and the judges for these courts review the decisions of the federal district courts. Generally, a panel of three judges reviews the cases. However, some decisions, called ***en banc*** decisions, are made by the circuit's full panel of judges. **For Example,** in 2003, the Ninth Circuit heard an appeal on a father's right to challenge the requirement that his daughter recite the Pledge of Allegiance in the public school she attended. The contentious case had so many issues that the Ninth Circuit issued three opinions and the third opinion was issued after the case was heard *en banc.*[5]

(c) **U.S. Supreme Court.** The final court in the federal system is the U.S. Supreme Court. The U.S. Supreme Court has appellate jurisdiction over cases that are appealed from the federal courts of appeals as well as from state supreme courts

[5] *Newdow v U.S. Congress,* 292 F3d 597, 602 (CA 9 2002) (*Newdow I*); *Newdow v U.S. Congress,* 313 F3d 500, 502 (CA 9 2002) (*Newdow II*); and *Newdow v U.S. Congress,* 328 F3d 466, 468 (CA 9 2003) (*Newdow III*). The U.S. Supreme Court eventually heard the case. *Elkgrove Unified School District v Newdow,* 542 US 1 (2004). Another *en banc* hearing occurred at the Ninth Circuit over the issues in the California gubernatorial recall election. The three-judge panel held that the voting methods in California violated the rights of voters and therefore placed a stay on the election. However, the Ninth Circuit then heard the case *en banc* and reversed the decision of the original three-judge panel. The recall election then proceeded.

FIGURE 2-2 | *The Thirteen Federal Judicial Circuits*

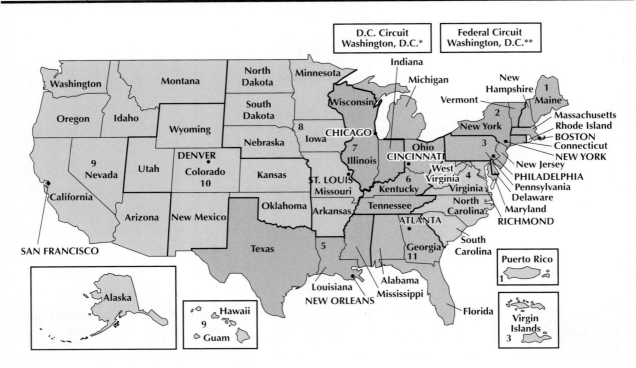

*A sizable portion of the caseload of the D.C. Circuit comes from the federal administrative agencies and offices located in Washington, D.C., such as the Securities and Exchange Commission, the National Labor Relations Board, the Federal Trade Commission, the Secretary of the Treasury, and the Labor Department, as well as appeals from the U.S. District Court of the District of Columbia.

**Rather than being defined by geography like the regional courts of appeals, the Federal Circuit is defined by subject matter, having jurisdiction over such matters as patent infringement cases, appeals from the Court of Federal Claims and the Court of International Trade, and appeals from administrative rulings regarding subject matter such as unfair import practices and tariff schedule disputes.

writ of *certiorari*–order by the U.S. Supreme Court granting a right of review by the court of a lower court decision.

when a constitutional issue is involved in the case or a state court has reversed a federal court ruling. The U.S. Supreme Court does not hear all cases from the federal courts of appeals but has a process called granting a **writ of *certiorari*,** which is a preliminary review of those cases appealed to decide whether a case will be heard or allowed to stand as ruled on by the lower courts.[6]

The U.S. Supreme Court is the only court expressly created in the U.S. Constitution. All other courts in the federal system were created by Congress pursuant to its Constitutional power. The Constitution also makes the U.S. Supreme Court a court of original jurisdiction. The U.S. Supreme Court serves as the trial court for cases involving ambassadors, public ministers, or consuls and for cases in which two states are involved in a lawsuit. **For Example,** the U.S. Supreme

[6] For example, the Supreme Court refused to grant *certiorari* in a Fifth Circuit case on law school admissions at the University of Texas. However, it granted *certiorari* in a later case involving law school admissions at the University of Michigan. *Gratz v Bollinger*, 539 US 244 (2003).

Court has served for a number of years as the trial court for a Colorado River water rights case in which California, Nevada, and Arizona are parties.

3. State Court Systems

(A) GENERAL TRIAL COURTS. Most states have trial courts of general jurisdiction that may be called superior courts, circuit courts, or county courts. These courts of general and original jurisdiction usually hear both criminal and civil cases. Cases that do not meet the jurisdictional requirements for the federal district courts would be tried in these courts. Figure 2.3 illustrates a sample state court system.

(B) SPECIALTY COURTS. Most states also have courts with limited jurisdiction, sometimes referred to as *specialty courts.* **For Example,** most states have juvenile courts, or courts with limited jurisdiction over criminal matters that involve defendants who are under the age of 18. Other specialty courts or lesser courts in state systems are probate and family law courts.

FIGURE 2-3 | *Sample State Court System*

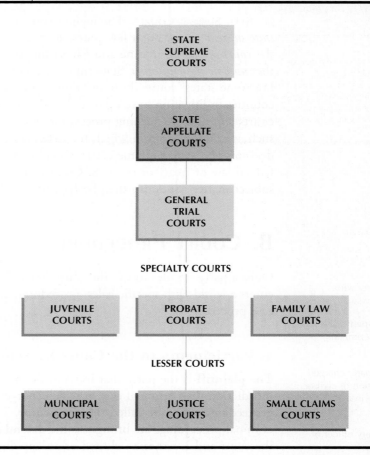

(C) City, Municipal, and Justice Courts. Cities and counties may also have lesser courts with limited jurisdiction, which may be referred to as *municipal courts* or *justice courts.* These courts generally handle civil matters in which the claim made in the suit is an amount below a certain level, such as $5,000 or $10,000. These courts may also handle misdemeanor types of offenses, such as traffic violations or violations of noise ordinances, and the trials for them.

small claims courts–courts that resolve disputes between parties when those disputes do not exceed a minimal level; no lawyers are permitted; the parties represent themselves.

(D) Small Claims Courts. Most states also have **small claims courts** at the county or city level. These are courts of limited jurisdiction where parties with small amounts in dispute may come to have a third party, such as a justice of the peace or city judge, review their disputes and determine how they should be resolved. A true small claims court is one in which the parties are not permitted to be represented by counsel. Rather, the parties present their cases to the judge in an informal manner without the strict procedural rules that apply in courts of general jurisdiction. Small claims courts provide a faster and inexpensive means for resolving a dispute that does not involve a large amount of claimed damages.

(E) State Appellate Courts. Most states also have intermediate-level courts similar to the federal courts of appeals. They are courts with appellate jurisdiction that review the decisions of lower courts in that state. Decisions of the general trial courts in a state would be appealed to these courts.

(F) State Supreme Courts. The highest court in most states is generally known as the *state supreme court,* but a few states, such as New York, may call their highest court the *court of appeals;* Maine and Massachusetts, for example, call their highest court the *supreme judicial court.* State supreme courts primarily have appellate jurisdiction, but some states' courts do have original jurisdiction, such as in Arizona, where counties in litigation have their trial at the supreme court level. Most state supreme courts also have a screening process for cases. They are required to hear some cases, such as criminal cases in which the defendant has received the death penalty. A decision of a state supreme court is final except in those circumstances in which a federal law or treaty or the U.S. Constitution is involved. Cases with these federal subject matter issues can then be appealed to the U.S. Supreme Court.

B. Court Procedure

Once a party decides to use the court system for resolution of a dispute, that party enters a world with specific rules, procedures, and terms that must be used to have a case proceed.

4. Participants in the Court System

plaintiff–party who initiates a lawsuit.

prosecutor–party who originates a criminal proceeding.

defendant–party charged with a violation of civil or criminal law in a proceeding.

judge–primary officer of the court.

The **plaintiff** is the party that initiates the proceedings in a court of original jurisdiction. In a criminal case in which charges are brought, the party initiating the proceedings would be called the **prosecutor**. The party against whom the civil or criminal proceedings are brought is the **defendant**. A **judge** is the primary officer of the court and is either an elected or an appointed official who presides over the matters brought before the court. Attorneys or lawyers are representatives for the plaintiff and the defendant for purposes of presenting their cases. Lawyers and clients have a privilege of confidentiality know as the **attorney-client privilege**. Lawyers cannot disclose what their clients tell them unless the client is committing, or plans to commit, a crime.

A **jury** is a body of citizens sworn by a court to reach a verdict on the basis of the case presented to them. Jurors are chosen for service based on lists compiled from voter registration and driver's license records.

attorney-client privilege— right of individual to have discussions with his/her attorney kept private and confidential

jury—a body of citizens sworn by a court to determine by verdict the issues of fact submitted to them.

5. Which Law Applies—Conflicts of Law

When a lawsuit is brought, there is not just the question of where a case will be tried but also of what law will be applied in determining the rights of the parties. The principle that determines when a court applies the law of its own state—the law of the forum—or some foreign law is called *conflict of laws*. Because there are 50 state court systems and a federal court system, as well as a high degree of interstate activity, conflicts of law questions arise frequently.

Some general rules apply. For example, the law of the state in which the court is located governs the case on procedural issues and rules of evidence. In contract litigation, the court applies the law of the state in which the contract was made for determining issues of formation. Performance disputes and damages for non-performance are generally governed by the law of the state where the contract is to be performed. International contracts follow similar rules. **For Example,** a California court will apply Swiss law to a contract made in Switzerland that is to be performed in that country.

However, it is becoming more common for the parties to specify their choice of law in their contract. In the absence of a law-selecting provision in the contract, there is a growing acceptance of the rule that a contract should be governed by the law of the state that has the most significant contacts with the transaction. **For Example,** assume the buyer's place of business and the seller's plant are located in Nebraska, and the buyer is purchasing goods from the seller to resell to Nebraska customers. Many courts will hold that this is a contract governed by the law of Nebraska. In determining which state has the most significant contacts, the court considers the place of contracting, negotiating, and performing; the location of the subject matter of the contract; and the domicile (residence), states of incorporation, and principal place of business of the parties.

6. Initial Steps in a Lawsuit

The following steps in a lawsuit generally apply in cases brought in courts of original jurisdiction. Not every step applies in every case, but understanding litigation steps and terms is important for businesspeople.

complaint—the initial pleading filed by the plaintiff in many actions, which in many states may be served as original process to acquire jurisdiction over the defendant.

(A) COMMENCEMENT OF A LAWSUIT. A lawsuit begins with the filing of a **complaint**. The complaint generally contains a description of the wrongful conduct and a request for damages, such as a monetary amount. **For Example,** a plaintiff in a contract suit would describe the contract, when it was entered into, and when the defendant stopped performance on the contract. A copy of the contract would be attached to the complaint.

(B) SERVICE OF PROCESS. Once the plaintiff has filed the complaint with the proper court, the plaintiff has the responsibility of notifying the defendant that the lawsuit has been filed. The defendant must be served with **process**. Process, often called a *writ, notice,* or *summons,* is delivered to the defendant and includes a copy of the complaint and notification that the defendant must appear and respond to the allegations in the complaint.

(C) THE DEFENDANT'S RESPONSE AND THE PLEADINGS. After the defendant is served with process in the case, the defendant is required to respond to or **answer** the complaint within the time provided under the court's rules. In answering the plaintiff's complaint, the defendant has several options. For example, the defendant could make a **motion to dismiss**, which is a request to the court to dismiss the lawsuit on the grounds that, even if everything the plaintiff said in the complaint were true, there is still no right of recovery. A motion to dismiss is also called a **demurrer**.

A defendant could also respond and deny the allegations. **For Example,** in a contract lawsuit, the defendant-seller could say he did not breach the contract but stopped shipment of the goods because the plaintiff-buyer did not pay for the goods in advance as the contract required. A defendant could also **counterclaim** in the answer, which is asking the court for damages as a result of the underlying dispute. **For Example,** the defendant-seller in the contract lawsuit might ask for damages for the plaintiff-buyer's failure to pay as the contract required.

All documents filed in this initial phase of the case are referred to as the **pleadings**. The pleadings are a statement of the case and the basis for recovery if all the facts alleged can be proved.

(D) DISCOVERY. The Federal Rules of Civil Procedure and similar rules in all states permit one party to obtain from the adverse party information about all witnesses, documents, and any other items relevant to the case. **Discovery** requires each side to name its potential witnesses and to provide each side the chance to question those witnesses in advance of the trial. Each party also has the opportunity to examine, inspect, and photograph books, records, buildings, and machines. Even examining the physical or mental condition of a party is part of discovery when it has relevance in the case. The scope of discovery is extremely broad because the rules permit any questions that are likely to lead to admissible evidence.

Deposition.
A **deposition** is the testimony of a witness taken under oath outside the courtroom; it is transcribed by a court reporter. Each party is permitted to question the witness. If a party or a witness gives testimony at the trial that is inconsistent with her deposition testimony, the prior inconsistent testimony can be used to **impeach** the witness's credibility at trial

Depositions can be taken either for discovery purposes or to preserve the testimony of a witness who will not be available during the trial. Some states now permit depositions to be videotaped. A videotape is a more effective way of

---

process–paperwork served personally on a defendant in a civil case.

answer–what a defendant must file to admit or deny facts asserted by the plaintiff.

motion to dismiss–a pleading that may be filed to attack the adverse party's pleading as not stating a cause of action or a defense.

demurrer–a pleading to dismiss the adverse party's pleading for not stating a cause of action or a defense.

counterclaim–a claim that the defendant in an action may make against the plaintiff.

pleadings–the papers filed by the parties in an action in order to set forth the facts and frame the issues to be tried, although, under some systems, the pleadings merely give notice or a general indication of the nature of the issues.

discovery–procedures for ascertaining facts prior to the time of trial in order to eliminate the element of surprise in litigation.

deposition–the testimony of a witness taken out of court before a person authorized to administer oaths.

impeach–using prior inconsistent evidence to challenge the credibility of a witness.

presenting deposition testimony than reading that testimony at trial from a reporter's transcript because jurors can see the witness and the witness's demeanor and hear the words as they were spoken, complete with inflection.[7]

Other Forms of Discovery.

interrogatories–written questions used as a discovery tool that must be answered under oath.

Other forms of discovery include written **interrogatories** (questions) and written **requests for production of documents**. These discovery requests can be very time consuming to the answering party and often lead to pretrial legal disputes between the parties and their attorneys as a result of the legal expenses involved.

request for production of documents–discovery tool for uncovering paper evidence in a case.

(E) MOTION FOR SUMMARY JUDGMENT. If a case has no material facts in dispute, either party can file a **motion for summary judgment**. Using affidavits or deposition testimony obtained in discovery, the court can find that there are no factual issues and decide the case as a matter of law. **For Example,** suppose that the parties can agree that they entered into a life insurance contract but dispute whether the policy applies when there is a suicide. The facts are not in dispute; the law on payment of insurance proceeds in the event of a suicide is the issue. Such a case is one that is appropriate for summary judgment.

motion for summary judgment–request that the court decide a case on basis of law only because there are no material issues disputed by the parties.

(F) DESIGNATION OF EXPERT WITNESSES. In some cases, such as those involving product safety, the parties may want to designate an expert witness. An **expert witness** is a witness who has some special expertise, such as an economist who gives expert opinion on the value of future lost income or a scientist who testifies about the safety of a prescription drug. There are rules for naming expert witnesses as well as for admitting into evidence any studies or documents of the expert.[8] The purpose of these rules is to avoid the problem of what has been called *junk science,* or the admission of experts' testimony and research that has not been properly conducted or reviewed by peers.

expert witness–one who has acquired special knowledge in a particular field as through practical experience or study, or both, whose opinion is admissible as an aid to the trier of fact.

7. The Trial

(A) SELECTING A JURY. Jurors drawn for service are questioned by the judge and lawyers to determine whether they are biased or have any preformed judgments about the parties in the case. Jury selection is called *voir dire* **examination. For Example,** in the trial of Martha Stewart, the multimedia home and garden diva, it took a great deal of time for the lawyers to question the potential jurors about their prior knowledge concerning the case, which had received nationwide attention and much media coverage. Lawyers have the opportunity to remove jurors who know parties in the case or who indicate they have already formed opinions about guilt or innocence. The attorneys question the potential jurors to determine if a juror should be *challenged for cause* (e.g., when the prospective juror states he is employed by the plaintiff's company). Challenges for cause are unlimited, but each side can also

voir dire examination–the preliminary examination of a juror or a witness to ascertain fitness to act as such.

---

[7] At the civil trial of O.J. Simpson for the wrongful death of Nicole Brown Simpson and Ronald Goldman, Daniel Petrocelli used a videotape of Mr. Simpson's deposition very effectively in impeaching Mr. Simpson's testimony at trial. Daniel Petrocelli, *Triumph of Justice: The Final Judgment on the Simpson Saga* (New York: Crown, 1998).

[8] *Daubert v Merrell Dow Pharmaceuticals, Inc.,* 509 US 579 (1993).

exercise six to eight peremptory challenges.[9] A peremptory challenge is an arbitrary challenge that may be used to strike (remove) a juror except for racial reasons.

(B) OPENING STATEMENTS. After the jury is called, the opposing attorneys make their **opening statements** to the jury. An opening statement, as one lawyer has explained, makes a puzzle frame for the case so jurors can follow the witnesses and place the pieces of the case—the various forms of evidence—within the frame.

(C) THE PRESENTATION OF EVIDENCE. Following the opening statements, the plaintiff then begins to present his case with witnesses and other evidence. A judge rules on the **admissibility** of evidence. Evidence can consist of documents, testimony, and even physical evidence.

In the case of testimony, the attorney for the plaintiff conducts **direct examination** of his witnesses during his case, and the defense attorney conducts **cross-examination** of the plaintiff's witnesses. The plaintiff's attorney can then ask questions again of his witnesses in what is called **redirect examination**. Finally, the defense attorney may question the plaintiff's witnesses again in **recross-examination**. This procedure is followed with all of the plaintiff's witnesses, and then the defendant presents her case after the plaintiff's case concludes. During the defendant's case, the lawyer for the defendant conducts direct examination of the defendant's witnesses, and the plaintiff's lawyer can then cross-examine the defendant's witnesses.

(D) MOTION FOR A DIRECTED VERDICT. A motion for a **directed verdict** asks the court to grant a verdict because even if all the evidence that has been presented by each side were true, there is either no basis for recovery or no defense to recovery. For example, in some states, the defendant can make a motion for a directed verdict after the plaintiff's case is concluded. The defendant's motion argues that even if the plaintiff's case were 100 percent true, there is no basis in law for recovery. It is also possible for either side to move for a directed verdict after both sides have presented their cases. The defendant is arguing the same position as stated earlier, that there is no basis for recovery even assuming all facts to be true. The plaintiff is arguing that even if everything the defendant presented were 100 percent true, there was nothing in the defense case that challenged the plaintiff's right to recovery.

(E) SUMMATION. After the witnesses for both parties have been examined and all the evidence has been presented, each attorney makes another address to the jury. These statements are called **summations** or *closing arguments;* they summarize the case and suggest that a particular verdict be returned by the jury.

(F) MOTION FOR MISTRIAL. During the course of a trial, when necessary to avoid great injustice, the trial court may declare that there has been a **mistrial**. The declaration of a mistrial terminates the trial and requires that it start over with a new jury. A mistrial can be declared for jury or attorney misconduct. **For Example,** if a juror were caught fraternizing with one of the lawyers in the case, objectivity would be compromised and the court would most likely declare a mistrial.

---

[9] The number of peremptory challenges varies from state to state and may also vary within a particular state depending on the type of case. For example, in Arizona, peremptory challenges are unlimited in capital cases.

opening statements– statements by opposing attorneys that tell the jury what their cases will prove.

admissibility–the quality of the evidence in a case that allows it to be presented to the jury.

direct examination– examination of a witness by his or her attorney.

cross-examination–the examination made of a witness by the attorney for the adverse party.

redirect examination– questioning after cross-examination, in which the attorney for the witness testifying may ask the same witness other questions to overcome effects of the cross-examination.

recross-examination–an examination by the other side's attorney that follows the redirect examination.

directed verdict–a direction by the trial judge to the jury to return a verdict in favor of a specified party to the action.

summation–the attorney address that follows all the evidence presented in court and sums up a case and recommends a particular verdict be returned by the jury.

mistrial–a court's declaration that terminates a trial and postpones it to a later date; commonly entered when evidence has been of a highly prejudicial character or when a juror has been guilty of misconduct.

ethics&the law

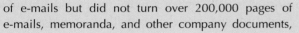

Qualcomm filed suit against Broadcom for alleged patent infringement. Broadcom made a discovery request from Qualcomm for copies of e-mail and other correspondence among and between Qualcomm employees and others in their industry. Qualcomm lawyers turned over a handful of e-mails but did not turn over 200,000 pages of e-mails, memoranda, and other company documents, all of which had important information that undercut Qualcomm's patent infringement claim. In fact, Qualcomm's legal counsel, while preparing a key Qualcomm witness for her testimony, stripped over 50 pages of e-mails from her email archives. Evaluate the ethics of Qualcomm's lawyer **[Qualcomm, Inc. v Broadcom, Inc., 539 F Supp 2d 1214 SD Cal 2007]**

thinking things through

Why Do We Require Sworn Testimony?

There is a difference between what people say in conversation (and even what company executives say in speeches and reports) and what they are willing to say under oath. Speaking under oath often means that different information and recollections emerge. The oath is symbolic and carries the penalty of criminal prosecution for perjury if the testimony given is false.

The *Wall Street Journal* has reported that the testimony of executives in the Microsoft antitrust trial and their statements regarding their business relationships outside the courtroom are quite different. For example, the following quotations indicate some discrepancies. Eric Benhamou, the chief executive officer (CEO) of Palm, Inc., said:

> *We believe that the handheld opportunity remains wide open…. Unlike the PC industry, there is no monopoly of silicon, there is no monopoly of software.*

However, at the Microsoft trial, another officer of Palm, Michael Mace, offered the following testimony:

> *We believe that there is a very substantial risk that Microsoft could manipulate its products and its standards in order to exclude Palm from the marketplace in the future.*

Likewise, Microsoft has taken different positions inside and outside the courtroom. For example, an attorney for Microsoft stated that Microsoft had "zero deployments of its interactive TV middleware products connected to cable systems in the United States." However, Microsoft's marketing materials provide as follows:

> *Microsoft's multiple deployments around the world now including Charter-show Microsoft TV is ready to deploy now and set the standard for what TV can be.*[*]

Explain why the executives had differing statements. For more information on the Microsoft antitrust cases, go to **www.usdoj.gov** or **www.microsoft.com**.

[*] Rebecca Buckman and Nicholas Kulish, "Microsoft Trial Prompts an Outbreak of Doublespeak," *Wall Street Journal*, April 15, 2002, B1, B3.

instruction–summary of the law given to jurors by the judge before deliberation begins.

(G) JURY INSTRUCTIONS AND VERDICT. After the summation by the attorneys, the court gives the jurors **instructions** on the appropriate law to apply to the facts presented. The jury then deliberates and renders its verdict. After the jury verdict, the court enters a judgment. If the jury is deadlocked and unable to reach a verdict, the case is reset for a new trial at some future date.

judgment n.o.v.–*or non obstante veredicto* (notwithstanding the verdict), a judgment entered after verdict upon the motion of the losing party on the ground that the verdict is so wrong that a judgment should be entered the opposite of the verdict.

(H) MOTION FOR NEW TRIAL; MOTION FOR JUDGMENT N.O.V. A court may grant a judgment *non obstante veredicto* or a **judgment n.o.v.** (notwithstanding the verdict) if the verdict is clearly wrong as a matter of law. The court can set aside the verdict and enter a judgment in favor of the other party. Perhaps one of the most famous judgments n.o.v. occurred in Boston in 1997 when a judge reversed the murder conviction of nanny Louise Woodward, who was charged with the murder of one of her young charges.

8. Posttrial Procedures

(A) RECOVERY OF COSTS/ATTORNEY FEES. Generally, the prevailing party is awarded costs. Costs include filing fees, service-of-process fees, witness fees, deposition transcript costs, and jury fees. Costs do not include compensation spent by a party for preparing the case or being present at trial, including the time lost from work because of the case and the fee paid to the attorney, although lost wages from an injury are generally part of damages.

Attorney fees may be recovered by a party who prevails if a statute permits the recovery of attorney fees or if the complaint involves a claim for breach of contract and the contract contains a clause providing for recovery of attorney fees.

execution–the carrying out of a judgment of a court, generally directing that property owned by the defendant be sold and the proceeds first be used to pay the execution or judgment creditor.

garnishment–the name given in some states to attachment proceedings.

(B) EXECUTION OF JUDGMENT. After a judgment has been entered or all appeals or appeal rights have ended, the losing party must pay that judgment. The winning party can also take steps to execute, or carry out, the judgment. The **execution** is accomplished by the seizure and sale of the losing party's assets by the sheriff according to a writ of execution or a writ of possession.

Garnishment is a common method of satisfying a judgment. When the judgment debtor is an employee, the appropriate judicial authority in the state garnishes (by written notice to the employer) a portion of the employee's wages on a regular basis until the judgment is paid.

C. ALTERNATIVE DISPUTE RESOLUTION (ADR)

Parties can use means other than litigation to resolve disagreements or disputes. Litigation takes significant time and money, so many businesses use alternative methods for resolving disputes. Those methods, which include arbitration, mediation, and several other formats, are enjoying increasing popularity. Figure 2.4 provides an overall view of dispute resolution procedures.

FIGURE 2-4 | *Dispute Resolution Procedures*

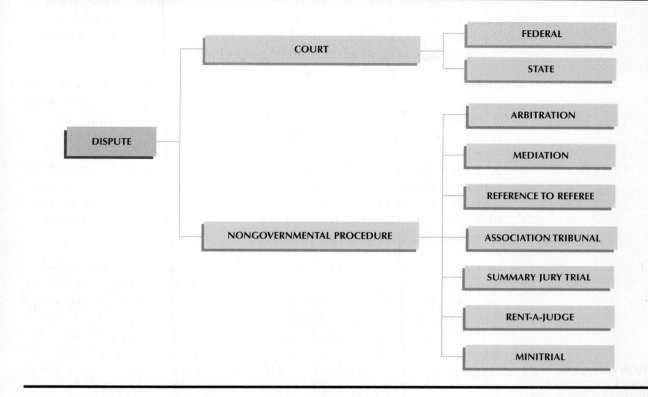

9. Arbitration

arbitration–the settlement of disputed questions, whether of law or fact, by one or more arbitrators by whose decision the parties agree to be bound.

In **arbitration**, arbitrators (disinterested persons selected by the parties to the dispute) hear evidence and determine a resolution. Arbitration enables the parties to present the facts before trained experts familiar with the industry practices that may affect the nature and outcome of the dispute. Arbitration first reached extensive use in the field of commercial contracts and is encouraged as a means of avoiding expensive litigation and easing the workload of courts.[10]

A number of states have adopted the Uniform Arbitration Act.[11] Under this act and similar statutes, the parties to a contract may agree in advance that all disputes arising under it will be submitted to arbitration. In some instances, the contract will name the arbitrators for the duration of the contract. The uniform act requires a written agreement to arbitrate.[12]

[10] *Warfield v Beth* Israel Deaconess Medical Center, Inc., 910 NE2d 317, 454 Mass 390 (2009). Arbitration has existed in the United States since 1920 when New York passed an arbitration statute. For a look at the history of arbitration, see Charles L. Knapp, "Taking Contracts Private: The Quiet Revolution in Contract Law," 71 *Fordham L. Rev.* 761 (2002).
[11] On August 3, 2000, the National Conference of Commissioners on Uniform State Laws unanimously passed major revisions to the Uniform Arbitration Act (UAA). These revisions were the first major changes in 45 years to the UAA, which is the basis of arbitration law in 49 states, although not all states have adopted it in its entirety. Thirty-five states and the District of Columbia have adopted the 1955 version. Only 13 states have adopted the UAA 2000 revisions. Donald L. Carpo & John B. LaRocco, "A Comparison of Litigation, Arbitration, and Mediation," 63 *Dispute Resolution* J. 48 (2008).
[12] Fawzy v Fawzy, 973 A2d 347 (NJ 2009).

The Federal Arbitration Act[13] provides that an arbitration clause in a contract relating to an interstate transaction is valid, irrevocable, and enforceable. When a contract subject to the Federal Arbitration Act provides for the arbitration of disputes, the parties are bound to arbitrate in accordance with the federal statute even if the agreement to arbitrate would not be binding under state law.

(A) **MANDATORY ARBITRATION.** In contrast with statutes that merely regulate arbitration when it is selected voluntarily by the parties, some statutes require that certain kinds of disputes be submitted to arbitration. In some states, by rule or statute, the arbitration of small claims is required.

(B) **SCOPE OF ARBITRATION.** When arbitration is required by statute, the terms of the statute will define the scope of the arbitration. When the parties have voluntarily agreed to arbitrate, their agreement will control the scope of the dispute. Because arbitration is now favored, any doubt as to its scope will be decided in favor of arbitration by the arbitrator.[14]

(C) **FINALITY OF ARBITRATION.** Most parties provide, within their arbitration agreements, that the decision of the arbitrator will be final. Such a clause is binding on the parties, even when the decision seems to be wrong, and can be set aside only if there is clear proof of fraud, arbitrary conduct, or a significant procedural error.[15]

If the arbitration is mandatory under statute or rule, the losing party generally may appeal such arbitration to a court.[16] The appeal proceeds just as though there had never been any prior arbitration. This new court proceeding is called a **trial *de novo*** and is necessary to preserve the constitutional right to a jury trial. As a practical matter, however, relatively few appeals are taken from arbitration decisions.

trial *de novo*–a trial required to preserve the constitutional right to a jury trial by allowing an appeal to proceed as though there never had been any prior hearing or decision.

10. Mediation

mediation–the settlement of a dispute through the use of a messenger who carries to each side of the dispute the issues and offers in the case.

In **mediation**, a neutral person acts as a messenger between opposing sides of a dispute, carrying to each side the latest settlement offer made by the other. The mediator has no authority to make a decision, although in some cases the mediator may make suggestions that might ultimately be accepted by the disputing parties.

The use of mediation has the advantage of keeping discussions going when the disputing parties have developed such fixed attitudes or personal animosity that direct discussion between them has become impossible.

11. MedArb

In this new form of alternative dispute resolution (ADR), the arbitrator is also empowered to act as a mediator. Beyond just hearing a case, the arbitrator acts as a messenger for the parties on unresolved issues.

---

[13] 9 USC § 114 *et. seq.*
[14] *First Options v Kaplan,* 514 US 938 (1995). See also *Hialeah Automotive, LLC v Basulto*— So2d —, 2009 WL 187584 (Fla App).
[15] *Apache Bohai Corp. LDC v Texaco China BV,* 480 F.3d 397 (CA 5 2007).
[16] *U.S. v Park Place Associates,* 563 F3d 907 (CA 9 2009).

12. Reference To a Third Person

reference to a third person—settlement that allows a nonparty to resolve the dispute.

Many types of transactions provide for **reference to a third person**, in which a third person or a committee makes an out-of-court determination of the rights of persons. **For Example,** employees and an employer may have agreed as a term of the employment contract that claims of employees under retirement plans will be decided by a designated board or committee. In a sales contract, the seller and buyer can select a third person to determine the price to be paid for goods. Construction contracts often include a provision for disputes to be referred to the architect in charge of the construction with the architect's decision being final.

These referrals often eliminate the disputes or pursuit of remedies. **For Example,** fire insurance policies commonly provide that if the parties cannot agree on the amount of the loss, each will appoint an appraiser, the two appraisers will appoint a third appraiser, and the three will determine the amount of the loss the insurer is required to pay.

13. Association Tribunals

association tribunal—a court created by a trade association or group for the resolution of disputes among its members.

Many disputes never reach the courts because both parties to a dispute belong to a group or an association, and the **association tribunal** created by the group or association disposes of the matter. Trade associations commonly require their members to employ out-of-court methods of dispute settlement. **For Example,** the National Association of Home Builders requires its member builders to employ arbitration. The National Automobile Dealers Association provides for panels to determine warranty claims of customers. The decision of such panels is final as to the builder or dealer, but the consumer can still bring a regular lawsuit after losing before the panel. Members of an association must use the association tribunal, which means they cannot bypass the association tribunal and go directly to a law court.[17]

14. Summary Jury Trial

summary jury trial—a mock or dry-run trial for parties to get a feel for how their cases will play to a jury.

A **summary jury trial** is a dry-run or mock trial in which the lawyers present their claims before a jury of six persons. The object is to get the reaction of a sample jury. No evidence is presented before this jury, and it bases its opinion solely on what the lawyers state. The determination of the jury has no binding effect, but it has value in that it gives the lawyers some idea of what a jury might think if there were an actual trial. This type of ADR has special value when the heart of a case is whether something is reasonable under all circumstances. When the lawyers and their clients see how the sample jury reacts, they may moderate their positions and reach a settlement.

15. Rent-A-Judge

rent-a-judge plan—dispute resolution through private courts with judges paid to be referees for the cases.

Under the **rent-a-judge plan**, the parties hire a judge to hear the case. In many states, the parties voluntarily choose the judge as a "referee," and the judge acts under a statute authorizing the appointment of referees. Under such a statute, the referee hears all evidence just as though there were a regular trial, and the rented judge's determination is binding on the parties unless reversed on appeal if such an appeal

[17] The securities industry follows this process as well.

e-commerce&cyberlaw

Referred to as the "Google Mistrial," a federal judge in Florida declared a mistrial after a juror told that judge that he had been doing research on the Internet on the drug trial in which he was serving When the judge declared the mistrial, eight other jurors confessed that they had been doing the same thing.

Judges have long warned jurors about using outside sources, including the Internet, but BlackBerries and iPhones have proven to be mighty tempting for jurors. Some jurors are using Facebook to announce when verdicts are coming. One juror even looked up evidence that had been excluded by the judge in the case. When asked why he violated the judge's order, the juror said simply, "Well, I was curious."

A judge in Arkansas is reviewing a request for a reversal of a $12.6 million jury verdict against a company from one of the company's lawyers based on the court's discovery that one of the jurors was using Twitter to send out postings about how the trial was proceeding. An excerpt from the posting follows:

"Oh, and nobody buy Stoam. It's bad mojo and they'll probably cease to Exist now that their wallet is $12m lighter … So, Jonathan, what did you do today? Oh nothing really, I just gave away TWELVE MILLION DOLLARS of somebody else's money."

What is the problem with jurors using these electronic tools during their cases?

** John Schwartz, "As Jurors Turn to Google and Twitter, Mistrials Are Popping Up," *New York Times*, March 18, 2009, A1.*

(like a court trial) is permitted under the parties' agreement. In some jurisdictions, the parties can agree that the decision of the judge selected as referee will be final.

16. Minitrial

minitrial—a trial held on portions of the case or certain issues in the case.

When only part of a case is disputed, the parties may stay within the framework of a lawsuit but agree that only the disputed issues will be taken to trial and submitted to a jury. When there is no real dispute over the liability of the defendant but the parties disagree as to the damages, the issue of damages alone may be submitted to the jury. This shortened trial is often called a **minitrial**. A minitrial may use a retired judge to listen to the evidence on just the disputed issues and decide the case. The agreement of the parties for the minitrial may specify whether this decision will be binding on the parties. As a practical matter, the evaluation of a case by a neutral person often brings the opposing parties together to reach a settlement.

17. Judicial Triage

judicial triage—court management tool used by judges to expedite certain cases in which time is of the essence, such as asbestos cases in which the plaintiffs are gravely ill.

The court systems, experiencing heavy caseloads, now practice **judicial triage**. Judges examine cases from a timeliness perspective. For example, in asbestos cases, judges are now evaluating plaintiffs on the basis of "how sick they are" and expediting trials for those plaintiffs who are the most ill from the alleged effects of asbestos that are the subject of their suits. The trials of those who do not have medical documentation of current illness are postponed and placed on the inactive docket until the court can get to them or until the plaintiffs become sick. Using triage, one judge has been able to bring to trial 40 percent of all asbestos cases brought since 1992.[18]

[18] Susan Warren, "Swamped Courts Practice Plaintiff Triage," *Wall Street Journal*, January 27, 2003, B1, B3.

18. Contract Provisions

The parties' contract may pave the way for the settlement of future disputes by containing clauses requiring the parties to use one of the procedures already described. In addition, contracts may provide that no action may be taken until after the expiration of a specified cooling-off period. Contracts may also specify that the parties should continue in the performance of their contract even though a dispute between them still exists.

19. Disposition of Complaints and Ombudsmen

ombudsman–a government official designated by a statute to examine citizen complaints.

In contrast with the traditional and alternative procedures for resolving disputes are the procedures aimed at removing the grounds for a complaint before it develops into a dispute that requires resolution. **For Example,** the complaint department in a department store is often be able to iron out a difficulty before the customer and the store are locked in an adversarial position that could end in a lawsuit. Some states have a public official, called an **ombudsman**, who receive complaints and then make recommendations for improvements.

lawflix

Class Action (1991) (R)

Here is a good movie to illustrate discovery and the ethics of withholding paperwork.

Twelve Angry Men (1957) G

A movie that shows the jury process, rights of parties in court, jury instructions, and group think, all wrapped up in terrific dialogue.

Check out LawFlix at **www.cengage.com/blaw/dvl** to access movie clips that illustrate business law concepts.

MAKE THE CONNECTION

SUMMARY

Courts have been created to hear and resolve legal disputes. A court's specific power is defined by its jurisdiction. Courts of original jurisdiction are trial courts, and courts that review the decisions of trial courts are appellate courts. Trial courts may have general jurisdiction to hear a wide range of civil and criminal matters, or they may be courts of limited jurisdiction—such as a probate court or the Tax Court—with the subject matter of their cases restricted to certain areas.

The courts in the United States are organized into two different systems: the state and federal court systems. There are three levels of courts, for the most part, in each system, with trial courts, appellate courts, and a supreme court in each. The federal courts are federal district courts, federal courts of appeals, and the U.S. Supreme Court. In the states, there may be specialized courts, such as municipal, justice, and small claims courts, for trial courts. Within the courts of original jurisdiction, there are rules for procedures in all matters brought before them. A civil case begins with the filing of a complaint by a plaintiff, which is then answered by a defendant. The parties may be represented by their attorneys. Discovery is the pretrial process used by the parties to find out the evidence in the case. The parties can use depositions, interrogatories, and document requests to uncover relevant information.

The case is managed by a judge and may be tried to a jury selected through the process of *voir dire,* with the parties permitted to challenge jurors on the basis of cause or through the use of their peremptory challenges. The trial begins following discovery and involves opening statements and the presentation of evidence, including the direct examination and cross-examination of witnesses. Once a judgment is entered, the party who has won can collect the judgment through garnishment and a writ of execution.

Alternatives to litigation for dispute resolution are available, including arbitration, mediation, MedArb, reference to a third party, association tribunals, summary jury trials, rent-a-judge plans, minitrials, judicial triage, and the use of ombudsmen. Court dockets are relieved and cases consolidated using judicial triage, a process in which courts hear the cases involving the most serious medical issues and health conditions first. Triage is a blending of the judicial and alternative dispute resolution mechanisms.

LEARNING OUTCOMES

After studying this chapter, you should be able to clearly explain:

A. THE COURT SYSTEM

LO.1 Explain the federal and state court systems

    See Figure 2-1 on p. 19 and accompanying text.

    See Figure 2-3 on p. 21 and accompanying text.

B. COURT PROCEDURE

LO.2 Describe court procedures

    See the discussion of steps in litigation that begins on p. 23.

    See the **For Example** discussion of the Martha Stewart *voir dire* example on p. 25.

C. ALTERNATIVE DISPUTE RESOLUTION (ADR)

LO.3 List the forms of alternative dispute resolution and distinguish among them

    See the discussion of arbitration that begins on p. 29.

    See the discussion of other forms of ADR, mediation, minitrials, rent-a-judge, MedArb, judicial triage, and referral to a third party that begins on p. 28.

    See the discussion of employee and employer referrals of disputes to a designated board or committee on p. 31.

KEY TERMS

admissibility	federal district courts	plaintiff
affirm	garnishment	pleadings
answer	general jurisdiction	process
appeal	impeach	prosecutor
appellate jurisdiction	instructions	recross-examination
arbitration	interrogatories	redirect examination
association tribunal	judge	reference to a third person
attorney-client privilege	judgment n.o.v.	remand
complaint	judicial triage	rent-a-judge plan
counterclaim	jurisdiction	requests for production of
court	jury	documents
cross-examination	limited jurisdiction	reverse
defendant	mediation	reversible error
demurrer	minitrial	small claims courts
deposition	mistrial	special jurisdiction
direct examination	motion for summary	subject matter jurisdiction
directed verdict	judgment	summary jury trial
discovery	motion to dismiss	summations
en banc	ombudsman	trial *de novo*
execution	opening statements	*voir dire* examination
expert witness	original jurisdiction	writ of *certiorari*

QUESTIONS AND CASE PROBLEMS

1. List the steps in a lawsuit. Begin with the filing of the complaint, and explain the points at which there can be a final determination of the parties' rights in the case.

2. Distinguish between mandatory and voluntary arbitration. What is the difference between mediation and arbitration?

3. Ralph Dewey has been charged with a violation of the Electronic Espionage Act, a federal statute that prohibits the transfer, by computer or disk or other electronic means, of a company's proprietary data and information. Ralph is curious. What type of court has jurisdiction? Can you determine which court?

4. Jerry Lewinsky was called for jury duty. When *voir dire* began, Jerry realized that the case involved his supervisor at work. Can Jerry remain as a juror on the case? Why or why not?

5. Carolyn, Elwood, and Isabella are involved in a real estate development. The development is a failure, and Carolyn, Elwood, and Isabella want to have their rights determined. They could bring a lawsuit, but they are afraid the case is so complicated that a judge and jury not familiar with the problems of real estate development would not reach a proper result. What can they do?

6. Larketta Randolph purchased a mobile home from Better Cents Home Builders, Inc., and financed her purchase through Green Tree Financial Corporation. Ms. Randolph signed a standard form contract that required her to buy Vendor's Single Interest insurance, which protects the seller against the costs of repossession in the event of default. The agreement also provided that all disputes arising from the contract would be resolved by binding arbitration. Larketta found that there was an additional $15 in finance charges that were not disclosed in the contract. She and other Green Tree customers filed a class-action suit to recover the fees. Green Tree moved to dismiss the suit because Larketta had not submitted the issue to arbitration. Larketta protests, "But I want the right to go to court!" Does she have that right? What are the rights of parties under a contract with an arbitration clause? [*Green Tree Financial Corp. v Randolph*, 531 US 79]

7. John Watson invested $5,000,000 in SmartRead, Inc., a company that was developing an electronic reading device. Within a few months, the $5,000,000 was spent but SmartRead never developed the reading device. John filed suit against directors of SmartRead for their failure to supervise SmartRead's CEO in his operation of the company. The directors used an expert on corporate governance to testify that the directors had done all that they could to oversee the company. The expert did not disclose that he had served as a director of a company and had been found to be negligent in his role there and had been required to pay $370,000 to shareholders. The directors won the case. Is there anything Watson can do?

8. Indicate whether the following courts are courts of original, general, limited, or appellate jurisdiction:

   a. Small claims court

   b. Federal bankruptcy court

   c. Federal district court

   d. U.S. Supreme Court

   e. Municipal court

   f. Probate court

   g. Federal court of appeals

9. The Nursing Home Pension Fund filed suit against Oracle Corporation alleging that Larry Ellison, the company's CEO, misled investors in 2001 about the true financial condition of the company. During the time of the alleged misrepresentation, Mr. Ellison was working with a biographer on his life story and there are videotapes of Mr. Ellison's interviews with his biographer as well as e-mails between the two that discuss Oracle. Could the Nursing Home Pension Fund have access to the tapes and e-mails? Explain how. [*Nursing Home Pension Fund, Local 144 v Oracle Corp.*, 380 F3d 1226 (CA 9)]

10. Mostek Corp., a Texas corporation, made a contract to sell computer-related products to North American Foreign Trading Corp., a New York corporation.

North American used its own purchase order form, on which appeared the statement that any dispute arising out of an order would be submitted to arbitration, as provided in the terms set forth on the back of the order. Acting on the purchase order, Mostek delivered almost all of the goods but failed to deliver the final installment. North American then demanded that the matter be arbitrated. Mostek refused to do so. Was arbitration required? [*Application of Mostek Corp.,* 120 App Div 2d 383, 502 NYS2d 181]

11. Ceasar Wright was a longshoreman in Charleston, South Carolina, and a member of the International Longshoremen's Association (AFL-CIO). Wright used the union hiring hall. The collective bargaining agreement (CBA) of Wright's union provides for arbitration of all grievances. Another clause of the CBA states: "It is the intention and purpose of all parties hereto that no provision or part of this Agreement shall be violative of any Federal or State Law."

    On February 18, 1992, while Wright was working for Stevens Shipping and Terminal Company (Stevens), he injured his right heel and back. He sought permanent compensation from Stevens and settled his claims for $250,000 and another $10,000 in attorney fees. Wright was also awarded Social Security disability benefits.

    In January 1995, Wright, whose doctor had approved his return to work, returned to the hiring hall and asked to be referred for work. Wright did work between January 2 and January 11, 1995, but when the companies realized Wright had been certified as permanently disabled, they deemed him not qualified for longshoreman work under the CBA and refused to allow him to work for them.

    Wright did not file a grievance under the union agreement but instead hired a lawyer and proceeded with a claim under the Americans with Disabilities Act. The district court dismissed the case because Wright had failed to pursue the grievance procedure provided by the CBA. Must Wright pursue the dispute procedure first, or can he go right to court on the basis of his federal rights under the Americans with Disabilities Act? [*Wright v Universal Maritime Service Corp.,* 525 US 70]

12. Winona Ryder was arrested for shoplifting from Saks Fifth Avenue in California. One of the members of the jury panel for her trial was Peter Guber, a Hollywood executive in charge of the production of three films in which Ms. Ryder starred, including *Bram Stoker's Dracula, The Age of Innocence,* and *Little Women.* If you were the prosecuting attorney in the case, how could you discover such information about this potential juror, and what are your options for excluding him from selection? [Rick Lyman, "For the Ryder Trial, a Hollywood Script," *New York Times,* November 3, 2002, SL-1]

13. What is the difference between the role of a trial court and the role of an appellate court? What functions do they perform, and how do they perform them?

14. Martha Simms is the plaintiff in a contract suit she has brought against Floral Supply, Inc., for its failure to deliver the green sponge Martha needed in

building the floral designs she sells to exclusive home decorators. Martha had to obtain the sponge from another supplier and was late on seven deliveries. One of Martha's customers has been called by Martha's lawyer as a witness and is now on the witness stand, testifying about Martha's late performance and the penalty she charged. The lawyer for Floral Supply knows that Martha's customer frequently waives penalties for good suppliers. How can Floral Supply's lawyer get that information before the jury?

Chapter 3

BUSINESS ETHICS, SOCIAL FORCES, AND THE LAW

E ach day businesspeople work together on contracts and projects. Their completion of the work is partially the result of the laws that protect contract rights. Much of what businesspeople do, however, is simply a matter of their word. Executives arrive at a 9:00 A.M. meeting because they promised they would be there. An employee meets a deadline for an ad display board because she said she would. Business transactions are completed through a combination of the values of the parties and the laws that reflect those values and the importance of one's word in business.

This chapter takes you behind the rules of law to examine the objectives in establishing rules for business conduct. Both social forces and business needs contribute to the standards that govern businesses and their operations.

A. WHAT IS BUSINESS ETHICS?

ethics–a branch of philosophy dealing with values that relate to the nature of human conduct and values associated with that conduct.

business ethics–balancing the goal of profits with values of individuals and society.

Ethics is a branch of philosophy dealing with values that relate to the nature of human conduct and values associated with that conduct. Balancing the goal of profits with the values of individuals and society is the focus of **business ethics**. Some economists make the point that insider trading is an efficient way to run that market. To an economist, inside information allows those with the best information to make the most money. This view ignores some issues: What about those who trade stock who do not have access to that information? Is the philosophy fair to them? What will happen to the stock market if investors perceive there is not a level playing field? In the U.S. Supreme Court decision *United States v O'Hagan*[1] on insider trading, Justice Ruth Ginsburg noted, "Investors likely wouldn't invest in a market where trading based on misappropriated nonpublic information is unchecked." The field of business ethics deals with the balance between society's values and the need for businesses to remain profitable.

1. The Law as the Standard for Business Ethics

positive law–law enacted and codified by governmental authority.

Philosophers debate the origin of moral and ethical standards as well as which of those standards should be applied. One view of ethics is simply following what codified or **positive law** requires. The test of whether an act is legal is a common moral standard used frequently in business. Codified law, or law created by governmental authority, is used as the standard for ethical behavior. Absent illegality, all behavior is ethical under this simple standard. The phrase "AS IS," on a contract (see Chapter 25 for further discussion), means by law that there are no warranties for the goods being sold. **For Example,** if a buyer purchases a used car and the phrase "AS IS" is in the contract, the seller has no legal obligation, in most states, if the transmission falls apart the day after the buyer's purchase. Following a positive law standard, the seller who refuses to repair the transmission has acted ethically. However, ethical standards are different. We know there was no legal obligation to fix the transmission, but was it fair that the car fell apart the day after it was purchased?

[1] 521 US 657 (1997).

2. The Notion of Universal Standards for Business Ethics

Another view of ethics holds that standards exist universally and cannot be changed or modified by law. In many cases, universal standards stem from religious beliefs. In some countries today, the standards for business are still determined by religious tenets. **Natural law** imposes higher standards of behavior than those required by positive law and they must be followed even if those higher standards run contrary to codified law. **For Example,** in the early nineteenth century when slavery was legally permissible in the United States, a positive law standard supported slavery. However, slavery violates the natural law principle of individual freedom and would be unethical. **Civil disobedience** is the remedy natural law proponents use to change positive law.

Former Supreme Court Justice Sandra Day O'Connor, who was second in her class at Stanford Law School (the late Chief Justice William Rehnquist was first), was offered a job as a receptionist for a law firm while her male classmates were hired as attorneys. At that time, no law prohibited discrimination against women, so law firms' hiring practices, using only a positive law standard, were ethical. However, if the natural law standard of equality is applied, the refusal to hire Sandra O'Connor as a lawyer, a position for which she was qualified, was a violation of the natural law principle of equality and unethical.

3. The Standard of Situational Business Ethics or Moral Relativism

Situational ethics or **moral relativism** is a flexible standard of ethics that considers circumstances and motivation before attaching the label of right or wrong to conduct. The classic example of moral relativism: Would it be unethical to steal a loaf of bread to feed a starving child? A question a Florida court faced was whether to go forward with the prosecution for arson of a man who set fire to an abandoned property in his neighborhood that was used as a crack-cocaine house. In both cases, the law has been broken. The first crime is theft, and the second crime is arson. Neither person, either the bread thief or the arsonist, denied committing the crime. The issue in both cases is not whether the crime was committed but whether the motivation and circumstances excuse the actions and eliminate the punishment. An employee embezzles money from her employer because she is a single parent trying to make ends meet. Was her conduct unethical? The conduct is illegal, but moral relativism would consider the employee's personal circumstances in determining whether it is ethical.

Businesses use moral relativism standards frequently in their international operations. Bribery is illegal in the United States, but, as many businesses argue, it is an accepted method of doing business in other countries.[2] The standard of moral relativism is used to allow behavior in international business transactions that would be a violation of the law in the United States. **For Example,** Google and other Internet service providers have agreed to do business in China despite the

---

natural law–a system of principles to guide human conduct independent of, and sometimes contrary to, enacted law and discovered by man's rational intelligence.

civil disobedience–the term used when natural law proponents violate positive law.

situational ethics–a flexible standard of ethics that permits an examination of circumstances and motivation before attaching the label of right or wrong to conduct.

moral relativism–takes into account motivation and circumstance to determine whether an act was ethical.

---

[2] The United States, Mexico, Korea, and most of the countries in the European Union have joined together and signed a resolution denouncing bribery, specifically noting that its practice is neither legally nor culturally accepted in their nations.

thinking things through

Corrupt Climates: Good or Bad for Business?

As you examine the following list of countries, those in the column labeled "Least Corrupt" (countries in which government officials are least likely to accept bribes) and those in the column marked

"Most Corrupt" (countries in which government officials are most likely to accept bribes), can you comment on the business climates in them?

Least Corrupt (Least Likely to Accept Bribes)		Most Corrupt (Most Likely to Accept Bribes)	
• Denmark	• Luxembourg	• Somalia	• Zimbabwe
• New Zealand	• Austria	• Myanmar	• Uzbekistan
• Sweden	• Hong Kong	• Iraq	• Turkmenistan
• Singapore	• Germany	• Haiti	• Kyrgyzstan
• Finland	• Norway	• Afghanistan	• Cambodia
• Switzerland	• Ireland	• Sudan	• Venezuela
• Iceland	• United Kingdom	• Guinea	• Sierra Leone
• Netherlands	• Belgium	• Chad	• Guinea-Bissou
• Australia	• Japan	• Equatorial Guinea	• Gambia
• Canada	• USA	• Congo, Democratic Republic	• Congo Republic

*From 2008 Transparency International annual survey, **http://www.transparency.org**.

---

restrictions the Chinese government places on the use of the Internet and the content of search engines. Such restrictions in the United States would be an unconstitutional violation of our First Amendment. In China, however, government control of information is legal. Google and others testified before Congress that some entry, however restricted, was better for the Chinese people than no access at all. Their decision weighed the conflicting values and concluded that they would use the standard of honoring the law of China despite the censorship.

4. The Business Stakeholder Standard of Behavior

Businesses have different constituencies, referred to as **stakeholders**, often with conflicting goals for the business. Shareholders, for example, may share economists' view that earnings, and hence dividends, should be maximized. Members of the community where a business is located are also stakeholders in the business and have an interest in preserving jobs. The employees of the business itself are stakeholders and certainly wish to retain their jobs. Balancing the interests of these stakeholders is a standard used in resolving ethical dilemmas in business.

As Figure 3-1 indicates, stakeholder analysis requires a view of an issue from different perspectives in the light of day. **Stakeholder analysis** requires measurement of the impact of a decision on various groups but also requires that public

stakeholders—those who have a stake, or interest, in the activities of a corporation; stakeholders include employees, members of the community in which the corporation operates, vendors, customers, and any others who are affected by the actions and decisions of the corporation.

stakeholder analysis—the term used when a decision maker views a problem from different perspectives and measures the impact of a decision on various groups.

FIGURE 3-1 | *Guidelines for Analyzing a Contemplated Action*

1. DEFINE THE PROBLEM FROM THE DECISION MAKER'S POINT OF VIEW.
2. IDENTIFY WHO COULD BE INJURED BY THE CONTEMPLATED ACTION.
3. DEFINE THE PROBLEM FROM THE OPPOSING POINT OF VIEW.
4. WOULD YOU (AS THE DECISION MAKER) BE WILLING TO TELL YOUR FAMILY, YOUR SUPERVISOR, YOUR CEO, AND THE BOARD OF DIRECTORS ABOUT THE PLANNED ACTION?
5. WOULD YOU BE WILLING TO GO BEFORE A COMMUNITY MEETING, A CONGRESSIONAL HEARING, OR A PUBLIC FORUM TO DESCRIBE THE ACTION?
6. WITH FULL CONSIDERATION OF THE FACTS AND ALTERNATIVES, REACH A DECISION ABOUT WHETHER THE CONTEMPLATED ACTION SHOULD BE TAKEN.

disclosure of that decision be defensible. The questions provide insight in a variety of situations and ethical dilemmas. For example, if a lender gives a loan to a debtor without checking income, the lapse seems harmless. But, suppose someone purchases that loan believing the debtor met the standards and the lender verified income. The debtor defaults on the loan. The purchaser has to write down or write off the loan. If enough loans that were not documented go into default, you create the kind of ripples in the real estate and stock markets that occurred in late 2008. Stakeholder analysis helps you to see that the decisions we make in business are not made in isolation or limited in their impact.

In other ethical dilemmas, a business faces the question of taking voluntary action or simply complying with the law. Some experts maintain that the shareholders' interest is paramount in resolving these conflicts among stakeholders. Others maintain that a business must assume some responsibility for social issues and their resolution. Economist Milton Friedman expresses his views on resolving the conflicts among stakeholders as follows:

A corporate executive's responsibility is to make as much money for the shareholders as possible, as long as he operates within the rules of the game. When an executive decides to take action for reasons of social responsibility, he is taking money from someone else—from the stockholders, in the form of lower dividends; from the employees, in the form of lower wages; or from the consumer, in the form of higher prices. The responsibility of the corporate executive is to fulfill the terms of his contract. If he can't do that in good conscience, then he should quit his job and find another way to do good. He has the right to promote what he regards as desirable moral objectives only with his own money.[3]

Many businesses feel an obligation to solve social problems because those problems affect their stakeholders. For example, programs such as flextime, job sharing, and telecommuting as work are not legal requirements but voluntary options businesses offer their employees to accommodate family needs. These

---

[3] "Interview: Milton Friedman," *Playboy*, February 1973. ©1973 *Playboy*.

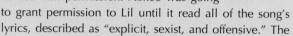

ethics & the law

Rapper Lil Wayne used lyrics from the Rolling Stones' 1965 song, "Playing With Fire," in his "Playing With Fire" song that was part of his *The Carter III* CD. Abkco Music filed an infringement suit against Lil Wayne for using the lyrics after it had denied him permission. Abkco was going to grant permission to Lil until it read all of the song's lyrics, described as "explicit, sexist, and offensive." The suit was settled when Lil Wayne agreed to remove the song from the CD and from iTunes. The Rolling Stones did not seek damages, only that the song be removed. Why did Abkco and the Rolling Stones take this position? Who are the stakeholders? Are there any constitutional issues here?

Source: Ethan Smith, "Rapper to Pull Song in Copyright Fight," *Wall Street Journal,* January 30, 2009, B8.

options are a response to larger societal issues surrounding children and their care but may also serve as a way to retain a quality workforce that is more productive without the worry of poor child care arrangements.

Some businesses are also involved in their communities through employees' volunteer work and companies' charitable donations. For example, Bill Gates, the CEO of Microsoft who is ranked as the richest man in the United States, in 2003 pledged $3 billion for fighting AIDS and providing childhood vaccine programs around the world. In 2008, corporations gave a total of $15.6 billion to charity. Overall charitable giving in the United States in 2008 reached over $300 billion for the first time. Many companies also provide support for employees to participate in volunteer programs in their communities.

B. WHY IS BUSINESS ETHICS IMPORTANT?

Ethics and values represent an important part of business success. Business ethics is important for more than the simple justification that "it's the right thing to do." This section covers the significance of ethics in business success.

5. The Importance of Trust

Capitalism succeeds because of trust. Investors provide capital for a business because they believe the business will provide a return on their investment. Customers are willing to purchase products and services from businesses because they believe the businesses will honor their commitments to deliver quality and then stand behind their product or service. Businesses are willing to purchase equipment and hire employees on the assumption that investors will continue to honor their commitment to furnish the necessary funds and will not withdraw their promises or funds. Business investment, growth, and sales are a circle of trust. Although courts provide remedies for breaches of agreements, no economy could grow if it were based solely on positive law and court-mandated performance. It is the reliance on promises, not the reliance on litigation, that produces good business relationships.

6. Business Ethics and Financial Performance

Studies centering on a business's commitment to values and its financial performance suggest that those with the strongest value systems survive and do so successfully. According to the book *Building and Growing a Business Through Good Times and Bad* by Louis Grossman and Marianne Jennings,[4] an in-depth look at companies with 100 years of consistent dividends produced a common thread: the companies' commitment to values. All firms studied had focused on high standards for product quality, employee welfare, and customer service.

Poor value choices do have an effect on financial performance. A study of the impact of just breaches of federal law by companies showed that for five years after their regulatory or legal misstep, these companies were still struggling to recover the financial performances they had achieved prior to their legal difficulties.[5]

Over the past five years, there have been devastating stories of companies' fates after ethical lapses. After Enron announced that it would restate its income because it had been spinning off its debt obligations into off-the-book-entities, its price per share dropped from $83 on January 14, 2001, to $0.67 on January 14, 2002.[6] By the time former Enron CEO Jeffrey Skilling and its former chairman, the late Kenneth Lay, were convicted of multiple federal felonies, Enron stock was trading at $0.15 per share, a figure that was up four cents from the pre-verdict value of $0.11. Columbia Health Care's share price dropped 58 percent and it experienced a 93 percent drop in earnings after it was charged with overbilling for Medicare reimbursements. Its share price dropped from $40 to $18. The nation's largest hospital chain had to spin off 100 hospitals and has paid record fines to settle the charges.[7] When the subprime lender New Century Financial announced that it was finally writing down all the subprime loans it had made that had gone into default but that it had been concealing, it was forced to declare bankruptcy because it was insolvent. On January 1, 2007, New Century had $1.75 billion in market capitalization, but by the middle of March, that figure was $55 million and its stock was delisted by the New York Stock Exchange.

Insurance broker Marsh & McLennan paid $850 million to former clients to settle price-fixing charges brought by then- New York Attorney General Eliot Spitzer. The 134-year-old company saw a drop in both its earnings (64 percent) and its share price (40 percent).[8] The financial crunch resulted in 3,000 employees losing their jobs. AIG, the insurance giant, paid $1.64 billion, the largest penalty ever by a U.S. company, to settle charges that it smoothed its earnings over time. The fine came after the company was forced to reduce its reported earnings by $1.3 billion.[9] The company also issued an apology as part of the settlement: "Providing incorrect information to the investing public and regulators was wrong and is

---

[4] Greenwood Press (2002).
[5] Melinda S. Baucus and David A. Baucus, "Paying the Piper: An Empirical Examination of Longer-Term Financial Consequences of Illegal Corporate Behavior," 40 *Academic Management Journal* 129 (1997).
[6] From stock price chart, **www.enron.com**.
[7] Lucette Lagnado, "Columbia/HCA Warns of Profit Decline," *Wall Street Journal*, September 10, 1987, A3.
[8] Ian McDonald, "After Spitzer Probe, Marsh CEO Tries Corporate Triage," *Wall Street Journal*, August 29, 2005 A1, A5.
[9] Ian McDonald and Liam Pleven, "AIG Reaches Accord with Regulators, Stock Rises But May Still Be a Bargain," *Wall Street Journal*, February 10, 2006, C1, C4.

against the values of our current leadership and employees."[10] Its $73 share price dropped to $50 before the financial reporting allegations were settled. But AIG continued to underestimate its needed reserves and losses for the subprime mortgage market it had insured. By the fall of 2008, AIG had to be rescued by the federal government with a funds bailout. The company continues to struggle as its dependence on federal funding draws attention to all of its activities.

ethics & the law

In March 2009, after it received government assistance, AIG announced the payment of $100 million in bonuses to various executives and managers in the company. There was a great hue and cry from regulators, legislators, and the public. However, AIG maintained it was contractually obligated to pay the bonuses. For a time, AIG had to cover its name on its New York office building because of public protests. The executives who received the bonuses received death threats. Evaluate the ethical issues related to the bonus payments. Evaluate the ethical issues in the public response to those bonuses. Be sure to discuss AIG's argument on the legal requirements for the bonuses.

7. The Importance of A Good Reputation

Richard Teerlink, the CEO of Harley-Davidson, once said, "A reputation, good or bad, is tough to shake."[11] A breach of ethics is costly to a firm not only in the financial sense of drops in earnings and possible fines. A breach of ethics also often carries with it a lasting memory that affects the business and its sales for years to come. **For Example,** the Peanut Corporation of America had to declare bankruptcy in 2009 after government officials discovered that its plant was the source of salmonella poisonings among those customers who had eaten peanut products that used Peanut Corporation's product as their base. Records showed that Peanut Corporation continued to produce the product even after salmonella warnings and questions arose. The company's name and image became so damaged that it could not continue to make sales. When an ethical breach occurs, businesses lose that component of trust important to customers' decisions to buy and invest.

8. Business Ethics and Business Regulation: Public Policy, Law, and Ethics

When business behavior results in complaints from employees, investors, or customers, laws or regulations are often used to change the behavior. **For Example,** the bankruptcy of Lehman Brothers, the near-collapse of Bear Stearns, and the losses

---

[10] Gretchen Morgenson, "AIG Apologizes and Agrees to $1.64 Billion Settlement," *New York Times,* February 10, 2006, C1, C5.

[11] David K. Wright, *The Harley-Davidson Motor Co.: An Official Ninety-Year History* (Milwaukee: Motorbook International, 1993).

at Merrill Lynch and AIG in 2008-2009 all resulted from the subprime mortgage financial derivative investment market, a market that had previously been a relatively regulation-free environment. The companies had billions of dollars of exposure because of their sales and purchases of financial instruments that were tied to the subprime mortgage market that ultimately resulted in high rates of foreclosure and nearly worthless loans. Congress, the Securities and Exchange Commission (SEC), and the Federal Reserve all stepped in to regulate virtually all aspects of mortgage transactions, including the lenders and others who were involved in packaging the loans into financial products.

Confusion among consumers about car leasing and its true costs and the fees applicable at the end of the lease terms caused the Federal Reserve to expand its regulation of credit to car leases. Figure 3-2 depicts the relationships among ethics, the social forces of customers and investors, and the laws that are passed to remedy the problems raised as part of the social forces movement.

From the nutrition facts that appear on food packages to the type of pump at the gas station, government regulation of business activity is evident. Legislation and regulation are responses to activities of businesses that are perfectly legal but raise questions of fairness that cause customer and investor protests.

Businesses that act voluntarily on the basis of value choices often avoid the costs and the sometimes arbitrariness of legislation and regulation. Voluntary change by businesses is less costly and is considered less intrusive.

Businesses that respond to social forces and the movements of the cycle of societal interaction often gain a competitive advantage. Businesses that act irresponsibly and disregard society's views and desire for change speed the transition from value choice to enforceable law. Businesses should watch the cycle of social forces and follow trends there to understand the values attached to certain activities and

FIGURE 3-2 | *The Endless Cycle of Societal Interaction*

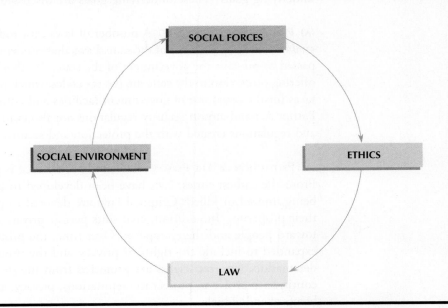

ethics & the law

Ethics, Trust, and Markets

The cover of *Fortune* magazine from May 14, 2001, featured a picture of Wall Street financial analyst Mary Meeker and the words, "Can we ever trust again?"* The inside story focused on the relationship of underwriters, analysts, and brokerage houses with the high-tech companies whose stocks they were touting and selling. They had continued to pump the virtues of stock shares they knew had overinflated prices. When the dot-com market bubble burst, the losses to shareholders were catastrophic. The analysts, underwriters, and brokers had not violated the law. Those in the financial markets had too much at stake to be honest with investors.

In 2002, when companies beyond the dot-coms, such as Enron, WorldCom, and Tyco, experienced write-downs for some fairly creative accounting practices gone awry, the market once again looked at

analysts, wondering how they had failed to catch the accounting issues. The cover of *Fortune* read, "In Search of the Last Honest Analyst."**

During 2007, *Fortune* ran a cover with the pictures of the CEOs of the major Wall Street investment firms (such as Merrill Lynch, Bear Stearns, and Lehman Brothers) who had managed to lose trillions of investors' pension and 401 (k) plans to risky investments in subprime mortgages that were marketed as low-risk investments. The cover's headline asked, "What Were They Smoking?"***

What do the covers of this business magazine convey about the importance of trust and its role in markets?

* "Can We Ever Trust Again?" *Fortune*, May 14, 2000 (cover).

** "In Search of the Last Honest Analyst," *Fortune*, June 10, 2002 (cover).

*** Cover, *Fortune*, November 26, 2007.

responses. These values motivate change either in the form of voluntary business activity or legislation. All values that precipitate change have one of several basic underlying goals. These underlying goals are discussed in the following sections.

(A) PROTECTION OF THE STATE. A number of laws exist today because of the underlying goal or value of protection of the state. Laws that condemn treason are examples of laws passed to preserve the government of the state. Another less dramatic set of laws offering protection to the state are the tax codes, which provide authority for collecting taxes for the operation of government facilities and enforcement agencies. The U.S Patriot Act and airport security regulations are also examples of government programs and regulations created with the protection and security of the state as the goal.

(B) PROTECTION OF THE PERSON. A second social force is protection of the person. From the earliest times, laws have been developed to protect the individual from being injured or killed. Criminal laws are devoted to protection of individuals and their properties. In addition, civil suits permit private remedies for wrongful acts toward people and their property. Over time, the protection of personal rights has expanded to include the rights of privacy and the protection of individuals from defamation. Contract rights are protected from interference by others. Laws continue to evolve to protect the reputations, privacy, and mental and physical well-being of individuals.

(c) PROTECTION OF PUBLIC HEALTH, SAFETY, AND MORALS. Food-labeling regulations are an example of laws grounded in the value of protecting the safety and health of individuals. Food and restaurant inspections, mandatory inoculation, speed limits on roadways, mandatory smoke detectors and sprinkler systems in hotels, and prohibitions on the sale of alcohol to minors are all examples of laws based on the value of safety for the public. Zoning laws that prohibit the operation of adult bookstores and movie theaters near schools and churches are examples of laws based on moral values.

(d) PROTECTION OF PROPERTY: ITS USE AND TITLE. Someone who steals another's automobile is a thief and is punished by law with fines and/or imprisonment. A zoning law that prohibits the operation of a steel mill in a residential area also provides protection for property. A civil suit brought to recover royalties lost because of another's infringement of one's copyrighted materials is based on federal laws that afford protection for property rights in nontangible or intellectual property (see Chapter 10). Laws afford protection of title for all forms of property. The deed recorded in the land record is the legal mechanism for protecting the owner's title. The copyright on a software program or a song protects the creator's rights in that intellectual property. The title documents issued by a department of motor vehicles afford protection of title for the owner of a vehicle.

Those who have title to property are generally free to use the property in any manner they see fit. However, even ownership has restrictions imposed by law. A landowner cannot engage in activities on his property that damage another's land or interfere with another's use of land. A business may operate a factory on its real property, but if the factory creates a great deal of pollution, adjoining landowners may successfully establish it as a nuisance (see Chapter 49) that interferes with their use and enjoyment of their land. The law affords remedies for such a nuisance that might include an injunction, or court order, limiting the hours of the factory's operation or requiring scrubbers on the emissions towers.. Environmental laws also emerged as regulation of land use in response to concerns about legal, but harmful, emissions by companies.

(e) PROTECTION OF PERSONAL RIGHTS. The desire for individual freedom to practice religion and to enjoy freedom from political domination gave rise to the colonization of the United States and, eventually, the American Revolution. The desire for freedom from economic domination resulted in the free enterprise philosophy that exists in the United States today. Individual freedoms and personal rights continue as a focus of value discussions followed by legislation if those individual rights are violated.

(f) ENFORCEMENT OF INDIVIDUAL INTENT. When we voluntarily enter into a contract, we have a responsibility to fulfill the promises made in that agreement. Principles of honesty and the honoring of commitments are the ethical values at the heart of the parties' conduct in carrying out contracts. If, however, the parties do not keep their promises, the law does enforce transactions through sets of rules governing requirements for them. **For Example,** the law will carry out the intentions of the parties to a business transaction.

Laws exist to honor the intent of parties because not all commitments are fulfilled voluntarily. The law may impose requirements that a transaction or agreement be in writing to ensure that the intent of the parties is adequately documented and fulfilled (see Chapter 17). The law may also place restrictions on honoring intentions. A contract to commit a murder may be evidenced by intent and fully documented in writing. However, the intent of the parties will not be honored because of the social values manifested in the protection of individuals and individuals' rights and safety.

(G) PROTECTION FROM EXPLOITATION, FRAUD, AND OPPRESSION. Many laws have evolved because businesses took advantage of another group. The law has given some groups or individuals protection because of excesses by businesses in dealing with them. Minors, or persons under legal age (see Chapter 14), are given special protections under contract laws that permit them to disaffirm their contracts so they are not disadvantaged by excessive commitments without the benefit of the wisdom of age and with the oppressive presence of an adult party.

The federal laws on disclosure in the sales of securities and shareholder relations (see Chapters 45 and 46) were developed following the 1929 stock market crash when many investors lost all they had because of the lack of candor and information by the businesses in which they were investing.

(H) FURTHERANCE OF TRADE. Some laws are the result of social forces seeking to simplify business and trade. Installment sales and credit transactions, and their accompanying laws and regulations, have made additional capital available for businesses and provided consumers with alternatives to cash purchases. The laws on checks, drafts, and notes have created instruments used to facilitate trade.

(I) PROTECTION OF CREDITORS AND REHABILITATION OF DEBTORS. Society seeks to protect the rights of creditors and to protect them from dishonest or fraudulent acts of debtors. Statutes that make it a fraud for a debtor to conceal property from a creditor also protect creditors. Mortgages, security interests, and surety relationships (see Chapters 32, 34, and 49) are mechanisms created by law to provide creditors the legal mechanisms for collecting their obligations.

When collection techniques became excessive and exploitative, new laws on debtors' rights were enacted. Debtors' prisons were abolished. Congress mandated disclosure requirements for credit contracts. The Fair Debt Collections Practices Act (see Chapter 33) limited collection techniques. The remedy of bankruptcy was afforded debtors under federal law to provide them an opportunity to begin a new economic life when their existing debts reached an excessive level and could no longer be paid in a timely fashion (see Chapter 35).

(J) STABILITY AND FLEXIBILITY. Stability is particularly important in business transactions. When you buy a house, for example, you want to know not only what the exact meaning of the transaction is under today's law but also that the transaction will have the same meaning in the future.

Because of the desire for stability, courts will ordinarily follow former decisions unless there is a strong reason to depart from them. Similarly, when no former case bears on the point involved, a court will try to reach a decision that is a logical extension of some former decision or that follows a former decision by analogy rather than strike out on a new path to reach a decision unrelated to the past.

The typical modern statute, particularly in the area of business regulation, often contains an escape clause by which a person can "escape" from the operation of the statute under certain circumstances. **For Example,** a rent control law may impose a rent ceiling, that is, a maximum rent a landlord can charge a tenant. The same law may also authorize a higher charge when special circumstances make it just and fair to allow such an exception. For example, the landlord may have made expensive repairs to the property or taxes on the property may have increased substantially.

C. How to Recognize and Resolve Ethical Dilemmas

Business managers often find themselves in circumstances in which they are unclear about right and wrong and are confused about how to resolve the dilemmas they face. A recent survey showed that 98 percent of all Fortune 500 companies have codes of ethics designed to help their employees recognize and resolve ethical dilemmas. Nearly 90 percent of those firms provide their employees some form of training in ethics.[12] Almost 80 percent of companies now have an ethics officer. These codes of ethics provide employees information about categories of behavior that constitute ethical breaches. Regardless of the industry, the type of business, or the size of the company, certain universal categories can help managers recognize ethical dilemmas. Figure 3-3 provides a list of those categories.

9. Categories of Ethical Behavior

(A) Integrity and Truthfulness. Mark Twain once wrote, "Always tell the truth. That way you don't have to remember anything." As discussed earlier, trust is a key component of business relationships and of the free enterprise system. Trust begins

FIGURE 3-3 | *Categories of Ethical Behavior*

1. INTEGRITY AND TRUTHFULNESS
2. PROMISE KEEPING
3. LOYALTY—AVOIDING CONFLICTS OF INTEREST
4. FAIRNESS
5. DOING NO HARM
6. MAINTAINING CONFIDENTIALITY

[12] Survey of the Society for Human Resource Management and Ethics Resource Center (2005).

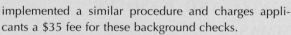

ethics&the law

Lying to Get into a Top School

The University of California at Berkeley has implemented a new step in its admission process. The Haas School of Business has begun running background checks on students who have applied to determine whether the information in their applications is correct. The Wharton School implemented a similar procedure and charges applicants a $35 fee for these background checks.

Of the 100 students admitted to Berkeley in the fall of 2003, 5 students were found to have offered false information on their admissions applications. The most common type of false information was the job titles they held, and the second most common type was their number of years of work experience. Haas admissions officers indicated that had the students not lied, they otherwise met the GMAT score and GPA standards for admission to Haas.

What risk do the students take in lying on their applications? What are the long-term consequences?

Source: "Cheaters Don't Make the Grade at Berkeley Business School," **www.azcentral.com**, March 14, 2003, AP wire reports.

---

with the belief that honesty is at the heart of relationships. Many contract remedies in law are based on the failure of the parties to be truthful with each other. If you purchase a home that has been certified as termite free but you discover termites in the home shortly after you move in, someone has not been truthful. If you also discover that two termite inspections were conducted and that the first one, which revealed there were termites, was concealed from you, your trust in both the sellers and their exterminators is diminished.

An assurance that a seller has the expertise to handle your project is important in building that relationship. If you discover later that the seller lacks the expertise, you are harmed by the delay and possible poor work that has been done. Investors become skeptical when offerings do not carry with them a very basic level of honesty in their disclosures. Honesty is necessary for the wheels of commerce to turn.

integrity–the adherence to one's values and principles despite the costs and consequences.

Integrity is the adherence to one's values and principles despite the costs and consequences. **For Example,** an executive contracted with a variety of companies to sell his hard-to-find computer components. When he was approached by one of his largest customers to break a contract with a small customer, the executive refused. The customer assured the executive it would be his last order with the company if he did not get more components. Despite facing the threat of losing a multimillion-dollar customer, the executive fulfilled his promises to the small purchasers. The executive kept his word on all of his contracts and demonstrated integrity.

(B) PROMISE KEEPING. If we examine the types of things we do in a day, we would find that most of them are based on promises. We promise to deliver goods either with or without a contract. We promise to pay the dentist for our dental work. We promise to provide someone with a ride. Keeping those promises, regardless of whether there is a legal obligation to do so, is a key component of

sports & entertainment law

Image, Morals, and Cereal

Olympic champion Michael Phelps was photographed apparently smoking a bong pipe at a party at the University of South Carolina. When the picture made its way onto the Internet, the companies that carry Mr. Phelps's image for their products were listed on the Internet. Those companies include the following:

- Kellogg's
- Subway*
- Speedo
- Visa

- Omega
- PureSport
- 505 Games*
- Mazda (China only)

After the picture appeared, Kellogg's canceled its contract with Mr. Phelps. What legal right would a company have to cancel its agreement with Mr. Phelps? What is a "morals clause" and how is it used?

* Indicates that endorsement was signed after the Olympics.

being an ethical person and practicing ethical business. Keeping promises is also evidence of integrity.

The issue of employee downsizing is debated with the underlying question of whether the downsized employees had a promise from their company of continued employment. As we consider stakeholder analysis the ethical issue surrounding the question is whether there are promises to others who are at risk. Weren't shareholders promised a return on their investment? Weren't suppliers promised payment? In many circumstances, the question is not *whether* a promise will be kept but rather *which* promise will be kept. The strategic issue is whether businesses should make commitments and promises in circumstances that create a very thin margin of profit and perhaps even thinner margin for error. Over the long term, the importance of a company's keeping its promises to all stakeholders translates into its reputation.

(c) LOYALTY—AVOIDING CONFLICTS OF INTEREST. An employee who works for a company owes allegiance to that company. Conduct that compromises that loyalty is a **conflict of interest**. **For Example,** suppose that your sister operates her own catering business. Your company is seeking a caterer for its monthly management meetings. You are responsible for these meetings and could hire your sister to furnish the lunches for the meetings. Your sister would have a substantial contract, and your problems with meal logistics would be solved. Nearly all companies have a provision in their codes of ethics covering this situation. An employee cannot hire a relative, friend, or even her own company without special permission because it is a conflict of interest. Your loyalty to your sister conflicts with the loyalty to your employer, which requires you to make the best decision at the best price.

conflict of interest– conduct that compromises an employee's allegiance to that company.

A conflict of interest arises when a purchasing agent accepts gifts from suppliers, vendors, or manufacturers' representatives. The purchasing agent has introduced into the buy-sell relationship an element of *quid pro quo,* or the supplier's expectation that the gift will bring about a return from the agent in the form of a contract. Some companies have zero tolerance for conflicts and establish a complete prohibition on employees accepting any gifts from suppliers and manufacturers. **For Example,** Wal-Mart buyers are not permitted to accept even a cup of coffee from potential merchandise suppliers, and Amgen's buyers can go out to dinner with a supplier only if Amgen pays.

(D) FAIRNESS. In business transactions in which the buyer was not told about the crack in the engine block or the dry well on the property, a typical response is "That's not fair. I wouldn't have bought it if I'd known." A question often posed to the buyer in response is "Wouldn't you have done the same thing?" We feel differently about such situations, depending on whether we are the victims of unfairness or whether we hold the superior knowledge in the transaction. The ethical standard of fairness requires both sides to ask these questions: "How would I want to be treated? Would this information make a difference to me?" Imposing our own standards and expectations on our own behavior in business transactions produces fairness in business.

(E) DOING NO HARM. Imagine selling a product that your company's internal research shows presents significant health dangers to its users. Selling the product without disclosure of the information is unfair. There is the additional ethical breach of physical harm to your customers and users. Ford designed and sold its Pinto with a fundamental flaw in the placement of the car's gas tank. Rear-end collisions in which a Pinto was involved resulted, even at very low speeds, in fires that engulfed the car so quickly that occupants could not always escape from it. An internal memo from engineers at Ford revealed that employees had considered doing an analysis of the risk of the tanks versus the cost of redesign but never did. The late Peter Drucker's advice on ethics for businesses is ***primum non nocere***, or "above all, do no harm." Such a rule might have helped Ford.

***primum non nocere*–**above all do no harm.

(F) MAINTAINING CONFIDENTIALITY. Often the success of a business depends on the information or technology that it holds. If the competitive edge that comes from the business's peculiar niche or knowledge is lost through disclosure, so are its profits. Employees not only owe a duty of loyalty to their employers, but they also owe an obligation of confidentiality. Employees should not use, either personally or through a competitor, information they have obtained through their employer's work or research. Providing customer lists or leads is a breach of employees' obligation of confidentiality.

In addition, managers have responsibilities regarding their employees' privacy. Performance evaluations of individual employees are private and should never be disclosed or revealed, even in one-on-one conversations outside the lines of authority and the workplace.

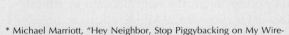

e-commerce&cyberlaw

Piggybacking on Wireless Networks

A new issue that has evolved because of technology could require legal steps to stop it. People are "piggybacking" or tapping onto their neighbors' wireless Internet connection. The original subscriber pays a monthly fee for the service, but without security, people located in the area are able to tap into the wireless network, which bogs down the speed of the service. Once limited to geeks and hackers, the practice is now common among the ordinary folk who just want free Internet service.

One college student said, "I don't think it's stealing. I always find people out there who aren't protecting their connection, so I just feel free to go ahead and use it."* According to a recent survey, only about 30 percent of the 4,500 wireless networks onto which the surveyors logged were encrypted.

An apartment dweller said she leaves her connection wide open because "I'm sticking it to the man. I open up my network, leave it wide open for anyone to jump on." One of the users of another's wireless network said, "I feel sort of bad about it, but I do it anyway. It just seems harmless." She said that if she gets caught, "I'm a grandmother. They're not going to yell at an old lady. I'll just play the dumb card."

Some neighbors offer to pay those with wireless service in exchange for their occasional use rather than paying a wireless company for full-blown service. However, the original subscribers do not really want to run their own Internet service.

Do you think we need new legislation to cover this activity? What do you think of the users' statements? Is their conduct legal? Is it ethical?

---

* Michael Marriott, "Hey Neighbor, Stop Piggybacking on My Wireless," *New York Times*, March 5, 2006, A1, A23.

10. Resolving Ethical Dilemmas

Recognizing an ethical dilemma is perhaps the easiest part of business ethics. Resolution of that dilemma is more difficult. The earlier section on stakeholders offers one model for resolution of ethical dilemmas (see Figure 3-1). Other models have been developed to provide managers analytical methods for resolving dilemmas in a timely fashion.

(A) BLANCHARD AND PEALE THREE-PART TEST. Dr. Kenneth Blanchard, author of books on the *One-Minute Manager,* and the late Dr. Norman Vincent Peale developed a model for evaluating ethical breaches that is widely used among Fortune 500 companies.[13] To evaluate situations, ask the following three questions: Is it legal? Is it balanced? How does it make me feel?

In answering the questions on legality, a manager should look to positive law both within and outside the company. If the proposed conduct would violate antitrust laws, the manager's analysis can stop there. If the proposed conduct would violate company policy, the manager's analysis can stop. In the field of business ethics, there is little room for civil disobedience. Compliance with the law is a critical component of a successful ethics policy in any company.

---

[13] Kenneth Blanchard and Norman Vincent Peale, *The Power of Ethical Management* (New York: William Morrow, 1986).

The second question on balance forces the manager to examine the ethical value of fairness. Perhaps the decision to downsize must be made, but couldn't the company offer the employees a severance package and outplacement assistance to ease the transition?

The final question of the Blanchard and Peale model is conscience based. Although some managers may employ any tactics to maximize profits, this final question forces a manager to examine the physical impact of a decision: Does it cause sleeplessness or appetite changes? Personalizing business choices often helps managers to see the potential harm that comes from poor ethical choices.

(B) THE FRONT-PAGE-OF-THE-NEWSPAPER TEST. This simple but effective model for ethical evaluation helps a manager visualize the public disclosure of proposed conduct. When he temporarily took over as the leader of Salomon Brothers after its bond-trading controversy, Warren Buffett described the newspaper test as follows:

Contemplating any business act, an employee should ask himself whether he would be willing to see it immediately described by an informed and critical reporter on the front page of his local paper, there to be read by his spouse, children, and friends. At Salomon, we simply want no part of any activities that pass legal tests but that we, as citizens, would find offensive. [14]

(C) LAURA NASH MODEL. In her work, business ethicist Laura Nash has developed a series of questions to help businesspeople reach the right decision in ethical dilemmas. These are her questions: Have you defined the problem accurately? How would you define the problem if you stood on the other side of the fence? How did this situation occur in the first place? What is your intention in making this decision? How does the intention compare with the probable results? Whom could your decision or action injure? Can you discuss your decision with the affected parties? Are you confident that your position will be as valid over a long period of time as it seems now? Could you discuss your decision with your supervisor, coworkers, officers, board, friends, and family?

The Nash model requires an examination of the dilemma from all perspectives. Defining the problem and how the problem arose provides the business assistance in avoiding the dilemma again. **For Example,** suppose that a supervisor is asked to provide a reference for a friend who works for her. The supervisor is hesitant because the friend has not been a very good employee. The ethical dilemma the manager believes she faces is whether to lie or tell the truth about the employee. The real ethical dilemma is why the supervisor never provided evaluation or feedback indicating the friend's poor performance. Avoiding the problem in the future is possible through candid evaluations. Resolving the problem requires that the supervisor talk to her friend now about the issue of performance and the problem with serving as a reference.

One final aspect of the Nash model that businesspeople find helpful is a question that asks for a perspective on an issue from family and friends. The problem of groupthink in business situations is very real. As businesspeople sit together in a room and discuss an ethical dilemma, they can persuade each other to think the same way. The power of consensus can overwhelm each person's concerns and values. There is a

---

[14] Janet Lowe, *Warren Buffett Speaks: Wit and Wisdom from the World's Greatest Investor* (New York: Wiley, 1997).

ethics&the law

Burger King, Coke, and Numbers

Coca-Cola has admitted that it paid a consultant $10,000 to drive up the demand for its Frozen Coke beverage being test-marketed in Burger Kings in the Richmond, Virginia, area. The consultant used the money to make donations to Boys and Girls Clubs. The clubs then provided meal  coupons to the children in exchange for them doing their homework. The impressive demand that resulted from the Richmond area test market led Burger King to invest $65 million to put the machines in restaurants around the country. However, the demand was not what it had been falsely alleged to be, and the result is that, following a six-week investigation by a law firm hired by the Coca-Cola board, Coca-Cola admitted that the marketing studies were inflated.

The board investigation followed an allegation in a lawsuit filed by a former employee, Matthew Whitley. Whitley was terminated following his questioning of an expense claim by the consultant and his resulting investigation that produced an internal memo describing the consultant's work on driving up the demand.

Coca-Cola also issued an earnings restatement of $9 million based on an investigation of those allegations. The *Wall Street Journal* was following the Whitley lawsuit when the underlying issues emerged, and it reported the marketing scheme.* Coca-Cola settled with Burger King by paying $21 million.

Was this conduct ethical? Was it fraud? What does Mr. Whitley's termination say about the company? Does he have protection? Why do you think the marketing managers decided to involve the consultant and report the false demand? What effect does this incident have on Burger King's relationship with Coke? How do you think the story played on the front page of the *Wall Street Journal?***

---

* Chad Terhune, "Coke Employees Acted Improperly in Marketing Test," *Wall Street Journal*, June 18, 2003, A3, A6;Sherri Day, "Coke Confirms Product Test Was Rigged," *New York Times*, June 18, 2003, C1, C10.

** Marianne Jennings, one of the authors of this text, has done consulting work for Coca-Cola since this incident. Why is this disclosure important?

---

certain fear in bringing up a different point of view in a business meeting. Proper perspective is often lost as the discussion centers around numbers. Therefore, bringing in the views of an outsider is often helpful. For example, when McNeil, the manufacturer of Tylenol, faced the cyanide poisonings from contaminated capsules sold in the Chicago area, it had to make a decision about the existing Tylenol inventory. It was clear to both insiders and outsiders that the poison had not been put in the capsules at McNeil but after delivery to the stores. Despite the huge numbers involved in the recall and the destruction of inventory, the McNeil managers made the decision easily because they viewed the risk to their own families, that is, from the outside. From this standpoint, the issue became a question of human life, not of numbers.[15]

(D) *WALL STREET JOURNAL* MODEL. The *Wall Street Journal* presented a simple, three-prong test for resolving ethical dilemmas known as the three-C model: (1) Will this conduct be in compliance with the law? (2) What contribution does this decision make to the shareholders? To the community? To the employees? (3) What are the consequences of this decision? This model requires an examination of the impact of a choice, which then produces a different perspective on a course of conduct.

---

[15] "Brief History of Johnson & Johnson" (company pamphlet, 1992).

For Example, Sears paid $475 million in fines and penalties for its unauthorized collection of debts from debtors who were in bankruptcy or had debts discharged in bankruptcy. Such collection beyond what the law allows did not comply with the law.[16] The contribution to the company was more collections and hence more cash, but the consequences were the large fine and the damage to Sears's reputation for putting its interests above the law and above the interests of other creditors who conducted themselves within the limits of the bankruptcy law. Sears may have resented the fact that debtors had not paid, but the company was not justified in taking the law into its own hands or profiting at the expense of other creditors.

lawflix

Breaking Away (1979) (PG)

In this story about "cutters" (a nickname for natives of Bloomington, Indiana), a recent high school graduate trains to be a first-class bike rider. He idolizes the Italian world racing team and enters an Indiana race to have the opportunity to compete with them. He does well in the race and manages to catch up and keep pace with the Italian team. As he rides alongside his idols, one of the members of the Italian team places a tire pump in his spoke. His bike crashes, he loses the race and is injured. He becomes disillusioned. Is this experience like business? Do unethical tactics get you ahead? Do nice guys finish last? Are there sanctions for unethical conduct?

Jaws (1975) (PG 13)

The movie that shot Steven Spielberg to directorial legend brings us the classic business dilemma of what to do when you have a high-risk/low-probability event that you know about but about which the public has no knowledge. Do you stop? But what about the economic losses?

Hoosiers (1986) (PG)

Often called the "greatest sports movie ever made," this story of a coach with a history and a small-town team presents several life-defining ethical moments. In one, with advancement to the finals on the table, Coach Norman Dale grapples with whether he should allow one of his injured players to continue when he has no depth on his bench. What do you do when your values are in conflict?

The Family Man (2000) (PG 13)

Nicolas Cage plays a Wall Street billionaire who is suddenly given a suburban life in New Jersey with all of its family life and financial constraints. He is forced to examine who he really is and what is important.

You can view a clip of these movies and others that illustrate business law concepts at the LawFlix site, located at **www.cengage.com/blaw/dvl**.

---

[16] Leslie Kaufman, "Sears Settles Suit on Raising of Its Credit Card Rates," *New York Times*, March 11, 1999, C2.

MAKE THE CONNECTION

SUMMARY

Business ethics is the application of values and standards to business conduct and decisions. These values originate in various sources from positive (codified) law to natural law to stakeholder values. Business ethics is important because trust is a critical component of good business relationships and free enterprise. A business with values will enjoy the additional competitive advantage of a good reputation and, over the long term, better earnings. When businesses make decisions that violate basic ethical standards, they set into motion social forces and cause the area of abuse to be regulated, resulting in additional costs and restrictions for business. Voluntary value choices by businesses position them for a competitive advantage.

The categories of ethical values in business are truthfulness and integrity, promise keeping, loyalty and avoiding conflicts of interest, fairness, doing no harm, and maintaining confidentiality.

Resolution of ethical dilemmas is possible through the use of various models that require a businessperson to examine the impact of a decision before it is made. These models include stakeholder analysis, the Blanchard and Peale test, the front-page-of-the-newspaper test, the Laura Nash model, and the *Wall Street Journal* model.

LEARNING OUTCOMES

After studying this chapter, you should be able to clearly explain:

A. WHAT IS BUSINESS ETHICS?

LO.1 Define business ethics

    See the discussion of the definition, balancing the goal of profits with the values of individuals and society, on p. 40.

B. WHY IS BUSINESS ETHICS IMPORTANT?

LO.2 Discuss why ethics are important in business

    See "The Importance of Trust" on p. 44.

    See "Business Ethics and Financial Performance" on p. 45.

    See "The Importance of a Good Reputation" on p. 46.

C. HOW TO RECOGNIZE AND RESOLVE ETHICAL DILEMMAS

LO.3 Describe how to recognize and resolve ethical dilemmas

    See "Integrity and Truthfulness" on p. 51

    See "Promise Keeping" on p. 52

    See "Loyalty—Avoiding Conflicts of Interest" on p. 53.

    See "Fairness" on p. 54.

    See "Doing No Harm" on p. 54.

    See "Maintaining Confidentiality" on p. 54.

    See "Resolving Ethical Dilemmas" on p. 55.

    See "Blanchard and Peale Three-Part Test" on p. 55.

See "The Front-Page-of-the-Newspaper Test" on p. 56.
See "Laura Nash Model" on p. 56.
See "*Wall Street Journal* Model" on p. 57.

KEY TERMS

business ethics	integrity	*primum non nocere*
civil disobedience	moral relativism	situational ethics
conflict of interest	natural law	stakeholder analysis
ethics	positive law	stakeholders

QUESTIONS AND CASE PROBLEMS

1. Marty Mankamyer, the president of the United States Olympic Committee (USOC), resigned in early February 2003 following reports in *The Denver Post* that indicated she had demanded a commission from a fellow real estate broker in the Colorado Springs area, the home of the USOC, who had sold property to Lloyd Ward, the CEO of the USOC. Mr. Ward had purchased a 1.3-acre lot in Colorado Springs for $475,000 and had paid the listing broker, Brigette Ruskin, a commission. Ms. Mankamyer allegedly demanded a portion of the commission from Ms. Ruskin, and Ms. Ruskin sent her a check. Ms. Mankamyer had shown Mr. Ward and his wife properties in the area when they were being considered for the job and when he was considering taking the job. However, Mrs. Ward indicated that Ms. Mankamyer did not identify herself as a real estate agent and that she assumed that Ms. Mankamyer was showing the properties as a "goodwill gesture."[17] What conflicts of interest do you see here?

2. Ann Elkin, who works for Brill Co., has been sent out to conduct two customer evaluations, which have gone much more quickly than Ann anticipated. Her supervisor does not expect Ann back until after lunch. It is now 10:30 A.M., and Ann would like to run some personal errands and then go to lunch before returning to work at 1:00 P.M. Should Ann take the time? Would you? Why or why not? Be sure to consider the categories of ethical values and apply one or two models before reaching your conclusion.

3. Fred Sanguine is a New York City produce broker. Ned Santini is a 19-year-old college student who works for Sanguine from 4:00 A.M. until 7:00 A.M. each weekday before he attends classes at Pace University. Fred has instructed Ned on the proper packing of produce as follows: "Look, put the bad and small cherries at the bottom. Do the same with the strawberries and blueberries. Put the best fruit on top and hide the bad stuff at the bottom. This way I get top dollar on all that I sell." Ned is uncomfortable about the instructions, but, as he explains to his roommate, "It's not me doing it. I'm just following orders. Besides, I need the job." Should Ned just follow instructions? Is the manner in

---

[17] Richard Sandomir, "U.S. Olympic Chief Resigns in a Furor Over Ethics Issues," *New York Times*, February 5, 2003, A1, C17; Bill Briggs, *Realtor Waving Red Flag*, **www.denverpost.com**, February 4, 2003.

which the fruit is packed unethical? Would you do it? Why or why not? Is anyone really harmed by the practice?

4. Alan Gellen is the facilities manager for the city of Milwaukee and makes all final decisions on purchasing items such as chairs, lights, and other supplies and materials. Alan also makes the final decisions for the award of contracts to food vendors at event sites. Grand Beef Franks has submitted a bid to be one of the city's vendors. Alan went to school with Grand Beef's owner, Steve Grand, who phones Alan and explains that Grand Beef owns a condominium in Maui that Alan could use. Steve's offer to Alan is: "All it would cost you for a vacation is your airfare. The condo is fully stocked with food. Just let me know." Should Alan take the offer? Would you? Be sure to determine which category of ethical values this situation involves and to apply several models as you resolve the question of whether Alan should accept the invitation.

5. Television network CNBC and other television networks have been working to develop policies for their business correspondents and guests on their business shows because of a practice known as *pump-and-dump,* the practice of a Wall Street professional or network business correspondent appearing on television to tout a particular stock as being a good buy. Often, unbeknown to the viewing audience, the guest or correspondent promoting the stock has a large holding in it and, after the television show runs and the stock price creeps up, sells his or her interest at a higher price than would have been possible before the show on which the person raved about the stock. What category of ethical issue exists here? If you were a network executive, what would you do to remedy the problem? Could the government regulate such practices? What kind of regulation could it impose?

6. Adam Smith wrote the following in *The Theory of Moral Sentiments:*

   In the practice of the other virtues, our conduct should rather be directed by a certain idea of propriety, by a certain taste for a particular tenor of conduct, than by any regard to a precise maxim or rule; and we should consider the end and foundation of the rule, more than the rule itself.[18]

   Do you think Adam Smith adhered to positive law as his ethical standard? Was he a moral relativist? Does his quote match stakeholder analysis? What would his ethical posture be on violating the law?

7. A new phenomenon for admissions to MBA programs is hiring consultants to help applicants hone their applications. About 20 percent of those who apply to the top MBA programs have hired consultants at a cost of $150 to $200 per hour to help them say and do the right things to be admitted. The total cost for most who use a consultant is $5,000. The consultants help with personal essays and applications. One admissions officer points out that one function of the consultant is to draw out and emphasize skills that the applicant may not see as important. For example, playing the piano is looked upon favorably because it shows discipline and focus. However, admissions committees are becoming adept at spotting the applications via consultant because, as the faculty describe

---

[18] Adam Smith, *The Theory of Moral Sentiments* (Arlington House, 1969; originally published in 1769).

it, these essays and applications have a certain "sameness" to them. The Fuqua School at North Carolina suggests that students simply call the admissions office and get comparable advice for free. Is it ethical to use an admissions consultant? When would you cross a line in using the consultant on the essay?

8. Oprah Winfrey named James Frey's autobiographical book, *A Million Little Pieces,* to her television book club. The impact of the book's inclusion in the Oprah Book Club was the sale of 10 million copies, making it the fastest-selling book in the club's history. The book allegedly addressed Mr. Frey's addictions and recovery. However, on January 8, 2006, the Web site The Smoking Gun found significant and multiple discrepancies between Frey's accounts of his life experiences in the book and what really happened. For example, Frey wrote that he spent 87 days in prison. In reality, he spent 3 hours. When the discrepancies initially emerged, Ms. Winfrey defended Mr. Frey, saying the book was the "essential truth" about his life. She also called the controversy "much ado about nothing."

   The public reaction was different, and Ms. Winfrey had Mr. Frey on her show, or, as some critics labeled it, "had him into the woodshed." Ms. Winfrey told Mr. Frey, "I feel really duped. You betrayed millions of readers. Why would you lie?"

   In the week following his Oprah appearance, Mr. Frey sold 50,000 copies of *A Million Little Pieces*, but the publisher for his next book canceled his contract. However, Mr. Frey rebounded and found another publisher for a book released in 2008. Was there truthfulness in his book? Mr. Frey said the book was a "creative novel memoir" that had not been intended to be autobiographical. Does this clarification help? Were Mr. Frey's actions ethical? Evaluate Ms. Winfrey's initial response.

9. The state of Arizona mandates emissions testing for cars before drivers can obtain updated registrations. The state hires a contractor to conduct the emissions tests in the various emissions-testing facilities around the state. In October 1999, the Arizona attorney general announced the arrest of 13 workers at one of the emissions-testing facilities for allegedly taking payoffs of between $50 to $200 from car owners to pass their cars on the emissions tests when those cars fell below emissions standards and would not have been registered. Nearly half of the staff at the emissions facility were arrested.

   Why is it a crime for someone working in a government-sponsored facility to accept a payment for a desired outcome? Do the payoffs to the workers really harm anyone?

10. The president and athletic director at the University of California at Los Angeles (UCLA) fired the school's basketball coach because an expense form he had submitted for reimbursement had the names of two students he said had joined him for a recruiting dinner. The students had not been to the dinner. The coach was stunned because he had been at UCLA for eight years and had established a winning program. He said, "And to throw it all away on a meal?" Do you agree with the coach's assessment? Was it too harsh to fire him for one inaccurate expense form? Did the coach commit an ethical breach?

11. A new trend is emerging in health insurance: premium increases based on claims. It is common practice in the auto insurance industry, for example, for insurers to revisit your premium each year and adjust it based on factors such as your driving record or number of accidents. However, health insurers have generally evaluated their insured's health only once, at the outset, when issuing a policy. The reevaluation of health and premiums was a practice that ended in the 1950s because the insurers feared regulators would impose limitations on premiums. At least one health insurer, however, has begun to evaluate the health of its insureds annually and to adjust policy premiums accordingly. Even without examination of insureds, some insurers have increased the insureds' premiums based simply on the nature of their claims for the year and the possibility that more claims will arise. Those who are healthy are in favor of this annual review. Perceiving themselves as the equivalent of good drivers, they want to pay less when they stay healthy. The health discount is, in their minds, the equivalent of the safe driver discount. However, those who are less healthy argue that people buy insurance so it will be there when they need it, and the coverage should apply without regard to claims. Consider the ethical issues in this type of pricing for health insurance.

12. David A. Vise, a Pulitzer Prize winner and a reporter for the *Washington Post,* wrote the book *The Bureau and the Mole.* When the book hit the market, Mr. Vise purchased 20,000 copies via Barnes & Noble.com, taking advantage of both free shipping offered by the publisher and a discounted initial price. Mr. Vise's book had already hit the *New York Times'* bestseller list in the week before the purchases. He used the books he purchased to conduct online sales of autographed copies of the books, and then returned 17,500 books and asked for his money back. However, that return of 17,500 books represented more books than a publisher generally runs for a book. Mr. Vise said that he did not intend to manipulate the market or profit from the transactions. He said his only intent was to "increase awareness of *The Bureau and the Mole.*" Mr. Vise's editor offered to pay Barnes & Noble for any expenses it incurred. Was it ethical to do what Mr. Vise did? Was he within his rights to return the books? What are his remedies? Does Barnes & Noble have any rights?

13. Suzy Wetlaufer, editor of the *Harvard Business Review,* interviewed former General Electric CEO Jack Welch for a piece in the business magazine. In December 2001, she asked that the piece be withdrawn because her objectivity might have been compromised. Those at the magazine did another interview and published that interview in the February issue of the magazine. Editorial director of the magazine, Walter Kiechel, who supervised Ms. Wetlaufer, acknowledged as true a report in the *Wall Street Journal* about an alleged affair between Ms. Wetlaufer and Mr. Welch and that Mr. Welch's wife had called to protest the article's objectivity. Mr. Welch refused to confirm or deny an affair with Ms. Wetlaufer, who was divorced. Some staff members asked that Ms. Wetlaufer resign from her $277,000-per-year job, but she refused. Their objections were that she compromised her journalistic integrity. Mr. Kiechel, on

the other hand, noted that she did "the right thing in raising her concerns."[19] About six weeks later, Ms. Wetlaufer did resign from her position as editor, announcing that she would be spending time with her four children. Do you think there was a conflict of interest because of the affair between Welch and Wetlaufer?[20] Note: Mr. Welch and Ms. Wetlaufer have married and have written a book together. They now write a semiweekly column for *BusinessWeek* magazine.

14. Piper High School in Piper, Kansas, a town located about 20 miles west of Kansas City, experienced national attention because of questions about students and their term papers for a botany class. Christine Pelton, a high school science teacher, had warned students in her sophomore class not to use papers posted on the Internet for their projects. When their projects were turned in, Ms. Pelton noticed that the writing in some of the papers was well above the students' usual quality and ability. She found that 28 of her 118 students had taken substantial portions of their papers from the Internet. She gave these students a zero grade on their term paper projects with the result that many of the students were going to fail the course for that semester. The students' parents protested, and the school board ordered Ms. Pelton to raise the grades. She resigned in protest. She received a substantial number of job offers from around the country following her resignation. Nearly half of the high school faculty as well as its principal announced their plans to resign at the end of the year. Several of the parents pointed to the fact that there was no explanation in the Piper High School handbook on plagiarism. They also said that the students were unclear about what could be used, when they had to reword, and when quotations marks were necessary. The annual Rutgers University survey on academic cheating has revealed that 15 percent of college papers turned in for grades are completely copied from the Internet. Do you think such copying is unethical? Why do we worry about such conduct? Isn't this conduct just a function of the Internet? Isn't it accepted behavior?

15. Pharmaceutical companies, faced with the uphill battle of getting doctors to take a look at their new products, have created complex systems and programs for enticing doctors to come, sit, and absorb information about the new products. Following is a list of the various type of benefits and gifts that drug companies have given doctors over the past few years to entice them to consider prescribing their new offerings:

- An event called "Why Cook?" in which doctors were given the chance to review drug studies and product information at a restaurant as their meals were being prepared—they could leave as soon as their meals were ready, and they were treated to appetizers and drinks as they waited

- Events at Christmas tree lots where doctors can come and review materials and pick up a free Christmas tree

- Flowers sent to doctors' offices on Valentine's Day with materials attached

[19] Del Jones, "Editor Linked with Welch Finds Job at Risk," *USA Today*, March 5, 2002, 3B.
[20] Ms. Wetlaufer and Mr. Welch were engaged to be married after Mr. Welch divorced Jane Welch.

- Manicures as they study materials on new drugs

- Pedicures as they study materials on new drugs

- Free car washes during which they study materials

- Free books with materials enclosed

- Free CDs with materials attached

- Bottles of wine with materials attached

- Events at Barnes & Noble where doctors can browse and pick out a book for themselves for free as long as they also take some materials on a new drug

Some doctors say that they can enjoy dinner on a drug company as often as five times per week. The American Medical Association (AMA) frowns on the "dine-and-dash" format because its rules provide that dinners are acceptable only as long as the doctors sit and learn something from a featured speaker. The AMA also limits gifts to those of a "minimal value" that should be related to their patients, such as note pads and pens with the new drug's name imprinted on them. The chairman of the AMA Committee on Ethics says the following about gifts, "There are doctors who say, 'I always do what's best for my patients, and these gifts and dinners and trips do not influence me.' They are wrong."[21] In which category of ethical issues do these gifts fall? Do you think doctors act ethically in accepting gifts, meals, and favors? The Food and Drug Administration recently issued rules about such favors and perks. Why?

---

[21] Chris Adams, "Doctors on the Run Can 'Dine 'n' Dash' in Style in New Orleans," *Wall Street Journal*, May 14, 2001, A1, A6.

Chapter 4

THE CONSTITUTION AS THE FOUNDATION OF THE LEGAL ENVIRONMENT

This chapter introduces you to the powers of government and to the protections that you have for your rights. The Constitution of the United States establishes the structure and powers of government but also the limitations on those powers. This Constitution forms the foundation of our legal environment.

A. THE U.S. CONSTITUTION AND THE FEDERAL SYSTEM

By establishing a central government to coexist with the governments of the individual states, the U.S. Constitution created a federal system. In a **federal system**, a central government has power to address national concerns, while the individual states retain the power to handle local concerns.

1. What a Constitution is

A **constitution** is the written document that establishes the structure of the government and its relationship to the people. The U.S. Constitution was adopted in 1789 by the 13 colonies that had won their independence from King George.[1]

2. The Branches of Government

The U.S. Constitution establishes a **tripartite** (three-part) government: a **legislative branch** (Congress) to make the laws, an **executive branch** (the president) to execute or enforce the laws, and a **judicial branch** (courts) to interpret the laws. The national legislature or Congress is a **bicameral** (two-house) body consisting of the Senate and the House of Representatives. Members of the Senate are popularly elected for a term of six years. Members of the House of Representatives are popularly elected for a term of two years. The president is elected by an electoral college whose membership is popularly elected. The president serves for a term of four years and is eligible for reelection for a second term. Judges of the United States are appointed by the president with the approval of the Senate and serve for life, subject to removal only by impeachment because of misconduct. (See Chapter 2 for a discussion of the federal court system.)

B. THE U.S. CONSTITUTION AND THE STATES

The Constitution created certain powers within the national government that would have been exercised by the individual states, which are given their powers by the people of the state. Figure 4-1 illustrates the delegation of powers. Likewise, the states, as the power-granting authorities, reserved certain powers for themselves.

federal system–the system of government in which a central government is given power to administer to national concerns while individual states retain the power to administer to local concerns.

constitution–a body of principles that establishes the structure of a government and the relationship of the government to the people who are governed.

tripartite–three-part division (of government).

legislative branch–the branch of government (e.g., Congress) formed to make the laws.

executive branch–the branch of government (e.g., the president) formed to execute the laws.

judicial branch–the branch of government (e.g., the courts) formed to interpret the laws.

bicameral–a two-house form of the legislative branch of government.

---

[1] To examine the U.S. Constitution, go to **www.constitution.org** and click on "Founding Documents," or refer to Appendix 2.

FIGURE 4-1 | *Governments of the United States*

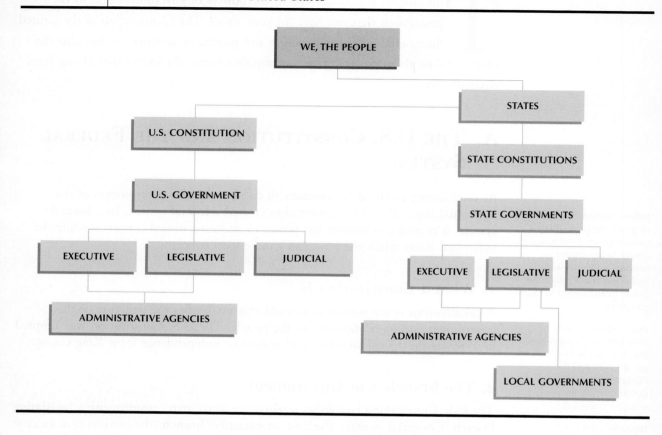

3. Delegated and Shared Powers

delegated powers–powers expressly granted the national government by the Constitution.

(A) DELEGATED POWERS. The powers given by the states to the national government are described as *delegated powers*. Some of these **delegated powers** are given exclusively to the national government. For example, the national government alone may declare war or establish a currency.

shared powers–powers that are held by both state and national governments.

(B) SHARED POWERS. The powers delegated to the national government that may still be exercised by the states are **shared powers**. **For Example,** the grant of power to the national government to impose taxes did not destroy the state power to tax. In other cases, a state may provide regulation along with, but subject to the supremacy of, federal law. **For Example,** regulation of the use of navigable waterways within a state is an example of joint state and federal regulation.

4. Other Powers

police power–the power to govern; the power to adopt laws for the protection of the public health, welfare, safety, and morals.

(A) STATE POLICE POWER. The states possess the power to adopt laws to protect the general welfare, health, safety, and morals of the people. This authority is called the **police power. For Example,** states may require that businesses be licensed with state agencies to protect persons dealing with the business. State exercise of the police power may not unreasonably interfere with federal powers.

(B) PROHIBITED POWERS. The Constitution also prohibits both states and the federal government from doing certain things. **For Example,** neither states nor the national government may adopt *ex post facto* **laws**, which make criminal an act that has already been committed but was not criminal when it was committed. Laws that increase the penalty for an act already committed above the penalty in force when the act was committed are also *ex post facto* laws.

ex post facto **law**–a law making criminal an act that was lawful when done or that increases the penalty when done. Such laws are generally prohibited by constitutional provisions.

5. Federal Supremacy

Federal law bars or preempts conflicting state regulation when a federal law regulates that particular subject. Federal law also preempts state action when congressional intent to regulate exclusively can be inferred from the details of congressional regulation. **Preemption** means that the federal regulatory scheme is controlling.

preemption–the federal government's superior regulatory position over state laws on the same subject area.

(A) EXPRESS FEDERAL REGULATION. The Constitution and statutes passed by Congress are the supreme law of the land. They cancel out any conflicting state law.[2] When a direct conflict exists between federal and state statutes, federal law prevails.

In some cases, however, no obvious conflict occurs because the federal statute covers only part of the subject matter. In such cases, the question becomes whether a state law can regulate the areas not regulated by Congress or whether the partial regulation made by Congress preempts, or takes over, the field so as to preclude state legislation.

CASE SUMMARY

The Folk Singer Who Staged a Protest against Preemption

FACTS: Diana Levine, a folk singer from Vermont, suffered from migraine headaches. She was being administered Wyeth Laboratory's Phenergan through a drip IV. Either because the IV needle entered Levine's artery or the drug escaped from the vein into her surrounding tissue, Ms. Levine developed gangrene. Doctors amputated her right hand and eventually her forearm. Levine could no longer work as a professional musician. Levine filed suit against both the clinic that administered the drug and Wyeth. She was awarded $7.4 million and Wyeth appealed on the grounds that the FDA approval of the drug preempted state tort suits by patients.

DECISION: In a 6 to 3 decision that departed from past precedent on preemption, the U.S. Supreme Court held that federal regulation did not preempt Levine's state tort suit against Wyeth. Wyeth argued that it could not change the label to warn against IV use of Phenergan without FDA approval—and the FDA had approved the drug as safe for use. The Court held that Wyeth could move to change the label with the FDA in a timely fashion and that federal regulation did not preempt responsible follow-up by manufacturers with regard to their drugs. **[Wyeth v Levine, 129 S Ct 1187 (2009)]**[3]

[2] U.S. Const., Art VI, cl 2. *Cuomo v Clearinghouse Ass'n, LLC,* 129 S Ct 2710 (2009).
[3] For an earlier decision that concluded differently on another preemption case involving medical and FDA issues, see *Riegel v Medtronic,* 552 US 312 (2008).

(B) SILENCE OF CONGRESS. In some situations, the silence of Congress in failing to cover a particular subject area indicates that Congress does not want any law on the matter. However, when national uniformity is essential, the silence of Congress generally means that the subject has been preempted for practical reasons by Congress and that no state law on the subject may be adopted.

(C) EFFECT OF FEDERAL DEREGULATION. The fact that the federal government removes the regulations from a regulated industry does not automatically give the states the power to regulate that industry. If under the silence-of-Congress doctrine the states cannot regulate, they are still barred from regulating after deregulation. **For Example,** deregulation of banks in the 1980s did not mean that the states could step in and regulate those banks.[4]

C. INTERPRETING AND AMENDING THE CONSTITUTION

The Constitution as it is interpreted today has changed greatly from the Constitution as originally written. The change has been brought about by interpretation, amendment, and practice.

6. Conflicting Theories

Shortly after the Constitution was adopted, conflict arose over whether it was to be interpreted strictly, so as to give the federal government the least power possible, or broadly, so as to give the federal government the greatest power that the words would permit. These two views may be called the *bedrock view* and the *living-document view*, respectively.

bedrock view—a strict constructionist interpretation of a constitution.

In the **bedrock view**, or strict constructionist or originalist view, the purpose of a constitution is to state certain fundamental principles for all time. In the **living-document view**, a constitution is merely a statement of goals and objectives and is intended to grow and change with time.

living-document view—the term used when a constitution is interpreted according to changes in conditions.

Whether the Constitution is to be liberally interpreted under the living-document view or narrowly interpreted under the bedrock view has a direct effect on the Constitution. For the last century, the Supreme Court has followed the living-document view. This view has resulted in strengthening the power of the federal government, permitting the rise of administrative agencies, and expanding the protection of human rights.

One view is not selected to the exclusion of the other. As contradictory as these two views sound, the Constitution remains durable. We do not want a set of New Year's resolutions that will soon be forgotten. At the same time, we know that the world changes, and therefore, we do not want a constitution that will hold us tied in a straitjacket of the past.

In terms of social forces that make the law, we are torn between our desire for stability and our desire for flexibility. We want a constitution that is stable. At the same time, we want one that is flexible.

[4] *New York v Trans World Airlines*, 556 NYS2d 803 (1990). See also footnote 2 and the *Cuomo* case from 2009.

7. Amending the Constitution

The U.S. Constitution has been amended in three ways: (1) expressly, (2) by interpretation, and (3) by practice. Figure 4-2 illustrates these three methods of amendment.

(A) CONSTITUTIONAL METHOD OF AMENDING. Article V of the Constitution gives the procedure to be followed for amending the Constitution. Relatively few changes have been made to the Constitution by this formal process, although thousands of proposals have been made. Since the time of its adoption, there have been only 27 amendments to the Constitution.

(B) AMENDMENT BY JUDICIAL INTERPRETATION. The U.S. Supreme Court has made the greatest changes to the written Constitution by interpreting it. Generally, interpretation is used to apply the Constitution to a new situation that could not have been foreseen when the written Constitution was adopted.

(C) AMENDMENT BY PRACTICE. In practice, the letter of the Constitution is not always followed. Departure from the written Constitution began as early as 1793 when George Washington refused to make treaties as required by the Constitution, by and with the consent of the Senate. Washington began the practice of the president's negotiating a treaty with a foreign country and then submitting it to the Senate for approval. This practice has been followed since that time. Similarly, the electoral college was originally intended to exercise independent judgment in selecting the president, but it now automatically elects the official candidate of the party that elected the majority of the members of the electoral college.

8. The Living Constitution

The living Constitution has the following characteristics.

(A) STRONG GOVERNMENT. One of the characteristics of the new Constitution is strong government. Business enterprises are highly regulated and the economy is controlled through monetary policy.

(B) STRONG PRESIDENT. Instead of being merely an officer who carries out the laws, the president has become the political leader of a party, exerting strong influence on the lawmaking process.

FIGURE 4-2 | *Amending the U.S. Constitution*

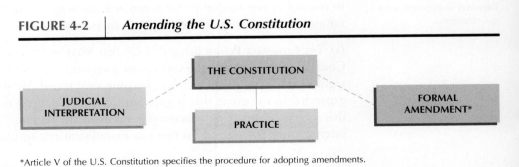

*Article V of the U.S. Constitution specifies the procedure for adopting amendments.

(C) **ECLIPSE OF THE STATES.** Under constitutional interpretations, all levels of government have powers that they never possessed before, but the center of gravity has shifted from the states to the nation. When the Constitution was adopted in 1789, the federal government was to have only the very limited powers specified in Article I, Section 8, of the Constitution. Whatever regulation of business was permissible was to be imposed by the states. Today, the great bulk of the regulation of business is adopted by the federal government through Congress or its administrative agencies. As the U.S. economy moved from the local community stage to the nationwide and then international stages, individual states could no longer provide effective regulation of business. Regulation migrated to the central government.

(D) **ADMINISTRATIVE AGENCIES.** These units of government were virtually unheard of in 1789, and the Constitution made no mention of them. The vast powers of the new Constitution are exercised to a very large degree by administrative agencies. They are in effect a fourth branch of the government, not provided for in the written Constitution. More importantly, the administrative agencies are the ones that come in contact with the majority of businesspersons and citizens.

Agencies have had a significant amount of power delegated to them. The members and heads of the agencies, boards, or commissions are not elected by the voters (see Chapter 6). They are appointed by the president and, at certain levels of appointment in the agency, must be approved by Congress.

D. FEDERAL POWERS

The federal government possesses powers necessary to administer matters of national concern.

9. The Power to Regulate Commerce

The desire to protect commerce from restrictions and barriers set up by the individual states was a prime factor leading to the adoption of the Constitution of 1789. To protect commerce, Congress was given Article I, Section 8, Clause 3—now known as the **commerce clause**—the power "to regulate commerce with foreign nations, and among the several states, and with the Indian tribes."[5]

Until 1937, the Supreme Court held that this provision gave Congress the power to control or regulate only that commerce crossing a state line, such as an interstate railway train or an interstate telegraph message.

commerce clause–that section of the U.S. Constitution allocating business regulation between federal and state governments.

(A) **THE COMMERCE POWER BECOMES A GENERAL WELFARE POWER.** In 1937, the Supreme Court began expanding the concept of interstate commerce. By 1946, the power to regulate interstate commerce had become very broad. By that year, the power had expanded to the point that it gave authority to Congress to adopt regulatory laws that were "as broad as the economic needs of the nation."[6] By virtue of this broad interpretation, Congress can regulate manufacturing, agriculture, mining, stock

---

[5] For more details on the actual language in the U.S. Constitution, go to **www.constitution.org** and click on "Founding Documents," or refer to Appendix 2.
[6] *American Power & Light Co. v Securities and Exchange Commission*, 329 US 90 (1946).

exchanges, insurance, loan sharking, monopolies, and conspiracies in restraint of trade. The far reach of the interstate commerce power is seen in the Freedom of Access to Clinic Entrances Act,[7] which prohibits obstruction of entrances to clinics.[8]

The case that was the beginning point in the transition of the commerce clause was *NLRB v Jones & Laughlin Steel*, 301 US 1 (1937). The "affectation" doctrine expanded the authority of the federal government under the commerce clause. At that time, the Court concluded, "If it is interstate commerce that feels the pinch, it does not matter how local the squeeze."

(B) **THE COMMERCE CLAUSE TODAY.** Today, judicial review of the commerce clause typically finds some connection between the legislation and congressional authority. However, in the past five years, the U.S. Supreme Court has found some areas Congress may not regulate and has placed some limitations on the commerce clause. These constraints on the commerce clause focus on the nature of the underlying activity being regulated. So long as the federal regulation relates to economic/commercial activity, it is constitutional. If, however, the underlying activity is not economic and has only an economic impact, the Supreme Court has imposed restrictions on congressional authority under the commerce clause.

C A S E   S U M M A R Y

The Commerce Clause Meets Violence

FACTS: Christy Brzonkala filed a suit under the federal Violence Against Women Act (VAWA) after she was raped by two of her fellow students at the Virginia Polytechnic Institute. The VAWA gives women who are the victims of violence a civil rights action against their assailants. The district court dismissed the suit because it found Congress lacked authority under the commerce clause for the VAWA. The court of appeals reversed. Because a lower court invalidated a federal statute, the Supreme Court granted *certiorari*.

DECISION: Congress does not have authority under the commerce clause for the VAWA. The Court held that neither the activity regulated by the VAWA nor the settings in which violence against women occur constitute interstate commerce. The VAWA did not regulate either the channels or instrumentalities of interstate commerce and must therefore rely on aggregating activities to show a substantial effect on interstate commerce. Because the commerce clause requires the aggregating of economic activities for substantial effect cases, the VAWA's underlying conduct of violence was insufficient to survive constitutional scrutiny. **[United States v Morrison, 529 US 598 (2000)]**

(C) **THE COMMERCE POWER AS A LIMITATION ON STATES.** The federal power to regulate commerce not only gives Congress the power to act but also prevents states from acting in any way that interferes with federal regulation or burdens interstate commerce. **For Example,** if the federal government establishes safety device regulations for interstate carriers, a state cannot require different devices.

---

[7] 18 USC § 248.
[8] The act is constitutional. *United States v Wilson*, 73 F3d 675 (7th Cir 1995), *cert denied*, 519 US 806 (1996).

CASE SUMMARY

Minors in Maine and a Major Commerce Clause Decision

FACTS: Maine passed a law that prohibited anyone other than a Maine-licensed tobacco retailer from accepting an order for delivery of tobacco. The law required the retailer to arrange for delivery with a special receipt showing that someone over the age of 18 had received and signed for the tobacco products delivered. Out-of-state shippers and tobacco sellers challenged the law as one that favored Maine tobacco retailers. The state of Maine argued that its law was passed to prevent the public health hazard of minors becoming addicted to tobacco. The federal district court granted summary judgment for the shippers, and the court of appeals affirmed. The state of Maine appealed.

DECISION: In a 9 to 0 decision, the Court held that the Maine law may have been passed with health benefits in mind, but it clearly gave Maine businesses an economic benefit. In addition, other states had managed to fight teen smoking using programs other than discrimination between in-state and out-of-state tobacco retailers. [**Rowe v New Hampshire Motor Transport Association, 552 US 364 (2008)**]

States may not use their tax power for the purpose of discriminating against interstate commerce, because such commerce is within the protection of the national government. **For Example,** a state cannot impose a higher tax on goods imported from another state than it imposes on the same kind of goods produced in its own territory.

State regulations designed to advance local interests may conflict with the commerce clause. Such regulations are invalid. A state cannot refuse to allow an interstate waste collector to conduct business within the state on the grounds that the state already has enough waste collectors.

CASE SUMMARY

Whining about Wine

FACTS: Michigan and New York regulate the sale and importation of alcoholic beverages, including wine, through a three-tier distribution system. Separate licenses are required for producers, wholesalers, and retailers. Both New York and Michigan prohibit out-of-state wine producers from selling their wines directly to consumers there. In-state wineries can sell directly to consumers. The impact of the prohibition on the out-of-state wine producers is that they are required to pay wholesaler fees and thus cannot compete with in-state wine producers on direct-to-consumer sales.

The wine producers challenging the New York and Michigan statutes are small wineries that rely on direct consumer sales as an important part of their businesses. If they did business through wholesalers in the state, the price of their wines would have to be increased to a level that would be noncompetitive.

CASE SUMMARY

Continued

The district court granted summary judgment for the state of Michigan. The Sixth Circuit Court of Appeals reversed on the grounds that the out-of-state restrictions violated the commerce clause. The state of Michigan appealed. In the New York case, the district court found that the out-of-state restrictions violated the commerce clause, and the Second Circuit Court of Appeals reversed and upheld the New York statute as constitutional. The out-of-state wine producers appealed.

DECISION: State laws violate the commerce clause if they treat in-state and out-of-state economic interests differently with the result that one benefits and the other is burdened. The mere fact that a wine producer is not a resident of the state should not foreclose access to markets there. The Michigan statutes prohibiting out-of-state wineries from shipping wine directly to in-state consumers, but permitting in-state wineries to do so if licensed, discriminated against interstate commerce. New York statutes imposing additional burdens on out-of-state wineries seeking to ship wine directly to New York consumers discriminated against interstate commerce. The effect of both statutes was to favor in-state wine producers and create the economic Balkanization that the commerce clause was intended to prevent. Both statutes violated the commerce clause. **[Granholm v Heald, 544 US 460 (2005)]**

10. The Financial Powers

The financial powers of the federal government include the powers to tax and to borrow, spend, and coin money.

(A) THE TAXING POWER. The federal Constitution provides that "Congress shall have power to lay and collect taxes, duties, imposts and excises, to pay the debts and provide for the common defence and general welfare of the United States."[9] Subject to the express and implied limitations arising from the Constitution, the states may impose such taxes as they desire and as their own individual constitutions and statutes permit. In addition to express constitutional limitations, both national and local taxes are subject to the unwritten limitation that they be imposed for a public purpose. Taxes must also be apportioned. A business cannot be taxed for all of its revenues in all 50 states. There must be apportionment of taxes, and there must be sufficient connection with the state.

(B) THE SPENDING POWER. The federal government may use tax money and borrowed money "to pay the debts and provide for the common defence and general welfare of the United States."[10]

(C) THE BANKING POWER. The Constitution is liberally interpreted to allow the federal government to create banks and to regulate banks created under state laws. For example, the Federal Reserve System is responsible for this regulatory oversight of banks.

---

[9] U.S. Const., Art 1, § 8, cl 1. To read more of the U.S. Constitution, refer to Appendix 2, or go to **www.constitution.org** and click on "Founding Documents."

[10] U.S. Const., Art 1, § 8, cl 1. See **www.constitution.org**, or Appendix 2.

CASE SUMMARY

A Quill in Your State Means Taxes in the Coffer

FACTS: Quill is a Delaware corporation with offices and warehouses in Illinois, California, and Georgia. None of its employees works or lives in North Dakota, and Quill owns no property in North Dakota.

Quill sells office equipment and supplies; it solicits business through catalogs and flyers, advertisements in national periodicals, and telephone calls. Its annual national sales exceed $200 million, of which almost $1 million are made to about 3,000 customers in North Dakota. The sixth-largest vendor of office supplies in the state, it delivers all of its merchandise to its North Dakota customers by mail or common carriers from out-of-state locations.

North Dakota requires every "retailer maintaining a place of business in" the state to collect the tax from the consumer and remit it to the state. In 1987, North Dakota amended its statutory definition of the term "retailer" to include "every person who engages in regular or systematic solicitation of a consumer market in the state." State regulations in turn define "regular or systematic solicitation" to mean three or more advertisements within a 12-month period.

Quill has taken the position that North Dakota does not have the power to compel it to collect a use tax from its North Dakota customers. Consequently, the state, through its tax commissioner, filed this action to require Quill to pay taxes (as well as interest and penalties) on all such sales made after July 1, 1987. The trial court ruled in Quill's favor.

The North Dakota Supreme Court reversed, and Quill appealed.

DECISION: The Court held that the issue is one of whether the company has intentionally placed itself within a state. Whether it does so with offices and salespeople or deluges the citizens with catalogs is irrelevant. So long as the company has voluntarily placed itself within the state, the taxation is neither unfair nor unconstitutional. **[Quill v North Dakota, 504 US 298 (1992)]**

E. CONSTITUTIONAL LIMITATIONS ON GOVERNMENT

The constitutional limitations discussed in the following sections afford protections of rights for both persons and businesses.

11. Due Process

The power of government is limited by both the Fifth and Fourteenth Amendments to the Constitution. Those amendments respectively prohibit the national government and state governments from depriving any person "of life, liberty, or property without due process of law."[11]

(A) WHEN DUE PROCESS RIGHTS ARISE. As a result of liberal interpretation of the Constitution, the **due process clause** now provides a guarantee of protection against the loss of property or rights without the chance to be heard. These amendments also guarantee that all citizens are given the same protections. **For Example,** the Supreme Court has extended the due process clause to protect the record or standing of a student.[12] A student cannot lose credit in a course or be suspended or expelled without some form of a hearing.

due process clause–a guarantee of protection against the loss of property or rights without the chance to be heard.

---

[11] For more information on the language of the Fifth and Fourteenth Amendments, see the U.S. Constitution in Appendix 2, or go to **www.constitution.org**.

[12] That is, a student cannot be expelled without a chance to have his or her side of the story reviewed.

quasi-judicial proceedings—
forms of hearings in which
the rules of evidence and
procedure are more relaxed
but each side still has a
chance to be heard.

Because there are so many areas in which due process rights exist and require a chance to be heard, speeding up due process has resulted in the creation of **quasi-judicial proceedings**. In these types of proceedings, the parties need not go through the complex, lengthy, and formal procedures of a trial (described in Chapter 2). Rather, these proceedings have a hearing officer or administrative law judge (see Chapter 6) who conducts an informal hearing in which the rules of evidence and procedure are relaxed.

For Example, a student taking a grade grievance beyond a faculty member's decision will generally have his case heard by a panel of faculty and students as established by college or university rules. An employer appealing its unemployment tax rate will have the appeal heard by an administrative law judge.

(b) What Constitutes Due Process? Due process does not require a trial on every issue of rights. Shortcut procedures, such as grade grievance panels, have resulted as a compromise for providing the right to be heard along with a legitimate desire to be expeditious in resolving these issues.

12. Equal Protection of the Law

The Constitution prohibits the states and the national government from denying any person the equal protection of the law.[13] This guarantee prohibits a government

---

e-commerce&cyberlaw
Internet and Interstate

Collection of sales tax from Internet stores has been a stickler of an issue for businesses, state revenue officials, and the U.S. Supreme Court. All three were grappling with how to collect, what to collect, and whether anybody had any authority to collect. Internet sales represent a large, untapped source of revenue. A study from the Center for Business and Economic Research at the University of Tennessee estimates the lost tax revenue from untaxed Internet sales as $21 billion in 2008.

The merchants involved fell into several different legal groups in terms of their theories on whether tax was owed and whether they should just pay it, with or without the states having the authority to tax:

1. Those stores with physical presences in states (Wal-Mart and J.C. Penney) that just collected sales tax as if they were collecting it in a store in that state where the Internet purchaser was located

2. Those stores without a physical presence (Amazon) that did collect taxes, particularly in those states known for taking a hard-line approach

3. Those stores without a physical presence that do not collect taxes and maintain that it is unconstitutional to do so

4. Those stores with or without a physical presence that have collected taxes but held them until everyone could figure out the legal status of the companies.

What are the constitutional issues in this taxation question?

Note: Amazon.com filed suit in 2008 challenging New York's statute that authorized the collection of sales taxes from online company sales to New York residents.

Source: Robery Guy Matthews, "Some States Push to Collect Sales Tax from Internet Stores," *Wall Street Journal,* Sept. 30, 2005, B1–B4.

---

[13] U.S. Constitution, Fourteenth Amendment as to the states; modern interpretation of due process clause of the Fifth Amendment as to national government. Congress adopted the Civil Rights Act to implement the concept of equal protection.

from treating one person differently from another when there is no reasonable ground for classifying them differently.

(A) REASONABLE CLASSIFICATION. Whether a classification is reasonable depends on whether the nature of the classification bears a reasonable relation to the wrong to be remedied or to the object to be attained by the law. The judicial trend is to permit the classification to stand as long as there is a rational basis for the distinction made.[14] Whether a rational basis exists is determined by answering whether the lawmaking body has been arbitrary or capricious.

The equal protection clause is the basis of many of the U.S. Supreme Court's most complicated decisions. **For Example,** during the 2000 presidential election, the U.S. Supreme Court faced an issue of equal protection with regard to the challenge then–vice president and presidential candidate Al Gore made to the undervotes in Florida's ballots. However, then-presidential candidate George W. Bush argued that counting the undervotes in some counties and not in others and applying different standards for counting or not counting the infamous dimpled chads, hanging chads, and other undervotes was unconstitutional because it deprived other Florida voters of equal protection because each vote is intended to count equally. Recounts in only some counties while using varying standards resulted in some counties being given greater weight in Florida's presidential election. The U.S. Supreme Court agreed in a 7–2 decision that the recounts were unconstitutional on equal protection grounds.[15] However, the justices split 5–4 on the correct remedy for the unconstitutional recounts.

(B) IMPROPER CLASSIFICATION. Laws that make distinctions in the regulation of business, the right to work, and the right to use or enjoy property on the basis of race, national origin, or religion are invalid. Also invalid are laws that impose restrictions on some, but not all, persons without any justification for the distinction.[16] **For Example,** a state statute taxing out-of-state insurance companies at a higher rate than in-state insurance companies violates the equal protection clause.[17]

13. Privileges and Immunities

The federal Constitution declares that "the citizens of each state shall be entitled to all privileges and immunities of citizens in the several states."[18] The so-called **privileges and immunities clause** means that a person going into another state is entitled to make contracts, own property, and engage in business to the same extent as the citizens of that state. **For Example,** a state cannot bar someone who comes from another state from engaging in local business or from obtaining a hunting or fishing license merely because the person is not a resident of that state.

privileges and immunities clause–a clause that entitles a person going into another state to make contracts, own property, and engage in business to the same extent as citizens of that state.

14. Protection of the Person

The Constitution has no general provision declaring that the government shall not impair rights of persons. The Constitution does not mention the phrase

---

[14] Ileto v Glock, Inc., 565 F3d 1126 (CA 9 2009)
[15] *Bush v Gore*, 531 US 98 (2000).
[16] *Associated Industries of Missouri v Lohman*, 511 US 641 (1994).
[17] *Metropolitan Life Ins. Co. v Ward*, 470 US 869 (1985).
[18] U.S. Const., Art IV, § 2, cl 1. See **www.constitution.org** and click on "Founding Documents" to access more language of the Constitution, or see Appendix 2.

"unalienable right" that was part of the Declaration of Independence.[19] However, the Bill of Rights, the first 10 amendments to the Constitution, does provide protections for freedom of speech, jury trials, and freedom of religion and association.[20] The Bill of Rights provides for the due process protections discussed earlier as well as those that prohibit unlawful searches and seizures. The Second Amendment provides for the right to keep and bear arms, an issue that has resulted in some conflicting decisions that the U.S. Supreme Court has begun to address.[21]

During the last six decades, the Supreme Court has been interpreting the rights in these amendments and has been finding constitutional protection for a wide array of rights of the person that are not expressly protected by the Constitution. **For Example,** judicial interpretations have concluded that the Constitution provides for the right of privacy, the right to marry the person one chooses,[22] protection from unreasonable zoning, protection of parental control, protection from discrimination because of poverty, and protection from gender discrimination.[23]

15. The Bill of Rights and Businesses as Persons

The Bill of Rights provides protections for individuals and also for corporations. **For Example,** the Fourth Amendment (see Chapter 8) provides protections against unreasonable searches. Individuals enjoy that protection in their homes, and corporations enjoy that protection with their files, offices, and business records. Businesses also enjoy freedom of speech protections under the First Amendment. The First Amendment provides that "Congress shall make no law ... abridging the freedom of speech ..."[24]

The U.S. Supreme Court has clarified the free speech rights of business through classification of the types of business speech. One form of business or commercial speech is advertising. This form of speech in which businesses tout their products is subject to regulation and restriction on form, content, and placement, and such regulation has been deemed constitutional. (See Chapters 25 and 33 for more information on the regulation of advertising.) However, there are other forms of commercial speech. Businesses do have the right to participate in political processes such as creating political action committees and supporting or opposing ballot initiatives. Businesses often take positions and launch campaigns on ballot initiatives that will affect the taxes they will be required to pay.

---

[19] The term *unalienable right* is employed in reference to natural right, fundamental right, or basic right. Apart from the question of scope of coverage, the adjective *unalienable* emphasizes the fact that the people still possess the right rather than having surrendered or subordinated it to the will of society. The word *alien* is the term of the old common law for transferring title or ownership. Today, we would say *transfer* and, instead of saying unalienable rights, would say *nontransferable* rights. Unalienable rights of the people were therefore rights that the people not only possessed but also could not give up even if they wanted to. Thus, these rights are still owned by everyone. It is important to note that the Declaration of Independence actually uses the word "unalienable" when describing the rights eventually placed in the Constitution as Amendments I–X, the Bill of Rights, not "inalienable."

[20] *North Coast Women's Care Medical Group, Inc. v San Diego County Superior Court*, 189 P 3d 959 (Ca 2008).

[21] *District of Columbia v Heller*, 128 S Ct 2783 (2008).

[22] *Akron v Akron Center for Reproductive Health, Inc.*, 462 US 416 (1983); but see *Colorado v Hill, cert granted*, 527 US 1068 (2000). For more on commercial speech, see *Greater New Orleans Broadcasting Association, Inc., v U.S.* 527 US 173 (1999) and U.S. v Philip Morris USA Inc., 566 F3d 1095 (CA DC 2009).

[23] In some cases, the courts have given the due process and equal protection clauses a liberal interpretation in order to find a protection of the person, thereby making up for the fact that there is no express constitutional guarantee of protection of the person. *Davis v Passman* 442 US 228 (1979) (due process); *Orr v Orr*, 440 US 268 (1979) (equal protection).

[24] To read the full language of the First Amendment, go to Appendix 2, or to **www.constitution.org** and click on "Founding Documents."

CASE SUMMARY

Banks Are People Too: First Amendment Political Speech

FACTS: Massachusetts had passed a statute that prohibited businesses and banks from making contributions or expenditures for the purpose of influencing or affecting the vote on any question submitted to the voters other than one materially affecting any of the property, business, or assets of the corporation. The statute also stated that taxation ballot questions did not materially affect the property, business, or assets of the corporation. The statute carried a fine of up to $50,000 for the corporation and $10,000 and/or one-year imprisonment for corporate officers.

First National Bank and other banks and corporations wanted to spend money to publicize their views on an upcoming ballot proposition that would give the legislature the right to impose a graduated tax on individual income. Frances X. Bellotti, the attorney general for Massachusetts, told First National and the others that he intended to enforce the statute against them. First National and the others brought suit to have the statute declared unconstitutional, and First National appealed.

DECISION: The worth of speech is not determined by the source. The First Amendment provides protection to all forms of speech. Further, neither the Court nor the Constitution is in a position to restrict the speech of corporations on the grounds that the speech is not about business. That corporate advertising on ballot issues may be influential is not grounds for restricting the ability to advertise on political issues and social concerns. The regulation was also determined to be selective in that it would limit corporate participation on ballot initiatives but placed no controls on lobbying for legislation. The purpose of the regulation was not compelling nor sufficiently narrowly drawn to justify its constitutionality. **[First National Bank of Boston v Bellotti, 435 US 765 (1978)]**

thinking things through

Sweating It Out on Free Speech

In 1996, Nike was inundated with allegations about its labor practices in shoe factories around the world. Nike responded to the negative reports and allegations with a series of releases, advertisements, and op-ed pieces in newspapers around the country. *New York Times* columnist Bob Herbert wrote two columns that were sharply critical of Nike's conditions in plants throughout Asia. The columns compared then-CEO Philip Knight's compensation with the $2.20 per day wages of Nike workers in Indonesia.

After the columns appeared, CEO Knight wrote a letter to the editor in response to them. In that letter, he wrote, "Nike has paid, on average, double the minimum wage as defined in countries where its products are produced under contract. History shows that the best way out of poverty for such countries is through exports of light manufactured goods that provide the base for more skilled production."*

Marc Kasky filed suit against Nike in California, alleging that the op-ed pieces and letters in response

thinking things through

Continued

to negative op-ed pieces about Nike violated the False Advertising Act of California. The act permits state agencies to take action to fine corporate violators of the act as well as to obtain remedies such as injunctions to halt the ads.

Nike challenged the suit on the grounds that such an interpretation and application of the advertising regulation violated its rights of free speech. The lower court agreed with Kasky and held that the advertising statute applied to Nike's defense of its labor practices, even on the op-ed pages of newspapers. The California Supreme Court, 45 P.3d 243 (Cal. 2002),

ruled that Nike could be subject to regulatory sanctions for false advertising. Nike appealed to the U.S. Supreme Court. Should Nike's editorial be protected by the First Amendment? Discuss where this type of speech fits.

The opinion handed down in this case is only one sentence: "The writ of certiorari is dismissed as improvidently granted." 539 US 654 (2003). Is this letter protected speech?

*Roger Parloff, "Can We Talk?" Fortune, September 2, 2002, 102–110.

lawflix

The Candidate (1972) (PG)

The movie depicts an idealist running for office who finds himself caught in the political process of fundraising, image-building, and winning. A number of scenes with speeches, fundraising, and principles in conflict provide excellent discussion issues with respect to government structure, the First Amendment, and campaign contributions.

Check out LawFlix at **www.cengage.com/blaw/dvl** to access movie clips that illustrate business law concepts.

MAKE THE CONNECTION

SUMMARY

The U.S. Constitution created the structure of our national government and gave it certain powers. It also placed limitations on those powers. It created a federal system with a tripartite division of government and a bicameral national legislature.

The national government possesses some governmental powers exclusively, while both the states and the federal government share other powers. In areas of conflict, federal law is supreme.

The U.S. Constitution is not a detailed document. It takes its meaning from the way it is interpreted. In recent years, liberal interpretation has expanded the powers of the federal government. Among the powers of the federal government that directly affect business are the power to regulate commerce; the power to tax and to borrow, spend, and coin money; and the power to own and operate businesses.

Among the limitations on government that are most important to business are the requirements of due process and the requirement of equal protection of the law. In addition, government is limited by the rights given to individuals such as freedom of speech, freedom of religion, and equal protection. The equal protection concept of the U.S. Constitution prohibits both the federal government and the state governments from treating one person differently from another unless there is a legitimate reason for doing so and unless the basis of classification is reasonable.

LEARNING OUTCOMES

After studying this chapter, you should be able to clearly explain:

A. THE U.S. CONSTITUTION AND THE FEDERAL SYSTEM

LO.1 Describe the U.S. Constitution and the Federal System
See the discussion of the **tripartite** (three-part) government on p. 67.

B. THE U.S. CONSTITUTION AND THE STATES

LO.2 Explain the relationship between the U.S. Constitution and the States
See the discussion of the federal system on p. 67.
See Figure 4-1 for an illustration of the delegation of powers.

C. INTERPRETING AND AMENDING THE CONSTITUTION

LO.3 Discuss interpreting and amending the Constitution
See the discussion of the bedrock and constructionist views on p. 70.

D. FEDERAL POWERS

LO.4 List and describe the significant federal powers
See the discussion of the commerce power on p. 72.
See the discussion of the taxing power on p. 76.
See the discussion of the banking power on p. 77.

E. CONSTITUTIONAL LIMITATIONS ON GOVERNMENT

LO.5 Discuss constitutional limitations on governmental power
See the discussion of the Bill of Rights on p. 79.
See the discussion of the Fourth Amendment on p. 79.
See the discussion of due process on p. 77.
See the **For Example** discussion of a student taking a grade grievance beyond a faculty member's decision on p. 77.

KEY TERMS

bedrock view	constitution	*ex post facto* laws
bicameral	delegated powers	executive branch
commerce clause	due process clause	federal system

judicial branch

preemption

shared powers

legislative branch

privileges and immunities

tripartite

living-document view

clause

police power

quasi-judicial proceedings

QUESTIONS AND CASE PROBLEMS

1. Federal law requires most interstate truckers to obtain a permit that reflects compliance with certain federal requirements. The 1965 version of the law authorized states to require proof that a truck operator had such a permit. By 1991, 39 states had demanded such proof, requiring a $10 per truck registration fee and giving each trucker a stamp to affix to a multistate "bingo card" carried in the vehicle. Finding this scheme inefficient and burdensome, Congress created the current Single State Registration System (SSRS), which allows a trucking company to fill out one set of forms in one state, thereby registering in every participating state through which its trucks travel.

   A subsection of Michigan's Motor Carrier Act imposes on truck companies operating in interstate commerce an annual fee of $100 for each self-propelled motor vehicle operated by or on behalf of the motor carrier. The American Truckers Association (ATA) and others challenged the $100 fee as preempted by the extensive federal regulation of interstate trucking and trucking companies. The ATA and others appealed to the U.S. Supreme Court. What should the U.S. Supreme Court do? Be sure to discuss what portion of the Constitution applies to this issue. [*American Trucking Associations, Inc. v Michigan Public Service Com'n*, 545 US 429]

2. J.C. Penney, a retail merchandiser, has its principal place of business in Plano, Texas. It operates retail stores in all 50 states, including 10 stores in Massachusetts, and a direct mail catalog business. The catalogs illustrated merchandise available for purchase by mail order. The planning, artwork, design, and layout for these catalogs were completed and paid for outside of Massachusetts, primarily in Texas, and Penney contracted with independent printing companies located outside Massachusetts to produce the catalogs. The three major catalogs were generally printed in Indiana, while the specialty catalogs were printed in South Carolina and Wisconsin. Penney supplied the printers with paper, shipping wrappers, and address labels for the catalogs; the printers supplied the ink, binding materials, and labor. None of these materials was purchased in Massachusetts. Printed catalogs, with address labels and postage affixed, were transported by a common carrier from the printer to a U.S. Postal Service office located outside Massachusetts, where they were sent to Massachusetts addressees via third- or fourth-class mail. Any undeliverable catalogs were returned to Penney's distribution center in Connecticut.

   Purchases of catalog merchandise were made by telephoning or returning an order form to Penney at a location outside Massachusetts, and the merchandise was shipped to customers from a Connecticut distribution center. The Massachusetts Department of Revenue audited Penney in 1995 and assessed a use tax, penalty, and interest on the catalogs that had been shipped into Massachusetts.

The position of the department was that there was a tax due of $314,674.62 on the catalogs that were used by Penney's Massachusetts customers. Penney said such a tax was unconstitutional in that it had no control or contact with the catalogs in the state. Can the state impose the tax? Why or why not? [*Commissioner of Revenue v J.C. Penney Co., Inc.*, 730 NE2d 266 (Mass)]

3. Alfonso Lopez, Jr., a 12th-grade student at Edison High School in San Antonio, Texas, went to school carrying a concealed .38-caliber handgun and five bullets. School officials, acting on an anonymous tip, confronted Lopez. Lopez admitted that he had the gun. He was arrested and charged with violation of federal law, the Gun-Free School Zones Act of 1990. Lopez moved to dismiss his indictment on the grounds that the provision of the Gun-Free School Zones Act with which he was charged was unconstitutional in that it was beyond the power of Congress to legislate controls over public schools. The district court found the statute to be a constitutional exercise of congressional authority.

   Lopez was found guilty and sentenced to two years in prison. He appealed and challenged his conviction on the basis of the commerce clause. The Court of Appeals agreed with Lopez, found the Gun-Free School Zones Act an unconstitutional exercise of congressional authority, and reversed the conviction. The U.S. Attorney appealed. Who should win at the U.S. Supreme Court and why? [*United States v Lopez*, 514 US 549]

4. The University of Wisconsin requires all of its students to pay, as part of their tuition, a student activity fee. Those fees are used to support campus clubs and activities. Some students who objected to the philosophies and activities of some of the student clubs filed suit to have the fees halted. What constitutional basis do you think they could use for the suit? [*Board of Regents of Wisconsin System v Southworth*, 529 US 217]

5. The Crafts' home was supplied with gas by the city gas company. Because of some misunderstanding, the gas company believed that the Crafts were delinquent in paying their gas bill. The gas company had an informal complaint procedure for discussing such matters, but the Crafts had never been informed that such a procedure was available. The gas company notified the Crafts that they were delinquent and that the company was shutting off the gas. The Crafts brought an action to enjoin the gas company from doing so on the theory that a termination without any hearing was a denial of due process. The lower courts held that the interest of the Crafts in receiving gas was not a property interest protected by the due process clause and that the procedures the gas company followed satisfied the requirements of due process. The Crafts appealed. Were they correct in contending that they had been denied due process of law? Why or why not? [*Memphis Light, Gas and Water Division v Craft*, 436 US 1]

6. Alexis Geier was injured in an accident while driving a 1987 Honda Accord that did not have passive safety restraints. When her Honda Accord was manufactured, the U.S. Department of Transportation required passive safety restraints on some, but not all, vehicles. Geier and her parents filed suit against Honda for its negligence in not equipping the Honda Accord with a driver's-side airbag. Geier alleged that because Honda knew of the safety standard but

did not voluntarily comply with it (it was not required to do so under the federal regulations), it was negligent under state negligence standards for liability and should be held liable. The district court granted Honda summary judgment based on Honda's argument that safety requirements for cars were set exclusively by the federal government. The Court of Appeals affirmed, and Geier appealed. What would be the effect of a decision that requires a car company to comply with state-by-state standards of negligence? Would a state court finding of negligence be a constitutional exercise of state power? Should the U.S. Supreme Court affirm or reverse the summary judgment for Honda? [*Geier v American Honda Motor Co.*, 529 US 1913]

7. Montana imposed a severance tax on every ton of coal mined within the state. The tax varied depending on the value of the coal and the cost of production. It could be as high as 30 percent of the price at which the coal was sold. Montana mine operators and some out-of-state customers claimed that this tax was unconstitutional as an improper burden on interstate commerce. Decide. [*Commonwealth Edison Co. v Montana*, 453 US 609]

8. Ollie's Barbecue is a family-owned restaurant in Birmingham, Alabama, specializing in barbecued meats and homemade pies, with a seating capacity of 220 customers. It is located on a state highway 11 blocks from an interstate highway and a somewhat greater distance from railroad and bus stations. The restaurant caters to a family and white-collar trade, with a take-out service for "Negroes." (Note: This term is used by the Court in its opinion in the case.) In the 12 months preceding the passage of the Civil Rights Act, the restaurant purchased locally approximately $150,000 worth of food, $69,683 or 46 percent of which was meat that it bought from a local supplier who had procured it from outside the state. Ollie's has refused to serve Negroes in its dining accommodations since opening in 1927, and since July 2, 1964, it has been operating in violation of the Civil Rights Act. A lower court concluded that if it were required to serve Negroes, it would lose a substantial amount of business. The lower court found that the Civil Rights Act did not apply because Ollie's was not involved in "interstate commerce." Will the commerce clause permit application of the Civil Rights Act to Ollie's? [*Katzenbach v McClung*, 379 US 294]

9. Ellis was employed by the city of Lakewood. By the terms of his contract, he could be discharged only for cause. After working for six years, he was told that he was going to be discharged because of his inability to generate safety and self-insurance programs, because of his failure to win the confidence of employees, and because of his poor attendance. He was not informed of the facts in support of these conclusions and was given the option to resign. He claimed that he was entitled to a hearing. Is he entitled to one? Why or why not? [*Ellis v City of Lakewood*, 789 P 2d 449 (Colo. App.)]

10. The Federal Food Stamp Act provided for the distribution of food stamps to needy households. In 1971, section 3(e) of the statute was amended to define households as limited to groups whose members were all related to each other. This was done because of congressional dislike for the lifestyles of unrelated hippies who were living together in hippie communes. Moreno and others

applied for food stamps but were refused them because the relationship requirement was not satisfied. An action was brought to have the relationship requirement declared unconstitutional. Is it constitutional? Discuss why or why not. [*USDA v Moreno*, 413 US 528]

11. New Hampshire adopted a tax law that in effect taxed the income of nonresidents working in New Hampshire only. Austin, a nonresident who worked in New Hampshire, claimed that the tax law was invalid. Was he correct? Explain. [*Austin v New Hampshire*, 420 US 656]

12. Following a boom in cruise ship construction, the ships are now looking for ports at which they can dock in order to begin voyages, most of which begin in the United States. With so many new ships, the companies are trying to establish connections with cities that are not ordinarily considered cruise ship docks. The companies pursue these alternatives because the traditional docking cities of New York, Seattle, Miami, Los Angeles, and Houston have become crowded with cruise ship traffic. The following issues have arisen:

- Without proper scheduling and departures, cruise ships often end up waiting in the harbor for three to eight hours; as a result, ports such as Tampa, a nontraditional cruise ship port, are experiencing traffic jams of ships waiting to dock.

- The presence of the large boats and the resulting number of tourists cause overwhelming flooding of the often-quaint alternative ports such as Charleston, South Carolina. Charleston residents worry that tourists from the cruise ships flooding their city will result in irreversible destruction of the town's preserved landmarks and quaint looks.

- Rising water levels in ports such as New Orleans mean that the tall ships cannot clear power lines and have to be redirected to ports nearby that are not prepared, as when New Orleans had to redirect a 2,974-passenger cruise ship to Gulfport, Mississippi.

- The port facilities are not adequate to handle all of the boats, the passengers, and even the ships' fueling needs.

Most cruise ship lines are incorporated outside of the United States, and they do not pay federal income taxes and are certainly not subject to state income taxes even though the most passengers come from the United States.[25] Can the ships be taxed to cover the harbor expenses? Can they be required by states and cities to pay docking fees, or are they internationally exempt companies?

13. A federal statute prohibited granting federal funds to libraries that did not control access to pornographic Internet sites on library computers so that children did not gain access and were not exposed to such sites as they used the public facilities. The American Library Association challenged the prohibition as a violation of First Amendment rights.

Are free speech rights violated with the funding regulation? [*U.S. v American Library Association*, 539 US 194; lower court decision at 201 F Supp 2d 401]

---

[25] Nicole Harris, "Big Cruise Ships Cause Traffic Jams in Ports," *Wall Street Journal*, August 20, 2003, B1–B6.

Chapter 5

GOVERNMENT REGULATION OF COMPETITION AND PRICES

T he government can regulate not just businesses but also business competition and prices. Antitrust legislation and a regulatory scheme help to ensure that businesses compete fairly.

A. POWER TO REGULATE BUSINESS

The federal government may regulate any area of business to advance the nation's economic needs.[1] Under the police power, states may regulate all aspects of business so long as they do not impose an unreasonable burden on interstate commerce or any activity of the federal government. (See Chapter 4 for a discussion of the protections and limits of the commerce clause.) Local governments may also exercise this police power to the extent a state permits them to do so.

1. Regulation, Free Enterprise, and Deregulation

Milton Friedman, the Nobel economist, has written that government regulation of business interferes with the free enterprise system. Under a true free enterprise system, market forces would provide the necessary protections for airline safety, food purity, and safe drugs through the forces of demand and supply. Sometimes, however, the demand response, or market reaction, to problems or services is not rapid enough to prevent harm, and government regulation steps in to stop abuses. For example, the Federal Trade Commission (FTC) stepped in to curb the tactics and practices of telemarketers when the number of consumer complaints increased dramatically without any industry self-regulation.

There has been some deregulation in certain industries. The collapse of companies such as Lehman Brothers and New Century Financial as well as the financial woes of companies such as Merrill Lynch and Bear Stearns (situations that stemmed from the meltdown of the subprime mortgage markets) have revealed that more oversight is necessary for Wall Street investment firms, financial analysts, and mortgage lenders. Consequently, Congress is in the process of regulating bond rating agencies, the mortgage process, appraisals, and investment banking operations.

2. Regulation of Production, Distribution, and Financing

To protect the public from harm, government may prohibit false advertising and labeling, and establish health and purity standards for cosmetics, foods, and drugs. Licenses may be required to be able to deal in certain goods, and these licenses may be revoked for improper conduct or violations of statutes and regulations.[2] The government may also regulate markets themselves: the quantity of a product that may be produced or grown and the price at which the finished product may be sold. For example, agricultural products markets and commodities have significant government constraints. Government may also engage in competition with private

---

[1] *SKF, USA, Inc. v Customs and Border Protection*, 556 F3d 1337 (CA 9 2009).
[2] *Culver v Maryland Ins. Com'r*, 931 A2d 537 (Md App 2007).

enterprises or own and operate an industry. **For Example,** the U.S. Postal Service competes directly with UPS and FedEx for the delivery of packages as well as for overnight delivery services.

The financing of business is directly affected by the national government, which creates a national currency and maintains the Federal Reserve banking system. State and other national laws may also affect financing by regulating financing contracts and documents, such as bills of lading and commercial paper.

3. Regulation of Unfair Competition

Each of the states and the federal government have statutes and regulations that prohibit unfair methods of competition. Unfair competition is controlled by both statutes and administrative agencies and regulations.

Congress has enacted the Federal Trade Commission Act,[3] which makes all "unfair methods of competition ... and unfair or deceptive acts or practices"[4] unlawful and created the Federal Trade Commission (FTC) to administer the act. The FTC has taken enforcement steps against refusals to sell, boycotts, market restrictions, disparagement of competitors' products, and unlawful methods of billing and collection. The FTC regulates false and misleading advertising and controls even the statements on packaged foods to ensure that the nutritional content of the food described on the label is accurate **For Example,** Beech-Nut Baby Food Company paid significant fines in the late 1980s for representing its baby apple juice to actually contain apple juice. The product was made from a very good-tasting chemical concoction, but it had no apple juice. Such misrepresentation on the label was a violation of Section 5 of the Federal Trade Commission Act that prohibits unfair methods of competition. Business missteps, from false advertising to boycotts, constitute unfair methods of competition prohibited under the FTC Act.[5]

B. Regulation of Markets and Competition

4. Regulation of Prices

Governments, both national and state, may regulate prices. Price regulation may be delegated to an administrative officer or agency. Prices in various forms are regulated, including not only what a buyer pays for goods purchased from a store (through controls on price fixing—see discussion that follows) but also through limits on interest rates and rent controls.

CPA

(A) **Prohibition on Price Fixing.** Agreements among competitors, as well as "every contract, combination ... or conspiracy" to fix prices, violate Section 1 of the Sherman Act.[6] Known as *horizontal price-fixing,* any agreements to charge an agreed-upon price or to set maximum or minimum prices between or among competitors are *per se*—in, through, or by themselves—a violation of the Sherman

---

[3] 15 USC § 41 *et seq.*
[4] To review the Federal Trade Commission Act, go to **www.ftc.gov**.
[5] In many states, such a seller would also be guilty of committing a deceptive trade practice or violating a consumer protection statute.
[6] To view the full language of Section 1 of the Sherman Act, see 15 USC § 1.

Act. An agreement among real estate brokers to never charge below a 6 percent commission is price-fixing.[7] **For Example,** in 2001, Christie's and Sotheby's auction houses settled an antitrust lawsuit for charging the same commissions for many years.[8]

Clayton Act–a federal law that prohibits price discrimination.

Robinson-Patman Act–a federal statute designed to eliminate price discrimination in interstate commerce.

price discrimination–the charging practice by a seller of different prices to different buyers for commodities of similar grade and quality, resulting in reduced competition or a tendency to create a monopoly.

(B) PROHIBITED PRICE DISCRIMINATION. The **Clayton Act** and **Robinson-Patman Act** prohibit price discrimination.[9] **Price discrimination** occurs when a seller charges different prices to different buyers for "commodities of like grade and quality," with the result being reduced competition or a tendency to create a monopoly.[10]

Price discrimination prohibits charging different prices to buyers as related to marginal costs. That is, volume discounts are permissible because the marginal costs are different on the larger volume of goods. However, the Robinson-Patman Act makes it illegal to charge different prices to buyers when the marginal costs of the seller for those goods are the same. Any added incentives or bonuses are also considered part of the price.

C A S E   S U M M A R Y

Bagging Customers for Having Sales

FACTS: Leegin Creative Leather Products, Inc. designs, manufactures, and distributes leather goods and accessories under the brand name "Brighton." The Brighton brand is sold across the United States in over 5,000 retail stores. PSKS, Inc., runs Kay's Kloset, a Brighton retailer in Lewisville, Texas, that carries about 75 different product lines, but was known as the place in that area to go for Brighton.

Leegin's president, Jerry Kohl, who also has an interest in about 70 stores that sell Brighton products, believes that small retailers treat customers better, provide customers more services, and make their shopping experience more satisfactory than do larger, often impersonal retailers. In 1997, Leegin instituted the "Brighton Retail Pricing and Promotion Policy," which banished retailers that discounted Brighton goods below suggested prices.

In December 2002, Leegin discovered that Kay's Kloset had been marking down Brighton's entire line by 20 percent. When Kay's would not stop marking the Brighton products prices down, Leegin stopped selling to the store.

PSKS sued Leegin for violation of the antitrust laws. The jury awarded PSKS $1.2 million in damages and the judge trebled the damages and reimbursed PSKS for its attorney's fees and costs–for a judgment against Leegin of $3,975,000.80. The Court of Appeals affirmed. Leegin appealed.

DECISION: The Court held that the goal of providing customers with information and service through the smaller boutiques was a competitive strategy that offered consumers choices. It was not a *per se* violation for Leegin to require minimum prices. Resale price maintenance increases the choices consumers have by providing them with a full-service retailer. Each case on resale price maintenance requires examination of the market and the effect on competition, but it is not automatically anticompetitive. The decision was reversed. **[Leegin Creative Leather Products, Inc. v PSKS, Inc., 551 US 877 (2007)]**

---

[7] *McClain v Real Estate Board of New Orleans, Inc.*, 441 US 942 (1980).
[8] Carol Vogel and Ralph Blumenthall, "Ex-Chairman of Sotheby's Gets a Year and a Day for Price-Fixing," *New York Times*, April 12, 2002, A26.
[9] 15 USC §§ 1, 2, 3, 7, 8.
[10] 15 USC § 13a. To read the full Clayton Act, go to **www.usdoj.gov** or **www.justice.gov** and plug in "Clayton Act" in a site search.

For Example, offering one buyer free advertising while not offering it to another as an incentive to buy would be a violation of the Robinson-Patman Act. The Clayton Act makes both the giving and the receiving of any illegal price discrimination a crime.

CPA

State statutes frequently prohibit favoring one competitor by giving a secret discount when the effect is to harm the competition.[11] A state may prohibit either selling below cost to harm competitors or selling to one customer at a secret price that is lower than the price charged other customers when there is no economic justification for the lower price.[12] Some state statutes specifically permit sellers to set prices so that they can match competitive prices, but not to undercut a competitor's prices.[13] The issue of state antitrust regulation and wide variations in state laws and decisions prompted the creation of the Antitrust Modernization Commission,

C A S E   S U M M A R Y

Getting a Piece of the Pie Market

FACTS: Utah Pie Company is a Utah corporation that for 30 years has been baking pies in its plant in Salt Lake City and selling them in Utah and surrounding states. It entered the frozen pie business in 1957 and was immediately successful with its new line of frozen dessert pies—apple, cherry, boysenberry, peach, pumpkin, and mince.

Continental Baking Company, Pet Milk, and Carnation, all based in California, entered the pie market in Utah. When these companies entered the Utah market, a price war began. In 1958 Utah Pie was selling pies for $4.15 per dozen. By 1961, as all the pie companies competed, it was selling the same pies for $2.75 per dozen. Continental's price went from $5.00 per dozen in 1958 to $2.85 in 1961. Pet's prices went from $4.92 per dozen to $3.46, and Carnation's from $4.82 per dozen to $3.30.

Utah Pie filed suit, charging price discrimination. The district court found for Utah Pie. The Court of Appeals reversed, and Utah Pie appealed.

DECISION: There was price discrimination. Pet was selling its pies in Utah through Safeway at prices that were lower than its prices in other markets and also much lower than its own brand pie in the Salt Lake City market. Pet also introduced a 20-ounce economy pie under the Swiss Miss label and began selling the new pie in the Salt Lake market in August 1960 at prices ranging from $3.25 to $3.30 for the remainder of the period. This pie was at times sold at a lower price in the Salt Lake City market than it was sold in other markets. For 7 of the 44 months in question for price discrimination, Pet's prices in Salt Lake were lower than prices charged in the California markets. This was true even though selling in Salt Lake involved a 30- to 35-cent freight cost.

Also, Pet had predatory intent to injure Utah Pie. Pet admitted that it sent into Utah Pie's plant an industrial spy to seek information. Pet suffered substantial losses on its frozen pie sales during the greater part of time involved in this suit. Pet had engaged in predatory tactics in waging competitive warfare in the Salt Lake City market. Coupled with the price discrimination, Pet's behavior lessened competition and violated Robinson-Patman. [**Utah Pie Co. v Continental Baking Co., 386 US 685 (1967)**]

---

[11] *Eddins v Redstone*, 35 Cal Rptr 3d 863 (2006).

[12] In *Weyerhaeuser v Ross-Simons*, 549 US 312 (2007), the U.S. Supreme Court ruled that predatory bidding is also a price discrimination issue. In a monopsony, a buyer tries to control a market by overbidding all its competitors and thereby cornering the market for supplies it needs to produce goods. However, if the bidder is actually just in need of the goods and bids higher for them, there is no anticompetitive conduct.

[13] *Home Oil Company, Inc. v Sam's East, Inc.*, 252 F Supp 1302 (MD Ala 2003).

a group likely to recommend changes in laws and judicial review standards at both the state and federal levels.[14]

(c) **Permitted Price Discrimination.** Price discrimination is expressly permitted when it can be justified on the basis of (1) a difference in grade, quality, or quantity; (2) the cost of transportation involved in performing the contract; (3) a good-faith effort to meet competition; (4) differences in methods or quantities, i.e., marginal cost differences; (5) deterioration of goods; or (6) a close-out sale of a particular line of goods. The Robinson-Patman Act[15] reaffirms the right of a seller to select customers and refuse to deal with anyone. The refusal, however, must be in good faith, not for the purpose of restraining trade.

5. Prevention of Monopolies and Combinations

Monopolies and combinations that restrain trade are prohibited under the federal antitrust laws.

Sherman Antitrust Act–a federal statute prohibiting combinations and contracts in restraint of interstate trade, now generally inapplicable to labor union activity.

(a) **The Sherman Act.** The **Sherman Antitrust Act** includes two very short sections that control anticompetitive behavior. They provide:

> *[§ 1] Every contract, combination in the form of trust or otherwise, or conspiracy, in restraint of trade or commerce among the several states, or with foreign nations, is declared to be illegal.*
>
> *[§ 2] Every person who shall monopolize or attempt to monopolize, or combine or conspire with any other person or persons to monopolize any part of the trade or commerce among the several states, or with foreign nations, shall be deemed guilty of a felony.*[16]

The Sherman Act applies not only to buying and selling activities but also to manufacturing and production activities. Section 1 of the Sherman Act applies to agreements, conduct, or conspiracies to restrain trade, which can consist of price-fixing, tying, and monopolization. Section 2 prohibits monopolizing or attempting to monopolize by companies or individuals.

market power–the ability to control price and exclude competitors.

(b) **Monopolization.** To determine whether a firm has engaged in monopolization or attempts to monopolize, the courts determine whether the firm has **market power**, which is the ability to control price and exclude competitors. Market power is defined by looking at both the geographic and product markets. **For Example,** a cereal manufacturer may have 65 percent of the nationwide market for its Crispy Clowns cereal (the product market), but it may have only 10 percent of the Albany, New York, market because of a local competitor, Crunchy Characters. Crispy Clowns may have market power nationally, but in Albany, it would not reach monopoly levels.

---

[14] 21st Century Department of Justice Appropriations Authorization Act, Pub. L. No. 107-273, 116 Stat. 1758 (2002), available at **http://amc.gov/pdf/statute/amc_act.pdf**.

[15] 15 USC §§ 13, 21.

[16] 15 USC § 1. Free competition has been advanced by the Omnibus Trade and Competitiveness Act of 1988, 19 USC § 2901 *et seq.*

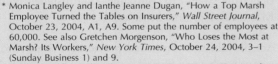

ethics & the law

Marsh & McLennan

Marsh & McLennan (MMC) is best known as the world's largest insurance broker with 43,000 employees in its global operations.* MMC had a different way of achieving growth.

MMC should have been obtaining competing bids on employee insurance plans for the companies it represented. However, MMC developed a "pay-to-play" format for obtaining bids that allowed the insurers and MMC to profit. To be sure (1) that the policies were renewed and (2) that the renewal bonus was a given, MMC had all of its insurers agree to roll over on renewals. For example, if Insurer A was up for renewal, Insurers B and C would submit fake and higher bids that MMC would then take to the corporate client and, of course, recommend renewal at the lower rate. In some cases, MMC did not even have official bids from the competing insurers. MMC sent bids forward that had not even been signed by the insurers who were playing along to receive the same treatment when their renewals came along. Once MCC implemented the "pay-to-play system," its insurance revenue became 67.1 percent of its revenue.** Commissions from these arrangements represented one-half of MMC's 2003 income of $1.5 billion.***

One of the companies to complain about MMC's practices was Munich RE. One of its e-mails to an MMC executive (whose name was blacked out) wrote, "I am not some Goody Two Shoes who believes that truth is absolute, but I do feel I have a pretty strict ethical code about being truthful and honest. This idea of 'throwing the quote' by quoting artificially high numbers in some predetermined arrangement for us to lose is repugnant to me, not so much because I hate to lose, but because it is basically dishonest. And I basically agree with the comments of others that it comes awfully close to collusion and price-fixing."

Without admitting or denying guilt, MMC settled antitrust charges by agreeing to drop the commission system and pay $850 million to its clients as a means of compensating for what might have been overcharges. MMC also agreed to hire a new CEO. The value of MMC's shares dropped almost 50 percent within 10 days following the mid-October filing of suit by then New York Attorney General Spitzer against the company.[†]

MMC's new CEO fired several senior executives despite the fact that there was no evidence that they had broken the law. When asked why he would fire them, Michael G. Cherkasky, a former district attorney in New York, said, "Freedom from criminal culpability is not our standard for executive leadership."[‡]

* Monica Langley and Ianthe Jeanne Dugan, "How a Top Marsh Employee Turned the Tables on Insurers," *Wall Street Journal*, October 23, 2004, A1, A9. Some put the number of employees at 60,000. See also Gretchen Morgenson, "Who Loses the Most at Marsh? Its Workers," *New York Times*, October 24, 2004, 3–1 (Sunday Business 1) and 9.

** Monica Langley and Ianthe Jeanne Dugan, "How a Top Marsh Employee Turned the Tables on Insurers," *Wall Street Journal*, October 23, 2004, A1, A9.

*** Id.

[†] "The Chatter," *New York Times*, November 14, 2004, BU2.

[‡] Ian McDonald, "After Spitzer Probe, Marsh CEO Tries Corporate Triage," *Wall Street Journal*, August 29, 2005, A1.

Having a large percentage of a market is not necessarily a monopoly. The Sherman Act requires that the monopoly position be gained because of a superior product or consumer preference, not because the company has engaged in purposeful conduct to exclude competitors by other means, such as preventing a competitor from purchasing a factory. Perhaps one of the best known monopolization cases involved Microsoft. In the case, the Justice Department alleged that because Microsoft had 90 percent of the market for operating systems it had and used monopoly power to control and market

CASE SUMMARY

Fill It Up: The Price Is Right and Fixed

FACTS: Barkat U. Khan and his corporation entered into an agreement with State Oil to lease and operate a gas station and convenience store owned by State Oil. The agreement provided that Khan would obtain the gasoline supply for the station from State Oil at a price equal to a suggested retail price set by State Oil, less a margin of $3.25 per gallon. Khan could charge any price he wanted, but if he charged more than State Oil's suggested retail price, the excess went to State Oil. Khan could sell the gasoline for less than State Oil's suggested retail price, but the difference would come out of his allowed margin.

After a year, Khan fell behind on his lease payments, and State Oil gave notice of, and began, eviction proceedings. The court had Khan removed and appointed a receiver to operate the station. The receiver did so without the price constraints and received an overall profit margin above the $3.25 imposed on Khan.

Khan filed suit, alleging that the State Oil agreement was a violation of Section 1 of the Sherman Act because State Oil was controlling price. The district court held that there was no *per se* violation and that Khan had failed to demonstrate antitrust injury. The Court of Appeals reversed, and State Oil appealed.

DECISION: In what was a reversal of prior decisions, the Court held that vertical maximum prices (as in this case in which a retailer was prohibited from charging above a certain amount) are not a *per se* violation of the Sherman Act. The Court noted that benefits can come from retailers' not being able to charge above a certain amount. At a minimum, such controls on maximum prices were not an automatic violation of the Sherman Act and need to be examined in light of what happens to competition. In determining whether such prices might affect competition, the Court noted that maximum prices might have an impact on the survival of inefficient dealers, as was the case here. However, encouraging inefficiency is not the purpose of either the market or the laws on anticompetitive behavior. **[State Oil v Khan, 522 US 3 (1997)]**

and did so by refusing to sell its operating system to companies that installed Netscape in lieu of or in addition to the Microsoft Explorer browser.[17]

CPA (c) PRICE-FIXING. The Sherman Act prohibits, as discussed previously, competitors agreeing to set prices. Price-fixing can involve competitors: agreeing to not sell below a certain price, agreeing on commission rates, agreeing on credit terms, or exchanging cost information. Price is treated as a sensitive element of competition, and discussion among competitors has also been deemed to be an attempt to monopolize.

(d) TYING. It is a violation of the Sherman Act to force "tying" sales on buyers. **Tying** occurs when the seller makes a buyer who wants to purchase one product buy an additional product that he or she does not want.

tying–the anticompetitive practice of requiring buyers to purchase one product in order to get another.

The essential characteristic of a tying arrangement that violates Section 1 of the Sherman Act is the use of control over the tying product within the relevant market to compel the buyer to purchase the tied article that either is not wanted or could be purchased elsewhere on better terms. **For Example,** in the Microsoft antitrust case,

[17] *United States v Microsoft*, 253 F3d 34 (CA DC 2001).

sports&entertainment law

Celebrity Issues and Antitrust

Public Interest Corporation (PIC) owned and operated television station WTMV-TV in Lakeland, Florida. MCA Television Ltd. (MCA) owns and licenses syndicated television programs. In 1990, the two companies entered into a licensing contract for several first-run television shows. With respect to all but one of these shows, MCA exchanged the licenses on a "barter" basis for advertising time on WTMV. However, MCA conditioned this exchange on PIC's agreeing to license the remaining show, *Harry and the Hendersons,* for cash as well as for barter. *Harry and the Hendersons* was what some in the industry would call a "dog," a show that was not very good that attempted to capitalize on a hit movie. PIC agreed to

this arrangement, although it did not want *Harry and the Hendersons*. The shows that PIC did want were *List of a Lifetime, List of a Lifetime II, Magnum P.I.,* and 17 other miscellaneous features.

The relationship between the parties was strained over nonpayment, poor ratings performance of *Harry,* and other issues. When litigation resulted, PIC alleged that it had been subjected to an illegal tying arrangement. PIC requested damages for MCA's violation of the Sherman Act. What violation do you think occurred?

Source: Adapted from *MCA Television Ltd. v Public Interest Corp.,* 171 F3d 1265 (CA 11 1998).

Microsoft is accused of requiring the purchase and use of its browser as a condition for purchasing its software. The Sherman Act also prohibits professional persons, such as doctors, from using a peer review proceeding to pressure another professional who competes with them in private practice and refuses to become a member of a clinic formed by them.

(E) BUSINESS COMBINATIONS. The Sherman Antitrust Act does not prohibit bigness. However, Section 7 of the Clayton Act provides that "no corporation ... shall acquire the whole or any part of the assets of another corporation ... where in any line of commerce in any section of the country, the effect of such acquisition may be substantially to lessen competition, or to tend to create a monopoly." If the Clayton Act is violated through ownership or control of competing enterprises, a court may order the violating defendant to dispose of such interests by issuing a decree called a **divestiture order.**[18]

divestiture order– a court order to dispose of interests that could lead to a monopoly.

(1) Premerger Notification

When large-size enterprises plan to merge, they must give written notice to the FTC and to the head of the Antitrust Division of the Department of Justice. This advance notice gives the department the opportunity to block the merger and thus avoid the loss that would occur if the enterprises merged and were then required to separate.[19] **For Example,** Time Warner was required to notify the Justice Department and seek

[18] *California v American Stores Co.,* 492 US 1301 (1989).
[19] Antitrust Improvement Act of 1976, PL 94-435, § 201, PL 94-435, 90 Stat 1383, 15 USC § 1311 *et seq.*

e-commerce&cyberlaw

E-mail's Revelations

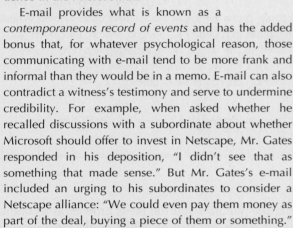

In the U.S. Justice Department's case against Microsoft, a lawyer commented, "The Government does not need to put Mr. Gates on the stand because we have his e-mail and memoranda." There were 30 million pages of e-mail used as evidence in the Microsoft trial.

E-mail provides what is known as a *contemporaneous record of events* and has the added bonus that, for whatever psychological reason, those communicating with e-mail tend to be more frank and informal than they would be in a memo. E-mail can also contradict a witness's testimony and serve to undermine credibility. For example, when asked whether he recalled discussions with a subordinate about whether Microsoft should offer to invest in Netscape, Mr. Gates responded in his deposition, "I didn't see that as something that made sense." But Mr. Gates's e-mail included an urging to his subordinates to consider a Netscape alliance: "We could even pay them money as part of the deal, buying a piece of them or something."

E-mail is discoverable, admissible as evidence, and definitely not private. Employees should follow the admonition of one executive whose e-mail was used to fuel a million-dollar settlement by his company with a former employee: "If you wouldn't want anyone to read it, don't send it in e-mail."

The impact of e-mail in the Microsoft antitrust case on companies and their e-mail policies was widespread. For example, Amazon.com launched a companywide program called "Sweep and Keep," under which employees were instructed to purge e-mail messages no longer needed for conducting business. Amazon.com offered employees who immediately purged their e-mail free lattes in the company cafeteria. The company had a two-part program. The first portion included instructions on document retention and deletion. The second part of the program was on document creation and included the following warning for employees: "Quite simply put, there are some communications that should not be expressed in written form. Sorry, no lattes this time."

Source: Adapted from Marianne M. Jennings, *Business: Its Legal, Ethical and Global Environment*, 8th ed. (Cincinnati, OH:: West Legal Studies in Business, 2009), ch. 16.

---

approval for its merger with AOL, which the Justice Department eventually gave. However, when WorldCom proposed its merger with Sprint, the Justice Department refused approval because it believed this would reduce competition in telecommunications too much.[20]

(2) Takeover Laws

takeover laws—laws that guard against unfairness in corporate takeover situations.

Antitrust laws usually focus on whether the combination or agreement is fair to society or to a particular class, such as consumers. Some legislation aims to protect the various parties directly involved in combining different enterprises. Concern arises that one enterprise may in effect be raiding another enterprise. Congress and four-fifths of the states have adopted **takeover laws**, which seek to guard against unfairness in such situations. State laws apply only to corporations chartered in their state.

[20] Rebecca Blumenstein and Jared Sandberg, "WorldCom CEO Quits Amid Probe of Firm's Finances," *Wall Street Journal*, April 30, 2002, A1, A9.

C. Power to Protect Business

In addition to controlling business combinations, the federal government protects others. By statute or decision, associations of exporters, marine insurance associations, farmers' cooperatives, and labor unions are exempt from the Sherman Act with respect to agreements between their members. Certain pooling and revenue-dividing agreements between carriers are exempt from the antitrust law when approved by the appropriate federal agency. The Newspaper Preservation Act of 1970 grants an antitrust exemption to operating agreements entered into by newspapers to prevent financial collapse. The Soft Drink Interbrand Competition Act[21] grants the soft drink industry an exemption when it is shown that, in fact, substantial competition exists in spite of the agreements.

The general approach of the U.S. Supreme Court has been that these types of agreements should not be automatically, or *per se*, condemned as a restraint of interstate commerce merely because they create the power or potential to monopolize interstate commerce. It is only when the restraint imposed is unreasonable that the practice is unlawful. The Court applies the rule of reason in certain cases because the practice may not always harm competition.

6. Remedies for Anticompetitive Behavior

(A) **Criminal Penalties.** A violation of either section of the Sherman Act is punishable by fine or imprisonment or both at the discretion of the court. The maximum fine for a corporation is $100 million. A natural person can be fined a maximum of $1,000,000 or imprisoned for a maximum term of ten years or both.

(B) **Civil Remedies.** In addition to these criminal penalties, the law provides for an injunction to stop the unlawful practices and permits suing the wrongdoers for damages.

(1) Individual Damage Suit

treble damages—three times the damages actually sustained.

Any person or enterprise harmed may bring a separate action for **treble damages** (three times the damages actually sustained).

(2) Class-Action Damage Suit by State Attorney General

When the effect of an antitrust violation is to raise prices, the attorney general of a state may bring a class-action suit to recover damages on behalf of those who have paid the higher prices. This action is called a *parens patriae* action on the theory that the state is suing as the parent of its people.

---

[21] Act of July 9, 1980, PL 96-308, 94 Stat 939, 15 USC § 3501 *et seq.*

lawflix

Antitrust (2001) (R)

This movie is based on Bill Gates and Microsoft.
Check out LawFlix at **www.cengage.com/blaw/dvl** to access movie clips that illustrate business law concepts.

MAKE THE CONNECTION

SUMMARY

Regulation by government has occurred primarily to protect one group from the improper conduct of another group. The police power is the basis for government regulation. Regulation is passed when the free enterprise system fails to control abuses, as with the recent passage of investment banking regulations. Unfair methods of competition are prohibited.

Prices have been regulated both by prohibiting setting the exact price or a maximum price and discrimination in pricing. Price discrimination between buyers is prohibited when the effect of such discrimination could tend to create a monopoly or lessen competition. Price discrimination occurs when the prices charged different buyers are different despite the same marginal costs. However, resale price maintenance is not illegal *per se* if the control is for purposes of providing customer service.

The Sherman Antitrust Act prohibits conspiracies in restraint of trade and the monopolization of trade. The Clayton Act prohibits mergers or the acquisition of the assets of another corporation when this conduct would tend to lessen competition or create a monopoly. The Justice Department requires premerger notification for proposed mergers. Violation of the federal antitrust statutes subjects the wrongdoer to criminal prosecution and possible civil liability that can include treble damages.

LEARNING OUTCOMES

After studying this chapter, you should be able to clearly explain:

A. POWER TO REGULATE BUSINESS

LO.1 State the extent to which government can regulate business
See the **For Example** discussion of the subprime mortgage market on p. 88
See the Ethics & the Law discussion of Marsh & McLennan on p. 93

B. REGULATION OF MARKETS AND COMPETITION

LO.2 Explain what laws regulate the markets and protect competition
See the *Utah Pie* case on predatory pricing, p. 91
See the *Kahn* oil case on price controls, p. 94
See the *Leegin* case on resale price maintenance, p. 90
See the Sports & Entertainment Law feature on tying, p. 95

C. POWER TO PROTECT BUSINESS

LO.3 Discuss the powers and remedies available to protect business competition
See Section 6 for a list of the penalties and remedies on p. 97

KEY TERMS

Clayton Act	price discrimination	takeover laws
divestiture order	Robinson-Patman Act	treble damages
market power	Sherman Antitrust Act	tying

QUESTIONS AND CASE PROBLEMS

1. American Crystal Sugar Co. was one of several refiners of beet sugar in northern California, and it distributed its product in interstate commerce. American Crystal and the other refiners had a monopoly on the seed supply and were the only practical market for the beets. In 1939, all of the refiners began using identical form contracts that computed the price paid to the sugar beet growers using a "factor" common to all the refiners. As a result, all refiners paid the same price for beets of the same quality. Though there was no hard evidence of an illegal agreement, the growers brought suit under the Sherman Act against the refiners, alleging that they conspired to fix a single uniform price among themselves to hold down the cost of the beets. The growers sued for the treble damages available under the Sherman Act. Can they recover? [*Mandeville Island Farms v American Crystal Sugar Co.*, 334 US 219]

2. A Wisconsin statute prohibits "the secret payment or allowance of rebates, refunds, commissions, or unearned discounts" to some customers without allowing them to all customers on the same conditions when such practices injure or tend to injure competition or a competitor. Kolbe generally gave dealers a 50 percent discount, but it gave Stock Lumber Co. a discount of 54 percent. Other dealers were not informed of this or of the conditions that had to be satisfied to obtain the same discount. Kolbe gave Jauquet, another lumber dealer, only a 50 percent discount and, when asked, expressly stated that it did not give any other dealer a higher discount. When Jauquet learned of the higher discount given to Stock, it brought suit against Kolbe for violation of the Wisconsin statute. Did Kolbe violate the statute? [*Jauquet Lumber Co., Inc. v Kolbe & Kolbe Millwork, Inc.*, 476 NW2d 305 (Wis App)]

3. The major record companies settled an antitrust suit brought by 40 state attorneys general against them for alleged price-fixing in the sale of CDs. The

record companies agreed to pay $67.4 million to consumers who purchased CDs during the period from 1995 to 2000. The consent decree stipulated that the record companies had required retailers that accepted subsidies from record companies for advertising CDs not to advertise CDs for sale at a price agreed upon in advance. The record companies said that the policy helped keep independent retailers in business because they could not afford to price at Wal-Mart levels. Wal-Mart always advertised CDs for sale at a price below the floor agreed to by the subsidized independent retailers and the record companies. The record companies did not admit any wrongdoing and, in addition to agreeing to the $67.4 million, also agreed to provide 5.5 million CDs to libraries, schools, and nonprofit organizations (worth $75.7 million).[22] What antitrust violation were the attorneys general alleging? Is a minimum price a violation of antitrust laws?

4. The Three Tenors (Luciano Pavarotti, Placido Domingo, and Jose Carreras) made a record of their live performances together once every four years. The first two CDs and videos in the series, made by Time Warner, sold millions, with both becoming two of the highest-volume opera recordings in history. However, by the third performance and CD and video, the public demand was not as great, and Time Warner believed the first two releases would cannibalize the sales for the third. As a result, all parties involved in the sales of these CDs and tapes had to agree not to discount the first two performance tapes so that the third would have an opportunity to sell. The Federal Trade Commission (FTC) stumbled across the information on the pricing program when its staff members located a memo on the marketing plan and advertising constraints as it was reviewing documents for the proposed Time Warner/EMI Music merger proposal, a merger that fell through after European officials balked at the idea. The FTC pursued the case, and Time Warner settled the charges by agreeing not to restrain competition or set prices in the future. Is establishing a minimum price a violation of the Sherman Act? Is restricting advertising a violation of the Sherman Act?

5. Hines Cosmetic Co. sold beauty preparations nationally to beauty shops at a standard or fixed-price schedule. Some of the shops were also supplied with a free demonstrator and free advertising materials. The shops that were not supplied with them claimed that giving the free services and materials constituted unlawful price discrimination. Hines replied that there was no price discrimination because it charged everyone the same. What it was giving free was merely a promotional campaign that was not intended to discriminate against those who were not given anything free. Was Hines guilty of unlawful price discrimination? Explain.

6. Moore ran a bakery in Santa Rosa, New Mexico. His business was wholly intrastate. Meads Fine Bread Co., his competitor, engaged in an interstate business. Meads cut the price of bread in half in Santa Rosa but made no price cut in any other place in New Mexico or in any other state. This price-cutting

[22] Claudia Deutsch, "Suit Settled over Pricing of Recordings at Big Chains," *New York Times*, October 1, 2002, C1, C10; David Lieberman, "States Settle CD Price-fixing Case," *USA Today*, October 1, 2002, 3B.

drove Moore out of business. Moore then sued Meads for damages for violating the Clayton and Robinson-Patman Acts. Meads claimed that the price-cutting was purely intrastate and, therefore, did not constitute a violation of federal statutes. Was Meads correct? Why or why not? [*Moore v Meads Fine Bread Co.*, 348 US 115]

7. A&P Grocery Stores decided to sell its own brand of canned milk (referred to as *private label* milk). A&P asked its longtime supplier, Borden, to submit an offer to produce the private label milk. Bowman Dairy also submitted a bid, which was lower than Borden's. A&P's Chicago buyer then contacted Borden and said, "I have a bid in my pocket. You people are so far out of line it is not even funny. You are not even in the ballpark." The Borden representative asked for more details but was told only that a $50,000 improvement in Borden's bid "would not be a drop in the bucket." A&P was one of Borden's largest customers in the Chicago area. Furthermore, Borden had just invested more than $5 million in a new dairy facility in Illinois. The loss of the A&P account would result in underutilization of the plant. Borden lowered its bid by more than $400,000. The Federal Trade Commission charged Borden with price discrimination, but Borden maintained it was simply meeting the competition. Did Borden violate the Robinson-Patman Act? Does it matter that the milk was a private label milk, not its normal trade name Borden milk? [*Great Atlantic & Pacific Tea Co., Inc. v FTC*, 440 US 69]

8. Department 56 is a company that manufactures and sells collectible Christmas village houses and other replica items to allow collectors to create the whimsical "Snow Village" town or "Dickens Christmas." Department 56 has only authorized dealers. Sam's Club, a division of Wal-Mart Stores, Inc., began selling Department 56 pieces from the Heritage Village Collection. Susan Engel, president and CEO of Department 56, refused to sell Department 56 products to Wal-Mart. Does her refusal violate any antitrust laws?

9. Dr. Edwin G. Hyde, a board-certified anesthesiologist, applied for permission to practice at East Jefferson Hospital in Louisiana. An approval was recommended for his hiring, but the hospital's board denied him employment on grounds that the hospital had a contract with Roux & Associates for Roux to provide all anesthesiological services required by the hospital's patients. Dr. Hyde filed suit for violation of antitrust laws. Had the hospital done anything illegal? [*Jefferson Parish Hosp. Dist. No. 2 v Hyde*, 466 US 2]

10. BRG of Georgia, Inc. (BRG), and Harcourt Brace Jovanovich Legal and Professional Publications (HJB) are the nation's two largest providers of bar review materials and lectures. HJB began offering a Georgia bar review course on a limited basis in 1976 and was in direct, and often intense, competition with BRG from 1977 to 1979 when the companies were the two main providers of bar review courses in Georgia. In early 1980, they entered into an agreement that gave BRG an exclusive license to market HJB's materials in Georgia and to use its trade name "Bar/Bri." The parties agreed that HJB would not compete with BRG in Georgia and that BRG would not compete with HJB outside of Georgia. Under the agreement, HJB received $100 per student

enrolled by BRG and 40 percent of all revenues over $350. Immediately after the 1980 agreement, the price of BRG's course was increased from $150 to more than $400. Is their conduct illegal under federal antitrust laws? [*Palmer v BRG of Georgia, Inc.*, 498 US 46]

11. Favorite Foods Corp. sold its food to stores and distributors. It established a quantity discount scale that was publicly published and made available to all buyers. The top of the scale gave the highest discount to buyers purchasing more than 100 freight cars of food in a calendar year. Only two buyers, both national food chains, purchased in such quantities, and therefore, they alone received the greatest discount. Favorite Foods was prosecuted for price discrimination in violation of the Clayton Act. Was it guilty?

12. Run America, Inc., manufactures running shoes. Its shoe is consistently rated poorly by *Run Run Run* magazine in its annual shoe review. The number one shoe in *Run Run Run*'s review is the Cheetah, a shoe that Run America has learned is manufactured by the parent company of the magazine. Is this conduct a violation of the antitrust laws? Do you think it is ethical to run the shoe review without disclosing ownership?

13. The Quickie brand wheelchair is the most popular customized wheelchair on the market. Its market share is 90 percent. Other manufacturers produce special-use wheelchairs that fold, that are made of mesh and lighter frames, and that are easily transportable. These manufacturers do not compete with Quickie on customized chairs. One manufacturer of the alternative wheelchairs has stated, "Look, it's an expensive market to be in, that Quickie market. We prefer the alternative chairs without the headaches of customizations." Another has said, "It is such a drain on cash flow in that market because insurers take so long to pay. We produce chairs that buyers purchase with their own money, not through insurers. Our sales are just like any other product." Quickie entered the market nearly 40 years ago and is known for its quality and attention to detail. Buying a Quickie custom chair, however, takes time, and the revenue stream from sales is slow but steady because of the time required to produce custom wheelchairs. Has Quickie violated the federal antitrust laws with its 90 percent market share? Discuss.

14. Gardner-Denver is the largest manufacturer of ratchet wrenches and their replacement parts in the United States. Gardner-Denver had two different lists of prices for its wrenches and parts. Its blue list had parts that, if purchased in quantities of five or more, were available for substantially less than its white list prices. Did Gardner-Denver engage in price discrimination with its two price lists? [*D. E. Rogers Assoc., Inc. v Gardner-Denver Co.*, 718 F2d 1431 (6th Cir)]

15. The Aspen ski area consisted of four mountain areas. Aspen Highlands, which owned three of those areas, and Aspen Skiing, which owned the fourth, had cooperated for years in issuing a joint, multiple-day, all-area ski ticket. After repeatedly and unsuccessfully demanding an increased share of the proceeds, Aspen Highlands canceled the joint ticket. Aspen Skiing, concerned that skiers would bypass its mountain without some joint offering, tried a variety of

increasingly desperate measures to recreate the joint ticket, even to the point of in effect offering to buy Aspen Highland's tickets at retail price. Aspen Highlands refused even that. Aspen Skiing brought suit under the Sherman Act, alleging that the refusal to cooperate was a move by Aspen Highlands to eliminate all competition in the area by freezing it out of business. Is there an antitrust claim here in the refusal to cooperate? What statute and violation do you think Aspen Skiing alleged? What dangers do you see in finding the failure to cooperate to be an antitrust violation? [*Aspen Skiing Co. v Aspen Highlands Skiing Corp.*, 472 US 585]

Chapter 6

ADMINISTRATIVE AGENCIES

Late in the nineteenth century, a new type of governmental structure began to develop to meet the highly specialized needs of government regulation of business: the administrative agency. The administrative agency is now typically the instrument through which government makes and carries out its regulations.

A. NATURE OF THE ADMINISTRATIVE AGENCY

administrative agency–government body charged with administering and implementing legislation.

An **administrative agency** is a government body charged with administering and implementing legislation. An agency may be a department, independent establishment, commission, administration, authority, board, or bureau. Agencies exist on the federal and state levels. One example of a federal agency is the Federal Trade Commission (FTC), whose structure is shown in Figure 6.1.

1. Purpose of Administrative Agencies

Federal administrative agencies are created to carry out general policies specified by Congress. Federal agencies include the Securities Exchange Commission (SEC), the Consumer Product Safety Commission (CPSC), and the Food and Drug Administration (FDA). The law governing these agencies is known as **administrative law**.

administrative law–law governing administrative agencies.

State administrative agencies also exist and may have jurisdiction over areas of law affecting business, such as workers' compensation claims, real estate licensing, and unemployment compensation.

2. Uniqueness of Administrative Agencies

The federal government and state governments alike are divided into three branches: executive, legislative, and judicial. Many offices in these branches are filled by

FIGURE 6-1 | *Structure of the Federal Trade Commission*

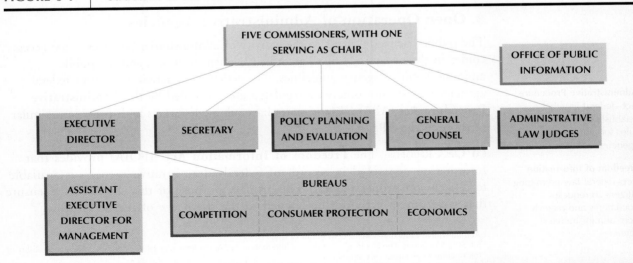

FIGURE 6-2 | *The Administrative Chain of Command*

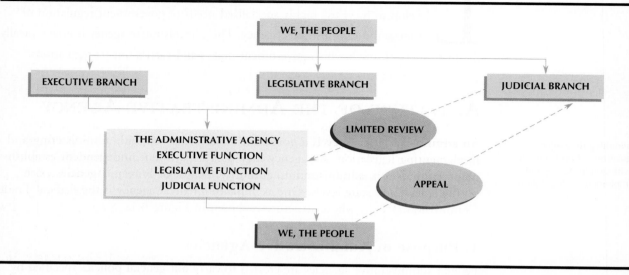

persons who are elected. In contrast, members of administrative agencies are ordinarily appointed (in the case of federal agencies, by the president of the United States with the consent of the Senate).

In the tripartite structure, the judicial branch reviews actions of the executive and legislative branches to ensure that they have not exceeded their constitutional powers. However, the major governmental agencies combine legislative, executive, and judicial powers (see Figure 6.2). These agencies make the rules, conduct inspections to see that the rules have been or are being obeyed, and sit in judgment to determine whether there have been violations of their rules. Because agencies have broad powers, they are subject to strict procedural rules as well as disclosure requirements (discussed in the following section).

3. Open Operation of Administrative Agencies

The public has ready access to the activity of administrative agencies. That access comes in three ways: (1) open records, (2) open meetings, and (3) public announcement of agency guidelines. The actions and activities of most federal agencies that are not otherwise regulated are controlled by the **Administrative Procedure Act** (APA).[1] Many states have adopted statutes with provisions similar to those of the APA.

Administrative Procedure Act–federal law that establishes the operating rules for administrative agencies.

Freedom of Information Act–federal law permitting citizens to request documents and records from administrative agencies.

(A) OPEN RECORDS. The **Freedom of Information Act**[2] (FOIA) provides that information contained in records of federal administrative agencies is available to citizens on proper request. The primary purpose of this statute is "to ensure that government activities be opened to the sharp eye of public scrutiny."[3]

[1] Administrative Procedures Act 5 USC § 550 *et seq.*
[2] 5 USC § 552 *et seq.* The Electronic Freedom of Information Act Amendments of 1996 extend the public availability of information to electronically stored data.
[3] *Brady-Lunny v Massey,* 185 F Supp 2d 928 (CD III 2002).

To ensure that members of the public understand how to obtain records, the FOIA provides that "[e]ach agency shall ... publish in the *Federal Register* for the guidance of the public ... the methods whereby the public may obtain information, make submittals or requests, or obtain decisions.[4] There are exceptions to this right of public scrutiny. They prevent individuals and companies from obtaining information that is not necessary to their legitimate interests and might harm the person or company whose information is being sought.[5] State statutes typically exempt from disclosure any information that would constitute an invasion of the privacy of others. However, freedom of information acts are broadly construed, and unless an exemption is clearly given, the information in question is subject to public inspection. Moreover, the person claiming that there is an exemption that prohibits disclosure has the burden of proving that the exemption applies to the particular request made. Exemptions include commercial or financial information not ordinarily made public by the person or company that supplies the information to the agency as part of the agency's enforcement role.[6]

The FOIA's primary purpose is to subject agency action to public scrutiny. Its provisions are liberally interpreted, and agencies must make good-faith efforts to comply with its terms.

open meeting law—law that requires advance notice of agency meeting and public access.

(B) OPEN MEETINGS. Under the Sunshine Act of 1976,[7] called the **open meeting law**, the federal government requires most meetings of major administrative agencies to be open to the public. The Sunshine Act[8] applies to those meetings involving "deliberations" of the agency or those that "result in the joint conduct or disposition of official agency business." The object of this statute is to enable the public to know what actions agencies are taking and to prevent administrative misconduct by having open meetings and public scrutiny. Many states also have enacted Sunshine laws.

(C) PUBLIC ANNOUNCEMENT OF AGENCY GUIDELINES. To inform the public of the way administrative agencies operate, the APA, with certain exceptions, requires that each federal agency publish the rules, principles, and procedures that it follows.[9]

B. LEGISLATIVE POWER OF THE AGENCY

An administrative agency has the power to make laws and does so by promulgating regulations with public input.

4. Agency's Regulations as Law

An agency may adopt regulations within the scope of its authority. The power of an agency to carry out a congressional program "necessarily requires the formulation of

---

[4] 5 USC § 552(a)(1)(a).
[5] Additional protection is provided by the Privacy Act of 1974, 5 USC § 552a(b); *Doe v U.S. Dept. of Treasury,* 2009 WL 1949119 (DDC).
[6] *Sun-Sentinel Company v U.S. Dept. of Homeland Security,* 431 F Supp 2d 1258 (SD Fla 2006).
[7] The Government in the Sunshine Act can be found at 5 USC § 552b.
[8] 5 USC § 552b(a)(2).
[9] APA codified at 5 USC § 552. See Section 5(c) of this chapter for a description of the *Federal Register,* the publication in which these agency rules, principles, and procedures are printed.

policy and the making of rules to fill any gap left by Congress."[10] If the regulation is not authorized by the law creating the agency, anyone affected by it can challenge the regulation on the basis that the agency has exceeded its authority. [See Section 11(c), "Beyond the Jurisdiction of the Agency."]

An administrative agency cannot act beyond the scope of the authority in the statute that created it or assigned a responsibility to it.[11] However, the authority of an agency is not limited to the technology in existence at the time the agency was created or assigned jurisdiction for enforcement of laws. The sphere in which an agency may act expands with new scientific developments.[12]

When an agency's proposed regulation deals with a policy question that is not specifically addressed by statute, the agency that was created or given the discretion to administer the statute may establish new policies covering such issues. This power is granted regardless of whether the lawmaker intentionally left such matters to the agency's discretion or merely did not foresee the problem. In either case, the matter is one to be determined within the agency's discretion, and courts defer to agencies' policy decisions.[13] For example, the FCC has authority to deal with cell phones and cell phone providers even though when the agency was created, there were only the traditional types of land-line telephones.

Today, regulations adopted by an agency may interpret or clarify the law. In effect, many regulations have the feel of legislation. Courts have come to recognize the authority of an agency even though the lawmaker creating the agency did nothing more than state the goal or objective to be attained by the agency. The modern approach is to regard the administrative agency as holding all powers necessary to effectively perform the duties entrusted to it. When the agency establishes a rational basis for its rule, courts accept the rule and do not substitute their own judgment.[14]

Legislatures have met the judicial standard for approval with various types of agencies created for different purposes such as licensing to protect the public, prohibiting unfair methods of competition, or administering the registration of autos and other vehicles. The purposes in these types of statutes include the typical public safety and welfare areas such as ensuring competence and integrity of professionals through the licensing process or ensuring that there are free markets that allow open competition.[15]

5. Agency Adoption of Regulations

(A) CONGRESSIONAL ENABLING ACT. Before an agency can begin rulemaking proceedings, it must be given jurisdiction by congressional enactment in the form of a statute. For example, Congress has enacted broad statutes governing discrimination in

---

[10] *Virginia v Browner*, 80 F3d 869 (4th Cir 1996).

[11] *Zuni Public School Dist. No. 89 v Department of Educ.*, 550 US 81 (2007).

[12] *United States v Midwest Video Corp.*, 406 US 649 (1972) (sustaining a commission regulation that provided that "no CATV system having 3,500 or more subscribers shall carry the signal of any television broadcast station unless the system also operates to a significant extent as a local outlet by cablecasting and has available facilities for local production and presentation of programs other than automated services").

[13] *Chevron, U.S.A., Inc. v National Resources Defense Council, Inc.*, 467 US 837 (1984).

[14] *Covad Communications Co. v FCC*, 430 F3d 528 (DC Cir 2006).

[15] All of these are examples of the general legislative authority given to agencies. Agencies are given generic commands of law and then create the law's specifics.

employment practices and has given authority to the Equal Employment Opportunity Commission (EEOC) to establish definitions, rules, and guidelines for compliance with those laws. Sometimes an existing agency is assigned the responsibility for new legislation implementation and enforcement. **For Example,** the Department of Labor has been assigned the responsibility to handle the whistle-blower protection provisions of Sarbanes-Oxley that provide protection against retaliation and/or termination to those who report financial chicanery at their companies. The Department of Labor has been in existence for almost a century, but it was assigned a new responsibility and given new jurisdiction by Congress.

(B) AGENCY RESEARCH OF THE PROBLEM. After jurisdiction is established, the agency has the responsibility to research the issues and various avenues of regulation for implementing the statutory framework. As the agency does so, it determines the cost and benefit of the problems, issues, and solutions. The study may be done by the agency itself, or it may be completed by someone hired by the agency. **For Example,** before red lights were required equipment in the rear windows of all cars, the Department of Transportation developed a study using taxicabs with the red lights in the rear windows and found that the accident rate for rear-end collisions with taxicabs was reduced dramatically. The study provided justification for the need for regulation as well as the type of regulation itself.

ethics & the law

Flush with Regulation: How Many Gallons and Where

The Energy Policy Act of 1992 requires that toilets installed after the act took effect (1994) use only 1.6 gallons of water rather than the nearly century-old standard of 3.5 gallons. As of 2000, about one-fourth of the nation's toilets were the 1.6-gallon types. The EPA mandated that permits be conditioned on the use of the 1.6-gallon toilets and that inspection approvals be denied if anything but a 1.6-gallon toilet had been installed.

As homeowners have remodeled and replaced older toilets, they have learned that the 3.5-gallon toilets are no longer sold in the United States. However, just across the U.S./Canadian border near Detroit, Canadian hardware stores are doing a land-office business selling 3.5-gallon tanks to U.S. citizens.

Those who are remodeling, and even some who are building new homes, provide for 1.6-gallon toilets in their plans and generally install $100 1.6-gallon toilets from Home Depot in order to pass inspection. They then purchase a standard fixture Canadian toilet for anywhere from $500 to $1,000 because of the high demand, and install it. Plumbing stores all over Canada report that sales are brisk. In a survey conducted in May 2000, the Canadian plumbing store owners said that they sell, on average, one toilet per day to U.S. citizens either via direct sale or shipment.

Do the citizens break any laws by what they do? Is what they do ethical? How could the regulation be challenged? What foundation in administrative law might be used?

Federal Register Act–
federal law requiring agencies to make public disclosure of proposed rules, passed rules, and activities.

Federal Register–
government publication issued five days a week that lists all administrative regulations, all presidential proclamations and executive orders, and other documents and classes of documents that the president or Congress direct to be published.

(c) **PROPOSED REGULATIONS.** Following a study, the agency proposes regulations, which must be published. To provide publicity for all regulations, the **Federal Register Act**[16] provides that proposed administrative regulation be published in the *Federal Register*. This is a government publication published five days a week that lists all administrative regulations, all presidential proclamations and executive orders, and other documents and classes of documents that the president or Congress directs to be published.

The Federal Register Act provides that printing an administrative regulation in the *Federal Register* is public notice of the contents of the regulation to persons subject to it or affected by it, but in addition, the Regulatory Flexibility Act,[17] passed during the Reagan administration, requires that all proposed rules be published in the trade journals of those trades that will be affected by the proposed rules. **For Example,** any changes in federal regulations on real property closings and escrows have to be published in real estate broker trade magazines. In addition to the public notice of the proposed rule, the agency must also include a "regulatory

CASE SUMMARY

Seats Belts and Air Bags and Rules, Oh My!

FACTS: The U.S. Department of Transportation (DOT), charged with enforcing the National Traffic and Motor Vehicle Safety Act of 1966 and reducing auto accidents, passed Standard 208 in 1967, which required that all cars be equipped with seat belts. When another study showed the DOT that people did not use the belts, the department began a study of passive restraint systems which showed that these devices—automatic seat belts and air bags— could prevent approximately 12,000 deaths a year and over 100,000 serious injuries.

In 1972, after many hearings and comments, the DOT passed a regulation requiring some type of passive restraint system on all vehicles manufactured after 1975. Because of changes in directors of the DOT and the unfavorable economic climate in the auto industry, the requirements for passive restraints were postponed. In 1981, the department proposed a rescission of the passive restraint rule. After receiving written comments and holding public hearings, the agency concluded there was no longer a basis for reliably predicting that passive restraints increased safety levels or decreased accidents. Furthermore, the agency found it would cost $1 billion to implement the rule, and it was unwilling to impose such substantial costs on auto manufacturers.

State Farm filed suit on the rescission of the rule on the basis that it was arbitrary and capricious. The Court of Appeals held that the rescission was, in fact, arbitrary and capricious. The auto manufacturers appealed.

DECISION: Just as an agency cannot pass regulations without studies, comments, and hearings, an agency cannot withdraw a regulation without going through the same process. In this case, the regulation was eliminated without any prior study of the issues and the impact of its elimination. The withdrawal of a regulation requires the same procedural steps as the promulgation of a rule. [**Motor Vehicles Manufacturers Ass'n v State Farm Mutual Ins. Co., 463 US 29 (1983)**]

[16] 44 USC § 1505 *et seq.*
[17] 5 USC § 601 *et seq.*

flexibility analysis" that "shall describe the impact of the proposed rule on small entities."[18] The goal of this portion of the APA was to be certain that small businesses were aware of proposed regulatory rules and their cost impact.

(D) PUBLIC COMMENT PERIOD. Following the publication of the proposed rules, the public has the opportunity to provide input on the proposed rules. Called the *public comment period,* this time must last at least 30 days (with certain emergency exceptions) and can consist simply of letters written by those affected that are filed with the agency or of hearings conducted by the agency in Washington, D.C., or at specified locations around the country. An emergency exemption for the 30-day comment period was made when airport security measures and processes were changed following the September 11, 2001, attacks on the World Trade Center and the Pentagon that used domestic, commercial airliners.

(E) OPTIONS AFTER PUBLIC COMMENT. After receiving the public input on the proposed rule, an agency can decide to pass, or promulgate, the rule. The agency can also decide to withdraw the rule. **For Example,** the EEOC had proposed rules on

C A S E   S U M M A R Y

Get Off of My Cloud, er, Parachute

FACTS: San Diego Air Sports (SDAS) Center operates a sports parachuting business in Otay Mesa, California. SDAS offers training to beginning parachutists and facilitates recreational jumping for experienced parachutists. It indicates that the majority of SDAS jumps occur at altitudes in excess of 5,800 feet. The jump zone used by SDAS overlaps the San Diego Traffic Control Area (TCA). Although the aircraft carrying the parachutists normally operate outside the TCA, the parachutists themselves are dropped through it. Thus, the air traffic controllers must approve each jump.

In July 1987, an air traffic controller in San Diego filed an Unsatisfactory Condition Report with the Federal Aviation Administration (FAA), complaining of the strain that parachuting was putting on the controllers and raising safety concerns. The report led to a staff study of parachute jumping within the San Diego TCA. This was followed by a letter in March 1988 from the FAA to SDAS informing SDAS that "[e]ffective immediately parachute jumping within or into the San Diego TCA in the Otay Reservoir Jump Zone will not be authorized." The FAA stated that the letter was final and appealable.

SDAS challenged the letter in federal court on grounds that it constituted rulemaking without compliance with required Administrative Procedure Act (APA) procedures.

DECISION: The effect of the FAA letter was to promulgate a rule. Although the FAA characterized the ban on parachutes as simply a safety issue, it was a new rule for operation in the air space around San Diego, and SDAS had the right to participate and be heard in the process that led to the letter. No process was followed here at all in terms of the release of the findings or a public comment period. The FAA was required to follow the same steps for this new rule and could not circumvent that process by labeling a fundamental change in the rules as simply an interpretation. [**San Diego Air Sports Center, Inc. v FAA, 887 F2d 966 (9th Cir 1989)**]

---

[18] 5 USC § 603(a).

handling religious discrimination in the workplace. The proposed rules, which would have required employers to police those wearing a cross or other religious symbol, met with so much public and employer protest that they were withdrawn. Finally, the agency can decide to modify the rule based on comments and then promulgate or, if the modifications are extensive or material, modify and put the proposed rule back out for public comment again. A diagram of the rule-making process can be found in Figure 6.3.

---

e-commerce&cyberlaw

Complying with Regulations Online

Federal agencies have been adapting to online business. For example, the IRS offers electronic filing of income tax returns. The SEC permits electronic submission of various forms and reports due from companies. Corporations are using the Web to telecast their discussions with

analysts to comply with SEC rules on uniform disclosure of all company information to all investors in the same time frame. All federal agencies are accepting e-mail comments on proposed rules as valid public comments during the public comment periods for proposed rules.

C. EXECUTIVE POWER OF THE AGENCY

The modern administrative agency has the power to execute the law and to bring proceedings against violators.

6. Enforcement or Execution of the Law

An agency has the power to investigate, to require persons to appear as witnesses, to require witnesses to produce relevant papers and records, and to bring proceedings against those who violate the law. In this connection, the phrase *the law* embraces regulations adopted by an agency as well as statutes and court decisions.

An agency may investigate to determine whether any violation of the law or of its rules generally has occurred. An agency may also investigate to determine whether additional rules need to be adopted, to ascertain the facts with respect to a particular suspected or alleged violation, and to see whether the defendant in a proceeding before it is complying with its final order. An agency may issue subpoenas to obtain information reasonably required by its investigation.[19]

7. Constitutional Limitations on Administrative Investigation

Although administrative agencies have broad enforcement authority, they remain subject to the constitutional protections afforded individuals and businesses.

---

[19] *EEOC v Sidley, Austen, Brown and Wood*, 35 F3d 696 (CA 7 2002).

FIGURE 6-3 | *Steps in Agency Rulemaking*

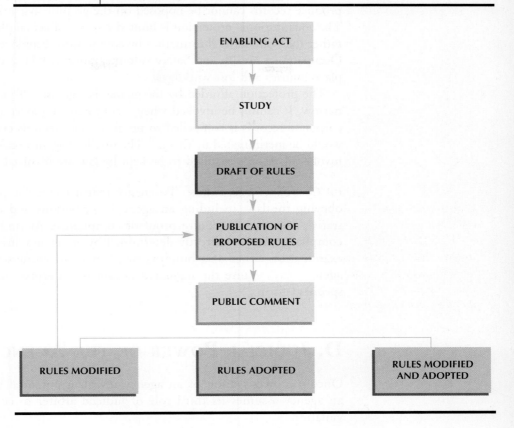

(A) Inspection of Premises. In general, a person has the same protection against unreasonable searches and seizures by an administrative officer as by a police officer. In contrast, when the danger of concealment is great, a warrantless search can be made of the premises of a highly regulated business, such as one selling liquor or firearms. Likewise, when violation of the law is dangerous to health and safety, the law may authorize inspection of the workplace without advance notice or a search warrant when such a requirement could defeat the purpose of the inspection.

(B) Aerial Inspection. A search warrant is never required when the subject matter can be seen from a public place. **For Example,** when a police officer walking on a public sidewalk can look through an open window and see illegal weapons, a search warrant is not required to enter the premises and seize the weapons. Using airplanes and helicopters, law enforcement officers can see from the air; an agency, too, can gather information in this manner.[20]

(C) Production of Papers. For the most part, the constitutional guarantee against unreasonable searches and seizures does not afford much protection for papers and

---

[20] *Dow Chemical Co. v United States,* 476 US 1819 (1986).

records being investigated by an agency. **For Example,** a subpoena to testify or to produce records cannot be opposed on the ground that it is a search and seizure. The constitutional protection is limited to cases of actual physical search and seizure rather than obtaining information by compulsion. Employers must turn over to the Occupational Health and Safety Administration (OSHA) their records on workplace injuries and lost workdays.

The protection afforded by the guarantee against self-incrimination is likewise narrow. It cannot be invoked when a corporate employee or officer in control of corporate records is compelled to produce those records even though he or she would be incriminated by them.[21] The privilege against self-incrimination cannot be invoked if records required to be kept by law are involved.

(D) COMPLIANCE VERIFICATION. To ensure that a particular person or business is obeying the law, including an agency's regulations and orders, the administrative agency may require proof of compliance. At times, the question of compliance may be directly determined by an agency investigation, involving an examination either of a building or plant or of witnesses and documents. An agency may require the regulated person or enterprise to file reports in a specified form.[22]

D. JUDICIAL POWER OF THE AGENCY

Once the investigation of an agency reveals a potential violation of the law, an agency assumes its third role of judicial arbiter to conduct hearings on violations.

8. The Agency as a Specialized Court

An agency, although not a court by law, may be given power to sit as a court and to determine whether any violations of the law or of agency regulations have occurred. The National Labor Relations Board (NLRB) determines whether a prohibited labor practice has been committed. The Federal Trade Commission (FTC) acts as a court to determine whether someone has engaged in unfair competition.

(A) BEGINNING ENFORCEMENT—PRELIMINARY STEPS. Either a private individual or company or an agency may file a written complaint alleging some violation of law or regulation that is within the agency's jurisdiction. This complaint is then served on the company or individual named in the complaint, who then has the opportunity to file an answer to the allegations. There may be other phases of pleading between the parties and the agency, but eventually, the matter comes before the agency to be heard. After a hearing, the agency makes a decision and enters an order either dismissing the complaint or directing remedies or resolutions.

---

[21] *Braswell v United States,* 487 US 99 (1988), see also *Armstrong v Guccione,* 470 F3d 89 (CA 2 2006).
[22] *United States v Morton Salt Co.,* 338 US 632 (1950).

(B) THE ADMINISTRATIVE HEARING. To satisfy the requirements of due process, an agency handling a complaint must generally give notice and hold a hearing at which all persons affected may be present. A significant difference between an agency hearing and a court hearing is that there is no right of trial by jury before an agency. **For Example,** a workers' compensation board may decide a claim without any jury. Similarly, a case in which an employer protests the unemployment tax rate assigned to her company by a state agency has no right to a jury trial. The lack of a jury does not deny due process (see Chapter 4). An administrative law judge (ALJ) hears the complaint and has the authority to swear witnesses, take testimony, make evidentiary rulings, and make a decision to recommend to the agency heads for action.

An agency hearing is ordinarily not subject to the rules of evidence. Another difference between an administrative hearing and a judicial determination is that an agency may be authorized to make an initial determination without holding a hearing. If its conclusion is challenged, the agency then holds a hearing. A court, on the other hand, must have a trial before it makes a judgment. This difference has important practical consequences because the party objecting to the agency's initial determination has the burden of proof and the cost of going forward. The result is that fewer persons go to the trouble of seeking such a hearing, which reduces the number of hearings and the amount of litigation in which an agency becomes involved. The government saves money and time with this abbreviated process.

When an administrative action involves only the individuals directly affected rather than a class of persons or the community in general, the agency must have some form of hearing before it makes a decision. The Supreme Court has held that because a civil service employee may be removed only for cause, it is a denial of due process for a statute to authorize an agency to remove the employee without a hearing.[23] Just giving the employee the right to appeal such action is not sufficient. Because the employee has a significant interest in continued employment, there must be some form of hearing prior to removing the employee to determine that there were not errors in the administrative action.

informal settlements—negotiated disposition of a matter before an administrative agency, generally without public sanctions.

consent decrees—informal settlements of enforcement actions brought by agencies.

(C) STREAMLINED PROCEDURE: CONSENT DECREES. **Informal settlements** or **consent decrees** are practical devices to cut across the procedures already outlined. In many instances, an alleged wrongdoer informally notified that a complaint has been made is willing to change. An agency's informing an alleged wrongdoer of the charge before filing any formal complaint is sound public relations, as well as expeditious policy. A matter that has already gone into the formal hearing stage may also be terminated by agreement, and a stipulation or consent decree may be filed setting forth the terms of the agreement. The Administrative Dispute Resolution Act of 1990 encourages the streamlining of the regulatory process and authorizes federal agencies to use alternative means of dispute resolution.[24]

(D) FORM OF ADMINISTRATIVE DECISION. When an administrative agency makes a decision, it usually files an opinion that sets forth the findings of facts and reasons

[23] *Cleveland Board of Education v Loudermill,* 470 US 532 (1985); *Darr v Town of Telluride, Colo.,* 495 F3d 1243 (CA 10 2007).
[24] 5 USC § 571 *et. seq.*

on which the decision is based. In some instances, a statute expressly requires this type of opinion, but an agency should always file one so that the parties and the court (in the event of an appeal) will understand the agency's action and reasoning.[25]

9. Punishment and Enforcement Powers of Agencies

(A) PENALTY. Within the last few decades, agencies have increasingly been given the power to impose a penalty and to issue orders that are binding on a regulated party unless an appeal is taken to a court, which reverses the administrative decision. As an illustration of the power to impose penalties, the Occupational Safety and Health Act of 1970 provides for the assessment of civil penalties against employers who fail to end dangerous working conditions when ordered to do so by the administrative agency created by that statute.[26]

cease-and-desist order – order issued by a court or administrative agency to stop a practice that it decides is improper.

(B) CEASE-AND-DESIST ORDER. Environmental protection statutes adopted by states commonly give a state agency the power to assess a penalty for violating environmental protection regulations. As an illustration of the issuance of binding orders, the FTC can issue a **cease-and-desist order** to stop a practice that it decides is improper. This order to stop is binding unless reversed on an appeal. **For Example,** the FTC can order a company to stop making claims in ads that have been determined by that agency to be deceptive.

10. Exhaustion of Administrative Remedies

All parties interacting with an agency must follow the procedure specified by the law. No appeal to a court is possible until the agency has acted on the party's matter before it. As a matter of policy, parties are required to exhaust administrative remedies before they may go into court or take an appeal.

As long as an agency is acting within the scope of its authority or jurisdiction, a party cannot appeal before the agency has made a final decision. The fact that the complaining party does not want the agency to decide the matter or is afraid that the agency will reach a wrong decision is not grounds for bypassing the agency by going to court before the agency has acted.

exhaustion of administrative remedies – requirement that an agency make its final decision before the parties can go to court.

Exceptions to the **exhaustion-of-administrative remedies** requirement are (1) available remedies that provide no genuine opportunity for adequate relief; (2) irreparable injury that could occur if immediate judicial relief is not provided; (3) an appeal to the administrative agency that would be useless; or (4) a substantial constitutional question that the plaintiff has raised.

11. Appeal from Administrative Action and Finality of Administrative Determination

The statute creating the modern administrative agency generally provides that an appeal may be taken from the administrative decision to a particular court. The statute may provide the basis for an appeal. However, judicial precedent holds that

---

[25] *Jordan v Civil Service Bd., Charlotte,* 570 SE 2d 912 (CA NC 2002).
[26] 29 USC § 651 *et seq.*

courts may review administrative agency decisions on the bases covered in the following sections.

(A) Procedural Issues. If the procedure that an agency is to follow is specified by law, a decision of the agency that was made without following that procedure will be set aside and the matter sent back to the agency to proceed according to the required law.[27] An agency's actions, whether enforcement or rule promulgation, can be set aside if the agency has not followed the procedures required for rule-making or, in the case of enforcement, the due process rights of the charged business or individual.

(B) Substantive Law or Fact Issues. When the question that an agency decides is a question of law, the court on appeal will reverse the agency if the court disagrees with the legal interpretation.[28] This concept is being eroded to some extent by technical aspects of regulation. Courts now accept an agency's interpretation of a statute that involves a technical matter. Courts now tend to accept the agency's interpretation so long as it was reasonable even though it was not the only interpretation that could have been made.

In contrast with an agency's decision on matters of law, a controversy may turn on a question of fact or a mixed question of law and fact. In such cases, a court accepts an agency's conclusion if it is supported by substantial evidence. This means that the court must examine the entire record of the proceedings before the administrative agency to determine if there was substantial evidence to support the administrative findings. So long as reasonable minds could have reached the same conclusion as the agency after considering all of the evidence as a whole, the court must sustain the agency's findings of fact.[29]

A court will not reverse an agency's decision merely because the court would have made a different decision based on the same facts.[30] Because most disputes before an agency are based on questions of fact, the net result is that the agency's decision will be final in most cases.

Courts must give administrative agencies the freedom to do the work delegated to them and should not intervene unless the agency action is clearly unreasonable or arbitrary (see below). The agency action is presumed proper, and a person seeking reversal of the agency action has the burden to prove a basis for reversal.[31]

(C) Beyond the Jurisdiction of the Agency. When the question is whether an administrative action is in harmony with the policy of the statute creating the agency, an appellate court will sustain the administrative action if substantial evidence supports it.

(D) Arbitrary and Capricious. When an agency changes its prior decisions and customary actions, it must give its reasons. In the absence of such an explanation, a reviewing court cannot tell whether the agency changed its interpretation of the law

---

[27] *Tingler v State Board of Cosmetology*, 814 SW2d 683 (Mo App 1991).

[28] *Wallace v Iowa State Bd. of Educ.*, 770 NW2d 344 (Iowa 2009).

[29] *Dorchester Associates LLC v District of Columbia Bd. of Zoning Adjustment*, 976 A2d 200 (DC 2009).

[30] *In re Smith*, 121 P3d 150 (Wyo. 2005). An appellate court cannot review the evidence to determine the credibility of witnesses who testified before the administrative agency. *Hammann v City of Omaha*, 17 NW2d 323 (Neb. 1987).

[31] See note 29.

C A S E   S U M M A R Y

I'll Call You—Maybe During Dinner: The FCC and the National Do-Not-Call List Regulation

FACTS: The Telephone Consumer Protection Act of 1991 (TCPA) granted the FCC the authority to promulgate rules creating a procedure to protect telephone subscribers from receiving unwanted telemarketing calls. In 1994, Congress enacted the Telemarketing Act, which granted the FTC the authority to promulgate rules prohibiting "deceptive or abusive telemarketing practices." Congress specifically found that consumers were being increasingly victimized by telemarketing fraud and other abuses, and it required the FTC in promulgating its rules to (1) define "deceptive telemarketing acts or practices," (2) prohibit abusive patterns of unsolicited telephone calls, (3) restrict the hours of the day when telemarketing calls may be placed, and (4) require telemarketers to promptly disclose to call recipients the nature of their call.

In December 2002, the FTC issued amended rules that prohibit "deceptive or abusive telemarketing acts or practices."

Under the TCPA, the FCC announced its intention to adopt rules similar to the FTC's, enforcing the do-not-call list.

Mainstream Marketing and TMG, independent telemarketing companies based in Colorado, brought suit challenging the FTC's authority to create a national do-not-call list that allows consumers to opt out, alleging that the do-not-call list violates the First Amendment and the APA. The District Court for Colorado held that the FTC's do-not-call rules were unconstitutional on First Amendment grounds, and the District Court for the Western District of Oklahoma held that FTC lacked statutory authority to enact its do-not-call rules. The two appeals by the FCC and FTC were consolidated in the Tenth Circuit.

DECISION: The court held that Congress has granted clear authority under the statutes for both agencies to engage in the regulation of telemarketing. The enabling legislation gave the agencies the authority to create such a list as a means of controlling the telemarketing practices throughout the country. The court also held that the do-not-call registry did not violate the First Amendment because the government has a substantial interest in protecting the privacy of its citizens and the do-not-call list directly advances that governmental interest. The Congress, FTC, and FCC all determined that commercial calls affected by the registry were most to blame for the problems that the regulations remedied and the proposed alternative of company-specific approach had proven extremely burdensome to consumers. [**Mainstream Marketing Services, Inc. v F.T.C., 358 F3d 1228 (10th Cir 2004); 529** *cert. denied* **543 US 812 (2004).**]

for a valid reason or has made a mistake. The absence of an explanation condemns the agency action as arbitrary and requires reversal.[32]

The greatest limitation on court review of administrative action is the rule that a decision involving discretion will not be reversed in the absence of an error of law or a clear abuse of, or the arbitrary or capricious exercise of, discretion. The courts reason that because agency members were appointed on the basis of expert ability, it would be absurd for the court, which is unqualified technically to make a decision in the matter, to step in and determine whether the agency made the proper choice.

[32] *Lorillard Tobacco Co. v Roth,* 786 NE2d 7 (CA NY 2003).

Courts will not do so unless the agency has clearly acted wrongly, arbitrarily, or capriciously. As a practical matter, an agency's action is rarely found to be arbitrary or capricious. As long as an agency has followed proper procedure, the fact that the court disagrees with the agency's conclusion does not make that conclusion arbitrary or capricious. In areas in which economic or technical matters are involved, it is generally sufficient that the agency had a reasonable basis for its decision. A court will not attempt to second-guess the agency about complex criteria with which an administrative agency is intimately familiar. The judicial attitude is that for protection from laws and regulations that are unwise, improvident, or out of harmony with a particular school of thought, the people must resort to the ballot box, not to the court.

Because of limited funding and staff, an agency must exercise discretion in deciding which cases it should handle. Ordinarily, a court will not reverse an agency's decision to do nothing about a particular complaint.[33] That is, the courts will not override an agency's decision to do nothing. Exceptions include acting arbitrarily in those enforcement actions as when an agency refuses to act in circumstances in which action is warranted and necessary.

C A S E   S U M M A R Y

Foul Mouths Can Get You a Foul

FACTS: During the 2002 Billboard Music Awards, which were broadcast over the Fox Television Stations, singer Cher exclaimed, "I've also had critics for the last 40 years saying that I was on my way out every year. Right. So f* * * 'em." During a segment of the similarly broadcast 2003 Billboard Music Awards, when Nicole Richie and Paris Hilton, principals in a Fox television series called "The Simple Life" were presenting an award, Ms. Hilton began their interchange by reminding Ms. Richie to "watch the bad language," but Ms. Richie proceeded to ask the audience, "Why do they even call it 'The Simple Life?' Have you ever tried to get cow s* * * out of a Prada purse? It's not so f* * *ing simple."

Following each of these broadcasts, the Federal Communications Commission (FCC) received numerous complaints from parents whose children were exposed to the language. The FCC found that Fox Television had violated the FCC's indecency standards that prohibited use of the "F word" and discussion of excrement. The FCC issued a notice of fine. Fox and other broadcasters appealed the order. The court of appeals reversed the order, finding that the FCC's reasoning on its standards for indecency was not consistent or grounded in logic. The FCC appealed.

DECISION: The U.S. Supreme Court held that the FCC had the authority to determine what was and what was not indecent use of language in broadcasts. The case-by-case basis was neither arbitrary nor capricious because it had established that it was concerned about the impact of the use of such indecent language on children and needed to evaluate the use within context. The statute giving the FCC authority to regulate the content of broadcasts for indecent content gave broad authority to the agency and discretion. [**F.C.C. v Fox Television Stations, Inc. 129 S. Ct. 1800 (2009)**]

---

[33] *Heckler v Chaney,* 470 US 821 (1985).

12. Liability of the Agency

The decision of an agency may cause substantial loss to a business by increasing its operating costs or by making a decision that later is shown to be harmful to the economy. An agency is not liable for such loss when it has acted in good faith in the exercise of discretionary powers. An administrator who wrongly denies a person the benefit of a government program is not personally liable to that person.

lawflix

Clear and Present Danger (1994) PG-13

The struggles of Jack Ryan involve more than Colombian drug lords; he must battle the political appointees and their overstepping of their agency's authority. The relationship between agencies and congress is also depicted in the film.

    Check out LawFlix at **www.cengage.com/blaw/dvl** to access movie clips that illustrate business law concepts.

MAKE THE CONNECTION

SUMMARY

The administrative agency is unique because it combines the three functions that are kept separate under our traditional governmental system: legislative, executive, and judicial. By virtue of legislative power, an agency adopts regulations that have the force of law, although agency members are not elected by those subject to the regulations. By virtue of the executive power, an agency carries out and enforces the regulations, makes investigations, and requires the production of documents. By virtue of the judicial power, an agency acts as a court to determine whether a violation of any regulation has occurred. To some extent, an agency is restricted by constitutional limitations in inspecting premises and requiring the production of papers. These limitations, however, have a very narrow application in agency actions. When an agency acts as a judge, a jury trial is not required, nor must ordinary courtroom procedures be followed. Typically, an agency gives notice to the person claimed to be acting improperly, and a hearing is then held before the agency. When the agency has determined that there has been a violation, it may order that the violation stop. Under some statutes, the agency may go further and impose a penalty on the violator.

An appeal to a court may be taken from any decision of an agency by a person harmed by the decision. Only a person with a legally recognized interest can appeal from the agency ruling. No appeal can be made until every step available before the agency has been taken; that is, the administrative remedy must first be exhausted. An agency's actions can be reversed by a court if the agency exceeded its authority, the decision is not based in law or fact, the decision is arbitrary and capricious, or, finally, the agency violated procedural steps.

Protection from secret government is provided by Sunshine laws that afford the right to know what most administrative agency records contain; by the requirement that most agency meetings be open to the public; by the invitation to the public to take part in rulemaking; and by publicity given, through publication in the *Federal Register* and trade publications, to the guidelines followed by the agency and the regulations it has adopted.

LEARNING OUTCOMES

After studying this chapter, you should be able to clearly explain:

A. NATURE OF THE ADMINISTRATIVE AGENCY

LO.1 Describe the nature and purpose of administrative agencies
See Section A(2) for a discussion of the unique nature of agencies, p. 105.

B. LEGISLATIVE POWER OF THE AGENCY

LO.2 Discuss the legislative or rulemaking power of administrative agencies
See the *State Farm* case on p. 110.
See the *San Diego Air Sports* case on p. 111.
See the National Do-Not-Call case on p. 118.

C. EXECUTIVE POWER OF THE AGENCY

LO.3 Explain the executive or enforcement function of administrative agencies
See the *CBS* case on p. 125.

D. JUDICIAL POWER OF THE AGENCY

LO.4 Discuss the judicial power of administrative agencies including the rule on exhaustion of administrative remedies
See the *Mainstream Marketing* case on p. 118.

KEY TERMS

administrative agency
administrative law
Administrative
  Procedure Act
cease-and-desist order

consent decrees
exhaustion of
  administrative remedies
Federal Register Act
Federal Register

Freedom of
  Information Act
informal settlements
open meeting law

QUESTIONS AND CASE PROBLEMS

1. Following the events of September 11, 2001, in which four airplanes crashed as a result of the presence of terrorists on those flights, the FAA concluded that it needed to implement new procedures for airports and flights. The new procedures for security and flights took effect when the airports reopened five days later. Why did the FAA not need to go through the promulgation and public comment processes and time periods to have the new rules take effect?

2. Reserve Mining Co. obtained a permit from the Minnesota Pollution Control Agency to dump wastewater into the nearby Beaver River. The permit specified that no more than 1 million fibers per liter could be discharged in the company's wastewater. The agency did not make or file any explanation as to how or why that maximum was selected. Normally, the wastewater that the company generated was kept in a tailings dam with a discharge in the river necessary only in an emergency. Because of a sudden economic downturn, the company foresaw the need to dispose of wastewater in the river and discovered that the discharge it would have to make would likely be between 10 to 15 times the amount of fiber allowed by the permit. Reserve Mining appealed the maximum limitation imposed by the agency. How could Reserve Mining challenge the 1-million-fibers standard? [*Reserve Mining Co. v Minnesota Pollution Control Agency*, 364 NW2d 411 (Minn App)]

3. The Tacoma-Pierce County Health Department conducted an investigation into the quality of care provided by ambulance service providers in its jurisdiction. On the basis of that investigation, the department issued a set of temporary rules and regulations that established minimum requirements for equipment, drugs, and service availability for ambulance service providers in Pierce County. The *Tacoma News* wanted to publish an article on the matter and sought discovery of everything that had led to the adoption of the regulations, including all details of the investigation made by the health department. The health department objected to disclosing the names of the persons who had volunteered information on which the department had based its action and the names of the ambulance companies. Were the names subject to a Freedom of Information Act (FOIA) request? [*Tacoma News, Inc. v Tacoma-Pierce County Health Dept.*, 778 P2d 1066 (Wash App)]

4. Congress adopted a law to provide insurance to protect wheat farmers. The agency in charge of the program adopted regulations to govern applications for this insurance. These regulations were published in the *Federal Register*. Merrill applied for insurance, but his application did not comply with the regulations. He claimed that he was not bound by the regulations because he never knew they had been adopted. Is he bound by the regulations? [*Federal Crop Ins. Corp. v Merrill*, 332 US 380]

5. Santa Monica adopted a rent control ordinance authorizing the Rent Control Board to set the amount of rents that could be charged. At a hearing before it, the board determined that McHugh was charging his tenants a rent higher than the maximum allowed. McHugh claimed that the action of the board was

improper because there was no jury trial. Is McHugh correct? Why or why not? [*McHugh v Santa Monica Rent Control Board*, 49 Cal 3d 348, 777 P2d 91]

6. New York City's charter authorized the New York City Board of Health to adopt a health code that it declared to have the force and effect of law. The board adopted a code that provided for the fluoridation of the public water supply. A suit was brought to enjoin the carrying out of this program on the grounds that it was unconstitutional and that money could not be spent to carry out such a program in the absence of a statute authorizing the expenditure. It was also claimed that the fluoridation program was unconstitutional because there were other means of reducing tooth decay; fluoridation was discriminatory by benefiting only children; it unlawfully imposed medication on children without their consent; and fluoridation was or may be dangerous to health. Was the code's provision valid? [*Paduano v City of New York*, 257 NYS2d 531]

7. What is the *Federal Register?* What role does it play in rulemaking? What is the difference between the *Federal Register* and the Code of Federal Regulations?

8. The Consumer Product Safety Commission is reconsidering a rule it first proposed in 1997 that would require child-resistant caps on household products, including cosmetics. When the rule was first proposed in 1997, it was resisted by the cosmetics industry and abandoned. However, in May 2001, a 16-month-old baby died after drinking baby oil from a bottle with a pull-tab cap.

   The proposed rule would cover products such as baby oil and suntan lotion and any products containing hydrocarbons such as cleansers and spot removers. The danger, according to the commission, is simply the inhalation by children, not necessarily the actual ingestion of the products. Five children have died from inhaling such fumes since 1993, and 6,400 children under the age of five were brought into emergency rooms and/ or hospitalized for treatment after breathing in hydrocarbons. There is no medical treatment for the inhalation of hydrocarbons.

   Several companies in the suntan oil/lotion industry have supported the new regulations. The head of a consumer group has said, "We know these products cause death and injury. That is all we need to know."[34]

   What process must the CPSC follow to promulgate the rules? What do you think of the consumer group head's statement? Will that statement alone justify the rulemaking?

9. The *Federal Register* contained the following provision from the Environmental Protection Agency on January 14, 2002:

   We, the U.S. Fish and Wildlife Service (Service), announce the re-opening of the comment period on the proposed listing of Lomatium cookii *(Cook's lomatium) and* Limnanthes floccosa ssp. grandiflora *(large-flowered wooly meadowfoam) as endangered species under the Endangered Species Act of 1973, as amended (Act). We are re-opening the comment period to provide the public an opportunity to review additional information on the status, abundance, and distribution of these plants, and to request additional information and comments from the public regarding the proposed rule. Comments previously submitted need not be*

---

[34] Julian E. Barnes, "Safety Caps Are Considered for Cosmetics," *New York Times*, October 10, 2001, C1, C8.

resubmitted as they will be incorporated into the public record as part of this extended comment period; all comments will be fully considered in the final rule.

DATES: We will accept public comments until March 15, 2002.

What was the EPA doing and why? What could those who had concerns do at that point?

10. Macon County Landfill Corp. applied for permission to expand the boundaries of its landfill. Tate and others opposed the application. After a number of hearings, the appropriate agency granted the requested permission to expand. Tate appealed and claimed that the agency had made a wrong decision on the basis of the evidence presented. Will the court determine whether the correct decision was made? [*Tate v Illinois Pollution Control Board*, 188 Ill App 3d 994, 544 NE2d 1176]

11. The planning commissioner and a real estate developer planned to meet to discuss rezoning certain land that would permit the real estate developer to construct certain buildings not allowed under the then-existing zoning law. A homeowners association claimed it had the right to be present at the meeting. This claim was objected to on the theory that the state's Open Meetings Act applied only to meetings of specified government units and did not extend to a meeting between one of them and an outsider. Was this objection valid?

12. The Michigan Freedom of Information Act declares that it is the state's policy to give all persons full information about the actions of the government and that "the people shall be informed so that they may participate in the democratic process." The union of clerical workers at Michigan State University requested the trustees of the university to give them the names and addresses of persons making monetary donations to the university. Michigan State objected because the disclosure of addresses was a violation of the right of privacy. Decide. [*Clerical-Technical Union of Michigan State University v Board of Trustees of Michigan State University*, 475 NW2d 373 (Mich)]

13. The Department of Health and Human Services has proposed new guidelines for the interpretation of federal statutes on gifts, incentives, and other benefits bestowed on physicians by pharmaceutical companies. The areas on which the interpretation focused follow:

- Paying doctors to act as consultants or market researchers for prescription drugs

- Paying pharmacies fees to switch patients to new drugs

- Providing grants, scholarships, and anything more than nominal gifts to physicians for time, information sessions, and so on, on new drugs[35]

The Office of Inspector General is handling the new rules interpretation and has established a public comment period of 60 days. Explain the purpose of the public comment period. What ethical issues do the regulations attempt to address?

[35] See 67 *Federal Register* 62057, October 3, 2002. Go to **www.oig.hhs.gov**. See also Robert Pear, "U.S. Warning to Drug Makers Over Payments," *New York Times*, October 1, 2002, A1, A23; Julie Appleby, "Feds Warn Drugmakers: Gifts to Doctors May Be Illegal," *USA Today*, October 2, 2002, 1A.

14. On February 1, 2004, CBS presented a live broadcast of the National Football League's Super Bowl XXXVIII, which included a halftime show produced by MTV Networks. Nearly 90 million viewers watched the Halftime Show, which began at 8:30 p.m. Eastern Standard Time and lasted about 15 minutes. The Halftime Show featured a performance with Janet Jackson and Justin Timberlake as a "surprise guest" for the final minutes of the show.

    Timberlake and Jackson performed his popular song "Rock Your Body" as the show's finale. Their performance, which involved sexually suggestive choreography, portrayed Timberlake seeking to dance with Jackson, and Jackson alternating between accepting and rejecting his advances. The performance ended with Timberlake singing, "gonna have you naked by the end of this song," and simultaneously tearing away part of Jackson's bustier. CBS had implemented a five-second audio delay to guard against the possibility of indecent language being transmitted on air, but it did not employ similar precautionary technology for video images. As a result, Jackson's bare right breast was exposed on camera for nine-sixteenths of one second.

    On September 22, 2004, the Commission issued a Notice of Apparent Liability, finding that CBS had apparently violated federal law and FCC rules restricting the broadcast of indecent material. After its review, the Commission determined that CBS was liable for a forfeiture penalty of $550,000 because its actions were willful..

    CBS filed with the FCC for a reconsideration, which was denied. CBS then appealed the case to the federal Court of Appeals on the grounds that the finding of willfulness as well as the penalty were arbitrary and capricious and violated First Amendment rights. Based on the *Fox Televisions Stations* case, what do you think the decision should be and why. [*CBS Corporation, Inc. v FCC*, 535 F3d 167 (CA 3 2006)]

15. The Endangered Species Act (ESA) charges the National Marine Fisheries Service (a federal agency) with the duty to "ensure" that any proposed action by the Council does not "jeopardize" any threatened or endangered species. The Steller sea lion is on the list of endangered species. The agency developed a North Pacific marine fishery plan that permitted significant harvest of fish by commercial fisheries in the area. Greenpeace, an environmental group, challenged the agency on the grounds that the plan was not based on a sufficient number of biological studies on the impact of the allowed fishing on the Steller sea lion. Greenpeace's biologic opinion concluded that the fishery plan would reduce the level of food for the sea lions by about 40 percent to 60 percent, if the juvenile fish were not counted in that figure. Greenpeace's expert maintained that counting juvenile fish was misleading because they were not capable of reproducing and the government agency's figure was, as a result, much lower at 22 percent. What would Greenpeace need to show to be successful in challenging the agency's fishery plan? [*Greenpeace, American Oceans Campaign v National Marine Fisheries Service*, 237 F Supp 2d 1181 (WD Wash)]

Chapter 7

THE LEGAL ENVIRONMENT OF INTERNATIONAL TRADE

The success or failure of the U.S. firms doing business in foreign countries may well depend on accurate information about the laws and customs of the host countries. In their domestic operations, U.S. business firms compete against imports from other nations. Such imported goods include Canadian lumber, Mexican machinery, Japanese automobiles, German steel, French wine, Chinese textiles, and Chilean copper. To compete effectively, U.S. firms should learn about the business practices of foreign firms. They should be alert to unfair trade practices that will put U.S. firms at a disadvantage. Such practices may include the violation of U.S. antitrust and antidumping laws or violation of international trade agreements. Individuals from all over the world participate in the U.S. securities markets. Special problems exist in the regulation and enforcement of U.S. securities laws involving financial institutions of countries with secrecy laws.

A. General Principles

Nations enter into treaties and conferences to further international trade. The business world has developed certain forms of organizations for conducting that trade.

1. The Legal Background

Because of the complexity and ever-changing character of the legal environment of international trade, this section will focus on certain underlying elements.

(A) WHAT LAW APPLIES. When there is a sale of goods within the United States, one law typically applies to the transaction. Some variation may be introduced when the transaction is between parties in different states, but for the most part, the law governing the transaction is the U.S. law of contracts and the Uniform Commercial Code (UCC). In contrast, when an international contract is made, it is necessary to determine whether it is the law of the seller's country or the law of the importer's country that will govern. The parties to an international contract often resolve that question themselves as part of their contract, setting forth which country's law will govern should a dispute arise. Such a provision is called a **choice-of-law clause**. **For Example,** U.S. investors Irmgard and Mitchell Lipcon provided capital to underwriters at Lloyd's of London and signed choice-of-law clauses in their investment agreements binding them to proceed in England under English law should disputes arise. When the Lipcons realized that their investments were exposed to massive liabilities for asbestos and pollution insurance claims, they sued in U.S. district court in Florida for alleged U.S. securities acts violations. However, their complaints were dismissed based on the choice-of-law clauses in their contracts. The U.S. court of appeals stated that the Lipcons must "honor their bargains" and attempt to vindicate their claims in English courts under English law. [1]

choice-of-law clause – clause in an agreement that specifies which law will govern should a dispute arise.

---

[1] *Lipcon v Underwriters at Lloyd's, London,*148 F2d 1285, 1299 (11th Cir 1998).

The major trading countries of the world have entered into a number of treaties. When their citizens deal with each other and their respective rights are not controlled in their contract, their rights and liabilities are determined by looking at the treaty. These treaties are discussed in Section 7 of this chapter, including the United Nations Convention on Contracts for the International Sale of Goods (CISG), which deals with certain aspects of the formation and performance of international commercial contracts for the sale of goods.

(B) **THE ARBITRATION ALTERNATIVE.** Traditional litigation may be considered too time consuming, expensive, and divisive to the relationships of the parties to an international venture. The parties, therefore, may agree to arbitrate any contractual disputes that may arise according to dispute resolution procedures set forth in the contract.

Pitfalls exist for U.S. companies arbitrating disputes in foreign lands. **For Example,** were a U.S. company to agree to arbitrate a contractual dispute with a Chinese organization in China, it would find that the arbitrator must be Chinese. Also, under Chinese law, only Chinese lawyers can present an arbitration case, even if one party is a U.S. company. Because of situations like this, it is common for parties to international ventures to agree to arbitrate their disputes in neutral countries.

An arbitration agreement gives the parties more control over the decision-making process. The parties can require that the arbitrator have the technical, language, and legal qualifications to best understand their dispute. While procedures exist for the prearbitration exchange of documents, full "discovery" is ordinarily not allowed. The decision of the arbitrator is final and binding on the parties with very limited judicial review possible.

(C) **CONFLICTING IDEOLOGIES.** Law, for all people and at all times, is the result of the desire of the lawmaker to achieve certain goals. These are the social forces that make the law. In the eyes of the lawmaker, the attainment of these goals is proper and therefore ethical. This does not mean that we all can agree on what the international law should be because different people have different ideas as to what is right. This affects our views as to ownership, trade, and dealings with foreign merchants. **For Example,** a very large part of the world does not share the U.S. dislike of cartels. Other countries do not have our antitrust laws; therefore, their merchants can form a trust to create greater bargaining power in dealing with U.S. and other foreign merchants.

(D) **FINANCING INTERNATIONAL TRADE.** There is no international currency. This creates problems as to what currency to use and how to make payment in international transactions. Centuries ago, buyers used precious metals, jewels, or furs in payment. Today, the parties to an international transaction agree in their sales contract on the currency to be used to pay for the goods. They commonly require that the buyer furnish the seller a **letter of credit**, which is a commercial device used to guarantee payment to a seller in an international transaction. By this, an issuer, typically a bank, agrees to pay the drafts drawn against the buyer for the purchase price. In trading with merchants in some countries, the foreign country itself will promise that the seller will be paid.

letter of credit– commercial device used to guarantee payment to a seller, primarily in an international business transaction.

2. International Trade Organizations, Conferences, and Treaties

A large number of organizations exist that affect the multinational markets for goods, services, and investments. A survey of major international organizations, conferences, and treaties follows.

(A) **GATT** AND **WTO.** The *General Agreement on Tariffs and Trade* 1994 (GATT 1994) is a multilateral treaty subscribed to by 126 member governments, including the United States.[2] It consists of the original 1947 GATT, numerous multilateral agreements negotiated since 1947, the Uruguay Round Agreements, and the agreement establishing the *World Trade Organization* (WTO). On January 1, 1995, the WTO took over responsibility for policing the objectives of the former GATT organization. Since 1947 and the end of the World War II era, the goal of the GATT has been to liberalize world trade and make it secure for furthering economic growth and human development. The current round of WTO negotiations began in Doha, Qatar, in 2001. As the talks continued in Cancun in 2003, the developed countries and developing countries divided on key issues such as agricultural subsidies. The Doha Round continues in an effort to meet the WTO's objectives of liberalizing world trade.

most-favored-nation clause–clause in treaties between countries whereby any privilege subsequently granted to a third country in relation to a given treaty subject is extended to the other party to the treaty.

The GATT is based on the fundamental principles of (1) trade without discrimination and (2) protection through tariffs. The principle of trade without discrimination is embodied in its **most-favored-nation clause**. In treaties between countries, a most-favored-nation clause is one whereby any privilege subsequently granted to a third country in relation to a given treaty subject is extended to the other party to the treaty. In the application and administration of import and export duties and charges under the GATT most-favored-nation clause, all member countries grant each other equal treatment. Thus, no country gives special trading advantages to another. All member countries are equal and share the benefits of any moves toward lower trade barriers. Exceptions to this basic rule are allowed in certain special circumstances involving regional trading arrangements, such as the European Union (EU) and the North American Free Trade Agreement (NAFTA). Special preferences are also granted to developing countries. The second basic principle is protection for domestic industry, which should be extended essentially through a tariff, not through other commercial measures. The aim of this rule is to make the extent of protection clear and to make competition possible.

Dispute Settlement Body– means, provided by the World Trade Organization, for member countries to resolve trade disputes rather than engage in unilateral trade sanctions or a trade war.

The WTO provides a **Dispute Settlement Body (DSB)** to enable member countries to resolve trade disputes rather than engage in unilateral trade sanctions or a trade war. The DSB appoints panels to hear disputes concerning allegations of GATT agreement violations, and it adopts (or rejects) the panels' decisions. If a GATT agreement violation is found and not removed by the offending country, trade sanctions authorized by a panel may be imposed on that country in an amount equal to the economic injury caused by the violation.

---

[2] Russia has applied to join the GATT and is in the final phase of accession to the World Trade Organization. However, to attain this goal, it is widely accepted that Russia will have to provide meaningful market access to member countries in goods and services and have a solid legal and administrative framework that will guarantee the implementation of contractual commitments.

(B) **CISG.** The *United Nations Convention on Contracts for the International Sale of Goods* (CISG or convention) sets forth uniform rules to govern international sales contracts. National law, however, is sometimes required to fill gaps in areas not covered by the CISG. The CISG became effective on January 1, 1988, between the United States and the 60 other nations that had approved it.[3] The provisions of the CISG have been strongly influenced by Article 2 of the UCC.

However, as set forth in Chapter 23 on sales, several distinct differences exist between the convention and the UCC. Excluded from the coverage of the convention under Article 2 are the sale of goods for personal, family, or household uses and the sale of watercraft, aircraft, natural gas, or electricity; letters of credit; and auctions and securities.[4] The CISG is often viewed by foreign entities as a neutral body of law, the utilization of which can be a positive factor in successfully concluding negotiations of a contract. The parties to an international commercial contract may opt out of the convention. However, absent an express "opt-out provision," the CISG is controlling and preempts all state actions.

(c) **UNCTAD.** The *United Nations Conference on Trade and Development* (UNCTAD) represents the interests of the less developed countries. Its prime objective is the achievement of an international redistribution of income through trade. Through UNCTAD pressure, the developed countries agreed to a system of preferences, with quota limits, for manufactured imports from the developing countries.

(D) **EU.** The *European Economic Community* (EEC) was established in 1958 by the Treaty of Rome to remove trade and economic barriers between member countries and to unify their economic policies. It changed its name and became the *European Union* (EU) after the Treaty of Maastricht was ratified on November 1, 1993. The Treaty of Rome containing the governing principles of this regional trading group was signed by the original six nations of Belgium, France, West Germany, Italy, Luxembourg, and the Netherlands. Membership expanded by the entry of Denmark, Ireland, and Great Britain in 1973; Greece in 1981; Spain and Portugal in 1986; and Austria, Sweden, and Finland in 1995. Ten countries joined the EU in 2004: Cyprus, the Czech Republic, Estonia, Hungary, Latvia, Lithuania, Malta, Poland, Slovakia, and Slovenia. Bulgaria, Romania, Croatia, and Turkey expect to join in the coming years.

Four main institutions make up the formal structure of the EU. The first, the European Council, consists of the heads of state of the member countries. The council sets broad policy guidelines for the EU. The second, the European Commission, implements decisions of the council and initiates actions against individuals, companies, or member states that violate EU law. The third, the European Parliament, has an advisory legislative role with limited veto powers. The fourth, the European Court of Justice (ECJ) and the lower Court of First Instance make up the judicial arm of the EU. The courts of member states may refer cases involving questions on the EU treaty to these courts.

[3] 52 Fed Reg 6262.
[4] CISG art. 2(a)–(f).

The Single European Act eliminated internal barriers to the free movement of goods, persons, services, and capital between EU countries. The Treaty on European Union, signed in Maastricht, Netherlands (the Maastricht Treaty), amended the Treaty of Rome with a focus on monetary and political union. It set goals for the EU of (1) single monetary and fiscal policies, (2) common foreign and security policies, and (3) cooperation in justice and home affairs.

(E) NAFTA. The *North American Free Trade Agreement* (NAFTA) is an agreement between Mexico, Canada, and the United States, effective January 1, 1994, that included Mexico in the arrangements previously initiated under the United States–Canada Free Trade Agreement of 1989. NAFTA eliminates all tariffs among the three countries over a 15-year period. Side agreements exist to prevent the exploitation of Mexico's lower environmental and labor standards.

Products are qualified for NAFTA tariff preferences only if they originate in one or more of the three member countries.

CASE SUMMARY

A Reason to Assemble Cars in Mexico

FACTS: DaimlerChrysler assembles trucks in Mexico utilizing sheet metal components manufactured in the United States. The sheet metal is subject to painting in Mexico, consisting of primer coats followed by a color-treated coat and a clear coat, referred to as the top coats. After the assembly is completed, the trucks are shipped to and sold in the United States. The U.S. Customs Service believes the top coats are subject to duty payments. DaimlerChrysler asserts that the entire painting process is duty free. Subheading 9802.00.80 of the Harmonized Tariffs Schedule of the U.S. (HTSUS) provides duty-free treatment for:

> Articles ... assembled abroad in whole or in part of fabricated components, the product of the United States, which (a) were exported in condition ready for assembly without further fabrication, (b) have not lost their physical identity in such articles by change in form, shape or otherwise, and (c) have not been advanced in value or improved in condition abroad except by being assembled and except by operations incidental to the assembly process such as cleaning, lubricating and painting. [emphasis added by the court]

From a judgment by the Court of International Trade in favor of the United States, DaimlerChrysler appealed.

DECISION: Judgment for DaimlerChrysler. Because subheading HTSUS 9802.00.80 unambiguously covers painting operations broadly, DaimlerChrysler's entire painting process, including the application of the top coats, qualifies for duty-free treatment. [**DaimlerChrysler Corp. v U.S., 361 F3d 1378 (Fed Cir 2004)**]

Documentation is required in a NAFTA *Certificate of Origin*, except for certain "low-value" items for which the statement of North American origin is recorded on an invoice. NAFTA ensures nondiscriminatory and open markets for a wide range of services and lowers barriers to U.S. investments in both Canada and Mexico. Although NAFTA does not create a common labor market, as does the European Union, the agreement provides temporary access for businesspersons across borders.

(F) **REGIONAL TRADING GROUPS OF DEVELOPING COUNTRIES.** In recent years, numerous trading arrangements between groups of developing countries have been established.

(G) **IMF—WORLD BANK.** The *International Monetary Fund* (IMF) was created after World War II by a group of nations meeting in Bretton Woods, New Hampshire. The Articles of Agreement of the IMF state that its purpose is "to facilitate the expansion and balanced growth of international trade" and to "shorten the duration and lessen the disequilibrium in the international balance of payments of members." The IMF helps to achieve such purposes by administering a complex lending system. A country can borrow money from other IMF members or from the IMF by means of **special drawing rights (SDRs)** sufficient to permit that country to maintain the stability of its currency's relationship to other world currencies. The Bretton Woods conference also set up the *International Bank for Reconstruction and Development* (World Bank) to facilitate the lending of money by capital surplus countries—such as the United States—to countries needing economic help and wanting foreign investments after World War II.

special drawing rights (SDRs)–rights that allow a country to borrow enough money from other International Money Fund (IMF) members to permit that country to maintain the stability of its currency's relationship to other world currencies.

(H) **OPEC.** The *Organization of Petroleum Exporting Countries* (OPEC) is a producer cartel or combination. One of its main goals was to raise the taxes and royalties earned from crude oil production. Another major goal was to take control over production and exploration from the major oil companies. Its early success in attaining these goals led other nations that export raw materials to form similar cartels. **For Example,** copper and bauxite- producing nations have formed cartels.

3. Forms of Business Organizations

The decision to participate in international business transactions and the extent of that participation depend on the financial position of the individual firm, production and marketing factors, and tax and legal considerations. There are a number of forms of business organizations for doing business abroad.

export sale–direct sale to customers in a foreign country.

(A) **EXPORT SALES.** A direct sale to customers in a foreign country is an **export sale**. A U.S. firm engaged in export selling is not present in the foreign country in such an arrangement. The export is subject to a tariff by the foreign country, but the exporting firm is not subject to local taxation by the importing country.

agent–person or firm who is authorized by the principal or by operation of law to make contracts with third persons on behalf of the principal.

principal–person or firm who employs an agent; the person who, with respect to a surety, is primarily liable to the third person or creditor; property held in trust.

(B) **AGENCY REQUIREMENTS.** A U.S. manufacturer may decide to make a limited entry into international business by appointing an agent to represent it in a foreign market. An **agent** is a person or firm with authority to make contracts on behalf of another—the **principal**. The agent will receive commission income for sales made on behalf of the U.S. principal. The appointment of a foreign agent commonly constitutes "doing business" in that country and subjects the U.S. firm to local taxation.

distributor–entity that takes title to goods and bears the financial and commercial risks for the subsequent sale of the goods.

(C) **FOREIGN DISTRIBUTORSHIPS.** A **distributor** takes title to goods and bears the financial and commercial risks for the subsequent sale. To avoid making a major financial investment, a U.S. firm may decide to appoint a foreign distributor. A U.S. firm may also appoint a foreign distributor to avoid managing a foreign operation with its complicated local business, legal, and labor conditions. Care is required in designing an exclusive distributorship for an EU country lest it would violate EU antitrust laws.

licensing—transfer of technology rights to a product so that it may be produced by a different business organization in a foreign country in exchange for royalties and other payments as agreed.

(D) LICENSING. U.S. firms may select licensing as a means of doing business in other countries. **Licensing** involves the transfer of technology rights in a product so that it may be produced by a different business organization in a foreign country in exchange for royalties and other payments as agreed. The technology being licensed may fall within the internationally recognized categories of patents, trademarks, and "know-how" (trade secrets and unpatented manufacturing processes outside the public domain). These intellectual property rights, which are legally protectable, may be licensed separately or incorporated into a single, comprehensive licensing contract. **Franchising**, which involves granting permission to use a trademark, trade name, or copyright under specified conditions, is a form of licensing that is now very common in international business.

franchising—granting of permission to use a trademark, trade name, or copyright under specified conditions; a form of licensing.

(E) WHOLLY OWNED SUBSIDIARIES. A firm seeking to maintain control over its own operations, including the protection of its own technological expertise, may choose to do business abroad through a wholly owned subsidiary. In Europe the most common choice of foreign business organization, similar to the U.S. corporate form of business organization, is called the *société anonyme* (S.A.). In German-speaking countries, this form is called *Aktiengesellschaft* (A.G.). Small and medium-sized companies in Europe now utilize a newly created form of business organization called the limited liability company (*Gesellschaft mit beschränkter Haftung,* or "GmbH" in Germany; *Società a responsabilità limitata,* or "S.r.l." in Spain). It is less complicated to form but is restrictive for accessing public capital markets.

A corporation doing business in more than one country poses many taxation problems for the governments in those countries where the firm does business. The United States has established tax treaties with many countries granting corporations relief from double taxation. Credit is normally given by the United States to U.S. corporations for taxes paid to foreign governments.

There is a potential for tax evasion by U.S. corporations from their selling goods to their overseas subsidiaries. Corporations could sell goods at less than the fair market value to avoid a U.S. tax on the full profit for such sales. By allowing the foreign subsidiaries located in countries with lower tax rates to make higher profits, a company as a whole would minimize its taxes. Section 482 of the Internal Revenue Code (IRC), however, allows the Internal Revenue Service (IRS) to reallocate the income between the parent and its foreign subsidiary. The parent corporation is insulated from such a reallocation if it can show, based on independent transactions with unrelated parties, that its charges were at arm's length.[5]

[5] *Bausch & Lomb Inc. v Commissioner,* 933 F2d 1084 (2d Cir 1991).

CASE SUMMARY

A Taxing Case

FACTS: E. I. Du Pont de Nemours created a wholly owned Swiss marketing and sales subsidiary: Du Pont International S.A. (DISA). Most of the Du Pont chemical products marketed abroad were first sold to DISA, which then arranged for resale to the ultimate consumer through independent distributors. Du Pont's tax strategy was to sell the goods to DISA at prices below fair market value so that the greater part of the total corporate profit would be realized by DISA upon resale. DISA's profits would be taxed at a much lower level by Switzerland than Du Pont would be taxed in the United States. The IRS, however, under Section 482 of the IRC, reallocated a substantial part of DISA's income to Du Pont, increasing Du Pont's taxes by a considerable amount. Du Pont contended that the prices it charged DISA were valid under the IRC.

DECISION: Judgment for the IRS. The reallocation of DISA's income to Du Pont was proper. Du Pont's prices to DISA were set wholly without regard to the factors that normally enter into the setting of intercorporate prices on an arm's-length basis. For example, there was no correlation of prices to cost. Du Pont set prices for the two years in question based solely on estimates of the greatest amount of profits that could be shifted without causing IRS intervention. [**E.I. Du Pont de Nemours & Co. v United States, 608 F2d 445 (Ct Cl 1979)**]

---

joint venture–relationship in which two or more persons or firms combine their labor or property for a single undertaking and share profits and losses equally unless otherwise agreed.

(F) JOINT VENTURES. A U.S. manufacturer and a foreign entity may form a **joint venture**, whereby the two firms agree to perform different functions for a common result. The responsibilities and liabilities of such operations are governed by contract. **For Example,** Hughes Aircraft Co. formed a joint venture with two Japanese firms, C. Itoh & Co. and Mitsui, and successfully bid on a telecommunications space satellite system for the Japanese government.

China has two forms of joint ventures: a *contract joint venture,* which allows the parties to operate as separate entities governed by a contract, and an *equity joint venture* whereby each party owns a portion of the business. Such an arrangement is governed by the Chinese Foreign Equity Joint Venture Law. This law requires a Chinese limited liability company to be formed and requires the foreign participant to contribute at least 25 percent of the firm's capital.

B. GOVERNMENTAL REGULATION

Nations regulate trade to protect the economic interests of their citizens or to protect themselves in international relations and transactions.

4. Export Regulations

For reasons of national security, foreign policy, or short supply of domestic products, the United States controls the export of goods and technology. The Export Administration Act[6] imposes export controls on goods and technical data from the U.S. Since April 2002, the Bureau of Industry and Security (BIS) of the Department

---

[6] The Export Administration Act of 1979 expired in August 1994 and was extended by Executive Orders signed by Presidents Clinton and G. W. Bush. The EAA is now extended annually by presidential notice.

of Commerce has issued Export Administration Regulations to enforce export controls.

Export Administration Regulations effective in 1996 simplify the process and enhance export trade by U.S. citizens.[7] The new regulations eliminate the former system of general and validated licenses under which every export required a license. Under the 1996 *Simplification Regulations,* no license is required unless the regulations affirmatively require a license. However, when no license is required, the exporter must fill out a Shipper's Export Declaration and attach it to the bill of lading for shipment with the goods being exported.

(A) DETERMINING IF A LICENSE IS NEEDED. To determine whether a product requires a BIS export license, the exporter should review the Commerce Control List (CCL) to see whether the product to be exported is listed. Listed products have Export Control Classification Numbers (ECCNs) that conform to those used by the EU. If a product is on the list, the ECCN code will provide the reason for control, such as national security, missile technology, nuclear nonproliferation, chemical and/or biological weapons, antiterrorism, crime control, short supply, or UN sanctions.[8] The exporter should then consult the Commerce Country Chart to *determine whether* a license is needed to send the product to its proposed destination. **For Example,** domestic crude petroleum products and western red cedar are on the Commerce Control List because of the "short supply" of these products. As a result, they are controlled to all destinations, and no reference to the Commerce Country Chart is necessary.

(B) SANCTIONS. Export licenses are required for the export of certain high-technology and military products. a company intending to ship "maraging 350 steel" to a user in Pakistan would find by checking the CCL and the ECCN code for the product that such steel is used in making high-technology products and has nuclear applications. Thus, an export license would be required. Because Pakistan is a nonsignatory nation of the Nuclear Non-Proliferation Treaty, the Department of Commerce would be expected to deny a license application for the use of this steel in a nuclear plant. However, a license to export this steel for the manufacture of high-speed turbines or compressors might be approved. The prospective purchaser must complete a "Statement of Ultimate Consignee and Purchaser" form with the application for an export license. The prospective purchaser must identify the "end use" for the steel and indicate where the purchaser is located and the location in Pakistan where a U.S. embassy official can make an on-site inspection of the product's use. Falsification of the information in the license application process is a criminal offense. Thus, if the exporter of maraging 350 steel asserted that it was to be used in manufacturing high-speed turbines when in fact the exporter knew it was being purchased for use in a nuclear facility, the exporter would be guilty of a criminal offense.[9]

Civil charges may also be brought against U.S. manufacturers who fail to obtain an export license for foreign sales of civilian items that contain any components that

---

[7] Simplification of Export Regulations, 61 Fed Reg 12,714 (1996).
[8] *Id.*
[9] See *United States v Perez,* 871 F2d 310 (3d Cir 1989), on the criminal application of the Export Administration Regulations to an individual who stated a false end use for maraging 350 steel on his export application to ship this steel to Pakistan.

have military applications under the Arms Control Export Act. For example. between 2000 and 2003, Boeing Co. shipped overseas 94 commercial jets that carried a gyrochip used as a backup system in determining a plane's orientation in the air. This 2-ounce chip that costs less than $2,000 also has military applications and can be used to stabilize and steer guided missiles. Boeing is asserted to have made false statements on shipping documents to get around the export restrictions. Boeing argued that the State Department is without legal authority to regulate its civilian rather than military items. However, Boeing agreed to pay a $15 million fine for the violations.[10]

(c) EXPERT ASSISTANCE. The Department of Commerce's Exporter Assistance Staff provides assistance to exporters needing help in determining whether an export license is needed.[11] Licensed foreign-**freight forwarders** are in the business of handling the exporting of goods to foreign destinations. They are experts on U.S. Department of Commerce export license requirements. Licensed foreign-freight forwarders can attend to all of the essential arrangements required to transport a shipment of goods from the exporter's warehouse to the overseas buyer's specified port and inland destination. They are well versed in all aspects of ocean, air, and inland transportation as well as banking, marine insurance, and other services relating to exporting.

freight forwarder—one who contracts to have goods transported and, in turn, contracts with carriers for such transportation.

5. Protection of Intellectual Property Rights

U.S. laws protect **intellectual property rights**, which consist of trademarks, copyrights, and patents.

intellectual property rights—trademark, copyright, and patent rights protected by law.

(A) COUNTERFEIT GOODS. The importation of counterfeit compact discs, tapes, computer software, and movies into the United States violates U.S. copyright laws. Importing goods, such as athletic shoes, jeans, or watches, bearing counterfeits of U.S. companies' registered trademarks violates the Lanham Act. Importing machines or devices that infringe on U.S. patents violates U.S. patent laws. A full range of remedies is available to U.S. firms under U.S. laws. Possible remedies include injunctive relief, seizure and destruction of counterfeit goods that are found in the United States, damages, and attorney fees. U.S. firms injured by counterfeit trademarks may recover triple damages from the counterfeiters.[12]

Intellectual property rights are also protected by international treaties, such as the Berne Convention, which protects copyrights; the Patent Cooperation Treaty; and the Madrid System of International Registration of Marks (the Madrid Protocol), a treaty providing for the international registration of marks applicable to more than 60 signatory countries, including the United States as of November 2003.[13]

(B) GRAY MARKET GOODS. A U.S. trademark holder may license a foreign business to use its trademark overseas. If a third party imports these foreign-made goods into

---

[10] Associated Press, "Boeing to Pay $15 Million Fine for Export of Military Technology," *The Boston Globe*, April 10, 2006, E3.

[11] Exporter Assistance Staff, U.S. Department of Commerce, Washington, DC 20230.

[12] 15 USC § 1117(b); *Nintendo of America v NTDEC*, 822 F Supp 1462 (D Ariz 1993).

[13] The Agreement on Trade-Related Aspects of Intellectual Property (TRIPS) is a WTO agreement that requires WTO members to adhere to certain treaties and guidelines in respecting copyright, trademark, and patent rights. Enforcement of such rights, however, varies, depending on national law.

gray market goods–
foreign-made goods with U.S. trademarks brought into the United States by a third party without the consent of the trademark owners to compete with these owners.

the United States to compete against the U.S. manufacturer's goods, the foreign-made goods are called **gray market goods**. The Tariff Act of 1930 prevents importation of foreign-made goods bearing a U.S. registered trademark owned by a U.S. firm unless the U.S. trademark owner gives written consent.[14] The Lanham Act may also be used to exclude gray market goods.[15]

A gray market situation also arises when foreign products made by affiliates of U.S. companies have trademarks identical to U.S. trademarks but the foreign products are physically different from the U.S. products.

CASE SUMMARY

Barring Imported Soap!

FACTS: Lever Brothers (Lever U.S.) manufactures a soap under the trademark Shield and a dishwashing liquid under the trademark Sunlight for sale in the United States. A British affiliate, Lever U.K., also makes products using the marks Shield and Sunlight. Because of different tastes of U.S. and U.K. consumers, the products have physical differences. Third parties imported these U.K. products into the United States. The Lanham Act prohibits "copying or simulating a trademark." The U.S. Customs Service refused to bar these foreign products because a markholder cannot "copy or simulate" its own trademark. That is, Lever U.K. could not copy the marks of its affiliated company, Lever U.S. Lever U.S. sought an injunction against the U.S. Customs Service, requiring it to bar these foreign products.

DECISION: Judgment for Lever U.S. American consumers desiring to purchase Shield and Sunlight may end up with different products not suited to their tastes and needs if the U.K. products continue to be allowed into the United States. Because of the confusion and dissatisfaction, the importation of foreign goods that bear trademarks identical to valid U.S. trademarks but that are physically different, regardless of the affiliation of markholders, are prohibited from import under Section 42 of the Lanham Act. [**Lever Brothers Co. v United States, 796 F Supp 1 (DDC 1992)**]

6. Antitrust

Antitrust laws exist in the United States to protect the U.S. consumer by ensuring the benefits of competitive products from foreign competitors as well as domestic competitors. Competitors' agreements designed to raise the price of imports or to exclude imports from our domestic markets in exchange for not competing in other countries are restraints of trade in violation of our antitrust laws.[16]

The antitrust laws also exist to protect U.S. export and investment opportunities against privately imposed restrictions, whereby a group of competitors seeks to

---

[14] 19 USC § 1526(1). The Copyright Act of 1976 may also apply to gray market goods. One provision of this act gives the copyright holder exclusive right to distribute copies of the copyrighted work. Still another section states that once a copyright owner sells an authorized copy of the work, subsequent owners may do what they like with it. The gray market issue occurs when U.S. manufacturers sell their products overseas at deep discounts, and other firms reimport the products back to the United States for resale. The Supreme Court held that a copyrighted label on the products would not protect a U.S. manufacturer's claim of unauthorized importation because the copyright owner's rights cease upon the original sale to the overseas buyer. *Quality King v L'Anza Research*, 523 US 135 (1998).

[15] *Bourdeau Bros. v International Trade Commission*, 444 F3d 1314 (Fed Cir 2006).

[16] *United States v Nippon Paper Industries Co. Ltd.*, 64 F Supp 2d 173 (1999).

exclude another competitor from a particular foreign market. Antitrust laws exist in other countries where U.S. firms compete. These laws are usually directed not at breaking up cartels to further competition but at regulating them in the national interest.

(A) JURISDICTION. In U.S. courts, the U.S. antitrust laws have a broad extraterritorial reach. Our antitrust laws must be reconciled with the rights of other interested countries as embodied in international law.

(1) The Effects Doctrine

effects doctrine–doctrine that states that U.S. courts will assume jurisdiction and will apply antitrust laws to conduct outside of the United States when the activity of business firms has direct and substantial effect on U.S. commerce; the rule has been modified to require that the effect on U.S. commerce also be foreseeable.

Judge Learned Hand's decision in *United States v Alcoa* established the **effects doctrine**.[17] Under this doctrine, U.S. courts assume jurisdiction and apply the antitrust laws to conduct outside of the United States where the activity of the business firms outside the United States has a direct and substantial effect on U.S. commerce. This basic rule has been modified to require that the effect on U.S. commerce also be foreseeable.

(2) The Jurisdictional Rule of Reason

jurisdictional rule of reason–rule that balances the vital interests, including laws and policies, of the United States with those of a foreign country.

The jurisdictional rule of reason applies when conduct taking place outside the United States affects U.S. commerce but a foreign state also has a significant interest in regulating the conduct in question. The **jurisdictional rule of reason** balances the vital interests, including laws and policies, of the United States with those of the foreign country involved. This rule of reason is based on **comity**, a principle of international law, that means that the laws of all nations deserve the respect legitimately demanded by equal participants in international affairs.

comity–principle of international and national law that the laws of all nations and states deserve the respect legitimately demanded by equal participants.

(B) DEFENSES. Three defenses are commonly raised to the extraterritorial application of U.S. antitrust laws. These defenses are also commonly raised to attack jurisdiction in other legal actions involving international law.

(1) Act-of-State Doctrine

act-of-state doctrine– doctrine whereby every sovereign state is bound to respect the independence of every other sovereign state, and the courts of one country will not sit in judgment of another government's acts done within its own territory.

By the **act-of-state doctrine**, every sovereign state is bound to respect the independence of every other sovereign state, and the courts of one country will not sit in judgment of another government's acts done within its own territory.[18] The act-of-state doctrine is based on the judiciary's concern over its possible interference with the conduct of foreign relations. Such matters are considered to be political, not judicial, questions.

(2) The Sovereign Compliance Doctrine

sovereign compliance doctrine–doctrine that allows a defendant to raise as an affirmative defense to an antitrust action the fact that the defendant's actions were compelled by a foreign state.

The **sovereign compliance doctrine** allows a defendant to raise as an affirmative defense to an antitrust action the fact that the defendant's actions were compelled by a foreign state. To establish this defense, compulsion by the foreign government is required. The Japanese government uses informal and formal contacts within an industry to establish a consensus on a desired course of action. Such governmental action is not a defense for a U.S. firm, however, because the activity in question is not compulsory.

---

[17] 148 F2d 416 (2d Cir 1945).
[18] *Underhill v Hernandez,* 108 US 250, 252 (1897).

(3) The Sovereign Immunity Doctrine

sovereign immunity doctrine–doctrine that states that a foreign sovereign generally cannot be sued unless an exception to the Foreign Sovereign Immunities Act of 1976 applies.

The **sovereign immunity doctrine** states that a foreign sovereign generally cannot be sued unless an exception to the Foreign Sovereign Immunities Act of 1976 applies.[19] The most important exception covers the commercial conduct of a foreign state.[20] **For Example,** receivers for various insurance companies brought suit against the Vatican City State, contending that the Vatican's conduct fell within the commercial activity exception to the FSIA. Martin Frankel had engaged in a massive insurance fraud scheme, using front organizations to acquire and loot several insurance agencies. Masquerading as "David Rose," a philanthropist, he met Monsignor Emilio Cologiovani and convinced him to create a Vatican-affiliated entity, the St. Francis of Assisi Foundation (SFAF), which was used as part of Frankel's scam. The Court of Appeals held, however, that Cologiovani, acting with only apparent authority of the state, could not trigger the commercial activity doctrine.[21]

(C) LEGISLATION. In response to business uncertainty as to when the antitrust laws apply to international transactions, Congress passed the Foreign Trade Antitrust Improvements Act of 1982. This act, in essence, codified the effects doctrine. The act requires a direct, substantial, and reasonably foreseeable effect on U.S. domestic commerce or exports by U.S. residents before business conduct abroad may come within the purview of U.S. antitrust laws.[22]

(D) FOREIGN ANTITRUST LAWS. Attitudes in different countries vary toward cartels and business combinations. Because of this, antitrust laws vary in content and application. **For Example,** Japan has stressed consumer protection against such practices as price-fixing and false advertising. However, with regard to mergers, stock ownership, and agreements among companies to control production, Japanese law is much less restrictive than U.S. law.

Europe is a major market for U.S. products, services, and investments. U.S. firms doing business in Europe are subject to the competition laws of the EU.[23] The Treaty of Rome uses the term *competition* rather than *antitrust*. Articles 85 and 86 of the Treaty of Rome set forth the basic regulation on business behavior in the EU.[24] Article 85(1) expressly prohibits agreements and concerted practices that

1. even indirectly fix prices of purchases or sales or fix any other trading conditions;

2. limit or control production, markets, technical development, or investment;

---

[19] See *Verlinden B.V. v Central Bank of Nigeria,* 461 US 574 (1983).

[20] See *Dole Food Co. v Patrickson,* 538 US 468 (2003), for a limited discussion of when a foreign state can assert a defense of sovereign immunity under the Foreign Sovereign Immunities Act of 1976 (FSIA). The FSIA allows certain foreign-state commercial entities not entitled to sovereign immunity to have the merits of a case heard in federal court. The U.S. Supreme Court held in the *Dole Food* case that a foreign state must itself own a majority of the shares of a corporation if the corporation is to be deemed an instrumentality of the state under the FSIA, and the instrumentality status is determined at the time of the filing of the complaint.

[21] *Dale v Cologiovani,* 443 F3d 425 (5th Cir 2006).

[22] PL 97-290, 96 Stat 1233, 15 USC § 6(a).

[23] The European Commission is the executive branch of the EU government and performs most of the EU's regulatory work. The Competition Commission oversees antitrust and mergers for the European Commission. New merger regulations took effect on May 1, 2004. The regulations require the Competition Commission to review proposed mergers and prohibit those mergers when the effects may "significantly impede effective competition" (called the *SIEC test*). The U.S. test prohibits mergers when the effect "may substantially lessen competition. …" 15 USC § 18 (2005). The wording of the EU and U.S. tests is relatively similar.

[24] See *Osakeyhtio v EEC Commission,* 1988 Common Mkt Rep (CCH) ¶ 14,491 for discussion of the extraterritorial reach of the European Commission.

3. share markets or sources of supply;

4. apply unequal terms to parties furnishing equivalent considerations, thereby placing one at a competitive disadvantage; or

5. make a contract's formation depend on the acceptance of certain additional obligations that, according to commercial usage, have no connection with the subject of such contracts.

Article 85(3) allows for an individual exemption if the agreement meets certain conditions, such as improving the production or distribution of goods, promoting technical or economic progress, and reserving to consumers a fair share of the resulting economic benefits.

Article 86 provides that it is unlawful for one or more enterprises having a dominant market position within at least a substantial part of the EU to take improper advantage of such a position if trade between the member states may be affected. **For Example,** the European Commission fined computer chip maker Intel $1.45 billion for abusing its dominance in the computer chip market by offering rebates which were conditioned on buying less of a rival's products, or not buying them at all. Intel disagrees with the decision and will appeal the matter to the Court of First Instance.[25]

7. Securities and Tax Fraud Regulation in an International Environment

Illegal conduct in the U.S. securities markets, whether this conduct is initiated in the United States or abroad, threatens the vital economic interests of the United States. Investigation and litigation concerning possible violations of the U.S. securities laws often have an extraterritorial effect. Conflicts with the laws of foreign countries may occur.

(A) JURISDICTION. U.S. district courts have jurisdiction over violations of the antifraud provisions of the Securities Exchange Act of 1934 when losses occur from sales to Americans living in the United States.[26] U.S. district courts also have jurisdiction when losses occur to Americans living abroad if the acts occurred in the United States. The antifraud provisions do not apply, however, to losses from sales of securities to foreigners outside the United States unless acts within the United States caused the losses.

secrecy laws–
confidentiality laws applied to home-country banks.

blocking laws–laws that prohibit the disclosure, copying, inspection, or removal of documents located in the enacting country in compliance with orders from foreign authorities.

(B) IMPACT OF FOREIGN SECRECY LAWS IN SEC ENFORCEMENT. **Secrecy laws** are confidentiality laws applied to home-country banks. These laws prohibit the disclosure of business records or the identity of bank customers. **Blocking laws** prohibit the disclosure, copying, inspection, or removal of documents located in the enacting country in compliance with orders from foreign authorities. These laws impede, and sometimes foreclose, the SEC's ability to police its securities markets properly.

[25] James Kanter, "Europe Fines Intel $1.45 Billion in Antitrust Case," *New York Times,* **www.nytimes.com/2009/05/14/bussiness/global/14/compete.html**.
[26] *Kauthar Sdn Bhd v Sternberg,*149 F3d 659 (7th Cir 1998).

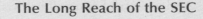

CASE SUMMARY

The Long Reach of the SEC

FACTS: Banca Della Suizzera Italiana (BSI), a Swiss bank with an office in the United States, purchased certain call options and common stock of St. Joe Minerals Corporation (St. Joe), a New York corporation, immediately prior to the announcement on March 11, 1981, of a cash tender offer by Joseph Seagram & Sons Inc. for all St. Joe common stock at $45 per share. On March 11, 1981, when BSI acted, the stock moved sharply higher in price. BSI instructed its broker to close out the purchases of the options and sell most of the shares of stock, resulting in an overnight profit of $2 million. The SEC noticed the undue activity in the options market and initiated suit against BSI. The SEC, through the Departments of State and Justice, and the Swiss government sought without success to learn the identity of BSI's customers involved in the transactions. The SEC believed that the customers had used inside information in violation of the Securities Exchange Act of 1934. The SEC brought a motion to compel disclosure. BSI objected on the ground that it might be subject to criminal liability under Swiss penal and banking laws if it disclosed the requested information.

DECISION: Judgment for the SEC. BSI made deliberate use of Swiss nondisclosure law to evade the strictures of U.S. securities law against insider trading. Whether acting solely as an agent or also as a principal (something that can be clarified only through disclosure of the requested information), BSI voluntarily engaged in transactions in U.S. securities markets and profited in some measure thereby. It cannot rely on Swiss nondisclosure law to shield this activity. [**SEC v Banca Della Suizzera Italiana, 92 FRD 111 (SDNY 1981)**]

The SEC is not limited to litigation when a securities law enforcement investigation runs into secrecy or blocking laws. For example, the SEC may rely on the 1977 Treaty of Mutual Assistance in Criminal Matters between the United States and Switzerland.[27] Although this treaty has served to deter the use of Swiss secrecy laws to conceal fraud in the United States, its benefits for securities enforcement have been limited. It applies only where there is a dual criminality— that is, the conduct involved constitutes a criminal offense under the laws of both the United States and Switzerland.

(c) *OFFSHORE TAX EVASION.* Switzerland and other countries with histories of banking secrecy have yielded somewhat to United States and EU pressures to help cut down on tax evaders. The U.S. and Switzerland have agreed in an amended tax treaty to increase the amount of tax information they share. Swiss banks have been reluctant to provide client information, asserting that it would violate Swiss Privacy laws. **For Example,** For Example, Swiss Bank UBS AG admitted that its bankers and managers referred U.S. clients to lawyers and accountants who set up secret offshore entities to conceal assets from the IRS, and it agreed to pay $780 million to settle the federal investigation in the U.S. and the Swiss government's investigations. Subsequently the Swiss Financial Markets Supervising Authority ordered UBS to reveal account details to the U.S. authorities for some 250 customers, asserting that "banking secrecy remains intact," while it "doesn't protect tax fraudsters."[28]

[27] 27 UST 2021.
[28] See "The Swiss Bank UBS Is Set to Open Its Secret Files," *New York Times,* **www.nytimes.com/2009/02/19/business/ worldbusiness/19ubs.htm**.

8. Barriers to Trade

The most common barrier to the free movement of goods across borders is a tariff. A wide range of nontariff barriers also restricts the free movement of goods, services, and investments. Government export controls used as elements of foreign policy have proven to be a major barrier to trade with certain countries.

tariff—(1) domestically—government-approved schedule of charges that may be made by a regulated business, such as a common carrier or warehouser; (2) internationally—tax imposed by a country on goods crossing its borders, without regard to whether the purpose is to raise revenue or to discourage the traffic in the taxed goods.

(A) TARIFF BARRIERS. A **tariff** is an import or export duty or tax placed on goods as they move into or out of a country. It is the most common method used by countries to restrict foreign imports. The tariff raises the total cost, and thus the price, of an imported product in the domestic market. Thus, the price of a domestically produced product not subject to the tariff is more advantageous.

The U.S. Customs and Border Protection Service (Customs) imposes tariffs on imported goods at the port of entry. The merchandise is classified under a tariff schedule, which lists each type of merchandise and the corresponding duty rate (or percentage). Customs also determines the "computed value" of the imported goods under very precise statutory formulas.[29] The total amount of the duty is calculated by applying the duty percentage to the computed value figure.[30] Customs also has authority to investigate fraudulent schemes to avoid or underpay customs' duties.[31]

CASE SUMMARY

Customs Crunch!

FACTS: Frito-Lay, Inc., owns a Mexican affiliate, Sabritas, S.A. de C.V., and it imports taco shells and *Munchos* potato chips from Mexico to the United States. Customs classified these products as "other bakers' wares" under Section 1905.90.90 of the Tariff Schedule subject to a 10 percent duty rate. Frito-Lay contends before the Court of International Trade that the import of taco shells is properly classified as "bread," which carries duty-free status. It also contends that *Munchos* are properly classified as potato chips and entitled to duty-free treatment.

DECISION: Classification disputes are resolved by (1) ascertaining the proper meaning of the specified terms in the tariff provision; and (2) determining whether the article comes within the meaning of the terms as properly construed. The term "bread" is not specifically defined in the tariff provision or in the legislative history. Customs' food expert, Dr.Pintauro, explained the leavening, loaf forming, and baking process of dough in his definition of bread. Such a narrow definition, however, ignores the reality that flat, fried, usually ethnic breads exist in the U.S. market and are generally accepted forms of bread. Therefore, hard, corn-based taco shells

---

[29] See Tariff Act of 1930, as amended, 19 USC § 1401a(e).

[30] It is common for importers to utilize customs brokers who research the tariff schedules to see whether a product fits unambiguously under one of the Customs Service's classifications. A broker will also research the classifications given to similar products. It may find that a fax switch may be classified as "other telephonic switching apparatus" at a tariff rate of 8.5 percent or "other telegraphic switching apparatus" with a tariff of 4.7 percent. Obviously, the importer desires to pay the lower rate, and the broker with the assistance of counsel will make a recommendation to the Customs Service for the lower rate, and Customs will make a ruling. The decisions of the Customs Service are published in the *Customs Bulletin*, the official weekly publication of the Customs Service. See *Command Communications v Fritz Cos.*, 36 P3d 182 (Colo App 2001).

[31] *U.S. v Inn Foods, Inc.*, 560 F3d 1338 (Fed Cir 2009).

CASE SUMMARY

Continued

are properly classified as bread under the tariff provisions and are duty-free. *Munchos,* however, are composed of cornmeal, dehydrated potato flakes, and potato starch, while potato chips are produced entirely from sliced raw whole potatoes. As such, Customs properly classified the plaintiffs' *Munchos.* [**Sabritas v United States, 998 F Supp 1123 (Ct Int'l Trade 1998)**]

(B) NONTARIFF BARRIERS. Nontariff barriers consist of a wide range of restrictions that inhibit the free movement of goods between countries. An import quota, such as a limitation on the number of automobiles that can be imported into one country from another, is such a barrier. More subtle nontariff barriers exist in all countries. **For Example,** Japan's complex customs procedures resulted in the restriction of the sale of U.S.-made aluminum baseball bats in Japan. The customs procedures required the individual uncrating and "destruction testing" of bats at the ports of entry. Government subsidies are also nontariff barriers to trade.

One U.S. law—the Turtle Law—prohibits the importation of shrimp from countries that allow the harvesting of shrimp with commercial fishing technology that could adversely affect endangered sea turtles. **For Example,** two U.S. importers sought an exemption, representing that their Brazilian supply of shrimp was caught in the wild by vessels using turtle excluder devices (TEDs). Because Brazil had failed to comply with the U.S. Turtle Law by requiring TEDs on its commercial shrimp fleet, even though it had seven years to do so, the exemption was not granted.[32]

(C) EXPORT CONTROLS AS INSTRUMENTS OF FOREIGN POLICY. U.S. export controls have been used as instruments of foreign policy in recent years. **For Example,** the United States has sought to deny goods and technology of strategic or military importance to unfriendly nations. The United States has also denied goods such as grain, technology, and machine parts, to certain countries to protest or to punish activities considered violative of human rights or world peace.

9. Relief Mechanisms for Economic Injury Caused by Foreign Trade

Certain U.S. industries may suffer severe economic injury because of foreign competition. U.S. law provides protection against unfair competition from foreigners' goods and provides economic relief for U.S. industries, communities, firms, and workers adversely affected by import competition. U.S. law also provides certain indirect relief for U.S. exporters and producers who encounter unfair foreign import restrictions.

---

[32] *Earth Island Institute v Christopher,* 948 F Supp 1062 (Ct Int'l Trade 1996). See *Turtle Island Restoration Network v Evans,* 284 F3d 1282 (Fed Cir 2002), on the continuing litigation on this topic and the clash between statutory enforcement and political and diplomatic considerations.

dumping–selling goods in another country at less than their fair value.

(A) ANTIDUMPING LAWS AND EXPORT SUBSIDIES. Selling goods in another country at less than their fair value is called **dumping**. The dumping of foreign goods in the United States is prohibited under the Tariff Act of 1930, as amended including the antidumping laws contained in the Uraguay Round Agreement Act of 1994.[33] Proceedings in antidumping cases are conducted by two federal agencies, which separately examine two distinct components. The International Trade Administration (ITA) of the Department of Commerce (commonly referred to in cases as simply "Commerce") investigates whether specified foreign goods are being sold in the United States at less than fair value (LTFV). The International Trade Commission (ITC) conducts proceedings to determine if there is an injury to a domestic industry as a result of such sales. Findings of both LTFV sales and injury must be present before remedial action is taken. Remedial action might include the addition of duties to reflect the difference between the fair value of the goods and the price being charged in the U.S. Commerce and ITC decisions may be appealed to the Court of International Trade. Decisions of this court are reviewable by the U.S. Court of Appeals for the Federal Circuit and then the U.S. Supreme Court.

A settlement may be reached through a suspension agreement, whereby prices are revised to eliminate any LTFV sales and other corrective measures are taken.

American producers have to take the initiative and shoulder the expense of assisting government's enforcement of antidumping laws, and when antidumping laws are violated, producers are entitled to a reward as injured parties.[34]

CASE SUMMARY

Q. P-l-e-a-s-e. We Just Want to Share.

A. No. You're Not on the List.

FACTS: The Byrd Amendment to the Tariff Act, enacted in 2000, requires that antidumping duties collected by Customs be distributed to "affected domestic producers" for "qualifying expenditures." Starting in 1998, the Torrington Company filed a petition with the ITA (Commerce department) and the ITC requesting imposition of antidumping duties on imported antifriction bearings. Through the gathering of extensive data and representation at hearings before Commerce and the ITC, it expended significant economic resources leading to the ITC's material injury determination and Commerce's antidumping duty order on antifriction bearings imported from Japan and several other countries. SKF USA sought to have its name added to the list of affected domestic producers requesting Byrd Amendment distributions for 2005—which request was denied since it had not indicated support for the original petition. SKF USA appealed, raising constitutional issues.

DECISION: Judgment for U.S. Customs and the ITC. The Byrd Amendment is not unconstitutional because it directly advanced substantial governmental interests in preventing dumping by rewarding parties that assisted enforcement of the antidumping statutes. [**SKF USA v U.S. Customs, 556 F3d 1337 (Fed Cir 2009)**].

---

[33] 19 USC § 1675b (2000). See *Allegheny Ludlum Corp. v United States*, 287 F3d 1365 (Fed Cir 2002).
[34] The Continued Dumping and Subsidy Offset Act of 2000 (the Byrd Amendment), 19 USC 1679c(a) (2000).

The 1979 act also applies to subsidy practices by foreign countries. If subsidized goods are sold in the United States at less than their fair value, the goods may be subject to a countervailing duty.

Canada and Mexico may appeal countervailing duty assessments by the United States to an arbitration panel established under NAFTA. The NAFTA panel, however, can determine only whether the U.S. determinations were made in accordance with U.S. law. An appeal can also be made by member states to the WTO Dispute Settlement Body, which can determine whether the United States breached its obligations under the WTO.

(B) RELIEF FROM IMPORT INJURIES. Title II of the Trade Act of 1974[35] provides relief for U.S. industries, communities, firms, and workers when any one or more of them are substantially adversely affected by import competition. The Department of Commerce, the secretary of labor, and the president have roles in determining eligibility. The relief provided may be temporary import relief through the imposition of a duty or quota on the foreign goods. Workers, if eligible, may obtain readjustment allowances, job training, job search allowances, or unemployment compensation.

For Example, trade adjustment assistance, including unemployment compensation and training and relocation allowances, was provided for former employees of Johnson Controls Battery Group plants in Garland, Texas; Bennington, Vermont; and Owosso, Michigan; because surveys of the customers of those plants by the Department of Labor indicated that increased imports of aftermarket batteries, the products produced at these closed plants, caused the shutdowns. Former workers of the closed Louisville battery plant were not provided assistance because this plant produced new car batteries, and the work was shifted to another Johnson Controls plant in the United States.[36]

(C) RETALIATION AND RELIEF AGAINST FOREIGN UNFAIR TRADE RESTRICTIONS. U.S. exporters of agricultural or manufactured goods or of services may encounter unreasonable, unjustifiable, or discriminatory foreign import restrictions. At the same time, producers from the foreign country involved may be benefiting from trade agreement concessions that allow producers from that country access to U.S. markets. Prior trade acts and the Omnibus Trade and Competitiveness Act of 1988 contain broad authority to retaliate against "unreasonable," "unjustifiable," or "discriminatory" acts by a foreign country.[37] The authority to retaliate is commonly referred to as "Section 301 authority." The fear or actuality of the economic sting of Section 301 retaliation often leads offending foreign countries to open their markets to imports. Thus, indirect relief is provided to domestic producers and exporters adversely affected by foreign unfair trade practices.

---

[35] PL 93-618, 88 Stat 1978, 19 USC §§ 2251, 2298.
[36] 20 F Supp 2d 1288 (Ct Int'l Trade 1998). See also *Former Employees of Merrill Corp. v U.S.*, 387 F Supp 2d 1336 (Ct Int'l Trade 2005).
[37] PL 100-418, 102 Stat 1346, 15 USC § 4727.

Enforcement of the act is entrusted to the U.S. trade representative (USTR), who is appointed by the president. Under the 1988 act, mandatory retaliatory action is required if the USTR determines that (1) rights of the United States under a trade agreement are being denied or (2) actions or policies of a foreign country are unjustifiable and a burden or restrict U.S. commerce. The overall thrust of the trade provisions of the 1988 act is to open markets and liberalize trade.

10. Expropriation

A major concern of U.S. businesses that do business abroad is the risk of expropriation of assets by a host government. Firms involved in the extraction of natural resources, banking, communications, or defense-related industries are particularly susceptible to nationalization. Multinational corporations commonly have a staff of full-time political scientists and former Foreign Service officers studying the countries relevant to their operations to monitor and calculate risks of expropriation. Takeovers of U.S.-owned businesses by foreign countries may be motivated by a short-term domestic political advantage or the desire to demonstrate political clout in world politics. Takeovers may also be motivated by long-term considerations associated with planned development of the country's economy.

Treaty commitments, or provisions in other international agreements between the United States and the host country, may serve to narrow expropriation uncertainties. Treaties commonly contain provisions whereby property will not be expropriated except for public benefit and with the prompt payment of just compensation.

One practical way to mitigate the risk of investment loss as a result of foreign expropriation is to purchase insurance through private companies, such as Lloyd's of London. Commercial insurance is also available against such risks as host governments' arbitrary recall of letters of credit and commercial losses resulting from embargoes.

The Overseas Private Investment Corporation (OPIC) is a U.S. agency under the policy control of the secretary of state. OPIC supports private investments in less developed, friendly countries. OPIC also offers asset protection insurance against risk of loss to plant and equipment as well as loss of deposits in overseas bank accounts to companies that qualify on the basis of the involvement of a "substantial U.S. interest."

11. The Foreign Corrupt Practices Act

There are restrictions on U.S. firms doing business abroad that disallow payments to foreign government officials for getting business from their governments. The Foreign Corrupt Practices Act of 1977 requires strict accounting standards and internal control procedures to prevent the hiding of improper payments to foreign officials. The act prohibits any offers, payments, or gifts to foreign officials—or third parties who might have influence with foreign officials—to influence a decision on behalf of the firm making the payment. It provides for sanctions of up to $1 million against the company and fines and imprisonment for the employees involved. Moreover, the

ethics&the law

Combating Bribery of Foreign Public Officials in International Business Transactions

Prior to 1999, German law prohibited bribery of domestic public officials (and did not prohibit bribery of foreign officials). Siemens AG, headquartered in Germany and Europe's largest engineering conglomerate, conducts business throughout the world. Employees were allowed to withdraw up to €1 million for bribes from three "cash desks" set up at Siemens's offices to facilitate the obtaining of government contracts throughout the world. And, until 1999, Siemens claimed tax deductions for these bribes, many of which were listed as "useful expenditures."

The Organization for Economic Cooperation and Development (OECD) works on global issues, endeavoring to help member countries sustain economic growth and employment. OECD adopted its Anti-Bribery Convention on November 21, 1997; its regulations came into effect in 1999. In 1999, member countries, including Germany, adopted laws combating bribery of foreign public officials in international business transactions. However, between 2001 and 2004 some $67 million was withdrawn from the Siemens "cash desks." The bribery had continued! Mark Pieth, chairman of the working group on bribery at the OECD, said: "People felt confident that they were doing nothing wrong."* With some 470,000 employee jobs at Siemens depending on the ability to obtain engineering and high-tech contracts throughout the world, were Siemens contracting agents justified in continuing to make "useful expenditures" to save jobs and their company from ruin? How could these expenditures be a bad thing?

On December 11, 2008, Siemens AG pleaded guilty to criminal violations of the United States Foreign Corrupt Practices Act and received a total criminal fine of $450 million. It also reached a settlement with the U.S. Securities and Exchange Commission for violation of the FCPA's antibribery, books and records, and internal control provisions and agreed to pay $350 million in disgorgement of profits. Moreover, it agreed to fines and disgorgement of profits of $569 million to settle an investigation by the Munich Public Prosecutor's Office. Seimens's bribery was a bad thing because bribery and corruption were criminal acts. Moreover, it allowed the corporation to have an inherently unfair competitive advantage over other contract bidders. The convention helps ensure that public works projects are awarded on the basis of sound economic judgment rather than on the basis of who offers the biggest bribe. The notoriety of the Siemens prosecutions should send a strong and clear message to all trading partners that parties to the convention must not engage in bribery to obtain business deals.** Siemens's current board member Peter Solmssen believes it is a myth that firms have to pay bribes to do business in developing countries, and believes that Siemens can increase sales without paying bribes.***

** The current members of the Anti-Bribery Convention are Argentina, Australia, Austria, Belgium, Brazil, Bulgaria, Canada, Chile, Czech Republic, Denmark, Estonia, Finland, France, Germany, Greece, Hungary, Iceland, Ireland, Israel, Italy, Japan, Korea, Luxemburg, Mexico, Netherlands, New Zealand, Norway, Poland, Portugal, Slovak Republic, Slovenia, South Africa, Spain, Sweden, Switzerland, Turkey, United Kingdom, and the United States.

* "The Siemens Scandal: Bavarian Baksheesh," *The Economist*, **www.economist.com/business/displaystory.cfm?story_id=12814642**.

*** "Siemens Settlement: Relief, But Is It Over?" *Business Week*, **www.businessweek.com/print/globalbiz/content/dec2008/gb20081215_941906.htm**.

individuals involved may be responsible for damages as a result of civil actions brought by competitors under federal and state antiracketeering acts.[38]

The act does not apply to payments made to low-level officials for expediting the performance of routine government services.

[38] PL 95-213, 94 Stat 1494, 15 USC § 78a nt.

C A S E   S U M M A R Y

You Just Can't Do That!

FACTS: Harry Carpenter, CEO of Kirkpatrick Company, agreed to pay Nigerian government officials a "commission" equal to 20 percent of the contract price if Kirkpatrick obtained the contract to build an aeromedical center in Nigeria. Kirkpatrick was awarded the contract, and the "commission" was paid to the Nigerian officials. A competitor for the project, ETC, International (ETC), learned of the "20 percent commission" and informed U.S. officials. Kirkpatrick and Carpenter pleaded guilty to violations of the Foreign Corrupt Practices Act by paying bribes to get the Nigerian contract. ETC then brought this civil action against Kirkpatrick, Carpenter, and others for damages under the Racketeer Influenced and Corrupt Organizations Act (RICO) and the New Jersey Antiracketeering Act. The district court ruled the suit was barred by the act-of-state doctrine, the Court of Appeals reversed, and the U.S. Supreme Court granted *certiorari*.

DECISION: Judgment for ETC. The act-of-state doctrine does not establish an exception for cases that may embarrass foreign governments. The doctrine merely requires that, in the process of deciding cases, the acts of foreign governments, taken in their own jurisdictions, shall be deemed valid. The doctrine has no application to the present case: The validity of a foreign sovereign act is not at issue because the payment and receipt of bribes are prohibited by Nigerian law. [**Kirkpatrick v ETC, International, 493 US 400 (1990)**]

lawflix

The In-Laws (1979) (PG)

Review the segment in the film in which money is paid by a dictator for the sale of U.S. currency plates. The dictator's plan is to create worldwide inflation. List the various laws and conventions Peter Falk and Alan Arkin violate through their sale of the plates.

 Check out LawFlix at **www.cengage.com/blaw/dvl** to access movie clips that illustrate business law concepts.

MAKE THE CONNECTION

SUMMARY

The World Trade Organization, a multilateral treaty subscribed to by the United States and most of the industrialized countries of the world, is based on the principle of trade without discrimination. The United Nations Convention on Contracts for the International Sale of Goods provides uniform rules for international sales contracts between parties in contracting nations. The European Union is a regional trading group that includes most of western Europe. The North American Free Trade Agreement involves Mexico, Canada, and the United States and eliminates all tariffs between the three countries over a 15-year period.

U.S. firms may choose to do business abroad by making export sales or contracting with a foreign distributor to take title to their goods and sell them abroad. U.S. firms may also license their technology or trademarks for foreign use. An agency arrangement or the organization of a foreign subsidiary may be required to participate effectively in foreign markets. This results in subjecting the U.S. firm to taxation in the host country. However, tax treaties commonly eliminate double taxation.

The Export Administration Act is the principal statute imposing export controls on goods and technical data.

In choosing the form for doing business abroad, U.S. firms must be careful not to violate the antitrust laws of host countries. Anticompetitive foreign transactions may have an adverse impact on competition in U.S. domestic markets. U.S. antitrust laws have a broad extraterritorial reach. U.S. courts apply a "jurisdictional rule of reason," weighing the interests of the United States against the interests of the foreign country involved in making a decision on whether to hear a case. Illegal conduct may occur in U.S. securities markets. U.S. enforcement efforts sometimes run into foreign countries' secrecy and blocking laws that hinder effective enforcement.

Antidumping laws offer relief for domestic firms threatened by unfair foreign competition. In addition, economic programs exist to assist industries, communities, and workers injured by import competition.

The Foreign Corrupt Practices Act restricts U.S. firms doing business abroad from paying public officials "commissions" for getting business contracts from the foreign governments.

LEARNING OUTCOMES

After studying this chapter, you should be able to clearly explain:

A. GENERAL PRINCIPLES

LO.1 Explain which country's law will govern an international contract should a dispute arise

See the choice of law example where the U.S. Court required the Lipcons to "honor their bargains" and vindicate their claims in an English Court on p. 127.

LO.2 Identify seven major international organizations, conferences, and treaties that affect the multinational markets for goods, services, and investments

See the discussion of the GATT-WTO, CISG, UNCTAD, EU, NAFTA, IMF-World Bank, and OPEC beginning on p. 129.

LO.3 List the forms of business organizations for doing business abroad

See the discussion of export sales, appointing of an agent, foreign distributorships, licensing, subsidiaries, and joint ventures beginning on p. 132.

B. GOVERNMENTAL REGULATION

LO.4 Explain the tariff barriers and nontariff barriers to the free movements of goods across borders

> See the *Sabritas* case on the applicability of tariff barriers on p. 142.
> See the U.S. embargo on all Brazilian shrimp example because of Brazil's failure to require turtle excluder devices on its shrimp boats p. 143.

LO.5 Explain U.S. law regarding payment to foreign government officials as a means of obtaining business contracts with other governments, and compare U.S. law to laws and treaties applicable to most First World nations

> See the Ethics & the Law discussion of the tax deductions for "useful expenditures" (bribes) claimed by Siemens AG, p. 147.

KEY TERMS

act-of-state doctrine
agent
blocking laws
choice-of-law clause
comity
Dispute Settlement Body (DSB)
distributor
dumping
effects doctrine

export sale
franchising
freight forwarders
gray market goods
intellectual property rights
joint venture
jurisdictional rule of reason
letter of credit
licensing
most-favored-nation clause

principal
secrecy laws
sovereign compliance doctrine
sovereign immunity doctrine
special drawing rights (SDRs)
tariff

QUESTIONS AND CASE PROBLEMS

1. How does the selling of subsidized foreign goods in the United States adversely affect free trade?

2. Able Time Inc. imported a shipment of watches into the United States. The watches bore the mark "TOMMY," which is a registered trademark owned by Tommy Hilfiger. U.S. Customs seized the watches pursuant to the Tariff Act, which authorizes seizure of any "merchandise bearing a counterfeit mark." Tommy Hilfiger did not make or sell watches at the time of the seizure. Able argues that because Tommy Hilfiger did not make watches at the time of the seizure, the watches it imported were not counterfeit, and the civil penalty imposed by Customs was unlawful. The government argues that the mark was counterfeit and the Tariff Act does not require the owner of the registered mark to make the same type of goods as those bearing the offending mark. Decide. [*U.S. v Able Time, Inc.*, 545 F3d 824 (9th Cir 2008)].

3. PepsiCo has registered its PEPSI trademarks in the U.S. Patent and Trademark Office. PEPSI products are bottled and distributed in the United States by PepsiCo and by authorized bottlers pursuant to Exclusive Bottling

Appointment agreements, which authorize local bottlers to bottle and distribute PEPSI products in their respective territories. Similarly, PepsiCo has appointed local bottlers to bottle and distribute PEPSI products in Mexico within particular territories. Pacific Produce, Ltd., has been engaged in the sale and distribution within the United States and Nevada of PEPSI products that were manufactured and bottled in Mexico and intended for sale in Mexico ("Mexican product"). The Mexican product sold by Pacific Products in the United States has certain material differences from domestic PEPSI products sold by PepsiCo: (1) it contains inferior paper labels that improperly report nutritional information; (2) it does not comply with the labeling standards followed by PepsiCo in the United States; (3) it is sold in channels of trade different from PepsiCo's authorized distribution channels without "drink by" notice dates on the Mexican product and monitoring on the Mexican product for proper shipment and storage conditions; and (4) it conflicts with the bottle return policies of PepsiCo. The Mexican product with its "Marca Reg" and Spanish language bottle caps is well received by consumers in Pacific Produce distribution channels. Classify the goods being sold by Pacific Produce. State the applicable law governing a dispute between PepsiCo and Pacific Produce. How would you decide this case? [*PepsiCo, Inc. v Pacific Produce, Ltd.*, 2001 US Dist LEXIS 12085]

4. Ronald Sadler, a California resident, owned a helicopter distribution company in West Germany, Delta Avia. This company distributed U.S.-made Hughes civilian helicopters in western Europe. Sadler's German firm purchased 85 helicopters from Hughes Aircraft Co. After export licenses were obtained in reliance on the purchaser's written assurance that the goods would not be disposed of contrary to the export license, the helicopters were exported to Germany for resale in western Europe. Thereafter, Delta Avia exported them to North Korea, which was a country subject to a trade embargo by the United States. The helicopters were converted to military use. Sadler was charged with violating the Export Administration Regulations. In Sadler's defense, it was contended that the U.S. regulations have no effect on what occurs in the resale of civilian helicopters in another sovereign country. Decide.

5. Mirage Investments Corp. (MIC) planned a tender offer for the shares of Gulf States International Corp. (GSIC). Archer, an officer of MIC, placed purchase orders for GSIC stock through the New York office of the Bahamian Bank (BB) prior to the announcement of the tender offer, making a $300,000 profit when the tender offer was made public. The Bahamas is a secrecy jurisdiction. The bank informed the SEC that under its law, it could not disclose the name of the person for whom it purchased the stock. What, if anything, may the SEC do to discover whether the federal securities laws have been violated?

6. United Overseas, Ltd. (UOL), is a U.K. firm that purchases and sells manufacturers' closeouts in Europe and the Middle East. UOL's representative, Jay Knox, used stationery listing a UOL office in New York to solicit business from Revlon, Inc., in New York. On April 1, 1992, UOL faxed a purchase order from its headquarters in England to Revlon's New York offices for the

purchase of $4 million worth of shampoo. The purchase order on its face listed six conditions, none of which referred to a forum selection clause. When Revlon was not paid for the shampoo it shipped, it sued UOL in New York for breach of contract. UOL moved to dismiss the complaint because of a forum selection clause, which it stated was on the reverse side of the purchase order and provided that "the parties hereby agree to submit to the jurisdiction of the English Courts disputes arising out of the contract." The evidence did not show that the reverse side of the purchase order had been faxed with the April 1992 order. Should the court dismiss the complaint based on the "forum selection clause"? Read Chapter 32 on letters of credit and advise Revlon how to avoid similar litigation in the future. [*Revlon, Inc. v United Overseas, Ltd.,* 1994 WL 9657 (SDNY)]

7. Reebok manufactures and sells fashionable athletic shoes in the United States and abroad. It owns the federally registered Reebok trademark and has registered this trademark in Mexico as well. Nathan Betech is a Mexican citizen residing in San Diego, California, with business offices there. Reebok believed that Betech was in the business of selling counterfeit Reebok shoes in Mexican border towns, such as Tijuana, Mexico. It sought an injunction in a federal district court in California ordering Betech to cease his counterfeiting activity and to refrain from destroying certain documents. It also asked the court to freeze Betech's assets pending the outcome of a Lanham Act lawsuit. Betech contended that a U.S. district court has no jurisdiction or authority to enter the injunction for the activities allegedly occurring in Mexico. Decide. [*Reebok Int'l, Ltd. v Marnatech Enterprises, Inc.,* 970 F2d 552 (9th Cir)]

8. Assume that before the formation of the European Union, the lowest-cost source of supply for a certain product consumed in France was the United States. Explain the basis by which, after the EU was formed, higher-cost German producers could have replaced the U.S. producers as the source of supply.

9. A complaint was filed with the U.S. Commerce Department's ITA by U.S. telephone manufacturers AT&T, Comidial Corp., and Eagle Telephones, Inc., alleging that 12 Asian manufacturers of small business telephones, including the Japanese firms Hitachi, NEC, and Toshiba and the Taiwanese firm Sun Moon Star Corp., were dumping their small business phones in the U.S. market at prices that were from 6 percent to 283 percent less than those in their home markets. The U.S. manufacturers showed that the domestic industry's market share had dropped from 54 percent in 1985 to 33 percent in 1989. They asserted that it was doubtful if the domestic industry could survive the dumping. Later, in a hearing before the ITC, the Japanese and Taiwanese respondents contended that their domestic industry was basically sound and that the U.S. firms simply had to become more efficient to meet worldwide competition. They contended that the United States was using the procedures before the ITA and ITC as a nontariff barrier to imports. How should the ITC decide the case? [*American Telephone and Telegraph Co. v Hitachi,* 6 ITC 1511]

10. Campbell Soup Co. imports tomato paste from a wholly owned Mexican subsidiary, Sinalopasta, S.A. de C.V. It deducted $416,324 from the computed value of goods shipped to the United States, which was the cost of transportation of the finished tomato paste from Sinalopasta's loading dock in Mexico to the U.S. border. The deduction thus lowered the computed value of the goods and the amount of duty to be paid the U.S. government by Campbell Soup Co. United States Customs questioned this treatment of freight costs. Tariff Act § 140a(e)(1)(B) requires that profits and general expenses be included in calculating the computed value of goods, which in part quantify the value of the merchandise in the country of production. Is Campbell's position correct? [*Campbell Soup Co., Inc. v United States,* 107 F3d 1556 (Fed Cir)]

11. Roland Staemphfli was employed as the chief financial officer of Honeywell Bull, S.A. (HB), a Swiss computer company operating exclusively in Switzerland. Staemphfli purportedly arranged financing for HB in Switzerland through the issuance of promissory notes. He had the assistance of Fidenas, a Bahamian company dealing in commercial paper. Unknown to Fidenas, the HB notes were fraudulent. The notes were prepared and forged by Staemphfli, who lost all of the proceeds in a speculative investment and was convicted of criminal fraud. HB denied responsibility for the fraudulently issued notes when they came due. Fidenas's business deteriorated because of its involvement with the HB notes. It sued HB and others in the United States for violations of U.S. securities laws. HB defended, arguing that the U.S. court did not have jurisdiction over the transactions in question. Decide. [*Fidenas v Honeywell Bull, S.A.,* 606 F2d 5 (2d Cir)]

12. Marc Rich & Co., A.G., a Swiss commodities trading corporation, refused to comply with a grand jury subpoena requesting certain business records maintained in Switzerland and relating to crude oil transactions and possible violations of U.S. income tax laws. Marc Rich contended that a U.S. court has no authority to require a foreign corporation to deliver to a U.S. court documents located abroad. The court disagreed and imposed fines, froze assets, and threatened to close a Marc Rich wholly owned subsidiary that did business in the state of New York. The fines amounted to $50,000 for each day the company failed to comply with the court's order. Marc Rich appealed. Decide. [*Marc Rich v United States,* 707 F2d 633 (2d Cir)]

13. U.S. Steel Corp. formed Orinoco Mining Co., a wholly owned corporation, to mine large deposits of iron ore that U.S. Steel had discovered in Venezuela. Orinoco, which was incorporated in Delaware, was subject to Venezuela's maximum tax of 50 percent on net income. Orinoco was also subject to U.S. income tax, but the U.S. foreign tax credit offset this amount. U.S. Steel purchased the ore from Orinoco in Venezuela. U.S. Steel formed Navios, Inc., a wholly owned subsidiary, to transport the ore. Navios, a Liberian corporation, was subject to a 2.5 percent Venezuelan excise tax and was exempt from U.S. income tax. Although U.S. Steel was Navios's primary customer, it charged other customers the same price it charged U.S. Steel. U.S. Steel's investment in Navios was $50,000. In seven years, Navios accumulated nearly $80 million in

cash but had not paid any dividends to U.S. Steel. The IRS used IRC § 482 to allocate $52 million of Navios's income to U.S. Steel. U.S. Steel challenged this action, contending Navios's charges to U.S. Steel were at arm's length and the same it charged other customers. Decide. [*United States Steel Corp. v Commissioner,* 617 F2d 942 (2d Cir)]

14. National Computers, Inc., a U.S. firm, entered into a joint venture with a Chinese computer manufacturing organization, TEC. A dispute arose over payments due the U.S. firm under the joint venture agreement with TEC. The agreement called for disputes to be arbitrated in China, with the arbitrator being chosen from a panel of arbitrators maintained by the Beijing arbitration institution, Cietac. What advantages and disadvantages exist for the U.S. firm under this arbitration arrangement? Advise the U.S. firm on negotiating future arbitration agreements with Chinese businesses.

15. Sensor, a Netherlands business organization wholly owned by Geosource, Inc., of Houston, Texas, made a contract with C.E.P. to deliver 2,400 strings of geophones to Rotterdam by September 20, 1982. The ultimate destination was identified as the USSR. Thereafter, in June 1982, the president of the United States prohibited shipment to the USSR of equipment manufactured in foreign countries under license from U.S. firms. The president had a foreign policy objective of retaliating for the imposition of martial law in Poland, and he was acting under regulations issued under the Export Administration Act of 1979. Sensor, in July and August of 1982, notified C.E.P. that as a subsidiary of a U.S. corporation, it had to respect the president's embargo. C.E.P. filed suit in a district court of the Netherlands asking that Sensor be ordered to deliver the geophones. Decide. [*Compagnie Européenne des Pétroles v Sensor Nederland,* 22 ILM 66]

Chapter 8

CRIMES

S ociety sets certain standards of conduct and punishes a breach of those standards as a crime. This chapter introduces the means by which government protects people and businesses from prohibited conduct.

A. GENERAL PRINCIPLES

Detailed criminal codes and statutes define crimes and specify their punishment. Crimes vary from state to state but still show the imprint of a common law background through similar elements and structure.

1. Nature and Classification of Crimes

crime–violation of the law that is punished as an offense against the state or government.

misdemeanor–criminal offense with a sentence of less than one year that is neither treason nor a felony.

felony–criminal offense that is punishable by confinement in prison for more than one year or by death, or that is expressly stated by statute to be a felony.

A **crime** is conduct that is prohibited and punished by a government. Crimes are classified as *common law* or *statutory* according to their origin. Offenses punishable by less than one year in prison are called **misdemeanors**. More serious crimes are called **felonies**, including serious business crimes such as bribery and embezzlement, which are punishable by confinement in prison for more than one year. Misdemeanors include weighing goods with uninspected scales or operating without a sales tax license. An act may be a felony in one state and a misdemeanor in another.[1]

2. Basis of Criminal Liability

A crime generally consists of two elements: (1) a mental state (scienter or intent) and (2) an act or omission. Harm may occur as a result of a crime, but harm is not an essential element of a crime.

(A) MENTAL STATE. Mental state, or intent, does not require an awareness or knowledge of guilt. In most crimes, the voluntary commission of the act is sufficient for proving mental state. Ignorance that a law is being broken does not mean there is not mental state. **For Example,** dumping waste without a permit is still a criminal act even when the party releasing the waste did not know about the permit requirement.

(B) ACT OR OMISSION. Specific statutes define the conduct that, when coupled with sufficient mental state, constitutes a crime. **For Example,** writing a check knowing you do not have the funds available is conduct that is a crime.

3. Responsibility for Criminal Acts

In some cases, persons who did not necessarily commit the criminal act itself are still held criminally responsible for acts committed by others.

(A) CORPORATE LIABILITY. Corporations are held responsible for the acts of their employees. A corporation may also be held liable for crimes based on the failure of its employees to act. In the past decade, some of the nation's largest corporations have paid fines for crimes based on employees' failure to take action or for the

---

[1] Some states further define crimes by seriousness with different degrees of a crime, such as first-degree murder, second-degree murder, and so on. Misdemeanors may be differentiated by giving special names to minor misdemeanors.

CASE SUMMARY

Making Stuff Up for the Grand Jury

FACTS: Kathryn Erickson was the general manager of the Uintah Special Services District (USSD), an entity created to use federal-mineral-lease revenues for road projects. She, along with her secretary, Cheryl McCurdy, administered the USSD from a small office in Vernal, Utah. Ms. Erickson's authority was limited and she was not permitted to enter into or modify contracts for or to expend more than $1,000 of USSD funds, without board approval.

Mitchell Construction was a major contractor for USSD. In 1998, USSD awarded Mitchell Construction a contract to haul gravel from a site called Hamaker Bottoms and another contract to carry out small asphalt-paving projects. Both contracts were to be completed within the 1998 construction year.

During 1999 and 2000 Mitchell Construction continued to perform work on the projects covered by its 1998 contracts with USSD, despite their expiration. It submitted invoices to USSD and was paid for this work.

In June 1999 a federal grand jury began to investigate contracting irregularities at USSD and the Uintah County Road Department and issued a subpoena duces tecum to USSD requesting copies of "project contracts, invoices" between USSD and contractors.

While the office was preparing the response for the grand jury subpoena, Ms. McCurdy saw Ms. Erickson prepare a handwritten change order for the Hamaker Bottoms contract and saw Ms. Erickson and Gilman N. Mitchell both sign it. The change order, which was backdated to January 13, 1999, extended the contract through December 31, 2000.

Ms. McCurdy later discovered that two other change orders had been created and backdated. She spent a day copying documents for the grand jury and recording, on a handwritten list, all of the documents that she had copied. However, she left Ms. Erickson in the office while she was working on the list in order to go home for dinner. Ms. Erickson called her and told her not to come back because all the copying was done. Later, Ms. McCurdy found on Ms. Erickson's desk a photocopy of the grand jury document list and saw that two entries not in her handwriting had been added. These entries were for change orders for contracts between Mitchell Construction and USSD. Ms. McCurdy reported the change to the government.

Ms. Erickson and Mr. Mitchell were each indicted by a grand jury in the U.S. District Court for the District of Utah on three counts of obstruction of justice by knowingly falsifying a document with the knowledge and intent that the grand jury would rely on it.

The jury returned a verdict of guilty against both Ms. Erickson and Mr. Mitchell on all three counts. The two appealed.

DECISION: The court affirmed the decision. There are three requirements for conviction of obstruction of justice: (1) There must be a pending judicial proceeding; (2) the defendant must have knowledge or notice of the pending proceeding; and (3) the defendant must have acted corruptly with the specific intent to obstruct or impede the administration of justice. The two had backdated the documents in order to cover up the fact that the contracts had expired. They had continued the contracts without authority and authorized or received payments above the $1,000 limit. They were responding to a grand jury subpoena and gave it false change orders. They did so in order to protect Ms. Erickson's job and Mr. Mitchell's company's contracts and relationship with USSD. [**U.S. v Erickson, 561 F3d 1150 CA 10 2009**]

actions they did take. **For Example,** AIG, the world's largest insurer, paid the largest fine in corporate history in the United States, $1.6 billion, for its questionable accounting practices and alleged sham insurance contracts undertaken for the purpose of boosting its earnings. [2]

(B) **OFFICERS AND AGENTS OF CORPORATIONS.** One of the main differences between nonbusiness and business crimes is that more people in a company can be convicted for the same business crime. For nonbusiness crimes, only those who are actually involved in the act itself can be convicted of the crime. For business crimes, however, managers of firms whose employees commit criminal acts can be held liable if the managers authorized the conduct of the employees or knew about their conduct and did nothing or failed to act reasonably in their supervisory positions to prevent the employees from engaging in criminal conduct.

CASE SUMMARY

Rats in the Warehouse and a CEO with a Fine

FACTS: Acme Markets, Inc., was a national food retail chain headquartered in Philadelphia. John R. Park was president of Acme, which, in 1970, employed 36,000 people and operated 16 warehouses.

In 1970, the Food and Drug Administration (FDA) forwarded a letter to Park describing, in detail, problems with rodent infestation in Acme's Philadelphia warehouse facility. In December 1971, the FDA found the same types of conditions in Acme's Baltimore warehouse facility. In January 1972, the FDA's chief of compliance for its Baltimore office wrote to Park about the inspection:

> We note with much concern that the old and new warehouse areas used for food storage were actively and extensively inhabited by live rodents. Of even more concern was the observation that such reprehensible conditions obviously existed for a prolonged period of time without any detection, or were completely ignored.
>
> We trust this letter will serve to direct your attention to the seriousness of the problem and formally advise you of the urgent need to initiate whatever measures are necessary to prevent recurrence and ensure compliance with the law.

After Park received the letter, he met with the vice president for legal affairs for Acme and was assured that he was "investigating the situation immediately and would be taking corrective action."

When the FDA inspected the Baltimore warehouse in March 1972, there was some improvement in the facility, but there was still rodent infestation. Acme and Park were both charged with violations of the federal Food, Drug and Cosmetic Act. Acme pleaded guilty. Park was convicted and fined $500; he appealed.

DECISION: Officers of a corporation can be held criminally liable for the conduct of others within the company if it can be shown that the officers knew of the issue and failed to take the steps necessary to eliminate the criminal activity. In this case, Park had been warned and had been given several opportunities to remedy the problem. Part of his responsibility as an officer is following up to be certain that tasks he has assigned are completed. Failure to follow through can be a basis for criminal liability. [**United States v Park, 421 US 658 (1975)**]

[2] **www.sec.gov**.

(c) **PENALTY FOR CRIME: FORFEITURE.** When a defendant is convicted of a crime, the court may also declare that the defendant's rights in any property used or gained from a crime (an instrument of that crime) be confiscated. Some types of instruments of the crime are automatically forfeited, such as the tools of a crime. **For Example,** the U.S. government confiscated from confessed $50-billion-Ponzi schemer, Bernie Madoff, everything from his yacht to his bank accounts to his seat on NASDAQ. Confiscation is, in effect, an increased penalty for the defendant's crime.

(d) **PENALTIES FOR BUSINESS AND WHITE-COLLAR CRIMES.** Most common law criminal penalties were created with "natural" persons in mind, as opposed to "artificial" or corporate persons. A $100,000 fine may be significant to an individual but to a corporation with $3 billion in assets and hundreds of millions in income, such a fine could be viewed as a minimal cost of doing business.

Criminal penalties for corporations have been reformed to address this need for deterrence. Rather than using fixed-amount fines, statutes and courts apply percentage of revenue penalties. **For Example,** a bad decision on a product line would cost a company 10 percent to 20 percent of its earnings. A criminal penalty could be imposed in the same percentage fashion with the idea that the company simply made a bad legal decision that should be reflected in earnings.

Another change in penalties for business and white-collar crimes has been the requirement for mandatory prison sentences for officers and directors who are convicted of crimes committed as they led their corporations. In 2009, a federal judge required an executive who entered a guilty plea to spend his two years of probation writing a book about what he did and offer guidance to business executives so that they can avoid his missteps. He is then required to publish and distribute the book.[3] The human element of the corporation is then punished for the crimes that the business committed. The U.S. Sentencing Commission, established by Congress in 1984, has developed both federal sentencing guidelines and a carrot-and-stick approach to fighting business crime. If the managers of a company are involved and working to prevent criminal misconduct in the company and a crime occurs, the guidelines permit sentence reductions for the managers' efforts. If the managers do not adequately supervise conduct and do not encourage compliance with the law, the guidelines require judges to impose harsher sentences and fines. The guidelines, referred to as the **Federal Sentencing Guidelines** (or the *U.S. Sentencing Guidelines*), apply to federal crimes such as securities fraud, antitrust violations, racketeering, theft (embezzlement), Medicare fraud, and other business crimes. The sentencing guidelines permit a judge to place a guilty company on probation, with the length of the probation controlled by whether the company had prevention programs in place.

Federal Sentencing Guidelines – federal standards used by judges in determining mandatory sentence terms for those convicted of federal crimes.

Following the collapse of companies such as Enron, WorldCom, and Adelphia, the U.S. Sentencing Commission (USSC) piloted the passage of the 2001 Economic Crime Package: Consolidation, Clarification, and Certainty. Amended guidelines, post-Enron, address the increased corporate and white-collar criminal penalties enacted under Sarbanes-Oxley (SOX), and consider the seriousness of the offense,

---

[3] Natasha Singer, "Judge Orders Former Bristol-Myers Executive to Write Book," *New York Times*, June 9, 2009, p. B3.

the company's history of violations, its cooperation in the investigation, the effectiveness of its compliance program (often called an *ethics program*), and the role of senior management in the wrongdoing. Corporate managers found to have masterminded any criminal activity must be sentenced to prison time.[4] Figure 8.1 is a summary of the current penalties for federal crimes. Under a U.S. Supreme Court decision in 2005, *U.S. v Booker,* judges may only use the guidelines as just that, guidelines; the sentencing ranges are no longer mandatory for judges.[5] Going outside those ranges, however, is carefully reviewed by appellate courts.[6] Federal judges can consider only the evidence presented at trial and may not consider evidence of previous convictions, but not evidence that has not been proven at trial.[7]

FIGURE 8-1 | *Roster of White-Collar Criminal Charges*

COMPANY/PERSON	ISSUE	STATUS
Andrew Fastow, former CFO of Enron (2004)	Multimillion-dollar earnings from serving as principal in SPEs of Enron created to keep debts off the company books; significant sales of shares during the time frame preceding company collapse	Resigned as CFO; appeared before Congress and took the Fifth Amendment; entered guilty plea to securities and wire fraud; sentence of 6 years
Bear Stearns	Sale of mortgage-based securities without full disclosure of risk	Two of its long-term fund managers under indictment; company's demise
Bernie Ebbers (2005) Former CEO, WorldCom	Fraud	Convicted; sentenced to 25 years
Computer Associates (2004)	Criminal investigation pending on securities fraud and obstruction following $2.2 billion restatement in sales	Pending investigations; former CEO entered guilty plea to felony charges
Countrywide Mortgage (2009)	Insider trading; securities fraud	Former CEO Angelo Mozilo charged with insider trading, CFO and COO charged with failure to disclose firm's relaxed lending standards
Enron (2001)	Earnings overstated through mark-to-market accounting; off-the-book/special-purpose entities (SPEs) carried significant amounts of Enron debt not reflected in the financial statements; significant offshore SPEs (881 of 3,000 SPEs were offshore, primarily in Cayman Islands)	Company in bankruptcy; impetus for SOX; CFO Andrew Fastow and others entered guilty pleas; see Lea Fastow, Kenneth Lay, and Jeffrey Skilling

[4] *U.S. v Booker,* 543 US 220 (2005).
[5] *U.S. v Skilling,* 554 F3d 529(C.A. 5 2009).
[6] *Gall v U.S.,* 552 US 38 (2007).
[7] Mary Kreiner Ramirez, "Just in Crime: Guiding Economic Crime Reform after the Sarbanes-Oxley Act of 2002," 34 *Loyola University of Chicago Law Journal* 359, 387 (2003).

FIGURE 8-1 | *Continued*

COMPANY/PERSON	ISSUE	STATUS
HealthSouth (2003)	$2.7 billion accounting fraud; overstatement of revenues	16 former executives indicted; 5 plead guilty; see Richard Scrushy
KPMG (2006)	Tax shelter fraud	Settled by paying a penalty of $456 million fine in lieu of indictment; 16 former partners and employees indicted; most charges dismissed
L. Dennis Kozlowski, former CEO of Tyco (2003)	Accused of improper use of company funds	Indicted in New York for failure to pay sales tax on transactions in fine art; hung jury on charges of looting Tyco; convicted on retrial with 15-25-year sentence
Bernard Madoff (2009)	Ran a $50-billion Ponzi scheme through Madoff Securities	Entered guilty plea to all charges and refused to cooperate with investigators; 150-year sentence (at age of 71 in 2009, it is the equivalent of a life sentence)
Marsh & McLennan (2005)	Price-fixing	Paid $850 million in restitution to end investigation of its brokerage practices
Martha Stewart, CEO of Martha Stewart Living, Omnimedia, Inc., and close friend of Dr. Waksal (2003)	Sold 5,000 shares of ImClone one day before public announcement of negative FDA action on Erbitux	Indicted and convicted, along with her broker at Merrill Lynch, of making false statements and conspiracy; served sentence and probation
Richard Scrushy (2003)	Indicted for fraud and bribery for HealthSouth accounting fraud	Acquitted of all charges related to HealthSouth; convicted of bribing former governor of Alabama
Stanford Securities (2009)	$9 billion Ponzi scheme	Indictments of 4 top officers, including Stanford, the controller, the chief accounting officer, the chief investment officer, and an official from Antigua for mail, wire, and securities fraud

White-Collar Crime Penalty Enhancement Act of 2002—federal reforms passed as a result of the collapses of companies such as Enron; provides for longer sentences and higher fines for both executives and companies.

(E) SARBANES-OXLEY REFORMS TO CRIMINAL PENALTIES. Part of SOX, passed by Congress following the collapses of Enron and WorldCom corporations, was the **White-Collar Crime Penalty Enhancement Act of 2002**.[8] This act increases penalties substantially. **For Example,** the penalties for mail and wire fraud are increased from a maximum of

[8] 18 USC § 1314 *et seq.*

thinking things through

Employees Obeying Orders—Employer Liable?

Lauro Ortega was digging a foundation at a Lattarulo construction site. The Lattarulo site involved digging a foundation next to another building, but the Lattarulo building required a deeper dig. The result was that the foundation of the building next to the site was weakened and required support until the Lattarulo concrete was poured to provide the substitute for the former ground support. A consultant working nearby did warn Mr. Williams Lattarulo, the owner, about the foundation's risk of collapse once the digging went deeper. Mr. Ortega also raised his concerns to Mr. Lattarulo. Mr. Lattarulo told him to keep digging. Mr. Ortega's co-workers also warned Mr. Lattarulo that the trench was unsafe and needed to have some supports placed in it to prevent a collapse. When he was warned a second time by his workers he said, "Don't worry about it."

Shortly thereafter, the adjoining building's foundation collapsed onto Mr. Ortega. Mr. Ortega's head was all that was uncovered when the foundation collapsed, but the pressure of the dirt and debris that rendered him immobile constricted his chest and made him unable to

breathe. He suffocated to death as his co-workers tried to dig him out from the debris.

While Mr. Lattarulo listed a company as a safety consultant for the site (something required by code), he did not actually have or pay a consultant, something that saved him $90,000 on the job. On the day of the collapse, a building inspector for the city visited the site where the fatality had occurred and said there were "shoddy work conditions." She also found eight violations of city code at the site.

The city brought manslaughter charges against Mr. Lattarulo. Mr. Lattarulo maintained that there was just an accident on a job site and he cannot be held criminally liable. However, the Building Department commissioner said that when there are clear rules and warnings—as there were in the case for the required support for digging trenches—and those rules and warnings are not followed, there will be criminal sanctions. When is an owner criminally liable for actions and work conducted by employees?

Source: Michael Wilson, "Manslaughter Charge for Builder in Brooklyn Collapse," *New York Times*, October 12, 2008, A24.

---

5 years to a maximum of 20 years. Penalties for violation of pension laws increased from 1 year to 10 years and the fines increased from $5,000 to $100,000. [9]

4. Indemnification of Crime Victims

Penalties are paid to the government. Typically, the victim of a crime does not benefit from the criminal prosecution and conviction of the wrongdoer, although courts can order that restitution be paid to victims.

Several states have adopted statutes providing a limited degree of indemnification to victims of crime to compensate them for the harm or loss sustained. [10] Under

---

[9] 18 USC §§ 1341 and 1343; 29 USC § 1131.

[10] A 1973 Uniform Crime Victims Reparations Act was adopted in Kansas, Louisiana, Montana, North Dakota, Ohio, and Utah. This act has been superseded by the Uniform Victims of Crime Act of 1992 adopted only in Montana, with variations.

some criminal victim indemnification statutes, dependents of a deceased victim are entitled to recover the amount of support they were deprived of by the victim's death. The Victims of Crime Act of 1984 creates a federal Crime Victims Fund. Using the fines paid into the federal courts as well as other monies, the federal government makes grants to the states to assist them in financing programs to provide assistance for victims of crime.[11] The Victim and Witness Protection Act of 1982 authorizes the sentencing judge in a federal district court to order, in certain cases, that the defendant make restitution (restoration) to the victim or pay the victim the amount of medical expenses or loss of income caused by the crime.[12]

(A) Action for Damages. The criminal prosecution of a wrongdoer is not undertaken primarily for the financial benefit of the victim of the crime, but the victim is typically entitled to bring a civil action for damages against the wrongdoer for the harm sustained. Statutes creating business crimes often give the victim the right to sue for damages. **For Example,** a company or individual violating federal antitrust laws is liable to the victim for three times the damages actually sustained.

(B) Indemnification of Unjustly Convicted. If an innocent person is convicted of a crime, the state legislature typically pays the person damages to compensate for the wrong that has been done. In some states, this right to indemnity is expressly established by statute, as in the case of the New York Unjust Conviction and Imprisonment Act. The fact that a person has been imprisoned while awaiting trial and is then acquitted does not entitle that person to compensation under such a statute because an acquittal does not mean that the person was found innocent. It means only that the government was not able to prove guilt beyond a reasonable doubt.[13]

B. White-Collar Crimes

white-collar crimes – crimes that do not use nor threaten to use force or violence or do not cause injury to persons or property.

White-collar crime is generally considered business crime, the type committed without physical threats or acts.

5. Conspiracies

conspiracy – agreement between two or more persons to commit an unlawful act.

Prior to the commission of an intended crime, a person may engage in conduct that is itself a crime, such as a conspiracy. A **conspiracy** is an agreement between two or more persons to commit an unlawful act or to use unlawful means to achieve an otherwise lawful result. The crime is the agreement itself; generally, it is immaterial that nothing is done to carry out the agreement, although some conspiracy statutes do require that some act is done to carry out the agreement before the crime of conspiracy is committed.

[11] 18 USC § 1401 *et seq.*
[12] 18 USC § 3579, as amended by 18 USC § 18.18; see *Hughey v United States,* 495 US 411 (1990). Some states likewise provide for payment into a special fund. *Ex parte* Lewis, 556 So 2d 370 (Ala 1989). In 2002, Congress passed another victims' compensation statute, with this one providing relief and assistance to the victims of terrorist attacks in the United States. 42 USCA § 10603b.
[13] *People v Neff,* 731 NY S2d 269 (2001).

6. Crimes Related to Production, Competition, and Marketing

(A) IMPROPER USE OF INTERSTATE COMMERCE. The shipment of improper goods or the transmission of improper information in interstate commerce is a federal crime. **For Example,** knowingly shipping food with salmonella would be a violation of the federal law that prohibits shipping adulterated foods, drugs, or cosmetics in interstate commerce.

The Communications Act of 1934, as amended, makes it a crime to manufacture or sell devices knowing their primary use is to unscramble satellite telecasts without having paid for the right to do so.[14]

(B) SECURITIES CRIMES. To protect the investing public, both state and federal laws have regulated the issuance and public sale of stocks and bonds. Between 1933 and 1940, Congress adopted seven such regulatory statutes. These statutes and the crimes associated with sales of securities are covered in Chapter 46.

7. Money Laundering

The federal government has adopted a Money Laundering Control Act (MLCA).[15] The act prohibits the knowing and willful participation in a financial transaction involving unlawful proceeds when the transaction is designed to conceal or disguise the source of the funds. The so-called *USA Patriot Act* that was passed on October 26, 2001, less than two months after the destruction of the World Trade Center and the damage to the Pentagon on September 11, 2001, includes a substantial number of changes and amendments to the Money Laundering Control Act and the Bank Secrecy Act (BSA).[16] Both statutes have been used as means to control bribery, tax evasion, and money laundering. Their changes and amendments were designed to curb the funding of terrorist activities in the United States.

The Patriot Act expands the coverage of the law from banks and financial institutions to anyone involved in financial transactions, which includes securities brokers; travel agents; those who close real estate transactions; insurance companies; loan or finance companies; casinos; currency exchanges; check-cashing firms; auto, plane, and boat dealers; and branches and agencies of foreign banks located in the United States. The amendments make even small businesses subject to the requirements of disclosure under MLCA and BSA, such as reporting cash transactions in excess of $10,000.

In addition, the types of accounts covered have been expanded. The accounts covered are not only securities accounts but also money market accounts. Furthermore, banks are now more actively involved in supervising accounts and following through on government information furnished to the bank on suspicious transactions and activities as well as individuals. Banks are required to implement new policies to prevent the types of transactions tagged by the government and conduct internal investigations for suspicious transactions. Because of the required

---

[14] 47 USC § 705(d)(1), (e)(4), 47 USC § 605 (d)(1), (e)(4); *United States v Harrell,* 983 F2d 36 (5th Cir 1993); but see *DIRECTV, Inc. v Robson,* 420 F3d 532 (5th Cir 2005).
[15] 18 USC §§ 1956–1957 (2000). *U.S. v Prince,* 214 F3d 740 (6th Cir 2000).
[16] 31 USC § 531(h).

close-watch provisions of these laws, banks and others covered under the federal statutes have developed anti-money-laundering programs. These programs must include a "Know Your Customer" training segment that teaches employees how to spot suspicious customers and transactions.

8. Racketeering

Racketeer Influenced and Corrupt Organizations (RICO) Act – federal law, initially targeting organized crime, that has expanded in scope and provides penalties and civil recovery for multiple criminal offenses, or a pattern of racketeering.

Congress passed the **Racketeer Influenced and Corrupt Organizations (RICO) Act**[17] in 1970 as part of the Organized Crime Control Act. The law was designed primarily to prevent individuals involved in organized crime from investing money obtained through racketeering in legitimate businesses. However, the broad language of the act, coupled with a provision that allows individuals and businesses to sue for treble damages, has resulted in an increasing number of lawsuits against ordinary businesspersons not associated with organized crime.

(A) CRIMINAL AND CIVIL APPLICATIONS. RICO authorizes criminal and civil actions against persons who use any income derived from racketeering activity to invest in, control, or conduct an enterprise through a pattern of *racketeering activity*.[18] In criminal and civil actions under RICO, a pattern of racketeering activity must be established by proving that at least two acts of racketeering activity—so-called *predicate acts*—have been committed within 10 years.[19] Conviction under RICO's criminal provisions may result in a $25,000 fine and up to 20 years' imprisonment as well as forfeiture of the property involved. A successful civil plaintiff may recover three times the actual damages suffered and attorney fees.[20]

predicate act – qualifying underlying offense for RICO liability.

(B) EXPANDING USAGE. Civil RICO actions have been successful against business entities, such as accounting firms, labor unions, insurance companies, commercial banks, and stock brokerage firms. However, under the Private Securities Litigation Reform Act of 1995, securities fraud is eliminated as a **predicate act**, or a qualifying underlying offense, for private RICO actions, absent a prior criminal conviction.[21]

---

[17] 18 USC §§ 1961–1968.

[18] § 1961. Definitions:
   (1) "Racketeering activity" means any act or threat involving murder, kidnapping, gambling, arson, robbery, bribery, extortion, dealing in obscene matter, dealing in a controlled substance or listed chemical, or sports bribery; counterfeiting; theft from interstate shipment; embezzlement from pension and welfare funds; extortionate credit transactions; fraud; wire fraud; mail fraud; procurement of citizenship or nationalization unlawfully; reproduction of naturalization or citizenship papers; obstruction of justice; tampering with a witness, victim, or an informant; retaliating against a witness, victim, or an informant; false statement in application and use of passport; forgery or false use of passport; fraud and misuse of visas, permits, and other documents; racketeering; unlawful welfare fund payments; laundering of monetary instruments; use of interstate commerce facilities in the commission of murder-for-hire; sexual exploitation of children; interstate transportation of stolen motor vehicles; interstate transportation of stolen property; trafficking in counterfeit labels of phonorecords, computer programs or computer program documentation, or packaging and copies of motion pictures or other audiovisual works; criminal infringement of a copyright; trafficking in contraband cigarettes; and white slave traffic.

[19] Brian Slocum, "RICO and the Legislative Supremacy Approach to Federal Criminal Lawmaking," 31 *Loyola Univ. Chicago Law Journal* 639 (2000).

[20] 18 U.S.C. § 1963.

[21] Connecticut's commercial bribery statute is a good example. It provides: *A person is guilty of commercial bribery when he confers, or agrees to confer, any benefit upon any employee, agent or fiduciary without the consent of the latter's employer or principal, with intent to influence his conduct in relation to his employer's or principal's affairs.* CGSA § 53a-160 (2002). Other examples of commercial bribery statues can be found at Minn. Stat Ann § 6-9.86 (Minnesota 2001); NH Rev Stat § 638:8 (New Hampshire 2001); Alaska Stat 11.45.670 (Alaska 2001); and Ala. Code § 13A-11-120 (Alabama 2001). Mississippi prohibits commercial bribery as well as sports bribery, which is paying the agent of a sports team in order to influence the outcome of a sporting event. Miss. Code Ann § 97-9-10 (2001).

9. Bribery

Bribery is the act of giving money, property, or any benefit to a particular person to influence that person's judgment in favor of the giver. At common law, the crime was limited to doing such acts to influence a public official.

The giving and the receiving of a bribe constitute separate crimes. In addition, the act of trying to obtain a bribe may be a crime of solicitation of bribery in some states, while in other states bribery is broadly defined to include solicitation of bribes.

10. Commercial Bribery

Commercial bribery is a form of bribery in which an agent for another is paid or given something of value in order to make a decision on behalf of his or her principal that benefits the party paying the agent. **For Example,** a napkin supplier who pays a restaurant agent $500 in exchange for that agent's decision to award the restaurant's napkin contract to that supplier has engaged in commercial bribery.[22]

11. Extortion and Blackmail

Extortion and *blackmail* are crimes in which money is exchanged for either specific actions or restraint in taking action.

extortion–illegal demand by a public officer acting with apparent authority.

(A) EXTORTION. When a public officer makes an illegal demand, the officer has committed the crime of **extortion**. **For Example,** if a health inspector threatens to close down a restaurant on a false sanitation law charge unless the restaurant pays the inspector a sum of money, the inspector has committed extortion. (If the restaurant voluntarily offers the inspector the money to prevent the restaurant from being shut down because of actual violations of the sanitation laws, the crime committed would be bribery.) Extortion has been expanded beyond the public law officer requirement of the common law. Most states have expanded extortion to include obtaining anything of value by threat, which might be, for example, loan sharking. In a number of states, statutes extend the extortion concept to include making terrorist threats.[23]

blackmail–extortion demands made by a nonpublic official.

(B) BLACKMAIL. In jurisdictions where extortion is limited to the conduct of public officials, a nonofficial commits **blackmail** by making demands that would be extortion if made by a public official. Ordinarily, blackmail is the act of threatening someone with publicity about a matter that would damage the victim's personal or business reputation.

12. Corrupt Influence

Legislative bodies have increasingly outlawed certain practices that exert a corrupting influence on business transactions.

(A) IMPROPER POLITICAL INFLUENCE. At the federal and state levels, it is a crime for one who holds public office to hold a financial interest in or to receive money from an

---

[22] 15 USC § 78(a), (n)–(t).
[23] *Pennsylvania v Bunting,* 426 A2d 130 (Pa 1981).

enterprise that seeks to do business with the government. Such conduct is a conflict of interest between the official's duty to citizens and his or her personal financial interests. **For Example,** the former governor of Illinois, Rod Blagojevich, was charged with seeking funds, fundraisers, and positions in exchange for political favors. To keep officials' conduct transparent, lobbyists must register in Washington, D.C.,[24] and adhere to statutory limits on gifts and contributions to political campaigns. Public officials must file annual disclosure forms about their financial positions as well as provide a disclosure of all gifts and their value.

(B) FOREIGN CORRUPT PRACTICES ACT. The **Foreign Corrupt Practices Act (FCPA)** is a federal criminal statute that applies to businesses whose principal offices are in the United States; it is an antibribery and anticorruption statute covering these companies' international operations.[25] The FCPA prohibits making, authorizing, or promising payments or gifts of money or anything of value with the intent to corrupt. This prohibition applies to payments or gifts designed to influence official acts of foreign officials, parties, party officials, candidates for office, nongovernmental organizations (NGOs), or any person who transmits the gift or money to these types of persons.

The FCPA does not prohibit **grease** or **facilitation payments**. These are payments made only to get officials to perform their normal duties or to perform them in a timely manner. Facilitation payments are those made to (1) secure a permit or a license, (2) obtain paper processing, (3) secure police protection, (4) provide phone, water, or power services, or (5) obtain any other similar action.

Foreign Corrupt Practices Act (FCPA)–federal law that makes it a felony to influence decision makers in other countries for the purpose of obtaining business, such as contracts for sales and services; also imposes financial reporting requirements on certain U.S. corporations.

grease payments–(facilitation payments) legal payments to speed up or ensure performance of normal government duties.

facilitation payments–(grease payments) legal payments to speed up or ensure performance of normal government duties.

ethics&the law
Why Regulate Bribes?

In 1999, a scandal involving the International Olympic Committee (IOC) erupted when it was discovered that members of the Salt Lake City Olympic Committee had given extensive gifts to members of the IOC to win the 2002 Winter Olympics for Salt Lake City. The gifts included everything from college tuition to medical care to entertainment. The attitude at the time toward the Salt Lake City revelations was, "It's always been done this way," or

"Everybody does this," or "It doesn't really hurt anyone."

Why should criminal indictments be brought against the U.S. citizens who bribed IOC members?* Why do we care?

* The criminal charges against two members of the Salt Lake City Olympic Committee were dismissed by the court but were reinstated by the Tenth Circuit. *U.S. v Welch*, 327 F3d 1081 (10th Cir 2003). The federal charges were again dismissed for lack of evidence.

13. Counterfeiting

Counterfeiting is making, with fraudulent intent, a document or coin that appears to be genuine but is not because the person making it did not have the authority to make it.

[24] Foreign Agents Registration Act, 22 USC § 611 *et seq.*, as amended.
[25] 15 USC § 78dd-1 *et seq.*

It is a federal crime to make, to possess with intent to transfer, or to transfer counterfeit coins, bank notes, or obligations or other securities of the United States. Various states also have statutes prohibiting the making and passing of counterfeit coins and bank notes. These statutes often provide, as does the federal statute, a punishment for the mutilation of bank notes or the lightening (of the weight) or mutilation of coins.

14. Forgery

Forgery consists of the fraudulent making or material altering of an instrument, such as a check, that attempts to create or changes a legal liability of another person.[26] Ordinarily, **forgery** consists of signing another's name with intent to defraud, but it may also consist of making an entire instrument or altering an existing one. It may result from signing a fictitious name or the offender's own name with the intent to defraud.

forgery–fraudulently making or altering an instrument that apparently creates or alters a legal liability of another.

The issuing or delivery of a forged instrument to another person constitutes the crime of **uttering** a forged instrument. Any sending of a forged check through the channels of commerce or of bank collection constitutes an uttering of a forged instrument. The act of depositing a forged check into the forger's bank account by depositing it in an automatic teller machine constitutes uttering within the meaning of a forgery statute.[27]

uttering–crime of issuing or delivering a forged instrument to another person.

15. Perjury

Perjury consists of knowingly giving false testimony in a judicial proceeding after having been sworn to tell the truth. Knowingly making false answers on any form filed with a government typically constitutes perjury or is subjected to the same punishment as perjury. In some jurisdictions, the false answers given in a situation other than in court or the litigation process is called the crime of *false swearing*. The penalties for perjury were increased substantially following the collapse of Enron with the passage of SOX.

16. False Claims and Pretenses

Many statutes make it a crime to submit false claims or to obtain goods by false pretenses.

(A) FALSE CLAIMS. Some statutes provide that making a false claim to an insurance company or government office is a crime. The federal false statement statute makes it a crime to knowingly and willfully make a false material statement about any matter within the jurisdiction of any department or agency of the United States. For example, it is a crime for a contractor to make a false claim against the United States for payment for work that was never performed. It is also a crime to make false statements about income and assets on a student's application for federal financial aid.

---

[26] Misrepresenting the nature of a document in order to obtain their signature on it is forgery. *State v Martinez*, 74 Cal Rptr 3d 409 (2008).

[27] *Wisconsin v Tolliver*, 440 NW2d 571 (Wis App 1989).

(B) **Obtaining Goods by False Pretenses.** Almost all states have statutes that forbid obtaining money or goods under false pretenses.[28] Sometimes they are directed against a particular form of deception, such as using a bad check. An intent to defraud is an essential element of obtaining property by false pretenses.[29]

Examples of false pretense include delivering a check knowing that there is insufficient money in the bank account to cover the check.[30] False representations as to future profits in a business are also forms of false pretenses.

Failing to perform on a contract is not a false pretense crime unless the contract had been entered into with the intent of not performing it.[31]

(C) **Unauthorized Use of Automated Teller Machine.** Obtaining money from an automated teller machine (ATM) by the unauthorized use of the depositor's ATM card is a federal crime.

(D) **False Information Submitted to Banks.** Knowingly making false statements in a loan application to a federally insured bank is a federal crime.[32] It is also a crime for a landowner to put a false value on land transferred to a bank as security for a loan.[33] **For Example,** many of the initial criminal charges in the subprime mortgage market collapse have involved mortgage brokers and appraisers who misrepresented property value or applicants' income in their mortgage applications for federally insured loans.

17. Bad Checks

The use of a bad check is commonly made a crime by statute. In the absence of a bad check statute, the use of a bad check could generally be prosecuted under a false pretenses statute.

Under a bad check statute, it is a crime to use or pass a check with the intent to defraud with the knowledge that there are insufficient funds in the bank to pay the check when it is presented for payment. Knowledge that the bad check will not be paid when presented to the bank is an essential element of the crime. The bad check statutes typically provide that if the check is not made good within a specified number of days after payment by the bank is refused, it is presumed that the defendant acted with the intent to defraud.[34] For more information on checks, see Chapter 28.

18. Credit Card Crimes

It is a crime to steal a credit card and, in some states, to possess the credit card of another person without that person's consent. Using a credit card without the permission of the card owner is the crime of obtaining goods or services by false pretenses or with the intent to defraud. Likewise, a person who continues to use a

---

[28] *Mass. v Cheromcka,* 850 NE2d 1088 (Mass App 2006).
[29] *State v Moore,* 903 A2d 669 (Conn App 2006).
[30] *U.S. v Tudeme,* 457 F3d 577 (Fed App 2006).
[31] *Jacobs v State,* (230 SW3d 225 Tex App 2006).
[32] 18 USC § 1014. See *United States v Autorino,* 381 F3d 48 (2d Cir 2004).
[33] *United States v Faulkner,* 17 F3d 745 (5th Cir 1994).
[34] *McMillan v First Nat. Bank of Berwick,* A2d, 2009 WL 1966952 (Pa Super).

credit card with the knowledge that it has been canceled is guilty of the crime of obtaining goods by false pretenses.

When, without permission, someone signs the name of the card owner for the credit card transaction, she has committed the crime of forgery.

The Credit Card Fraud Act of 1984[35] makes it a federal crime to obtain anything of value in excess of $1,000 in a year by means of a counterfeit credit card, to make or sell such cards, or to possess more than 15 counterfeit cards at one time.

19. Embezzlement

embezzlement–statutory offense consisting of the unlawful conversion of property entrusted to the wrongdoer.

Embezzlement is the fraudulent conversion of another's property or money by a person to whom it has been entrusted.[36] Employees who take their employer's property or funds for personal use have committed the crime of embezzlement. An agent employee commits embezzlement when he receives and keeps payments from third persons—payments the agent should have turned over to the principal. **For Example,** when an insured gives money to an insurance agent to pay the insurance company but the insurance agent uses the money to pay premiums on the policies of other persons, the agent is guilty of embezzlement. Generally, the fact that the defendant intends to return the property or money embezzled or does in fact do so is no defense.

Today, every jurisdiction has not only a general embezzlement statute but also various statutes applicable to particular situations. **For Example,** statutes cover embezzlement by government officials and employees.

20. Obstruction of Justice: Sarbanes-Oxley

Another Sarbanes-Oxley Act of 2002 provision clarifies what constitutes obstruction of justice and increases the penalties for such an act. The new section makes it a felony for anyone, including company employees, auditors, attorneys, and consultants,

> to alter, destroy, mutilate, conceal, cover up, falsify or make a false entry with the "intent to impede, obstruct, or influence the investigation or proper administration of any matter within the jurisdiction of any department or agency of the United States."[37]

The statute goes on to address audit records specifically and requires auditors to retain their work papers related to a client's audit for at least five years. Any destruction of documents prior to that time constitutes a felony and carries a penalty of up to 10 years. The statute was passed in response to the conduct of Arthur Andersen, the audit firm for the collapsed Enron Corporation. Many of the firm's audit papers on Enron were destroyed, but the firm and partner-in-charge escaped criminal liability because the government could not establish that the senior managers in Andersen were aware of the shredding.[38]

---

[35] 18 USC § 1029.
[36] *State v Weaver,* 607 SE2d 599 (NC 2005).
[37] 18 USC § 1519. The newly defined and expanded crime of obstruction carries an unspecified fine and a sentence of up to 20 years.
[38] *Arthur Andersen LLP v U.S.,* 544 US 696 (2005).

21. Corporate Fraud: Sarbanes-Oxley

SOX also created a new form of mail and wire fraud. Ordinarily, mail or wire fraud consists of the use of the mail or telephones for purposes of defrauding someone of money and/or property. However, the SOX form of mail or wire fraud is based on new requirements imposed on corporate officers to certify their financial statements when they are issued. If a corporate officer fails to comply with all requirements for financial statement certification or certifies financial statements that contain false material information, the officer and company have committed corporate fraud with penalties that range from fines of $1,000,000 and/or 10 years to $5,000,000 and/or 20 years for willful violation of the certification requirements.

sports&entertainment law

The NBA Referee, Gambling, and Some Tossed Games

Tim Donaghy, a referee for the NBA, entered a guilty plea to two federal felony charges in connection with his bets and tips on NBA games. The charges are conspiracy to engage in wire fraud and transmitting betting information via interstate commerce. Mr. Donaghy picked teams to win

in games he was scheduled to referee. Experts have said that Donaghy committed the equivalent of insider trading on Wall Street by providing outsiders with information about games, players, and referees. He got $5,000 from his tippees for correct picks.

According to the indictments, Donaghy began betting on games in 2003, but in December 2006 began passing along inside information to others who were also charged in the conspiracy. The communication was in code via cell phone. Through his lawyer, Donaghy indicated that he had a gambling addiction problem and was currently on medication and under the treatment of a psychiatrist.

The NBA Commissioner, David Stern, referred to Donaghy as a "rogue referee," but said that the gambling charges were a wake-up call for the NBA and that it must not be "complacent."*

Mr. Donaghy's missteps were discovered as the federal government was conducting an investigation into the Gambino crime family, based in Brooklyn.

Commissioner Stern said that the NBA would be looking at the checks and balances that the NFL has built into its system including Las Vegas travel prohibitions on referees. The NFL also has significant background checks and ongoing monitoring of its referees.

Mr. Donaghy ran a basketball clinic for developmentally disabled boys in Springfield, P.A. (Mr. Donaghy's hometown) for almost a decade. He was a graduate of Villanova and had worked his way up to being one of the NBA's top referees, coming through the ranks of refereeing in both high school and the Continental Basketball Association. Mr. Donaghy had a wife and four children. His salary with the NBA during 2006 was $260,000. Mr. Donaghy was sentenced to 15 months in prison.

Why do you think Mr. Donaghy was engaged in gambling? Doesn't his civic activity paint a different picture of his character?

* Roscoe Nance, "Scandal Is a 'Wakeup Call,' Stern Says," *USA Today*, August 16, 2007, 2C.

22. The Common Law Crimes

In contrast to white-collar crimes, *common law crimes* are crimes that involve the use of force or the threat of force or cause injury to persons or damage to property. The following sections discuss crimes of force and crimes against property that affect businesses.

(A) LARCENY. *Larceny* is the wrongful or fraudulent taking of the personal property of another by any person with fraudulent intent. Shoplifting is a common form of larceny. In many states, shoplifting is made a separate crime. In some states, all forms of larceny and robbery are consolidated into a statutory crime of theft. At common law, there was no crime known as theft.

(B) ROBBERY. *Robbery* is the taking of personal property from the presence of the victim by use of force or fear. Most states have aggravated forms of robbery, such as robbery with a deadly weapon. Snatching a necklace from the neck of the victim involves sufficient force to constitute robbery. When the unlawful taking is not by force or fear, as when the victim does not know that the property is being taken, the offense is larceny, but it cannot be robbery.

Some statutes may be aimed at a particular kind of robbery. **For Example,** carjacking is a federal crime under the Anti-Car Theft Act of 1992.[39]

(C) BURGLARY. At common law, *burglary* was the breaking and entering during the night into the dwelling house of another with the intent to commit a felony. Inserting the automatic teller card of another, without their knowledge or permission, into an automatic teller machine set in the wall of the bank may constitute an entry into the bank for the purpose of committing burglary.[40] Some states word their burglary statutes, however, so that there is no burglary in this automatic teller case. This act would be covered by other criminal statutes.

Modern statutes have eliminated many of the elements of the common law definition so that under some statutes it is now immaterial when or whether there was an entry to commit a felony. The elements of breaking and entering are frequently omitted. Under some statutes, the offense is aggravated and the penalty is increased, depending on the place where the offense was committed, such as a bank building, freight car, or warehouse. Related statutory offenses, such as the crime of possessing burglars' tools, have been created.

(D) ARSON. At common law, *arson* was the willful and malicious burning of another's dwelling. The law was originally designed to protect human life, although arson has been committed just with the burning of the building even if no one is actually hurt. In most states, arson is a felony, so if someone is killed in the resulting fire, the offense is considered a felony-murder. Under the felony-murder rule, homicide, however unintended, occurring in the commission of a felony is automatically classified as murder. Virtually every state has created a special offense of burning to defraud an insurer.

(E) RIOTS AND CIVIL DISORDERS. Damage to property in the course of a riot or civil disorder is ordinarily covered by other types of crimes such as the crime of larceny

[39] 18 USC § 2119. See *U.S. v Bell*, 608, F Supp 2d 1257 (Kan 2009).
[40] *California v Ravenscroft*, 243 Cal Rptr 827 (Ct App 1988).

or arson. In addition, the act of assembling as a riotous mob and engaging in civil disorders is generally some form of crime in itself under either common law concepts of disturbing the peace or modern antiriot statutes, even without destruction or theft of property. However, statutes on civil disorders must be carefully drawn to avoid infringing on constitutionally protected free speech.

C. CRIMINAL LAW AND THE COMPUTER

In some situations, ordinary crimes cover computer crimes situations. In other situations, new criminal law statutes are required.

23. What is a Computer Crime?

computer crimes–wrongs committed using a computer or with knowledge of computers.

Generally, the term **computer crime** is used to refer to a crime that can be committed only by a person having some knowledge of the operation of a computer. Just as stealing an automobile requires knowledge of how to operate and drive a car, so the typical computer crime requires the knowledge of how the computer works.

Because the more serious and costly wrongs relating to computers do not fit into the ordinary definitions of crime, there are now computer-specific criminal statutes: Computer crimes can be committed against the computer, using the computer, or through the computer.

24. The Computer as Victim

A traditional crime may be committed by stealing or intentionally damaging a computer.

(A) THEFT OF HARDWARE. When a computer itself is stolen, the ordinary law relating to theft crimes should apply. Theft of a computer is subject to the same law as the theft of a truck or a desk.

(B) THEFT OF SOFTWARE. When a thief takes software, whether in the form of a program written on paper or a program on a disk or memory stick, something has been taken, but it is not tangible property as larceny requires. At common law, the value of stolen software would be determined by the value of the tangible substance on which the program was recorded. Under a traditional concept of property, which would ignore the value of the intangible program, theft of software would be only petty larceny. Now, however, virtually every state makes stealing software a crime. Chapter 11 provides more information on crimes, software, and the Internet.

(C) INTENTIONAL DAMAGE. The computer may be the "victim" of a crime when it is intentionally destroyed or harmed. In the most elementary form of damage, the computer could be harmed if it was smashed with an ax or destroyed in an explosion or a fire. In such cases, the purpose of the intentional damage is to cause the computer's owner the financial loss of the computer and the destruction of the information that is stored in it.

Intentional damage can result from more subtle means. Gaining access to the computer and then erasing or altering the data is also the crime of intentional damage. Likewise, interfering with the air conditioning so computers are damaged or malfunction would also be covered under intentional damage statutes. Planting a bug or virus in the software, causing the program to malfunction or to give incorrect output, is a form of intentional damage. Angry employees, former employees, and competitors have all been convicted of intentional damage.

25. Unauthorized Use of Computers

The unlawful use of a computer belonging to someone else is also a crime in some states. There are specific statutes at the state and federal levels that make it unlawful to use government computers without permission.

26. Computer Raiding

Taking information from a computer without the consent of the owner is a crime. Whether theft is accomplished by instructing the computer to make a printout of stored information or by tapping into its data bank by electronic means is not important. In some states, taking information is known as the crime of "computer trespass."[41]

Both Congress and state legislatures have adopted statutes that make it a crime to gain unauthorized access to a computer or use information so gained to cause harm to the computer or its rightful user.[42]

27. Diverted Delivery by Computer

In many industries, a computer controls the delivery of goods. The person in charge of that computer or someone unlawfully gaining access to it may cause the computer to direct delivery to an improper place. That is, instead of shipping goods to the customers to whom they should go, the wrongdoer diverts the goods to a different place, where the wrongdoer or a confederate receives them.

In precomputer days, written orders were sent from the sales department to the shipping department. The shipping department then sent the ordered goods to the proper places. If the person in the sales department or the person in the shipping department was dishonest, either one could divert the goods from the proper destination. Today, instructing the computer to give false directions can cause this fraudulent diversion of goods. Basically, the crime has not changed. The computer is merely the new instrument by which the old crime is committed. This old crime has taken on a new social significance because of the amazingly large dollar value of the thefts. In one case, several hundred loaded freight cars disappeared. In another case, a loaded oil tanker was diverted to unload into a fleet of tank trucks operated by an accomplice of the computer operator.

---

[41] *Washington v Riley,* 846 P2d 1365 (Wash 1993).

[42] The Counterfeit Access Device and Computer Fraud Act of 1984, 18 USC § 1030 *et seq.;* Computer Fraud and Abuse Act of 1986, as amended in 1999, 18 USC § 1001; Electronic Communications Privacy Act of 1986, Act of 1986, 18 USC § 2510; Computer Fraud Act of 1987, 15 USC §§ 272, 278, 40 USC § 759; National Information Infrastructure Protection Act, 18 USC § 1030 (protecting confidentiality and integrity on the Internet).

e-commerce&cyberlaw

They Were Bullies: Mean Girls in Cyberspace

It has been called the MySpace suicide case. On May 14, 2008, a federal grand jury indicted Lori Drew, 49, of Missouri, the so-called cyber bully. Ms. Drew had created a MySpace site for Josh Evans, a fictitious teen boy she used as a means of getting information from Megan Meier, a 13-year-old girl with whom Ms. Drew's daughter had had a falling-out. Josh pretended to be interested in Megan, but then said that she was "fat" and that the world would be a better place without her. Megan hanged herself within an hour of receiving the final comments from "Josh."

Ms. Drew was charged with one count of conspiracy and two counts of accessing computers without authorization and was convicted of three lesser charges.

When the indictment was made public, Salvador Hernandez, assistant director of the FBI in Los Angeles, said, "Whether we characterize this tragic case as 'cyber-bullying,' cyberabuse, or illegal computer access, it should serve as a reminder that our children use the Internet for social interaction and that technology has altered the way they conduct their daily activities. As adults, we must be sensitive to the potential dangers posed by the use of the Internet by our children."*

Some states have now passed specific statutes to make cyber-bullying a crime.

Is there a computer crime statute that covers Ms. Drew's conduct?

* K. C. Jones, "Missouri Mom Indicted in MySpace Cyber-Bullying Suicide Case," **www.informationweek.com**. May 15, 2008.

28. Economic Espionage by Computer

Economic Espionage Act (EEA) – federal law that makes it a felony to copy, download, transmit, or in any way transfer proprietary files, documents, and information from a computer to an unauthorized person.

The **Economic Espionage Act (EEA)** is a federal law[43] passed in response to several cases in which high-level executives took downloaded proprietary information from their computers to their new employers. The EEA makes it a felony to steal, appropriate, or take a trade secret as well as to copy, duplicate, sketch, draw, photograph, download, upload, alter, destroy, replicate, transmit, deliver, send, mail, or communicate a trade secret. The penalties for EEA violations are up to $500,000 and 15 years in prison for individuals and $10 million for organizations. When employees take new positions with another company, their former employers are permitted to check the departing employees' computer e-mails and hard drives to determine whether the employees have engaged in computer espionage.

29. Electronic Fund Transfer Crimes

The Electronic Fund Transfers Act (EFTA)[44] makes it a crime to use any counterfeit, stolen, or fraudulently obtained card, code, or other device to obtain money or goods in excess of a specified amount through an electronic fund transfer system. The EFTA also makes it a crime to ship in interstate commerce devices or

---

[43] 18 USC § 1831.
[44] 15 USC § 1693(n).

ethics & the law

Ethics and the Tobacco Class-Action Lawyer

Class-action lawyer Dickie Scruggs was portrayed in the 1999 movie "The Insider," which starred Russell Crowe as Jeffrey Wigand, the tobacco industry whistle-blower who obtained a $206 billion settlement from the tobacco companies (Mr. Scruggs's fee for the case was $1 billion). Almost a decade after the movie that made him a hero came out, Scruggs entered a guilty plea to bribery and was sentenced to five years in prison for his role in an attempt to bribe a federal judge.

Mr. Scruggs was representing insurance claimants against insurers for their damages from Hurricane Katrina. The judge presiding over the case contacted the FBI about a bribery attempt. One of the four lawyers working with Scruggs was approached by the FBI and agreed to wear a wire to catch Scruggs. The content of the tapes revealed both *actus reus* and *scienter*. Zachary Scruggs, Dickie's son, also entered a guilty plea. All of

the remaining lawyers involved in the bribery scheme entered guilty pleas as well.

Those in the legal profession said they did not understand Scruggs's actions because he had the skill to win any case. "He didn't need to cheat," was the comment of a representative from the American Trial Lawyers Association. Scruggs's words at his sentencing were poignant: "I could not be more ashamed to be where I am today, mixed up in a judicial bribery scheme.... I realized I was getting mixed up in it. And I will go to my grave wondering why. I have disappointed everyone in my life—my wife, my family, my son, particularly.... I deeply regret my conduct. It is a scar and a stain on my soul that will be there forever."

Source: Abha Bhattarai, "Class-Action Lawyer Given 5 Years in a Bribery Case," New York Times, June 28, 2008, B3.

goods so obtained or to knowingly receive goods that have been obtained by means of the fraudulent use of the transfer system.

30. Circumventing Copyright Protection Devices Via Computer

The Digital Millennium Copyright Act (DMCA)[45] makes it a federal offense to circumvent or create programs to circumvent encryption devices that copyright holders place on copyrighted material to prevent unauthorized copying. **For Example,** circumventing the encryption devices on software or CDs or DVDs is a violation of the DMCA.

For example, Dmitry Sklyarov, a Russian computer programmer, was the first person to be charged with a violation of the DMCA. Mr. Sklyarov was arrested in early 2002 at a computer show after giving a speech in Las Vegas at the Defcon convention on his product that he had developed to permit the circumvention of security devices on copyrighted materials. His program unlocks password-protected e-books and PDF files. He gave his speech and was returned to Russia in exchange for his agreement to testify in a case that will determine the constitutionality of DMCA.

[45] 17 USC § (1998).

31. Spamming

More states are addressing the use of computers to send unsolicited e-mails. Nevada was the first state to regulate spam and California, Washington, and Virginia followed shortly after. Criminal regulation began with very narrowly tailored statutes such as one in Washington that made it a crime to send an e-mail with a misleading title line.[46] The specific criminal statutes on spamming are evolving, and Virginia became the first state to pass a criminal antispamming law. The statute prohibits sending "unsolicited bulk electronic mail" or spam and makes the offense a felony based on the level of activity.[47] Thirty-six states now have some form of spamming regulation. The penalties range from fines to imprisonment.

D. CRIMINAL PROCEDURE RIGHTS FOR BUSINESSES

Business criminals are treated the same procedurally as other criminals. They have the same rights under the criminal justice system. The U.S. Constitution guarantees the protection of individual rights within the criminal justice system.

32. Fourth Amendment Rights for Businesses

Fourth Amendment— privacy protection in the U.S. Constitution; prohibits unauthorized searches and seizures.

search warrant—judicial authorization for a search of property where there is the expectation of privacy.

(A) SEARCH AND SEIZURE: WARRANTS. The **Fourth Amendment** of the U.S. Constitution provides that "the right of the people to be secure in their persons, houses, papers, and effects, against unreasonable searches and seizures, shall not be violated." This amendment protects individual privacy by preventing unreasonable searches and seizures. Before a government agency can seize the property of individuals or businesses, it must obtain a valid **search warrant** issued by a judge or magistrate, based on probable cause, or an exception to this warrant requirement must apply. In other words, there must be good reason to search the location named. The Fourth Amendment applies equally to individuals and corporations. If an improper search is conducted, evidence obtained during the course of that search may be inadmissible in the criminal proceedings for the resulting criminal charges.[48]

(B) EXCEPTIONS TO THE WARRANT REQUIREMENT. Exceptions to the warrant requirement are emergencies, such as a burning building, and the "plain-view" exception, which allows law enforcement officials to take any property that anyone can see, for no privacy rights are violated when items and property are left in the open for members of the public to see. **For Example,** you have an expectation of privacy in the garbage in your garbage can when it is in your house. However, once you move that garbage can onto the public sidewalk for pickup, you no longer have the expectation of privacy because you have left your garbage out in plain view of the public.

Another exception allows officers to enter when they are needed to give aid because of an ongoing criminal act. **For Example,** officers who are able to see a fight

---

[46] Saul Hansell, "Total Up the Bill for Spam," *New York Times*, July 28, 2003, C1, C4.
[47] *Id.*
[48] See, *Arizona v Gant*, 129 SCt 1710 (2009) in which the U.S. Supreme Court held that evidence obtained searching the vehicle of a suspect who is handcuffed and locked in a police car cannot be used. A search warrant is needed when the suspect has no access to the evidence to destroy it.

C A S E   S U M M A R Y

Low-Flying Aircraft Bearing Federal Agents with Cameras

FACTS: Dow Chemical (petitioner) operates a 2,000-acre chemical plant at Midland, Michigan. The facility, with numerous buildings, conduits, and pipes, is visible from the air. Dow has maintained ground security at the facility and has investigated flyovers by other, unauthorized aircraft. However, none of the buildings or manufacturing equipment is concealed.

In 1978, the Environmental Protection Agency (EPA) conducted an inspection of Dow. The EPA requested a second inspection, but Dow denied the request. The EPA then employed a commercial aerial photographer to take photos of the plant from 12,000, 3,000, and 1,200 feet. The EPA had no warrant, but the plane was always within navigable air space when the photos were taken.

When Dow became aware of the EPA photographer, it brought suit in federal district court and challenged the action as a violation of its Fourth Amendment rights. The district court found that the EPA had violated Dow's rights and issued an injunction prohibiting further use of the aircraft. The Court of Appeals reversed and Dow appealed.

DECISION: The Court ruled against Dow, finding that the EPA did not need explicit statutory provisions to use methods of observation commonly available to the public. There was no expectation of privacy in an area that was not covered. [**Dow Chemical Co. v United States, 476 US 1819 (1986)**]

---

through the windows of a house and resulting injuries can enter to render help. Another exception would be that the person who lives in the property to be searched has given permission for the search.

(C) BUSINESS RECORDS AND SEARCHES. In many business crimes, the records that prove a crime was committed are not in the hands of the person who committed that crime. Accountants, attorneys, and other third parties may have the business records in their possession. In addition to the Fourth Amendment issues involved in seizing these records (a warrant is still required), there may be protections for the business defendants. The next section covers those protections.

(D) PROTECTIONS FOR PRIVILEGED RECORDS AND DOCUMENTS. All states recognize an attorney-client privilege, which means that an individual's conversations with her lawyer and the notes of those conversations are not subject to seizure unless the privilege is waived. In many of the prosecutions of companies, the Justice Department has asked companies to waive the attorney/client privilege so that it can have access to information that is then used to find other companies that may have participated in criminal activity. Some states recognize an accountant-client privilege and other privileges, such as those between priest and parishioner or doctor and patient. A privileged relationship is one in which the records and notes resulting from the contact between individuals cannot be seized even with a warrant (with some exceptions).

33. Fifth Amendment Self-Incrimination Rights for Businesses

Fifth Amendment – constitutional protection against self-incrimination; also guarantees due process.

(A) SELF-INCRIMINATION. The words "I take the Fifth" are used to invoke the constitutional protections against self-incrimination provided under the **Fifth Amendment** that prevents compelling a person to be a witness against himself. **For Example,** Mark McGwire, the former St. Louis baseball player, invoked the Fifth Amendment in his testimony during Congressional hearings on steroid use. Ken Lay, former CEO and chairman of Enron, took the Fifth Amendment before Congress when asked to testify—as did Bernie Ebbers, former CEO of WorldCom. However, both Lay and Ebbers took the witness stand in their own trials. They were not required to, but hoped to help their cases. The Fifth Amendment protection applies only to individuals; corporations are not given Fifth Amendment protection. A corporation cannot prevent the disclosure of its books and records on the grounds of self-incrimination. The officers and employees of a corporation can assert the Fifth Amendment, but the records of the corporation belong to the corporation, not to them.

CASE SUMMARY

A Man's Home Is His Castle, but His Wife Can Still Turn on Him

FACTS: Scott Randolph and his wife, Janet, separated in late May 2001, when she left their Americus, Georgia, home and went to stay with her parents in Canada, taking their son and some belongings. In July, she returned to the Americus house with the child. No one is sure whether she had returned to reconcile or whether she had come to gather her remaining possessions.

On July 6, 2001, Janet called police and told them that there were "items of drug evidence" in the house. Sergeant Murray asked Scott Randolph for permission to search the house, which he refused.

The sergeant turned to Janet for consent to search, which she readily gave. She led the officer upstairs to a bedroom that she identified as Scott's, where the sergeant noticed a section of a drinking straw with a powdery residue he suspected was cocaine. He then left the house to get an evidence bag from his car and to call the district attorney's office, which instructed him to stop the search and apply for a warrant. When Sergeant Murray returned to the house, Janet Randolph withdrew her consent. The police took the straw and the Randolphs to the police station. After getting a search warrant, the police returned to the house and seized further evidence of drug use, which served as the basis of Scott's indictment for possession of cocaine.

Scott Randolph moved to suppress the evidence, as products of a warrantless search. The trial court denied the motion, ruling that Janet had common authority to consent to the search.

The Court of Appeals of Georgia reversed, and the Georgia Supreme Court sustained the reversal. The state of Georgia appealed, and the U.S. Supreme Court granted *certiorari*.

DECISION: The Court held that "a man's home is his castle" and that when he objects to a search, his spouse could not overrule his decision. Co-ownership of property does not necessarily mean that individuals are willing to waive their rights of privacy for purposes for warrantless searches. The dissent argued that sharing necessarily means waiving privacy. The fact that they are betrayed by a spouse, roommate, or others does not affect the consent exception to the Fourth Amendment because underlying that protection is the right to privacy and that right has been waived through the shared ownership or living arrangement. [**Georgia v Randolph, 547 US 103 (2006)**]

Miranda warnings–
warnings required to
prevent self-incrimination
in a criminal matter.

(B) **Miranda Rights.** The famous **Miranda warnings** come from a case interpreting the extent of Fifth Amendment rights. In *Miranda v Arizona*,[49] the U.S. Supreme Court ruled that certain warnings must be given to persons who face custodial interrogation for the purposes of possible criminal proceedings. The warnings consist of an explanation to individuals that they have the right to remain silent; that if they do speak, anything they say can be used against them; that they have the right to have an attorney present; and that if they cannot afford an attorney, one will be provided for them. Failure to give the *Miranda* warnings means that any statements, including a confession, obtained while the individual was being interrogated cannot be used as evidence against that individual. The prosecution will have to rely on evidence other than the statements made in violation of *Miranda,* if such evidence exists.

34. Due Process Rights for Businesses

due process–the
constitutional right to be
heard, question witnesses,
and present evidence.

Also included in the Fifth Amendment is the language of due process. **Due process** is the right to be heard, question witnesses, and present evidence before any criminal conviction can occur. Due process in criminal cases consists of an initial appearance at which the charges and the defendant's rights are outlined; a preliminary hearing or grand jury proceeding in which the evidence is determined to be sufficient to warrant a trial; an arraignment for entering a plea and setting a trial date when the defendant pleads innocent; a period of discovery for obtaining evidence; and a trial at which witnesses for the prosecution can be cross-examined and evidence presented to refute the charges. In addition to these procedural steps, the **Sixth Amendment** guarantees that the entire process will be completed in a timely fashion because this amendment guarantees a speedy trial.

Sixth Amendment–the U.S.
constitutional amendment
that guarantees a speedy
trial.

C A S E   S U M M A R Y

I Confess, but Without *Miranda* You Can't Use It against Me

FACTS: Dickerson confessed to robbing a bank at a field office of the Federal Bureau of Investigation (FBI). At the time he confessed, he was not a suspect, was free to leave, and was not in custody. He was not, however, given his *Miranda* warnings before the FBI agents interrogated him about the robbery. Dickerson's lawyer moved to have his confession excluded from his trial because it was obtained in violation of *Miranda.* The federal district court suppressed the confession. The Court of Appeals reversed, noting that while the warnings had not been given, the confession was clearly voluntary. Dickerson appealed.

DECISION: The U.S. Supreme Court held that the confession could not be used because Dickerson had not been given his warnings. The judicial decision is complex because it focuses on the difference between questioning in custody and the need to give *Miranda* warnings even when there is no custody of the person. The majority of the Court ruled that *Miranda* warnings must still be given as a way to prevent those being questioned from unknowingly waiving their rights. [**Dickerson v United States, 530 US 428 (2000)**]

[49] 384 US 436 (1966).

lawflix

Double Jeopardy (2000) R

Ashley Judd plays a woman on the run for false charges of killing her husband. But her husband faked his death and then she finds and kills him – can she be tried again?

Columbo (Seasons 1–6)

Detective Columbo is the bumbling, brilliant sleuth who crosses a few Fourth and Fifth Amendment lines here and there.

Check out LawFlix at **www.cengage.com/blaw/dvl** to access movie clips that illustrate business law concepts.

MAKE THE CONNECTION

SUMMARY

When a person does not live up to the standards set by law, this punishable conduct, called *crime,* may be common law or statutory in origin. Crimes are classified as *felonies,* which generally carry greater sentences and more long-term consequences, and *misdemeanors.*

Employers and corporations may be criminally responsible for their acts and the acts of their employees. The federal sentencing guidelines provide parameters for sentences for federal crimes and allow judges to consider whether the fact that a business promotes compliance with the law is a reason to reduce a sentence.

White-collar crimes include those relating to financial fraud. Sarbanes-Oxley reforms increased the penalties for financial fraud and added fraudulent financial statement certification as a crime. Other white-collar crimes include bribery, extortion, blackmail, and corrupt influence in politics and in business. Also included as white-collar crimes are counterfeiting, forgery, perjury, making false claims against the government, obtaining goods or money by false pretenses, using bad checks, false financial reporting, and embezzlement. The common law crimes include those that involve injury to person and/or property, such as arson and murder.

Statutes have expanded the area of criminal law to meet situations in which computers are involved. Both federal and state statutes make the unauthorized taking of information from a computer a crime. The diversion of deliveries of goods and the transfer of funds, the theft of software, and the raiding of computers are made crimes to some extent by federal laws. Newer federal statutes that apply to computers are the Economic Espionage Act, which prohibits downloading or copying information via computer to give to a competitor, and the Digital

Millennium Copyright Act that prohibits circumventing or designing programs to circumvent encryption devices.

Criminal procedure is dictated by the Fourth, Fifth, and Sixth Amendments. The Fourth Amendment protects against unreasonable searches, the Fifth Amendment protects against self-incrimination and provides due process, and the Sixth Amendment guarantees a speedy trial.

LEARNING OUTCOMES

After studying this chapter, you should be able to clearly explain:

A. GENERAL PRINCIPLES

LO.1 Discuss the nature and classification of crimes
See the discussion of crimes and misdemeanors on p. 156

LO.2 Describe the basis of criminal liability
See the **For Example,** discussion of dumping waste and intent on p. 156
See *U.S. v Erickson* on p. 157

LO.3 Identify who is responsible for criminal acts
See *U.S. v Park* on p. 158
See Thinking Things Through on p. 162

LO.4 Explain the penalties for crimes and the sentencing for corporate crimes
See the discussion of the sentencing guidelines and the various cases related to them on p. 159

B. WHITE-COLLAR CRIMES

LO.5 List examples of white-collar crimes and their elements
See the discussion that begins on p. 163
See the Sports & Entertainment Law discussion of the NBA referee on p. 171

LO.6 Describe the common law crimes
See the discussion that begins on p. 172
See the E-Commerce & Cyberlaw discussion of cyber-bullying on p. 175

C. CRIMINAL LAW AND THE COMPUTER

LO.7 Discuss crimes related to computers
See the discussion that begins on p. 173

D. CRIMINAL PROCEDURE RIGHTS FOR BUSINESSES

LO.8 Describe the rights of businesses charged with crimes and the constitutional protections afforded them
See the *Dow* case on p. 178
See the *Dickerson* case on p. 180

KEY TERMS

blackmail	due process	extortion
computer crime	Economic Espionage Act	facilitation payments
conspiracy	(EEA)	Federal Sentencing
crime	embezzlement	Guidelines

felonies
Fifth Amendment
Foreign Corrupt Practices
  Act (FCPA)
forgery
Fourth Amendment
grease payment

Miranda warnings
misdemeanors
predicate act
Racketeer Influenced and
  Corrupt Organizations
  (RICO) Act
search warrant

Sixth Amendment
uttering
white-Collar Crime
  Penalty Enhancement
  Act of 2002
white-collar crime

QUESTIONS AND CASE PROBLEMS

1. Bernard Flinn operated a business known as Harvey Investment Co., Inc./High Risk Loans. Flinn worked as a loan broker, matching those who came to him with lenders willing to loan them money given their credit history and the amount involved. From 1982 through 1985, Flinn found loans for five people. Indiana requires that persons engaged in the business of brokering loans obtain a license from the state. Flinn was prosecuted for brokering loans without having a license. He raised the defense that he did not know that a license was required and that, accordingly, he lacked the criminal intent to broker loans without having a license. Does Flinn have a good defense? [*Flinn v Indiana*, 563 NE2d 536 (Ind)]

2. H. J., Inc., and other customers of Northwestern Bell Corp. alleged that Northwestern Bell had furnished cash and tickets for air travel, plays, and sporting events and had offered employment to members of the Minnesota Public Utilities Commission in exchange for favorable treatment in rate cases before the commission. A Minnesota statute makes it a felony to bribe public officials. H. J. and other customers brought suit against Northwestern for violating the criminal bribery statute. Can the customers bring a criminal action? [*H. J., Inc. v Northwestern Bell Corp.*, 420 NW2d 673 (Minn App)]

3. Baker and others entered a Wal-Mart store shortly after 3:00 A.M. by cutting through the metal door with an acetylene torch. They had moved some of the merchandise in the store to the rear door, but the police arrived before the merchandise could be taken from the store. Baker was prosecuted for larceny. He raised the defense that he was not guilty of larceny because no merchandise had ever left the store. Is there enough intent and action for a crime? [*Tennessee v Baker*, 751 SW2d 154 (Tenn App)]

4. Gail drove her automobile after having had dinner and several drinks. She fell asleep at the wheel and ran over and killed a pedestrian. Prosecuted for manslaughter, she raised the defense that she did not intend to hurt anyone and because of the drinks did not know what she was doing. Was this a valid defense?

5. Dr. Doyle E. Campbell, an ophthalmologist, established his practice in southern Ohio in 1971. Many of Dr. Campbell's patients are elderly people who qualify for federal Medicare benefits and state Medicaid benefits. Under the existing financing system, a doctor who treats a Medicare patient is required to submit a "Medicare Health Insurance Claim Form" (HCFA Form 1500). The doctor is required to certify that "the services shown on this form were

medically indicated and necessary for the health of the patient and were personally rendered by me or were rendered incident to my professional service by my employees." Claims Dr. Campbell submitted for his elderly patients ranged from $900 to $950, of which $530 to $680 were covered by the Medicare program. The government alleged that Dr. Campbell billed Medicare for several treatments that were either not performed or not necessary. Dr. Campbell was charged with fraud for the paperwork he submitted. Has he committed a crime? [*United States v Campbell*, 845 F2d 1374 (6th Cir)]

6. In the late 1980s, Life Energy Resources, Ltd. (LER), a New York corporation, was a multilevel marketing network. LER's marketing plan provided that members of the general public could purchase its products only through an official LER distributor or by becoming LER distributors themselves. Each potential distributor had to be sponsored by an existing distributor and was required to sign a distributorship agreement with LER stating that he or she would not make medical claims or use unofficial literature or marketing aids to promote LER products.

   Ballistrea and his partner Michael Ricotta were at the top of the LER distribution network. Two products sold by LER were the REM SuperPro Frequency Generator (REM) and the Lifemax Miracle Cream (Miracle Cream). The REM, which sold for $1,350 to distributors, was a small box powered by electricity that ran currents through the feet and body of the user.

   Ballistrea and Ricotta distributed literature and audiotapes to many potential downstream distributors and customers—some of whom were undercover government agents—touting the REM and the Miracle Cream. Other literature claimed that the Miracle Cream could alleviate the discomforts of premenstrual syndrome and reverse the effects of osteoporosis. The Food and Drug Administration charged Ballistrea and Ricotta with violating federal law for making medical claims concerning LER products. Their defense is that they never sold any of the products. They simply earned commissions as part of the marketing scheme and could not be held criminally liable on the charges. Are they correct? [*United States v Ballistrea*, 101 F3d 827 (2d Cir)]

7. Carriage Homes, Inc. was a general contractor that built multifamily residential and land-development projects in Minnesota. John Arkell was Carriage Homes' chief executive officer, president, and sole shareholder. Carriage Homes built Southwinds, a condominium development of 38 residential units in Austin, Minnesota. The foundation elevations of some of the Southwinds units were lower than permitted under the State Building Code, causing storm water to pool in the units' driveways and garages. The city of Austin's development director sent Arkell a series of seven letters in 1999 and 2001 concerning the elevation problems, and Arkell gave the letters to the project managers, who failed to resolve the problems.

   Minnesota makes a violation of the State Building Code a misdemeanor. On May 30, 2001, the state charged Carriage Homes and Arkell with three misdemeanor counts each, alleging a violation of the Uniform Building Code (UBC).

Carriage Homes pleaded guilty and was sentenced to a $1,000 fine. But Arkell pleaded not guilty, asserting that he could not be held criminally responsible for the violation. After a bench trial, the district court found Arkell guilty. He was sentenced to pay a fine, pay restitution to the condominium owners, and serve 90 days in jail, with 80 days stayed pending his compliance with sentencing conditions. Mr. Arkell appealed on the grounds that the employees and subcontractors had simply not followed his orders and he was not responsible for their failures. Is he correct? [*State v Arkell*, 657 NW2d 883 (Minn. App. 2003)]

8. James Durham runs an art gallery. He has several paintings from unknown artists that he has listed for sale. The paintings always sell at his weekly auction for $20,000 to $50,000 above what James believes them to be worth. James learns that the bidders at the auctions are employed by an olive distributor located near the shipping yards of the city. What concerns should Durham have about the art, the bidders and the large purchase prices?

9. Jennings operated a courier service to collect and deliver money. The contract with his customers allowed him a day or so to deliver the money that had been collected. Instead of holding collections until delivered, Jennings made short-term investments with the money. He always made deliveries to the customers on time, but because he kept the profit from the investments for himself, Jennings was prosecuted for embezzlement. Was he guilty? [*New York v Jennings*, 504 NE2d 1079 (NY)]

10. In 2000, former investment banker Frank Quattrone was head of the technology division of Credit Suisse First Boston Corporation (CSFB), earning about $120 million per year. Quattrone and his Tech Group did the initial public offerings (IPOs) for a great many of the dot-coms. Because of questions about those IPOs, there were several state and federal grand jury investigations of CSFB pending in the fall of 2000. On December 5, 2000, Quattrone sent the following e-mail "endorsement":

    [H]aving been a key witness in a securities litigation case in south texas (miniscribe) i strongly advise you to follow these procedures.

    Quattrone then added an e-mail from Richard Char, another investment banker, that read:

    Subject: Time to clean up those files ...

    With the recent tumble in stock prices, and many deals now trading below issue price, the securities litigation bar is expected to [sic] an all out assault on broken tech IPOs.

    In the spirit of the end of the year (and the slow down in corporate finance work), we want to remind you of the CSFB document retention policy [the policy was reproduced here].

    Note that if a lawsuit is instituted, our normal document retention policy is suspended and any cleaning of files is prohibited under the CSFB guidelines (since it constitutes the destruction of evidence). We strongly suggest that before you leave for the holidays, you should catch up on file cleanup.

    As a result of the Quattrone e-mail, at least some Tech Group bankers began or continued "cleaning" their files. Quattrone was indicted for obstruction of justice in connection with the investigations. Did he obstruct justice? [*U.S. v Quattrone*, 441 F3d 153 (2d Cir 2006)]

11. Grabert ran Beck's, an amusement center in Louisiana. He held a license for video gambling machines. Louisiana makes it illegal to allow a minor to play a video gambling machine. A mother came into Grabert's center carrying her 23-month-old baby in her arms. She sat at the video poker machine with her child on her lap and proceeded to play. State troopers witnessed the baby pushing the buttons on the machine at least three times. The Department of Public Safety and Corrections revoked Grabert's video gaming license because a minor had been allowed to play the machines, and Grabert sought judicial review. The trial court reversed, and the department appealed. Has Grabert committed the crime of allowing a minor to engage in gaming? Is this the crime of allowing a minor to gamble? [*Grabert v Department of Public Safety & Corrections*, 680 So2d 764 (La App) *cert. denied; Grabert v State through Dept. of Public Safety and Corrections*, 685 So2d 126 (La.)]

12. The Banco Central administered a humanitarian plan for the government of Ecuador. Fernando Banderas and his wife presented false claims that the bank paid. After the fraud was discovered, the bank sued Banderas and his wife for damages for fraud and treble damages under the Florida version of RICO. Banderas and his wife asserted that they were not liable for RICO damages because there was no proof that they were related to organized crime and because the wrong they had committed was merely ordinary fraud. They had not used any racketeering methods. Is involvement with organized crime a requirement for liability under RICO? [*Banderas v Banco Central del Ecuador*, 461 So2d 265 (Fla App)]

13. Kravitz owned 100 percent of the stock of American Health Programs, Inc. (AHP). To obtain the Philadelphia Fraternal Order of Police as a customer for AHP, Kravitz paid money bribes to persons who he thought were officers of that organization but who in fact were federal undercover agents. He was prosecuted for violating RICO. He was convicted, and the court ordered the forfeiture of all of Kravitz's shares of AHP stock. Can a forfeiture be ordered? [*United States v Kravitz*, 738 F2d 102 (3d Cir)]

14. Howell made long-distance telephone calls through the telephone company's computer-controlled switching system to solicit funding for a nonexistent business enterprise. What crimes did Howell commit? [*New Mexico v Howell*, 895 P2d 232 (NM App)]

Chapter 9

TORTS

T he law of torts permits individuals and companies to recover from other individuals and companies for wrongs committed against them. Tort law provides rights and remedies for conduct that meets the elements required to establish that a wrong has occurred.

A. GENERAL PRINCIPLES

Civil, or noncriminal, wrongs that are not breaches of contract are governed by tort law. This chapter covers the types of civil wrongs that constitute torts and the remedies available for those wrongs.

1. What is a Tort?

tort–civil wrong that interferes with one's property or person.

Tort comes from the Latin term *tortus,* which means "crooked, dubious, twisted." Torts are actions that are not straight but are crooked, or civil, wrongs. A tort is an interference with someone's person or property. **For Example,** entering someone's house without his or her permission is an interference and constitutes the tort of trespass. Causing someone's character to be questioned is a wrong against the person and is the tort of defamation. The law provides protection against these harms in the form of remedies awarded after the wrongs are committed. These remedies are civil remedies for the acts of interference by others.

2. Tort and Crime Distinguished

A *crime* is a wrong that arises from a violation of a public duty, whereas a *tort* is a wrong that arises from a violation of a private duty. A crime is a wrong of such a serious nature that the appropriate level of government steps in to prosecute and punish the wrongdoer to deter others from engaging in the same type of conduct. However, whenever the act that is committed as a crime causes harm to an identifiable person, that person may recover from the wrongdoer for monetary damages to compensate for the harm. For the person who experiences the direct harm, the act is called a *tort*; for the government, the same act is called a *crime.*

When the same act is both a crime and a tort, the government may prosecute the wrongdoer for a violation of criminal law, and the individual who experiences the direct harm may recover damages. **For Example,** O. J. Simpson was charged by the state of California with the murder of his ex-wife, Nicole Brown Simpson, and her friend Ron Goldman. A criminal trial was held in which O. J. Simpson was acquitted. Simpson was subsequently sued civilly by the families of Nicole Simpson and Ron Goldman for the tort of wrongful death. The jury in the civil case found Simpson civilly liable and the court ordered him to pay nearly $20 million in damages plus interest. Only $382,000 of this judgment has actually been paid to the families.

3. Types of Torts

intentional tort–civil wrong that results from intentional conduct.

There are three types of torts: intentional torts, negligence, and strict liability. **Intentional torts** are those that occur when wrongdoers engage in intentional conduct. **For Example,** striking another person in a fight is an intentional act and would be the tort of battery and possibly also the crime of battery. Your arm striking another person's nose in a fast-moving crowd of people at a rock concert is not a tort or crime because your arm was pushed unintentionally by the force of the crowd. If you stretched out your arms in that crowd or began to swing your arms about and struck another person, you would be behaving carelessly in a crowd of people; and, although you may not have committed an intentional tort, it is possible that your careless conduct constitutes the tort of **negligence**. Careless actions, or actions taken without thinking through their consequences, constitute negligence. The harm to the other person's nose may not have been intended, but there is liability for these accidental harms under negligence. **For Example,** if you run a red light, hit another car, and injure its driver, you did not intend the result. However, your careless behavior of disregarding a traffic signal resulted in the injury, and you would have liability for your negligence to that driver.

negligence–failure to exercise due care under the circumstances in consequence of which harm is proximately caused to one to whom the defendant owed a duty to exercise due care.

strict liability–civil wrong for which there is absolute liability because of the inherent danger in the underlying activity, for example, the use of explosives.

Strict liability is another type of tort that imposes liability without regard to whether there was any intent to harm or any negligence occurred. Strict liability is imposed without regard to fault. Strict or absolute liability is imposed because the activity involved is so dangerous that there must be full accountability. Nonetheless, the activity is necessary and cannot be prohibited. The compromise is to allow the activity but ensure that its dangers and resulting damages are fully covered through the imposition of full liability for all injuries that result. **For Example,** contractors often need to use dynamite to take a roadway through a mountainside or demolish a building that has become a hazard. When the dynamite is used, noise, debris, and possibly dangerous pieces of earth and building will descend on others' land and possibly on people. In most states, contractors are held strictly liable for the resulting damage from the use of dynamite. The activity is necessary and not illegal, but those who use dynamite must be prepared to compensate those who are injured as a result.

Other areas in which there is strict liability for activity include the storage of flammable materials and crop dusting. The federal government and the states have pure food laws that impose absolute liability on manufacturers who fail to meet the statutory standards for their products. Another area of strict liability is *product liability,* which is covered in Chapter 25.

B. Intentional Torts

4. Assault

An *assault* is intentional conduct that threatens a person with a well-founded fear of imminent harm coupled with the present ability to carry out the threat of harm. **For Example,** the angry assertion "I'm going to kick your butt" along with aggressive movement in the direction of the victim with the intent to carry out the threat is an assault, even though a third person intervenes to stop the intended action. Mere words, however, although insulting, are ordinarily insufficient to constitute an assault.

5. Battery

A *battery* is the intentional, wrongful touching of another person without that person's consent. Thus, a threat to use force is an assault, and the actual use of force is the battery. The single action of striking an individual can be both a crime and a tort. A lawsuit for the tort of battery provides a plaintiff with the opportunity to recover damages resulting from the battery. The plaintiff must prove damages, however.

C A S E   S U M M A R Y

An Exchange of Unpleasantries ...

FACTS: Moore and Beye had an altercation after a public meeting regarding airport expansion. Moore owns a ranch near the airport and staunchly opposes expansion. Beye owns a flying service and avidly supports expansion. Moore and Beye exchanged unpleasantries while leaving the meeting. Beye then punched Moore on the left side of the jaw. Moore stumbled but caught himself before falling. He then exclaimed to the crowd, "You saw that. You are my witnesses. I've been assaulted. I want that man arrested." Ravalli County deputies took Beye into custody, and the state charged him with misdemeanor assault. Moore visited the hospital complaining of back and neck pain two days later and contended that he had injured his back while reeling from Beye's punch. He filed a civil complaint against Beye for damages. Moore's evidence mostly concerned his alleged back injury. Beye did not contest that he had punched Moore. His evidence countered that Moore's back problems had existed before the altercation. The judge instructed the jury that Beye had committed a battery as a matter of law and directed that they answer the question, "Was Moore damaged as a result of the battery?" The jury voted 11 to 1 that the battery did not injure Moore, and Moore appealed.

DECISION: Judgment for Beye. Beye presented the testimony of several eyewitnesses and a medical expert that Moore had sustained no damages. Although Moore presented considerable evidence to the contrary, it was not the court's function to agree or disagree with the verdict. Beye presented sufficient evidence to uphold the jury's verdict. [**Moore v Beye, 122 P3d 1212 (Mont 2005)**]

6. False Imprisonment

false imprisonment–
intentional detention of a person without that person's consent; called the *shopkeeper's tort* when shoplifters are unlawfully detained.

False imprisonment is the intentional detention of a person without that person's consent.[1] The detention need not be for any specified period of time, for any detention against one's will is false imprisonment. False imprisonment is often called the *shopkeeper's tort* because so much liability has been imposed on store owners for their unreasonable detention of customers suspected of shoplifting. Requiring a customer to sit in the manager's office or not allowing a customer to

[1] *Forgie-Buccioni v Hannaford Bros. Inc.*, 413 F3d 175 (1st Cir 2005).

leave the store can constitute the tort of false imprisonment. Shop owners do, however, need the opportunity to investigate possible thefts in their stores. As a result, all states have some form of privilege or protection for store owners called a *shopkeeper's privilege.*

shopkeeper's privilege—
right of a store owner to detain a suspected shoplifter based on reasonable cause and for a reasonable time without resulting liability for false imprisonment.

The **shopkeeper's privilege** permits the store owner to detain a suspected shoplifter based on reasonable suspicion for a reasonable time without resulting liability for false imprisonment to the accused customer.[2] The privilege applies even if the store owner was wrong about the customer being a shoplifter, so long as the store owner acted based on reasonable suspicions and treated the accused shoplifter in a reasonable manner. These privilege statutes do not protect the store owner from liability for unnecessary physical force or for invasion of privacy.

C A S E   S U M M A R Y

Officer Rivera Flagged for Unnecessary Roughness?

FACTS: Dillard Department Stores, Inc. (Dillard), detained hairstylist Lyndon Silva at its Houston, Texas, store. Silva testified that he was stopped by security guard Kevin Rivera, an off-duty Houston police officer who was in uniform with his "gun on his hip," and he was accused of theft of three shirts. Silva testified that Rivera placed him on the floor, handcuffed him, and emptied his shopping bag onto the floor. Silva testified people were around him when he was taken upstairs in handcuffs and when he was later escorted to the police car. He further stated that the officer and a woman made fun of him while he was being detained upstairs. Silva stated that when the city police came to take him into custody, Rivera again placed him on the floor with his knee in his back and exchanged handcuffs with the city police. He further testified that he asked Rivera many times to check his car for the receipt for the three shirts he was returning, but these requests were ignored, and that during the entire time he was detained, no one asked him for any explanation.

Officer Rivera's testimony was in direct conflict with Silva's, stating that Silva offered no excuse for not having a receipt for the shirts, and disputing that there were a lot of people watching, stating that the store was a "ghost town" at that time of day, 1:30 P.M. Silva later produced a receipt for three shirts. A jury returned a verdict for Silva for $13,121 in damages for physical pain, mental anguish, and attorney fees for false imprisonment and $50,000 in punitive damages. Dillard appealed, contending its employee had a shopkeeper's privilege to detain a customer to investigate the ownership of property.

DECISION: Judgment for Silva. The shopkeeper's privilege is applicable so long as (1) the employee has a reasonable belief that the customer is attempting to steal store merchandise (2) the detention is for a reasonable period of time, and (3) the detention is in a reasonable manner. In this case there was a reasonable belief by a store employee that items were being stolen. The detention for approximately an hour while store employees and Silva were questioned and the police department was called was a reasonable period of time. Regarding the third component, however, the jury found that Silva's story was more credible than Rivera's. It concluded that the detention was not in a reasonable manner and, accordingly, the shopkeeper's privilege did not apply. Since Silva's testimony supported the jury's finding, Dillard's appeal was denied. [**Dillard Department Stores, Inc. v Silva, 106 SW3d 789 (Tex App 2003)**]

---

[2] *Limited Stores, Inc. v Wilson-Robinson*, 876 SW2d 248 (Ark 1994); see also *Wal-Mart Stores, Inc. v Binns*, 15 SW3d 320 (Ark 2000).

7. Intentional Infliction of Emotional Distress

The **intentional infliction of emotional distress** (IIED) is a tort involving conduct that goes beyond all bounds of decency and produces mental anguish in the harmed individual. This tort requires proof of outrageous conduct and resulting emotional distress in the victim. **For Example,** Erica Schoen, a 16-year employee of Freightliner, returned to work on light duty after surgery for a work-related shoulder injury. She was assigned to work out of the nurse's station under two employees who intentionally worked her beyond her restrictions, assigned her to humiliating work, repeatedly called her worthless, and used her as a personal servant—ordering her to get snacks, sodas, and lunches for them and not reimbursing her. After five months of this treatment, Erica brought the matter to the human resources manager, who told her, in part, "Nobody wants you. You're worthless. We build trucks down here…." Erica became hysterical and thereafter required psychiatric care. The jury awarded $250,000 for IIED, and it was upheld on appeal because the repetitive misconduct and its duration, ratified by the human resource manager, was intolerable.[3]

8. Invasion of Privacy

The right of privacy is the right to be free of unreasonable intrusion into one's private affairs. The tort of **invasion of privacy** actually consists of three different torts: (1) intrusion into the plaintiff's private affairs (for example, planting a microphone in an office or home); (2) public disclosure of private facts (for example, disclosing private financial information, such as a business posting returned checks from customers near its cash register in a public display); and (3) appropriation of another's name, likeness, or image for commercial advantage. This form of invasion of privacy is generally referred to as the *right to publicity*. The elements of this tort are (1) appropriation of the plaintiff's name or likeness for the value associated with it, and not in an incidental manner or for a newsworthy purpose, (2) identification of the plaintiff in the publication, and (3) an advantage or benefit to the defendant. The right to publicity is designed to protect the commercial interest of celebrities in their identities. **For Example,** popular and critically acclaimed rock and roll musician Don Henley, the founder and member of the band The Eagles, successfully sued a department store chain that ran an international newspaper advertisement for its Henley shirt, which stated in large letters as the focus of the ad "This is Don's henley." The ad (1) used the value associated with the famous name Don Henley to get consumers to read it, (2) the plaintiff was identifiable in the ad, and (3) the ad was created with the belief that use of the words "Don's henley" would help sell the product.[4]

---

[3] *Schoen v Freightliner LLC*, 199 P3d 332 (Or App 2008).
[4] *Henley v Dillard Department Stores*, 46 F Supp 2d 587 (ND Tex 1999).

CASE SUMMARY

Cashing in on Catherine's Vacation

FACTS: Catherine Bosley worked as a television news anchor for WKBN, Channel 27, in Youngstown, Ohio. While on vacation with her husband in Florida, she participated in a "wet t-shirt" contest that was videotaped without her consent by DreamGirls, Inc., and licensed to Marvad Corp., which runs a Web site for adult entertainment through a subscription service on the Internet. Marvad used depictions of her in advertisements to promote the materials and services it markets. Web site searches related to Catherine Bosley in 2004 were the most popular search on the World Wide Web. Due to the publicity, she resigned from her position at WKBN and was prevented from seeking other employment. Bosley sought an injunction under the right to publicity theory against the defendants from using her image in any manner that promotes the sale of their goods or services. The defendants contended that an injunction would violate their First Amendment rights.

DECISION: Judgment for Bosley. The First Amendment does not immunize defendants from damages for infringement of the right to publicity. No significant editorial comment or artistic expression involving First Amendment protections applies in this case. If any "speech" interest is involved, it is commercial speech. At its core, the defendants are selling Bosley's image for a profit without her consent. It is in violation of her right to publicity, which protects one's right to be free from the appropriation of one's persona. The injunction sought was granted. [**Bosley v Wildwett.com, 310 F Supp 2d 914 (ND Ohio 2004)**]

9. Defamation

defamation–untrue statement by one party about another to a third party.

slander–defamation of character by spoken words or gestures.

libel–written or visual defamation without legal justification.

Defamation is an untrue statement by one party about another to a third party. **Slander** is oral or spoken defamation, and **libel** is written (and in some cases broadcast) defamation. The elements for defamation are (1) a statement about a person's reputation, honesty, or integrity that is untrue; (2) publication (accomplished when a third party hears or reads the defamatory statement); (3) a statement directed at a particular person; and (4) damages that result from the statement.

For Example, a false statement by the owner of a business that the former manager was fired for stealing when he was not would be defamation, and the former manager's damages could be his inability to find another position because of the statement's impact on his reputation.

In cases in which the victim is a public figure, such as a Hollywood celebrity or a professional sports player, another element is required, the element of malice, which means that what was said or written was done with the knowledge that the information was false or with reckless disregard for whether it was true or false.

The defenses to defamation include the truth. If the statement is true, even if it is harmful to the victim, it is not the tort of defamation.[5]

Some statements are privileged, and this privilege provides a full or partial defense to the tort of defamation. **For Example,** members of Congress enjoy an

---

[5] See Stark v Zeta Phi Beta Sorority Inc., 587 F Supp 2d 170 (D DC 2008).

absolute privilege – complete defense against the tort of defamation, as in the speeches of members of Congress on the floor and witnesses in a trial.

absolute privilege when they are speaking on the floor of the Senate or the House because public policy requires a free dialogue on the issues pending in a legislative body. The same absolute privilege applies to witnesses in court proceedings to encourage witnesses with information to come forward and testify. Where a witness granted immunity from prosecution testifies before a governmental agency, the witness is entitled to immunity from defamation lawsuits.

C A S E   S U M M A R Y

Roger Clemens Strikes Out in Texas Court

FACTS: Roger Clemens sued his former trainer Brian McNamee for defamation. He alleged that McNamee falsely stated to the "Mitchell Commission," a congressional investigatory body looking into the use of performance-ehancing drugs in major league baseball, that Clemens had used steroids and human growth hormones during his professional baseball career. Clemens's complaint alleged that McNamee's statements to the Commissioner "injured Clemens's reputation and exposed him to public hatred, contempt, ridicule, and financial injuries." McNamee filed a motion to dismiss for lack of personal jurisdiction and privilege.

DECISION: Motion to dismiss granted in part. McNamee was interviewed by federal agents investigating the use of steroids, human growth hormones, and money laundering; he was given immunity from prosecution for his cooperation, but could be subject to prosecution for making false statements. McNamee's interviews with the Mitchell's Commission were scheduled by U.S. Attorneys and he was told by U.S. Attorneys that his immunity and truth obligations continued to apply to Mitchell interviews. Under Texas law, statements made to government agencies as part of legislative, judicial, or quasi-judicial proceedings may be entitled to absolute immunity, because the proper administration of justice requires full disclosure from witnesses without fear of retaliatory lawsuits for defamation.* [**Clemens V McNamee, 608 F Supp 2d 811 (SDTex, 2009)**]

* The court dismissed for lack of personal jurisdiction Clemens's allegations regarding statements made by McNamee to *Sports Illustrated* because they were not made in Texas. A charge of defamation regarding alleged statements made by McNamee to pitcher Andy Pettitte in Texas is still pending before the court.

qualified privilege – media privilege to print inaccurate information without liability for defamation, so long as a retraction is printed and there was no malice.

The media enjoy a **qualified privilege** for stories that turn out to be false. Their qualified privilege is a defense to defamation so long as the information was released without malice and a retraction or correction is made when the matter is brought to their attention.

A *qualified privilege* to make a defamatory statement in the workplace exists when the statement is made to protect the interests of the private employer on a work-related matter, especially when reporting actual or suspected wrongdoing.

For Example, Neda Lewis was fired from her job at Carson Oil Company for allegedly stealing toilet paper. The employee in charge of supplies noticed toilet paper was regularly missing from the ladies room, and one evening from a third-floor window overlooking the parking lot, she observed that the plaintiff's bag contained two rolls of toilet paper. She reported the matter to the executive secretary, who reported it to both the president and the CEO of the firm, who decided to fire her. Two other employees were also informed. The employer was able to successfully raise the defense of a qualified privilege to Ms. Lewis' defamation action for "false accusations of theft" since all of the employees involved were participants in the investigation and termination of the employee.[6]

A new statutory privilege has been evolving with respect to letters of recommendation and references given by employers for employees who are applying for jobs at other companies. Most companies, because of concerns about liability for defamation, will only confirm that a former employee did work at their firm and will provide the time period during which the person was employed. However, many employees who had histories that should have been revealed for safety reasons have been hired because no negative information was released. Numerous states now have statutes that provide employers a qualified privilege with respect to references and recommendations. So long as the employer acts in good faith in providing information, there is no liability for defamation to the former employee as a result of the information provided.

CASE SUMMARY

Putting in an Exaggerated Good Word

FACTS: Randi W., a 13-year-old who attended the Livingston Middle School, was molested and sexually touched by Robert Gadams, a vice principal at the school, in his office at the school. Gadams's prior employer was Muroc Unified School District, where disciplinary actions were taken against him for sexual harassment. When allegations of "sexual touching" of female students were made, Gadams was forced to resign from Muroc. Nonetheless, Gary Rice and David Malcolm, officials at Muroc, provided a letter of recommendation for Gadams that described him as "an upbeat, enthusiastic administrator who relates well to the students" and who was responsible "in large part" for making Boron Junior High School (located in Muroc) "a safe, orderly and clean environment for students and staff." Randi W. filed suit against the school districts, alleging that her injuries from Gadams's sexual touching were proximately caused by their failure to provide full and accurate information about Gadams to the placement service. The trial court dismissed the case, and the Court of Appeals reversed. The districts appealed.

DECISION: One of society's highest priorities is to protect children from sexual or physical abuse. On the other hand, a rule imposing liability in a case like this where a letter of recommendation fails to disclose material information could greatly inhibit the preparation and distribution of reference letters, to the general detriment of employers and employees alike. However, the balancing of these two competing policy issues simply requires that employers prepare recommendation letters stating all "material" facts, positive and negative, and simply decline to write a reference letter or, at most, merely confirm the former employee's position, salary, and dates of employment. Misleading letters of recommendation for potentially dangerous employees present foreseeable risks of harms to others, like the young person harmed here.

The judgment of the Court of Appeals is affirmed as to liability for negligent misrepresentation and fraud. [**Randi W. v Muroc Joint Unified School District, 929 P2d 582 Cal 1997**]

---

[6] *Lewis v Carson Oil Co.*, 127 P3d 1207 (Or App 2006).

10. Product Disparagement

slander of title–malicious making of false statements as to a seller's title.

trade libel–written defamation about a product or service.

product disparagement–false statements made about a product or business.

Although the comparison of products and services is healthy for competition, false statements about another's products constitute a form of slander called **slander of title** or libel called **trade libel**; collectively, these are known as **product disparagement**, which occurs when someone makes false statements about another business, its products, or its abilities.[7] The elements of product disparagement are (1) a false statement about a particular business product or about its service in terms of honesty, reputation, ability, or integrity; (2) communication of the statement to a third party; and (3) damages.

11. Wrongful Interference with Contracts

contract interference–tort in which a third party interferes with others' freedom to contract.

The tort of **contract interference** or (tortious interference with contracts) occurs when parties are not allowed the freedom to contract without interference from third parties. While the elements required to establish the tort of contract interference are complex, a basic definition is that the law affords a remedy when a third party intentionally causes another to break a contract already in existence. **For Example,** Nikke Finke, a newspaper reporter who had a contract with the *New York Post* to write stories about the entertainment industry for the *Post's* business section, wrote two articles about a lawsuit involving a literary agent and the Walt Disney Company over merchandising rights to the Winnie-the-Pooh characters. Finke reported that the trial court sanctioned Disney for engaging in "misuse of the discovery process" and acting in "bad faith" and ordered Disney to pay fees and costs of $90,000. Disney's president, Robert Iger, sent a letter to the *Post's* editor-in-chief, Col Allan, calling Finke's reporting an "absolute distortion" of the record and "absolutely false." Approximately two weeks after the Pooh articles were published, the *Post* fired Finke; her editor told her she was being fired for the Pooh articles. She sued Disney on numerous tort theories, including interference with her contract with the *Post*. Disney sought to have the complaint dismissed, which motion was denied by the court. The Court of Appeals concluded that Finke demonstrated a reasonable probability of proving that Iger's allegations that she made false statements in her article were themselves false; and it concluded that a jury could find Disney liable for intentional interference with contractual relations based on circumstantial evidence and negligent interference with contractual relations because it was reasonably foreseeable to Disney that the nature of its accusations against Finke would result in her termination from employment.[8]

12. Trespass

trespass–unauthorized action with respect to person or property.

A **trespass** is an unauthorized action with respect to land or personal property. A *trespass to land* is any unpermitted entry below, on, across, or above the land of another. **For Example,** Joyce Ameral's home abuts the mid-way point of the 240-yard, par-4 ninth hole of the public Middlebrook Country Club. Balls sliced

---

[7] *Sannerud v Brantz*, 879 P2d 341 (Wyo 1994). See *Suzuki Motor Corp. v Consumers Union*, 230 F3d 1110 (9th Cir 2003), *cert denied* 540 US 983 (2003), for an example of the complexity of a product disparagement action.
[8] *Finke v The Walt Disney Co.*, 2 Cal Rptr 3d 436 (Cal App 2003).

and hooked by golfers have damaged her windows and screens, dented her car, and made her deck too dangerous for daytime use. Her landscapers are forced to wear hard hats when cutting her lawn. In her lawsuit against the country club owner, the court ruled that the projection of golf balls onto Ameral's property constituted a continuing trespass and it enjoined the trespass.[9]

A *trespass to personal property* is the invasion of personal property without the permission of the owner. **For Example,** the use of someone's car without that person's permission is a trespass to personal property.

C. NEGLIGENCE

The widest range of tort liability today arises in the field of negligence. Accidents happen! Property is damaged, and/or injuries result. The fact that an individual suffers an injury does not necessarily mean that the individual will be able to recover damages for the injury. **For Example,** Rhonda Nichols was shopping in the outdoor garden center at a Lowe's Home Center when a "wild bird" flew into the back of her head, causing injuries. Her negligence lawsuit against Lowe's was dismissed because the owner did not have a duty to protect her from a wild bird attack because it was not reasonably foreseeable.[10] Jane Costa was passively watching a Boston Red Sox baseball game at Fenway Park when a foul ball struck her in the face, causing severe and permanent injuries. Her negligence lawsuit against the Boston Red Sox was unsuccessful because it was held that the owners had no duty to warn Ms. Costa of the obvious danger of foul balls being hit into the stands.[11] Although cases involving injury to spectators at baseball games in other jurisdictions have turned on other tort doctrines, injured fans, like Ms. Costa, are left to bear the costs of their injuries. Only when an injured person can demonstrate the following four elements of negligence is a right to recover established: (1) a duty, (2) breach of duty, (3) causation, and (4) damages.[12] Several defenses may be raised in a negligence lawsuit.

13. Elements of Negligence

(A) DUTY TO EXERCISE REASONABLE CARE. The first element of negligence is a *duty*. There is a general duty of care imposed to act as a reasonably prudent person would in similar circumstances. **For Example,** Gustavo Guzman worked for a subcontractor as a chicken catcher at various poultry farms where a Tyson Foods employee, Brian Jones, operated a forklift and worked with the catchers setting up cages to collect birds for processing at a Tyson plant. Contrary to Tyson's instructions "never to allow catchers to move behind the forklift or otherwise out of sight," Brian moved his forklift and struck Guzman, who suffered a serious spinal injury. A general contractor, Tyson Foods, owes a duty to exercise reasonable care to a subcontractor's employee, Gustavo Guzman.[13]

---

[9] *Ameral v Pray*, 831 NE2d 915 (Mass App 2005).
[10] *Nichols v Lowe's Home Center, Inc.*, 407 F Supp 2d 979 (SD Ill 2006).
[11] *Costa v Boston Red Sox Baseball Club*, 809 NE2d 1090 (Mass App 2004).
[12] *Alfred v Capital Area Soccer League, Inc.*, 669 SE2d 277 (NC App 2008).
[13] *Tyson Foods Inc. v Guzman*, 116 SW3d 233 (Tex App 2003).

Professionals have a duty to perform their jobs at the level of a reasonable professional. For a professional such as an accountant, doctor, lawyer, dentist, or architect to avoid liability for **malpractice,** the professional must perform his or her skill in the same manner as, and at the level of, other professionals in the same field.

malpractice—when services are not properly rendered in accordance with commonly accepted standards; negligence by a professional in performing his or her skill.

Those who own real property have a duty of care to keep their property in a condition that does not create hazards for guests. Businesses have a duty to inspect and repair their property so that their customers are not injured by hazards, such as spills on the floor or uneven walking areas. When customer safety is a concern, businesses have a duty to provide adequate security, such as security patrols in mall parking lots.

(B) Breach of Duty. The second element of negligence is the breach of duty imposed by statute or by the application of the reasonable person standard. The defendant's conduct is evaluated against what a reasonable person would have done under the circumstances. That is, when there is sufficient proof to raise a jury question, the jury decides whether the defendant breached the duty to the injured person from a reasonable person's perspective.[14] **For Example,** the jury in Guzman's lawsuit against Tyson Foods (the *Tyson* case), after weighing all of the facts and circumstances, determined that Tyson's employee's operation of the forklift constituted a breach of Tyson's duty of care to Guzman.

(C) Causation. A third element of negligence is *causation,* the element that connects the duty and the breach of duty to the injuries to the plaintiff. **For Example,** in Guzman's lawsuit, the forklift operator's careless conduct was the cause in fact of this worker's injuries. A "but for" test for causation is used. *But for* Tyson employee Brian Jones' negligent conduct in moving the forklift under the circumstances surrounding the accident, Guzman would not have been injured.

Once the cause in fact is established, the plaintiff must establish *proximate cause.* That is, it must establish that the harm suffered by the injured person was a foreseeable consequence of the defendant's negligent actions. Foreseeability requires only the general danger to be foreseeable. In the *Tyson* case, the court determined that while there was some evidence that a jury could possibly infer that Tyson could not foresee an accident similar to the one involving Guzman, the evidence was legally sufficient to support the jury's finding that Tyson's negligence was foreseeable and the cause in fact of Guzman's injuries.

The landmark *Palsgraf v Long Island Rail Road Co.* case established a limitation on liability for unforeseeable or unusual consequences following a negligent act.

(D) Damages. The plaintiff in a personal injury negligence lawsuit must establish the actual losses caused by the defendant's breach of duty of care and is entitled to be made whole for all losses. The successful plaintiff is entitled to compensation for (1) past and future pain and suffering (mental anguish), (2) past and future physical impairment, (3) past and future medical care, and (4) past and future loss of earning capacity. Life and work life expectancy are critical factors to consider in assessing

---

[14] A breach of duty may be established by the very nature of the harm to the plaintiff. The doctrine of *res ipsa loquitur* ("the event speaks for itself") provides a rebuttable presumption that the defendant was negligent when a defendant owes a duty to the plaintiff, the nature of the harm caused the plaintiff is such that it ordinarily does not happen in the absence of negligence, and the instrument causing the injury was in the defendant's exclusive control. An example of the doctrine is a lawsuit against a surgeon after a surgical device is discovered in a former patient months after the surgery by another physician seeking the cause of the patient's continuing pain subsequent to the operation.

CASE SUMMARY

The Scales Tipped on Causation

FACTS: Helen Palsgraf lived in Brooklyn. On a summer's day, she purchased tickets to travel to Rockaway Beach on the Long Island Rail Road (LIRR) with her two daughters. She was standing on a platform on the LIRR's East New York station when two men ran to catch another train. One of the men made it onto the train, but the other man, who was carrying a package, was unsteady as the train was about to pull out of the station. The LIRR conductor pulled him up, while the LIRR platform guard pushed him in the train, but in the process, he dropped the package. It contained fireworks and exploded! The concussion from the explosion caused the scales located next to Mrs. Palsgraf to fall over, striking and injuring her. Mrs. Palsgraf sued LIRR for the negligence of the two employees who had assisted the passenger with the package to board the train. A jury awarded her $6,000, which was upheld 3-2 by the Appellate Division. Thereafter the state's highest court considered the railroad's appeal.

DECISION: Recovery for negligence is not available unless there has been some violation of a right. Helen Palsgraf was too remote in distance from the accident for any invasion of rights. To reach a different decision would mean that there could be no end to those who might be harmed. By helping someone onto a moving train, the train employees can anticipate that the passenger himself might be injured, that other passengers might be injured, and that those around the immediate scene might be injured. But Mrs. Palsgraf was too remote for her injuries to be reasonably foreseeable as a consequence of the action of helping a passenger onto a moving train. She was 25 to 30 feet away from the scene, and the explosion cannot be called the proximate cause of her concussion and other injuries. [**Palsgraf v Long Island RR. Co., 162 NE 99 (NY 1928)**]

damage involving permanent disabilities with loss of earning capacity. Expert witnesses are utilized at trial to present evidence based on worklife tables and present value tables to deal with these economic issues. The jury considers all of the evidence in the context of the elements necessary to prove negligence and all defenses raised, and it renders a verdict. **For Example,** in the *Tyson* case, the defendant presented evidence and argued that Gustavo Guzman was himself negligent regarding the accident. The jury found that both parties were negligent and attributed 80 percent of the fault to Tyson and 20 percent to Guzman (this is called *comparative negligence* and is discussed in the following section). The jury awarded Guzman $931,870.51 in damages ($425,000.00 for past physical pain and mental anguish, $150,000.00 for future physical pain and mental anguish, $10,000.00 for past physical impairment, $10,000.00 for future physical impairment, $51,870.51 for past medical care, $5,000.00 for future medical care, $70,000.00 for past lost earning capacity, and $210,000.00 for future lost earning capacity). After deducting 20 percent of the total jury award for Guzman's own negligence, the trial court's final judgment awarded Guzman $745,496.41.

In some situations, the independent actions of two defendants occur to cause harm. **For Example,** Penny Shipler was rendered a quadriplegic as a result of a Chevrolet S-10 Blazer rollover accident. She sued the driver Kenneth Long for negligence and General Motors for negligent design of the Blazer's roof. She was awarded $18.5 million in damages. Because two causes provided a single indivisible injury, the two defendants were held jointly and severally liable.[15] Under *joint and several liability,* each defendant may be held liable to pay the entire judgment. However, should one defendant pay the entire judgment, that party may sue the other for "contribution" for its proportionate share.

In some cases in which the breach of duty was shocking, plaintiffs may be awarded *punitive damages.* However, punitive (also called *exemplary*) damages are ordinarily applied when the defendant's tortious conduct is attended by circumstances of fraud, malice, or willful or wanton conduct.[16]

14. Defenses to Negligence

(A) CONTRIBUTORY NEGLIGENCE. A plaintiff who is also negligent gives the defendant the opportunity to raise the defense of **contributory negligence,** which the defendant establishes by utilizing the elements of negligence previously discussed, including the plaintiff's duty to exercise reasonable care for his or her own safety, the breach of that duty, causation, and harm. Under common law, the defense of contributory negligence, if established, is a complete bar to recovery of damages from the defendant.

contributory negligence– negligence of the plaintiff that contributes to injury and at common law bars from recovery from the defendant although the defendant may have been more negligent than the plaintiff.

CASE SUMMARY

Keep Your Eye on the Ball in Sports: Keep Your Eye on the 300-Pound Boxes in Trucking

FACTS: Lawrence Hardesty is an over-the-road tractor-trailer truck driver who picked up a load of stadium seating equipment for the NFL stadium under construction in Baltimore. The equipment was packaged in large corrugated cardboard boxes weighing several hundred pounds. The shipper, American Seating Co., loaded the trailer while Hardesty remained in the cab of his truck doing "paperwork" and napping. Considerable open space existed between the boxes and the rear door of the trailer. The evidence showed that Hardesty failed to properly examine the load bars used to secure the boxes from movement during transit. When Hardesty arrived at the Baltimore destination, he opened the rear trailer door and boxes at the end of the trailer fell out and injured him. Hardesty brought a personal injury negligence action against the shipper. American Seating Co. responded that Hardesty was contributorily negligent, thus barring his negligence claim.

DECISION: Judgment for American Seating Co. because the claim is barred by Hardesty's contributory negligence. His decision to ignore the loading process by remaining in his truck, oblivious to the manner and means of the loading of the trailer, coupled with his own failure to examine the load bars sufficiently to confirm that they would "adequately secure" the cargo, together with his decision, in the face of his prior omissions, to open the doors of the trailer upon his arrival in Baltimore while standing within the zone of danger created by the possibility (of which he negligently failed to inform himself) of injury from cargo falling out of the trailer, cohered to rise to the level of a cognizable breach of duty—contributory negligence. [**Hardesty v American Seating Co., 194 F Supp 2d 447 D Md 2002**]

---

[15] *Shipler v General Motors Corp.,* 710 NW2d 807 (Neb 2006).

[16] See *Eden Electrical, Ltd. v Amana Co.,* 370 F3d 824 (8th Cir 2004); and *University of Colorado v American Cyanamid Co.,* 342 F3d 1298 (Fed Cir 2003).

The contributory negligence defense has given way to the defense of comparative negligence in most states.

(B) Comparative Negligence. Because contributory negligence produced harsh results with no recovery of damages for an injured plaintiff, most states have adopted a fairer approach to handling situations in which both the plaintiff and the defendant are negligent; it is called *comparative negligence.* Comparative negligence is a defense that permits a negligent plaintiff to recover some damages but only in proportion to the defendant's degree of fault.[17] **For Example,** in the *Tyson* case, both the defendant and the plaintiff were found to be negligent. The jury attributed 80 percent of the fault for the plaintiff's injury to Tyson and 20 percent of the fault to the plaintiff, Guzman. While Guzman's total damages were $931,870, they were reduced by 20 percent, and the final judgment awarded Guzman was $745,496.

Some comparative negligence states refuse to allow the plaintiff to recover damages if the plaintiff's fault was more than 50 percent of the cause of the harm.[18]

(C) Assumption of the Risk. The assumption of the risk defense has two categories. *Express assumption of the risk* involves a written exculpatory agreement under which a plaintiff acknowledges the risks involved in certain activities and releases the defendant from prospective liability for personal injuries sustained as a result of the defendant's negligent conduct. Examples include ski lift tickets, white water rafting contracts, permission for high school cheerleading activities, and parking lot claim checks. In most jurisdictions these agreements are enforceable as written. However, in some jurisdictions they may be considered unenforceable because they violate public policy. **For Example,** Gregory Hanks sued the Powder Ridge Ski Resort for negligence regarding serious injuries he sustained while snowtubing at the defendant's facility. He had signed a release which explicitly provided that the snowtuber: *["fully] assume[s] all risks associated with [s]nowtubing,* even if due to the NEGLIGENCE" of the defendants [emphasis in original]. The Supreme Court of Connecticut found that the release was unenforceable because it violated the public policy by shifting the risk of negligence to the weaker bargainer.[19]

Implied primary assumption of the risk arises when a plaintiff has impliedly consented, often in advance of any negligence by the defendant, to relieve a defendant of a duty to the plaintiff regarding specific known and appreciated risks. It is a subjective standard, one specific to the plaintiff and his or her situation. **For Example,** baseball mom Delinda Taylor took her two boys to a Seattle Mariners baseball game and was injured during the pregame warm-up when a ball thrown by José Mesa got past Freddie Garcia, striking Taylor in the face and causing serious injuries. The defendant baseball team successfully raised the affirmative defense of implied primary assumption of the risk by showing that Mrs. Taylor had full subjective understanding of the specific risk of getting hit by a thrown baseball, and she voluntarily chose to encounter that risk.[20]

---

[17] *City of Chicago v M/V Morgan,* 375 F3d 563 (7th Cir 2004).
[18] *Davenport v Cotton Hope Plantation,* 482 SE2d 569 (SC App 1997).
[19] *Hanks v Powder Ridge,* 885 A2d 734 (Conn 2005).
[20] *Taylor v Baseball Club of Seattle,* 130 P3d 835 (Wash App 2006).

A number of states have either abolished the defense of assumption of the risk, reclassifying the defense as comparative negligence so as not to completely bar a plaintiff's recovery of damages, or have eliminated the use of the assumption of the risk terminology and handle cases under the duty, breach of duty, causation, and harm elements of negligence previously discussed.[21]

(D) **IMMUNITY.** Governments are generally immune from tort liability.[22] This rule has been eroded by decisions and in some instances by statutes, such as the Federal Tort Claims Act. Subject to certain exceptions, this act permits the recovery of damages from the United States for property damage, personal injury, or death action claims arising from the negligent act or omission of any employee of the United States

sports&entertainment law

Liability for Injuries Under the Sports Exception Doctrine

Charles "Booby" Clark played football for the Cincinnati Bengals as a running back on offense. Dale Hackbart played defensive free safety for the Denver Broncos. As a consequence of an interception by the Broncos, Hackbart became an offensive player, threw a block, and was watching the play with one knee on the ground when Clark "acting out of anger and frustration, but without a specific intent to injure," stepped forward and struck a blow to the back of Hackbart's head and neck, causing a serious neck fracture. Is relief precluded for injuries occurring during a professional football game? The answer is no. While proof of mere negligence is insufficient to establish liability during such an athletic contest, liability must instead be premised on heightened proof of reckless or intentional conduct on the part of the defendant. In the *Hackbart* case, the court determined that if the evidence established that the injury was the result of acts of Clark that were in reckless disregard of Hackbart's safety, Hackbart is

entitled to damages.* Why didn't Hackbart pursue recovery under negligence law, contending that Clark had a general duty of care to act as a reasonably prudent person would in similar circumstances? Because football and other contact sports contain within the rules of the games inherent *unreasonable* risks of harm, a negligence theory is not applicable. What contact sports do you believe qualify under this "sports exception" doctrine for which proof of negligence is insufficient to establish liability for injuries sustained during the athletic contest?

PGA golfer Walter Mallin sued PGA golfer John Paesani for injuries that Mallin sustained while competing in a PGA golf tournament when Paesani drove a golf ball that struck Mallin in the head on his right temple. Paesani contends that the "sports exception" doctrine applies and the negligence case must be dismissed. How would you decide this case?**

* *Hackbart v Cincinnati Bengals, Inc.*, 601 F2d 516 (10th Cir 1979).
** *Mallin v Paesani*, 892 A2d 1043 (Conn Super, 2005).

[21] See, for example, *Costa v The Boston Red Sox Baseball Club*, 809 NE2d 1090 (Mass App 2004), where the court cites state precedent that"… the abolishment of assumption of the risk as an affirmative defense did not alter the plaintiff's burden … to prove the defendant owed [the plaintiff] a duty of care … and thus left intact the open and obvious damages rule, which operates to negate the existence of a duty to care."
[22] *Kirby v Macon County*, 892 SW2d 403 (Tenn 1994).

under such circumstances that the United States, if a private person, would be liable to the claimant in accordance with the law of the place where the act or omission occurred. A rapidly growing number of states have abolished governmental immunity, although many still recognize it.

Until the early 1900s, charities were immune from tort liability, and children and parents and spouses could not sue each other. These immunities are fast disappearing. **For Example,** if a father's negligent driving of his car causes injuries to his minor child passenger, the child may recover from the father for his injuries.[23]

D. STRICT LIABILITY

The final form of tort liability is known as *strict liability*. When the standards of strict liability apply, very few defenses are available. Strict liability was developed to provide guaranteed protection for those who are injured by conduct the law deems both serious and inexcusable.

---

thinking things through

Torts and Public Policy

Over a decade ago, a jury awarded 81-year-old Stella Liebeck nearly $3 million because she was burned after she spilled a cup of McDonald's coffee on her lap. Based on these limited facts, a national discussion ensued about a need for tort reform, and to this day "Stella Awards" are given on Web sites for apparently frivolous or excessive lawsuits. Consider the following additional facts and the actual damages awarded Stella Liebeck. Decide whether her recovery was just.

- McDonald's coffee was brewed at 195 to 205 degrees.

- McDonald's quality assurance manager "was aware of the risk [of burns] … and had no plans to turn down the heat."

- Mrs. Liebeck spent seven days in the hospital with third degree burns and had skin grafts. Gruesome photos of burns of the inner thighs, groin, and buttocks were entered as evidence.

- The compensatory damages were $200,000, which were reduced to $160,000 because Mrs. Liebeck was determined to be 20 percent at fault.

- The jury awarded $2.7 million in punitive damages. The trial court judge reduced this amount to $480,000.

- The total recovery at the trial court for Mrs. Liebeck was $640,000. Both parties appealed, and a settlement was reached at what is believed to be close to the $640,000 figure.

Tort remedies have evolved because of public policy incentives for the protection of individuals from physical, mental, and economic damage. Tort remedies provide economic motivation for individuals and businesses to avoid conduct that could harm others.

The amount of the compensation and the circumstances in which compensation for torts should be paid are issues that courts, juries, and legislatures review.

---

[23] *Cates v Cates*, 588 NE2d 330 (Ill App 1992); see also *Doe v McKay*, 700 NE2d 1018 (Ill 1998).

thinking things through

Continued

Many legislatures have examined and continue to review the standards for tort liability and damages.

The U.S. Supreme Court devoted several decisions in recent years to dealing with excessive punitive damages in civil litigation, and it has set "guideposts" to be used by courts in assessing punitive damages.* In *State Farm Mutual Automobile Insurance Co. v Campbell*, compensatory damages for the plaintiffs at the trial court

* *BMW of North America v Gore*, 517 US 559 (1996); *Cooper Industries v Leatherman Tool Group, Inc.*, 532 US 424 (2001); *State Farm Insurance v Campbell*, 538 US 408 (2003); and *Exxon Shipping Co. v Baker*, 128 S Ct 2605, 2621 (2008).

level were $1 million, and punitive damages, based in part on evidence that State Farm's nationwide policy was to underpay claims regardless of merit to enhance profits, were assessed at $145 million. The Supreme Court concluded that the facts of *Campbell* would likely justify a punitive damages award only at or near the amount of compensatory damages. Thus, even those who act very badly as State Farm Insurance did have a constitutionally protected right under the Due Process Clause of the Fourteenth Amendment to have civil law damages assessed in accordance with the Supreme Court's guideposts.

15. What is Strict Liability?

Strict liability is an absolute standard of liability imposed by the law in circumstances the courts or legislatures have determined require a high degree of protection. When strict liability is imposed, the result is that the company or person who has caused injury or damages by the conduct will be required to compensate for those damages in an absolute sense. Few, if any, defenses apply in a situation in which the law imposes a strict liability standard. **For Example,** as noted earlier in the chapter, engaging in ultrahazardous activities, such as using dynamite to excavate a site for new construction, results in strict liability for the contractor performing the demolition. Any damages resulting from the explosion are the responsibility of that contractor, so the contractor is strictly liable.

16. Imposing Strict Liability

Strict liability arises in a number of different circumstances, but the most common are in those situations in which a statutory duty is imposed and in product liability. For example at both the state and federal levels, there are requirements for the use, transportation, and sale of radioactive materials, as well as the disposal of biomedical materials and tools. Any violation of these rules and regulations would result in strict liability for the company or person in violation.

Product liability, while more fully covered in Chapter 25, is another example of strict liability. A product that is defective through its design, manufacture, or instructions and that injures someone results in strict liability for the manufacturer.

lawflix

Class Action (1991) (R)

This movie depicts the magnitude of damages and recovery when multiple injuries occur. The film provides insights on tort reform and the ethics of lawyers. You can learn about the magnitude of discovery and evidence.

Check out LawFlix at [**www.cengage.com/blaw/dvl**] to access movie clips that illustrate business law concepts.

Notting Hill (1999) (PG-13)

A story of famous star gets guy, dumps guy, gets guy back, dumps guy again, and then guy dumps famous star, and on and on. But, the guy owns a bookstore that sells travel books and he has a shoplifter. Hugh Grant, as the guy, illustrates perfection in exercising the shopkeeper's privilege.

You can view a clip of this movie and others that illustrate business law concepts at the LawFlix site, located at **www.cengage.com/blaw/dvl**.

MAKE THE CONNECTION

SUMMARY

A *tort* is a civil wrong that affords recovery for damages that result. The three forms of torts are intentional torts, negligence, and strict liability. A tort differs from a crime in the nature of its remedy. Fines and imprisonment result from criminal violations, whereas money damages are paid to those who are damaged by conduct that constitutes a tort. An action may be both a crime and a tort, but the tort remedy is civil in nature.

Selected intentional torts are false imprisonment, defamation, product disparagement, contract interference or tortious interference, and trespass. False imprisonment is the detention of another without his or her permission. False imprisonment is often called the *shopkeeper's tort* because store owners detain suspected shoplifters. Many states provide a privilege to store owners if they detain shoplifting suspects based on reasonable cause and in a reasonable manner. Defamation is slander (oral) or libel (written) and consists of false statements about another that damage the person's reputation or integrity. Truth is an absolute defense to defamation, and there are some privileges that protect against defamation, such as those for witnesses at trial and for members of Congress during debates on the floor. There is a developing privilege for employers when they give references for former employees. Invasion of privacy is intrusion into private affairs; public disclosure of private facts; or appropriation of someone's name, image, or likeness for commercial purposes.

To establish the tort of negligence, one must show that there has been a breach of duty in the form of a violation of a statute or professional competency standards or of behavior that does not rise to the level of that of a reasonable person. That breach of duty must have caused the foreseeable injuries to the plaintiff, and the plaintiff must be able to quantify the damages that resulted. Possible defenses to negligence include contributory negligence, comparative negligence, and assumption of risk.

Strict liability is absolute liability with few defenses.

LEARNING OUTCOMES

After studying this chapter, you should be able to clearly explain:

A. GENERAL PRINCIPLES

LO.1 Explain the difference between torts and crimes

See the discussion on wrongs that are a violation of a private duty as torts, and wrongs that are a violation of a public duty of crimes, p. 188. See the O.J. Simpson example of his acquittal of the crime of murder and his civil liability for the torts of wrongful death on p. 188.

B. INTENTIONAL TORTS

LO.2 Distinguish between an assault and a battery

See the "kick your butt" threat example of an assault on p. 189.

LO.3 Explain the three different torts of invasion of privacy

See the discussion of the intrusion into a person' private affairs, public disclosure of private facts, and right to publicity torts beginning on p. 192.

LO.4 Explain the torts of defamation and defenses

See the discussion of slander, libel, and trade libel beginning on p. 193. See the discussion of the requirement of the enhanced element of malice for cases in which the victim is a public figure, p. 193. See the defense of privilege raised in the *Clemens* case on p. 194.

C. NEGLIGENCE

LO.5 Explain the elements of negligence and defenses

See the discussion of the elements of negligence: duty, breach of duty, and causation and damages beginning on p. 197. See the discussion of the defenses of contributory negligence, comparative negligence, assumption of risk, and immunity beginning on p. 200.

D. STRICT LIABILITY

LO.6 Explain the tort of strict liability and why very few defenses are avaliable

See the dynamite excavation example, holding the contractor liable for any damages with no defenses because of the hazardous activity, p. 204.

KEY TERMS

absolute privilege

contract interference

contributory negligence,

defamation

false imprisonment

intentional infliction of
  emotional distress

intentional torts

invasion of privacy

libel

malpractice,

negligence

product disparagement

qualified privilege

shopkeeper's privilege

slander of title

slander

strict liability

tort

trade libel

trespass

QUESTIONS AND CASE PROBLEMS

1. Christensen Shipyards built a 155-foot yacht for Tiger Woods at its Vancouver, Washington, facilities. It used Tiger's name and photographs relating to the building of the yacht in promotional materials for the shipyard without seeking his permission. Was this a right to publicity tort because Tiger could assert that his name and photos were used to attract attention to the shipyard to obtain commercial advantage? Did the shipyard have a First Amendment right to present the truthful facts regarding their building of the yacht and the owner's identity as promotional materials? Does the fact that the yacht was named *Privacy* have an impact on this case? Would it make a difference as to the outcome of this case if the contract for building the yacht had a clause prohibiting the use of Tiger's name or photo without his permission?

2. ESPN held its Action Sports and Music Awards ceremony in April, at which celebrities in the fields of extreme sports and popular music such as rap and heavy metal converged. Well-known musicians Ben Harper and James Hetfield were there, as were popular rappers Busta Rhymes and LL Cool J. Famed motorcycle stuntman Evel Knievel, who is commonly thought of as the "father of extreme sports," and his wife Krystal were photographed. The photograph depicted Evel, who was wearing a motorcycle jacket and rose-tinted sunglasses, with his right arm around Krystal and his left arm around another young woman. ESPN published the photograph on its "extreme sports" Web site with a caption that read "Evel Knievel proves that you're never too old to be a pimp." The Knievels brought suit against ESPN, contending that the photograph and caption were defamatory because they accused Evel of soliciting prostitution and implied that Krystal was a prostitute. ESPN contends that the caption was a figurative and slang usage and was not defamatory as a matter of law. Decide. [*Knievel v ESPN*, 393 F3d 1068 (9th Cir)]

3. While snowboarding down a slope at Mammoth Mountain Ski Area (Mammoth), 17-year-old David Graham was engaged in a snowball fight with his 14-year-old brother. As he was "preparing to throw a snowball" at his

brother, David slammed into Liam Madigan, who was working as a ski school instructor for Mammoth, and injured him. Madigan sued Graham for damages for reckless and dangerous behavior. The defense contended that the claim was barred under the doctrine of assumption of the risk, applicable in the state, arising from the risk inherent in the sport that allows for vigorous participation and frees a participant from a legal duty to act with due care. Decide. [*Mammoth Mountain Ski Area v Graham*, 38 Cal Rptr 3d 422 (Cal App)]

4. Following a visit to her hometown of Coalinga, Cynthia wrote "An Ode to Coalinga" (Ode) and posted it in her online journal on MySpace.com. Her last name did not appear online. Her page included her picture. The Ode opens with "The older I get, the more I realize how much I despise Coalinga" and then proceeds to make a number of extremely negative comments about Coalinga and its inhabitants. Six days later, Cynthia removed the Ode from her journal. At the time, Cynthia was a student at UC Berkeley, and her parents and sister were living in Coalinga. The Coalinga High School principal, Roger Campbell, submitted the Ode to the local newspaper, the *Coalinga Record*, and it was published in the Letters to the Editor section, using Cynthia's full name. The community reacted violently to the Ode, forcing the family to close its business and move. Cynthia and her family sued Campbell and the newpaper on the right-of-privacy theory of public disclosure of private facts. What are the essential element of this theory? Was Cynthia and her family's right of privacy violated? [*Moreno v Hanford Sentinel, Inc.*, 91 Cal Rptr 3d 858 (Cal App)]

5. JoKatherine Page and her 14-year-old son Jason were robbed at their bank's ATM at 9:30 P.M. one evening by a group of four thugs. The thieves took $300, struck Mrs. Page in the face with a gun, and ran. Mrs. Page and her son filed suit against the bank for its failure to provide adequate security. Should the bank be held liable? [*Page v American National Bank & Trust Co.*, 850 SW2d 133 (Tenn)]

6. A Barberton Glass Co. truck was transporting large sheets of glass down the highway. Elliot Schultz was driving his automobile some distance behind the truck. Because of the negligent way that the sheets of glass were fastened in the truck, a large sheet fell off the truck, shattered on hitting the highway, and then bounced up and broke the windshield of Shultz's car. He was not injured but suffered great emotional shock. He sued Barberton to recover damages for this shock. Barberton denied liability on the ground that Schultz had not sustained any physical injury at the time or as the result of the shock. Should he be able to recover? [*Schultz v Barberton Glass Co.*, 447 NE2d 109 (Ohio)]

7. Mallinckrodt produces nuclear and radioactive medical pharmaceuticals and supplies. Maryland Heights Leasing, an adjoining business owner, claimed that low-level radiation emissions from Mallinckrodt damaged its property and caused a loss in earnings. What remedy should Maryland Heights have? What torts are involved here? [*Maryland Heights Leasing, Inc. v Mallinckrodt, Inc.*, 706 SW2d 218 (Mo App)]

8. An owner abandoned his van in an alley in Chicago. In spite of repeated complaints to the police, the van was allowed to remain in the alley. After several months, it was stripped of most of the parts that could be removed. Jamin Ortiz, age 11, was walking down the alley when the van's gas tank exploded. The flames from the explosion set fire to Jamin's clothing, and he was severely burned. Jamin and his family brought suit brought against the city of Chicago to recover damages for his injuries. Could the city be held responsible for injuries caused by property owned by someone else? Why or why not? [*Ortiz v Chicago*, 398 NE2d 1007 (Ill App)]

9. Carrigan, a district manager of Simples Time Recorder Co., was investigating complaints of mismanagement of the company's Jackson office. He called at the home of Hooks, the secretary of that office, who expressed the opinion that part of the trouble was caused by the theft of parts and equipment by McCall, another employee. McCall was later discharged and sued Hooks for slander. Was she liable? [*Hooks v McCall*, 272 So2d 925 (Miss)]

10. Defendant no. 1 parked his truck in the street near the bottom of a ditch on a dark, foggy night. Iron pipes carried in the truck projected nine feet beyond the truck in back. Neither the truck nor the pipes carried any warning light or flag, in violation of both a city ordinance and a state statute. Defendant no. 2 was a taxicab owner whose taxicab was negligently driven at an excessive speed. Defendant no. 2 ran into the pipes, thereby killing the passenger in the taxicab. The plaintiff brought an action for the passenger's death against both defendants. Defendant no. 1 claimed he was not liable because it was Defendant no. 2's negligence that had caused the harm. Was this defense valid? [*Bumbardner v Allison*, 78 SE2d 752 (NC)]

11. Carl Kindrich's father, a member of the Long Beach Yacht Club before he died, expressed a wish to be "buried at sea." The Yacht Club permitted the Kindrich family the use of one of its boats, without charge, for the ceremony, and Mr. Fuller—a good friend of Carl's father—piloted the boat. Portable stairs on the dock assisted the attendees in boarding. Upon returning, Fuller asked for help to tie up the boat. The steps were not there, and Carl broke his leg while disembarking to help tie up the boat. Carl sued the Yacht Club for negligence in failing to have someone on the dock to ensure that the portable steps were available. The Yacht Club contended that it was not liable because Carl made the conscious decision to jump from the moving vessel to the dock, a primary assumption of risk in the sport of boating. The plaintiff contended that he was not involved in the sport of boating, and at most his actions constituted minimal comparative negligence, the type which a jury could weigh in conjunction with the defendant's negligence in assessing damages. Decide. [*Kindrich v Long Beach Yacht Club*, 84 Cal Rptr 3d 824 (Cal App)]

12. Hegyes was driving her car when it was negligently struck by a Unjian Enterprises truck. She was injured, and an implant was placed in her body to counteract the injuries. She sued Unjian, and the case was settled. Two years later Hegyes became pregnant. The growing fetus pressed against the implant,

making it necessary for her doctor to deliver the child 51 days prematurely by Cesarean section. Because of its premature birth, the child had a breathing handicap. Suit was brought against Unjian Enterprises for the harm sustained by the child. Was the defendant liable? [*Hegyes v Unjian Enterprises, Inc.*, 286 Cal Rptr 85 (Cal App)]

13. Kendra Knight took part in a friendly game of touch football. She had played before and was familiar with football. Michael Jewett was on her team. In the course of play, Michael bumped into Kendra and knocked her to the ground. He stepped on her hand, causing injury to a little finger that later required its amputation. She sued Michael for damages. He defended on the ground that she had assumed the risk. Kendra claimed that assumption of risk could not be raised as a defense because the state legislature had adopted the standard of comparative negligence. What happens if contributory negligence applies? What happens if the defense of comparative negligence applies?

14. A passenger on a cruise ship was injured by a rope thrown while the ship was docking. The passenger was sitting on a lounge chair on the third deck when she was struck by the weighted end of a rope thrown by an employee of Port Everglades, where the boat was docking. These ropes, or heaving lines, were being thrown from the dock to the second deck, and the passenger was injured by a line that was thrown too high.

    The trial court granted the cruise line's motion for directed verdict on the ground there was no evidence that the cruise line knew or should have known of the danger. The cruise line contended that it had no notice that this "freak accident" could occur. What is the duty of a cruise ship line to its passengers? Is there liability here? Does it matter that an employee of the port city, not the cruise lines, caused the injury? Should the passenger be able to recover? Why or why not? [*Kalendareva v Discovery Cruise Line Partnership*, 798 So2d 804 (Fla App)]

15. Blaylock was a voluntary psychiatric outpatient treated by Dr. Burglass, who became aware that Blaylock was violence prone. Blaylock told Dr. Burglass that he intended to do serious harm to Wayne Boynton, Jr., and shortly thereafter he killed Wayne. Wayne's parents then sued Dr. Burglass on grounds that he was liable for the death of their son because he failed to give warning or to notify the police of Blaylock's threat and nature. Was a duty breached here? Should Dr. Burglass be held liable? [*Boynton v Burglass*, 590 So2d 446 (Fla App)]

Chapter 10

INTELLECTUAL PROPERTY RIGHTS AND THE INTERNET

I ntellectual property comes in many forms: the writing by an author or the software developed by an employee, the new product or process developed by an inventor, the company name Hewlett-Packard, and the secret formula used to make Coca-Cola. Federal law provides rights to owners of these works, products, company names, and secret formulas that are called *copyrights, patents, trademarks,* and *trade secrets.* State laws provide protection for trade secrets. These basic legal principles are also applicable in an Internet and e-commerce context. This chapter discusses the federal and state laws governing intellectual property rights and their Internet context.

A. TRADEMARKS AND SERVICE MARKS

The Lanham Act, a federal law, grants a producer the exclusive right to register a trademark and prevent competitors from using that mark. This law helps assure a producer that it, not an imitating competitor, will reap the financial, reputation-related rewards of a desirable product. And trademarks reduce consumers' search costs, allowing them to make decisions that more closely coincide with their preferences.

1. Introduction

A mark is any word, name, symbol, device, or combination of these used to identify a product or service.[1] If the mark identifies a product, such as an automobile or soap, it is called a **trademark**. If it identifies a service, such as an airline or dry cleaner, it is called a **service mark**.

trademark–mark that identifies a product.

service mark–mark that identifies a service.

The owner of a mark may obtain protection from others using it by registering the mark in accordance with federal law at the Patent and Trademark Office (PTO) in Washington, D.C.[2] To be registered, a mark must distinguish the goods or services of the applicant from those of others. Under the federal Lanham Act, a register, called the Principal Register, is maintained for recording such marks. Inclusion on the Principal Register grants the registrant the exclusive right to use the mark. Challenges may be made to the registrant's right within five years of registration, but after five years, the right of the registrant is incontestable.

A mark may be "reserved" before starting a business by filing an application for registration on the basis of the applicant's good-faith intent to use the mark. Once the mark is used in trade, then the PTO will actually issue the registration with a priority date retroactive to the date the application was filed. The applicant has a maximum period of 36 months to get the business started and demonstrate that the mark is in "use in commerce."

---

[1] 15 USC § 1127.
[2] Lanham Act, 15 USC §§ 1050–1127.

2. International Registration

Under the Madrid System of International Registration of Marks (the Madrid Protocol), the United States became a party to a treaty providing for the international registration of marks in November 2003. Now U.S. companies that sell products and provide services in foreign countries may register their marks and obtain protection for them in more than 60 signatory countries by filing a single application in English for each mark with the U.S. Patent and Trademark Office.[3] Before the mark can be the subject of an international application, it must have already been registered or applied for with the U.S. Patent and Trademark Office (PTO). A change in ownership of a mark can be accomplished by a single filing. Renewal is required every 10 years by paying a single renewal fee.

3. Registrable Marks

distinctiveness—capable of serving the source-identifying function of a mark

Trademark law categorizes marks along a spectrum of **distinctiveness**, based on their capacity to serve a source-identifying function. A mark is classified as (1) coined or fanciful (most distinctive), (2) arbitrary, (3) suggestive, (4) descriptive, and (5) generic (least distinctive). **For Example,** the mark EXXON is fanciful because it was designed by its owner to designate petroleum and related products. The name KODAK is a coined creation of the owner of this trademark and has no other meaning in English, but it serves to distinguish the goods of its owner from all others. The mark APPLE for computers, an arbitrary mark, consists of a word in common usage that is arbitrarily applied in such a way that it is not descriptive or suggestive. The mark COPPERTONE for suntan lotion is a suggestive mark—requiring some imagination to reach a conclusion about the nature of the product. Coined or fanciful, arbitrary, and suggestive marks may be registered on the Principal Register under the Lanham Act without producing any actual evidence of the source-identifying attribution or the public perception of these marks.

acquired distinctiveness—through advertising, use and association, over time, an ordinary descriptive word or phase has taken on a new source-identifying meaning and functions as a mark in the eyes of the public

Descriptive marks are those that convey an immediate idea of the ingredients, qualities, or characteristics of the goods or service, such as SPORTS ILLU-STRATED for a sports magazine. Because descriptive marks are not inherently capable of serving as source identifiers, such marks may only be registered on the Principal Register after the owner has provided sufficient evidence to establish that the public associates the term or phrase not only with a specific feature or quality, but also with a single commercial source. When a descriptive phrase becomes associated with a single commercial source, the phrase is said to possess "**acquired distinctiveness**" or "**secondary meaning,**" and therefore functions as a trademark. **For Example,** when the public perceives the phrase SPORTS ILLUSTRATED as a particular sports magazine in addition to its primary meaning as a description of a specific feature or element, the phrase has "acquired distinctiveness" or "secondary meaning" and may receive trademark protection.

secondary meaning—is a legal term signifying the words in question have taken on a new meaning with the public, capable of serving a source-identifying function of a mark

Generic terms that describe a "genus" or class of goods such as soap, car, cola, or rosé wine are never registrable because they do not have a capacity to serve as a source identifier.

---

[3] Signatory countries include most U.S. trading partners with the exception of Canada and Mexico.

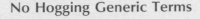

CASE SUMMARY

No Hogging Generic Terms

FACTS: Beginning in the late 1960s and thereafter, the word *hog* was used by motorcycle enthusiasts to refer to large motorcycles. Into the early 1980s, motorcyclists came to use the word *hog* when referring to Harley-Davidson (Harley) motorcycles. In 1981, Harley itself began using *hog* in connection with its merchandise. In 1983, it formed Harley Owners Group, used the acronym H.O.G., and registered the acronym in conjunction with various logos in 1987.

Since 1909, Harley has used variations of its bar-and-shield logo. Ronald Grottanelli opened a motorcycle repair shop under the name The Hog Farm in 1969. At some point after 1981, he sold products such as Hog Wash engine degreaser and a Hog Trivia board game. Grottanelli had used variants of Harley's bar-and-shield logo since 1979 on signs and T-shirts, dropping the name Harley-Davidson from the bar of the logo in 1982 after receiving a letter of protest from the company. He continued to use the bar-and shield, however, and featured a drawing of a pig wearing sunglasses and a banner with the words "Unauthorized Dealer." From a judgment for Harley for infringement of the bar-and-shield trademark and an injunction prohibiting the use of the word *hog* in reference to some of his products and services, Grottanelli appealed.

DECISION: *Hog* was a generic word in the language as applied to large motorcycles before segments of the public began using it to refer to Harley-Davidson motorcycles. Neither a manufacturer nor the public can withdraw from the language a generic term, already applicable to a category of products, and accord it trademark significance as long as the term retains some generic meaning. It was an error to prohibit Grottanelli from using the word *hog*. Harley must rely on a portion of its trademark to identify the brand of motorcycles, for example, Harley Hogs. Grottanelli was properly enjoined from using the bar-and-shield logo. Grottanelli's mark uses Harley's mark in a somewhat humorous manner to promote his own products, which is not a permitted trademark parody use. The use of the prefix "UN" before "AUTHORIZED DEALER" is no defense. The courts have ordinarily found the use of such disclaimers insufficient to avoid liability for infringement. [**Harley-Davidson v Grottanelli, 164 F3d 806 (2d Cir 1999)**]

Ordinarily geographic terms are not registrable on the Principal Register. **For Example,** BOSTON BEER was denied trademark protection because it was a geographic term.[4] However if a geographic term has acquired a secondary meaning, it would be registrable. **For Example,** the geographic term *Philadelphia* has acquired secondary meaning when applied to cream cheese products.

A personal name can acquire trademark protection if the name has acquired secondary meaning. **For Example,** the name "Paul Frank" is a personal name and as a trademark had acquired significant recognition and fame in the sale of t-shirts, clothing, and accessories designed by Paul Frank Sunich. Mr. Sunich had a falling out with Paul Frank Industries Inc. (PFI), and started his own t-shirt business using his own personal name, Paul Frank Sunich. The court rejected Mr. Sunich's contention that he had a right to use his full name as a trademark, because it was likely to cause consumer confusion with the established famous mark, and the court preliminarily enjoined him from using his "Paul Frank Sunich" mark with the sale of clothing or accessories. It did, however, permit him to use his full name, Paul Frank Sunich, in signatures, business meetings, and other such contexts where the name did not resemble a trademark or trade name, and did not appear on goods

---

[4] *Boston Beer Co. v Slesar Bros. Brewing Co.,* 9 F3d 812 (1st Cir 1994).

similar to those sold by PFI. Where Mr. Sunich's full name was used, there also had to be some clear explanation that Mr. Sunich was no longer affiliated with PFI. For example, his use of the Web site domain name ***www.paulfranksunich.com*** was not enjoined so long as it maintained a message explaining that Mr. Sunich no longer worked for or with PFI.[5]

With a limited number of colors available for use by competitors, along with possible shade confusion, courts had held for some 90 years that color alone could not function as a trademark. The U.S. Supreme Court has overturned this rule, and now if a color serves as a symbol that distinguishes a firm's goods and identifies their source without serving any other significant function, it may, sometimes at least, meet the basic legal requirements for use as a trademark.[6] **For Example,** Owens-Corning Fiberglass Corp. has been allowed to register the color pink as a trademark for its fiberglass insulation products.

4. Remedies for Improper Use of Marks

A person who has the right to use a mark may obtain an injunction prohibiting a competitor from imitating or duplicating the mark. The basic question in such litigation is whether the general public is likely to be confused by the mark of the defendant and to believe wrongly that it identifies the plaintiff's mark.[7] If there is this danger of confusion, the court will enjoin the defendant from using the particular mark.

In some cases, the fact that the products of the plaintiff and the defendant did not compete in the same market was held to entitle the defendant to use a mark that would have been prohibited as confusingly similar if the defendant manufactured the same product as the plaintiff. **For Example,** it has been held that Cadillac, as applied to boats, is not confusingly similar to Cadillac as applied to automobiles; therefore, its use cannot be enjoined.[8]

In addition to broad injunctive relief, the prevailing party may recover lost profits and other actual damages. In cases of willful violations, the court has full discretion to award the plaintiff up to treble damages. In "exceptional cases" the court has discretion to award attorney's fees.

C A S E   S U M M A R Y

But ... What's Wrong with Diverting Traffic?

FACTS: In 1996, Venture Tape Corporation, a manufacturer of specialty adhesive tapes and foils used in the stained-glass industry, procured two federal trademark registrations for products called "Venture Tape" and "Venture Foil," respectively. Over the next 15 years, Venture expended hundreds of thousands of dollars to promote the two marks in both print and Internet advertising.

[5] *Paul Frank Industries Inc. v Paul Sunich*, 502 F Supp 2d 1094 (CD Cal 2007).
[6] *Qualitex Co. v Jacobson Products Co., Inc.*, 514 US 159 (1995).
[7] *Resource Lenders, Inc. v Source Solutions, Inc.*, 404 F Supp 2d 1232 (ED Cal 2005).
[8] *General Motors Corp. v Cadillac Marine and Boat Co.*, 140 USPQ (BNA) 447 (1964). See also *Amstar Corp. v Domino's Pizza Inc.*, 615 F2d 252 (5th Cir 1980), where the mark Domino as applied to pizza was not held to be confusingly similar to Domino as applied to sugar.

Continued

Consequently, its products gained considerable popularity, prestige, and goodwill in the worldwide stained-glass market.

Through its Internet Web site, McGills Glass Warehouse also sells adhesive tapes and foils that directly compete with "Venture Tape" and "Venture Foil." Beginning in 2000, and without obtaining Venture's permission or paying it any compensation, McGills owner Donald Gallagher intentionally "embedded" the Venture marks in the McGills Web site, both by including the marks on the Web site's metatags—a component of a Web page's programming containing descriptive information about the Web page that is typically not observed when the Web page is displayed in a Web browser—and in white lettering on a white background screen, similarly invisible to persons viewing the Web page. Gallagher admittedly took these actions because he had heard that Venture's marks would attract people using Internet search engines to the McGills Web site, people who might buy McGills products. Upon discovery, Venture sued McGills for trademark infringement. McGills contends that it had no way of knowing whether the Venture marks had lured any Internet consumers to the Web site, and so there was no proven confusion of source, and thus no liability. And it asserts that Gallagher was unaware that the use of the marks was illegal.

DECISION: Judgment for Venture Tape Corp. Venture proved that (1) it owns the marks in question, (2) McGills used the same marks without permission, and (3) McGills' use of the Venture marks likely confused Internet customers, thereby causing Venture lost sales. Venture was awarded an equitable share of the defendant's profits, some $230,339.17, as a rough measure of the likely harm incurred, along with attorney's fees of $188,583.06 and $7,564.75 in costs. [**Venture Tape Corp. v McGills Glass Warehouse, 540 F3d 56 (1ˢᵗ Cir 2008)**]

5. Abandonment of Exclusive Right to Mark

An owner who has an exclusive right to use a mark may lose that right. If other persons are permitted to use that mark, it loses its exclusive character and is said to pass into the English language and become generic. Examples of formerly enforceable marks that have made this transition into the general language are *aspirin, thermos, cellophane,* and *shredded wheat.* Nonuse for three consecutive years is prima facie evidence of abandonment.[9]

6. Trade Dress Protection

Firms invest significant resources to develop and promote the appearance of their products and the packages in which these products are sold so that they are clearly recognizable by consumers.

trade dress–product's total image including its overall packaging look.

Trade dress involves a product's total image and, in the case of consumer goods, includes the overall packaging look in which each product is sold.

When a competitor adopts a confusingly similar trade dress, it dilutes the first user's investment and goodwill and deceives consumers, hindering their ability

[9] *Doeblers' Pennsylvania Hybrids, Inc. v Doebler,* 442 F3d 812 (3rd Cir 2006).

to distinguish between competing brands. The law of trade dress protection was initially settled by the U.S. Supreme Court in 1992,[10] and courts have subsequently become more receptive to claims of trade dress infringement under Section 43(a) of the Lanham Act. To prevail, a plaintiff must prove that its trade dress is distinctive and nonfunctional and the defendant's trade dress is confusingly similar to the plaintiff's.[11] Thus a competitor who copied the Marlboro cigarettes package for its Gunsmoke brand of cigarettes was found to have infringed on the trade dress of the Marlboro brand.[12] Trade dress protection under the Lanham Act is the same as that provided a qualified unregistered trademark and does not provide all the protection available to the holder of a registered trademark.

7. Limited Lanham Act Protection of Product Design

Trade dress originally included only the packaging and "dressing" of a product, but in recent years, federal courts of appeals' decisions have expanded trade dress to encompass the design of a product itself. Some manufacturers have been successful in asserting Section 43(a) Lanham Act protection against "knockoffs"—that is, copies of their furniture designs, sweater designs, and handbag designs. In this context Samara Brothers, Inc., discovered that Wal-Mart Stores, Inc., had contacted a supplier to manufacture children's outfits based on photographs of Samara garments, and Wal-Mart was selling these so-called knockoffs. Samara sued Wal-Mart, claiming infringement of unregistered trade dress under Section 43(a) of the Lanham Act. The matter progressed to the U.S. Supreme Court, which considered whether a product's design can be distinctive and, therefore, protectable under Section 43(a) of the Lanham Act. The Court set aside the trial court's decision in favor of Samara Brothers and concluded that a product's design is not inherently distinctive and can only meet the "distinctiveness" element required in a Section 43(a) case by a showing of secondary meaning. That is, the manufacturer must show that the design has come to be known by the public as identifying the product in question and its origin. The matter was remanded for further proceeding consistent with the Court's decision.[13]

It is clear from the Supreme Court's *Wal-Mart Stores, Inc. v Samara Bros, Inc.* decision that ordinarily only famous designers whose works are widely recognized by the public by their design alone, such as certain Tommy Hilfiger and Ralph Lauren garments, Dooney & Bourke handbags, and Movado watches, will be able to successfully pursue Section 43(a) trade dress protection for their designs against knockoff versions of their work sold under Wal-Mart or other private labels. Of course if a manufacturer's design is copied along with the manufacturer's labels or logo, the makers and sellers of these counterfeit goods are always in clear violation of the Lanham Act. As discussed later, design patents also have limited applicability and protect new and nonobvious ornamental features of a product.

---

[10] *Two Pesos, Inc. v Taco Cabana, Inc.*, 505 US 763 (1992).
[11] *Clicks Billiards v Sixshooters, Inc.*, 251 F3d 1252 (9th Cir 2001); and *Woodsland Furniture, LLC v Larsen*, 124 P3d, 1016 (Idaho 2005).
[12] *Philip Morris, Inc. v Star Tobacco Corp.*, 879 F Supp 379 (SDNY 1995).
[13] *Wal-Mart Stores, Inc. v Samara Bros, Inc.*, 529 US 205 (2000).

8. Prevention of Dilution of Famous Marks

The Federal Trademark Dilution Act of 1995 (FTDA)[14] provides a cause of action against the "commercial use" of another's famous mark or trade name when it results in a "dilution of the distinctive quality of the mark." The act protects against discordant uses, such as Du Pont shoes, Buick aspirin, and Kodak pianos. Unlike an ordinary trademark infringement action, a dilution action applies in the absence of competition and likelihood of confusion. The act was amended in 2005 to provide that a plaintiff need not prove actual injury to the economic value of the famous mark to prevail in the lawsuit. In addition, the revised act permits truthful comparative advertising and a "fair use" defense for parodying a famous mark.[15]

9. Internet Domain Names and Trademark Rights

An *Internet domain name* is a unique address by which an Internet resource can be identified and found by a Web browser accessing the Internet. Examples of commercial Internet domain names are "Amazon.com," "Priceline.com," and the publisher of this book, "Cengage.com." These domain names match the names of their respective businesses, and these domain names are also trademarks.

Any unused domain name can be registered on a first-come, first-served basis for a rather modest fee, so long as the name differs from a previously registered name by at least one character. With such quick and inexpensive registration and with the addition of new registrars and new global suffixes such as ".biz" (small businesses), ".info" (resources), ".name" (individuals), and ".pro" (professionals) to relieve ".com" (commerce) overcrowding, there exists an ever-increasing chance of intentional and unintentional trademark infringement.

cybersquatters—term for those who register and set up domain names on the Internet for resale to the famous users of the names in question.

(A) CYBERSQUATTERS. **Cybersquatters** are individuals who register and set up domain names on the Internet that are identical, or confusingly similar, to existing trademarks that belong to others or are the personal names of famous persons. The cybersquatter hopes to sell or "ransom" the domain name to the trademark owner or the famous individual.

Because the extent of the legal remedies available to famous companies or famous individuals who have been victims of cybersquatters has not always been certain, Congress passed the Federal Anticybersquatting Consumer Protection Act (ACPA)[16] in 1999 to prohibit the practice of cybersquatting and cyberpiracy and to provide clear and certain remedies. However, to be successful in a ACPA lawsuit, the plaintiff must prove that the name is famous and that the domain name was registered in bad faith.[17] Remedies include (1) injunctive relief preventing the use of the name, (2) forfeiture of the domain name, and (3) attorney fees and costs. In addition, trademark owners may obtain damages and the profits that cybersquatters made from the use of the name.

---

[14] 15 USC § 125(c)(1).
[15] Trademark Dilution Revision Act (2005).
[16] Pub L 106, 113 Stat 1536, 15 USC § 1051.
[17] A plaintiff must meet the burden of proof, however that its mark is "famous," in order to come within the protection of the ACPA, with the courts requiring the marks be highly distinctive and thus well known throughout the country. Among the marks courts have ruled not to be distinctive are "Blue Man Group," the performing group; "Clue," the board game; and "Trek," for bicycles. In contrast, marks that have been ruled famous include "Nike," "Pepsi," and "Victoria's Secret." See *Philbrick v eNom Inc.*, 593 F Supp 2d 352, 367 (D NH 2009).

A safe harbor exists under the ACPA for defendants who both "believed and had reasonable grounds to believe that the use of the domain name was fair use or otherwise lawful."[18] A defendant who acts even partially in bad faith in registering a domain name is not entitled to the shelter of the safe harbor provision. **For Example,** Howard Goldberg, the president of Artco, is an operator of Web sites that sell women's lingerie and other merchandise. He registered a domain name **http://www. victoriassecrets.net** to divert consumers to his Web sites to try to sell them his goods. The court rejected his ACPA safe harbor defense that he intended in good faith to have customers compare his company's products with those of Victoria's Secret. The fact that Victoria's Secret is a distinctive or famous mark deserving of the highest degree of trademark protection, coupled with the fact that the defendant added a mere *s* to that mark and gave false contact information when he requested the domain name, indicates that he and his company acted in bad faith and intended to profit from the famous mark.[19]

(B) Dispute Avoidance. To avoid the expense of trademark litigation, it is prudent to determine whether the Internet domain name selected for your new business is an existing registered trademark or an existing domain name owned by another. Commercial firms provide comprehensive trademark searches for less than $500.

e-commerce&cyberlaw

Metatags describe the contents of a Web site using keywords. Some search engines search metatags to identify Web sites related to a search. In *Playboy Enterprises, Inc. (PEI) v WELLES,** PEI sued "Playmate of the year 1981" Terri Welles for using that and other phrases involving PEI's trademarks on her Internet Web site metatags. Some search engines that use their own summaries of Web sites, or that search the entire text of sites, would be likely to identify Welles's site as relevant to a search for "Playboy" or "Playmate," thus allowing Welles to trade on PEI's marks, PEI asserted. Remembering that the purpose of a trademark is not to provide a windfall monopoly to the mark owner but to prevent confusion over the source of products or services, the court applied a three-factor test for normative use to this case: (1) the product or service

must be one not readily identifiable without the use of the mark, (2) only so much of the mark may be used as reasonably necessary to identify the product or service, and (3) the user must not suggest sponsorship or endorsement by the trademark holder.

Welles had no practical way of describing herself without using the trademark terms. The court stated, "We can hardly expect someone searching for Welles's site… to describe Welles without referring to Playboy—as the nude model selected by Mr. Hefner's organization."

The court stated that there is no descriptive substitute for the trademarks used in Welles's metatags, and to preclude their use would inhibit the free flow of information on the Internet, which is not a goal of trademark law. Moreover, the metatag use was reasonable use to identify her products and services and did not suggest sponsorship, thus satisfying the second and third elements of the court's test.

* *Playboy Enterprises, Inc. v Welles*, 279 F3d 796 (9th Cir 2002). See *ESS Entertainment 2000, Inc. v Rockstar Videos Inc.*, 2008 US App, LEXIS 23294 (9th Cir).

---

[18] 15 USC § 1125(d)(1)(B)(ii).
[19] *Victoria's Secret Stores v Artco*, 194 F Supp 2d 204 (SD Ohio 2002).

Determining whether a domain name is owned by another may be done online at **www.internic.net/whois.html**.

The Internet Corporation for Assigned Names and Numbers (ICANN) provides fast-track arbitration procedures to protect trademark owners from conflicting online domain names under the auspices of the World Intellectual Property Organization (WIPO). **For Example,** Victoria's Secret stores arbitrated the "victoriassecrets.net" domain name held by Howard Goldberg's company, and the arbitration panel transferred the ownership of the name to Victoria's Secret stores. Victoria's Secret stores subsequently brought an action against Goldberg and Artco for damages and injunctive relief under trademark law and the ACPA.

B. COPYRIGHTS

copyright—exclusive right given by federal statute to the creator of a literary or an artistic work to use, reproduce, and display the work.

A **copyright** is the exclusive right given by federal statute to the creator of a literary or an artistic work to use, reproduce, and display the work. Under the international treaty called the *Berne Convention*, copyright of the works of all U.S. authors is protected automatically in all Berne Convention nations that have agreed under the treaty to treat nationals of other member countries like their own nationals.

A copyright prevents not the copying of an idea but only the copying of the way the idea is expressed.[20] That is, the copyright is violated when there is a duplication of the words, pictures, or other form of expression of the creator but not when there is just use of the idea those words, pictures, or other formats express.

The Copyright Act does not apply extraterritorially. However, if the infringement is completed in the United States and the copied work is then disseminated overseas, there is liability under the act for the resulting extraterritorial damages. **For Example,** the Los Angeles News Service (LANS), an independent news organization, produced two copyrighted videotapes of the beating of Reginald Denny during the Los Angeles riots of April 1992, and LANS licensed them to NBC for use on the *Today Show* in New York. Visnews taped the works and transmitted them by satellite to Reuters in London, which provided copies to its overseas subscribers. The infringement by Visnews occurred in New York, and Visnews was liable for the extraterritorial damages that resulted from the overseas dissemination of the work.[21]

It is a violation of U.S. copyright law for satellite carriers to capture signals of network stations in the United States and transmit them abroad. **For Example,** PrimeTime's satellite retransmission of copyrighted NFL football games to satellite dish owners in Canada was held to be a violation of U.S. copyright law, notwithstanding testimony of PrimeTime's CEO that a law firm in Washington, D.C., told him that U.S. law did not pertain to the distribution of products in Canada. The NFL was awarded $2,557,500 in statutory damages.[22]

---

[20] *Attia v New York Hospital*, 201 F3d 50 (2d Cir 2000).
[21] *Los Angeles News Service v Reuters*, 149 F3d 987 (9th Cir 1998).
[22] *National Football League v PrimeTime 24 Joint Venture*, 131 F Supp 2d 458 (SDNY 2001).

10. Duration of Copyright

Article 1, Section 8, of the U.S. Constitution empowered Congress to

> *promote the Progress of Science and useful Arts, by securing for limited times to Authors and Inventors the exclusive Right to their respective Writings and Discoveries.*

The first U.S. copyright statute was enacted soon after in 1790 and provided protection for any "book, map or chart" for 14 years, with a privilege to renew for an additional 14 years. In 1831, the initial 14-year term was extended to 28 years, with a privilege for an additional 14 years. Under the 1909 Copyright Act, the protection period was for 28 years, with a right of renewal for an additional 28 years.

The Copyright Act of 1976 set the duration of a copyright at the life of the creator of the work plus 50 years. Under the Sonny Bono Copyright Term Extension Act of 1998, the duration has been extended to the life of the creator plus 70 years.[23] If a work is a "work made for hire"—that is, a business pays an individual to create the work—the business employing the creator registers the copyright. Under the 1998 Extension Act, such a copyright has been extended by 20 years and now runs for 120 years from creation or 95 years from publication of the work, whichever period is shorter. After a copyright has expired, the work is in the public domain and may be used by anyone without cost.[24]

11. Copyright Notice

Prior to March 1, 1989, the author of an original work secured a copyright by placing a copyright notice on the work, consisting of the word *copyright* or the symbol©, the year of first publication, and the name or pseudonym of the author. The author was also required to register the copyright with the Copyright Office. Under the Berne Convention Implementation Act of 1988,[25] a law that adjusts U.S. copyright law to conform to the Berne Convention, it is no longer mandatory that works published after March 1, 1989, contain a notice of copyright. However, placing a notice of copyright on published works is strongly recommended. This notice prevents an infringer from claiming innocent infringement of the work, which would reduce the amount of damages owed. To bring a copyright infringement suit for a work of U.S. origin, the owner must have submitted two copies of the work to the Copyright Office in Washington, D.C., for registration.

12. What is Copyrightable?

Copyrights protect literary, musical, dramatic, and artistic work. Protected are books and periodicals; musical and dramatic compositions; choreographic works; maps; works of art, such as paintings, sculptures, and photographs; motion pictures and other audiovisual works; sound recordings; architectural works; and computer programs.

[23] PL 105-298, 112 Stat 2827, 17 USC § 302(b).
[24] Without the Sonny Bono Extension Act of 1998, the copyright on Mickey Mouse, created by Walt Disney Co. in 1928, was set to expire in 2003 and enter the public domain. Pluto, Goofy, and Donald Duck would have followed soon after.
[25] PL 100-568, 102 Stat 2854, 17 USC § 101 et seq.

The work must be original, independently created by the author, and possess at least some minimal degree of creativity.[26] **For Example,** William Darden, a Web page designer, challenged the Copyright Office's denial of a copyright registration for a series of existing maps with some changes in the nature of shading, coloring, or font. A court found that the Copyright Office acted within its discretion when it denied Darden's registration with the finding by the examiner from the Visual Arts Section that the maps were "representations of the preexisting census maps in which the creative spark is utterly lacking or so trivial as to be virtually nonexistent."[27]

13. Copyright Ownership and the Internet

Businesses today commonly use offsite programming services to create copyrightable software, with the delivery of code over the Internet. As set forth previously, when a business pays an employee to create a copyrightable work, it is a "work for hire" and the business employing the creator owns and may register the copyright. On the other hand, if a freelancer is employed offsite to create software for a fixed fee without a contract setting forth the ownership of the work, the freelancer owns the work product and the company utilizing the freelancer has a license to use the work product but does not have ownership of it. To avoid disputes about ownership of custom software, a written contract that addresses these ownership and license questions is necessary.

14. Rights of Copyright Holders

A copyright holder has the exclusive right to (1) reproduce the work; (2) prepare derivative works, such as a script from the original work; (3) distribute copies of recordings of the work; (4) publicly perform the work, in the case of plays and motion pictures; and (5) publicly display the work, in the case of paintings, sculptures, and photographs.

The copyright owner may assign or license some of the rights listed and will receive royalty payments as part of the agreement. The copyright law also ensures royalty payments. **For Example,** Jessie Riviera is a songwriter whose songs are sung at public performances and are recorded by performers on records, tapes, and CDs. Jessie is entitled to royalties from the public performance of her works. Such royalties are collected by two performing rights societies, the American Society of Composers, Authors, and Publishers (ASCAP) and Broadcast Music, Inc. (BMI), who act on behalf of the copyright holders. Jessie is also entitled to so-called mechanical royalties that refer to the royalty stream derived from "mechanically" reproduced records, tapes, and CDs.[28] The principal payers of mechanical royalties are record companies, and the rates are set by the Copyright Royalty Tribunal.

In addition to rights under the copyright law and international treaties, federal and state laws prohibit record and tape piracy.

---

[26] *Feist Publications Inc. v Rural Telephone Services Co.*, 499 US 340 (1991).
[27] *Darden v Peters*, 402 F Supp 2d 638 (ED NC 2005).
[28] The ASCAP was formed in 1914 by eminent American composers including Victor Herbert and John Philip Sousa. BMI was formed in 1939. Public performance royalties collected by these societies exceed $1.5 billion per year and are distributed according to elaborate formulas.

15. Limitation on Exclusive Character of Copyright

A limitation on the exclusive rights of copyright owners exists under the principle of *fair use*, which allows limited use of copyrighted material in connection with criticism, news reporting, teaching, and research. Four important factors to consider when judging whether the use made in a particular case is fair use include the following:

1. The purpose and character of the use, including whether such use is of a commercial nature or is for nonprofit educational purposes[29]

2. The nature of the copyrighted work

3. The amount and substantiality of the portion used in relation to the copyrighted work as a whole

4. The effect of the use on the potential market for or value of the copyrighted work[30]

CASE SUMMARY

Fair Use or Not Fair Use—That is the Question

FACTS: The American Geophysical Union and 82 other publishers of scientific and technical journals brought a class-action lawsuit against Texaco, claiming that Texaco's unauthorized photocopying of articles from their journals constituted a copyright infringement. Texaco's defense was that the copying was fair use under Section 107 of the Copyright Act of 1976. To avoid extensive discovery, the parties agreed to focus on one randomly selected Texaco scientist, Dr Donald Chickering, who had photocopies of eight articles from the *Journal of Catalysis* in his files. The trial court judge held that the copying of the eight articles did not constitute fair use, and Texaco appealed.

DECISION: Judgment for the publishers. Applying the four statutory standards to determine whether Texaco's photocopying of the scientific journal articles was fair use, three of the four factors favor the publishers. The first factor, purpose and character of use, favors the publishers because the purpose of Texaco's use was to multiply the number of copies for the benefit of its scientists, which is the same purpose for which additional subscriptions are normally sold. The second factor, the nature of the copyrighted work, which in this case is scientific articles, favors Texaco. The third factor, the amount and substantiality of the portion used, favors the publishers because Texaco copied the entire works. The fourth factor, effect on the potential market or value of the work, favors the publishers because they have shown substantial harm due to lost licensing revenue and lost subscription revenue. The aggregate assessment is that the photocopying was not fair use. [**American Geophysical Union v Texaco Inc., 60 F3d 913 (2d Cir 1995)**]

---

[29] In *Princeton University Press v Michigan Document Services, Inc.*, 99 F3d 1381 (6th Cir 1996), a commercial copyshop reproduced "coursepacks" and sold them to students attending the University of Michigan. The court refused to consider the "use" as one for nonprofit educational purposes because the use challenged was that of the copyshop, a for-profit corporation that had decided to duplicate copyrighted material for sale to maximize its profits and give itself a competitive edge over other copyshops by declining to pay the royalties requested by the holders of the copyrights.

[30] See fair use analysis in *Perfect 10 v Amazon.com,Inc.*, 487 F3d 701, 719 – 725 (9th Cir 2007).

First Amendment privileges of freedom of speech and the press are preserved through the doctrine of *fair use*, which allows for use of portions of another's copyrighted work for matters such as comment and criticism. Parodies and caricatures are the most penetrating forms of criticism and are protected under the fair use doctrine. Moreover, while injunctive relief is appropriate in the vast majority of copyright infringement cases because the infringements are simply piracy, in the case of parodies and caricatures where there are reasonable contentions of fair use, preliminary injunctions to prevent publication are inappropriate. The copyright owner can be adequately protected by an award of damages should infringement be found. **For Example,** Suntrust Bank, the trustee of a trust that holds the copyright to Margaret Mitchell's *Gone with the Wind*, one of the all-time best-selling books in the world, obtained a preliminary injunction preventing Houghton Mifflin Co. from publishing Alice Randall's *The Wind Done Gone*. The Randall book is an irreverent parody that turns old ideas upside down. The Court of Appeals set aside the injunction of the federal district court because Houghton Mifflin had a viable fair use defense.[31]

16. Secondary Liability for Infringement

An entity that distributes a device with the object of promoting its use to infringe copyrights as shown by clear expression or other active steps taken to foster the resulting acts of infringement is liable for these acts of infringement by third parties,

---

ethics & the law

The Death of Journalism?

Washington Post columnist Ian Shapira wrote a column entitled "How Gawker Ripped off My Newspaper Story"*. He had written a profile on Washington based "business coach" Anne Loehr, an expert on how people in their 20s and late teens behave in the workplace. He conducted an extensive phone interview with Loehr, attended one of her "Get Wise with Gen Ys" sessions and spent an additional day writing the story. Shapira is provided a living wage, health care, and retirement benefits by The Post. Gawker's eight paragraph posting condensed Loehr's biography with a link to Shapira's story, and

utilized Loehr's own words on various points of interest, followed by a "cut and paste" of Shapira's "stuff". It ended with the hyperlinked words "Washington Post."

The newspaper industry is in financial peril. Is there a line that can be drawn between the "fair use" doctrine allowing appropriate quoting and linking, and "parasitic" free-rider Web sites? Shapira asserts that current law allows "the Gawker's of the world to appropriate others' work, repurpose it and sell ads against it with no payment to or legal recourse for the company that [paid the originator of the story]." Should the copyright law be amended to require those who sell ads against heavily excerpted articles to pay a fee to the originator? Is this payment the ethical thing to do?

* **http://www.washingtonpost.com/wp-dyn/content/ article/2009/07/31/...**

---

[31] *Suntrust Bank v Houghton Mifflin Co.*, 268 F3d 1257 (11th Cir 2001).

regardless of the device's lawful uses. **For Example,** Grokster, Ltd., and StreamCast Networks, Inc., distributed free software products that allow all computer users to share electronic files through peer-to-peer networks, so called because users' computers communicate directly with each other, not through central servers. When these firms distributed their free software, each clearly voiced the objective that the recipients use the software to download copyrighted works. These firms derived profits from selling advertising space and streaming ads to the software users. Liability for infringement was established under the secondary liability doctrines of contributory or vicarious infringement.[32]

17. Digital Millennium Copyright Act

The Digital Millennium Copyright Act of 1998 (DMCA)[33] was enacted to curb the pirating of software and other copyrighted works, such as books, films, videos, and recordings, by creating civil and criminal penalties for anyone who circumvents encryption software. The law also prohibits the manufacture, import, sale, or distribution of circumvention devices.

Title II of the DMCA provides a "safe harbor" for Internet Service Providers (ISP) from liability for direct, vicarious, and contributory infringement of copyrights provided the ISP (1) does not have actual knowledge of the infringing activity or expeditiously removed access to the problematic material upon obtaining knowledge of infringing activity, (2) does not receive financial benefit directly attributable to the infringing activity, and (3) responded expeditiously upon notification of the claimed infringement.

C. PATENTS

Under Article 1, Section 8, of the U.S. Constitution, the founding fathers of our country empowered Congress to promote the progress of science by securing for limited times to inventors the exclusive rights to their discoveries. Federal patent laws established under Article 1, Section 8, protect inventors just as authors are protected under copyright law authorized by the same section of the U.S. Constitution.

18. Types, Duration, and Notice

There are three types of patents, the rights to which may be obtained by proper filing with the Patent and Trademark Office (PTO) in Washington, D.C. The types and duration of patents are as follows.

(A) UTILITY PATENTS. Inventions classified as *utility* or *functional patents* grant inventors of any new and useful process, machine, manufacture, or composition of matter or any new and useful improvement of such devices the right to obtain a patent.[34] Prior to 1995, utility patents had a life of 17 years from the date of grant. Under the Uruguay Round Trade Agreement Act, effective June 8, 1995, the

---

[32] *Metro-Goldwyn-Mayer Studios, Inc. v Grokster, Ltd.*, 545 US 913 (2005).
[33] 17 USC § 1201.
[34] 35 USC § 101.

duration of U.S. utility patents was changed from 17 years from the date of grant to 20 years from the date of filing to be consistent with the patent law of World Trade Organization (WTO) member states.

(B) DESIGN PATENTS. A second kind of patent exists under U.S. patent law that protects new and nonobvious ornamental features that appear in connection with an article of manufacture.[35] These patents are called *design patents* and have a duration of 14 years. In order to establish design patent infringement, the patent holder has the difficult task of proving, by a preponderance of the evidence, that an ordinary observer (and not the eye of an expert) taking into account the prior art would believe the accused design to be the same as the patented design.[36] **For Example,** the Court of Appeals for the Federal Circuit (CAFC) held that defendant Swisa's Nail Buffer, which features buffer surfaces on all four of its sides, was not "the same as" and thus did not infringe on Egyptian Goddess, Inc.'s patented nail buffer design, which features buffer surfaces on three of its four sides.[37]

(C) PLANT PATENTS. A third type of patent, called a *plant patent*, protects the inventors of asexually reproduced new varieties of plants. The duration is 20 years from the date of filing, the same duration applied to utility patents.

(D) NOTICE. The owner of a patent is required to mark the patented item or device using the word *patent* and must list the patent number on the device to recover damages from an infringer of the patent.

19. Patentability

Section 101 of the 1952 Patent Act recognizes four categories of subject matter for patent eligibility: (1) processes, (2) machines, (3) manufactures, and (4) compositions of matter. However, even if a claim may be deemed to fit one of these categories, it may not be patent eligible. Phenomena of nature, though just discovered; mental processes; and abstract intellectual concepts are not patentable because they are the basic tools of scientific and technological work.[38]

Once it is established that an invention is patent eligible, a patent may be obtained if the invention is something that is *new and not obvious* to a person of ordinary skill and knowledge in the art or technology to which the invention is related. Whether an invention is new and not obvious in its field may lead to highly technical proceedings before a patent examiner, the PTO's Board of Patent Appeals, and the U.S. Court of Appeals for the Federal Circuit (CAFC). **For Example,** Thomas Devel's application for a patent on complementary DNA (cDNA) molecules encoding proteins that stimulated cell division was rejected by a patent examiner as "obvious" and the rejection was affirmed by the PTO's Board of Patent Appeals. However, after a full hearing before the CAFC, which focused on the state of research in the field as applied to the patent application, Devel's patent claims were determined to be "not invalid because of obviousness."[39]

[35] 35 USC § 173.
[36] *Gorham v White*, 81 US 511 (1871).
[37] *Egyptian Goddess, Inc. v SWISA, Inc.*, 545 F3d 665 (Fed Cir 2008).
[38] *Gottschalk v. Benson*, 409 US 63, 67 (1972).
[39] *In re Devel*, 51 F3d 1552 (Fed Cir 1995).

Once approved by the Patent and Trademark Office, a patent is presumed valid. However, a defendant in a patent infringement lawsuit may assert a patent's invalidity as a defense to an infringement claim by showing the invention as a whole would have been obvious to a person of ordinary skill in the art when the invention was patented. This showing is called **prior art**. **For Example,** Ron Rogers invented and patented a tree-trimming device that is essentially a chain saw releasably mounted on the end of a telescoping pole. Rogers sued Desa International, Inc. (DIA) for patent infringement after DIA introduced the Remington Pole Saw, a chain saw releasably mounted on the end of a telescoping pole. DIA provided evidence of prior art, citing four preexisting patents dealing with "trimming tools on extension poles" that correlated with Rogers's patent. The court nullified Rogers's patent because it concluded the DIA had met its heavy burden of proof that releasably mounting a lightweight chain saw on the end of a telescoping pole assembly to trim trees would be obvious to a person of ordinary skill in the art.[40]

prior art–a showing that an invention as a whole would have been obvious to a person of ordinary skill in the art when the invention was patented

Patent law has expanded to include human-made microorganisms as patent-eligible subject matter, since such compositions are not nature's handiwork, but the inventor's own work.

CASE SUMMARY

Crude Life Forms Can Be Patented

FACTS: Chakrabarty was a microbiologist. He found a way of creating a bacterium that would break down crude oil. This could not be done by any bacteria that exist naturally. His discovery had a great potential for cleaning up oil spills. When he applied for a patent for this process, the commissioner of patents refused to grant it because what he had done was not a "manufacture" or "composition of matter" within the meaning of the federal statute and because a patent could not be obtained on something that was living. Chakrabarty appealed.

DECISION: Judgment for Chakrabarty. Discovering a way to produce a living organism that is not found in nature is within the protection of the patent laws. The fact that this kind of invention was not known when the patent laws were first adopted has no effect on the decision. The patent laws are to be interpreted according to the facts existing when an application for a patent is made. [**Diamond v Chakrabarty, 447 US 303 (1980)**]

20. Patentable Business Methods

A 1998 Court of Appeals for the Federal Circuit (CAFC) decision recognized "business methods" as a patent-eligible "process" under Section 101 of the Patent Act.[41] A burgeoning number of business-method patents followed, with the U.S.

---

[40] *Rogers v Desa International, Inc.,* 166 F Supp 2d 1202 (ED Mich 2001). See *KRS International Co. v Teleflex, Inc.,* 127 S Ct 1727, 1731 (2007) for the Supreme Court's recent "obviousness" patent decision, where the Court held that mounting an available sensor on a fixed pivot point of the prior art pedal was a design step well within the grasp of a person of ordinary skill in the relevant art and that the benefit of doing so would be obvious.

[41] *State Street Bank v Signature Financial Group* 149 F3d 1368 (Fed Cir 1998).

Supreme Court referencing in its *eBay v MercExchange* decision the "potential vagueness and suspect validity of some of these patents." A pure business-method patent consists basically of a series of steps related to performing a business process. **For Example,** Patent No. 6,846,131 sets forth a method of doing business with steps for Producing Revenue from Gypsum-Based Refuse Sites. So-called junk patents have also been issued as business-method patents. **For Example,** Patent No. 4,022,227, Method of Concealing Baldness, contains a series of steps for combing one's hair that amount to what is best known as a *comb-over*. Business methods are often in the form of software programs and encompass e-commerce applications.

Recent decisions of the Federal Circuit Court of Appeals contain a much more restrictive approach to evaluating the patentability of business methods under Section 101 of the Patent Act. **For Example,** Bernard Bilski's "business method" of hedging risk in the field of commodities trading was found not to be patent eligible because it was neither "tied to a machine or apparatus," nor did it transform anything.[42]

CASE SUMMARY

The *Bilski* Bolt: A More Restrictive Approach to Business-Method Patents

FACTS: Lewis Ferguson and other applicants filed for a business-method patent that read, in part,

A method of marketing a product comprising:

Developing a shared marketing force, said shared marketing force including at least marketing channels, which enable marketing a number of related products;

Using said shared marketing force to market a plurality of different products that are made by a plurality of different autonomous producing companies, so that different autonomous companies, having different ownerships, respectively produce said related products;

Obtaining a share of total profits from each of said plurality of different autonomous producing companies in return for said using; and

Obtaining an exclusive right to market of said plurality of products in return for said using.

The applicants also sought a business-method patent for marketing software for multiple software companies. The applicants contended that the claims fell within one of the four categories of statutory subject matter—processes—and were thus patentable. The Board of Patent Appeals concluded that a "marketing company" cannot be considered a process, a machine, a manufacture, or a composition of matter under Section 101 of the act. The applicants appealed the matter to the CAFC.

DECISION: Judgment against Ferguson and the other applicants. In the *Bilski* decision, the court phrased the machine-or-transformation test as follows:

A claimed process is surely patent eligible under §101 if: (1) it is tied to a particular machine or apparatus, or (2) it transforms a particular article into a different state or thing.

---

[42] *In re Bilski,* 545 F3d 943 (Fed Cir 2008) *(en banc).*

C A S E   S U M M A R Y

Continued

The applicants' method claims are not tied to any particular machine or apparatus. Although the applicants argue that the method claims are tied to the use of a shared marketing force, a marketing force is not a machine or apparatus, nor do the claims transform a particular article into a different state or thing. As the court stated in *Bilski,* "[p]urported transformations or manipulations simply of public or private legal obligations or relationships, business risks, or other such abstractions cannot meet the test because they are not physical objects or substances, and they are not representative of physical objects or substances." **[In re Ferguson, 558 F3d 1359 (Fed Cir 2009)]**

Believing that many business-method patents are obvious to persons of ordinary skill in their respective fields and have a chilling effect on consumer and public interests, a number of organizations have filed multiple reexamination requests with the PTO to invalidate these patents.[43]

21. Infringement

The patent owner has the exclusive right to make, use, or sell the invention. The owner may bring suit for patent infringement for unauthorized use of a patent and obtain appropriate monetary damages and injunctive relief. The Patent Act provides for the enhancement of damages upon proof of willful infringement and the award of reasonable attorney's fees in "exceptional cases."[44]

Under the act, the owner has "the right to exclude others from making, using, offering for sale or selling the invention."[45] In *eBay, Inc. v MercExchange, LLC,* the U.S. Supreme Court dealt with the question of whether the patent holder had the right to obtain the permanent injunctive relief of stopping a business entity from "using" the patented technology in addition to obtaining damages for the patent violation. The threat of a court order may be used to seek high and often unreasonable licensing fees. Major technology companies contended that trial courts should consider multiple factors in deciding whether to issue a permanent injunction.

C A S E   S U M M A R Y

"Squeeze Play" Averted

FACTS: eBay and its subsidiary half.com operate popular Internet Web sites that allow private sellers to list goods they wish to sell at either an auction or a fixed price (its "Buy It Now" feature). MercExchange, LLC, sought to license its business-method patent to eBay, but no agreement was reached. In MercExchange's subsequent patent infringement suit, a jury found that its patent

---

[43] See Electronic Frontier Foundation, Patent Busting Project at **www.eff.org/patent/wanted** (April 2009).
[44] *See In re Seagate Technology, LLC,* 497 F3d 1360 (Fed. Cir. 2007), where the CAFC set a higher "willfulness" standard, requiring at least a showing of objective recklessness on the part of the infringer.
[45] 35 USC § 154(a)(1).

C A S E   S U M M A R Y

Continued

was valid, eBay had infringed the patent, and $29.5 million in damages were appropriate. However, the District Court denied MercExchange's motion for permanent injunctions against patent infringement absent exceptional circumstances. MercExchange appealed. The Federal Circuit Court of Appeals reversed, and the U.S. Supreme Court granted *certiorari*.

DECISION: Judgment against MercExchange's position. The traditional four-factor test of equity applied by courts when considering whether to award permanent injunctive relief to a prevailing plaintiff applies to disputes arising under the Patent Act. That test requires a plaintiff to demonstrate that (1) it has suffered an irreparable injury, (2) remedies available at law are inadequate to compensate for that injury, (3) considering the balance of hardships between the plaintiff and defendant, a remedy in equity is warranted, and (4) the public interest would not be disserved by a permanent injunction. The decision to grant or deny such relief is an act of equitable discretion by the district court, reviewable on appeal for abuse of discretion. The Federal Circuit's ruling was vacated and remanded to the district court to apply the four-factor test. [A concurring opinion written by Justice Kennedy and joined by Justices Stevens, Souter, and Breyer stated that "an industry has developed in which firms use patents not as a basis for producing and selling goods but, instead, primarily for obtaining licensing fees. For these firms, an injunction, and the potentially serious sanctions arising from its violation, can be employed as a bargaining tool to charge exorbitant fees to companies that seek to buy licenses to practice the patent." Such may be considered under the four-factor test.] [**eBay, Inc. v MercExchange, LLC, 547 US 388 (2006)**]

Under the Supreme Court's "doctrine of equivalents," infringers may not avoid liability for patent infringement by substituting insubstantial differences for some of the elements of the patented product or process. The test for infringement requires an essential inquiry: Does the accused product or process contain elements identical or equivalent to each claimed element of the patented invention?[46]

D. SECRET BUSINESS INFORMATION

A business may have developed information that is not generally known but that cannot be protected under federal law, or a business may want to avoid the disclosure required to obtain a patent or copyright protection of computer software. As long as such information is kept secret, it will be protected under state law relating to trade secrets.[47]

22. Trade Secrets

trade secret—any formula, device, or compilation of information that is used in one's business and is of such a nature that it provides an advantage over competitors who do not have the information.

A **trade secret** may consist of any formula, device, or compilation of information that is used in one's business and is of such a nature that it provides an advantage

---

[46] *Warner-Jenkinson v Hilton Davis Chemical Co.*, 520 US 17 (1997). But see *Festo Corp. v Shoketsu*, 493 F3d 1368 (Fed Cir 2007).

[47] The Uniform Trade Secrets Act was officially amended in 1985. It is now in force in Alabama, Alaska, Arizona, Arkansas, California, Colorado, Connecticut, Delaware, Florida, Georgia, Hawaii, Idaho, Illinois, Indiana, Iowa, Kansas, Kentucky, Louisiana, Maine, Minnesota, Mississippi, Montana, Nebraska, Nevada, New Hampshire, New Mexico, North Dakota, Ohio, Oklahoma, Oregon, Rhode Island, South Carolina, South Dakota, Utah, Vermont, Virginia, Washington, West Virginia, and Wisconsin. Trade secrets are protected in all states either under the uniform act or common law and under both criminal and civil statutes.

over competitors who do not have the information. It may be a formula for a chemical compound; a process of manufacturing, treating, or preserving materials; or, to a limited extent, certain confidential customer lists.[48]

Courts will not protect customer lists if customer identities are readily ascertainable from industry or public sources or if products or services are sold to a wide group of purchasers based on their individual needs.[49]

23. Loss of Protection

When secret business information is made public, it loses the protection it had while secret. This loss of protection occurs when the information is made known without any restrictions. In contrast, there is no loss of protection when secret information is shared or communicated for a special purpose and the person receiving the information knows that it is not to be made known to others.

When a product or process is unprotected by a patent or a copyright and is sold in significant numbers to the public, whose members are free to resell to whomever they choose, competitors are free to reverse engineer (start with the known product and work backward to discover the process) or copy the article. **For Example,** Crosby Yacht Co., a boatbuilder on Cape Cod, developed a hull design that is not patented. Maine Boatbuilders, Inc. (MBI), purchased one of Crosby's boats and copied the hull by creating a mold from the boat it purchased. MBI is free to build and sell boats utilizing the copied hull.

24. Defensive Measures

Employers seek to avoid the expense of trade secret litigation by limiting disclosure of trade secrets to employees with a "need to know." Employers also have employees sign nondisclosure agreements, and they conduct exit interviews when employees with confidential information leave, reminding the employees of the employer's intent to enforce the nondisclosure agreement. In addition, employers have adopted industrial security plans to protect their unique knowledge from "outsiders," who may engage in theft, trespass, wiretapping, or other forms of commercial espionage.

25. Criminal Sanctions

Under the federal Industrial Espionage Act of 1996,[50] knowingly stealing, soliciting, or obtaining trade secrets by copying, downloading, or uploading via electronic means or otherwise with the intention that it will benefit a foreign government or agent is a crime. This act also applies to the stealing or purchasing of trade secrets by U.S. companies or individuals who intend to convert trade secrets to the economic benefit of anyone other than the owner. The definition of trade secret is closely modeled on the Uniform Trade Secrets Act and includes all forms and types of financial, business, scientific, technical, economic, and engineering information. The law requires the owner to have taken "reasonable and proper" measures to keep

---

[48] Restatement (Second) of Torts § 757 cmt b. See *Home Pride Foods, Inc. v Johnson*, 634 NW2d 774 (Neb 2001).
[49] *Xpert Automation Systems Corp. v Vibromatic Co.*, 569 NE2d 351 (Ind App 1990).
[50] PL 104–294, 18 USC § 1831 et seq. (1996).

the information secret. Offenders are subject to fines of up to $500,000 or twice the value of the proprietary information involved, whichever is greater, and imprisonment for up to 15 years.

Corporations may be fined up to $10,000,000 or twice the value of the secret involved, whichever is greater. In addition, the offender's property is subject to forfeiture to the U.S. government, and import-export sanctions may be imposed.

E. PROTECTION OF COMPUTER SOFTWARE AND MASK WORKS

Computer programs, chip designs, and mask works are protected from infringement with varying degrees of success by federal statutes, restrictive licensing, and trade secrecy.

CPA **26. Copyright Protection of Computer Programs**

Under the Computer Software Copyright Act of 1980,[51] a written program is given the same protection as any other copyrighted material regardless of whether the program is written in source code (ordinary language) or object code (machine language). **For Example,** Franklin Computer Corp. copied certain operating-system computer programs that had been copyrighted by Apple Computer, Inc. When Apple sued Franklin for copyright infringement, Franklin argued that the object code on which its programs had relied was an uncopyrightable "method of operation." The Third Circuit held that computer programs, whether in source code or in object code embedded on ROM chips, are protected under the act.[52]

In determining whether there is a copyright violation under the Computer Software Copyright Act, courts will examine the two programs in question to compare their structure, flow, sequence, and organization. Moreover, the courts in their infringement analysis look to see whether the most *significant* steps of the program are similar rather than whether most of the program's steps are similar. To illustrate a copyright violation, substantial similarity in the structure of two computer programs for dental laboratory record-keeping was found—even though the programs were dissimilar in a number of respects—because five particularly important subroutines within both programs performed almost identically."[53]

The protection afforded software by the copyright law is not entirely satisfactory to software developers because of the distinction made by the copyright law of protecting expressions but not ideas. Also, Section 102(b) of the 1980 Computer Software Copyright Act does not provide protection for "methods of operation." A court has allowed a competitor to copy the identical menu tree of a copyrighted spreadsheet program because it was a noncopyrightable method of operation.[54]

[51] Act of December 12, 1980, PL 96–517, 94 Stat 3015, 17 USC §§ 101, 117.
[52] *Apple Computer Inc. v Franklin Computer Corp.*, 714 F2d 1240 (3d Cir 1983).
[53] *Whelen Associates v Jaslow Dental Laboratory*, 797 F2d 1222 (3d Cir 1986).
[54] *Lotus Development Corp. v Borland International Inc.*, 49 F3d 807 (1st Cir 1995), aff'd, 516 US 233 (1996).

As set forth previously, the Digital Millennium Copyright Act of 1998 was enacted to curb the pirating of a wide range of works, including software.

CPA   ## 27. Patent Protection of Programs

Patents have been granted for computer programs; for example, a method of using a computer to translate from one language to another has been held patentable.

The disadvantage of patenting a program is that the program is placed in the public records and may thus be examined by anyone. This practice poses a potential danger that the program will be copied. To detect patent violators and bring legal action is difficult and costly.[55]

28. Trade Secrets

While primary protection for computer software is found in the Computer Software Copyright Act, industry also uses trade secret law to protect computer programs. When software containing trade secrets is unlawfully appropriated by a former employee, the employee is guilty of trade secret theft.[56]

29. Restrictive Licensing

To retain greater control over proprietary software, it is common for the creator of the software to license its use to others rather than selling it to them. Such licensing agreements typically include restrictions on the use of the software by the licensee and give the licensor greater protection than that provided by copyright law. These restrictions commonly prohibit the licensee from providing, in any manner whatsoever, the software to third persons or subjecting the software to reverse engineering.[57]

30. Semiconductor Chip Protection

mask work–specific form of expression embodied in a chip design, including the stencils used in manufacturing semiconductor chip products.

semiconductor chip product–product placed on a piece of semiconductor material in accordance with a predetermined pattern that is intended to perform electronic circuitry functions.

The Semiconductor Chip Protection Act (SCPA) of 1984[58] created a new form of industrial intellectual property by protecting mask works and the semiconductor chip products in which they are embodied against chip piracy. A **mask work** refers to the specific form of expression embodied in chip design, including the stencils used in manufacturing semiconductor chip products. A **semiconductor chip product** is a product placed on a piece of semiconductor material in accordance with a predetermined pattern that is intended to perform electronic circuitry functions. These chips operate microwave ovens, televisions, computers, robots, x-ray machines, and countless other devices. This definition of semiconductor chip products includes such products as analog chips, logic function chips like microprocessors, and memory chips like RAMS and ROMs.

[55] The PTO has adopted guidelines for the examination of computer-related inventions, 61 CFR §§ 7478–7502.
[56] The National Conference of Commissioners on Uniform State Laws (NCCUSL) has promulgated a new uniform law, the Uniform Computer Information Transactions Act (UCITA), to govern contracts involving the sale, licensing, maintenance, and support of computer software and books in digital form. This uniform act had been identified as Article 2B and was part of the comprehensive revisions to Article 2 of the Uniform Commercial Code. The act is supported by software publishers and opposed by software developers and buyers. The act can be obtained from the NCCUSL at **www.nccusl.org.** Information for and against the UCITA can be found at **www.ucitaonline.com.** The act has been adopted by Maryland and Virginia.
[57] See *Fonar Corp. v Domenick*, 105 F3d 99 (2d Cir 1997).
[58] PL 98-620, 98 Stat 3347, 17 USC § 901.

FIGURE 10-1 | *Summary Comparison of Intellectual Property Rights*

TYPE OF INTELLECTUAL PROPERTY	TRADEMARKS	COPYRIGHTS	PATENTS	TRADE SECRETS
PROTECTION	WORDS, NAMES, SYMBOLS, OR DEVICES USED TO IDENTIFY A PRODUCT OR SERVICE	ORIGINAL CREATIVE WORKS OF AUTHORSHIP, SUCH AS WRITINGS, MOVIES, RECORDS, AND COMPUTER SOFTWARE	UTILITY, DESIGN, AND PLANT PATENTS	ADVANTAGEOUS FORMULAS, DEVICES, OR COMPILATION OF INFORMATION
APPLICABLE STANDARD	IDENTIFIES AND DISTINGUISHES A PRODUCT OR SERVICE	ORIGINAL CREATIVE WORKS IN WRITING OR IN ANOTHER FORMAT	NEW AND NONOBVIOUS, ADVANCED IN THE ART	NOT READILY ASCERTAINABLE, NOT DISCLOSED TO THE PUBLIC
WHERE TO APPLY	PATENT AND TRADEMARK OFFICE	REGISTER OF COPYRIGHTS	PATENT AND TRADEMARK OFFICE	NO PUBLIC REGISTRATION NECESSARY
DURATION	INDEFINITE SO LONG AS IT CONTINUES TO BE USED	LIFE OF AUTHOR PLUS 70 YEARS, OR 95 YEARS FROM PUBLICATION FOR "WORKS FOR HIRE"	UTILITY AND PLANT PATENTS, 20 YEARS FROM DATE OF APPLICATION; DESIGN PATENTS, 14 YEARS	INDEFINITE SO LONG AS SECRET IS NOT DISCLOSED TO PUBLIC

(A) DURATION AND QUALIFICATIONS FOR PROTECTION. The SCPA provides the owner of a mask work fixed in semiconductor chip products the exclusive right for 10 years to reproduce and distribute the products in the United States and to import them into the United States. The protection of the act applies only to those works that, when considered as a whole, are not commonplace, staple, or familiar in the semiconductor industry.

(B) LIMITATION ON EXCLUSIVE RIGHTS. Under the SCPA's reverse engineering exemption, competitors may not only study mask works but may also use the results of that study to design their own semiconductor chip products embodying their own original masks even if the masks are substantially similar (but not substantially identical) so long as their products are the result of substantial study and analysis, not merely the result of plagiarism.

Innocent infringers are not liable for infringements occurring before notice of protection is given them and are liable for reasonable royalties on each unit distributed after notice has been given them. However, continued purchase of infringing semiconductors after notice has been given can result in penalties of up to $250,000.

(c) **REMEDIES.** The SCPA provides that an infringer will be liable for actual damages and will forfeit its profits to the owner. As an alternative, the owner may elect to receive statutory damages of up to $250,000 as determined by a court. The court may also order destruction or other disposition of the products and equipment used to make the products. **For Example,** Altera Corporation manufactures programmable logic devices. It was successful in the lawsuit against its competitor Clear Logic, Inc., which works from a different business model. Altera was successful in its lawsuit against Clear Logic under the SCPA, asserting that Clear Logic had copied the layout design of its registered mask works. It also was successful in its claim that Clear Logic induced breach of software licenses with Altera customers. Damages were assessed at $36 million.[59]

lawflix

The Jerk (1979) (R)

Steve Martin invents a special handle for eyeglasses that is mass marketed by a businessman who gives him a percentage of the royalties from sales. Should Martin be paid?

You can view a clip of this movie and others that illustrate business law concepts at the LawFlix site, located at **www.cengage.com/blaw/dvl**.

MAKE THE CONNECTION

SUMMARY

Property rights in trademarks, copyrights, and patents are acquired as provided primarily in federal statutes. A trademark or service mark is any word, symbol, design, or combination of these used to identify a product (in the case of a trademark) or a service (in the case of a service mark). Terms will fall into one of four categories: (1) generic, (2) descriptive, (3) suggestive, or (4) arbitrary or fanciful. Generic terms are never registrable. However, if a descriptive term has acquired a secondary meaning, it is registrable. Suggestive and arbitrary or fanciful marks are registrable as well. If there is likelihood of confusion, a court will enjoin the second user from using a particular mark.

A copyright is the exclusive right given by federal statute to the creator of a literary or an artistic work to use, reproduce, or display the work for the life of the creator and 70 years after the creator's death.

[59] *Altera Corp. v Clear Logic Inc.,* 424 F3d 1079 (9th Cir 2005).

A patent gives the inventor an exclusive right for 20 years from the date of application to make, use, and sell an invention that is new and useful but not obvious to those in the business to which the invention is related. Trade secrets that give an owner an advantage over competitors are protected under state law for an unlimited period so long as they are not made public.

Protection of computer programs and the design of computer chips and mask works is commonly obtained, subject to certain limitations, by complying with federal statutes, by using the law of trade secrets, and by requiring restrictive licensing agreements. Many software developers pursue all of these means to protect their proprietary interests in their programs.

LEARNING OUTCOMES

After studying this chapter, you should be able to clearly explain:

A. TRADEMARKS AND SERVICE MARKS

LO.1 Explain the spectrum of distinctiveness used to classify trademarks and explain why distinctiveness is important

See the Kodak example, a coined most distinctive mark, p. 213.

See the Sports Illustrated example, a descriptive mark with acquired distinctiveness.

See the *Harley Davidson* case where H.O.G. was found to be generic and not distinctive at all.

LO.2 Explain how personal names can acquire trademark protection

See the Paul Frank example on p. 214.

LO.3 List the remedies available for improper use of trademarks

See the remedies applied in the *Venture Tape* case, injunctive relief, lost profits, and attorney's fees.

B. COPYRIGHTS

LO.4 Explain what is and is not copyrightable; explain the fair use defense

See the discussion on what is copyrightable on p. 221.

See the Darden example of a denial of a copyright because of lack of creativity, p. 222.

See the *Wind Done Gone* example of fair use parody.

C. PATENTS

LO.5 Explain the "new and not obvious" requirement necessary to obtain a patent

See the cDNA "not obvious" example on p. 226.

See the mounted chain saw "obvious" example on p. 226.

D. SECRET BUSINESS INFORMATION

LO.6 List and explain the defensive measures employers take to preserve confidential business information

See the discussion on signing and enforcing nondisclosure agreements on p. 231.

E. PROTECTION OF COMPUTER SOFTWARE AND MASK WORKS

LO.7 Explain the extent of protection provided owners of software

See the *Apple Computer* example on p. 232.

KEY TERMS

acquired distinctiveness
copyright
cybersquatters
distinctiveness
mask work

prior art
secondary meaning
semiconductor chip
  product
service mark

trade dress
trade secret
trademark

QUESTIONS AND CASE PROBLEMS

1. China is a signatory country to the Madrid Protocol on the international registration of trademarks. Starbucks opened its first café in China in 1999 and has added outlets in numerous locations including Shanghai and at the Great Wall and the imperial palace in Beijing. Xingbake Café Corp. Ltd. has imitated the designs of Starbuck's cafés in its business coffee café locations in Shanghai. *Xing* (pronounced "Shing") means star, and *bake*, or "bak kuh" is pronounced like "bucks." Does the Seattle, Washington, Starbucks Corporation have standing to bring suit in China against Xingbake Café Corp. Ltd? If so, on what theory? Decide. (*Boston Globe*, January 3, 2006, 1)

2. Cable News Network with its principal place of business in Atlanta, Georgia, is the owner of the trademark CNN in connection with providing news and information services to people worldwide through cable and satellite television networks, Web sites, and news services. Its services are also available worldwide on the Internet at the domain name CNN.com. Maya Online Broadband Network (Maya HK) is a Chinese company. It registered the domain name CNNEWS. com with Network Solutions, Inc. The CNNews.com Web site was designed to provide news and information to Chinese-speaking individuals worldwide, making significant use of the terms *CNNews* and *CNNews.com* as brand names and logos that the Atlanta company contends resembles its logos. Maya HK has admitted that CNNews in fact stands for China Network News abbreviated as CNN. The Atlanta company had notified Maya HK of its legal right to the CNN mark before the Chinese company registered the CNNews.com domain name. Does the federal Anticybersquatting Consumer Protection Act apply to this case? If so, does a "safe harbor" exist under the ACPA for Maya HK in that most people who access its Web site in China have never heard of CNN? Decide. [*Cable News Network v CNN News.com*, 177 F Supp 2d 506 (ED Va)]

3. Banion manufacturers semiconductor chips. He wants to obtain protection for his mask works under federal law, particularly so that competitors will be prohibited from reverse engineering these works. Advise Banion of his legal options, if any, to accomplish his objective.

4. Jim and Eric work for Audio Visual Services (AVS) at Cramer University in Casper, Wyoming. For "expenses" of $5, Jim and Eric used AVS facilities after hours to burn discs of Pearl Jam's CD *Vitology* for 25 friends or friends of friends from school. When Mrs. Mullen, who is in charge of AVS, discovered this and confronted them, Jim, a classics major, defended their actions, telling

her, "It's *de minimis*... I mean, who cares?" Explain to Jim and Eric the legal and ethical ramifications of their actions.

5. Sullivan sold t-shirts with the name *Boston Marathon* and the year of the race imprinted on them. The Boston Athletic Association (BAA) sponsors and administers the Boston Marathon and has used the name *Boston Marathon* since 1917. The BAA registered the name *Boston Marathon* on the Principal Register. In 1986, the BAA entered into an exclusive license with Image, Inc., to use its service mark on shirts and other apparel. Thereafter, when Sullivan continued to sell shirts imprinted with the name *Boston Marathon*, the BAA sought an injunction. Sullivan's defense was that the general public was not being misled into thinking that his shirts were officially sponsored by the BAA. Without this confusion of source, he contended, no injunction should be issued. Decide. [*Boston Athletic Ass'n v Sullivan*, 867 F2d 22 (1st Cir)]

6. The University of Georgia Athletic Association (UGAA) brought suit against beer wholesaler Bill Laite for marketing Battlin' Bulldog Beer. The UGAA claimed that the cans infringed its symbol for its athletic teams. The symbol, which depicted an English Bulldog wearing a sweater with a G and the word BULLDOGS on it, had been registered as a service mark. Soon after the beer appeared on the market, the university received telephone calls from friends of the university who were concerned that Battlin' Bulldog Beer was not the sort of product that should in any way be related to the University of Georgia. The university's suit was based on the theory of false designation of origin in violation of the Lanham Act. Laite contended that there was no likelihood of confusion because his bulldog was different from the university's and his cans bore the disclaimer "Not associated with the University of Georgia." Decide. [*University of Georgia Athletic Ass'n v Laite*, 756 F2d 1535 (11th Cir)]

7. Twentieth Century Fox (Fox) owned and distributed the successful motion picture *The Commitments*. The film tells the story of a group of young Irish men and women who form a soul music band. In the film, the leader of the band, Jimmy, tries to teach the band members what it takes to be successful soul music performers. Toward that end, Jimmy shows the band members a videotape of James Brown's energetic performance of the song "Please, Please, Please." This performance came from Brown's appearance in 1965 on a television program called the *TAMI Show*. Portions of the 1965 performance are shown in *The Commitments* in seven separate "cuts" for a total of 27 seconds. Sometimes the cuts are in the background of a scene, and sometimes they occupy the entire screen. Brown's name is not mentioned at all during these relatively brief cuts. His name is mentioned only once later in the film, when Jimmy urges the band members to abandon their current musical interests and tune in to the great soul performers, including James Brown: "Listen, from now on I don't want you listening to Guns & Roses and The Soup Dragons. I want you on a strict diet of soul. James Brown for the growls, Otis Redding for the moans, Smokey Robinson for the whines, and Aretha for the whole lot put together." Would it be fair use under U.S. copyright law for Fox to use just 27 seconds of James Brown cuts in the film without formally

obtaining permission to use the cuts? Advise Fox as to what, if anything, would be necessary to protect it from a lawsuit. [See *Brown v Twentieth Century Fox Film Corp.*, 799 F Supp 166 (DDC)]

8. The Greenwich Bank & Trust Co. (GB&T) opened in 1998 and by 2008 had expanded to a total of four branches in the Greenwich, Connecticut, community of 62,000 residents. A competitor using the name Bank of Greenwich (BOG) opened in December 2006. GB&T's parent entity sued BOG for trademark violation under the Lanham Act. BOG argued that GB&T's service mark is generic and is simply not entitled to Lanham Act protection because it combines the generic term "bank" and the geographic term "Greenwich." GB&T asserted that it had been the only bank in Greenwich using the word *Greenwich* in its name and had done so exclusively for nine years. It asserted that a geographic term is entitled to protection if it acquires secondary meaning. GB&T introduced evidence regarding its advertising expenditures, sales success, and length of exclusivity of use along with evidence of actual consumer confusion. Decide. [*Connecticut Community Bank v The Bank of Greenwich*, 578 F Supp 2d 405 (D Conn)].

9. The menu commands on the Lotus 1-2-3 spreadsheet program enable users to perform accounting functions by using such commands as "Copy," "Print," and "Quit." Borland International, Inc., released its Quattro spreadsheet, a program superior to Lotus 1-2-3 that did, however, use an identical copy of the entire Lotus 1-2-3 menu tree but did not copy any of Lotus's computer code. Lotus believed that its copyright in Lotus 1-2-3 had been violated. Borland insisted that the Lotus menu command was not copyrightable because it is a method of operation foreclosed from protection under Section 102(b) of the Copyright Act of 1976. Decide. [*Lotus Development Corp. v Borland International, Inc.*, 49 F3d 807 (1st Cir), aff'd, 516 US 233 116 S Ct 904]

10. Diehr devised a computerized process for curing rubber that was based on a well-known mathematical formula related to the cure time, and he devised numerous other steps in his synthetic rubber-curing process. The patent examiner determined that because abstract ideas, the laws of nature, and mathematical formulas are not patentable subject matter, the process in this case (based on a known mathematical formula) was also not patentable. Diehr contended that all of the steps in his rubber-curing process were new and not obvious to the art of rubber curing. He contended also that he did not seek an exclusive patent on the mathematical formula, except for its use in the rubber-curing process. Decide. [*Diamond v Diehr*, 450 US 175]

11. Aries Information Systems, Inc., develops and markets computer software specifically designed to meet the financial accounting and reporting requirements of such public bodies as school districts and county governments. One of Aries's principal products is the POBAS III accounting program. Pacific Management Systems Corporation was organized by Scott Dahmer, John Laugan, and Roman Rowan for marketing a financial accounting and budgeting system known as FAMIS. Dahmer, Laugan, and Rowan were Aries employees before, during, and shortly after they organized Pacific.

As employees, they each gained access to Aries's software materials (including the POBAS III system) and had information about Aries's existing and prospective clients. Proprietary notices appeared on every client contract, source code list, and magnetic tape. Dahmer, Laugan, and Rowan signed an Employee Confidential Information Agreement after beginning employment with Aries. While still employees of Aries, they submitted a bid on behalf of Pacific to Rock County and were awarded the contract. Pacific's FAMIS software system is substantially identical to Aries's proprietary POBAS III system. Aries sued Pacific to recover damages for misappropriation of its trade secrets. Pacific's defense was that no "secrets" were misappropriated because many employees knew the information in question. Decide. [*Aries Information Systems, Inc. v Pacific Management Systems Corp.*, 366 NW2d 366 (Minn App)]

12. The plaintiff, Herbert Rosenthal Jewelry Corporation, and the defendant, Kalpakian, manufactured jewelry. The plaintiff obtained a copyright registration of a jeweled pin in the shape of a bee. Kalpakian made a similar pin. Rosenthal sued Kalpakian for infringement of copyright registration. Kalpakian raised the defense that he was only copying the idea, not the way the idea was expressed. Was he liable for infringement of the plaintiff's copyright? [*Herbert Rosenthal Jewelry Corp. v Kalpakian*, 446 F2d 738 (9th Cir)]

13. Mineral Deposits, Ltd. (MD, Ltd.), an Australian company, manufactures the Reichert Spiral, a device used for recovering gold particles from sand and gravel. The spiral was patented in Australia, and MD, Ltd., had applied for a patent in the United States. Theodore Zigan contacted MD, Ltd., stating he was interested in purchasing up to 200 devices for use in his gravel pit. MD, Ltd., agreed to lend Zigan a spiral for testing its efficiency. Zigan made molds of the spiral's components and proceeded to manufacture 170 copies of the device. When MD, Ltd., found out that copies were being made, it demanded the return of the spiral. MD, Ltd., also sought lost profits for the 170 spirals manufactured by Zigan. Recovery was sought on a theory of misappropriation of trade secrets. Zigan offered to pay for the spiral lent him by MD, Ltd. He argued that trade secret protection was lost by the public sale of the spiral. What ethical values are involved? Was Zigan's conduct a violation of trade secret law? [*Mineral Deposits, Ltd. v Zigan*, 773 P2d 609 (Colo App)]

14. Village Voice Media, owners of the famous *Village Voice* newspaper in New York City, sent a letter to *The Cape Cod Voice*, a year-old publication located in Orleans, Massachusetts, objecting to the use of the word *Voice* in the title of its publication. It warned that the Cape Cod publication could cause "confusion as to the source affiliation with the famous Village Voice marks." The publisher of *The Cape Cod Voice* responded that "small places have a right to their own voices." The use of the word *Voice* was thus in dispute between these parties. Would you classify it as generic, descriptive, suggestive, arbitrary, or fanciful? How would you resolve this controversy? [*Cape Cod Times* Business Section, Amy Zipkin, *The New York Times*, October 16, 2004, G-1].

CPA QUESTIONS

1. Multicomp Company wishes to protect software it has developed. It is concerned about others copying this software and taking away some of its profits. Which of the following is true concerning the current state of the law?

   a. Computer software is generally copyrightable.

   b. To receive protection, the software must have a conspicuous copyright notice.

   c. Software in human readable source code is copyrightable but machine language object code is not.

   d. Software can be copyrighted for a period not to exceed 20 years.

2. Which of the following is not correct concerning computer software purchased by Gultch Company from Softtouch Company? Softtouch originally created this software.

   a. Gultch can make backup copies in case of machine failure.

   b. Softtouch can typically copyright its software for at least 75 years.

   c. If the software consists of compiled computer databases, it cannot be copyrighted.

   d. Computer programs are generally copyrightable.

3. Using his computer, Professor Bell makes 15 copies (to distribute to his accounting class) of a database in some software he has purchased for his personal research. The creator of this software is claiming copyright. Which of the following is correct?

   a. This is an infringement of copyright, since he bought the software for personal use.

   b. This is not an infringement of copyright, since databases cannot be copyrighted.

   c. This is not an infringement of copyright because the copies were made using a computer.

   d. This is not an infringement of copyright because of the fair use doctrine.

4. Intellectual property rights included in software may be protected under which of the following?

   a. Patent law

   b. Copyright law

   c. Both of the above

   d. None of the above

Chapter 11

CYBERLAW

A. Introduction to Cyberlaw

1. What is Cyberlaw?

The World Wide Web has enabled businesses to move goods and services through commerce at lightning speed. In many ways, the changes in technology and resulting changes in business practices have occurred at speeds that have not permitted the law to keep pace with them. As a result, this new world of business has caused some distress among managers, law professors, and students as they wonder, "Are there laws that cover this new way of doing business?"

The answer to the question is both yes and no. Although certainly some new laws govern aspects of using and operating systems in the new economy and cyberspace, body of law and precedent—the same body of law and precedent that has seen businesses through many economic and technological revolutions—remains. This same body of law and its characteristics are again a resource for resolving the new economy's legal issues. Examining how the law applies to the new technology provides further evidence of the law's stability, innovation, and flexibility. (See Chapter 1 for more discussion of the characteristics of law.) The rise of the Internet and its pervasive use in business is not the first time the law has had to change to keep pace with technological revolutions. **For Example,** the new clarity of satellite pictures and observation techniques such as thermal scanning have raised new issues concerning searches and the requirements for warrants. The law adjusts and survives through a balancing of the interests at stake as issues arise from the use of new technologies.

Even though the law that is applied to resolve the problems of the new technologies and the new economy is often referred to as **cyberlaw**, you need not fear that you will be required to learn a whole new body of law. There have been and will continue to be changes in the law to accommodate new ways of doing business, but there has also been and will continue to be reliance on the fundamental principles that underlie our laws and the rights they protect. This chapter simply examines the issues and concerns in cyberspace and covers their resolution through a brief overview of new and existing laws. Other chapters provide more details on these rights and protections. This chapter provides a framework for both the challenges of legal issues in **cyberspace** as well as how the law is adjusting to and absorbing the changes business brings through innovation.

cyberlaw–laws and precedent applicable to Internet transactions and communications.

cyberspace–World Wide Web and Internet communication.

tort–civil wrong that interferes with one's property or person.

2. What are the Issues in Cyberlaw?

The legal issues of cyberspace can be broken down into six areas: **tort** issues, contract issues, intellectual property issues, criminal law issues, constitutional restraints and protections, and securities law issues. Within each of these six areas of existing law are a number of new legal issues that have arisen because of the nature of cyberspace and the conduct of business there. That various cyberlaw issues can be grouped into traditional areas of law demonstrates the not-so-new nature of cyberlaw in the new economy. The following sections focus on these six main areas.

B. Tort Issues in Cyberspace

The tort issues in cyberlaw are privacy, appropriation, and defamation.

3. Employer/Employee Privacy Issues in Cyberlaw

E-mail use and Internet surfing for personal reasons in the workplace is a nearly universal practice. A 2007 study found that employees spend about 20 percent of their work day on social use of the Internet, which includes personal e-mails and Web surfing.[1] An earlier survey concluded that 30 percent of employees have used company e-mail systems to send racist, pornographic, sexist, or otherwise discriminatory messages.[2] Blogging has introduced yet another way the Internet is used by employees—often to disclose private and/or negative information about their companies. Tweeting is instant and ongoing communication that could reveal, prematurely, information that the company does not want public. E-mails, Internet surfing, and blogging require a delicate balancing of rights and interests.

(A) EMPLOYERS ARE ACCOUNTABLE FOR EMPLOYEE E-MAIL CONTENT. Employers are held responsible for the content of employee e-mails and employers must have access and control rights as a result. For example, e-mails that contain off-color jokes or suggestive comments create an atmosphere of harassment. (See Chapter 40 for more information on sexual harassment).[3] Employers are also responsible when employees use e-mail or the Internet at work to violate intellectual property rights (see pp. 249 and 253 in this chapter for more discussion on this topic). Employers are also held accountable when employees use e-mails and blogs to defame fellow employees or competitors, vendors, or even customers.

Employee e-mail is spontaneous, candid, and discoverable. As a result, the content of employees' e-mail is often fertile territory for prosecutors who can find evidence of intent in employee e-mails and blogs. For example, in 2008, investigators uncovered e-mails of employees at Standard & Poor's, the investment rating agency, that indicated that while the employee/analysts were rating debt instruments as AAA, they were also having their doubts about them. One employee wrote, "These deals could have been structured by cows and we would still rate them."[4] Another e-mail read, "Rating agencies continue to create [an] even bigger monster—the CDO market. Let's hope we are all wealthy and retired by the time this house of cards falters."[5] These candid e-mails were a foundation for settlements paid by the analysts' firms and resulted in general reforms of the analyst industry.

---

[1] **www.salary.com**, July 2007.

[2] W. Michael Hoffman, Laura P. Hartman, and Mark Rowe, "You've Got Mail . . . And the Boss Knows: A Survey by the Center for Business Ethics of Companies' Email and Internet Monitoring," 108 Business and Society 285 (2003). See also **http://www.elronsoftware.com** for more information on employee use of e-mail.

[3] See *Garrity v John Hancock Mut. Life Ins. Co.*, (D Mass 2002) (memorandum opinion), in which an employer's termination of an employee for sending an e-mail entitled, "The Top Ten Reasons Cookie Dough Is Better Than Men" was upheld on grounds that such content created an atmosphere of harassment.

[4] Summary Report of Issues Identified in the Commission's Examination of Select Credit Rating Agencies, July 8, 2008.

[5] Summary Report of Issues Identified in the Commission's Examination of Select Credit Rating Agencies, July 8, 2008.

In 2005, Marsh & McLennan settled its price-fixing case with New York's attorney general after e-mails showing that employees were concerned about possible antitrust violations emerged. One employee had written, "I am not some Goody Two Shoes who believes that truth is absolute, but I do feel I have a pretty strict ethical code about being truthful and honest. This idea of 'throwing the quote' by quoting artificially high numbers in some predetermined arrangement for us to lose is repugnant to me, not so much because I hate to lose, but because it is basically dishonest. And I basically agree with the comments of others that it comes awfully close to collusion and price-fixing."[6] Marsh settled the case for $850 million.

(B) **TYPES OF EMPLOYER MONITORING: WHAT'S LEGAL.** Because they are held accountable for what employees do in cyberspace, employers use various methods for monitoring employees including using key-stroking software that allows the employer to see those messages employees typed but did not send, using blocking software that limits sites employees can visit, monitoring and searching e-mails, checking blogs for content, and examining items posted on Facebook and YouTube.

There were some efforts in the early days of cyberspace to apply existing law to ensure e-mail privacy. The Electronic Communications Privacy Act of 1986 (ECPA) prohibits the unauthorized access of "live" communications, as when someone uses a listening device to intercept a telephone conversation. However, e-mail is stored information, and the question of this act's application for resolving the privacy issue is doubtful.[7] ECPA also has an exception for consensual interception. The Stored Communication Act (SCA) prohibits the unauthorized interception of electronic communications, generally meaning stored communication, not ongoing communication such as text messaging, tweeting, and instant messaging. However, the courts have held consistently that employees give consent to such monitoring, and there are no statutory violations when employers do live listening, interception, or recovery of sent communication that is stored and available electronically.[8] When employers have informal policies or policies that allow employees to reimburse their employers for private use of text services, the courts have held that monitoring and disclosure of those messages is a violation of the law.

(C) **PRIVACY AND EMPLOYER SCREENING OF APPLICANTS.** If the employer will be doing prehiring monitoring, such as looking at MySpace.com and Facebook—and/or "Googling" the applicant's name—the applicant must be told of this monitoring at the time of the application. The information that we post on publicly available sites is not considered private, so employers, as long as they are maintaining consistent standards for all applicants, can examine what you have posted on the Internet.

Employers are also using Google and other Internet sources to track employee work excuses. One company's human resources official was on the phone with the

[6] Alex Berenson, "Once Again, Spitzer Follows E-Mail Trail," *New York Times*, Oct. 18, 2004, C1, C2.
[7] "Every circuit court to have considered the matter has held that an 'intercept' under the ECPA must occur contemporaneously with transmission." See *Fraser v Nationwide Mut. Ins. Co.*, 352 F3d 107, 113 (3d Cir 2003).
[8] Meir S. Hornung, "Think Before You Type: A Look at E-mail Privacy in the Workplace," 11 *Fordham Journal of Corporate & Financial Law*, 115, 154 (2005).

company employment lawyer seeking to determine what action could be taken against an employee who was absent frequently but who claimed he was absent to care for his ill grandmother. While they were talking, the lawyer "Googled" the employee's name and found that he was being arraigned in federal court.

Schools, employment counselors, and lawyers are offering the following warnings about the dangers of Internet personal postings:[9]

1. Nothing is private on the Internet. People can see everything.

2. Be careful what you blog.

3. Protect your identity when in chat rooms.

4. Assume that everything you write and post will be seen.

5. You can clean up your name on Google using several services, but having no hits at all can lead to suspicions.

6. Think before you write, blog, post, or do anything on the Internet.

(D) PRIVACY TORTS AND EMPLOYERS' RIGHT OF ACCESS TO EMPLOYEE E-MAILS AND INTERNET USE. Because employers are accountable for the content of employee e-mail, it is not a breach of privacy for employers to monitor employee e-mail and Internet usage. Monitoring the content of employee e-mails is important for keeping companies out of legal difficulties. However, employees may believe they have an expectation of privacy in their e-mails, even when those e-mails are sent from work. That belief may spring from the tort standards that protect private lives, communications, and information. The tort of **invasion of privacy**, or intrusion into private affairs, has application to cyberspace communication. Internet disclosure, without permission, of private information is a breach of privacy. Employers generally require employees to sign a document in which they acknowledge that by working at the company and using the company's e-mail and server that they have waived their right to privacy. Former Sun Microsoft Systems CEO, Scott McNealy, summed up employee rights to privacy when it comes to Internet use: "You have zero privacy. Get over it."[10]

> **invasion of privacy**–tort of intentional intrusion into the private affairs of another.

Employers can monitor electronic communications from employees that are marked as private; e-mails that are sent from home and from private computers that use the company server; e-mails that do not involve company business; text messages sent using company phones; and tweets sent over company iPhones, BlackBerries, and other phone communication systems. Even an employee's communications to his or her lawyer are not private if the company has a "no personal use" policy that employees agree to follow.[11]

---

[9] From Michelle Conlin, "You Are What You Post," *Business Week*, March 27, 2006, 52–53. For a discussion of research on blogging, see Rainie, "The State of Blogging," Pew Internet and American Life Project, November 2005; available at **www.pewinternet.org/pdfs/PIP_blogging_data.pdf**, and **www.technorati.com**.

[10] A. Michael Froomkin, "The Death of Privacy," 52 *Stanford Law Review*, 1461, 1462 (2000). Presented at the *Cyberspace and Privacy: A New Legal Paradigm? Symposium*, Stanford, CA, 2000.

[11] *Scott v Beth Israel Med. Ctr.*, 847 NYS2d 436 (2007).

CASE SUMMARY

When You Pay for the Texting, It Belongs to You

FACTS: Jeff Quon, a sergeant and member of the city of Ontario's SWAT team used the city's Arch Wireless system for both professional and personal text messages.

The city had no official policy directly addressing the use of text messaging. However, the city did have a general "Computer Usage, Internet, and E-mail Policy" applicable to all employees. The policy provided that all software, programs, networks, Internet, e-mail, and other systems were to be used only for city of Ontario–related business. The policy also provided, "Users should have no expectation of privacy or confidentiality when using these resources," and indicated that usages were monitored and recorded. Quon attended a meeting during which SWAT team members and others were told that text messages would fall under the city's policy as public information, and be therefore eligible for auditing.

Under the city's contract with Arch Wireless, each pager was allotted 25,000 characters, after which the city was required to pay overage charges. Quon's supervisor told him that he was over by more than 15,000 characters and that he should reimburse the city for the overage charges so that he (the supervisor) would not have to audit the transmission and see how many messages were non–work related. Quon refused to pay and was told to cut down on his transmissions.

When Quon and another officer again exceeded the 25,000-character limit, his supervisor stated that he was "tired of being a bill collector with guys going over the allotted amount of characters on their text pagers." Ontario's chief of police, Chief Scharf, then requested an audit of the text messages.

Because city officials were not able to access the text messages themselves, they requested and obtained the messages from Arch Wireless. The audit of the messages revealed abuse of on-the-clock time through sheer numbers of personal texts and their sexually explicit content. The officers were disciplined and subsequently challenged the discipline by claiming violation of their Fourth Amendment rights. The trial court found that there was a Fourth Amendment violation, but granted Arch Wireless a summary judgment on Quon's claims of invasion of privacy.

DECISION: The wireless provider was an "electronic communication service" (ECS) under SCA, and had violated SCA by releasing archived transcripts to the city. The police employees had the expectation of privacy in the content of their text messages—because the city had an informal policy of not auditing those messages if the employees paid for their usage overage. . The scope of the department's search of text messages was unreasonable and violative of the Fourth Amendment. [**Quon v Arch Wireless Operating Co., Inc., 529 F3d 892 (CA 9 2008)**]

4. Web User Information and Privacy

A second privacy issue in cyberlaw is the use of information that Web sites have gleaned from their users. **For Example,** if you use an airline's Web site to book your travel arrangements, that Web site has a profile of your travel habits. The airline knows how frequently you travel and where you travel. That type of targeted customer information is something other Web sites and retailers are willing to pay dearly for because they know their product is being considered by those most likely to purchase it. If you use Amazon.com to buy books, that Web site has relevant information about the types of books you read, your interests, and even some indications about your income level based on your spending habits.

Even though this issue of privacy may seem new and peculiar to cyberspace, it is, in fact, a rather old issue that has long been a concern of credit card companies.

e-commerce&cyberlaw

Ten Commandments for Avoiding Workplace Exposure

1. Publish policies regarding employee use of e-mail, the Internet, and any employer-issued hardware or software.

2. Have employees sign off on the policy each year.

3. Tell employees that the company will monitor e-mail, Internet use, and any other use of employer-issued computers. Be sure to cover all new technology, such as Palm Pilots, BlackBerries, and two-way text-messaging systems.

4. Create a style guide for writing business e-mails.

5. Train all employees on how to write appropriate business e-mails.

6. Develop a document/e-mail retention policy.

7. Tell employees you will cooperate with law enforcement officials and turn over any evidence of illegal activities.

8. Enforce all policies in an even-handed manner.

9. Keep current on new technology in the marketplace and how it can be used and monitored.

10. Reevaluate all technology-related policies annually.*

* Frank C. Morris, Jr., "The Electronic Platform: Email and Other Privacy Issues in the Workplace," 20 *Computer & Internet Law* (no. 8), 1–20.

These companies' use and sale of information about their customers are restricted. Customers must be given the right to refuse such use of their names and other information for sale as part of lists for target marketing. Some state attorneys general are utilizing these credit card privacy rights to enforce privacy rights against Web site owners who sell information about their users. The Federal Trade Commission (FTC) has begun to take positions that are identical to its stances on other types of commerce issues. **For Example,** if catalog companies are required to provide notice to customers about delays in shipment of goods to customers, Internet companies must comply with the same notification rules.

(A) Freedom of Speech, Screen Names, and Privacy. Another privacy issue that has arisen is whether plaintiffs in suits for defamation can successfully subpoena Internet Service Providers (ISPs) to obtain the identity of individuals who post statements in chat rooms and across the Internet, make defamatory remarks over the Internet, facilitate the downloading of music through their sites, and even allow the sharing of exam information that is proprietary. Music companies' actions against individuals who download music but do not pay for their songs requires the discovery of the identity of those who are doing the downloading. Can the music companies require the ISPs to disclose the names of their customers for purposes of preventing copyright infringement? There are now clear standards for determining disclosure of identity that tend to favor disclosure.[12] Access to ISP identity information is now relatively routine.[13]

[12] *Columbia Pictures, Inc. v Bunnell*, 245 FRD 443 (CD Cal 2007).
[13] See, e.g., *Laface Records, LLC v Atlantic Recording Corp.*, 2007 WL 4286189, (WD Mich Sept. 27, 2007).

C A S E   S U M M A R Y

The Ratfink ISP: Telling Who's Doing the Downloading

FACTS: Sony and others own the copyrights and exclusive licenses to their various sound recordings. Without permission, 40 unidentified individuals (called Does) used "Fast Track," an online media distribution system—or "peer to peer" ("P2P") file-copying network —to download hundreds or thousands of copyrighted sound recordings. Sony was able to identify Cablevision as the Internet service provider (ISP) to which the Does subscribed. Sony did so by using a publicly available database to trace the Internet Protocol (IP) address for each Doe.

As a condition of providing its Internet service, Cablevision requires its subscribers to agree to its "Terms of Service" under which "[t]ransmission or distribution of any material in violation of any applicable law or regulation is prohibited. This includes, without limitation, material protected by copyright, trademark, trade secret or other intellectual property right used without proper authorization."

On January 26, 2004, the court issued an order granting Sony the right to serve a subpoena upon Cablevision to obtain the identity of each Doe by requesting the name, address, telephone number, e-mail address, and Media Access Control address for each defendant.

On February 23, 2004, Cablevision complied with the subpoena and provided relevant identifying information for 36 Does, who filed a motion to quash the subpoena.

DECISION: The court held for Sony, finding that there are five relevant factors when weighing privacy and First Amendment rights with the issue of copyright infringement. These factors include (1) the concrete showing of a prima facie claim of actionable harm, (2) the specificity of the discovery request, (3) the absence of alternative means to obtain the subpoenaed information, (4) a central need for the subpoenaed information to advance the claim, and (5) the party's expectation of privacy. The court found that the infringement was a substantial harm to Sony, that Sony had narrowed its request specifically based on the public information about who was doing the downloading, that the request for identification was specific, that there was no other source for the information and identity and that Sony had done as much as it could to determine the identities, and that the right to privacy was clearly waived by the customer's agreement not to be involved in copyright infringement. [**Sony Music Entertainment Inc. v Does 1–40, 326 F Supp 2d 556 (SDNY 2004)**]

(B) **COOKIES AND PRIVACY.** Technology has permitted companies to plant "cookies" on the computers of those who are using certain Internet sites. With those "cookies" in place, the Web site owner has a way to track the computer owner's activity. At least one court has held that a Web site operator's placing cookies on a user's computer is a violation of an unauthorized access statute that would provide the computer owner a right of action for that breach of the statute and privacy.[14]

(C) **STATUTORY PROTECTIONS FOR PRIVACY IN CYBERSPACE.** Several federal laws and some state laws provide privacy protections, although somewhat limited, for Internet users. The Privacy Act of 1974 controls the use of information gathered about

---

[14] *In re Intuit Privacy Litigation,* 138 F Supp 2d 1272 (CD Cal 2001); see also *In re Toys R Us, Inc., Privacy Litig.,* 2001 WL 34517252 (ND Cal), in which the court reached a different conclusion. However, tapping into sites to gain competitive or proprietary information is a breach of privacy. *Creative Computing v Getloaded.com LLC,* 386 F3d 930 (CA 9 2004).

consumers, but it applies only to government-collected data such as information gathered by the Social Security Administration or the Internal Revenue Service. Furthermore, there are exceptions for the agencies for "routine use."[15] Some segments of the Computer Fraud and Abuse Act (CFAA) and the ECPA provide privacy protection for certain types of communications, such as financial information and its use and transfer.[16] These privacy laws are not general protections but address specific issues. For example, the Children's Online Privacy Protection Act (COPPA) targets online informational privacy but applies only to Web sites that collect information from children.[17]

Numerous state laws on privacy exist; the problem comes in enforcing those laws against Web site sponsors who have no presence in the state. (See the discussion of long-arm jurisdiction over these Internet players in Section 13, "Due Process Issues in Cyberspace.")

5. Appropriation in Cyberspace

appropriation–taking of an image, likeness, or name for commercial advantage.

The tort of **appropriation** involves taking an image, likeness, or name for purposes of commercial advantage. A business cannot use someone's name or likeness for advertising or endorsement without permission. The use of that name or image in cyberspace does not change the nature of the protection that this form of the privacy tort provides. **For Example,** the use of Tiger Woods's name or picture on the website of a yacht company, without his permission, is appropriation, even if Mr. Woods actually owns one of the companys' yachts. a screen saver program that uses a likeness of Richard, the million-dollar winner on the CBS television program *Survivor,* without his permission has violated his privacy rights. The use of his likeness for the Conniver screen saver program with the *Survivor* logo was appropriation. The method of appropriation may be different, but the elements are the same. Appropriation in cyberspace is still the tort of appropriation.

6. Defamation in Cyberspace

defamation–untrue statement by one party about another to a third party.

(A) DEFAMATION AND DAMAGES. The elements of **defamation** remain the same in cyberspace. (See Chapter 9 for more details.) You must show that someone said or wrote something false that portrayed you in a bad light and that the statement, written or oral, was published, heard, or read by others. That the defamation occurs in a chat room does not change the application of tort law. However, the pervasive nature of the Internet could increase the damages for defamation because of the large number of people who obtain the information quickly, and damage can be done rapidly. **For Example,** Mark S. Jakob, a securities trader who had lost $100,000 in August 2000 with poor trades in Emulex, Inc., decided to correct his declining earnings trend by posting a false press release on the Internet that Emulex's earnings were overstated and that its CEO would resign. The fake news release resulted in an overall loss in the value of Emulex stock of $2.5 billion before

---

[15] 5 USC § 552a (2000).
[16] 18 USC § 1030 and 18 USC §§ 2510–2520, 2701 (1997).
[17] 15 USC §§ 6501–6506.

trading was stopped. As a result of this action, Jakob made $240,000 through a short position.[18] The tort of defamation would permit the investors to recover their losses.

(B) **Defamation and Blogging.** By 2009, there were approximately 112.5 million blogs, not including the 72 million in China. While blogs may be personal, there are tort issues that arise when employees begin posting information about their companies or their companies' competitors on their personal blogs. Even when employees discuss what has happened at work, the company can be portrayed in a negative or untruthful way that could be defamatory. For example, an employee discussing disciplinary action at work might present a view of what happened that leaves out information and results in damage to the company.

Because the blogging phenomenon is so new, there is scant case law on the rights of companies against blogging employees. However, there are some situations in which employees have been fired or disciplined because of their postings on their blogs. **For Example,** a Delta flight attendant was suspended and later fired because she had posted a photo on her "Queen of the Sky" blog that showed her in her Delta flight attendant uniform.[19] Delta's reasons for her termination, also known as "doocing," or being fired for blogging, were related to its logo and name being associated with the content of the blog, something over which it had no control. A Starbucks employee who was not permitted to leave work when he was sick was also terminated by the company for his posting of a negative story about his rugged boss.

Concealed identity bloggers can wreak havoc on competitors. John Mackey, the CEO of Whole Foods, using the name Rahodeb (his wife's name, Deborah, jumbled), posted over 1,000 messages in chat rooms that were dedicated to stock trading. During the period that Mr. Mackey was posting messages, Whole Foods stock quadrupled in value. The messages were flattering to Whole Foods and negative about Wild Oats, a competitor. On February 24, 2005, Mackey posted the following comment about Wild Oats CEO Perry Odak: "Perhaps the OATS Board will wake up and dump

ethics & the law

The Blogger Who Kissed and Told on Capitol Hill

Jessica Cutler, a staff member for Senator Mike DeWine, began a blog that detailed her sexual encounters with various government officials in Washington, D.C. Ms. Cutler did not identify anyone by name in her blog, but the level of detail in her posts had most of Washington figuring out who was who in the Cutler blog. Ms. Cutler was fired for "misusing an office computer." What ethical issues

exist in Ms. Cutler's public revelations? Was it legal for the senator to terminate her employment? What advice could you offer employers that would come from this experience? What about defamation if her partners are not identified by name?

Source: April Witt, "Blog Interrupted," *Washington Post,* Apr. 15, 2004, W12.

---

[18] Alex Berenson, "Man Charged in Stock Fraud Based on Fake News," *New York Times,* September 1, 2000, C1, C2.
[19] *Simonetti v Delta Air Lines Inc.,* No. 1: 05-CV-2321, 2005 WL 2407621 (ND Ga 2005).

Odak and bring in a visionary and highly competent CEO [like Mackey]." Referred to as "sock-puppeting," this common practice also raises ethical issues.

C. CONTRACT ISSUES IN CYBERSPACE

7. Formation of Contracts in Cyberspace

contract–binding agreement based upon the genuine assent of the parties, made for a lawful object, between competent parties, in the form required by law, and generally supported by consideration.

Formation of a **contract** in cyberspace is simply the result of the desire for speed and better communication in business. If you wanted to form a contract with a New York seller 20 years ago and you were in Los Angeles, you drafted a proposal and mailed it to the seller. The back-and-forth negotiations took time through the mail. Then overnight delivery service arrived to speed up your cross-country negotiations. Next came faxes and their instantaneous exchanges of terms and negotiations. The amount of paperwork involved in transactions was still unchanged. Paperless contracts were born with the availability of electronic digital interchange (EDI). EDI is simply the electronic exchange of business forms. Contracts are formed using purchase orders and invoices submitted via computer.[20]

With the Internet, e-mail, and the ability to attach documents, cyberspace has provided business yet another method for forming contracts. And while the method is different, the rules for formation have not changed. The same laws that apply when contracts are formed in a business office govern the formation of contracts in cyberspace: there must be offer and acceptance.

Some issues that arise in contract formation in the new economy are, for example, whether a contract is formed when someone downloads a program from the Internet. The person may have paid for the program by credit card and simply downloaded it on the computer. Acceptance occurs when the click occurs—a contract is formed.[21] (See Chapters 12–17 for more information on contracts in cyberspace.)

E-sign–signature over the Internet.

The Electronic Signatures in Global and National Commerce Act (called **E-sign**) is a federal law that recognizes digital signatures as authentic for purposes of contract formation. Even though E-sign recognizes the validity of electronic signatures, states laws regulate the authenticity and security of signatures. The Uniform Electronic Transactions Act (UETA) and the Uniform Computer Information Transaction Act (UCITA) are two model laws drafted to allow states to adopt a uniform position. UETA is a uniform law that 46 states plus the District of Columbia have adopted;[22] two states have adopted UCITA.[23]

8. Misrepresentation and Fraud in Cyberspace

misrepresentation–false statement of fact, although made innocently without any intent to deceive.

The types of **misrepresentation** and fraud on the Internet range from promises of delivery not fulfilled to promises of performance not met. The majority of the fraud complaints received by the FBI relate to Internet auctions. These issues are not new legal issues; only the form of misrepresentation or fraud has changed. **For Example,** seven retailers signed a consent decree with the FTC, which requires

---

[20] L. J. Kutten, Bernard D. Reams, and Allen E. Strehler, *Electronic Contracting Law* (Clark Boardman, 1991).
[21] A.V. *v iParadigms, Ltd. Liability Co.*, 544 F Supp 2d 473 (ED Va 2008).
[22] Forty-six jurisdictions have adopted UETA. The states that have not adopted it are Georgia, Illinois, New York, and Washington.
[23] Maryland Commercial Law §§ 22-101 to 22-816, and Virginia Code §§ 59.1-501.1 to 59.1-509.2. Both laws can be found online: **www.uetaonline.com** and **www.ucitaonline.com**.

them to pay fines totaling $1.5 million to settle a complaint against them for late delivery of Christmas merchandise ordered over the Web. Macys.com, Toysrus.com, and CDNOW all signed the consent decree that was based on the FTC mail-and-telephone rule requiring retailers to let customers know when they do not have a product or that there will be a delay in the shipment. The existing notification rule was simply applied to Internet transactions.

search engine–Internet service used to locate Web sites.

In marketing **search engines**, some companies have misrepresented the capabilities of their products or have failed to disclose the methods they use to give preference to certain links and their order of listing when the search engine is used. The remedy for such misrepresentations and fraud on the Internet is the same as the remedy in situations with paper contracts. Misrepresentation and fraud are defenses to formation and entitle the party who was misled or defrauded to rescind the agreement and/or collect money damages.

In addition to contract remedies available for misrepresenting the nature of the search engine product and capabilities, a small group of search engine companies has proposed a code of ethics for search engine firms. Headed by Mike Adams, founder and owner of WebSeed.com, the rules are called "Search Engine Promotion Code of Ethics." Adams says that his industry needs reform and gave the following example of Dotsubmit.com, a former company that claimed it would submit its clients' Web sites to 10,000 search engines. Other problems include the lack of limitations on the number of pages from any domain, which means there is so much space used that consumers have difficulty finding what they are looking for.

Key provisions of the search engine code of ethics cover claims about search engine performance as well as the honoring of submission guidelines that impose requirements on Web sites seeking to be listed.

D. Intellectual Property Issues in Cyberspace

intellectual property rights–trademark, copyright, and patent rights protected by law.

Intellectual property rights have not changed—simply because the Internet has facilitated the ability to copy everything from trademarks to songs with great ease. As noted in Chapter 10, intellectual property rights are protected for the sake of innovation. As in the other areas of law discussed to this point, the Internet simply presents new challenges for interpretation of copyright law. The ease of posting items to the Internet and the ability to copy them quickly does not change the rights of copyright ownership. As with all other reproductions of work, permission to reproduce copyrighted work, either using a copy machine or the Internet, is required.[24]

Perhaps no case has brought to a head the discussion of intellectual property rights and their application to cyberspace than that of Napster. Shawn Fanning and Sean Parker, two college students who were then 19 and 20 years old, respectively, founded this company. Napster developed a software program that enabled users to download music files over the Internet at no cost. The music industry filed suit

---

[24] See *Lowry's Reports, Inc. v Legg Mason, Inc.*, 271 F Supp 2d 737 (D Md 2003) in which the employer was found liable for copyright infringement by its employees who posted subscription e-mail of financial newsletter on employer's intranet using employer's equipment and on company time, even though employees violated employer's policy not to do so.

against Napster, Grokster, and other companies and all have either been settled or fully litigated with arrangements for music companies to charge fees for access to music and then pay those fees to the copyright holders.

The Recording Industry Association of America (RIAA) has undertaken an aggressive litigation strategy against music downloaders. The RIAA estimates that 11 million home computers actively share music files in one month. The RIAA and others have moved into international markets as well. Gottfrid Svartholm Warg, Peter Sunde, Fredrik Neij, and Carl Lundstrom, the four Swedish lads who were the operators and financiers of the Pirate Bay Web site, were convicted in Sweden of copyright infringement in April 2009. Pirate Bay, a site that allows free access to copyrighted movies, music, and more, has been shut down.

fair use–principle that allows the limited use of copyrighted material for teaching, research, and news reporting.

The legal question in the music cases, as with all other Internet infringement cases, is: Is it **fair use** or **infringement** to provide a link on a Web site to another Web site for copyrighted materials there? The Digital Millennium Copyright Act (DMCA)[25] was enacted as an amendment to federal copyright laws and makes it a federal offense to circumvent or create programs to circumvent encryption devices placed in copyrighted material to prevent unauthorized copying. **For Example,** circumventing the encryption devices on software or DVDs violates the DMCA. (See Chapter 10 for more information.)

infringement–violation of trademarks, patents, or copyrights by copying or using material without permission.

Another issue that has resulted because of the universal access and availability of the Internet is that of disputes over names for Internet sites. In October 1999, the Internet Corporation for Assigned Names and Numbers (ICANN) approved the Uniform Domain Name Dispute Resolution Policy (UDRP). Prior to this policy, Network Solutions Inc. (NSI) had followed a policy of allowing trademark holders to halt the use of trademarked names for Web sites until the issue of ownership was resolved.

Under UDRP, the parties go through arbitration, and the current user continues to use the name until the matter is resolved. The UDRP also does not require a registration for a complainant to bring proceedings—the party can bring the action without registration and can base a complaint on a Web site's name being deceptively similar.

In addition to the use of this international registration system, existing U.S. laws can help protect the identity and property of businesses. **For Example,** the Federal Trademark Dilution Act permits a company whose name is harmed or diluted through its use by another to bring suit for injunctions and damages. Also, the FTC's rules on trademark protection are equally applicable to the Internet.

E. Criminal Law Issues in Cyberspace

9. Nature and Types of Cyberspace Crimes

cybercrime–crimes committed via the Internet.

The FBI has labeled **cybercrime** "epidemic."[26] More than 25 percent of the Fortune 500 companies have fallen victim to computer crime.[27] As one expert put it, computer viruses cost the United States more than the total cost of the war in Afghanistan. One virus, known as the "Love Letter" virus, cost U.S. businesses

[25] 17 USC § 1201 *et seq.*
[26] **http://www.emergency.com**
[27] **http://www.jaring.my**

$10 billion.[28] In 1999, one man was able to perpetrate a fraud of $45 million by simply making credit card charges to various credit cards from around the world with information he had gleaned by searching Web sites with consumer information.[29]

Computer crime is simply a more conventional crime carried out through the use of a computer. In other words, using someone else's credit card is fraud, whether you steal the credit card and hand it to the clerk or you use the card number through a transaction on the Web. Some crimes, however, owe their existence to the Internet. **For Example,** rerouting users from the domain they were trying to access to a pornographic Web site does not fit the elements of any particular common law crime, but it is a wrongful use of a computer and its systems. Likewise, using a computer to ensure that your call to a radio station will be answered before other callers' calls is wrong and an unlawful trespass into the radio station's system, but no common law crime covers it. Special computer crime statutes must be developed to deal with the use of computers to carry out new forms of fraud and unfair advantage.[30] Computers can be tools of the crime (**identity theft**), targets of crime (hacking into a system of another), or incidental to a crime (as when they are used for money laundering). Several new crimes have arisen as technology has evolved that are variations of the theft statutes. *Phishing* refers to sending e-mails that appear to be from banks and other account sources to get consumers to respond with their private financial information. *Pharming* is the term for a new tool that redirects consumers to another Web site (even when they have correctly entered the right address) so the redirected site can obtain financial information from the consumers.

Finally, the *evil twins phenomenon* consists of wireless networks that lure consumers to the networks by appearing to be legitimate Wi-Fi networks available in locations such as Starbucks, airports, and hotels. The Wi-Fi networks seem to be original and legitimate. However, they are simply created by hackers as the evil twin of the good Wi-Fi sites. The evil twin manipulators/hackers are just seeking financial information and passwords. Evil twins have also been known to infect computers with viruses.

There are criminal laws that are specifically applicable to computer crime that were covered in Chapter 8 and include the Computer Fraud and Abuse Act[31] and the Economic Espionage Act (EEA).[32]

10. Criminal Procedure and Rights in Cyberspace

Another issue that arises because of cyberspace relates to **warrants**. The Fourth Amendment applies not only to searches of offices and homes but also to searches of computers. Indeed, when a warrant specifies that the officers search computers and files, at least one court has ordered that the warrant be specific as to whether it includes home and/or office computers and files.[33] The protection against unlawful

identity theft—use of another's credit tools, social security number, or other IDs to obtain cash, goods, or credit without permission.

warrant—authorization via court order to search private property for tools or evidence of a crime.

---

[28] **http://www.computereconomics.com**
[29] **http://www.computerworld.com/news/1999/**
[30] *United States v Peterson*, 98 F3d 502 (9th Cir 1996).
[31] 18 USC § 1030 (2002).
[32] 18 USC § 1831 et seq. (2002).
[33] *United States v Hunter*, 13 F Supp 2d 574 (D Vt 1998).

thinking things through

Free-Riders and Piggybacking

A new issue that has evolved because of technology could require legal steps. Neighbors are *piggybacking* or tapping into their neighbors' wireless Internet connection. The original subscriber pays a monthly fee for the service but, without security, people in the area are able to tap into the wireless network and bog down the speed of the service. Once limited to geeks and hackers, the practice is now common among ordinary folk who just want free Internet service.

One college student said, "I don't think it's stealing. I always find people out there who aren't protecting their connection, so I just feel free to go ahead and use it."* According to a recent survey, only about 30 percent of the 4,500 wireless networks onto which the surveyors logged were encrypted.

An apartment dweller said she leaves her connection wide open because, "I'm sticking it to the man. I open up my network, leave it wide open for anyone to jump on." One of the users of another's wireless network said, "I feel sort of bad about it, but I do it anyway. It just seems harmless." She said that if she gets caught, "I'm a grandmother. They're not going to yell at an old lady. I'll just play the dumb card."

Some neighbors offer to pay those with wireless service in exchange for their occasional use rather than paying a wireless company for full-blown service. However, the original subscribers do not really want to run their own Internet service.

What possible crimes could be committed here? Do you think we need new legislation to cover this activity? What do you think of the users' statements?

* Michael Marriott, "Hey Neighbor, Stop Piggybacking on My Wireless," *New York Times*, March 5, 2006, A1, A23.

---

searches and seizures has not changed; only the objects being searched have become more sophisticated, and a warrant can include them as well, so long as it specifies the extent of the computer and file search. Just as in the case of the employer access and the music downloaders, the question for the courts is whether Internet users who are identified only by their screen names have an expectation of privacy.

CASE SUMMARY

Shared Drive + Shared Access= NO PRIVACY

FACTS: In February 2003, while serving as a civilian contractor, Michael D. King resided in a dormitory at the Prince Sultan Air Base in Saudi Arabia. During his stay in the dormitory, King kept his personal laptop computer in his room and connected it to the base network. All users of the base network signed agreements indicating that they understood their communications over and use of the base network were subject to monitoring.

An enlisted airman was searching the base network for music files when he came across King's computer on the network. The airman was able to access King's hard drive because it was a "shared" drive. The airman discovered a pornographic movie and text files "of a pornographic nature." The airman reported his discovery to a military investigator who in turn referred the

Continued

matter to a computer specialist. This specialist located King's computer and hard drive on the base network and verified the presence of pornographic videos and explicit text files on the computer. She also discovered a folder on the hard drive labeled "pedophilia."

Military officials seized King's computer and also found CDs containing child pornography.

Two years later, the government obtained an indictment charging King with possession of child pornography. After his arrest, the government searched his residence pursuant to a search warrant and found additional CDs and hard drives containing over 30,000 images of child pornography.

King entered a guilty plea and was sentenced to 108 months in prison. King then appealed his conviction on the grounds that there had been an illegal search and seizure of his computer and files.

DECISION: The court held that there was no Fourth Amendment violation because the investigators did not search King's files or computer initially to discover the pornographic materials. They merely had to access the universally accessible files of the military base. King had no expectation of privacy in whatever was posted on the shared drive. The search of his home computer and files in his room was with a warrant that was based on probable cause obtained from public access to the files. [**U.S. v King, 509 F3d 1338 (CA 11 2007)**]

F. CONSTITUTIONAL RESTRAINTS AND PROTECTIONS IN CYBERSPACE

The constitutional issues that have arisen as a result of Internet technology cover everything from the First Amendment to the commerce clause and involve issues ranging from pornography to taxation.

11. First Amendment Rights in Cyberspace

Some speech on the Internet is commercial, but other forms of speech involve communications relating to voting and ballot initiatives. Speech on the Internet enjoys constitutional protection, but the Internet has also facilitated the transport of pornography with great ease because photos can be sent from computer to computer. The presence of pornography on the Internet and the ease of access that children have to that material have presented challenges for regulation. The Child Pornography Prevention Act[34] made it a crime to knowingly sell, possess, or distribute child pornography on the Web. However, the U.S. Supreme Court ruled that the statute was void for both vagueness and violating First Amendment rights.[35]

Other First Amendment issues in cyberspace include whether a blogger is a journalist for purposes of asserting the defense of protecting a source. At least one court has held that bloggers are entitled to that journalistic defense.[36]

---

[34] 18 USC § 2252 *et seq.* (2002).
[35] *United States v Hilton*, 167 F3d 61 (1st Cir 1999), *cert denied*, 528 US 844 (1999); *United States v Acheson*, 195 F3d 645 (11th Cir 1999); and *Free Speech Coalition v Reno*, 220 F3d 1113 (9th Cir 1999), *cert granted as Ashcroft v Free Speech Coalition*, 535 US 234 (2002).
[36] *Doe v Cahill*, 884 A2d 451 (Del 2005).

12. Commerce Clause Issues in Cyberspace

The commerce clause has also come into play with the Internet because of the desire of both the states and the federal government to tax the transactions taking place via the Internet. The U.S. Constitution requires that there be some "nexus" between the taxing authority and the business paying the tax (see Chapter 4 for more information on constitutional issues in taxation), and many questions arise about the constitutionality of taxing Internet sales because of the lack of "bricks and mortar" in these businesses. Some Internet retailers are located in one state and have no contact, physically, with any other states. Their only contact is through the computers of their customers, who may be located in all 50 states. Is it constitutional for Colorado to tax a New Jersey company operating out of a small office in Trenton? Courts will simply apply the standards of fairness and allocation that they have relied on in other eras as businesses grew in reach even though their physical locations did not change.

The Internet Tax Freedom Act (ITFA)[37] has been renewed. The ITFA provides that states and local governments cannot tax Internet access. Contrary to popular belief, ITFA does not suspend sales taxes on transactions over the Internet. To tax Internet sales, the seller must have some physical presence in the state or a pattern of distribution and doing business there. **For Example,** Nordstrom might not have stores located in a particular state, but it would be required to collect sales taxes from sales to residents of that state if it had warehouse facilities in that state. Refer to Chapter 3 for a full discussion of the Internet and sales tax.

13. Due Process Issues in Cyberspace

Related to the nexus doctrine and taxation of Internet sales is the issue of whether an Internet business site with few physical facilities and no real presence in other states can be required to travel to the states where its customers are to litigate cases brought by those customers. The notion of long-arm jurisdiction (see Chapter 4) becomes even more critical because of the Internet. When does a company have a sufficient presence in a state that requires it to defend a lawsuit in that state? The answer is the same as the answer for the presence of a "bricks and mortar" business. Is requiring the Internet retailer to come to a state to defend a lawsuit fair, or does it offend notions of justice and fair play? Is reaching out to customers in a state through the Internet sufficient to require the Internet company to come to that state and defend lawsuits brought by those customers, or should the customers be required to travel to the state where the Internet company is located?

G. SECURITIES LAW ISSUES IN CYBERSPACE

The Internet has facilitated access to the capital markets. The existence of computers has led to *day traders,* investors who have online second-by-second financial information about companies as well as the ability to track trades in order to buy

---

[37] Pub. L. No. 105-277, originally enacted on October 21, 1998, and renewed on November 16, 2001.

and sell stock. However, this universal access means an increase in the players in the market, and those players have often used tactics not entirely within the boundaries of the existing legal framework or the level playing field so important in the stock markets.

pump-and-dump–self-touting a stock to drive its price up and then selling it.

One practice that has begun is **pump-and-dump** through which a trader buys a certain stock and then posts information on the Web to increase interest in it, which drives up its price. When the price has climbed to a sufficiently high level, the trader sells it and walks away with the profits earned by the hype created on the Web. The tactic is new and the response time faster, but the practice of pump-and-dump is nothing more than securities fraud. Pump-and-dump allowed 15-year-old Jonathan Lebed to turn his $8,000 in savings into $800,000 in stock gains. He became the first minor ever charged by the Securities and Exchange Commission (SEC) with securities fraud. His penalty was to repay the gains that he made.[38]

Many CEOs and CFOs have developed their own blogs or have begun "tweeting" as a means of staying in touch with concerned shareholders and employees. However, securities lawyers have been monitoring the blogs and tweets closely because of the concern that these executives would unwittingly disclose information that was not yet ready for public disclosure. For example, a tweet that discloses a luncheon meeting might prematurely reveal merger discussions.

Existing securities laws also cover other issues that have emerged with cyberspace companies. **For Example,** America Online entered into a consent decree with the SEC for its accounting practices in which the company predicted sales and booked income on the basis of advertising expenses. The SEC found the model for predicting sales untested and misleading. Even though doing business on the Internet was new with no historical financial data, , the SEC held that financial projections must be based on adequate information.[39]

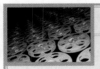

lawflix

The Net 1995 PG 13

In a movie that was ahead of its time, a computer programmer becomes a victim of identity theft when she holds too much information about the software companies for which she has done consulting work.

Check out LawFlix at **www.cengage.com/blaw/dvl** to access movie clips that illustrate business law concepts.

---

[38] Gretchen Morgenson, "S.E.C. Says Teenager Had After-School Hobby: Online Stock Fraud," *New York Times*, September 21, 2000, A1, C10.
[39] Floyd Norris, "AOL Pays a Fine to Settle a Charge That It Inflated Profits," *New York Times*, May 16, 2000, C6.

MAKE THE CONNECTION

SUMMARY

The term *cyberlaw* seems to indicate a new body of law that exists or is being created to manage all of the legal issues of the cybereconomy, cyberspace, and cybertechnology. Even though some new criminal statutes have been enacted to address specific types of computer crimes, the law, with its great flexibility, has been able to easily adapt to address many of the legal issues that affect the new economy in cyberspace.

Six existing areas of law apply to cyberspace: tort issues, contract issues, intellectual property issues, criminal violations, constitutional restraints and protections, and securities law issues.

In tort law, the issues that arise on the Internet relate to privacy and defamation. In contracts, the issues center on formation and signatures, as well as the need for diligence in handling fraud and misrepresentation in the course of formation of contracts. Infringement and fair use are the key topics of intellectual property law that arise through the Internet. Although some peculiar issues such as linking Web sites and copyrighted materials or the types of domain names that may be used exist, the laws to address these new ways of possible infringement of others' intellectual property rights are in place. Criminal violations remain centered on the crimes of trespass and theft. Computers are either used to commit crimes or become the object of crimes, and both old criminal statutes and new ones protect property from harm, even on the Internet. The Constitution still applies to questions of jurisdiction and taxation. The standards of fairness still apply, and courts simply face the issue of whether a company is present because the Internet is available in every state and country. Finally, securities fraud is securities fraud whether committed face-to-face, by paper, by phone, or by chat room.

LEARNING OUTCOMES

After studying this chapter, you should be able to clearly explain:

A. INTRODUCTION TO CYBERLAW

LO.1 Identify the privacy rights of employees and obligations of employees with regard to the Internet, their e-mails, and servers

See the Standard & Poor's example on p. 244.
See E-Commerce & Cyberlaw, "Ten Commandments for Avoiding Workplace Exposure," on p. 248.
See *Quon v Arch Wireless Operating Co., Inc.,* on p. 247.

B. TORT ISSUES IN CYBERSPACE

LO.2 Discuss the issue of defamation on the Web

See the Ethics & the Law discussion of the blogger who kissed and told, p. 251.

C. CONTRACT ISSUES IN CYBERSPACE

LO.3 Explain the obligations of service providers to reveal identity and content

See, *Sony Music Entertainment Inc. v Does 1– 40* on p. 249.

LO.4 ▶ Discuss the constitutional law issues that have resulted from cyberspace
See *U.S. v King* on p. 256.

D. INTELLECTUAL PROPERTY ISSUES IN CYBERSPACE

LO.5 ▶ Describe the intellectual property issues in cyberspace
See *Sony Music Entertainment Inc. v Does* on p. 249.

E. CRIMINAL LAW ISSUES IN CYBERSPACE

F. CONSTITUTIONAL RESTRAINTS AND PROTECTIONS IN CYBERSPACE

LO.6 ▶ Explain the concerns and legal issues blogging raises
See the John Mackey example on p. 251.
See the Delta and Starbucks examples on p. 251.

G. SECURITIES LAW ISSUES IN CYBERSPACE

See the AOL example on booking ad revenues on p. 259.

KEY TERMS

appropriation
contract
cybercrime
cyberlaw
cyberspace
defamation
E-sign

fair use
identity theft
infringement
intellectual property
 rights
invasion of privacy

misrepresentation
pump-and-dump
search engines
tort
warrants

QUESTIONS AND CASE PROBLEMS

1. Discuss whether employees would have the right of privacy in the following e-mail situations:

   1. E-mail sent in a company in which there is no warning given about the lack of privacy in e-mails. [*Smyth v Pillsbury*, 914 F Supp 97 (ED Pa 1996)]

   2. An e-mail sent to co-workers from home using the employee's AOL account.

   3. An e-mail sent from a laptop while the employee is traveling for the company.

   4. An e-mail sent to a coworker over a company Internet system in a company in which the employer has promised privacy in e-mail. [*Commonwealth v Proetto*, 771 A2d 823 (Pa Super Ct 2001)]

   5. Employer monitoring of the e-mails of any employee when those e-mails were stored in a file folder marked "Personal." [*Mclaren v Microsoft Corp.*, 1999 WL 339015 (Tex App–Dallas 1999)]

   6. Employees using company e-mail for union organization purposes. [*Pratt & Whitney*, National Labor Relations Board General Counsel Advisory

Memorandum Cases 12-CA-18446, 12-CA-18722, 12-CS-18863 (February 23, 1998)]

2. In the midst of the litigation surrounding its program for downloading music, Napster, Inc., discovered that a company was selling t-shirts with its logo on them. Can Napster do anything to prevent the use of its logo? Is the use of the logo for t-shirts any different from the use of songs for purposes of downloading for individual listening?

3. The *New York Times* discovered that 24 of the employees in its payroll processing center were sending "inappropriate and offensive e-mail in violation of corporate policy." Do the employees have any right to privacy with regard to the jokes they send over their e-mail accounts at work? Applying what you have learned about the nature of cyberlaw, determine whether, under existing sexual harassment laws, a company could be held liable for harassment via e-mails.

4. Daniel Dagesse suffered serious injuries when he slipped and fell in his hotel room at the Aruba Marriott Resort (the Plant Hotel). He sued Plant Hotel N. V., the limited liability company that owns the resort; Oranjestad Property Management N.V., Plant Hotel's parent company; Marriott Aruba N.V., the company that manages the resort; and Marriott International, Inc., a corporation that was the agent and management company for Plant Hotel and Oranjestad. Elaine Dagesse, Daniel's wife, also filed suit against the same companies alleging loss of consortium. The Dagesses filed suit in federal district court in New Hampshire, seeking to have the companies come and defend the lawsuit there. The companies filed a motion to dismiss on the grounds that they had no physical presence in the state of New Hampshire. The Dagesses contended that all of the companies operated an interactive Web site to which they went and through which they made their reservations as they sat in their home in New Hampshire, and that this Web site resulted in New Hampshire's jurisdiction over the companies. Were they correct? [*Dagesse v Plant Hotel N.V.*, 113 F Supp 2d 211 (D NH)]

5. Colleges and universities continue to work to help students understand that what they post on the Web is not private information and can often have unintended consequences. The following examples resulted in student disciplinary proceedings:

- Several students at The Ohio State University boasted on Facebook (a networking/socializing site) that they had stormed the field after Ohio State beat Penn State and had taken part in what erupted into a riot. Law enforcement officials were able to trace the students through the university system, and 50 Ohio State students were referred to the office of judicial affairs.

- Students at the University of Mississippi stated on an open site that they wanted to have sex with a professor.

- A student at Fisher College threatened to take steps to silence a campus police officer.

Another problem with the open sites is that the students are posting personal information with which stalkers and others can access them. These nefarious individuals can then easily obtain students' cell phone numbers, addresses, whereabouts, and other information.

The most popular college site, Facebook, indicates that students spend an average of 17 minutes per day on the site. A great deal of information can be conveyed during that time period. Students do so without thinking through the possibility that outsiders with bad intentions could be seeking and using information about them that is posted there.

What legal and ethical issues do you see in the types of comments that students make on these sites and in the sites themselves? Why and how can the colleges and universities obtain information from these sites without a warrant?

6. On July 24, 2002, the Recording Industry Association of America (RIAA) served its first subpoena to obtain the identity of a Verizon subscriber alleged to have made more than 600 copyrighted songs available for downloading over the Internet through peer-to-peer file transfer software provided by KaZaA. Verizon claimed that because RIAA's subpoena related to material transmitted over Verizon's network—rather than stored on it—it fell outside the scope of the subpoena power. Should the subpoena be quashed as Verizon requests, or should it be honored? [*In re Verizon Internet Services, Inc.*, 257 F Supp 2d 244 (DDC)]

7. Glenayre Electronics announced to its employees that it could inspect the laptops it furnished for its employees to use. An employee challenged the inspection of his laptop as a violation of his privacy. Could the company search the laptops? [*Muick v Glenayre Electronics*, 280 F3d 741 (7th Cir)]

8. A state university provided a written notice to employees that their computers could be monitored and added a splash screen with the same notice that appears on the computers each time employees start their computers. Has the university done enough to allow monitoring without invading employee privacy? Would it make any difference if the employees had a password for their e-mail access and computer access? What about state public records law? Would employee e-mails be subject to public disclosure because the e-mails would be considered public record? [*U.S. v Angevine*, 281 F3d 1130 (10th Cir)]

9. APTC, a publicly traded corporation, filed a complaint, captioned *"Anonymous Publicly Traded Company v John Does 1 through 5,"* asserting that the John Doe defendants, whose identities and residences were unknown, "made defamatory and disparaging material misrepresentations" about APTC in Internet chat rooms. APTC asserted its belief that the John Doe defendants were current and/or former employees who breached their fiduciary duties and contractual obligations by publishing "confidential material insider information" about APTC on the Internet. Although it did not specify what harm would be incurred by identifying itself, APTC contended that it had to proceed anonymously "because disclosure of its true company name will cause it irreparable harm." APTC wanted the court to issue subpoenas to the ISP to determine the identity of the John Does. How do you think the court will

decide on the issue of the John Does' identity? [*America Online, Inc. v Anonymous Publicly Traded Co.*, 542 SE2d 377 (Va)]

10. In response to legal cases in which companies have had their internal e-mails used to their disadvantage, several companies have developed programs that automatically destroy e-mails once they have been opened and read on the other end. Is it legal and ethical to destroy e-mails on a regular basis such as this? To visit an e-mail destruction site, go to **www.authentica.com** or **www.qvtech.com**.

11. Immunomedics, Inc., has discovered sensitive information about its technology posted on various Web sites and chat rooms. The information is so proprietary that it could have come only from company employees, all of whom have signed agreements not to disclose such information. Those who posted the information used screen names, and Immunomedics has asked the court to issue a subpoena to the ISP so that it can determine the identity of those posting the information and recover for breach of contract and trade secret infringement. Should the court issue the subpoena? [*Immunomedics, Inc. v Does 1–10*, 2001 WL 770389 (NJ Super 2001)]

12. Jane Doe filed a complaint against Richard Lee Russell and America Online (AOL) to recover for alleged emotional injuries suffered by her son, John Doe. Doe claimed that in 1994, Russell lured John Doe, who was then 11 years old, and two other minor males to engage in sexual activity with each other and with Russell. She asserted that Russell photographed and videotaped these acts and used AOL's chat rooms to market the photographs and videotapes and to sell a videotape. In her six-count complaint, Doe claimed that AOL violated criminal statutes and that AOL was negligent *per se* in distributing an advertisement offering "a visual depiction of sexual conduct involving [John Doe]" and by allowing Russell to sell or arrange to sell child pornography, thus aiding in the sale and distribution of child pornography, including obscene images of John Doe. Does Mrs. Doe have a cause of action? What laws discussed in this chapter apply? [*Doe v America Online, Inc.*, 783 So2d 1010 (Fla)]

13. Customers of a chat room are using the chat room, Maphia, for access to each other and to transfer Sega games to each other. They are able to avoid paying the $19 to $60 the games cost for purchase in the stores. The users say they are simply transferring files and that there is no crime. The chat room says it cannot stop customers from interacting. Do you think there are any civil or criminal law violations in their conduct? [*Sega Enterprises, Ltd. v Maphia*, 857 F Supp 679 (ND Cal)]

Part 2

CONTRACTS

Chapter 12

Nature and Classes of Contracts: Contracting on the Internet

P ractically every business transaction affecting people involves a contract.

A. Nature of Contracts

This introductory chapter will familiarize you with the terminology needed to work with contract law. In addition, the chapter introduces quasi contracts, which are not true contracts but obligations imposed by law.

1. Definition of a Contract

contract—a binding agreement based on the genuine assent of the parties, made for a lawful object, between competent parties, in the form required by law, and generally supported by consideration.

A **contract** is a legally binding agreement.[1] By one definition, "a contract is a promise or a set of promises for the breach of which the law gives a remedy, or the performance of which the law in some way recognizes as a duty."[2] Contracts arise out of agreements, so a contract may be defined as an agreement creating an obligation.

The substance of the definition of a contract is that by mutual agreement or assent, the parties create enforceable duties or obligations. That is, each party is legally bound to do or to refrain from doing certain acts.

2. Elements of a Contract

The elements of a contract are (1) an agreement (2) between competent parties (3) based on the genuine assent of the parties that is (4) supported by consideration, (5) made for a lawful objective, and (6) in the form required by law, if any. These elements will be considered in the chapters that follow.

3. Subject Matter of Contracts

The subject matter of a contract may relate to the performance of personal services, such as contracts of employment to work developing computer software or to play professional football. A contract may provide for the transfer of ownership of property, such as a house (real property) or an automobile (personal property), from one person to another.

4. Parties to a Contract

promisor—person who makes a promise.

promisee—person to whom a promise is made.

obligor—promisor.

obligee—promisee who can claim the benefit of the obligation.

privity—succession or chain of relationship to the same thing or right, such as privity of contract, privity of estate, privity of possession.

The person who makes a promise is the **promisor**, and the person to whom the promise is made is the **promisee**. If the promise is binding, it imposes on the promisor a duty or obligation, and the promisor may be called the **obligor**. The promisee who can claim the benefit of the obligation is called the **obligee**. The parties to a contract are said to stand in **privity** with each other, and the relationship

---

[1] The Uniform Commercial Code defines *contract* as "the total legal obligation which results from the parties' agreement as affected by [the UCC] and any other applicable rules of law." UCC § 1–201(11).
[2] Restatement (Second) of Contracts § 1.

privity of contract–
relationship between a
promisor and the promisee.

between them is termed **privity of contract**. **For Example,** when the state of North Carolina and the architectural firm of O'Brien/Atkins Associates executed a contract for the construction of a new building at the University of North Carolina, Chapel Hill, these parties were in privity of contract. However, a building contractor, RPR & Associates, who worked on the project did not have standing to sue on the contract between the architect and the state because the contractor was not in privity of contract.[3]

In written contracts, parties may be referred to by name. More often, however, they are given special names that better identify each party. For example, consider a contract by which one person agrees that another may occupy a house upon the payment of money. The parties to this contract are called *landlord* and *tenant*, or *lessor* and *lessee*, and the contract between them is known as a *lease*. Parties to other types of contracts also have distinctive names, such as *vendor* and *vendee* for the parties to a sales contract, *shipper* and *carrier* for the parties to a transportation contract, and *insurer* and *insured* for the parties to an insurance policy.

A party to a contract may be an individual, a partnership, a limited liability company, a corporation, or a government.[4] One or more persons may be on each side of a contract. Some contracts are three-sided, as in a credit card transaction, which involves the company issuing the card, the holder of the card, and the business furnishing goods and services on the basis of the credit card.

If a contract is written, the persons who are the parties and who are bound by it can ordinarily be determined by reading what the document says and seeing how it is signed. A contract binds only the parties to the contract. It cannot impose a duty on a person who is not a party to it. Ordinarily, only a party to a contract has any rights against another party to the contract.[5] In some cases, third persons have rights on a contract as third-party beneficiaries or assignees. A person cannot be bound, however, by the terms of a contract to which that person is not a party.[6]

CPA   ## 5. How a Contract Arises

offeror–person who makes
an offer.

offeree–person to whom
an offer is made.

A contract is based on an agreement. An agreement arises when one person, the **offeror**, makes an offer and the person to whom the offer is made, the **offeree**, accepts. There must be both an offer and an acceptance. If either is lacking, there is no contract.

6. Intent to Make a Binding Agreement

Because a contract is based on the consent of the parties and is a legally binding agreement, it follows that the parties must have an intent to enter into an agreement

---

[3] *RPR & Associates v O'Brien/Atkins Associates, P.A.*, 24 F Supp 2d 515 (MDNC 1998). See also *Roof Techs Int. Inc. v State*, 57P3d 538 (Kan App 2002), where a layer of litigation was avoided regarding lawsuits involving the renovation of the Farrell Library at Kansas State University. The state was the only party in privity of contract with the architectural firm and would thus have to bring claims against the architectural firm on behalf of all of the contractors. Two subcontractors, the general contractor, and the owner of the library, the state of Kansas, used a settlement and liquidation agreement assigning all of the state's claims against the architect to the general contractor.
[4] See *Purina Mills, LLC v Less*, 295 F Supp 2d 1017 (ND Iowa 2003) in which the pig-seller plaintiff, which converted from a corporation to a limited liability company (LLC) while the contract was in effect, was a proper party in interest and could maintain a contract action against defendant buyers.
[5] *Hooper v Yakima County*, 904 P2d 1193 (Wash App 1995).
[6] *Walsh v Telesector Resources Group, Inc.*, 662 NE2d 1043 (Mass App 1996).

that is binding. Sometimes the parties are in agreement, but their agreement does not produce a contract. Sometimes there is merely a preliminary agreement, but the parties never actually make a contract, or there is merely an agreement as to future plans or intentions without any contractual obligation to carry out those plans or intentions.

7. Freedom of Contract

In the absence of some ground for declaring a contract void or voidable, parties may make such contracts as they choose. The law does not require parties to be fair, or kind, or reasonable, or to share gains or losses equitably.

B. CLASSES OF CONTRACTS

formal contracts–written contracts or agreements whose formality signifies the parties' intention to abide by the terms.

Contracts may be classified according to their form, the way in which they were created, their binding character, and the extent to which they have been performed.

CPA   8. Formal and Informal Contracts

Contracts can be classified as formal or informal.

contract under seal– contract executed by affixing a seal or making an impression on the paper or on some adhering substance such as wax attached to the document.

(A) FORMAL CONTRACTS. **Formal contracts** are enforced because the formality with which they are executed is considered sufficient to signify that the parties intend to be bound by their terms. Formal contracts include (1) **contracts under seal** where a person's signature or a corporation's name is followed by a scroll, the word *seal*, or the letters *L.S.*;[7] (2) contracts of record, which are obligations that have been entered before a court of record, sometimes called a **recognizance**; and (3) negotiable instruments.

CPA

recognizance–obligation entered into before a court to do some act, such as to appear at a later date for a hearing. Also called a *contract of record*.

(B) INFORMAL CONTRACTS. All contracts other than formal contracts are called **informal** (or simple) **contracts** without regard to whether they are oral or written. These contracts are enforceable, not because of the form of the transaction but because they represent agreement of the parties.

informal contract–simple oral or written contract.

9. Express and Implied Contracts

Simple contracts may be classified as express *contracts* or *implied contracts* according to the way they are created.

express contract– agreement of the parties manifested by their words, whether spoken or written.

(A) EXPRESS CONTRACTS. An **express contract** is one in which the terms of the agreement of the parties are manifested by their words, whether spoken or written.

implied contract–contract expressed by conduct or implied or deduced from the facts.

(B) IMPLIED CONTRACTS. An **implied contract** (or, as sometimes stated, a *contract implied in fact*) is one in which the agreement is shown not by words, written or spoken, but by the acts and conduct of the parties.[8] Such a contract arises when (1) a person renders services under circumstances indicating that payment for them

---

[7] Some authorities explain *L.S.* as an abbreviation for *locus sigilium* (place for the seal).
[8] *Lindquist Ford, Inc. v Middleton Motors, Inc.*, 557 F3d 469, 481 (7th Cir 2009).

FIGURE 12-1 | *Contractual Liability*

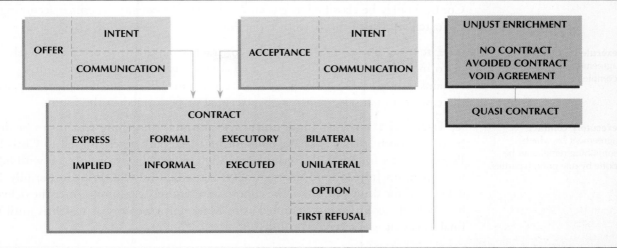

is expected and (2) the other person, knowing such circumstances, accepts the benefit of those services. **For Example,** when a building owner requests a professional roofer to make emergency repairs to the roof of a building, an obligation arises to pay the reasonable value of such services, although no agreement has been made about compensation.

An implied contract cannot arise when there is an existing express contract on the same subject.[9] However, the existence of a written contract does not bar recovery on an implied contract for extra work that was not covered by the contract.

CPA   ## 10. Valid and Voidable Contracts and Void Agreements

Contracts may be classified in terms of enforceability or validity.

valid contract–agreement that is binding and enforceable.

(A) VALID CONTRACTS. A **valid contract** is an agreement that is binding and enforceable.

voidable contract– agreement that is otherwise binding and enforceable but may be rejected at the option of one of the parties as the result of specific circumstances.

(B) VOIDABLE CONTRACTS. A **voidable contract** is an agreement that is otherwise binding and enforceable, but because of the circumstances surrounding its execution or the lack of capacity of one of the parties, it may be rejected at the option of one of the parties. **For Example,** a person who has been forced to sign an agreement that that person would not have voluntarily signed may, in some instances, avoid the contract.

void agreement–agreement that cannot be enforced.

(C) VOID AGREEMENTS. A **void agreement** is without legal effect. An agreement that contemplates the performance of an act prohibited by law is usually incapable of enforcement; hence it is void. Likewise, it cannot be made binding by later approval or ratification.

[9] *Pepsi-Cola Bottling Co. of Pittsburgh, Inc., v PepsiCo, Inc.,* 431 F3d 1241 (10th Cir 2000).

11. Executed and Executory Contracts

Contracts may be classified as *executed contracts* and *executory contracts* according to the extent to which they have been performed.

executed contract– agreement that has been completely performed.

(A) EXECUTED CONTRACTS. An **executed contract** is one that has been completely performed. In other words, an executed contract is one under which nothing remains to be done by either party.[10] A contract may be executed immediately, as in the case of a cash sale, or it may be executed or performed in the future.

executory contract– agreement by which something remains to be done by one or both parties.

(B) EXECUTORY CONTRACTS. In an **executory contract**, something remains to be done by one or both parties.[11] **For Example,** on July 10, Mark agreed to sell to Chris his Pearl drum set for $600, the terms being $200 upon delivery on July 14, with $200 to be paid on July 21, and the final $200 being due July 28. Prior to the July 14 delivery of the drums to Chris, the contract was entirely executory. After the delivery by Mark, the contract was executed as to Mark and executory as to Chris until the final payment was received on July 28.

12. Bilateral and Unilateral Contracts

In making an offer, the offeror is in effect extending a promise to do something, such as pay a sum of money, if the offeree will do what the offeror requests. Contracts are classified as *bilateral* or *unilateral*. Some bilateral contracts look ahead to the making of a later contract. Depending on their terms, these are called *option contracts* or *first-refusal contracts*.

CPA

bilateral contract– agreement under which one promise is given in exchange for another.

(A) BILATERAL CONTRACT. If the offeror extends a promise and asks for a promise in return and if the offeree accepts the offer by making the promise, the contract is called a **bilateral contract**. One promise is given in exchange for another, and each party is bound by the obligation. **For Example,** when the house painter offers to paint the owner's house for $3,700 and the owner promises to pay $3,700 for the job, there is an exchange of promises, and the agreement gives rise to a bilateral contract.

unilateral contract– contract under which only one party makes a promise.

(B) UNILATERAL CONTRACT. In contrast with a bilateral contract, the offeror may promise to do something or to pay a certain amount of money only when the offeree does an act.[12] Examples of where **unilateral contracts** commonly appear are when a reward is offered, a contest is announced, or changes are made and disseminated in an employee manual. The offeree does not accept the offer by express agreement, but rather by performance.

option contract– contract to hold an offer to make a contract open for a fixed period of time.

(C) OPTION AND FIRST-REFUSAL CONTRACTS. The parties may make a contract that gives a right to one of them to enter into a second contract at a later date. If one party has an absolute right to enter into the later contract, the initial contract is called an **option contract**. Thus, a bilateral contract may be made today giving one of the parties the right to buy the other party's house for a specified amount. This is an option contract because the party with the privilege has the freedom of choice, or

---

[10] *Marsh v Rheinecker*, 641 NE2d 1256 (Ill App 1994).
[11] *DiGeneraro v Rubbermaid, Inc.*, 214 F Supp 2d 1354 (SO Fla 2002).
[12] See *Young v Virginia Birth-Related Neurological Injury Compensation Program*, 620 SE2d 131 (Va App 2005).

CASE SUMMARY

Unilateral Contract: Pretty Good Bonus!

FACTS: Aon Risk Services, Inc. (ARS Arkansas), and Combined Insurance Companies are subsidiaries of Aon Corporation. The parent corporation issued a "Interdependency Memo" dated February 2000, which encouraged ARS brokerage offices to place insurance business with Aon-affiliated companies. It also set up a bonus pool for revenues generated under the plan, with Combined agreeing to pay "30% of annualized premium on all life products over 15-year term plus 15% 1st year for all other products." John Meadors saw the memo in February 2000, and believed it would entitle him to this compensation over and above his employment contract. Meadors put Combined in touch with Dillard's Department Stores and on March 24, 2000, Dillard's and Combined executed a five-year agreement whereby Dillard's employees could purchase life, disability, and other insurance policies through workplace enrollment. When Meadors did not receive bonus-pool money generated by the transaction, he sued his employer for breach of a unilateral contract. The employer's defense was that the memo was not sufficiently definite to constitute an offer.

DECISION: Judgment for Meadors for $2,406,522.60. A unilateral contract is composed of an offer that invites acceptance in the form of actual performance. For example, in the case of a reward, the offeree accepts by performing the particular task, such as the capture of the fugitive for which the reward is offered. In this case the offer contained in the Interdependency Memo set out specific percentages of provisions that would go into the bonus pool, and required that the pool be distributed annually. It was sufficiently definite to constitute an offer. Meadors was responsible for the production of the Dillard's account, and was entitled to the bonus promised in the memo. [**Aon Risk Services, Inc. v Meadors, 267 SW3d 603 (Ark App 2007)**]

---

option, to buy or not buy. If the option is exercised, the other party to the contract must follow the terms of the option and enter into the second contract. If the option is never exercised, no second contract ever arises, and the offer protected by the option contract merely expires.

In contrast with an option contract, a contract may merely give a **right of first refusal**. This imposes only the duty to make the first offer to the party having the right of first refusal.

> **right of first refusal**—right of a party to meet the terms of a proposed contract before it is executed, such as a real estate purchase agreement.

13. Quasi Contracts

In some cases, a court will impose an obligation even though there is no contract.[13] Such an obligation is called a **quasi contract**, which is an obligation imposed by law.

> **quasi contract**—court-imposed obligation to prevent unjust enrichment in the absence of a contract.

(A) PREVENTION OF UNJUST ENRICHMENT. A quasi contract is not a true contract reflecting all of the elements of a contract set forth previously in this chapter. The court is not seeking to enforce the intentions of the parties contained in an agreement. Rather, when a person or enterprise receives a benefit from another, even

---

[13] *Thayer v Dial Industrial Sales, Inc.*, 85 F Supp 2d 263 (SDNY 2000).

FIGURE 12-2 | *Contract*

CONTRACT

Parties

This contract is executed between the Lookout Alarm System, herein called "System," of 276 West Jackson Street, Phoenix, Arizona, and ___A. J. ARMSTRONG___, herein called "Homeowner," of 737 Inwood Drive, Phoenix, Arizona_____.

} 1

Installation

System agrees to install a burglar alarm system at the above address of the homeowner, in accordance with the specifications that are attached hereto.

} 2

Payment

Homeowner agrees to pay system for the above installation the sum of ___$4,863.00___, ___$663.00___ being paid upon execution of this contract and the balance of ___$4,200.00___ being paid within 90 days following satisfactory completion of the work by System.

} 3

4

Lookout Alarm System

By ___S. J. Mc Rory___
S.J. McRory, President

___July 1, 2010___
Date

___a. J. Armstrong___
A.J. Armstrong

___July 1, 2010___
Date

5

Note that this contract includes the following important information: (1) the name and address of each party, (2) the promise or consideration of the seller, (3) the promise or consideration of the buyer, (4) the signature of the two parties, and (5) the date.

---

in the absence of a promise to pay for the benefit, a court may impose an obligation to pay for the reasonable value of that benefit, to avoid *unjust enrichment.*

A successful claim for unjust enrichment usually requires (1) a benefit conferred on the defendant, (2) the defendant's knowledge of the benefit, and (3) a finding that it would be unjust for the defendant to retain the benefit without payment. The burden of proof is on the plaintiff to prove all of the elements of the claim.

For Example, Hiram College sued Nicholas Courtad for $6,000 plus interest for tuition and other expenses. Because no evidence of a written contract was produced, the court considered it an unjust enrichment claim by the college. Courtad had attended classes for a few weeks and had not paid his tuition due to a problem with his financial aid package. Because he did not receive any credit hours toward a degree, which is the ultimate benefit of attending college, the court found that he did not receive a benefit and that a finding of unjust enrichment was not appropriate.[14]

Sometimes a contract may be unenforceable because of a failure to set forth the contract in writing in compliance with the statute of frauds. In other circumstances, no enforceable contract exists because of a lack of definite and certain terms. Yet in both situations, one party may have performed services for the benefit of the other party and the court will require payment of the reasonable value of services to avoid the unjust enrichment of the party receiving the services without paying for them. These damages are sometimes referred to as *restitution damages*. Some courts refer to this situation as an action or recovery in **quantum meruit** (as much as he or she deserved).

quantum meruit–as much as deserved; an action brought for the value of the services rendered the defendant when there was no express contract as to the purchase price.

For Example, Arya Group, Inc. (Arya), sued the entertainer Cher for unjust enrichment. In June 1996, Cher negotiated an oral agreement with Arya to design and construct a house on her Malibu property for $4,217,529. The parties' oral agreement was set forth in a written contract with an August 1997 date and was delivered to Cher in October 1997. She never signed it. However, between June 1996 and November 1997, Arya performed and received payment for a number of services discharged under the unsigned contract. In August 1997, Cher requested Arya to meet with a home designer named Bussell who had previously worked with Cher on a Florida project, and Arya showed Bussell the plans and designs for the Malibu property and introduced her to his subcontractors. In November 1997, Cher terminated her agreement with Arya without paying the balance then due, as asserted by Arya, of $415,169.41. Arya claims that Cher and Bussell misappropriated the plans and designs Arya had prepared. Cher and the other defendants demurred to Arya's unjust enrichment complaint, pointing out that construction contracts must be evidenced in a writing signed by both parties under state law in order to be enforceable in a court of law. The appeals court determined that Arya's noncompliance with the state law requiring a signed written contract did not absolutely foreclose Arya from seeking damages for unjust enrichment if he could

CASE SUMMARY

No Free Rides

FACTS: PIC Realty leased farmland to Southfield Farms. After Southfield harvested its crop, it cultivated the land in preparation for the planting in the following year. However, its lease expired, so it did not plant that crop. It then sued PIC for reimbursement for the reasonable value of the services and materials used in preparing the land because this was a benefit to PIC. There was evidence that it was customary for landlords to compensate tenants for such work.

DECISION: Southfield was entitled to recover the reasonable value of the benefit conferred upon PIC. This was necessary in order to prevent the unjust enrichment of PIC. [**PIC Realty Corp. v Southfield Farms, Inc., 832 SW2d 610 (Tex App 1992)**]

[14] *Hiram College v Courtad*, 834 NE2d 432 (Ohio App 2005).

prove the assertions in the complaint that Cher was a sophisticated homeowner with previous involvement in residential construction who had legal representation in negotiating the agreement with Arya, and that Cher would be unjustly enriched if she were not required to compensate Arya for the reasonable value of the work already performed.[15]

A situation may arise over the mistaken conference of a benefit. **For Example,** Nantucket Island has a few approved colors for houses in its historic district. Using the approved gray color, Martin Kane and his crew began painting Sheldon Adams's house in the historic district as the result of a mistaken address. Adams observed the initiation of the work from his office across the street but did nothing to stop the painters. At the end of the day when the work was done, Adams refused to pay for the work, saying, "I signed no contract and never approved this work." The law deems it inequitable that Adams should have received the benefit of this work, having observed the benefit being conferred and knowing that the painters expected payment. Adams would be unjustly enriched if he were allowed to retain the benefit without payment for the reasonable value of the work. If Adams did not have knowledge that the work was being done and thus that payment was expected, quasi-contractual liability would not be imposed.

The mistake that benefits the defendant may be the mistake of a third party.

C A S E   S U M M A R Y

Who Pays the Piper?

FACTS: When improvements or buildings are added to real estate, the real estate tax assessment is usually increased to reflect the increased value of the property. Frank Partipilo and Elmer Hallman owned neighboring tracts of land. In 1977 Hallman made improvements to his land, constructing a new building and driveway on the tract. The tax assessor made a mistake about the location of the boundary line between Partipilo's and Hallman's land and thought the improvements were made on Partipilo's property. Instead of increasing the taxes on Hallman's land, the assessor wrongly increased the taxes on Partipilo's land. Partipilo paid the increased taxes for three years. When he learned why his taxes had been increased, he sued Hallman for the amount of the increase that Partipilo had been paying. Hallman raised the defense that he had not done anything wrong and that the mistake had been the fault of the tax assessor.

DECISION: Judgment for Partipilo. Because the improvements were made to Hallman's land, Hallman should be the one to pay the tax increase. When Partipilo paid it, Hallman received a benefit to which he was not entitled. This was an unjust enrichment. Therefore, Partipilo could recover the amount of the increased taxes without regard to the fact that Hallman was free of any fault and that the only fault in the case was the fault of the tax assessor. [**Partipilo v Hallman, 510 NE2d 8 (Ill App 1987)**]

---

[15] *Arya Group, Inc. v Cher*, 91 Cal Rptr 2d 815 (Cal App 2d 2000). See also *Fischer v Flax*, 816 A2d 1 (2003).

thinking things through

Twelve Years of Litigation

Brown University accepted the bid of Marshall Contractors, Inc. (Marshall), to build the Pizzitola Sports Facility on its Providence, Rhode Island, campus. The parties intended to execute a formal written contract. Brown decided to pay $7,157,051 for the project, but Marshall sought additional payment for items it deemed extras and not contemplated in its bid. Because the parties were unable to agree on the scope of the project as compared to the price Brown was willing to pay, they never executed the formal written contract. Nevertheless, in the context of this disagreement over terms and price, construction began in May 1987. When the parties could not resolve their disagreements as the project neared completion in January 1989, Marshall sued Brown University, seeking to recover the costs for what it deemed "changes." Brown asserted that an implied-in-fact contract existed for all work at the $7,157,051 figure because the contractor went ahead with the project knowing the money Brown would pay. The litigation ended up in the Supreme Court of Rhode Island, and in 1997, the court concluded that no express or implied-in-fact contract had ever been reached by the parties concerning the scope of the project and what costs were to be included in the price stipulated by Brown. The case was remanded to the trial court for a new trial. After a trial on the theories of *quantum meruit* and unjust enrichment, a jury awarded Marshall $1.2 million dollars, which was some $3.1 million less than Marshall sought. Brown University appealed, and on November 21, 2001, the Supreme Court of Rhode Island affirmed the jury verdict for the contractor, determining that the proper measure of damages on unjust enrichment and *quantum meruit* theories was "the reasonable value of the work done."*

In May 1987 when the parties could not reach agreement enabling the execution of a formal written contract, thinking things through at that point in time should have exposed the potential for significant economic uncertainties to both parties in actually starting the building process under such circumstances. In the spring of 1987 when all parties were unable to reach agreement, mediation or expedited arbitration by construction experts may well have resolved the controversy and yielded an amicable written contract with little or no delay to the project. Instead, the unsettled cost issues during the building process could have had an adverse impact on the "job chemistry" between the contractor and the owner, which may have adversely affected the progress and quality of the job. The 12 years of litigation that, with its economic and human resource costs, yielded just $1.2 million for the contractor was a no-win result for both sides. A primary rule for all managers in projects of this scope is to make sure the written contracts are executed before performance begins! Relying on "implied-in-fact" or quasi-contract legal theories is simply a poor management practice.

* *ADP Marshall, Inc. v Brown University*, 784 A2d 309 (RI 2001).

(B) **EXTENT OF RECOVERY.** When recovery is allowed in quasi contract, the plaintiff recovers the reasonable value of the benefit conferred on the defendant,[16] or the fair and reasonable[17] value of the work performed, depending on the jurisdiction and the circumstances of the case itself. The customary method of calculating damages in construction contract cases is actual job costs plus an allowance for overhead and profits minus amount paid.[18]

[16] *Ramsey v Ellis*, 484 NW2d 331 (Wis 1992).
[17] *ADP Marshall, Inc. v Brown University*, 784 A2d 309 (RI 2001).
[18] *Mirano Contracting, Inc. v Perel*, 871 NYS2d 310 (AD 2008).

C. CONTRACTING ON THE INTERNET

Doing business online for consumers is very similar to doing business through a catalog purchase or by phone. Before placing an order, a buyer is commonly concerned about the reputation of the seller. The basic purchasing principle of *caveat emptor* still applies: buyer beware! The Internet provides valuable tools to allow a buyer to research the reputation of the seller and its products. Online evaluations of companies and their products can be found at Web sites, such as Consumer Reports (**www.consumerreports.org**), Consumers Digest (**www.consumersdigest.com**), or the Better Business Bureau (**www.bbb.org**). E-consumers may have access to categorized histories of comments by other e-consumers, such as Planet Feedback ratings at **www.planetfeedback.com**.

The intellectual property principles set forth in Chapter 10—as well as the contractual principles, the law of sales, and privacy laws you are about to study—all apply to e-commerce transactions. When you are purchasing an item online, you must carefully read all of the terms and conditions set forth on the seller's Web site when assessing whether to make a contemplated purchase. The proposed terms may require that any disputes be litigated in a distant state or be resolved through arbitration with restricted remedies, or there may be an unsatisfactory return policy, warranty limitations, or limitation of liability. Generally, the Web site terms become the contract of the parties and are legally enforceable.

The laws you have studied that prevent deceptive advertising by brick-and-mortar businesses also apply to Internet sites.[19] If an in-state site is engaging in false advertising, you may be able to exercise consumer protection rights through your state's attorney general's office, or you may find some therapeutic relief by reporting the misconduct to the Internet Scambusters site (**www.scambusters.com**).

From a seller's perspective, it is exceedingly helpful to have as much information as possible on your potential customers' buying habits. Federal law prohibits the collection of personal information from children without parental consent, and some states restrict the unauthorized collection of personal information. European Union countries have strict laws protecting the privacy of consumers. Sellers intending to collect personal information should obtain the consent of their customers, make certain that children are excluded, and make sure that the information is stored in a secure environment.

Advanced encryption technology has made the use of credit card payments through the Internet very safe. No computer system connected to the Internet is totally secure however. In the worst-case scenario, credit card issuers will not charge a user for more than the first $50 of unauthorized activity.

Internet contracts involve the same types of issues that are addressed in contracts offline but with certain technology-related nuances. The parties to the e-contracts must still negotiate their obligations in clear and unambiguous language, including such terms as quantity, quality, and price as well as warranties, indemnification responsibilities, limitations on liability, and termination procedures. The federal Electronic Signatures in Global and National Commerce Act (E-Sign) and the

---

[19] See *MADCAP I, LLC v McNamee*, 702 NW2d 16 (Wis App 2005) in which the court found genuine issues of material fact as to whether a business Web site falsely represented the size and nature of its business to induce the public to purchase products and services described on its Web site in violation of the state's fraudulent representations statute.

Uniform Electronic Transactions Act (UETA) mandate parity between paper and electronic contracts. The basic legal rules that govern contracts offline are the very same rules that govern online contracts, and basic civil procedure rules apply. **For Example,** California buyer Paul Boschetto bought a 1964 Ford Galaxy that had been advertised on eBay to be "in awesome condition" from a Milton, Wisconsin resident, J. Hansing, for $34,106. On delivery Boschetto discovered that the car had rust, extensive dents, and would not start. His lawsuit against Hansing in U.S. District Court in California was dismissed for lack of personal jurisdiction.[20] (The formation of a contract with a nonresident defendant was not, standing alone, sufficient to create personal jurisdiction in California.)

Boxes identifying special Internet e-commerce topics are strategically placed throughout these chapters.

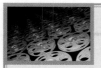

lawflix

Paper Moon (1973) (PG)

In this movie for which Tatum O'Neal was given an Oscar, the ongoing issue between Annie and her alleged father is her recoupment of the money she says he promised. Discuss the contract issues (voidable [minor], formation, unilateral vs. bilateral, express, informal, etc.).

Check out LawFlix at **www.cengage.com/blaw/dvl** to access movie clips that illustrate business law concepts.

MAKE THE CONNECTION

SUMMARY

A contract is a binding agreement between two or more parties. A contract arises when an offer is accepted with contractual intent (the intent to make a binding agreement).

Contracts may be classified in a number of ways according to form, the way in which they were created, validity, and obligations. With respect to form, a contract may be either informal or formal, such as those under seal or those appearing on the records of courts. Contracts may be classified by the way they were created as those that are expressed by words— written or oral—and those that are implied or deduced from conduct. The question of validity requires distinguishing between contracts that are valid, those that are voidable, and those that are not contracts at all but are merely void agreements. Contracts can be distinguished on the basis of the obligations created as executed contracts, in which everything has been

---

[20] *Boschetto v. Hansing*, 539 F3d 1011 (9th Cir 2008).

performed, and executory contracts, in which something remains to be done. The bilateral contract is formed by exchanging a promise for a promise, so each party has the obligation of thereafter rendering the promised performance. In the unilateral contract, which is the doing of an act in exchange for a promise, no further performance is required of the offeree who performed the act.

In certain situations, the law regards it as unjust for a person to receive a benefit and not pay for it. In such a case, the law of quasi contracts allows the performing person to recover the reasonable value of the benefit conferred on the benefited person even though no contract between them requires any payment. Unjust enrichment, which a quasi contract is designed to prevent, sometimes arises when there was never any contract between the persons involved or when there was a contract, but for some reason it was avoided or held to be merely a void agreement.

LEARNING OUTCOMES

After studying this chapter, you should be able to clearly explain:

A. NATURE OF CONTRACTS

LO.1 Explain the meaning and importance of privity of a contract
See the example of the subcontractor, RPR & Associates, who worked on a project but could not sue the owner for payment, p. 269.

LO.2 Describe the way in which a contract arises
See the discussion on offer and acceptance on p. 269.

B. CLASSES OF CONTRACTS

LO.3 Distinguish between bilateral and unilateral contracts
See the example of the Nantucket painters on p. 276.
See the *AON Risk Services* case where an insurance agent won his case based on a unilateral contract theory, p. 273.

LO.4 Explain the reasoning behind quasi-contract recovery
See the example whereby Cher had to pay a home designer for certain work even though there was no contract, p. 275.

C. CONTRACTING ON THE INTERNET

LO.5 Explain how Internet contracts involve the same types of issues as offline contracts.
See the eBay example on p. 279.

KEY TERMS

bilateral contract	obligee	quantum meruit
contract	obligor	quasi contract
contracts under seal	offeree	recognizance
executed contract	offeror	right of first refusal
executory contract	option contract	unilateral contract
express contract	privity	valid contract
formal contracts	privity of contract	void agreement
implied contract	promisee	voidable contract
informal contract	promisor	

QUESTIONS AND CASE PROBLEMS

1. What is a contract?

2. Fourteen applicants for a city of Providence, Rhode Island, police academy training class each received from the city a letter stating that it was a "conditional offer of employment" subject to successful completion of medical and psychological exams. The 14 applicants passed the medical and psychological exams. However, these applicants were replaced by others after the city changed the selection criteria. Can you identify an offer and acceptance in this case? Can you make out a bilateral or unilateral contract? [*Ardito et al. v City of Providence,* 213 F Supp 2d 358 (D RI)]

3. Compare an implied contract with a quasi contract.

4. The Jordan Keys law firm represented the Greater Southeast Community Hospital of Washington, D.C., in a medical malpractice suit against the hospital. The hospital was self-insured for the first $1,000,000 of liability and the St. Paul Insurance Co. provided excess coverage up to $4,000,000. The law firm was owed $67,000 for its work on the malpractice suit when the hospital went into bankruptcy. The bankruptcy court ordered the law firm to release its files on the case to St. Paul to defend under the excess coverage insurance, and the Jordan Keys firm sued St. Paul for its legal fees of $67,000 expended prior to the bankruptcy under an "implied-in-fact contract" because the insurance company would have the benefit of all of its work. Decide. [*Jordan Keys v St. Paul Fire*, 870 A2d 58 (DC)]

5. Beck was the general manager of Chilkoot Lumber Co. Haines sold fuel to the company. To persuade Haines to sell on credit, Beck signed a paper by which he promised to pay any debt the lumber company owed Haines. He signed this paper with his name followed by "general manager." Haines later sued Beck on this promise, and Beck raised the defense that the addition of "general manager" showed that Beck, who was signing on behalf of Chilkoot, was not personally liable and did not intend to be bound by the paper. Was Beck liable on the paper? [*Beck v Haines Terminal and Highway Co.,* 843 P2d 1229 (Alaska)]

6. *A* made a contract to construct a house for *B*. Subsequently, *B* sued *A* for breach of contract. *A* raised the defense that the contract was not binding because it was not sealed. Is this a valid defense? [*Cooper v G. E. Construction Co.*, 158 SE2d 305 (Ga App)]

7. Edward Johnson III, the CEO and principal owner of the world's largest mutual fund company, Fidelity Investments, Inc., was a longtime tennis buddy of Richard Larson. In 1995, Johnson asked Larson, who had construction experience, to supervise the construction of a house on Long Pond, Mount Desert Island, Maine. Although they had no written contract, Larson agreed to take on the project for $6,700 per month plus lodging. At the end of the project in 1997, Johnson made a $175,000 cash payment to Larson, and he made arrangements for Larson to live rent-free on another Johnson property in the area called Pray's Meadow in exchange for looking after Johnson's extensive property interests inMaine. In the late summer of 1999, Johnson initiated a new project

on the Long Pond property. Johnson had discussions with Larson about doing this project, but Larson asked to be paid his former rate, and Johnson balked because he had already hired a project manager. According to Johnson, at a later date he again asked Larson to take on the "shop project" as a favor and in consideration of continued rent-free use of the Pray's Meadow home. Johnson stated that Larson agreed to do the job "pro bono" in exchange for the use of the house, and Johnson acknowledged that he told Larson he would "take care" of Larson at the end of the project, which could mean as much or as little as Johnson determined. Larson stated that Johnson told him that he would "take care of" Larson if he would do the project and told him to "trust the Great Oracle" (meaning Johnson, the highly successful businessperson). Larson sought payment in March 2000 and asked Johnson for "something on account" in April. Johnson offered Larson a loan. In August during a tennis match, Larson again asked Johnson to pay him. Johnson became incensed, and through an employee, he ended Larson's participation in the project and asked him to vacate Pray's Meadow. Larson complied and filed suit for payment for work performed at the rate of $6,700 per month. Did Larson have an express contract with Johnson? What legal theory or theories could Larson utilize in his lawsuit? How would you decide this case if you believed Larson's version of the facts? How would you decide the case if you believed Johnson's version of the facts? [*Larson v Johnson*, 196 F Supp 2d 38 (D.Me 2002)]

8. While Clara Novak was sick, her daughter Janie helped her in many ways. Clara died, and Janie then claimed that she was entitled to be paid for the services she had rendered her mother. This claim was opposed by three brothers and sisters who also rendered services to the mother. They claimed that Janie was barred because of the presumption that services rendered between family members are gratuitous. Janie claimed that this presumption was not applicable because she had not lived with her mother but had her own house. Was Janie correct? [*In re Estate of Novak*, 398 NW2d 653 (Minn App)]

9. Dozier and his wife, daughter, and grandson lived in the house Dozier owned. At the request of the daughter and grandson, Paschall made some improvements to the house. Dozier did not authorize these, but he knew that the improvements were being made and did not object to them. Paschall sued Dozier for the reasonable value of the improvements, but Dozier argued that he had not made any contract for such improvements. Was he obligated to pay for such improvements?

10. When Harriet went away for the summer, Landry, a house painter, painted her house. He had a contract to paint a neighbor's house but painted Harriet's house by mistake. When Harriet returned from vacation, Landry billed her for $3,100, which was a fair price for the work. She refused to pay. Landry claimed that she had a quasi-contractual liability for that amount. Was he correct?

11. Margrethe and Charles Pyeatte, a married couple, agreed that she would work so that he could go to law school and that when he finished, she would go back to school for her master's degree. After Charles was admitted to the bar and before Margrethe went back to school, the two were divorced. She sued Charles, claiming that she was entitled to quasi-contractual recovery of the money that

she had paid for Charles's support and law school tuition. He denied liability. Was she entitled to recover for the money she spent for Charles's maintenance and law school tuition? [*Pyeatte v Pyeatte*, 661 P2d 196 (Ariz App)]

12. Carriage Way was a real estate development of approximately 80 houses and 132 apartments. The property owners were members of the Carriage Way Property Owners Association. Each year, the association would take care of certain open neighboring areas, including a nearby lake, that were used by the property owners. The board of directors of the association would make an assessment or charge against the property owners to cover the cost of this work. The property owners paid these assessments for a number of years and then refused to pay any more. In spite of this refusal, the association continued to take care of the areas in question. The association then sued the property owners and claimed that they were liable for the benefit that had been conferred on them. Were the owners liable? [*Board of Directors of Carriage Way Property Owners Ass'n v Western National Bank*, 487 NE2d 974 (Ill App)]

13. Lombard insured his car, and when it was damaged, the insurer sent the car to General Auto Service for repairs. The insurance company went bankrupt and did not pay the repair bill. General Auto Service then sued Lombard for the bill because he had benefited from the repair work. Was he liable?

14. When a college student complained about a particular course, the vice president of the college asked the teacher to prepare a detailed report about the course. The teacher did and then demanded additional compensation for the time spent in preparing the report. He claimed that the college was liable to provide compensation on an implied contract. Was he correct? [*Zadrozny v City Colleges of Chicago*, 581 NE2d 44 (Ill App)]

15. Smith made a contract to sell automatic rifles to a foreign country. Because the sale of such weapons to that country was illegal under an act of Congress, the U.S. government prosecuted Smith for making the contract. He raised the defense that because the contract was illegal, it was void and there is no binding obligation when a contract is void; therefore, no contract for which he could be prosecuted existed. Was he correct?

CPA QUESTIONS

1. Kay, an art collector, promised Hammer, an art student, that if Hammer could obtain certain rare artifacts within two weeks, Kay would pay for Hammer's postgraduate education. At considerable effort and expense, Hammer obtained the specified artifacts within the two-week period. When Hammer requested payment, Kay refused. Kay claimed that there was no consideration for the promise. Hammer would prevail against Kay based on:

   a. Unilateral contract

   b. Unjust enrichment

   c. Public policy

   d. Quasi contract

Chapter 13

FORMATION OF CONTRACTS: OFFER AND ACCEPTANCE

A *contract* consists of enforceable obligations that have been voluntarily assumed. Thus, one of the essential elements of a contract is an agreement. This chapter explains how the basic agreement arises, when there is a contract, and how there can be merely unsuccessful negotiations without a resulting contract.

A. Requirements of an Offer

offer–expression of an offeror's willingness to enter into a contractual agreement.

An **offer** expresses the willingness of the offeror to enter into a contractual agreement regarding a particular subject. It is a promise that is conditional upon an act, a forbearance (a refraining from doing something one has a legal right to do), or a return promise.

CPA ## 1. Contractual Intention

To make an offer, the offeror must appear to intend to create a binding obligation. Whether this intent exists is determined by objective standards.[1] This intent may be shown by conduct.

For Example, when one party signs a written contract and sends it to the other party, such action is an offer to enter into a contract on the terms of the writing.

There is no contract when a social invitation is made or when an offer is made in obvious jest or excitement. A reasonable person would not regard such an offer as indicating a willingness to enter into a binding agreement.

(A) INVITATION TO NEGOTIATE. The first statement made by one of two persons is not necessarily an offer. In many instances, there may be a preliminary discussion or an invitation by one party to the other to negotiate or to make an offer. Thus, an inquiry by a school as to whether a teacher wished to continue the following year was merely a survey or invitation to negotiate and was not an offer that could be accepted. Therefore, the teacher's affirmative response did not create a contract.

Ordinarily, a seller sending out circulars or catalogs listing prices is not regarded as making an offer to sell at those prices. The seller is merely indicating a willingness to consider an offer made by a buyer on those terms. The reason for this rule is, in part, the practical consideration that because a seller does not have an unlimited supply of any commodity, the seller cannot possibly intend to make a contract with everyone who sees the circular. The same principle is applied to merchandise that is displayed with price tags in stores or store windows and to most advertisements. An advertisement in a newspaper is ordinarily considered an invitation to negotiate and is not an offer that can be accepted by a reader of the paper.[2] However, some court decisions have construed advertisements as offers that called for an act on the part of the customer thereby forming a unilateral contract, such as the advertisement of a reward for the return of lost property.

Quotations of prices, even when sent on request, are likewise not offers unless the parties have had previous dealings or unless a trade custom exists that would give the recipient of the quotation reason to believe that an offer was being made. Whether a

---

[1] *Glass Service Co. v State Farm Mutual Automobile Ins. Co.*, 530 NW2d 867 (Minn App 1995).
[2] *Pico v Cutter Dodge, Inc.*, 98 Hawaii 309 (2002).

price quotation is to be treated as an offer or merely an invitation to negotiate is a question of the intent of the party giving the quotation.[3]

(B) Agreement to Make a Contract at a Future Date. No contract arises when the parties merely agree that at a future date they will consider making a contract or will make a contract on terms to be agreed on at that time. In such a case, neither party is under any obligation until the future contract is made. Unless an agreement is reached on all material terms and conditions and nothing is left to future negotiations, a contract to enter a contract in the future is of no effect. **For Example,** Hewitt Associates provided employee benefits administrative services to Rollins, Inc. under a contract negotiated in 2001 to run through 2006. Prior to its expiration, the parties negotiated—seeking to agree to a multiyear extension of the 2001 agreement. They agreed to all of the material terms of the contract, except that Rollins balked at a $1.8 million penalty clause. Rollins's employees told Hewitt that the extension "was going to be signed." However, Rollins did not sign and the 2001 agreement expired. Hewitt's contention that the agreement was enforceable at the moment Rollins told Hewitt it was going to sign the new agreement was rejected by the court, stating that an agreement to reach an agreement is a contradiction in terms and imposes no obligation on the parties.[4]

2. Definiteness

An offer, and the resulting contract, must be definite and certain.[5] If an offer is indefinite or vague or if an essential provision is lacking,[6] no contract arises from an attempt to accept it. The reason is that courts cannot tell what the parties are to do. Thus, an offer to conduct a business for as long as it is profitable is too vague to be a valid offer. The acceptance of such an offer does not result in a contract that can be enforced. Statements by a bank that it was "with" the debtors and would "support" them in their proposed business venture were too vague to be regarded as a promise by the bank to make necessary loans to the debtors.

CASE SUMMARY

What is the Meaning of an Agreement for a "Damn Good Job"?

FACTS: Larry Browneller made an oral contract with Hubert Plankenhorn to restore a 1963 Chevrolet Impala convertible. The car was not in good condition. Hubert advised the owner that his work would not yield a car of "show" quality because of the condition of the body, and he accordingly believed that the owner merely wanted a presentable car. Larry, on the other hand, having told Hubert that he wanted a "damn good job," thought this statement would yield a car that would be competitive at the small amateur car shows he attended. When the finished car had what Larry asserted were "waves" in the paint as a result of an uneven surface on the body, Larry brought suit against Hubert for breach of the oral contract.

---

[3] Statutes prohibiting false or misleading advertising may require adherence to advertised prices.
[4] *Hewitt Associates, LLC v Rollins, Inc.,* 669 SE2d 551 (Ga App 2008).
[5] *Graziano v Grant,* 744 A2d 156 (NJ Super AD 1999).
[6] *Peace v Doming Holdings Inc.,* 554 SE2d 314 (Ga App 2001).

CASE SUMMARY

Continued

DECISION: There was clearly a misunderstanding between the parties over the quality of work that could and would be obtained. *Quality* was a material term of the oral contract between the parties, on which there was no shared understanding. Accordingly, a court will not find an individual in breach of a term of the contract where the term did not exist. [**In re Hubert Plankenhorn 228 BR 638 (ND Ohio 1998)**]

The fact that minor, ministerial, and nonessential terms are left for future determination does not make an agreement too vague to be a contract.[7]

CASE SUMMARY

Offer to Purchase Is Controlling Legal Document

FACTS: John McCarthy executed an offer to purchase (OTP) real estate on a preprinted form generated by the Greater Boston Real Estate Board. The OTP contained a description of the property, the price to be paid, deposit requirements, limited title requirements, and the time and place for closing. The OTP required the parties to execute the applicable Standard Form Purchase and Sale Agreement recommended by the Greater Boston Real Estate Board that, when executed, was to be the agreement between the parties. An unnumbered paragraph immediately above the signature line stated: "NOTICE: This is a legal document that creates binding obligations. If not understood, consult an attorney." The seller, Ann Tobin, signed the OTP. While lawyers for the parties exchanged drafts of a purchase and sale agreement (PSA), a much higher offer for the property was made to Tobin by the Diminicos. Because she had not yet signed the purchase and sale agreement, Tobin accepted the Diminicos's offer and executed a purchase and sales agreement with them. Before that deal closed, McCarthy filed an action for specific performance of the OTP. McCarthy contended he and Tobin intended to be bound by the OTP and that the execution of a PSA was merely a formality. Tobin contended the OTP language contemplated the execution of a final written document, thus clearly indicating that the parties had not agreed to all material aspects of the transaction, and thus the parties did not intend to be bound until the PSA was signed. From a judgment for Tobin and the Diminicos, McCarthy appealed.

DECISION: Judgment for McCarthy. Although the provisions of the purchase and sale agreement can be the subject of negotiation, norms exist for their customary resolution. The inference that the OTP was legally binding is bolstered by the notice printed on the form. McCarthy and Tobin were alerted to the fact that the OTP "creates binding obligations." The OTP employed familiar contractual language. It stated that McCarthy "hereby offers to buy" the property, and Tobin's signature indicates that "this Offer is hereby accepted." The OTP also details the amount to be paid and when, describes the property bought, and specifies for how long the offer was open. This was a firm offer, the acceptance of which bound Tobin to sell and McCarthy to buy the subject property. [**McCarthy v Tobin, 706 NE2d 629 (Mass 1999)**]

---

[7] *Hsu v Vet-A-Mix, Inc.*, 479 NW2d 336 (Iowa App 1991). But see *Ocean Atlantic Development Corp v Aurora Christian Schools, Inc.*, 322 F3d 983 (7th Cir 2003), where letter offers to purchase (OTP) real estate were signed by both parties, but the offers conditioned the purchase and sale of each property upon the subsequent execution of a purchase and sale agreement. The court held that the parties thus left themselves room to walk away from the deal under Illinois law, and the OTPs were not enforced.

thinking things through

The Rules of Negotiations

Business agreements are often reached after much discussion, study, and posturing by both sides. Many statements may be made by both sides about the price or value placed on the subject of the transaction. Withholding information or presenting selective, self-serving information may be perceived by a party to the negotiations as protective self-interest. Does the law of contracts apply a duty of good faith and fair dealing in the negotiation of contracts? Does the Uniform Commercial Code provide for a general duty of good faith in the negotiation of contracts? Are lawyers under an ethical obligation to inform opposing counsel of relevant facts? The answer to all of these questions is no.

The Restatement (Second) of Contracts applies the duty of good faith and fair dealing to the performance and enforcement of contracts, not their negotiation[*]; so also does the UCC.[**] The American Bar Association's Model Rules of Professional Conduct, Rule 4.1 Comment 1 requires a lawyer to be "truthful" when dealing with others on a client's behalf, but it also states that generally a lawyer has "no affirmative duty to inform an opposing party of relevant facts."[***] Comment 2 to Rule 4.1 contains an example of a "nonmaterial" statement of a lawyer as "estimates of price or value placed on the subject of a transaction."

The legal rules of negotiations state that—in the absence of fraud, special relationships, or statutory or contractual duties—negotiators are not obligated to divulge pertinent information to the other party to the negotiations. The parties to negotiations themselves must demand and analyze pertinent information and ultimately assess the fairness of the proposed transaction. Should a party conclude that the elements of a final proposal or offer are excessive or dishonest, that party's legal option is to walk away from the deal. Generally, the party has no basis to bring a lawsuit for lack of good faith and fair dealing in negotiations.

However, THINKING THINGS THROUGH, the ethical standards for negotiations set forth in Chapter 3 indicate that establishing a reputation for trustworthiness, candor, and reliability often leads to commercial success for a company's continuing negotiations with its customers, suppliers, distributors, lenders, unions, and employees.[****]

[*] Restatement (Second) of Contracts § 105, comment (c).
[**] Uniform Commercial Code § 1-203.
[***] American Bar Association Model Rule of Professional Conduct 4.1 (a) Comment 1.

[****] For a contrary example, consider the following story. The Atlanta Braves baseball team's general manager Frank Wren negotiated with free agent baseball player Rafael Furcal's agent Paul Kinzer. When all terms had been negotiated, Kinzer asked for a written terms-of-agreement sheet signed by the Braves, which to Wren meant an agreement had been reached. Kinzer took the sheet to the L.A. Dodgers, who then reached an agreement to sign the shortstop. Braves President John Schuerholz said, "The Atlanta Braves will no longer do business with that company—ever. I told Arn Tellem that we can't trust them to be honest and forthright." "Braves GM Blasts Furcal's Agents," Associated Press, *The Boston Globe*, December 20, 2008, C-7.

The law does not favor the destruction of contracts because that would go against the social force of carrying out the intent of the parties.[8] Consequently, when it is claimed that a contract is too indefinite to be enforced, a court will do its best to find the intent of the parties and thereby reach the conclusion that the contract is not too indefinite. **For Example,** boxing promoter Don King had both a Promotional Agreement and a Bout Agreement with boxer Miguel Angel Gonzalez. The Bout Agreement for a boxing match held on March 7, 1998, with Julio Cesar Chavez gave King the option to promote the next four of Gonzalez's matches. The contract made clear that if Gonzalez won the Chavez match, he would receive at

[8] *Mears v Nationwide Mut, Inc. Co.*, 91 F3d 1118 (8th Cir 1996).

FIGURE 13-1 | *Offer and Acceptance*

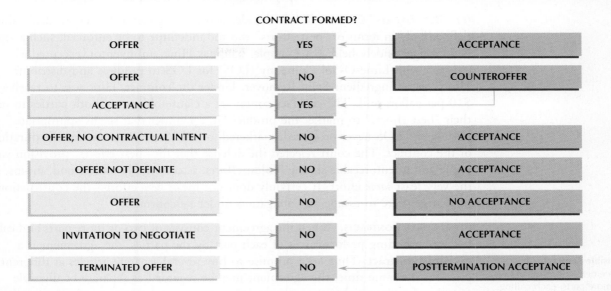

least $75,000 for the next fight unless the parties agreed otherwise, and if he lost, he would receive at least $25,000 for the subsequent fight unless otherwise agreed. The agreement did not explicitly state the purse for the subsequent match in the event of a draw. The Chavez match ended in a draw, and Gonzalez contended that this omission rendered the contract so indefinite that it was unenforceable. The court disagreed, stating that striking down a contract as indefinite and in essence meaningless is at best a last resort. The court held that although the contract was poorly drafted, the Promotional Agreement contained explicit price terms for which a minimum purse for fights following a draw may be inferred.[9] A court may not rewrite the agreement of the parties in order to make it definite.

(A) DEFINITE BY INCORPORATION. An offer and the resulting contract that by themselves may appear "too indefinite" may be made definite by reference to another writing. **For Example,** a lease agreement that was too vague by itself was made definite because the parties agreed that the lease should follow the standard form with which both were familiar. An agreement may also be made definite by reference to the prior dealings of the parties and to trade practices.

(B) IMPLIED TERMS. Although an offer must be definite and certain, not all of its terms need to be expressed. Some omitted terms may be implied by law. **For Example,** an offer "to pay $400" for a certain Movado timepiece does not state the terms of payment. A court, however, would not condemn this provision as too vague but would hold that it required that cash be paid and that the payment be made on delivery of the watch. Likewise, terms may be implied from conduct. As an illustration, when borrowed money was given to the borrower by a check on which

[9] *Gonzalez v Don King Productions, Inc.,* 17 F Supp 2d 313 (SDNY 1998); see also *Echols v Pelullo,* 377 F3d 272 (3rd Cir 2004).

the word *loan* was written, the act of the borrower in endorsing the check constituted an agreement to repay the amount of the check.

(c) "BEST EFFORTS" CLAUSES. While decades ago it was generally accepted that a duty defined only in terms of "best efforts" was too indefinite to be enforced, such a view is no longer widely held. **For Example,** Thomas Hinc, an inventor, executed a contract with Lime-O-Sol Company (LOS) for LOS to produce and distribute Hinc's secret ingredient Stain Remover. Under the contract, Hinc was to receive $10 per gallon sold. The contract contained a clause obligating both parties to use their "best efforts" to market the product "in a manner that seems appropriate." Ultimately, LOS never produced, marketed, or sold Stain Remover for the duration of the contract. The court rejected the defense that the "best efforts" provision was vague and unenforceable stating "[b]est efforts, as commonly understood, means, at the very least *some* effort. It certainly does not mean *zero* effort—the construction LOS urges here to escape any obligation under its contract."[10]

(d) DIVISIBLE CONTRACTS. When the agreement consists of two or more parts and calls for corresponding performances of each part by the parties, the agreement is a **divisible contract**. Thus, in a promise to buy several separate articles at different prices at the same time, the agreement may be regarded as separate or divisible promises for the articles.

(e) EXCEPTIONS TO DEFINITENESS. The law has come to recognize certain situations in which the practical necessity of doing business makes it desirable to have a contract, yet the situation is such that it is either impossible or undesirable to adopt definite terms in advance. In these cases, the indefinite term is often tied to the concept of good-faith performance or to some independent factor that will be definitely ascertainable at some time in the future. The indefinite term might be tied to market price, cost to complete, production, or sales requirements. Thus, the law recognizes binding contracts in the case of a **requirements contract**—that is, a contract to buy all requirements of the buyer from the seller.[11] **For Example,** an agreement between Honeywell International Inc. and Air Products and Chemicals Inc. whereby Air Products would purchase its total requirements of wet process chemicals from Honeywell was held to be an enforceable requirements contract.[12] The law also recognizes as binding an **output contract**—that is, the contract of a producer to sell

divisible contract–
agreement consisting of two or more parts, each calling for corresponding performances of each part by the parties.

requirements contract–
contract to buy all requirements of the buyer from the seller.

output contract–contract of a producer to sell its entire production or output to a given buyer.

C A S E   S U M M A R Y

GM—In The Driver's Seat On Quantity and Timing!

FACTS: Automodular entered into a series of purchase orders that obligated Delphi to purchase and Automodular to provide all of Delphi's requirements deliverable to the original equipment manufacturer (OEM), General Motors. Automodular receives directions from the OEM's final assembly plants, regardless of whether Automodular is under contract to the OEM or Delphi.

[10] *Hinc v Lime-O-Sol Company*, 382 F3d 716 (7th Cir 2004).
[11] *Simcala v American Coal Trade, Inc.*, 821 So2d 197 (Ala 2001).
[12] *Honeywell International Inc. v Air Products and Chemicals, Inc.*, 872 A2d 944 (Sup Ct Del 2005).

C A S E   S U M M A R Y

Continued

The purchase orders ("Contracts") incorporated Delphi's terms that the Buyer, GM, could require Automodular to implement changes to the specifications or design of the goods or to the scope of any services covered by the Contracts. GM informed Automodular that it needed fewer components and directed Automodular to, among other requirements, reduce shifts, change the assembly line speed, and change the length of workers' shifts. As a result, Automodular requested a price increase per unit assembled from Delphi because Automodular believed that such an increase was warranted pursuant to the Contract's change-in-scope provision. Delphi, however, refused to negotiate any price increase and the matter was litigated.

DECISION: Judgment for Delphi. In a requirements contract, the parties do not fix a quantity term, but instead, the quantity will be the buyer's needs of a specific commodity over the contract's life. Section 2.5 of the Contract states in relevant part that "[d]eliveries will be made in the quantities, on the dates, and at the times specified by Buyer in this Contract or any subsequent releases or instructions Buyer issues under this Contract," and that "[i]f the requirements of Buyer's customers or market, economic or other conditions require changes in delivery schedules, Buyer may change the rate of scheduled shipments or direct temporary suspension of scheduled shipments without entitling [Automodular] to a price adjustment or other compensation." This provision demonstrates the intent of the parties to allow the buyer to effectively control the timing and quantity of deliveries without entitling Automodular to an adjustment in price. [**In re Delphi Corp., 2009 WL 803598, (SDNY 2009).**]

the entire production or output to a given buyer. These are binding contracts even though they do not state the exact quantity of goods that are to be bought or sold.

CPA **3. Communication of Offer to Offeree**

An offer must be communicated to the offeree. Otherwise, the offeree cannot accept even though knowledge of the offer has been indirectly acquired. Internal management communications of an enterprise that are not intended for outsiders or employees do not constitute offers and cannot be accepted by them. Sometimes, particularly in the case of unilateral contracts, the offeree performs the act called for by the offeror without knowing of the offer's existence. Such performance does not constitute an acceptance. Thus, without knowing that a reward is offered for information leading to the arrest of a particular criminal, a person may provide information that leads to the arrest of the criminal. In most states, if that person subsequently learns of the reward, the reward cannot be recovered.[13]

Not only must the offer be communicated but also it must be communicated by the offeror or at the offeror's direction.

CPA **B. TERMINATION OF OFFER**

An offeree cannot accept a terminated offer. Offers may be terminated by revocation, counteroffer, rejection, lapse of time, death or disability of a party, or subsequent illegality.

---

[13] With respect to the offeror, it should not make any difference, as a practical matter, whether the services were rendered with or without knowledge of the existence of the offer. Only a small number of states have adopted this view, however.

CPA   4. Revocation of Offer by Offeror

Ordinarily, an offeror can revoke the offer before it is accepted. If this is done, the offeree cannot create a contract by accepting the revoked offer. Thus, the bidder at an auction sale may withdraw (revoke) a bid (offer) before it is accepted, and the auctioneer cannot accept that bid later.

An ordinary offer may be revoked at any time before it is accepted even though the offeror has expressly promised that the offer will be good for a stated period and that period has not yet expired. It may also be revoked even though the offeror has expressly promised to the offeree that the offer would not be revoked before a specified later date.

The fact that the offeror expressly promised to keep the offer open has no effect when no consideration was given for that promise.

(A) WHAT CONSTITUTES A REVOCATION? No particular form or words are required to constitute a revocation. Any words indicating the offeror's termination of the offer are sufficient. A notice sent to the offeree that the property that is the subject of the offer has been sold to a third person is a revocation of the offer. A customer's order for goods, which is an offer to purchase at certain prices, is revoked by a notice to the seller of the cancellation of the order, provided that such notice is communicated before the order is accepted.

(B) COMMUNICATION OF REVOCATION. A revocation of an offer is ordinarily effective only when it is made known to the offeree.[14] Until it is communicated to the offeree, directly or indirectly, the offeree has reason to believe that there is still an offer that may be accepted, and the offeree may rely on this belief. A letter revoking an offer made to a particular offeree is not effective until the offeree receives it. It is not a revocation when the offeror writes it or even when it is mailed or dispatched. A written revocation is effective, however, when it is delivered to the offeree's agent or to the offeree's residence or place of business under such circumstances that the offeree may be reasonably expected to be aware of its receipt.

It is ordinarily held that there is a sufficient communication of the revocation when the offeree learns indirectly of the offeror's revocation. This is particularly true in a land sale when the seller-offeror, after making an offer to sell the land to the offeree, sells the land to a third person and the offeree indirectly learns of such sale. The offeree necessarily realizes that the seller cannot perform the original offer and therefore must be considered to have revoked it.

If the offeree accepts an offer before it is effectively revoked, a valid contract is created.

(C) OPTION CONTRACTS. An *option contract* is a binding promise to keep an offer open for a stated period of time or until a specified date. An option contract requires that the promisor receive consideration—that is, something, such as a sum of money—as the price for the promise to keep the offer open. In other words, the option is a contract to refrain from revoking an offer.

(D) FIRM OFFERS. As another exception to the rule that an offer can be revoked at any time before acceptance, statutes in some states provide that an offeror cannot revoke

---

[14] *MD Drilling and Blasting, Inc. v MLS Construction, LLC,* 889 A2d 850 (Conn App 2006).

firm offer–offer stated to be held open for a specified time, which must be so held in some states even in the absence of an option contract, or under the UCC, with respect to merchants.

an offer prior to its expiration when the offeror makes a firm offer. A **firm offer** is an offer that states that it is to be irrevocable, or irrevocable for a stated period of time. Under the Uniform Commercial Code, this doctrine of firm offer applies to a merchant's signed, written offer to buy or sell goods but with a maximum of three months on its period of irrevocability.[15]

5. Counteroffer by Offeree

counteroffer–proposal by an offeree to the offeror that changes the terms of, and thus rejects, the original offer.

The offeree rejects the offer when she ignores the original offer and replies with a different offer.[16] If the offeree purports to accept an offer but in so doing makes any change to the terms of the offer, such action is a **counteroffer** that rejects the original offer. An "acceptance" that changes the terms of the offer or adds new terms is a rejection of the original offer and constitutes a counteroffer.[17]

Ordinarily, if *A* makes an offer, such as to sell a used automobile to *B* for $3,000, and *B* in reply makes an offer to buy at $2,500, the original offer is terminated. *B* is in effect indicating refusal of the original offer and in its place is making a different offer. Such an offer by the offeree is known as a *counteroffer*. No contract arises unless the original offeror accepts the counteroffer.

Counteroffers are not limited to offers that directly contradict the original offers. Any departure from or addition to the original offer is a counteroffer even though the original offer was silent on the point added by the counteroffer.

6. Rejection of Offer by Offeree

If the offeree rejects the offer and communicates this rejection to the offeror, the offer is terminated. Communication of a rejection terminates an offer even though the period for which the offeror agreed to keep the offer open has not yet expired. It may be that the offeror is willing to renew the offer, but unless this is done, there is no longer any offer for the offeree to accept.

7. Lapse of Time

When the offer states that it is open until a particular date, the offer terminates on that date if it has not yet been accepted. This is particularly so when the offeror declares that the offer shall be void after the expiration of the specified time. Such limitations are strictly construed.

If the offer contains a time limitation for acceptance, an attempted acceptance after the expiration of that time has no effect and does not give rise to a contract.[18] When a specified time limitation is imposed on an option, the option cannot be exercised after the expiration of that time, regardless of whether the option was exercised within what would have been held a reasonable time if no time period had been specified.

---

[15] UCC § 2-205.
[16] *Bourque v FDIC*, 42 F3d 704 (1st Cir 1994).
[17] *McLaughlin v Heikkila*, 697 NW2d 731 (Minn App 2005).
[18] *Century 21 Pinetree Properties, Inc. v Cason*, 469 SE2d 458 (Ga App 1996).

If the offer does not specify a time, it will terminate after the lapse of a reasonable time. What constitutes a reasonable time depends on the circumstances of each case—that is, on the nature of the subject matter, the nature of the market in which it is sold, the time of year, and other factors of supply and demand. If a commodity is perishable or fluctuates greatly in value, the reasonable time will be much shorter than if the subject matter is of a stable value. An offer to sell a harvested crop of tomatoes would expire within a very short time. When a seller purports to accept an offer after it has lapsed by the expiration of time, the seller's acceptance is merely a counteroffer and does not create a contract unless the buyer accepts that counteroffer.

8. Death or Disability of Either Party

If either the offeror or offeree dies or becomes mentally incompetent before the offer is accepted, the offer is automatically terminated. **For Example,** Chet Wilson offers to sell his ranch to Interport, Inc., for $2.5 million. Five days later, Chet is killed in an aviation accident. Interport, Inc., subsequently writes to Chet Wilson Jr., an adult, that his father's offer is accepted. No contract is formed because the offer made by Chet died with him.

CPA 9. Subsequent Illegality

If the performance of the contract becomes illegal after the offer is made, the offer is terminated. **For Example,** if an offer is made to sell six semiautomatic handguns to a commercial firing range for $550 per weapon but a new law prohibiting such sales is enacted before the offer is accepted, the offer is terminated.

CPA C. ACCEPTANCE OF OFFER

acceptance—unqualified assent to the act or proposal of another; as the acceptance of a draft (bill of exchange), of an offer to make a contract, of goods delivered by the seller, or of a gift or deed.

An **acceptance** is the assent of the offeree to the terms of the offer. Objective standards determine whether there has been an agreement of the parties.

10. What Constitutes an Acceptance?

No particular form of words or mode of expression is required, but there must be a clear expression that the offeree agrees to be bound by the terms of the offer. If the offeree reserves the right to reject the offer, such action is not an acceptance.[19]

11. Privilege of Offeree

Ordinarily, the offeree may refuse to accept an offer. If there is no acceptance, by definition there is no contract. The fact that there had been a series of contracts between the parties and that one party's offer had always been accepted before by the other does not create any legal obligation to continue to accept subsequent offers.

[19] *Pantano v McGowan*, 530 NW2d 912 (Neb 1995).

CPA   12. Effect of Acceptance

The acceptance of an offer creates a binding agreement or contract,[20] assuming that all of the other elements of a contract are present. Neither party can subsequently withdraw from or cancel the contract without the consent of the other party. **For Example,** James Gang refused to honor an oral stock purchase agreement he made with Moshen Sadeghi under terms he assented to and that were announced on the record to a court as a mutual settlement of a dispute. Gang was not allowed subsequently to withdraw from the agreement, because it was an enforceable contract.[21]

CPA   13. Nature of Acceptance

An *acceptance* is the offeree's manifestation of intent to enter into a binding agreement on the terms stated in the offer. Whether there is an acceptance depends on whether the offeree has manifested an intent to accept. It is the objective or outward appearance that is controlling rather than the subjective or unexpressed intent of the offeree.[22]

In the absence of a contrary requirement in the offer, an acceptance may be indicated by an informal "okay," by a mere affirmative nod of the head, or in the case of an offer of a unilateral contract, by performance of the act called for.

The acceptance must be absolute and unconditional. It must accept just what is offered.[23] If the offeree changes any terms of the offer or adds any new term, there is no acceptance because the offeree does not agree to what was offered.

When the offeree does not accept the offer exactly as made, the addition of any qualification converts the "acceptance" into a counteroffer, and no contract arises unless the original offeror accepts such a counteroffer.

CPA   14. Who May Accept?

Only the person to whom an offer is directed may accept it. If anyone else attempts to accept it, no agreement or contract with that person arises.

If the offer is directed to a particular class rather than a specified individual, anyone within that class may accept it. If the offer is made to the public at large, any member of the public at large having knowledge of the existence of the offer may accept it.

When a person to whom an offer was not made attempts to accept it, the attempted acceptance has the effect of an offer. If the original offeror is willing to accept this offer, a binding contract arises. If the original offeror does not accept the new offer, there is no contract.

---

[20] *Ochoa v Ford*, 641 NE2d 1042 (Ind App 1994).
[21] *Sadeghi v Gang*, 270 SW2d 773 (Tex App 2008).
[22] *Cowan v Mervin Mewes, Inc.*, 546 NW2d 104 (SD 1996).
[23] *Jones v Frickey*, 618 SE2d 29 (Ga App 2005).

CASE SUMMARY

There's No Turning Back

FACTS: As a lease was about to expire, the landlord, CRA Development, wrote the tenant, Keryakos Textiles, setting forth the square footage and the rate terms on which the lease would be renewed. Keryakos sent a reply stating that it was willing to pay the proposed rate but wanted different cancellation and option terms in the renewal contract. CRA rejected Keryakos's terms, and on learning this, Keryakos notified CRA that it accepted the terms of its original letter. CRA sought to evict Keryakos from the property, claiming that no lease contract existed between it and Keryakos.

DECISION: The lease contract is governed by ordinary contract law. When the tenant offered other terms in place of those made by the landlord's offer, the tenant made a counteroffer. This had the effect of rejecting or terminating the landlord's offer. The tenant could not then accept the rejected offer after the tenant's counteroffer was rejected. Therefore, there was no contract. [**Keryakos Textiles, Inc. v CRA Development, Inc. 563 NYS2d 308 (App Div 1990)**]

CPA ___ **15. Manner and Time of Acceptance**

The offeror may specify the manner and time for accepting the offer. When the offeror specifies that there must be a written acceptance, no contract arises when the offeree makes an oral acceptance. If the offeror calls for acceptance by a specified time and date, a late acceptance has no legal effect, and a contract is not formed. Where no time is specified in the offer, the offeree has a reasonable period of time to accept the offer. After the time specified in the offer or a reasonable period of time expires (when no time is specified in the offer), the offeree's power to make a contract by accepting the offer "lapses."

When the offeror calls for the performance of an act or of certain conduct, the performance thereof is an acceptance of the offer and creates a unilateral contract.

When the offeror has specified a particular manner and time of acceptance, generally, the offeree cannot accept in any other way. The basic rule applied by the courts is that the offeror is the master of the offer![24]

CPA ___ (A) SILENCE AS ACCEPTANCE. In most cases, the offeree's silence and failure to act cannot be regarded as an acceptance. Ordinarily, the offeror is not permitted to frame an offer in such a way as to make the silence and inaction of the offeree operate as an acceptance. Nor can a party to an existing contract effect a modification of that agreement without the other party's actual acceptance or approval. **For Example,** H. H. Taylor made a contract with Andy Stricker, a civil engineer, to design a small hotel. The parties agreed on an hourly rate with "total price not to exceed $7,200," and required that additional charges be presented to Taylor prior to proceeding with any changes. Andy was required to dedicate more hours to the project than anticipated but could not present the additional charges to

[24] See *1-800 Contacts, Inc v Weigner,* 127 P3d 1241 (Utah App 2005).

e-commerce&cyberlaw
Contract Formation On The Internet

It is not possible for an online service provider or seller to individually bargain with each person who visits its Web site. The Web site owner, therefore, as offeror, places its proposed terms on its Web site and requires visitors to assent to these terms in order to access the site, download software, or purchase a product or service.

In a written contract, the parties sign a paper document indicating their intention to be bound by the terms of the contract. Online, however, an agreement may be accomplished by the visitor-offeree simply typing the words "I Accept" in an onscreen box and then clicking a "send" or similar button that indicates acceptance. Or the individual clicks an "I Agree" or "I Accept" icon or check box. Access to the site is commonly denied those who do not agree to the terms. Such agreements have come to be known as *clickwrap* agreements and in the case of software license agreements, *SLAs*. The agreements contain fee schedules and other financial terms and may contain terms such as a notice of the proprietary nature of the material contained on the site and of any limitations on the use of the site and the downloading of software. Moreover, the clickwrap agreements may contain limitations on liability, including losses associated with the use of downloaded software or products or services purchased from the site.

To determine whether a clickwrap agreement is enforceable, courts apply traditional principles of contract law and focus on whether the plaintiffs had reasonable notice of and manifested assent to the clickwrap agreement. Failure to read an enforceable clickwrap agreement, as with any binding contract, will not excuse compliance with its terms.

In *Specht v Netscape Communications Corp.,** the Internet users were urged to click on a button to download free software, but the offer did not make clear to the user that clicking the download button would signify assent to restrictive contractual terms and conditions. The court, in its 2002 decision, declined to enforce this clickwrap agreement. Internet sellers and service providers generally learned from the *Specht* decision, and most clickwrap agreements now provide sufficient notice and means for clear assent. For example, in *Feldman v Google, Inc.,*** decided in 2007, the user was unsuccessful in challenging the terms of Google's "AdWords" Program clickwrap agreement. In order to activate an AdWords account, the user had to visit a Web page that displayed the agreement in a scrollable text box. The text of the agreement was immediately visible to the user, as was a prominent admonition in boldface to read the terms and conditions carefully, and with instructions to indicate assent if the user agreed to the terms.

Unlike the impermissible agreement in *Specht*, the user here had to take affirmative action and click the "Yes, I agree to the above terms and conditions" button in order to proceed to the next step. Clicking "Continue" without clicking the "Yes" button would have returned the user to the same Web page. If the user did not agree to all of the terms, he could not have activated his account, placed ads, or incurred charges.

* 306 F3d 17 (2d Cir 2002).
** *Feldman v Google. Inc.*, 513 F Supp 2d 229 (ED Pa 2007). See also *A. V. v Iparadigms, LLC*, 554 F Supp 2d 473 (ED Va 2008).

Taylor because Taylor would not return his phone calls. He billed Taylor $9,035 for his services. Taylor's failure to act in not returning phone calls is not a substitute for the assent needed to modify a contract. Stricker is thus only entitled to $7,200. [25]

(B) Unordered Goods and Tickets. Sometimes a seller writes to a person with whom the seller has not had any prior dealings, stating that unless notified to the contrary, the seller will send specified merchandise and the recipient is obligated to pay for it at stated prices. There is no acceptance if the recipient of the letter ignores the offer

[25] *Stricker v Taylor*, 975 P2d 930 (Or App 1999).

and does nothing. The silence of the person receiving the letter is not an acceptance, and the sender, as a reasonable person, should recognize that none was intended.

This rule applies to all kinds of goods, books, magazines, and tickets sent through the mail when they have not been ordered. The fact that the items are not returned does not mean that they have been accepted; that is, the offeree is required neither to pay for nor to return the items. If desired, the recipient of the unordered goods may write "Return to Sender" on the unopened package and put the package back into the mail without any additional postage. The Postal Reorganization Act provides that the person who receives unordered mailed merchandise from a commercial sender has the right "to retain, use, discard, or dispose of it in any manner the recipient sees fit without any obligation whatsoever to the sender."[26] It provides further that any unordered merchandise that is mailed must have attached to it a clear and conspicuous statement of the recipient's right to treat the goods in this manner.

CPA   16. Communication of Acceptance

Acceptance by the offeree is the last step in the formation of a bilateral contract. Intuitively, the offeror's receipt of the acceptance should be the point in time when the contract is formed and its terms apply. When the parties are involved in face-to-face negotiations, a contract is formed upon the offeror's receipt of the acceptance. When the offeror hears the offeree's words of acceptance, the parties may shake hands, signifying their understanding that the contract has been formed.

CPA   (A) MAILBOX RULE. When the parties are negotiating at a distance from each other, special rules have developed as to when the acceptance takes effect based on the commercial expediency of creating a contract at the earliest period of time and the protection of the offeree. Under the so-called *mailbox rule,* a properly addressed, postage-paid mailed acceptance takes effect when the acceptance is placed into the control of the U.S. Postal Service[27] or, by judicial extension, is placed in the control of a private third-party carrier such as Federal Express or United Parcel Service.[28] That is, the acceptance is effective upon dispatch even before it is received by the offeror.

C A S E   S U M M A R Y

When the Mailbox Bangs Shut

FACTS: The Thoelkes owned land. The Morrisons mailed an offer to the Thoelkes to buy their land. The Thoelkes agreed to this offer and mailed back a contract signed by them. While this letter was in transit, the Thoelkes notified the Morrisons that their acceptance was revoked. Were the Thoelkes bound by a contract?

---

[26] Federal Postal Reorganization Act § 3009.

[27] See *Adams v Lindsell,* 106 Eng Rep 250 (KB 1818). Common law jurisdictions have unanimously adopted the mailbox rule, as has the Restatement (Second) of Contracts § 63, and the UCC [see UCC § 1-201(26),(38)].

[28] But see *Baca v. Trejo,* 902 NE2d 1108 (III App 2009) whereby an Illinois Court determined that a statute deeming a document to be filed with a state court on the date shown by the U.S. Postal Service cancellation mark—the mailbox rule—does not apply to documents consigned to a private carrier, UPS. The court reasoned that courts should not have the task of deciding which carriers are acceptable.

C A S E   S U M M A R Y

Continued

DECISION: The acceptance was effective when mailed, and the subsequent revocation of the acceptance had no effect. [**Morrison v Thoelke, 155 So 2d 889 (Fla App 1963)**]

The offeror may avoid the application of this rule by stating in the offer that acceptance shall take effect upon receipt by the offeror.

CPA (B) DETERMINING THE APPLICABLE MEANS OF COMMUNICATION. The modern rule on the selection of the appropriate medium of communication of acceptance is that unless otherwise unambiguously indicated in the offer, it shall be construed as inviting acceptance in any manner and by any medium reasonable under the circumstances.[29] A medium of communication is normally reasonable if it is one used by the offeror or if it is customary in similar transactions at the time and place the offer is received. Thus, if the offeror uses the mail to extend an offer, the offeree may accept by using the mail. Indeed, acceptance by mail is ordinarily reasonable when the parties are negotiating at a distance even if the offer is not made by mail.

C A S E   S U M M A R Y

Just Be Reasonable

FACTS: Maria Cantu was a special education teacher under a one-year contract with the San Benito School District for the 1990–1991 school year. On Saturday, August 18, just weeks before fall-term classes were to begin, she hand delivered a letter of resignation to her supervisor. Late Monday afternoon the superintendent put in the mail a properly stamped and addressed letter to Cantu accepting her offer of resignation. The next morning at 8:00, before the superintendent's letter reached her, Cantu hand delivered a letter withdrawing her resignation. The superintendent refused to recognize the attempted rescission of the resignation.

DECISION: Cantu was wrong. The resignation became binding when the acceptance of the resignation was mailed. The fact that the offer to resign had been delivered by hand did not require that the offer be accepted by a hand delivery of the acceptance. The use of mail was reasonable under the circumstances, and therefore the mailing of the acceptance made it effective. [**Cantu v Central Education Agency, 884 SW2d 563 (Tex App 1994)**]

CPA (C) TELEPHONE AND ELECTRONIC COMMUNICATION OF ACCEPTANCE. Although telephonic communication is very similar to face-to-face communication, most U.S. courts, nevertheless, have applied the mailbox rule, holding that telephoned acceptances are effective where and when dispatched.

[29] Restatement (Second) of Contracts § 30; UCC § 2-206(1) (a).

The courts have yet to address the applicability of the mailbox rule to e-mail. However, when the offeree's server is under the control of an independent entity, such as an online service provider, and the offeree cannot withdraw the message, it is anticipated that the courts will apply the mailbox rule, and acceptance will take effect on proper dispatch. In the case of companies that operate their own servers, the acceptance will take effect when the message is passed onto the Internet.

Facsimile transmissions are substantially instantaneous and could be treated as face-to-face communications. However, it is anticipated that U.S. courts, when called upon to deal with this issue, will apply the mailbox acceptance-upon-dispatch rule as they do with telephoned acceptances.

(D) **Effects of the Mailbox Rule.** If an offer requires that acceptance be communicated by a specific date and the acceptance is properly dispatched by the offeree on the final date, the acceptance is timely and the contract is formed, even though the offeror actually receives the acceptance well after the specified date has passed. **For Example,** by letter dated February 18, 1999, Morton's of Chicago mailed a certified letter to the Crab House accepting the Crab House's offer to terminate its restaurant lease. The Crab House, Inc., sought to revoke its offer to terminate the lease in a certified letter dated February 18, 1999 and by facsimile transmission to Morton's dated February 19, 1999. On February 22, 1999, the Crab House received Morton's acceptance letter; and on the same date Morton's received Crab House's letter revoking the offer to terminate the lease. Acceptance of an offer is effective upon dispatch to the Postal Service, and the contract springs into existence at the time of the mailing. Offers, revocations, and rejections are generally effective only upon the offeree's receipt. Morton's dispatch of its acceptance letter on February 18 formed an agreement to terminate the lease, and the fax dispatched on February 19 was too late to revoke the offer to terminate the lease. [30]

17. Auction Sales

At an auction sale, the statements made by the auctioneer to draw forth bids are merely invitations to negotiate. Each bid is an offer, which is not accepted until the auctioneer indicates that a particular offer or bid is accepted. Usually, this is done by the fall of the auctioneer's hammer, indicating that the highest bid made has been accepted.[31] Because a bid is merely an offer, the bidder may withdraw the bid at any time before it is accepted by the auctioneer.

Ordinarily, the auctioneer who is not satisfied with the amounts of the bids that are being made may withdraw any article or all of the property from the sale. Once a bid is accepted, however, the auctioneer cannot cancel the sale. In addition, if it had been announced that the sale was to be made "without reserve," the property must be sold to the person making the highest bid regardless of how low that bid may be.

In an auction "with reserve," the auctioneer takes bids as agent for the seller with the understanding that no contract is formed until the seller accepts the transaction.[32]

---

[30] *Morton's of Chicago v Crab House Inc.*, 746 NYS2d 317 (2002). *Kass v Grais*, 2007 NY Misc LEXIS 9017.
[31] *Dry Creek Cattle Co. v Harriet Bros. Limited Partnership,* 908 P2d 399 (Wyo 1995).
[32] *Marten v Staab,* 543 NW2d 436 (Neb 1996). Statutes regulate auctions and auctioneers in all states. For example, state of Maine law prohibits an auctioneer from conducting an auction without first having a written contract with the consignor of any property to be sold, including (1) whether the auction is with reserve or without reserve, (2) the commission rate, and (3) a description of all items to be sold. See *Street v Board of Licensing of Auctioneers,* 889 A2d 319 ([Me] 2006).

lawflix

Funny Farm (1988) (PG)

Near the end of this Chevy Chase movie, two couples face a formation issue as one couple attempts to purchase a home. An offer, presented around a friendly kitchen table setting, is declined by the sellers. Do the buyers' threats to sue the sellers have any legal basis? While the buyers had made a special trip to see the land and felt that since they were offering more than the asking price that they had a contract, the sellers were free to reject the offer. Listing a house for a price is not an offer; it is an invitation for an offer.

Check out LawFlix at **www.cengage.com/blaw/dvl** to access movie clips that illustrate business law concepts.

MAKE THE CONNECTION

SUMMARY

Because a contract arises when an offer is accepted, it is necessary to find that there was an offer and that it was accepted. If either element is missing, there is no contract.

An offer does not exist unless the offeror has contractual intent. This intent is lacking if the statement of the person is merely an invitation to negotiate, a statement of intention, or an agreement to agree at a later date. Newspaper ads, price quotations, and catalog prices are ordinarily merely invitations to negotiate and cannot be accepted.

An offer must be definite. If an offer is indefinite, its acceptance will not create a contract because it will be held that the resulting agreement is too vague to enforce. In some cases, an offer that is by itself too indefinite is made definite because some writing or standard is incorporated by reference and made part of the offer. In some cases the offer is made definite by implying terms that were not stated. In other cases, the indefinite part of the offer is ignored when that part can be divided or separated from the balance of the offer.

Assuming that there is in fact an offer that is made with contractual intent and that it is sufficiently definite, it still does not have the legal effect of an offer unless it is communicated to the offeree by or at the direction of the offeror.

In some cases, there was an offer but it was terminated before it was accepted. By definition, an attempted acceptance made after the offer has been terminated has no effect. The offeror may revoke the ordinary offer at any time. All that is required is the showing of the intent to revoke and the communication of that intent to the offeree. The offeror's power to revoke is barred by the existence of an option contract under common law or a firm offer under the Uniform Commercial Code. An offer is also terminated by the express rejection of the offer or by the making of a counteroffer, by the lapse of the time stated in the offer or of a reasonable time when none is stated, by the death or disability of either party, or by a change of law that makes illegal a contract based on the particular offer.

When the offer is accepted, a contract arises. Only the offeree can accept an offer, and the acceptance must be of the offer exactly as made without any qualification or change. Ordinarily, the offeree may accept or reject as the offeree chooses.

The acceptance is any manifestation of intent to agree to the terms of the offer. Ordinarily, silence or failure to act does not constitute acceptance. The recipient of unordered goods and tickets may dispose of the goods or use the goods without such action constituting an acceptance. An acceptance does not exist until the words or conduct demonstrating assent to the offer is communicated to the offeror. Acceptance by mail takes effect at the time and place when and where the letter is mailed or the fax is transmitted.

In an auction sale, the auctioneer asking for bids makes an invitation to negotiate. A person making a bid is making an offer, and the acceptance of the highest bid by the auctioneer is an acceptance of that offer and gives rise to a contract. When the auction sale is without reserve, the auctioneer must accept the highest bid. If the auction is not expressly without reserve, the auctioneer may refuse to accept any of the bids.

LEARNING OUTCOMES

After studying this chapter, you should be able to clearly explain:

A. REQUIREMENTS OF AN OFFER

LO.1 Decide whether an offer contains definite and certain terms
> See the *Plankenhorn* case for the meaning of a "damn good job" on p. 286.
> See the legal impact of a party's statement that the contract "was going to be signed" in the *Hewitt* example on p. 286.

B. TERMINATION OF AN OFFER

LO.2 Explain the exceptions the law makes to the requirement of definiteness
> See the *Delphi* case on requirements contracts, p. 290.

LO.3 Explain all the ways an offer can be terminated
> See the discussion of revocation, counteroffer, rejection, lapse of time, death or disability of a party, or subsequent illegality, starting on p. 291.

C. ACCEPTANCE OF AN OFFER

LO.4 Explain what constitutes the acceptance of an offer
> See the *Sadeghi* example where acceptance of an offer created a binding contract, p. 295.
> See the *Keryakos Textiles* case on the impact of a counteroffer, p. 296.

LO.5 Explain the implications of failing to read a clickwrap agreement
> See the *Feldman* case as an example of an enforceable clickwrap agreement containing notice and manifested assent, p. 297.

KEY TERMS

acceptance	firm offer	requirements contract
counteroffer	offer	
divisible contract	output contract	

QUESTIONS AND CASE PROBLEMS

1. Bernie and Phil's Great American Surplus store placed an ad in the *Sunday Times* stating, "Next Saturday at 8:00 A.M. sharp, 3 brand new mink coats worth $5,000 each will be sold for $500 each! First come, First served." Marsha Lufklin was first in line when the store opened and went directly to the coat department, but the coats identified in the ad were not available for sale. She identified herself to the manager and pointed out that she was first in line in conformity with the store's advertised offer and that she was ready to pay the $500 price set forth in the store's offer. The manager responded that a newspaper ad is just an invitation to negotiate and that the store decided to withdraw "the mink coat promotion." Review the text on unilateral contracts in Section 12(b) of Chapter 12. Decide.

2. Brown made an offer to purchase Overman's house on a standard printed form. Underneath Brown's signature was the statement: "ACCEPTANCE ON REVERSE SIDE." Overman did not sign the offer on the back but sent Brown a letter accepting the offer. Later, Brown refused to perform the contract, and Overman sued him for breach of contract. Brown claimed there was no contract because the offer had not been accepted in the manner specified by the offer. Decide. [*Overman v Brown,* 372 NW2d 102 (Neb)]

3. Katherine mailed Paul an offer with definite and certain terms and that was legal in all respects stating that it was good for 10 days. Two days later she sent Paul a letter by certified mail (time stamped by the Postal Service at 1:14 P.M.) stating that the original offer was revoked. That evening Paul e-mailed acceptance of the offer to Katherine. She immediately phoned him to tell him that she had revoked the offer that afternoon, and he would surely receive it in tomorrow's mail. Was the offer revoked by Katherine?

4. Nelson wanted to sell his home. Baker sent him a written offer to purchase the home. Nelson made some changes to Baker's offer and wrote him that he, Nelson, was accepting the offer as amended. Baker notified Nelson that he was dropping out of the transaction. Nelson sued Baker for breach of contract. Decide. What social forces and ethical values are involved? [*Nelson v Baker,* 776 SW2d 52 (Mo App)]

5. Lessack Auctioneers advertised an auction sale that was open to the public and was to be conducted with reserve. Gordon attended the auction and bid $100 for a work of art that was worth much more. No higher bid, however, was

made. Lessack refused to sell the item for $100 and withdrew the item from the sale. Gordon claimed that because he was the highest bidder, Lessack was required to sell the item to him. Was he correct?

6. Willis Music Co. advertised a television set at $22.50 in the Sunday newspaper. Ehrlich ordered a set, but the company refused to deliver it on the grounds that the price in the newspaper ad was a mistake. Ehrlich sued the company. Was it liable? Why or why not? [*Ehrlich v Willis Music Co.,* 113 NE2d 252 (Ohio App)]

7. When a movement was organized to build Charles City College, Hauser and others signed pledges to contribute to the college. At the time of signing, Hauser inquired what would happen if he should die or be unable to pay. The representative of the college stated that the pledge would then not be binding and that it was merely a statement of intent. The college failed financially, and Pappas was appointed receiver to collect and liquidate the assets of the college corporation. He sued Hauser for the amount due on his pledge. Hauser raised the defense that the pledge was not a binding contract. Decide. What ethical values are involved? [*Pappas v Hauser,* 197 NW2d 607 (Iowa)]

8. *A* signed a contract agreeing to sell land he owned but reserved the right to take the hay from the land until the following October. He gave the contract form to *B*, a broker. *C*, a prospective buyer, agreed to buy the land and signed the contract but crossed out the provision regarding the hay crop. Was there a binding contract between *A* and *C*?

9. A. H. Zehmer discussed selling a farm to Lucy. After a 40-minute discussion of the first draft of a contract, Zehmer and his wife, Ida, signed a second draft stating: "We hereby agree to sell to W. O. Lucy the Ferguson farm complete for $50,000 title satisfactory to buyer." Lucy agreed to purchase the farm on these terms. Thereafter, the Zehmers refused to transfer title to Lucy and claimed they had made the contract for sale as a joke. Lucy brought an action to compel performance of the contract. The Zehmers claimed there was no contract. Were they correct? [*Lucy v Zehmer,* 84 SE2d 516 (Va App)]

10. Wheeler operated an automobile service station, which he leased from W. C. Cornitius, Inc. The lease ran for three years. Although the lease did not contain any provision for renewal, it was in fact renewed six times for successive three-year terms. The landlord refused to renew the lease for a seventh time. Wheeler brought suit to compel the landlord to accept his offer to renew the lease. Decide. [*William C. Cornitius, Inc. v Wheeler,* 556 P2d 666 (Or)]

11. Buster Cogdill, a real estate developer, made an offer to the Bank of Benton to have the bank provide construction financing for the development of an outlet mall, with funds to be provided at prime rate plus two percentage points. The bank's president Julio Plunkett thanked Buster for the proposal and said, "I will start the paperwork." Did Cogdill have a contract with the Bank of Benton? [*Bank of Benton v Cogdill,* 454 NE2d 1120 (Ill App)]

12. Ackerley Media Group, Inc., claimed to have a three-season advertising Team Sponsorship Agreement (TSA) with Sharp Electronics Corporation to promote Sharp products at all Seattle Supersonics NBA basketball home games. Sharp contended that a valid agreement did not exist for the third season (2000–2001) because a material price term was missing, thus resulting in an unenforceable "agreement to agree." The terms of the TSA for the 2000–2001 third season called for a base payment of $144,200 and an annual increase "not to exceed 6% [and] to be mutually agreed upon by the parties." No "mutually agreed" increase was negotiated by the parties. Ackerley seeks payment for the base price of $144,200 only. Sharp contends that since no price was agreed upon for the season, the entire TSA is unenforceable, and it is not obligated to pay for the 2000–2001 season. Is Sharp correct? [*Ackerley Media Group, Inc. v Sharp Electronics Corp.*, 170 F Supp 2d 445 (SDNY)]

13. L. B. Foster invited Tie and Track Systems Inc. to submit price quotes on items to be used in a railroad expansion project. Tie and Track responded by e-mail on August 11, 2006, with prices for 9 items of steel ties. The e-mail concluded, "The above prices are delivered/Terms of Payment—to be agreed/Delivery—to be agreed/We hope you are successful with your bid. If you require any additional information please call." Just 3 of the 9 items listed in Tie and Track's price quote were "accepted" by the project. L. B. Foster demanded that Tie and Track provide the items at the price listed in the quote. Tie and Track refused. L. B. Foster sued for breach of contract. Did the August 11 e-mail constitute an offer, acceptance of which could bind the supplier to a contract? If so, was there a valid acceptance? [*L. B. Foster v Tie and Track Systems, Inc.*, 2009 WL 900993 (ND Ill 2009)]

14. On August 15, 2003, Wilbert Heikkila signed an agreement with Kangas Realty to sell eight parcels of Heikkila's property. On September 8, 2003, David McLaughlin met with a Kangas agent who drafted McLaughlin's offer to purchase three of the parcels. McLaughlin signed the offer and gave the agent checks for each parcel. On September 9 and 10, 2003, the agent for Heikkila prepared three printed purchase agreements, one for each parcel. On September 14, 2003, David's wife, Joanne McLaughlin, met with the agent and signed the agreements. On September 16, 2003, Heikkila met with his real estate agent. Writing on the printed agreements, Heikkila changed the price of one parcel from $145,000 to $150,000, the price of another parcel from $32,000 to $45,000, and the price of the third parcel from $175,000 to $179,000. Neither of the McLaughlins signed an acceptance of Heikkila's changes to the printed agreements before Heikkila withdrew his offer to sell. The McLaughlins learned that Heikkila had withdrawn his offer on January 1, 2004, when the real estate agent returned the checks to them. Totally shocked at Heikkila's conduct, the McLaughlins brought action to compel specific performance of the purchase agreement signed by Joanne McLaughlin on their behalf. Decide. [*McLaughlin v Heikkila*, 697 NW2d 231 (Minn App)]

CPA QUESTIONS

1. Able Sofa, Inc., sent Noll a letter offering to sell Noll a custom-made sofa for $5,000. Noll immediately sent a telegram to Able purporting to accept the offer. However, the telegraph company erroneously delivered the telegram to Abel Soda, Inc. Three days later, Able mailed a letter of revocation to Noll, which was received by Noll. Able refused to sell Noll the sofa. Noll sued Able for breach of contract. Able:

   a. Would have been liable under the deposited acceptance rule only if Noll had accepted by mail

   b. Will avoid liability since it revoked its offer prior to receiving Noll's acceptance

   c. Will be liable for breach of contract

   d. Will avoid liability due to the telegraph company's error (Law, #2, 9911)

2. On September 27, Summers sent Fox a letter offering to sell Fox a vacation home for $150,000. On October 2, Fox replied by mail agreeing to buy the home for $145,000. Summers did not reply to Fox. Do Fox and Summers have a binding contract?

   a. No, because Fox failed to sign and return Summers's letter

   b. No, because Fox's letter was a counteroffer

   c. Yes, because Summers's offer was validly accepted

   d. Yes, because Summers's silence is an implied acceptance of Fox's letter (Law, #2, 0462)

3. On June 15, Peters orally offered to sell a used lawn mower to Mason for $125. Peters specified that Mason had until June 20 to accept the offer. On June 16, Peters received an offer to purchase the lawn mower for $150 from Bronson, Mason's neighbor. Peters accepted Bronson's offer. On June 17, Mason saw Bronson using the lawn mower and was told the mower had been sold to Bronson. Mason immediately wrote to Peters to accept the June 15 offer. Which of the following statements is correct?

   a. Mason's acceptance would be effective when received by Peters.

   b. Mason's acceptance would be effective when mailed.

   c. Peters's offer had been revoked and Mason's acceptance was ineffective.

   d. Peters was obligated to keep the June 15 offer open until June 20. (Law, #13, 3095)

Chapter 14

CAPACITY AND GENUINE ASSENT

A *contract* is a binding agreement. This agreement must be made between parties who have the capacity to do so. They must also truly agree so that all parties have really consented to the contract. This chapter explores the elements of contractual capacity of the parties and the genuineness of their assent.

A. CONTRACTUAL CAPACITY

Some persons lack contractual capacity, a lack that embraces both those who have a status incapacity, such as minors, and those who have a factual incapacity, such as persons who are insane.

1. Contractual Capacity Defined

contractual capacity –
ability to understand that a contract is being made and to understand its general meaning.

Contractual capacity is the ability to understand that a contract is being made and to understand its general meaning. However, the fact that a person does not understand the full legal meaning of a contract does not mean that contractual capacity is lacking. Everyone is presumed to have capacity unless it is proven that capacity is lacking or there is status incapacity.[1] **For Example,** Jacqueline, aged 22, entered into a contract with Sunrise Storage Co. but later claimed it was not binding because she did not understand several clauses in the printed contract. The contract was binding. No evidence supported her claim that she lacked capacity to contract or to understand its subject. Contractual capacity can exist even though a party does not understand every provision of the contract.

(A) STATUS INCAPACITY. Over the centuries, the law has declared that some classes of persons lack contractual capacity. The purpose is to protect these classes by giving them the power to get out of unwise contracts. Of these classes, the most important today is the class identified as minors.

Until recent times, some other classes were held to lack contractual capacity in order to discriminate against them. Examples are married women and aliens.

C A S E   S U M M A R Y

We Really Mean Equal Rights

FACTS: An Alabama statute provided that a married woman could not sell her land without the consent of her husband. Montgomery made a contract to sell land she owned to Peddy. Montgomery's husband did not consent to the sale. Montgomery did not perform the contract and Peddy sued her. The defense was raised that the contract was void and could not be enforced because of the statute. Peddy claimed that the statute was unconstitutional.

DECISION: The statute was unconstitutional. Constitutions, both federal and state, guarantee all persons the equal protection of the law. Married women are denied this equal protection when they are treated differently than married men and unmarried women. The fact that such unequal treatment had once been regarded as proper does not justify its modern continuation. [**Peddy v Montgomery 345 So 2d 631 (Ala 1977)**]

---

[1] *In re Adoption of Smith*, 578 So 2d 988 (La App 1991).

Still other classes, such as persons convicted of and sentenced for a felony, were held to lack contractual capacity in order to punish them. Today, these discriminatory and punitive incapacities have largely disappeared. Married women have the same contractual capacity as unmarried persons.[2]

By virtue of international treaties, the discrimination against aliens has been removed.

(B) **FACTUAL INCAPACITY.** A *factual incapacity* contrasts with incapacity imposed because of the class or group to which a person belongs. A factual incapacity may exist when, because of a mental condition caused by medication, drugs, alcohol, illness, or age, a person does not understand that a contract is being made or understand its general nature. However, mere mental weakness does not incapacitate a person from contracting. It is sufficient if the individual has enough mental capacity to understand, to a reasonable extent, the nature and effect of what he is doing.[3]

2. Minors

Minors may make contracts.[4] To protect them, however, the law has always treated minors as a class lacking contractual capacity.

(A) **WHO IS A MINOR?** At common law, any person, male or female, under 21 years of age was a minor. At common law, minority ended the day before the twenty-first birthday. The "day before the birthday" rule is still followed, but the age of majority has been reduced from 21 years to 18 years.

CPA (B) **MINOR'S POWER TO AVOID CONTRACTS.** With exceptions that will be noted later, a contract made by a minor is voidable at the election of the minor. The minor may affirm or ratify the contract on attaining majority by performing the contract, by expressly approving the contract, or by allowing a reasonable time to lapse without avoiding the contract.

CPA *(1) What Constitutes Avoidance?*
A minor may avoid or *disaffirm* a contract by any expression of an intention to repudiate the contract. Any act inconsistent with the continuing validity of the contract is also an avoidance.

CPA *(2) Time for Avoidance.*
A minor can disaffirm a contract only during minority and for a reasonable time after attaining majority. After the lapse of a reasonable time, the contract is deemed ratified and cannot be avoided by the minor.

CPA *(3) Minor's Misrepresentation of Age.*
Generally, the fact that the minor has misrepresented his or her age does not affect the minor's power to disaffirm the contract. Some states hold that such fraud of a

---

[2] A few states have a limitation that a married woman cannot make a binding contract to pay the debt of her husband if he fails to.
[3] *Fisher v Schefers,* 656 NW2d 591 (Minn App 2003).
[4] *Buffington v State Automobile Mut. Ins. Co.,* 384 SE2d 873 (Ga App 1989).

minor bars contract avoidance. Some states permit the minor to disaffirm the contract in such a case but require the minor to pay for any damage to the property received under the contract.

In any case, the other party to the contract may disaffirm it because of the minor's fraud.

CPA (c) RESTITUTION BY MINOR AFTER AVOIDANCE. When a minor disaffirms a contract, the question arises as to what the minor must return to the other contracting party.

(1) Original Consideration Intact.
When a minor still has what was received from the other party, the minor, on avoiding the contract, must return it to the other party or offer to do so. That is, the minor must put things back to the original position or, as it is called, restore the **status quo ante**.

status quo ante–original positions of the parties.

(2) Original Consideration Damaged or Destroyed.
What happens if the minor cannot return what has been received because it has been spent, used, damaged, or destroyed? The minor's right to disaffirm the contract is not affected. The minor can still disaffirm the contract and is required to return only what remains. The fact that nothing remains or that what remains is damaged does not bar the right to disaffirm the contract. In states that follow the common law rule, minors can thus refuse to pay for what has been received under a contract or can get back what had been paid or given even though they do not have anything to return or return property in a damaged condition. There is, however, a trend to limit this rule.

(D) RECOVERY OF PROPERTY BY MINOR ON AVOIDANCE. When a minor disaffirms a contract, the other contracting party must return the money received. Any property received from the minor must also be returned. If the property has been sold to a third person who did not know of the original seller's minority, the minor cannot get the property back. In such cases, however, the minor is entitled to recover the property's monetary value or the money received by the other contracting party.

CPA (E) CONTRACTS FOR NECESSARIES. A minor can disaffirm a contract for necessaries but must pay the reasonable value for furnished necessaries.

(1) What Constitutes Necessaries?
Originally, **necessaries** were limited to those things absolutely necessary for the sustenance and shelter of the minor. Thus limited, the term would extend only to food, clothing, and lodging. In the course of time, the rule was relaxed to extend generally to things relating to the health, education, and comfort of the minor. Thus, the rental of a house used by a married minor is a necessary.

necessaries–things indispensable or absolutely necessary for the sustenance of human life.

(2) Liability of Parent or Guardian.
When a third person supplies the parents or guardian of a minor with goods or services that the minor needs, the minor is not liable for these necessaries because the third person's contract is with the parent or guardian, not with the minor.

When necessary medical care is provided a minor, a parent is liable at common law for the medical expenses provided the minor child. However, at common law, the child can be held contractually liable for her necessary medical expenses when the parent is unable or unwilling to pay.

C A S E   S U M M A R Y

The Concussion and Legal Repercussions

FACTS: Sixteen-year-old Michelle Schmidt was injured in an automobile accident and taken to Prince George's Hospital. Although the identities of Michelle and her parents were originally unknown, the hospital provided her emergency medical care for a brain concussion and an open scalp wound. She incurred hospital expenses of $1,756.24. Ms. Schmidt was insured through her father's insurance company. It issued a check to be used to cover medical expenses. However, the funds were used to purchase a car for Ms. Schmidt. Since she was a minor when the services were rendered, she believed that she had no legal obligation to pay. After Ms. Schmidt attained her eighteenth birthday and failed to pay the hospital, it brought suit against her.

DECISION: Judgment for the hospital. The prevailing modern rule is that minors' contracts are voidable except for necessaries. The doctrine of necessaries states that a minor may be held liable for necessaries, including medical necessaries when parents are unwilling to pay. The court concluded that Ms. Schmidt's father demonstrated a clear unwillingness to pay by using the insurance money to purchase a car rather than pay the hospital. The policy behind the necessaries exception is for the benefit of minors because the procurement of such is essential to their existence, and if they were not permitted to bind themselves, they might not be able to obtain the necessaries. [**Schmidt v Prince George's Hospital 784 A2d 1112 (Md 2001)**]

CPA (F) RATIFICATION OF FORMER MINOR'S VOIDABLE CONTRACT. A former minor cannot disaffirm a contract that has been ratified after reaching majority.[5]

CPA *(1) What Constitutes Ratification?*
Ratification consists of any words or conduct of the former minor manifesting an intent to be bound by the terms of a contract made while a minor.

CPA *(2) Form of Ratification.*
Generally, no special form is required for ratification of a minor's voidable contract, although in some states a written ratification or declaration of intention is required.

CPA *(3) Time for Ratification.*
A person can disaffirm a contract any time during minority and for a reasonable time after that but, of necessity, can ratify a contract only after attaining majority. The minor must have attained majority, or the ratification would itself be regarded as voidable.

[5] *Fletcher v Marshall*, 632 NE2d 1105 (Ill App 1994).

(G) **CONTRACTS THAT MINORS CANNOT AVOID.** Statutes in many states deprive a minor of the right to avoid an educational loan;[6] a contract for medical care; a contract made while running a business; a contract approved by a court; a contract made in performance of a legal duty; and a contract relating to bank accounts, insurance policies, or corporate stock.

(H) **LIABILITY OF THIRD PERSON FOR A MINOR'S CONTRACT.** The question arises as to whether parents are bound by the contract of their minor child. The question of whether a person cosigning a minor's contract is bound if the contract is avoided also arises.

(1) Liability of Parent.

Ordinarily, a parent is not liable on a contract made by a minor child. The parent may be liable, however, if the child is acting as the agent of the parent in making the contract. Also, the parent is liable to a seller for the reasonable value of necessaries supplied by the seller to the child if the parent had deserted the child.

(2) Liability of Cosigner.

When the minor makes a contract, another person, such as a parent or a friend, may sign along with the minor to make the contract more acceptable to the third person.

With respect to the other contracting party, the cosigner is bound independently of the minor. Consequently, if the minor disaffirms the contract, the cosigner remains bound by it. When the debt to the creditor is actually paid, the obligation of the cosigner is discharged.

If the minor disaffirms a sales contract but does not return the goods, the cosigner remains liable for the purchase price.

3. Mentally Incompetent Persons

A person with a mental disorder may be so disabled as to lack capacity to make a contract. If the person is so mentally incompetent as to be unable to understand that a contract is being made or the general nature of the contract, the person lacks contractual capacity.

(A) **EFFECT OF INCOMPETENCY.** An incompetent person may ordinarily avoid a contract in the same manner as a minor. Upon the removal of the disability (that is, upon becoming competent), the formerly incompetent person can either ratify or disaffirm the contract.

A mentally incompetent person or his estate is liable for the reasonable value of all necessaries furnished that individual.

A current trend in the law is to treat an incompetent person's contract as binding when its terms and the surrounding circumstances are reasonable and the person is unable to restore the other contracting party to the status quo ante.

---

[6] A Model Student Capacity to Borrow Act makes educational loans binding on minors in Arizona, Mississippi, New Mexico, North Dakota, Oklahoma, and Washington. This act was reclassified from a uniform act to a model act by the Commissioners on Uniform State Law, indicating that uniformity was viewed as unimportant and that the matter was primarily local in character.

CASE SUMMARY

Friends Should Tell Friends About Medical Leaves

FACTS: Wilcox Manufacturing Group, Inc., did business under the name of Superior Automation Co., and Howard Wilcox served as Superior's president. As part of a loan "lease agreement" of $50,000 executed on December 5, 2000, Superior was to repay Marketing Services of Indiana (MSI) $67,213.80 over the course of 60 months. Wilcox gave a personal guarantee for full and prompt payment. Wilcox had been a patient of psychiatrist Dr. Shaun Wood since May 21, 1999, and was diagnosed as suffering from bipolar disorder during the period from June 2000 to January 2001. On June 9, 2000, Wilcox told Dr. Wood he was having problems functioning at work, and Dr. Wood determined that Wilcox was experiencing lithium toxicity, which lasted for 10 months, during which time he suffered from impaired cognitive functions that limited his capacity to understand the nature and quality of his actions and judgments. Superior made monthly payments though to October 28, 2003, and the balance owed at that time was $33,031.37. MSI sued Wilcox personally and the corporation for breach of contract. The defendants raise the defense of lack of capacity and contend that they are not liable on the loan signed by the corporate president when he was incapacitated.

DECISION: Judgment for MSI. The acts or deeds of a person of unsound mind whose condition has not been judicially ascertained and who is not under guardianship are voidable and not absolutely void. The acts are subject to ratification or disaffirmance on removal of the disability. The latest Wilcox could have been experiencing the effects of lithium toxicity was October 2001. Wilcox thus regained his capacity by that date. No attempt was made to disaffirm the contract. Rather, monthly payments continued to be made for a year and one-half before the payments ceased. The contract was thus ratified by the conduct of the president of Superior after he recovered his ability to understand the nature of the contract. [**Wilcox Manufacturing, Inc. v Marketing Services of Indiana, Inc. 832 NE2d 559 (Ind App 2005)**]

(B) APPOINTMENT OF GUARDIAN. If a court appoints a guardian for the incompetent person, a contract made by that person before the appointment may be ratified or, in some cases, disaffirmed by the guardian. If the incompetent person makes a contract after a guardian has been appointed, the contract is void and not merely voidable.

4. Intoxicated Persons

The capacity of a party to contract and the validity of the contract are not affected by the party's being impaired by alcohol at the time of making the contract so long as the party knew that a contract was being made.

If the degree of intoxication is such that a person does not know that a contract is being made, the contract is voidable by that person. The situation is the same as though the person were insane at the time and did not know what he or she was doing. On becoming sober, the individual may avoid or rescind the contract. However, an unreasonable delay in taking steps to set aside a known contract entered into while intoxicated may bar the intoxicated person from asserting this right.[7]

---

[7] *Diedrich v Diedrich*, 424 NW2d 580 (Minn App 1988).

For Example, Edward made a contract while intoxicated. When he sobered up, he immediately disaffirmed the contract for lack of capacity as the result of his intoxication. The other contracting party claimed that voluntary intoxication cannot void a contract, but Edward could disaffirm the contract because he lacked the legal capacity to enter a contract.

The courts treat impairment caused by the use of drugs the same as impairment caused by the excessive use of alcohol.

---

ethics & the law

Globe Life Insurance Company undertook a new sales program that targets neighborhoods in Los Angeles where drive-by shootings were a nightly occurrence. In two such shootings, children were killed as they sat in their living rooms.

Globe salespeople were instructed to "hit" the houses surrounding those where children were victims. They were also told to contact the parents of those children to sell policies for their other children.

Tom Raskin, an experienced Globe salesman, read of a drive-by shooting at Nancy Leonard's home, in which Leonard's five-year-old son was killed. The *Los Angeles Times* reported that Leonard was a single parent with four other children.

Raskin traveled to Leonard's home and described the benefits of a Globe policy for her other children. He offered her the $10,000 term life policy for each of the children for a total cost of $21 per month. Leonard was in the process of making funeral arrangements for her son, and Raskin noted, "See how much it costs for a funeral."

Leonard had been given several tranquilizers the night before by a physician at the hospital's emergency room. The physician had also given her 15 more tranquilizers to help her through the following week. She had taken one additional tranquilizer an hour before Raskin arrived, using a Coors Lite beer to take the pill.

Leonard signed the contract for the policy. After her son's funeral, she received the first month's bill for it and exclaimed, "I didn't buy any life insurance! Where did this come from?"

After you discuss Leonard's legal standing, discuss the ethical issues involved in Globe's sales program. Discuss the legal issues involved in Raskin's decision to target Leonard the day after her son's death.

CPA ## B. MISTAKE

The validity of a contract may be affected by the fact that one or both of the parties made a mistake. In some cases, the mistake may be caused by the misconduct of one of the parties.

5. Unilateral Mistake

A *unilateral mistake*—that is, a mistake by only one of the parties—as to a fact does not affect the contract when the mistake is unknown to the other contracting party.[8] When a contract is made on the basis of a quoted price, the validity of the contract is not affected by the fact that the party furnishing the quotation made a mathematical mistake in computing the price if there was no reason for the other

---

[8] *Truck South Inc. v Patel,* 528 SE2d 424 (SC 2000).

party to recognize that there had been a mistake.[9] The party making the mistake may avoid the contract if the other contracting party knew or should have known of the mistake.

C A S E   S U M M A R Y

Bumper Sticker: "Mistakes Happen!" (or words to that effect)

FACTS: Lipton-U City, LLC (Lipton), and Shurgard Storage Centers discussed the sale of a self-storage facility for approximately $7 million. Lipton became concerned about an existing environmental condition and as a result, the parties agreed to a lease with an option to buy rather than an outright sale. The contract specified a 10-year lease with an annual rent starting at $636,000 based on a property valuation of $7 million. Section 2.4 of the contract contained the purchase option. Shurgard representatives circulated an e-mail with a copy to Lipton representatives that a purchase option price would be based on six months of *annualized* net operating income. When the lease was submitted to Lipton, inexplicably any language regarding multiplying by 2 or annualizing the net income was omitted. Donn Lipton announced to his attorneys that the lease reflected his successful negotiation of a purchase option based on six months of *unannualized* net operating income. Eight months after signing the lease, Lipton sought to exercise the purchase option under Section 2.4 and stated a price of $2,918,103. Shurgard rejected the offer and filed suit for rescission, citing the misunderstanding about the price terms.

DECISION: Judgment for Shurgard. Under state law, if a material mistake made by one party is known to the other party or is of such a character or circumstances that the other party should know of it, the mistaken party has a right to rescission. Lipton knew or should have known of the mistake of the lessor (Shurgard) in believing that the purchase price would be based on a full year of net operating income rather than six months of net operating income. Lipton was notified by e-mail that the six-month figure was to be annualized and knew that the property was valued at approximately $7 million. [**Shurgard Storage Centers v Lipton-U City, LLC 394 F3d 1041 (8th Cir 2005)**]

---

6. Mutual Mistake

When both parties enter into a contract under a mutually mistaken understanding concerning a basic assumption of fact or law on which the contract is made, the contract is voidable by the adversely affected party if the mistake has a material effect on the agreed exchange.[10]

A contract based on *a mutual mistake in judgment* is not voidable by the adversely affected party. **For Example,** if both parties believe that a colt is not fast enough to develop into a competitive race horse and effect a sale accordingly, when the animal later develops into the winner of the Preakness as a three-year-old, the seller cannot rescind the contract based on mutual mistake because the mutual mistake was a mistake in judgment. In contrast, when two parties to a contract believe a cow to be barren at the time they contract for its sale, but before delivery of

---

[9] *Procan Construction Co. v Oceanside Development Corp.*, 539 NYS2d 437 (App Div 2d 1989).
[10] See *Browning v Howerton*, 966 P2d 367 (Wash App 1998).

FIGURE 14-1 | *Avoidance of Contract*

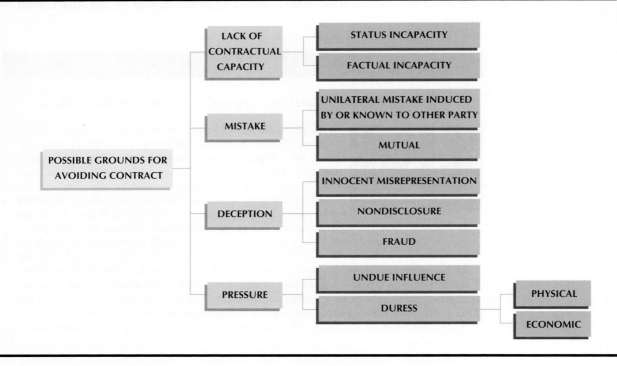

the animal to the buyer, it is discovered that the assumption was mistaken, such is a mutual mistake of fact making the contract void.[11]

7. Mistake in the Transcription or Printing of the Contract: Reformation

In some instances, the parties make an oral agreement, and in the process of committing it to writing or printing it from a manuscript, a phrase, term, or segment is inadvertently left out of the final, signed document. The aggrieved party may petition the court to **reform** the contract to reflect the actual agreement of the parties. However, the burden of proof is heightened to clear and convincing evidence that such a mistake was made. **For Example,** the Printers International Union reached agreement for a new three-year contract with a large regional printing company. As was their practice, the union negotiators then met with Sullivan Brothers Printers, Inc., a small specialty shop employing 10 union printers, and Sullivan Brothers and the union agreed to follow the contractual pattern set by the union and the large printer. That is, Sullivan Brothers agreed to give its workers all of the benefits negotiated for the employees of the large printing company. When the contract was typed, a new benefit of 75 percent employer-paid coverage for a dental plan was inadvertently omitted from the final contract that the parties signed. The mistake was not discovered until later, and Sullivan Brothers, Inc., is now reluctant to

reformation–remedy by which a written instrument is corrected when it fails to express the actual intent of both parties because of fraud, accident, or mistake.

[11] See *Sherwood v Walker*, 66 Mich 568 (1887).

assume the additional expense. Based on the clear and convincing evidence of a practice of following the contractual pattern set by the large printer and Sullivan's assent to again follow the pattern, a court or arbitrator will reform the contract.

C. DECEPTION

One of the parties may have been misled by a fraudulent statement. In such situations, there is no true or genuine assent to the contract, and it is voidable at the innocent party's option.

8. Intentional Misrepresentation

Fraud is a generic term embracing all multifarious means that human ingenuity can devise and that are resorted to by one individual to get advantage over another. It is classified in the law as a *tort*. However, where a party is induced into making a contract by a material misrepresentation of fact, this form of fraudulent activity adversely affects the genuineness of the assent of the innocent party, and this type of fraud is the focus of our discussion in the chapters on contracts.

9. Fraud

fraud–making of a false statement of a past or existing fact, with knowledge of its falsity or with reckless indifference as to its truth, with the intent to cause another to rely thereon, and such person does rely thereon and is harmed thereby.

Fraud is the making of a material misrepresentation (or false statement) of fact with (1) knowledge of its falsity or reckless indifference to its truth, (2) the intent that the listener rely on it, (3) the result that the listener does so rely, and (4) the consequence that the listener is harmed.[12]

To prove fraud, there must be a material misrepresentation of fact. Such a misrepresentation is one that is likely to induce a reasonable person to assent to a contract. **For Example,** Traci Hanson-Suminski purchased a used Honda Civic from Arlington Acura for $10,899. On a test drive with salesperson Mike Dobin, Traci noticed a vibration in the steering wheel and asked if the car had been in an accident. Dobin said, "No, it's fine." The dealer put new tires on the car and Traci bought it. Traci testified that she would not have purchased the car if she had known it had been in an accident. Eight months later when she sought to trade the car for another car, she was shown a Carfax Vehicle History Report which indicated the car had been in an accident. The dealer testified that all its sales associates are trained to respond to questions about vehicle history with "I don't know." It asserted that Dobin's statement was mere puffery. The court found that Dobin's statement was a material misrepresentation of the car's history, inducing the plaintiff to purchase the car. It rejected outright the dealer's assertion of puffery, which it defined as meaningless superlatives that no reasonable person would take seriously.[13]

(A) STATEMENT OF OPINION OR VALUE. Ordinarily, matters of opinion of value or opinions about future events are not regarded as fraudulent. Thus, statements that a building was "very good," it "required only normal maintenance," and the "deal was excellent" were merely matters of opinion. Therefore, a court considered the

---

[12] *Maack v Resource Design & Construction, Inc.*, 875 P2d 570 (Utah 1994); *Bortz v Noon*, 729 A2d 555 (Pa 1999).
[13] *Hanson-Suminski v. Rohrman Midwest Motors Inc.*, 858 NE2d 194 (Ill App 2008).

CASE SUMMARY

Watch Out! Some People Have a Lot of Nerve

FACTS: German citizens Klaus and Gerda Tschira brought suit against Corim, Inc., a U.S. real estate investment firm and its president, Ben Willingham Jr., for fraudulent misrepresentation during a real estate transaction between the Tschiras and Corim. Klaus attended a meeting in Walldorf, Germany, in which Willingham, who speaks fluent German, made a presentation. Willingham explained that Corim proposed to obtain buildings for investors to purchase at a "fair market price"; Corim then intended to enter into management contracts with the new owners. By the terms of the management contracts, Corim and Willingham would lease the buildings from the investors and, in return, would then pay the investors a contractually established rent. The Tschiras subsequently purchased a Nashville, Tennessee, commercial property on December 14, 1990, for $1,985,000. The Tschiras did not visit the property, secure independent counsel, or obtain an appraisal. They later discovered that two closings occurred on December 14, 1990. In the first, One Church Street, Inc., a shell corporation owned by Corim and Willingham, purchased the property from its owner, First Atlanta Services Corporation. The selling price in this deal was $774,000. In the second transaction, One Church Street, Inc., sold the building to the Tschiras for $1,985,000. The title insurance policy Willingham forwarded to the Tschiras indicated that the Ticor Title Insurance Company had provided protection up to $1,985,000. In actuality, Lisa Wilson, the branch manager of Ticor, testified that the policy the company extended for the property was for only $774,000. Willingham and Corim contended that any representations were not material because they "guaranteed" a return on the investment. From a judgment for the Tschiras in the amount of $1,420,000 in compensatory damages and $1,750,000 in punitive damages, Corim and Willingham appealed.

DECISION: Judgment for the Tschiras. Willingham and Corim argue that there was no fraudulent misrepresentation because the representations made were not material because they provided a "guaranteed" return on the Tschiras' investment through the rental income. However, the jury could have reasonably found otherwise. The Tschiras believed they were paying "fair market price" for the purchase of the property in addition to receiving a guaranteed return on their investment. The Tschiras believed, and the jury could have reasonably concluded, that the Tschiras actually paid $1,211,000 over the fair market price of the property and therefore lost that amount on their investment at the time of purchase. The Tschiras reasonably relied on the representations and suffered the damages as a result of that reliance. [**Tschiras v Willingham 133 F3d 1077 (6th Cir 1998)**]

sophistication and expertise of the parties and the commercial setting of the transaction and enforced the contract "as is." The theory is that the person hearing the statement recognizes or should recognize that it is merely the speaker's personal opinion, not a statement of fact. A statement that is mere sales talk cannot be the basis of fraud liability. **For Example,** CEO Bernard Ellis sent a memo to shareholders of his Internet-related services business some four days before the expiration of a lockup period during which these shareholders had agreed not to sell their stock. In the memo, he urged shareholders not to sell their stock on the release date because in the event of a massive sell-off "our stock could plummet." He also stated, "I think our share price will start to stabilize and then rise as our company's strong performance continues." Based on Ellis's "strong performance" statement, a major corporate shareholder did not sell. The price of the stock fell from $40 a share to 29 cents a share over the subsequent nine-month period. The shareholder sued Ellis for fraud, seeking $27 million in damages. The court held that the first half of the sentence in question was framed as a mere opinion as to future events and thus was nonactionable; and as to the characterization of the company's performance as "strong," such a self-congratulatory comment constituted mere puffery on which no reasonable investor would rely.[14]

A statement of opinion may be fraudulent when the speaker knows of past or present facts that make the opinion false. **For Example,** Biff Williams, the sales manager of Abrasives International (AI), sold an exclusive dealership selling AI products to Fred Farkas for $100,000 down and a 3 percent royalty on all gross proceeds. Williams told Farkas, "You have the potential to earn $300,000 to $400,000 a year in this territory." He later added, "We have four dealerships making that kind of money today." Farkas was thus persuaded by the business potential of the territory and executed the purchase contract. He later found out AI had a total of just four distributorships at that time, and the actual earnings of the highest producer was $43,000. Assertions of opinions about the future profit potential alone may not amount to fraud, but the assertion of present fact—that four dealerships were presently earning $300,000 to $400,000 a year—was a material misstatement of fact that made the forecast sales potential for Farkas's territory a material misstatement of fact as well. Because there were reliance and damages, Farkas can rescind the contract based on fraud and recover all damages resulting from it.[15]

(B) Reliance on Statement. A fraudulent statement made by one party has no importance unless the other party relies on the statement's truth. **For Example,** after making thorough tests of Nagel Company's pump, Allstate Services Company ordered 100 pumps. It later sued Nagel on the ground that advertising statements made about the pumps were false. Allstate Services cannot impose fraud liability on Nagel for the advertisements, even if they were false, because it had not relied on them in making the purchase but had acted on the basis of its own tests.

If the alleged victim of the fraud knew that the statements were false because the truth was commonly known, the victim cannot rely on the false statements. When the statements of a seller are so "indefinite and extravagant" that reasonable persons would not rely on them, the statements cannot be the basis of a claim of fraud.[16]

(C) Proof of Harm. For an individual to recover damages for fraud, proof of harm to that individual is required. The injured party may recover the actual losses suffered as a result of the fraud as well as punitive damages when the fraud is gross or oppressive. The injured party has the right to have the court order the rescission or cancellation of the contract that has been induced by fraud.[17]

[14] *Next Century Communications v Ellis,* 318 F3d 1023 (11th Cir 2003).
[15] The Federal Trade Commission and state agencies have franchise disclosure rules that will penalize the franchisor in this case. See Chapter 41.
[16] *Eckert v Flair Agency, Inc.,* 909 P2d 1201 (Okla App 1995) (seller's statement that house would never be flooded again).
[17] *Paden v Murray,* 523 SE2d 75 (Ga App 2000).

10. Negligent Misrepresentation

While fraud requires the critical element of a known or recklessly made falsity, a claim of negligent misrepresentation contains similar elements except it is predicated on a negligently made false statement. That is, the speaker failed to exercise due care regarding material information communicated to the listener but did not intend to deceive. When the negligent misrepresentation of a material fact that the listener relies on results in harm to the listener, the contract is voidable at the option of the injured party. If fraud is proven, as opposed to misrepresentation, recovery of punitive damages in addition to actual damages can occur. Because it may be difficult to prove the intentional falsity required for fraud, it is common for a lawsuit to allege both a claim of fraud and a claim of negligent misrepresentation. **For Example,** Marshall Armstrong worked for Fred Collins, owner of Collins Entertainment, Inc., a conglomerate that owns and operates video games. Collins Entertainment's core product video poker was hurt by a court ruling that prohibited cash payouts, which adversely affected its business and resulted in a debt of $13 to $20 million to SouthTrust bank. Chief operating officer Armstrong, on his own time, came up with the idea of modifying bingo machines as a new venture. To exploit this idea, Collins agreed to form a corporation called Skillpins Inc., that was unencumbered by the SouthTrust debt and to give Armstrong a 10 percent ownership interest. After a period, with some 300 Skillpins machines producing income, Armstrong discovered the revenues from the new venture on the debt-laden Collins Entertainment profit and loss statement, not that of Skillpins, Inc. Armstrong's suit for both fraud and intentional misrepresentation was successful. In addition to actual damages, he received $1.8 million in punitive damages for fraud.[18]

11. Nondisclosure

Under certain circumstances, nondisclosure serves to make a contract voidable, especially when the nondisclosure consists of active concealment.

(A) GENERAL RULE OF NONLIABILITY. Ordinarily, a party to a contract has no duty to volunteer information to the other party. **For Example,** if Fox does not ask Tehan any questions, Tehan is not under any duty to make a full statement of material facts. Consequently, the nondisclosure of information that is not asked for does not impose fraud liability or impair the validity of a contract.

C A S E   S U M M A R Y

Welcome to the Seesaw: Buyer versus Seller

FACTS: Dalarna Management Corporation owned a building constructed on a pier on a lake. There were repeated difficulties with rainwater leaking into the building, and water damage was visible in the interior of the building. Dalarna made a contract to sell the building to Curran. Curran made several inspections of the building and had the building inspected twice by a

18 621 SE2d 368 (SC App 2005).

C A S E   S U M M A R Y

Continued

licensed engineer. The engineer reported there were signs of water leaks. Curran assigned his contract to Puget Sound Service Corporation, which then purchased the building from Dalarna. Puget Sound spent approximately $118,000 attempting to stop the leaks. Puget Sound then sued Dalarna for damages, claiming that Dalarna's failure to disclose the extent of the water leakage problem constituted fraud.

DECISION: Judgment for Dalarna. Curran was aware there was a water leakage problem, and therefore the burden was on the buyer to ask questions to determine the extent of the problem. There was no duty on the seller to volunteer the extent of the water damage merely because it had been a continuing problem that was more than just a simple leak. The court reached this conclusion because the law "balances the harshness of the former rule of caveat emptor [let the buyer beware] with the equally undesirable alternative of courts standing in loco parentis [in the place of a parent] to parties transacting business." [**Puget Sound Service Corp. v Dalarna Management Corp. 752 P2d 1353 (Wash App 1988)**]

(B) Exceptions. The following exceptions to the general rule of nonliability for nondisclosure exist.

(1) Unknown Defect or Condition.

A duty may exist in some states for a seller who knows of a serious defect or condition to disclose that information to the other party where the defect or condition is unknown to the other person and is of such a nature that it is unlikely that the other person would discover it. However, a defendant who had no knowledge of the defect cannot be held liable for failure to disclose it.[19]

(2) Confidential Relationship.

confidential relationship – relationship in which, because of the legal status of the parties or their respective physical or mental conditions or knowledge, one party places full confidence and trust in the other.

If parties stand in a **confidential relationship**, failure to disclose information may be regarded as fraudulent. For example, in an attorney-client relationship,[20] the attorney has a duty to reveal anything that is material to the client's interest when dealing with the client. The attorney's silence has the same legal consequence as a knowingly made false statement that there was no material fact to be told the client.

(3) Active Concealment.

Nondisclosure may be more than the passive failure to volunteer information. It may consist of a positive act of hiding information from the other party by physical concealment, or it may consist of knowingly or recklessly furnishing the wrong information. Such conduct constitutes fraud. **For Example,** when Nigel wanted to sell his house, he covered the wooden cellar beams with plywood to hide extensive termite damage. He sold the house to Kuehne, who sued Nigel for damages on later discovering the termite damage. Nigel claimed he had no duty to volunteer information about the termites, but by covering the damage with plywood, he committed active fraud as if he had made a false statement that there were no termites.

---

[19] *Nesbitt v Dunn*, 672 So 2d 226 (La App 1996).
[20] *In re Boss Trust*, 487 NW2d 256 (Minn App 1992).

D. Pressure

What appears to be an agreement may not in fact be voluntary because one of the parties entered into it as the result of undue influence or physical or economic duress.

CPA   ## 12. Undue Influence

An aged parent may entrust all business affairs to a trusted child; a disabled person may rely on a nurse; a client may follow implicitly whatever an attorney recommends. The relationship may be such that for practical purposes, one person is helpless in the hands of the other. When such a confidential relationship exists, it is apparent that the parent, the disabled person, or the client is not exercising free will in making a contract suggested by the child, nurse, or attorney but is merely following the will of the other person. Because of the great possibility of unfair advantage, the law presumes that the dominating person exerts **undue influence** on the other person whenever the dominating person obtains any benefit from a contract made with the dominated person. The contract is then voidable. It may be set aside by the dominated person unless the dominating person can prove that, at the time the contract was made, no unfair advantage had been taken.

The class of confidential relationships is not well defined. It ordinarily includes the relationships of parent and child, guardian and ward, physician and patient, and attorney and client, and any other relationship of trust and confidence in which one party exercises a control or influence over another.

Whether undue influence exists is a difficult question for courts (ordinarily juries) to determine. The law does not regard every influence as undue.

An essential element of undue influence is that the person making the contract does not exercise free will. In the absence of a recognized type of confidential relationship, such as that between parent and child, courts are likely to take the attitude that the person who claims to have been dominated was merely persuaded and there was therefore no undue influence.

undue influence–influence that is asserted upon another person by one who dominates that person.

CASE SUMMARY

Cards and Small Talk Sometimes Make the Sale

FACTS: John Lentner owned the farm adjacent to the Schefers. He moved off the farm to a nursing home in 1999. In the fall of 2000, Kristine Schefers visited Lentner at the nursing home some 15 times, engaging in small talk and watching him play cards. In the spring of 2001, Lentner agreed to sell his farm to Kristine and her husband Thomas for $50,000 plus $10,000 for machinery and tools. Kristine drove Lentner to the bank to get the deed from his safe deposit box. She also took him to the abstractor who drafted the transfer documents. Soon after the sale, Earl Fisher was appointed special conservator of Lentner. Fisher sought to set aside the transaction, asserting that Kristine's repeated visits to the nursing home and her failure to involve Lentner's other family members in the transaction unduly influenced Lentner.

C A S E   S U M M A R Y

Continued

DECISION: Judgment for Thomas and Kristine Schefers. Undue influence is shown when the person making the contract ceased to act of his own free volition and became a mere puppet of the wielder of that influence. Mere speculation alone that Lentner was a "puppet" acting according to the wishes of Schefers is insufficient to set aside the sale. Undue influence was not established. [**Fisher v Schefers 656 NW2d 592 (Minn App 2003)**]

CPA   13. Duress

physical duress–threat of physical harm to person or property.

economic duress–threat of financial loss.

duress–conduct that deprives the victim of free will and that generally gives the victim the right to set aside any transaction entered into under such circumstances.

A party may enter into a contract to avoid a threatened danger. The danger threatened may be a physical harm to person or property, called **physical duress**, or it may be a threat of financial loss, called **economic duress**.

(A) Physical Duress. A person makes a contract under **duress** when there is such violence or threat of violence that the person is deprived of free will and makes the contract to avoid harm. The threatened harm may be directed either at a near relative of the contracting party or against the contracting party. If a contract is made under duress, the resulting agreement is voidable at the victim's election.

Agreements made to bring an end to mass disorder or violence are ordinarily not binding contracts because they were obtained by duress.

One may not void a contract on grounds of duress merely because it was entered into with great reluctance and proves to be very disadvantageous to that individual.[21]

(B) Economic Duress. Economic duress is a condition in which one is induced by a wrongful act or threat of another to make a contract under circumstances that deprive one of the exercise of his own free will.[22] **For Example,** Richard Case, an importer of parts used to manufacture high-quality mountain bicycles, had a contractual duty to supply Katahdin Manufacturing Company's needs for specifically manufactured stainless steel brakes for the 2010 season. Katahdin's president, Bill Read, was in constant contact with Case about the delay in delivery of the parts and the adverse consequences it was having on Katahdin's relationship with its retailers. Near the absolute deadline for meeting orders for the 2010 season, Case called Read and said, "I've got the parts in, but I'm not sure I'll be able to send them to you because I'm working on next year's contracts, and you haven't signed yours yet." Case's 2011 contract increased the cost of parts by 38 percent. Read signed the contract to obtain the delivery but later found a new supplier and gave notice to Case of this action. The defense of economic duress would apply in a breach of contract suit brought by Case on the 2011 contract because Case implicitly threatened to commit the wrongful act of not delivering parts due under the prior contract, and Katahdin Company had no means available to obtain parts elsewhere to prevent the economic loss that would occur if it did not receive those parts.

[21] *Miller v Calhoun Johnson Co.*, 497 SE2d 397 (Ga App 1998).
[22] *Hurd v Wildman, Harrold, Allen, and Dixon*, 707 NE2d 609 (Ill App 1999).

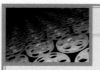

lawflix

Jerry Maguire (1996) (R)

Consider the marriage proposal, its validity, and Dorothy's later statement, "I did this. I made this happen. And the thing is, I can do something about it." What was Maguire's state of mind at the time of the proposal? Consider its possible hypothetical nature and the issues of whether it was a joke and the possible presence of undue influence (the young boy).

Matilda (1996)(PG)

A brilliant little girl with a strong moral compass who tries to instruct her family on many things erudite and her father specifically on what constitutes misrepresentation in selling used cars.

You can view a clip of this movie and others that illustrate business law concepts at the LawFlix site, located at **www.cengage.com/blaw/dvl**.

MAKE THE CONNECTION

SUMMARY

An agreement that otherwise appears to be a contract may not be binding because one of the parties lacks contractual capacity. In such a case, the contract is ordinarily voidable at the election of the party who lacks contractual capacity. In some cases, the contract is void. Ordinarily, contractual incapacity is the inability, for mental or physical reasons, to understand that a contract is being made and to understand its general terms and nature. This is typically the case when it is claimed that incapacity exists because of insanity, intoxication, or drug use. The incapacity of minors arises because society discriminates in favor of that class to protect them from unwise contracts.

The age of majority is 18. Minors can disaffirm most contracts. If a minor received anything from the other party, the minor, on avoiding the contract, must return what had been received from the other party if the minor still has it.

When a minor disaffirms a contract for a necessary, the minor must pay the reasonable value of any benefit received.

Minors only are liable for their contracts. Parents of a minor are not liable on the minor's contracts merely because they are the parents. Frequently, an adult enters into the contract as a coparty of the minor and is then liable without regard to whether the minor has avoided the contract.

The contract of an insane person is voidable to much the same extent as the contract of a minor. An important distinction is that if a guardian has been appointed for the insane person, a contract made by the insane person is void, not merely voidable.

An intoxicated person lacks contractual capacity if the intoxication is such that the person does not understand that a contract is being made.

The consent of a party to an agreement is not genuine or voluntary in certain cases of mistake, deception, or pressure. When this occurs, what appears to be a contract can be avoided by the victim of such circumstances or conduct.

As to mistake, it is necessary to distinguish between unilateral mistakes that are unknown to the other contracting party and those that are known. Mistakes that are unknown to the other party usually do not affect the binding character of the agreement. A unilateral mistake of which the other contracting party has knowledge or has reason to know makes the contract avoidable by the victim of the mistake.

The deception situation may be one of negligent misrepresentation or fraud. The law ordinarily does not attach any significance to nondisclosure. Contrary to this rule, there is a duty to volunteer information when a confidential relationship exists between the possessor of the knowledge and the other contracting party.

When concealment goes beyond mere silence and consists of actively taking steps to hide the truth, the conduct may be classified as fraud. A statement of opinion or value cannot ordinarily be the basis for fraud liability.

The voluntary character of a contract may be lacking because the agreement had been obtained by pressure. This may range from undue influence through the array of threats of extreme economic loss (called *economic duress*) to the threat of physical force that would cause serious personal injury or damage to property (called *physical duress*). When the voluntary character of an agreement has been destroyed by deception, or pressure, the victim may avoid or rescind the contract or may obtain money damages from the wrongdoer.

LEARNING OUTCOMES

After studying this chapter, you should be able to clearly explain:

A. CONTRACTUAL CAPACITY

LO.1 Define contractual capacity

See the example where Jacqueline, age 22, did not understand parts of a storage contract, p. 308.

LO.2 Explain the extent and effect of avoidance of a contract by a minor.

See the *Prince George's Hospital* case where a minor had to pay for medical necessaries, p. 311.

B. MISTAKE

LO.3 Distinguish unilateral mistakes and mutual mistakes

See the *Shurgard Storage* case where the "other party" should have known of the unilateral mistake, p. 315.

See the example of the mutual mistake of fact regarding the fertility of a cow on p. 315.

C. DECEPTION

LO.4 Explain the difference between intentional misrepresentation, negligent misrepresentation and puffery.

See the example of the purchase of the used Honda where the misrepresentation was found to be fraud not puffery on p. 317.

D. PRESSURE

LO.5 Explain the difference between undue influence and duress

See the *Fisher v. Schefers* undue influence litigation, p. 322.

See the Katahdin bicycle example on economic duress, p. 323.

KEY TERMS

confidential relationship	fraud	status quo ante
contractual capacity	necessaries	undue influence
duress	physical duress	
economic duress	reform	

QUESTIONS AND CASE PROBLEMS

1. Lester purchased a used automobile from MacKintosh Motors. He asked the seller if the car had ever been in a wreck. The MacKintosh salesperson had never seen the car before that morning and knew nothing of its history but quickly answered Lester's question by stating: "No. It has never been in a wreck." In fact, the auto had been seriously damaged in a wreck and, although repaired, was worth much less than the value it would have had if there had been no wreck. When Lester learned the truth, he sued MacKintosh Motors and the salesperson for damages for fraud. They raised the defense that the salesperson did not know the statement was false and had not intended to deceive Lester. Did the conduct of the salesperson constitute fraud?

2. Helen, age 17, wanted to buy a Harley-Davidson "Sportster" motorcycle. She did not have the funds to pay cash but persuaded the dealer to sell the cycle to her on credit. The dealer did so partly because Helen said that she was 22 and showed the dealer an identification card that falsely stated her age as 22. Helen drove the motorcycle away. A few days later, she damaged it and then returned it to the dealer and stated that she disaffirmed the contract because she was a minor. The dealer said that she could not because (1) she had misrepresented her age and (2) the motorcycle was damaged. Can she avoid the contract?

3. Paden signed an agreement dated May 28 to purchase the Murrays' home. The Murrays accepted Paden's offer the following day, and the sale closed on June 27. Paden and his family moved into the home on July 14, 1997. Paden had the home inspected prior to closing. The report listed four minor repairs

needed by the home, the cost of which was less than $500. Although these repairs had not been completed at the time of closing, Paden decided to go through with the purchase. After moving into the home, Paden discovered a number of allegedly new defects, including a wooden foundation, electrical problems, and bat infestation. The sales agreement allowed extensive rights to inspect the property. The agreement provided:

> *Buyer…shall have the right to enter the property at Buyer's expense and at reasonable times…to thoroughly inspect, examine, test, and survey the Property…. Buyer shall have the right to request that Seller repair defects in the Property by providing Seller within 12 days from Binding Agreement Date with a copy of inspection report(s) and a written amendment to this agreement setting forth the defects in the report which Buyer requests to be repaired and/or replaced…. If Buyer does not timely present the written amendment and inspection report, Buyer shall be deemed to have accepted the Property "as is."*

Paden sued the Murrays for fraudulent concealment and breach of the sales agreement. If Mr. Murray told Paden on May 26 that the house had a concrete foundation, would this be fraud? Decide. [*Paden v Murray*, 523 SE2d 75 (Ga App)]

4. High-Tech Collieries borrowed money from Holland. High-Tech later refused to be bound by the loan contract, claiming the contract was not binding because it had been obtained by duress. The evidence showed that the offer to make the loan was made on a take-it-or-leave-it basis. Was the defense of duress valid? [*Holland v High-Tech Collieries, Inc.*, 911 F Supp 1021 (DC WA)]

5. Thomas Bell, a minor, went to work in the Pittsburgh beauty parlor of Sam Pankas and agreed that when he left the employment, he would not work in or run a beauty parlor business within a 10-mile radius of downtown Pittsburgh for a period of two years. Contrary to this provision, Bell and another employee of Pankas's opened a beauty shop three blocks from Pankas's shop and advertised themselves as Pankas's former employees. Pankas sued Bell to stop the breach of the noncompetition, or restrictive, covenant. Bell claimed that he was not bound because he was a minor when he had agreed to the covenant. Was he bound by the covenant? [*Pankas v Bell*, 198 A2d 312 (Pa)]

6. Aldrich and Co. sold goods to Donovan on credit. The amount owed grew steadily, and finally Aldrich refused to sell any more to Donovan unless Donovan signed a promissory note for the amount due. Donovan did not want to but signed the note because he had no money and needed more goods. When Aldrich brought an action to enforce the note, Donovan claimed that the note was not binding because it had been obtained by economic duress. Was he correct? [*Aldrich & Co. v Donovan*, 778 P2d 397 (Mont)]

7. James Fitl purchased a 1952 Mickey Mantle Topps baseball card from baseball card dealer Mark Strek for $17,750 and placed it in a safe deposit box. Two years later, he had the card appraised, and he was told that the card had been refinished and trimmed, which rendered it valueless. Fitl sued Strek and testified

that he had relied on Strek's position as a sports card dealer and on his representations that the baseball card was authentic. Strek contends that Fitl waited too long to give him notice of the defects that would have enabled Strek to contact the person who sold him the card and obtain relief. Strek asserts that he therefore is not liable. Advise Fitl concerning possible legal theories that apply to his case. How would you decide the case? [See *Fitl v Strek*, 690 NW2d 605 (Neb)]

8. An agent of Thor Food Service Corp. was seeking to sell Makofske a combination refrigerator-freezer and food purchase plan. Makofske was married and had three children. After being informed of the eating habits of Makofske and his family, the agent stated that the cost of the freezer and food would be about $95 to $100 a month. Makofske carefully examined the agent's itemized estimate and made some changes to it. Makofske then signed the contract and purchased the refrigerator-freezer. The cost proved to be more than the estimated $95 to $100 a month, and Makofske claimed that the contract had been obtained by fraud. Decide. [*Thor Food Service Corp. v Makofske*, 218 NYS2d 93]

9. Blubaugh was a district manager of Schlumberger Well Services. Turner was an executive employee of Schlumberger. Blubaugh was told that he would be fired unless he chose to resign. He was also told that if he would resign and release the company and its employees from all claims for wrongful discharge, he would receive about $5,000 in addition to his regular severance pay of approximately $25,000 and would be given job-relocation counseling. He resigned, signed the release, and received about $40,000 and job counseling. Some time thereafter, he brought an action claiming that he had been wrongfully discharged. He claimed that the release did not protect the defendants because the release had been obtained by economic duress. Were the defendants protected by the release? [*Blubaugh v Turner*, 842 P2d 1072 (Wyo)]

10. Sippy was thinking of buying Christich's house. He noticed watermarks on the ceiling, but the agent showing the house stated that the roof had been repaired and was in good condition. Sippy was not told that the roof still leaked and that the repairs had not been able to stop the leaking. Sippy bought the house. Some time later, heavy rains caused water to leak into the house, and Sippy claimed that Christich was liable for damages. What theory would he rely on? Decide. [*Sippy v Christich*, 609 P2d 204 (Kan App)]

11. Pileggi owed Young money. Young threatened to bring suit against Pileggi for the amount due. Pileggi feared the embarrassment of being sued and the possibility that he might be thrown into bankruptcy. To avoid being sued, Pileggi executed a promissory note to pay Young the amount due. He later asserted that the note was not binding because he had executed it under duress. Is this defense valid? [*Young v Pileggi*, 455 A2d 1228 (Pa Super)]

12. Office Supply Outlet, Inc., a single-store office equipment and supply retailer, ordered 100 model RVX-414 computers from Compuserve, Inc. A new staff member made a clerical error on the order form and ordered a quantity that was

far in excess of what Office Supply could sell in a year. Office Supply realized the mistake when the delivery trucks arrived at its warehouse. Its manager called Compuserve and explained that it had intended to order just 10 computers. Compuserve declined to accept the return of the extra machines. Is the contract enforceable? What additional facts would allow the store to avoid the contract for the additional machines?

13. C&J Publishing Co. told a computer salesman that it wanted a computer system that would operate its printing presses. C&J specified that it wanted only new equipment and no used equipment would be acceptable. The seller delivered a system to C&J that was a combination of new and secondhand parts because it did not have sufficient new parts to fill the order. When C&J later learned what had happened, it sued the seller for fraud. The seller contended that no statement or warranty had been made that all parts of the system were new and that it would not therefore be liable for fraud. Decide.

14. The city of Salinas entered into a contract with Souza & McCue Construction Co. to construct a sewer. City officials knew unusual subsoil conditions (including extensive quicksand) existed that would make performance of the contract unusually difficult. This information was not disclosed when city officials advertised for bids. The advertisement for bids directed bidders to examine carefully the site of the work and declared that the submission of a bid would constitute evidence that the bidder had made an examination. Souza & McCue was awarded the contract, but because of the subsoil conditions, it could not complete on time and was sued by Salinas for breach of contract. Souza & McCue counterclaimed on the basis that the city had not revealed its information on the subsoil conditions and was thus liable for the loss. Was the city liable? [*City of Salinas v Souza & McCue Construction Co.*, 424 P2d 921 (Cal App 3d)]

15. Vern Westby inherited a "ticket" from Anna Sjoblom, a survivor of the sinking of the *Titanic*, which had been pinned to the inside of her coat. He also inherited an album of postcards, some of which related to the *Titanic*. The ticket was a one-of-a-kind item in good condition. Westby needed cash and went to the biggest antique dealer in Tacoma, operated by Alan Gorsuch and his family, doing business as Sanford and Sons, and asked about the value of these items. Westby testified that after Alan Gorsuch examined the ticket, he said, "It's not worth nothing." Westby then inquired about the value of the postcard album, and Gorsuch advised him to come back later. On Westby's return, Gorsuch told Westby, "It ain't worth nothing." Gorsuch added that he "couldn't fetch $500 for the ticket." Since he needed money, Westby asked if Gorsuch would give him $1,000 for both the ticket and the album, and Gorsuch did so.

Six months later, Gorsuch sold the ticket at a nationally advertised auction for $110,000 and sold most of the postcards for $1,200. Westby sued Gorsuch for fraud. Testimony showed that Gorsuch was a major buyer in antiques and collectibles in the Puget Sound area and that he would have had an understanding of the value of the ticket. Gorsuch contends that all elements of fraud are not present since there was no evidence that Gorsuch intended that

Westby rely on the alleged representations, nor did Westby rely on such. Rather, Gorsuch asserts, it was an arm's-length transaction and Westby had access to the same information as Gorsuch. Decide. [*Westby v Gorsuch*, 112 Wash App 558 (2002)]

CPA QUESTIONS

1. A building subcontractor submitted a bid for construction of a portion of a high-rise office building. The bid contained material computational errors. The general contractor accepted the bid with knowledge of the errors. Which of the following statements best represents the subcontractor's liability?

   a. Not liable, because the contractor knew of the errors

   b. Not liable, because the errors were a result of gross negligence

   c. Liable, because the errors were unilateral

   d. Liable, because the errors were material (5/95, Law, #17, 5351)

2. Egan, a minor, contracted with Baker to purchase Baker's used computer for $400. The computer was purchased for Egan's personal use. The agreement provided that Egan would pay $200 down on delivery and $200 thirty days later. Egan took delivery and paid the $200 down payment. Twenty days later, the computer was damaged seriously as a result of Egan's negligence. Five days after the damage occurred and one day after Egan reached the age of majority, Egan attempted to disaffirm the contract with Baker. Egan will:

   a. Be able to disaffirm despite the fact that Egan was *not* a minor at the time of disaffirmance

   b. Be able to disaffirm only if Egan does so in writing

   c. Not be able to disaffirm because Egan had failed to pay the balance of the purchase price

   d. Not be able to disaffirm because the computer was damaged as a result of Egan's negligence (11/93, Law, #21, 4318)

Chapter 15

CONSIDERATION

Will the law enforce every promise? Generally, a promise will not be enforced unless something is given or received for the promise.

A. GENERAL PRINCIPLES

As a general rule, one of the elements needed to make an agreement binding is consideration.

1. Consideration Defined and Explained

consideration–promise or performance that the promisor demands as the price of the promise.

Consideration is what each party to a contract gives up to the other in making their agreement.

(A) BARGAINED-FOR EXCHANGE. *Consideration* is the bargained-for exchange between the parties to a contract. In order for consideration to exist, something of value must be given or promised in return for the performance or promise of performance of the other.[1] The value given or promised can be money, services, property, or the forbearance of a legal right.

For Example, Beth offers to pay Kerry $100 for her used skis, and Kerry accepts. Beth has promised something of value, $100, as consideration for Kerry's promise to sell the skis, and Kerry has promised Beth something of value, the skis, as consideration for the $100. If Kerry offered to *give* Beth the used skis and Beth accepted, these parties would have an agreement but not an enforceable contract because Beth did not provide any consideration in exchange for Kerry's promise of the skis. There was no *bargained-for exchange* because Kerry was not promised anything of value from Beth.

(B) BENEFIT-DETRIMENT APPROACH. Some jurisdictions analyze consideration from the point of view of a *benefit-detriment approach,* defining *consideration* as a benefit received by the promisor or a detriment incurred by the promisee.

As an example of a unilateral contract analyzed from a benefit-detriment approach to consideration, Mr. Scully, a longtime summer resident of Falmouth, states to George Corfu, a college senior, "I will pay you $3,000 if you paint my summer home." George in fact paints the house. The work of painting the house by George, the promisee, was a legal detriment to him. Also, the painting of the house was a legal benefit to Scully, the promisor. There was consideration in this case, and the agreement is enforceable.

2. Gifts

Promises to make a gift are unenforceable promises under the law of contracts because of lack of consideration, as illustrated previously in the scenario of Kerry promising to give her used skis to Beth without charge. There was no bargained-for

---

[1] *Brooksbank v Anderson*, 586 NW2d 789 (Minn App 1998).

exchange because Kerry was not promised anything of value from Beth. A completed gift, however, cannot be rescinded for lack of consideration.[2]

Charitable subscriptions by which individuals make pledges to finance the construction of a college building, a church, or another structure for charitable purposes are binding to the extent that the donor (promisor) should have reasonably realized that the charity was relying on the promise in undertaking the building program. Some states require proof that the charity has relied on the subscription.[3]

C A S E   S U M M A R Y

You Can't Back Out Now

FACTS: Salsbury was attempting to establish a new college, Charles City College. Salsbury obtained a pledge from Northwestern Bell Telephone Company to contribute to the college. When the company did not pay, Salsbury sued the company. The company raised the defense that there was no consideration for its promise and that nothing had been done by the college in reliance on the promise.

DECISION: Judgment for Salsbury. As a matter of public policy, a promise of a charitable contribution is binding even though there is no consideration for the promise and without regard for whether the charity had done any acts in reliance on the promise. The company was therefore liable on its promise to contribute. [**Salsbury v Northwestern Bell Telephone Co., 221 NW2d 609 (Iowa 1974)**]

3. Adequacy of Consideration

Ordinarily, courts do not consider the adequacy of the consideration given for a promise. The fact that the consideration supplied by one party is slight when compared with the burden undertaken by the other party is immaterial. It is a matter for the parties to decide when they make their contract whether each is getting a fair return. In the absence of fraud or other misconduct, courts usually will not interfere to make sure that each side is getting a fair return.

C A S E   S U M M A R Y

Who's to Say?

FACTS: On the death of their aunt, a brother and sister became the owners of shares of stock of several corporations. They made an agreement to divide these shares equally between them, although the sister's shares had a value approximately seven times those of the brother. The brother died before the shares were divided. The sister then claimed that the agreement to divide was not binding because the consideration for her promise was not adequate.

---

[2] *Homes v O'Bryant,* 741 So2d 366 (Miss App 1999).
[3] *King v Trustees of Boston University,* 647 NE2d 1176 (Ma 1995).

C A S E   S U M M A R Y

Continued

DECISION: The value of stock cannot be determined precisely. It may change with time. In addition, the value that one person may see can be different than that seen by another. The court therefore will not make a comparison of the value that each party was to receive under the agreement. It was sufficient that a promise was exchanged for a promise. The adequacy of the consideration would not be examined. This sister was therefore bound by her promise to divide the shares. [**Emberson v Hartley 762 P2d 364 (Wash App 1988)**]

Because the adequacy of consideration is ignored, it is immaterial that consideration is so slight that the transaction is in part a "gift." However, the Internal Revenue Service may view a given transaction as part consideration, part gift, and assess a gift tax as appropriate.

The fact that the consideration turns out to be disappointing does not affect the binding character of the contract. Thus, the fact that a business purchased by a group of investors proves unprofitable does not constitute a failure of consideration that releases the buyers from their obligation to the seller.

C A S E   S U M M A R Y

Expectations versus Consideration

FACTS: Aqua Drilling Company made a contract to drill a well for the Atlas Construction Company. It was expected that this would supply water for a home being constructed by Atlas. Aqua did not make any guarantee or warranty that water would be produced. Aqua drilled the well exactly as required by the contract, but no water was produced. Atlas refused to pay. It asserted that the contract was not binding on the theory that there had been a failure of consideration because the well did not produce water.

DECISION: The contract was binding. Atlas obtained the exact performance required by the contract. While Atlas had expected that water would be obtained, Aqua did not make any guarantee or warranty that this would be so. Hence, there was no failure of consideration. [**Atlas Construction Co., Inc. v Aqua Drilling Co., 559 P2d 39 (Wyo 1977)**]

4. Forbearance as Consideration

In most cases, consideration consists of the performance of an act such as providing a service, or the making of a promise to provide a service or goods, or paying money.[4] Consideration may also consist of **forbearance**, which is refraining from doing an act that an individual has a legal right to do, or it may consist of a promise of forbearance. In other words, the promisor may desire to buy the inaction or a promise of inaction of the other party.

forbearance–refraining from doing an act.

---

[4] *Prenger v Baumhoer*, 914 SW2d 413 (Mo App 1996).

The giving up of any legal right can be consideration for the promise of the other party to a contract. Thus, the relinquishment of a right to sue for damages will support a promise for the payment of money given in return for the promise to relinquish the right, if such is the agreement of the parties.

The promise of a creditor to forbear collecting a debt is consideration for the promise of the debtor to modify the terms of the transaction.

5. Illusory Promises

In a bilateral contract, each party makes a promise to the other. For a bilateral contract to be enforceable, there must be *mutuality of obligation*. That is, both parties must have created obligations to the other in their respective promises. If one party's promise contains either no obligation or only an apparent obligation to the other, this promise is an **illusory promise**. The party making such a promise is not bound because he or she has made no real promise. The effect is that the other party, who has made a real promise, is also not bound because he or she has received no consideration. It is said that the contract fails for lack of mutuality.

For Example, Mountain Coal Company promises to sell Midwest Power Company all the coal it may order for $48 per ton for the year 2010, and Midwest Power agrees to pay $48 for any coal it orders from Mountain Coal. Mountain Coal in its promise to Midwest Power has obligated itself to supply all coal ordered at a stated price. However, Midwest Power's promise did not obligate it to buy any coal whatsoever from Mountain Coal (note that it was not a requirements contract). Because Midwest has no obligation to Mountain Coal under its promise, there is no mutuality of obligation, and Midwest cannot enforce Mountain Coal's promise when the market price of coal goes to $55 a ton in the winter of 2010 as the result of severe weather conditions.

Consider as well the example of the Jacksonville Fire soccer team's contract with Brazilian soccer star Edmundo. Edmundo signed a contract to play for the Jacksonville franchise of the new International Soccer League for five-years at $25 million. The extensive document signed by Edmundo set forth the details of the team's financial commitment and the details of Edmundo's obligations to the team and its fans. On page 4 of the document, the team inserted a clause reserving the right "to terminate the contract and team obligations at any time in its sole discretion." During the season, Edmundo received a $40 million five-year offer to play for Manchester United of the English Premier League, which he accepted. Because Jacksonville had a free way out of its obligation by the unrestricted cancellation provision in the contract, it thus made its promises to Edmundo illusory. Edmundo was not bound by the Jacksonville contract as a result of a lack of mutuality and was free to sign with Manchester United.

(A) **CANCELLATION PROVISIONS.** Although a promise must impose a binding obligation, it may authorize a party to cancel the agreement under certain circumstances on giving notice by a certain date. Such a provision does not make this party's promise illusory, for the party does not have a free way out and is limited to living up to the terms of the **cancellation provision**. **For Example,** actress Zsa Zsa Gabor made a contract with Hollywood Fantasy Corporation to appear at a fantasy vacation in San

illusory promise–promise that in fact does not impose any obligation on the promisor.

cancellation provision– crossing out of a part of an instrument or a destruction of all legal effect of the instrument, whether by act of party, upon breach by the other party, or pursuant to agreement or decree of court.

Antonio, Texas, on May 2–4, for a $10,000 appearance fee plus itemized (extravagant) expenses. The last paragraph of the agreement stated: "It is agreed that if a significant acting opportunity in a film comes up, Ms. Gabor will have the right to cancel her appearance in San Antonio by advising Hollywood Fantasy in writing by April 15, 1991." Ms. Gabor sent a telegram on April 15, 1991, canceling her appearance. During the May 2 through 4 period, Ms. Gabor's only acting activity was a 14-second cameo role during the opening credits of *Naked Gun 2½*. In a lawsuit for breach of contract that followed, the jury saw this portion of the movie and concluded that Ms. Gabor had not canceled her obligation on the basis of a "significant acting opportunity," and she was held liable for breach of contract.[5]

(B) Conditional Promises. A *conditional promise* is a promise that depends on the occurrence of a specified condition in order for the promise to be binding. **For Example,** Mary Sparks, in contemplation of her signing a lease to take over a restaurant at Marina Bay, wanted to make certain that she had a highly qualified chef to run the restaurant's food service. She made a contract with John "Grumpy" White to serve as executive chef for a one-year period at a salary of $150,000. The contract set forth White's responsibilities and was conditioned on the successful negotiation of the restaurant lease with Marina Bay Management. Both parties signed it. Although the happening of the condition was within Mary's control because she could avoid the contract with Grumpy White by not acquiring the restaurant lease, she limited her future options by the contract with White. Her promise to White was not illusory because after signing the contract with him, if she acquired the restaurant lease, she was bound to hire White as her executive chef. Before signing the contract with White, she was free to sign any chef for the position. The contract was enforceable.

CPA B. Special Situations

The following sections analyze certain common situations in which a lawsuit turns on whether the promisor received consideration for the promise sued on.

6. Preexisting Legal Obligation

Ordinarily, doing or promising to do what one is already under a legal obligation to do is not consideration.[6] Similarly, a promise to refrain from doing what one has no legal right to do is not consideration. This preexisting duty or legal obligation can be based on statute, on general principles of law, on responsibilities of an office held, or on a preexisting contract.

For Example, Officer Mary Rodgers is an undercover police officer in the city of Pasadena, California, assigned to weekend workdays. Officer Rodgers promised Elwood Farnsworth that she would diligently patrol the area of the Farnsworth estate on weekends to keep down the noise and drinking of rowdy young persons who gathered in this area, and Mr. Farnsworth promised to provide a $500 per month gratuity for this extra service. Farnsworth's promise is unenforceable because

---

[5] *Hollywood Fantasy Corp. v Gabor,* 151 F2d 203 (5th Cir 1998).
[6] *Gardiner, Kamya & Associates v Jackson,* 369 F3d 1318 (Fed Cir 2004).

Officer Rodgers has a preexisting official duty as a police officer to protect citizens and enforce the antinoise and public drinking ordinances.

CPA (A) **COMPLETION OF CONTRACT.** Suppose that a contractor refuses to complete a building unless the owner promises a payment or bonus in addition to the sum specified in the original contract, and the owner promises to make that payment. The question then arises as to whether the owner's promise is binding. Most courts hold that the second promise of the owner is without consideration.

C A S E   S U M M A R Y

You're Already Under Contract

FACTS: Crookham & Vessels had a contract to build an extension of a railroad for the Little Rock Port Authority. It made a contract with Larry Moyer Trucking to dig drainage ditches. The ditch walls collapsed because water would not drain off. This required that the ditches be dug over again. Larry Moyer refused to do this unless extra money was paid. Crookham & Vessels agreed to pay the additional compensation, but after the work was done, it refused to pay. Larry Moyer sued for the extra compensation promised.

DECISION: Judgment against Moyer. Moyer was bound by its contract to dig the drainage ditches. Its promise to perform that obligation was not consideration for the promise of Crookham & Vessels to pay additional compensation. Performance of an obligation is not consideration for a promise by a party entitled to that performance. The fact that performance of the contract proved more difficult or costly than originally contemplated does not justify making an exception to this rule. [**Crookham & Vessels, Inc. v Larry Moyer Trucking, Inc. 699 SW2d 414 (Ark App 1985)**]

If the promise of the contractor is to do something that is not part of the first contract, then the promise of the other party is binding. **For Example,** if a bonus of $5,000 is promised in return for the promise of a contractor to complete the building at a date earlier than that specified in the original agreement, the promise to pay the bonus is binding.

CPA *(1) Good-Faith Adjustment*
A current trend is to enforce a second promise to pay a contractor a higher amount for the performance of the original contract when there are extraordinary circumstances caused by unforeseeable difficulties and when the additional amount promised the contractor is reasonable under the circumstances.

(2) Contract for Sale of Goods
When the contract is for the sale of goods, any modification made in good faith by the parties to the contract is binding without regard to the existence of consideration for the modification.

CPA (B) **COMPROMISE AND RELEASE OF CLAIMS.** The rule that doing or promising to do what one is already legally bound to do is not consideration applies to a part payment made in satisfaction of an admitted or *liquidated debt*. Thus, a promise to pay part of an amount that is admittedly owed is not consideration for a promise to discharge the balance. It will not prevent the creditor from demanding the remainder later. **For Example,** John owes Mark $100,000, which was due on March 1, 2010. On March 15, John offers to pay back $80,000 if Mark will agree to accept this amount as the discharge of the full amount owed. Mark agrees to this proposal, and it is set forth in writing signed by the parties. However, Mark later sues for the $20,000 balance. Mark will be successful in the lawsuit because John's payment of the $80,000 is not consideration for Mark's promise to discharge the full amount owed because John was doing only what he had a preexisting legal duty to do.

If the debtor pays the part payment before the debt is due, there is consideration because, on the day when the payment was made, the creditor was not entitled to demand any payment. Likewise, if the creditor accepts some article (even of slight value) in addition to the part payment, consideration exists.

A debtor and creditor may have a bona fide dispute over the amount owed or whether any amount is owed. Such is called an *unliquidated debt.* In this case, payment by the debtor of less than the amount claimed by the creditor is consideration for the latter's agreement to release or settle the claim. It is generally regarded as sufficient if the claimant believes in the merit of the claim.[7]

(C) **PART-PAYMENT CHECKS.** When there is a good-faith dispute about the amount of a debt and the debtor tenders a check that states on its face "paid in full" and references the transaction in dispute, but the amount of the check is less than the full amount the creditor asserts is owed, the cashing of the check by the creditor discharges the entire debt.

composition of creditors— agreement among creditors that each shall accept a part payment as full payment in consideration of the other creditors doing the same.

(D) **COMPOSITION OF CREDITORS.** In a **composition of creditors**, the various creditors of one debtor mutually agree to accept a fractional part of their claims in full satisfaction of the claims. Such agreements are binding and are supported by consideration. When creditors agree to extend the due date of their debts, the promise of each creditor to forbear is likewise consideration for the promise of other creditors to forbear.

7. Past Consideration

past consideration— something that has been performed in the past and which, therefore, cannot be consideration for a promise made in the present.

A promise based on a party's past performance lacks consideration.[8] It is said that **past consideration** is no consideration. **For Example,** Fred O'Neal came up with the idea for the formation of the new community bank of Villa Rica and was active in its formation. Just prior to the execution of the documents creating the bank, the organizers discussed that once the bank was formed, it would hire O'Neal, giving him a three-year contract at $65,000 the first year, $67,000 the second year, and $70,000 the third. In a lawsuit against the bank for breach of contract, O'Neal testified that the consideration he gave in exchange for the three-year contract was his past effort to organize the bank. The court stated that past consideration generally will not support a subsequent promise and that the purported consideration was not rendered to the bank, which had not yet been established

[7] *F. H. Prince & Co. v Towers Financial Corp.,* 656 NE2d 142 (Ill App 1995).
[8] *Smith v Locklear,* 906 So2d 1273 (Fla App 2005).

when his promotion and organization work took place.[9] The presence of a bargained-for exchange is not present when a promise is made in exchange for a past benefit.[10]

8. Moral Obligation

In most states, promises made to another based on "moral obligation" lack consideration and are not enforceable.[11] They are considered gratuitous promises and unenforceable. **For Example,** while on a fishing trip, Tom Snyder, a person of moderate means, met an elderly couple living in near-destitute conditions in a rural area of Texas. He returned to the area often, and he regularly purchased groceries for the couple and paid for their medical needs. Some two years later, the couple's son, David, discovered what Tom had been doing and promised to reimburse Snyder for what he had furnished his parents. This promise, based on a moral obligation, is unenforceable. A "past consideration" analysis also renders David's promise as unenforceable.

ethics & the law

Alan Fulkins, who owns a construction company that specializes in single-family residences, is constructing a small subdivision with 23 homes. Tretorn Plumbing, owned by Jason Tretorn, was awarded the contract for the plumbing work on the homes at a price of $4,300 per home.

Plumbing contractors complete their residential projects in three phases. Phase one consists of digging the lines for the plumbing and installing the pipes that are placed in the foundation of the house. Phase two consists of installing the pipes within the walls of the home, and phase three is installing of the surface plumbing, such as sinks and tubs. However, industry practice dictates that the plumbing contractor receive one-half of the contract amount after completion of phase one.

Tretorn completed the digs of phase one for Fulkins and received payment of $2,150. Tretorn then went to Fulkins and demanded an additional $600 per house to complete the work. Fulkins said, "But you already have a contract for $4,300!" Tretorn responded, "I know, but the costs are killing me. I need the additional $600."

Fulkins explained the hardship of the demand, "Look, I've already paid you half. If I hire someone else, I'll have to pay them two-thirds for the work not done. It'll cost me $5,000 per house."

Tretorn responded, "Exactly. I'm a bargain because the additional $600 I want only puts you at $4,900. If you don't pay it, I'll just lien the houses and then you'll be stuck without a way to close the sales. I've got the contract all drawn up. Just sign it and everything goes smoothly."

Should Fulkins sign the agreement? Does Tretorn have the right to the additional $600? Was it ethical for Tretorn to demand the $600? Is there any legal advice you can offer Fulkins?

[9] *O'Neal v Home Town Bank of Villa Rica,* 514 SE2d 669 (Ga App 1999).

[10] But see *United Resource Recovery Corp v Ranko Venture Management Inc.,* 854 F Supp 2d 645 (SDNY 2008) where a past work agreement was unenforceable because it was based on past consideration—however, the individual could recover under a signed consulting agreement for which no compensation had been paid. See also *Travis v Paepke,* 3 So3d 131 (Miss App 2009).

[11] *Production Credit Ass'n of Manaan v Rub,* 475 NW2d 532 (ND 1991). As to the Louisiana rule of moral consideration, see *Thomas v Bryant,* 596 So2d 1065 (La App 1992).

FIGURE 15-1 | *Consideration and Promises*

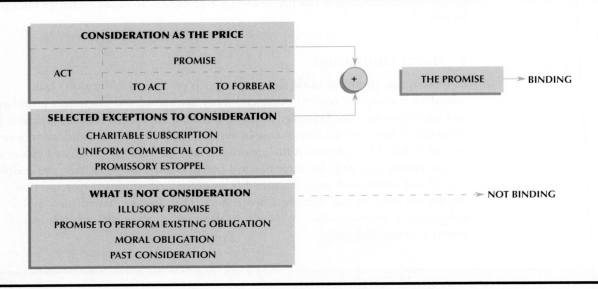

C. EXCEPTIONS TO THE LAWS OF CONSIDERATION

The ever-changing character of law clearly appears in the area of consideration as part of the developing law of contracts.

9. Exceptions to Consideration

By statute or decision, traditional consideration is not required in these situations:

(A) CHARITABLE SUBSCRIPTIONS. Where individuals made pledges to finance the construction of buildings for charitable purposes, consideration is lacking according to technical standards applied in ordinary contract cases. For public policy reasons, the reliance of the charity on the pledge in undertaking the project is deemed a substitute for consideration.

(B) UNIFORM COMMERCIAL CODE. In some situations, the Uniform Commercial Code abolishes the requirement of consideration. **For Example,** under the Code, consideration is not required for (1) a merchant's written, firm offer for goods stated to be irrevocable, (2) a written discharge of a claim for an alleged breach of a commercial contract, or (3) an agreement to modify a contract for the sale of goods. [12]

(C) PROMISSORY ESTOPPEL. Under the doctrine of **promissory estoppel**, a promisor may be prevented from asserting that his or her promise is unenforceable because the promisee gave no consideration for the promise. This doctrine, sometimes called the *doctrine of detrimental reliance,* is applicable when (1) the promisor makes a promise that lacks consideration, (2) the promisor intends or should reasonably expect that the promisee will rely on the promise, (3) the promisee in fact relies on

promissory estoppel– doctrine that a promise will be enforced although it is not supported by consideration when the promisor should have reasonably expected that the promise would induce action or forbearance of a definite and substantial character on the part of the promised and injustice can be avoided only by enforcement of the promise.

[12] UCC § 2-209(1).

the promise in some definite and substantial manner, and (4) enforcement of the promise is the only way to avoid injustice.[13]

Damages recoverable in a case of promissory estoppel are not the profits that the promisee expected, but only the amount necessary to restore the promisee to the position he or she would have been in had the promisee not relied on the promise.[14]

Legal difficulties often arise because parties take certain things for granted. Frequently, they will be sure that they have agreed to everything and that they have a valid contract. Sometimes, however, they do not. The courts are then faced with the problem of leaving them with their broken dreams or coming to their rescue when promissory estoppel can be established.

C A S E   S U M M A R Y

Brits Rescued by Promissory Estoppel

FACTS: Portman Lamborghini, Ltd. (Portman), was owned by Chaplake Holdings, Ltd., a United Kingdom company, which was owned by David Jolliffe and David Lakeman as equal shareholders. Between 1984 and 1987, Portman sold approximately 30 new Lamborghinis each year through its exclusive concession contract with the car maker. It was then the largest Lamborghini dealer in the world since Lamborghini's production was just 250 cars per year. These cars sold at a retail price between $200,000 and $300,000. In 1987, Chrysler Corporation bought Lamborghini, and its chairman, Lee Iacocca, presented a plan to escalate production to 5,000 units within five years. The plan included the introduction of a new model, the P140, with a retail price of $70,000. Between 1987 and 1991, *all* of the Chrysler/ Lamborghini top executives with whom Jolliffe and Lakeman and their top advisors came in contact provided the same message to them: Chrysler was committed to the Expansion Plan, and in order for Portman to retain its exclusive U.K. market, it must expand its operational capacity from 35 cars in 1987 to 400 cars by 1992. Accordingly, Portman acquired additional financing, staff, and facilities and built a new distribution center. An economic downturn in the United States and major development and production problems at Lamborghini led Chrysler to reduce its expansion investment by two-thirds. Factory production delays eroded Portman's profitability and success, and it entered into receivership in April 1992. Suit was brought on behalf of the Portman and Chaplake entities on a promissory estoppel theory against Chrysler, a Delaware corporation.

DECISION: Judgment for Portman and Chaplake on the promissory estoppel theory. (1) A promise was made by Chrysler that the Lamborghini line would expand tenfold and that Portman would retain its exclusivity deal *only* if it expanded its operational capacity. (2) The promisor, Chrysler, should have reasonably expected that Portman would rely on this promise. (3) Lakeman and Jolliffe were given the same message and promise by *all* of the top executives involved, and it was therefore not unreasonable for them to rely upon the promises made by these executives and to undertake the detriment of major expansion activity that would have been unnecessary but for the Expansion Plan and the role they were promised. (4) The prevention of injustice is the "fundamental idea" underlying the doctrine of promissory estoppel, and injustice can be avoided in this case only by the enforcement of Chrysler's promise. Portman is entitled to £ 569,321 for its costs to implement its Expansion Plan, and Chaplake is entitled to £ 462,686 for its investment in Portman's expansion. [**Chrysler Corp. v Chaplake Holdings, Ltd. 822 A2d 1024 (Del 2003)**]

---

[13] *Neuhoff v Marvin Lumber and Cedar Co.,* 370 F3d 197 (1st Cir 2004).
[14] *Medistar Corp. v Schmidt,* 267 SW3d 150 (Tex App 2008).

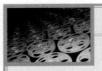

lawflix

Baby Boom (1987) (PG)

Review the scene near the end of the movie when Diane Keaton is presented with an offer for the purchase of her company, Country Baby. List the elements of consideration that Food Giant is paying for the company. Explain what Ms. Keaton's consideration is in exchange.

Check out LawFlix at **www.cengage.com/blaw/dvl** to access movie clips that illustrate business law concepts.

MAKE THE CONNECTION

SUMMARY

A promise is not binding if there is no consideration for the promise. Consideration is what the promisor requires as the price for his promise. That price may be doing an act, refraining from the doing of an act, or merely promising to do or to refrain. In a bilateral contract, it is necessary to find that the promise of each party is supported by consideration. If either promise is not so supported, it is not binding, and the agreement of the parties in not a contract. Consequently, the agreement cannot be enforced. When a promise is the consideration, it must be a binding promise. The binding character of a promise is not affected by the circumstance that there is a condition precedent to the performance promised. A promise to do what one is already obligated to do is not consideration, although some exceptions are made. Such exceptions include the rendering of a partial performance or a modified performance accepted as a good-faith adjustment to a changed situation, a compromise and release of claims, a part-payment check, and a compromise of creditors. Because consideration is the price that is given to obtain the promise, past benefits conferred on the promisor cannot be consideration.

A promise to refrain from doing an act can be consideration. A promise to refrain from suing or asserting a particular claim can be consideration. When consideration is forbearance to assert a claim, it is immaterial whether the claim is valid as long as the claim has been asserted in the good-faith belief that it was valid.

When the promisor obtains the consideration specified for the promise, the law is not ordinarily concerned with the value or adequacy of that consideration.

Under the doctrine of promissory estoppel a court may enforce a promise lacking consideration where it is the only way to avoid injustice.

LEARNING OUTCOMES

After studying this chapter, you should be able to clearly explain:

A. GENERAL PRINCIPLES—CONSIDERATION

LO.1 Explain what constitutes consideration

See the "bargained for exchange" example involving Beth and Kerry, p. 332.
See the "benefit-detriment" approach to consideration example, p. 332.
See the discussion on forbearance as consideration on p. 334.

B. SPECIAL SITUATIONS

LO.2 Distinguish between a "preexisting legal obligation" and "past consideration"

See the preexisting duty example involving Officer Rogers on p. 336.
See the example involving Fred O'Neal where he found out the past consideration is no consideration rule, p. 338.

LO.3 Explain why promises based on moral obligations lack consideration.

See the example of the gratuitous deeds of Tom Synder on p. 336.

C. EXCEPTIONS TO THE LAWS OF CONSIDERATION

LO.4 List the exceptions to the requirement of consideration

See the discussion on charitable subscriptions, the UCC, and promissory estoppel starting on p. 340.

LO.5 Explain the "fundamental idea" underlying promissory estoppel

See the *Chaplake Holdings* case where the court enforced Chrysler's promise in order to correct an injustice, p. 341.

KEY TERMS

cancellation provision	forbearance	past consideration
composition of creditors	illusory promise	promissory estoppel
consideration		

QUESTIONS AND CASE PROBLEMS

1. Sarah's house caught on fire. Through the prompt assistance of her neighbor Odessa, the fire was quickly extinguished. In gratitude, Sarah promised to pay Odessa $1,000. Can Odessa enforce this promise?

2. William E. Story agreed to pay his nephew, William E. Story II, a large sum of money (roughly equivalent to $50,000 in 2007 dollars) "if he would refrain from drinking liquor, using tobacco, swearing, and playing cards or billiards for money until he should come to be 21 years of age." William II had been using tobacco and occasionally drank liquor but refrained from using these stimulants over several years until he was 21 and also lived up to the other requirements of his uncle's offer. Just after William II's 21st birthday, Story acknowledged that

William II had fulfilled his part of the bargain and advised that the money would be invested for him with interest. Story died, and his executor, Sidway, refused to pay William II because he believed the contract between Story and William II was without consideration. Sidway asserted that Story received no benefit from William II's performance and William II suffered no detriment (in fact, by his refraining from the use of liquor and tobacco, William II was not harmed but benefited, Sidway asserted). Is there any theory of consideration that William II can rely on? How would you decide this case? [*Hamer v Sidway,* 124 NY 538]

3. Dale Dyer, who was employed by National By-Products, Inc., was seriously injured at work as the result of a job-related accident. He agreed to give up his right to sue the employer for damages in consideration of the employer's giving him a lifetime job. The employer later claimed that this agreement was not binding because Dyer's promise not to sue could not be consideration for the promise to employ on the ground that Dyer in fact had no right to sue. Dyer's only remedy was to make a claim under workers' compensation. Was the agreement binding? [*Dyer v National By-Products, Inc.,* 380 NW2d 732 (Iowa)]

4. Charles Sanarwari retained Stan Gissel to prepare his income tax return for the year 2006. The parties agreed on a fee of $400. Charles had done a rough estimate based on last year's return and believed he would owe the IRS approximately $2,000. When Stan's work was completed, it turned out that Charles would receive a $2,321 tax refund. Stan explained how certain legitimate advantages were used to reduce Charles's tax obligation. Charles paid for Stan's services and was so pleased with the work that he promised to pay Stan an additional $400 for the excellent job on the tax return when he received his tax refund. Thereafter, Stan and Charles had a falling out over a golf tournament where Charles was late for his tee time and Stan started without him, causing Charles to lose an opportunity to win the club championship. Stan was not paid the $400 promised for doing an excellent job on the tax return, and he sued Charles as a matter of principle. Decide.

5. Medistar is a real estate development company specializing in the development of medical facilities. Dr. Schmidt, the team physician for the San Antonio Spurs basketball team, sought to develop "The Texas Center for Athletes" medical center next to the Spurs facility and urged Medistar to obtain the real estate and develop the project on his group's behalf. Medistar spent more than $1 million and thousands of man-hours on the project from 2000 to July 12, 2004 when Dr. Schmidt's new group of investors purchased the property next to the Spur's facility for the project; subsequently, Medistar was informed that it would have no role in the project. Medistar asserts that it relied on Dr. Schmidt's assurances that it would be the developer of the project—and after four years and the $1 million in time and expenses it spent, it is unconscionable to be excluded from the project. Dr. Schmidt and associates contend that Medistar has presented no contractual agreement tying it to any legal obligation to Medistar. Is there a viable legal theory available to Medistar? If so what is the remedy? [*Medistar v Schmidt,* 267 SW3d 150 (Tex App)]

6. Fedun rented a building to Gomer, who did business under the name of Mike's Cafe. Later, Gomer was about to sell the business to Brown and requested Fedun to release him from his liability under the lease. Fedun agreed to do so. Brown sold the business shortly thereafter. The balance of the rent due by Gomer under the original lease agreement was not paid, and Fedun sued Gomer on the rent claim. Could he collect after having released Gomer? [*Fedun v Mike's Cafe,* 204 A2d 776 (Pa Super)]

7. Alexander Proudfoot Co. was in the business of devising efficiency systems for industry. It told Sanitary Linen Service Co. that it could provide an improved system for Sanitary Linen that would save Sanitary Linen money. It made a contract with Sanitary Linen to provide a money-saving system. The system was put into operation, and Proudfoot was paid the amount due under the contract. The system failed to work and did not save money. Sanitary Linen sued to get the money back. Was it entitled to do so? [*Sanitary Linen Service Co. v Alexander Proudfoot Co.,* 435 F2d 292 (5th Cir)]

8. Sears, Roebuck and Co. promised to give Forrer permanent employment. Forrer sold his farm at a loss to take the job. Shortly after beginning work, he was discharged by Sears, which claimed that the contract could be terminated at will. Forrer claimed that promissory estoppel prevented Sears from terminating the contract. Was he correct? [*Forrer v Sears, Roebuck & Co.,* 153 NW2d 587 (Wis)]

9. Kemp leased a gas filling station from Baehr. Kemp, who was heavily indebted to Penn-O-Tex Oil Corp., transferred to it his right to receive payments on all claims. When Baehr complained that the rent was not paid, he was assured by the corporation that the rent would be paid to him. Baehr did not sue Kemp for the overdue rent but later sued the corporation. The defense was raised that there was no consideration for the promise of the corporation. Decide. [*Baehr v Penn-O-Tex Corp.,* 104 NW2d 661 (Minn)]

10. Bogart owed several debts to Security Bank & Trust Co. and applied to the bank for a loan to pay the debts. The bank's employee stated that he would take the application for the loan to the loan committee and "within two or three days, we ought to have something here, ready for you to go with." The loan was not made. The bank sued Bogart for his debts. He filed a counterclaim on the theory that the bank had broken its contract to make a loan to him and that promissory estoppel prevented the bank from going back on what the employee had said. Was this counterclaim valid?

11. Kelsoe worked for International Wood Products, Inc., for a number of years. One day Hernandez, a director and major stockholder of the company, promised Kelsoe that the corporation would give her 5 percent of the company's stock. This promise was never kept, and Kelsoe sued International for breach of contract. Had the company broken its contract? [*Kelsoe v International Wood Products, Inc.,* 588 So2d 877 (Ala)]

12. Kathy left her classic 1978 Volkswagen convertible at Freddie's Service Station, requesting a "tune-up." When she returned that evening, Freddie's bill was

$374. Kathy stated that Firestone and Sears advertise tune-ups for $70, and she asked Freddie, "How can you justify this bill?" Freddie responded, "Carburator work." Kathy refused to pay the bill and left. That evening, when the station closed, she took her other set of keys and removed her car, after placing a check in the station's mail slot. The check was made out to Freddie's Service Station for $200 and stated on its face: "This check is in full payment of my account with you regarding the tune-up today on my 1978 Volkswagen convertible." Freddie cashed the check in order to meet his business expenses and then sued Kathy for the difference owed. What result?

13. On the death of their mother, the children of Jane Smith gave their interests in their mother's estate to their father in consideration of his payment of $1 to each of them and his promise to leave them the property on his death. The father died without leaving them the property. The children sued their father's second wife to obtain the property in accordance with the agreement. The second wife claimed that the agreement was not a binding contract because the amount of $1 and future gifts given for the children's interests were so trivial and uncertain. Decide.

14. Radio Station KSCS broadcast a popular music program. It announced that it would pay $25,000 to any listener who detected that it did not play three consecutive songs. Steve Jennings listened to and heard a program in which two songs were followed by a commercial program. He claimed the $25,000. The station refused to pay on the ground that there was no consideration for its promise to pay that amount. Was the station liable? [*Jennings v Radio Station KSCS,* 708 SW2d 60 (Tex App)]

15. Hoffman wanted to acquire a franchise for a Red Owl grocery store. (Red Owl was a corporation that maintained a system of chain stores.) An agent of Red Owl informed Hoffman and his wife that if they would sell their bakery in Wautoma, acquire a certain tract of land in Chilton (another Wisconsin city), and put up $6,000, they would be given a franchise. In reliance on the agent's promise, Hoffman sold his business and acquired the land in Chilton, but he was never granted a franchise. He and his wife sued Red Owl. Red Owl raised the defense that there had been only an assurance that Hoffman would receive a franchise, but because there was no promise supported by consideration, there was no binding contract to give him a franchise. Decide. [*Hoffman v Red Owl Stores, Inc.,* 133 NW2d 267 (Wis)]

Chapter 16

LEGALITY AND PUBLIC POLICY

A court will not enforce a contract if it is illegal, contrary to public policy, or unconscionable.

A. GENERAL PRINCIPLES

An agreement is illegal either when its formation or performance is a crime or a tort or when it is contrary to public policy or unconscionable.

1. Effect of Illegality

Ordinarily, an illegal agreement is void. When an agreement is illegal, the parties are usually not entitled to the aid of the courts. Examples of illegal contracts where the courts have left the parties where they found them include a liquor store owner not being allowed to bring suit for money owed for goods (liquor) sold and delivered on credit in violation of statute and an unlicensed home improvement contractor not being allowed to enforce his contract for progress payments due him. If the illegal agreement has not been performed, neither party can sue the other to obtain performance or damages. If the agreement has been performed, neither party can sue the other to obtain damages or to set the agreement aside.[1]

C A S E   S U M M A R Y

The Illegal Paralegal

FACTS: Brian Neiman was involved in the illegal practice of law for over seven years. Having been found guilty of illegally practicing law, he sought to collect disability benefits under his disability insurance policy with Provident Life due to an alleged bipolar disorder, the onset of which occurred during the pendency of criminal and bar proceedings against him. Neiman contends that his bipolar disorder prevents him from working as a paralegal. Provident contends that Neiman should not be indemnified for the loss of income generated from his illegal practice of law.

DECISION: Because all of Neiman's income was derived from the unlawful practice of law in the seven years preceding his claim, as a matter of public policy, a court will not enforce a disability benefits policy that compensates him for his loss of income he was not entitled to earn. Neiman's own wrongdoing caused the contract to be void. Accordingly, Neiman was *in pari delicto* [equally guilty], if not more at fault than the insurance company, in causing the contract to be void and will recover neither benefits nor the premiums he paid. The court must leave the parties where it found them. [**Neiman v Provident Life & Accident Insurance Co., 217 F Supp 2d 1281 SD Fla 2002**]

---

[1] *Sabia v Mattituck Inlet Marina, Inc.*, 805 NYS2d 346 (AD 2005).

Even if a contract appears to be legal on its face, it may be unenforceable if it was entered into for an illegal purpose. **For Example,** if zoning regulations in the special-purpose district of Washington, D.C., require that only a professional can lease space in a given building, and the rental agent suggests that two nonprofessionals take out the lease in their attorney's name, but all parties realize that the premises will be used only by the nonprofessionals, then the lease in question is illegal and unenforceable.[2]

2. Exceptions to Effect of Illegality

To avoid hardship, exceptions are made to the rules stated in Section 1.

(A) **PROTECTION OF ONE PARTY.** When the law that the agreement violates is intended to protect one of the parties, that party may seek relief. **For Example,** when, in order to protect the public, the law forbids the issuance of securities by certain classes of corporations, a person who has purchased them may recover the money paid.

(B) **UNEQUAL GUILT.** When the parties are not *in pari delicto*—equally guilty—the least guilty party is granted relief when public interest is advanced by doing so. **For Example,** when a statute is adopted to protect one of the parties to a transaction, such as a usury law adopted to protect borrowers, the person to be protected will not be deemed to be *in pari delicto* with the wrongdoer when entering into a transaction that the statute prohibits.

in pari delicto—equally guilty; used in reference to a transaction as to which relief will not be granted to either party because both are equally guilty of wrongdoing.

3. Partial Illegality

An agreement may involve the performance of several promises, some of which are illegal and some legal. The legal parts of the agreement may be enforced provided that they can be separated from the parts that are illegal.

When the illegal provision of a contract may be ignored without defeating the contract's basic purpose, a court will merely ignore the illegal provision and enforce the balance of the contract. Consequently, when a provision for the payment of an attorney's fee in a car rental agreement was illegal because a local statute prohibited it, the court would merely ignore the fee provision and enforce the balance of the contract.[3]

If a contract is susceptible to two interpretations, one legal and the other illegal, the court will assume that the legal meaning was intended unless the contrary is clearly indicated.

4. Crimes and Civil Wrongs

An agreement is illegal, and therefore void, when it calls for the commission of any act that constitutes a crime. To illustrate, one cannot enforce an agreement by which the other party is to commit an assault, steal property, burn a house, or kill a person.

[2] *McMahon v A, H, & B,* 728 A2d 656 (DC 1999).
[3] *Harbour v Arelco, Inc.,* 678 NE2d 381 (Ind 1997).

A contract to obtain equipment for committing a crime is illegal and cannot be enforced. Thus, a contract to manufacture and sell illegal slot machines is void.

An agreement that calls for the commission of a civil wrong is also illegal and void. Examples are agreements to slander a third person; defraud another; infringe another's patent, trademark, or copyright; or fix prices.

5. Good Faith and Fairness

Every contract has an implied obligation that neither party shall do anything that will have the effect of destroying or injuring the right of the other party to receive the fruits of the contract. This means that in every contract there exists an implied covenant of **good faith** and fair dealing. **For Example,** Katy Lesser entered into a 10-year lease of retail space to operate a natural food store in South Burlington, Vermont. Her business prospered and in April of 1999 she signed a lease for additional space. For five years, the landlord continually rebuffed her efforts to meet and discuss plans to renovate the 1999 space to expand the grocery store, motivated solely by a desire to pressure the tenant to pay a portion of his legal fees in an unrelated zoning case. The court found that the landlord breached the obligation of good faith and fair dealing, causing the 1999 space to be essentially unusable from 1999 to 2004. The court awarded the tenant the rent she paid for this period less a storage fee adjustment.[4]

good faith–absence of knowledge of any defects or problems.

6. Unconscionable Clauses

Ordinarily, a court will not consider whether a contract is fair or unfair, is wise or foolish, or operates unequally between the parties. **For Example,** the Kramper Family Farm sold 17.59 acres of land to Dakota Industrial Development, Inc. (DID), for $35,000 per acre if the buyer constructed a paved road along the property by December 31. The contract also provided that if the road was not completed by the date set forth in the contract, the price per acre would be $45,000. When the road was not completed by the December 31 date, Family Farm sued DID for the additional $10,000 per acre. DID defended that to apply the contract according to its plain language would create an unconscionable result and was an unenforceable penalty provision contrary to public policy. The court refused to allow DID to escape its contractual obligations on the pretext of unconscionability and public policy arguments. The parties are at liberty to contract as they see fit, the court concluded, and generally, a court will not inquire into the adequacy of consideration inasmuch as the value of property is a matter of personal judgment by the parties to the contract. In this case, the price consisted of either $45,000 per acre, or $35,000 per acre with the road by a certain date.[5]

However, in certain unusual situations, the law may hold a contract provision unenforceable because it is too harsh or oppressive to one of the parties. This

---

[4] *Century Partners, LP v Lesser Goldsmith Enterprises*, 958 A2d 627 (Vt 2008).
[5] *Kramper Family Farm v Dakota Industrial Development, Inc.*, 603 NW2d 463 (Neb App 1999).

principle may be applied to invalidate a clause providing for the payment by one party of an excessive penalty on the breaking of a contract or a provision inserted by the dominant party that it shall not be liable for the consequences of intentional torts, fraud, or gross negligence. This principle is extended in connection with the sale of goods to provide that "if the court … finds the contract or any clause of the contract to have been unconscionable at the time it was made, the court may refuse to enforce the contract, or it may enforce the remainder of the contract without the unconscionable clause, or it may so limit the application of any unconscionable clause as to avoid any unconscionable result."[6]

(A) What Constitutes Unconscionability? A provision in a contract that gives what the court believes is too much of an advantage over a buyer may be held void as unconscionable.

(B) Determination of Unconscionability. Some jurisdictions analyze unconscionability as having two separate elements: procedural and substantive. Both elements must be present for a court to refuse to enforce a contract provision. Other jurisdictions analyze unconscionability by considering the doctrine of adhesion and whether the clause in question is unduly oppressive.

Procedural unconscionability has to do with matters of freedom of assent resulting from inequality of bargaining power and the absence of real negotiations and meaningful choice or a surprise resulting from hiding a disputed term in an unduly long document or fine print. Companywide standardized form contracts imposed on a take-it-or-leave-it basis by a party with superior bargaining strength are called **contracts of adhesion**, and they may sometimes be deemed procedurally unconscionable.

contract of adhesion–
contract offered by a dominant party to a party with inferior bargaining power on a take-it-or-leave-it basis.

Substantive unconscionability focuses on the actual terms of the contract itself. Such unconscionability is indicated when the contract terms are so one-sided as to shock the conscience or are so extreme as to appear unconscionable according to the mores and business practices of the time and place.

The U.S. Supreme Court has made clear that arbitration is an acceptable forum for the resolution of employment disputes between employees and their employers, including employment-related claims based on federal and state statutes.[7] The controlling arbitration agreement language is commonly devised and implemented by the employer. Under the Federal Arbitration Act (FAA), the employer can obtain a court order to stay court proceedings and compel arbitration according to the terms of the controlling arbitration agreement. The Supreme Court also made clear that in agreeing to arbitration of a statutory claim, a party does not forgo substantive rights afforded by the statute. In a growing number of court decisions, in effect employers are finding that courts will not enforce arbitration agreements in which the employer has devised an arbitration agreement that functions as a thumb on the employer's side of the scale.[8]

[6] UCC § 2-302(1).
[7] *Gilmer v Interstate/Johnson Lane Corp.*, 500 US 20 (1991); *Circuit City Stores, Inc. v Adams,* 532 US 105 (2001).
[8] See *Vassi/Kouska v Woodfield Nissan Inc.*, 830 NE2d 619 (Ill App 2005).

C A S E   S U M M A R Y

Arbitration Agreement Short-Circuited

FACTS: Saint Clair Adams completed an application to work as a salesperson at Circuit City. As part of the application, Adams signed the "Circuit City Dispute Resolution Agreement" (DRA). The DRA requires employees to submit all claims and disputes to binding arbitration. Incorporated into the DRA is a set of "Dispute Resolution Rules and Procedures" that defines the claims subject to arbitration, discovery rules, allocation of fees, and available remedies. Under these rules, the amount of damages is restricted: Back pay is limited to one year, front pay to two years, and punitive damages to the higher of the amount of front and back pay awarded or $5,000. In addition, the employee is required to split the cost of the arbitration, including the daily fees of the arbitrator, the cost of a reporter to transcribe the proceedings, and the expense of renting the room in which the arbitration is held, unless the employee prevails and the arbitrator decides to order Circuit City to pay the employee's share of the costs. Circuit City is not required under the agreement to arbitrate any claims against the employee. An employee cannot work at Circuit City without signing the DRA.

Adams filed a state court lawsuit against Circuit City and three coworkers alleging sexual harassment and related charges. Circuit City responded by filing a petition in federal district court to compel arbitration pursuant to the FAA. The petition was granted by the trial court, reversed by the Ninth Circuit Court of Appeals, which court was reversed by the U.S. Supreme Court (*Circuit City 1*) and the case remanded to the Ninth Circuit Court of Appeals.

DECISION: Judgment for Adams. The arbitration provision is unenforceable. The DRA is procedurally unconscionable because it is a contract of adhesion drafted by the party with superior bargaining power, which relegates to the other party the option of either adhering to its terms without modification or rejecting the contract entirely.

The DRA is substantively unconscionable because employees must arbitrate "any and all employment-related claims" while Circuit City is not obligated to arbitrate their claims against employees and may bring lawsuits against employees, thus depriving the DRA of any modicum of bilaterality. Moreover, the remedies are limited under the DRA, including a one-year back pay limit and a two-year front pay limit, with a cap on punitive damages of an amount up to the higher of the amount of back pay and front pay awarded or $5,000. By contrast, in a civil lawsuit under state law, a plaintiff is entitled to all forms of relief. Further, the DRA requires that the employee split the cost of the arbitrator's fees with the employer while an individual would not be required to split the cost of a judge. [**Circuit City Stores, Inc. v Adams (Circuit City II), 279 F3d 889 9th Cir 2002**]

B. Agreements Affecting Public Welfare

Agreements that may harm the public welfare are condemned as contrary to public policy and are not binding. Agreements that interfere with public service or the duties of public officials, obstruct legal process, or discriminate against classifications of individuals may be considered detrimental to public welfare and, as such, are not enforceable.

7. Agreements Contrary to Public Policy

A given agreement may not violate any statute but may still be so offensive to society that the courts feel that enforcing the contract would be contrary to public policy.

public policy–certain objectives relating to health, morals, and integrity of government that the law seeks to advance by declaring invalid any contract that conflicts with those objectives even though there is no statute expressly declaring such a contract illegal.

Public policy cannot be defined precisely but is loosely described as protection from that which tends to be injurious to the public or contrary to the public good or which violates any established interest of society. Contracts that may be unenforceable as contrary to public policy frequently relate to the protection of the public welfare, health, or safety; to the protection of the person; and to the protection of recognized social institutions. **For Example,** a woman entered into a services contract with a male in exchange for financial support. The record disclosed, however, that the association between the parties was one founded upon the exchange of money for sex. The court determined that the agreement for financial support in exchange for illicit sexual relations was violative of public policy and thus was unenforceable.[9] Courts are cautious in invalidating a contract on the ground that it is contrary to public policy because courts recognize that, on the one hand, they are applying a very vague standard and, on the other hand, they are restricting the freedom of the contracting parties to contract freely as they choose.[10]

8. Gambling, Wagers, and Lotteries

lottery–any plan by which a consideration is given for a chance to win a prize; it consists of three elements: (1) there must be a payment of money or something of value for an opportunity to win, (2) a prize must be available, and (3) the prize must be offered by lot or chance.

Gambling contracts are illegal. Largely as a result of the adoption of antigambling statutes, wagers or bets are generally illegal. Private **lotteries** involving the three elements of prize, chance, and consideration (or similar affairs of chance) are also generally held illegal. In many states, public lotteries (lotteries run by a state government) have been legalized by statute. Raffles are usually regarded as lotteries.

C A S E   S U M M A R Y

Horseplay Prohibited

FACTS: Robert Bovard contracted to sell American Horse Enterprises, Inc., to James Ralph. When Ralph did not make payments when due, Bovard brought suit against him. The trial judge raised the question whether the contract was void for illegality. American Horse Enterprises was predominantly engaged in manufacturing devices for smoking marijuana and tobacco, and to a lesser degree in manufacturing jewelry. When the contract was made, there was no statute prohibiting the manufacture of any of these items, but there was a statute making it illegal to possess, use, or transfer marijuana.

DECISION: Although the question of illegality had not been raised by the parties, the trial judge had the duty to question the validity of the contract when it appeared that the contract might be illegal. Although there was no statute expressly making the contract illegal, the statute prohibiting the possession and sale of marijuana manifested a public policy against anything that would further the use of marijuana. It was therefore against public policy to make the devices used in smoking marijuana or to sell a business that engaged in such manufacture. The sales contract was therefore contrary to public policy and void and could not be enforced. [**Bovard v American Horse Enterprises, Inc. 247 Cal Rptr 340 Cal App 1988**]

---

[9] *Anonymous v Anonymous*, 740 NYS2d 341 (App Div 2002).
[10] *Beacon Hill Civic Ass'n v Ristorante Toscano, Inc.*, 662 NE2d 1015 (Mass 1996).

In some states, bingo games, lotteries, and raffles are legalized by statute when the funds raised are used for a charitable purpose.

Sales promotion schemes calling for the distribution of property according to chance among the purchasers of goods are held illegal as lotteries without regard to whether the scheme is called a *guessing contest,* a *raffle,* or a *gift.*

Giveaway plans and games are lawful so long as it is not necessary to buy anything or give anything of value to participate. If participation is free, the element of consideration is lacking, and there is no lottery.

An activity is not gambling when the result is solely or predominantly a matter of skill. In contrast, it is gambling when the result is solely a matter of luck. Rarely is any activity 100 percent skill or 100 percent luck.

C. Regulation of Business

Local, state, and national laws regulate a wide variety of business activities and practices.

9. Effect of Violation

Whether an agreement made in connection with business conducted in violation of the law is binding or void depends on how strongly opposed the public policy is to the prohibited act. Some courts take the view that the agreement is not void unless the statute expressly specifies this. In some instances, a statute expressly preserves the validity of the contract. **For Example,** if someone fails to register a fictitious name under which a business is conducted, the violator, after registering the name as required by statute, is permitted to sue on a contract made while illegally conducting business.

10. Statutory Regulation of Contracts

To establish uniformity or to protect one of the parties to a contract, statutes frequently provide that contracts of a given class must follow a statutory model or must contain specified provisions. **For Example,** statutes commonly specify that particular clauses must be included in insurance policies to protect the persons insured and their beneficiaries. Other statutes require that contracts executed in connection with credit buying and loans contain particular provisions designed to protect the debtor.

Consumer protection legislation gives the consumer the right to rescind the contract in certain situations. Laws relating to truth in lending, installment sales, and home improvement contracts commonly require that an installment-sale contract specify the cash price, the down payment, the trade-in value (if any), the cash balance, the insurance costs, and the interest and finance charges.

CPA   11. Licensed Callings or Dealings

Statutes frequently require that a person obtain a license, certificate, or diploma before practicing certain professions, such as law and medicine.[11] A license may also

---

[11] *Hakimi v Cantwell,* 855 NYS2d 273 (App Div 2008).

be required before carrying on a particular business or trade, such as that of a real estate broker, stockbroker, hotel keeper, or pawnbroker.

If a license is required to protect the public from unqualified persons, a contract made by an unlicensed person is unenforceable. **For Example,** a corporation that does not hold a required real estate broker's license cannot sue to recover fees for services as a broker. An unlicensed insurance broker who cannot recover a fee because of the absence of a license cannot evade the statutory requirement by having a friend who is a licensed broker bill for the services and collect the payment for him.

CASE SUMMARY

How Much for a Brokerage License? How Much Commission Was Lost?

FACTS: Thompson Halbach & Associates, Inc., an Arizona corporation, entered into an agreement with Meteor Motors, Inc., the owner of Palm Beach Acura, to find a buyer for the dealership, and Meteor agreed to pay a 5 percent commission based on the closing price of the sale. Working out of Scottsdale, Arizona, Thompson solicited potential Florida purchasers for the Florida business by phone, fax, and e-mail. Among those contacted was Craig Zinn Automotive Group, which ultimately purchased Palm Beach Acura from Meteor Motors for $5,000,000. Thompson was not paid its $250,000 commission and brought suit against Meteor for breach of contract. Meteor defended that Thompson was an unlicensed broker and that a state statute declares a contract for a commission with an unlicensed broker to be invalid. Thompson responded that the Florida state statue did not apply because it worked out of Scottsdale.

DECISION: Judgment for Meteor. The Florida statute clearly applies to a foreign broker who provides brokerage activities in Florida. Thompson solicited potential Florida purchasers for the Florida business and that purchaser was a Florida corporation. [**Meteor Motors v Thompson Halbach & Associates, 914 So2d 479 Fla App 2005**]

CPA ## 12. Contracts in Restraint of Trade

An agreement that unreasonably restrains trade is illegal and void on the ground that it is contrary to public policy. Such agreements take many forms, such as a combination to create a monopoly or to obtain a corner on the market or an association of merchants to increase prices. In addition to the illegality of the agreement based on general principles of law, statutes frequently declare monopolies illegal and subject the parties to various civil and criminal penalties.[12]

CPA ## 13. Agreements Not to Compete

In the absence of a valid restrictive covenant, the seller of a business may compete with the buyer, or an ex-employee may solicit customers of the former employer.

[12] Sherman Antitrust Act, 15 USC §§ 1–7; Clayton Act, 15 USC §§ 12–27; Federal Trade Commission Act, 15 USC §§ 41–58.

A noncompetition covenant may be held invalid because of vagueness concerning the duration and geographic area of the restriction.[13] Moreover, if the agreement not to compete is not properly executed in accordance with state law, it will not be enforced. **For Example,** Holly Martinez worked for Avis Rent-A-Car at the New Bern, North Carolina, airport. When hired, she printed her name on the top of the form containing an agreement not to compete but did not sign it. On December 17, she resigned her position to return to school, saying that she planned to get a part-time job. The next day, she began working for Hertz Rent-A-Car at the counter adjacent to the Avis counter. Avis was unsuccessful in obtaining a restraining order to prevent Holly from working for its competitor because the agreement was not signed as required by state law.[14]

CPA   (A) SALE OF BUSINESS. When a going business is sold, it is commonly stated in the contract that the seller shall not go into the same or a similar business again within a certain geographic area or for a certain period of time, or both. In early times, such agreements were held void because they deprived the public of the service of the person who agreed not to compete, impaired the latter's means of earning a livelihood, reduced competition, and exposed the public to monopoly. To modern courts, the question is whether, under the circumstances, the restriction imposed on one party is reasonably necessary to protect the other party. If the restriction is reasonable, it is valid and enforceable. **For Example,** when Scott Gaddy, the majority stockholder of GWC Insurance Brokers, sold his business to Alliant for $4.1million he agreed to refrain from competing in the insurance business in California for five years. Under California law, contracts not to compete are void, except for noncompetition covenants in connection with the sale of a business. The reason for the exception is to prevent the seller from depriving the buyer of the full value of the acquisition, including the sold company's goodwill. The court enforced the covenant against Gaddy.[15]

(B) EMPLOYMENT CONTRACT. Restrictions to prevent competition by a former employee are held valid when reasonable and necessary to protect the interest of the former employer. **For Example,** a noncompete clause executed by Dr. Samuel Keeley that prohibited his "establishing a competing cardiovascular surgery practice within a 75-mile radius of Albany, Georgia, for a period of two years following the date of termination" was upheld in court and did not include more territory than necessary to protect the professional corporation's business interests.[16]

Public policy requires that noncompetition covenants be strictly construed in favor of freedom of action of the employee.[17] A restrictive covenant is not binding when it places a restriction on the employee that is broader than reasonably necessary to protect the employer. **For Example,** Illinois manufacturer Arcor's noncompete clause, which had a restricted area of "the United States and Canada" precluding competition by a former employee for a one-year period, was found to

[13] *Vukovich v Coleman*, 789 NE2d 520 (Ind App 2003).
[14] *New Hanover Rent-A-Car, Inc. v Martinez*, 525 SE2d 487 (NC App 2000).
[15] 72 Cal Rptr 3d 259 (Cal App 2008).
[16] *Keeley v CSA, P.C.*, 510 SE2d 880 (Ga App 1999).
[17] Noncompetition covenants are not valid in California. However, confidentiality agreements protecting trade secrets are enforceable in that state.

be unenforceable as an industrywide ban that constituted a "blanket prohibition on competition."[18] In determining the validity of a restrictive covenant binding an employee, the court balances the aim of protecting the legitimate interests of the employer with the right of the employee to follow gainful employment and provide services required by the public and other employers.

thinking things through

Noncompete Clauses, Cause for Concern?

Some 10 states do not enforce noncompete clauses in employment contracts, according to the research of Matt Marx who has dedicated his doctoral studies at Harvard to this topic. The states are (from west to east): California, Washington, Nevada, Montana, North Dakota, Minnesota, Oklahoma, West Virginia, and Connecticut. (New York and Oregon have significantly limited their applicability). Marx had naively signed a two-year noncompete agreement out of MIT at SpeechWorks, a voice recognition start-up, and when he wanted to leave and continue in the voice recognition field, his options were to sit out the two-year noncompete period or go to work at a California firm, which he did. He is now researching whether enforcing noncompetes in a state can spur inventors, engineers, and entrepreneurs to move elsewhere to pursue development of their ideas.*

Does a state's innovation suffer when noncompete clauses handcuff employees to an employer, or force employees to take an unpaid leave for the noncompete period before continuing in their field with a new or start-up employer? THINKING THINGS THROUGH, prospective employees should carefully consider the impact noncompetes would have on their lives, and if they must sign one, carefully negotiate its duration and scope.

* *See* Scott Kirsner, "Why 'Noncompete' Means 'Don't Thrive,'" *Boston Globe*, December 30, 2007, E-1; Scott Kirsner, "Start-ups Stifled by Noncompetes," *Boston Globe*, June 21, 2009, G-1.

(c) **EFFECT OF INVALIDITY.** When a restriction of competition agreed to by the parties is invalid because its scope as to time or geographic area is too great, how does this affect the contract? Some courts trim the restrictive covenant down to a scope they deem reasonable and require the parties to abide by that revision.[19] This rule is nicknamed the "blue-pencil rule." **For Example,** Julie Murray signed a noncompete agreement, which was validly assigned to the purchaser of the Accounting Center of Lucas County, Inc. When the new owner changed from an hourly wage to commission pay for her tax preparation work, she objected and was terminated. The court found the 24-month noncompete restriction exceeded what was reasonable to protect the employer's legitimate business interests, and modified the time period to one year.[20] In the *Arcor* case, the court refused to "blue pencil" the covenant because to render the clause

---

[18] *Arcor, Inc. v Haas*, 842 NE2d 265 (Ill App 2005).
[19] *Unisource Worldwide, Inc. v Valenti*, 196 F Supp 2d 269 (EDNY 2002).
[20] *Murray v Accounting Center of Lucas County, Inc.*, 898 NE2d 89 (Ohio App 2008).

ethics&the law

William Stern and his wife were unable to have children because the wife suffered from multiple sclerosis and pregnancy posed a substantial health risk. Stern's family had been killed in the Holocaust, and he had a strong desire to continue his bloodline.

The Sterns entered into a surrogacy contract with Mary Beth Whitehead through the Infertility Center of New York (ICNY). William Stern and the Whiteheads (husband and wife) signed a contract for Mary Beth to be artificially inseminated and carry Stern's child to term, for which Stern was to pay Mary Beth $10,000 and ICNY $7,500.

Mary Beth was successfully artificially inseminated in 1985, and Baby M was born on March 27, 1986. To avoid publicity, the parents of Baby M were listed as "Mr. and Mrs. Whitehead," and the baby was called Sara Elizabeth Whitehead. On March 30, 1986, Mary Beth turned Baby M over to the Sterns at their home. They renamed the little girl Melissa.

Mary Beth became emotionally distraught and was unable to eat or sleep. The Sterns were so frightened by her behavior that they allowed her to take Baby M for one week to help her adjust. The Whiteheads took the baby and traveled throughout the East, staying in 20 different hotels and motels. Florida authorities found Baby M with Mary Beth's parents and returned her to the Sterns.

Mary Beth said the contract was one to buy a baby and was against public policy and therefore void. She also argued that the contract violated state laws on adoption and the severance of parental rights. The Sterns brought an action to have the contract declared valid and custody awarded to them.

Should the contract be valid or void? What types of behavior would be encouraged if the contract were declared valid? Is it ethical to "rent a womb"? Is it ethical to sell a child? See **In re Baby M, 537 A2d 15 (NJ 1988).**

---

reasonable, the court would in effect be writing a new agreement, which is inappropriate.[21]

Other courts refuse to apply the blue-pencil rule and hold that the restrictive covenant is void or that the entire contract is void.[22] There is also authority that a court should refuse to apply the blue-pencil rule when the restrictive covenant is manifestly unfair and would virtually keep the employee from earning a living.

14. Usurious Agreements

usury–lending money at an interest rate that is higher than the maximum rate allowed by law.

Usury is committed when money is loaned at a higher rate of interest than the law allows. Most states prohibit by statute charging more than a stated amount of interest. These statutes provide a maximum annual contract rate of interest that can be exacted under the law of a given state. In many states, the usury law does not apply to loans made to corporations.

When a lender incurs expenses in making a loan, such as the cost of appraising property or making a credit investigation of the borrower, the lender will require the

---

[21] *Arcor Inc.,* 847 NE2d at 374.
[22] *SWAT 24 v Bond,* 759 So2d 1047 (La App 2000). Under California law, any "contract by which anyone is restrained from engaging in a lawful profession, trade or business is to that extent void." Cal B&P Code § 16600. A noncompete provision is permitted, however, when "necessary to protect the employer's trade secrets." See *Lotona v Aetna U.S. Healthcare Inc.,* 82 F Supp 2d 1089 (CD Cal 1999), where Aetna was liable for wrongful termination when it fired a California employee for refusing to sign a noncompete agreement.

thinking things through

Legality and Public Policy

Karl Llewellyn, the principal drafter of the law that governs nearly all sales of goods in the United States—the Uniform Commercial Code (UCC)—once wrote, "Covert tools are never reliable tools." He was referring to unfairness in a contract or between the contracting parties.

The original intent of declaring certain types of contracts void because of issues of imbalance was based in equity. Courts stepped in to help parties who found themselves bound under agreements that were not fair and open in both their written terms and the communications between the parties. One contracts scholar wrote that the original intent could be described as courts stepping in to help "presumptive sillies like sailors and heirs…" and others who, if not crazy, are "pretty peculiar."

However, as the sophistication of contracts and commercial transactions increased, the importance of accuracy, honesty, and fairness increased. Unconscionability is a contracts defense that permits courts to intervene where contracts, if enforced, would "affront the sense of decency." UNCONSCIONABILITY is a term of ethics or moral philosophy used by courts to prevent exploitation and fraud.

borrower to pay the amount of such expenses. Any fee charged by a lender that goes beyond the reasonable expense of making the loan constitutes "interest" for the purposes of determining whether the transaction is usurious.[23]

Penalites for violating usury laws vary from state to state, with a number of states restricting the lender to the recovery of the loan but no interest whatsoever; other states allow recovery of the loan principal and interest up to the maximum contract rate. Some states also impose a penalty on the lender such as the payment of double the interest paid on a usurious loan.

C A S E   S U M M A R Y

Would You Recommend Karen Canzoneri as an Investment Advisor?

FACTS: Karen Canzoneri entered into two agreements with Howard Pinchuck. Under the first agreement, Canzoneri advanced $50,000 to be repaid at 12 percent per month for 12 consecutive months "as an investment profit." The second agreement required "$36,000 to be repaid on or before 6/1/01 with an investment profit of $36,000, total being $72,000." The annualized rate of return for the first transaction was 144 percent and for the second transaction was 608 percent. The civil penalty for violating the state's maximum interest rate of 25 percent per annum is forfeiture of the entire principal amount. Canzoneri contends that the transactions were investments not subject to the usury law.

[23] *Lentimo v Cullen Center Bank and Trust Co.*, 919 SW2d 743 (Tex App 1996).

CASE SUMMARY

Continued

DECISION: Judgment for Pinchuck. The four elements of a usurious transaction are present: (1) the transaction was a loan, (2) the money loaned required that it be returned, (3) an interest rate higher than allowed by law was required, and (4) a corrupt intention to take more than the legal rate for the use of the money loaned exists. Even though the terms called for "profit," not "interest," the courts looked to the substance, not the form, of the transaction. [**Pinchuck v Canzoneri, 920 So2nd 713 (Fla App 4 Dist 2006)**]

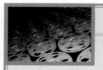

lawflix

Midnight Run (1988) (R)

Is the contract Robert DeNiro has for bringing in Charles Grodin, an embezzler, legal? Discuss the issues of consideration and ethics as the bail bondsman puts another bounty hunter on the case and DeNiro flees from law enforcement agents in order to collect his fee. And finally, discuss the legality of DeNiro's acceptance of money from Grodin and his release of Grodin at the end of the movie.

You can view a clip of this movie and others that illustrate business law concepts at the LawFlix site, located at **www.cengage.com/blaw/dvl**.

MAKE THE CONNECTION

SUMMARY

When an agreement is illegal, it is ordinarily void and no contract arises from it. Courts will not allow one party to an illegal agreement to bring suit against the other party. There are some exceptions to this, such as when the parties are not equally guilty or when the law's purpose in making the agreement illegal is to protect the person who is bringing suit. When possible, an agreement will be interpreted as being lawful. Even when a particular provision is held unlawful, the balance of the agreement may be saved so that the net result is a contract minus the clause that was held illegal.

The term *illegality* embraces situations in unconscionable contract clauses in which the courts hold that contract provisions are unenforceable because they are too harsh or oppressive to one of the parties to a transaction. If the clause is part of a standard form contract drafted by the party having superior bargaining power and is presented on a take-it-or-leave-it basis (a contract of adhesion) and the substantive terms of the clause itself are unduly oppressive, the clause will be found to be unconscionable and not enforced.

Whether a contract is contrary to public policy may be difficult to determine because public policy is not precisely defined. That which is harmful to the public welfare or general good is contrary to public policy. Contracts condemned as contrary to public policy include those designed to deprive the weaker party of a benefit that the lawmaker desired to provide, agreements injuring public service, and wagers and private lotteries. Statutes commonly make the wager illegal as a form of gambling. The private lottery is any plan under which, for a consideration, a person has a chance to win a prize.

Illegality may consist of the violation of a statute or administrative regulation adopted to regulate business. An agreement not to compete may be illegal as a restraint of trade except when reasonable in its terms and when it is incidental to the sale of a business or to a contract of employment.

The charging by a lender of a higher rate of interest than allowed by law is usury. Courts must examine transactions carefully to see whether a usurious loan is disguised as a legitimate transaction.

LEARNING OUTCOMES

After studying this chapter, you should be able to clearly explain:

A. GENERAL PRINCIPLES

LO.1 Explain the general contract principles on "illegality"
> See the unenforceable illegal lease to nonprofessionals example on p. 348. See the example where a contract to manufacture and sell illegal slot machines is void, p. 350.

LO.2 Explain the implied obligation on all parties of good faith and fair dealing
> See the example of the Vermont landlord who deprived a tenant of her rights under a lease, p. 350.

B. AGREEMENTS AFFECTING PUBLIC WELFARE

LO.3 Understand that it is only in unusual situations that a contract provision will be unenforceable because it is unconscionable
> See the *Kramper Family Farm* example where the court refused to consider whether the contract was fair or unfair, wise or foolish, p. 350.

C. REGULATION OF BUSINESS

LO.4 Explain the rationale for requiring licenses to carry on as a business, trade, or profession
> See the discussion requiring licenses to protect the public from unqualified persons, p. 355.

LO.5 Distinguish between noncompete clauses after the sale of a business and noncompete clauses in employment contracts

See the example where the California court enforced a 5 year noncompete clause against the seller of a business, p. 356.
See the example involving Julie Murray's noncompete clause and why it was modified from 24 months to one year, p. 357.

KEY TERMS

contracts of adhesion   *in pari delicto*   public policy
good faith   lotteries   usury

QUESTIONS AND CASE PROBLEMS

1. When are the parties to an illegal agreement *in pari delicto*?

2. John Iwen sued U.S. West Direct because of a negligently constructed yellow pages advertisement. U.S. West Direct moved to stay litigation and compel arbitration under the yellow pages order form, which required advertisers to resolve all controversies through arbitration, but allowed U.S. West (the publisher) to pursue judicial remedies to collect amounts due it. Under the arbitration provision, Iwen's sole remedy was a pro rata reduction or refund of the cost of the advertisement. The order form language was drafted by U.S. West Direct on a take-it-or-leave-it basis and stated in part:

   Any controversy or claim arising out of or relating to this Agreement, or breach thereof, other than an action by Publisher for the collection of amounts due under this Agreement, shall be settled by final, binding arbitration in accordance with the Commercial Arbitration rules of the American Arbitration Association.

   If forced to arbitration, Iwen would be unable to recover damages for the negligently constructed yellow pages ad, nor could he recover damages for infliction of emotional distress and punitive damages related to his many efforts to adjust the matter with the company, which were ignored or rejected. Must Iwen have his case resolved through arbitration rather than a court of law? [*Iwen v U.S. West Direct*, 977 P2d 989 (Mont)]

3. Sutcliffe Banton, dba Nemard Construction, furnished labor and materials (valued at $162,895) for improving Vicky Deafeamkpor's New York City residential property. She paid only $41,718, leaving $121,987 unpaid. Banton sued her and the jury awarded $90,000 in damages. Deafeamkpor moved for an order setting aside the jury's verdict because Banton was not properly licensed by New York City. Under NYC Code an unlicensed contractor may neither enforce a home improvement contract against an owner or recover in *quantum meruit*. The jury heard all the evidence regarding the materials and labor expended on Deafeamkpor's residence and concluded that the plaintiff

performed satisfactory work valued at $90,000 for which he was not paid. Should the court allow the owner to take advantage of Banton and his employees and suppliers? What public policy would support such an outcome? Decide. [*Nemard Construction Corp. v Deafeamkpor*, 863 NY S2d 846]

4. Eugene McCarthy left his position as director of sales for Nike's Brand Jordan division in June 2003 to become vice president of U.S. footwear sales and merchandising at Reebok, one of Nike's competitors. Nike sought a preliminary injunction to prevent McCarthy from working for Reebok for a year, invoking a noncompete agreement McCarthy had signed in Oregon in 1997 when Nike had promoted him to his earlier position as a regional footwear sales manager. The agreement stated in pertinent part:

> *During EMPLOYEE'S employment by NIKE ... and for one (1) year thereafter, ("the Restriction Period"), EMPLOYEE will not directly or indirectly ... be employed by, consult for, or be connected in any manner with, any business engaged anywhere in the world in the athletic footwear, athletic apparel or sports equipment and accessories business, or any other business which directly competes with NIKE or any of its subsidiaries or affiliated corporations.*

McCarty contends that such a contract is a restraint of trade and should not be enforced. Nike contends that the agreement is fair and should be enforced. Decide. [*Nike, Inc. v McCarthy*, 379 F3d 576 (9th Cir)]

5. Ewing was employed by Presto-X-Co., a pest exterminator. His contract of employment specified that he would not solicit or attempt to solicit customers of Presto-X for two years after the termination of his employment. After working several years, his employment was terminated. Ewing then sent a letter to customers of Presto-X stating that he no longer worked for Presto-X and that he was still certified by the state. Ewing set forth his home address and phone number, which the customers did not previously have. The letter ended with the statement, "I thank you for your business throughout the past years." Presto-X brought an action to enjoin Ewing from sending such letters. He raised the defense that he was prohibited only from soliciting and there was nothing in the letters that constituted a seeking of customers. Decide. What ethical values are involved? [*Presto-X-Co. v Ewing*, 442 NW2d 85 (Iowa)]

6. The Minnesota adoption statute requires that any agency placing a child for adoption make a thorough investigation and not give a child to an applicant unless the placement is in the best interests of the child. Tibbetts applied to Crossroads, Inc., a private adoption agency, for a child to adopt. He later sued the agency for breach of contract, claiming that the agency was obligated by contract to supply a child for adoption. The agency claimed that it was required only to use its best efforts to locate a child and was not required to supply a child to Tibbetts unless it found him to be a suitable parent. Decide. [*Tibbetts v Crossroads, Inc.*, 411 NW2d 535 (Minn App)]

7. Siddle purchased a quantity of fireworks from Red Devil Fireworks Co. The sale was illegal, however, because Siddle did not have a license to make the

purchase, which the seller knew because it had been so informed by the attorney general of the state. Siddle did not pay for the fireworks, and Red Devil sued him. He defended on the ground that the contract could not be enforced because it was illegal. Was the defense valid? [*Red Devil Fireworks Co. v Siddle*, 648 P2d 468 (Wash App)]

8. Onderdonk entered a retirement home operated by Presbyterian Homes. The contract between Onderdonk and the home required Onderdonk to make a specified monthly payment that could be increased by the home as the cost of operations increased. The contract and the payment plan were thoroughly explained to Onderdonk. As the cost of operations rose, the home continually raised the monthly payments to cover these costs. Onderdonk objected to the increases on the ground that the increases were far more than had been anticipated and that the contract was therefore unconscionable. Was his objection valid?

9. Smith was employed as a salesman for Borden, Inc., which sold food products in 63 counties in Arkansas, 2 counties in Missouri, 2 counties in Oklahoma, and 1 county in Texas. Smith's employment contract prohibited him from competing with Borden after leaving its employ. Smith left Borden and went to work for a competitor, Lady Baltimore Foods. Working for this second employer, Smith sold in 3 counties of Arkansas. He had sold in 2 of these counties while he worked for Borden. Borden brought an injunction action against Smith and Lady Baltimore to enforce the noncompete covenant in Smith's former contract. Was Borden entitled to the injunction? [*Borden, Inc. v Smith*, 478 SW2d 744 (Ark)]

10. Central Water Works Supply, a corporation, had a contract with its shareholders that they would not compete with it. There were only four shareholders, of whom William Fisher was one, but he was not an employee of the corporation. When he sold his shares in the corporation and began to compete with it, the corporation went to court to obtain an injunction to stop such competition. Fisher claimed that the corporation was not entitled to an injunction because he had not obtained any confidential information or made customer contacts. The corporation claimed that such matters were relevant only when an employee had agreed not to compete but were not applicable when there was a noncompetitive covenant in the sale of a business and that the sale-of-a-business rule should be applied to a shareholder. Who was correct?

11. Vodra was employed as a salesperson and contracting agent for American Security Services. As part of his contract of employment, Vodra signed an agreement that for three years after leaving this employment, he would not solicit any customer of American. Vodra had no experience in the security field when he went to work for American. To the extent that he became known to American's customers, it was because of being American's representative rather than because of his own reputation in the security field. After some years, Vodra left American and organized a competing company that solicited American's customers. American sued him to enforce the restrictive covenant. Vodra

claimed that the restrictive covenant was illegal and not binding. Was he correct? [*American Security Services, Inc. v Vodra*, 385 NW2d 73 (Neb)]

12. Potomac Leasing Co. leased an automatic telephone system to Vitality Centers. Claudene Cato signed the lease as guarantor of payments. When the rental was not paid, Potomac Leasing brought suit against Vitality and Cato. They raised the defense that the rented equipment was to be used for an illegal purpose—namely, the random sales solicitation by means of an automatic telephone in violation of state statute; that this purpose was known to Potomac Leasing; and that Potomac Leasing could therefore not enforce the lease. Was this defense valid? [*Potomac Leasing Co. v Vitality Centers, Inc.*, 718 SW2d 928 (Ark)]

13. The English publisher of a book called *Cambridge* gave a New York publisher permission to sell that book any place in the world except in England. The New York publisher made several bulk sales of the book to buyers who sold the book throughout the world, including England. The English publisher sued the New York publisher and its customers for breach of the restriction prohibiting sales in England. Decide.

14. A state law required builders of homes to be licensed and declared that an unlicensed contractor could not recover compensation under a contract made for the construction of a residence. Although Annex Construction, Inc., did not have a license, it built a home for French. When he failed to pay what was owed, Annex sued him. He raised the defense that the unlicensed contractor could not recover for the contract price. Annex claimed that the lack of a license was not a bar because the president of the corporation was a licensed builder and the only shareholder of the corporation, and the construction had been properly performed. Was Annex entitled to recover?

15. Yarde Metals, Inc., owned six season tickets to New England Patriots football games. Gillette Stadium, where the games are played, had insufficient men's restrooms in use for football games at that time, which was the subject of numerous newspaper columns. On October 13, 2002, a guest of Yarde Metals, Mikel LaCroix, along with others, used available women's restrooms to answer the call of nature. As LaCroix left the restroom, however, he was arrested and charged with disorderly conduct. The Patriots organization terminated all six of Yarde's season ticket privileges, incorrectly giving as a reason that LaCroix was ejected "for throwing bottles in the seating section." Yarde sued, contending that "by terminating the plaintiff's season tickets for 2002 and for the future arbitrarily, without cause and based on false information," the Patriots had violated the implicit covenant of good faith and fair dealing of the season tickets contract. The back of each Patriots ticket states:

> *This ticket and all season tickets are revocable licenses. The Patriots reserve the right to revoke such licenses, in their sole discretion, at any time and for any reason.*

How would you decide this case? [*Yarde Metals, Inc. v New England Patriots Ltd.*, 834 NE2d 1233 (Mass App Ct)]

CPA QUESTIONS

1. West, an Indiana real estate broker, misrepresented to Zimmer that West was licensed in Kansas under the Kansas statute that regulates real estate brokers and requires all brokers to be licensed. Zimmer signed a contract agreeing to pay West a 5 percent commission for selling Zimmer's home in Kansas. West did not sign the contract. West sold Zimmer's home. If West sued Zimmer for nonpayment of commission, Zimmer would be:

   a. Liable to West only for the value of services rendered

   b. Liable to West for the full commission

   c. Not liable to West for any amount because West did not sign the contract

   d. Not liable to West for any amount because West violated the Kansas licensing requirements (5/92, Law, #25)

2. Blue purchased a travel agency business from Drye. The purchase price included payment for Drye's goodwill. The agreement contained a covenant prohibiting Drye from competing with Blue in the travel agency business. Which of the following statements regarding the covenant is *not* correct?

   a. The restraint must be *no* more extensive than is reasonably necessary to protect the goodwill purchased by Blue.

   b. The geographic area to which it applies must be reasonable.

   c. The time period for which it is to be effective must be reasonable.

   d. The value to be assigned to it is the excess of the price paid over the seller's cost of all tangible assets. (11/87, Law, #2)

Chapter 17

WRITING, ELECTRONIC FORMS, AND INTERPRETATION OF CONTRACTS

When must a contract be written? What is the effect of a written contract? These questions lead to the statute of frauds and the parol evidence rule.

A. STATUTE OF FRAUDS

A *contract* is a legally binding agreement. Must the agreement be evidenced by a writing?

1. Validity of Oral Contracts

In the absence of a statute requiring a writing, a contract may be oral or written. Managers and professionals should be more fully aware that their oral communications, including telephone conversations and dinner or breakfast discussions, may be deemed legally enforceable contracts. **For Example,** suppose that Mark Wahlberg, after reviewing a script tentatively entitled *The Bulger Boys*, meets with Steven Spielberg to discuss Mark's playing mobster James "Whitey" Bulger in the film. Steven states, "You *are* 'Whitey,' Marky! The nuns at Gate of Heaven Grammar School in South Boston—or maybe it was St. Augustine's—they don't send for the Boston Police when they are troubled about drug use in the schools; they send for you to talk to the kids. Nobody messes with you, and the kids know it. This is true stuff, I think, and this fugitive's brother Bill comes out of the Southie projects to be president of U Mass." Mark likes the script. Steven and Mark block out two months of time for shooting the film this fall. They agree on Mark's usual fee and a "piece of the action" based on a set percentage of the net income from the film. Thereafter, Mark's agent does not like the deal. He believes there are better scripts for Mark. Incredibly brutal things are coming out about "Whitey" that could severely tarnish the film. And with Hollywood accounting, a percentage of the "net" take is usually of little value. However, all of the essential terms of a contract have been agreed on, and such an oral agreement would be legally enforceable. As set forth in the following text, no writing is required for a services contract that can be performed within one year after the date of the agreement.

Certain contracts, on the other hand, must be evidenced by a writing to be legally enforceable. These contracts are covered by the **statute of frauds**.[1]

Because many oral contracts are legally enforceable, it is a good business practice in the preliminary stages of discussions to stipulate that no binding agreement is intended to be formed until a written contract is prepared and signed by the parties.

statute of frauds–statute that, in order to prevent fraud through the use of perjured testimony, requires that certain kinds of transactions be evidenced in writing in order to be binding or enforceable.

---

[1] The name is derived from the original English Statute of Frauds and Perjuries, which was adopted in 1677 and became the pattern for similar legislation in America. The 17th section of that statute governed the sale of goods, and its modern counterpart is § 2-201 of the UCC. The 4th section of the English statute provided the pattern for U.S. legislation with respect to contracts other than for the sale of goods described in this section of the chapter. The English statute was repealed in 1954 except as to land sale and guarantee contracts. The U.S. statutes remain in force, but the liberalization by UCC § 2-201 of the pre-Code requirements with respect to contracts for the sale of goods lessens the applicability of the writing requirement. Additional movement away from the writing requirement is seen in the 1994 Revision of Article 8, Securities, which abolishes the statute of frauds provision of the original UCC § 8-319 and goes beyond by declaring that the one-year performance provision of the statute of frauds is not applicable to contracts for securities. UCC § 8-113 [1994 Revision].

2. Contracts that Must be Evidenced by a Writing

The statute of frauds requires that certain kinds of contracts be evidenced by a writing or they cannot be enforced. This means that either the contract itself must be in writing and signed by both parties or there must be a sufficient written memorandum of the oral contract signed by the person being sued for breach of contract. A *part performance* doctrine or exception to the statute of frauds may exist when the plaintiff's part performance is "unequivocally referable" to the oral agreement.[2]

(A) AGREEMENT THAT CANNOT BE PERFORMED WITHIN ONE YEAR AFTER THE CONTRACT IS MADE. A writing is required when the contract, by its terms or subject matter, cannot be performed within one year after the date of the agreement. An oral agreement to supply a line of credit for two years cannot be enforced because of the statute of frauds. Likewise, a joint venture agreement to construct a condominium complex was subject to the one-year provision of the statute of frauds when the contract could not reasonably have been performed within one year. The plans of the parties projected a development over the course of three years.

The year runs from the time the oral contract is made rather than from the date when performance is to begin. In computing the year, the day on which the contract was made is excluded.

No *part performance* exception exists to validate an oral agreement not performable within one year. **For Example,** Babyback's Foods negotiated a multiyear oral agreement to comarket its barbecue meat products with the Coca-Cola Co. nationwide and arranged to have several coolers installed at area grocery stores in Louisville under the agreement. Babyback's faxed to Coca-Cola a contract that summarized the oral agreement but Coca-Cola never signed it. Because Coca-Cola did not sign and no part performance exception exists for an oral agreement not performable within one year, Babyback's lawsuit was unsuccessful.[3]

When no time for performance is specified by the oral contract and complete performance could "conceivably occur" within one year, the statute of frauds is not applicable to the oral contract.[4]

When a contract may be terminated at will by either party, the statute of frauds is not applicable because the contract may be terminated within a year. **For Example,** David Ehrlich was hired as manager of Gravediggaz pursuant to an oral management agreement that was terminable at will by either Ehrlich or the group. He was entitled to receive 15 percent of the gross earnings of the group and each of its members, including rap artist Robert Diggs, professionally known as RZA, for all engagements entered into while he was manager under this oral agreement. Such an at-will contract is not barred by the statute of frauds.[5]

---

[2] *Carey & Associates v Ernst,* 802 NYS2d 160 (AD 2005).
[3] *Coca-Cola Co. v Babyback's International Inc.,* 841 NE2d 557 (Ind 2006).
[4] *El Paso Healthcare System v Piping Rock Corp.,* 939 SW2d 695 (Tex App 1997).
[5] See *Ehrlich v Diggs,* 169 F Supp 2d 124 (EDNY 2001). See also *Sterling v Sterling,* 800 NYS2d 463 (AD 2005), in which the statute of frauds was no bar to an oral partnership agreement, deemed to be at will, that continued for an indefinite period of time.

FIGURE 17-1 | *Hurdles in the Path of a Contract*

WRITING REQUIRED	
STATUTE OF FRAUDS	**EXCEPTIONS**
MORE THAN ONE YEAR TO PERFORM **SALE OF LAND** **ANSWER FOR ANOTHER'S DEBT OR DEFAULT** **PERSONAL REPRESENTATIVE TO PAY DEBT OF DECEDENT FROM PERSONAL FUNDS** **PROMISE IN CONSIDERATION OF MARRIAGE** **SALE OF GOODS FOR $500 OR MORE** **MISCELLANEOUS**	**PART PERFORMANCE** **PROMISOR BENEFIT** **DETRIMENTAL RELIANCE**
PAROL EVIDENCE RULE	**EXCEPTIONS**
EVERY COMPLETE, FINAL WRITTEN CONTRACT	**INCOMPLETE CONTRACT** **AMBIGUOUS TERMS** **FRAUD, ACCIDENT, OR MISTAKE** **TO PROVE EXISTENCE OR NONBINDING CHARACTER OF CONTRACT** **MODIFICATION OF CONTRACT** **ILLEGALITY**

(1) Oral Extension of a Contract.

A contract in writing, but not required to be so by the statute of frauds because it is terminable at will, may be varied by a new oral contract, even if the original written contract provided that it should not be varied except by writing. However, the burden of proof on the party asserting the oral modification is a heavy one. The modification must be shown by "clear, unequivocal and convincing evidence, direct or implied." **For Example,** John Boyle is the sole shareholder of numerous entertainment-related companies called the Cellar Door Companies, valued at some $106,000,000. Through these companies, he controls much of the large concert business at outdoor amphitheaters in Virginia and North Carolina. Bill Reid worked for Boyle beginning in 1983 as president of one of Boyle's companies. Boyle conducted financial affairs with an "air of informality." Reid proposed to Boyle the need for an amphitheater in Virginia Beach, and Boyle promised him a "33 percent interest" "if he pulled it off." As a result of Reid's efforts, the 20,000-seat Virginia Beach Amphitheater opened in 1996. The Supreme Court of Virginia determined that clear and convincing evidence did support the oral modification of Reid's written contract, including the following excerpt from the Court's opinion:

> *Thomas J. Lyons, Jr., Boyle's friend for over 35 years, testified on behalf of Reid. Lyons and his wife attended a concert in July 1996 at the newly constructed Virginia Beach Amphitheater as guests of Boyle and his wife. Lyons complimented Boyle for the excellent work and effort that Reid had undertaken in making the amphitheater a reality. According to Lyons, Boyle stated: "Well that's why he's my partner... that's why he owns 35 percent in this—in the Amphitheater or this project." After Lyons finished his testimony, the chancellor remarked on the record that Boyle stood up from his seat and "hugged" Lyons, even though Lyons had just provided testimony detrimental to Boyle.*

Reid was thus entitled to a judgment equivalent to the value of his interest in the project, $3,566,343.[6]

(B) AGREEMENT TO SELL OR A SALE OF AN INTEREST IN LAND. All contracts to sell land, buildings, or interests in land, such as mortgages, must be evidenced by a writing.[7] Leases are also interests in land and must be in writing, except in some states where leases for one year or less do not have to be in writing.[8] **For Example,** if Mrs. O'Toole orally agrees to sell her house to the Gillespies for $250,000 and, thereafter, her children convince her that she could obtain $280,000 for the property if she is patient, Mrs. O'Toole can raise the defense of the statute of frauds should she be sued for breach of the oral agreement. Under the *part performance doctrine,* an exception exists by which an oral contract for the sale of land will be enforced by a court of equity in a suit for specific performance if the buyer has taken possession of the land under an oral contract and has made substantial improvements, the value of which cannot easily be ascertained, or has taken possession and paid part of the purchase price.

(C) PROMISE TO ANSWER FOR THE DEBT OR DEFAULT OF ANOTHER. If an individual *I* promises a creditor *C* to pay the debt of *D* if *D* does not do so, *I* is promising to answer for the debt of another. Such a promise is sometimes called a **suretyship** contract, and it must be in writing to be enforceable. *I*, the promisor, is obligated to pay only if *D* does not pay. *I*'s promise is a *collateral* or *secondary* promise, and such promises must be in writing under the statute of frauds.[9]

suretyship–undertaking to pay the debt or be liable for the default of another.

(1) Main Purpose of Exception.

When the main purpose of the promisor's promise to pay the debt of another is to benefit the promisor, the statute of frauds is not applicable, and the oral promise to pay the debt is binding.

---

[6] *Reid v Boyle,* 527 SE2d 137 (Va 2000).

[7] *Magnum Real Estate Services, Inc. v Associates, LLC,* 874 NYS2d 435 (App Div 2009).

[8] See, however, *BBQ Blues Texas, Ltd. v Affiliated Business,* 183 SW3d 543 (Tex App 2006), in which Eddie Calagero of Affiliated Business and the owners of BBQ Blues Texas, Ltd. entered an oral commission agreement to pay a 10 percent commission if he found a buyer for the restaurant, and he did so. The oral agreement was held to be outside the statute of frauds because this activity of finding a willing buyer did not involve the transfer of real estate. The second contract between the buyer and seller of the restaurant, which involved the transfer of a lease agreement, was a separate and distinct agreement over which Calagero had no control.

[9] See *Martin Printing, Inc. v Sone,* 873 A2d 232 (Conn App 2005), in which James Kuhe in writing personally guaranteed Martin Printing, Inc, to pay for printing expenses of *Pub Links Golfer Magazine,* if his corporation, Abbey Inc., failed to do so. When Abbey, Inc., failed to pay, the court enforced Kuhe's promise to pay.

For Example, an individual *I* hires a contractor *C* to repair *I* 's building, and the supplier *S* is unwilling to extend credit to *C*. In an oral promise by *I* to pay *S* what is owed for the supplies in question if *C* does not pay, *I* is promising to pay for the debt of another, *C*. However, the *main purpose* of *I*'s promise was not to aid *C* but to get his own house repaired. This promise is not within the statute of frauds.[10]

CASE SUMMARY

"I Personally Guarantee" Doesn't Mean I'm Personally Liable, Does It?

FACTS: Joel Burgower owned Material Partnerships Inc. (MPI), which supplied Sacos Tubulares del Centro, S.A. de C.V. (Sacos), a Mexican bag manufacturer, essential materials to make its products. When MPI was not paid for shipments, it insisted that Jorge Lopez, Sacos's general manager, personally guarantee all past and future obligations to MPI. In a letter to Burgower dated September 25, 1998, Lopez wrote:

I… want to certify you [sic] that I, personally, guaranty all outstanding [sic] and liabilities of Sacos Tubulares with Material Partnerships as well as future shipments.

Lopez drafted the letter himself and signed it over the designation "Jorge Lopez Venture, General Manager."

After receiving the September 25th letter, MPI resumed shipping product to Sacos, sending additional shipments valued at approximately $200,000. MPI subsequently received one payment of approximately $60,000 from Sacos. When Sacos did not pay for the additional shipments, MPI stopped shipping to it. The Sacos plant closed, and MPI brought suit in a Texas court against Lopez, claiming he was individually liable for the corporate debt of more than $900,000 under the terms of the personal guarantee. Lopez contended that he signed the letter in his capacity as general manager of Sacos as a corporate guarantee and that it was not an enforceable personal guarantee. MPI contended that the letter was a clear personal guarantee.

DECISION: The essential terms of a guarantee agreement required by the statute of frauds were present in this case. Lopez stated in his September 25th letter that "I, personally, guaranty," manifesting an intent to guarantee, and described the obligation being guaranteed as "all outstandings and liabilities of Sacos," as well as "future shipments." Lopez's signature over his corporate office does not render the document ambiguous because the clear intent was expressed in the word "personally." [**MPI v Jorge Lopez Ventura, 102 SW2d 252 (Tex App 2003)**]

(D) Promise by the Executor or Administrator of a Decedent's Estate to Pay a Claim Against the Estate from Personal Funds. The **personal representative** (**executor** or **administrator**) has the duty of handling the affairs of a deceased person, paying the debts from the proceeds of the estate and distributing any balance remaining. The executor or administrator is not personally liable for the claims against the estate of the **decedent**. If the personal representative promises to pay the decedent's debts

---

personal representative – administrator or executor who represents decedents under UPC.

executor, executrix – person (man, woman) named in a will to administer the estate of the decedent.

administrator, administratrix – person (man, woman) appointed to wind up and settle the estate of a person who has died without a will.

decedent – person whose estate is being administered.

---

[10] See *Christian v Smith*, 759 NW2d 447 (Neb 2008).

with his or her own money, the promise cannot be enforced unless it is evidenced by a writing.

If the personal representative makes a contract on behalf of the estate in the course of administering the estate, a writing is not required. The representative is then contracting on behalf of the estate. Thus, if the personal representative employs an attorney to settle the estate or makes a burial contract with an undertaker, no writing is required.

(e) Promises Made in Consideration of Marriage. Promises to pay a sum of money or give property to another in consideration of marriage must be in writing under the statute of frauds.

For Example, if Mr. John Bradley orally promises to provide Karl Radford $20,000 on Karl's marriage to Mr. Bradley's daughter Michelle—and Karl and Michelle marry—the agreement is not enforceable under the statute of frauds because it was not in writing.

Prenuptial or *antenuptial* agreements are entered into by the parties before their marriage. After full disclosure of each party's assets and liabilities, and in some states, income,[11] the parties set forth the rights of each partner regarding the property and, among other things, set forth rights and obligations should the marriage end in a separation or divorce. Such a contract must be in writing.

For Example, when Susan DeMatteo married her husband M. J. DeMatteo in 1990, she had a 1977 Nova and $5,000 in the bank. M. Joseph DeMatteo was worth as much as $112 million at that time, and he insisted that she sign a prenuptial agreement before their marriage. After full disclosure of each party's assets, the prenuptial agreement was signed and videotaped some five days before their marriage ceremony. The agreement gave Susan $35,000 a year plus cost-of-living increases, as well as a car and a house, should the marriage dissolve. After the couple divorced, Susan argued before the state's highest court that the agreement was not "fair or reasonable" because it gave her less than 1 percent of her former husband's wealth. The court upheld the agreement, however, pointing out that Susan was fully informed about her fiancé's net worth and was represented by counsel.[12] When there is full disclosure and representation, prenuptial agreements, like other contracts, cannot be set aside unless they are unconscionable, which in a domestic relations setting means leaving a former spouse unable to support herself or himself.

(f) Sale of Goods. As will be developed in Chapter 23, Nature and Form of Sales, contracts for the sale of goods priced at $500 or more must ordinarily be in writing under UCC § 2-201.[13]

(g) Promissory Estoppel. The statute of frauds may be circumvented when the party seeking to get around the statute of frauds is able to prove an enhanced promissory estoppel. While one element a of routine promissory estoppel case requires that the promisee rely on the promise in some definite and substantial manner, an enhanced level of reasonable reliance is necessary in order to have enhanced promissory

---

[11] See FLA, STAT § 732·702 (2).
[12] *DeMatteo v DeMatteo*, 762 NE2d 797 (Mass 2002). See also *Waton v Waton*, 887 So2d 419 (Fla App 2004).
[13] As will be presented in Chapter 23, under Revised Article 2, § 2-201, the $500 amount is increased to $5,000. This revision has not yet been adopted by any states.

estoppel, along with proof of an unconscionable injury or unjust enrichment. **For Example,** an Indiana bakery, Classic Cheesecake Inc., was able to interest several hotels and casinos in Las Vegas in buying its products. On July 27, 2004, its principals sought a loan from a local branch office of J. P. Morgan Chase Bank in order to establish a distribution center in Las Vegas. On September 17, local bank officer Dowling told Classic that the loan was a "go." When credit quality issues surfaced, Dowling continued to make assurances that the loan would be approved. On October 12, however, she told Classic that the loan had been turned down. Classic claimed that the bank's breach of its oral promise to make the loan and Classic's detrimental reliance on the promise caused it to lose more than $1 million. The Indiana statute of frauds requires agreements to lend money to be in writing. Classic contended that the oral agreement in this case must be enforced on the basis of promissory estoppel and the company's unconscionable injury. Judge Posner of the Seventh Circuit upheld the dismissal of the claim, writing (in part):

> *…For the plaintiff to treat the bank loan as a certainty because they were told by the bank officer whom they were dealing with that it would be approved was unreasonable, especially if, as the plaintiffs' damages claim presupposes, the need for the loan was urgent. Rational businessmen know that there is many a slip 'twixt cup and lips,' that a loan is not approved until it is approved, that if a bank's employee tells you your loan application will be approved that is not the same as telling you it has been approved, and that if one does not have a loan commitment in writing yet the need for the loan is urgent one had better be negotiating with other potential lenders at the same time….*[14]

CPA   3. Note or Memorandum

The statute of frauds requires a writing to evidence those contracts that come within its scope. This writing may be a note or memorandum as distinguished from a contract.[15] The statutory requirement is, of course, satisfied if there is a complete written contract signed by both parties.

(A) SIGNING. The note or memorandum must be signed by the party sought to be bound by the contract. **For Example,** in the previous scenario involving Mark Wahlberg and Steven Spielberg, suppose the parties agreed to do the film according to the same terms but agreed to begin shooting the film a year from next April, and Mark wrote the essential terms on a napkin, dated it, and had Steven sign it "to make sure I got it right." Mark then placed the napkin in his wallet for his records. Because the contract could not be performed within one year after the date of the agreement, a writing would be required. If Steven thereafter decided not to pursue the film because of new murder indictments against Whitey Bulger, Mark could enforce the contract against him because the napkin-note had been signed by the party to be bound or "sought to be charged," Steven. However, if Mark later decided not to appear in the film, the agreement to do the film could not be enforced against Mark because no writing existed signed by Mark, the party sought to be charged.

[14] *Classic Cheesecake Co. Inc. v J. P. Morgan Chase Bank*, 546 F3d 839 (7th Cir 2008).
[15] *McLinden v Coco*, 765 NE2d 606 (Ind App 2002).

Some states require that the authorization of an agent to execute a contract coming within the statute of frauds must also be in writing. In the case of an auction, it is usual practice for the auctioneer to be the agent of both parties for the purpose of signing the memorandum.

e–commerce&cyberlaw

Electronic Signatures in the Internet Age

A SIGNATURE authenticates a writing by identifying the signers through their distinctive marks. The act of signing a document calls to the attention of the signing parties the legal significance of their act and expresses authorization and assent to the body of the signed writing. An ELECTRONIC SIGNATURE, including technology having digital or wireless capabilities, means any electronic sound, symbol, or process attached to, or logically associated with, a contract or other electronic record and executed with the intent to sign the record. An ELECTRONIC RECORD means any contract or other record created or stored in an electronic medium and retrievable in a perceivable form.

Conducting business electronically over the Internet has many advantages for consumers, businesses, and governments by allowing the instant purchase of goods, information, and services, and the reduction of sales, administrative, and overhead expenses. To facilitate the expansion of electronic commerce and place electronic signatures and electronic contracts on an equal footing with written signatures and paper contracts, Congress enacted a federal electronic signatures law.

Under the Electronic Signatures in Global and National Commerce Act (E-Sign),* electronically signed contracts cannot be denied legal effect because the signatures are in electronic form, nor can they be denied legal effect because they are delivered electronically. Contracts or documents requiring a notarized signature can be satisfied by the electronic signatures of the notaries coupled with the enclosure of all other required information as part of the record.

One of the goals of E-Sign was to spur states to enact the Uniform Electronic Transactions Act (UETA). Under E-Sign, a state may "modify, limit or supersede" the provisions of the federal act by enacting UETA "as approved and recommended for enactment in all the states" by the National Conference of Commissioners on Uniform State Laws or enacting a law that is consistent with E-Sign.** Thus, for those states that enacted the official version of UETA or one consistent with E-Sign, the federal law is superceded by the state law. UETA is similar to E-Sign. It specifies that e-signatures and e-records can be used in contract formation, in audits, and as evidence. Selective differences between E-Sign and UETA are identified below. **For Example,** inventor Stewart Lamle sued toy maker Mattel, Inc., for breach of contract. The U.S. Court of Appeals for the Federal Circuit remanded the case for trial after resolving the motions before it. The facts reveal that after a June 11, 1997, meeting of the parties, Mattel employee Mike Bucher sent an e-mail dated June 26 to Lamle, which set forth the terms agreed to in principle at the meeting with the salutation "Best regards, Mike Bucher" appearing at the end of the e-mail. The court resolved the issue of whether an e-mail is a writing "subscribed by the party to be charged or the party's agent" in Lamle's favor. The court stated that under the UETA, the e-signature satisfies the state's (California's) Statute of Frauds. Because the e-mail was sent in 1997 prior to the effective date on the UETA, January 1, 2000, an evaluation of state common law was necessary. The court stated that it

* Pub L 106-229, 114 Stat 464, 15 USC § 7001.

** § 102(a) and 102(a)(2). Forty-eight states and the District of Columbia have enacted the UETA in some form.

e-commerce&cyberlaw

continued

could see no meaningful difference between a type-written signature on a telegram, which is sufficient to be a signature under state law, and the typed signature on the June 26 e-mail. It concluded that the e-mail satisfies the Statute of Frauds, assuming that there was a binding oral agreement on June 11. ***

(a) General Rule of Parity. E-Sign provides for parity of electronic and paper signatures, contracts, and records. Electronic signatures and contracts satisfy the statute of frauds to the same extent they would if embodied as paper contracts with handwritten signatures. Internet contracts are neither more nor less valid, legal, and binding than are offline paper contracts. The rules are the same! The UETA is comparable to E-Sign in that it treats e-signatures and e-records as if they were handwritten.[†]

(b) Identity Verification. Neither E-Sign nor UETA is a digital signature law in that neither requires security procedures or a certification authority for the verification of electronic signatures. The parties themselves determine how they will verify each other's identity. Some options are a credit card, a password or PIN, public-key cryptographic exchange of digital signatures, or biometric signatures.

(c) Exceptions. The E-Sign Act exempts documents and records on trust and estate law so that it does not cover wills, codicils, and testamentary trusts or commercial law matters such as checks, negotiable instruments, and letters of credit. The act also does not cover court documents and cancellation of health and life insurance. Generally, the UETA also does not apply to these documents and records set forth previously.

(d) Consumer Protection and Notice and Consent Requirements. Consumer protection laws remain intact under E-Sign. Protections exist for consumers to consent to receiving electronic contracts, records, and documents; and businesses must tell consumers of their right to receive hardcopy documents.

Consumers must consent to receiving documents electronically or confirm consent electronically. For example, a consumer and a business may have negotiated terms of a contract by telephone and agreed to execute their agreement by e-mail. The consumer is then sent an e-mail that contains a consent disclosure, which contains a hypertext markup language (HTML) link the consumer can use to test her ability to view the contract in HTML. The consumer then returns the e-mail message to the business, thereby confirming electronically her consent to use this electronic means.

The UETA, like E-Sign, defers to existing substantive law regarding consumer protection.

(e) Time and Place of Sending and Receipt. E-Sign does not contain a provision addressing basic contract requirements such as sending and delivery, leaving such matters to existing contract law. However, the UETA provides that an electronic record is sent when it (1) is properly directed to an information processing system designated or used by the recipient to receive such records and from which the recipient may recover that record; (2) is in a form that the recipient's system is able to process; and (3) enters an information processing system that is in the control of the recipient but outside the control of the sender. An electronic record is received when (1) it enters an information processing system designated or used by the recipient to receive such records and from which the recipient is able to obtain the record and (2) it is in a form that the recipient's system can process.[††]

(f) Errors. Unlike E-Sign, which leaves matters relating to errors to be resolved by existing state contract law, UETA creates a system for dealing with errors. For example, when Marv Hale clicks on "buy" to make an online purchase of 12 bottles of Napa Valley Supreme Chardonnay at $12.90 per bottle, the computer will produce the equivalent of an invoice that includes the product's name, description, quantity, and price to enable Marv to avoid possible error when forming the electronic contract. This procedure gives the buyer an opportunity to identify and immediately correct an error. When such a procedure is not in effect and an error is later discovered, prompt notice to the other party can cure the error under Section 10 of the UETA.[†††]

*** *Lamle v Mattel, Inc.*, 394 F3d 1355 (Fed Cir 2005); see also *Payout v Coral Mortgage Bankers*, 2009 LEXIS 14190 (D Colo 2009).
[†]   UETA § 7(a) and 7(b).

[††]   UETA § 15.
[†††] UETA § 10(2)(A)-(C).

The signature may be an ordinary one or any symbol that is adopted by the party as a signature. It may consist of initials, figures, or a mark. In the absence of a local statute that provides otherwise, a signature may be made by pencil, pen, typewriter, print, or stamp. As will be discussed, electronic signatures have parity with on-paper signatures.

(B) CONTENT. The note or memorandum must contain all of the essential terms of the contract so the court can determine just what was agreed. If any essential term is missing, the writing is not sufficient. A writing evidencing a sale of land that does not describe the land or identify the buyer does not satisfy the statute of frauds. The subject matter must be identified either within the writing itself or in other writings to which it refers. A deposit check given by the buyer to the seller does not take an oral land sales contract out of the statute of frauds. This is so because the check does not set forth the terms of the sale.

The note or memorandum may consist of one writing or of separate papers, such as letters, or a combination of such papers. Separate writings cannot be considered together unless they are linked. Linkage may be express reference in each writing to the other or by the fact that each writing clearly deals with the same subject matter.

4. Effect of Noncompliance

The majority of states hold that a contract that does not comply with the statute of frauds is not enforceable.[16] If an action is brought to enforce the contract, the defendant can raise the defense that the alleged contract is not enforceable because it is not evidenced by a writing, as required by the statute of frauds.

(A) RECOVERY OF VALUE CONFERRED. In most instances, a person who is prevented from enforcing a contract because of the statute of frauds is nevertheless entitled to recover from the other party the value of any services or property furnished or money given under the oral contract. Recovery is not based on the terms of the contract but on a quasi-contractual obligation. The other party is to restore to the plaintiff what was received in order to prevent unjust enrichment at the plaintiff's expense. **For Example,** when an oral contract for services cannot be enforced because of the statute of frauds, the person performing the work may recover the reasonable value of the services rendered.

C A S E   S U M M A R Y

Limited Effect of Oral Contract under Statute of Frauds

FACTS: Richard Golden orally agreed to sell his land to Earl Golden, who paid a deposit of $3,000. The transaction was never completed, and Earl sued for the return of his deposit. Richard claimed that the statute of frauds prevented Earl from proving that there ever was an oral contract under which a deposit of money had been paid.

---

[16] The UCC creates several statutes of frauds of limited applicability, in which it uses the phrase "not enforceable": § 1-206 (sale of intangible personal property); § 2-201 (sale of goods); and § 8-319 (sale of securities).

DECISION: Judgment for Earl. The statute of frauds bars enforcement of an oral contract for the sale of land. It does not prevent proof of the contract for the purpose of showing that the seller has received a benefit that would unjustly enrich him if he retained it. Earl could therefore prove the existence of the unperformed oral contract to show that Richard had received a deposit that should be returned. [**Golden v Golden, 541 P2d 1397 (Or 1975)**]

(B) WHO MAY RAISE THE DEFENSE OF NONCOMPLIANCE? Only a party to the oral contract may raise a defense that it is not binding because there is no writing that satisfies the statute of frauds. Third persons, such as an insurance company or the Internal Revenue Service, cannot claim that a contract is void because the statute of frauds was not satisfied.

B. PAROL EVIDENCE RULE

When the contract is evidenced by a writing, may the contract terms be changed by the testimony of witnesses?

5. Exclusion of Parol Evidence

The general rule is that parol or extrinsic evidence will not be allowed into evidence to add to, modify, or contradict the terms of a written contract that is fully integrated or complete on its face.[17] Evidence of an alleged earlier oral or written agreement within the scope of the fully integrated written contract or evidence of an alleged contemporaneous oral agreement within the scope of the fully integrated written contract is inadmissible as *parol evidence.*

Closing the Door on Different Terms

FACTS: Airline Construction, Inc., made a contract with William Barr to build a hotel within 240 calendar days. Barr completed the work 57 days late. Airline Construction sued for damages for delay, and the contractor raised the defense that he had been induced to enter into the contract because it had been agreed that he would have additional time in which to complete the work. Airline Construction objected to the admission of evidence of this agreement.

[17] *Speed v Muhana*, 619 SE2d 324 (Ga App 2005).

C A S E   S U M M A R Y

Continued

DECISION: Parol evidence could not be admitted to show that there was a prior oral agreement that was inconsistent with the terms of the written contract. It was immaterial that the contractor had been "induced" to make the contract because of the alleged agreement. The fact remained that the written contract signed by him specified the time for performance and the parol evidence rule barred proof of any prior inconsistent oral agreement. [**Airline Construction, Inc. v Barr, 807 SW2d 247 (Tenn App 1990)**]

Parol evidence is admissible, however, to show fraud, duress, or mistake and under certain other circumstances to be discussed in the following paragraphs.

The **parol evidence rule** is based on the theory that either there never was an oral agreement or, if there was, the parties abandoned it when they reached the stage in negotiations of executing their written contract. The social objective of the parol evidence rule is to give stability to contracts and to prevent the assertion of terms that did not exist or did not survive the bargaining of the parties so as to reach inclusion in the final written contract.

parol evidence rule–rule that prohibits the introduction into evidence of oral or written statements made prior to or contemporaneously with the execution of a complete written contract, deed, or instrument, in the absence of clear proof of fraud, accident, or mistake causing the omission of the statement in question.

For Example, *L* (landlord), the owner of a new development containing a five-store mall, discusses leasing one of the stores to *T* (tenant), who is viewing the property with his sister *S*, a highly credible poverty worker on leave from her duties in Central America. *L*, in the presence of *S*, agrees to give *T* the exclusive right to sell coffee and soft drinks in the five-store mall. Soon *L* and *T* execute a detailed written lease for the store, which makes no provision for *T*'s exclusive right to sell soft drinks and coffee in the mall. Subsequently, when two of the mall's new tenants begin to sell soft drinks and coffee, *T* brings suit against *L* for the breach of the oral promise granting him exclusive rights to sell soft drinks and coffee. *T* calls *S* as his first witness to prove the existence of the oral promise. *L*, through his attorney, will object to the admission of any evidence of a prior oral agreement that would add to or amend the fully integrated written lease, which set forth all restrictions on the landlord and tenant as to uses of the premises. After study of the matter, the court, based on the parol evidence rule, will not hear testimony from either *S* or *T* about the oral promise *L* made to *T*. In order to preserve his exclusive right to sell the drinks in question, *T* should have made certain that this promise was made part of the lease. His lawsuit will not be successful.

6. When the Parol Evidence Rule Does Not Apply

The parol evidence rule will not apply in certain cases. The most common of these are discussed in the following paragraphs.

ambiguous–having more than one reasonable interpretation.

(A) AMBIGUITY. If a written contract is **ambiguous** or may have two or more different meanings, parol evidence may generally be admitted to clarify the meaning.[18]

---

[18] *Berg v Hudesman*, 801 P2d 222 (Wash 1990). This is also the view followed by UCC § 2-202(a), which permits terms in a contract for the sale of goods to be "explained or supplemented by a course of dealing or usage of trade... or by course of performance." Such evidence is admissible not because there is an ambiguity but "in order that the true understanding of the parties as to the agreement may be reached." Official Code Comment to § 2-202.

Parol evidence may also be admitted to show that a word used in a contract has a special trade meaning or a meaning in the particular locality that differs from the common meaning of that word.

(B) Fraud, Duress, or Mistake. A contract apparently complete on its face may have omitted a provision that should have been included. Parol evidence may be admitted to show that a provision was omitted as the result of fraud, duress, or mistake and to further show what that provision stated. Parol evidence is admissible to show that a provision of the written contract was a mutual mistake even though the written provision is unambiguous.[19] When one party claims to have been fraudulently induced by the other to enter into a contract, the parol evidence rule does not bar proof that there was a fraud. **For Example,** the parol evidence rule does not bar proof that the seller of land intentionally misrepresented that the land was zoned to permit use as an industrial park. Such evidence does not contradict the terms of the contract but shows that the agreement is unenforceable.[20]

(C) Modification of Contract. The parol evidence rule prohibits only the contradiction of a complete written contract. It does not prohibit proof that the contract was thereafter modified or terminated.

CASE SUMMARY

All Sail and No Anchor

FACTS: On April 2, 1990, Christian Bourg hired Bristol Boat Co., Inc., and Bristol Marine Co. (defendants) to construct and deliver a yacht on July 1, 1990. However, the defendants did not live up to their promises and the contract was breached. On October 22, 1990, the defendants executed a written settlement agreement whereby Bourg agreed to pay an additional sum of $135,000 for the delivery of the yacht and to provide the defendants a loan of $80,000 to complete the construction of the vessel. Referencing the settlement agreement, the defendants at the same time executed a promissory note obliging them to repay the $80,000 loan plus interest in annual installments due on November 1 of each year, with the final payment due on November 1, 1994. The court stated in presenting the facts: "However, like the yacht itself, the settlement agreement soon proved to be just another hole in the water into which the plaintiff threw his money." Bourg sued the defendants after they failed to make certain payments on the note, and the court granted a motion for summary judgment in favor of Bourg for $59,081. The defendants appealed.

DECISION: Judgment for Bourg. Because the defendants' affidavit recites that an alleged oral side agreement was entered into at the same time as the settlement agreement and promissory note—the oral side agreement allegedly stated "that the note would be paid for by services rendered by the defendants"—the oral side agreement would have constituted a contemporaneous modification that would merge into the integrated promissory note and settlement agreement and thus be barred from admission into evidence under the parol evidence rule. Although parties to an integrated written contract can modify their understanding by a subsequent oral pact, to be legally effective, there must be evidence of mutual assent to the essential terms of the modification and adequate consideration. Here the defendants adduced no

[19] *Thompson v First Citizens Bank & Trust Co,* 151 NC App 704 (2002).
[20] *Edwards v Centrex Real Estate Corp.,* 61 Cal Rptr 518 (Cal App 1997).

C A S E   S U M M A R Y

Continued

competent evidence of either mutual assent to particular terms or a specific consideration that would be sufficiently definite to constitute an enforceable subsequent oral modification to the parties' earlier written agreements. Thus, legally this alleged oral agreement was all sail and no anchor. [**Bourg v Bristol Boat Co., 705 A2d 969 (RI 1998)**]

C. Rules of Construction and Interpretation

In interpreting contracts, courts are aided by certain rules.

7. Intention of the Parties

When persons enter into an agreement, it is to be presumed that they intend for their agreement to have some effect. A court will strive to determine the intent of the parties and to give effect to it. A contract, therefore, is to be enforced according to its terms.[21] A court cannot remake or rewrite the contract of the parties under the pretense of interpreting.[22]

No particular form of words is required, and any words manifesting the intent of the parties are sufficient. In the absence of proof that a word has a peculiar meaning or that it was employed by the parties with a particular meaning, a common word is given its ordinary meaning.

(A) MEANING OF WORDS. Ordinary words are to be interpreted according to their ordinary meaning.[23] **For Example,** when a contract requires the gasoline dealer to pay the supplier for "gallons" supplied, the term *gallons* is unambiguous and does not require that an adjustment of the gallonage be made for the temperature.[24] When a contract calls for a businessperson to pay a builder for the builder's "costs," the term *costs* is unambiguous, meaning actual costs, not a lesser amount based on the builder's bid.[25]

If there is a common meaning to a term, that meaning will be followed even though the dictionary may contain additional meanings. If technical or trade terms are used in a contract, they are to be interpreted according to the area of technical knowledge or trade from which the terms are taken.

(B) INCORPORATION BY REFERENCE. The contract may not cover all of the agreed terms. The missing terms may be found in another document. Frequently, the parties executing the contract for storage will simply state that a storage contract is entered into and that the contract applies to the goods listed in the schedule attached to and

---

[21] See *Greenwald v Kersh*, 621 SE2d 463 (Ga App 2005).
[22] *Abbot v Schnader, Harrison, Segal & Lewis, LLP*, 805 A2d 547 (Pa Super 2002).
[23] *Thorton v D.F.W. Christian Television, Inc.*, 925 SW2d 17 (Tex App 1995).
[24] *Hopkins v BP Oil, Inc.*, 81 F3d 1070 (11th Cir 1996).
[25] *Batzer Construction, Inc. v Boyer*, 125 P3d 773 (Or App 2006).

made part of the contract. Likewise, a contract for the construction of a building may involve plans and specifications on file in a named city office. The contract will simply state that the building is to be constructed according to those plans and specifications that are "incorporated herein and made part of this contract." When there is such an **incorporation by reference**, the contract consists of both the original document and the detailed statement that is incorporated in it.

When a contract refers to another document, however, the contract must sufficiently describe the document or so much of it as is to be interpreted as part of the contract.

incorporation by reference–contract consisting of both the original or skeleton document and the detailed statement that is incorporated in it.

C A S E   S U M M A R Y

Specificity Required

FACTS: Consolidated Credit Counseling Services, Inc. (Consolidated), sued Affinity Internet, Inc., doing business as SkyNet WEB (Affinity), for breach of its contract to provide computer and Web-hosting services. Affinity moved to compel arbitration, and Consolidated argued that the contract between the parties did not contain an arbitration clause. The contract between the parties stated in part: "This contract is subject to all of SkyNet WEB's terms, conditions, user and acceptable use policies located at **http://www.skynetweb.com/company/legal/legal.php**." By going to the Web site and clicking to paragraph 17 of the User Agreement, an arbitration provision can be found. The contract itself, however, makes no reference to an agreement to arbitrate, nor was paragraph 17 expressly referred to or described in the contract. Nor was a hard copy of the information on the Web site either signed by or furnished to Consolidated.

DECISION: Judgment for Consolidated. Mere reference to another document is not sufficient to incorporate that document into the contract absent specificity describing the portion of the writing to apply to the contract. [**Affinity Internet v Consolidated Credit, 920 So2d 1286 (Fla App 2006)**]

8. Whole Contract

The provisions of a contract must be construed as a whole in such a way that every part is given effect.

Every word of a contract is to be given effect if reasonably possible. The contract is to be construed as a whole, and if the plain language of the contract thus viewed solves the dispute, the court is to make no further analysis.[26]

9. Contradictory and Ambiguous Terms

One term in a contract may conflict with another term, or one term may have two different meanings. It is then necessary for the court to determine whether there is a contract and, if so, what the contract really means.

---

[26] *Covensky v Hannah Marine Corp.*, 903 NE2d 422 (Ill App 2009).

C A S E   S U M M A R Y

Who Pays the Piper?

FACTS: Olander Contracting Co., developer Gail Wachter, and the City of Bismarck, North Dakota, entered into a water and sewer construction contract including, among other things, connecting a 10-inch sewer line from Wachter's housing development to the city's existing 36-inch concrete sewer main and installing a manhole at the connection, to be paid for by Wachter. Olander installed the manhole, but it collapsed within a few days. Olander installed a second manhole, with a large base supported by pilings, but it too failed a few days after it was installed. Olander then placed a rock bedding under the city's sewer main, replaced 78 feet of the existing concrete pipe with PVC pipe, and installed a manhole a third time on a larger base. Olander sued Wachter and the City of Bismarck for damages of $456,536.25 for extra work it claims it was required to perform to complete its contract. Both defendants denied they were responsible for the amount sued under the contract. The jury returned a special verdict, finding that Olander performed "extra work/unforeseen work… for which it is entitled to be compensated in excess of the contract price" in the amount of $220,849.67, to be paid by the City of Bismarck. Appeals were taken.

DECISION: Judgment for Olander. The trial judge properly made the initial determination that the contract language was ambiguous. That is, the language used by the parties could support good arguments for the positions of both parties. This resolved a question of law. Once this determination had been made, the judge allowed extrinsic evidence from all parties as to what they meant when they negotiated the contract. This evidence related to the questions of fact, which were left to the jury. Testimony was taken from the parties who negotiated the contract, and testimony was also heard about the role of each of the parties in the actual construction of the manhole, the cause for the collapses, and why the contractor had to replace the city's existing concrete pipe with PVC pipe and the city's role in making this determination. The jury then fulfilled its role answering the question whether or not Olander had performed extra work in the affirmative, concluding that the city was required to pay for it. [**Olander Contracting v Wachter, 643 NW2d 29 (2002))**]

In some instances, apparent conflict between the terms of a contract is eliminated by the introduction of parol evidence or by the application of an appropriate rule of construction.[27]

(A) NATURE OF WRITING. When a contract is partly a printed form or partly typewritten and partly handwritten and the written part conflicts with the printed or typewritten part, the written part prevails. When there is a conflict between a printed part and a typewritten part, the latter prevails. Consequently, when a clause typewritten on a printed form conflicts with what is stated by the print, the conflicting print is ignored and the typewritten clause controls. This rule is based on

---

[27] See *Wilkie v Eutice 36747, LLC*, 669 SE2d 155 (Ga App 2008) where the courts in this jurisdiction resolve contract interpretation issues by first determining whether the language is ambiguous. (1) If it is not, the trial court judge enforces the contract as written; (2) if the contract is ambiguous, the trial court judge will apply the rules of contract construction to resolve this ambiguity; and (3) if the ambiguity cannot be resolved in Step 2, a jury must decide what the parties intended and what the ambiguous language means.

the belief that the parties had given greater thought to what they typed or wrote for the particular contract as contrasted with printed words already in a form designed to cover many transactions. Thus, a typewritten provision to pay 90 cents per unit overrode a preprinted provision setting the price as 45 cents per unit.

When there is a conflict between an amount or quantity expressed both in words and figures, as on a check, the amount or quantity expressed in words prevails. Words control because there is less danger that a word will be wrong than a number.

(B) AMBIGUITY. A contract is *ambiguous* when the intent of the parties is uncertain and the contract is capable of more than one reasonable interpretation.[28] The background from which the contract and the dispute arose may help in determining the intention of the parties. **For Example,** when suit was brought in Minnesota on a Canadian insurance policy, the question arose whether the dollar limit of the policy referred to Canadian or U.S. dollars. The court concluded that Canadian dollars were intended. Both the insurer and the insured were Canadian corporations; the original policy, endorsements to the policy, and policy renewals were written in Canada; over the years, premiums had been paid in Canadian dollars; and a prior claim on the policy had been settled by the payment of an amount computed on the basis of Canadian dollars.

(C) STRICT CONSTRUCTION AGAINST DRAFTING PARTY. An ambiguous contract is interpreted strictly against the party who drafted it.[29] **For Example,** an insurance policy containing ambiguous language regarding coverage or exclusions is interpreted against the insurer and in favor of the insured when two interpretations are reasonably possible. This rule is a secondary rule that may be invoked only after all of the ordinary interpretive guides have been exhausted. The rule basically assigns the risk of an unresolvable ambiguity to the party creating it.[30]

10. Implied Terms

In some cases, a court will imply a term to cover a situation for which the parties failed to provide or, when needed, to give the contract a construction or meaning that is reasonable.

The court often implies details of the performance of a contract not expressly stated in the contract. In a contract to perform work, there is an implied promise to use such skill as is necessary to properly perform the work. When a contract does not specify the time for performance, a reasonable time is implied.

In every contract, there is an implied obligation that neither party shall do anything that will have the effect of destroying or injuring the right of the other party to receive the fruits of the contract. This means that in every contract there exists an implied covenant of **good faith** and fair dealing. When a contract may reasonably be interpreted in different ways, a court should make the interpretation

good faith—absence of knowledge of any defects or problems.

---

[28] *Kaufman & Stewart v Weinbrenner Shoe Co.,* 589 NW2d 499 (Minn App 1999).
[29] *Idaho Migrant Council, Inc. v Warila,* 89 P2d 39 (Wyo 1995).
[30] *Premier Title Co. v Donahue,* 765 NE2d 513 (Ill App 2002).

that is in harmony with good faith and fair dealing. **For Example,** when a contract is made subject to the condition that one of the parties obtain financing, that party must make reasonable, good-faith efforts to obtain financing. The party is not permitted to do nothing and then claim that the contract is not binding because the condition has not been satisfied. Likewise, when a contract requires a party to obtain government approval, the party must use all reasonable means to obtain it.[31]

The Uniform Commercial Code imposes an obligation of good faith in the performance or enforcement of every contract.[32]

11. Conduct and Custom

The conduct of the parties and the customs and usages of a particular trade may give meaning to the words of the parties and thus aid in the interpretation of their contract.

(A) CONDUCT OF THE PARTIES. The conduct of the parties in carrying out the terms of a contract is the best guide to determine the parties' intent. When performance has been repeatedly tendered and accepted without protest, neither party will be permitted to claim that the contract was too indefinite to be binding. **For Example,** a travel agent made a contract with a hotel to arrange for trips to the hotel. After some 80 trips had already been arranged and paid for by the hotel at the contract price without any dispute about whether the contract obligation was satisfied, any claim by the travel agent that it could charge additional fees must be rejected.

usage of trade–language and customs of an industry.

(B) CUSTOM AND USAGE OF TRADE. The customs and **usages of trade** or commercial activity to which the contract relates may be used to interpret the terms of a contract.[33] **For Example,** when a contract for the construction of a building calls for a "turn-key construction," industry usage is admissible to show what this means: a construction in which all the owner needs to do is to turn the key in the lock to open the building for use and in which all construction risks are assumed by the contractor.[34]

Custom and usage, however, cannot override express provisions of a contract that are inconsistent with custom and usage.

12. Avoidance of Hardship

As a general rule, a party is bound by a contract even though it proves to be a bad bargain. If possible, a court will interpret a contract to avoid hardship. Courts will, if possible, interpret a vague contact in a way to avoid any forfeiture of a party's interest.

When hardship arises because the contract makes no provision for the situation that has occurred, the court will sometimes imply a term to avoid the hardship.

---

[31] *Kroboth v Brent,* 625 NYS2d 748 (App Div 1995).
[32] UCC §§ 1-201(19), 1-203.
[33] *Affiliated FM Ins. Co. v Constitution Reinsurance Corp.,* 626 NE2d 878 (Mass 1994).
[34] *Blue v R.L. Glossen Contracting, Inc.,* 327 SE2d 582 (Ga App 1985).

CASE SUMMARY

Court Glides with Clyde

FACTS: Standard Oil Company made a nonexclusive jobbing or wholesale dealership contract with Perkins, which limited him to selling Standard's products and required Perkins to maintain certain minimum prices. Standard Oil had the right to approve or disapprove Perkins's customers. To be able to perform under his contract, Perkins had to make a substantial monetary investment, and his only income was from the commissions on the sales of Standard's products. Standard Oil made some sales directly to Perkins's customers. When Perkins protested, Standard Oil pointed out that the contract did not contain any provision making his rights exclusive. Perkins sued Standard Oil to compel it to stop dealing with his customers.

DECISION: Judgment for Perkins. In view of the expenditure required of Perkins to operate his business and to perform his part of the contract and because of his dependence on his customers, the interpretation should be made that Standard Oil would not solicit customers of Perkins. This is true even though the contract did not give Perkins an exclusive dealership within the given geographic area. [**Perkins v Standard Oil Co., 383 P2d 107 (Or 1963)**]

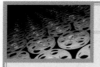

lawflix

The Santa Clause (1996) (PG)

When Scott Calvin (Tim Allen) tries on a Santa suit, he discovers that he has assumed all of Santa's responsibility. Calvin tries to challenge his acceptance of the terms of the agreement. Analyze the problems with offer, acceptance, and terms in very fine print (a magnifying glass is required). Do the terms of the suit contract apply when Calvin did not know them at the time he put on the suit?

For movie clips that illustrate business law concepts, see LawFlix at **www.cengage.com/blaw/dvl**.

MAKE THE CONNECTION

SUMMARY

An oral agreement may be a contract unless it is the intention of the parties that they should not be bound by the agreement without a writing executed by them. Certain contracts must be evidenced by a writing, however, or else they cannot be enforced. The statutes that declare this exception are called *statutes of frauds*. Statutes of frauds commonly require that a contract be evidenced by writing in the case of (1) an agreement that cannot be performed within one year after the contract is made, (2) an agreement to sell any interest in land, (3) a promise to answer for the debt or default of another, (4) a promise by the executor or administrator of a decedent's estate to pay a claim against the estate from personal funds, (5) a promise made in consideration of marriage, and (6) a contract for the sale of goods for a purchase price of $500 or more.

To evidence a contract to satisfy a statute of frauds, there must be a writing of all essential terms. The writing must be signed by the defendant against whom suit is brought for enforcement of the contract.

If the applicable statute of frauds is not satisfied, the oral contract cannot be enforced. To avoid unjust enrichment, a plaintiff barred from enforcing an oral contract may in most cases recover from the other contracting party the reasonable value of the benefits conferred by the plaintiff on the defendant.

When there is a written contract, the question arises whether that writing is the exclusive statement of the parties' agreement. If the writing is the complete and final statement of the contract, parol evidence as to matters agreed to before or at the time the writing was signed is not admissible to contradict the writing. This is called the *parol evidence rule.* In any case, the parol evidence rule does not bar parol evidence when (1) the writing is ambiguous, (2) the writing is not a true statement of the agreement of the parties because of fraud, duress, or mistake, or (3) the existence, modification, or illegality of a contract is in controversy.

Because a contract is based on the agreement of the parties, courts must determine the intent of the parties manifested in the contract. The intent that is to be enforced is the intent as it reasonably appears to a third person. This objective intent is followed.

In interpreting a contract, ordinary words are to be given their ordinary meanings. If trade or technical terms have been used, they are interpreted according to their technical meanings. The court must consider the whole contract and not read a particular part out of context. When different writings are executed as part of the same transaction, or one writing refers to or incorporates another, all of the writings are to be read together as the contract of the parties.

When provisions of a contract are contradictory, the court will try to reconcile or eliminate the conflict. If this cannot be done, the conclusion may be that there is no contract because the conflict makes the agreement indefinite as to a material matter. In some cases, conflict is solved by considering the form of conflicting terms. Handwriting prevails over typing and a printed form, and typing prevails over a printed form. Ambiguity will be eliminated in some cases by the admission of parol evidence or by interpreting the provision strictly against the party preparing the contract, particularly when that party has significantly greater bargaining power.

LEARNING OUTCOMES

After studying this chapter, you should be able to clearly explain:

A. STATUTE OF FRAUDS

LO.1 Explain when a contract must be evidenced by a writing
See the discussion and examples beginning on p. 368.

LO.2 Explain the effect of noncompliance with the statute of frauds
See the example in which an oral contract cannot be enforced because it is not in writing, but the plaintiff may recover the reasonable value of the services rendered, p. 377.

B. PAROL EVIDENCE RULE

LO.3 Explain the parol evidence rule and the exceptions to this rule

See the example in which the tenant is not allowed to call a witness to testify about a prior oral agreement that would add to and alter the written lease, p. 379.

See the exceptions based on ambiguity, fraud, duress, and mistake discussed on p. 379.

C. RULES OF CONSTRUCTION AND INTERPRETATION

LO.4 Understand the basic rule of contract construction that a contract is enforced according to its terms

See the example of the interpretation of the word "costs" on p. 381.

LO.5 State the rules for interpreting ambiguous terms in a contract

See the discussion on the nature of the writing beginning on p. 383.

KEY TERMS

administrator
ambiguous
decedent
executor
good faith

incorporation by
 reference
parol evidence rule
personal representative
statute of frauds

suretyship
usages of trade

QUESTIONS AND CASE PROBLEMS

1. Kelly made a written contract to sell certain land to Brown and gave Brown a deed to the land. Thereafter, Kelly sued Brown to get back a 20-foot strip of the land. Kelly claimed that before making the written contract, it was agreed that Kelly would sell all of his land to Brown to make it easier for Brown to get a building permit, but after that was done, the 20-foot strip would be reconveyed to Kelly. Was Kelly entitled to the 20-foot strip? What ethical values are involved? [*Brown v Kelly*, 545 So2d 518 (Fla App)]

2. Martin made an oral contract with Cresheim Garage to work as its manager for two years. Cresheim wrote Martin a letter stating that the oral contract had been made and setting forth all of its terms. Cresheim later refused to recognize the contract. Martin sued Cresheim for breach of the contract and offered Cresheim's letter in evidence as proof of the contract. Cresheim claimed that the oral contract was not binding because the contract was not in writing and the letter referring to the contract was not a contract but only a letter. Was the contract binding?

3. Lawrence loaned money to Moore, who died without repaying the loan. Lawrence claimed that when he mentioned the matter to Moore's widow, she promised to pay the debt. She did not pay it, and Lawrence sued her on her promise. Does she have any defense? [*Moore v Lawrence*, 480 SW2d 941 (Ark)]

4. Jackson signed an agreement to sell 79 acres of land to Devenyns. Jackson owned 80 acres and was apparently intending to keep for himself the acre on which his home was located. The written agreement also stated that "Devenyns shall have the option to buy on property _____," but nothing was stated in the blank space. Devenyns sued to enforce the agreement. Was it binding? [*In re Jackson's Estate*, 892 P2d 786 (Wyo)]

5. Boeing Airplane Co. contracted with Pittsburgh–Des Moines Steel Co. for the latter to construct a supersonic wind tunnel. R.H. Freitag Manufacturing Co. sold materials to York-Gillespie Co., which subcontracted to do part of the work. To persuade Freitag to keep supplying materials on credit, Boeing and the principal contractor both assured Freitag that he would be paid. When Freitag was not paid by the subcontractor, he sued Boeing and the contractor. They defended on the ground that the assurances given Freitag were not written. Decide. What ethical values are involved? [*R.H. Freitag Mfg. Co. v Boeing Airplane Co.*, 347 P2d 1074 (Wash)]

6. Louise Pulsifer owned a farm that she wanted to sell and ran an ad in the local newspaper. After Russell Gillespie agreed to purchase the farm, Pulsifer wrote him a letter stating that she would not sell it. He sued her to enforce the contract, and she raised the defense of the statute of frauds. The letter she had signed did not contain any of the terms of the sale. Gillespie, however, claimed that the newspaper ad could be combined with her letter to satisfy the statute of frauds. Was he correct? [*Gillespie v Pulsifer*, 655 SW2d 123 (Mo)]

7. In February or March, Corning Glass Works orally agreed to retain Hanan as management consultant from May 1 of that year to April 30 of the next year for a present value fee of $200,000. Was this agreement binding? Is this decision ethical? [*Hanan v Corning Glass Works*, 314 NYS2d 804 (App Div)]

8. Catherine (wife) and Peter (husband) Mallen had lived together unmarried for some four years when Catherine got pregnant and a marriage was arranged. Peter asked Catherine to sign a prenuptial agreement. Although his financial statement attached to the agreement did not state his income at $560,000 per year, it showed he was wealthy, and she had lived with him for four years and knew from their standard of living that he had significant income. Catherine contends that failure to disclose Peter's income was a nondisclosure of a material fact when the agreement was drawn up and that accordingly the agreement is not valid. Peter contends that he fully disclosed his net worth and that Catherine was well aware of his significant income. Further, he contends that disparities in the parties' financial status and business experience did not make the agreement unconscionable. Decide. [*Mallen v Mallen*, 622 SE2d 812 (Ga Sup Ct)]

9. Panasonic Industrial Co. (PIC) created a contract making Manchester Equipment Co., Inc. (MECI), a nonexclusive wholesale distributor of its products. The contract stated that PIC reserved the unrestricted right to solicit and make direct sales of the products to anyone, anywhere. The contract also stated that it contained the entire agreement of the parties and that any prior agreement or statement was superseded by the contract. PIC subsequently began to make direct sales to two of MECI's established customers. MECI

claimed that this was a breach of the distribution contract and sued PIC for damages. Decide. What ethical values are involved? [*Manchester Equipment Co. Inc. v Panasonic Industrial Co.*, 529 NYS2d 532 (App Div)]

10. A contract made for the sale of a farm stated that the buyer's deposit would be returned "if for any reason the farm cannot be sold." The seller later stated that she had changed her mind and would not sell, and she offered to return the deposit. The buyer refused to take the deposit back and brought suit to enforce the contract. The seller contended that the "any reason" provision extended to anything, including the seller's changing her mind. Was the buyer entitled to recover? [*Phillips v Rogers*, 200 SE2d 676 (W Va)]

11. Integrated, Inc., entered into a contract with the state of California to construct a building. It then subcontracted the electrical work to Alec Fergusson Electrical Contractors. The subcontract was a printed form with blanks filled in by typewriting. The printed payment clause required Integrated to pay Fergusson on the 15th day of the month following the submission of invoices by Fergusson. The typewritten part of the contract required Integrated to pay Fergusson "immediately following payment" (by the state) to the general contractor. When was payment required? [*Integrated, Inc. v Alec Fergusson Electrical Contractors*, 58 Cal Rptr 503 (Cal App)]

12. Norwest Bank had been lending money to Tresch to run a dairy farm. The balance due the bank after several years was $147,000. The loan agreement stated that Tresch would not buy any new equipment in excess of $500 without the express consent of the bank. Some time later, Tresch applied to the bank for a loan of $3,100 to purchase some equipment. The bank refused to make the loan because it did not believe the new equipment would correct the condition for which it would be bought and would not result in significant additional income. Tresch then sued the bank, claiming that its refusal to make the loan was a breach of the implied covenant of good faith and fair dealing. Decide. [*Tresch v Norwest Bank of Lewistown*, 778 P2d 874 (Mont)]

13. Physicians Mutual Insurance Co. issued a policy covering Brown's life. The policy declared that it did not cover any deaths resulting from "mental disorder, alcoholism, or drug addiction." Brown was killed when she fell while intoxicated. The insurance company refused to pay because of the quoted provision. Her executor, Savage, sued the insurance company. Did the insurance company have a defense? [*Physicians Mutual Ins. Co. v Savage*, 296 NE2d 165 (Ind App)]

14. The Dickinson Elks Club conducted an annual Labor Day golf tournament. Charbonneau Buick-Pontiac offered to give a new car as a prize to anyone making "a hole in one on hole no. 8." The golf course of the club was only nine holes. To play 18 holes, the players would go around the course twice, although they would play from different tees or locations for the second nine holes. On the second time around, what was originally the eighth hole became the seventeenth hole. Grove was a contestant in the tournament. He scored 3 on the no. 8 hole, but on approaching it for the second time as the seventeenth hole, he made a hole in one. He claimed the prize car from Charbonneau. The latter claimed that Grove had not won the prize because he did not make the

hole in one on the eighth hole. Decide. [*Grove v Charbonneau Buick-Pontiac, Inc.*, 240 NW2d 8533 (ND)]

15. Tambe Electric Inc. entered into a written agreement with Home Depot to provide copper wire to Tambe at a price set forth in the writing, and allowing the contractor the option of paying for the wire over a period of time. Home Depot did not fulfill this written agreement and Tambe sued for $68,598, the additional cost it had to subsequently pay to obtain copper wire for its work. Home Depot defended that it had made an oral condition precedent requiring payment in full by Tambe at the time it accepted the price quoted in the written agreement. Decide. [*Tambe Electric v Home Depot*, 856 NYS2d 373]

CPA QUESTIONS

1. Which of the following statements is true with regard to the statute of frauds?

   a. All contracts involving consideration of more than $500 must be in writing.

   b. The written contract must be signed by all parties.

   c. The statute of frauds applies to contracts that can be fully performed within one year from the date they are made.

   d. The contract terms may be stated in more than one document.

2. With regard to an agreement for the sale of real estate, the statute of frauds:

   a. Requires that the entire agreement be in a single writing

   b. Requires that the purchase price be fair and adequate in relation to the value of the real estate

   c. Does *not* require that the agreement be signed by all parties

   d. Does *not* apply if the value of the real estate is less than $500

3. In negotiations with Andrews for the lease of Kemp's warehouse, Kemp orally agreed to pay one-half of the cost of the utilities. The written lease, later prepared by Kemp's attorney, provided that Andrews pay all of the utilities. Andrews failed to carefully read the lease and signed it. When Kemp demanded that Andrews pay all of the utilities, Andrews refused, claiming that the lease did not accurately reflect the oral agreement. Andrews also learned that Kemp intentionally misrepresented the condition of the structure of the warehouse during the negotiations between the parties. Andrews sued to rescind the lease and intends to introduce evidence of the parties' oral agreement about sharing the utilities and the fraudulent statements made by Kemp. Will the parol evidence rule prevent the admission of evidence concerning each of the following?

	Oral agreement regarding who pays the utilities	*Fraudulent statements by Kemp*
a.	Yes	Yes
b.	No	Yes
c.	Yes	No
d.	No	No

Chapter 18

THIRD PERSONS AND CONTRACTS

A. Third-Party Beneficiary Contracts

Generally, only the parties to a contract may sue on it. However, in some cases a third person who is not a party to the contract may sue on the contract.

CPA

1. Definition

intended beneficiary – third person of a contract whom the contract is intended to benefit.

third-party beneficiary – third person whom the parties to a contract intend to benefit by the making of the contract and to confer upon such person the right to sue for breach of contract.

When a contract is intended to benefit a third person, such a person is an **intended beneficiary** and may bring suit on and enforce the contract. In some states, the right of the intended **third-party beneficiary** to sue on the contract is declared by statute. **For Example,** Ibberson Co., the general contractor hired by AgGrow Oils, LLC to design and build an oilseed processing plant, contracted with subcontractor Anderson International Corp. to supply critical seed processing equipment for the project. Anderson's formal proposal to Ibberson identified the AgGrow Oils Project, and the proposal included drawings of the planned AgGrow plant. Under state law, this contract made between the contractor and subcontractor for the express benefit of the third-party AgGrow Oils could be enforced by the intended third-party beneficiary AgGrow Oils. The project was a failure. AgGrow was successful in the lawsuit against Anderson under the Anderson-Ibberson contract, having the standing to sue as an intended third-party beneficiary of that contract.[1]

(A) Creditor Beneficiary. The intended beneficiary is sometimes classified as a *creditor beneficiary* when the promisee's primary intent is to discharge a duty owed to the third party.[2] **For Example,** when Max Giordano sold his business, Sameway Laundry, to Harry Phinn, he had three years of payments totaling $14,500 owing to Davco, Inc., on a commercial Davco shirt drying and pressing machine purchased in 2006. Max (the promisee) made a contract with Harry to sell the business for a stipulated sum. A provision in this contract selling the business called for Harry (the promisor) to make the Davco machine payments when due over the next three years. Should Harry fail to make payments, Davco, Inc., as an intended creditor beneficiary under the contract between Max and Harry, would have standing to sue Harry for breach of the payment provision in the contract.

CPA

(B) Donee Beneficiary. The second type of intended beneficiary is a *donee beneficiary* to whom the promisee's primary intent in contracting is to give a benefit. A life insurance contract is such an intended third-party beneficiary contract. The promisee-insured pays premiums to the insurer under the contract of insurance so that, upon the death of the insured, the promisor-insurer would pay the sum designated in the contract to the beneficiary. The beneficiary's rights vest upon the insured's death, and the beneficiary can sue the insurance company upon the insured's death even though the insurance company never made any agreement directly with the beneficiary.

---

[1] *AgGrow Oils, LLC v National Union Fire Ins.*, 420 F3d 751 (8th Cir 2005).
[2] The Restatement (Second) of Contracts § 302 substitutes "intended beneficiary" for the terms "creditor" and "donee" beneficiary. However, some courts continue to use the classifications of creditor and donee third-party beneficiaries. Regardless of the terminology, the law continues to be the same. See *Continental Casualty v Zurich American Insurance*, 2009 WL 455285 (DC Or 2009).

(c) Necessity of Intent. A third person does not have the status of an intended third-party beneficiary unless it is clear at the time the contract was formed that the parties intended to impose a direct obligation with respect to the third person.[3] In determining whether there is intent to benefit a third party, the surrounding circumstances as well as the contract may be examined.[4] There is a strong presumption that the parties to a contract intend to benefit only themselves.[5]

CASE SUMMARY

The Pest Control Case

FACTS: Admiral Pest Control had a standing contract with Lodging Enterprises to spray its motel every month to exterminate pests. Copeland, a guest in the motel, was bitten by a spider. She sued Admiral on the ground that she was a third-party beneficiary of the extermination contract.

DECISION: Judgment against Copeland. There was no intent manifested in the contract that guests of the motel were beneficiaries of the contract. The contract was made by the motel to protect itself. The guests were incidental beneficiaries of that contract and therefore could not sue for its breach. [**Copeland v Admiral Pest Control Co., 933 P2d 937 (Okla App 1996)**]

(d) Description. It is not necessary that the intended third-party beneficiary be identified by name. The beneficiary may be identified by class, with the result that any member of that class is a third-party beneficiary. **For Example,** a contract between the promoter of an automobile stock car race and the owner of the racetrack contains a promise by the owner to pay specified sums of money to each driver racing a car in certain races. A person driving in one of the designated races is a third-party beneficiary and can sue the owner on the contract for the promised compensation.

2. Modification or Termination of Intended Third-Party Beneficiary Contract

Can the parties to the contract modify or terminate it so as to destroy the right of the intended third-party beneficiary? If the contract contains an express provision allowing a change of beneficiary or cancellation of the contract without the consent

---

[3] *American United Logistics, Inc. v Catellus,* 319 F3d 921 (7th Cir 2003).
[4] See *Becker v Crispell-Synder, Inc.,* 763 NW2d 192 (Wisc App 2009) for an example of complex circumstances surrounding a third-party beneficiary contract. The town of Somers, Wisconsin, entered into a contract with engineering firm Crispell-Synder (C-S) because it needed an engineering firm to oversee a new subdivision to be developed by the Beckers. Under this contract C-S would submit bills to the town for overseeing the development, and the town would pay C-S through a line of credit from the Beckers. The court held that the Beckers were third-party beneficiaries entitled to sue C-S for overcharging change orders.
[5] *Barney v Unity Paving, Inc.,* 639 NE2d 592 (Ill App 1994).

of the intended third-party beneficiary, the parties to the contract may destroy the rights of the intended beneficiary by acting in accordance with that contract provision.[6]

For Example, Roy obtained a life insurance policy from Phoenix Insurance Company that provided the beneficiary could be changed by the insured. Roy named his son, Harry, as the beneficiary. Later, Roy had a falling out with Harry and removed him as beneficiary. Roy could do this because the right to change the beneficiary was expressly reserved by the contract that created the status of the intended third-party beneficiary.

In addition, the rights of an intended third-party beneficiary are destroyed if the contract is discharged or ended by operation of law, for example, through bankruptcy proceedings.

3. Limitations on Intended Third-Party Beneficiary

Although the intended third-party beneficiary rule gives the third person the right to enforce the contract, it obviously gives no more rights than the contract provides. That is, the intended third-party beneficiary must take the contract as it is. If there is a time limitation or any other restriction in the contract, the intended beneficiary cannot ignore it but is bound by it.

If the contract is not binding for any reason, that defense may be raised against the intended third-party beneficiary suing on the contract.[7]

CPA 4. Incidental Beneficiaries

Not everyone who benefits from the performance of a contract between other persons is entitled to sue as a third-party beneficiary. If the benefit was intended, the third person is an intended beneficiary with the rights described in the preceding sections. If the benefit was not intended, the third person is an *incidental beneficiary*.

For Example, Ensil International (EI), a New York firm, entered a repair agreement in 1998 with a Canadian company (EC) to perform repair work relating to medical imaging devices. EI solicited repair business in the U.S. and shipped the items for repair to the Canadian firm. In 2001 BC Technical (BCT) shipped items for repair to EI who shipped them to EC for the actual repairs. The repair work was not successful and BCT sued both EI and EC under the 1998 repair agreement for damages. BC Technical was not an intended third-party beneficiary of the 1998 agreement that was undertaken several years before BCT and EI contracted for the repairs in 2001. BCT had no standing to sue the Canadian firm under the 1998 contract. BCT was an incidental beneficiary of the 1998 agreement.[8]

Whether or not a third party is an *intended* or *incidental* beneficiary, therefore, comes down to determining whether or not a reasonable person would believe that

---

[6] A common form of reservation is the life insurance policy provision by which the insured reserves the right to change the beneficiary. Section 142 of the Restatement (Second) of Contracts provides that the promisor and the promisee may modify their contract and affect the right of the third-party beneficiary thereby unless the agreement expressly prohibits this or the third-party beneficiary has changed position in reliance on the promise or has manifested assent to it.

[7] *XL Disposal Corp. v John Sexton Contractors Co.,* 659 NE2d 1312 (Ill App 1995).

[8] *BC Technical Inc. v Ensil International,* 2007 WL 2908282 (D Utah 2007).

the promisee intended to confer on the beneficiary an enforceable benefit under the contract in question. The intent must be clear and definite or expressed in the contract itself or in the circumstances surrounding the contract's execution.

CASE SUMMARY

Third Party Must Be Identified in the Four Corners of the Contract

FACTS: Novus International, Inc., manufactures a poultry-feed supplement named Alimet at its plant in Chocolate Bayou, Texas. A key component of Alimet is the chemical MMP. Novus contracted with Union Carbide to secure MMP from Carbide's plant in Taft, Louisiana. Sometime later, Carbide entered into a major rail-transportation contract with the Union Pacific Railroad (UP). The rail contract consisted of nearly 100 pages. Exhibit 2 of the contract delineated inbound and outbound shipments to and from all of Carbide's Texas and Louisiana facilities. Among the hundreds of shipments listed in Exhibit 2 were three outbound MMP shipments from Taft, Louisiana, to Chocolate Bayou, Texas. These shipments were described as "Taft outbound liquid chemicals." Due to difficulties that arose from its merger with the Southern Pacific Railroad, UP experienced severe disruptions in its rail service over parts of two years and was unable to transport sufficient MMP to Chocolate Bayou. As a result, Novus had to utilize more expensive methods of transportation to obtain Alimet. It sued UP to recover the increased costs of premium freight resulting from UP's breach of its rail contract with Carbide. UP asserts that Novus did not have standing to sue; and Novus contends that it had standing to sue as an intended third-party beneficiary.

DECISION: Judgment for UP. Third-party beneficiary claims succeed or fail according to the provisions of the contact upon which suit is brought. The intention to confer a direct benefit on a third party must be clearly and fully spelled out in the four corners of the contract. Otherwise, enforcement of the contract by a third party must be denied. After reviewing the rail contract, no intent to confer a direct benefit on Novus is evident. Novus is never named in the contract, and all obligations flow between UP and Carbide. Nor is it stated anywhere in the contract that the parties are contracting for the benefit of Carbide's customers. Novus, thus, is an incidental beneficiary without standing to sue. [**Union Pacific Railroad v Novus International, Inc., 113 SW3d 418 (Tex App 2003)**]

B. Assignments

The parties to a contract have both rights and duties. Can rights be transferred or sold to another person or entity? Can duties be transferred to another person?

5. Definitions

Contracts create **rights** and **duties** between the parties to the contract. An **assignment** is a transfer of contractual rights to a third party. The party owing a duty or debt under the contract is the **obligor** or **debtor**, and the party to whom the obligation is owed is the **obligee**. The party making the assignment is the **assignor**. The third party to whom the assignment is made is the **assignee**. **For Example,** Randy Marshall and Marilee Menendez own Huntington Beach Board (HBB) Company,

---

right–legal capacity to require another person to perform or refrain from an action.

duty–obligation of law imposed on a person to perform or refrain from performing a certain act.

assignment–transfer of a right; generally used in connection with personal property rights, as rights under a contract, commercial paper, an insurance policy, a mortgage, or a lease. (Parties—assignor, assignee.)

obligor–promisor.

debtor–buyer on credit (i. e., a borrower).

obligee–promisee who can claim the benefit of the obligation.

assignor–party who assigns contract rights to a third party.

assignee–third party to whom contract benefits are transferred.

FIGURE 18-1 | *Surfboard Transaction Diagram*

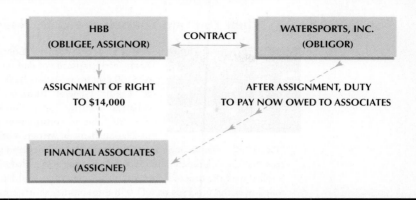

LLC, a five-employee start-up company making top-of-the line surfboards. Marilee was able to sell 100 Duke Kahanamoku–inspired "longboards" to Watersports, Inc., a large retail sporting goods chain, for $140 per board. However, the best payment terms she could obtain were payment in full in 90 days. A contract containing these terms was executed, and the goods were delivered. To meet internal cash flow needs, HBB assigned its right to receive the $14,000 payment from the buyer to West Coast Financial Associates (Associates) and received $12,800 cash from Associates on execution of the assignment documents. Notice was given at that time to Watersports, Inc., of the assignment. The right to receive the payment due in 90 days under the sales contract has thus been transferred by the seller HBB (assignor) to the third party, Associates (the assignee), to whom the buyer, Watersports, Inc. (obligor), now owes the duty of payment. Under the law of assignments, Associates, the assignee, now has direct rights against the obligor, Watersports, Inc. (See Figure 18.1.)

6. Form of Assignment

Generally, an assignment may be in any form. Statutes, however, may require that certain kinds of assignments be in writing or be executed in a particular form. Any words, whether written or spoken, that show an intention to transfer or assign will be given the effect of an assignment.[9]

7. Notice of Assignment

An assignment, if otherwise valid, takes effect the moment it is made. The assignee should give immediate notice of the assignment to the obligor, setting forth the obligor's duty to the assignee, in order to prevent improper payment.[10]

---

[9] *Jom Investments, LLC v Callahan Industries, Inc.*, 667 SE2d 429 (Ga App 2008).
[10] In some cases, an assignee will give notice of the assignment to the obligor in order to obtain priority over other persons who claim the same right or in order to limit the defenses that the obligor may raise against the assignee. UCC § 9-318.

C A S E   S U M M A R Y

When You Find Yourself in a Hole, NationsBank, Stop Digging

FACTS: L & S General Contractors, LLC (L & S), purchased a book-entry certificate of deposit (CD 005) in the principal amount of $100,000 from NationsBank, N.A. L & S later assigned CD 005 to Credit General Insurance Company (Credit General) as collateral security for performance and payment bonds on a Howard Johnson construction project. Credit General forwarded to NationsBank a written notice of the assignment that stated, "Please hold this account as assigned to use until demanded or released by us." NationsBank recorded the assignment and executed a written acknowledgment. When CD 005 matured, L & S rolled over the proceeds into a short-term certificate of deposit (CD 058) and, upon maturity, rolled over the proceeds of CD 058 into another short-term certificate of deposit (CD 072).

The bank book entries of CD 058 and CD 072 recorded L & S as the only principal/payee and did not reflect Credit General's assignment interest. NationsBank admitted its failure to show Credit General as assignee on the rollover book entries for CD 058 and CD 072 was a mistake.

Upon maturity, L & S withdrew the proceeds of CD 072 without the knowledge or consent of Credit General. Later Credit General made written demand on NationsBank for the proceeds of CD 005, and NationsBank informed Credit General that CD 005 had been redeemed and refused payment. Credit General sued NationsBank for wrongful payment of proceeds. NationsBank argues that the assignment was limited in time to the completion of the Howard Johnson project.

DECISION: Judgment for the assignee, Credit General. Upon notice and acknowledgment of the assignment, NationsBank incurred a legal duty to pay the account proceeds only to the assignee, Credit General, in whom the account was vested by the terms of the assignment. The assignment was absolute and unambiguous on its face and clearly was not limited as NationsBank proposes. The assignment language controls. [**Credit General Insurance Co. v NationsBank, 299 F3d 943 (8th Cir 2002)**]

If the obligor is notified in any manner that there has been an assignment and that any money due must be paid to the assignee, the obligor's obligation can be discharged only by making payment to the assignee.

If the obligor is not notified that there has been an assignment and that the money due must be paid to the assignee, any payment made by the obligor to the assignor reduces or cancels that portion of the debt. The only remedy for the assignee is to sue the assignor to recover the payments that were made by the obligor.

The Uniform Consumer Credit Code (UCCC) protects consumer-debtors making payments to an assignor without knowledge of the assignment[11] and imposes a penalty for using a contract term that would destroy this protection of consumers.[12]

[11] UCCC § 2.412.
[12] UCCC § 5.202.

8. Assignment of Right to Money

Assignments of contracts are generally made to raise money. **For Example,** an automobile dealer assigns a customer's credit contract to a finance company and receives cash for it. Sometimes assignments are made when an enterprise closes and transfers its business to a new owner.

A person entitled to receive money, such as payment for goods sold to a buyer or for work done under a contract, may generally assign that right to another person.[13] A **claim** or **cause of action** against another person may be assigned. Isaac Hayes, an Academy Award®–winning composer, producer, and the original voice of Chef in the television series South Park, assigned his copyright interests in several musical works in exchange for royalties from Stax Records.[14] A contractor entitled to receive payment from a building's owner can assign that right to a bank as security for a loan or can assign it to anyone else.

For Example, Celeste owed Roscoe Painters $5,000 for painting her house. Roscoe assigned this claim to the Main Street Bank. Celeste later refused to pay the bank because she had never consented to the assignment. The fact that Celeste had not consented is irrelevant. Roscoe was the owner of the claim and could transfer it to the bank. Celeste, therefore, is obligated to pay the assignee, Main Street Bank.

(A) Future Rights. By the modern rule, future and expected rights to money may be assigned. Thus, prior to the start of a building, a building contractor may assign its rights to money not yet due under an existing contract's payment on completion-phase schedule.

(B) Purpose of Assignment. The assignment of the right to money may be a complete transfer of the right that gives the assignee the right to collect and keep the money. In contrast, the assignment may be held for security. In this case, the assignee may hold the money only as a security for some specified obligation.

(C) Prohibition of Assignment of Rights. A clear and specific contractual prohibition against the assignment of rights is enforceable at common law. However, the UCC favors the assignment of contracts, and express contractual prohibitions on assignments are ineffective against (1) the assignment of rights to payment for goods or services, including accounts receivable,[15] and (2) the assignment of the rights to damages for breach of sales contracts.[16]

9. Nonassignable Rights

If the transfer of a right would materially affect or alter a duty or the rights of the obligor, an assignment is not permitted.[17]

(A) Assignment Increasing Burden of Performance. When the assignment of a right would increase the burden of the obligor in performing, an assignment is ordinarily not permitted. To illustrate, if the assignor has the right to buy a certain quantity of

---

claim–right to payment.

cause of action–right to damages or other judicial relief when a legally protected right of the plaintiff is violated by an unlawful act of the defendant.

---

[13] *Pravin Banker Associates v Banco Popular del Peru,* 109 F3d 850 (2d Cir 1997).
[14] *Hayes v Carlin America, Inc.,* 168 F Supp 3d 154 (SDNY 2001).
[15] UCC § 9-318(4). This section of the UCC is applicable to most commercial assignments.
[16] UCC § 2-210(2).
[17] *Aslakson v Home Savings Ass'n,* 416 NW2d 786 (Minn App 1987) (increase of credit risk).

FIGURE 18-2 | *Limitations on Transfer of Rights and Duties*

ASSIGNMENT OF RIGHT TO MONEY	ASSIGNMENT OF RIGHT TO PERFORMANCE	DELEGATION OF DUTIES
GENERALLY NO LIMITATION	INCREASE OF BURDEN PERSONAL SERVICES CREDIT TRANSACTION	PERSONAL OR NONSTANDARDIZED PERFORMANCE

a stated article and to take such property from the seller's warehouse, this right can be assigned. However, if the sales contract stipulates that the seller should deliver to the buyer's premises and the assignee's premises are a substantial distance from the assignor's place of business, the assignment would not be given effect. In this case, the seller would be required to give a different performance by providing greater transportation if the assignment were permitted.

(B) PERSONAL SERVICES. Contracts for personal services are generally not assignable. **For Example,** were golf instructor David Ledbetter to sign a one-year contract to provide instruction for professional golfer Davis Love III, David Ledbetter could not assign his first assistant to provide the instruction, nor could Davis Love assign a protégé to receive instruction from Ledbetter. Professional athletes and their agents commonly deal with assignment or trading rights of the athletes in their contracts with professional sports franchises.

There is a split among jurisdictions regarding whether employee noncompetition covenants are assignable to the new owner of a business absent employee consent. That is, some courts permit a successor employer to enforce an employee's noncompetition agreement as an assignee of the original employer. However, a majority of states that have considered this issue have concluded that restrictive covenants are personal in nature and not assignable. **For Example,** in September 2000, Philip Burkhardt signed a noncompetition agreement with his employer, NES Trench Shoring. On June 30, 2002, United Rentals Purchased NES with all contracts being assigned to United Rentals. Burkhardt stayed on with the new owner for five weeks and thereafter went to work for Traffic Control Services, a direct competitor of United. United was unsuccessful in its action to enforce the noncompetition covenant Burkhardt had signed with NES. Burkhardt's covenant with NES did not contain a clause allowing the covenant to be assigned to a new owner, and the court refused to enforce it, absent an express clause permitting assignment.[18]

(C) CREDIT TRANSACTION. When a transaction is based on extending credit, the person to whom credit is extended cannot assign any rights under the contract to another. **For Example,** Jack Aldrich contracted to sell his summer camp on Lake

[18] *Traffic Control Sources, Inc. v United Rentals Northwest, Inc.*, 87 P3d 1054 (Nov 2004).

Sunapee to Pat Norton for $200,000, with $100,000 in cash due at the closing and the balance due on an installment basis secured by a mortgage on the property to be executed by Norton. Several days later, Norton found a more desirable property, and her sister Meg was very pleased to take over the Sunapee contract. Pat assigned her rights to Meg. Jack Aldrich, having received a better offer after contracting with Pat, refused to consent to the assignment. In this situation, the assignment to Meg is prohibited because the assignee, Meg, is a different credit risk even though the property to serve as security remained unchanged.

CPA 10. Rights of Assignee

Unless restricted by the terms of the assignment or applicable law, the assignee acquires all the rights of the assignor.[19]

An assignee stands exactly in the position of the assignor. The assignee's rights are no more or less than those of the assignor. If the assigned right to payment is subject to a condition precedent, that same condition exists for the assignee. **For Example,** when a contractor is not entitled to receive the balance of money due under the contract until all bills of suppliers of materials have been paid, the assignee to whom the contractor assigns the balance due under the contract is subject to the same condition. As set forth previously, in some states the assignee of a business purchasing all of the assets and rights of the business has the right to enforce a confidentiality and noncompetition agreement against a former employee of the assignor, just as though it were the assignor.[20]

11. Continuing Liability of Assignor

The making of an assignment does not relieve the assignor of any obligation of the contract. In the absence of a contrary agreement, an assignor continues to be bound by the obligations of the original contract. **For Example,** boatbuilder Derecktor NY's assignment of obligations to a Connecticut boatbuilder did not release it from all liabilities under its boatbuilding contract with New York Water Taxi (NYWT); and NYWT was allowed to proceed against Derecktor NY for breach of contract–design and breach of contract–workmanship.[21]

When a lease is assigned, the assignee becomes the principal obligor for rent payments, and the leasee becomes a surety toward the lessor for the assignee's performance. **For Example,** Tri-State Chiropractic (TSC) held a five-year lease on premises at 6010 East Main Street in Columbus, Ohio. Without the leasor's consent, TSC assigned that lease to Dr. T. Wilson and Buckeye Chiropractic, LLC, prior to the expiration of the lease. TSC continues to be liable for rent as surety during the term of the lease, even if the leasor (owner) had consented to the assignment or accepted payment from the assignee.[22] In order to avoid liability as a surety, TSC would have to obtain a discharge of the lease by **novation**, in which all three parties agree that the original contract (the lease) would be discharged and a

novation–substitution for an old contract with a new one that either replaces an existing obligation with a new obligation or replaces an original party with a new party.

---

[19] *Puget Sound National Bank v Washington Department of Revenue*, 868 P2d 127 (Wash 1994).
[20] *Artromick International, Inc. v Koch*, 759 NE2d 385 (Ohio App 2001).
[21] *New York Trans Harbor, LLC v Derecktor Shipyards*, 841 NYS2d 821 (2007).
[22] *Schottenstein Trustees v Carano*, 2000 WL 1455425 (Ohio App 2000).

new lease between Dr. Wilson and the owner would take effect. A novation allows for the discharge of a contractual obligation by the substitution of a new contract involving a new party.[23]

12. Liability of Assignee

It is necessary to distinguish between the question of whether the obligor can assert a particular defense against the assignee and the question of whether any person can sue the assignee. Ordinarily, the assignee is not subject to suit by virtue of the fact that the assignment has been made.

(A) CONSUMER PROTECTION LIABILITY OF ASSIGNEE. The assignee of the right to money may have no direct relationship to the original debtor except with respect to receiving payments. Consumer protection laws in most states, however, may subject the assignee to some liability for the assignor's misconduct.

CASE SUMMARY

The Pool and the Agreement Will Not Hold Any Water

FACTS: Homeowner Michael Jackson entered into a contract with James DeWitt for the construction of an in-ground lap pool. The contract provided for a 12 ft. 60 ft. pool at an estimated cost of $21,000. At the time the contract was signed, Jackson paid DeWitt $11,400 in cash and financed $7,500 through a Retail Installment Security Agreement (RISA). Associates Financial Services Company (Associates) provided DeWitt with all of the forms necessary to document the financing of the home improvements. Consumer requests for financing were subject to Associates's approval, which was given for Jackson's lap pool. When the RISA was completed, DeWitt assigned it to Associates. Jackson made two monthly payments of $202.90 and a final payment of $7,094.20 while the lap pool was still under construction. When the pool was filled, it failed to hold water and Jackson had the pool and deck removed. Jackson sued DeWitt for breach of contract. He asserted that all valid claims and defenses he had against DeWitt were also valid against the assignee, Associates. Jackson sought the return of the $7,500 he had financed from Associates. The trial court held that because Jackson had paid the entire balance of the loan before Associates knew of Jackson's claim, he could not obtain relief from Associates under the consumer protection law, section ATCP 110.06 of the Wisconsin Administrative Code. Jackson appealed this decision.

DECISION: Judgment for Jackson. As one commentator has noted, "ch. ATCP 110 deals with virtually a laundry list of unfair or deceptive home improvement practices that have resulted from substantial financial losses to home owners over the years. Jeffries, 57 MARQ. L. REV at 578." Associates is an assignee of a "home improvement contract" that is governed by section ATCP 110.06. The regulation provides that "[e]very assignee of a home improvement contract takes subject to all claims and defenses of the buyer or successors in interest." Therefore, as the assignee of the RISA, Associates is subject to any claims without regard to the negotiability of the contract. [**Jackson v DeWitt, 592 NW2d 262 (Wis App 1999)**]

---

[23] See *Quicksilver Resources, Inc. v Eagle Drilling, LLC*, 2009 LEXIS 39176 (SD Tex 2009).

FIGURE 18-3 | *Can a Third Person Sue on a Contract?*

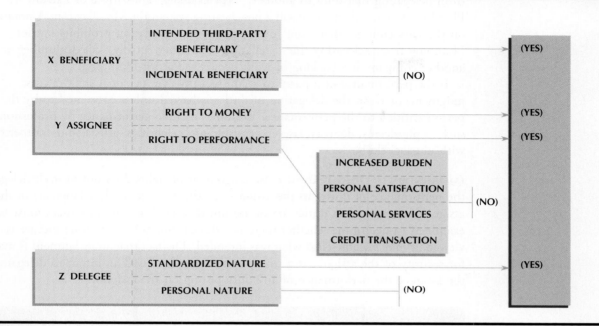

(B) **DEFENSES AND SETOFFS.** The assignee's rights are no greater than those of the assignor.[24] If the obligor could successfully defend against a suit brought by the assignor, the obligor will also prevail against the assignee.

The fact that the assignee has given value for the assignment does not give the assignee any immunity from defenses that the other party, the obligor, could have asserted against the assignor. The rights acquired by the assignee remain subject to any limitations imposed by the contract.

13. Warranties of Assignor

implied warranty–warranty that was not made but is implied by law.

When the assignment is made for a consideration, the assignor is regarded as providing an **implied warranty** that the right assigned is valid. The assignor also warrants that the assignor is the owner of the claim or right assigned and that the assignor will not interfere with the assignee's enforcement of the obligation.

14. Delegation of Duties

delegation of duties– transfer of duties by a contracting party to another person who is to perform them.

delegation–transfer to another of the right and power to do an act.

A **delegation of duties** is a transfer of duties by a contracting party to another person who is to perform them. Under certain circumstances, a contracting party may obtain someone else to do the work. When the performance is standardized and nonpersonal, so that it is not material who performs, the law will permit the **delegation** of the performance of the contract. In such cases, however, the contracting party remains liable in the case of default of the person doing the work just as though no delegation had been made.[25]

---

[24] *Shoreline Communications, Inc. v Norwich Taxi, LCC,* 70 Conn App 60 (2002).
[25] *Orange Bowl Corp. v Warren,* 386 SE2d 293 (SC App 1989).

A contract may prohibit a party owing a duty of performance under a contract from delegating that duty to another.[26] **For Example,** Tom Joyce of Patriot Plumbing Co. contracts to install a new heating system for Mrs. Lawton. A notation on the sales contract that Tom Joyce will do the installation prohibits Patriot Plumbing from delegating the installation to another equally skilled plumber or to another company if a backlog of work occurs at Patriot Plumbing.

If the performance of a party to a contract involves personal skill, talents, judgment, or trust, the delegation of duties is barred unless consented to by the person entitled to the performance. Examples include performance by professionals such as physicians, dentists, lawyers, consultants, celebrities, artists, and craftpersons with unusual skills.

(A) INTENTION TO DELEGATE DUTIES. An assignment of rights does not in itself delegate the performance of duties to the assignee. In the absence of clear language in the assignment stating that duties are or are not delegated, all circumstances must be examined to determine whether there is a delegation. When the total picture is viewed, it may become clear what was intended. The fact that an assignment is made for security of the assignee is a strong indication there was no intent to delegate to the assignee the performance of any duty resting on the assignor.[27]

CASE SUMMARY

Duties were Delegated Too, Dude

FACTS: Smith, who owned the Avalon Apartments, a condominium, sold individual apartments under contracts that required each purchaser to pay $15 a month extra for hot and cold water, heat, refrigeration, taxes, and fire insurance. Smith assigned his interest in the apartment house under various contracts to Roberts. When Roberts failed to pay the taxes on the building, the purchasers of the individual apartments sued to compel Roberts to do so.

DECISION: Judgment against Roberts. In the absence of a contrary indication, it is presumed that an assignment of a contract delegates the performance of the duties as well as transfers the rights. Here, there was no indication that a package transfer was not intended, and the assignee was therefore obligated to perform in accordance with the contract terms. [**Radley v Smith and Roberts, 313 P2d 465 (Utah 1957)**]

(B) DELEGATION OF DUTIES UNDER THE UCC. With respect to contracts for the sale of goods, "an assignment of 'the contract' or of 'all my rights under the contract' or an assignment in similar general terms is an assignment of rights and, unless the language or the circumstances (as in an assignment for security) indicate the contrary, it is a delegation of performance of the duties of the assignor, and its acceptance by the assignee constitutes a promise ... to perform those duties. This promise is enforceable by either the assignor or the other party to the original contract."[28]

---

[26] See *Physical Distribution Services, Inc. v R. R. Donnelley*, 561 F3d 792 (8th Cir 2009).
[27] *City National Bank of Fort Smith v First National Bank and Trust Co. of Rogers*, 732 SW2d 489 (Ark App 1987).
[28] UCC § 2-210(4).

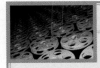

lawflix

It Could Happen to You (1996) (PG)

Discuss the legal, ethical and contract issues involved in the first portion of the film in which a police officer (Nicholas Cage) promises to split a lottery ticket with a coffee shop waitress (Bridget Fonda) as her tip because he does not have enough money. The lottery ticket (purchased by Cage and his wife, Rosie Perez) is a winner, and Cage wrestles with his obligation to tell Fonda. You could discuss whether there was an assignment or whether Fonda was added as a third-party beneficiary after the fact.

Check out LawFlix at **www.cengage.com/blaw/dvl** to access movie clips that illustrate business law concepts.

MAKE THE CONNECTION

SUMMARY

Ordinarily, only the parties to contracts have rights and duties with respect to such contracts. Exceptions are made in the case of third-party beneficiary contracts and assignments.

When a contract shows a clear intent to benefit a third person or class of persons, those persons are called *intended third-party beneficiaries,* and they may sue for breach of the contract. A third-party beneficiary is subject to any limitation or restriction found in the contract. A third-party beneficiary loses all rights when the original contract is terminated by operation of law or if the contract reserves the right to change the beneficiary and such a change is made.

In contrast, an incidental beneficiary benefits from the performance of a contract, but the conferring of this benefit was not intended by the contracting parties. An incidental beneficiary cannot sue on the contract.

An assignment is a transfer of a right; the assignor transfers a right to the assignee. In the absence of a local statute, there are no formal requirements for an assignment. Any words manifesting the intent to transfer are sufficient to constitute an assignment. No consideration is required. Any right to money may be assigned, whether the assignor is entitled to the money at the time of the assignment or will be entitled or expects to be entitled at some time in the future.

A right to a performance may be assigned except when (1) it would increase the burden of performance, (2) the contract involves the performance of personal services, or (3) the transaction is based on extending credit.

When a valid assignment is made, the assignee has the same rights—and only the same rights—as the assignor. The assignee is also subject to the same defenses and setoffs as the assignor had been.

The performance of duties under a contract may be delegated to another person except when a personal element of skill or judgment of the original contracting party is involved. The intent to delegate duties may be expressly stated. The intent may also be found in an "assignment" of "the contract" unless the circumstances make it clear that only the right to money was intended to be transferred. The fact that there has been a delegation of duties does not release the assignor from responsibility for performance. The assignor is liable for breach of the contract if the assignee does not properly perform the delegated duties. In the absence of an effective delegation or the formation of a third-party beneficiary contract, an assignee of rights is not liable to the obligee of the contract for its performance by the assignor.

Notice is not required to effect an assignment. When notice of the assignment is given to the obligor together with a demand that future payments be made to the assignee, the obligor cannot discharge liability by payment to the assignor.

When an assignment is made for a consideration, the assignor makes implied warranties that the right assigned is valid and that the assignor owns that right and will not interfere with its enforcement by the assignee.

LEARNING OUTCOMES

After studying this chapter, you should be able to clearly explain:

A. THIRD-PARTY BENEFICIARY CONTRACTS

LO.1 Explain the two types of intended third-party beneficiaries
> See the Sameway Laundry example that illustrates how the "intended creditor beneficiary" can sue the buyer, p. 393.
> See the text discussion explaining that a life insurance contract is an "intended" donee third-party beneficiary contract, p. 393.

LO.2 Explain why an incidental beneficiary does not have the right to sue as a third-party beneficiary
> See the *Ensil* case in which the owner had no standing to sue as an incidental beneficiary, p. 395.

B. ASSIGNMENTS

LO.3 Define an assignment
> See the text discussion explaining that an assignment is the transfer of contractual rights to a third party, p. 396.
> See the Hunington *Beach Board* example that discusses the assignee's direct rights against the obligor, p. 396.

LO.4 Explain the general rule that a person entitled to receive money under a contract may generally assign that right to another person
> See the example of an automobile dealer assigning a customer's credit contract to a finance company in order to raise cash to buy more inventory, p. 399.

LO.5 List the nonassignable rights to performance
See the text discussion regarding increase of burden, personal services, and credit transactions beginning on p. 399.

KEY TERMS

assignee	delegation of duties	obligee
assignment	delegation	obligor
assignor	duties	rights
cause of action	implied warranty	third-party beneficiary
claim	intended beneficiary	
debtor	novation	

QUESTIONS AND CASE PROBLEMS

1. Give an example of a third-party beneficiary contract.

2. A court order required John Baldassari to make specified payments for the support of his wife and child. His wife needed more money and applied for Pennsylvania welfare payments. In accordance with the law, she assigned to Pennsylvania her right to the support payments from her husband. Pennsylvania then increased her payments. Pennsylvania obtained a court order directing John, in accordance with the terms of the assignment from his wife, to make the support-order payments directly to the Pennsylvania Department of Public Welfare. John refused to pay on the ground that he had not been notified of the assignment or the hearing directing him to make payment to the assignee. Was he correct? [*Pennsylvania v Baldassari*, 421 A2d 306 (Pa Super)]

3. Lee contracts to paint Sally's two-story house for $2,500. Sally realizes that she will not have sufficient money, so she transfers her rights under this agreement to her neighbor Karen, who has a three-story house. Karen notifies Lee that Sally's contract has been assigned to her and demands that Lee paint Karen's house for $2,500. Is Lee required to do so?

4. Assume that Lee agrees to the assignment of the house-painting contract to Karen as stated in question 3. Thereafter, Lee fails to perform the contract to paint Karen's house. Karen sues Sally for damages. Is Sally liable?

5. Jessie borrows $1,000 from Thomas and agrees to repay the money in 30 days. Thomas assigns the right to the $1,000 to Douglas Finance Co. Douglas sues Jessie. Jessie argues that she had agreed to pay the money only to Thomas and that when she and Thomas had entered into the transaction, there was no intention to benefit Douglas Finance Co. Are these objections valid?

6. Washington purchased an automobile from Smithville Motors. The contract called for payment of the purchase price in installments and contained the defense preservation notice required by the Federal Trade Commission regulation. Smithville assigned the contract to Rustic Finance Co. The car was always in need of repairs, and by the time it was half paid for, it would no longer run. Washington canceled the contract. Meanwhile, Smithville had gone out of

business. Washington sued Rustic for the amount she had paid Smithville. Rustic refused to pay on the grounds that it had not been at fault. Decide.

7. Helen obtained an insurance policy insuring her life and naming her niece Julie as beneficiary. Helen died, and about a year later the policy was found in her house. When Julie claimed the insurance money, the insurer refused to pay on the ground that the policy required that notice of death be given to it promptly following the death. Julie claimed that she was not bound by the time limitation because she had never agreed to it, as she was not a party to the insurance contract. Is Julie entitled to recover?

8. Lone Star Life Insurance Co. agreed to make a long-term loan to Five Forty Three Land, Inc., whenever that corporation requested one. Five Forty Three wanted this loan to pay off its short-term debts. The loan was never made, as it was never requested by Five Forty Three, which owed the Exchange Bank & Trust Co. on a short-term debt. Exchange Bank then sued Lone Star for breach of its promise on the theory that the Exchange Bank was a third-party beneficiary of the contract to make the loan. Was the Exchange Bank correct? [*Exchange Bank & Trust Co. v Lone Star Life Ins. Co.,* 546 SW2d 948 (Tex App)]

9. The New Rochelle Humane Society made a contract with the city of New Rochelle to capture and impound all dogs running at large. Spiegler, a minor, was bitten by some dogs while in her schoolyard. She sued the school district of New Rochelle and the Humane Society. With respect to the Humane Society, she claimed that she was a third-party beneficiary of the contract that the Humane Society had made with the city. She claimed that she could therefore sue the Humane Society for its failure to capture the dogs that had bitten her. Was she entitled to recover? [*Spiegler v School District of the City of New Rochelle,* 242 NYS2d 430]

10. Zoya operated a store in premises rented from Peerless. The lease required Zoya to maintain liability insurance to protect Zoya and Peerless. Caswell entered the store, fell through a trap door, and was injured. She then sued Zoya and Peerless on the theory that she was a third-party beneficiary of the lease requirement to maintain liability insurance. Was she correct? [*Caswell v Zoya Int'l,* 654 NE2d 552 (Ill App)]

11. Henry was owed $10,000 by Jones Corp. In consideration of the many odd jobs performed for him over the years by his nephew, Henry assigned the $10,000 claim to his nephew Charles. Henry died, and his widow claimed that the assignment was ineffective so that the claim was part of Henry's estate. She based her assertion on the ground that the past performance rendered by the nephew was not consideration. Was the assignment effective?

12. Industrial Construction Co. wanted to raise money to construct a canning factory in Wisconsin. Various persons promised to subscribe the needed amount, which they agreed to pay when the construction was completed. The construction company assigned its rights and delegated its duties under the agreement to Johnson, who then built the cannery. Vickers, one of the subscribers, refused to pay the amount that he had subscribed on the ground that the contract could not be assigned. Was he correct?

13. The Ohio Department of Public Welfare made a contract with an accountant to audit the accounts of health care providers who were receiving funds under the Medicaid program. Windsor House, which operated six nursing homes, claimed that it was a third-party beneficiary of that contract and could sue for its breach. Was it correct? [*Thornton v Windsor House, Inc.,* 566 NE2d 1220 (Ohio)]

CPA QUESTIONS

1. On August 1, Neptune Fisheries contracted in writing with West Markets to deliver to West 3,000 pounds of lobster at $4.00 a pound. Delivery of the lobsters was due October 1, with payment due November 1. On August 4, Neptune entered into a contract with Deep Sea Lobster Farms that provided as follows: "Neptune Fisheries assigns all the rights under the contract with West Markets dated August 1 to Deep Sea Lobster Farms." The best interpretation of the August 4 contract would be that it was:

   a. Only an assignment of rights by Neptune

   b. Only a delegation of duties by Neptune

   c. An assignment of rights and a delegation of duties by Neptune

   d. An unenforceable third-party beneficiary contract

2. Graham contracted with the city of Harris to train and employ high school dropouts residing in Harris. Graham breached the contract. Long, a resident of Harris and a high school dropout, sued Graham for damages. Under the circumstances, Long will:

   a. Win, because Long is a third-party beneficiary entitled to enforce the contract

   b. Win, because the intent of the contract was to confer a benefit on all high school dropouts residing in Harris

   c. Lose, because Long is merely an incidental beneficiary of the contract

   d. Lose, because Harris did not assign its contract rights to Long

3. Union Bank lent $200,000 to Wagner. Union required Wagner to obtain a life insurance policy naming Union as beneficiary. While the loan was outstanding, Wagner stopped paying the premiums on the policy. Union paid the premiums, adding the amounts paid to Wagner's loan. Wagner died, and the insurance company refused to pay the policy proceeds to Union. Union may:

   a. Recover the policy proceeds because it is a creditor beneficiary

   b. Not recover the policy proceeds because it is a donee beneficiary

   c. Not recover the policy proceeds because it is not in privity of contract with the insurance company

   d. Not recover the policy proceeds because it is only an incidental beneficiary

Chapter 19

DISCHARGE OF CONTRACTS

I n the preceding chapters, you studied how a contract is formed, what a contract means, and who has rights under a contract. In this chapter, attention is turned to how a contract is ended or discharged. In other words, what puts an end to the rights and duties created by a contract?

A. Conditions Relating to Performance

As developed in the body of this chapter, the ordinary method of discharging obligations under a contract is by performance. Certain promises may be less than absolute and instead come into effect only upon the occurrence of a specified event, or an existing obligation may be extinguished when an event happens. These are conditional promises.

1. Classifications of Conditions

condition–stipulation or prerequisite in a contract, will, or other instrument.

When the occurrence or nonoccurrence of an event, as expressed in a contract, affects the duty of a party to the contract to perform, the event is called a **condition**. Terms such as *if, provided that, when, after, as soon as, subject to,* and *on the condition that* indicate the creation of a condition.[1] Conditions are classified as *conditions precedent, conditions subsequent,* and *concurrent conditions*.

condition precedent–event that if unsatisfied would mean that no rights would arise under a contract.

(A) CONDITION PRECEDENT. A **condition precedent** is a condition that must occur before a party to a contract has an obligation to perform under the contract. **For Example,** a condition precedent to a contractor's (MasTec's) obligation to pay a subcontractor (MidAmerica) under a "pay-if-paid" by the owner (PathNet) clause in their subcontract agreement is the receipt of payment by MasTec from PathNet. The condition precedent—payment by the owner—did not occur due to bankruptcy, and therefore MasTec did not have an obligation to pay MidAmerica.[2]

C A S E   S U M M A R Y

A Blitz on Offense?

FACTS: Richard Blitz owns a piece of commercial property at 4 Old Middle Street. On February 2, 1998, Arthur Subklew entered into a lease with Blitz to rent the rear portion of the property. Subklew intended to operate an auto sales and repair business. Paragraph C of the lease was a zoning contingency clause that stated, "Landlord [plaintiff] will use Landlord's best efforts to obtain a written verification that Tenant can operate [an] Auto Sales and Repair Business at the demised premises. If Landlord is unable to obtain such

---

[1] *Harmon Cable Communications v Scope Cable Television, Inc.,* 468 NW2d 350 (Neb 1990).
[2] *MidAmerica Construction Management, Inc. v MasTec North America, Inc.,* 436 F3d 1257 (10th Cir 2006).

C A S E   S U M M A R Y

Continued

commitment from the municipality, then this agreement shall be deemed null and void and Landlord shall immediately return deposit monies to Tenant." The zoning paraboard approved the location only as a general repair business. When Subklew refused to occupy the premises, Blitz sued him for breach of contract.

DECISION: Judgment for Subklew. A condition precedent is a fact or event that the parties intend must exist before there is right to a performance. If the condition is not fulfilled, the right to enforce the contract does not come into existence. Blitz's obligation to obtain written approval of a used car business was a condition precedent to the leasing agreement. Since it was not obtained, Blitz cannot enforce the leasing agreement. [**Blitz v Subklew, 74 Conn App 183 (2002)**]

---

condition subsequent–
event whose occurrence or lack there of terminates a contract.

(B) CONDITION SUBSEQUENT. The parties to a contract may agree that a party is obligated to perform a certain act or pay a certain sum of money, but the contract contains a provision that relieves the obligation on the occurrence of a certain event. That is, on the happening of a **condition subsequent**, such an event extinguishes the duty to thereafter perform. **For Example,** Chad Newly served as the weekend anchor on *Channel 5 News* for several years. The station manager, Tom O'Brien, on reviewing tapes in connection with Newly's contract renewal, believed that Newly's speech on occasion was slightly slurred, and he suspected that it was from alcohol use. In the parties' contract discussions, O'Brien expressed his concerns about an alcohol problem and offered help. Newly denied there was a problem. O'Brien agreed to a new two-year contract with Newly at $167,000 for the first year and $175,000 for the second year with other benefits subject to "the condition" that the station reserved the right to make four unannounced drug-alcohol tests during the contract term; and should Newly test positive for drugs or alcohol under measurements set forth in the contract, then all of Channel 5's obligations to Newly under the contract would cease. When Newly subsequently failed a urinalysis test three months into the new contract, the happening of this event extinguished the station's obligation to employ and pay him under the contract.

---

sports&entertainment law

Endorsement Contracts

Sports marketing involves the use of famous athletes to promote the sale of products and services in our economy. Should an athlete's image be tarnished by allegations of immoral or illegal conduct, a company could be subject to financial losses and

corporate embarrassment. Endorsement contracts may extend for multiyear periods, and should a "morals" issue arise, a company would be well served to have had a broad morals clause in its contract that would allow the company at its sole

sports&entertainment law

continued

discretion to summarily terminate the endorsement contract. Representatives of athletes, on the other hand, seek narrow contractual language that allows for termination of endorsement contracts only upon the indictment for a crime, and they seek the right to have an arbitrator, as opposed to the employer, make the determination as to whether the morals clause was violated. NBA player Latrell Spreewell's endorsement contract with Converse Athletic Shoe Co. was terminated by the company following his altercation with his coach P.J. Carlisimo; John Daly's endorsement contract with Callaway Golf was terminated by the company when he violated his good conduct clause that restricted gambling and drinking activities; and when a photograph of Olympic gold medal swimmer Michael Phelps showed him with a marijuana pipe at a party at the University of South Carolina, Kellogg Co. dropped Phelps's endorsement deal.

Can the courts be utilized to resolve controversies over whether a "morals clause" has been violated? If so, is the occurrence of a morals clause violation a condition precedent or a condition subsequent?

(C) **Concurrent Condition.** In most bilateral contracts, the performances of the parties are *concurrent conditions*. That is, their mutual duties of performance under the contract are to take place simultaneously. **For Example,** concerning a contract for the sale and delivery of certain goods, the buyer must tender to the seller a certified check at the time of delivery as set forth in the contract, and the seller must tender the goods to the buyer at the same time.

B. Discharge by Performance

When it is claimed that a contract is discharged by performance, questions arise as to the nature, time, and sufficiency of the performance.

2. Normal Discharge of Contracts

A contract is usually discharged by the performance of the terms of the agreement. In most cases, the parties perform their promises and the contract ceases to exist or is thereby discharged. A contract is also discharged by the expiration of the time period specified in the contract.[3]

3. Nature of Performance

Performance may be the doing of an act or the making of payment.

tender–goods have arrived, are available for pickup, and buyer is notified.

(A) **Tender.** An offer to perform is known as a **tender**. If performance of the contract requires the doing of an act, the refusal of a tender discharges the party offering to perform and is a basis for that party to bring a lawsuit.

---

[3] *Washington National Ins. Co. v Sherwood Associates*, 795 P2d 665 (Utah App 1990).

A valid tender of payment consists of an unconditional offer of the exact amount due on the date when due. A tender of payment is not just an expression of willingness to pay; it must be an actual offer to perform by making payment of the amount owed.

(B) **PAYMENT.** When the contract requires payment, performance consists of the payment of money.

(1) Application of Payments

If a debtor owes more than one debt to the creditor and pays money, a question may arise as to which debt has been paid. If the debtor specifies the debt to which the payment is to be applied and the creditor accepts the money, the creditor is bound to apply the money as specified.[4] Thus, if the debtor specifies that a payment is to be made for a current purchase, the creditor may not apply the payment to an older balance.

(2) Payment by Check

Payment by commercial paper, such as a check, is ordinarily a conditional payment. A check merely suspends the debt until the check is presented for payment. If payment is then made, the debt is discharged; if not paid, the suspension terminates, and suit may be brought on either the debt or the check. Frequently, payment must be made by a specified date. It is generally held that the payment is made on time if it is mailed on or before the final date for payment.

C A S E   S U M M A R Y

The Mailed-Check Payment

FACTS: Thomas Cooper was purchasing land from Peter and Ella Birznieks. Cooper was already in possession of the land but was required to pay the amount owed by January 30; otherwise, he would have to vacate the property. The attorney handling the transaction for the Birznieks told Cooper that he could mail the payment to him. On January 30, Cooper mailed to the attorney a personal check drawn on an out-of-state bank for the amount due. The check arrived at the Birznieks' attorney's office on February 1. The Birznieks refused to accept the check on the grounds that it was not a timely payment and moved to evict Cooper from the property.

DECISION: Because of the general custom to regard a check mailed to a creditor as paying the bill that is owed, payment was made by Cooper on January 30 when he mailed the check. Payment was therefore made within the required time even though received after the expiration of the required time. [**Birznieks v Cooper, 275 NW2d 221 (Mich 1979)**]

4. Time of Performance

When the date or period of time for performance is specified in the contract, performance should be made on that date or within that time period.

---

[4] *Oakes Logging, Inc. v Green Crow, Inc.,* 832 P2d 894 (Wash App 1992).

(A) No Time Specified. When the time for performance is not specified in the contract, an obligation to perform within a reasonable time is implied.[5] The fact that no time is specified neither impairs the contract on the ground that it is indefinite nor allows an endless time in which to perform. What constitutes a reasonable time is determined by the nature of the subject matter of the contract and the facts and circumstances surrounding the making of the contract.

(B) When Time is Essential. If performance of the contract on or within the exact time specified is vital, it is said that "time is of the essence." Time is of the essence when the contract relates to property that is perishable or that is fluctuating rapidly in value. When a contract fixes by unambiguous language a time for performance and where there is no evidence showing that the parties did not intend that time should be of the essence, failure to perform within the specified time is a breach of contract entitling the innocent party to damages. **For Example,** Dixon and Gandhi agreed that Gandhi would close on the purchase of a motel as follows: "Closing Date. The closing shall be held … on the date which is within twenty (20) days after the closing of Nomura Financing." Gandhi did not close within the time period specified, and Dixon was allowed to retain $100,000 in prepaid closing costs and fees as liquidated damages for Gandhi's breach of contract.[6]

(C) When Time is Not Essential. Unless a contract so provides, time is ordinarily not of the essence, and performance within a reasonable time is sufficient. In the case of the sale of property, time is not regarded as of the essence when there has not been any appreciable change in the market value or condition of the property and when the person who delayed does not appear to have done so for the purpose of speculating on a change in market price.

(D) Waiver of Essence of Time Limitation. A provision that time is of the essence may be waived. It is waived when the specified time has expired but the party who could complain requests the delaying party to take steps necessary to perform the contract.

5. Adequacy of Performance

When a party renders exactly the performance called for by the contract, no question arises as to whether the contract has been performed. In other cases, there may not have been a perfect performance, or a question arises as to whether the performance satisfies the standard set by the contract.

CPA

substantial performance– equitable rule that if a good-faith attempt to perform does not precisely meet the terms of the agreement, the agreement will still be considered complete if the essential purpose of the contract is accomplished.

(A) Substantial Performance. Perfect performance of a contract is not always possible when dealing with construction projects. A party who in good faith has provided **substantial performance** of the contract may sue to recover the payment specified in the contract. However, because the performance was not perfect, the performing party is subject to a counterclaim for the damages caused the other party. When a building contractor has substantially performed the contract to construct a building, the contractor is responsible for the cost of repairing or correcting the defects as an offset from the contract price.[7]

---

[5] *First National Bank v Clark,* 447 SE2d 558 (W Va 1994).
[6] *Woodhull Corp. v Saibaba Corp.,* 507 SE2d 493 (Ga App 1998).
[7] Substantial performance is not a defense to a breach of contract claim, however. See *Bentley Systems Inc. v Intergraph Corp.,* 922 So2d 61 (Ala 2005).

FIGURE 19-1 | *Causes of Contract Discharge*

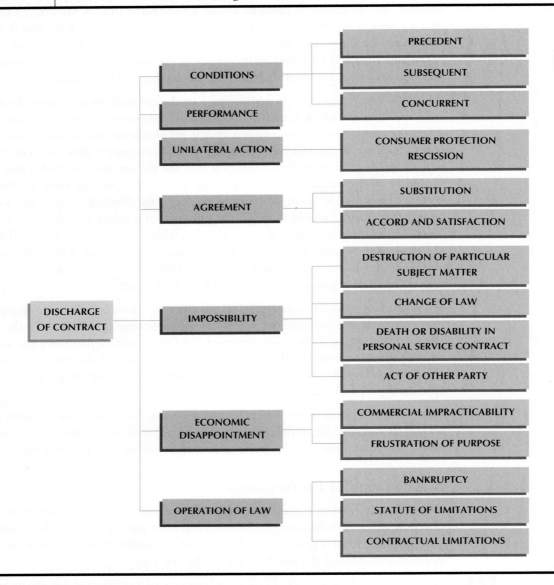

The measure of damages under these circumstances is known as "cost of completion" damages.[8] If, however, the cost of completion would be unreasonably disproportionate to the importance of the defect, the measure of damages is the diminution in value of the building due to the defective performance.

Whether there is substantial performance is a question of degree to be determined by all of the facts, including the particular type of structure involved, its intended purpose, and the nature and relative expense of repairs.

[8] *Hammer Construction Corp. v Phillips,* 994 So2d 1135 (Fla App 2008).

For Example, a certain building contractor (BC) and a certain owner (O) made a contract to construct a home overlooking Vineyard Sound on Martha's Vineyard according to plans and specifications that clearly called for the use of General Plumbing Blue Star piping. The contract price was $1,100,000. Upon inspecting the work before making the final $400,000 payment and accepting the building, O discovered that BC had used Republic piping throughout the house. O explained to BC that his family had made its money by investing in General Plumbing, and he, therefore, would not make the final payment until the breach of contract was remedied. BC explained that Republic pipes were of the same industrial grade and quality as the Blue Star pipes. Moreover, BC estimated that it would cost nearly $300,000 to replace all of the pipes because of the destruction of walls and fixtures necessary to accomplish such a task. BC may sue O for $400,000 for breach of contract, claiming he had substantially performed the contract, and O may counterclaim for $300,000, seeking an offset for the cost of remedying the breach. The court will find in favor of the contractor and will not allow the $300,000 offset but will allow a "nominal" offset of perhaps $100 to $1,000 for the amount by which the Republic pipes diminished the value of the building. [9]

In most jurisdictions, the willfulness of the departure from the specifications of the contract does not by itself preclude some recovery for the contractor on the "cost of completion" basis but rather is a factor in consideration of whether there was substantial performance by the contractor.[10]

C A S E   S U M M A R Y

When Perfection is Not Required

FACTS: Beeson Company made a contract to construct a shopping center for Sartori. Before the work was fully completed, Sartori stopped making the payments to Beeson that the contract required. The contract provided for liquidated damages of $1,000 per day if Beeson failed to substantially complete the project within 300 days of the beginning of construction. The contract also provided for a bonus of $1,000 for each day Beeson completed the project ahead of schedule. Beeson then stopped working and sued Sartori for the balance due under the contract, just as though it had been fully performed. Sartori defended on the ground that Beeson had not substantially completed the work. Beeson proved that Sartori had been able to rent most of the stores in the center.

DECISION: The fact that the shopping center could be used for its intended purpose, that of renting stores to others, showed that there had been a substantial performance of the contract. The contractor therefore could recover the contract price less any amount required to complete the construction. [**J.M. Beeson Co. v Sartori, 553 So2d 180 (Fla App 1989)**]

[9] See *Jacob & Youngs, Inc. v Kent,* 230 NY 239 (1921).
[10] But see *USX Corp. v M. DeMatteo Construction Co.,* 315 F3d 43 (1st Cir 2002), for application of a common law rule that prohibits a construction contractor guilty of a willful breach of contract from maintaining any suit on the contract against the other party.

(B) FAULT OF COMPLAINING PARTY. A party cannot complain that a performance was defective when the performance follows the terms of the contract required by the complaining party. Thus, a homeowner who supplied the specifications for poured cement walls could not hold a contractor liable for damages when the walls that were poured in exact compliance with those specifications proved defective.

(C) PERFORMANCE TO THE SATISFACTION OF THE CONTRACTING PARTY OR A THIRD PARTY. Sometimes an agreement requires performance to the satisfaction, taste, or judgment of the other party to the contract. When the contract specifically stipulates that the performance must satisfy the contracting party, the courts will ordinarily enforce the plain meaning of the language of the parties and the work must satisfy the contracting party—subject, of course, to the requirement that dissatisfaction be made in good faith. **For Example,** the Perrones' written contract to purchase the Hills' residence contained a clause making performance subject to inspection to the Perrones' satisfaction. During the house inspection, the inspector found a piece of wood in a crawl space that appeared to have been damaged by termites and had possibly been treated some 18 years before with chlordane. At the end of the inspection Mr. Perrone indicated that he would perform on the contract. Thereafter, he went on the Internet and found that chlordane is a highly toxic pesticide now banned from use as a termite treatment. As a result, the Perrones rescinded the contract under the buyer satisfaction clause. The Hills sued, believing that speculation about a pesticide treatment 18 years ago was absurd. They contended that the Perrones had breached the contract without a valid reason. The court decided for the Perrones, since they exercised the "satisfaction clause" in good faith.[11] Good-faith personal satisfaction is generally required when the subject matter of the contract is personal, such as interior design work, tailoring, or the painting of a portrait.

With respect to things mechanical or routine performances, courts require that the performance be such as would satisfy a reasonable person under the circumstances.

When work is to be done subject to the approval of an architect, engineer, or another expert, most courts apply the reasonable person test of satisfaction.

C. DISCHARGE BY ACTION OF PARTIES

Contracts may be discharged by the joint action of both contracting parties or, in some cases, by the action of one party alone.

6. Discharge by Unilateral Action

Ordinarily, a contract cannot be discharged by the action of either party alone. In some cases, however, the contract gives one of either party the right to cancel the

---

[11] *Hill v Perrones,* 42 P3d 210 (Kan App 2002).

contract by unilateral action, such as by notice to the other party. Insurance policies covering loss commonly provide that the insurer may cancel the policy upon giving a specified number of days' notice.

(A) Consumer Protection Rescission. A basic principle of contract law is that once made, a contract between competent persons is a binding obligation. Consumer protection legislation introduces into the law a contrary concept—that of giving the consumer a chance to think things over and to rescind the contract. Thus, the federal Consumer Credit Protection Act (CCPA) gives the debtor the right to rescind a credit transaction within three business days when the transaction would impose a lien on the debtor's home. **For Example,** a homeowner who mortgages his or her home to obtain a loan may cancel the transaction for any reason by notifying the lender before midnight of the third full business day after the loan is made.[12]

A Federal Trade Commission regulation gives the buyer three business days in which to cancel a home-solicited sale of goods or services costing more than $25.[13]

7. Discharge by Agreement

A contract may be discharged by the operation of one of its provisions or by a subsequent agreement. Thus, there may be a discharge by (1) the terms of the original contract, such as a provision that the contract should end on a specified date; (2) a mutual cancellation, in which the parties agree to end their contract; (3) a mutual **rescission**, in which the parties agree to annul the contract and return both parties to their original positions before the contract had been made; (4) the **substitution** of a new contract between the same parties; (5) a novation or substitution of a new contract involving a new party;[14] (6) an **accord and satisfaction**; (7) a release; or (8) a **waiver**.

(A) Substitution. The parties may decide that their contract is not the one they want. They may then replace it with another contract. If they do, the original contract is discharged by substitution.[15]

(B) Accord and Satisfaction. When the parties have differing views as to the performance required by the terms of a contract, they may agree to a different performance. Such an agreement is called an *accord*. When the accord is performed or executed, there is an accord and satisfaction, which discharges the original obligation. To constitute an accord and satisfaction, there must be a bona fide dispute, a proposal to settle the dispute, and performance of the agreement.

rescission–action of one party to a contract to set the contract aside when the other party is guilty of a breach of the contract.

substitution–substitution of a new contract between the same parties.

accord and satisfaction–agreement to substitute for an existing debt some alternative form of discharging that debt, coupled with the actual discharge of the debt by the substituted performance.

waiver–release or relinquishment of a known right or objection.

---

[12] If the owner is not informed of this right to cancel, the three-day period does not begin until that information is given. Consumer Credit Protection Act § 125, 15 USC § 1635(a), (e), (f).

[13] CFR § 429.1. This displaces state laws making similar provisions for rescission, such as UCCC § 2.502.

[14] *Eagle Industries, Inc. v Thompson,* 900 P2d 475 (Or 1995). In a few jurisdictions, the term *novation* is used to embrace the substitution of any new contract, whether between the original parties or not.

[15] *Shawnee Hospital Authority v Dow Construction, Inc.,* 812 P2d 1351 (Okla 1990).

FACTS: In September 2002, La Crosse Litho Supply, LLC (La Crosse) entered into a distribution agreement with MKL Pre-Press Electronics (MKL) for the distribution of a printing system. La Crosse purchased a 7000 System unit from MKL for its end user Printing Plus. MKL technicians were to provide service and training for the unit. The 7000 System at Printing Plus failed on three occasions, and ultimately repairs were unsuccessful. On September 30, 2003, La Crosse cancelled the distribution agreement. On October 2, 2003, La Crosse sent a letter to MKL's sales vice president Bill Landwer setting forth an itemized accounting of what it owed MKL Pre-Press with deductions for the purchase price of the failed 7000 System and other offsets. MKL sent a subsequent bill for repairs and services, to which La Crosse objected and stated that it would not pay. MKL's attorney sent a demand letter for $26,453.31. La Crosse's president, Randall Peters, responded by letter dated December 30, 2003, explaining that with an offset for training and warranty work it had performed, "we are sending you the final payment in the amount of $1,696.47." He added, "[w]ith this correspondence, we consider all open issues between La Crosse Litho Supply and MKL Pre-Press closed." Enclosed with the letter was a check for $1,696.47 payable to MKL Pre-Press. In the remittance portion of the check, under the heading "Ref," was typed "FINAL PAYM." The check was endorsed and deposited on either January 26 or 27, 2004. MKL sued La Crosse for $24,756.84. La Crosse defended that the tender and subsequent deposit of the check for $1,696.47 constituted an accord and satisfaction. Jill Fleming, MKL's office manager, stated that it was her duty to process checks and that she did not read Peters' letter. From a judgment for La Crosse, MKL appealed.

DECISION: Judgment for La Crosse. There was an honest dispute as to the amount owed, as evident from the exchange of letters. La Crosse tendered an amount with the explicit understanding that it was the "final payment" of all demands, and the creditor MKL's acceptance and negotiation of a check for that amount constitutes an accord and satisfaction. Ms. Fleming had the authority to endorse checks and deposit them, and her doing so can and should be imputed to her employer, thereby constituting an accord and satisfaction. [**MKL Pre-Press Electronics v La Crosse Litho Supply, LLC, 840 NE2d 687 (Ill App 2005)**]

D. DISCHARGE BY EXTERNAL CAUSES

Circumstances beyond the control of the contracting parties may discharge the contract.

8. Discharge by Impossibility

To establish impossibility a party must show (1) the unexpected occurrence of an intervening act; (2) that the risk of the unexpected occurrence was not allocated by agreement or custom; and (3) that the occurrence made performance impossible. The doctrine of impossibility relieves nonperformance only in extreme circumstances.[16] The party asserting the defense of impossibility bears the burden of proving "a real impossibility and not a mere inconvenience or unexpected difficulty."[17] Moreover, courts will generally only excuse nonperformance where

---

[16] *Island Development Corp. v District of Columbia*, 933 A2d 340, 350 (DC 2007).
[17] *Bergmann v Parker*, 216 A2d 581 (DC 1966).

performance is objectively impossible—that is, incapable performance by anyone. Financial inability to perform a contract that a party voluntarily entered into will rarely, if ever, excuse nonperformance. **For Example,** Ms. Robinson was employed by East Capital Community Development Group under a written employment contract for one year, but was terminated early for lack of funding. The contract did not reference that her continued employment was contingent on continued grant funding. The contract was objectively capable of performance. The defense of impossibility was rejected by the court.[18]

(A) Destruction of Particular Subject Matter. When parties contract expressly for, or with reference to, a particular subject matter, the contract is discharged if the subject matter is destroyed through no fault of either party. When a contract calls for the sale of a wheat crop growing on a specific parcel of land, the contract is discharged if that crop is destroyed by blight.

On the other hand, if there is merely a contract to sell a given quantity of a specified grade of wheat, the seller is not discharged when the seller's crop is destroyed by blight. The seller had made an unqualified undertaking to deliver wheat of a specified grade. No restrictions or qualifications were imposed as to the source. If the seller does not deliver the goods called for by the contract, the contract is broken, and the seller is liable for damages.

(B) Change of Law. A contract is discharged when its performance is made illegal by a subsequent change in the law. Thus, a contract to construct a nonfireproof building at a particular place is discharged by the adoption of a zoning law prohibiting such a building within that area. Mere inconvenience or temporary delay caused by the new law, however, does not excuse performance.

(C) Death or Disability. When the contract obligates a party to render or receive personal services requiring peculiar skill, the death, incapacity, or illness of the party that was either to render or receive the personal services excuses both sides from a duty to perform. It is sometimes said that "the death of either party is the death of the contract."

The rule does not apply, however, when the acts called for by the contract are of such a character that (1) the acts may be as well performed by others, such as the promisor's personal representatives, or (2) the contract's terms contemplate continuance of the obligations after the death of one of the parties. **For Example,** Lynn Jones was under contract to investor Ed Jenkins to operate certain Subway sandwich shops and to acquire new franchises with funding provided by Jenkins. After Jenkins's death, Jones claimed he was no longer bound under the contract and was free to pursue franchise opportunities on his own. The contract between Jones and Jenkins expressed that it was binding on the parties' "heirs and assigns" and that the contract embodied property rights that passed to Jenkins's widow. The agreement's provisions thus established that the agreement survived the death of Jenkins, and Jones was therefore obligated to remit profits from the franchise he acquired for himself after Jenkins's death.[19]

(D) Act of Other Party. Every contract contains "an implied covenant of good faith and fair dealing." As a result of this covenant, a promisee is under an obligation to

[18] *East Capital View Community Development Corp. v Robinson*, 941 A2d 1036 (DC 2008).
[19] *Jenkins Subway, Inc. v Jones*, 990 SW2d 713 (Tenn App 1998).

do nothing that would interfere with the promisor's performance. When the promisee prevents performance or otherwise makes performance impossible, the promisor is discharged from the contract. Thus, a subcontractor is discharged from any obligation when it is unable to do the work because the principal contractor refuses to deliver the material, equipment, or money required by the subcontract. When the default of the other party consists of failing to supply goods or services, the duty may rest on the party claiming a discharge of the contract to show that substitute goods or services could not be obtained elsewhere.

9. Developing Doctrines

Commercial impracticability and frustration of purpose may excuse performance.

(A) COMMERCIAL IMPRACTICABILITY. The doctrine of *commercial impracticability* was developed to deal with the harsh rule that a party must perform its contracts unless it is absolutely impossible. However, not every type of impracticability is an excuse for nonperformance. **For Example,** I. Patel was bound by his franchise agreement with Days Inn, Inc., to maintain his 60- room inn on old Route 66 in Lincoln, Illinois, to at least minimum quality assurance standards. His inn failed five consecutive quality inspections over two years, with the inspector noting damaged guest rooms, burns in the bedding, and severely stained carpets. Patel's defense when his franchise was cancelled after the fifth failed inspection was that bridge repairs on the road leading from I-55 to his inn had adversely affected his business and made it commercially impractical to live up to the franchise agreement. The court rejected his defense, determining that while the bridge work might have affected patronage, it had no effect on his duty to comply with the quality assurance standards of his franchise a greement.[20] Commercial impracticability is available only when the performance is made impractical by the subsequent occurrence of an event whose nonoccurrence was a basic assumption on which the contract was made.[21]

C A S E   S U M M A R Y

A Bolt Out of the Blue

FACTS: CIT, a major equipment leasing company, entered into a sale/leaseback contract with Condere Tire Corporation for 11 tire presses at Condere's tire plant in Natchez, Mississippi. Condere ceased making payments on these presses owned by CIT, and Condere filed for Chapter 11 bankruptcy. CIT thereafter contracted to sell the presses to Specialty Tires, Inc., for $250,000. When the contract was made, CIT, Condere, and Specialty Tires believed that CIT was the owner of the presses and was entitled to immediate possession. When CIT attempted to gain access to the presses to have them shipped, Condere changed its position and refused to allow the equipment to be removed from the plant. When the presses were not delivered, Specialty sued CIT for damages for nondelivery of the presses to date, and CIT asserted the defense of impracticability.

---

[20] *Days Inn of America, Inc. v Patel*, 88 F Supp 2d 928 (CD Ill 2000).
[21] See Restatement (Second) of Contracts § 261; UCC § 2-615.

DECISION: Summary judgment for CIT. The delivery of the presses to Specialty Tires Company was made impracticable by the actions of Condere in refusing to give up the presses. Condere's change of its position and refusal to give up the presses was "a bolt out of the blue" for both CIT and Specialty. It was not a risk that CIT should have expected to either bear or contract against. CIT is excused by the doctrine of impracticability from damages for nondelivery of the presses to date. The impracticability relieves the obligation for only so long as the impracticability lasts. CIT asserts it will perform when it receives possession of the presses. **[Specialty Tires, Inc. v CIT, 82 F Supp 2d 434 (WD Pa 2000)]**

If a subsequent event occurs involving a severe shortage of raw materials or supplies that results in a marked increase in the cost of the materials or supplies and this event was foreseeable, the defense of commercial impracticability is not available.

(B) FRUSTRATION OF PURPOSE DOCTRINE. Because of a change in circumstances, the purpose of the contract may have no value to the party entitled to receive performance. In such a case, performance may be excused if both parties were aware of the purpose and the event that frustrated the purpose was unforeseeable.[22]

For Example, National Southern Bank rents a home near Willowbend Country Club on the southeastern shore of North Carolina for $75,000 a week to entertain business guests at the Ryder Cup matches scheduled for the week in question. Storm damage from Hurricane David the week before the event caused the closing of the course and the transfer of the tournament to another venue in a different state. The bank's duty to pay for the house may be excused by the doctrine of *frustration of purpose,* because the transfer of the tournament fully destroyed the value of the home rental, both parties were aware of the purpose of the rental, and the cancellation of the golf tournament was unforeseeable.

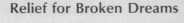

C A S E   S U M M A R Y

Relief for Broken Dreams

FACTS: John J. Paonessa Company made a contract with the state of Massachusetts to reconstruct a portion of highway. Paonessa then made a contract with Chase Precast Corporation to obtain concrete median barriers for use in the highway. Thereafter, the state highway department decided that such barriers would not be used. Paonessa therefore had no reason to go through with the contract to purchase the barriers from Chase because it could not

[22] The defense of frustration of purpose, or commercial frustration, is very difficult to invoke because the courts are extremely reluctant to allow parties to avoid obligations to which they have agreed. See *Wal-Mart Stores, Inc. v AIG Life Insurance Co., 872 A2d 611 (Del Ch 2005),* denying application of the commercial frustration doctrine when the supervening event, the invalidation of hundreds of millions in tax deductions by the IRS, was reasonably foreseeable and could have been provided for in the contract.

C A S E   S U M M A R Y

Continued

use them and could not get paid for them by the state. Chase sued Paonessa for the profit Chase would have made on the contract for the barriers.

DECISION: Judgment for Paonessa. The change to the highway construction plan made by the State Department of Highways made the barriers worthless. There was accordingly a frustration of the purpose for which the contract had been made to purchase the barriers. Therefore, the contract for the median barriers was discharged by such frustration of purpose and did not bind Paonessa. [**Chase Precast Corp. v John J. Paonessa Co., Inc. 566 NE2d 603 (Mass 1991)**]

(c) **COMPARISON TO COMMON LAW RULE.** The traditional common law rule refuses to recognize commercial impracticability or frustration of purpose. By the common law rule, the losses and disappointments against which commercial impracticability and frustration of purpose give protection are merely the risks that one takes in entering into a contract. Moreover, the situations could have been guarded against by including an appropriate condition subsequent in the contract. A condition subsequent declares that the contract will be void if a specified event occurs.[23] The contract also could have provided for a readjustment of compensation if there was a basic change of circumstances. The common law approach also rejects these developing concepts because they weaken the stability of a contract.

An indication of a wider recognition of the concept that "extreme" changes of circumstances can discharge a contract is found in the Uniform Commercial Code. The UCC provides for the discharge of a contract for the sale of goods when a condition that the parties assumed existed, or would continue, ceases to exist.[24]

(d) **FORCE MAJEURE.** To avoid litigation over impossibility and impractability issues, modern contracting parties often contract around the doctrine of impossibility, specifying the failures that will excuse performance in their contracts. The clauses in which they do this are called *force majeure*—uncontrollable event—clauses. And they are enforced by courts as written.

C A S E   S U M M A R Y

WEPCO Was Not Railroaded, It Was *Force Majeured!*

FACTS: WEPCO, an electric utility, sued the Union Pacific Railroad Co. alleging that the railroad breached the *force majeure* provision of the parties' long-term coal-hauling contract, which ran from 1999 to 2005. The provision at issue provides that if the railroad is prevented by "an event of Force Majeure" from reloading its empty cars (after it has delivered coal to WEPCO) with iron ore destined for Geneva, Utah, it can charge the higher

---

[23] *Wermer v ABI,* 10 SW3d 575 (Mo App 2000).
[24] UCC § 2-615.

Continued

C A S E   S U M M A R Y

rate that the contract makes applicable to shipments that do not involve backhauling. The rate for coal shipped from one of the Colorado coal mines to WEPCO was specified as $13.20 per ton if there was a backhaul shipment but $15.63 if there was not. The iron ore that the railroad's freight trains would have picked up in Minnesota was intended for a steel mill in Utah. The steel company was bankrupt when the parties signed the contract. In November 2001 the steel mill shut down, and closed for good in February 2004. Two months later the railroad wrote WEPCO to declare "an event of Force Majeure" and that henceforth it would be charging WEPCO the higher rate applicable to shipments without a backhaul. WEPCO sued the railroad for breach of the force majeure provision in the contract.

DECISION: Judgment for the railroad. The provision dealt with the foreseeable situation of the steel mill shutdown and the possibility of hauling back to the mine empty coal cars, thereby generating no revenue. The contract clause is enforced as written. [**Wisconsin Electric Power Co. v Union Pacific Railroad Co., 557 F3d 504 (7th Cir 2009)**]

10. Temporary Impossibility

Ordinarily, a temporary impossibility suspends the duty to perform. If the obligation to perform is suspended, it is revived on the termination of the impossibility. If, however, performance at that later date would impose a substantially greater burden on the party obligated to perform, some courts discharge the obligor from the contract.

After the September 11, 2001, terrorist attack on the World Trade Center, New York City courts followed wartime precedents that had developed the law of temporary impossibility. Such impossibility, when of brief duration, excuses performance until it subsequently becomes possible to perform rather than excusing performance altogether. Thus, an individual who was unable to communicate her cancellation of travel 60 days prior to her scheduled travel as required by her contract, which needed to occur on or before September 14, 2001, could expect relief from a cancellation penalty provision in the contract based on credible testimony of attempted phone calls to the travel agent on and after September 12, 2001, even though the calls did not get through due to communication problems in New York City.[25]

(A) **WEATHER.** Acts of God, such as tornadoes, lightning, and floods, usually do not terminate a contract even though they make performance difficult. Thus, weather conditions constitute a risk that is assumed by a contracting party in the absence of a contrary agreement. Consequently, extra expense sustained by a contractor because of weather conditions is a risk that the contractor assumes in the absence of an express provision for additional compensation in such a case. **For Example,** Danielo Contractors made a contract to construct a shopping mall for the Rubicon Center, with construction to begin November 1. Because of abnormal cold and blizzard

[25] See *Bugh v Protravel International, Inc.,* 746 NYS2d 290 (Civ Ct NYC 2002).

conditions, Danielo was not able to begin work until April 1 and was five months late in completing the construction of the project. Rubicon sued Danielo for breach of contract by failing to perform on schedule. Danielo is liable. Because the contract included no provision covering delay caused by weather, Danielo bore the risk of the delay and resulting loss.

Modern contracts commonly contain a "weather clause" and reflect the parties' agreement on this matter. When the parties take the time to discuss weather issues, purchasing insurance coverage is a common resolution.

11. Discharge by Operation of Law

operation of law—attaching of certain consequences to certain facts because of legal principles that operate automatically as contrasted with consequences that arise because of the voluntary action of a party designed to create those consequences.

A contract is discharged by **operation of law** by (1) an alteration or a material change made by a party, (2) the destruction of the written contract with intent to discharge it, (3) bankruptcy, (4) the operation of a statute of limitations, or (5) a contractual limitation.

(A) **BANKRUPTCY.** As set forth in the chapter on bankruptcy, even though all creditors have not been paid in full, a discharge in **bankruptcy** eliminates ordinary contract claims against the debtor.

CPA

bankruptcy—procedure by which one unable to pay debts may surrender all assets in excess of any exemption claim to the court for administration and distribution to creditors, and the debtor is given a discharge that releases him from the unpaid balance due on most debts.

(B) **STATUTE OF LIMITATIONS.** A **statute of limitations** provides that after a certain number of years have passed, a contract claim is barred. The time limitation provided by state statutes of limitations varies widely. The time period for bringing actions for breach of an oral contract is two to three years. The period may differ with the type of contract—ranging from a relatively short time for open accounts (ordinary customers' charge accounts) to four years for sales of goods.[26] A somewhat longer period exists for bringing actions for breach of written contracts (usually four to ten years). **For Example,** Prate Installations, Inc., sued homeowners Richard and Rebecca Thomas for failure to pay for a new roof installed by Prate. Prate had sent numerous invoices to the Thomases over a four-year period seeking payment to no avail. The Thomases moved to dismiss the case under a four-year limitation period. However, the court concluded that the state's ten-year limitations period on written contracts applied. [27] The maximum period for judgments of record is usually 10 to 20 years.

statute of limitations—statute that restricts the period of time within which an action may be brought.

(C) **CONTRACTUAL LIMITATIONS.** Some contracts, particularly insurance contracts, contain a time limitation within which suit must be brought. This is in effect a private statute of limitations created by the agreement of the parties.

A contract may also require that notice of any claim be given within a specified time. A party who fails to give notice within the time specified by the contract is barred from suing on the contract.

A contract provision requiring that suit be brought within one year does not violate public policy, although the statute of limitations would allow two years in the absence of such a contract limitation.[28]

---

[26] UCC § 2-725(1).
[27] *Prate Installations, Inc. v Thomas*, 842 NE2d 1205 (Ill App 2006).
[28] *Keiting v Skauge*, 543 NW2d 565 (Wis App 1995).

lawflix

Uncle Buck (1989) (PG-13)

John Candy plays ne'er-do-well Uncle Buck who promises to go to work at his girlfriend's tire store and marry her. When his brother calls in the middle of the night seeking help with his children, Buck tells his girlfriend (Chenise) that he can no longer honor his promise because he must go to the suburbs to care for his brother's children while his brother and sister-in-law travel to Indiana to be with his sister-in-law's very ill father.

Discuss Buck's excuse. Is it impossibility? Does the change in circumstances excuse Buck?

Check out LawFlix at **www.cengage.com/blaw/dvl** to access movie clips that illustrate business law concepts.

MAKE THE CONNECTION

SUMMARY

A party's duty to perform under a contract can be affected by a condition precedent, which must occur before a party has an obligation to perform; a condition subsequent, that is, a condition or event that relieves the duty to thereafter perform; and concurrent conditions, which require mutual and often simultaneous performance.

Most contracts are discharged by performance. An offer to perform is called a *tender of performance*. If a tender of performance is wrongfully refused, the duty of the tenderer to perform is terminated. When the performance called for by the contract is the payment of money, it must be legal tender that is offered. In actual practice, it is common to pay and to accept payment by checks or other commercial paper.

When the debtor owes the creditor on several accounts and makes a payment, the debtor may specify which account is to be credited with the payment. If the debtor fails to specify, the creditor may choose which account to credit.

When a contract does not state when it is to be performed, it must be performed within a reasonable time. If time for performance is stated in the contract, the contract must be performed at the time specified if such time is essential (is of the essence). Ordinarily, a contract must be performed exactly in the manner specified by the contract. A less-than-perfect performance is allowed if it is a substantial performance and if damages are allowed the other party.

A contract cannot be discharged by unilateral action unless authorized by the contract itself or by statute, as in the case of consumer protection rescission.

Because a contract arises from an agreement, it may also be terminated by an agreement. A contract may also be discharged by the substitution of a new contract for the original contract; by a novation, or making a new contract with a new party; by accord and satisfaction; by release; or by waiver.

A contract is discharged when it is impossible to perform. Impossibility may result from the destruction of the subject matter of the contract, the adoption of a new law that prohibits performance, the death or disability of a party whose personal action was required for performance of the contract, or the act of the other party to the contract. Some courts will also hold that a contract is discharged when its performance is commercially impracticable or there is frustration of purpose. Temporary impossibility, such as a labor strike or bad weather, has no effect on a contract. It is common, though, to include protective clauses that excuse delay caused by temporary impossibility.

A contract may be discharged by operation of law. This occurs when (1) the liability arising from the contract is discharged by bankruptcy, (2) suit on the contract is barred by the applicable statute of limitations, or (3) a time limitation stated in the contract is exceeded.

LEARNING OUTCOMES

After studying this chapter, you should be able to clearly explain:

A. CONDITIONS RELATING TO PERFORMANCE

LO.1 List the three types of conditions that affect a party's duty to perform
See the "pay-if-paid" condition-precedent example on p. 411.
See the TV anchor's "failed urinalysis test" condition-subsequent example on p. 412.

B. DISCHARGE BY PERFORMANCE

LO.2 Explain the on-time performance rule
See the "mailed payment" example on p. 414.
See the "time is of the essence" example on p. 415.

C. DISCHARGE BY ACTION OF PARTIES

LO.3 Explain four ways a contract can be discharged by agreement of the parties
See the text discussion on recession, cancellation, substitution, and novation on p. 419.

D. DISCHARGE BY EXTERNAL CAUSES

LO.4 State the effect on a contract of the death or disability of one of the contracting parties
See the Subway Sandwich Shops example on p. 421.

LO.5 Explain when impossibility or impracticability may discharge a contract
See the *Specialty Tire* impracticability case on p. 422.
See the Ryder Cup frustration-of-purpose example on p. 423.

KEY TERMS

accord and satisfaction	operation of law	tender
bankruptcy	rescission	waiver
condition precedent	statute of limitations	
condition subsequent	substantial performance	
condition	substitution	

QUESTIONS AND CASE PROBLEMS

1. McMullen Contractors made a contract with Richardson to build an apartment house for a specific price. A number of serious apartment house fires broke out in the city, and the city council adopted an ordinance increasing the fire precautions that had to be taken in the construction of a new building. Compliance with these new requirements would make the construction of the apartment house for Richardson more expensive than McMullen had originally contemplated. Is McMullen discharged from the contract to build the apartment house?

2. Lymon Mitchell operated a Badcock Home Furnishings dealership, under which as dealer he was paid a commission on sales and Badcock retained title to merchandise on display. Mitchell sold his dealership to another and to facilitate the sale, Badcock prepared a summary of commissions owed with certain itemized offsets it claimed that Mitchell owed Badcock. Mitchell disagreed with the calculations, but he accepted them and signed the transfer documents closing the sale on the basis of the terms set forth in the summary and was paid accordingly. After pondering the offsets taken by Badcock and verifying the correctness of his position, he brought suit for the additional funds owed. What defense would you expect Badcock to raise? How would you decide the case? Explain fully. [*Mitchell v Badcock Corp.,* 496 SE2d 502 (Ga App)]

3. American Bank loaned Koplik $50,000 to buy equipment for a restaurant about to be opened by Casual Citchen Corp. The loan was not repaid, and Fast Foods, Inc., bought out the interest of Casual Citchen. As part of the transaction, Fast Foods agreed to pay the debt owed to American Bank, and the parties agreed to a new schedule of payments to be made by Fast Foods. Fast Foods did not make the payments, and American Bank sued Koplik. He contended that his obligation to repay $50,000 had been discharged by the execution of the agreement providing for the payment of the debt by Fast Foods. Was this defense valid? [*American Bank & Trust Co. v Koplik,* 451 NYS2d 426 (App Div)]

4. Metalcrafters made a contract to design a new earth-moving vehicle for Lamar Highway Construction Co. Metalcrafters was depending on the genius of Samet, the head of its research department, to design a new product. Shortly after the contract was made between Metalcrafters and Lamar, Samet was killed in an automobile accident. Metalcrafters was not able to design the product without Samet. Lamar sued Metalcrafters for damages for breach of the contract. Metalcrafters claimed that the contract was discharged by Samet's death. Is it correct?

5. The Tinchers signed a contract to sell land to Creasy. The contract specified that the sales transaction was to be completed in 90 days. At the end of the 90 days, Creasy requested an extension of time. The Tinchers refused to grant an extension and stated that the contract was terminated. Creasy claimed that the 90-day clause was not binding because the contract did not state that time was of the essence. Was the contract terminated? [*Creasy v Tincher,* 173 SE2d 332 (W Va)]

6. Christopher Bloom received a medical school scholarship created by the U.S. Department of Health and Human Services to increase the number of doctors serving rural areas. In return for this assistance, Bloom agreed to practice four years in a region identified as being underserved by medical professionals. After some problem with his postgraduation assignment, Bloom requested a repayment schedule from the agency. Although no terms were offered, Bloom tendered to the agency two checks totaling $15,500 and marked "Final Payment." Neither check was cashed, and the government sued Bloom for $480,000, the value of the assistance provided. Bloom claimed that by tendering the checks to the agency, his liability had been discharged by an accord and satisfaction. Decide. [*United States v Bloom,* 112 F3d 200 (7th Cir)]

7. Dickson contracted to build a house for Moran. When it was approximately 25 percent to 40 percent completed, Moran would not let Dickson work any more because he was not following the building plans and specifications and there were many defects. Moran hired another contractor to correct the defects and finish the building. Dickson sued Moran for breach of contract, claiming that he had substantially performed the contract up to the point where he had been discharged. Was Dickson correct? [*Dickson v Moran,* 344 So2d 102 (La App)]

8. A lessor leased a trailer park to a tenant. At the time, sewage was disposed of by a septic tank system that was not connected with the public sewage system. The tenant knew this, and the lease declared that the tenant had examined the premises and that the landlord made no representation or guarantee as to the condition of the premises. Some time thereafter, the septic tank system stopped working properly, and the county health department notified the tenant that he was required to connect the septic tank system with the public sewage system or else the department would close the trailer park. The tenant did not want to pay the additional cost involved in connecting with the public system. The tenant claimed that he was released from the lease and was entitled to a refund of the deposit that he had made. Was he correct? [*Glen R. Sewell Street Metal v Loverde,* 451 P2d 721 (Cal App)]

9. Oneal was a teacher employed by the Colton Consolidated School District. Because of a diabetic condition, his eyesight deteriorated so much that he offered to resign if he would be given pay for a specified number of "sick leave" days. The school district refused to do this and discharged Oneal for nonperformance of his contract. He appealed to remove the discharge from his record. Decide. What ethical values are involved? [*Oneal v Colton Consolidated School District,* 557 P2d 11 (Wash App)]

10. Northwest Construction, Inc., made a contract with the state of Washington for highway construction. Part of the work was turned over under a subcontract to

Yakima Asphalt Paving Co. The contract required that any claim be asserted within 180 days. Yakima brought an action for damages after the expiration of 180 days. The defense was that the claim was too late. Yakima replied that the action was brought within the time allowed by the statute of limitations and that the contractual limitation of 180 days was therefore not binding. Was Yakima correct?

11. The Metropolitan Park District of Tacoma gave Griffith a concession to run the district's parks. The agreement gave the right to occupy the parks and use any improvements found therein. The district later wished to set this agreement aside because it was not making sufficient money from the transaction. While it was seeking to set the agreement aside, a boathouse and a gift shop in one of the parks were destroyed by fire. The district then claimed that the concession contract with Griffith was discharged by impossibility of performance. Was it correct? [*Metropolitan Park District of Tacoma v Griffith,* 723 P2d 1093 (Wash)]

12. Suburban Power Piping Corp., under contract to construct a building for LTV Steel Corp., made a subcontract with Power & Pollution Services, Inc., to do some of the work. The subcontract provided that the subcontractor would be paid when the owner (LTV) paid the contractor. LTV went into bankruptcy before making the full payment to the contractor, who then refused to pay the subcontractor on the ground that the "pay-when-paid" provision of the subcontract made payment by the owner a condition precedent to the obligation of the contractor to pay the subcontractor. Was the contractor correct? [*Power & Pollution Services, Inc. v Suburban Power Piping Corp.,* 598 NE2d 69 (Ohio App)]

13. Ellen borrowed money from Farmers' Bank. As evidence of the loan, she signed a promissory note by which she promised to pay to the bank in installments the amount of the loan together with interest and administrative costs. She was unable to make the payments on the scheduled dates. She and the bank then executed a new agreement that gave her a longer period of time for making the payments. However, after two months, she was unable to pay on this new schedule. The bank then brought suit against her under the terms of the original agreement. She raised the defense that the original agreement had been discharged by the execution of the second agreement and could not be sued on. Decide.

14. Acme Hydraulic Press Co. manufactured large presses and sold them throughout the United States. The agreement-of-sale contract that Acme executed with its customers specified that they could make no claim for breach of contract unless notice of the breach was given within 10 days after the delivery of a press in question to the buyer and that no lawsuit could thereafter be brought if notice had not been given. Was this time limitation valid?

15. New Beginnings provides rehabilitation services for alcohol and drug abuse to both adults and adolescents. New Beginnings entered into negotiation with Adbar for the lease of a building in the city of St. Louis, and subsequently entered into a three-year lease. The total rent due for the three-year term was $273,000. After the lease was executed, the city denied an occupancy permit because Alderman Bosley and residents testified at a hearing in vigorous opposition to the presence

of New Beginnings in the neighborhood. A court ordered the permit issued. Alderman Bosley thereafter contacted the chair of the state's appointment committee and asked her to pull the agency's funding. He received no commitment from her on this matter. After a meeting with the state director of Alcohol and Drug Abuse where it was asserted that the director said the funding would be pulled if New Beginnings moved into the Adbar location, New Beginnings's board decided not to occupy the building. Adbar brought suit for breach of the lease, and New Beginnings asserted it was excused from performance because of commercial impracticability and frustration of purpose. Do you believe the doctrine of commercial impracticability should be limited in its application so as to preserve the certainty of contracts? What rule of law applies to this case? Decide. [*Adbar v New Beginnings,* 103 SW2d 799 (Mo App)]

CPA QUESTIONS

1. Parc hired Glaze to remodel and furnish an office suite. Glaze submitted plans that Parc approved. After completing all the necessary construction and painting, Glaze purchased minor accessories that Parc rejected because they did not conform to the plans. Parc refused to allow Glaze to complete the project and refused to pay Glaze any part of the contract price. Glaze sued for the value of the work performed. Which of the following statements is correct?

   a. Glaze will lose because Glaze breached the contract by not completing performance.

   b. Glaze will win because Glaze substantially performed and Parc prevented complete performance.

   c. Glaze will lose because Glaze materially breached the contract by buying the accessories.

   d. Glaze will win because Parc committed anticipatory breach.

2. Ordinarily, in an action for breach of a construction contract, the statute of limitations time period would be computed from the date the contract is:

   a. Negotiated

   b. Breached

   c. Begun

   d. Signed

3. Which of the following will release all original parties to a contract but will maintain a contractual relationship?

	Novation	Substituted contract
a.	Yes	Yes
b.	Yes	No
c.	No	Yes
d.	No	No

Chapter 20

BREACH OF CONTRACT AND REMEDIES

W hat can be done when a contract is broken?

A. WHAT CONSTITUTES A BREACH OF CONTRACT?

The question of remedies does not become important until it is first determined that a contract has been violated or breached.

1. Definition of Breach

breach–failure to act or perform in the manner called for in a contract.

A **breach** is the failure to act or perform in the manner called for by the contract. When the contract calls for performance, such as painting an owner's home, the failure to paint or to paint properly is a *breach of contract*. If the contract calls for a creditor's forbearance, the creditor's action in bringing a lawsuit is a breach of the contract.

2. Anticipatory Breach

When the contract calls for performance, a party may make it clear before the time for performance arrives that the contract will not be performed. This is referred to as an **anticipatory breach**.

anticipatory breach– promisor's repudiation of the contract prior to the time that performance is required when such repudiation is accepted by the promisee as a breach of the contract.

(A) ANTICIPATORY REPUDIATION. When a party expressly declares that performance will not be made when required, this declaration is called an **anticipatory repudiation** of the contract. To constitute such a repudiation, there must be a clear, absolute, unequivocal refusal to perform the contract according to its terms.

anticipatory repudiation– repudiation made in advance of the time for performance of the contract obligations.

For Example, Procter & Gamble (P&G) sought payment on four letters of credit issued by a Serbian bank, Investbanka. P&G presented two letters by June 8, prior to their expiration dates, with the necessary documentation for payment to Beogradska Bank New York, Investbanka's New York agent. A June 11 letter from Beogradska Bank broadly and unequivocally stated that the bank would not pay the letters of credit. Two additional letters of credit totaling $20,000 issued by Investbanka that expired by June 30 were not thereafter submitted to the New York agent bank by P&G. However, a court found that the bank had anticipatorily breached its obligations under those letters of credit by its broad renouncements in the June 11 letter, and judgments were rendered in favor of P&G.[1]

C A S E   S U M M A R Y

Splitting Tips—Contract Price Less Cost of Completion

FACTS: Hartland Developers, Inc., agreed to build an airplane hangar for Robert Tips of San Antonio for $300,000, payable in three installments of $100,000, with the final payment due upon the completion of the building and the issuance of a certificate of completion by the engineer representing Tips. The evidence shows

---

[1] *Procter & Gamble v Investbanka*, 2000 WL 520630 (SDNY 2000).

C A S E   S U M M A R Y

Continued

that Tips's representative, Mr. Lavelle, instructed Hartland to cease work on the building because Tips could no longer afford to make payments. Hartland ceased work as instructed before the final completion of the building, having been paid $200,000 at the time. He sued Tips for breach of contract. On May 6, 1996, the trial court allowed Hartland the amount owing on the contract, $100,000, less the cost of completing the building according to the contract, $65,000, plus attorney fees and prejudgment interest. Tips appealed, pointing out, among other assertions, that he was required to spend $23,000 to provide electrical outlets for the hangar, which were contemplated in the contract.

DECISION: Judgment for Tips, subject to offsets. The trial judge based his damages assessment on anticipatory repudiation of contract. The evidence that Tips's representative, Lavelle, instructed Hartland to cease work on the project because Tips no longer could afford to make payments was sufficient to support this finding. However, Tips is entitled to an offset for electrical connections of $23,000 under a breach of contract theory. [**Tips v Hartland Developers, Inc., 961 SW2d 618 (Tex App 1998)**]

A refusal to perform a contract that is made before performance is required unless the other party to the contract does an act or makes a concession that is not required by the contract, is an anticipatory repudiation of the contract.[2]

sports&entertainment law

Get It While You Can?

In 2000, the cast of *Friends*, one of the hottest shows on television, demanded a pay increase. The demand was made with a valid contract in place and near the time NBC was to announce its fall lineup. The six stars demanded $1,000,000 each per episode. NBC settled for $750,000 per star, up from the stars' $150,000 per episode figure renegotiated in 1998.

When stars seek to renegotiate contracts before their expiration, the network can replace them if they fail to live up to their contracts, and it can enforce the standard contractual clause, which prohibits them from doing other television work until the expiration of their contracts. Recasting six stars for a highly successful show would not be feasible. To offset the stars' bargaining power, NBC prepared a television promotion that would relabel the last show for that season as the "series finale" and announce "See how it all ends on *Friends*." The cast were informed of NBC's threat to end the series in this manner. Renegotiations quickly ensued and led to the $750,000 agreement. Two years later the six stars obtained their goal of $1 million per episode paychecks. Was it ethical for the stars to threaten to strike just before the fall lineup announcements? When Jay Leno was asked about the tactics of the *Friends* stars, he responded, "You have to get what you can while you can in this business." Is Mr. Leno right? Is such an attitude ethical? When the new agreement was reached, was there a mutual rescission of the existing contract and the substitution of a new contract, or did the new contract fail for lack of consideration?

[2] *Chamberlain v Puckett Construction*, 921 P2d 1237 (Mont 1996).

A party making an anticipatory repudiation may retract or take back the repudiation if the other party has not changed position in reliance on the repudiation. However, if the other party has changed position, the party making the anticipatory repudiation cannot retract it. **For Example,** if a buyer makes another purchase when the seller declares that the seller will not perform the contract, the buyer has acted in reliance on the seller's repudiation. The seller will therefore not be allowed to retract the repudiation.

(B) **ANTICIPATORY REPUDIATION BY CONDUCT.** The anticipatory repudiation may be expressed by conduct that makes it impossible for the repudiating party to perform subsequently. To illustrate, there is a repudiation by conduct if a farmer makes a contract to sell an identified quantity of potatoes nearly equivalent to his entire crop and then sells and delivers them to another buyer before the date specified for the delivery to the first buyer.

B. WAIVER OF BREACH

The breach of a contract may have no importance because the other party to the contract waives the breach.

3. Cure of Breach by Waiver

The fact that one party has broken a contract does not necessarily mean that there will be a lawsuit or a forfeiture of the contract. For practical business reasons, one party may be willing to ignore or waive the breach. When it is established that there has been a **waiver** of a breach, the party waiving the breach cannot take any action on the theory that the contract was broken. The waiver, in effect, erases the past breach. The contract continues as though the breach had not existed.

The waiver may be express or it may be implied from the continued recognition of the existence of the contract by the aggrieved party.[3] When the conduct of a party shows an intent to give up a right, it waives that right.[4]

waiver–release or relinquishment of a known right or objection.

4. Existence and Scope of Waiver

It is a question of fact whether there has been a waiver.

CASE SUMMARY

Have You Driven a Ford Lately, Jennifer?

FACTS: In 1995, Northland Ford Dealers, an association of dealerships, offered to sponsor a "hole in one" contest at Moccasin Creek Country Club. A banner announced that a hole in one would win a car but gave no other details, and the local dealer parked a Ford Explorer near the banner. Northland paid a $4,602

---

[3] *Huger v Morrison*, 2000 La App LEXIS 241.
[4] *Stronghaven Inc. v Ingram*, 555 SE2d 49 (Ga App 2001).

CASE SUMMARY

Continued

premium to Continental Hole-In-One, Inc., to ensure the award of the contest prize. The insurance application stated in capital letters that "ALL AMATEUR MEN AND WOMEN WILL UTILIZE THE SAME TEE." And Continental established the men/women yardage for the hole to be 170 yards, but did not make this known to the participants. Jennifer Harms registered for the tournament and paid her entrance fee. At the contest hole, she teed off from the amateur women's red marker, which was a much shorter distance to the pin than the 170 yards from the men's marker— and she made a hole in one. When she inquired about the prize, she was told that because of insurance requirements, all amateurs had to tee off from the amateur men's tee box, and because she had not done so, she was disqualified. Harms, a collegiate golfer at Concordia College, returned there to complete her last year of athletic eligibility and on graduation sued Northland for breach of contract. Northland contends that under NCAA rules, accepting a prize or agreeing to accept a prize would have disqualified Harms from NCAA competition. It also asserts that her continuation of her NCAA competition evinced intent to waive acceptance of the car.

DECISION: Judgment for Harms. Northland must abide by the rules it announced, not by the ones it left unannounced that disqualified all amateur women from the contest. This was a vintage unilateral contract with performance by the offeree as acceptance. Harms earned the prize when she sank her winning shot. Waiver is a volitional relinquishment, by act or word, of a known existing right conferred in law or contract. Harms could not disclaim the prize; it was not hers to refuse. She was told her shot from the wrong tee disqualified her. One can hardly relinquish what was never conferred. Northland's waiver defense is devoid of merit. [**Harms v Northland Ford Dealers, 602 NW2d 58 (SD 1999)**]

(A) **EXISTENCE OF WAIVER.** A party may express or declare that the breach of a contract is waived. A waiver of a breach is more often the result of an express forgiving of a breach. Thus, a party allowing the other party to continue performance without objecting that the performance is not satisfactory waives the right to raise that objection when sued for payment by the performing party.

For Example, a contract promising to sell back a parcel of commercial property to Jackson required Jackson to make a $500 payment to Massey's attorney on the first of the month for five months, December through April. It was clearly understood that the payments would be "on time without fail." Jackson made the December payment on time. New Year's Day, a holiday, fell on a Friday, and Jackson made the second payment on January 4. He made $500 payments on February 1, March 1, and March 31, respectively, and the payments were accepted and a receipt issued on each occasion. However, Massey refused to convey title back to Jackson because "the January 4 payment was untimely and the parties' agreement had been breached." The court held that the doctrine of waiver applied due to Massey's acceptance of the late payment and the three subsequent payments without objection, and the court declared that Jackson was entitled to possession of the land.[5]

---

[5] *Massey v Jackson*, 726 So2d 656 (Ala Civ App 1998).

(B) **Scope of Waiver.** The waiver of a breach of contract extends only to the matter waived. It does not show any intent to ignore other provisions of the contract.

(c) **Antimodification Clause.** Modern contracts commonly specify that the terms of a contract shall not be deemed modified by waiver as to any breaches. This means that the original contract remains as agreed to. Either party may therefore return to, and insist on, compliance with the original contract.

In the example involving Jackson and Massey's contract, the trial court reviewed the contract to see whether the court was restricted by the contract from applying the waiver. It concluded: "In this case, the parties' contract did not contain any terms that could prevent the application of the doctrine of waiver to the acceptance of late payments."[6]

5. Reservation of Rights

It may be that a party is willing to accept a defective performance but does not wish to surrender any claim for damages for the breach. **For Example,** Midwest Utilities, Inc., accepted 20 carloads of Powder River Basin coal (sometimes called *Western coal*) from its supplier, Maney Enterprises, because its power plants were in short supply of coal. Midwest's requirements contract with Maney called for Appalachian coal, a low-sulfur, highly efficient fuel, which is sold at a premium price per ton. Midwest, in accepting the tendered performance with a **reservation of rights**, gave notice to Maney that it reserved all rights to pursue damages for the tender of a nonconforming shipment.

C. Remedies for Breach of Contract

One or more **remedies** may be available to the innocent party in the case of a breach of contract. There is also the possibility that arbitration or a streamlined out-of-court alternative dispute resolution procedure is available or required for determining the rights of the parties.

6. Remedies Upon Anticipatory Repudiation

When an anticipatory repudiation of a contract occurs, the aggrieved person has several options. He may (1) do nothing beyond stating that performance at the proper time will be required, (2) regard the contract as having been definitively broken and bring a lawsuit against the repudiating party without waiting to see whether there will be proper performance when the performance date arrives, or (3) regard the repudiation as an offer to cancel the contract. This offer can be accepted or rejected. If accepted, there is a discharge of the original contract by the subsequent cancellation agreement of the parties.

7. Remedies in General and the Measure of Damages

Courts provide a *quasi-contractual* or *restitution* remedy in which a contract is unenforceable because it lacked definite and certain terms or was not in compliance with the statute of frauds, yet one of the parties performed services for the other.

reservation of rights–
assertion by a party to a contract that even though a tendered performance (e.g., a defective product) is accepted, the right to damages for nonconformity to the contract is reserved.

remedy–action or procedure that is followed in order to enforce a right or to obtain damages for injury to a right.

[6] Id., at 659.

FIGURE 20-1 | *What Follows the Breach*

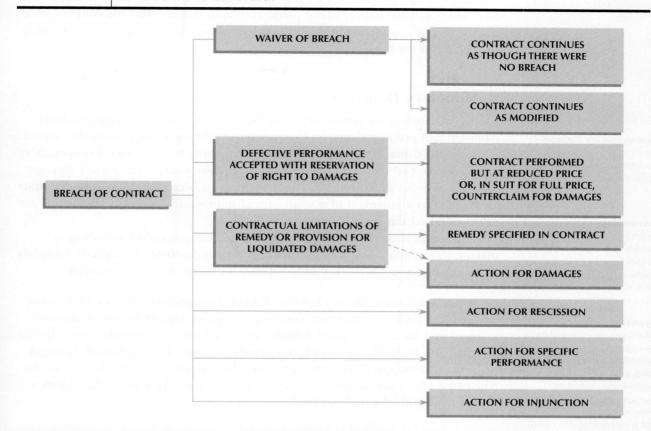

The measure of damages in these and other quasi-contract cases is the reasonable value of the services performed, not an amount derived from the defective contract.

In cases when a person retains money or when a contemplated contract is not properly formed and no work is performed, the party retaining the benefit is obligated to make restitution to the person conferring the benefit. **For Example,** Kramer Associates, Inc. (KAI), a Washington D.C., consulting firm, accepted $75,000 from a Ghana-based corporation, Ikam, Ltd., to secure financing for a Ghana development project. No contract was ever executed, and KAI did virtually nothing to secure financing for the project. Restitution of the $75,000 was required.[7]

When there is a breach of contract, the regular remedy is an award of *monetary damages*. In unusual circumstances, when monetary damages are inadequate, the injured party may obtain **specific performance**, whereby the court will order that the contract terms be carried out.

The measure of monetary damages when there has been a breach of contract is the sum of money that will place the injured party in the same position that would have been attained if the contract had been performed.[8] That is, the injured party

specific performance–
action brought to compel the adverse party to perform a contract on the theory that merely suing for damages for its breach will not be an adequate remedy.

[7] *Kramer Associates, Inc. v IKAM, Ltd.,* 888 A2d 247 (DC 2005).
[8] *Leingang v City of Mandan Weed Board,* 468 NW2d 397 (ND 1991).

will be given the *benefit of the bargain* by the court. As seen in the *Tips v Hartland Developers* case, the nonbreaching party, Hartland, was awarded the contract price less the cost of completion of the project, which had the effect of giving the builder the benefit of the bargain.

8. Monetary Damages

compensatory damages–sum of money that will compensate an injured plaintiff for actual loss.

Monetary damages are commonly classified as compensatory damages, nominal damages, and punitive damages. **Compensatory damages** compensate the injured party for the damages incurred as a result of the breach of contract. Compensatory damages have two branches, *direct damages* and *consequential* (or *special*) *damages*.

Injured parties that do not sustain an actual loss because of a breach of contract are entitled to a judgment of a small sum of money such as $1; these damages are called **nominal damages**.

nominal damages–nominal sum awarded the plaintiff in order to establish that legal rights have been violated although the plaintiff in fact has not sustained any actual loss or damages.

Damages in excess of actual loss, imposed for the purpose of punishing or making an example of the defendant, are known as **punitive damages** or *exemplary damages*. In contract actions, punitive damages are not ordinarily awarded.[9]

punitive damages–damages, in excess of those required to compensate the plaintiff for the wrong done, that are imposed in order to punish the defendant because of the particularly wanton or willful character of wrongdoing; also called *exemplary damages*.

(A) **DIRECT AND CONSEQUENTIAL DAMAGES.** **Direct damages** (sometimes called *general damages*) are those that naturally flow from the given type of breach of contract involved and include *incidental damages*, which are extra expenditures made by the injured party to rectify the breach or mitigate damages. **Consequential damages** (sometimes called *special damages*) are those that do not necessarily flow from the type of breach of contract involved but happen to do so in a particular case as a result of the injured party's particular circumstances.

direct damages–losses that are caused by breach of a contract.

consequential damages–damages the buyer experiences as a result of the seller's breach with respect to a third party, also called *special damages*.

CASE SUMMARY

Who Pays the Expenses?

FACTS: Jerry Birkel was a grain farmer. Hassebrook Farm Service, Inc., made a contract with Jerry to sell to him and install a grain storage and drying bin. Jerry traded in his old dryer to the seller. The new equipment did not work properly, and Jerry had to pay other persons for drying and storing his grain. Jerry sued Hassebrook for damages and claimed the right to be repaid what he had paid to others for drying and storage.

DECISION: Jerry was entitled to recover what he had paid others for drying and storage. Because Jerry had traded in his old dryer to the seller, it was obvious to the seller that if the new equipment did not work properly, Jerry would be forced to pay for alternative drying and storage to prevent the total loss of his crops. The cost of such an alternative was therefore within the seller's contemplation when the contract was made, and so the buyer could recover this cost as an element of damages for the seller's breach of contract. [**Birkel v Hassebrook Farm Service, Inc., 363 NW2d 148 (Neb 1985)**]

[9] A party who is not awarded actual damages but wins nominal damages can be considered a "prevailing party" for the purposes of a contractual attorney fee-shifting provision. *Brock v King*, 629 SE2d 829 (Ga App 2006).

Consequential damages may be recovered only if it was reasonably foreseeable to the defendant that the kind of loss in question could be sustained by the nonbreaching party if the contract were broken.

For Example, in early August, Spencer Adams ordered a four-wheel-drive GMC truck with a rear-end hydraulic lift for use on his Aroostook County, Maine, potato farm. The contract price was $58,500. He told Brad Jones, the owner of the dealership, that he had to have the truck by Labor Day so he could use it to bring in his crop from the fields before the first frost, and Brad nodded that he understood. The truck did not arrive by Labor Day as promised in the written contract. After a two-week period of gradually escalating recriminations with the dealership, Adams obtained the same model GMC truck at a dealership 40 minutes away in Houlton but at the cost of $60,500. He was also able to rent a similar truck from the Houlton dealer for $250 for the day while the new truck was being prepared. Farmhands had used other means of harvesting, but because of the lack of the truck, their work was set back by five days. As a result of the delays, 30 percent of the crop was still in the fields when the first frost came, causing damages expertly estimated at $320,000. The *direct damages* for the breach of contract in this case would be the difference between the contract price for the truck of $58,500 and the market price of $60,500, or $2,000. These direct damages naturally flow from the breach of contract for the purchase of a truck. Also, the *incidental damages* of $250 for the truck rental are recoverable direct damages. The $320,000 loss of the potato crop was a consequence of not having the truck, and this sum is arguably recoverable by Spencer Adams as *consequential or special damages.* Adams notified Brad Jones of the reason he needed to have the truck by Labor Day, and it should have been reasonably foreseeable to Jones that loss of a portion of the crop could occur if the truck contract was breached. However, because of Spencer Adams's obligation to mitigate damages (as discussed below), it is unlikely that Adams will recover the full consequential damages. Truck rental availability or the lack of availability within the rural area, alternative tractor usage, and the actual harvesting methods used by Adams all relate to the mitigation issue to be resolved by the jury.

(B) **MITIGATION OF DAMAGES.** The injured party is under the duty to mitigate damages if reasonably possible.[10] In other words, damages must not be permitted to increase if an increase can be prevented by reasonable efforts. This means that the injured party must generally stop any performance under the contract to avoid running up a larger bill. The duty to mitigate damages may require an injured party to buy or rent elsewhere the goods that the wrongdoer was obligated to deliver under the contract. In the case of breach of an employment contract by the employer, the employee is required to seek other similar employment. The wages earned from other employment must be deducted from the damages claimed. The discharged employee, however, is not required to take employment of less-than-comparable work.

---

[10] *West Pinal Family Health Center, Inc. v McBride*, 785 P2d 66 (Ariz 1989).

(1) Effect of Failure to Mitigate Damages.

The effect of the requirement of mitigating damages is to limit recovery by the nonbreaching party to the damages that would have been sustained had this party mitigated the damages where it was possible to do so. **For Example,** self-described "sports nut" Gary Baker signed up for a three-year club-seat "package" that entitled him and a companion to tickets for 41 Boston Bruins hockey games and 41 Boston Celtics basketball games at the New Boston Garden Corporation's Fleet Center for approximately $18,000 per year. After one year, Baker stopped paying for the tickets, thinking that he would simply lose his $5,000 security deposit. Baker, a CPA, tried to work out a compromise settlement to no avail. New Boston sued Baker for breach of contract, seeking the balance due on the tickets of $34,866. At trial, Baker argued to the jury that although he had breached his contract, New Boston had an obligation to mitigate damages, for example, by treating his empty seats and those of others in the same situation as "rush seats" shortly before game time and selling them at a discount. New Boston argued that just as a used luxury car cannot be returned for a refund, a season ticket cannot be canceled without consequences. The jury accepted Baker's position on mitigation and reduced the amount owed New Boston by $21,176 to $13,690.[11]

9. Rescission

When one party commits a material breach of the contract, the other party may rescind the contract; if the party in default objects, the aggrieved party may bring an action for rescission. A breach is *material* when it is so substantial that it defeats the object of the parties in making the contract.[12]

An injured party who rescinds a contract after having performed services may recover the reasonable value of the performance rendered under restitutionary or quasi-contractual damages. Money paid by the injured party may also be recovered. The purpose is to restore the injured party to the position occupied before the contract was made. However, the party seeking restitutionary damages must also return what this party has received from the party in default.

For Example, Pedro Morena purchased real estate from Jason Alexander after Alexander had assured him that the property did not have a flooding problem. In fact, the property regularly flooded after ordinary rainstorms. Morena was entitled to the return of the purchase price and payment for the reasonable value of the improvements he made to the property. Alexander was entitled to a setoff for the reasonable rental value of the property during the time Morena was in possession of this property.

10. Action for Specific Performance

Under special circumstances, an injured party may obtain the equitable remedy of specific performance, which compels the other party to carry out the terms of a contract. Specific performance is ordinarily granted only if the subject matter of the

---

[11] Sacha Pfeiffer, "Disenchanted Fan Scores Win in Ticket Fight," *Boston Globe*, August 28, 1999, B-4.
[12] *Greentree Properties, Inc. v Kissee*, 92 SW3d 289 (Mo App 2003).

contract is "unique," thereby making an award of money damages an inadequate remedy. Contracts for the purchase of land will be specifically enforced.[13]

Specific performance of a contract to sell personal property can be obtained only if the article is of unusual age, beauty, unique history, or other distinction. **For Example,** Maurice owned a rare Revolutionary War musket that he agreed to sell to Herb. Maurice then changed his mind because of the uniqueness of the musket. Herb can sue and win, requesting the remedy of specific performance of the contract because of the unique nature of the goods.

When the damages sustained by the plaintiff can be measured in monetary terms, specific performance will be refused. Consequently, a contract to sell a television station will not be specifically enforced when the buyer had made a contract to resell the station to a third person; the damages caused by the breach of the first contract would be the loss sustained by being unable to make the resale, and such damages would be adequate compensation to the original buyer.[14]

Ordinarily, contracts for the performance of personal services are not specifically ordered. This is because of the difficulty of supervision by the court and the restriction of the U.S. Constitution's Thirteenth Amendment prohibiting involuntary servitude except as criminal punishment.

11. Action for an Injunction

injunction–order of a court of equity to refrain from doing (negative injunction) or to do (affirmative or mandatory injunction) a specified act. Statute use in labor disputes has been greatly restricted.

When a breach of contract consists of doing an act prohibited by the contract, a possible remedy is an **injunction** against doing the act. **For Example,** when the obligation in an employee's contract is to refrain from competing after resigning from the company and the obligation is broken by competing, a court may order or enjoin the former employee to stop competing. Similarly, when a vocalist breaks a contract to record exclusively for a particular label, she may be enjoined from recording for any other company. This may have the indirect effect of compelling the vocalist to record for the plaintiff.

12. Reformation of Contract by a Court

At times, a written contract does not correctly state the agreement already made by the parties. When this occurs, either party may seek to have the court reform or correct the writing to state the agreement actually made.

A party seeking reformation of a contract must clearly prove both the grounds for reformation and what the agreement actually was. This burden is particularly great when the contract to be reformed is written. This is so because the general rule is that parties are presumed to have read their written contracts and to have intended to be bound by them when they signed the contracts.

When a unilateral mistake is made and it is of such consequence that enforcing the contract according to its terms would be unreasonable, a court may reform the contract to correct the mistake.

---

[13] *English v Muller*, 514 SE2d 195 (Ga 1999).
[14] *Miller v LeSea Broadcasting, Inc.*, 87 F3d 224 (7th Cir 1996).

Will a Court Correct a Huge Mistake?

FACTS: New York Packaging Corp. (NYPC) manufactured plastic sheets used by Owens Corning (OC) at its asphalt plants throughout the country as dividers to separate asphalt containers and prevent them from sticking to one another. Janet Berry, a customer service representative at Owens Corning, called and received a price from NYPC of "$172.50 per box," with a box containing 200 plastic sheets. Ms. Berry put the information into OC's computer systems, which in turn generated a purchase order. She mistakenly believed that the unit of measurement designated as "EA" on the purchase order was per box when it in fact was per sheet. As a result, the purchase orders likewise reflected a price of $172.50 per sheet rather than per box. The computer automatically calculated the total price of the purchase order and faxed it to NYPC as $1,078,195, without Ms. Berry seeing the huge total price. NYPC filled the order, which included overrun sheets, and billed OC $1,414,605.60. NYPC sought payment at the contract price of $172.50 per sheet. It points out that the purchase order contained a "no oral modification" clause and, by its terms, the order was binding when NYPC accepted. The buyer contends that NYPC is attempting to take advantage of this huge and obvious mistake and that the contract should be reformed.

DECISION: Ms. Berry made a unilateral mistake that was, or should have been, known by NYPC. OC used the sheets after its offer to return them to NYPC was refused. Therefore, the contract could not be rescinded. The drafting error in this case was so huge that to enforce the written contract would be unconscionable. Accordingly, the unit of measurement is amended to read "per box" rather than "EA"; the "Order Qty" is amended to read "41 boxes of 200 sheets per box"; and the overall price is modified to read $7,072.50, not $1,078,195. [**In re Owens Corning et al., Debtors in Possession, 91 BR 329 (2003)**]

D. CONTRACT PROVISIONS AFFECTING REMEDIES AND DAMAGES

The contract of the parties may contain provisions that affect the remedies available or the recovery of damages.

13. Limitation of Remedies

The contract of the parties may limit the remedies of the aggrieved parties. **For Example,** the contract may give one party the right to repair or replace a defective item sold or to refund the contract price. The contract may require both parties to submit any dispute to arbitration or another streamlined out-of-court dispute resolution procedure.

14. Liquidated Damages

liquidated damages–
provision stipulating the amount of damages to be paid in the event of default or breach of contract.

The parties may stipulate in their contract that a certain amount should be paid in case of a breach. This amount is known as liquidated damages and may be variously measured by the parties. When delay is possible, **liquidated damages** may be a fixed sum, such as $1,000 for each day of delay. When there is a total default, damages may be a percentage of the contract price or the amount of the down payment.

valid–legal.

liquidated damages clause–specification of exact compensation in case of a breach of contract.

(A) **VALIDITY.** To be **valid**, a **liquidated damages clause** must satisfy two requirements: (1) The situation must be one in which it is difficult or impossible to determine the actual damages and (2) the amount specified must not be excessive when compared with the probable damages that would be sustained.[15] The validity of a liquidated damages clause is determined on the basis of the facts existing when the clause was agreed to.

C A S E   S U M M A R Y

Can We Freeze the Damages?

FACTS: Manny Fakhimi agreed to buy an apartment complex for $697,000 at an auction from David Mason. Fakhimi was obligated to put up 10 percent of the agreed-to price at the auction as a deposit. The agreement signed by Fakhimi allowed Mason to keep this deposit should Fakhimi fail to come up with the remaining 90 percent of the auction price as liquidated damages for the default. Shortly after the auction, Fakhimi heard a rumor that the military base located near the apartment complex might be closing. Fakhimi immediately stopped payment on the check and defaulted on the agreement. Mason sued Fakhimi for the liquidated damages specified in the sales contract.

DECISION: Because of the difficulty of forecasting the loss that might be caused by the breach of a real estate purchase contract, it is held that a liquidated damage clause of 10 percent of the sale price is valid and is not a penalty. The fact that the damages sustained thereafter were less than 10 percent does not convert the 10 percent into an unreasonable forecast. The 10 percent clause remained valid as it would have remained had the damages on resale been more than 10 percent. [**Mason v Fakhimi, 865 P2d 333 (Neb 1993)**]

(B) **EFFECT.** When a liquidated damages clause is held valid, the injured party cannot collect more than the amount specified by the clause. The defaulting party is bound to pay such damages once the fact is established that there has been a default. The injured party is not required to make any proof as to damages sustained, and the defendant is not permitted to show that the damages were not as great as the liquidated sum.

(C) **INVALID CLAUSES.** If the liquidated damages clause calls for the payment of a sum that is clearly unreasonably large and unrelated to the possible actual damages that might be sustained, the clause will be held to be void as a penalty. **For Example,** a settlement agreement between 27 plaintiffs seeking recovery for injuries resulting from faulty breast implants and the implants' manufacturer, Dow Corning Corp., called for seven $200,000 payments to each plaintiff. The agreement also called for a $100 per day payment to each plaintiff for any time when the payments were late as "liquidated damages." The court held that the $100 per day figure was not a reasonable estimate of anticipated damages. Rather, it was an unenforceable "penalty" provision.[16]

---

[15] *Southeast Alaska Construction Co. v Alaska*, 791 P2d 339 (Alaska 1990).
[16] *Bear Stearns v Dow Corning Corp.*, 419 F3d 543 (6th Cir 2005). See *RKR Motors Inc. v Associated Uniform Rentals*, 995 So2d 588 (Fla App 2008).

When a liquidated damages clause is held invalid, the effect is merely to erase the clause from the contract, and the injured party may proceed to recover damages for breach of the contract. Instead of recovering the liquidated damages amount, the injured party will recover whatever actual damages he can prove. **For Example,** JRC

CASE SUMMARY

Could We Make It Any Clearer?

FACTS: Woodside Homes made a contract to build a house for Russ. He and his wife later visited the construction site, where his wife slipped and fell into a hole in the driveway in front of the house. The fall caused a blood clot to form, which caused the wife's death. Russ sued Woodside for damages for his wife's death, claiming that she had been harmed because of Woodside's negligence. There was no evidence of negligence. Woodside raised the defense that the construction contract stated that "the construction site is a dangerous place to visit" and that Woodside would not be liable for any accident, injury, or death resulting from a visit to the jobsite.

DECISION: Judgment for Woodside. The contractor gave adequate warning of the danger, and the wife assumed the risk in visiting the site. The exculpation clause therefore shielded the contractor from liability. [**Russ v Woodside Homes, Inc., 905 P2d 901 (Utah App 1995)**]

Trading Corp (JRC) bought computer software and hardware from Progressive Data Systems (PDS) for $167,935, which it paid in full, to track the movement of its trucks with inventory and to process transactions. The purchase agreement also called for a $7,500 per year licensing fee for an 18-year period, and it stated that in the event of default, PDS could "accelerate and declare all obligations of Customer as a liquidated sum." A dispute arose between the parties, and when the case was litigated, the only actual contract charges owed PDS were license fees of $7,500 for two years. The application of the liquidated damages clause would yield an additional $120,000 cash for PDS for the future fees for 16 years without any reduction for expenses or the present cash value for the not-yet-earned fees. Actual damages were clearly ascertainable and not difficult to determine, and the amount sought was excessive. The court deemed the liquidated damages clause an unenforceable penalty and PDS was relegated to recovering its actual contractual damages.[17]

15. Attorneys' Fees

Attorneys' fees are a very significant factor in contract litigation. In Medistar Corporation's suit against Dr. David Schmidt, the jury awarded it $418,069 in damages under its promissory estoppel claim and in addition thereto the trial court judge allowed Medistar to recover $408,412 for its attorneys' fees. A state statute

[17] *Jefferson Randolf Corporation v PDS*, 553 SE2d 304 (Ga App 2001).

allows recovery of attorneys' fees for the prevailing party in a breach of partnership claim. On appeal the recovery of $408,412 in attorneys' fees was reversed since the jury awarded zero damages on Medistars' fees was reveresed since ther jury awareded zero damages on Medistars' breach of partnership claim. The net result after payment of attorneys' fees—and not counting attorneys' fees for the appeal—was $9657 for Medistar, after four years of "successful" litigation.[18]

The so-called "American rule" states that each party is responsible for its own attorneys' fees in the absence of an express contractual or statutory provision to the contrary.[19] Even in the event of a valid contractual provision for attorneys' fees, a trial court has the discretion to exercise its equitable control to allow only such sum as is reasonable, or the court may properly disallow attorneys' fees altogether on the basis that such recovery would be inequitable. **For Example,** although Evergreen Tree Care Services was awarded some monetary damages in its breach of contract suit against JHL, Inc., it was unsuccessful in its claim for attorneys' fees under a provision for attorneys' fees in the contract because the trial court exercised its equitable discretion, finding that both parties to the litigation came to court with "unclean hands," and that Evergreen failed to sufficiently itemize and exclude fees to discovery abuses.[20]

16. Limitation of Liability Clauses

A contract may contain a provision stating that one of the parties shall not be liable for damages in case of breach. Such a provision is called an **exculpatory clause**, or when a monetary limit to damages for breach of contract is set forth in the contract, it may be referred to as a **limitation-of-liability clause**.

(A) CONTENT AND CONSTRUCTION. If an exculpatory clause or a limitation-of-liability clause limits liability for damages caused only by negligent conduct, liability is neither excluded nor limited if the conduct alleged is found to be grossly negligent, willful, or wanton. **For Example,** Security Guards Inc. (SGI) provided services to Dana Corporation, a truck frame manufacturer under a contract that contained a limitation-of-liability clause capping losses at $50,000 per occurrence for damages "caused solely by the negligence" of SGI or its employees. When a critical alarm was activated by a fire in the paint shop at 5:39 P.M., the SGI guard on duty did not follow appropriate procedures, which delayed notification to the fire department for 15 minutes. Royal Indemnity Co., Dana's insurer, paid Dana $16,535,882 for the fire loss and sued SGI for $7 million, contending that the SGI guard's actions were grossly negligent and caused the plant to suffer increased damages. The court held that if SGI were to be found grossly negligent, the liability would not be limited to $50,000, and a jury could find damages far exceeding that amount.[21]

(B) VALIDITY. As a general rule, experienced businesspersons are free to allocate liability in their contracts as they see fit. They have freedom to contract—even to make bad bargains or relinquish fundamental rights. However, courts in most states

exculpatory clause– provision in a contract stating that one of the parties shall not be liable for damages in case of breach; also called a *limitation-of-liability clause.*

limitation-of-liability clause–provision in a contract stating that one of the parties shall not be liable for damages in case of breach; also called an *exculpatory clause.*

[18] *Medistar Corp. v Schmidt*, 267 SW3d 150 (Tex App 2008).
[19] *Centimark v Village Manor Associates, Ltd.*, 967 A2d 550 (Conn App 2009).
[20] *Stafford v JHL, Inc.*, 194 P3d 315 (Wyo 2008). See also *FNBC v Jennessey Group, LLC*, 759 NW2d 808 (Iowa App 2008).
[21] *Royal Indemnity Co. v Security Guards, Inc.*, 255 F Supp 2d 497 (ED Pa 2003).

will not enforce a contract provision that *completely exonerates* a party from gross negligence or intentional acts.

(c) **RELEASES.** Release forms signed by participants in athletic and sporting events declaring that the sponsor, proprietor, or operator of the event shall not be liable for injuries sustained by participants because of its negligence are generally binding.[22] **For Example,** when Merav Sharon sued the city of Newton for negligence as a result of an injury received while participating in a high school cheerleading practice, the city successfully raised a signed exculpatory release as a defense.[23] So also the exculpatory contract Nathan Henderson signed releasing a white-water rafting expedition operator from liability for its negligence barred Henderson's negligence claim against the operator for an injury suffered disembarking from the operator's bus.[24]

lawflix

The Goodbye Girl (1977) (PG)

Richard Dreyfuss plays Elliott Garfield, a struggling Shakespearean actor who lands in New York with a sublease on an apartment still occupied by divorcee Marsha Mason and her daughter. The two work out living arrangements, split rent and food, and deal with the issue of whether Mason has any rights. Review all aspects of contracts as the characters discuss subleases, rent payment, living arrangements, and food costs.

Check out LawFlix at **www.cengage.com/blaw/dvl** to access movie clips that illustrate business law concepts.

MAKE THE CONNECTION

SUMMARY

When a party fails to perform a contract or performs improperly, the other contracting party may sue for damages caused by the breach. What may be recovered by the aggrieved person is stated in terms of being direct or consequential damages. Direct damages are those that ordinarily will result from the breach. Direct damages may be recovered on proof of causation and amount. Consequential

---

[22] But see *Woodman v Kera, LLC,* 760 NW2d 641 (Mich App 2008) where the Court of Appeals of Michigan held that a preinjury waiver signed by a parent on behalf of a five-year-old child was invalid.
[23] *Sharon v City of Newton,* 437 Mass 99 (2002).
[24] *Henderson v Quest Expeditions, Inc.,* 174 SW3d 730 (Tenn App 2005).

damages can be recovered only if, in addition to proving causation and amount, it is shown that they were reasonably within the contemplation of the contracting parties as a probable result of a breach of the contract. The right to recover consequential damages is lost if the aggrieved party could reasonably have taken steps to avoid such damages. In other words, the aggrieved person has a duty to mitigate or reduce damages by reasonable means.

In any case, the damages recoverable for breach of contract may be limited to a specific amount by a liquidated damages clause.

In a limited number of situations, an aggrieved party may bring an action for specific performance to compel the other contracting party to perform the acts called for by the contract. Specific performance by the seller is always obtainable for the breach of a contract to sell land or real estate on the theory that such property has a unique value. With respect to other contracts, specific performance will not be ordered unless it is shown that there was some unique element present so that the aggrieved person would suffer a damage that could not be compensated for by the payment of money damages.

The aggrieved person also has the option of rescinding the contract if (1) the breach has been made concerning a material term and (2) the aggrieved party returns everything to the way it was before the contract was made.

Although there has been a breach of the contract, the effect of this breach is nullified if the aggrieved person by word or conduct waives the right to object to the breach. Conversely, an aggrieved party may accept a defective performance without thereby waiving a claim for breach if the party makes a reservation of rights. A reservation of rights can be made by stating that the defective performance is accepted "without prejudice," "under protest," or "with reservation of rights."

LEARNING OUTCOMES

After studying this chapter, you should be able to clearly explain:

A. WHAT CONSTITUTES A BREACH OF CONTRACT

LO.1 Explain what constitutes a breach of contract and an anticipatory breach of contract

> See the illustration of a painting contractor's failure to properly paint a house, p. 434.
>
> See the *Tips* case in which damages are assessed for anticipatory repudiation of a contract, p. 434.

B. WAIVER OF BREACH

LO.2 Describe the effect of a waiver of a breach

> See the application of the waiver doctrine as applied in the Massey example on p. 438.

C. REMEDIES FOR BREACH OF CONTRACT

LO.3 Explain the range of remedies available for breach of contract

> See Figure 20.1, "What Follows the Breach," on p. 439.
>
> See the *Spenser Adams* example involving a range of monetary damages on p. 441.
>
> See the *Pedro Morena* example involving rescission of a contract on p. 442.

See the rare Revolutionary War musket example of specific performance, p. 443.

D. CONTRACT PROVISIONS AFFECTING REMEDIES AND DAMAGES

LO.4 Explain when liquidated damages clauses are valid and invalid

See the Dow Corning faulty breast implants settlement agreement example in which liquidated damages of a $100 per day late payment were found to be unenforceable penalty provision, p. 445.

LO.5 State when liability-limiting clauses and releases are valid

See the example in which the city of Newton successfully raised a signed exculpatory release as a defense in a high school cheerleading injury case, p. 448.

KEY TERMS

anticipatory breach
anticipatory repudiation
breach
compensatory damages
consequential damages
direct damages
exculpatory clause

injunction
limitation-of-liability
    clause
liquidated damages
liquidated damages clause
nominal damages
punitive damages

remedies
reservation of rights
specific performance
valid
waiver

QUESTIONS AND CASE PROBLEMS

1. The Forsyth School District contracted with Textor Construction, Inc., to build certain additions and alter school facilities, including the grading of a future softball field. Under the contract, the work was to be completed by August 1. Various delays occurred at the outset of the project attributable to the school district, and the architect's representative on the job, Mr. Hamilton, told Textor's vice president, William Textor, not to be concerned about a clause in the contract of $250 per day liquidated damages for failure to complete the job by August 1. Textor sued the school district for breach of contract regarding payment for the grading of the softball field, and the District counterclaimed for liquidated damages for 84 days at $250 per day for failure to complete the project by the August 1 date. What legal basis exists for Textor to defend against the counter-claim for failure to complete the job on time? Was it ethical for the school district to bring this counterclaim based on the facts before you? [*Textor Construction, Inc. v Forsyth R-III School District*, 60 SW3d 692 (Mo App)]

2. Anthony makes a contract to sell a rare painting to Laura for $100,000. The written contract specifies that if Anthony should fail to perform the contract, he will pay Laura $5,000 as liquidated damages. Anthony fails to deliver the painting and is sued by Laura for $5,000. Can she recover this amount?

3. Rogers made a contract with Salisbury Brick Corp. that allowed it to remove earth and sand from land he owned. The contract ran for four years with provision to renew it for additional four-year terms up to a total of 96 years. The contract provided for compensation to Rogers based on the amount of earth and sand removed. By an unintentional mistake, Salisbury underpaid Rogers the amount of $863 for the months of November and December 1986. Salisbury offered this amount to Rogers, but he refused to accept it and claimed that he had been underpaid in other months. Rogers claimed that he was entitled to rescind the contract. Was he correct? [*Rogers v Salisbury Brick Corp.*, 882 SE2d 915 (SC)]

4. A contractor departed from the specifications at a number of points in a contract to build a house. The cost to put the house in the condition called for by the contract was approximately $14,000. The contractor was sued for $50,000 for breach of contract and emotional disturbance caused by the breach. Decide.

5. Protein Blenders, Inc., made a contract with Gingerich to buy from him the shares of stock of a small corporation. When the buyer refused to take and pay for the stock, Gingerich sued for specific performance of the contract on the ground that the value of the stock was unknown and could not be readily ascertained because it was not sold on the general market. Was he entitled to specific performance? [*Gingerich v Protein Blenders, Inc.*, 95 NW2d 522 (Iowa)]

6. The buyer of real estate made a down payment. The contract stated that the buyer would be liable for damages in an amount equal to the down payment if the buyer broke the contract. The buyer refused to go through with the contract and demanded his down payment back. The seller refused to return it and claimed that he was entitled to additional damages from the buyer because the damages that he had suffered were more than the amount of the down payment. Decide. [*Waters v Key Colony East, Inc.*, 345 So2d 367 (Fla App)]

7. Kuznicki made a contract for the installation of a fire detection system by Security Safety Corp. for $498. The contract was made one night and canceled at 9:00 the next morning. Security then claimed one-third of the purchase price from Kuznicki by virtue of a provision in the contract that "in the event of cancellation of this agreement… the owner agrees to pay $33^{1/3}$ percent of the contract price, as liquidated damages." Was Security Safety entitled to recover the amount claimed? [*Security Safety Corp. v Kuznicki*, 213 NE2d 866 (Mass)]

8. FNBC is a business brokerage firm that assits in the purchase and sale of businesses. Jennings and Hennessey were independent contractors working for FNBC. They left FNBC, and FNBC sued them for breach of their contracts with FNBC. The trial court issued a permanent injuction prohibiting the former contractors from using proprietary information and the court awarded attorneys' fees under a clause in the contract that would obligate Jennings and Hennessey to indemnify FNBC against claims "brought by persons not a party to the provision." Jennings and Hennessey appealed the decision on attorneys' fees. Decide. [*FNBC v Jennessey Group, LLC*, 759 NW2d 808 (Iowa Ap)]

9. Melodee Lane Lingerie Co. was a tenant in a building that was protected against fire by a sprinkler and alarm system maintained by the American District Telegraph Co. (ADT). Because of the latter's fault, the controls on the system were defective and allowed the discharge of water into the building, which damaged Melodee's property. When Melodee sued ADT, its defense was that its service contract limited its liability to 10 percent of the annual service charge made to the customer. Was this limitation valid? [*Melodee Lane Lingerie Co. v American District Telegraph Co.*, 218 NE2d 661 (NY)]

10. In May, a homeowner made a contract with a roofer to make repairs to her house by July 1. The roofer never came to repair the roof, and heavy rains in the fall damaged the interior of the house. The homeowner sued the roofer for breach of contract and claimed damages for the harm done to the interior of the house. Is the homeowner entitled to recover such damages?

11. Ken Sulejmanagic, aged 19, signed up for a course in scuba diving taught by Madison at the YMCA. Before the instruction began, Ken was required to sign a form releasing Madison and the YMCA from liability for any harm that might occur. At the end of the course, Madison, Ken, and another student went into deep water. After Ken made the final dive required by the course program, Madison left him alone in the water while he took the other student for a dive. When Madison returned, Ken could not be found, and it was later determined that he had drowned. Ken's parents sued Madison and the YMCA for negligence in the performance of the teaching contract. The defendants raised the defense that the release Ken signed shielded them from liability. The plaintiffs claimed that the release was invalid. Who was correct? [*Madison v Superior Court*, 250 Cal Rptr 299 (Cal App)]

12. Wassenaar worked for Panos under a three-year contract stating that if the contract were terminated wrongfully by Panos before the end of the three years, he would pay as damages the salary for the remaining time that the contract had to run. After three months, Panos terminated the contract, and Wassenaar sued him for pay for the balance of the contract term. Panos claimed that this amount could not be recovered because the contract provision for the payment was a void penalty. Was this provision valid? [*Wassenaar v Panos*, 331 NW2d 357 (Wis)]

13. Soden, a contractor, made a contract to build a house for Clevert. The sales contract stated that "if either party defaults in the performance of this contract," that party would be liable to the other for attorneys' fees incurred in suing the defaulter. Soden was 61 days late in completing the contract, and some of the work was defective. In a suit by the buyer against the contractor, the contractor claimed that he was not liable for the buyer's attorneys' fees because he had made only a defective performance and because "default" in the phrase quoted meant "nonperformance of the contract." Was the contractor liable for the attorneys' fees? [*Clevert v Soden*, 400 SE2d 181 (Va)]

14. Protection Alarm Co. made a contract to provide burglar alarm security for Fretwell's home. The contract stated that the maximum liability of the alarm

company was the actual loss sustained or $50, whichever was the lesser, and that this provision was agreed to "as liquidated damages and not as a penalty." When Fretwell's home was burglarized, he sued for the loss of approximately $12,000, claiming that the alarm company had been negligent. The alarm company asserted that its maximum liability was $50. Fretwell claimed that this was invalid because it bore no relationship to the loss that could have been foreseen when the contract was made or that in fact "had been sustained." Decide.

15. Shepherd-Will made a contract to sell Emma Cousar:

    5 acres of land adjoining property owned by the purchaser and this being formerly land of Shepherd-Will, Inc., located on north side of Highway 223. This 5 acres to be surveyed at earliest time possible at which time plat will be attached and serve as further description on property.

    Shepherd-Will owned only one 100-acre tract of land that adjoined Emma's property. This tract had a common boundary with her property of 1,140 feet. Shepherd-Will failed to perform this contract. Emma sued for specific performance of the contract. Decide. [*Cousar v Shepherd-Will, Inc.*, 387 SE2d 723 (SC App)]

CPA QUESTIONS

1. Master Mfg., Inc., contracted with Accur Computer Repair Corp. to maintain Master's computer system. Master's manufacturing process depends on its computer system operating properly at all times. A liquidated damages clause in the contract provided that Accur pay $1,000 to Master for each day that Accur was late responding to a service request. On January 12, Accur was notified that Master's computer system had failed. Accur did not respond to Master's service request until January 15. If Master sues Accur under the liquidated damages provision of the contract, Master will:

   a. Win, unless the liquidated damage provision is determined to be a penalty

   b. Win, because under all circumstances liquidated damages provisions are enforceable

   c. Lose, because Accur's breach was *not* material

   d. Lose, because liquidated damage provisions violate public policy
      (5/93, Law, #25)

2. Jones, CPA, entered into a signed contract with Foster Corp. to perform accounting and review services. If Jones repudiates the contract prior to the date performance is due to begin, which of the following is *not* correct?

   a. Foster could successfully maintain an action for breach of contract after the date performance was due to begin.

   b. Foster can obtain a judgment ordering Jones to perform.

    c. Foster could successfully maintain an action for breach of contract prior to the date performance is due to begin.

    d. Foster can obtain a judgment for the monetary damages it incurred as a result of the repudiation. (5/89, Law, #35)

3. Which of the following concepts affect(s) the amount of monetary damages recoverable by the nonbreaching party when a contract is breached?

	Forseeability of damages	Mitigation of damages
a.	Yes	Yes
b.	Yes	No
c.	No	Yes
d.	No	No

Chapter 22

LEGAL ASPECTS OF SUPPLY CHAIN MANAGEMENT

Alll bailments are not created equal. Because of the circumstances under which possession of the bailed property is transferred, the law imposes special duties in some cases on warehouses, common carriers, factors, and hotelkeepers. Documents of title facilitate the transportation, storage, and financing of goods in commerce.

A. WAREHOUSES

The storage of goods in a warehouse is a special bailment.

1. Definitions

warehouse–entity engaged in the business of storing the goods of others for compensation.

public warehouses–entities that serve the public generally without discrimination.

A **warehouse** is an entity engaged in the business of storing the goods of others for compensation. **Public warehouses** hold themselves out to serve the public generally, without discrimination.

A building is not essential to warehousing. Thus, an enterprise that stores boats outdoors on land is engaged in warehousing, for it is engaged in the business of storing goods for hire.

2. Rights and Duties of Warehouses

The rights and duties of a warehouse are for the most part the same as those of a bailee under a mutual benefit bailment.[1] A warehouse is not an insurer of goods. A warehouse is liable for loss or damage to goods stored in its warehouse when the warehouse is negligent.[2]

(A) STATUTORY REGULATION. The rights and duties of warehouses are regulated by the UCC, Article 7. Article 7 was revised in 2003 and 32 states have adopted the revised version.[3] The purpose of revision was to provide a framework for the future development of electronic documents of title and to update the article for modern times in light of state, federal, and international developments, including the need for medium and gender neutrality. For example, the term utilized to designate a person engaged in storing goods for hire under Article 7 is *warehouseman*.[4] The revised act uses the term *warehouse*.[5] In addition, most states have passed warehouse acts defining the rights and duties of warehouses and imposing regulations. Regulations govern charges and liens, bonds for the protection of patrons, maintenance of storage facilities in a suitable and safe condition, inspections, and general methods of transacting business.

---

[1] UCC § 7-204.

[2] General contract principles also apply. For example, in *Williamson v Strictland & Smith Inc.*, 673 SE2d 858 (Ga App 2009), a warehouser successfully sued an onion farmer for breach of contract when the warehouser was unable to fill a large order because the majority of the farmer's onions stored at the warehouse were rotten.

[3] Revised Article 7 (2003) has been adopted by Alabama, Arizona, Arkansas, California, Colorado, Connecticut, Delaware, Hawaii, Idaho, Illinois, Indiana, Iowa, Kansas, Maryland, Minnesota, Mississippi, Montana, Nebraska, Nevada, New Hampshire, New Jersey, New Mexico, North Carolina, North Dakota, Oklahoma, Pennsylvania, Rhode Island, Tennessee, Texas, Utah, Virginia, and West Virginia. For more modern statutory drafting, the revised edition converts subparagraph designations from numbers to letters. For example, UCC § 7-307(1) is designated as Rev. UCC § 7-307(a).

[4] UCC § 7-102(1)(h).

[5] Rev. UCC § 7-102(a)(13).

specific lien–right of a creditor to hold particular property or assert a lien on particular property of the debtor because of the creditor's having done work on or having some other association with the property, as distinguished from having a lien generally against the assets of the debtor merely because the debtor is indebted to the lien holder.

warehouse receipt–receipt issued by the warehouse for stored goods. Regulated by the UCC, which clothes the receipt with some degree of negotiability.

depositor–person, or bailor, who gives property for storage.

issuer–warehouse that prepares a receipt of goods received for storage.

document of title– document treated as evidence that a person is entitled to receive, hold, and dispose of the document and the goods it covers.

(B) **LIEN OF WAREHOUSE.** The public warehouse has a lien against the goods for reasonable storage charges.[6] It is a **specific lien** in that it attaches only to the property on which the charges arose and cannot be asserted against any other property of the same owner in the possession of the warehouse. However, the warehouse may make a lien carry over to other goods by noting on the receipt for one lot of goods that a lien is also claimed for charges on the other goods. The warehouse's lien for storage charges may be enforced by sale after due notice has been given to all persons who claim any interest in the stored property.

3. Warehouse Receipts

A **warehouse receipt** is a written acknowledgment or record of an acknowledgment by a warehouse (bailee) that certain property has been received for storage from a named person called a **depositor** (bailor). The warehouse receipt is a memorandum of the contract between the **issuer**, the warehouse that prepares the receipt, and the depositor. No particular form is required, but usually the receipt (record) will provide:

> *(1) the location of the warehouse where the goods are stored, (2) the date of issuance of the receipt, (3) the consecutive number of the receipt, (4) information on the negotiability of the receipt, (5) the rate of storage and handling charges, (6) a description of the goods or the packages containing them, and (7) a statement of any liabilities incurred for which the warehouse claims a lien or security interest.[7]*

A warehouse receipt (as well as a bill of lading, discussed at a later point in this chapter) is considered a **document of title**—that is, a document that in the regular course of business or financing is treated as evidence that a person is entitled to receive, hold, and dispose of the document and the goods it covers.[8] Under revised Article 7 of the UCC, the term *record* is used in the definition of document of title, reflecting the present commercial reality of the use of electronic records as documents of title, in addition to traditional "written" documents of title inscribed on a tangible medium.[9] The person holding a warehouse receipt or the person specified in the receipt is entitled to the goods represented by the receipt. A warehouse receipt as a document of title can be bought or sold and can be used as security for a loan.

4. Rights of Holders of Warehouse Receipts

The rights of the holders of warehouse receipts differ depending on whether the receipts are nonnegotiable or negotiable.

---

[6] UCC § 7-209(1). The warehouse's lien provision of the UCC is constitutional as a continuation of the common law lien.
[7] UCC § 7-202(2)(a)–(i).
[8] UCC § 1-201(15).
[9] Rev. UCC § 1-201(b)(16). An "electronic" document of title is evidenced by a record consisting of information stored in an electronic medium. A "tangible" document of title is evidenced by a record consisting of information that is inscribed on a tangible medium.

CPA

nonnegotiable warehouse receipt–receipt that states the covered goods received will be delivered to a specific person.

(A) NONNEGOTIABLE WAREHOUSE RECEIPTS. A warehouse receipt in which it is stated that the goods received will be delivered to a specified person is a **nonnegotiable warehouse receipt**. A transferee of a nonnegotiable receipt acquires only the title and rights that the transferor had actual authority to transfer. Therefore, the transferee's rights may be defeated by a good-faith purchaser of the goods from the transferor of the receipt.

(B) NEGOTIABLE WAREHOUSE RECEIPTS. A warehouse receipt stating that the goods will be delivered "to the bearer" or "to the order of" any named person is a **negotiable warehouse receipt**.

negotiable warehouse receipt–receipt that states the covered goods will be delivered "to the bearer" or "to the order of."

(1) Negotiation

If the receipt provides for the delivery of the goods "to the bearer," the receipt may be negotiated by transfer of the document. If the receipt provides for delivery of the goods "to the order of" a named individual, the document must be indorsed[10] and delivered by that person in order for the document to be negotiated.

(2) Due Negotiation

If a receipt is duly negotiated, the person to whom it is negotiated may acquire rights superior to those of the transferor. A warehouse receipt is "duly negotiated" when the holder purchases the document in good faith without notice of any defense to it, for value, in an ordinary transaction in which nothing appears improper or irregular.[11] The holder of a duly negotiated document acquires title to the document and title to the goods.[12] The holder also acquires the direct obligation of the issuer to hold or deliver the goods according to the terms of the warehouse receipt. The rights of a holder of a duly negotiated document cannot be defeated by the surrender of the goods by the warehouse to the depositor.[13]

---

[10] The spelling *endorse* is commonly used in business. The spelling *indorse* is used in the UCC.

[11] UCC § 7-501(4).

[12] UCC § 7-502(1).

[13] For electronic documents of title, Revised Article 7, Section 7-106, includes a list of how a party becomes a holder, and the result is that Article 7 creates a new concept of "control." That is, a holder who has control of a document of title (as evidenced by a record that may be electronic) has all the rights of a holder. The Revised Article states:

  a. A person has control of an electronic document of title if a system employed for evidencing the transfer of interests in the electronic document reliably establishes that person as the person to which the electronic document was issued or transferred,

  b. A system satisfies subsection (a) and a person is deemed to have control of an electronic document of title, if the electronic document is created, stored, and assigned in such a manner that:

    1. a single authoritative copy of the document exists which is unique, identifiable, and, except as otherwise provided in paragraphs (4), (5), and (6), unalterable.

    2. the authoritative copy identifies the person asserting control as:

      A. the person to which the document was issued; or

      B. if the authoritative copy indicates that the document has been transferred, the person to which the document was most recently transferred;

    3. the authoritative copy is communicated to and maintained by the person asserting control or its designated custodian;

    4. copies or amendments that add or change an identified assignee of the authoritative copy can be made only with the consent of the person asserting control;

    5. each copy of the authoritative copy and any copy of a copy is readily identifiable as a copy that is not the authoritative copy; and

    6. any amendment of the authoritative copy is readily identifiable as authorized or unauthorized.

It is the duty of the warehouse to deliver the goods only to the holder of the negotiable receipt and to cancel this receipt on surrendering the goods.[14]

The rights of a purchaser of a warehouse receipt by due negotiation are not cut off by the fact that (1) an original owner was deprived of the receipt in "bearer" form by misrepresentation, fraud, mistake, loss, theft, or conversion or (2) a bona fide purchaser bought the goods from the warehouse.

A purchaser of a warehouse receipt who takes by due negotiation does not cut off all prior rights. If the person who deposited the goods with the warehouse did not own the goods or did not have power to transfer title to them, the purchaser of the receipt is subject to the title of the true owner. Accordingly, when goods are stolen and delivered to a warehouse and a warehouse receipt is issued for them, the owner of the goods prevails over the due-negotiation purchaser of the warehouse receipt.

Study Figure 22.1, and note all of the features of a negotiable warehouse receipt in the context of the following. **For Example,** Latham and Loud (L&L) sporting goods manufacturers' representatives in Cleveland, Ohio, hijacked a truckload of ice skates from Bartlett Shoe and Skate Company of Bangor, Maine. L&L warehoused the skates at the Northern Transfer Company warehouse, and received a negotiable warehouse receipt. Jack Preston, a large sporting goods retailer who had had previous business dealings with L&L and believed it to be operated by honest individuals, made a bona fide purchase of the receipt. Bartlett, the true owner, discovered that the skates were at Northern's warehouse and informed Northern of the hijacking. Northern delivered the skates to Bartlett; Latham and Loud have fled the country. Preston believed he was entitled to delivery of the skates because he acquired the negotiable receipt by due negotiation and informed Northern of his status before delivery of the skates to Bartlett. He contemplated legal action against Northern. Preston, however, is not entitled to the skates. Ordinarily, a purchaser of a warehouse receipt obtained by due negotiation takes title to the document and title to the goods. However, an exception exists in the case of theft. Thus, because of the theft by L&L, Preston's rights have been cut off by the true owner in this case. When conflicting claims exist, the warehouse can protect itself by instituting proceedings under UCC § 7-603 to ascertain the validity of the conflicting claims.

CPA   (c) Warranties. The transferor of a negotiable or nonnegotiable warehouse receipt makes certain implied warranties for the protection of the transferee. These warranties are that (1) the receipt is genuine, (2) its transfer is rightful and effective, and (3) the transferor has no knowledge of any facts that impair the validity or worth of the receipt.[15]

5. Field Warehousing

Ordinarily, stored goods are placed in a warehouse belonging to the warehouse company. In other instances, the owner of goods, such as a manufacturer, keeps the goods in the owner's own storage area or building. The warehouse may then take exclusive control over the area in which the goods are stored and issue a receipt for

---

[14] UCC § 7–403(3).

[15] UCC § 7-507. These warranties are in addition to any that may arise between the parties by virtue of the fact that the transferor is selling the goods represented by the receipt to the transferee. See Chapter 25 for a discussion of seller's warranties.

FIGURE 22-1 | *Negotiable Warehouse Receipt*

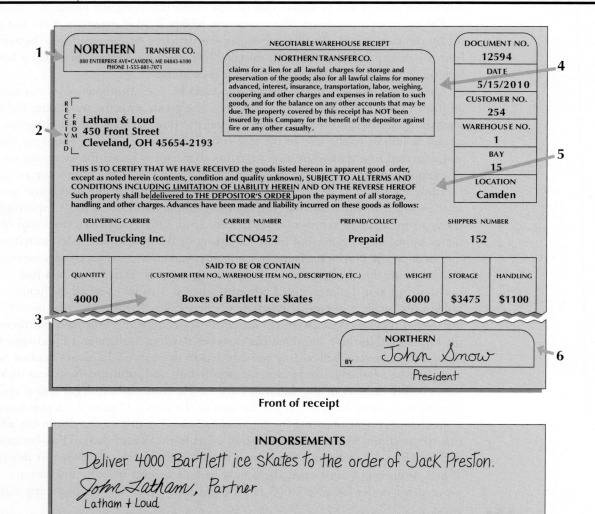

Front of receipt

INDORSEMENTS

Deliver 4000 Bartlett ice skates to the order of Jack Preston.

John Latham, Partner
Latham + Loud

Reverse side

(1) Warehouse, (2) depositor, (3) goods, (4) warehouse's lien, (5) negotiable delivery terms, (6) warehouse's authorized agent. A negotiable warehouse receipt contains a promise to deliver the goods to the bearer or to the order of the depositor, unlike a nonnegotiable warehouse receipt, which promises only to deliver them to the depositor.

field warehousing—stored goods under the exclusive control of a warehouse but kept on the owner's premises rather than in a warehouse.

the goods just as though they were in the warehouse. Such a transaction has the same legal effect with respect to other persons and purchasers of the warehouse receipts as though the property were in fact in the warehouse. This practice is called **field warehousing** because the goods are not taken to the warehouse but remain "in the field."

The purpose of field warehousing is to create warehouse receipts that the owner of the goods may pledge as security for loans. The owner could, of course, have done this by actually placing the goods in a warehouse, but this would have involved the expense of transportation and storage.

CPA 6. Limitation of Liability of Warehouses

A warehouse may limit liability by a provision in the warehouse receipt specifying the maximum amount for which the warehouse can be held liable. This privilege is subject to two qualifications. First, the customer must be given the choice of storing the goods without such limitation if the customer pays a higher storage rate, and, second, the limitation must be stated for each item or for each unit of weight.[16] **For Example,** a limitation is proper when it states that the maximum liability for a piano is $5,000 or that the maximum liability per bushel of wheat is a stated amount. Conversely, there cannot be a blanket limitation of liability, such as "maximum liability $100," when the receipt covers more than one item.

General contract law determines whether a limitation clause is a part of the contract between the warehouse and the customer. **For Example,** warehouse Eastern Warehousing, Inc., and customer Delavau, Inc., executed a comprehensive contract for storage of a nutritional supplement after extensive negotiations between Eastern's chief operating officer and Delavau's president. The goods were damaged due to a leaking warehouse roof. Eastern was unsuccessful in its argument that the contract was formed when the goods were subsequently delivered to the warehouse and a preprinted warehouse receipt containing a limitation-of-liability provision was given to the customer's driver. The court ruled that the terms of the receipt were not part of the contract of the parties, and awarded Delavau $1,358,601 in damages.[17]

B. Common Carriers

The purpose of a bailment may be transportation. In this case, the bailee may be a common carrier.

carrier—individual or organization undertaking the transportation of goods.

consignor—(1) person who delivers goods to the carrier for shipment, (2) party with title who turns goods over to another for sale.

consignee—(1) person to whom goods are shipped, (2) dealer who sells goods for others.

common carrier—carrier that holds out its facilities to serve the general public for compensation without discrimination.

7. Definitions

A **carrier** of goods is an individual or organization undertaking the transportation of goods regardless of the method of transportation or the distance covered. The **consignor** or shipper is the person who delivers goods to the carrier for shipment. The **consignee** is the person to whom the goods are shipped and to whom the carrier should deliver the goods.

A carrier may be classified as a common carrier, a contract carrier, or a private carrier. A **common carrier** holds itself out as willing to furnish transportation for compensation without discrimination to all members of the public who apply, assuming that the goods to be carried are proper and facilities of the carrier are

[16] UCC § 7-204(2); *Lobel v Samson Moving & Storage, Inc.,* 737 NYS2d 24 (App Div 2002).
[17] *Delavau v Eastern American Trading & Warehousing, Inc.,* 810 A2d 672 (Pa Super 2002).

contract carrier–carrier that transports on the basis of individual contracts that it makes with each shipper.

private carrier–carrier owned by the shipper, such as a company's own fleet of trucks.

available. A **contract carrier** transports goods under individual contracts, and a **private carrier** is owned and operated by the shipper. **For Example,** a truck fleet owned and operated by an industrial firm is a private carrier. Common carrier law or special bailment law applies to common carriers, ordinary bailment law to contract carriers, and the law of employment to private carriers.

The Federal Motor Carrier Safety Administration is the successor agency to the Interstate Commerce Commission and was created under the Interstate Commerce Commission Termination Act (ICCTA).[18] Under the ICCTA, Congress merged

CASE SUMMARY

The Distinction Continues

FACTS: M. Fortunoff of Westbury operates a chain of department stores in New York and New Jersey. In March of 1997, the company entered into a contract with Frederickson Motor Express, whereby the carrier agreed "as contract carrier and independent contractor ... to transfer shipments ... as authorized in Carrier's contract carrier permit ... issued by the ICC." The contract further provided: "Although carrier is authorized to operate ... as a common carrier, each and every shipment tendered to carrier by shipper ... shall be deemed to be a tender to carrier as a motor contract carrier... ." Fortunoff's goods were damaged in transit, prompting it to make a claim against Frederickson. When the carrier went out of business, Fortunoff asserted the same claim against the carrier's insurer, Peerless Insurance Co., for $13,249.42 under the BMC-32 indorsement (the mandatory attachment to all common carrier insurance policies), which was part of Frederickson's insurance policy. From a judgment for Fortunoff, on the ground that the ICCTA mandated the extension of BMC-32 indorsements to all motor carriers, Peerless appealed.

DECISION: Judgment against the shipper, Fortunoff. Historically, many trucking companies obtained both a common carrier certificate and a contract carrier permit, meaning they were authorized to operate as either type of carrier. If the carrier agreed to transport a shipper's goods according to standard terms and at a fixed rate (i.e., without an individually negotiated contract) on a nonrecurring basis, the transportation was conducted under the carrier's common carrier certificate. Accordingly, common carrier rules, including the cargo liability insurance and the BMC-32 indorsement requirement, applied. If the carrier and the shipper wished to negotiate a bilateral contract for an ongoing course of shipping services, the carrier was required to operate under its contract carrier permit, and no cargo insurance was necessary.

Requiring cargo liability insurance for common carriage but not contract carriage is not an arbitrary distinction. Instead, it makes economic sense because of the different types of services performed and the customers served by common carriage. Although the ICCTA abolished the licensing distinction between common and contract carriers, it did so in large part because most carriers had a common carrier certificate and a contract carrier permit and provided both types of service anyway. But the functional distinction between the two types of carriage survives and is still highly relevant to deciding which motor carriers must have cargo liability insurance. The administrative agency's decision to require BMC-32 cargo insurance only when performing common carriage service is consistent with the ICCTA. The district court's ruling is reversed. [**M. Fortunoff of Westbury Corp. v Peerless Ins., 432 F3d 127 (2nd Cir 2005)**]

---

[18] 49 USC § 13906 (a)(3) (2000) (amended 2005).

the separate classifications of common and contract carrier into one classification termed "motor carrier." However, as is seen in the *Fortunoff* case, the fundamental distinction between the types of carriage remains explicit in the act.

8. Bills of Lading

bill of lading–document issued by a carrier reciting the receipt of goods and the terms of the contract of transportation. Regulated by the Federal Bills of Lading Act or the UCC.

airbill–document of title issued to a shipper whose goods are being sent via air.

When the carrier accepts goods for shipment or forwarding, the carrier ordinarily issues to the shipper a **bill of lading** in the case of land or water transportation or an **airbill** for air transportation. This instrument is a document of title and provides rights similar to those provided by a warehouse receipt. A bill of lading is both a receipt for the goods and a memorandum of a contract stating the terms of carriage. Title to the goods may be transferred by a transfer of the bill of lading made with that intention.

Bills of lading for intrastate shipments are governed by the Uniform Commercial Code. For interstate shipments, bills of lading are regulated by the Federal Bills of Lading Act (FBLA).[19]

CPA   (A) CONTENTS OF BILL OF LADING. The form of the bill of lading is regulated in varying degrees by administrative agencies. Prior to the revisions to Article 7, negotiable bills of lading were printed on yellow paper, and nonnegotiable or straight bills of lading were printed on white paper. This color-coding may continue as commercial practice for those documents reduced to written form, but new commercial practices will evolve regarding the use of "records.[20]

As against the good faith transferee of the bill of lading, a carrier is bound by the recitals in the bill as to the contents, quantity, or weight of goods.[21] This means that the carrier must produce the goods that are described or pay damages for failing to do so. This rule is not applied if facts appear on the face of the bill that should keep the transferee from relying on the recital.

negotiable bill of lading– document of title that by its terms calls for goods to be delivered "to the bearer" or "to the order of" a named person.

nonnegotiable bill of lading–see *straight bill of lading*.

straight (or nonnegotiable) bill of lading–document of title that consigns transported goods to a named person.

(B) NEGOTIATION. A bill of lading is a **negotiable bill of lading** when by its terms the goods are to be delivered "to the bearer" or "to the order of" a named person.[22] Any other bill of lading, such as one that consigns the goods to a named person, is a **nonnegotiable** or **straight bill of lading**. Like transferees of warehouse receipts who take by due negotiation, holders of bills of lading who take by due negotiation ordinarily also acquire title to the bills and title to the goods represented by them.

Rights of a transferee are defeated by the true owner, however, when a thief delivers the goods to the carrier and then negotiates the bill of lading. The thief had no title to the goods at any time.

---

[19] 49 USC § 81 *et seq.*

[20] The UCC contains no provision regulating the form of the bill of lading and the use of records, including electronic tracking, now covered under Revised Article 7. This means that new commercial practices will evolve.

[21] UCC § 7-301(1).

[22] UCC § 7-104(1)(a).

CASE SUMMARY

International Intrigue

FACTS: Banque de Depots, a Swiss bank, sued Bozel, a Brazilian corporation, for money owed the bank. Banque obtained a writ of attachment from the court against goods being shipped by Bozel from Rio de Janeiro through the port of New Orleans for transit to purchasers located in three states. Bozel claimed that the writ of attachment must be dissolved because the cargo was shipped under negotiable bearer bills of lading and the bills of lading had been sent to U.S. banks for collection from the purchasers.

DECISION: Judgment for Bozel. The writ of attachment must be dissolved. Goods shipped pursuant to a negotiable bill of lading cannot be seized unless the bill of lading is surrendered to the carrier or impounded by a court. On the day of the seizure of the cargo under the writ, the negotiable bills of lading were outstanding. The bills of lading were not in the hands of the carrier, and their negotiation had not been enjoined by the court. The law protects holders of duly negotiated bills of lading from purchasing such bills and then finding out that the goods have been seized by judicial process. The holder of a duly negotiated bill of lading acquires title to the document and title to the goods described in the document. [**Banque de Depots v Bozel, 569 So2d 40 (La App 1990)**]

(C) **WARRANTIES.** By transferring for value a bill of lading, whether negotiable or nonnegotiable, the transferor makes certain implied warranties to the transferee. The transferor impliedly warrants that (1) the bill of lading is genuine, (2) its transfer is rightful and is effective to transfer the goods represented by it, and (3) the transferor has no knowledge of facts that would impair the validity or worth of the bill of lading.[23]

9. Rights of Common Carrier

A common carrier of goods has the right to make reasonable and necessary rules for the conduct of its business. It has the right to charge such rates for its services to yield it a fair return on the property devoted to the business of transportation.

As security for unpaid transportation and service charges, a common carrier has a lien on goods that it transports. The carrier's lien also secures demurrage, the costs of preservation of the goods, and the costs of sale to enforce the lien.[24]

10. Duties of Common Carrier

A common carrier is required (1) to receive and carry proper and lawful goods of all persons who offer them for shipment as long as the carrier has space, (2) to furnish facilities that are adequate for the transportation of freight in the usual course of business and to furnish proper storage facilities for goods awaiting shipment or

---

[23] UCC § 7-507; FBLA, 49 USC §§ 114, 116. When the transfer of the bill of lading is part of a transaction by which the transferor sells the goods represented thereby to the transferee, there will also arise the warranties that are found in other sales of goods.

[24] UCC § 7-307(1); FBLA, 49 USC § 105.

awaiting delivery after shipment, (3) to follow the directions given by the shipper, (4) to load and unload goods delivered to it for shipment, but the shipper or consignee may assume this duty by contract or custom, and (5) to deliver the goods in accordance with the shipment contract.

Goods must be delivered at the usual place of delivery at the specified destination. When goods are shipped under a negotiable bill of lading, the carrier must not deliver the goods without obtaining possession of the bill, properly indorsed. When goods are shipped under a straight bill of lading, the carrier may deliver the goods to the consignee or the consignee's agent without receiving the bill of lading unless notified by the shipper to deliver the goods to someone else. If the carrier delivers the goods to the wrong person, the carrier is liable for breach of contract and for the tort of conversion.

CPA ## 11. Liabilities of Common Carrier

When goods are delivered to a common carrier for immediate shipment and while they are in transit, the carrier is absolutely liable for any loss or damage to the goods unless it can prove that the loss or damage was due solely to one or more of the following excepted causes: (1) an act of God, meaning a natural phenomenon that is not reasonably foreseeable, (2) an act of a public enemy, such as the military forces of an opposing government, as distinguished from ordinary robbers, (3) an act of a public authority, such as a health officer removing goods from the carrier, (4) an act of the shipper, such as fraudulent labeling or defective packing, or (5) the inherent nature of the goods, such as those naturally tending to spoil or deteriorate.

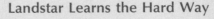

C A S E   S U M M A R Y

Landstar Learns the Hard Way

FACTS: Tempel Steel Corporation shipped a large machine press from Minster, Ohio, to Monterrey, Mexico, by Landstar Inway, Inc., a common carrier. Landstar issued Tempel a through bill of lading for this service. It then hauled the press to the U.S. border, where it hired a customs broker who utilized a local carrier, Teresa de Jesus Ortiz Obregon, to move the cargo through U.S. and Mexican customs to interchange with a Mexican carrier. It was determined that Obregon failed to secure the press properly and drove too fast, causing $300,000 damage to the press. Tempel sued Landstar to recover for this damage. Landstar defended that it was not responsible for causalities in Mexico and that the loss was the fault of Obregon.

DECISION: Landstar is financially responsible for the entire movement by having entered a competitive bid to transport goods from Ohio through to Mexico and having issued a through bill of lading. Tempel is thus entitled to hold Landstar liable for the damage, and Landstar then bears the responsibility for seeking compensation from the carrier actually responsible for the loss. Although Landstar had every legal right to issue a bill of lading that stopped at the U.S. border, it did not do so. Landstar must accept the legal consequences of the issuance of the through bill of lading without limitation of liability for losses. [**Temple Steel Corp. v Landstar Inway, Inc., 211 F3d 1029 (2000)**]

(A) **CARRIER'S LIABILITY FOR DELAY.** A carrier is liable for losses caused by its failure to deliver goods within a reasonable time. **For Example,** J.B. Hunt Transport, Inc., "lost" a shipment of boxed Christmas cards specially packaged for Target Stores, Inc., by the shipper, Paper Magic, Inc. The goods were shipped on October 16, 1998, and the invoice valued them at $130,080.48. Hunt located the shipment on February 5, 1999, and Target refused the goods because it was well after Christmas and the goods were worthless to Target. The cards were worthless to Paper Magic because they were packaged with Target's private label. The court found that awarding the shipper the invoice value was a permissible award under the Carmack Amendment to the Interstate Commerce Act.[25]

The carrier, however, is not liable for every delay. The shipper assumes the risk of ordinary delays incidental to transporting goods.

(B) **LIMITATION OF LIABILITY OF CARRIER.** In the absence of a constitutional or statutory prohibition, a common carrier generally has the right to limit its liability by contract.

Common carriers operating interstate may limit their liability for the negligent loss of consigned items to a stated dollar amount, such as $100 per package. Shippers, however, must be given a reasonable opportunity to select excess liability coverage for the higher value of their shipment, with payment of higher freight charges.[26]

The Carmack Amendment to the Interstate Commerce Act governs the liability of carriers for loss or damage in the interstate shipment of goods.[27] Shippers displeased with liability limitations permitted carriers under the Carmack Amendment may not sue a carrier under any state statute if the statute in any way enlarges the responsibility of a carrier for loss or damage to the goods.[28] The Carmack Amendment provides the exclusive remedy for loss or damage, and its purpose is to provide uniformity in the disposition of claims brought under a bill of lading or waybill.

C A S E   S U M M A R Y

Kroger's Calling American Foods: "Where's the Beef?"

FACTS: On November 14, 2006, American Foods retained Wayne Flandrich dba as J&W Transport to pick up a load of meat from American Foods. The load consisted of approximately 16,000 pounds of ground beef. J&W Transport was to deliver the load to The Kroger Company in Delaware, Ohio, and Meijer, Inc. in Tipp City, Ohio. In picking up the load, Flandrich signed bills

---

[25] *The Paper Magic Group, Inc. v J.B. Hunt Transport, Inc.*, 318 F3d 458 (3d Cir 2003). See also *National Hispanic Circus, Inc. v Rex Trucking*, 414 F3d 546 (5th Cir 2005).

[26] In *Sassy Doll Creations Inc. v Watkins Motor Lines Inc.*, 331 F3d 834 (11th Cir 2003), the carrier was held liable for the full value of a lost shipment of perfume, $28,273.60, rather than $10,000.00, the carrier's established limitation of its liability. The bill of lading prepared by the carrier contained a declared value box, which the shipper filled in. However, the document did not contain any space for requesting excess liability coverage and thus did not give the shipper a reasonable opportunity to select a higher level of coverage as required by the Carmack Amendment to the Interstate Commerce Act.

[27] 49 USC § 11707.

[28] *Dugan v FedEx Corp.*, 2002 WL 31305208 (CD Cal).

C A S E   S U M M A R Y

Continued

of lading attesting that the meat was in "apparent good order." On November 15, 2006, at approximately 1:45 A.M., the tractor-trailer overturned and the cargo was never delivered to the buyers. American Foods was never paid by the buyers for the value of the cargo. Pursuant to its cargo insurance policy, Great West Casualty Co. paid American Foods' damage claim of $31,813.85 when Flandrich failed to pay the claim. As the shipper's insurer, Great West sued the carrier under the Carmack Amendment and for breach of contract under state law. Flandrich did not believe that Great West had standing to sue under the Carmack Amendment.

DECISION: Judgment for Great West. The bills of lading were issued to American Foods and it had title to the cargo of meat at the time of the accident. It thus had an insurable interest in the cargo and its rights were subrogated to Great West; therefore, Great West had standing to bring a claim under the Carmack Amendment. To establish a prima facie case under the Carmack Amendment, Great West had to show (1) delivery of the meat in good condition to the carrier, (2) that the meat had arrived in damaged condition, and (3) the amount of damages. There was no issue of material fact as to any of the elements. The burden of proof then shifted to Flandrich who could not show both that he was free from negligence and that the damage to the cargo was due to one of the excepted causes relieving the carrier of liability. Accordingly, Great West was entitled to summary judgment on its Carmack Amendment claim. The breach of contract claim for consequential damages resulting from the failure to deliver the cargo was denied due to preemption, which eliminates all state law claims. [**Great West Casualty Co. v Flandrich, 605 F Supp 2d 955 (ED Ohio 2009)**]

(c) **NOTICE OF CLAIM.** The bill of lading and applicable government regulations may require that a carrier be given notice of any claim for damages or loss of goods within a specified time, generally within nine months.

(d) **COD SHIPMENT.** A common carrier transporting goods under a COD (cash on delivery) shipment may not make delivery of the goods without first receiving payment. If it does, it is liable to the shipper for any resulting loss. Thus, if a FedEx or UPS driver were to accept a bad check from a consignee on a COD shipment, the carrier would be liable to the shipper for the amount owed.

There are two forms of COD payments in addition to cash—certified and cashier's checks.

C A S E   S U M M A R Y

Cashier's Check Is King

FACTS: ABF Freight Systems, Inc., accepted a certified check for a COD fee owed upon delivery of 511 cartons of shoes to the location designated in the bill of lading. It turned out that the bank certification stamped on the face of the check was a forgery. The bill of lading included the specification that delivery be "COD Cashier's Check" and that ABF collect payment on behalf of

Continued

Imports, Ltd. Imports sued ABF for $53,180.90, the full value of the COD payment. From a judgment for Imports for the full amount plus interest, ABF appealed.

DECISION: Judgment for Imports, Ltd. The primary difference between a bank certified check and a cashier's check is in the ease with which one can create a fraudulent instrument. To forge a cashier's check, one would need to replicate all of the other features of the bank's form. To forge a bank check, on the other hand, one need only have a writing on the check indicating that the check is "certified." Imports had a right to believe that a cashier's check is a better form of payment than a certified check. The agreement that ABF would accept only a cashier's check reflected this belief. ABF broke its contract with Imports by accepting a bank certified check rather than a cashier's check for the COD payment. [**Imports, Ltd., v ABF Freight Systems, Inc., 162 F3d 528 (8th Cir 1998)**]

(E) **Rejected Shipments.** When a common carrier tenders delivery of consigned goods to a consignee that refuses to accept the delivery, the carrier is no longer a common carrier but becomes a warehouse. When the carrier-turned-warehouse receives new shipping instructions from the owner, its status again changes to that of a common carrier.

(F) **Complexities in Intercontinental and Domestic Shipping.** In intercontinental ocean-to-inland shipping, carriers may or may not know whether they are dealing with an intermediary, such as a freight forwarding company rather than a cargo owner, or what legal obligations the cargo owner and intermediary have agreed upon. Moreover, the number of times goods change hands in the course of this intermodal transportation of goods adds to the complexities regarding liability limitations and other bills-of-lading issues such as forum selection clauses. **For Example,** James Kirby, Ltd, an Australian manufacturer, hired International Cargo Control (ICC) to arrange for the delivery of machinery from Australia to Huntsville, Alabama. The bill of lading that ICC issued to Kirby designated Savannah, Georgia, as the discharge port and Huntsville, Alabama, as the ultimate destination, and set ICC's liability limitation lower than the cargo's true value, using the default liability rule in the Carriage of Goods by Sea Act (COGSA) of $500 per package for the sea leg and a higher amount for the land leg. The bill also contained what is known as the "Himalaya Clause," which extends liability limitations to downstream carriers and contractors. When ICC hired a German shipping company, Hamburg Süd, to transport the containers, Hamburg Süd issued its own bill of lading to ICC. That bill of lading also adopted COGSA's default rule, extended it to any land damages, and extended it in a Himalaya Clause to "all agents ... (including inland) carriers ...". Hamburg Süd hired Norfolk Southern Railway (NS) to transport the machinery some 366 miles from Savannah to Huntsville. The train derailed, causing some $1.5 million in damages. Kirby sued NS for the full value of its loss, and NS, claiming the protections of the ICC and Hamburg Süd bills of lading, asserted that it owed just $500 per container. The U.S. Supreme Court held that "when it comes to liability limitations for negligence resulting in damage, an intermediary [ICC and Hamburg Süd] can negotiate reliable and enforceable agreements with the carrier it engages,"[29] thus upholding NS's limited liability of $500 per container. U.S. courts have also recognized the rule that a freight forwarder has a limited agency to bind a cargo owner to a forum selection clause by accepting a carrier's bill of lading.[30]

C. FACTORS AND CONSIGNMENTS

factor—bailee to whom goods are consigned for sale.

A **factor** is a special type of bailee who sells consigned goods as though the factor were the owner of those goods.

12. Definitions

selling on consignment—entrusting a person with possession of property for the purpose of sale.

commission merchant—bailee to whom goods are consigned for sale.

commission or **factorage**—consignee's compensation.

Entrusting a person with the possession of property for the purpose of sale is commonly called **selling on consignment**.[31] The owner who consigns the goods for sale is the *consignor*. The person or agent to whom they are consigned is the factor or *consignee*; this individual may also be known as a **commission merchant**. A consignee's compensation is known as a **commission** or **factorage**. For Example, *consignor* Rolly Tasker Sails Co., Ltd. (RTS) would ship sails from Thailand to the *consignee*, Bacon & Associates of Annapolis, Maryland, with a bill of lading and an "invoice price" for each sail. Mrs. Bacon would then set her "retail fair market value price." Once a set of sails was sold, Mrs. Bacon would deposit a check to the consignor's account at Alex Brown Co. at the invoice price. Her *commission* was the difference between the retail price and the invoice price. This arrangement began in 1971, but began to unravel 27 years later. RTS was successful in its breach of *consignment agreement* lawsuit against Bacon for $345,327 in damages and $78,660 in interest.[32]

13. Effect of Factor Transaction

In a sale on consignment, the property remains the property of the owner-consignor, and the consignee acts as the agent of the owner to pass the owner's title to the buyer. A consignment sale is treated as a sale or return under Article 2 of the Uniform Commercial Code (UCC), and the factor-consignee has full authority to sell the goods for the consignor and can pass title to those goods. Thus, creditors of the consignee can obtain possession of the goods and have a superior right to them over the consignor. If, however, the owner-consignor complies with the security interest and perfection provisions of Article 9 of the UCC (Chapter 34), there is public notice of the consignment, and the goods will be subject to the claims of the owner's creditors, but not to those of the factor-consignee.[33]

---

[29] *Norfolk Southern Ry. Co. v Kirby*, 543 US 1433 (2004).
[30] *Maersk Sealand v Ocean Express Miami (Quality Print)*, 550 F Supp 2d 484 (SDNY 2008).
[31] *Amoco Oil Co. v DZ Enterprises, Inc.*, 607 F Supp 595 (SDNY 1985).
[32] *Bacon & Associates, Inc. v Rolly Tasker Sails Co. Ltd. (Thailand)*, 841 A2d 53 (Md App 2004).
[33] Revised Article 2 (1999) modifies the rules on consignments slightly in that all transactions are treated as sales or return or sales on approval unless steps are taken to identify a transaction as a consignment and to comply with state laws on consignment. The new UCC § 2-326(a), (b), and (c) provides as follows:

The provisions of this subsection are applicable even though an agreement purports to reserve title to the person making delivery until payment or resale or uses such words as "on consignment" or "on memorandum." However, this subsection is not applicable if the person making delivery

a. complies with an applicable law providing for a consignor's interest or the like to be evidenced by a sign, or
b. establishes that the person conducting the business is generally known by his creditors to be substantially engaged in selling the goods of others, or
c. complies with the filing provisions of the Article on Second Transactions (Article 9).

conversion–act of taking personal property by a person not entitled to it and keeping it from its true owner or prior possessor without consent.

If the consignor is not the owner, as when a thief delivers stolen goods to the factor, a sale by the factor passes no title and is an unlawful **conversion**.

D. HOTELKEEPERS

A hotelkeeper has a bailee's liability with respect to property specifically entrusted to the hotelkeeper's care. In addition, the hotelkeeper has special duties with respect to a guest's property brought into the hotel. The rules governing the special relationship between a hotelkeeper and a guest arose because of the special needs of travelers.

14. Definitions

The definitions of *hotelkeeper* and *guest* exclude lodging of a more permanent character, such as that provided by boardinghouse keepers to boarders.

hotelkeeper–one regularly engaged in the business of offering living accommodations to all transient persons.

(A) HOTELKEEPER. A **hotelkeeper** is an operator of a hotel, motel, or tourist home or anyone who is regularly engaged in the business of offering living accommodations to transient persons. In the early law, the hotelkeeper was called an *innkeeper* or a *tavernkeeper*.

guest–transient who contracts for a room or site at a hotel.

(B) GUEST. A **guest** is a transient. The guest need not be a traveler or come from a distance. A person living within a short distance of a hotel who engages a room at the hotel and remains there overnight is a guest.

In contrast, a person who enters a hotel at the invitation of a guest or attends a dance or a banquet given at the hotel is not a guest. Similarly, the guest of a registered occupant of a motel room who shares the room with the occupant without the knowledge or consent of the management is not a guest of the motel because there is no relationship between that person and the motel.

15. Duration of Guest Relationship

The relationship of guest and hotelkeeper does not begin until a person is received as a guest by the hotelkeeper. The guest–hotelkeeper relationship does not automatically end when the hotel bill is paid.[34]

The relationship terminates when the guest leaves or ceases to be a transient, as when the guest arranges for a more or less permanent residence at the hotel. The transition from the status of guest to the status of boarder or lodger must be clearly indicated. It is not established by the mere fact that one remains at the hotel for a long period, even though it runs into months.

Circumstances arise when a hotel assumes an obligation to deliver packages to a guest from a person who is not a guest of the hotel. The hotelkeeper has a bailee's liability for the care of such packages. **For Example,** Richard St. Angelo, vice president of sales for jewelry manufacturer Don-Linn Inc., left two boxes of jewelry prototypes at the front desk of the Westin Hotel with instructions to deliver the boxes to the hotel's guest from Dillard's Inc., a national department store. This delivery took place. Thereafter, a Dillard's representative notified St. Angelo that Dillard's review of the products was complete and he could pick up the boxes at the hotel but specified no location. St. Angelo and the Westin staff later searched for

---

[34] *Garrett v Impac Hotels, LLC,* 87 SW3d 870 (Mo App 2002).

the boxes, but they were never found. The manufacturer's lawsuit against the Westin asserting a breach of bailment was not successful. St. Angelo was not a guest at the Westin, thus the obligation assumed for the care of the packages initially left at the Westin was not as a hotelkeeper but a bailee. When the Westin surrendered the packages to Dillard's group, it completed its bailment agreement. No bailment or any other legal obligation between Don-Linn and the Westin was shown to exist with regard to the return of the jewelry prototypes.[35]

16. Hotelkeeper's Liability for Guest's Property

With respect to property expressly entrusted to the hotelkeeper's care, the hotelkeeper has a bailee's liability. At common law, the hotelkeeper was absolutely liable for damage to, or loss of, a guest's property unless the hotelkeeper could show that the damage or loss was caused solely by an act of God, a public enemy, an act of a public authority, the inherent nature of the property, or the fault of the guest.[36]

In most states, statutes limit or provide a method of limiting the common law liability of a hotelkeeper. The statutes may limit the extent of liability, reduce the liability of a hotelkeeper to that of an ordinary bailee, or permit the hotelkeeper to limit liability by contract or by posting a notice of the limitation. Some statutes relieve the hotelkeeper from liability when the guest has not complied with directions for depositing valuables with the hotelkeeper.[37] A hotelkeeper must substantially comply with such statutes in order to obtain their protection.

C A S E   S U M M A R Y

Problems of the Rich and Famous at a Five-Star Hotel

FACTS: Thelma Paraskevaides and others were guests at the Four Seasons Hotel in Washington, D.C. Upon arrival, they placed and locked their valuables in their room safe and left the room for the day. Upon their return, they found the room ransacked and the safe opened, and their valuables worth $1.2 million missing. Thelma theorized that the hotel's master key to the hotel's room safes had been missing, and she believed she should have been informed of this by the hotel. The hotel contends that it satisfied the conditions for the statutory bar to strict liability for the loss under District of Columbia law.

DECISION: Judgment for the hotel. Under the common law rule, an innkeeper is statutorily liable for loss or damage to a guest's property. In D.C. and many other jurisdictions, however, the common law rule has been modified. Section 34-101 of the D.C. Code frees hotels of liability when the host hotel conspicuously posts a copy or summary of § 34-101 and information that safety deposit boxes are maintained at the front desk. The plaintiffs admitted the hotel did post a summary of § 34-101 next to the room safe; and this was sufficient to place the plaintiffs on notice. The hotel is not liable for the plaintiffs' property loss. [**Paraskevaides v Four Seasons Washington, 148 F Supp 2d 20 (D DC 2002)**]

---

[35] *Don-Linn Jewelry Co. v The Westin Hotel Co.*, 877 A2d 621 (RI 2005).
[36] *Cook v Columbia Sussex Corp.*, 807 SW2d 567 (Tenn App 1991).
[37] *Chappone v First Florence Corp.*, 504 SE2d 761 (Ga App 1998). But see *World Diamond Inc. v Hyatt Corp.*, 699 NE2d 980 (Ohio App 1997), where the court held that when special arrangements have been made between the innkeeper and the guest, the innkeeper is liable for the loss of any property so received when the loss is caused by the innkeeper's negligence.

17. Hotelkeeper's Lien

The hotelkeeper has a lien on the baggage of guests for the agreed charges or, if no express agreement was made, for the reasonable value of the accommodations furnished. Statutes permit the hotelkeeper to enforce this lien by selling the goods of the guests at a public sale. The lien of the hotelkeeper is terminated by (1) the guest's payment of the hotel charges, (2) any conversion of the guest's goods by the hotelkeeper, or (3) final return of the goods to the guest.

18. Boarders or Lodgers

The hotelkeeper owes only the duty of an ordinary bailee of personal property under a mutual benefit bailment to those persons who are permanent boarders or lodgers rather than transient guests.

A hotelkeeper has no lien on property of boarders or lodgers, as distinguished from guests, in the absence of an express agreement creating such a lien. A number of states, however, have adopted legislation giving a lien to keepers of boarding-houses or lodging houses.

lawflix

Nine to Five (1980) (PG)

At the heart of the twists and turns in this boss/secretary caper are the warehouse receipts an executive is using to embezzle from his company. Analyze what the executive was doing with the documents.

Check out LawFlix at **www.cengage.com/blaw/dvl** to access movie clips that illustrate business law concepts.

MAKE THE CONNECTION

SUMMARY

A warehouse stores the goods of others for compensation and has the rights and duties of a bailee in an ordinary mutual benefit bailment. A warehouse issues a warehouse receipt to the depositor of the goods. This receipt is a document of title that ordinarily entitles the person in possession of the receipt to receive the goods. The warehouse receipt can be bought, sold, or used as security to obtain a loan. A nonnegotiable warehouse receipt states that the goods received will be delivered to a specified person. A negotiable warehouse receipt states that the goods will be delivered "to the bearer" or "to the order of" a named person. If a negotiable warehouse receipt is duly negotiated, the transferee may acquire rights superior to those of the transferor. A warehouse may limit its liability for loss or damage to goods resulting from its own negligence to an agreed valuation of the property stated in the warehouse receipt, provided the depositor is given the right to store the goods without the limitation at a higher storage rate.

A common carrier of goods is in the business of transporting goods received from the general public. It issues to the shipper a bill of lading or an airbill. Both of these are documents of title and provide rights similar to those provided by a warehouse receipt. A common carrier is absolutely liable for any loss or damage to the goods unless the carrier can show that the loss was caused solely by an act of God, an act of a public enemy, an act of a public authority, an act of the shipper, or the inherent nature of the goods. The carrier may limit its liability in the same manner as a warehouse.

A factor is a special type of bailee who has possession of the owner's property for the purpose of sale. The factor, or consignee, receives a commission on the sale.

A hotelkeeper is in the business of providing living accommodations to transient persons called guests. Subject to exceptions, at common law, hotelkeepers were absolutely liable for loss or damage to their guests' property. Most states, however, provide a method of limiting this liability. A hotelkeeper has a lien on the property of the guest for the agreed charges.

LEARNING OUTCOMES

After studying this chapter, you should be able to clearly explain:

A. WAREHOUSERS

LO.1 Identify and explain all of the features of a negotiable warehouse receipt
> See the example of the bona fide purchase of a warehouse receipt of 4,000 pairs of ice skates on p. 483.
> See Figure 22-1.

B. COMMON CARRIERS

LO.2 List and explain the differences between the three types of motor carriers of goods
> See the *Fortunoff* case and distinctions made between "common" and "contract" carriers, p. 486.

LO.3 Explain a common carrier's liability for loss or damage to goods
> See the *Great West Casualty* case applying the Carmack Amendment rule on carrier liability, p. 490.

C. FACTORS AND CONSIGNMENTS

LO.4 Identify and explain the role of each of the persons or business entities involved in the sale of goods on consignment
> See the Rolly Tasker Sails example involving breach of a consignment agreement on p. 493.

D. HOTELKEEPERS

LO.5   Describe a hotelkeeper's liability for loss of a guest's property

See the *Paraskevaides v Four Seasons Washington* case for a discussion of the common law rule on liability for loss of a guest's property and application of a statutory exemption, p. 495.

KEY TERMS

airbill	factorage	nonnegotiable warehouse
bill of lading	factor	receipt
carrier	field warehousing	private carrier
commission merchant	guest	public warehouses
commission	hotelkeeper	selling on consignment
common carrier	issuer	specific lien
consignee	negotiable bill of lading	straight bill of lading
consignor	negotiable warehouse	warehouse receipt
contract carrier	receipt	warehouse
conversion	nonnegotiable bill of	
depositor	lading	
document of title		

QUESTIONS AND CASE PROBLEMS

1. What social forces are involved in the rule of law governing the liability of a common carrier for loss of freight?

2. American Cyanamid shipped 7,000 vials of DPT—a vaccine for immunization of infants and children against diphtheria, pertussis, and tetanus—from its Pearl River, New York, facility to the U.S. Defense Department depot in Mechanicsburg, Pennsylvania, by New Penn Motor Express, a common carrier. Cyanamid's bill of lading included a "release value," which stated the value of the property was declared as not exceeding $1.65 per pound. Cyanamid's shipment weighed 1,260 pounds. The bill of lading accepted by New Penn on picking up the DPT vaccine on February 6 also clearly stated that the shipment contained drugs and clearly warned to "protect from freezing." The bill further recited "rush … must be delivered by February 8, 1989." New Penn permitted the vaccine to sit in an unheated uninsulated trailer while it gathered enough other merchandise to justify sending a truck to Mechanicsburg. The DPT vaccine was delivered on February 10 in worthless condition, having been destroyed by the cold. New Penn admitted it owed $2,079 in damages pursuant to the bill of lading ($1.65 1,260 lbs.). Cyanamid claimed that the actual loss was much greater, $53,936.75. It stated that because New Penn breached its contract with Cyanamid, it could not invoke the benefits of that same contract, namely, the release value clause.

   Was it ethical for New Penn to hold the vaccine while waiting for enough merchandise to justify the trip? How would you decide the case? [*American Cyanamid Co. v New Penn Motor Express, Inc.*, 979 F2d 301 (3d Cir)]

3. Compare the liens of carriers, warehouses, and hotels in terms of being specific.

4. Compare the limitations of the liability of a warehouse and of a hotelkeeper.

5. Compare warehouse receipts and bills of lading as to negotiability.

6. Doyle Harms applied to his state's Public Utilities Commission for a Class B permit authorizing performance as a common carrier. Doyle testified that it was not his intention to haul in a different direction than he was already going, stating in part:

   > *No way, that's not what I'm asking for. I've got enough business of my own, it's just the times when you get done with a sale at the end of the day and you've got a half load and somebody else has a half load, then you'd be able to help each other out. It's kind of the name of the game in my mind.*

   He also testified that the application was so he could haul cattle for his own customers. State law defines a common carrier as "a motor carrier which holds itself out to the general public as engaged in the business of transporting persons or property in intrastate commerce which it is accustomed to and is capable of transporting from place to place in this state, for hire." Its property is "devoted to the public service." Should Doyle Harms be issued a common carrier permit? [*In re Harms*, 491 NW2d 760 (SD)]

7. Motorola manufactured cell phones for Nextel of Mexico at its facility in Plantation, Florida. Nextel used Westwind International to arrange transportation of the cell phones. Westwind utilized Transpro Logistics to administer the transportation process and Transpro entered a Broker Transportation Agreement (BTA) with Werner Enterprises, a common carrier, to transport the phones from Florida to Texas on a regular basis. The BTA incorporated Werner's tariff giving shippers the option of selecting Carmack Liability full-value coverage or the carrier's limitation of liability of a maximum of $200,000 per truckload shipment. In its contract with Nextel, Westwind notified Nextel that third-party carriers might limit their liability for loss, and stated that it would request excess valuation coverage only upon specific written instructions from Nextel. Nextel simply relied on Westwind to handle shipping issues. On October 8, 2004, a shipment of 7,958 cell phones valued at $1,251,673 was stolen from one of Werner's trucks. Werner contended it owed a maximum liability of $200,000 under its tariff. Nextel's insurer, Ace Seguros SA, sued Werner for the full value of the shipment, contending that contracts downstream by Westwind and Transpro cannot be imputed back to Nextel—and that the cargo owner Nextel had not been give the opportunity to choose between two or more levels of liability as required by the Carmack Amendment. Can intermediaries like Westwind and/or Transpro negotiate an enforceable agreement with a carrier it engages? Was Nextel given a reasonable opportunity to choose between two or more levels of liability? Decide. [*Werner Enterprises, Inc. v Ace Seguros SA*, 554 F3d 1319 (11th Cir)]

8. Richard Schewe and others placed personal property in a building occupied by Winnebago County Fair Association, Inc. Prior to placing their property in the

building, they signed a "Storage Rental Agreement" prepared by the County Fair Association, which stated: "No liability exists for damage or loss to the stored equipment from the perils of fire... ." The property was destroyed by fire. Suit was brought against the County Fair Association to recover damages for the losses on the theory of negligence of a warehouse. The County Fair Association claimed that the language in the storage agreement relieved it of all liability. [*Allstate Ins. Co. v Winnebago County Fair Ass'n, Inc.*, 475 NE2d 230 (Ill App)]

9. Buffett sent a violin to Strotokowsky by International Parcel Service (IPS), a common carrier. Buffett declared the value of the parcel at $500 on the pick-up receipt given him by the IPS driver. The receipt also stated: "Unless a greater value is declared in writing on this receipt, the shipper hereby declares and agrees that the released value of each package covered by this receipt is $100.00, which is a reasonable value under the circumstance surrounding the transportation." When Strotokowsky did not receive the parcel, Buffett sued IPS for the full retail value of the violin—$2,000. IPS's defense was that it was liable for just $100. Decide.

10. Glen Smith contracted with Dave Watson, a common carrier, to transport 720 hives of live bees along with associated equipment from Idabel, Oklahoma, to Mandan, North Dakota. At 9:00 A.M. on May 24, 1984, while en route, Watson's truck skidded off the road and tipped over, severely damaging the cargo. Watson notified Smith about what had happened, and Smith immediately set out for the scene of the accident. He arrived at 6:00 P.M. with two bee experts and a Bobcat loader. They were hindered by the turned-over truck on top of the cargo, and they determined that they could not safely salvage the cargo that evening. The next day, an insurance adjuster determined that the cargo was a total loss. The adjuster directed a bee expert, Dr. Moffat, to conduct the cleanup; Moffat was allowed to keep the salvageable cargo, valued at $12,326, as compensation. Smith sued Watson for damages. Watson denied liability and further contended that Smith failed to mitigate damages. Decide. [*Smith v Watson*, 406 NW2d 685 (ND)]

11. A guest in a motel opened the bedroom window at night and went to sleep. During the night, a prowler pried open the screen, entered the room, and stole property of the guest. The guest sued the motel. The motel asserted that it was not responsible for property in the possession of the guest and that the guest had been contributorily negligent in opening the window. Could the guest recover damages? [*Buck v Hankin*, 269 A2d 344 (Pa Super)]

12. On March 30, Emery Air Freight Corp. picked up a shipment of furs from Hopper Furs, Inc. Hopper's chief of security filled in certain items in the airbill. In the box entitled ZIP Code, he mistakenly placed the figure "61,045," which was the value of the furs. The ZIP Code box was immediately above the Declared Value box. The airbill contained a clause limiting liability to $10 per pound of cargo lost or damaged unless the shipper makes a declaration of value in excess of the amount and pays a higher fee. A higher fee was not charged in this case, and Gerald Doane signed the airbill for the carrier and took possession of the furs. The furs were lost in transit by Emery, and Hopper sued

for the value of the furs, $61,045. Emery's offer to pay $2,150, the $10-per-pound rate set forth in the airbill, was rejected. Hopper claimed that the amount of $61,045, which was mistakenly placed in the ZIP Code box, was in fact part of the contract set forth in the airbill and that Emery, on reviewing the contract, must have realized a mistake was made. Decide. [*Hopper Furs, Inc., v Emery Air Freight Corp.*, 749 F2d 1261 (8th Cir)]

13. When de Lema, a Brazilian resident, arrived in New York City, his luggage consisted of three suitcases, an attaché case, and a cylindrical bag. The attaché case and the cylindrical bag contained jewels valued at $300,000. De Lema went from JFK Airport to the Waldorf Astoria Hotel, where he gave the three suitcases to hotel staff in the garage, and then he went to the lobby to register. The assistant manager, Baez, summoned room clerk Tamburino to assist him. De Lema stated, "The room clerk asked me if I had a reservation. I said, 'Yes. The name is José Berga de Lema.' And I said, 'I want a safety deposit box.' He said, 'Please fill out your registration.' " While de Lema was filling out the registration form, paying $300 in cash as an advance, and Tamburino was filling out a receipt for that amount, de Lema had placed the attaché case and the cylindrical bag on the floor. A woman jostled de Lema, apparently creating a diversion, and when he next looked down, he discovered that the attaché case was gone. De Lema brought suit against the hotel for the value of the jewels stolen in the hotel's lobby. The hotel maintained a safe for valuables and posted notices in the lobby, garage, and rooms as required by the New York law that modifies a hotelkeeper's common law liability. The notices stated in part that the hotel was not liable for the loss of valuables that a guest had neglected to deliver to the hotel for safekeeping. The hotel's defense was that de Lema had neglected to inform it of the presence of the jewels and to deliver the jewels to the hotel. Is the hotel liable for the value of the stolen jewels? [*De Lema v Waldorf Astoria Hotel, Inc.*, 588 F Supp 19 (SDNY)]

14. Frosty Land Foods shipped a load of beef from its plant in Montgomery, Alabama, to Scott Meat Co. in Los Angeles via Refrigerated Transport Co. (RTC), a common carrier. Early Wednesday morning, December 7, at 12:55 A.M., two of RTC's drivers left the Frosty Land plant with the load of beef. The bill of lading called for delivery at Scott Meat on Friday, December 9, at 6:00 A.M. The RTC drivers arrived in Los Angeles at approximately 3:30 P.M. on Friday, December 9. Scott notified the drivers that it could not process the meat at that time. The drivers checked into a motel for the weekend, and the load was delivered to Scott on Monday, December 12. After inspecting 65 of the 308 carcasses, Scott determined that the meat was in off condition and refused the shipment. On Tuesday, December 13, Frosty Land sold the meat, after extensive trimming, at a loss of $13,529. Frosty Land brought suit against RTC for its loss. Decide. [*Frosty Land Foods v Refrigerated Transport Co.*, 613 F2d 1344 (5th Cir)]

15. Tate hired Action-Mayflower Moving & Storage to ship his belongings. Action prepared a detailed inventory of Tate's belongings, loaded them on its truck, and received the belongings at its warehouse, where they would be stored until

Tate asked that they be moved. Months later, a dispute arose, and Tate asked Action to release his property to a different mover. Tate had prepaid more than enough to cover all charges to this point. Action refused to release the goods and held them in storage. After allowing storage charges to build up for 15 months, Action sold Tate's property under the warehouser's public sale law. Tate sued Action for damages. Decide. [*Tate v Action-Mayflower Moving & Storage, Inc.*, 383 SE2d 229 (NC App)]

CPA QUESTIONS

1. A common carrier bailee generally would avoid liability for loss of goods entrusted to its care if the goods are:

   a. Stolen by an unknown person

   b. Negligently destroyed by an employee

   c. Destroyed by the derailment of the train carrying them due to railroad employee negligence

   d. Improperly packed by the party shipping them

2. Under a nonnegotiable bill of lading, a carrier who accepts goods for shipment must deliver the goods to:

   a. Any holder of the bill of lading

   b. Any party subsequently named by the seller

   c. The seller who was issued the bill of lading

   d. The consignee of the bill of lading

3. Under the UCC, a warehouse receipt:

   a. Is negotiable if, by its terms, the goods are to be delivered to bearer or to the order of a named person

   b. Will not be negotiable if it contains a contractual limitation on the warehouse's liability

   c. May qualify as both a negotiable warehouse receipt and negotiable commercial paper if the instrument is payable either in cash or by the delivery of goods

   d. May be issued only by a bonded and licensed warehouser

4. Under the Documents of Title Article of the UCC, which of the following acts may limit a common carrier's liability for damages to the goods in transit?

   a. Vandalism

   b. Power outage

   c. Willful acts of third person

   d. Providing for a contractual dollar liability limitation

Chapter 28

KINDS OF INSTRUMENTS, PARTIES, AND NEGOTIABILITY

commercial paper—written, transferable, signed promise or order to pay a specified sum of money; a negotiable instrument.

For convenience and as a way to facilitate transactions, businesses began to accept certain kinds of paper called **commercial paper** or negotiable instruments as substitutes for money or as a means of offering credit. Negotiable commercial paper is special paper created for the special purpose of facilitating transfer of funds and payment. In addition, the use of this special paper for special purposes can create additional rights in a special person status known as a *holder in due course*. Although the details on holders in due course are covered in Chapters 29 and 30, it is important to understand that one of the purposes of the use of special paper is to allow parties to achieve the special status of holder in due course and its protections and rights. Taking each component of negotiable instruments in step-by-step sequences, from their creation to the rights associated with each, and to their transfer, helps in understanding how commercial paper is used for special purposes in order to create rights for special persons.

A. Types of Negotiable Instruments and Parties

Article 3 of the Uniform Commercial Code (UCC) defines the types of negotiable instruments and the parties for each.[1] Article 3 of the UCC was last amended in 2002 with those reforms adopted in some states and under consideration in others.[2] Those changes are explained in each of the relevant sections.

1. Definition

negotiable instruments— drafts, promissory notes, checks, and certificates of deposit that, in proper form, give special rights as "negotiable commercial paper."

Section 3-104(a)(1) and (2) of the UCC defines a **negotiable instrument** as "an unconditional promise or order to pay a fixed amount of money, ... if it (1) is payable to bearer or order...; (2) is payable on demand or at a definite time; and (3) does not state any other undertaking or instruction ... to do any act in addition to the payment of money...."[3] A *negotiable instrument* is a record of a signed promise or order to pay a specified sum of money.[4] The former requirement that the instrument be in writing to be valid has been changed to incorporate requirements of UETA (Uniform Electronic Transactions Act) and E-Sign (Electronic Signatures in Global and National Commerce Act of 2000). Many lenders now use electronic promissory notes.[5] In addition, we now have electronic checks, or those check withdrawals from your account that you authorize over the phone or via the Internet.

---

[1] The law covering negotiable instruments has been evolving and changing. The latest version of Article 3 was adopted in 1990. The 1990 version of Article 3 had been adopted in all 50 states by August 1999. States with variations are Alabama, Georgia, Montana, Ohio, South Dakota, and Wisconsin. The earlier version was called UCC-Commercial Paper, and the 1990 version is called UCCNegotiable Instruments.

[2] As of June 2006, Arkansas, Minnesota, Nevada, and Texas had adopted the amendments to Article 3, but by 2009 had repealed the adoption.

[3] UCC § 3-104(a)(1) and (2).

[4] See UCC § 3-104.

[5] Electronic Signatures in Global and National Commerce Act, 15 USCS § 7001 (Supp 2009);

Instruments are negotiable when they contain certain elements required by the UCC. These elements are listed and explained in Section 5 of this chapter. However, even those instruments that do not meet the requirements for negotiability may still be referred to by their UCC names or classifications.

CPA 2. Kinds of Instruments

There are two categories of negotiable instruments: (1) promises to pay, which include promissory notes and certificates of deposit,[6] and (2) orders to pay, including drafts and checks.

promissory note–
unconditional promise in writing made by one person to another, signed by the maker engaging to pay on demand, or at a definite time, a sum certain in money to order or to bearer. (Parties—maker, payee)

(A) PROMISSORY NOTES. A **promissory note** is a written promise made and signed by the maker to pay a *sum certain* in money to the holder of the instrument.[7] (See Figure 28.1.)

(B) CERTIFICATES OF DEPOSIT. A **certificate of deposit (CD)** is a promise to pay issued by a bank.[8] Through a CD, a bank acknowledges the customer's deposit of a specific sum of money and promises to pay the customer that amount plus interest when the certificate is surrendered.

certificate of deposit (CD)–promise-to-pay instrument issued by a bank.

draft or bill of exchange–
an unconditional order in writing by one person upon another, signed by the person giving it, and ordering the person to whom it is directed to pay upon demand or at a definite time a sum certain in money to order or to bearer.

(C) DRAFTS. A **draft, or bill of exchange**, is an order by one party to pay a sum of money to a second party. (See Figure 28.2.) The party who gives the order is called the *drawer*, and the party on whom the order to pay is drawn is the *drawee*.[9] The party to whom payment is to be made is the *payee*. The drawer may also be named as the payee, as when a seller draws a draft naming a buyer as the drawee. The draft is then used as a means to obtain payment for goods delivered to that buyer. A drawee is not bound to pay a draft simply because the drawer has placed his name on it. However, the drawee may agree to pay the draft by accepting it, which then attaches the drawee's liability for payment.

FIGURE 28-1 | *Promissory Note*

MARCH 31, 2010

Six months after date debtor undersigned hereby promises to pay to the order of Galactic Games, Inc., three thousand six hundred dollars with interest at the rate of 10.9%. This note is secured by the Video Arcade game purchased with its funds.

In the event of default, all sums due hereunder may be collected. Debtor agrees to pay all costs of collection including, but not limited to, attorney fees, costs of repossession, and costs of litigation.

JOHN R. HALDEHAND

VIDEO ARCADE, INC.

---

[6] UCC § 3-104(j).
[7] *IFC Credit Corp. v Specialty Optical Systems, Inc.*, 252 SW3d 761(Tex App 2008).
[8] UCC § 3-104(j).
[9] UCC § 3-103(a)(2)–(3).

FIGURE 28-2 | *Draft*

TO: _Topa Fabrics, Inc._   _March 17,_ 20 _10_
      1700 W. Lincoln
      Marina Del Rey, CA

      Thirty days from date _____ **PAY TO THE ORDER OF**
      Malden Mills, Inc.

THE SUM OF _sixteen thousand and no/100_ _____ **DOLLARS**

ACCEPTED BY: _Aaron Johnson_
_____   _Malden Mills, Inc._

DATE

---

check–order by a depositor on a bank to pay a sum of money to a payee; a bill of exchange drawn on a bank and payable on demand.

cashier's check–draft drawn by a bank on itself.

teller's check–draft drawn by a bank on another bank in which it has an account.

traveler's check–check that is payable on demand provided it is countersigned by the person whose specimen signature appears on the check.

money order–draft issued by a bank or a nonbank.

party–person involved in a legal transaction; may be a natural person, an artificial person (e.g., a corporation), or an unincorporated enterprise (e.g., a governmental agency).

maker–party who writes or creates a promissory note.

(D) **CHECKS.** Under UCC § 3-104(f), *check* means "a draft, other than a documentary draft, payable on demand and drawn on a bank."[10] A **check** is an order by a depositor (the drawer) on a bank or credit union (the drawee) to pay a sum of money to the order of another party (the payee).[11]

In addition to the ordinary checks just described, there are also cashier's checks, teller's checks, traveler's checks, and bank money orders. A **cashier's check** is a draft drawn by a bank on itself. UCC § 3-104(g) defines a cashier's check as "a draft with respect to which the drawer and drawee are the same bank or branches of the same bank."[12] A **teller's check** is a draft drawn by a bank on another bank in which it has an account.[13] A **traveler's check** is a check that is payable on demand, provided it is countersigned by the person whose signature was placed on the check at the time the check was purchased.[14] Money orders are issued by both banks and nonbanks. A **money order** drawn by a bank is also a check.[15]

3. Parties To Instruments

A note has two original parties: the *maker* and the *payee*.[16] A draft or a check has three original parties: the *drawer*, the *drawee*, and the *payee*. The names given to the parties to these instruments are important because the liability of the parties varies depending on the parties' roles. The rights and liabilities of the various parties to negotiable instruments are covered in Chapters 29 and 30.

A **party** to an instrument may be a natural person, an artificial person such as a corporation, or an unincorporated enterprise such as a government agency.

(A) **MAKER.** The **maker** is the party who writes or creates a promissory note, thereby promising to pay the amount specified in the note.

[10] UCC § 3-104(f).
[11] *Id.*
[12] UCC § 3-104(g).
[13] UCC § 3-104(h).
[14] UCC § 3-104(i).
[15] Some items are held to be checks for purposes other than Article 3 negotiability. For example, in *In re Armstrong* 291 F3d 517 (CA 8 2002), the court held that gambling markers were checks for purposes of the state's "bad check" law.
[16] UCC § 3-103(a)(5).

drawer–person who writes out and creates a draft or bill of exchange, including a check.

drawee–person to whom the draft is addressed and who is ordered to pay the amount of money specified in the draft.

payee–party to whom payment is to be made.

acceptor–drawee who has accepted the liability of paying the amount of money specified in a draft.

accommodation party–person who signs an instrument to lend credit to another party to the paper.

(B) **Drawer.** The **drawer** is the party who writes or creates a draft or check.

(C) **Drawee.** The **drawee** is the party to whom the draft is addressed and who is ordered to pay the amount of money specified in the draft. The bank is the drawee on a check, and the credit union is the drawee on a share draft. Again, a drawee on a draft has no responsibility under the draft until it has accepted that instrument.

(D) **Payee.** The **payee** is the person named in the instrument to receive payment. **For Example,** on a check with the words "Pay to the order of John Jones," the named person, John Jones, is the payee.

The payee has no rights in the instrument until the drawer or the maker has delivered it to the payee. Likewise, the payee is not liable on the instrument in any way until the payee transfers the instrument to someone else.

(E) **Acceptor.** When the drawee of a draft has indicated by writing or record a willingness to pay the amount specified in the draft, the drawee has accepted liability and is called the **acceptor.**[17]

(F) **Secondary Obligor (Accommodation Party).** When a party who is not originally named in an instrument allows her name to be added to it for the benefit of another party in order to add strength to the collectability of the instrument, that party becomes a secondary obligor (formerly called an **accommodation party**) and assumes a liability role.[18] Revised Article 3 now refers to drawer, indorsers, and accommodation parties as "secondary obligors."[19]

CPA   B. Negotiability

negotiability–quality of an instrument that affords special rights and standing.

nonnegotiable instrument–contract, note, or draft that does not meet negotiability requirements of Article 3.

An instrument is a form of contract that, if negotiable, affords certain rights and protections for the parties. **Negotiability** is the characteristic that distinguishes commercial paper and instruments from ordinary contracts or what makes such paper and instruments special paper.[20] That an instrument is negotiable means that certain rights and protections may be available to the parties to the instrument under Article 3. A **nonnegotiable instrument's** terms are enforceable, but the instrument is treated simply as a contract governed by contract law.[21]

4. Definition of Negotiability

If an instrument is negotiable, it is governed by Article 3 of the UCC, and it may be transferred by negotiation. This form of transfer permits the transferee to acquire rights greater than those afforded assignees of contracts under contract law. The quality of negotiability in instruments creates opportunities for transfers and financings that streamline payments in commerce. Transfers can be made with

---

[17] UCC § 3-103(a)(1).
[18] UCC § 3-419; *In re TML, Inc.*, 291 BR 400, 50 UCC Rep Serv 2d 511 (WD Mich 2003).
[19] Revised Article 3, § 3-103(12), has the following definition of a secondary obligor on an instrument: "an indorser, a drawer, an accommodation party, or any other party to the instrument that has a right of recourse against another party to the instrument...." This definition was changed to be consistent with the Restatement of Surety.
[20] UCC § 3-104.
[21] A note payable when "lessee is granted possession of the premises" is not a negotiable instrument, but it is an enforceable contract. *Schiffer v United Grocers, Inc.*, 989 P2d 10 (Or 1999). See also, *In re Bedrock Marketing, LLC*, 404 B 929 (Utah 2009), where court held that a note "payable upon completion" was indefinite, but was saved by clause that declared it payable "no later than three years after execution."

e-commerce&cyberlaw
The Check Is in the Internet

The Check Clearing for the 21st Century Act ("Check 21") allows banks to use electronic images of checks as full and complete records of transactions, the same status formerly used only for paper checks that had been canceled. You can also pay your monthly credit card bills by preauthorizing your credit card company to withdraw the amount you specify from your account. With the bank's routing number and your account number, the company can obtain payment on the due date or any date you authorize. PayPal allows you to do the same with your bank account when you purchase items on the Internet.

assurance of payment without the need for investigation of the underlying contract. The process of negotiation is covered in Chapter 29. For more information on the rights of assignees of contracts, refer to Chapter 18.

CPA

5. Requirements of Negotiability

To be negotiable, an instrument (1) must be evidenced by a record[22] and (2) must be signed (authenticated under Revised Article 3) by the maker or the drawer, (3) must contain an unconditional promise or order to pay, (4) must pay a sum certain, (5) must be payable in money, (6) must be payable on demand or at a definite time, and (7) must be payable to order or bearer, using what are known as words of negotiability.[23]

(A) A RECORD (WRITING). A negotiable instrument must be evidenced by a record. The requirement of a *record*, under Revised Article 3, is satisfied by handwriting, typing, printing, electronic record, and any other method of making a record. A negotiable instrument may be partly printed and partly typewritten. No particular form is required for an instrument to satisfy the record requirement, although customers of banks may agree to use the banks' forms as part of their contractual agreement with their banks. Telephonic checks are a complete record for purposes of Article 3 rights and obligations.

(B) AUTHENTICATED (SIGNED) BY THE MAKER OR DRAWER. The instrument must be authenticated (signed under old Article 3) by the maker or the drawer. When a signature is used as authentication, it usually appears at the lower right-hand corner of the face of the instrument, but there is no requirement for where the signature must be placed on the instrument.[24]

---

[22] Revised Article 3. Existing Article 3 requires a writing, but the revisions reflect electronic transactions and the federal mandate for recognizing electronic transactions as valid and on equal footing with paper transactions. The definition of a record is found in Revised UCC § 3-103(a)(14), which provides that *record* "means information that is inscribed on a tangible medium or which is stored in an electronic or other medium and is retrievable in perceivable form."

[23] UCC § 3-104.

[24] According to Revised UCC § 3-103, *authenticate* means (a) to sign or (b) to execute or otherwise adopt a symbol, or encrypt or similarly process a record in whole or in part, with the present intent of the authenticating person to identify the person and adopt or accept a record.

The authentication may consist of the full name or of any symbol placed with the intent to authenticate the instrument. Other means of authentication that are valid as signatures include initials, figures, and marks. Electronic security devices can be used as a means of authentication for electronic records. A person signing a trade name or an assumed name is liable just as if the signer's own name had been used.

(1) Agent

An authentication may be made by the drawer or the maker or by his or her authorized agent. **For Example,** Eileen Smith, the treasurer of Mills Company, could sign a note for her company as an agent. No particular form of authorization for an agent to authenticate an instrument is required. An authenticating agent should disclose on the instrument (1) the identity of the principal and (2) the fact that the authentication was done in a representative capacity. When this information appears on the face of the instrument, an authorized agent is not liable on it.

The representative capacity of an officer of an organization can be shown by the authentication of the officer along with the title of the office and the organization's name.[25] **For Example,** a signature of "James Shelton, Treasurer, NorWest Utilities, Inc.," or "NorWest Utilities, Inc., by James Shelton, Treasurer," on a note is enough to show Shelton's representative capacity. NorWest Utilities, not Shelton, would be liable on the note.

(2) Absence of Representative Capacity or Identification of Principal.

If an instrument fails to show the **representative capacity** of the person who is authenticating or fails to identify the person, then the individual who authenticates the instrument is personally liable on the instrument to anyone who acquires superior rights, such as the rights of a holder in due course (see Chapter 30). Because the instrument is a final agreement, the parol evidence rule applies, and the party who authenticated is not permitted to introduce extrinsic evidence that might clarify his or her representative capacity. The party who authenticated, in order to avoid personal liability, must indicate on the face of the instrument his or her role in the principal, such as president or vice president. (For more information about the parol evidence rule, see Chapter 17.)

However, an agent is not personally liable on a check that is drawn on the bank account of the principal and authenticated by him or her, even though the agent failed to disclose his or her representative capacity on the check. **For Example,** a check that is already imprinted with the employer's name is not the check of the employee, regardless of whether the employee only authenticates with his or her name or also adds a title such as "Payroll Clerk" or "Treasurer" near the signature.

(c) **PROMISE OR ORDER TO PAY.** A promissory note must contain a promise to pay money. A mere acknowledgment of a debt, such as a record stating "I.O.U.," is not a promise. A draft or check must contain an order or command to pay money.

(d) **UNCONDITIONAL PROMISE OR ORDER.** For an instrument to be negotiable, the promise or order to pay must be unconditional.[26]

representative capacity—
action taken by one on behalf of another, as the act of a personal representative on behalf of a decedent's estate, or action taken both on one's behalf and on behalf of others, as a shareholder bringing a representative action.

---

[25] UCC § 3-402.
[26] UCC § 3-109(c).

For Example, when an instrument makes the duty to pay dependent on the completion of the construction of a building, the promise is conditional and the instrument is nonnegotiable. The instrument is enforceable as a contract, but it is not a negotiable instrument given all the rights and protections afforded under Article 3.

An order for the payment of money out of a particular fund is negotiable. The instrument can refer to a particular account or merely indicate a source of reimbursement for the drawee, such as "Charge my expense account." Nor is an instrument conditional when payment is to be made only from an identified fund if the issuer is a government or governmental unit or agency, or when payment is to be made from the assets of a partnership, unincorporated association, trust, or estate.[27] However, the fund noted must in fact exist because payment from a fund to be created by a future event would be conditional. **For Example,** making an instrument "payable from the account I'll establish when the sale of my house occurs" is conditional because the fund's creation is tied to an event whose time of occurrence is unknown.

The standards for negotiability do not require that the issuer of the instrument be personally obligated to pay it.[28] An instrument's negotiability is not destroyed by a reference to a related document. Section 3-106(b) provides, "A promise or order is not made conditional (i) by a reference to another writing for a statement of

CASE SUMMARY

The Sticky Note That Was a Reminder of Personal Liability

FACTS: Northwest Harvest Products, Inc., fell behind on payments on its account with Major Products Company, Inc. Major requested a note for the debt, and Northwest sent a $78,445.24 note. The chief executive officer of Northwest at that time signed the note "Donald H. Eoll CEO," attached a Post-It fax transmittal memo indicating that the note came from Donald Eoll at Northwest, and sent the note via facsimile. The note was not paid, and Major sued both Eoll and Northwest for the debt. Only the facsimile copy of the note was presented at trial, and the trial court found that the writing on the Post-It note, coupled with the signature, identified Northwest as the principal on the note. The trial court held that Eoll was not personally liable for the debt because he signed the note as an agent for Northwest. Major appealed.

DECISION: The court held that Eoll was personally liable on the note. The Post-It note was separate from the document and anything that Eoll and Major wanted to be part of the promissory note should have been written on the promissory note. Without the Post-it, there is no indication of capacity on the promissory note, which leaves Eoll liable personally on that note. Reversed. [**Major Products Co., Inc. v Northwest Harvest Products, Inc., 979 P2d 905 (Wash App 1999)**]

---

[27] A check issued by a debtor in bankruptcy for payment of court-ordered obligations is not conditional because of the involvement of the court or ongoing conditions on debtor's payments. *In re Blasco*, 352 BR 888 (Bankr ND Ala E Div., 2006).

[28] UCC § 3-110(c)(1)–(2) (1990); *Ocwen Loan Servicing, LLC v. Branaman*, 554 F Supp 2d 645, (ND Miss 2008).

thinking things through

When Your John Hancock Is Enough

Work through the following examples of signatures on negotiable instruments, capacity, and personal liability.

1. Jonathan Beecham, CEO of Captains of the Guards (GC) wrote the checks to Payroll Control Systems (PCS) for providing payroll services that totaled $21,000. GC did not have enough money in its account to cover the checks so PCS filed suit against both GC and Beecham. Beecham says that he is not personally liable for the checks. The checks were printed with "Captains of the Guard" and the company's address and signed "J. Beecham." Can PCS collect from Beecham? [*Diversified Industries, Inc., d/b/a Payroll Control Systems v Captains of the Guards*, 2008 WL 1972925 (Minn App), 66 UCC Rep Serv 2d 58]

2. A corporate guaranty was signed as follows:
THE PRODUCERS GROUP OF FLA., INC. a Florida corporation, by the following officers solely on behalf of the corporation:

/s/ Eddie Beverly, as its President

CORPORATE PRESIDENT Eddie Beverly

/s/ Stephen Edman, as its Secretary

CORPORATE SECRETARY Steve Edman

/s/ John Bauder, as its Treasurer

CORPORATE TREASURER John Bauder

Are the officers personally liable on the guaranty? [*Tampa Bay Economic Development Corp. v Edman*, 598 So2d 172 (Fla App 1992)]

---

rights with respect to collateral, prepayment, or acceleration."[29] **For Example,** if a note includes the following phrase, "This note is secured by a mortgage on the property located at Hilding Lane," the note is still negotiable.[30]

money–medium of exchange.

(E) **PAYMENT IN MONEY.** A negotiable instrument must be payable in money. **Money** is defined to include any medium of exchange adopted or authorized by the United States, a foreign government, or an intergovernmental organization. The parties to an instrument are free to decide which currency will be used for payment even though their transaction may occur in a different country.[31] **For Example,** two parties in the United States are free to agree that their note will be paid in pesos.

If the order or promise is not for money, the instrument is not negotiable. **For Example,** an instrument that requires the holder to take stock or goods in place of money is nonnegotiable. The instrument is enforceable as a contract, but it cannot qualify as a negotiable instrument for purposes of Article 3 rights.

sum certain–amount due under an instrument that can be computed from its face with only reference to interest rates.

(F) **SUM CERTAIN.** Negotiable instruments must include a statement of a **sum certain**, or an exact amount of money. Without a definite statement as to how much is to be

---

[29] UCC § 3-106(b).
[30] Reference to a bill of lading does not affect negotiability. *Regent Corp., U.S.A. v Azmat Bangladesh, Ltd.*, 686 NYS2d 24 (1999).
[31] UCC § 3-107.

paid under the terms of the instrument, there is no way to determine how much the instrument is worth.

There are some minor variations from sum certain requirement. **For Example,** an instrument is not nonnegotiable because its interest rate provisions include changes in the rate at maturity or because it provides for certain costs and attorney fees to be recovered by the holder in the event of enforcement action or litigation.[32]

In most states, the sum payable under an instrument is certain even though it calls for the payment of a floating or variable interest rate.[33] An instrument is negotiable even though it provides for an interest rate of 1 percent above the prime rate of a named bank. It is immaterial that the exact amount of interest that will be paid cannot be determined at the time the paper is issued because the rate may later change. It is also immaterial that the amount due on the instrument cannot be determined without looking at records outside of the face of the instrument.[34]

(G) Time of Payment. A negotiable instrument must be payable on demand or at a definite time.[35] If an instrument is payable "when convenient," it is nonnegotiable because the day of payment may never arrive. An instrument payable only upon the happening of a particular event that may or may not happen is not negotiable. **For Example,** a provision in a note to pay the sum certain when a person marries is not payable at a definite time because that particular event may never occur. It is immaterial whether the contingency in fact has happened because from an examination of the instrument alone, it still appears to be subject to a condition that might not occur.

(1) Demand

An instrument is *payable on demand* when it expressly states that it is payable "on demand," at sight, or on presentation. UCC § 3-108(a) provides "A promise or order is 'payable on demand' if (i) it states that it is payable on demand or at sight, or otherwise indicates that it is payable at the will of the holder, or (ii) it does not state any time of payment."[36] Presentation occurs when a holder demands payment. Commercial paper is deemed to be payable on demand when no time for payment is stated in the instrument.[37]

(2) Definite Time

definite time–time of payment computable from the face of the instrument.

The time of payment is a **definite time** if an exact time or times are specified or if the instrument is payable at a fixed time after sight or acceptance or at a time that is readily ascertainable. The time of payment is definite even though the instrument provides for prepayment, for acceleration, or for extensions at the option of a party or automatically on the occurrence of a specified contingency.

---

[32] UCC § 3-106.

[33] *Means v Clardy*, 735 SW2d 6 (Mo App 1987); while revised Article 3 permits variable and market rates, notes entered into before the revised act was adopted will be governed under old Article 3; *YYY Corp. v Gazda*, 761 A2d 395 (NH 2000), *Barnsley v Empire Mortgage, Ltd. Partnership*, 720 A2d 63 (NH 1998).

[34] *SCADIF, S.A. v First Union Nat. Bank*, 208 F Supp 2d 1352 (SD Fla 2002), aff'd, 344 F3d 1123 (CA 11 2003). See also *Bankers Trust v 236 Beltway Investment*, 865 F Supp 1186 (ED Va 1994).

[35] UCC § 3-108.

[36] UCC § 3-108(a).

[37] UCC § 3-112; *Universal Premium Acceptance Corp. v York Bank's Trust Co.*, 69 F3d 695 (3d Cir 1995); *State v. McWilliams*, 178 P 3d 121(Mont 2008).

C A S E   S U M M A R Y

Whenever … Paying When You Can Does Not a Negotiable Instrument Make

FACTS: Gary Vaughn signed a document stating that Fred and Martha Smith were loaning him $9,900. As to when the loan was to be repaid, the document stated, "when you can." Approximately 18 months later, the Smiths sued Vaughn for the entire amount, claiming default on the note as well as unjust enrichment. The Smiths moved for summary judgment. They contended that Vaughn was immediately liable for the entire amount but that they were willing to work out a repayment schedule. Vaughn also moved for summary judgment, arguing that he did not have to repay the Smiths because he did not have the ability to do so. The trial court denied the Smiths' motion and granted Vaughn's. The Smiths appealed.

DECISION: The court held the following: a promissory note that calls for a borrower to repay "when you can" was not payable on demand and was not a negotiable instrument. However, an issue of fact remained as to when a debt payable "when you can" became payable. There were other issues of fact such as whether there was unjust enrichment and whether it was reasonable for the borrower to repay the debt. The language implied that there was an open-ended agreement. The parties might have a contract, but the Smiths could not demand payment as if the instrument were a demand negotiable instrument. Reversed for further factual determinations. [**Smith v Vaughn, 882 NE2d 941, 64 UCC Rep Serv 2d 757 (Ohio App 2007)**]

(3) Missing Date

An instrument that is not dated is deemed dated on the day it is issued to the payee. Any holder may add the correct date to the instrument.

(4) Effect of Date on a Demand Instrument

The date on a demand instrument controls the time of payment, and the paper is not due before its date. Consequently, a check that is postdated ceases to be demand paper and is not properly payable before the date on the check. A bank making earlier payment does not incur any liability for doing so unless the drawer has given the bank a postdated check notice.

(H) Words of Negotiability: Payable To Order or Bearer. An instrument that is not a check must be **payable to order** or **bearer**.[38] This requirement is met by such phrases as "Pay to the order of John Jones," "Pay to John Jones or order," "Pay to bearer," and "Pay to John Jones or bearer." The use of the phrase "to the order of John Jones" or "to John Jones or order" shows that the person executing the instrument had no intention of restricting payment of the instrument to John Jones. These phrases indicate that there is no objection to paying anyone to whom John Jones orders the paper to be paid. Similarly, if the person executing the instrument originally wrote that it will be paid "to bearer" or "to John Jones or bearer," there is no restriction on the payment of the paper to the original payee. However, if the instrument is not a check and it is payable on its face "to John Jones," the instrument is not negotiable.[39] Whether an instrument is bearer or order paper is important

payable to order–term stating that a negotiable instrument is payable to the order of any person described in it or to a person or order.

bearer–person in physical possession of commercial paper payable to bearer, a document of title directing delivery to bearer, or an investment security in bearer form.

[38] *Max Duncan Family Investments, Ltd. v. NTFN Inc.*, 267 SW3d 447 (Tex App 2008).
[39] UCC § 3-108.

ethics&the law

The Fancy Footwork to Avoid Payment Using Article 3

Do you think that Gary Vaughn, in *Smith v. Vaughn*, was trying to get out of paying?

Did he use Article 3 to avoid payment? Is his response and defense ethical?

CASE SUMMARY

The Lawyer Who Didn't Understand Negotiability

FACTS: On November 13, 1999, Bryce Erickson executed a promissory note payable to Sirius, which provided "[f]or value received, the undersigned Bryce H. Erickson promises to pay to SIRIUS LC … the sum of Twenty Nine Thousand One Hundred Seventy Three Dollars and Thirty Eight Cents ($29,173.38) bearing 10% interest due and payable on June 1, 2001." Sirius was an LLC owned by William Bagley and his wife. Bagley was also Erickson's lawyer. The note was payment to Bagley for filing a bankruptcy proceeding for Erickson. Erickson also executed a real estate mortgage securing the promissory note that same day. Thereafter, Bagley, on behalf of Erickson, filed a Chapter 12 bankruptcy proceeding.

Sirius then brought suit to foreclose on the mortgage property after Erickson refused to pay the note. Erickson alleged defenses for his nonpayment, including lack of consideration and misrepresentation. But Bagley said that he was the holder in due course of a negotiable note and Erickson's defenses were limited. The trial court found that Erickson could not raise his defenses under Article 3 because Bagley was the holder of a negotiable instrument. Erickson appealed.

DECISION: The instrument was not a negotiable note because it was made payable to only one person. It had no words of negotiability and could not be transferred further. But the note not being negotiable was good news for Erickson because it meant Bagley was not a holder in due course and was subject to defenses. Erickson could raise his defenses, just as he would under a contract, because a note without words of negotiability is governed by contract law, not Article 3. Bagley was subject to the defenses Erickson could prove. [**Sirius LC v Erickson, 144 Idaho 38, 156 P3d 539, 62 UCC Rep Serv 2d 411 (Id 2007)**]

because the two instruments are transferred in different ways and because the liability of the transfer or scan be different.

(1) Order Paper

order paper—instrument payable to the order of a party.

An instrument is payable to order, or **order paper**, when by its terms it is payable to the order of any person described in it ("Pay to the order of K. Read") or to a person or order ("Pay to K. Read or order").

(2) Bearer Paper

bearer paper—instrument with no payee, payable to cash or payable to bearer.

An instrument is payable to bearer, or **bearer paper**, when it is payable (1) to bearer or the order of bearer, (2) to a specified person or bearer, or (3) to "cash," "the order of cash," or any other designation that does not purport to identify a person or when (4) the last or only indorsement is a blank indorsement (an indorsement that does not name the person to whom the instrument is negotiated). An instrument that does not identify any payee is payable to bearer.[40]

Whether an instrument is bearer or order paper is important for determining how the instrument is transferred (see Chapter 28) and what the liability of the parties under the instrument is. Review Figure 28.3 for more background.

CASE SUMMARY

I May Be a Thief, But Under Article 3 Bearer Paper Rules, I Am Not a Forger

FACTS: Joshua Herrera found a purse in a dumpster near San Pedro and Kathryn Streets in Albuquerque. Herrera took the purse with him to a friend's house. Either Herrera or his friend called the owner of the purse and the owner retrieved the purse at some point. After the purse was returned to the owner, Herrera returned to the dumpster where he found a check and some other items. The check Herrera found was written out to "Cash" and he thought this meant that he "could get money for [the] check."

When he presented the check to the teller at a credit union to cash it, the teller instructed him to put his name on the payee line next to "Cash." Herrera added "to Joshua Herrera" next to the word "Cash" on the payee line of the check and indorsed the check.

Herrera had pleaded guilty to one count of forgery but moved to have the indictment dismissed on the grounds that adding his name to a bearer instrument was not forgery. He appealed the denial of the motion to dismiss the indictment.

DECISION: The court held that the instrument that Herrera originally found was bearer paper. By adding his named "to Joshua Herrera" to the "Pay to" line after "Cash" did not change the character of the instrument from bearer to order paper. At best, the addition of the words created an ambiguity and under the code interpretations should continue to be treated as bearer paper. Since he did not alter the nature of the instrument or convert it to a different instrument, he could not be charged with forgery. [**New Mexico v Herrera, 18 P3d 326 (NM App 2001);** *cert. den.* **20 P3d 810 (NM 2001)**]

6. Factors Not Affecting Negotiability

postdate—to insert or place on an instrument a later date than the actual date on which it was executed.

collateral—property pledged by a borrower as security for a debt.

Omitting a date of execution or antedating or **postdating** an instrument has no effect on its negotiability.

Provisions relating to **collateral**, such as specifying the collateral as security for the debt or a promise to maintain, protect, or give additional collateral, do not affect negotiability. **For Example,** the phrase "This note is secured by a first mortgage" does not affect negotiability.

[40] UCC § 3-104(d).

FIGURE 28-3 | *Bearer versus Order Paper*

"Pay to the order of ABC Corp."	ORDER
"Pay to the order of Bearer."	BEARER
"Pay to the order of ABC Corp. or Bearer"	BEARER
"Pay to the order of ABC Corp., Bearer"	ORDER
"Pay to the order of John Jones" (note)	NONNEGOTIABLE
"Pay to the order of John Jones" (check)	ORDER
"Pay to John Jones" (note)	NONNEGOTIABLE
"Pay to John Jones" (check)	NEGOTIABLE
"Pay to the order of John Jones or Bearer"	BEARER
"Pay to cash"	BEARER
"Pay to the order of cash"	BEARER

7. Ambiguous Language

ambiguous–having more than one reasonable interpretation.

The following rules are applied when **ambiguous** language exists in words or descriptions:

1. Words control figures where conflict exists.

2. Handwriting supersedes conflicting typewritten and printed terms.

3. Typewritten terms supersede preprinted terms.

4. If there is a failure to provide for the payment of interest or if there is a provision for the payment of interest but no rate is mentioned, the judgment rate at the place of payment applies from the date of the instrument.[41]

8. Statute of Limitations

Article 3 of the UCC establishes a three-year statute of limitations for most actions involving negotiable instruments. This limitation also applies to actions for the conversion of such instruments and for breach of warranty. There is a six-year statute of limitations for suits on certificates of deposit and accepted drafts.

MAKE THE CONNECTION

SUMMARY

An instrument or piece of commercial paper is a transferable, signed promise or order to pay a specified sum of money that is evidenced by a record. An instrument is negotiable when it contains the terms required by the UCC.

Negotiable instruments have two categories: (1) promises to pay and (2) orders to pay. Checks and drafts are orders to pay. Notes and certificates of deposits are promises to pay. In addition to ordinary checks, there are cashier's checks and teller's checks. A bank money order is a check even though it bears the words *money order.*

The original parties to a note are the maker and the payee. The original parties to a draft are the drawer, the drawee, and the payee. The term *party* may refer to a natural person or to an artificial person, such as a corporation. Indorsers and accommodation parties are considered secondary obligors.

The requirements of negotiability are that the instrument (1) be evidenced by a record, (2) be signed (authenticated) by the maker or the drawer, and (3) contain a promise or order (4) of an unconditional character (5) to pay in money (6) a sum certain (7) on demand or at a definite time (8) to order or bearer. A check may be negotiable without being payable to order or bearer.

If an instrument meets the requirements of negotiability, the parties have the rights and protections of Article 3. If it does not meet the requirements of negotiability, the rights of the parties are governed under contract law.

LEARNING OUTCOMES

After studying this chapter, you should be able to clearly explain:

A. TYPES OF NEGOTIABLE INSTRUMENTS AND PARTIES

LO.1 Explain the importance and function of negotiable instruments
See the discussion of negotiability on p. 625.
See *New Mexico v Herrera* on p. 633.

LO.2 Name the parties to negotiable instruments
See the list of parties to instruments on p. 624.

B. NEGOTIABILITY

LO.3 Describe the concept of negotiability and distinguish it from assignability
See *Sirius LC v Erickson* on p. 632 to see the effects of negotiability.

LO.4 List the requirements for a negotiable instrument
See the list of negotiability requirements on p. 626.
See *Smith v Vaughn* on p. 631.

KEY TERMS

acceptor	definite time	party
accommodation party	draft, or bill of exchange	payable to order
ambiguous	drawee	payee
bearer	drawer	postdating
bearer paper	maker	promissory note
cashier's check	money	representative capacity
certificate of deposit (CD)	money order	sum certain
check	negotiability	teller's check
collateral	negotiable instrument	traveler's check
commercial paper	nonnegotiable instrument	
	order paper	

QUESTIONS AND CASE PROBLEMS

1. Harold H. Heidingsfelder signed a credit agreement as vice president of J. O. H. Construction Co. for a line of credit with Pelican Plumbing Co. The credit agreement contained the following language:

   In consideration of an open account privilege, I hereby understand and agree to the above terms. Should it become necessary to place this account for collection I shall personally obligate myself and my corporation, if any, to pay the entire amount due including service charges (as outlined above terms) thirty-three and one-third (33 $^1/_3$%) attorney's fees, and all costs of collection, including court costs.

   Signed [Harold H. Heidingsfelder]
   Company J. O. H. Construction Co., Inc.

   When J. O. H. Construction failed to make payment, Pelican, claiming it was a holder of a negotiable instrument, sued Heidingsfelder to hold him personally liable for his failure to indicate a representative capacity on the credit agreement. He claims that a credit application is not a negotiable instrument and that he could not be held personally liable. Is he right? [*Pelican Plumbing Supply, Inc. v J. O. H. Construction Co., Inc.*, 653 So2d 699 (La)]

2. East Penn Broadcasting Co. borrowed money from Hershey National Bank. The promissory note representing the loan was made payable "to the Hershey National Bank." It also contained a provision authorizing confession of judgment against the borrower at any time. This provision allowed a judgment to be entered against East Penn without giving the defendant the opportunity to make a defense or to oppose the entry of such judgment. The note was signed with the typewritten name of the borrowing corporation and the handwritten signature of three individuals including the defendant, Frank. The loan was not paid. The bank sued Frank and the others on the note; they raised defenses under the UCC. Who is liable on the note? [*Frank v Hershey National Bank*, 306 A2d 207 (Md Ct Spec App)]

3. Charter Bank of Gainesville had in its possession a note containing the following provision: "This note with interest is secured by a mortgage on real estate, of even date herewith, made by the maker hereof in favor of said payee.... The terms of said mortgage are by this reference made a part hereof." When the bank sued on the note, it said it was a holder of a negotiable instrument. Is this instrument negotiable? [*Holly Hill Acres, Ltd. v Charter Bank of Gainesville*, 314 So2d 209 (Fla App)]

4. On October 14, 1980, United American Bank of Knoxville made a $1,700,000 loan to Frederic B. Ingram. William F. Earthman, the president of the bank and a beneficiary of the loan, had arranged for the loan and prepared the loan documents. Mr. Ingram and Mr. Earthman were old friends, and Mr. Ingram had loaned Mr. Earthman money in the past. Mr. Ingram was in jail at the time of this loan and was unable to complete the documents for the loan. Mr. Earthman says that Mr. Ingram authorized him to do the loan so long as it did not cost him anything to do it.

Also on October 14, 1980, Mr. Earthman prepared and executed a personal $1,700,000 note to Mr. Ingram, using a standard Commerce Union Bank note form. Mr. Earthman wrote "Frederic B. Ingram" in the space for identifying the lending bank and also filled in another blank stating that the note would be due "Eighteen Months after Date." With regard to the interest, Mr. Earthman checked a box signifying that the interest would be "At the Bank's 'Prime Rate' plus % per year."

Mr. Earthman then sold both of the notes, which ended up in the hands of third parties (holders in due course) who demanded payment. Mr. Ingram raised the defense that he had not authorized Mr. Earthman to handle the transactions. The third parties said the notes were negotiable instruments and they were entitled to payment without listening to Mr. Ingram's defenses. Mr. Earthman said his note to Mr. Ingram as well as the bank note from Mr. Ingram were not negotiable and that they could both raise defenses to the third parties seeking payment.

Who is correct? What do you think of Mr. Earthman's banking processes and procedures? What ethical issues do you see in these loan transactions? [*Ingram v Earthman*, 993 SW2d 611 (Tenn)]

5. The state of Alaska was a tenant in a large office building owned by Univentures, a partnership. The state made a lease payment of $28,143.47 to Univentures with state treasury warrant No. 21045102. Charles LeViege, the managing partner of Univentures, assigned the warrant to Lee Garcia. A dispute then arose among the Univentures partners, and the company notified the state that it should no longer pay LeViege the rent. The state placed a stop payment order on the warrant. Garcia claimed that he was a holder of a negotiable instrument and that the state owed him the money. The state claimed that a warrant did not qualify as a negotiable instrument. The warrant was in writing, was signed by the governor of the state, provided a definite sum of $28,143.47, and stated that "it will be deemed paid unless redeemed within two years after the date of issue." The warrant stated that it was "payable to the order of Univentures." Does the warrant meet the requirements for a negotiable instrument? [*National Bank v Univentures*, 824 P2d 1377 (Alaska)]

6. Nation-Wide Check Corp. sold money orders through local agents. A customer would purchase a money order by paying an agent the amount of the desired money order plus a fee. The customer would then sign the money order as the remitter or sender and would fill in the name of the person who was to receive the money following the printed words "Payable to." In a lawsuit between Nation-Wide and Banks, a payee on some of these orders, the question was raised as to whether these money orders were checks and could be negotiable even though not payable to order or to bearer. Are the money orders negotiable instruments? [*Nation-Wide Check Corp. v Banks*, 260 A2d 367 (DC)]

7. George S. Avery signed a letter regarding the unpaid balance on a $20,000 promissory note owed to Jim Whitworth in the form of a letter addressed to Whitworth stating: "This is your note for $45,000.00, secured individually and by our Company for your security, due February 7, 1984." The letter was signed: "Your friend, George S. Avery." It was typed on stationery with the

name of Avery's employer, V & L Manufacturing Co., Inc., printed at the bottom and the words "George Avery, President" printed at the top. Avery says he is not personally liable on the note. The court granted summary judgment for Whitworth and Avery appealed. Who is liable? [*Avery v Whitworth*, 414 SE2d 725 (Ga App)]

8. Bellino made a promissory note that was payable in installments and contained the provision that on default of the payment of any installment, the holder had the option to declare the entire balance due and payable on demand. The note was negotiated to Cassiani, who sued Bellino for the full debt when there was a default on the installment. Is a note with an acceleration clause still negotiable? [*Cassiani v Bellino*, 157 NE2d 409 (Mass)]

9. A corporation borrowed money from a bank after the president negotiated the loan and signed the promissory note. On the first blank signature line of the note, the president wrote the name of the corporation. On the second such line, he signed his own name. The note was negotiated by the lending bank to the Federal Reserve Bank. The note was not paid when due, and the Federal Reserve Bank sued the corporation and its president. The president claimed that he was not bound on the note because he did not intend to bind himself and because the money obtained by the loan was used by the corporation. Is the president liable on the note? [*Talley v Blake*, 322 So2d 877 (La App) (non-Code); *Geer v Farquhar*, 528 P2d 1335 (Or)]

10. Lloyd and Mario Spaulding entered into a contract to purchase property from Richard and Robert Krajcir. The two Spaulding brothers signed a promissory note to the Krajcir brothers with the following language: "The amount of $10,000 [is] to be paid sellers at the time of the initial closing [delivery of the deed]; plus, the principal amount payable to sellers at the time of the final indorsement of the subject H.U.D. loan." In litigation over the note, the Spauldings said it was not a negotiable instrument. The lower court found it to be a negotiable promissory note and the Spaulding partners appealed. Is the note negotiable? [*Krajcir v Egid*, 712 NE2d 917 (Ill App)]

11. Is the following instrument negotiable?

I, Richard Bell, hereby promise to pay to the order of Lorry Motors Ten Thousand Dollars ($10,000) upon the receipt of the final distribution from the estate of my deceased aunt, Rita Dorn. This negotiable instrument is given by me as the down payment on my purchase of a 1986 Buick to be delivered in three weeks.

Richard Bell (signature).

12. Smith has in his possession the following instrument:

September 1, 2003
    I, Selma Ray, hereby promise to pay Helen Savit One Thousand Dollars ($1,000) one year after date. This instrument was given for the purchase of Two Hundred (200) shares of Redding Mining Corporation, Interest 6%.
                                                    Selma Ray (signature).

What is this instrument? Is it negotiable?

13. Master Homecraft Co. received a promissory note with a stated face value from Sally and Tom Zimmerman. The note was payment for remodeling their home and contained unused blanks for installment payments but contained no maturity date. When Master Homecraft sued the Zimmermans on the note, the couple argued that they should not be liable on the note because it is impossible to determine from its face the amount due or the date of maturity. Decide. [*Master Homecraft Co. v Zimmerman*, 22 A2d 440 (Pa)]

14. A note from Mark Johnson with HealthCo International as payee for $28,979.15 included the following language:

    [p]ayable in _____, Successive Monthly Installments of $ Each, and in 11 Successive Monthly Installments of $2,414.92 Each thereafter, and in a final payment of $2,415.03 thereafter. The first installment being payable on the _____ day of _____ 20 _____, and the remaining installments on the same date of each month thereafter until paid.

    Johnson signed the note. Is it negotiable? [*Barclays Bank, P.L.C. v Johnson*, 499 SE2d 769 (NC App)]

15. The text of a handwritten note stated simply that "'I Robert Harrison owe Peter Jacob $25,000 …,' /s/ Robert Harrison." Peter Jacob sought to use the handwritten note as a negotiable promissory note. Can he? [*Jacob v Harrison*, 49 UCC Rep Serv 2d 554 (Del Super)]

CPA QUESTIONS

1. A company has in its possession the following instrument:

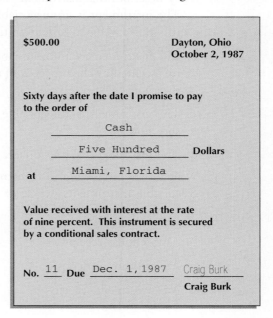

This instrument is:

a. Not negotiable until December 1, 1987

b. A negotiable bearer note

c. A negotiable time draft

d. A nonnegotiable note because it states that it is secured by a conditional sales contract

2. The instrument shown here is a:

a. Draft

b. Postdated check

c. Trade acceptance

d. Promissory note

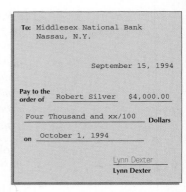

To: Middlesex National Bank
    Nassau, N.Y.

September 15, 1994

Pay to the order of ___ Robert Silver ___ $4,000.00

Four Thousand and xx/100 ___ Dollars

on ___ October 1, 1994 ___

Lynn Dexter
Lynn Dexter

3. Under the commercial paper article of the UCC, for an instrument to be negotiable, it must:

a. Be payable to order or to bearer

b. Be signed to the payee

c. Contain references to all agreements between the parties

d. Contain necessary conditions of payment

4. An instrument reads as follows:

Which of the following statements correctly describes this instrument?

a. The instrument is nonnegotiable because it is not payable at a definite time.

b. The instrument is nonnegotiable because it is secured by the proceeds of the sale of the ring.

c. The instrument is a negotiable promissory note.

d. The instrument is a negotiable sight draft payable on demand.

$10,000   Ludlow, Vermont
                           February 1, 1993

I promise to pay to the order of Custer Corp. $10,000 within 10 days after the sale of my two-carat diamond ring. I pledge the sale proceeds to secure my obligation hereunder.

R. Harris
R. Harris

5. Which of the following instruments is subject to the provisions of the Negotiable Instruments Article of the UCC?

a. A bill of lading

b. A warehouse receipt

c. A certificate of deposit

d. An investment security

Chapter 35

BANKRUPTCY

hat can a person or business do when overwhelmed by debts? Bankruptcy proceedings can provide temporary and sometimes permanent relief from those debts.

A. Bankruptcy Law

Bankruptcy is a statutory proceeding with detailed procedures and requirements.

1. The Federal Law

Bankruptcy law is based on federal statutes that have been refined over the years. In October 2005, the Bankruptcy Abuse Prevention and Consumer Protection Act of 2005 (BAPCPA) took effect.[1] The BAPCPA was passed more than 10 years after the Bankruptcy Reform Commission was created, and the changes in bankruptcy law reflect an expressed congressional desire to curb a 15-year trend of increases in the number of bankruptcies.

Jurisdiction over bankruptcy proceedings is vested in the federal district courts. The district courts have the authority to transfer such matters to courts of special jurisdiction called **bankruptcy courts**.

bankruptcy courts – court of special jurisdiction to determine bankruptcy issues.

2. Types of Bankruptcy Proceedings

The three types of bankruptcy proceedings that existed before the 2005 reforms are still available to individuals and businesses.

CPA

(A) Liquidation or Chapter 7 Bankruptcy. A **Chapter 7 bankruptcy** is one in which all of the debtor's assets (with some exemptions) will be **liquidated** to pay debts. Those debts that remain unpaid or are paid only partially are discharged, with some exceptions. The debtor who declares Chapter 7 bankruptcy begins again with a nearly clean slate.

Chapter 7 bankruptcy – liquidation form of bankruptcy under federal law.

liquidation – process of converting property into money whether of particular items of property or of all the assets of a business or an estate.

Chapter 7 bankruptcy is available to individuals, partnerships, and corporations. However, farmers, insurance companies, savings and loans, municipalities, Small Business Administration companies, and railroads are not entitled to declare Chapter 7 bankruptcy because they are specifically governed by other statutes or specialized sections of the Bankruptcy Code.[2]

Under the BAPCPA, consumers generally cannot go directly to a Chapter 7 liquidation bankruptcy because they must demonstrate that they do not have the means to repay the debts before they can do a Chapter 7 liquidation.[3] The means test, which is discussed later, considers the disposable income that is available after the

---

[1] Pub. L. No. 109-8, 119 Stat. 23 (2005); the act is codified at 11 USC § 101 *et. seq.*

[2] For example, the Small Business Investment Act governs the insolvency of small business investment companies, 11 USC § 109(b). Municipalities' bankruptcies are governed by Chapter 9 of the Bankruptcy Code, and farmers' bankruptcies are covered under Chapter 12.

[3] 11 USC §707(C)(2)(a). There are exceptions to the requirements of establishing no means, such as those who incurred their debts while on active military service.

ethics&the law

Bankruptcy Records

According to **www.bankruptcydata.com**, the following are the largest bankruptcies in the history of the United States:

Company	Bankruptcy Date	Total Assets Prebankruptcy
Lehman Brothers	9/15/08	$691,063,000,000
WaMu	9/26/08	$327,913,000,000
WorldCom, Inc.	7/21/02	$103,914,000,000
Enron Corp.	12/02/01	$63,392,000,000
Conseco, Inc.	12/18/02	$61,392,000,000
Chrysler LLC	4/09/09	$39,300,000,000
Thornburg Mgt.	5/01/09	$36,521,000,000
PG&E	4/06/01	$36,152,000,000
Texaco, Inc.	4/12/87	$35,892,000,000
Financial Corporation of America	9/9/88	$33,864,000,000
Refco	10/17/05	$33,333,172,000
IndyMac	7/31/08	$32,734,000,000
Global Crossing.	1/28/02	$30,185,000,000

Total bankruptcy filings in the United States from 2003 to 2008 were as follows. Note the significant drop following the 2005 reforms, followed by the spike in 2008 because of the economic crisis.

Year	Total Business	Total Nonbusiness
2008	43,546	1,074,225
2007	28,322	822,590
2006	19,695	597,695
2005	39,201	2,039,214
2004	34,317	1,563,145
2003	35,037	1,660,245

Do you think, as many federal regulators and representatives and senators did in enacting the reforms, that the bankruptcy laws were being abused and that too many people were declaring bankruptcy just to avoid paying obligations? Is there an ethical component to declaring bankruptcy?

bankruptcy court has deducted allowable expenses that are listed as part of the means section of the BAPCPA, including items such as health insurance and child support.

CPA

Chapter 11 bankruptcy— reorganization form of bankruptcy under federal law.

(B) Reorganization or Chapter 11 Bankruptcy. **Chapter 11 bankruptcy** is a way for a debtor to reorganize and continue a business with protection from overwhelming debts and without the requirement of liquidation. Chrysler, General Motors, United Airlines, and Delta are all examples of companies that have done through Chapter 11 bankruptcies. Stockbrokers, however, are not eligible for Chapter 11 bankruptcy.

CPA

Chapter 13 bankruptcy— proceeding of consumer debt readjustment plan bankruptcy.

(C) Chapter 13 Bankruptcy or Payment Plans or Consumer Debt Adjustment Plans. Chapter 13 of the federal Bankruptcy Code provides consumers an individual form of reorganization. Chapter 13 works with consumer debtors to develop a plan to repay debt. To be eligible for **Chapter 13 bankruptcy**, the individual must owe unsecured debts of less than $336,900 and secured debts of less than $1,010,650 and have regular income.[4] Chapter 13 plays an expanded role in bankruptcy because reforms require debtors with the means to pay their debts to go first into Chapter 13 bankruptcy rather than automatically declaring Chapter 7 bankruptcy.

[4] 11 USC §109(e).

B. How Bankruptcy is Declared

Bankruptcy can be declared in different ways. The federal Bankruptcy Code spells out in detail the exact requirements and process for declaration.

CPA

3. Declaration of Voluntary Bankruptcy

voluntary bankruptcy– proceeding in which the debtor files the petition for relief.

A **voluntary bankruptcy** is begun when the debtor files a petition with the bankruptcy court. A joint petition may be filed by a husband and wife. When a voluntary case is begun, the debtor must file a schedule of current income and current expenditures unless the court excuses this filing.

means test– new standard under the Reform Act that requires that court to find that the debtor does not have the means to repay creditors; goes beyond the past requirement of petitions being granted on the simple assertion of the debtor saying, "I have debts."

Under the 2005 reforms, a court can dismiss an individual debtor's (consumer's) petition for abuse if the debtor does not satisfy the **means test**, which measures the debtor's ability to pay by computing the debtor's disposable income. Only those debtors who fall below their state's median disposable income will be able to continue in a Chapter 7 proceeding. Individual debtors who meet the means test are required to go into Chapter 13 bankruptcy because they have not qualified for Chapter 7 bankruptcy. The formula for applying the means test is as follows:

Debtor's current monthly income less
Allowable expenses under the Bankruptcy Code = Disposable income
Disposable income × 60

The debtor is guilty of bankruptcy abuse if this number is not less than the lower of the following:

- 25 percent of the debtor's unsecured claims or $6,000, whichever is greater
- $10,000

A finding of abuse means that the debtor's Chapter 7 voluntary petition is dismissed. Previously, the law required the judge to find "substantial abuse" before dismissing the petition; now the standard reads only "abuse."[5]

Under the BAPCPA, the bankruptcy judge also has the discretion to order the debtor's lawyer to reimburse the trustee for costs and attorney's fees and to assess a civil penalty against the lawyer if the court finds that the lawyer has not acted in good faith in filing the debtor's bankruptcy petition.[6] As part of this change, lawyers must declare themselves (in public ads as well as in any individual meetings with clients) to be "debt relief agencies" or state that they "help people file for relief under the Bankruptcy Code." The Code now requires those who help consumers deal with their creditors to disclose that part of the assistance could include filing for bankruptcy. Lawyers who advertise their credit/bankruptcy expertise are subject to the laws and regulations that apply to debt relief agencies. If the agency/lawyer advises them to do something that causes the court to declare that there has been bankruptcy abuse, the lawyer/debt relief agency is responsible as well. As part of their role as a debt counselor, lawyers are prohibited under the changes in the law from advising clients to undertake more debt in contemplation of filing bankruptcy.[7]

[5] 11 USC § 707(b).
[6] 11 USC § 707(b)(4).
[7] 11 USC §§ 526–528.

Debtors are required to undergo credit counseling (from an approved nonprofit credit counseling agency) within the 180 days prior to declaring a bankruptcy. In addition, the court applies the means test described earlier to determine whether the debtor qualifies for bankruptcy.[8]

---

ethics&the law

The Nonprofit Credit Counselors with Ties to Profits

The credit counseling business is funded in one of two ways, the most common of which is that the agency works with debtors to develop a debt management plan (DMP) and then receives from the creditor a percentage of any payments the debtor makes to the creditor as part of the plan. A second way is that the debtor pays a fee to the agency for the service. For the most part, debtors have not been counseled on creditor relationships but have been convinced to develop a DMP. Under a DMP, the debtor pays one monthly payment to the credit counseling agency, the agency negotiates payments with the debtor's creditors (generally a reduced amount), and the agency keeps a percentage (generally 12 to 15 percent) of each payment made to each creditor.

The Federal Trade Commission (FTC) cited a third possible funding arrangement: Although it can collect a donation from the debtor, the agency is primarily funded through for-profit collection agencies that earn a percentage fee of the total amount collected from the debtor. In late 2003, the FTC had filed a complaint against AmeriDebt, alleging that the credit counseling

agency duped new clients into making a "voluntary contribution" to enroll in the program, which allowed AmeriDebt to keep these "contributions" as fees without consumers' knowledge. Furthermore, the FTC alleged that AmeriDebt was not a charitable organization as it had advertised but was really a front organization for two for-profit agencies, DebtWorks and Andris Pukke, to which AmeriDebt funneled profits of approximately $170 million. By mid-2004, AmeriDebt had declared bankruptcy, and the FTC case was settled.

Discuss the ethics of AmeriDebt's operations. Was it fair to make these arrangements without telling the debtors of its ties to profit agencies? Do you think that the mandatory counseling requirement for bankruptcy will cause more problems such as AmeriDebt?*

* In re AmeriDebt Inc., Case No. 04-23649-PM (D Md); Federal Trade Commission v AmeriDebt, Inc., DebtWorks, Inc., Andris Pukke, and Pamela Pukke, also known as Pamela Shuster, File No. 0223171 (D Md 2003); In re AmeriDebt Inc., Case No. 04-23649-PM (D Md 2005).

There is significant disagreement among the bankruptcy courts about the meaning of "projected income." The disagreement results from the differing situations of the debtors. **For Example,** how do courts deal with debtors who are about to experience a large drop in disposable income? And do courts then consider what happens when debtors' incomes are expected to go up? If the projected income test used is applied, the bankruptcy could be dismissed. Debtors and creditors take different positions depending on which way the income goes, and the courts continue to debate the definition of projected income.[9]

---

[8] 11 USC § 109(h)(2). There are exceptions to the counseling requirements; for example, active military duty, disability, and emergencies.

[9] For cases that disagree with *Jass*, see *In re Musselman*, 379 BR 583, 586+, 58 Collier Bankr Cas 2d 2037 (Bankr EDNC Nov 30, 2007) (NO. 07-00701-8-RDD); and *In re Frederickson*, 375 BR 829, 833, 58 Collier Bankr Cas 2d 719, 719, Bankr L Rep P 81,022 (8th Cir BAP Ark Sep 24, 2007) (NO. 07-6025EA).

CASE SUMMARY

Disposable Income and Predisposed Not to Pay

FACTS: The Jasses filed for Chapter 13 bankruptcy relief. Their Form B22C indicated that their yearly household aggregate income was $143,403.96 based on income they received during the six-month period before filing. After deducting allowed expenses and deductions from their income, the Jasses' Statement of Current Monthly Income showed a "disposable income" of $3,625.63 per month.

The Jasses filed a Chapter 13 plan which proposed to return $790.00 per month to unsecured creditors. At the hearing, the trustee objected to confirmation because the Jasses' "disposable income," as calculated on their Form B22C, was $3,625.63, and they proposed to pay only $790.00 to unsecured creditors. The trustee argued that because the Jasses were not proposing to pay their full disposable income of $3,625.63 to unsecured creditors, their plan did not comply with this "disposable income test."

The Jasses argued that the word "projected" in the statute modifies the definition of "disposable income." Mrs. Jass testified that beginning in December 2005, her husband experienced serious medical problems involving injuries to his intestines. She testified that her family incurred $12,000 in medical expenses. In light of these expenses and medical problems, the Jasses argued that their income in the future would not be commensurate with the "disposable income" shown on Form B22C. They argued that the changes under the BAPCPA did not require them to pay unsecured creditors the amount resulting from their Form B22C, so long as they could show that the income and expenses reported on the Form were inadequate representations of their future budget.

DECISION: The court held that the word *projected* modifies *disposable income* and that the Code intended that the disposable income figure be based on "projected income." The court acknowledged that the debtor would need to provide testimony regarding the change in circumstances that would result in a reduction of the income but also noted that without the word *projected* being used, the parties to a bankruptcy would be deprived of the fresh-start purpose the laws were intended to provide. They could not pay more money to creditors than they would be earning and their change in health and financial circumstances meant that they would simply not have the funds available to pay all that the form computed; the testimony on the future established the notion of *projected*. [**In re Jass, 340 BR 411 (Utah 2006)**]

CPA   ## 4. Declaration of Involuntary Bankruptcy

involuntary bankruptcy–
proceeding in which a
creditor or creditors file the
petition for relief with the
bankruptcy court.

(A) ELIGIBILITY. An **involuntary bankruptcy** is begun when creditors file a petition with the bankruptcy court. An involuntary case may be commenced against any individual, partnership, or corporation, except those excluded from filing voluntary petitions. Nonprofit corporations are also exempt from involuntary proceedings.[10]

CPA   (B) NUMBER AND CLAIMS OF PETITIONING CREDITORS. If there are 12 or more creditors, at least 3 of those creditors whose unsecured and undisputed claims total $13,475 or more must sign the involuntary petition.[11] If there are fewer than 12 creditors,

---

[10] 11 USC § 303(a).
[11] 11 USC § 303. The term "undisputed" was added to this section and commentators are unclear as to whether this addition will make it easier for debtors to challenge involuntary bankruptcies.

excluding employees or insiders (that is, the debtor's relatives, partners, directors, and controlling persons), any creditor whose unsecured claim is at least $13,475 may sign the petition. In the case of involuntary consumer petitions, there is disagreement as to whether the debtor will still be required to complete the credit counseling requirement prior to the granting of the automatic stay.

If a creditor holds security for a claim, only the amount of the claim in excess of the value of the security is counted. The holder of a claim that is the subject of a **bona fide** dispute may not be counted as a petitioning creditor.[12]

bona fide–in good faith; without any fraud or deceit.

---

sports&entertainment law

Hip-Hop to the Top: Bankruptcy to the Bottom

TLC was an Atlanta rhythm, blues, and hip-hop band that performed at clubs in 1991. The three-woman group signed a recording contract with LaFace Records. The group's first album that LaFace produced, *Oooooooohhh on the TLC Tip*, sold almost 3 million albums in 1992. The group's second album, *Crazysexycool*, also produced by LaFace, sold 5 million albums through June 1996. The two albums together had six top-of-the-chart singles.

LaFace had the right to renew TLC's contract in 1996 following renegotiation of the contract terms. In the industry, royalty rates for unknown groups, as TLC was in 1991, are generally 7 percent of the revenues for the first 500,000 albums and 8 percent for sales on platinum albums (albums that sell over 1 million copies). The royalty rate increases to 9.5 percent for all sales on an eighth album. Established artists in the industry who renegotiate often have royalty rates of 13 percent, and artists with two platinum albums can command an even higher royalty.

The three women in TLC—Tionne Watkins (T-Boz), Lisa Lopes (Left-Eye, who has since died), and Rozonda Thomas (Chili)—declared bankruptcy in July 1995. All three listed debts that exceeded their assets, which included sums owed to creditors for their cars and to Zale's and The Limited for credit purchases. Lopes was being sued by Lloyd's of London, which claimed she owed it $1.3 million it had paid on a policy held by her boyfriend on his home that was destroyed by fire. Lopes pleaded guilty to one count of arson in the destruction of the home but denied that she intended to destroy it. She was sentenced to five years probation and treatment at a halfway house.

Lopes asked that the Lloyd's claim be discharged in her bankruptcy. All three members of TLC asked that their contract with LaFace be discharged in bankruptcy because being bound to their old contract could impede their fresh financial starts.

Did the three women meet the standards for declaring bankruptcy? Evaluate whether Lopes's Lloyd's claim should be discharged. Determine whether the record contract should be discharged.

Pop singer Billy Joel also had a record contract with a small company during the initial stages of his career. When the company refused, during renegotiations, to increase his royalty rate, Joel did not produce another album during the period of the contract renewal option. Instead, he used a clause in the contract that limited him to nightclub and piano bar appearances in the event another album was not produced. For three years, Joel played small clubs and restaurants and did not produce an album. At the end of that period when his contract had expired, he negotiated a contract with Columbia. His first album with Columbia was *Piano Man,* a multiplatinum album. Did Joel take an ethical route? Is his solution more ethical than bankruptcy?

---

[12] 11 USC § 303(b)(1).

thinking things through

Means Test Justifying the End of Debt

The following excerpt is a hypothetical case an experienced bankruptcy attorney worked through to illustrate the application of the means test because no bankruptcy means cases have made their way through to appellate decision.

The Brokes, a married couple in their early 40s, have two children in private schools. They are residents of Memphis, Shelby County, Tennessee; their annual gross income is $86,496. Like many debtors, the Brokes lost their home following an unsuccessful Chapter 13 case three years ago. They now rent a house for $2,000 a month. They owe back federal taxes in the amount of $9,000. They have secured debt on two cars with remaining balances of $10,000 and $6,000 and unsecured, consumer debt totaling $28,000. They desire to seek relief under Chapter 7 of the Bankruptcy Code.

The Brokes' gross monthly income is $7,208. After deducting taxes and other mandatory payroll deductions of $1,509, the couple has $5,699 in monthly income. The means test requires several additional deductions from the Brokes' gross monthly income. Section 707(b)(A)(2)(ii) provides a deduction for living and housing expenses using National Standards and Local Standards and additional Internal Revenue Service (IRS) figures. Allowable living expenses for a family of four in Ura and Ima Brokes' income bracket, based on national standards, total $1,564, while housing and utility figures for Shelby County, Tennessee, allow $1,354. In addition, there are allowable expenses for transportation. Based on IRS figures, the Brokes can subtract national ownership costs of $475 for the first car and $338 for the second, as well as regional operating and public transportation costs of $242 and

$336, respectively. They can also deduct their reasonably necessary health insurance costs, here the sum of $600, and $250 a month for private school tuition. Subtracting all of these figures from the Brokes' monthly income leaves $540.

Under § 707(b)(2)(A)(iii), the Brokes can subtract payments on secured debt. The amount contractually due on their two automobiles over the next 60 months is $16,000. After dividing this total by 60 and rounding to the nearest dollar, the monthly allowable deduction for secured debt is $267. Subtracting this amount from $540 leaves $273.

Next come priority claim deductions. The Brokes are not subject to any child support or alimony claims, but they do owe $9,000 in back taxes. Again, dividing this amount by 60 yields a deductible amount of $150. Subtracting this from $273 leaves $123 in disposable monthly income. This figure would be multiplied by 60, amounting to a total of $7,380 in disposable income over the five-year period. Abuse is thus statutorily presumed because the debtors' current monthly income reduced by allowable amounts is not less than either $7,000 (25 percent of their nonpriority unsecured claims of $28,000) or $6,000. The Brokes' Chapter 7 case will therefore be dismissed (or they will be allowed voluntarily to convert their Chapter 7 case to a case under Chapter 13).

Does the means test make it more difficult for debtors to declare bankruptcy?*

---

* Robert J. Landry III and Nancy Hisey Mardis, "Consumer Bankruptcy Reform: Debtors' Prison without Bars or 'Just Desserts' for Deadbeats?" 36 *Golden Gate U L Rev* 91 (2006).

For Example, David, a CPA, is an unsecured creditor of Arco Company for $15,000. Arco has a total of 10 creditors, all of whom are unsecured. Arco has not paid any of the creditors for three months. The debtor has fewer than 12 creditors. Any one of the creditors may file the petition if the unsecured portion of the amount due that creditor is at least $13,475.[13] Because David is owed $15,000 in unsecured debts, he may file the petition alone.

CPA   (C) GROUNDS FOR RELIEF FOR INVOLUNTARY CASE. The mere filing of an involuntary case petition does not result in an order of relief. The debtor may contest the bankruptcy petition. If the debtor does not contest the petition, the court will enter an order of relief if at least one of the following grounds exists: (1) The debtor is generally not paying debts as they become due or (2) within 120 days before the filing of the petition, a custodian has been appointed for the debtor's property.

CPA   ## 5. Automatic Stay

automatic stay–order to prevent creditors from taking action such as filing suits or seeking foreclosure against the debtor.

Just the filing of either a voluntary or an involuntary petition operates as an **automatic stay**, which prevents creditors from taking action, such as filing suits or foreclosure actions, against the debtor.[14] The stay freezes all creditors in their filing date positions so that no one creditor gains an advantage over other creditors. This automatic stay ends when the bankruptcy case is closed or dismissed (for example, on a finding of abuse by the debtor who has failed to survive the means-to-pay test) or when the debtor is granted a discharge. An automatic stay means that all activity by creditors with respect to collection must stop, with some exceptions incorporated for child support and other family support issues under the 2005 reforms. All litigation with the debtor is halted, and any judgments in place cannot be executed.[15]

FIGURE 35-1 | *Declaration of Bankruptcy*

	CHAPTER 7	CHAPTER 11	CHAPTER 13
TRUSTEE	YES	NO	YES
ELIGIBLE PERSONS:			
INDIVIDUALS	YES (CONSUMER RESTRICTIONS)	YES (INDIVIDUAL RESTRICTIONS)	YES (CONSUMER RESTRICTIONS)
PARTNERSHIPS	YES	YES	NO
CORPORATIONS	YES	YES	NO
VOLUNTARY	YES	YES	YES
INVOLUNTARY	YES, EXCEPT FOR FARMERS AND NONPROFITS**	YES, EXCEPT FOR FARMERS AND NONPROFITS	NO
EXEMPTIONS	S & L's, CREDIT UNIONS, SBA, RAILROADS, MUNICIPALITIES	SAME AS CHAPTER 7 PLUS STOCKBROKERS*	ONLY INDIVIDUALS ALLOWED
REQUIREMENTS-VOLUNTARY	DEBTS; MEANS TEST APPLIES TO CONSUMERS	DEBTS; MEANS TEST APPLIES TO CONSUMERS	INCOME: <$336,900 UNSECURED; <$1,010,650 SECURED
REQUIREMENTS-INVOLUNTARY	<12 = 1/$13,475 ≥12 = 3/$13,475	<12 = 1/$13,475 ≥12 = 3/$13,475	N/A

*RAILROADS ARE ELIGIBLE
**CHAPTER 9 — MUNICIPALITIES; CHAPTER 12 — FARMERS

[13] The amount was $10,000 originally, but the bankruptcy reforms had a built-in clause for increases in this figure.
[14] 11 USC § 362.
[15] The reforms exempt dissolution, custody, child support, and other related litigation from the stay.

6. If the Creditors are Wrong: Rights of Debtor in an Involuntary Bankruptcy

If an involuntary petition is dismissed other than by consent of all petitioning creditors and the debtor, the court may award costs, reasonable attorney fees, or damages to the debtor. The damages are those that were caused by taking possession of the debtor's property. The debtor may also recover damages against any creditor who filed the petition in bad faith.[16]

Figure 35.1 provides a summary of the requirements for declaration of bankruptcy and the standards for relief.

C. Administration of the Bankruptcy Estate

The administration of the bankruptcy estate varies according to the type of bankruptcy declared. This section of the chapter focuses on the process for liquidation or Chapter 7 bankruptcy. Figure 35.2 provides a flowchart view of the Chapter 7 liquidation process.

7. The Order of Relief

order of relief–The order from the bankruptcy judge that starts the protection for the debtor; when the order of relief is entered by the court, the debtor's creditors must stop all proceedings and work through the bankruptcy court to recover debts (if possible). Court finding that creditors have met the standards for bankruptcy petitions.

The **order of relief** is granted by the bankruptcy court and is the procedural step required for the case to proceed in bankruptcy court.[17] An order of relief is entered automatically in a voluntary case and in an involuntary case when those filing the petition have established that the debtor is unable to pay his, her, or its debts as they become due. In consumer cases and Chapter 11 cases that involve an individual, the bankruptcy court must apply the means test to determine whether the individual is eligible for declaring bankruptcy or whether there has been an abuse of the bankruptcy court and system.

8. List of Creditors

It is the debtor's responsibility to furnish the bankruptcy court a list of creditors. Although imposing the responsibility for disclosing debts on the debtor may not seem to be effective, the debtor has an incentive for full disclosure. Those debts not disclosed by the debtor will not be discharged in bankruptcy.

9. Trustee in Bankruptcy

trustee in bankruptcy– impartial person elected to administer the debtor's estate.

The **trustee in bankruptcy** is elected by the creditors. The court or the U.S. trustee will appoint an interim trustee if the creditors do not elect a trustee.

The trustee is the successor to the property rights of the debtor. By operation of law, the trustee automatically becomes the owner of all of the debtor's property in excess of the property to which the debtor is entitled under exemption laws. The trustee holds all of the rights formerly owned by the debtor.

---

[16] *Arizona Public Service v Apache County*, 847 P2d 1339 (Ariz App 1993).
[17] 11 USC § 301.

FIGURE 35-2 | *Anatomy of Bankruptcy Case*

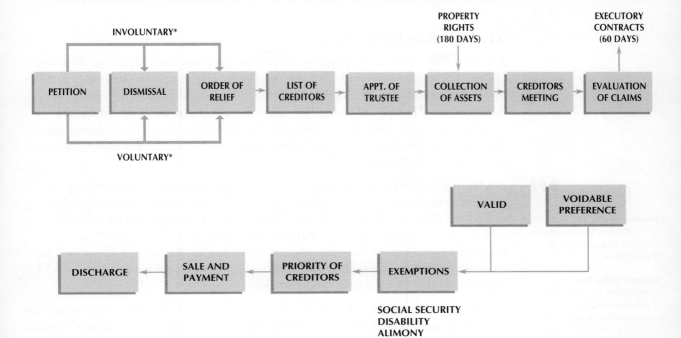

VOIDABLE PREFERENCES

1. 2 YR. FRAUD
2. 1 YR. INSOLVENT** AND UNFAIR
3. 1 YR. INSIDER
4. 90 DAYS—PRESUMED INSOLVENT**—NOT ORDINARY COURSE OF BUSINESS
5. SECURITY FOR ANTECEDENT DEBT

OK (NOT VOIDABLE)

1. UP TO $600 CONSUMER DEBT
2. CONTEMPORANEOUS EXCHANGE
3. REGULAR PAYMENTS
4. UP TO $5,475 FOR NON-CONSUMER CREDITORS***

*MEANS TEST FOR CONSUMERS
**INSOLVENT = "BANKRUPTCY" SENSE (LIABILITIES > ASSETS)
***AMOUNTS ARE ADJUSTED ANNUALLY

CPA   10. The Bankrupt's Estate

All of the debtor's property, with certain exceptions discussed later, is included in the *bankrupt's estate.* Property inherited by the debtor within six months after the filing of the petition also passes to the trustee.

In many cases, when a debtor knows that insolvency is a problem and bankruptcy is imminent, the debtor attempts to hang onto property or reputation by making transfers of assets to friends, relatives, and creditors. However, trustees have the authority to set aside or void (1) transfers by the debtor that a creditor holding a valid claim under state law could have avoided at the commencement of the bankruptcy case, (2) **preferences**, that is, transfers of property by the debtor to a creditor, the effect of which is to enable the creditor to obtain payment of a higher percentage of the creditor's claim than the creditor would have received if the

preferences–transfers of property by a debtor to one or more specific creditors to enable these creditors to obtain payment for debts owed.

debtor's assets had been liquidated in bankruptcy, and (3) statutory liens that became effective against the debtor at the commencement of the bankruptcy.

11. Voidable Preferences

A debtor may not transfer property to prevent creditors from satisfying their legal claims. The trustee may void any such transfer, known as a *fraudulent transfer,* made or obligation incurred by the debtor within two years of bankruptcy when the debtor's actual intent was to hinder, delay, or defraud creditors by doing so.[18]

The trustee may also void certain transfers of property made by a debtor merely because their effect is to make the debtor insolvent or to reduce the debtor's assets to an unreasonably low amount.[19]

CPA

insolvency–excess of debts and liabilities over assets, or inability to pay debts as they mature.

balance sheet test– comparison of assets to liabilities made to determine solvency.

preferential transfers– certain transfers of money or security interests in the time frame just prior to bankruptcy that can be set aside if voidable.

insider–full-time corporate employee or a director or their relatives.

(A) THE INSOLVENT DEBTOR. A debtor is insolvent for purposes of determining voidable transfers when the total fair value of all of the debtor's assets does not exceed the debts owed by the debtor. This test for **insolvency** under voidable transfers is commonly called the **balance sheet test** because it is merely a comparison of assets to liabilities without considering whether the debtor will be able to meet future obligations as they become due. The debtor is presumed to be insolvent in the 90 days prior to declaration of bankruptcy.

(B) PREFERENTIAL TRANSFERS. A transfer of property by the debtor to a creditor may be set aside as **preferential transfers** and the property recovered by the debtor's trustee in bankruptcy if (1) the transfer was made to pay a debt incurred at some earlier time, (2) the transfer was made when the debtor was insolvent and within 90 days before the filing of the bankruptcy petition, and (3) the transfer resulted in the creditor receiving more than the creditor would have received in a liquidation of the debtor's estate. A debtor is presumed to be insolvent on and during the 90 days immediately preceding the date of the filing of the bankruptcy petition.[20]

Transfers made to **insiders** within the 12 months prior to the filing of the petition may be set aside.[21] **For Example,** if a building contractor transferred title to one of his model homes to the company accountant just six months before declaring bankruptcy, the transfer would be a preferential one that would be set aside. However, a transfer by an insider to a noninsider is not subject to recovery by the trustee. The sale of that same model home to a good faith buyer just three days before bankruptcy would be valid. **For Example,** the trustee in the Bernie Madoff case sought to set aside several transfers made to companies and individuals just prior to the time Mr. Madoff admitted that he had an insolvent, $50-billion Ponzi scheme. The trustee used several of the voidable preferences theories to seek a return of funds.

The trustee may not set aside certain transfers by a debtor as preferences. A transaction for a present consideration, such as a cash sale, is not set aside.[22] A payment by a debtor in the ordinary course of business, such as the payment of a utility bill, will not be set aside. Under the prior bankruptcy law, a payment was not a

---

[18] Prior to the reforms, the time period for fraudulent transfers was one year.
[19] 11 USC § 548.
[20] 11 USC § 547(f).
[21] 11 USC § 547(b)(4)(B).
[22] *In re Smith Min. and Material, LLC*, 405 BR 589 (WDKy 2009).

voidable preference if it was made in the ordinary course of business and it was made according to industry terms and practices. Under the 2005 reforms, the *and* is changed to *or,* and it is now easier for creditors to show that they were not the recipients of a voidable preference. Also under the 2005 reforms, nonconsumer debt payments that have a value of less than $5,475 are not subject to the voidable preference standards. The expectation is that the time and effort spent by bankruptcy trustees and courts will be reduced because of the minimum amount required before a challenge can be made. In nonconsumer debts, transfers of less than $5,475 within the voidable preference period are not considered voidable preferences.

(C) SELF-SETTLED TRUST. Under the Reform Act, the trustee has the ability to set aside the transfer of property into a "self-settled" (a self-created personal trust) any time within the past 10 years if the trustee can establish that the trust was created with actual intent to hinder, delay, or defraud existing or future creditors.[23] This section was added to address the problem of the many assets of individuals being in personal trusts for which those individuals serve as trustees.

12. Proof of Claim

Bankruptcy law regulates the manner in which creditors present their claims and the way in which the debtor's assets are distributed in payment of these claims.

After the debtor has filed a list of creditors, the court then sends a notice of the bankruptcy proceedings to listed creditors. The creditors who wish to participate in the distribution of the proceeds of the liquidation of the debtor's estate must file a proof of claim. A **claim** is a right to payment, whether liquidated (certain and not disputed), unliquidated, contingent, unmatured, disputed, legal, or equitable. A **proof of claim** is a written statement, signed by the creditor or an authorized representative, setting forth any claim made against the debtor and the basis for it. It must ordinarily be filed within 90 days after the first meeting of creditors.[24] A creditor must file within that time even though the trustee in bankruptcy in fact knows of the existence of the creditor's claim.

claim–creditor's right to payment.

proof of claim–written statement, signed by the creditor or an authorized representative, setting forth any claim made against the debtor and the basis for it.

CPA 13. Priority of Claims

Creditors who hold security for payment, such as a lien or a mortgage on the debtor's property, are not affected by the debtor's bankruptcy. Secured creditors may enforce their security interest to obtain payment of their claims up to the value of their security, the collateral in which they hold an interest. **For Example,** suppose that First Bank holds a mortgage on a company's office building. The mortgage amount is $750,000. The building is sold for $700,000. First Bank is entitled to the $700,000 from the sale. For the remaining portion of the debt, First Bank drops down in priority to wait with the other unsecured creditors for its remaining $50,000. Unsecured creditors with unsecured debts that have priority and their order of priority following the secured creditors' rights in their collateral are covered in the following list.[25] Once the bottom of the priority list is reached, any remaining

[23] 11 USC § 548(e).
[24] 11 USC § 302(c).
[25] 11 USC § 507(1)–(6).

unsecured creditors share on a pro rata basis any remaining assets of the debtor. Any balance remaining after all creditors have been paid goes to the debtor. However, in 98 to 99 percent of all bankruptcies, no unsecured creditors receive any payments, so it is highly unlikely that the debtor would ever receive anything from the bankruptcy litigation of the debtor's property and funds.

The following is a list of the priorities for unsecured creditors following the payment to any secured creditors from the debtors' pledged property:[26]

1. Allowed claims for debts to a spouse, former spouse, or child of the debtor and for alimony to, maintenance for, or support of such spouse or child (that were obligations at the time of the filing of the bankruptcy petition).

2. Costs and expenses of administration of the bankruptcy case, including fees to trustees, attorneys, and accountants, and the reasonable expenses of creditors in recovering property transferred or concealed by the debtor.

3. Claims arising in the ordinary course of a debtor's business or financial affairs after the commencement of the case but before the order of relief (involuntary).

4. Claims for wages, salaries, or commissions, including vacation, severance, or sick leave pay earned within 180 days before the filing of the petition or the date of cessation of the debtor's business, whichever occurred first, limited, however, to $10,950 for each person.[27]

5. Claims arising for contributions to employee benefit plans, based on services rendered within 180 days before the filing of the petition or when the debtor ceased doing business, whichever occurred first; the maximum amount is $5,400. Under the 2005 reforms (especially in Chapter 11 reorganizations), payments of key-employee retention plans are not permitted unless the plans are "essential" to keeping the key employee at the company that is in bankruptcy. Proving that they are essential requires the key employee actually to have a "bona fide" offer of employment from another company. In addition, there are limits on how much can be paid under key-employee retention plans.

6. Farm producers (up to $10,950) and fishers against debtors who operate grain storage facilities or fish produce storage or processing facilities, up to $5,400 per claim.

7. Claims by consumer creditors, not to exceed $2,425 for each claimant, arising for the purchase of consumer goods or services when such property or services were not delivered or provided.

8. Certain taxes and penalties due government, such as income and property taxes.

9. All other unsecured creditors.

10. Remainder (if any) to debtor.

Each claim must be paid in full before any lower claim is paid anything. If a class of claims cannot be paid in full, the claims in that case are paid on a pro rata basis. **For Example,** suppose that following the payment of all secured creditors,

---

[26] 11 USCA § 507.
[27] Prior to the 2005 reforms, the amount limit was $4,650 and the time period was 90 days.

$10,000 is left to be distributed. The accountants who performed work on the bankruptcy are owed $15,000, and the lawyers who worked on it are owed $10,000. Because there is not enough to pay two parties in the same priority ranking, the $10,000 is split proportionately. The accountants will receive 15/25, or 3/5, of the $10,000, or $6,000, and the lawyers will receive 10/25, or 2/5, of the $10,000, or $4,000.

D. Debtor's Duties and Exemptions

Bankruptcy law imposes certain duties on the debtor and provides for specific exemptions of some of the debtor's estate from the claims of creditors.

14. Debtor's Duties

A debtor must file with the court a list of creditors, a schedule of assets and liabilities, and a statement of her financial affairs. The debtor must also appear for examination under oath at the first meeting of creditors.

CPA | 15. Debtor's Exemptions

A debtor is permitted to claim certain property of the estate in the trustee's possession and keep it free from claims of creditors. Exemptions are provided under federal law, but state laws also provide for exemptions. In 14 states (examples are Massachusetts, New Jersey, Pennsylvania, and Connecticut), debtors can elect either federal or state exemption. In the other states (New York, California, Florida, and Delaware are examples), debtors are permitted to use only the state exemptions.[28] Examples of exempt property from the federal code include wedding rings, property used to earn a living, one VCR, and one car. New York exemptions include "all stoves in the home, one sewing machine, the family Bible, a pew in a public house of worship, enough food for sixty days, a wedding ring, and a watch not exceeding thirty-five dollars in value."[29] California exempts tools of the trade and the family cemetery plot.[30]

The principal exemptions provided by the Bankruptcy Code are the debtor's interest in real or personal property used as a residence.[31] The Reform Act has greatly limited the homestead exemption and, in effect, preempts state law on this debtor exemption. Debtors are required to have lived in the home for two years prior to bankruptcy, and the amount of the homestead exemption would be limited to $136,875.[32] To be able to use a higher state homestead exemption, the debtor must have lived in the home for 1215 days (40 months).[33] Labeled as the most flagrant abuse of the existing bankruptcy system, debtors have used the homestead exemption to shift their assets into expensive homes to shield everything from bankruptcy. Known as the "mansion loophole," the changes in the Reform Act

[28] 11 USC § 522.
[29] NY CPLR § 5205 (McKinney 2009).
[30] Cal Civ Proc Code § 704.010-704.210 (West 2009).
[31] A married couple gets a single homestead exemption. Gay couples who have registered under state domestic partner rights statutes are also entitled to only one homestead exemption. *In re Rabin*, 359 BR 242 (2007).
[32] The time requirement is at 11 USC § 522(b)(3)(A), and the amount limitation is at 11 USC § 522(o)(1). This amount refers to those who elect state exemptions. In the absence of state exemptions, the federal maximum is $20,200.
[33] 11 USC § 522(b)(2).

related to the homestead exemption were among the most debated and the most dramatic.[34] **For Example,** prior to the reforms actor Burt Reynolds declared bankruptcy in Florida and was relieved of millions in debt, but he was able to keep his $2.5 million Valhalla estate there. Corporate raider Paul Bilzerian, who was convicted of securities fraud, also declared bankruptcy in Florida but kept his mansion, the largest home in Hillsborough County, Florida. Former WorldCom CFO Scott Sullivan (who entered a guilty plea to fraud and other charges and is serving a five-year sentence) built a multimillion-dollar home in Florida to gain homestead protections. Wendy Gramm, who sat on Enron's board, purchased 200 acres of land in Texas and constructed a large home with her husband, former senator Phil Gramm, to take advantage of homestead exemptions then available in Texas. However, the Reform Act closed this corporate executive loophole by requiring that the $136,875 exemption apply to debtors who are convicted of securities fraud or bankruptcy fraud.[35]

Other exemptions include payments under a life insurance contract, alimony and child support payments, and awards from personal injury litigation.[36] Under the Reform Act, college savings accounts and IRAs are exempt property under the federal exemptions and can be used even by those debtors who are using state exemptions. The IRA exemption is limited to $1,095,000.[37]

Businesses that declare bankruptcy would not have included in their bankruptcy estates employee pension plan contributions. Those contributions would be returned to the employees. The proposed changes are the result of the numerous large corporate bankruptcies, such as the one involving United Airlines and the pensions of its employees.[38]

16. Debtor's Protection Against Discrimination

Federal, state, and local law may not discriminate against anyone on the basis of a discharge in bankruptcy. For example, a state cannot refuse to issue a new license to an individual if the license fees on a previous one have been discharged as a debt in the individual's declaration of bankruptcy.

E. DISCHARGE IN BANKRUPTCY

discharge in bankruptcy— order of the bankruptcy court relieving the debtor from obligation to pay the unpaid balance of most claims.

The main objectives of a bankruptcy proceeding are to collect and distribute the debtor's assets and the subsequent **discharge in bankruptcy** of the debtor from obligations. The decree terminating the bankruptcy proceeding is generally a discharge that releases the debtor from most debts. Under the BAPCPA, a discharge is available only once every eight years.

17. Denial of Discharge

The court will refuse to grant a discharge if the debtor has (1) within one year of the filing of the petition fraudulently transferred or concealed property with intent to

---

[34] 11 USC § 522(p).
[35] 11 USC § 522(q).
[36] 11 USC § 522(d) (including automatic adjustments effective April 1, 1998).
[37] 11 USC § 522(n).
[38] 11 USC § 541(b).

ethics&the law

The Skies are Not So Friendly to Employee Pensions

As part of its Chapter 11 bankruptcy, United Airlines was relieved of its pension liabilities. Employees and unions wonder how a company can be permitted to renege on those benefits when so many protections were built into the law under ERISA. Congressional hearings now reveal that there were loopholes in the accounting processes for pension fund reporting that permitted United, and many others, to report pension numbers that made the pension funds look healthy when they really were not. The loopholes were Enronesque in nature. Companies could spin the pension obligations off the books so that the existing levels of obligations of the plan looked small and the assets very rich. Because of United's pension bailout, Congress will be examining and changing the accounting for pension plans to avoid the problem of the rosy picture when the funds really

need further funding. One interesting approach to protecting pension plans is to require companies to fund the pension plans according to the numbers they have reported to the SEC in their financials. The numbers reported to the SEC for company pensions are accurate whereas the numbers reported for ERISA purposes are inflated. If United had funded its plans when its SEC numbers indicated it needed to (e.g., in 1998), the plan would have been sufficiently funded. Under ERISA guidelines, it was not required to kick in funds until 2002 when it was grossly underfunded.

Were companies acting ethically on their pension accounting? Were they acting legally?*

* Marry Williams Walsh, "Pension Law Loopholes Helped United Hide Its Troubles," *New York Times*, June 7, 2005, C1.

---

hinder, delay, or defraud creditors, (2) failed to keep proper financial records, (3) made a false oath or account,[39] (4) failed to explain satisfactorily any loss of assets, (5) refused to obey any lawful order of the court or refused to testify after having been granted immunity, (6) obtained a discharge within the last eight years,[40] (7) filed a written waiver of discharge that is approved by the court,[41] or (8) in the case of a consumer debtor, has failed to complete a personal financial management instructional course.[42]

A discharge releases the debtor from the unpaid balance of most debts except for taxes, customs duties, child support obligations, and tax penalties.[43] Student loan obligations are not discharged in bankruptcy unless the loan first became due more than seven years before bankruptcy or unless not allowing a discharge would impose undue hardship on the debtor.

In addition, the following debts are not discharged by bankruptcy: (1) loans obtained by use of a false financial statement made with intent to deceive and on which the creditor reasonably relied, (2) debts not scheduled or listed with the court

---

[39] The debtor must actually make a false statement. In *In re Mercer*, 211 F3d 214 (5th Cir 2000), the debtor ran up $3,186.82 on a credit card she was given by AT&T with a $3,000 credit limit. The credit card was issued to the debtor on a preapproved basis, so there was no fraud, just a great deal of spending.

[40] 11 USC § 727(a)(8).

[41] 11 USC § 523.

[42] 11 USC § 727(a)(11). The financial management course requirement applies to both Chapter 7 and Chapter 13 consumer bankruptcies.

[43] Child support obligations enjoy additional protections and priorities in bankruptcy. 11 USC § 507(a).

in time for allowance, (3) debts arising from fraud while the debtor was acting in a fiduciary capacity or by reason of embezzlement or larceny, (4) alimony and child support, (5) a judgment for willful and malicious injury, (6) a consumer debt to a single creditor totaling more than $5550 for luxury goods or services (within 90 days of the order of relief) and cash advances exceeding $825 based on consumer open-end credit, such as a credit card (within 70 days of the order of relief),[44] (7) damages arising from drunk driving or the operation of vessels and aircrafts by people who are inebriated,[45] (8) loans used to pay taxes (including credit cards),[46] (9) taxes not paid as a result of a fraudulent return, although other unpaid taxes beyond the past three years can be discharged,[47] (10) prebankruptcy fees and assessments owed to homeowners associations, and (11) debts owed to tax-qualified retirement plans. **For Example,** in regard to (5), the finding of malice in *Goldman v O. J. Simpson* precluded the discharge by bankruptcy of the $8.5 million damage award from Simpson to the Goldmans and Browns. See Figure 35.3 for a listing of nondischargeable debts.

FIGURE 35-3 | *Nondischargeable Debts in Bankruptcy*

1. **TAXES WITHIN THREE YEARS OF FILING BANKRUPTCY PETITION**
2. **LIABILITY FOR OBTAINING MONEY OR PROPERTY BY FALSE PRETENSES**
3. **WILLFUL AND MALICIOUS INJURIES**
4. **DEBTS INCURRED BY DRIVING DWI***
5. **ALIMONY, MAINTENANCE, OR CHILD SUPPORT**
6. **UNSCHEDULED DEBTS (UNLESS ACTUAL NOTICE)**
7. **DEBTS RESULTING FROM FRAUD AS A FIDUCIARY (EMBEZZLEMENT)**
8. **GOVERNMENT FINES OR PENALTIES IMPOSED WITHIN THREE YEARS PRIOR**
9. **EDUCATIONAL LOANS DUE WITHIN SEVEN PRIOR YEARS (UNLESS HARDSHIP)**
10. **PRIOR BANKRUPTCY DEBTS IN WHICH DEBTOR WAIVED DISCHARGE**
11. **PRESUMPTION ON LUXURY GOODS: $550 GOODS; $825 CASH**
12. **REAFFIRMATION AGREEMENTS** ┬ **WRITING**
    ├ **FILED WITH COURT**
    └ **NOT RESCINDED PRIOR TO DISCHARGE**

*****INCLUDES VESSELS AND AIRCRAFT**

F. REORGANIZATION PLANS UNDER CHAPTER 11

In addition to liquidation under Chapter 7, the Bankruptcy Code permits debtors to restructure the organization and finances of their businesses so that they may continue to operate. In these rehabilitation plans, the debtor keeps all of the assets

---

[44] 11 USC § 523(a)(2)(c)(i). (Amounts are adjusted each year).
[45] 11 USC § 523(a)(9).
[46] 11 USC § 523(a)(14A),(14B).
[47] 11 USC §§ 1129(a)(9)(c), (D), 1129(b)(2)(B), 1141(d)(6)(B).

(exempt and nonexempt), continues to operate the business, and makes a settlement that is acceptable to the majority of the creditors. This settlement is binding on the minority creditors.

Individuals, partnerships, and corporations in business may all be reorganized under the Bankruptcy Code. The first step is to file a plan for the debtor's reorganization. This plan may be filed by the debtor, any party in interest, or a committee of creditors. If the debtor wishes to move from a Chapter 11 proceeding (in the case of an individual debtor), the debtor must survive the means test that is now a requirement for determining eligibility for bankruptcy.

18. Contents of the Plan

The plan divides ownership interests and debts into those that will be affected by the adoption of the plan and those that will not be. It then specifies what will be done to those interests and claims that are affected. **For Example,** when mortgage payments are too high for the income of a corporation, a possible plan would be to reduce the mortgage payments and give the mortgage holder preferred stock to compensate for the loss sustained.

All creditors, shareholders, and other interest holders within a particular class must be treated the same way. **For Example,** the holders of first mortgage bonds must all be treated similarly. The treatment of the bondholders in the Chrysler and

---

C A S E   S U M M A R Y

Your Living Expenses are Fairly Minimal in Maximum Security

FACTS: Bryan Anthony Looper had over $300,000 in student loans that were used to finance his education at Mercer University where he obtained an A.B., an M.B.A, and another unspecified graduate degree as well as a large number of courses toward his J.D. degree. He did not make payments on these student loans.

In 1996, he was elected assessor for Putnam County, Tennessee, a position he held for two years and four months. He was then convicted of the first-degree murder of state senator Tommy Burks. He exhausted all of his appeals and is currently serving a life sentence without the possibility of parole. The debtor has one dependent, a son born in August 1998. The circuit court for Putnam County, Tennessee, ordered Looper to pay child support of $161.00 per month plus $7,254.20 in medical expenses. Looper did not make any of the court-ordered child support payments and was in arrears by more than $23,515.00.

Looper asked to have his student loans discharged on the basis of his hardship.

DECISION: The court refused to discharge the student loans. Looper had all of his living expenses covered by the Tennessee Department of Corrections. Looper had made no effort to make any payments on any of his student loans and had also not made attempts to try and work with his lenders or apply to programs set up to help with student loans. The court also noted that Looper's circumstances were the result of his choices and conduct, not the result of unforeseen and uncontrollable events. He had three degrees and the capability of earning a living but, through poor choices, produced his own difficult circumstances. [**In re Looper, 2007 WL 1231700 (B ED Tenn 2007)**]

GM bankruptcies has been a point of contention and negotiation in those reorganizations.

A plan can also provide for the assumption, rejection, or assignment of executory contracts. The trustee or debtor can, under certain circumstances, suspend performance of a contract not yet fully performed. **For Example,** collective bargaining agreements may be rejected with the approval of the bankruptcy court.[48]

19. Confirmation of the Plan

After the plan is prepared, the court must approve or confirm it. A plan will be confirmed if it has been submitted in good faith and if its provisions are reasonable.[49] After the plan is confirmed, the owners and creditors of the enterprise have only the rights that are specified in the plan. They cannot go back to their original contract positions.

CPA   G. Payment Plans Under Chapter 13

The Bankruptcy Code also provides for the adoption of extended-time payment plans for individual debtors who have regular income. These debtors must owe unsecured debts of less than $336,900 and secured debts of less than $1,010,650.

An individual debtor who has a regular income may submit a plan for the installment payment of outstanding debts. If the court approves it, the debtor may then pay the debts in the installments specified by the plan even if the creditors had not originally agreed to such installment payments.

20. Contents of the Plan

The individual debtor plan is, in effect, a budget of the debtor's future income with respect to outstanding debts. The plan must provide for the eventual payment in full of all claims entitled to priority under the Bankruptcy Code. All creditors holding the same kind or class of claim must be treated the same way.

21. Confirmation of the Plan

The plan has no effect until the court approves or confirms it. A plan will be confirmed if it was submitted in good faith and is in the best interests of the creditors.[50] When the plan is confirmed, debts are payable in the manner specified in the plan.

22. Discharge of the Debtor

After all of the payments called for by the plan have been made, the debtor is given a discharge. The discharge releases the debtor from liability for all debts except those

---

[48] 11 USC § 1113.
[49] 11 USC § 1129.
[50] 11 USC § 1325.

that would not be discharged by an ordinary bankruptcy discharge.[51] Under the bankruptcy reforms, the court cannot grant a discharge until the debtor has completed an instructional course concerning personal financial management.[52] If the debtor does not perform under the plan, the creditors can move to transfer the debtor's case to a Chapter 7 proceeding, but they would still face the means test in qualifying for Chapter 7.

MAKE THE CONNECTION

SUMMARY

Jurisdiction over bankruptcy cases is in U.S. district courts, which may refer all cases and related proceedings to adjunct bankruptcy courts.

Three bankruptcy proceedings are available: liquidation (Chapter 7), reorganization (Chapter 11), and extended-time payment (Chapter 13). A liquidation proceeding under Chapter 7 may be either voluntary or involuntary. A *voluntary case* is commenced by the debtor's filing a petition with the bankruptcy court. A voluntary petition is subject to the means test to determine if the debtor meets the standard for declaring bankruptcy. An involuntary case is commenced by the creditors' filing a petition with the bankruptcy court. If there are 12 or more creditors, at least 3 whose unsecured claims total $13,475 or more must sign the involuntary petition. If there are fewer than 12 creditors, any creditor whose unsecured claim is at least $13,475 may sign the petition. If the debtor contests the bankruptcy petition, it must be shown that the debtor is not paying debts as they become due. Eligibility for Chapters 7 and 11 bankruptcy excludes railroads, municipalities, and Small Business Administration companies. Individual debtors are restricted on Chapter 7 and 11 filings by their ability to repay. If found to have the means to pay, they go into a Chapter 13 proceeding. Chapter 13 eligibility is limited to consumers with $336,900 in unsecured debt and $1,010,650 in secured debt.

An automatic stay prevents creditors from taking legal action against the debtor after a bankruptcy petition is filed. The trustee in bankruptcy is elected by the creditors and is the successor to, and acquires the rights of, the debtor. In certain cases, the trustee can avoid transfers of property to prevent creditors from satisfying their claims. Preferential transfers may be set aside. A transfer for a present consideration, such as a cash sale, is not a preference.

Bankruptcy law regulates the way creditors present their claims and how the assets of the debtor are to be distributed in payment of the claims. Some assets of

---

[51] 11 USC § 1328.
[52] 11 USC § 1328(g)(1).

the debtor are exempt from the bankruptcy estate, such as a portion of the value of the debtor's home.

Secured claims are not affected by the debtor's bankruptcy. Unsecured claims are paid in the following order of priority:

1. Support or maintenance for a spouse, former spouse, or child.

2. Costs and expenses of administration of the bankruptcy case.

3. Claims arising in the ordinary course of a debtor's business or financial affairs after the commencement of the case but before the order of relief (involuntary).

4. Claims for wages, salaries, or commissions, including vacation, severance, or sick leave pay earned within 180 days before the filing of the petition or the date of cessation of the debtor's business, limited to $10,950 for each person.

5. Claims arising for contributions (up to $5,400) to employee benefit plans based on services rendered within 180 days before the filing of the petition or when the debtor ceased doing business.

6. Farm producers (up to $10,950) and fishers against debtors who operate grain storage facilities or fish produce storage or processing facilities, up to $5,400 per claim.

7. Claims by consumer creditors, not to exceed $2,425 for each claimant.

8. Certain taxes and penalties due government units, such as income and property taxes.

9. All other unsecured creditors.

10. Remainder (if any) to debtor.

The decree terminating bankruptcy proceedings is generally a discharge that releases the debtor from most debts. Certain debts, such as income taxes, student loans, loans obtained by use of a false financial statement, alimony, and debts not listed by the debtor, are not discharged.

Under Chapter 11 bankruptcy, individuals, partnerships, and corporations in business may be reorganized so that the business can continue to operate. A plan for reorganization must be approved by the court. Under a Chapter 13 bankruptcy proceeding, individual debtors with a regular income may adopt extended-time payment plans for the payment of debts. A plan for extended-time payment must also be confirmed by the court. Federal, state, and local law may not discriminate against anyone on the basis of a discharge in bankruptcy.

LEARNING OUTCOMES

After studying this chapter, you should be able to clearly explain:

A. BANKRUPTCY LAW

B. HOW BANKRUPTCY IS DECLARED

LO.1 List the requirements for the commencement of a voluntary bankruptcy case and an involuntary bankruptcy case

See the Ethics & the Law discussion of recording artists on p. 797.

See *In re Jass* on p. 798.

C. ADMINISTRATION OF THE BANKRUPTCY ESTATE

LO.2 Explain the procedure for the administration of a debtor's estate
See the list of priorities on p. 806.

D. DEBTOR'S DUTIES AND EXEMPTIONS

LO.3 List a debtor's duties and exemptions
See the discussion of the homestead exemptions on p. 807.

E. DISCHARGE IN BANKRUPTCY

LO.4 Explain the significance of a discharge in bankruptcy
See *In re Looper* on p. 811.

F. REORGANIZATION PLANS UNDER CHAPTER 11.

See Ethics & the Law, The Skies Are not So friendly on p. 809.

G. PAYMENT PLANS UNDER CHAPTER 13

LO.5 Explain when a business reorganization plan or an extended-time payment
plan might be used
See the Ethics & the Law discussion of United Airlines on p. 809.
See the discussion of Chrysler and GM on p. 811.

KEY TERMS

automatic stay
balance sheet test
bankruptcy courts
bona fide
Chapter 7 bankruptcy
Chapter 11 bankruptcy
Chapter 13 bankruptcy

claim
discharge in bankruptcy
insiders
insolvency
involuntary bankruptcy
liquidated
means test

order of relief
preferences
preferential transfers
proof of claim
trustee in bankruptcy
voluntary bankruptcy

QUESTIONS AND CASE PROBLEMS

1. Hall-Mark regularly supplied electronic parts to Peter Lee. On September 11, 1992, Lee gave Hall-Mark a $100,000 check for parts it had received. Hall-Mark continued to ship parts to Lee. On September 23, 1992, Lee's check was dishonored by the bank. On September 25, 1992, Lee delivered to Hall-Mark a cashier's check for $100,000. Hall-Mark shipped nothing more to Lee after receipt of the cashier's check. On December 24, 1992, Lee filed a voluntary petition for bankruptcy. The trustee filed a complaint to have the $100,000 payment to Hall-Mark set aside as a voidable preference. Hall-Mark said it was entitled to the payment because it gave value to Lee. The trustee said that the payment was not actually made until the cashier's check was delivered on September 25, 1992, and that Hall-Mark gave no further value to Lee after that check was paid. Who was correct? [*In re Lee*, 108 F3d 239 (9th Cir)]

2. Orso, who had declared bankruptcy, received a structured tort settlement in a personal injury claim he had pending. The settlement would pay him an annuity each year for 30 years because the claim was the result of an auto accident that left him permanently and severely brain damaged with an IQ of

about 70. His wife had a pending claim for $48,000 in arrearages on Orso's $1,000 per month child support payments. His wife wanted the annuity included in the bankruptcy estate. Would this property have been included in Orso's bankruptcy estate? [*In re Orso*, 214 F3d 637 (5th Cir)]

3. Harold McClellan sold ice-making machinery to Bobbie Cantrell's brother for $200,000 to be paid in installment payments. McClellan took a security interest in the ice machine but did not perfect it by filing a financing statement. The brother defaulted when he owed $100,000, and McClellan brought suit. With the suit pending, the brother "sold" the ice machine to Bobbie Cantrell for $10. Bobbie then sold the machine to someone for $160,000 and refused to explain what happened to that money. McClellan added Bobbie as a defendant in his suit against her brother. Bobbie then declared bankruptcy. McClellan sought to have the various transfers set aside. The trial court refused to do so, and McClellan appealed. Should the transfers be set aside? Why or why not? [*McClellan v Cantrell*, 217 F3d 890 (7th Cir)]

4. Okamoto owed money to Hornblower & Weeks-Hemphill, Noyes (a law firm and hereafter Hornblower). Hornblower filed an involuntary bankruptcy petition against Okamoto, who moved to dismiss the petition on the ground that he had more than 12 creditors and the petition could not be filed by only one creditor. Hornblower replied that the other creditors' claims were too small to count and, therefore, the petition could be filed by one creditor. Decide. [*In re Okamoto*, 491 F2d 496 (9th Cir)]

5. Jane Leeves declared voluntary Chapter 7 bankruptcy. The trustee included the following property in her bankruptcy estate:

   • Jane's wedding ring

   • Jane's computer for her consulting business that she operated from her home

   • Jane's car payment from a client in the amount of $5,000 that was received 91 days after Jane filed bankruptcy

   After collecting all of Jane's assets, the bankruptcy trustee was trying to decide how to distribute the assets. Jane had the following creditors:

   • Mortgage company—owed $187,000 (the trustee sold Jane's house for $190,000)

   • Expenses of the bankruptcy—$3,000

   • Federal income taxes—$11,000

   • Utility bills—$1,000

   • Office supply store open account—$1,000

   The trustee had $11,500 in cash, including the $3,000 additional cash left from the sale of the house after the mortgage company was paid. How should the trustee distribute this money? What if the amount were $14,500; how should that be distributed?

6. Kentile sold goods over an extended period of time to Winham. The credit relationship began without Winham's being required to furnish a financial

statement. After a time, payments were not made regularly, and Kentile requested a financial statement. Winham submitted a statement for the year just ended. Kentile requested a second statement. The second statement was false. Kentile objected to Winham's discharge in bankruptcy because of the false financial statement. Should the discharge be granted? Why or why not?

7. Essex is in serious financial difficulty and is unable to meet current unsecured obligations of $40,000 to some 20 creditors, who are demanding immediate payment. Essex owes Stevens $5,000, and Stevens has decided to file an involuntary petition against Essex. Can Stevens file the petition?

8. Sonia, a retailer, has the following assets: a factory worth $1 million; accounts receivable amounting to $750,000, which fall due in four to six months; and $20,000 cash in the bank. Sonia's sole liability is a $200,000 note falling due today, which she is unable to pay. Can Sonia be forced into involuntary bankruptcy under the Bankruptcy Code?

9. Samson Industries ceased doing business and is in bankruptcy proceedings. Among the creditors are five employees seeking unpaid wages. Three of the employees are owed $3,500 each, and two are owed $1,500 each. These amounts became due within 90 days preceding the filing of the petition. Where, in the priority of claims, will the employees' wage claims fall?

10. Carol Cott, doing business as Carol Cott Fashions, is worried about an involuntary bankruptcy proceeding being filed by her creditors. Her net worth, using a balance sheet approach, is $8,000 ($108,000 in assets minus $100,000 in liabilities). However, her cash flow is negative, and she has been hard pressed to meet current obligations as they mature. She is in fact some $12,500 in arrears in payments to her creditors on bills submitted during the past two months. Will the fact that Cott is solvent in the balance-sheet sense result in the court's dismissing the creditors' petition if Cott objects to the petition? Explain.

11. On July 1, Roger Walsh, a sole proprietor operating a grocery, was involuntarily petitioned into bankruptcy by his creditors. At that time, and for at least 90 days prior to that time, Walsh was unable to pay current obligations. On June 16, Walsh paid the May electric bill for his business. The trustee in bankruptcy claimed that this payment was a voidable preference. Was the trustee correct? Explain.

12. Steven and Teresa Hornsby are married and have three young children. On May 25, 1993, the Hornsbys filed a voluntary Chapter 7 petition. They had by that date accumulated more than $30,000 in debt, stemming almost entirely from student loans. They wanted a discharge of their student loans on grounds of undue hardship. The Hornsbys attended a succession of small Tennessee state colleges. Both studied business and computers, but neither graduated. Although they received several deferments and forbearances on the loans, they ultimately defaulted before making any payments. Interest had accumulated on the loans to the extent that Steven was indebted to the Tennessee Student Assistance Corporation (TSAC) for $15,058.52, and Teresa was indebted to TSAC for $18,329.15.

Steven was working for AT&T in Dallas, Texas; he made $6.53 per hour, occasionally working limited overtime hours. Teresa was employed by KinderCare Learning Center. Although she had begun work in Tennessee, she had transferred to become the director of a child care facility in Dallas. Teresa was earning $17,500 per year with medical benefits at the time of the hearing. In monthly net income, Steven earned approximately $1,083.33, and Teresa earned $1,473.33, amounting to $2,556.66 of disposable income per month. The Hornsbys' reported monthly expenses came to $2,364.90. They operated with a monthly surplus of $191.76 to $280.43, depending on whether Steven earned overtime for a particular month. Under the federal bankruptcy laws, are the Hornsbys entitled to a discharge on their student loans? Explain your answer. [*In re Hornsby*, 144 F3d 433 (6th Cir)]

13. On March 19, 1997, Jairath, as seller, and Bletnitsky, as buyer, entered into a real estate contract for sale of an apartment building located at 930 Ontario in Oak Park, Illinois, for a price of $3.1 million. The contract closed on June 4, 1997. Jairath represented to Bletnitsky that the building contained 21 apartments. Jairath's real estate broker had told Bletnitsky that the building contained 21 units, and the real estate broker's package also stated that the building contained 21 units.

    While neither Jairath nor his realtor were shown to have stated expressly that all 21 units in the building were legally available to be converted to condos, Jairath's real estate broker represented that the building was suitable for conversion into condominiums. Also, the real estate broker's package provided "for condo developer, this opportunity provides an opportunity with substantial returns. See Real Estate Broker Package, Investment Property Description."

    Prior to the closing on June 4, 1997, Bletnitsky received a copy of an inspection report prepared by an agency of the Village of Oak Park. The report stated that an inspection had taken place May 27, 1997, and that the apartment building contained only 20 units. On May 30, 1999, Bletnitsky wrote a letter to Jairath and indicated that he had received and read the Oak Park inspection report. In this letter, Bletnitsky stated that the inspection uncovered several violations, listed each violation, and estimated the repair costs at $88,595.

    Bletnitsky claims that he would not have paid $3.1 million dollars for the building had he known that it only contained 20 legal units. Bletnitsky claims that as a result of Jairath's representation that the building contained 21 units, he sustained a loss of $100,000. An arbitration proceeding awarded Bletnitsky damages for misrepresentation.

    Jairath filed for Chapter 7 bankruptcy. Bletnisky has filed to have the obligation on damages from the arbitration not be discharged in the bankruptcy because fraud was involved. Does Beltnisky have grounds for the obligation surviving Jairath's bankruptcy? [*In re Jairath*, 259 BR 308 (ND Ill)]

14. Place the following in order for a bankruptcy proceeding:

    a. Order of relief

    b. Collection of bankrupt's estate

    c. List of creditors

d. Petition

e. Evaluation of claims

f. Voidable preferences

g. Discharge

15. Three general unsecured creditors are owed $45,000 as follows: *A*, $15,000; *B*, $5,000; and *C*, $25,000. After all other creditors were paid, the amount left for distribution to general unsecured creditors was $9,000. How will the $9,000 be distributed?

CPA QUESTIONS

1. Which of the following statements is correct concerning the voluntary filing of a petition of bankruptcy?

   a. If the debtor has 12 or more creditors, the unsecured claims must total at least $13,475.

   b. The debtor must be solvent.

   c. If the debtor has less than 12 creditors, the unsecured claims must total at least $13,475.

   d. The petition may be filed jointly by spouses. (AICPA adapted)

2. On February 28, Master, Inc., had total assets with a fair market value of $1,200,000 and total liabilities of $990,000. On January 15, Master made a monthly installment note payment to Acme Distributors Corp., a creditor holding a properly perfected security interest in equipment having a fair market value greater than the balance due on the note. On March 15, Master voluntarily filed a petition in bankruptcy under the liquidation provisions of Chapter 7 of the federal Bankruptcy Code. One year later, the equipment was sold for less than the balance due on the note to Acme.

   If a creditor challenged Master's right to file, the petition would be dismissed:

   a. If Master had less than 12 creditors at the time of filing

   b. Unless Master can show that a reorganization under Chapter 11 of the federal Bankruptcy Code would have been unsuccessful

   c. Unless Master can show that it is unable to pay its debts in the ordinary course of business or as they come due

   d. If Master is an insurance company

3. A voluntary petition filed under the liquidation provisions of Chapter 7 of the federal Bankruptcy Code:

   a. Is not available to a corporation unless it has previously filed a petition under the reorganization provisions of Chapter 11 of the federal Bankruptcy Code

   b. Automatically stays collection actions against the debtor except by secured creditors for collateral only

c. Will be dismissed unless the debtor has 12 or more unsecured creditors whose claims total at least $13,475

d. Does not require the debtor to show that the debtor's liabilities exceed the fair market value of assets

4. Which following conditions, if any, must a debtor meet to file a voluntary bankruptcy petition under Chapter 7 of the federal Bankruptcy Code?

	Insolvency	*Three or More Creditors*
a.	Yes	Yes
b.	Yes	No
c.	No	Yes
d.	No	No

5. On July 15, 1988, White, a sole proprietor, was involuntarily petitioned into bankruptcy under the liquidation provisions of the Bankruptcy Code. White's nonexempt property has been converted to $13,000 cash, which is available to satisfy the following claims:

Unsecured claim for 1986 state income tax	$10,000
Fee owed to Best & Co., CPAs, for services rendered from April 1, 1988, through June 30, 1988	$6,000
Unsecured claim by Stieb for wages earned as an employee of White during March 1988	$3,000
There are no other claims.	

What is the maximum amount that will be distributed for the payment of the 1986 state income tax?

a. $4,000   b. $5,000   c. $7,000   d. $10,000

6. On May 1, 1997, two months after becoming insolvent, Quick Corp., an appliance wholesaler, filed a voluntary petition for bankruptcy under the provisions of Chapter 7 of the federal Bankruptcy Code. On October 15, 1996, Quick's board of directors had authorized and paid Erly $50,000 to repay Erly's April 1, 1996, loan to the corporation. Erly is a sibling of Quick's president. On March 15, 1996, Quick paid Kray $100,000 for inventory delivered that day. Which of the following is not relevant in determining whether the repayment of Erly's loan is a voidable preferential transfer?

a. That Erly is an insider

b. That Quick's payment to Erly was made on account of an antecedent debt

c. Quick's solvency when the loan was made by Erly

d. That Quick's payment to Erly was made within one year of the filing of the bankruptcy petition

Chapter 37

AGENCY

O ne of the most common business relationships is that of agency. By
virtue of the agency device, one person can make contracts at numerous
places with many different parties at the same time.

A. Nature of the Agency Relationship

Agency is ordinarily based on the consent of the parties, and for that reason is called
a *consensual relationship*. However, the law sometimes imposes an agency relationship. If consideration is present, the agency relationship is contractual.

1. Definitions and Distinctions

agency–relationship that
exists between a person
identified as a principal and
another by virtue of which
the latter may make
contracts with third persons
on behalf of the principal.
(Parties—principal, agent,
third person)

agent–person or firm who
is authorized by the
principal or by operation of
law to make contracts with
third persons on behalf of
the principal.

principal–person or firm
who employs an agent;
person who, with respect to
a surety, is primarily liable
to the third person or
creditor; property held in
trust.

Agency is a relationship based on an express or implied agreement by which one
person, the **agent**, is authorized to act under the control of and for another, the
principal, in negotiating and making contracts with third persons.[1] The acts of the
agent obligate the principal to third persons and give the principal rights against
third persons. (See Figure 37.1.)

The term *agency* is frequently used with other meanings. It is sometimes used
to denote the fact that one has the right to sell certain products, such as when a
dealer is said to possess an automobile agency. In other instances, the term is used to
mean an exclusive right to sell certain articles within a given territory. In these
cases, however, the dealer is not an agent in the sense of representing the
manufacturer.

It is important to be able to distinguish agencies from other relationships
because certain rights and duties in agencies are not present in other
relationships.

(A) Employees and Independent Contractors. Control and authority are
characteristics that distinguish ordinary employees and independent contractors
from agents.

(1) Employees
An agent is distinguished from an ordinary employee who is not hired to represent
the employer in making contracts with third persons. It is possible, however, for the
same person to be both an agent and an employee. **For Example,** the driver for a
spring water delivery service is an agent in making contracts between the company
and its customers but is an employee with respect to the work of delivering
products.

independent contractor–
contractor who undertakes
to perform a specified task
according to the terms of a
contract but over whom the
other contracting party has
no control except as
provided for by the
contract.

(2) Independent Contractors
An **independent contractor** is bound by a contract to produce a certain result—for
example, to build a house. The actual performance of the work is controlled by the

---

[1] Restatement (Second) of Agency § 1; *Union Miniere, S.A. v Parday Corp.*, 521 NE2d 700 (Ind App 1988).

FIGURE 37-1 | *Agency Relationships*

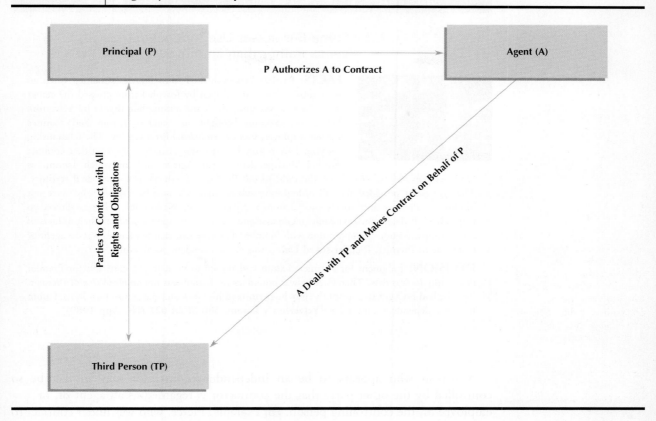

contractor, not the owner. An agent or employee differs from an independent contractor in that the principal or employer has the right to control the agent or employee, but not the contractor, in the performance of the work. **For Example,** Ned and Tracy Seizer contract with Fox Building Company to build a new home on Hilton Head Island, South Carolina, according to referenced plans and specifications. Individuals hired by Fox to work on the home are subject to the authority and control of Fox, the independent contractor, not the Seizers. However, Ned and Tracy could decide to build the home themselves, hiring two individuals from nearby Beaufort, Ted Chase and Marty Bromley, to do the work the Seizers will direct each day. Because Ted and Marty would be employees of the Seizers, the Seizers would be held responsible for any wrongs committed by these employees within the scope of their employment. As a general rule, on the other hand, the Seizers are not responsible for the torts of Fox, the independent contractor, and the contractor's employees. A "right to control" test determines whether an individual is an agent, an employee, or an independent contractor.[2]

---

[2] *NE Ohio College of Massotherapy v Burek*, 759 NE2d 869 (Ohio App 2001).

CASE SUMMARY

Why Some Businesses Use Independent Agents Rather than Employees!

FACTS: Patricia Yelverton died from injuries sustained when an automobile owned and driven by Joseph Lamm crossed the center line of a roadway and struck the automobile driven by Yelverton. Yelverton's executor brought suit against Lamm and Lamm's alleged employer, Premier Industrial Products Inc. The relationship between Lamm and Premier was governed by a written contract entitled "Independent Agent Agreement," in which Lamm, as "Independent Agent," was given the right to sell Premier's products in a designated territory. The agreement provided that all orders were subject to acceptance by Premier and were not binding on Premier until so accepted. Lamm was paid by commission only. He was allowed to work on a self-determined schedule, retain assistants at his own expense, and sell the products of other companies not in competition with Premier. The executor claimed Lamm was an agent or employee of Premier. Premier stated Lamm was an independent contractor.

DECISION: Judgment for Premier. Lamm had no authority to make contracts for Premier but simply took orders. Therefore, he was not an agent. Lamm was not an employee of Premier. Premier had no right to control the way he performed his work and did not in fact do so. Lamm was an independent contractor. [**Yelverton v Lamm, 380 SE2d 621 (NC App 1989)**]

A person who appears to be an independent contractor may in fact be so controlled by the other party that the contractor is regarded as an agent of, or employee of, the controlling person. **For Example,** Pierce, who was under contract to Brookville Carriers, Inc., was involved in a tractor-trailer/car collision with Rich and others. Pierce owned the tractor involved in the accident on a lease from Brookville but could use it only to haul freight for Brookville; he had no authority to carry freight on his own, and all of his operating authority belonged to Brookville. The "owner/operator" was deemed an employee rather than independent contractor for purposes of assessing the liability of the employer.[3] The separate identity of an independent contractor may be concealed so that the public believes that it is dealing with the principal. When this situation occurs, the principal is liable as though the contractor were an agent or employee.

2. Classification of Agents

special agent–agent authorized to transact a specific transaction or to do a specific act.

A **special agent** is authorized by the principal to handle a definite business transaction or to do a specific act. One who is authorized by another to purchase a particular house is a special agent.

general agent–agent authorized by the principal to transact all affairs in connection with a particular type of business or trade or to transact all business at a certain place.

A **general agent** is authorized by the principal to transact all affairs in connection with a particular type of business or trade or to transact all business at a certain place. To illustrate, a person who is appointed as manager by the owner of a store is a general agent.

[3] *Rich v Brookville Carriers, Inc.,* 256 F Supp 2d 26 (D Me 2003).

universal agent – agent authorized by the principal to do all acts that can lawfully be delegated to a representative.

A **universal agent** is authorized by the principal to do all acts that can be delegated lawfully to a representative. This form of agency arises when a person absent because of being in the military service gives another person a blanket power of attorney to do anything that must be done during such absence.

CPA

3. Agency Coupled with an Interest

interest in the authority – form of agency in which an agent has been given or paid for the right to exercise authority.

An agent has an **interest in the authority** when consideration has been given or paid for the right to exercise the authority. To illustrate, when a lender, in return for making a loan of money, is given, as security, authority to collect rents due the borrower and to apply those rents to the payment of the debt, the lender becomes the borrower's agent with an interest in the authority given to collect the rents.

interest in the subject matter – form of agency in which an agent is given an interest in the property with which that agent is dealing.

An agent has an **interest in the subject matter** when, for a consideration, she is given an interest in the property with which she is dealing. Hence, when the agent is authorized to sell property of the principal and is given a lien on such property as security for a debt owed to her by the principal, she has an interest in the subject matter.

B. CREATING THE AGENCY

An agency may arise by appointment, conduct, ratification, or operation of law.

4. Authorization by Appointment

express authorization – authorization of an agent to perform a certain act.

The usual method of creating an agency is by **express authorization;** that is, a person is appointed to act for, or on behalf of, another.

In most instances, the authorization of the agent may be oral. However, some appointments must be made in a particular way. A majority of the states, by statute, require the appointment of an agent to be in writing when the agency is created to acquire or dispose of any interest in land. A written authorization of agency is called a **power of attorney.** An agent acting under a power of attorney is referred to as an **attorney in fact.**[4]

power of attorney – written authorization to an agent by the principal.

attorney in fact – agent authorized to act for another under a power of attorney.

5. Authorization by Conduct

Conduct consistent with the existence of an agency relationship may be sufficient to show authorization. The principal may have such dealing with third persons as to cause them to believe that the "agent" has authority. Thus, if the owner of a store places another person in charge, third persons may assume that the person in charge is the agent for the owner in that respect. The "agent" then appears to be authorized and is said to have *apparent authority*, and the principal is estopped from contradicting the appearance that has been created.[5]

---

[4] *Lamb v Scott,* 643 So2d 972 (Ala 1994).
[5] *Intersparex Leddin KG v AL-Haddad,* 852 SW2d 245 (Tenn App 1992).

C A S E   S U M M A R Y

The "Bulletproof Against Rust" Case. Oops: Now What?

FACTS: While constructing a hotel in Lincoln City, Oregon, the owner, Todd Taylor, became concerned about possible rusting in the exterior stucco system manufactured by ChemRex that was being installed at the hotel. The general contractor Ramsay-Gerding arranged a meeting with the owner, the installer, and ChemRex's territory manager for Oregon, Mike McDonald, to discuss Mr. Taylor's concerns. McDonald told those present that the SonoWall system was "bulletproof against rust," and stated that "you're getting a five-year warranty." He followed up with a letter confirming the five-year warranty on parts and labor. A year later rust discoloration appeared, and no one from ChemRex ever fixed the problem. Taylor sued ChemRex for breach of warranty. ChemRex defended that McDonald did not have actual or apparent authority to declare such a warranty.

DECISION: Judgment for Taylor. The evidence indicated that ChemRex clothed Mike McDonald with the title of "territory manager" and gave him the actual authority to visit job sites and resolve problems. Although it denies he had actual authority, ChemRex took sufficient steps to create apparent authority to provide the five-year warranty on the stucco system. **[Taylor v Ramsay-Gerding Construction Co., 196 P3d 532 (Or 2008)]**

The term *apparent authority* is used when there is only the appearance of authority but no actual authority, and that appearance of authority was created by the principal. The test for the existence of apparent authority is an objective test determined by the principal's outward manifestations through words or conduct that lead a third person reasonably to believe that the "agent" has authority. A principal's express restriction on authority not made known to a third person is no defense.

Apparent authority extends to all acts that a person of ordinary prudence, familiar with business usages and the particular business, would be justified in believing that the agent has authority to perform. It is essential to the concept of apparent authority that the third person reasonably believe that the agent has authority. The mere placing of property in the possession of another does not give that person either actual or apparent authority to sell the property.

CPA

6. Agency by Ratification

An agent may attempt, on behalf of the principal, to do an act that was not authorized, or a person who is not the agent of another may attempt to act as such an agent. Generally, in such cases, the principal for whom the agent claimed to act has the choice of ignoring the transaction or of ratifying it. Ordinarily, any unauthorized act may be ratified.

(A) INTENTION TO RATIFY. Initially, ratification is a question of intention. Just as in the case of authorization, when there is a question of whether the principal authorized the agent, there is a question of whether the principal intended to approve or ratify the action of the unauthorized agent.

The intention to ratify may be expressed in words, or it may be found in conduct indicating an intention to ratify.[6] **For Example,** James Reiner signed a five-year lease of commercial space on 320 West Main Street in Avon, Connecticut, because his father Calvin was away on vacation, and the owner, Robert Udolf, told James that if he did not come in and sign the lease, his father would lose the opportunity to rent the space in question. James was aware that his father had an interest in the space, and while telling Robert several times that he had no authority, James did sign his name to the lease. In fact, his father took occupancy of the space and paid rent for three years and then abandoned the space. James is not liable on the remainder of the lease because the owner knew at the time of signing that James did not have authority to act. Although he did not sign the lease, Calvin ratified the lease signed by James by his conduct of moving into the space and doing business there for three years with full knowledge of all material facts relating to the transaction. The owner, therefore, had to bring suit against Calvin, not James.[7]

CPA (B) CONDITIONS FOR RATIFICATION. In addition to the intent to ratify, expressed in some instances with a certain formality, the following conditions must be satisfied for the intention to take effect as a ratification:

1. The agent must have purported to act on behalf of or as agent for the identified principal.

2. The principal must have been capable of authorizing the act both at the time of the act and at the time it was ratified.

3. The principal must have full knowledge of all material facts.

It is not always necessary, however, to show that the principal had actual knowledge. Knowledge will be imputed if a principal knows of other facts that would lead a prudent person to make inquiries or if that knowledge can be inferred from the knowledge of other facts or from a course of business. **For Example,** Stacey, without authorization but knowing that William needed money, contracted to sell one of William's paintings to Courtney for $298. Stacey told William about the contract that evening; William said nothing and helped her wrap the painting in a protective plastic wrap for delivery. A favorable newspaper article about William's art appeared the following morning and dramatically increased the value of all of his paintings. William cannot recover the painting from Courtney on the theory that he never authorized the sale because he ratified the unauthorized contract made by Stacey by his conduct in helping her wrap the painting with full knowledge of the terms of the sale. The effect is a legally binding contract between William and Courtney.

(C) EFFECT OF RATIFICATION. When an unauthorized act is ratified, the effect is the same as though the act had been originally authorized. Ordinarily, this means that the principal and the third party are bound by the contract made by the agent.[8]

---

[6] *Streetscenes, LLC v ITC Entertainment Group, Inc.,* 126 Cal Rptr 2d 754 (Cal App 2002).
[7] *Udolf v Reiner,* 2000 WL 726953 (Conn Super 2000).
[8] *Bill McCurley Chevrolet v Rutz,* 808 P2d 1167 (Wash App 1991).

When the principal ratifies the act of the unauthorized person, such ratification releases that person from the liability that would otherwise be imposed for having acted without authority.

CPA ## 7. Proving the Agency Relationship

The burden of proving the existence of an agency relationship rests on the person who seeks to benefit by such proof. The third person who desires to bind the principal because of the act of an alleged agent has the burden of proving that the latter person was in fact the authorized agent of the principal and possessed the authority to do the act in question.[9]

C. AGENT'S AUTHORITY

When there is an agent, it is necessary to determine the scope of the agent's authority.

8. Scope of Agent's Authority

The scope of an agent's authority may be determined from the express words of the principal to the agent or it may be implied from the principal's words or conduct or from the customs of the trade or business.

(A) EXPRESS AUTHORITY. If the principal tells the agent to perform a certain act, the agent has express authority to do so. Express authority can be given orally or in writing.

incidental authority—
authority of an agent that is reasonably necessary to execute express authority.

(B) INCIDENTAL AUTHORITY. An agent has implied **incidental authority** to perform any act reasonably necessary to execute the express authority given to the agent. **For Example,** if the principal authorizes the agent to purchase goods without furnishing funds to the agent to pay for them, the agent has the implied incidental authority to purchase the goods on credit.[10]

customary authority—
authority of an agent to do any act that, according to the custom of the community, usually accompanies the transaction for which the agent is authorized to act.

(C) CUSTOMARY AUTHORITY. An agent has implied **customary authority** to do any act that, according to the custom of the community, usually accompanies the transaction for which the agent is authorized to act. An agent who has express authority to receive payments from third persons, for example, has the implied customary authority to issue receipts.

apparent authority—
appearance of authority created by the principal's words or conduct.

(D) APPARENT AUTHORITY. A person has **apparent authority** as an agent when the principal's words or conduct leads a third person to reasonably believe that the person has that authority and the third person relies on that appearance.[11]

---

[9] *Cummings, Inc. v Nelson*, 115 P3d 536 (Alaska 2005).
[10] *Badger v Paulson Investment Co.*, 803 P2d 1178 (Ore 1991).
[11] *Alexander v Chandler*, 179 SW2d 385 (Mo App 2005).

CASE SUMMARY

CSX Gets Railroaded by Albert Arillotta

FACTS: Recovery Express and Interstate Demolition (IDEC) are two separate corporations located at the same business address in Boston. On August 22, 2003, Albert Arillotta, a "partner" at IDEC, sent an e-mail to Len Whitehead, Jr. of CSX Transportation expressing an interest in buying "rail cars as scrap." Arillotta represented himself to be "from interstate demolition and recovery express" in the e-mail. The e-mail address from which he sent his inquiry was **albert@recoveryexpress.com**. Arillotta went to the CSX rail yard, disassembled the cars, and transported them away. Thereafter CSX sent invoices for the scrap rail cars totaling $115,757.36 addressed to IDEC at its Boston office shared with Recovery Express. Whitehead believed Arillotta was authorized to act for Recovery Express, based on the e-mail's domain name, recoveryexpress.com. Recovery claims that Arillotta never worked for it. Recovery's President Thomas Trafton allowed the "fledgling" company to use telephone, fax, and e-mail services at its offices but never shared anything—assets, funds, books of business, or financials with IDEC—CSX sued Recovery for the invoice amount on the doctrine of "apparent authority." IDEC is now defunct. Recovery claims that Arillotta never worked for it and that it is not liable.

DECISION: Judgment for Recovery. Issuance of an e-mail address with Recovery's domain name to an individual who shared office space with Recovery did not give the individual, Albert Arillotta, apparent authority to enter contracts on Recovery's behalf. No reasonable person could conclude that Arillotta had apparent authority on the basis of an e-mail domain name by itself. Given the anonymity of the Internet, the court warned businesses to take additional action to verify a purported agent's authority to make a deal. [**CSX Transportation, Inc. v Recovery Express, Inc., 415 F Supp 2d 6 (D Mass 2006)**].

9. Effect of Proper Exercise of Authority

When an agent with authority properly makes a contract with a third person that purports to bind the principal, there is by definition a binding contract between the principal and the third person. The agent is not a party to this contract. Consequently, when the owner of goods is the principal, the owner's agent is not liable for breach of warranty with respect to the goods "sold" by the agent. The owner-principal, not the agent, was the "seller" in the sales transaction.

CPA   10. Duty to Ascertain Extent of Agent's Authority

A third person who deals with a person claiming to be an agent cannot rely on the statements made by the agent concerning the extent of authority.[12] If the agent is not authorized to perform the act or is not even the agent of the principal, the transaction between the alleged agent and the third person will have no legal effect between the principal and the third person.

Third persons who deal with an agent whose authority is limited to a special purpose are bound at their peril to find out the extent of the agent's authority.

---

[12] *Breed v Hughes Aircraft Col.,* 35 Fed App 864 (Fed Cir 2002).

An attorney is such an agent. Unless the client holds the attorney out as having greater authority than usual, the attorney has no authority to settle a claim without approval from the client.

(A) AGENT'S ACTS ADVERSE TO PRINCIPAL. The third person who deals with an agent is required to take notice of any acts that are clearly adverse to the interest of the principal. Thus, if the agent is obviously using funds of the principal for the agent's personal benefit, persons dealing with the agent should recognize that the agent may be acting without authority and that they are dealing with the agent at their peril.

The only certain way that third persons can protect themselves is to inquire of the principal whether the agent is in fact the agent of the principal and has the necessary authority. **For Example,** Ron Fahd negotiated the sale of a fire truck to the Edinburg Volunteer Fire Company, on behalf of the manufacturer, Danko Company, at a price of $158,000. On Danko forms and letterhead Fahd drafted a "Proposal for Fire Apparatus" and it was signed by the president of the Fire Company and Fahd, as a dealer for Danko. Fahd gave a special $2,000 discount for prepayment of the cost of the chassis. Fahd directed that the prepayment check of $55,000 be made payable to "Ron Fahd Sales" in order to obtain the discount. The Fire Company's treasurer inquired of Fahd why the prepayment check was being made out to Fahd rather than Danko, and he accepted Fahd's answer without contacting Danko to confirm this unusual arrangement. Fahd absconded with the proceeds of the check. The Fire Company sued Danko claiming Fahd had apparent authority to receive the prepayment. While there was some indicia of agency, the court found that the Fire Company had failed to make reasonable inquiry with Danko to verify Fahd's authority to receive the prepayment in Fahd's name, and it rejected the claim that Fahd had apparent authority to accept the prepayment check made out to Fahd as opposed to Danko.[13]

11. Limitations on Agent's Authority

A person who has knowledge of a limitation on the agent's authority cannot ignore that limitation. When the third person knows that the authority of the agent depends on whether financing has been obtained, the principal is not bound by the act of the agent if the financing in fact was not obtained. If the authority of the agent is based on a writing and the third person knows that there is such a writing, the third person is charged with knowledge of limitations contained in it.

(A) "OBVIOUS" LIMITATIONS. In some situations, it may be obvious to third persons that they are dealing with an agent whose authority is limited. When third persons know that they are dealing with a representative of a government agency, they should recognize that such a person will ordinarily have limited authority. Third persons should recognize that a contract made with such an officer or representative may not be binding unless ratified by the principal.

The federal government places the risk on any individual making arrangements with the government to accurately ascertain that the government agent is within the bounds of his or her authority.

---

[13] *Edinburg Volunteer Fire Company v Danko,* 867 NYS2d 547 (App Div 2008).

CASE SUMMARY

Humlen was Had?

FACTS: The FBI approached Humlen for assistance in securing the conviction of a drug trafficker. Humlen executed an agreement with the FBI to formalize his status as an informant. The agreement he signed contained compensation figures significantly less than those he had been promised by the FBI agents with whom he was dealing. Humlen claims that five agents repeatedly assured him that he would receive the extra compensation they had discussed with him, despite the wording of the contract. It was explained that the agreement had to be "couched" in that way because it was a discoverable document in any future criminal prosecution and thus could be used to destroy his credibility. Based on the information provided by Humlen, an arrest was made, and Humlen sought the remainder of his promised monetary reward from the FBI. The FBI refused to pay him any more than the contract stipulated. When no additional payment was forthcoming, Humlen sued the U.S. government.

DECISION: Judgment for the United States. The government, unlike private parties, cannot be bound by the apparent authority of its agents. When an agent exceeds his or her authority, the government can disavow the agent's words and is not bound by an implied contract. As a general rule, FBI agents lack the requisite actual authority—either express or implied—to contractually bind the United States to remit rewards to confidential informants. Moreover, Humlen's claims directly collide with the plain language of the agreement. [**Humlen v United States, 49 Fed Cl 497 (2001)**]

(B) SECRET LIMITATIONS. If the principal has clothed an agent with authority to perform certain acts but the principal gives secret instructions that limit the agent's authority, the third person is allowed to take the authority of the agent at its face value. The third person is not bound by the secret limitations of which the third person has no knowledge.

D. DUTIES AND LIABILITIES OF PRINCIPAL AND AGENT

The creation of the principal-agent relationship gives rise to duties and liabilities.

12. Duties and Liabilities of Agent during Agency

While the agency relationship exists, the agent owes certain duties to the principal.

(A) LOYALTY. An agent must be loyal or faithful to the principal.[14] The agent must not obtain any secret benefit from the agency. If the principal is seeking to buy or rent property, the agent cannot secretly obtain the property and then sell or lease it to the principal at a profit.

---

[14] *Patterson Custom Homes v Bach*, 536 F Supp 2d 1026 (ED ILL 2008).

An agent who owns property cannot sell it to the principal without disclosing that ownership to the principal. If disclosure is not made, the principal may avoid the contract even if the agent's conduct did not cause the principal any financial loss. Alternatively, the principal can approve the transaction and sue the agent for any secret profit obtained by the agent.

A contract is voidable by the principal if the agent who was employed to sell the property purchases the property, either directly or indirectly, without full disclosure to the principal.

An agent cannot act as agent for both parties to a transaction unless both know of the dual capacity and agree to it. If the agent does act in this capacity without the consent of both parties, any principal who did not know of the agent's double status can avoid the transaction.

An agent must not accept secret gifts or commissions from third persons in connection with the agency. If the agent does so, the principal may sue the agent for those gifts or commissions. Such practices are condemned because the judgment of the agent may be influenced by the receipt of gifts or commissions.

It is a violation of an agent's duty of loyalty to make and retain secret profits.

C A S E   S U M M A R Y

Was Grappolini a "Bad Boy"?

FACTS: Arthur Frigo, an adjunct professor at the Kellogg Graduate School of Management, formed Lucini Italia Co. (Lucini) to import and sell premium extra virgin olive oil and other products from Italy. Lucini's officers hired Guiseppe Grappolini as their olive oil supplier. They also hired him as their consultant. Grappolini signed an exclusivity agreement and a confidentiality agreement acknowledging the confidential nature of Lucini's product development, plans, and strategies. Grappolini was "branded" as a "master cultivator" in Lucini's literature and commercials.

In 1998, Lucini and Grappolini, as his consultant, discussed adding a line of extra virgin olive oils blended with "essential oils," for example, natural extracts such as lemon and garlic. It spent more than $800,000 developing the market information, testing flavors, designing labels and packaging, creating recipes, and generating trade secrets for the new products. Vegetal-Progress s.r.l. (Vegetal) was identified as the only company in Italy that was capable of producing the superior products Lucini sought, and Grappolini was assigned responsibility to obtain an exclusive supply contract with Vegetal.

In direct contravention of his representations to Lucini, Grappolini secretly negotiated an exclusive supply contract for the Grappolini Co., not for Lucini. Moreover, Grappolini Co. began to sell flavored olive oils in the United States, which coincided with Lucini's market research and recipe development that had been disclosed to Grappolini. When Lucini officers contacted Vegetal, they acknowledged that Grappolini was a "bad boy" in procuring the contract for his own company rather than for Lucini, but they would not renege on the contract. Lucini sued Grappolini.

DECISION: Judgment for Lucini. Grappolini was Lucini's agent and owed Lucini a duty to advance Lucini's interests, not his own. When he obtained an exclusive supply agreement with Vegetal for the Grappolini Co. instead of Lucini, he was disloyal and breached his fiduciary duties. As a result, Lucini suffered lost profits and damages of $4.17 million. In addition to these damages, Grappolini was ordered to pay $1,000,000 in punitive damages to deter similar acts in the future. Additionally, a permanent injunction was issued prohibiting Grappolini from using Lucini's trade secrets. [**Lucini Italia Co. v Grappolini, 2003 WL 1989605 (ND Ill 2003)**]

An agent is, of course, prohibited from aiding the competitors of a principal or disclosing to them information relating to the business of the principal. It is also a breach of duty for the agent to knowingly deceive a principal.[15]

(B) **OBEDIENCE AND PERFORMANCE.** An agent is under a duty to obey all lawful instructions.[16] The agent is required to perform the services specified for the period and in the way specified. An agent who does not do so is liable to the principal for any harm caused. For example, if an agent is instructed to take cash payments only but accepts a check in payment, the agent is liable for the loss caused the principal if a check is dishonored by nonpayment.

(C) **REASONABLE CARE.** It is the duty of an agent to act with the care that a reasonable person would exercise under the circumstances. **For Example,** Ethel Wilson applied for fire insurance for her house with St. Paul Reinsurance Co., Ltd., through her agent Club Services Corp. She thought she was fully covered. Unbeknown to her, however, St. Paul had refused coverage and returned her premium to Club Services, who did not refund it to Ms. Wilson or inform her that coverage had been denied. Fire destroyed her garage and St. Paul denied coverage. Litigation resulted, and St. Paul ended up expending $305,406 to settle the Wilson matter. Thereafter, St. Paul successfully sued Club Services Corp. under basic agency law principles that an agent (Club Services) is liable to its principal for all damages resulting from the agent's failure to discharge its duties.[17] In addition, if the agent possesses a special skill, as in the case of a broker or an attorney, the agent must exercise that skill.

(D) **ACCOUNTING.** An agent must account to the principal for all property or money belonging to the principal that comes into the agent's possession. The agent must, within a reasonable time, give notice of collections made and render an accurate account of all receipts and expenditures. The agency agreement may state at what intervals or on what dates such accountings are to be made. An agent must keep the principal's property and money separate and distinct from that of the agent.

(E) **INFORMATION.** It is the duty of an agent to keep the principal informed of all facts relating to the agency that are relevant to protecting the principal's interests.[18]

---

[15] *Koontz v Rosener,* 787 P2d 192 (Colo App 1990).
[16] *Stanford v Neiderer,* 341 SE2d 892 (Ga App 1986).
[17] *St. Paul Reinsurance Co., Ltd. v Club Services Corp.,* 30 Fed Appx 834, 2002 WL 203343 (10th Cir 2002).
[18] Restatement (Second) of Agency § 381; *Lumberman's Mutual Ins. Co. v Franey Muha Alliant Ins.,* 388 F Supp 2d 292 (SDNY 2005).

13. Duties and Liabilities of Agent after Termination of Agency

When the agency relationship ends, the duties of the agent continue only to the extent necessary to perform prior obligations. For example, the agent must return to the former principal any property that had been entrusted to the agent for the purpose of the agency. With the exception of such "winding-up" duties, the agency relationship is terminated, and the former agent can deal with the principal as freely as with a stranger.[19]

14. Duties and Liabilities of Principal to Agent

The principal must perform the contract, compensate the agent for services, make reimbursement for proper expenditures and, under certain circumstances, must indemnify the agent for loss.

(A) EMPLOYMENT ACCORDING TO TERMS OF CONTRACT. When the contract is for a specified time, the principal is obligated to permit the agent to act as agent for the term of the contract. Exceptions are made for just cause or contract provisions that permit the principal to terminate the agency sooner. If the principal gives the agent an exclusive right to act in that capacity, the principal cannot give anyone else the authority to act as agent, nor may the principal do the act to which the exclusive agent's authority relates. **For Example,** if Jill Baker gives Brett Stamos the exclusive right for six months to sell her house, she cannot give another real estate agent the right to sell it during the six-month period or undertake to sell the house herself. If the principal or another agent sells the house, the exclusive agent is entitled to full compensation just as though the act had been performed by the exclusive agent.

(B) COMPENSATION. The principal must pay the agent the agreed compensation.[20] If the parties have not fixed the amount of the compensation by their agreement but intended that the agent should be paid, the agent may recover the customary compensation for such services. If there is no established compensation, the agent may recover the reasonable value of the services rendered.

(1) Repeating Transactions

In certain industries, third persons make repeated transactions with the principal. In these cases, the agent who made the original contract with the third person commonly receives a certain compensation or percentage of commissions on all subsequent renewal or additional contracts. In the insurance business, for example, the insurance agent obtaining the policyholder for the insurer receives a substantial portion of the first year's premiums and then receives a smaller percentage of the premiums paid by the policyholder in subsequent years.

(2) Postagency Transactions

An agent is not ordinarily entitled to compensation in connection with transactions, such as sales or renewals of insurance policies, occurring after the termination of the agency even if the postagency transactions are the result of the agent's former

---

[19] *Corron & Black of Illinois, Inc. v Magner*, 494 NE2d 785 (Ill App 1986).
[20] *American Chocolates, Inc. v Mascot Pecan Co., Inc.*, 592 So2d 93 (Miss 1992).

activities. However, if the parties' employment contract calls for such compensation, it must be paid. **For Example,** real estate agent Laura McLane's contract called for her to receive $1.50 for every square foot the Atlanta Committee for the Olympic Games, Inc. (ACOG), leased at an Atlanta building; and even though she had been terminated at the time ACOG executed a lease amendment for 164,412 additional square feet, she was contractually entitled to a $246,618 commission.[21]

E. TERMINATION OF AGENCY

An agency may be terminated by the act of one or both of the parties to the agency agreement or by operation of law. When the authority of an agent is terminated, the agent loses all right to act for the principal.

15. Termination by Act of Parties

The duration of the agency relationship is commonly stated in the contract creating the relationship. In most cases, either party has the power to terminate the agency relationship at any time. However, the terminating party may be liable for damages to the other if the termination is in violation of the agency contract.

When a principal terminates an agent's authority, it is not effective until the agent receives the notice. Because a known agent will have the appearance of still being an agent, notice must be given to third persons of the termination, and the agent may have the power to bind the principal and third persons until this notice is given.

16. Termination by Operation of Law

The agency relationship is a personal one, and anything that renders one of the parties incapable of performing will result in the termination of the relationship by operation of law. The death of either the principal or the agent ordinarily terminates the authority of an agent automatically even if the death is unknown to the other.[22]

An agency is also terminated by operation of law on the (1) insanity of the principal or agent, (2) bankruptcy of the principal or agent, (3) impossibility of performance, such as the destruction of the subject matter, or (4) when the country of the principal is at war with that of the agent.

C A S E   S U M M A R Y

Missing Out by Minutes

FACTS: William Moore, a fire chief for the city of San Francisco, suffered severe head injuries in a fall while fighting a fire. Moore sued the building owner, Lera, for negligence. The attorneys for the parties held a conference and reached a settlement at 5:15 P.M. Unknown to them, Moore had died at 4:50 P.M. on that day. Was the settlement agreement binding?

[21] *McLane v Atlanta Market Center Management Co.,* 486 SE2d 30 (Ga App 1997).
[22] *New York Life Ins. Co. v Estate of Haelen,* 521 NYS2d 970 (Sup Ct AD 1987).

C A S E   S U M M A R Y

Continued

DECISION: No. The death of either the principal or the agent terminates the agency. Thus, the death of a client terminates the authority of his agent to act on his behalf. Because Moore died at 4:50 P.M., his attorney no longer had authority to act on his behalf, and the settlement was not enforceable. [**Moore v Lera Development Inc., 274 Cal Rptr 658 (Cal App 1990)**]

17. Disability of the Principal Under the UDPAA

The Uniform Durable Power of Attorney Act (UDPAA) permits the creation of an agency by specifying that "this power of attorney shall not be affected by subsequent disability or incapacity of the principal." Alternatively, the UDPAA permits the agency to come into existence upon the disability or incapacity of the principal. For this to be effective, the principal must designate the attorney in fact in writing. The writing must contain words showing the intent of the principal that the authority conferred shall continue notwithstanding the disability or incapacity of the principal. The UDPAA, which has been adopted by most states,[23] changes the common law and the general rule that insanity of the principal terminates the agent's authority to act for the principal. Society today recognizes that it may be in the best interest of a principal and good for the business environment for a principal to designate another as an attorney in fact to act for the principal when the principal becomes incapacitated.[24] It may be prudent to grant durable powers of attorney to different persons for property matters and for health care decisions.

Durable powers of attorney grant only those powers that are specified in the instrument. A durable power of attorney may be terminated by revocation by a competent principal and by the death of the principal.

C A S E   S U M M A R Y

Broad Powers ... But There is a Limit, Lucille

FACTS: On May 31, 2000, Thomas Graham made his niece Lucille Morrison his attorney in fact by executing a durable power of attorney. It was notarized and filed at the Registry of Deeds. The power of attorney granted Lucille broad powers and discretion in Graham's affairs. However, it did not contain express authority to make gifts. On October 26, 2000, Lucille conveyed 11.92 acres of property valued at between $400,000 and $700,000 to herself

---

[23] The Uniform Durable Power of Attorney Act has been adopted in some fashion in all states except Connecticut, Florida, Georgia, Illinois, Indiana, Kansas, Louisiana, and Missouri.

[24] The Uniform Probate Code and the Uniform Durable Power of Attorney Act provide for the coexistence of durable powers and guardians or conservators. These acts allow the attorney in fact to continue to manage the principal's financial affairs while the court-appointed fiduciary takes the place of the principal in overseeing the actions of the attorney in fact. See *Rice v Flood*, 768 SW2d 57 (Ky 1989).

C A S E   S U M M A R Y

Continued

based on consideration of services rendered to the principal, Thomas Graham. On June 5, 2001, Lucille, as attorney in fact for Graham, conveyed Graham's house in Charlotte to her son Ladd Morrison. On June 20, 2001, she conveyed Graham's Oakview Terrace property to her brother John Hallman for $3,000 to pay for an attorney to defend Graham in a competency proceeding. Thomas Graham died on August 7, 2001, and his estate sued to set aside the deeds, alleging Lucille's breach of fiduciary duties. After a judgment for the defendants, the estate appealed.

DECISION: Judgment for the estate regarding the 11.92 acre parcel of land Lucille conveyed to herself. When an attorney in fact conveys property to herself based on consideration of services rendered to the principal, the consideration must reflect a fair and reasonable price when compared with the market value of the property. There was no testimony regarding the value of Lucille's services compared with the value of the real property. The deed must be set aside. The conveyance of Graham's home to Ladd Morrison was a gift that was not authorized by her power of attorney and must be set aside. Lucille had authority to sell the principal's property to John Hallman to obtain funds to pay an attorney to represent the principal. The estate's claim of conversion regarding this sale was denied. [**Estate of Graham v Morrison, 607 SE2d 295 (NC App 2005)**]

18. Termination of Agency Coupled with an Interest

An agency coupled with an interest is an exception to the general rule as to the termination of an agency. Such an agency cannot be revoked by the principal before the expiration of the interest. It is not terminated by the death or insanity of either the principal or the agent.

19. Protection of Agent from Termination of Authority

The modern world of business has developed several methods of protecting an agent from the termination of authority for any reason.[25]

These methods include the use of an exclusive agency contract, a secured transaction, an escrow deposit, a standby letter of agreement, or a guarantee agreement.

20. Effect of Termination of Authority

If the principal revokes the agency, the authority to act for the principal is not terminated until the agent receives notice of revocation. As between the principal and the agent, the right of the agent to bind the principal to third persons generally ends immediately upon the termination of the agent's authority. This termination is effective without giving notice to third persons.

When the agency is terminated by the act of the principal, notice must be given to third persons. If this notice is not given, the agent may have the power to make contracts that will bind the principal and third persons. This rule is predicated on

---

[25] These methods generally replace the concept of an agency coupled with an interest because of the greater protection given to the agent. Typically, the rights of the agent under these modern devices cannot be defeated by the principal, by operation of law, or by claims of other creditors.

the theory that a known agent will have the appearance of still being the agent unless notice to the contrary is given to third persons. **For Example,** Seltzer owns property in Boca Raton that he uses for the month of February and leases the remainder of the year. O'Neil has been Seltzer's rental agent for the past seven years, renting to individuals like Ed Tucker under a power of attorney that gives him authority to lease the property for set seasonal and off-season rates. O'Neil's right to bind Seltzer on a rental agreement ended when Seltzer faxed O'Neil a revocation of the power of attorney on March 1. A rental contract with Ed Tucker signed by O'Neil on behalf of Seltzer on March 2 will bind Seltzer, however, because O'Neil still appeared to be Seltzer's agent and Tucker had no notice to the contrary.

When the law requires giving notice in order to end the power of the agent to bind the principal, individual notice must be given or mailed to all persons who had prior dealings with the agent. In addition, notice to the general public can be given by publishing in a newspaper of general circulation in the affected geographic area a statement that the agency has been terminated.

If a notice is actually received, the power of the agent is terminated without regard to whether the method of giving notice was proper. Conversely, if proper notice is given, it is immaterial that it does not actually come to the attention of the party notified. Thus, a member of the general public cannot claim that the principal is bound on the ground that the third person did not see the newspaper notice stating that the agent's authority had been terminated.

MAKE THE CONNECTION

SUMMARY

An agency relationship is created by an express or implied agreement by which one person, the agent, is authorized to make contracts with third persons on behalf of, and subject to, the control of another person, the principal. An agent differs from an independent contractor in that the principal, who controls the acts of an agent, does not have control over the details of performance of work by the independent contractor. Likewise, an independent contractor does not have authority to act on behalf of the other contracting party.

A special agent is authorized by the principal to handle a specific business transaction. A general agent is authorized by the principal to transact all business affairs of the principal at a certain place. A universal agent is authorized to perform all acts that can be lawfully delegated to a representative.

The usual method of creating an agency is by express authorization. However, an agency relationship may be found to exist when the principal causes or permits a third person to reasonably believe that an agency relationship exists. In such a case, the "agent" appears to be authorized and is said to have apparent authority.

An unauthorized transaction by an agent for a principal may be ratified by the principal.

An agent acting with authority has the power to bind the principal. The scope of an agent's authority may be determined from the express words of the principal to the agent; this is called express authority. An agent has incidental authority to perform any act reasonably necessary to execute the authority given the agent. An agent's authority may be implied so as to enable the agent to perform any act in accordance with the general customs or usages in a business or an industry. This authority is often referred to as customary authority.

The effect of a proper exercise of authority by an agent is to bind the principal and third person to a contract. The agent, not being a party to the contract, is not liable in any respect under the contract. A third person dealing with a person claiming to be an agent has a duty to ascertain the extent of the agent's authority and a duty to take notice of any acts that are clearly adverse to the principal's interests. The third person cannot claim that apparent authority existed when that person has notice that the agent's conduct is adverse to the interests of the principal. A third person who has knowledge of limitations on an agent's authority is bound by those limitations. A third person is not bound by secret limitations.

While the agency relationship exists, the agent owes the principal the duties of (1) being loyal, (2) obeying all lawful instructions, (3) exercising reasonable care, (4) accounting for all property or money belonging to the principal, and (5) informing the principal of all facts relating to the agency that are relevant to the principal's interests. An agency relationship can be terminated by act of either the principal or the agent. However, the terminating party may be liable for damages to the other if the termination is in violation of the agency contract.

Because a known agent will have the appearance of still being an agent, notice must be given to third persons of the termination, and the agent may have the power to bind the principal and third persons until this notice is given.

An agency is terminated by operation of law upon (1) the death of the principal or agent, (2) insanity of the principal or agent, (3) bankruptcy of the principal or agent, (4) impossibility of performance, caused, for example, by the destruction of the subject matter, or (5) war.

In states that have adopted the Uniform Durable Power of Attorney Act (UDPAA), an agency may be created that is not affected by subsequent disability or incapacity of the principal. In UDPAA states, the agency may also come into existence upon the "disability or incapacity of the principal." The designation of an attorney in fact under the UDPAA must be in writing.

LEARNING OUTCOMES

After studying this chapter, you should be able to clearly explain:

A. NATURE OF THE AGENCY RELATIONSHIP

LO.1 Explain the difference between an agent and an independent contractor

See the Ned and Tracy Seizer example and the "right to control" test, beginning on p. 851.

B. CREATING THE AGENCY

LO.2 Explain three methods of creating an agency relationship

See the discussion on the usual method of creating an agency (which is by express authorization), p. 853.

See the *Taylor* case where actual authority to perform some tasks created apparent authority to perform other related tasks, p. 854.

See the agency by ratification example of James and Calvin Reiner on p. 855.

C. AGENT'S AUTHORITY

LO.3 Recognize that third persons who deal with an agent are required to take notice of acts contrary to the interests of the principal

See the example of the Fire Company that failed to verify with the principal an agent's authority to receive a prepayment check of $55,000 made out in the agent's name, p. 858.

D. DUTIES AND LIABILITIES OF PRINCIPAL AND AGENT

LO.4 List and explain the duties an agent owes the principal

See the discussion concerning an agent's duty of loyalty, obedience, reasonable care, accounting, and information beginning on p. 859.

E. TERMINATION OF AGENCY

LO.5 Explain how the Uniform Durable Power of Attorney Act changes the common law rule on incapacity of the principal

See the *Estate of Graham* case on the limits of a durable power of attorney, p. 864.

KEY TERMS

agency
agent
apparent authority
attorney in fact
customary authority
express authorization

general agent
incidental authority
independent contractor
interest in the authority
interest in the subject
   matter

power of attorney
principal
special agent
universal agent

QUESTIONS AND CASE PROBLEMS

1. How does an agent differ from an independent contractor?

2. Compare authorization of an agent by (a) appointment and (b) ratification.

3. Ernest A. Kotsch executed a durable power of attorney when he was 85 years old, giving his son, Ernie, the power to manage and sell his real estate and personal property "and to do all acts necessary for maintaining and caring for [the father] during his lifetime." Thereafter, Kotsch began "keeping company" with a widow, Margaret Gradl. Ernie believed that the widow was attempting to alienate his father from him, and he observed that she was exerting a great deal of influence over his father. Acting under the durable power of attorney and without informing his father, Ernie created the "Kotsch Family Irrevocable Trust," to which he transferred $700,000, the bulk of his father's liquid assets, with the father as

grantor and initial beneficiary and Ernie's three children as additional beneficiaries. Ernie named himself trustee. His father sued to avoid the trust. Ernie defended his action on the ground that he had authority to create the trust under the durable power of attorney. Decide. [*Kotsch v Kotsch,* 608 So2d 879 (Fla App)]

4. Ken Jones, the number-one-ranked prizefighter in his weight class, signed a two-year contract with Howard Stayword. The contract obligated Stayword to represent and promote Jones in all business and professional matters, including the arrangement of fights. For these services, Jones was to pay Stayword 10 percent of gross earnings. After a year, when Stayword proved unsuccessful in arranging a title match with the champion, Jones fired Stayword. During the following year, Jones earned $4 million. Stayword sued Jones for $400,000. Jones defended himself on the basis that a principal has the absolute power at any time to terminate an agency relationship by discharging the agent, so he was not liable to Stayword. Was Jones correct?

5. Paul Strich did business as an optician in Duluth, Minnesota. Paul used only the products of the Plymouth Optical Co., a national manufacturer of optical products and supplies with numerous retail outlets and some franchise arrangements in areas other than Duluth. To increase business, Paul renovated his office and changed the sign on it to read "Plymouth Optical Co." Paul did business this way for more than three years—advertised under that name, paid bills with checks bearing the name of Plymouth Optical Co., and listed himself in the telephone and city directories by that name. Plymouth immediately became aware of what Paul was doing. However, because Paul used only Plymouth products and Plymouth did not have a franchise in Duluth, it saw no advantage at that time in prohibiting Paul from using the name and losing him as a customer. Paul contracted with the *Duluth Tribune* for advertising, making the contract in the name of Plymouth Optical Co. When the advertising bill was not paid, the *Duluth Tribune* sued Plymouth Optical Co. for payment. Plymouth's defense was that it never authorized Paul to do business under the name, nor authorized him to make a contract with the newspaper. Decide.

6. Record owned a farm that was managed by his agent, Berry, who lived on the farm. Berry hired Wagner to bale the hay and told him to bill Record for this work. Wagner did so and was paid by Record. By the summer of the following year, the agency had been terminated by Record, but Berry remained in possession as tenant of the farm and nothing appeared changed. Late in the summer, Berry asked Wagner to bale the hay as he had done the previous year and bill Record for the work. He did so, but Record refused to pay on the ground that Berry was not then his agent. Wagner sued him. Decide. [*Record v Wagner,* 100 NH 419]

7. Gilbert Church owned Church Farms, Inc., in Manteno, Illinois. Church advertised its well-bred stallion Imperial Guard for breeding rights at $50,000, directing all inquiries to "Herb Bagley, Manager." Herb Bagley lived at Church Farms and was the only person available to visitors. Vern Lundberg answered the ad, and after discussions in which Bagley stated that Imperial Guard would remain in Illinois for at least a two-year period, Lundberg and Bagley executed a two-year breeding rights contract. The contract was signed by Lundberg and by Bagley as "Church Farms, Inc., H. Bagley, Mgr." When Gil Church moved

Imperial Guard to Oklahoma prior to the second year of the contract, Lundberg brought suit for breach of contract. Church testified that Bagley had no authority to sign contracts for Church Farms. Decide. [*Lundberg v Church Farms, Inc.,* 502 NE2d 806 (Ill)]

8. The Holzmans signed an exclusive listing agreement with the Blum real estate brokerage firm. The contract provided that the Holzmans had an obligation to pay a commission "if they enter into a written agreement to sell the property to any person during the term of this exclusive listing agreement." The Holzmans entered into a written agreement to sell their house for $715,000 to the Noravians. On the advice of their attorney, the Holzmans included a default provision in this contract stating that in the event of default by the Holzmans, the Noravians' only remedy would be a refund of their deposit. Subsequently, the Sterns offered $850,000 for the property and the Holzmans canceled their contract with the Noravians and returned their deposit. After the exclusive listing period expired, the Holzmans executed a contract to sell their property to the Sterns at the offered price of $850,000— with the contract calling for the Holzmans to pay half the real estate fee to Blum and half to a cooperating broker. Blum was paid this fee of $21,500. Blum brought suit against the Holzmans seeking the full commission for the Noravian contract under the exclusive listing agreement. Did Blum have a legal obligation or ethical duty to advise the Holzmans when considering the Sterns' offer that he believed they were obligated to him for the full commission under the Novarian contract? Decide. [*Holzman v Blum*, 726 A2d 818 (Md App)]

9. Tillie Flinn properly executed a durable power of attorney designating her nephew James C. Flanders and/or Martha E. Flanders, his wife, as her attorney in fact. Seven months later, Martha Flanders went to the Capitol Federal Savings and Loan Association office. She had the durable power of attorney instrument, five certificates of deposit, and a hand-printed letter identifying Martha as an attorney in fact and stating that Tillie wished to cash her five CDs that Martha had with her. At approximately 10:31 A.M., five checks were given to Martha in the aggregate amount of $135,791.34, representing the funds in the five CDs less penalties for early withdrawal. Some of the checks were drawn to the order of Martha individually and some to the order of James and Martha, as individuals. Tillie was found dead of heart disease later that day. The time of death stated on her death certificate was 11:30 A.M. The Flanderses spent the money on themselves. Bank IV, as administrator of Tillie's estate, sued Capitol Federal to recover the amount of the funds paid to the Flanderses. It contended that Capitol Federal breached its duty to investigate before issuing the checks. Capitol Federal contended that it did all that it had a duty to do. Decide. [*Bank IV v Capitol Federal Savings and Loan Ass'n,* 828 P2d 355 (Kan)]

10. Lew owns a store on Canal Street in New Orleans. He paid a person named Mike and other individuals commissions for customers brought into the store. Lew testified that he had known Mike for less than a week. Boulos and Durso, partners in a wholesale jewelry business, were visiting New Orleans on a business trip when Mike brought them into the store to buy a stereo. While Durso finalized the stereo transaction with the store's manager, Boulos and

Mike negotiated to buy 2 cameras, 3 videos, and 20 gold Dupont lighters. Unknown to the store's manager, Mike was given $8,250 in cash and was to deliver the merchandise later that evening to the Marriott Hotel, where Boulos and Durso were staying. Mike gave a receipt for the cash, but it showed no sales tax or indication that the goods were to be delivered. Boulos testified that he believed Mike was the store owner. Mike never delivered the merchandise and disappeared. Boulos and Durso contended that Lew is liable for the acts of his agent, Mike. Lew denied that Mike was his agent, and the testimony showed that Mike had no actual authority to make a sale, to use a cash register, or even to go behind a sales counter. What ethical principle applies to the conduct of Boulos and Durso? Decide. [*Boulos v Morrison*, 503 So2d 1(La)]

11. Martha Christiansen owns women's apparel stores bearing her name in New Seabury, Massachusetts; Lake Placid, New York; Palm Beach, Florida; and Palm Springs, California. At a meeting with her four store managers, she discussed styles she thought appropriate for the forthcoming season, advised them as always to use their best judgment in the goods they purchased for each of their respective stores, and cautioned "but no blue jeans." Later, Jane Farley, the manager of the Lake Placid store, purchased a line of high-quality blue denim outfits (designer jeans with jacket and vest options) from Women's Wear, Inc., for the summer season. The outfits did not sell. Martha refused to pay for them, contending that she had told all of her managers "no blue jeans" and that if it came to a lawsuit, she would fly in three managers to testify that Jane Farley had absolutely no authority to purchase denim outfits and was, in fact, expressly forbidden to do so. Women's Wear sued Martha, and the three managers testified for her. Is the fact that Martha had explicitly forbidden Farley to purchase the outfits in question sufficient to protect her from liability for the purchases made by Farley?

12. Fred Schilling, the president and administrator of Florence General Hospital, made a contract, dated August 16, 1989, on behalf of the hospital with CMK Associates to transfer the capacity to utilize 25 beds from the hospital to the Faith Nursing Home. Schilling, on behalf of the hospital, had previously made a contract with CMK Associates on May 4, 1987. Schilling had been specifically authorized by the hospital board to make the 1987 contract. The hospital refused to honor the 1989 contract because the board had not authorized it. CMK contended that Schilling had apparent authority to bind the hospital because he was president and administrator of the hospital and he had been the person who negotiated and signed a contract with CMK in 1987. Thus, according to CMK, the hospital had held out Schilling as having apparent authority to make the contract. The hospital disagreed. Decide. [*Pee Dee Nursing Home v Florence General Hospital*, 419 SE2d 843 (SC Ct App)]

13. Barbara Fox was the agent of Burt Hollander, a well-known athlete. She discovered that Tom Lanceford owned a 1957 Chevrolet convertible, which had been stored in a garage for the past 15 years. After demonstrating to Lanceford that she was the authorized agent of Hollander, she made a contract with Lanceford on behalf of Hollander to purchase the Chevrolet. Lanceford later discovered that the car was much more valuable than he originally

believed, and he refused to deliver the car to Fox. Fox sued Lanceford for breach of contract. Can she recover?

14. Francis Gagnon, an elderly gentleman, signed a power of attorney authorizing his daughter, Joan, "to sell any of my real estate and to execute any document needed to carry out the sale…and to add property to a trust of which I am grantor or beneficiary." This power was given in case Gagnon was not available to take care of matters personally because he was traveling. When Joan learned that Gagnon intended to sell his Shelburne property to Cosby for $750,000, she created an irrevocable trust naming Gagnon as beneficiary and herself as trustee. Acting then on the basis of the authority set forth in the power of attorney, she conveyed the Shelburne property to herself as trustee of the irrevocable trust, thus blocking the sale to Cosby. When Gagnon learned of this, he demanded that Joan return the Shelburne property to him, but she refused, saying she had acted within the authority set forth in the power of attorney. Did Joan violate any duty owed to Gagnon? Must she reconvey the property to Gagnon? [*Gagnon v Coombs*, 654 NE2d 54 (Mass App)]

15. Daniels and Julian were employed by the Marriott Hotel in New Orleans and were close personal friends. One day after work, Daniels and Julian went to Werlein's music store to open a credit account. Julian, with Daniels's authorization and in her presence, applied for credit using Daniels's name and credit history. Later, Julian went to Werlein's without Daniels and charged the purchase of a television set to Daniels's account, executing a retail installment contract by signing Daniels's name. Daniels saw the new television in Julian's home and was informed that it was charged to the Werlein's account. Daniels told Julian to continue making payments. When Werlein's credit manager first contacted Daniels to inform her that her account was delinquent, she claimed that a money order for the television was in the mail. On the second call, she asked for a "payment balance." Some four months after the purchase, she informed Werlein's that she had not authorized the purchase of the television nor ratified the purchase. Werlein's sued Daniels for the unpaid balance. Decide. [*Philip Werlein, Ltd. v Daniels,* 536 So 2d 722 (La App)]

CPA QUESTIONS

1. Generally, an agency relationship is terminated by operation of law in all of the following situations except the:

   a. Principal's death

   b. Principal's incapacity

   c. Agent's renunciation of the agency

   d. Agent's failure to acquire a necessary business license

2. Able, on behalf of Pix Corp., entered into a contract with Sky Corp., by which Sky agreed to sell computer equipment to Pix. Able disclosed to Sky that she was acting on behalf of Pix. However, Able had exceeded her actual authority

by entering into the contract with Sky. If Pix wishes to ratify the contract with Sky, which of the following statements is correct?

a. Pix must notify Sky that Pix intends to ratify the contract.

b. Able must have acted reasonably and in Pix's best interest.

c. Able must be a general agent of Pix.

d. Pix must have knowledge of all material facts relating to the contract at the time it is ratified.

3. Which of the following actions requires an agent for a corporation to have a written agency agreement?

a. Purchasing office supplies for the principal's business

b. Purchasing an interest in undeveloped land for the principal

c. Hiring an independent general contractor to renovate the principal's office building

d. Retaining an attorney to collect a business debt owed the principal

4. Simmons, an agent for Jensen, has the express authority to sell Jensen's goods. Simmons also has the express authority to grant discounts of up to 5 percent of list price. Simmons sold Hemple a 10 percent discount. Hemple had not previously dealt with either Simmons or Jensen. Which of the following courses of action may Jensen properly take?

a. Seek to void the sale to Hemple

b. Seek recovery of $50 from Hemple only

c. Seek recovery of $50 from Simmons only

d. Seek recovery of $50 from either Hemple or Simmons

5. Ogden Corp. hired Thorp as a sales representative for nine months at a salary of $3,000 per month plus 4 percent of sales. Which of the following statements is correct?

a. Thorp is obligated to act solely in Ogden's interest in matters concerning Ogden's business.

b. The agreement between Ogden and Thorp formed an agency coupled with an interest.

c. Ogden does not have the power to dismiss Thorp during the nine-month period without cause.

d. The agreement between Ogden and Thorp is not enforceable unless it is in writing and signed by Thorp.

6. Frost's accountant and business manager has the authority to:

a. Mortgage Frost's business property

b. Obtain bank loans for Frost

c. Insure Frost's property against fire loss

d. Sell Frost's business

Chapter 39

REGULATION OF EMPLOYMENT

E mployment law involves the law of contracts and the law established by lawmakers, courts, and administrative agencies.

A. THE EMPLOYMENT RELATIONSHIP

The relationship of an employer and an employee exists when, pursuant to an express or implied agreement of the parties, one person, the employee, undertakes to perform services or to do work under the direction and control of another, the employer, for compensation. In older cases, this relationship was called the *master-servant relationship.*

1. Characteristics of Relationship

An employee is hired to work under the control of the employer. An employee differs from an agent, who is to negotiate or make contracts with third persons on behalf of, and under the control of, a principal. However, a person may be both an employee and an agent for the other party. An employee also differs from an independent contractor, who is to perform a contract independent of, or free from, control by the other party.[1]

2. Creation of Employment Relationship

The relationship of employer and employee can be created only with the consent of both parties. Generally, the agreement of the parties is a contract. It is therefore subject to all of the principles applicable to contracts. The contract will ordinarily be express, but it may be implied, such as when the employer accepts the rendering of services that a reasonable person would recognize as being rendered with the expectation of receiving compensation.

(A) INDIVIDUAL EMPLOYMENT CONTRACTS. As in contracts generally, both parties must assent to the terms of an employment contract. Subject to statutory restrictions, the parties are free to make a contract on any terms they wish.

(B) COLLECTIVE BARGAINING CONTRACTS. Collective bargaining contracts govern the rights and obligations of employers and employees in many private and public areas of employment. Under collective bargaining, representatives of the employees bargain with a single employer or a group of employers for an agreement on wages, hours, and working conditions. The agreement worked out by the representatives of the employees, usually union officials, is generally subject to a ratification vote by the employees. Terms usually found in collective bargaining contracts are (1) identification of the work belonging exclusively to designated classes of employees, (2) wage and benefits clauses, (3) promotion and layoff clauses, which are generally tied in part to seniority, (4) a management's rights clause, and (5) a grievance procedure. A grievance procedure provides a means by which persons claiming that the contract was violated or that they were disciplined or discharged without just cause may have their cases decided by impartial labor arbitrators.

---

[1] *Ost v West Suburban Travelers Limousine, Inc.,* 88 F3d 435 (7th Cir 1996).

3. Duration and Termination of Employment Contract

In many instances, the employment contract does not state any time or duration. In such a case, it may be terminated at any time by either party. In contrast, the employment contract may expressly state that it shall last for a specified period of time; an example would be an individual's contract to work as general manager for five years. In some instances, a definite duration may be implied by the circumstances.

(A) EMPLOYMENT-AT-WILL DOCTRINE AND DEVELOPING EXCEPTIONS. Ordinarily, a contract of employment may be terminated in the same manner as any other contract. If it is to run for a definite period of time, the employer cannot terminate the contract at an earlier date without justification. If the employment contract does not have a definite duration, it is terminable at will. Under the **employment-at-will doctrine**, the employer has historically been allowed to terminate the employment contract at any time for any reason or for no reason.[2] Recent court decisions—and in some instances, statutes—have changed the rule in most states by limiting the power of the employer to discharge the employee. Some courts have carved out exceptions to the employment-at-will doctrine when the discharge violated an established public policy.[3]

Public policy exceptions are often made to the employment-at-will doctrine when an employee is discharged in retaliation for insisting that the employer comply with the state's food and drug act or for filing a workers' compensation claim.[4] In some states, so-called whistleblower laws have been enacted to protect employees who disclose employer practices that endanger public health or safety. Also, a statutory right exists for at-will employees who are terminated in retaliation for cooperating with a federal criminal prosecution or are terminated in violation of the public policy to provide truthful testimony.[5]

> **employment-at-will doctrine**–doctrine in which the employer has historically been allowed to terminate the employment contract at any time for any reason or for no reason.

C A S E   S U M M A R Y

Pretext at the Pizzeria

FACTS: While working his nighttime cooking shift at Pizzeria Uno, Gerald Adams noticed that the restaurant's kitchen floor was saturated with a foul-smelling liquid coming from the drains. Adams left work, complaining of illness, and contacted the Department of Health about the drainage problem in the restaurant's kitchen. Upon returning to the restaurant a few days

---

[2] *Payne v Western & Atlantic Railroad Co.*, 82 Tenn 507, 518–519 (1884).
[3] *Huang v Gateway Hotel Holdings*, 520 F Supp 2d 1137 (ED Mo 2007).
[4] *Brigham v Dillon Companies, Inc.*, 935 P2d 1054 (Kan 1997).
[5] *Fitzgerald v Salsbury Chemical, Inc.*, 613 NW2d 275 (Iowa 2000). In *Garcetti v Ceballos*, 547 US 410 (2006), the U.S. Supreme Court held that when public employees make statements pursuant to their official duties, the First Amendment of the Constitution does not insulate their communications from employer discipline because the employees are not speaking as citizens for First Amendment purposes. In his dissent, Justice Souter argued that a public employee should have constitutional protection when the employee acts as a whistleblower, pointing out the limitations of protections afforded public employee whistleblowers (at pages 1970 and 1971).

C A S E   S U M M A R Y

Continued

later, Adams was ordered into his manager's office. He was accused of stealing a softball shirt and taking home a work schedule. A shouting match ensued, and Adams was later arraigned on a criminal charge of disorderly conduct. The charges were eventually dropped and have since been expunged from his record. Adams contends that he was unlawfully terminated in violation of the state's whistleblower act because he notified the Board of Health regarding the unsanitary kitchen conditions. Uno contends he was fired for threatening the supervisor, which is an untenable act.

DECISION: Judgment for Adams in the amount of $7,500. The confrontation between Adams and his employer was calculated by the employer to provoke a reaction from Adams that would serve as an excuse to fire him, a pretext for the real reason—Adam's phone call to the Board of Health. The wrongful termination and criminal charges that ensued from the verbal altercation were sufficient to establish damages for emotional distress. Adams's loss of security clearance in the National Guard, which prevented him from participating in an overseas mission in Germany, also supported the jury's finding of compensable emotional distress. [**Adams v Uno Restaurants, Inc., 18 IER Cases 998 (RI 2002)**]

The contract of employment may be construed to bar a discharge of the employee except for cause. If so construed, good cause would then be required for the discharge of an at-will employee. Written personnel policies used as guidelines for supervisors have also been interpreted as being part of the employment contract. These policies have thus been held to restrict the employer's right to discharge at-will employees without proof of good or just cause. Moreover, employee handbooks that provide for "proper notice and investigation" before termination may bar employers from terminating employees without providing such notice and an investigation.[6]

Other courts still follow the common law at-will rule because they believe that a court should not rewrite the contract of the parties to provide employee protection that was never intended.[7]

(B) EMPLOYER REACTIONS. Employers have revised their personnel manuals and employee handbooks and have issued directives to all employees that no assurance of continued employment exists—that the employers are not obligated to have good cause to terminate employees, just as employees are free to leave their positions with the employers. While simultaneously reserving their at-will termination powers, many employers also may design specific, apparently fair termination procedures and promulgate antiharassment policies and procedures, as seen in the *Semple v FedEx* decision.

---

[6] *Carlson v Lake Chelan Community Hospital,* 66 P3d 1080 (Wash App 2003); but see *Trabing v Kinko's, Inc.,* 57 P3d 1248 (Wyo 2002) and *Williams v First Tennessee National Corp.,* 97 SW3d 798 (Tex App 2003).
[7] See *Texas Farm Bureau Mutual Insurance Co. v Sears,* 84 SW3d 604 (Tex 2002).

C A S E   S U M M A R Y

It's Not Easy to Get Around the Employment-at-Will Doctrine, Mr. Semple

FACTS: John Semple was terminated from his employment with FedEx for falsification of company documents. He appealed his termination through internal FedEx procedures without success and thereafter sued the employer in federal court, contending that his termination was in violation of the "public policy exception" to the employment-at-will doctrine in that his termination resulted from his filing internal grievances regarding harassment by his superiors and that he was protected by the employee handbook exception to the at-will doctrine. The employer disagreed.

DECISION: Judgment for FedEx. When he was hired, John Semple signed an employment contract that included the following statement:

I also agree that my employment and compensation can be terminated with or without cause and without notice or liability whatsoever, at any time, at the option of either the company or myself.

The employee handbook stated in part:

The employment relationship between the Company and employee may be terminated at the will of either party as stated in the employment agreement signed upon application for employment. As described in that agreement, the policies and procedures set forth in this manual provide guidelines for management and employees during employment, but do not create contractual rights regarding termination otherwise.

Semple was an employee at-will. No public policy prevented FedEx from terminating Semple's employment. Moreover, FedEx had not surrendered its statutory right to terminate at-will employees based on its employee handbook. [**Semple v Federal Express Corp, 2008 WL 1793481 D SD (2008)**]

Most employers have no interest in terminating employees without good and sufficient cause. They have taken steps to assure that terminations are in fact for good cause and that a solid case exists for each termination should the employee in question sue on an unjust dismissal theory. Employers have standardized their termination methods. Employers often require that every disciplined employee be advised in writing of the infraction, informed of the expected corrective action, and informed of the fact that further misconduct could lead to additional discipline up to and including discharge. When a termination appears to be warranted, most employers require that at least two supervisors be involved and that they take care to ensure that the reasons for the termination are accurate and consistent with the documentation concerning the employee's deficiencies. Moreover, employers should inform the employee of the basis of the proposed termination and give the employee an opportunity to be heard before the dismissal notice is issued.

(c) Justifiable Discharge. An employer may be justified in discharging an employee because of the employee's (1) nonperformance of duties, (2) misrepresentation or fraud in obtaining the employment, (3) disobedience of proper directions, (4) disloyalty, (5) theft or other dishonesty, (6) possession or use of drugs or intoxicants, (7) misconduct, or (8) incompetence.

Employers generally have the right to lay off employees because of economic conditions, including a lack of work. Such actions are sometimes referred to as *reductions in force (RIFs)*.

Employers, however, must be very careful not to make layoffs based on age, for that is a violation of the Age Discrimination in Employment Act.

In some states, a "service letter" statute requires an employer on request to furnish to a discharged employee a letter stating the reason for the discharge.

4. WhistleBlower Protection Under the Sarbanes-Oxley Act

The Sarbanes-Oxley Act (SOA or SOX Act) of 2002 was enacted to restore investor confidence in financial markets following the exposure in 2001–2002 of widespread misconduct by directors and officers of publicly held companies. The SOA contains reforms regarding corporate accountability, enhanced disclosure requirements, and enforcement and liability provisions. Title VIII of the act contains protections for corporate whistleblowers.[8]

(A) PROTECTION PROVIDED. The SOA prohibits a publicly traded company or any agent of it from taking an adverse employment action against an employee who provides information, testifies, or "otherwise assists" in proceedings regarding (1) mail, wire, bank, or securities fraud, (2) any violation of an SEC rule or regulation, or (3) any federal law protecting shareholders against fraud. The act sets forth the types of adverse employment actions that qualify for protection, specifically protecting employees from discharge, demotion, suspension, threats, harassment, failure to hire or rehire, blacklisting, or action otherwise discriminatory against employees in their terms and conditions of employment.

An employee who provides information to the SEC may be incorrect in the belief that an activity is illegal. Nevertheless, the employee is considered involved in a protected activity so long as the employee had an objectively "reasonable belief" that the reported activity was in violation of a federal law protecting shareholders from fraud. **For Example,** when an employee reported to the SEC what he believed to be a financial impropriety regarding delays in payments owed by the company to a subsequent quarter and an SEC investigation exonerated the employer, an administrative law judge found the whistleblower to have been engaged in "protected activities" because he had a reasonable belief that the company action was illegal.[9]

Case law cautions that SOX whistleblower protection provisions do not provide "whistleblower protection for all employee complaints about how a public company spends its money and pays its bills."[10] **For Example,** CFO David Welch had refused to certify an SEC quarterly report as required by SOX because of accounting irregularities and he was fired. The Court of Appeals held that the conduct in question was not shown to be in violation of any fraud or securities laws listed in SOX; thus, Welch was not protected.[11] Indeed, to date, SOX whistleblowers have not fared very well in administrative proceedings and the courts.[12]

---

[8] 18 USC § 1514A (2005).
[9] *Halloum v Intel Corp.,* 2003-SOX-7 (ALJ Mar. 4, 2004).
[10] *Platone v Flyi, Inc.,* DOL ARB No 04-154 (Sept. 29, 2006).
[11] *Welch v Choa,* 536 F3d 269 (4th Cir 2008).
[12] See V. Watnick, "Whistleblower Protections Under the Sarbanes-Oxley Act," *12 Fordham J. of Corp. and Financial Law* 831, 862 (2007), where as of June 2005, only 4 out of 119 total whistleblower complaints heard under SOX had been successful at a hearing.

(B) Procedures. An individual who believes that she has been subject to an adverse employment action because of whistleblowing activities must file a complaint with the Department of Labor's Occupational Safety and Health Administration (OSHA) within 90 days after the asserted adverse employment action. OSHA administers 13 other federal whistleblower laws and has experienced investigators to facilitate its responsibilities under the SOA.[13]

The burden of proof is on the complainant to demonstrate that the complainant's protected activity was a "contributing factor" in the adverse employment action. If this is established, the burden shifts to the employer to prove by "clear and convincing evidence"—a heavy burden of proof—that it would have taken the same adverse action in the absence of the protected activity.[14]

Whistleblowers are entitled to make whole relief including reinstatement with all rights unimpaired and compensatory damages, including back pay with interest, and "special damages" such as reasonable attorneys' fees and expert witness fees.

Criminal penalties may be imposed against the employer or its agents for retaliating against an informant who has provided truthful information relating to a federal offense.[15]

5. Duties of the Employee

The duties of an employee are determined primarily by the contract of employment with the employer. The law also implies certain obligations.

(A) Services. Employees are under the duty to perform such services as may be required by the contract of employment.

(B) Trade Secrets. An employee may be given confidential trade secrets by the employer but must not disclose this knowledge to others. An agreement by the employee to refrain from disclosing trade secrets is binding. If the employee violates this obligation, the employer may enjoin the use of the information by the employee and by any person to whom it has been disclosed by the employee.

Former employees who are competing with their former employer may be enjoined from using information about suppliers and customers that they obtained while employees when this information is of vital importance to the employer's business. Injunctive relief is denied, however, if the information is not important or not secret.

(C) Inventions. Employment contracts commonly provide that an employer will own any invention or discovery made by an employee, whether during work hours, after work hours, or for a period of one or two years after leaving the employment. In the absence of an express or implied agreement to the contrary, the inventions of an employee usually belong to the employee. This is true even though the employee

---

[13] In *Bechtel v Competitive Technologies, Inc.*, 448 F3d 469 (2d Cir 2006), the complainant, John Bechtel, applied to the U.S. District Court for the enforcement of the investigator's preliminary order of reinstatement, which was made before the Administrative Law Judge hearing. The court issued the requested injunction. On appeal, the Second Circuit determined that because the order of reinstatement was not a "final order" of the agency, the court lacked jurisdiction to enforce it. In his dissenting opinion, Judge Straub stated that the failure to enforce the preliminary reinstatement order negated congressional intent to provide a quick remedy for whistleblowers.

[14] 18 USC § 1514A(b)(2)(C), and 29 CFR § 1980.104.

[15] 18 USC § 1513(e) (2005).

shop right–right of an employer to use in business without charge an invention discovered by an employee during working hours and with the employer's material and equipment.

used the time and property of the employer in the discovery. In this case, however, the employer has what is known as a **shop right** to use the invention without cost in its operations.

6. Rights of the Employee

The rights of an employee are determined by the contract of employment and by the law as declared by courts, lawmakers, and administrative agencies.

(A) COMPENSATION. The rights of an employee with respect to compensation are governed in general by the same principles that apply to the compensation of an agent. In the absence of an agreement to the contrary, when an employee is discharged, whether for cause or not, the employer must pay wages to the expiration of the last pay period. State statutes commonly authorize employees to sue employers for wages improperly withheld and to recover penalties and attorney fees. In addition to hourly wages, payments due for vacations and certain bonuses are considered "wages" under state statutes.[16] **For Example,** Diane Beard worked for Summit Institute as a licensed practical nurse for 13 months when she walked off the job and terminated her employment. She requested her accrued vacation pay of $432, but Summit refused to pay her, claiming she had abandoned her job and thus forfeited her right to vacation pay under company policy. Accrued vacation qualifies as "wages," and she was entitled to the $432 vacation pay plus a penalty equal to 90 days' wages at the employee's rate of pay or $9,720, plus $2,400 in attorneys' fees for the trial and an additional $2,600 in attorneys' fees for the appeal. These statutes with their penalty provisions are designed as a coercive means to compel employers to promptly pay their employees.[17]

(B) FEDERAL WAGE AND HOUR LAW. Workers at enterprises engaged in interstate commerce are covered by the Fair Labor Standards Act (FLSA),[18] popularly known as the Wage and Hour Act. These workers cannot be paid less than a specified minimum wage.

CASE SUMMARY

What Is a "Willful" Violation?

FACTS: An action against an employer for violating the Fair Labor Standards Act must be brought within two years unless the violation was willful, in which case it may be brought within three years. McLaughlin, the secretary of labor, brought suit against Richland Shoe Company for failing to pay the minimum wage. Richland claimed that the suit was barred because more than two years had elapsed. McLaughlin claimed that the violation was

---

[16] *Knutson v Snyder Industries, Inc.,* 436 NW2d 496 (Neb 1989).
[17] *Beard v Summit Institute of Pulmonary Medicine and Rehabilitation, Inc.,* 707 So 2d 1233 (La 1998); see also *Beckman v Kansas Dep't. of Human Resources,* 43 P3d 891 (Kan App 2002).
[18] PL 75-718, 52 Stat 1060, 29 USC § 201 *et seq.*

C A S E   S U M M A R Y

Continued

willful, in which case the action was properly brought because three years had not expired. The parties disagreed as to what proof was required to establish that the violation was "willful."

DECISION: To be "willful" within the statute, the violation must be intentional or made with reckless indifference to whether the statute has been satisfied. Because the case had not been tried on the basis of this standard, the case was remanded to the lower court to determine the matter in the light of the new definition of *willful*. [**McLaughlin v Richland Shoe Co., 486 US 128 (1988)**]

The FLSA has been amended to cover domestic service workers, including housekeepers, cooks, and full-time babysitters. Executive, administrative, and professional employees and outside salespersons are exempt from both the minimum wage and overtime provisions of the law.

(1) Subminimum Wage Provisions.

The FLSA allows for the employment of full-time students at institutions of higher education at wage rates below the statutory minimum. Also, individuals whose productive capacity is impaired by age, physical or mental deficiency, or injury may be employed at less than the minimum wage to prevent the curtailment of work opportunities for these individuals. In these cases, however, a special certificate is needed by the employer from the Department of Labor's (DOL) Wage and Hour Division, which has offices throughout the United States.

(2) Wage Issues.

Deductions made from wages as a result of cash or merchandise shortages and deductions for tools of the trade are not legal if they reduce wages below the minimum wage. An employer's requirement that employees provide uniforms or tools of their own is a violation of the law to the extent that the expenses for these items reduce wages below the minimum wage.

Job-related training generally is compensable under the FLSA. However, an exception exists for voluntary training not directly related to an employee's job when the employee does not perform productive work. **For Example,** Hogar, Inc., operates a nursing home and required new employees to undergo two days of unpaid training before assuming paid duties as nurses' aides, maintenance/laundry workers, and kitchen workers. Little or no instruction was offered to these "trainees," and each individual would perform the regular duties of the position for the two-day period. Hogar's practices did not fall within the training exception because the trainees performed productive work with little or no actual training during a regular shift. In a lawsuit brought by the Secretary of Labor, Hogar was ordered by the court to pay 14 hours' pay (two days' pay) for each employee so "trained," plus liquidated damages of an additional 14 hours pay.[19]

[19] *Herman v Hogar Praderas De Amor, Inc.*, 130 F Supp 2d 257 (SD PR 2001).

A large Pennsylvania landscape contractor whose cash wages appeared to comply with all applicable laws was found to be in violation of the FLSA because his Guatemalan and Mexican seasonal workers were required to pay employment-related costs, such as point-of-hire transportation costs, visa costs, and recruiter's fees, which reduced their real wages to below the minimum wage.[20]

(3) Overtime Pay.

Overtime must be paid at a rate of one and a half times the employee's regular rate of pay for each hour worked in excess of 40 hours in a workweek.[21]

(4) Child Labor Provisions.

The FLSA child labor provisions are designed to protect educational opportunities for minors and prohibit their employment in occupations detrimental to their health and well-being. The FLSA restricts hours of work for minors under 16 and lists hazardous occupations too dangerous for minors to perform.

B. LABOR RELATIONS LAWS

Even if employers are not presently unionized, they are subject to certain obligations under federal labor relations law. It is important to both unionized and nonunionized employers to know their rights and obligations under the National Labor Relations Act (NLRA).[22] Employee rights and obligations are also set forth in this act. The Labor-Management Reporting and Disclosure Act regulates internal union affairs.[23]

7. The National Labor Relations Act

The National Labor Relations Act (NLRA), passed in 1935, was based on the federal government's power to regulate interstate commerce granted in Article 1, Section 8, of the Constitution. Congress, in enacting this law, explained that its purpose was to remove obstructions to commerce caused by employers who denied their employees the right to join unions and refused to accept collective bargaining.[24] Congress stated that these obstructions resulted in depression of wages, poor working conditions, and diminution of purchasing power.

Section 7 of the amended NLRA is the heart of the act, stating in part that "[e]mployees shall have the right to self-organization ... to bargain collectively through representatives of their own choosing and to engage in other concerted activities for the purpose of collective bargaining or other mutual aid or protection ... and shall have the right to refrain from such activities...."

Section 8 of the NLRA contains employer and union unfair labor practices, set forth in Figure 39.1, and authorizes the National Labor Relations Board to conduct proceedings to stop such practices.

---

[20] *Rivera v Brickman Group, Ltd.*, 2008 WL 81570 (ED Pa 2008).

[21] DOL regulations, referred to as the *white collar exemptions* from the overtime requirements of the FLSA took effect on August 23, 2004. Generally, executive, administrative, professional, outside sales, computer professional, and certain "highly compensated employees" are exempt from the overtime requirements if they meet the "tests" set forth in the new regulations.

[22] 29 USC §§ 141–169. Note that in the *Lechmere* and *Transportation Management* cases presented in this section, the employers were not unionized.

[23] 29 USC §§ 401–531.

[24] NLRA § 1; 29 USC § 141.

FIGURE 39-1 | *Employer and Union Unfair Labor Practices Charge*

UNFAIR LABOR PRACTICES CHARGES AGAINST EMPLOYERS	SECTION OF THE NLRA[*]
1. Restrain or coerce employees in the exercise of their rights under section 7; threat of reprisals or promise of benefits	8(a)(1); 8(c)
2. Dominate or interfere with the formation or administration of a labor organization or contribute financial or other support to it	8(a)(2)
3. Discriminate in regard to hire or tenure of employment or any term or condition of employment in order to encourage or discourage membership in any labor organization	8(a)(3)
4. Discharge or otherwise discriminate against employees because they have given testimony under the act	8(a)(4)
5. Refuse to bargain collectively with representatives of its employees	8(a)(5)

UNFAIR LABOR PRACTICES CHARGES AGAINST UNIONS	SECTION OF THE NLRA
1. Restrain or coerce employees in the exercise of their rights under section 7	8(b)(1)(A)
2. Restrain or coerce an employer in the selection of its representatives	8(b)(1)(B)
3. Cause or attempt to cause an employer to discriminate against an employee	8(b)(2)
4. Refuse to bargain collectively with the employer	8(b)(3)
5. Require employees to pay excessive fees for membership	8(b)(5)
6. Engage in "featherbed practices" of seeking pay for services not performed	8(b)(6)
7. Use secondary boycotts (banned, except for publicity proviso)	8(b)(4)
8. Allow recognitional and organizational picketing by an uncertified union	8(b)(7)
9. Enter into "hot cargo" agreements, except for construction and garment industries	8(e)

[*]**29 USC § 151.**

The act applies to private-sector employers with gross incomes of $500,000 or more. The Railway Labor Act applies to employees of railroad and air carriers.

8. National Labor Relations Board

Administration of the NLRA is entrusted to the five-member National Labor Relations Board (NLRB, or Board) and the general counsel of the Board. The general counsel is responsible for investigating and prosecuting all unfair labor practice cases. The five-member Board's major function is to decide unfair labor practice cases brought before it by the general counsel.

The Board is also responsible for conducting representation and decertification elections. This responsibility is delegated to the regional directors of the 32 regional offices located throughout the United States who (1) determine the appropriateness of each proposed bargaining unit for the purpose of collective bargaining, (2) investigate petitions for the certification or decertification of unions, and (3) conduct elections to determine the choice of the majority of those employees voting in the election. Should a majority of the employees voting select a union, the NLRB will certify that union as the exclusive representative of all employees within the unit for the purpose of bargaining with the employer to obtain a contract with respect to wages, hours, and other conditions of employment.

9. Election Conduct

The Board of the NLRB has promulgated preelection rules restricting electioneering activities so that the election will express the true desire of employees. The NLRA prohibits employer interference or coercion during the preelection period. The act also prohibits during this period employer statements that contain threats of reprisal or promises of benefits. **For Example,** it is a violation of section 8(c) of the NLRA for a Southern California manufacturer to make implied threats to relocate its plant to Mexico if the employees choose union representation. Furthermore, when the company announced its intent to move to Mexico one day after the union won a representation election, the Labor Board obtained an injunction against the move.[25]

The Board prohibits all electioneering activities at polling places and has formulated a "24-hour rule," which prohibits both unions and employers from making speeches to captive audiences within 24 hours of an election. The rationale is to preserve free elections and prevent any party from obtaining undue advantage.

10. Union Activity on Private Property

Although section 7 of the NLRA gives employees the statutory right to self-organization, employers have the undisputed right to make rules to maintain discipline in their establishments. Generally speaking, employers may prohibit union solicitation by employees during work periods. During nonworking time, employers may prohibit activity and communications only for legitimate efficiency and safety reasons and only if the prohibitions are not manifestly intended to impede employees' exercise of their rights under the law. Nonunion employers, moreover, may not refuse

---

[25] See *Quadrtech Corp.*, NLRB, No 21–CA–33997 (settlement Dec. 11, 2000).

to interview or retain union members because of their union membership. And even if a union pays an individual working for a nonunion employer to help organize the company, that individual is still protected under the NLRA.[26]

An employer may validly post its property against all nonemployee solicitations, including distribution of union literature, if reasonable efforts by the union through other available channels of communication would enable it to reach the employees with its message.

CASE SUMMARY

The Supreme Court Is Always Right

FACTS: Lechmere, Inc., owned and operated a retail store located in a shopping plaza in Newington, a suburb of Hartford, Connecticut. Lechmere was also part owner of the plaza's parking lot, which was separated from a public highway by a 46-foot-wide grassy strip. Almost all of the strip was public property. In a campaign to organize Lechmere employees, nonemployee union organizers from Local 919 of the United Food and Commercial Workers placed handbills on the windshields of cars parked in the employees' part of the parking lot. After Lechmere denied the organizers access to the lot, they picketed from the grassy strip. In addition, they were able to contact directly some 20 percent of the employees. The union filed an unfair labor practice charge with the Board, alleging that Lechmere had violated the NLRA by barring the organizers from its property. An administrative law judge ruled in the union's favor. The Board affirmed, and the Court of Appeals enforced the Board's order. The matter was heard by the Supreme Court.

DECISION: Judgment for Lechmere. A two-stage test is used in evaluating the accommodation between the employees' right to learn of the advantages of unionization from outside union organizers and an employer's property rights. Stage 1 considers whether the outsiders have reasonable access to employees off the employer's property. Stage 2 applies if the access is infeasible. In such a case, the employer's property rights must yield to the extent needed to communicate information on organizational rights. The Court majority determined that the outsiders had reasonable access from the grassy strip. The dissent believed that holding up signs from the grassy strip was not sufficient to learn of advantages of unionization. [**Lechmere, Inc. v NLRB, 502 US 527 (1992)**]

11. Firing Employees for Union Activity

Although employers and supervisors often feel betrayed by individual employees who take leadership roles in forming organizations, the NLRA prohibits discrimination against such employees because of their union activity.

The NLRB has found evidence of discrimination against active union supporters when the employer

1. Discharges on the strength of past misdeeds that were condoned;

2. Neglects to give customary warnings prior to discharge;

3. Discharges for a rule generally unenforced;

[26] *NLRB v Town & Country Electric, Inc.,* 516 US 85 (1995).

4. Applies disproportionately severe punishment to union supporters; or

5. Effects layoffs in violation of seniority status with disproportionate impact on union supporters.

The NLRA preserves the right of the employer to maintain control over the workforce in the interest of discipline, efficiency, and pleasant and safe customer relations. Employees, on the other hand, have the right to be free from coercive discrimination resulting from union activity.

At times these two rights may collide. For example, an employee may be discharged for apparently two reasons: (1) violation of a valid company rule and (2) union activity. The employer gives the former as the reason for termination; the latter remains unstated on the employer's part, causing the filing of a section 8(a)(3) unfair labor practice charge against the employer. These are known as *dual motive cases.* The general counsel must present on behalf of the dismissed employee a prima facie case that such protected conduct as union activity was a motivating factor in the dismissal. After this showing, the burden shifts to the employer, who must prove that the employee would have been dismissed for legitimate business reasons even absent the protected conduct.

C A S E S U M M A R Y

The Sam Santillo Story

FACTS: Prior to his discharge, Sam Santillo was a bus driver for Transportation Management Corporation. On March 19, Santillo talked to officials of the Teamsters Union about organizing the drivers who worked with him. Over the next four days, Santillo discussed with his fellow drivers the possibility of joining the Teamsters and distributed authorization cards. On the night of March 23, George Patterson, who supervised Santillo and the other drivers, told one of the drivers that he had heard of Santillo's activities. Patterson referred to Santillo as two-faced and promised to get even with him. Later that evening, Patterson talked to Ed West, who was also a bus driver. Patterson asked, "What's with Sam and the Union?" Patterson said that he took Santillo's actions personally, recounted several favors he had done for Santillo, and added that he would remember Santillo's activities when Santillo again asked for a favor. On Monday, March 26, Santillo was discharged. Patterson told Santillo that he was being fired for leaving his keys in the bus and taking unauthorized breaks. Santillo filed charges with the Board, and the general counsel issued a complaint, contending that Santillo was discharged because of his union activities in distributing authorization cards to fellow employees. The evidence revealed that the practice of leaving keys in buses was commonplace among company employees and the company tolerated the practice of taking coffee breaks. The company had never taken disciplinary action against an employee for the behavior in question.

DECISION: Judgment for Santillo and the NLRB. The general counsel established a prima facie case by showing that Santillo was involved in union-organizing activities just prior to his discharge. The employer did not meet its burden of proving that Santillo was fired for a legitimate business reason. The infractions involved were commonplace, and no discipline had ever been issued to any employee previously. The reasons given by the company were pretextual. Santillo would not have been fired had the employer not considered his effort to establish a union. [**NLRB v Transportation Management Corp., 462 US 393 (1983)**]

12. Duty of Employer to Bargain Collectively

Once a union wins a representative election, the Board certifies the union as the exclusive bargaining representative of the employees. The employer then has the obligation under the NLRA to bargain with the union in good faith over wages, hours, and working conditions. These matters are *mandatory subjects of bargaining* and include seniority provisions, promotions, layoff and recall provisions, no-strike no-lockout clauses, and grievance procedures. Employers also have an obligation to bargain about the "effects" of the shutdown of a part of a business[27] and may have an obligation to bargain over the decision to relocate bargaining unit work to other plants.[28]

Permissive subjects of bargaining are those over which an employer's refusal to bargain is not a section 8(a)(5) unfair labor practice. Examples are the required use of union labels, internal union affairs, union recognition clauses, and benefits for already retired workers.

C A S E   S U M M A R Y

To Bargain or Not To Bargain?

FACTS: Four subsidiaries of the Southern Company made modifications to the health care and life insurance benefits of their future retirees without negotiating with their employees' unions. The unions filed unfair labor practice charges with the NLRB claiming violations of Section 8(a)(5), refusal to bargain over mandatory subjects of bargaining. The employer defended that retirees are not employees under NLRA and such benefits are permissive subjects of bargaining.

DECISION: Judgment against the employer. While benefits of workers who have already retired are not mandatory subjects of bargaining, retirement benefits for current employees are mandatory subjects of bargaining. [**Southern Nuclear Operating Co. v NLRB, 524 F3d 1350 (DC Cir 2008)**]

13. Right to Work

The NLRA allows states to enact **right-to-work laws**. These laws restrict unions and employers from negotiating clauses in their collective bargaining agreements that make union membership compulsory.[29]

Advocates of such laws contend that compulsory union membership is contrary to the First Amendment right of freedom of association. Unions have attacked these laws as unfair because unions must represent all employees, and in right-to-work states where a majority of employees vote for union representation, nonunion

---

[27] *First National Maintenance v NLRB*, 452 US 666 (1981).
[28] *Dubuque Packing Co. and UFCWIU, Local 150A*, 303 NLRB 66 (1991).
[29] Right-to-work statutes declare unlawful any agreement that denies persons the right to work because of nonmembership in a union or the failure to pay dues to a union as a condition of employment. These laws have been adopted in Alabama, Arizona, Arkansas, Florida, Georgia, Idaho, Iowa, Kansas, Louisiana, Mississippi, Nebraska, Nevada, North Carolina, North Dakota, Oklahoma, South Carolina, South Dakota, Tennessee, Texas, Utah, Virginia, and Wyoming.

employees receive all of the benefits of collective bargaining contracts without paying union dues.

14. Strike and Picketing Activity

If the parties reach an impasse in the negotiation process for a collective bargaining agreement, a union may call a strike and undertake picketing activity to enforce its bargaining demands. Strikers in such a situation are called **economic strikers**. Although the strike activity is legal, the employers may respond by hiring temporary or permanent replacement workers.

(A) RIGHTS OF STRIKERS. Economic strikers who unconditionally apply for reinstatement when their positions are filled by permanent replacements are not entitled to return to work at the end of the economic strike. They are, however, entitled to full reinstatement when positions become available.

> **economic strikers**—union strikers trying to enforce bargaining demands when an impasse has been reached in the negotiation process for a collective bargaining agreement.

C A S E   S U M M A R Y

Avoiding the Sack—The Pilots Returned Before Their Positions Were Filled

FACTS: Striking pilots of Eastern Airlines made an unconditional offer to return to work on November 22, 1989. As of that date, some 227 new-hire replacement pilots were in training but had not obtained certificates from the Federal Aviation Administration permitting them to fly revenue flights. The striking pilots contended that the trainees were not permanent replacement pilots on the date they offered to go back to work because the trainees could not lawfully fly revenue flights. Eastern contended that the new-hire pilots were permanent employees and as such should not be displaced.

DECISION: The pilots' positions were not filled by permanent replacements at the time the striking pilots unconditionally applied to return to work. The new-hire replacement pilots were not qualified to fill the positions at that time. Giving preference to trainees over returning strikers would discourage employees from exercising their right to strike. [**Eastern Airlines Inc. v Airline Pilots Association Int'l, 970 F2d 722 (11th Cir 1990)**]

Strikers responsible for misconduct while out on strike may be refused reemployment by the employer.

When employees strike to protest an employer's unfair labor practice, such as firing an employee for union-organizing activity, these unfair labor practice strikers have a right to return to their jobs immediately at the end of the strike. This right exists even if the employer has hired permanent replacements.[30]

(B) PICKETING. Placing persons outside a business at the site of a labor dispute so that they may, by signs or banners, inform the public of the existence of a labor dispute

---

[30] *Poly America, Inc. v NLRB,* 260 F3d 465 (5th Cir 2001).

primary picketing–legal presentations in front of a business notifying the public of a labor dispute.

mass picketing–illegal tactic of employees massing together in great numbers to effectively shut down entrances of the employer's facility.

secondary picketing– picketing an employer with which a union has no dispute to persuade the employer to stop doing business with a party to the dispute; generally illegal under the NLRA.

is called **primary picketing** and is legal. Should the picketing employees mass together in great numbers in front of the gates of the employer's facility to effectively shut down the entrances, such coercion is called **mass picketing**; it is illegal. **Secondary picketing** is picketing an employer with whom a union has no dispute to persuade the employer to stop doing business with a party to the dispute. Secondary picketing is generally illegal under the NLRA. An exception exists for certain product picketing at supermarkets or other multiproduct retail stores provided that it is limited to asking customers not to purchase the struck product at the neutral employer's store.[31]

15. Regulation of Internal Union Affairs

To ensure the honest and democratic administration of unions, Congress passed the Labor-Management Reporting and Disclosure Act (LMRDA).[32] Title IV of the LMRDA establishes democratic standards for all elections for union offices, including

1. Secret ballots in local union elections;

2. Opportunity for members to nominate candidates;

3. Advance notice of elections;

4. Observers at polling and at ballot-counting stations for all candidates;

5. Publication of results and preservation of records for one year;

6. Prohibition of any income from dues or assessments to support candidates for union office; and

7. Advance opportunity for each candidate to inspect the membership name and address lists.

C. Pension Plans and Federal Regulation

The Employee Retirement Income Security Act (ERISA)[33] was adopted in 1974 to protect employee pensions and benefits.

16. Erisa

The act sets forth fiduciary standards and requirements for administration, vesting, funding, and termination insurance.

(A) **Administration.** Commonly a "benefits claims committee" is set up under the plan to make determinations about coverage issues, and courts will not disturb the finding of a benefits committee unless the determinations are "arbitrary and capricious." **For Example,** Joe Gustafson, who provided chauffeur services for senior

---

[31] *NLRB v Fruit and Vegetable Packers, Local 760 (Tree Fruits, Inc.),* 377 US 58 (1964); but see *NLRB v Retail Clerks, Local 1001 (Safeco Title Ins. Co.),* 477 US 607 (1980).
[32] 29 USC §§ 401–531.
[33] PL 93-406, 88 Stat 829, 29 USC §§ 1001–1381.

executives at NYNEX for a number of years while classified as an independent contractor, sought benefits under ERISA because he asserted he was a common law employee of NYNEX. While the court determined he was in fact an employee entitled to overtime compensation under the Fair Labor Standards Act, the court was compelled to defer to the benefits committee's determination that Gustafson was not an employee under the NYNEX plan because he was not "on the payroll" as required by the plan guidelines. The court found that such a determination was not arbitrary or capricious.[34] Nevertheless, individuals may successfully challenge determinations of the plan administrators. **For Example,** Bell South denied ERISA-covered benefits to Suzanne Lee under both its Short Term Disability Plan and its Long Term Disability Plan. She suffered from chronic pain syndrome, and the administrator determined that she had failed to submit "objective medical evidence" of her condition. The U.S. Court of Appeals reviewed the extensive medical record of pain care specialists supporting her diagnosis and determined that Bell South had acted arbitrarily and capriciously in denying Lee's claim of benefits.[35]

(B) FIDUCIARY STANDARDS AND REPORTING. Persons administering a pension fund must handle it to protect the interest of employees.[36]

CASE SUMMARY

Placing a Conglomerate's Money-Losing Eggs in One Financially Rickety Basket

FACTS: Charles Howe and others worked for Massey-Ferguson, a wholly owned subsidiary of Varity Corporation. These employees were beneficiaries of Massey-Ferguson's self-funded employee welfare benefit plan, an ERISA-protected plan that Massey-Ferguson itself administered. Varity became concerned that some of Massey-Ferguson's money-losing divisions were losing too much money, and it developed a business plan to deal with the problem that amounted to placing many of Varity's money-losing eggs in one financially rickety basket. It called for a transfer of Massey-Ferguson's money-losing divisions, along with other debts, to a newly created, separately incorporated subsidiary called Massey Combines. The plan foresaw the possibility that Massey Combines would fail, but it viewed such a failure, from Varity's business perspective, as closer to a victory than to a defeat because failure would eliminate several poorly performing divisions and eradicate various debts that Varity would transfer to Massey Combines. Among the obligations that Varity hoped the reorganization would eliminate were those arising from the benefit plan's promises to pay medical and other nonpension benefits to employees of Massey-Ferguson's money-losing divisions. Varity called employees together at a special meeting. The thrust of Varity's remarks was that the employees' benefits would remain secure if they voluntarily transferred to Massey Combines. As Varity knew, however, the reality was very different. The evidence showed that Massey Combines was insolvent from the day of its creation and that it hid its $46 million negative net worth by overvaluing its assets and underestimating its liabilities. After Massey Combines went into receivership, the employees lost

[34] *Gustafson v Bell Atlantic Corp.*, 171 F Supp 2d 311 (SDNY 2001).
[35] *Lee v Bell South Telecommunications Inc.*, 318 FedAppx 829, 2009 WL 596006 (11th Cir 2009).
[36] *John Hancock Mutual Life Ins. Co. v Harris Trust*, 510 US 86 (1993).

C A S E   S U M M A R Y

Continued

their benefits, and Howe and others sued for reinstatement of the old plan. Varity's defense was that individuals did not have a right to bring an ERISA lawsuit for individual relief.

DECISION: Judgment for Howe and the other employees restoring plan benefits. When an employer runs a benefits plan and its managers or agents, regardless of their job titles, talk about those benefits to employees, painting a false picture of security to induce them to transfer to a new company by saying "your benefits are secure," they are fiduciaries, and their breach of fiduciary duties in making false and misleading statements is binding on the employer. ERISA § 502(a)(3) authorizes lawsuits for individual equitable relief for breach of fiduciary duties. [**Varity Corp. v Howe, 516 US 489 (1996)**]

The fact that an employer contributed all or part of the money to the pension fund does not entitle it to use the fund as though the employer still owned it. Persons administering pension plans must make detailed reports to the Secretary of Labor.

(C) VESTING. *Vesting* is the right of an employee to pension benefits paid into a pension plan in the employee's name by the employer. Prior to ERISA, many pension plans did not vest accrued benefits until an employee had 20 to 25 years of service. Thus, an employee who was forced to terminate service after 18 years would have no pension rights or benefits. Under ERISA, employees' rights must be fully vested within five or seven years in accordance with the two vesting options available under the law.

In the past, it had been common for pension plans to contain break-in-service clauses, whereby employees who left their employment for a period longer than one year for any reason other than an on-the-job injury lost pension eligibility rights. Under the Retirement Equity Act of 1984,[37] an individual can leave the workforce for up to five consecutive years and still retain eligibility for pension benefits.

(D) FUNDING. ERISA requires that employers make contributions to their pension funds on a basis that is actuarially determined so that the pension fund will be large enough to make the payments that will be required of it.

(E) TERMINATION INSURANCE. ERISA established an insurance plan to protect employees when an employer goes out of business. To provide this protection, the statute created a Pension Benefit Guaranty Corporation (PBGC). In effect, this corporation guarantees that employees will receive benefits in much the same way as the Federal Deposit Insurance Corporation protects bank depositors. The PBGC is financed by small payments made by employers for every employee covered by a pension plan.

(F) ENFORCEMENT. ERISA authorizes the Secretary of Labor and employees to bring court actions to compel the observance of statutory requirements.

[37] PL 98-397, 29 USC § 1001.

D. Unemployment Benefits, Family Leaves, and Social Security

Generally, when employees are without work through no fault of their own, they are eligible for unemployment compensation benefits. Twelve-week maternity, paternity, or adoption leaves and family and medical leaves are available for qualifying employees. Social Security provides certain benefits, including retirement and disability benefits.

17. Unemployment Compensation

Unemployment compensation today is provided primarily through a federal-state system under the unemployment insurance provisions of the Social Security Act of 1935.[38] All states have laws that provide similar benefits, and the state agencies are loosely coordinated under the federal act. Agricultural employees, domestic employees, and state and local government employees are not covered by this federal-state system. Federal programs of unemployment compensation exist for federal civilian workers and former military service personnel. A separate federal unemployment program applies to railroad workers.

(A) Eligibility. In most states, an unemployed person must be available for placement in a similar job and willing to take such employment at a comparable rate of pay. Full-time students generally have difficulty proving that they are available for work while they are still going to school.

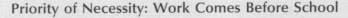

CASE SUMMARY

Priority of Necessity: Work Comes Before School

FACTS: Robert Evjen was a full-time employee of Boise Cascade. At the same time, he was a full-time student at Chemata Community College. He was laid off as part of a general economy move by the employer. He applied for unemployment compensation. His claim was opposed on the ground that he was not available for work because he was going to school. The referee found that Evjen never missed work to go to classes, that he could not afford to go to school without working, and that, in case of any conflict between work and school, work came first.

DECISION: Judgment for Evjen. To obtain unemployment benefits, an unemployed individual must prove, among other things, that she or he is "available for work" and is unable to obtain suitable work. A student's unavailability for work during school hours is contrary to the concept of "available for work," which requires availability for all shifts of suitable work. However, Evjen's uncontroverted testimony that his education was secondary to his employment was sufficient to overcome either an inference or a presumption of nonavailability. He was available for work and therefore entitled to unemployment compensation. [**Evjen v Employment Agency, 539 P2d 662 (Or App 1975)**]

[38] 42 USC §§ 301–1397e.

If an employee quits a job without cause or is fired for misconduct, the employee is ordinarily disqualified from receiving unemployment compensation benefits. **For Example,** stealing property from an employer constitutes misconduct for which benefits will be denied. Moreover, an employee's refusal to complete the aftercare portion of an alcohol treatment program has been found to be misconduct connected with work, disqualifying the employee from receiving benefits.

(B) FUNDING. Employers are taxed for unemployment benefits based on each employer's "experience rating" account. Thus, employers with a stable workforce with no layoffs, who therefore do not draw on the state unemployment insurance fund, pay lower tax rates. Employers whose experience ratings are higher pay higher rates. Motivated by the desire to avoid higher unemployment taxes, employers commonly challenge the state's payment of unemployment benefits to individuals who they believe are not properly entitled to benefits.

18. Family and Medical Leaves of Absence

The Family and Medical Leave Act of 1993 (FMLA)[39] entitles an eligible employee, whether male or female, to a total of 12 workweeks of unpaid leave during any 12-month period (1) because of the birth or adoption of the employee's son or daughter, (2) to care for the employee's spouse, son, daughter, or parent with a serious health condition, or (3) because of a serious health condition that makes the employee unable to perform the functions of his or her position. Notice should be given by the employer to an employee that the leave he or she is taking will count against FMLA entitlement in order to comply with the Secretary of Labor's regulations.[40] In the case of an employee's serious health condition or that of a covered family member, an employer may require the employee to use any accrued paid vacation, personal, medical, or sick leave toward any part of the 12-week leave provided by the act. When an employee requests leave because of the birth or adoption of a child, the employer may require the employee to use all available paid personal, vacation, and medical leave, but not sick leave, toward any FMLA leave.

To be eligible for FMLA leave, an employee must have been employed by a covered employer for at least 12 months and have worked at least 1,250 hours during the 12-month period preceding the leave. Covered employers are those that employ 50 or more employees.[41] Upon return from FMLA leave, the employee is entitled to be restored to the same or an equivalent position with equivalent pay and benefits. **For Example,** when Magda Brenlla returned to her position at LaSorsa Buick in the Bronx, New York, after quadruple bypass surgery, she was terminated by the owner who told her he had decided to consolidate the positions of office manager and controller, even though he had no business plan for restructuring, and soon thereafter had to hire additional help in the office. The judge upheld a jury verdict of $320,000, finding that the jury had ample evidence to conclude that the real reason for her termination was her FMLA leave.[42]

---

[39] 29 USC §§ 2601–2654.
[40] See *Ragsdale v Volverine World Wide, Inc.,* 535 US 81 (2002).
[41] *Bellum v PCE Constructors Inc.,* 407 F3d 734 (5th Cir 2005). Joint employers are obligated to honor FMLA-qualifying leaves. See *Grace v USCAR,* 521 F3d 655 (6th Cir 2008).
[42] *Brenlla v LaSorsa Buick,* 2002 WL 1059117 (SDNY 2002).

The FMLA provides specific statutory relief for violations of the provisions of the act, including pay to the employee for damages equal to lost wages and benefits or any actual monetary losses, plus interest, plus an equal amount in liquidated damages.[43]

19. Leaves for Military Service Under Userra

The Uniformed Services Employment and Re-Employment Rights Act (USERRA) was enacted in 1994 to encourage noncareer service in the armed services, minimize the disruption experienced in the civilian careers of reservists, and promote prompt reemployment of reservists upon return from military leave.[44] In the context of mobilizing more than 500,000 reservists between September 11, 2001, and the summer of 2006, the USERRA has and will have a broad impact on U.S. employers as it provides reemployment and benefit protection rights for returning military personnel and prohibits discrimination against individuals because of their application for or performance of military service.[45]

(A) PROTECTIONS. Section 4312 of the USERRA generally requires returning reservists to be "promptly reemployed" and returned to the same or comparable positions of like seniority, status, and pay they would have had if they had not been activated. Moreover, Section 4316(c) provides that persons reemployed under the act shall not be discharged from employment within a year of their reemployment if their period of service was more than 180 days. For service of more than 30 days, the protective period is 180 days. However, the employer may terminate an individual for cause regardless of the duration of service.

Sections 4312(a)(3) and (4) provide protection for those disabled while in the service and requires employers to make reasonable efforts to accommodate each employee's disability so that each individual may return to the same or comparable positions or, if no longer qualified for the position, allow for the transfer to a position the disabled individual can perform closest to the prior position in terms of seniority, status, and pay.

Section 4323 of the act provides a full range of remedies, including back pay for loss of wages and benefits as well as liquidated damages in an amount equal to the actual damages when the employer's failure to comply with the act was willful. The Department of Labor has issued USERRA regulations.[46] The act's enforcement is performed by the U.S. Justice Department's Division of Civil Rights.

(B) DEFENSES. In addition to an employer's right to terminate a reemployed service-person for cause, employers may be excused from reemploying or continuing employment of persons under § 4312(d)(1) of the act when the employer's circumstances have so changed as to make reemployment impossible, unreasonable, or an undue hardship. The burden of proof on the matter is on the employer.

---

[43] See *Arban v West Publishing Co.*, 345 F3d 390 (6th Cir 2003), in which the U.S. Court of Appeals required the doubling of a jury verdict of $130,000 under the FMLA provision providing for liquidated damages unless the employer is able to prove that it acted "in good faith..." and had reasonable grounds to believe it was not in violation of the FMLA. 29 USC § 2617(a)(iii).

[44] 38 USC.§ 4301 (2005).

[45] 38 USC § 4312, 4316, and 4317 (2005).

[46] 30 Federal Register Vol. 70 No. 242 (Dec 19, 2005).

For Example, Joseph Duarte was called to active duty in the Marine Corps Reserve to serve nine months' active duty from November to July. On his return in July he was given his same pay but diminished status by being assigned a temporary assignment rather than acting as a primary consultant to one of the employer's business groups. Faced with financial need to reduce its payroll, the employer eliminated Duarte's temporary assignment and terminated him four months later for what it believed was economic "cause." Duarte believed that his termination violated the USERRA. The court disagreed with the employer and determined that Duarte was within the act's one-year protective period and had been returned to work in the diminished status of a temporary assignment that was a direct result of his military service. Duarte was awarded back pay of $114,500 and front pay of $324,000, less $55,000 in severance benefits already paid him, for a total of $384,000 in damages.[47] Liquidated damages equal to $384,000 were declined because the employer's actions were not deemed willful.

(c) Discrimination and Retaliation Protection. As opposed to the protections contained in Section 4312, the act's Section 4311 provides separate and distinct statutory protection against discrimination of employees on the basis of military service and retaliation against individuals, whether military or not, who give testimony or statements on behalf of a USERRA claimant. **For Example,** a Section 4311 discrimination violation is made out that bakery driver Robert Mills was terminated by Multigrain Baking Co. because of his need to have time off for reserve duty training after the personnel director, Marsha Coyle, testified on cross-examination, "If we knew Bobby Mills was in the Guard, we would not have hired him. These drivers have to be available to protect their territories or we lose business."

20. Social Security

Employees and employers are required to pay Social Security taxes, which provide employees with four types of insurance protection: retirement benefits, disability benefits, life insurance benefits, and health insurance (Medicare). The federal Social Security Act established a federal program of aid for the aged, the blind, and the disabled. This is called the Supplemental Security Income (SSI) program. Payments are administered directly by the Social Security Administration, which became an independent government agency in 1995.

E. Employees' Health and Safety

The Occupational Safety and Health Act of 1970 (OSHA) was passed to assure every worker, so far as possible, safe and healthful working conditions and to preserve the country's human resources.[48] OSHA provides for (1) the establishment of safety and health standards and (2) effective enforcement of these standards and the other employer duties required by OSHA.

---

[47] *Duarte v Agilent Technologies, Inc.,* 366 F Supp 2d 1039 (D Colo 2005).
[48] 29 USC § 651 *et seq.*

21. Standards

The Secretary of Labor has broad authority under OSHA to promulgate occupational safety and health standards.[49] Except in emergency situations, public hearings and publication in the *Federal Register* are required before the secretary can issue a new standard. Any person adversely affected may then challenge the validity of the standard in a U.S. Court of Appeals. The secretary's standards will be upheld if they are reasonable and supported by substantial evidence. The secretary must demonstrate a need for a new standard by showing that it is reasonably necessary to protect employees against a "significant risk" of material health impairment. The cost of compliance with new standards may run into billions of dollars. The secretary is not required to do a cost-benefit analysis for a new standard but must show that the standard is economically feasible.

22. Employer Duties

Employers have a "general duty" to furnish each employee a place of employment that is free from hazards that are likely to cause death or serious physical injuries.

OSHA requires employers to maintain records of occupational illness and injuries if they result in death, loss of consciousness, or one or more lost workdays or if they require medical treatment other than first aid. Such records have proven to be a valuable aid in recognizing areas of risk. They have been especially helpful in identifying the presence of occupational illnesses.

23. Enforcement

The Occupational Safety and Health Administration (also identified as OSHA) is the agency within the Department of Labor that administers the act. OSHA has authority to conduct inspections and to seek enforcement action when noncompliance has occurred. Worksite inspections are conducted when employer records indicate incidents involving fatalities or serious injuries.[50] These inspections may also result from employee complaints. The act protects employees making complaints from employer retaliation. Employers have the right to require an OSHA inspector to secure a warrant before inspecting the employer's plant.

If OSHA issues a citation for a violation of workplace health or safety standards, the employer may challenge the citation before the Occupational Safety and Health Review Commission (OSHRC). Judicial review of a commission ruling is obtained before a U.S. Court of Appeals. **For Example,** after an accident at Staley Manufacturing Company's Decatur, Illinois, plant in which an employee was fatally asphyxiated, OSHA inspectors issued citations for multiple violations of the OSH Act. The employer challenged the citations before the OSHRC. Upon review by the U.S. Court of Appeals, the court affirmed OSHRC's decision, finding that the company's "plain indifference" to act on the hazards at the workplace and train

---

[49] *Martin v OSHRC*, 499 US 144 (1991).
[50] *Chao v Mallard Bay Drilling Co.*, 534 US 235 (2002).

employees how to handle the hazards was a willful violation of the act, allowing for civil penalty of no more than $70,000 for each violation.[51]

The Occupational Safety and Health Act provides that no employer shall discharge or in any manner discriminate against employees because they filed a complaint with OSHA, testified in any OSHA proceeding, or exercised any right afforded by the act. A regulation issued by the Secretary of Labor under the act provides that if employees with no reasonable alternative refuse in good faith to expose themselves to a dangerous condition, they will be protected against subsequent discrimination. The Secretary of Labor may obtain injunctive and other appropriate relief in a U.S. district court against an employer who discriminates against employees for testifying or exercising any right under the act.

thinking things through

Taking Chances or Shortcuts in Violation of OSHA Standards Is Bad Management

John Carlo, Inc. (JCI) was installing a sewer line down the middle of an existing roadway in Jacksonville, Florida. The new line crossed under an existing gas line that was perpendicular to the proposed sewer line. The JCI crew worked in two stacked trench boxes, laying pipe up to the location where the pipeline crossed the trench for the sewer line. OSHA regulations require protection of employees from cave-ins; trench boxes and sloping of trench walls provide this protection. The following day, the crew removed the top trench box because both boxes would not fit under the perpendicular gas line. The crew pulled the bottom box under the perpendicular gas line and prepared the bottom of the trench to lay one joint of the sewer pipe. Project superintendent Cox had discussed this move with his foreman Jacobs. Jacobs reminded Cox that this move would leave the top portion of the trench unprotected. Cox explained that he realized the problem, but because JCI had bid the project based on 6-foot-wide trenches, they could not slope the trenches. The supervisors anticipated that just 15 minutes was needed to lay the one joint of pipe. Two crew members entered the trench to lay the pipe. The trench walls above the box (approximately 6 feet) were not sloped or otherwise protected. A large clay ball dislodged, fell into the trench, and struck one employee, who eventually died as a result.

Thinking Things Through, was it a reasonable risk for the employer to utilize the two employees in the trench for just 15 minutes to lay one joint of pipe? Of course not! The ALJ found that both supervisors "knowingly and deliberately" violated the OSHA standard because it was "more expedient to place employees in an unprotected trench… than to take the time to adequately shore up or slope the trench to protect the employees." The $50,000 willful violation penalty was upheld by the U.S. Court of Appeals.*

In 1970, the year that OSHA became law, the American population was approximately 204,000,000; over 14,000 workers were killed in industrial accidents. For 2006, near the time of the JCI fatality, the population of the United States was approximately 300,000,000 and the number of fatal work injuries was 5,703. OSHA has drastically improved the safety and health of workers. OSHA standards are commonly devised as corrective responses to the occurrence of previous fatalities or injuries on often similarly situated work sites. Employees are empowered to refuse to expose themselves to dangerous duties under the *Whirlpool v Marshall* U.S. Supreme Court decision.** Management and employees must always be encouraged to take the safe course!

* *John Carlo, Inc. v Secretary of Labor*, 2008 CCH OSHD ¶32,929.
** 445 US 1 (1980).

[51] *A. E. Staley Manufacturing Co. v Chao*, 295 F3d 1341 (DC Cir 2002).

24. State "Right-To-Know" Legislation

Laws that guarantee individual workers the "right to know" if there are hazardous substances in their workplaces have been enacted by many states in recent years. These laws commonly require an employer to make known to an employee's physician the chemical composition of certain workplace substances in connection with the employee's diagnosis and treatment by the physician. Furthermore, local fire and public health officials, as well as local neighborhood residents, are given the right to know if local employers are working with hazardous substances that could pose health or safety problems.

F. COMPENSATION FOR EMPLOYEES' INJURIES

For most kinds of employment, workers' compensation statutes govern compensation for injuries. These statutes provide that an injured employee is entitled to compensation for accidents occurring in the course of employment from a risk involved in that employment.

25. Common Law Status of Employer

In some employment situations, common law principles apply. Workers' compensation statutes commonly do not apply to employers with fewer than a prescribed minimum number of employees or to agricultural, domestic, or casual employment. When an exempted area of employment is involved, it is necessary to consider the duties and defenses of employers apart from workers' compensation statutes.

(A) DUTIES. The employer is under the common law duty to furnish an employee with a reasonably safe place in which to work, reasonably safe tools and appliances, and a sufficient number of competent fellow employees for the work involved. The employer is also under the common law duty to warn the employee of any unusual dangers particular to the employer's business.

(B) DEFENSES. At common law, the employer is not liable to an injured employee if the employee is harmed by the act of a fellow employee. Similarly, an employer is not liable at common law to an employee harmed by an ordinary hazard of the work because the employee assumed such risks. If the employee is guilty of contributory negligence, regardless of the employer's negligence, the employer is not liable at common law to an injured employee.

26. Statutory Changes

The rising incidence of industrial accidents resulting from the increasing use of more powerful machinery and the growth of the industrial labor population led to a demand for statutory modification of common law rules relating to the liability of employers for industrial accidents.

(A) MODIFICATION OF EMPLOYER'S COMMON LAW DEFENSES. One type of change by statute was to modify the defenses that an employer could assert when sued by an employee for damages. **For Example,** under the Federal Employer's Liability Act (FELA), which covers railroad workers, the injured employee must still bring an action in court and prove the negligence of the employer or other employees. However, the burden of proving the case is made lighter by limitations on employers' defenses. Under FELA, contributory negligence is a defense only in mitigation of damages; assumption of the risk is not a defense.[52]

(B) **WORKERS' COMPENSATION.** A more sweeping development was made by the adoption of workers' compensation statutes in every state. In addition, civil employees of the U.S. government are covered by the Federal Employees' Compensation Act. When an employee is covered by a workers' compensation statute and the injury is job connected, the employee's remedy is limited to that provided in the workers' compensation statute.[53]

Workers' compensation proceedings are brought before a special administrative agency or workers' compensation board. In contrast, a common law action for damages or an action for damages under an employer's liability statute is brought in a court of law.

CASE SUMMARY

Locked in

FACTS: Bryant is the administrator of the estate of the deceased and the guardian of the deceased's minor child. Bryant sued Wal-Mart for damages following the death of the deceased based on the theory of false imprisonment. While working on the night restocking crew, the deceased suffered a stroke. Medical personnel arrived six minutes later but could not enter the store because management had locked all doors of the store for security reasons and no manager was present to open a door. By the time the medical crew entered the store to assist her, they were unable to revive her, and she died 15 hours later. Bryant contended that the false imprisonment occurred between the time the deceased became ill and the time the medical team was unable to enter the store. Wal-Mart contended that Bryant's exclusive remedy is the Workers' Compensation Act.

DECISION: Judgment for Wal-Mart. It is well settled that a claim under the Workers' Compensation Act is the sole and exclusive remedy for injury or occupational disease incurred in the course of employment. In exchange for the right to recover scheduled compensation without proof of negligence on the part of the employer, employees forgo other rights and remedies they once had. Injuries to an employee's peace, happiness, and feelings are not compensable under the act. [**Bryant v Wal-Mart Stores, Inc., 417 SE2d 688 (Ga App 1992)**]

For injuries arising within the course of the employee's work from a risk involved in that work, workers' compensation statutes usually provide (1) immediate medical

---

[52] 45 USC § 1 *et seq.*
[53] Immunity from a tort action based on workers' compensation law applies only to the injured employee's employer, not the owner of the work location. See *Peronto v Case Corp.,* 693 NW2d 133 (Wisc App 2005).

benefits, (2) prompt periodic wage replacement, often computed as a percentage of weekly wages (ranging from 50 percent to 80 percent of the injured employee's wage) for a specified number of weeks, and (3) a death benefit of a limited amount.[54] In such cases, compensation is paid without regard to whether the employer or the employee was negligent. However, no compensation is generally allowed for a willful, self-inflicted injury or one sustained while intoxicated.

There has been a gradual widening of the workers' compensation statutes, so compensation today is generally recoverable for both accident-inflicted injuries and occupational diseases.

G. Employee Privacy

Employers may want to monitor employee telephone conversations in the ordinary course of their business to evaluate employee performance and customer service; to document business transactions between employees and customers; or to meet special security, efficiency, or other needs. Employers may likewise want to monitor e-mail for what they perceive to be sound business reasons. Employers also may seek to test employees for drug use or search employee lockers for illicit drugs. Litigation may result because employees may believe that such activities violate their right to privacy.

27. Source of Privacy Rights

The Bill of Rights contained in the U.S. Constitution, including the Fourth Amendment, which protects against unreasonable search and seizure, provides a philosophical and legal basis for individual privacy rights for federal employees. The Fourteenth Amendment applies this privacy protection to actions taken by state and local governments that affect their employees. The privacy rights of individuals working in the private sector are not directly controlled by the Bill of Rights, however, because challenged employer actions are not government actions. Limited employee privacy rights in the private sector are provided by statute, case law, and collective bargaining agreements.

28. Monitoring Employee Telephone Conversations

The Federal Wiretapping Act[55] makes it unlawful to intercept oral and electronic communications and provides for both criminal liability and civil damages against the violator. There are two major exceptions, however. The first allows an employer to monitor a firm's telephones in the "ordinary course of business" through the use of extension telephones; a second exception applies when there is prior employee consent to the interception. If employer monitoring results in the interception of a business call, it is within the ordinary-course-of-business exception. Personal calls can be monitored, however, only to the extent necessary to determine that the call is personal, and the employer must then cease listening. **For Example,** Newell Spears taped all phone conversations at his store in trying to find out if an employee was

---

[54] *Union Light & Power Co. v DC Department of Employment Services,* 796 A2d 665 (DC App 2002).
[55] Title III of the Omnibus Crime Control and Safe Streets Act of 1968, 28 USC §§ 2510–2520.

connected to a store theft. He listened to virtually all 22 hours of intercepted and recorded telephone conversations between his employee Sibbie Deal and her boyfriend Calvin Lucas without regard to the conversations' relation to Spears's business interest. While Spears might well have legitimately monitored Deal's calls to the extent necessary to determine that the calls were personal and made or received in violation of store policy, the scope of the interception in this case was well beyond the boundaries of the ordinary-course-of-business exception and in violation of the act.[56]

Employer monitoring of employee phone calls can be accomplished without fear of violating the act if consent is established. Consent may be established by prior written notice to employees of the employer's monitoring policy. It is prudent, as well, for the employer to give customers notice of the policy through a recorded message as part of the employer's phone-answering system.

29. E-Mail Monitoring

Electronic mail (e-mail) is a primary means of communication in many of today's businesses, serving for some employers as an alternative to faxes, telephones, or the U.S. Postal Service. Employers may want to monitor employees' e-mail messages to evaluate the efficiency and effectiveness of their employees or for corporate security purposes, including the protection of trade secrets and other intangible property interests. When employees are disciplined or terminated for alleged wrongful activities discovered as a result of e-mail searches, however, the issue of privacy may be raised. (See Chapter 2 for a discussion of use of e-mail in litigation and discovery.)

The Electronic Communications Privacy Act of 1986 (ECPA)[57] amended the federal wiretap statute and was intended in part to apply to e-mail. However, ordinary-course-of-business and consent exceptions apply to e-mail, and it would appear that employers have broad latitude to monitor employee e-mail use. **For Example,** Alana Shoars, an e-mail administrator for Epson America, was fired after complaining about her supervisor's reading of employee e-mail messages. Her state court invasion of privacy case was unsuccessful.[58] Very few cases involving e-mail and Web site issues have been adjudicated so far under the ECPA. It has been held that for an employee's secure Web site to be "intercepted" in violation of the wiretap act, the electronic documents acquired must be acquired during transmission, not while in electronic storage.[59]

An employer can place itself within the consent exception of the act by issuing a policy statement to all employees that informs them of the monitoring program and its purposes and justification.

30. Property Searches

Protected by the Fourth Amendment, public-sector employees have a reasonable expectation of privacy with respect to their desks and file cabinets. However,

[56] *Deal v Spears,* 580 F2d 1153 (8th Cir 1992); *Arias v Mutual Central Alarm Services, Inc.,* 182 FRD 407 (SDNY 1998).
[57] 18 USC §§ 2510–2520.
[58] See *Shoars v Epson America, Inc.,* 1994 Cal LEXIS 3670 (June 29, 1994).
[59] *Konop v Hawaiian Airlines, Inc.,* 302 F3d 868 (9th Cir 2002); *Fraser v Nationwide Mutual Insurance Co.,* 352 F3d 107 (3d Cir 2003) (court held that the wiretaps act was not violated because the employer did not "intercept" the e-mail but retrieved it after it had been sent and received).

depending on the fact-specific purpose, justification, and scope of the search, the balance of interest should favor the public employer because its interests in supervision, control, and the efficient operation of the workplace outweigh a public employee's privacy interests.[60] Search of a postal service employee's locker was held not to be a Fourth Amendment violation because well-publicized regulations informed employees that their lockers were subject to search to combat pilferage and stealing. However, the warrantless search of the desk and files of a psychiatrist employed by a state hospital was found to be a Fourth Amendment violation, exceeding the scope of a reasonable work-related search when the search examined his private possessions, including purely personal belongings, and management sought to justify the search on false grounds.[61]

In the private sector, employers may create a reasonable expectation of privacy by providing an employee a locker and allowing the employee to provide his or her own lock. A search of that locker could be an invasion of privacy.[62] If, however, the employer provides a locker and lock but retains a master key and this is known to employees, the lockers may be subject to legitimate reasonable searches by the employer. If a private-sector employer notifies all employees of its policy on lockers, desks, and office searches and the employer complies with its own policy, employees will have no actionable invasion of privacy case.

Many businesses use overt or hidden video cameras as a security method in the workplace to enhance worker safety and to prevent and/or detect theft or other criminal conduct. To avoid state constitutional or statutory claims for invasion of privacy, employers should not set up video cameras in areas where employees have a reasonable expectation of privacy.[63] Utilizing signs to notify employees and members of the public that certain areas are under video surveillance is a common business practice not likely to initiate privacy claims. Additionally, employers should disseminate their written policy on surveillance and obtain a consent form from employees acknowledging that they received this notice to preserve their consent defense.

31. Drug and Alcohol Testing

Drug and alcohol testing is an additional source of privacy concerns for employees. Public-sector employees may see drug and alcohol testing as potentially infringing on their Fourth and Fifth Amendment rights, although they may be subject to this testing on the basis of reasonable suspicion. In ordinary circumstances, however, random drug testing is not permissible in the public sector except for mass transit workers and some safety-sensitive positions. The Federal Omnibus Transportation Employee Testing Act,[64] which covers certain classes of employees working in the airline, railroad, and trucking industries, makes covered employees subject to random drug and alcohol testing. Random drug and alcohol

---

[60] *O'Connor v Ortega*, 480 US 709 (1987).
[61] *Ortega v O'Connor*, 146 F3d 1149 (9th Cir 1998).
[62] *Kmart Corp. v Trotti*, 677 SW2d 632 (Tex App 1984).
[63] *See Kline v Security Guards, Inc.*, 386 F3d 246 (3rd Cir 2004). Some 370 employees of Dana Corporation's Reading, Pennsylvania, facility sued the corporation and its security guard company after employees learned that a new audio and video surveillance system at the entrance of the facility allowed what was said in the area where employees "punch in" for work to be observed and heard in the guard booth. The Third Circuit Court of Appeals rejected the employer's preemption claims and remanded the matter to the state court to handle the invasion of privacy and other tort claims.
[64] PL 102-143, 105 Stat 952, 49 USC § 1301 nt.

testing of employees working in safety-sensitive positions in the private sector also is permissible, as is the testing of private-sector employees on the basis of reasonable suspicion.

H. EMPLOYER-RELATED IMMIGRATION LAWS

The Immigration and Naturalization Act (INA), the Immigration Reform and Control Act of 1986 (IRCA), and the Immigration Act of 1990[65] are the principal employer-related immigration laws. Administration of these laws was formerly under the Immigration and Naturalization Service, and is now reorganized under the Department of Homeland Security as the United States Bureau of Citizenship and Immigration Services (USCIS).

32. Employer Liability

The IRCA sets criminal and civil penalties against employers who knowingly hire aliens who have illegally entered the United States. The IRCA was designed to stop illegal immigration by eliminating job opportunities for these aliens.

33. Employer Verification and Special Hiring Programs

Upon hiring a new employee, an employer must verify that the employee is legally entitled to work in the United States. Both the employer and the employee must fill out portions of Form I-9. Verification documents include a U.S. passport, a certificate of U.S. citizenship, or an Alien Registration Card ("green card"). In lieu of these documents, a state driver's license and a Social Security card are sufficient to prove eligibility to work. The Immigration Act of 1990 prohibits employers from demanding other documentation. Thus, if a prospective employee with a "foreign accent" offers a driver's license and Social Security card but the employer seeks a certificate of U.S. citizenship or a green card, the employer has committed an unfair immigration practice. The employer will be ordered to hire the individual and provide back pay.

H-1 classification visas allow aliens of "distinguished merit and ability" to enter and work in the United States on a temporary basis. These persons include architects, engineers, lawyers, physicians, and teachers. Temporary, foreign, high-tech, "highly skilled" workers are classified as H-1B visa employees. An annual cap of 65,000 visas is applied to the H-1B visa classification. The hiring employer must attest that it will not lay off an American employee 90 days before or after filing a petition to employ a foreign worker regarding any position to be filled by the foreign worker. H-1B professionals must be paid the higher of the actual or prevailing wage for each position in order to eliminate economic incentives to use this foreign workers program.

L-1 visas allow qualifying multinational businesses to make intracompany transfers of foreign persons to the United States when the individuals are employed

---

[65] PL 101-649, 8 USC § 1101.

in management or have "specialized knowledge." L-1 visas are good for up to seven years for executives and managers. "Specialized knowledge" personnel may stay for five years. There are no annual caps on the number of L-1 visas issued, and the employer is not required to attest that no American worker will be laid off. While the H-1B visa program requires employers to pay foreign workers the prevailing U.S. wage for a particular job, the L-1 visa has no such requirement.

The demand for the 65,000 H-1B visas far exceeded the supply in 2009 and prior years. Many technology companies are utilizing the L-1 visas as an alternative to the H-1B visas. However, U.S. Bureau of Citizenship and Immigration Services (USCIS), in compliance with the 1990 act, requires the transferee or his or her employer to demonstrate that the transferee's responsibilities are "primarily managerial." **For Example,** Brazilian corporation Granite Ebenezer established a U.S.-based affiliate, Brazil Quality Stones, Inc. (BQS), as a California corporation. Eugene dos Santos, a Brazilian citizen, served as President and CEO of both entities and owned 99 percent of the corporation's stock. Citizenship and Immigration Services determined that he was not entitled to an L-1 visa. Although BQS submitted an organizational chart with him at the top supervising five employees, only three had received pay during the quarter. The USCIS determined that BQS had not reached the level of development in which dos Santos could devote his primary attention to managerial duties as opposed to operational ones.[66]

MAKE THE CONNECTION

SUMMARY

The relationship of employer and employee is created by the agreement of the parties and is subject to the principles applicable to contracts. If the employment contract sets forth a specific duration, the employer cannot terminate the contract at an earlier date unless just cause exists. If no definite time period is set forth, the individual is an at-will employee. Under the employment-at-will doctrine, an employer can terminate the contract of an at-will employee at any time for any reason or for no reason. Courts in many jurisdictions, however, have carved out exceptions to this doctrine when the discharge violates public policy or is contrary to good faith and fair dealing in the employment relationship. The Fair Labor Standards Act regulates minimum wages, overtime hours, and child labor.

Under the National Labor Relations Act, employees have the right to form a union to obtain a collective bargaining contract or to refrain from organizational activities. The National Labor Relations Board conducts elections to determine whether employees in an appropriate bargaining unit desire to be represented by a

---

[66] *Brazil Quality Stones, Inc. v Chertoff*, 531 F3d 1063 (9th Cir 2008).

union. The NLRA prohibits employers' and unions' unfair labor practices and authorizes the NLRB to conduct proceedings to stop such practices. Economic strikes have limited reinstatement rights. Federal law sets forth democratic standards for the election of union offices.

The Employees Retirement Income Security Act (ERISA) protects employees' pensions by requiring (1) high standards of those administering the funds, (2) reasonable vesting of benefits, (3) adequate funding, and (4) an insurance program to guarantee payments of earned benefits.

Unemployment compensation benefits are paid to persons for a limited period of time if they are out of work through no fault of their own. Persons receiving unemployment compensation must be available for placement in a job similar in duties and comparable in rate of pay to the job they lost. Twelve-week maternity, paternity, and adoption leaves are available under the Family and Medical Leave Act. Employers and employees pay Social Security taxes to provide retirement benefits, disability benefits, life insurance benefits, and Medicare.

The Occupational Safety and Health Act provides for the (1) establishment of safety and health standards and (2) effective enforcement of these standards. Many states have enacted "right-to-know" laws, which require employers to inform their employees of any hazardous substances present in the workplace.

Workers' compensation laws provide for the prompt payment of compensation and medical benefits to persons injured in the course of employment without regard to fault. An injured employee's remedy is generally limited to the remedy provided by the workers' compensation statute. Most states also provide compensation to workers for occupational diseases.

The Bill of Rights is the source of public-sector employees' privacy rights. Private-sector employees may obtain limited privacy rights from statutes, case law, and collective bargaining agreements. Employers may monitor employee telephone calls, although once it is determined that the call is personal, the employer must stop listening or be in violation of the federal wiretap statute. The ordinary-course-of-business and consent exceptions to the Electronic Communications Privacy Act of 1986 (ECPA) give private employers a great deal of latitude to monitor employee e-mail. Notification to employees of employers' policies on searching lockers, desks, and offices reduces employees' expectations of privacy, and a search conducted in conformity with a known policy is generally not an invasion of privacy. Drug and alcohol testing is generally permissible if it is based on reasonable suspicion; random drug and alcohol testing may also be permissible in safety-sensitive positions.

Immigration laws prohibit the employment of aliens who have illegally entered the United States.

LEARNING OUTCOMES

After studying this chapter, you should be able to clearly explain:

A. THE EMPLOYMENT RELATIONSHIP

LO.1 Explain the contractual nature of the employment relationship

See the *FedEx* case in which the employment contract and the employee handbook both preserved the employer's at-will termination powers, p. 900.

LO.2 ▸ Explain how whistleblower protection under Sarbanes-Oxley is limited to conduct in violation of fraud or securities laws

See the example in which David Welch was *not* protected under SOX because he, as CFO, refused to sign an SEC quarterly report due to accounting irregularities that did not amount to fraud or a violation of securities laws, p. 901.

B. LABOR RELATIONS LAWS

LO.3 ▸ Explain how the National Labor Relations Act prohibits employers from firing employees attempting to form a union, and requires employers to bargain with unions in good faith over wages, hours, and working conditions

See the *Sam Santillo* case on wrongful termination of an employee because of his union activity, p. 909.

See the discussion of mandatory and permissive subjects of bargaining, p. 910.

C. PENSION PLANS AND FEDERAL REGULATION

LO.4 ▸ Explain how ERISA protects employee pensions and benefits

See the Bell South example in which Ms. Lee successfully sued for disability benefits, p. 913.

D. UNEMPLOYMENT BENEFITS, FAMILY LEAVES, AND SOCIAL SECURITY

LO.5 ▸ Explain the essentials of unemployment benefits, family and medical leaves, military leaves, and social security benefits

E. EMPLOYEE HEALTH AND SAFETYS

LO.6 ▸ Explain how OSHA is designed to ensure workers safe and healthful working conditions

See the Thinking Things Through discussion for reasons why taking chances or shortcuts in violation of OSHA standards is bad management, p. 920.

F. COMPENSATION FOR EMPLOYEE INJURIES

LO.7 ▸ Explain the three types of benefits provided by Workers' Compensation statutes

G. EMPLOYEE PRIVACY

LO.8 ▸ Explain the sources of privacy rights, and applications to telephone, e-mail, text-messaging, and property searches

H. EMPLOYER-RELATED IMMIGRATION LAWS

LO.9 ▸ Explain an employer's verification obligations when hiring new employees and discuss special hiring programs allowing aliens to work in the U.S.

See the Brazilian Quality Stones example of a CEO who did not meet his burden of proof that his responsibilities were "primarily managerial," p. 927.

KEY TERMS

economic strikers	mass picketing	secondary picketing
employment-at-will doctrine	primary picketing	shop right
	right-to-work laws	

QUESTIONS AND CASE PROBLEMS

1. What remedies does an employee who has been wrongfully discharged have against an employer?

2. Michael Smyth was an operations manager at Pillsbury Co., and his employment status was that of an employee at will. Smyth received certain e-mail messages at home, and he replied to his supervisor by e-mail. His messages contained some provocative language including the phrase "kill the backstabbing bastards" and a reference to an upcoming company party as the "Jim Jones Koolaid affair." Later, Smyth was given two weeks' notice of his termination, and he was told that his e-mail remarks were inappropriate and unprofessional. Smyth believes that he is the victim of invasion of privacy because the e-mail messages caused his termination, and the company had promised that e-mail communications would not be intercepted and used as a basis for discipline or discharge. The company denies that it intercepted the e-mail messages and points out that Smyth himself sent the unprofessional comments to his supervisor. Is Smyth entitled to reinstatement and back pay because of the invasion of privacy? [*Smyth v Pillsbury Co.*, 914 F Supp 97 (ED Pa)]

3. Michael Hauck claimed that he was discharged by his employer, Sabine Pilot Service, because he refused its direction to perform the illegal act of pumping the bilges of the employer's vessel into the waterways. Hauck was an employee at will, and Sabine contends that it therefore had the right to discharge him without having to show cause. Hauck brought a wrongful discharge action against Sabine. Decide. [*Sabine Pilot Service, Inc., v Hauck*, 687 SW2d 733 (Tex)]

4. Jeanne Eenkhoorn worked as a supervisor at a business office for the New York Telephone Co. While at work, she invented a process for terminating the telephone services of delinquent subscribers. The telephone company used the process but refused to compensate her for it, claiming a shop right. Eenkhoorn then sued for damages on a quasi-contract theory. Decide. [*Eenkhoorn v New York Telephone Co.*, 568 NYS2d 677]

5. One Monday, a labor organization affiliated with the International Ladies Garment Workers Union began an organizational drive among the employees of Whittal & Son. On the following Monday, six of the employees who were participating in the union drive were discharged. Immediately after the firings, the head of the company gave a speech to the remaining workers in which he made a variety of antiunion statements and threats. The union filed a complaint with the NLRB, alleging that the six employees were fired because they were engaging in organizational activity and were thus discharged in violation of the NLRA. The employer defended its position, arguing that it had a business to run and that it was barely able to survive in the global economy against cheap labor from third-world countries. It asserted that the last thing it needed was "union baloney." Was the NLRA violated?

6. David Stark submitted an application to the maintenance department of Wyman-Gordon Co. Stark was a journeyman millwright with nine years' experience at a neighboring company at the time of his application to

Wyman-Gordon. Stark was vice president of the local industrial workers' union. In his preliminary interview with the company, Ms. Peevler asked if Stark was involved in union activity, and Stark detailed his involvement to her. She informed Stark that Wyman-Gordon was a nonunion shop and asked how he felt about this. Peevler's notes from the interview characterize Stark's response to this question as "seems to lean toward third-party intervention." Company officials testified that Stark's qualifications were "exactly what we were looking for," but he was not hired. Stark claimed that he was discriminated against. Wyman-Gordon denied that any discrimination had occurred. Is a job applicant (as opposed to an employee) entitled to protection from antiunion discrimination? On the facts of this case, has any discrimination taken place? [*Wyman-Gordon Co. v NLRB*, 108 LRRM 2085 (1st Cir)]

7. Armenda Malone and Stephen Krantz were induced to leave other employment and join ABI's CD-Rom division as national account managers in part because of a favorable commission agreement at ABI. Their employment relationship with ABI had no set duration, and as such they were employees at will. For the first two quarters of their employment, their commission reports were approved by the president of the division and paid without incident. Thereafter, a new management team took over the division. When the mid-level manager presented third quarter commission reports based on the prior practice to the new vice president, Bruce Lowry, for approval, he was told, "You got to learn how to f— these people." Lowry then utilized severable variables—some of which the mid-level manager found "ridiculous"—to reduce the commission figures. After much discourse that carried on well into the fourth quarter, Lowry announced that a new model for determining commissions would be implemented. Commissions for both the third and fourth quarters, ending in December, were then calculated based on this model. ABI asserts that because Malone and Krantz were employees at will, the employer had the right to interpret or alter how it pays employees as it sees fit. Krantz and Malone left ABI and have sued for what they believe are the full commissions earned in the third and fourth quarters. Present a legal theory on behalf of Malone and Krantz for the payment of back commissions. Assess the strengths and weaknesses of Lowry's approach to employee relations. How would you decide this case? [*Malone v American Business Information, Inc.*, 647 NW2d 569 (Neb)]

8. Jane Richards was employed as the sole crane operator of Gale Corp. and held the part-time union position of shop steward for the plant. On May 15, Richards complained to OSHA concerning what she contended were seven existing violations of the Occupational Safety and Health Act that were brought to her attention by members of the bargaining unit. On May 21, she stated to the company's general manager at a negotiating session: "If we don't have a new contract by the time the present one expires on June 15, we will strike." On May 22, an OSHA inspector arrived at the plant, and Richards told her supervisor, "I blew the whistle." On May 23, the company rented and later purchased two large electric forklifts that were used to do the work previously performed by the crane, and the crane operator's job was abolished. Under the existing collective bargaining contract, the company had the right to lay off for

lack of work. The contract also provided for arbitration, and it prohibited discipline or discharge without "just cause." On May 23, Richards was notified that she was being laid off "for lack of work" within her classification of crane operator. She was also advised that the company was not planning on using the crane in the future and that, if she were smart, she would get another job. Richards claimed that her layoff violated the National Labor Relations Act, the Occupational Safety and Health Act, and the collective bargaining agreement. Was she correct?

9. Virgil Deemer and Thomas Cornwell, employees at a Whirlpool Corporation plant, refused to comply with a supervisor's order that they perform maintenance work on certain mesh screens located some 20 feet above the plant floor. Twelve days before a fellow employee had fallen to his death from the screens. Because they refused to do the work assigned them, they were told to punch out and go home; reprimands were placed in their files. Should employees be able to pick and choose what work they will perform? Do Deemer and Cornwell have any recourse? [*Whirlpool v Marshall*, 445 US 1]

10. In May, the nurses union at Waterbury Hospital went on strike, and the hospital was shut down. In mid-June, the hospital began hiring replacements and gradually opened many units. To induce nurses to take employment during the strike, the hospital guaranteed replacement nurses their choice of positions and shifts. If a preferred position was in a unit that was not open at that time, the hospital guaranteed that the individual would be placed in that position at the end of the strike. The strike ended in October and as the striking workers returned to work, the hospital began opening units that had been closed during the strike. It staffed many of these positions with replacement nurses. The nurses who had the positions prior to the strike and were waiting to return to work believed that they should have been called to fill these positions rather than the junior replacements who had held other positions during the strike. Decide. [*Waterbury Hospital v NLRB*, 950 F2d 849 (2d Cir)]

11. Buffo was employed by the Baltimore & Ohio Railroad. Along with a number of other workers, he was removing old brakes from railroad cars and replacing them with new brakes. In the course of the work, rivet heads and scrap from the brakes accumulated on the tracks under the cars. This debris was removed only occasionally when the workers had time. Buffo, while holding an air hammer in both arms, was crawling under a car when his foot slipped on scrap on the ground, causing him to strike and injure his knee. He sued the railroad for damages under the Federal Employers Liability Act. Decide. [*Buffo v Baltimore & Ohio Railroad Co.*, 72 A2d 593 (Pa)]

12. Mark Phipps was employed as a cashier at a Clark gas station. A customer drove into the station and asked him to pump leaded gasoline into her 1976 Chevrolet, an automobile equipped to receive only unleaded gasoline. The station manager told Phipps to comply with the request, but he refused, believing that his dispensing leaded gasoline into the gas tank was a violation of law. Phipps stated that he was willing to pump unleaded gas into the tank, but the manager immediately fired him. Phipps sued Clark for wrongful

termination. Clark contended that it was free to terminate Phipps, an employee at will, for any reason or no reason. Decide. [*Phipps v Clark Oil & Refining Corp.*, 396 NW2d 588 (Minn App)]

13. Reno, Nevada, police officers John Bohach and Jon Catalano communicated with each other on the Alphapage computer system, typing messages on a keyboard and sending them to each other by use of a "send" key. The computer dials a commercial paging company, which receives the message by modem, and the message is then sent to the person paged by radio broadcast. When the system was installed, the police chief warned that every Alphapage message was logged on the network, and he barred messages that were critical of department policy or discriminatory. The two police officers sought to block a department investigation into their messages and prevent disclosure of the messages' content. They claimed that the messages should be treated the same as telephone calls under federal wiretap law. The department contended that the system was essentially a form of e-mail whose messages are by definition stored in a computer, and the storage was itself not part of the communication. Was the federal wiretap law violated? [*Bohach v City of Reno*, 932 F Supp 1232 (D Nev)]

14. Michael Kittell was employed at Vermont Weatherboard. While operating a saw at the plant, Kittell was seriously injured when a splinter flew into his eye and penetrated his head. Kittell sued Vermont Weatherboard, seeking damages under a common law theory. His complaint alleged that he suffered severe injuries solely because of the employer's wanton and willful acts and omissions. The complaint stated that he was an inexperienced worker, put to work without instructions or warning on a saw from which the employer had stripped away all safety devices. Vermont Weatherboard made a motion to dismiss the complaint on the ground that the Workers' Compensation Act provided the exclusive remedy for his injury. Decide. [*Kittell v Vermont Weatherboard, Inc.*, 417 A2d 926 (Vt)]

Chapter 40

EQUAL EMPLOYMENT OPPORTUNITY LAW

L aws of the United States reflect our society's concern that all Americans, including minorities, women, and persons with disabilities, have equal employment opportunities and that the workplace is free from discrimination and harassment. Title VII of the Civil Rights Act of 1964, as amended in 1972, 1978, and 1991, is the principal law regulating equal employment opportunities in the United States. Other federal laws require equal pay for men and women doing substantially the same work and forbid discrimination because of age or disability.

CPA A. Title VII of the Civil Rights Act of 1964, as Amended

Title VII of the Civil Rights Act of 1964[1] seeks to eliminate employer and union practices that discriminate against employees and job applicants on the basis of race, color, religion, sex, or national origin. The law applies to the hiring process and to discipline, discharge, promotion, and benefits.

1. Theories of Discrimination

The Supreme Court has created, and the Civil Rights Act of 1991 has codified, two principal legal theories under which a plaintiff may prove a case of unlawful employment discrimination: disparate treatment and disparate impact.

A *disparate treatment* claim exists where an employer treats some individuals less favorably than others because of their race, color, religion, sex, or national origin. Proof of the employer's discriminatory motive is essential in a disparate treatment case.[2]

Disparate impact exists when an employer's facially neutral employment practices, such as hiring or promotion examinations, although neutrally applied and making no adverse reference to race, color, religion, sex, or national origin, have a significantly adverse or disparate impact on a protected group. In addition, the employment practice in question is not shown by the employer to be job related and consistent with business necessity. Under the disparate impact theory, it is not a defense for an employer to demonstrate that it did not intend to discriminate.

For Example, if plant manager Jones is heard telling the personnel director that the vacant welder's position should be filled by a male because "this is man's work," a qualified female applicant turned down for the job would prevail in a *disparate treatment* theory case against the employer because she was not hired because of her gender. Necessary evidence of the employer's discriminatory motive would be satisfied by testimony about the manager's "this is man's work" statement.

If the policy for hiring new pilots at Generic Airlines, Inc., required a minimum height of 5 feet 7 inches, and no adverse reference to gender was stated in this employment policy, nevertheless, the 5-feet-7-inch minimum height policy has an

---

[1] 42 USC § 2000(e) *et seq.*
[2] *Woodson v Scott Paper Co.,* 109 F3d 913 (3d Cir 1997).

adverse or disparate impact on women because far fewer women than men reach this height. Such an employment policy would be set aside on a *disparate impact* theory, and a minimum height for the position would be established by the court based on evidence of job-relatedness and business necessity. A 5-feet-5-inch height requirement was set by one court for pilots.

C A S E   S U M M A R Y

Number 1 on the Charts! The Case That Created the Disparate Impact Theory

FACTS: Griggs and other black employees of the Duke Power Company's Dan River Station challenged Duke Power's require-ment of a high school diploma and passing standardized general intelligence tests for transfer to more desirable "inside" jobs. The district court and Court of Appeals found no violation of Title VII because the employer did not adopt the diploma and test requirements with the purpose of intentionally discriminating against black employees. The Supreme Court granted *certiorari*.

DECISION: Judgment for Griggs. The absence of any intent on the part of the employer to discriminate was not a defense. Title VII prohibits not only overt discrimination but also practices that are fair in form but discriminatory in operation. If any employment practice, such as a diploma or testing requirement, that operates to exclude minorities at a substantially higher rate than white applicants cannot be shown to be "job-related" and consistent with "business necessity," the practice is prohibited. [**Griggs v Duke Power Co., 401 US 424 (1971)**]

"Disparate treatment" and "disparate impact" may both be at issue in the same case. **For Example,** as required by the city charter, the city of New Haven used objective examinations to identify those firefighters best qualified for promotion to fill vacant lieutenant and captain positions. On the basis of the examinations' results, no black candidates were eligible for immediate promotion. A rancorous public debate ensued. The city threw out the results based on the statistical racial disparity to avoid potential liability in a lawsuit based on *disparate impact* against the black candidates. White and Hispanic firefighters who passed the exams but were denied a chance for promotion by the city's refusal to certify the test results, sued the city, alleging a *disparate treatment* (intentional discrimination) case—that discarding the test results discriminated against them based on their race in violation of Title VII. The Supreme Court determined that the city rejected the test results because the higher-scoring candidates were white and that without some other justification this express race-based decision making is prohibited. The Court stated that "a strong basis in evidence" standard was necessary before the city could make an employment decision based on fear of liability under Title VII—and the Court held that the city did not meet this standard. The statistical disparity by itself was insufficient to constitute a strong basis in evidence of unlawful disparate impact. The examinations were job related and consistent with business necessity. And there was no strong basis in evidence of an equally valid, less-discriminating testing alternative. Thus, in a 5-4 decision, the U.S. Supreme Court ruled that the city had violated the civil rights of the white and Hispanic firefighters and remanded the case for further proceedings.[3]

2. The Equal Employment Opportunity Commission

The Equal Employment Opportunity Commission (EEOC) is a five-member body appointed by the president to establish equal employment opportunity policy under the laws it administers. The EEOC supervises the agency's conciliation and enforcement efforts.

The EEOC administers Title VII of the Civil Rights Act, the Equal Pay Act (EPA), the Age Discrimination in Employment Act (ADEA), section 501 of the Rehabilitation Act (which prohibits federal-sector discrimination against persons with disabilities), and Title I (the employment provisions) of the Americans with Disabilities Act (ADA).

(A) PROCEDURE. Where a state or local EEO agency with the power to act on claims of discriminatory practices exists, the charging party must file a complaint with that agency. The charging party must wait 60 days or until the termination of the state proceedings, whichever occurs first, before filing a charge with the EEOC. If no state or local agency exists, a charge may be filed directly with the EEOC so long as it is filed within 180 days of the occurrence of the discriminatory act. The commission conducts an investigation to determine whether reasonable cause exists to believe that the charge is true. If such cause is found to exist, the EEOC attempts to remedy the unlawful practice through conciliation. If the EEOC does not resolve the matter to the satisfaction of the parties, it may decide to litigate the case when systemic or unusual circumstances exist, including a "pattern or practice of discrimination." In most instances, however, the EEOC issues the charging party a *right-to-sue letter.* Thereafter, the individual claiming a violation of EEO law has 90 days to file a lawsuit in a federal district court.[4]

(B) DAMAGES. Title VII sets damages available to victims of discrimination (see Figure 40.1).

(C) THE ARBITRATION OPTION. With the exception of transportation employees, employers can craft arbitration agreements that require employees to arbitrate any employment dispute, including statutory discrimination claims, and these mandatory arbitration clauses can be enforced in federal courts under the Federal Arbitration Act.[5] Courts do, however, require that the arbitration clauses be "fair."

---

[3] *Ricci v DeStefano*, 129 SCt 2658 (2009). Contrary to the extensive presentation in the majority decision of the detailed steps taken to develop and administer the examinations, the dissent asserted that the Court had ignored substantial evidence of multiple flaws in the tests and that the Court had failed to acknowledge that better tests used in other cities have yielded less racially skewed outcomes. The decision, the dissent, and two concurrences provide an insight into the complexities of our judicial process.

[4] An individual who misses the filing deadline of Title VII may be able to bring a race discrimination case under the two-year time limit allowed under section 1981 of the Civil Rights Act of 1964, codified at 42 USC § 1981, and sometimes called a *section 1981 lawsuit.* In the *Edelman v Lynchburg College decision,* 535 US 106 (2002), the U.S. Supreme Court approved an EEOC regulation that allows certain defective charges to be cured, with the cured charge relating back to the date the EEOC first received the initial charge, which was within the 300-day filing period.

[5] *Circuit City Stores, Inc. v Adams,* 532 US 105 (2001).

Moreover, a party agreeing to arbitration does not forgo substantive rights afforded by Title VII or alter federal antidiscrimination statutes. A fair arbitration clause requires adequate discovery, mandates that the arbitrator have authority to apply the same types of relief available from a court, and should not preclude an employee from vindicating statutory rights because of arbitration costs.[6]

A union may negotiate a provision in a collective bargaining agreement requiring all employment-related discrimination claims to be resolved in arbitration.[7]

B. Protected Classes and Exceptions

To successfully pursue a Title VII lawsuit, an individual must belong to a protected class and meet the appropriate burden of proof. Exceptions exist for certain employment practices.

3. Race and Color

The legislative history of Title VII of the Civil Rights Act demonstrates that a primary purpose of the act is to provide fair employment opportunities for black Americans. The protections of the act are applied to blacks based on race or color.

The word *race* as used in the act applies to all members of the four major racial groupings: white, black, Native American, and Asian-Pacific. Native Americans can file charges and receive the protection of the act on the basis of national origin, race, or, in some instances, color. Individuals of Asian-Pacific origin may file discrimination charges based on race, color, or, in some instances, national origin. Whites are also protected against discrimination because of race and color.

For Example, two white professors at a predominately black university were successful in discrimination suits against the university when it was held that the university had discriminated against them on the basis of race and color in tenure decisions.[8]

4. Religion

Title VII requires employers to accommodate their employees' or prospective employees' religious practices. Most cases involving allegations of religious

---

[6] See *Circuit City II*, 279 F3d 889 (9th Cir 2002).

[7] For some 35 years it was widely understood that an individual may prospectively waive his or her own statutory right to a judicial forum and be compelled to resolve a statutory discrimination claim in arbitration, but a union may not prospectively waive that right for the individual in a collective bargaining agreement. [See *Alexander v Gardner-Denver Co.*, 485 US 36 (1974) and *Gilmer v Interstate/Johnson Lane Corp.*, 500 US 20 (1991)]. In *14 Penn Plaza, LLC v Pyett*, 129 S Ct 1456 (2009), the U.S. Supreme Court, in a 5-4 decision, held that a provision in a collective bargaining agreement (CBA) negotiated under the National Labor Relations Act between a union and employer group that requires union members to arbitrate Age Discrimination in Employment Act (ADEA) claims is enforceable as a matter of federal law. Thus, the petitioner union members were precluded from bringing their ADEA case in federal court and the matter had to be resolved under the arbitration provisions of the CBA.

[8] *Turgeon v Howard University*, 571 F Supp 679 (DDC 1983).

FIGURE 40-1 | *Unlawful Discrimination under Title VII of the Civil Rights Act of 1964 as Amended by the Civil Rights Act of 1991*

DISCRIMINATORY TREATMENT IN EMPLOYMENT DECISIONS ON THE BASIS OF RACE, COLOR, RELIGION, SEX, OR NATIONAL ORIGIN	
DISPARATE TREATMENT THEORY	**DISPARATE IMPACT THEORY**
NONNEUTRAL PRACTICE OR NONNEUTRAL APPLICATION	FACIALLY NEUTRAL PRACTICE AND NEUTRAL APPLICATION
REQUIRES PROOF OF DISCRIMINATORY INTENT	DOES NOT REQUIRE PROOF OF DISCRIMINATORY INTENT REQUIRES PROOF OF ADVERSE EFFECT ON PROTECTED GROUP AND EMPLOYER IS UNABLE TO SHOW THAT THE CHALLENGED PRACTICE IS JOB RELATED FOR THE POSITION IN QUESTION AND IS CONSISTENT WITH BUSINESS NECESSITY
EITHER PARTY HAS A RIGHT TO REQUIRE A JURY TRIAL WHEN SEEKING COMPENSATORY OR PUNITIVE DAMAGES	NO RIGHT TO A JURY TRIAL
REMEDY REINSTATEMENT, HIRING, OR PROMOTION BACK PAY LESS INTERIM EARNINGS RETROACTIVE SENIORITY ATTORNEY AND EXPERT WITNESS FEES PLUS COMPENSATORY* AND PUNITIVE DAMAGES DAMAGES CAPPED FOR CASES OF SEX AND RELIGIOUS DISCRIMINATION DEPENDING ON SIZE OF EMPLOYER:	**REMEDY** REINSTATEMENT, HIRING, OR PROMOTION BACK PAY LESS INTERIM EARNINGS RETROACTIVE SENIORITY ATTORNEY AND EXPERT WITNESS FEES

NUMBER OF EMPLOYEES	DAMAGES CAP
100 OR FEWER	$ 50,000
101 TO 200	100,000
201 TO 500	200,000
OVER 500	300,000
NO CAP ON DAMAGES FOR RACE CASES	

* COMPENSATORY DAMAGES INCLUDE FUTURE PECUNIARY LOSSES AND NONPECUNIARY LOSSES SUCH AS EMOTIONAL PAIN AND SUFFERING.

discrimination revolve around the determination of whether an employer has made reasonable efforts to accommodate religious beliefs.

If an employee's religious beliefs prohibit working on Saturday, an employer's obligation under Title VII is to try to find a volunteer to cover for the employee on Saturdays. The employer would not have an obligation to violate a seniority provision of a collective bargaining agreement or call in a substitute worker if such accommodation would require more than a *de minimis* or very small cost.

Many employers have work rules or grooming policies for employees who provide service to customers on behalf of the employers. Employees have challenged employer bans on body art as religious discrimination, asserting that the employers have not made reasonable efforts to accommodate religious beliefs. EEOC's 1980 Guidelines broadly define religion "to include moral or ethical beliefs as to what is right and wrong which are sincerely held with the strength of traditional religious views."[9] The Guidelines do not limit religion to theistic practices or to beliefs professed by organized religions. **For Example,** Kimberly Cloutier was a member of the Church of Body Modification. Costco's grooming policy prohibited any "visible facial or tongue jewelry" in order to present a professional image to its customers. Ms. Cloutier wore an eyebrow ring as a religious practice. Ms. Cloutier rejected Costco's offer to return her to work if she wore a bandage or plastic retainer over the jewelry because it would violate her religious beliefs. The U.S. Court of Appeals determined that her refusal to accept an accommodation short of an exemption was an undue hardship for the employer because an exemption would negatively impact the company's policy of professionalism.[10]

Some courts, however, look for actual proof of harm to the employer in assessing whether undue hardship exists for an employer. **For Example,** the EEOC brought an action against Red Robin Gourmet Burgers, Inc., for failure to provide an exemption from its grooming policy for an employee's religious tattoos surrounding his wrists. The federal district court looked for actual proof of the restaurant's assertion that the tattoos contravened the company's "family-oriented image," such as customer complaints or other evidence, as opposed to the mere assertion. The court concluded that the employer failed to provide sufficient evidence of undue hardship in accommodating an exemption for the employee.[11]

Title VII permits religious societies to grant hiring preferences in favor of members of their religion. It also provides an exemption for educational institutions to hire employees of a particular religion if the institution is owned, controlled, or managed by a particular religious society. The exemption is a broad one and is not restricted to the religious activities of the institution.

5. Sex

Employers who discriminate against female or male employees because of their sex are held to be in violation of Title VII. The EEOC and the courts have determined that the word *sex* as used in Title VII means a person's gender, not the person's sexual orientation. State and local legislation, however, may provide specific protection against discrimination based on sexual orientation.

---

[9] 29 CFR § 1605.1 (1980). The EEOC's definition of religion was derived from early Selective Service cases that moved beyond institutional religions and theistic belief structures in handling exemptions to the draft and military service. See *Welsh v U.S.*, 398 US 333, 343-44 (1970), which allows for expansion of belief systems to include nonreligious ethical or moral codes.

[10] *Cloutier v Costco*, 390 F3d 126 (1st Cir 2004).

[11] *EEOC v Red Robin Gourmet Burger, Inc.*, Not Reported in F Supp 2d, 2005 WL 2090677 (WD Wash).

(A) **Height, Weight, and Physical Ability Requirements.** Under the *Griggs v Duke Power* precedent, an employer must be able to show that criteria used to make an employment decision that has a disparate impact on women, such as minimum height and weight requirements, are in fact job related. All candidates for a position requiring physical strength must be given an opportunity to demonstrate their capability to perform the work. Women cannot be precluded from consideration just because they have not traditionally performed such work.

(B) **Pregnancy-Related Benefits.** Title VII was amended by the Pregnancy Discrimination Act (PDA) in 1978. The amendment prevents employers from treating pregnancy, childbirth, and related medical conditions in a manner different from the manner in which other medical conditions are treated. Thus, women unable to work as a result of pregnancy, childbirth, or related medical conditions must be provided the same benefits as all other workers. These include temporary and long-term disability insurance, sick leave, and other forms of employee benefit programs. An employer who does not provide disability benefits or paid sick leave to other employees is not required to provide them for pregnant workers.[12]

6. Sexual Harassment

Tangible employment action and hostile work environment are two classifications of sexual harassment.

(A) **Tangible Employment Action.** Sexual harassment classified as *tangible employment action* involves situations in which a supervisor performs an "official act" of the enterprise, such as discharge, demotion, or undesirable reassignment against a subordinate employee because of the employee's refusal to submit to the supervisor's demand for sexual favors. The employer is always vicariously liable for this harassment by a supervisor under the so-called aided-in-the-agency-relation standard. That is, the supervisor is aided in accomplishing the wrongful objective by the existence of the agency relationship. The employer empowered the supervisor as a distinct class of agent to make economic decisions affecting other employees under the supervisor's control. The employer can raise no affirmative defense based on the presence of an employer's antiharassment policy in such a case.

(B) **Hostile Work Environment.** A second type of sexual harassment classified as *hostile work environment* occurs when a supervisor's conduct does not affect an employee's economic benefits but causes anxiety and "poisons" the work

---

[12] In *AT&T Corporation v Hulteen*, 129 SCt 1962 (2009), the U.S. Supreme Court addressed a current effect of a pre-PDA personnel policy. Prior to the PDA of 1978, AT&T employees on "disability" leave received full-service credit towards retirement benefits for the entire period of absence. Pregnancy at that time was considered a "personal" leave of absence and women on this leave received a maximum service credit of 30 days. Upon retirement, Noreen Hulteen received seven months less service credit for the pre-PDA leave for a pregnancy than she would have had for the same leave time for a disability, and it resulted in a smaller pension benefit. The Court decided against Ms. Hulteen, determining that there was no intent to apply the PDA retroactively, and that AT&T's pre-PDA leave policy was not discriminatory when adopted.

environment for the employee. Such conduct may include unwelcome sexual flirtation, propositions, or other abuses of a sexual nature, including the use of degrading words or the display of sexually explicit pictures.[13] This type of sexual harassment applies to all cases involving supervisors in which the enterprise takes no official act, including constructive discharge cases. The plaintiff must prove severe and pervasive conduct on the supervisor's part to meet the plaintiff's burden of proof.[14] The employer may raise an affirmative defense to liability for damages by proving that (1) it exercised reasonable care to prevent and promptly correct any sexually harassing behavior at its workplace and (2) the plaintiff employee unreasonably failed to take advantage of corrective opportunities provided by the employer. The existence of an employer's sexual harassment policy and notification procedures (see Figure 40.2) will aid the employer in proving the affirmative defense in hostile working environment cases.

(C) RATIONALE. The "primary objective of Title VII, like that of any statute meant to influence primary conduct, is not to provide redress but to avoid harm."[15] When there is no "official act" of the employer, the employer may raise an affirmative defense. This approach fosters the preventative aspect of Title VII, encouraging employers to exercise reasonable care to prevent and correct sexual harassment while providing damages only when the conduct is clearly attributed to an official action of the enterprise or when the employer has not exercised reasonable care to prevent and correct misconduct. **For Example,** Kim Ellerth alleged that she was subject to constant sexual harassment by her supervisor, Ted Slowik, at Burlington Industries. Slowik made comments about her breasts, told her to "loosen up," and warned, "You know, Kim, I could make your life very hard or very easy at Burlington." When Kim was being considered for promotion, Slowik expressed reservations that she was not "loose enough" and then reached over and rubbed her knee. She received the promotion, however. After other such incidents, she quit and filed charges alleging that she was constructively discharged because of the unendurable working conditions resulting from the hostile work environment created by Slowik. She did not use Burlington's sexual harassment internal complaint procedures. Because she was not a victim of a tangible employment action involving an official act of the enterprise, because she received the promotion sought, the employer will be able to raise an affirmative defense. She will be able to prove severe and pervasive conduct on the part of a supervisor under a hostile work environment theory. However, the employer may defeat liability by proving both that it exercised reasonable care to prevent

---

[13] According to EEOC Guidelines § 1604.11(f), unwelcome sexual advances, requests for sexual favors, and other verbal or physical conduct of a sexual nature constitute sexual harassment when (1) submission to or rejection of such conduct has the purpose or effect of unreasonably interfering with an individual's work performance or creating an intimidating, hostile, or offensive working environment.

[14] *Oncale v Sundowner Offshore Services, Inc.*, 523 US 75 (1998). The Supreme Court stated in *Oncale* that it did not intend to turn Title VII into a civility code, and the Court set forth the standard for judging whether the conduct in question amounted to sexual harassment requiring that the conduct be judged from the perspective of a reasonable person in the plaintiff's position, considering all circumstances. The Court warned that "common sense" and "context" must apply in determining whether the conduct was hostile or abusive.

[15] *Faragher v City of Boca Raton*, 524 US 775 at 805, citing *Albemale Paper Co. v Moody*, 422 US 405, 418 (1975).

FIGURE 40-2 | *Employer Procedure—Sexual Harassment*

A. DEVELOP AND IMPLEMENT AN EQUAL EMPLOYMENT POLICY THAT SPECIFICALLY PROHIBITS SEXUAL HARASSMENT AND IMPOSES DISCIPLINE UP TO AND INCLUDING DISCHARGE. SET FORTH SPECIFIC EXAMPLES OF CONDUCT THAT WILL NOT BE TOLERATED SUCH AS;

- UNWELCOME SEXUAL ADVANCES, WHETHER OR NOT THEY INVOLVE PHYSICAL TOUCHING

- SEXUAL EPITHETS AND JOKES; WRITTEN OR ORAL REFERENCES TO SEXUAL CONDUCT; GOSSIP REGARDING ONE'S SEX LIFE; COMMENTS ON AN INDIVIDUAL'S BODY; AND COMMENTS ABOUT AN INDIVIDUAL'S SEXUAL ACTIVITY, DEFICIENCIES, OR PROWESS

- DISPLAY OF SEXUALLY SUGGESTIVE OBJECTS, PICTURES, AND CARTOONS

- UNWELCOME LEERING, WHISTLING, BRUSHING AGAINST THE BODY, SEXUAL GESTURES, AND SUGGESTIVE OR INSULTING COMMENTS

- INQUIRIES INTO ONE'S SEXUAL EXPERIENCES

- DISCUSSION OF ONE'S SEXUAL ACTIVITIES

B. ESTABLISH ONGOING EDUCATIONAL PROGRAMS, INCLUDING ROLE-PLAYING AND FILMS TO DEMONSTRATE UNACCEPTABLE BEHAVIOR.

C. DESIGNATE A RESPONSIBLE SENIOR OFFICIAL TO WHOM COMPLAINTS OF SEXUAL HARASSMENT CAN BE MADE. AVOID ANY PROCEDURE THAT REQUIRES AN EMPLOYEE TO FIRST COMPLAIN TO THE EMPLOYEE'S SUPERVISOR, BECAUSE THAT INDIVIDUAL MAY BE THE OFFENDING PERSON. MAKE CERTAIN COMPLAINANTS KNOW THAT THERE WILL BE NO RETALIATION FOR FILING A COMPLAINT.

D. INVESTIGATE ALL COMPLAINTS PROMPTLY AND THOROUGHLY.

E. KEEP COMPLAINTS AND INVESTIGATIONS AS CONFIDENTIAL AS POSSIBLE AND LIMIT ALL INFORMATION TO ONLY THOSE WHO NEED TO KNOW.

F. IF A COMPLAINT HAS MERIT, IMPOSE APPROPRIATE AND CONSISTENT DISCIPLINE.

and correct sexual harassing behavior through its internal company complaint policies and that Kim unreasonably failed to take advantage of the company procedures.[16]

(D) NONSUPERVISORS. An employer is liable for the sexual harassment caused its employees by coworkers or customers only when it knew or should have known of the misconduct and failed to take prompt remedial action.

---

[16] *Burlington Industries, Inc. v Ellerth*, 524 US 742 (1998); see also *Faragher v City of Boca Raton*, 524 US 775 (1998). In *Pennsylvania v Suders*, 542 US 129 (2004), the U.S. Supreme Court reviewed a decision of the Third Circuit Court of Appeals that held that a "constructive discharge," if proved, constituted a "tangible employment action" that renders the employer liable for damages and precludes an affirmative defense. The Supreme Court disagreed with the Third Circuit's reading of its *Ellerth/Faragher* decisions, and made it very clear that "an official act of the enterprise" is necessary for the plaintiff to defeat the employer's right to raise an affirmative defense.

7. Protection Against Retaliation

Section 704(a) of Title VII prohibits retaliation against an employee "because he [or she] has made a charge, testified, assisted or participated in any manner in an investigation, proceeding hearing under this subchapter." This antiretaliation provision prohibits employer actions that are "materially adverse" to a reasonable employee or applicant. The reference to "material adversity" is to separate significant harms that are prohibited by the act as opposed to trivial harms that are not actionable. As set forth in the *Burlington Northern Santa Fe Railroad Co. v White case*, a retaliation plaintiff must show that the challenged employer action "well might have dissuaded a reasonable worker from making or supporting a charge of discrimination."[17]

CASE SUMMARY

New Traction for the Antiretaliation Provisions Thanks to Track Laborer White

FACTS: BNSF Railway hired Shelia White as a track laborer at its Tennessee Yard. She was the only woman in the track department. When hired, she was given the job of operating forklifts as opposed to doing ordinary track labor tasks. Three months after being hired, she complained to the roadmaster that her foreman treated her differently than male employees and had twice made inappropriate remarks. The foreman was suspended without pay for 10 days and ordered to attend training on sexual harassment. Also at that time, the roadmaster reassigned the forklift duties to the former operator who was "senior" to White and assigned White to track labor duties. Six months into her employment, White refused to ride in a truck as directed by a different foreman, and she was suspended for insubordination. Thirty-seven days later, she was reinstated with full back pay, and the discipline was removed from her record. She filed a complaint with the EEOC, claiming that the reassignment to track laborer duties was unlawful gender discrimination and retaliation for her complaint about her treatment by the foreman. The 37-day suspension led to a second retaliation charge. A jury rejected her gender discrimination claim and awarded her compensatory damages for her retaliation claims. BNSF appealed, contending that Ms. White had been hired as a track laborer and it was not retaliatory to assign her to do the work she was hired to do. It also asserted that the 37-day suspension had been corrected and she had been made whole for her loss.

DECISION: Judgment for White. The Supreme Court held that the jury could reasonably conclude that the reassignment from forklift operator to track laborer duties would have been materially adverse to a reasonable employee, thus constituting retaliatory discrimination. Moreover, the Court held that an indefinite suspension without pay for a month, even if the employee later received back pay, could well act as a deterrent to filing a discrimination complaint. [**Burlington Northern Santa Fe Railway Co. v White, 548 US 133 (2006)**]

The EEOC takes the position that claims can be filed for retaliation not only under Title VII but also under the Americans with Disabilities Act, the Age Discrimination in Employment Act, and the Equal Pay Act.

---

[17] *Burlington Northern Santa Fe Railway Co. v White*, 548 US 133 (2006) 548 US 53.

8. National Origin

Title VII protects members of all nationalities from discrimination. The judicial principles that have emerged from cases involving race, color, and gender employment discrimination are generally applicable to cases involving allegations of discrimination related to national origin. Thus, physical standards, such as minimum height requirements, that tend to exclude persons of a particular national origin because of the physical stature of the group have been found unlawful when these standards cannot be justified by business necessity.

Adverse employment action based on an individual's lack of English language skills violates Title VII when the language requirement bears no demonstrable relationship to the successful performance of the job to which it is applied.

CASE SUMMARY

A Close Call

FACTS: Manuel Fragante applied for a clerk's job with the city and county of Honolulu. Although he placed high enough on a civil service eligibility list to be chosen for the position, he was not selected because of a perceived deficiency in oral communication skills caused by his "heavy Filipino accent." Fragante brought suit, alleging that the defendants had discriminated against him on the basis of his national origin in violation of Title VII of the Civil Rights Act.

DECISION: Judgment for the city and county of Honolulu. Accents and national origin are inextricably intertwined in many cases. Courts look carefully at nonselection decisions based on foreign accents because an employer may unlawfully discriminate against someone based on national origin by falsely stating that it was the individual's inability to measure up to the communication skills demanded of the job. Because the record showed that the ability to speak clearly was one of the most important skills required for the clerk's position and because the judge confirmed that Fragante was difficult to understand, the court dismissed his complaint.
[**Fragante v City and County of Honolulu, 888 F2d 591 (9th Cir 1989)**]

9. Title VII Exceptions

Section 703 of Title VII defines which employment activities are unlawful. This same section, however, also exempts several key practices from the scope of Title VII enforcement. The most important are the bona fide occupational qualification exception, the testing and educational requirement exception, and the seniority system exception.

(A) BONA FIDE OCCUPATIONAL QUALIFICATION EXCEPTION. It is not an unlawful employment practice for an employer to hire employees on the basis of religion, sex, or national origin in those certain instances where religion, sex, or national origin is a bona fide occupational qualification (BFOQ) reasonably necessary to the normal operation of a particular enterprise. **For Example,** a valid BFOQ is a men's clothing store's policy of hiring only males to do measurements for suit alterations. An airline's policy of hiring only female flight attendants is not a valid BFOQ because such a policy is not reasonably necessary to safely operate an airline.

CASE SUMMARY

It's a Woman's Choice

FACTS: Johnson Controls, Inc. (JCI), manufactures batteries. A primary ingredient in the battery-manufacturing process is lead. Occupational exposure to lead entails health risks, including the risk of harm to any fetus carried by a female employee. After eight of its employees became pregnant while maintaining blood lead levels exceeding those set by the Centers for Disease Control as dangerous for a worker planning to have a family, respondent JCI announced a policy barring all women, except those whose infertility was medically documented, from jobs involving lead exposure exceeding the OSHA standard. The United Auto Workers (UAW) brought a class action in the district court, claiming that the policy constituted sex discrimination violative of Title VII of the Civil Rights Act of 1964, as amended. The court granted summary judgment for JCI based on its BFOQ defense, and the Court of Appeals affirmed. The Supreme Court granted *certiorari*.

DECISION: Judgment for the UAW. JCI's fetal protection policy discriminated against women because the policy applied only to women and did not deal with the harmful effect of lead exposure on the male reproductive system. JCI's concerns about the welfare of the next generation do not suffice to establish a BFOQ of female sterility. Title VII, as amended, mandates that decisions about the welfare of future children be left to the parents who conceive, bear, support, and raise them rather than to the employers who hire those parents or to the courts. Moreover, an employer's tort liability for potential fetal injuries does not require a different result. If, under general tort principles, Title VII bans sex-specific fetal-protection policies, the employer fully informs the woman of the risk, and the employer has not acted negligently, the basis for holding an employer liable seems remote at best. [**UAW v Johnson Controls, Inc., 499 US 187 (1991)**]

(B) TESTING AND EDUCATIONAL REQUIREMENTS. Section 703(h) of the act authorizes the use of "any professionally developed ability test [that is not] designed, intended, or used to discriminate." Employment testing and educational requirements must be "job related"; that is, the employers must prove that the tests and educational requirements bear a relationship to job performance.

Courts will accept prior court-approved validation studies developed for a different employer in a different state or region so long as it is demonstrated that the job for which the test was initially validated is essentially the same job function for which the test is currently being used. **For Example,** a firefighters' test that has been validated in a study in California will be accepted as valid when later used in Virginia. Such application is called *validity generalization.*

The Civil Rights Act of 1991 makes it an unlawful employment practice for an employer to adjust scores or use different cutoff scores or otherwise alter the results of employment tests to favor any race, color, religion, sex, or national origin. This provision addresses the so-called race-norming issue, whereby the results of hiring and promotion tests are adjusted to ensure that a minimum number of minorities are included in application pools.

(c) SENIORITY SYSTEM. Section 703(h) provides that differences in employment terms based on a bona fide seniority system are sanctioned so long as the differences do not stem from an intention to discriminate. The term *seniority system is* generally understood to mean a set of rules that ensures that workers with longer years of continuous service for an employer will have a priority claim to a job over others with fewer years of service. Because such rules provide workers with considerable job security, organized labor has continually and successfully fought to secure seniority provisions in collective bargaining agreements.

10. Affirmative Action and Reverse Discrimination

Employers have an interest in affirmative action because it is fundamentally fair to have a diverse and representative workforce. Moreover, affirmative action is an effective means of avoiding litigation costs associated with discrimination cases while at the same time preserving management prerogatives and preserving rights to government contracts. Employers, under **affirmative action plans (AAPs)**, may undertake special recruiting and other efforts to hire and train minorities and women and help them advance within the company. However, the plan may also provide job preferences for minorities and women. Such aspects of affirmative action plans have resulted in numerous lawsuits contending that Title VII of the Civil Rights Act of 1964, the Fourteenth Amendment, or collective bargaining contracts have been violated. The Supreme Court has not been able to settle the many difficult issues before it with a clear and consistent majority. The Court has decided cases narrowly, with individual justices often feeling compelled to speak in concurring or dissenting opinions.

affirmative action plan (AAP) –plan to have a diverse and representative workforce.

(A) AFFIRMATIVE ACTION PROGRAMS. In its 1995 *Adarand Constructors, Inc. v Pena* [18] decision, the Supreme Court placed significant limits on the federal government's authority to implement programs favoring businesses owned by racial minorities over white-owned businesses. The decision reinstated a reverse discrimination challenge to a federal program designed to provide highway construction contracts to "disadvantaged" subcontractors in which race-based presumptions were used to identify such individuals. The Court found the program to be violative of the equal protection component of the Fifth Amendment's due process clause and announced a strict scrutiny standard for evaluating the racial classifications used in the federal government's Disadvantaged Business Enterprise (DBE) program. This standard can be satisfied only by narrowly tailored measures that further compelling governmental interests. The Court stated that programs based on disadvantage rather than race are subject only to the most relaxed judicial scrutiny. Six additional years of litigation ensued before the case involving Adarand Constructors, Inc., was finally concluded on procedural and jurisdictional grounds. *Adarand I*, as it is now

[18] 515 US 200 (1995).

called, is now the landmark Supreme Court decision setting forth the legal principles for evaluating affirmative action programs involving race and remedies.

Following the Court's *Adarand I* decision, the EEOC issued a statement on affirmative action, stating, in part:

> *Affirmative action is lawful only when it is designed to respond to a demonstrated and serious imbalance in the workforce, is flexible, is time limited, applies only to qualified workers, and respects the rights of nonminorities and men.*[19]

(B) REVERSE DISCRIMINATION. When an employer's AAP is not shown to be justified or "unnecessarily trammels" the interests of nonminority employees, it is often called *reverse discrimination.* **For Example,** a city's decision to rescore police promotional tests to achieve specific racial and gender percentages unnecessarily trammeled the interests of nonminority police officers.[20]

(C) EXECUTIVE ORDER. Presidential Executive Order 11246 regulates contractors and subcontractors doing business with the federal government. This order forbids discrimination against minorities and women and in certain situations requires affirmative action to be taken to offer better employment opportunities to minorities and women. The Secretary of Labor has established the Office of Federal Contract Compliance Programs (OFCCP) to administer the order.

C. OTHER EQUAL EMPLOYMENT OPPORTUNITY (EEO) LAWS

Major federal laws require equal pay for men and women doing equal work and forbid discrimination against older people and those with disabilities.

11. Equal Pay

The Equal Pay Act prohibits employers from paying employees of one gender a lower wage rate than the rate paid employees of the other gender for equal work, or substantially equal work, in the same establishment for jobs that require substantially equal skill, effort, and responsibility and that are performed under similar working conditions.[21] The Equal Pay Act does not prohibit all variations in wage rates paid men and women but only those variations based solely on gender. The act sets forth four exceptions. Variances in wages are allowed where there is (1) a seniority system, (2) a merit system, (3) a system that measures earnings by quantity or quality of production, or (4) a differential based on any factor other than gender.

---

[19] *The Steelworkers v Weber*, 443 US 193 (1979), and *Johnson v Santa Clara Transportation Agency*, 480 US 617 (1987), are very important U.S. Supreme Court decisions in the developing law on permissible affirmative action plans.

[20] *San Francisco Police Officers Ass'n v San Francisco*, 812 F2d 1125 (9th Cir 1987).

[21] 29 USC § 206 (d)(1).

12. Age Discrimination

The Age Discrimination in Employment Act (ADEA) forbids discrimination by employers, unions, and employment agencies against persons over 40 years of age.[22] Section 4(a) of the ADEA sets forth the employment practices that are unlawful under the act, including the failure to hire because of age and the discharge of employees because of age. Section 7(b) of the ADEA allows for doubling the damages in cases of willful violations of the act. Consequently, an employer who willfully violates the ADEA is liable not only for back wages and benefits but also for an additional amount as liquidated damages.[23]

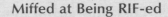

C A S E   S U M M A R Y

Miffed at Being RIF-ed

FACTS: Calvin Rhodes began his employment with Dresser Industries in 1955 as an oil industry salesman. In the throes of a severe economic downturn, Rhodes took a job selling oil field equipment at another Dresser company that became Guiberson Oil Tools. After seven months, he was discharged and told that the reason was a reduction in force (RIF) but that he would be eligible for rehiring. At that time, he was 56 years old. Within two months, Guiberson hired a 42-year-old salesperson to do the same job. Rhodes sued Guiberson for violating the ADEA. At the trial, Lee Snyder, the supervisor who terminated Rhodes, testified in part that Jack Givens, Snyder's boss who instructed Snyder to fire Rhodes, once said that he could hire two young salesmen for what some of the older salesmen were costing.

DECISION: Judgment for Rhodes. The official reason given Rhodes, that he was being terminated under a RIF, was false. Every other reason given by the employer was countered with evidence that Rhodes was an excellent salesman. Based on all of the evidence, including the statement about hiring two young salesmen for what some of the older salesmen were costing, a reasonable jury could find that Guiberson Oil discriminated against Rhodes on the basis of age.
[**Rhodes v Guiberson Oil Tools, 75 F3d 989 (5th Cir 1996)**]

The Older Workers Benefit Protection Act (OWBPA) of 1990[24] amends the ADEA by prohibiting age discrimination in employee benefits and establishing minimum standards for determining the validity of waivers of age claims. The OWBPA amends the ADEA by adopting an "equal benefit or equal cost" standard, providing that older workers must be given benefits at least equal to those provided for younger workers unless the employer can prove that the cost of providing an equal benefit would be more for an older worker than for a younger one.

---

[22] 29 USC § 623.

[23] In *Reeves v Sanderson Plumbing Products Co., Inc.*, 530 US 133 (2000), the Supreme Court reinstated a $98,490 judgment for Roger Reeves, which included $35,000 in back pay, $35,000 in liquidated damages, and $28,490.80 in front pay, and held that the plaintiff's evidence establishing a prima facie case and showing that the employer's stated reason for the termination was false was sufficient to prove that age was the motivation for the discharge.

[24] 29 USC § 623. This law reverses the Supreme Court's 1989 ruling in *Public Employees Retirement System of Ohio v Betts*, 492 US 158 (1989), which had the effect of exempting employee benefit programs from the ADEA.

Employers commonly require that employees electing to take early retirement packages waive all claims against their employers, including their rights or claims under the ADEA. The OWBPA requires that employees be given a specific period of time to evaluate a proposed package.

Enforcement of the ADEA is the responsibility of the EEOC. Procedures and time limitations for filing and processing ADEA charges are the same as those under Title VII.[25] However, Title VII is materially different from the ADEA with respect to burdens of persuasion, and Supreme Court decisions construing Title VII do not control the construction of the ADEA. Rather, in all cases of disparate treatment, including mixed-motive cases, the plaintiff has to prove, by a preponderance of the evidence, that age was the "but for" cause of the challenged adverse employment action.[26]

13. Discrimination against Persons with Disabilities

The right of persons with disabilities to enjoy equal employment opportunities was established on the federal level with the enactment of the Rehabilitation Act of 1973.[27]

Although not specifically designed as an employment discrimination measure but as a comprehensive plan to meet many of the needs of persons with disabilities, the act contains three sections that provide guarantees against discrimination in employment. Section 501 is applicable to the federal government itself, section 503 applies to federal contractors, and section 504 applies to the recipients of federal funds.

Title I of the Americans with Disabilities Act of 1990 extends employment protection for disabled persons beyond the federal level to state and local governmental agencies and to all private employers with 15 or more employees. The ADA refers to the term *qualified individuals with disabilities* rather than the term *handicapped persons*, which is used in the Rehabilitation Act. In drafting the ADA, Congress relied heavily on the language of the Rehabilitation Act and its regulations. It was anticipated that the body of case law developed under the Rehabilitation Act would provide guidance in the interpretation and application of the ADA. However, protections for individuals were eroded by U.S. Supreme Court decisions in 1999 and 2002. Under these precedents, numerous claims of ADA plaintiffs were extinguished at the threshold stage of proving the plaintiff had a disability. With the cooperation and agreement of both the employer and disability communities, the ADA Amendments Act of 2008 (ADAAA) became law (effective January 1, 2009), effectively overturning the Supreme Court decisions and restoring the

---

[25] In *Smith v City of Jackson, Mississippi*, 544 US 228 (2005), the U.S. Supreme Court determined that disparate impact claims of age discrimination are permitted under the ADEA. The Court relied on its Title VII *Griggs v Duke Power Co.* precedent, which interpreted text identical to that in the ADEA, with the substitution of the word "age" for the words "race, color, religion, sex or national origin," the narrowing of the coverage of the ADEA, which permits employers to take actions that would otherwise be prohibited based on "reasonable factors other than age" (called the *RFOA provision*) and the EEOC regulations permitting disparate impact claims. The dissenting justices asserted that in the nearly four decades since the law's enactment, the Court had never read it to impose liability on an employer without proof of discriminatory intent. The *Smith v City of Jackson* court decided the disparate impact case before it against the petitioning police officers, finding that the City's larger pay raises to younger employees were based on a RFOA that responded to the City's legitimate goal of retaining its new police officers.

[26] *Gross v FBL Financial Services, Inc.*, 129 S Ct 2343 (2009).

[27] 42 USC §§ 701–794.

original congressional intent of providing broad coverage to protect individuals who face discrimination on the basis of disability.[28] Under Title I of the ADA, an employer may make preemployment inquiries into the ability of a job applicant to perform job-related functions. Under "user-friendly" EEOC guidelines on pre-employment inquiries under the ADA, an employer may ask applicants whether they will need reasonable accommodations for the hiring process. If the answer is yes, the employer may ask for reasonable documentation of the disability. In general, the employer may not ask questions about whether an applicant will need reasonable accommodations to do the job. However, the employer may make preemployment inquiries regarding the job applicant's ability to perform job-related functions.

After making a job offer (contingent upon the applicant's passing a medical examination), the employer may rescind the offer if the position in question poses a direct threat to the worker's health or safety. **For Example,** Mario Echazabal was initially offered a job at Chevron's El Segundo, California, oil refinery but the offer was rescinded when the company doctors determined that exposure to chemicals on the job would further damage his already-reduced liver functions (due to hepatitis C) and might potentially kill him. An affirmative defense then exists for employers—not only in cases where hiring an individual poses a direct threat to the health or safety of other employees in the workplace, but also when there is a direct threat to the employee in question. However, the employer must make an individualized medical risk assessment of the employee's condition.[29]

(A) **PROVING A CASE.** The Americans with Disabilities Act, as amended in 2008, prohibits employers from discriminating "against a qualified individual on the basis of a disability." A qualified individual with a disability is one "who, with or without reasonable accommodation, can perform the essential functions of the employment position." To establish a viable claim under the act, a plaintiff must prove that (1) he or she has a disability; (2) he or she is qualified for the position; and (3) an employer has discriminated against him or her because of a disability.

The ADAAA defines the term "disability" in a three-pronged definition as follows:

> 1. *DISABILITY: The term "disability" means, with respect to an individual—*
>
>   A. *a physical or mental impairment that substantially limits one or more major life activities of such individual;*
>   B. *a record of such an impairment; or*
>   C. *being regarded as having such an impairment.*

The ADAAA sets forth in unmistakable language that the definition of disability "shall be construed in favor of broad coverage of individuals under this Act" and mandates that the term "substantially limits" be construed accordingly. Moreover, the determination of whether an impairment substantially limits a major life activity

---

[28] 42 USC §§ 12101-12117; PL 110-325, S3406 (Sept. 25, 2008).
[29] *Chevron v Echazabal*, 536 US 73 (2002).

must be made without regard to the ameliorative effects of mitigating measures (with the exception that ameliorative effects of ordinary eyeglasses or contact lenses are considered in determinations of whether an impairment substantially limits a major life activity).

The ADAAA includes a new expansive compilation of major life activities to confirm the congressional purpose of providing a broad scope of protection to individuals under the ADA.[30]

(B) Reasonable Accommodations under the ADA. Section 101(9) of the ADA defines an employer's obligation to make "reasonable accommodations" for individuals with disabilities to include (1) making existing facilities accessible to and usable by individuals with disabilities and (2) restructuring jobs, providing modified work schedules, and acquiring or modifying equipment or devices. An employer is not obligated under the ADA to make accommodations that would be an "undue hardship" on the employer.

For Example, before passage of the ADA, a supermarket meatcutter unable to carry meat from a refrigerator to a processing area might have been refused clearance to return to work after a back injury until he was able to perform all job functions. Today, under the ADA, it would be the employer's obligation to provide that worker with a cart to assist him in performing the job even if the cart cost $500. However, if the meatcutter was employed by a small business with limited financial resources, an "accommodation" costing $500 might be an undue hardship that the employer could lawfully refuse to make.

Seniority systems provide for a fair and uniform method of treating employees whereby employees with more years of service have a priority over employees with less years of service when it comes to layoffs, job selection, and other benefits such as days off and vacation periods. Seniority rules apply not only under collective bargaining agreements but also to many nonunion job classifications and to nonunion settings. An employer's showing that a requested accommodation conflicts with seniority rules is ordinarily sufficient to show that the requested "accommodation" is not "reasonable." **For Example,** Robert Barnett, a cargo handler for U.S. Airways, Inc., sought a less physically demanding job in the mailroom due to a back injury. Because a senior employee bid the job, U.S. Airways refused Barnett's request to accommodate his disability by allowing him to work the mailroom position. Barnett filed suit under the ADA, and the case progressed to the U.S. Supreme Court, which determined that ordinarily such a requested accommodation is not "reasonable." On remand to the trial court, Barnett was given the opportunity to show that the company allowed exceptions to the seniority rules and he fit within such exceptions.[31]

---

[30] Section 3(2) of the act provides:
  MAJOR LIFE ACTIVITIES—
  A. IN GENERAL.—For purposes of paragraph (1), major life activities include, but are not limited to, caring for oneself; performing manual tasks; seeing, hearing, eating, sleeping, walking, standing, lifting, bending, speaking, breathing, learning, reading, concentrating, thinking, communicating, and working.
  B. MAJOR BODILY FUNCTIONS.—For purposes of paragraph (1), a major life activity also includes the operation of major bodily functions, included but not limited to, functions of the immune system; normal cell growth; digestive, bowel, bladder, neurological, brain, respiratory, circulatory, endocrine, and reproductive functions.
[31] *U.S. Airways v Barnett*, 535 US 391 (2002).

(c) **Failure to Take Action.** With courts applying a less-demanding standard for coverage under the amended ADA, employers are finding requests to provide "reasonable accommodations" more common. Employers are liable for failure to take appropriate action regarding requests for reasonable accommodations. **For Example,** Jane Gagliardo had been diagnosed with multiple sclerosis that began affecting her work. The most severe symptom was fatigue, which affected her ability to think, focus, and remember. All of her symptoms were subject to being exacerbated by stress. She sought a "reasonable accommodation" under the ADA of having one major client removed from her job responsibilities. The employer took no action on this request. Moreover, while she continued to seek accommodation to no avail, the employer, began disciplining her for poor job performance and ultimately fired her. She was awarded $2.3 million in compensation and punitive damages.[32]

Where a disability is obvious and known to the employer, an employee is obligated to engage in an "interactive process" regarding accommodation of a disability, even when a formal request for accommodation is not made. **For Example,** 19-year-old Patrick Brady, who has cerebral palsy, was hired to work as a Wal-Mart pharmacy aide. After "a few days" on the job with no training, he was transferred to the job of collecting shopping carts and garbage in the parking lot. His supervisor, Ms. Chin, regarded Brady as "too slow" and stated that "she knew there was something wrong with him." While Brady did not request reasonable accommodations because his disability was obvious and known to the employer, Wal-Mart was found to be in violation of the ADA, and a judgment of $900,000—including $300,000 in punitive damages—was upheld by the U.S. Court of Appeals.[33]

(d) **Exclusions from Coverage of the Act.** The act excludes from its coverage employees or applicants who are "currently engaging in the illegal use of drugs." The exclusion does not include an individual who has been successfully rehabilitated from such use or is participating in or has completed supervised drug rehabilitation and is no longer engaging in the illegal use of drugs.

Title V of the act states that behaviors such as transvestitism, transsexualism, pedophilia, exhibitionism, compulsive gambling, kleptomania, pyromania, and psychoactive substance use disorders resulting from current illegal use of drugs are not in and of themselves considered disabilities.

D. Extraterritorial Employment

The Civil Rights Act of 1991 amended both Title VII and the ADA to protect U.S. citizens employed in foreign countries by American-owned or American-controlled companies against discrimination based on race, color, religion, national origin, sex, or disability.[34] The 1991 act contains an exemption if compliance with Title VII or the ADA would cause a company to violate the law of the foreign country in which it is located.

---

[32] *Gagliardo v Connaught Laboratories, Inc.*, 311 F3d 565 (3d Cir 2008). See also *Tobin v Liberty Mutual Insurance Co.*, 553 F3d 121 (1st Cir 2009).
[33] *Brady v Wal-Mart Stores, Inc.*, 531 F3d 127 (2d Cir. 2008).
[34] Section 109 of the Civil Rights Act of 1991, PL 102-166, 105 Stat 1071.

lawflix

Parenthood (1989) (PG)

A candid movie about raising children that has the added bonus of a scene involving Steve martin (Gil) and his boss, Dave, in which the two cross quite a few Title VII lines in their discussion about Gil's job and future at the company.

For movie clips that illustrate business law concepts, see LawFlix at **www.cengage.com/blaw/dvl.**

MAKE THE CONNECTION

SUMMARY

Title VII of the Civil Rights Act of 1964, as amended, forbids discrimination on the basis of race, color, religion, sex, or national origin. The EEOC administers the act. Intentional discrimination is unlawful when there is disparate treatment of individuals because of their race, color, religion, gender, or national origin. Also, employment practices that make no reference to race, color, religion, sex, or national origin, but that nevertheless have an adverse or disparate impact on the protected group, are unlawful. In disparate impact cases, the fact that an employer did not intend to discriminate is no defense. The employer must show that there is a job-related business necessity for the disparate impact practice in question. Employers have several defenses they may raise in a Title VII case to explain differences in employment conditions: (1) bona fide occupational qualifications reasonably necessary to the normal operation of the business, (2) job-related professionally developed ability tests, and (3) bona fide seniority systems. If a state EEO agency or the EEOC is not able to resolve the case, the EEOC issues a right-to-sue letter that enables the person claiming a Title VII violation to sue in a federal district court. An affirmative action plan is legal under Title VII provided there is a voluntary "plan" justified as a remedial measure and provided it does not unnecessarily trammel the interests of whites.

Under the Equal Pay Act (EPA), employers must not pay employees of one gender a lower wage rate than the rate paid to employees of the other gender for substantially equal work. Workers over 40 years old are protected from discrimination by the Age Discrimination in Employment Act (ADEA).

Employment discrimination against persons with disabilities is prohibited by the Americans with Disabilities Act (ADA). Under the ADA, employers must make reasonable accommodations without undue hardship on them to enable individuals with disabilities to work.

LEARNING OUTCOMES

After studying this chapter, you should be able to clearly explain:

A. TITLE VII OF THE CIVIL RIGHTS ACT OF 1964, AS AMENDED

LO.1 Explain the difference between the *disparate treatment* theory of employment discrimination and the *disparate impact* theory of employment discrimination

> See the discussion of the New Haven Firefighters case in which the city relied on a disparate impact theory and the firefighters asserted disparate treatment, p. 936.

B. PROTECTED CLASSES AND EXCEPTIONS

LO.2 List and explain the categories of individuals protected against unlawful employment discrimination under Title VII.

> See the discussion and examples of protections under Title VII applied to the categories of race and color, religion, sex, and national origin, beginning on p. 938.

LO.3 Recognize, and know the remedies for, sexual harassment in the workplace

> See the Ellerth example and the employer's affirmative defense on p. xxx. See Figure 40-2 for a presentation of an employer sexual harassment policy, p. 943.

LO.4 Explain the antiretaliation provision of Title VII

> See the *White* case, which sets forth the elements of retaliatory discrimination and the remedy provided, p. 944.

C. OTHER EQUAL EMPLOYMENT OPPORTUNITY

LO.5 List and explain the laws protecting equal pay for women and men for equal work, as well as the laws forbidding discrimination on the basis of age and against individuals with disabilities

> See the *Rhodes* case with facts and a remedy applicable to age discrimination on p. 949.
>
> See the Patrick Brady example of the attention-getting judgment in a case where the employer failed to recognize its obligation to make a reasonable accommodation, p. 953.

D. EXTRATERRITORIAL EMPLOYMENT

LO.6 Explain how both Title VII of the Civil Rights Act and the ADA protect from discrimination U.S. citizens working in foreign countries for American-owned and American-controlled businesses.

> See the discussion of the exemption for employers where compliance would cause a company to violate the law of the country in which it is located, p. 953.

KEY TERMS

affirmative action plans
(AAPs)

QUESTIONS AND CASE PROBLEMS

1. List the major federal statutes dealing with the regulation of equal rights in employment.

2. Casey Martin, a professional golfer with a circulatory disorder that makes walking an 18-hole golf course painfully difficult, was successful in his Title III of the Americans with Disabilities Act lawsuit against the PGA, and he was allowed to use a golf cart as a reasonable accommodation to the PGA rule requiring golfers on the professional tour to walk the course during professional rounds. Subsequently, Stephan Kuketz, a world-class wheelchair racquetball player, sued the Brockton Athletic Club under the ADA when the club refused to allow him to participate in nonhandicapped tournaments, with the only adjustment to the rules being that he be allowed two bounces rather than one, before he hit the ball from his wheelchair. Did the Casey Martin accommodation fundamentally alter the golf competition? Did the Kuketz proposed accommodation fundamentally alter the racquetball competition? Decide. [*Kuketz v Brockton Athletic Club*, *Boston Globe*, August 30, 2001, B-1]

3. Dial Corp. implemented a "work tolerance test," which all new employees were required to pass to obtain employment in its Armour Star brand sausage-making department. Of the applicants who passed the test, 97 percent were male and 38 percent were female. The EEOC "demonstrated" that the facially neutral work tolerance test "caused" a disparate impact on women. The defending employer did not deny that the employment practice in question caused the disparate impact. Rather, the employer responded that the test was "job related" and "necessary" to reduce job-related injuries at the plant and submitted evidence that the number of job injuries had been reduced after implementation of the testing program. The evidence showed that the company had initiated numerous other safety initiatives that had an impact on reducing injuries at the plant. After they failed the test, 52 women were denied jobs. Decide this case. [*EEOC v Dial Corp.*, 2005 WL 2839977 (SD Iowa)]

4. Continental Photo, Inc., is a portrait photography company. Alex Riley, a black man, applied for a position as a photographer with Continental. Riley submitted an application and was interviewed. In response to a question on a written application, Riley indicated that he had been convicted for forgery (a felony) six years before the interview, had received a suspended sentence, and was placed on five-year probation. He also stated that he would discuss the matter with his interviewer if necessary. The subject of the forgery conviction was subsequently not mentioned by Continental's personnel director in his interview with Riley. Riley's application for employment was eventually

rejected. Riley inquired about the reason for his rejection. The personnel director, Geuther, explained to him that the prior felony conviction on his application was a reason for his rejection. Riley contended that the refusal to hire him because of his conviction record was actually discrimination against him because of his race in violation of Title VII. Riley felt that his successful completion of a five-year probation without incident and his steady work over the years qualified him for the job. Continental maintained that because its photographers handle approximately $10,000 in cash per year, its policy of not hiring applicants whose honesty was questionable was justified. Continental's policy excluded all applicants with felony convictions. Decide. Would the result have been different if Riley had been a convicted murderer? [*Continental Photo, Inc.*, 26 Fair Empl Prac Cas (BNA) 1799 (EEOC)]

5. Beth Faragher worked part-time and summers as an ocean lifeguard for the Marine Safety Section of the city of Boca Raton, Florida. Bill Terry and David Silverman were her supervisors over the five-year period of her employment. During this period, Terry repeatedly touched the bodies of female employees without invitation and would put his arm around Faragher, with his hand on her buttocks. He made crudely demeaning references to women generally. Silverman once told Faragher, "Date me or clean the toilets for a year." She was not so assigned, however. The city adopted a sexual harassment policy addressed to all employees. The policy was not disseminated to the Marine Safety Section at the beach, however. Faragher resigned and later brought action against the city, claiming a violation of Title VII and seeking nominal damages, costs, and attorneys' fees. The city defended that Terry and Silverman were not acting within the scope of their employment when they engaged in harassing conduct, and the city should not be held liable for their actions. Are part-time employees covered by Title VII? Was Silverman's threat, "Date me or clean toilets for a year," a basis for *quid pro quo* vicarious liability against the city? Decide this case. [*Faragher v City of Boca Raton*, 524 US 775]

6. Mohen is a member of the Sikh religion whose practice forbids cutting or shaving facial hair and requires wearing a turban that covers the head. In accordance with the dictates of his religion, Mohen wore a long beard. He applied for a position as breakfast cook at the Island Manor Restaurant. He was told that the restaurant's policy was to forbid cooks to wear facial hair for sanitary and good grooming reasons and that he would have to shave his beard or be denied a position. Mohen contended that the restaurant had an obligation to make a reasonable accommodation to his religious beliefs and let him keep his beard. Is he correct?

7. Sylvia Hayes worked as a staff technician in the radiology department of Shelby Memorial Hospital. On October 1, Hayes was told by her physician that she was pregnant. When Hayes informed the doctor of her occupation as an X-ray technician, the doctor advised Hayes that she could continue working until the end of April so long as she followed standard safety precautions. On October 8, Hayes told Gail Nell, the director of radiology at Shelby, that she had discovered she was two months pregnant. On October 14, Hayes was

discharged by the hospital. The hospital's reason for terminating Hayes was its concern for the safety of her fetus given the X-ray exposure that occurs during employment as an X-ray technician. Hayes brought an action under Title VII, claiming that her discharge was unlawfully based on her condition of pregnancy. She cited scientific evidence and the practice of other hospitals where pregnant women were allowed to remain in their jobs as X-ray technicians. The hospital claimed that Hayes's discharge was based on business necessity. Moreover, the hospital claimed that the potential for future liability existed if an employee's fetus was damaged by radiation encountered at the workplace. Decide. [*Hayes v Shelby Memorial Hospital*, 546 F Supp 259 (ND Ala)]

8. Overton suffered from depression and was made sleepy at work by medication taken for this condition. Also, because of his medical condition, Overton needed a work area away from public access and substantial supervision to complete his tasks. His employer terminated him because of his routinely sleeping on the job, his inability to maintain contact with the public, and his need for supervision. Overton argued that he is a person with a disability under the ADA and the Rehabilitation Act, fully qualified to perform the essential functions of the job, and that the employer had an obligation to make reasonable accommodations, such as allowing some catnaps as needed and providing some extra supervision. Decide. [*Overton v Reilly*, 977 F2d 1190 (7th Cir)]

9. A teenage female high school student named Salazar was employed part-time at Church's Fried Chicken Restaurant. Salazar was hired and supervised by Simon Garza, the assistant manager of the restaurant. Garza had complete supervisory powers when the restaurant's manager, Garza's roommate, was absent. Salazar claimed that while she worked at the restaurant, Garza would refer to her and all other females by a Spanish term that she found objectionable. According to Salazar, Garza once made an offensive comment about her body and repeatedly asked her about her personal life. On another occasion, Garza allegedly physically removed eye shadow from Salazar's face because he claimed it was unattractive. Salazar also claimed that one night she was restrained in a back room of the restaurant while Garza and another employee fondled her. Later that night, when Salazar told a customer what had happened, she was fired. Salazar brought suit under Title VII against Garza and Church's Fried Chicken, alleging sexual harassment. Church's, the corporate defendant, maintained that it should not be held liable under Title VII for Garza's harassment. Church's based its argument on the existence of a published fair treatment policy. Decide. [*Salazar v Church's Fried Chicken, Inc.*, 44 Fair Empl Prac Cas (BNA) 472 (SD Tex)]

10. John Chadbourne was hired by Raytheon on February 4, 1980. His job performance reviews were uniformly high. In December 1983, Chadbourne was hospitalized and diagnosed with AIDS. In January 1984, his physician informed Raytheon that Chadbourne was able to return to work. On January 20, 1984, Chadbourne took a return-to-work physical examination required by

Raytheon. The company's doctor wrote the County Communicable Disease Control Director, Dr. Juels, seeking a determination of the appropriateness of Chadbourne's returning to work. Dr. Juels informed the company that "contact of employees to an AIDS patient appears to pose no risk from all evidence accumulated to date." Dr. Juels also visited the plant and advised the company doctor that there would be no medical risk to other employees at the plant if Chadbourne returned to work. Raytheon refused to reinstate Chadbourne to his position until July 19, 1984. Its basis for denying reinstatement was that coworkers might be at risk of contracting AIDS. Was Raytheon entitled to bar Chadbourne from work during the six-month period of January through July? [*Raytheon v Fair Employment and Housing Commission*, 261 Cal Rptr 197 (Ct App)]

11. Connie Cunico, a white woman, was employed by the Pueblo, Colorado, School District as a social worker. She and other social workers were laid off in seniority order because of the district's poor financial situation. However, the school board thereafter decided to retain Wayne Hunter, a black social worker with less seniority than Cunico because he was the only black on the administrative staff. No racial imbalance existed in the relevant workforce with black persons constituting 2 percent. Cunico, who was rehired over two years later, claimed that she was the victim of reverse discrimination. She stated that she lost $110,361 in back wages plus $76,000 in attorneys' fees and costs. The school district replied that it was correct in protecting with special consideration the only black administrator in the district under the general principles it set forth in its AAP. Did the employer show that its affirmative action in retaining Hunter was justified as a remedial measure? Decide. [*Cunico v Pueblo School District No. 6*, 917 F2d 431 (10th Cir)]

12. Della Janich was employed as a matron at the Yellowstone County Jail in Montana. The duties of the position of matron resemble those of a parallel male position of jailer. Both employees have the responsibility of booking prisoners, showering and dressing them, and placing them in the appropriate section of the jail depending on the offender's sex. Because 95 percent of the prisoners at the jail were men and 5 percent were women, the matron was assigned more bookkeeping duties than the jailer. At all times during Janich's employment at the jail, her male counterparts received $125 more per month as jailers. Janich brought an action under the Equal Pay Act, alleging discrimination against her in her wages because of her sex. The county sheriff denied the charge. Decide. [*Janich v Sheriff*, 29 Fair Empl Prac Cas (BNA) 1195 (D Mont)]

13. Following a decline in cigarette sales, L & M, Inc., hired J. Gfeller as vice president of sales and charged him to turn around the sales decline. After receiving an analysis of the ages of sales personnel and first-line management, Gfeller and his assistant, T. McMorrow, instituted an intensive program of personnel changes that led to the termination of many older managers and sales representatives. A top manager who sought to justify keeping an older manager was informed that he was "not getting the message." Gfeller and McMorrow

emphasized that they wanted young and aggressive people and that the older people were not able to conform or adapt to new procedures. R. E. Moran, who had been rated a first-rate division manager, was terminated and replaced by a 27-year-old employee. Gfeller and McMorrow made statements about employees with many years' experience: "It was not 20 years' experience, but rather 1 year's experience 20 times." The EEOC brought suit on behalf of the terminated managers and sales representatives. The company vigorously denied any discriminatory attitude with regard to age. Decide. [*EEOC v Liggett and Meyers, Inc.*, 29 FEP 1611 (EDNC)]

14. Mazir Coleman had driven a school bus for the Casey County, Kentucky, Board of Education for four years. After that time, Coleman's left leg had to be amputated. Coleman was fitted with an artificial leg and underwent extensive rehabilitation to relearn driving skills. When his driving skills had been sufficiently relearned over the course of four years, Coleman applied to the county board of education for a job as a school bus driver. The board refused to accept Coleman's application, saying that it had no alternative but to deny Coleman a bus-driving job because of a Kentucky administrative regulation. That regulation stated in part: "No person shall drive a school bus who does not possess both of these natural bodily parts: feet, legs, hands, arms, eyes, and ears. The driver shall have normal use of the above named body parts." Coleman brought an action under the Rehabilitation act, claiming discrimination based on his physical handicap. The county board of education denied this charge, claiming that the reason they rejected Coleman was because of the requirement of the state regulation. Could Coleman have maintained an action for employment discrimination in light of the state regulation on natural body parts? Decide. [*Coleman v Casey County Board of Education*, 510 F Supp 301 (ND Ky)]

15. Marcia Saxton worked for Jerry Richardson, a supervisor at AT&T's International Division. Richardson made advances to Saxton on two occasions over a three-week period. Each time Saxton told him she did not appreciate his advances. No further advances were made, but thereafter Saxton felt that Richardson treated her condescendingly and had stopped speaking to her on a social basis at work. Four months later, Saxton filed a formal internal complaint, asserting sexual harassment, and went on "paid leave." AT&T found inconclusive evidence of sexual harassment but determined that the two employees should be separated. Saxton declined a transfer to another department, so AT&T transferred Richardson instead. Saxton still refused to return to work. Thereafter, AT&T terminated Saxton for refusal to return to work. Saxton contended she had been a victim of hostile working environment sexual harassment. AT&T argued that while the supervisor's conduct was inappropriate and unprofessional, it fell short of the type of action necessary for sexual harassment under federal law (the *Harris* case). Decide. [*Saxton v AT&T Co.*, 10 F3d 526 (7th Cir)]

Part 7

BUSINESS ORGANIZATIONS

Chapter 41

TYPES OF BUSINESS ORGANIZATIONS

What form of legal organization should you have for your business? The answer will be found in your needs for money, personnel, control, tax and estate planning, and protection from liability.

A. Principal Forms of Business Organizations

The law of business organizations may be better understood if the advantages and disadvantages of proprietorships, partnerships, and corporations are first considered.

1. Individual Proprietorships

sole or individual proprietorship–form of business ownership in which one individual owns the business.

A **sole or individual proprietorship** is a form of business ownership in which one individual owns the business. The owner may be the sole worker of the business or employ as many others as needed to run the concern. Individual proprietorships are commonly used in retail stores, service businesses, and agriculture.

(A) ADVANTAGES. The proprietor or owner is not required to expend resources on organizational fees. The proprietor, as the sole owner, controls all decisions and receives all profits. The net earnings of the business are not subject to corporate income taxes but are taxed only as personal income.

(B) DISADVANTAGES. The proprietor is subject to unlimited personal liability for the debts of the business and cannot limit this risk. The investment capital in the business is limited by the resources of the sole proprietor. Because all contracts of the business are made by the owner or in the owner's name by agents of the owner, the authority to make contracts terminates on the death of the owner, and the business is subject to disintegration.

2. Partnerships, LLPs, and LLCs

partnership–pooling of capital resources and the business or professional talents of two or more individuals (partners) with the goal of making a profit.

limited liability partnership (LLP)–partnership in which at least one partner has a liability limited to the loss of the capital contribution made to the partnership.

A **partnership** involves the pooling of capital resources and the business or professional talents of two or more individuals whose goal is making a profit. Law firms, medical associations, and architectural and engineering firms may operate under the partnership form. Today, however, these firms may convert to a **limited liability partnership (LLP)**. A wide range of small manufacturing, retail, and service businesses operate as partnerships. These businesses may operate under the form of organization called *limited liability company (LLC)*, which allows tax treatment as a partnership with limited liability for the owners.

(A) ADVANTAGES. The partnership form of business organization allows individuals to pool resources and then initiate and conduct their business without the requirement of a formal organizational structure.

(B) DISADVANTAGES. Major disadvantages of a partnership are the unlimited personal liability of each partner and the uncertain duration of the business because the partnership is dissolved by the death of one partner. Unlimited personal liability is remedied by the LLC form of business organization. Professional partnerships that convert to an LLP shield innocent partners from personal liability beyond their investment in the firm.

3. Corporations

corporation–artificial being created by government grant, which for many purposes is treated as a natural person.

Business **corporations** exist to make a profit and are created by government grant. State statutes regulating the creation of corporations require a corporate structure consisting of shareholders, directors, and officers. The shareholders, as the owners of the business, elect a board of directors, which is responsible for managing the business. The directors employ officers, who serve as the agents of the business and run day-to-day operations. Corporations range in size from incorporated one-owner enterprises to large multinational concerns.

(A) **ADVANTAGES.** The major advantage to the shareholder, or investor, is that the shareholder's risk of loss from the business is limited to the amount of capital she invested in the business or paid for shares. This factor, coupled with the free transferability of corporate shares, makes the corporate form of business organization attractive to investors.

By purchasing shares, a large number of investors may contribute the capital assets needed to finance large business enterprises. As the capital needs of a business expand, the corporate form becomes more attractive.

A corporation is a separate legal entity capable of owning property, contracting, suing, and being sued in its own name. It has perpetual life. In other words, a corporation is not affected by the death of any of its shareholders or the transfer of their shares. In contrast to the case of a partnership or proprietorship, the death of an owner has no legal effect on the corporate entity.

(B) **DISADVANTAGES.** A corporation is required to pay corporate income taxes. Shareholders are required to pay personal income taxes on the amount received when they receive a distribution of profits from the corporation. This is a form of double taxation.

Incorporation involves the expenditure of funds for organizational expenses. Documents necessary for the formation of a corporation, which are required by state law, must be prepared, and certain filing fees must be paid. State corporation laws may also require filing an annual report and other reports.

B. SPECIALIZED FORMS OF ORGANIZATIONS

CPA   ### 4. Joint Ventures

joint venture–relationship in which two or more persons or firms combine their labor or property for a single undertaking and share profits and losses equally unless otherwise agreed.

A **joint venture**, or joint adventure, is a relationship in which two or more persons or entities combine their labor or property for a single business undertaking and share profits and losses equally or as otherwise agreed.[1] **For Example,** Front-Line Promotions and Insights Promotions formed a "joint venture" to produce two

---

[1] See *Abeles Inc. v Creekstone Farms Premium Beef*, LLC, 2009 WL 2495802 (EDNY 2009), for an in-depth discussion of the law of joint ventures. The court referenced a precedent, stating: "A joint venture has been described as a nebulous concept whose boundaries are not precisely drawn. Defining a joint venture is easier than identifying it, for each case depends upon its own facts."

events with musical and celebrity talent at the Sugar Mill in New Orleans on February 16 and February 17, 2008, the NBA All-Star Weekend in New Orleans. The entities agreed to split the costs and revenues from the events.[2]

A joint venture is similar in many respects to a partnership. It differs primarily in that the joint venture typically involves the pursuit of a single enterprise or transaction, although its accomplishment may require several years. A partnership is generally a continuing business or activity but may be expressly created for a single transaction. Because the distinction is so insubstantial, most courts hold that joint ventures are subject to the same principles of law as partnerships. **For Example,** the Virginia Uniform Partnership Act was utilized to enable PGI, Inc., to sue Rathe Productions, Inc., for conversion of its share of a settlement agreement with the Smithsonian Institute because PGI/Rathe was involved in a joint venture and the "rules of law governing the rights, duties and liabilities of joint ventures are substantially the same as those which govern partnerships."[3]

(A) DURATION OF JOINT VENTURE. A joint venture continues for the time specified in the agreement of the parties. In the absence of a fixed-duration provision, a joint venture is ordinarily terminable at the will of any participant. When the joint venture clearly relates to a particular transaction, such as the construction of a specified bridge, the joint venture ordinarily lasts until the particular transaction or project is completed or becomes impossible to complete.

(B) LIABILITY TO THIRD PERSONS. The conclusion that persons are joint venturers is important when a suit is brought by or against a third person for personal injuries or property damage. If there is a joint venture, the fault or negligence of one venturer will be imputed to the other venturers.[4]

5. Unincorporated Associations

unincorporated association–combination of two or more persons for the furtherance of a common nonprofit purpose.

An **unincorporated association** is a combination of two or more persons for the furtherance of a common purpose.[5] No particular form of organization is required. Any conduct or agreement indicating an attempt to associate or work together for a common purpose is sufficient.[6]

The authority of an unincorporated association over its members is governed by ordinary contract law. Except when otherwise provided by statute, an unincorporated association does not have any legal existence apart from its members. Thus, an unincorporated association cannot sue or be sued in its own name.

---

[2] Boxer Floyd "Money Mayweather" was to appear at the event on February 17, 2008, and be paid $25,000, but he did not appear. The joint venture sued him for breach of contract and consequential damages. In *Front-Line Inc. v Mayweather Promotions, LLC,* 2009 U.S. Lexis 27136, the U.S. District Court allowed Front-Line Promotions to pursue its claim against Mayweather Promotions, LLC.

[3] *PGI, Inc. v Rathe Productions, Inc.,* 576 SE2d 438 (Va 2003). See also *Pugliese v Mandello,* 871 NYS2d 174 (App Div 2008).

[4] *Kim v Chamberlain,* 504 So2d 1213 (Ala App 1987).

[5] The National Conference of Commissioners on Uniform State Laws has adopted a Uniform Unincorporated Nonprofit Association Act. In addition, community associations are being formed, primarily for the purpose of community planning and environmental protection.

[6] Under a policy of minimizing judicial involvement in private organizations, courts ordinarily will refrain from reviewing decisions on the internal-governance issues of unincorporated private associations where the organization's own adjudicatory procedures are followed. In *Tackney v United States Naval Academy Alumni Association Inc.,* 971 A2d 309 (Md App 2009), involving an incorporated private association, the court found that judicial intervention was not warranted regarding the election of trustees in 2006, because the alumni board's actions were not fraudulent or arbitrary.

Generally, the members of an unincorporated association are not liable for the debts or liabilities of the association by the mere fact that they are members. It must usually be shown that they authorized or ratified the act in question. If either authorization or ratification by a particular member can be shown, that member has unlimited liability for the act.

C A S E   S U M M A R Y

Batters with Two Strikes Should Never Trust the Umpire, and Their Parents Should Have Little Faith That the Association Will Pay the Bills

FACTS: Golden Spike Little League was an unincorporated association of persons who joined together to promote a Little League baseball team in Ogden, Utah. They sent one of their members to arrange for credit at Smith & Edwards, a local sporting goods store. After getting credit, various members went to the store and picked up and signed for different items of baseball equipment and uniforms, at a total cost of $3,900. When Smith, the owner, requested payment, the members arranged a fundraising activity that produced only $149. Smith sued the Golden Spike Little League as an entity and the members who had picked up and signed for the equipment individually. The individual defendants denied that they had any personal liability, contending that only the Golden Spike Little League could be held responsible.

DECISION: Judgment for Smith against the individual members. The association could not be held liable because it did not have any legal existence. The persons who purchased the goods from the seller were personally liable as buyers even though they had purported to act on behalf of the unincorporated association. [**Smith & Edwards v Golden Spike Little League, 577 P2d 132 (Utah 1978)**]

6. Cooperatives

cooperative–group of two or more persons or enterprises that acts through a common agent with respect to a common objective, such as buying or selling.

A **cooperative** consists of a group of two or more independent persons or enterprises that cooperate for a common objective or function. Thus, farmers may pool their farm products and sell them. Consumers may likewise pool their orders and purchase goods in bulk.

(A) INCORPORATED COOPERATIVES. Statutes commonly provide for the special incorporation of cooperative enterprises. Such statutes often provide that any excess of payments over the cost of operation shall be refunded to each participant member in direct proportion to the volume of business that the member has done with the cooperative. This contrasts with the payment of a dividend by an ordinary business corporation in which the payment of dividends is proportional to the number of shares held by the shareholder and is unrelated to the extent of the shareholder's business activities with the enterprise.

(B) ANTITRUST LAW EXEMPTION. The agreement by the members of sellers' cooperatives that all products shall be sold at a common price is an agreement to fix prices.

Therefore, the sellers' cooperative is basically an agreement in restraint of trade and a violation of antitrust laws. The Capper-Volstead Act of 1922 expressly exempts normal selling activities of farmers' and dairy farmers' cooperatives from the operation of the federal Sherman Antitrust Act so long as the cooperatives do not conspire with outsiders to fix prices.

C. The Franchise Business Format

In individual situations, *franchising* is a *method* of doing business, not a *form* of business organization. A franchisor or franchisee could be a sole proprietor, a partnership, a limited liability company, or a corporation. It is a *business format*, as opposed to a business organization. Franchising relies on contract law to set forth the rights and obligations of the parties. However, the Federal Trade Commission Act and certain state laws require disclosure. Any federal and/or state laws regulating securities, intellectual property, antitrust violations, sales, agency, and tort law apply to franchises.

Section 5 of the Federal Trade Commission Act prohibits deceptive, manipulative, or unfair business practices,[7] and state deceptive trade practices acts similarly prohibit such practice.

7. Definition and Types of Franchises

franchise–(1) privilege or authorization, generally exclusive, to engage in a particular activity within a particular geographic area, such as a government franchise to operate a taxi company within a specified city, or a private franchise as the grant by a manufacturer of a right to sell products within a particular territory or for a particular number of years; (2) right to vote.

franchisor–party granting the franchise.

franchisee–person to whom franchise is granted.

The Federal Trade Commission (FTC) has defined a **franchise** as "an arrangement in which the owner of a trademark, trade name, or copyright licenses others, under specified conditions or limitations, to use the trademark, trade name, or copyright in purveying goods or services." The **franchisor** is the party granting the franchise, and the **franchisee** is the person to whom the franchise is granted. There are three principal types of franchises. The first is a *manufacturing* or *processing franchise*, in which the franchisor grants the franchisee authority to manufacture and sell products under the trademark(s) of the franchisor. The franchisor may supply an essential ingredient in a processing franchise, such as the syrup for an independent regional Coca-Cola bottling company. The second type of franchise is a *service franchise*, whereby the franchisee renders a service to customers under the terms of a franchise agreement. The drain-cleaning service provided by Roto-Rooter is an example of a service franchise. The third type is a *distribution franchise*, in which the franchisor's products are sold to a franchisee, who then resells to customers in a geographical area. Exxon Mobil Oil Company's products are often sold to retail customers through independent distribution franchises.

A common issue in litigation under state laws protecting franchisees or dealers is whether the business arrangement is a franchise or dealership under the applicable state law.[8] The *Girl Scouts of Manitou* case dealt with such a question.

---

[7] 15 USC § 45.
[8] *Morrison v Chilton Professional Automotive, Inc.*, 984 F Supp 1018 (WD Tex 1997).

C A S E   S U M M A R Y

Are Girl Scouts "Dealers"?

FACTS: The Girl Scouts of the United States of America (GSUSA) is led by the National Council. Local councils are governed by their own independent boards of directors, and employ their own officers and professional staff and are responsible for their own financial health. For a nominal fee, GSUSA issues a charter to the local council, which grants to that council "the right to develop, manage, and maintain Girl Scouting throughout the areas of its jurisdiction, including the right to use GSUSA's names and protected marks." Plaintiff Manitou Council is one of GSUSA's local councils. It employs a full-time staff of 17 people. It owns significant real property, including two large Girl Scout camps and a corporate office building. Manitou asserts that nearly 100 percent of its annual revenues derive from the sale of Girl Scout merchandise and services, private donations, and investment income from Manitou's reserve funds. Girl Scout cookie sales alone generate more than $1 million in revenue each year. While the charter was still in effect, Manitou rejected the GSUSA merger directive, and GSUSA sought to unilaterally remove more than half of Manitou's jurisdiction. Manitou sued GSUSA under the Wisconsin Fair Dealership Law (WFDL), seeking a preliminary injunction. From a ruling in favor of GSUSA, Manitou appealed.

DECISION: GSUSA was enjoined from making any changes to Manitou's jurisdiction pending final resolution on the merits. Under the WFDL, it is illegal for any grantor to "terminate, cancel, fail to renew, or substantially change the competitive circumstances of a dealership agreement without good cause." GSUSA's argument that the Girl Scouts "are not 'dealers' of anything," emphasizing the word "dealer" as if its members are accused of selling drugs on the street corner, is unavailing. It matters not whether we would call the Girl Scouts "dealers" in everyday conversation; what matters is only how the statute defines the term, and the activities of Manitou clearly fall within its definition. Manitou is a business. It sells and distributes goods. It distributes services. It makes extensive use of GSUSA's marks and names. These requirements satisfy the statutes' plain language, which the Wisconsin Supreme Court has recognized was designed "to encompass an extraordinarily diverse set of business relationships not limited to the traditional franchise." [**Girl Scouts of Manitou v GSUSA, 549 F3d 1079 (7th Cir 2008)**]

---

franchise agreement–sets forth rights of franchisee to use trademarks, etc., of franchisor.

trademark–mark that identifies a product.

trade name–name under which a business is carried on and, if fictitious, must be registered.

trade dress–product's total image including its overall packaging look.

trade secret–formula, device, or compilation of information that is used in one's business and is of such a nature that it provides an advantage over competitors who do not have the information.

8. The Franchise Agreement

The relationship between the franchisor and the franchisee is ordinarily an arm's-length relationship between two independent contractors. Their respective rights are determined by the contract existing between them, called the **franchise agreement**.[9] The agreement sets forth the rights of the franchisee to use the **trademarks**, **trade name**, **trade dress**, and **trade secrets** of the franchisor. **For Example,** Burger King Corporation licenses franchisees to use the trademarks Burger King, Whopper, Croissanwich, and Whopper Jr.[10] The franchise agreement commonly requires the franchisor to provide training for the franchisee's employees, including processing or repair training. Thus, a new Chili's Bar and Grill franchise can expect to have its employees taught how to prepare and serve the food on its menu. In a distribution

---

[9] *See American Standard Inc. v Meehan*, 517 F Supp 2d 976 (ND Ohio 2007).
[10] *Burger King Corp. v Hinton, Inc.*, 2002 WL 31059465 (SD Fla 2002).

franchise, an Acura dealer can expect the franchisor to train its mechanics to repair the automobiles it sells. The franchise agreement also deals with terms for payment of various fees by the franchisee and sets forth compliance requirements for quality control set by the franchisor.

The duration of a franchise is a critical element of the franchise agreement. The franchise may last for as long as the parties agree. The laws in some states may require advance written notice of cancellation.[11] Franchise contracts generally specify the causes for which the franchisor may terminate the franchise, such as the franchisee's death, bankruptcy, failure to make payments, or failure to meet sales quotas. **For Example,** Burger King Corp. (BKC) instituted a required new item, value meals, "which must be sold in all U.S. restaurants … and failure to comply will be considered a default under the applicable franchise agreement." After due notice to franchisees Elizabeth and Luan Sadik and no compliance by the Sadiks with regard to the directive to sell the new value meal items, BKC cancelled the franchise, and the courts upheld BKC's action as proper under the franchise contract.[12]

Franchise agreements frequently contain an arbitration provision under which a neutral party is to make a final and binding determination whether there has been a breach of the contract sufficient to justify cancellation of the franchise.[13] The arbitration provision may provide that the franchisor can appoint a trustee to run the business of the franchisee while arbitration proceedings are pending.

9. Special Protections Under Federal Laws

Holders of automobile dealership franchises are protected from bad-faith termination of their dealerships by the federal Automobile Dealers' Day in Court Act (ADDCA).[14] **For Example,** Anthony Arciniaga was allowed to proceed with his ADDCA lawsuit against General Motors. The court refused to allow GM to create and apply a corporate structure that evades the ADDCA. Collectively, the court looked to the Dealer Sales and Service Agreement, the Shareholders' Agreement, and other documents that together made up the understanding between Arciniaga and GM, which made it possible for Arciniaga to become an automobile dealer. The court concluded that all of the agreements viewed together constituted a "motor vehicle franchise contract." The court refused to focus on just one document as asserted by GM because doing so would negate the protective features of the ADDCA.[15]

When an automobile manufacturer makes arbitrary and unreasonable demands and then terminates a dealer's franchise for failure to comply with the demands, the manufacturer is liable for the damages caused. The right of a franchisee to transfer its contractual rights in the franchise is protected by the state law subject to notice and approval by the franchisor.[16]

---

[11] See, for example, Mo Rev Stat § 407.405.

[12] *Burger King Corp. v E-Z Corporations*, 572 F3d 1306 (11th Cir 2009).

[13] *Central New Jersey Freightliner, Inc., v Freightliner Corp.*, 987 F Supp 289 (DNJ 1998).

[14] 15 USC §§ 1221–1225.

[15] *Arciniaga v General Motors Corp.*, 418 F Supp 2d 374 (SDNY 2005).

[16] *KMS Restaurant Corp. v Wendy's International*, 361 F3d 1321 (11th Cir 2004).

C A S E   S U M M A R Y

An Associate of Tony and Carmella Soprano? Prove It

FACTS: After a fire at its Audi dealership, Coast Automotive Group, Ltd., sought to transfer its contractual rights in the franchise to Aspen Knolles, Ltd. Applications were submitted to Volkswagen of America (VOA) and Audi of America (AOA), the franchisors, for approval. Under state law, a franchisor can reject a proposed transferee by giving material reasons relating to the character, financial ability, or business experience of the proposed transferee. However, it may not unreasonably withhold consent. VOA and AOA rejected the proposed corporate transferee, Aspen Knolles, Inc., because a principal of the group, Mr. Mazzuoccola, a race car enthusiast who sponsored a professional racing team and owned a Jeep dealership, was said by an individual to have associated with known organized crime figures. Coast sued VOA and AOA for specific performance. At the trial, Mr. Mazzuoccola took the witness stand to testify about his business experience.

DECISION: Judgment for Coast. The right of a franchisee to transfer its contractual rights in the franchise is protected by state law subject to notice and approval by the franchisor. The burden of proof is on the franchisor to present credible reasons for the refusal to consent. It is not a credible reason to turn down a transferee because of association with automobile racing. Association with organized crime figures is a valid reason to turn down a transferee; but there was no credible evidence presented to support such a contention at the trial. Indeed, Mr. Mazzuoccola took the stand giving VOA and AOA an opportunity to question him on character issues, and none were raised. Specific performance is the appropriate remedy. [**VW Credit, Inc. v Coast Automobile Group, Ltd., 787 A2d 950 (NJ Super 2002)**]

The Petroleum Marketing Practices Act (PMPA) gives gas station franchisees the opportunity to continue in business by purchasing the entire premises used in selling motor fuel when the franchisor decides to sell the property and not renew a lease. In some instances, the franchisor's intentions are unclear and its actions may be perceived as contrary to the PMPA. Litigation may be necessary to resolve the matter. **For Example,** eight independent gas station operators who leased stations from Shell Oil Co. and sold Shell products were successful in their PMPA lawsuit against Shell when Shell phased out rental subsidies provided franchisees under the parties' lease agreements and set the wholesale prices it charged dealers for gasoline so high that the increase would squeeze dealers' profits or force them to raise prices that competition could undercut. The dealers argued this was done to reduce the number of independent gas stations in the region. A jury awarded $3.3 million in compensatory damages.[17]

The PMPA prohibits early termination of a franchise, but only when the franchisee's failure to comply with a provision of the franchise is so serious as to undermine the entire relationship.[18]

---

[17] Kimberly Blanton, "Jury Rules for Franchisees in Shell Trial," *Boston Globe*, December 9, 2004, C-3.
[18] In *Chevron v El-Khoury*, 285 F3d 1159 (9th Cir. 2002), the Court of Appeals remanded a franchise termination case for trial on the materiality of a franchisee's failure to pay $15,000 in California sales taxes when the oil company had unsuccessfully attempted to buy out the dealer and, when the last buyout offer was rejected, had selected him to be audited. The dealer eventually paid all taxes due. One of Chevron's executives testified the failure to pay taxes was between "the dealer and the state" rather than the dealer and Chevron. However, Chevron contended that the failure to pay all taxes when due was a violation of the franchise agreement and tarnished the company's image.

10. Disclosure

The FTC has adopted a franchise disclosure rule that requires franchisors to give prospective franchisees a full disclosure statement 10 days before a franchisee signs a contract or pays any money for a franchise. Fourteen states also have protective regulations requiring disclosure in the sale of franchises. Effective on and after December 21, 1995, all 14 states and the FTC accepted the 1993 revised version of the Uniform Franchise Offering Circular as being in full compliance with state and FTC disclosure rules.

The disclosure statement must include (1) the business experience of the franchisor and its brokers, (2) any current and past litigation against the franchisor, (3) any previous bankruptcy, (4) the material terms of the franchise agreement, (5) initial and recurring payments, (6) restrictions on territories, (7) grounds for termination of the franchise, and (8) actual, average, or projected sales, profits, or earnings.

Under the FTC disclosure rule, a franchisor must pay a civil penalty of as much as $10,000 for each violation when it is shown that a sale of a franchise subject to the FTC rule was made, the franchisor knew or should have known of the disclosure rule, and no disclosure statement was given to the buyer. Also, the franchisor may be required to make the buyer whole for any losses suffered.

11. Vicarious Liability Claims Against Franchisors

In theory, a franchisor is not liable to a third person dealing with or affected by the franchise holder. This freedom from liability is one of the main reasons franchisors use franchises. If the negligence of the franchisee causes harm to a third person, the franchisor is not liable because the franchisee is an independent contractor. However, franchisors continue to be subject to lawsuits based on the wrongful conduct of their franchisees under the theory of either actual authority or apparent authority.[19]

CASE SUMMARY

Why Franchisors Use Franchises!

FACTS: William Roberts operated a McDonald's restaurant in Newcastle, Washington, under a franchise agreement with McDonald's Corporation. A thriving drug scene existed among employees and assistant managers at the restaurant. In May 2000, the restaurant hired 15-year-old D.L.S., and within weeks, she was part of the drug scene there. Thereafter, she left home to live with an assistant manager and use drugs. Her father, Clifford Street, and D.L.S. sued McDonald's Corp. and Roberts for introducing D.L.S. to drugs and sex. The trial court dismissed the claims against McDonald's Corp., and D.L.S. and her father appealed.

[19] *Smith-Hoy v AMC Property Evaluations, Inc.*, 826 NYS2d 513 (App Div 2008).

CASE SUMMARY

Continued

Mr. Street testified that "no person in their right mind would believe that McDonald's did not control what happened at the individual restaurants."

DECISION: The franchise agreement clearly provided that Roberts was not an agent of McDonald's Corporation and that McDonald's had no control over the daily operations of the restaurant. Thus, McDonald's has no liability as Roberts' actual principal. The court next considered an apparent authority theory to determine whether McDonald's created apparent authority that it operated the Newcastle restaurant and would ensure a safe working environment for young workers there. Beyond the general impression created by advertising that McDonald's restaurants offer a wholesome environment, no representations or acts of McDonald's existed to create an apparent employment relationship between McDonald's and D.L.S. She and her parents must pursue their claims against the franchisee. [**D.L.S. v Maybin, 121 P3d 1210 (Wash App 2005)**]

thinking things through

Ken Miyamoto was president and a shareholder of Bixby's Food Systems, Inc. (Bixby's), a franchisor of bagel restaurants. The business is incorporated and provides limited liability to Miyamoto and its other corporate investors. Bixby's hired a lawyer familiar with franchise disclosure laws in Illinois and drafted a franchise offering circular (FOC) in accordance with state laws. Jan and Phillip McKay attended a meeting of existing and prospective franchisees where Miyamoto spoke and said that prospective franchisees had signed and paid for 340 development agreements; a similar statement also appeared in a Bixby's newsletter. The McKays soon thereafter executed a franchise agreement. Based on Miyamoto's view that a lease of larger retail space than recommended in Bixby's circular would bring in larger revenues, the McKays executed the larger-than-recommended lease and spent $400,000 making their restaurant operational, which was a much higher investment than projected in the FOC. When the restaurant opened, sales did not come close to the figures estimated in the FOC. After eight months of operations, Bixby's terminated the McKays' franchise for their inability to pay Bixby's franchise royalty fees.

Bixby's sued the McKays for continuing to use its trademark, and the McKays counterclaimed against Bixby's, Inc. and Miyamoto as an individual for violation of the state Franchise Disclosure Act and the state Deceptive Business Practices Act.

Bixby's FOC was not shown to contain material misstatements of fact. However, the McKays listed a number of statements made by Miyamoto that were untrue concerning future events regarding costs, profitability, and financial success, like his encouraging them to rent larger-than-recommended retail space to bring in larger revenues, which did not materialize. The court held that such statements about future events, costs, and profitability are not actionable misrepresentations under the state Franchise Disclosure Act. Corporate executives selling franchises have latitude to take the facts set forth in franchise offering circulars and project a bright future in most respects. That is, they have a legal right to put their "spin" on the facts, just as society does in governmental and personal affairs. Of course, buyers must beware and view assertions about future events, costs, and profitability with critical analysis and informed skepticism.

thinking things through

Continued

With his business incorporated and his circulars drafted by competent counsel, was Miyamoto immune from personal liability in this case? The answer is no. When Miyamoto told the group of prospective franchisees that some 340 development agreements had been signed and paid for and later repeated this statement in a newsletter, he was not Thinking Things Through. Through the discovery process that preceded a trial, the McKays' attorney "discovered" that Bixby's had just 15 agreements executed and paid for at the time of Miyamoto's assertion that 340 agreements were

executed and paid for. Such a material misstatement of fact was a violation of the state franchising and deceptive practices laws.

The economic resources expended by Bixby's, Inc., to provide limited liability could not shield its shareholder-president from the consequences of his enormous lie. Along with Bixby's, Inc., Miyamoto was held personally liable to the McKays under the state statutes.*

* **Bixby's Food Systems, Inc. v McKay**, 193 F Supp 2d 1053 (ND Ill 2002).

To maintain uniform systems for processing or distributing goods or rendering services, franchisors often place significant controls on their franchisees' businesses. These controls are set forth in franchise agreements and operating manuals. In a lawsuit brought against a franchisor for the wrongful conduct of its franchisee, the franchise agreement and operations manuals may be used as evidence of the franchisor's right to control the franchisee and the existence of an agency relationship rather than an independent contractor relationship.[20]

To avoid negating its franchisees' independent contractor status and being liable for the wrongful conduct of a franchisee, the franchisor should make certain that the franchise agreement minimizes the number and kind of provisions that authorize the franchisor to control the "means" of operating the business. **For Example,** the franchisor should not exercise control over employment-related matters.[21]

Franchisors may also insulate themselves from liability by requiring individual franchisees to take steps to publicly maintain their own individual business identities.

For Example, a gas station may post a sign stating that it is "dealer owned and operated," or a real estate franchise may list on its business sign the franchise name and the name of the local owner, such as Century 21, L & K Realty Co. All

[20] *J. M. v Shell Oil Co.*, 1996 Bus. Franchise Guide (CCH) ¶ 10,817 (Mo App).
[21] Consider the degree of control exercised by McDonald's Corp. over its franchises. Only designated food and beverages may be served, and franchisees are required to use prescribed buildings and equipment. The franchisor dictates the level of quality, service, and cleanliness. All franchisees' employees must wear the uniforms designated by the franchisor with McDonald's logos. McDonald's dictates management, advertising, and personnel policies and requires that managers be trained at its "Hamburger University." The Illinois Court of Appeals held that the question of whether a franchise was an apparent agent of McDonald's was an issue of material fact that should go to a jury in a lawsuit involving a customer's slip and fall on ice in the franchised restaurant's bathroom. The court stated that the employees responsible for maintaining the bathroom wore "McDonald's uniforms" and were required to follow McDonald's standards of "quality, service, and cleanliness." *O'Banner v McDonald's Corp.*, 653 NE2d 1267 (Ill App 1995). On further appeal to the Supreme Court of Illinois, the Court of Appeals was reversed because in order to recover on an apparent agency theory, the customer had to show that he actually relied on the apparent agency in going to the restaurant where he was injured. The customer failed to do so, thus losing the right to hold McDonald's Corp. liable for his injuries. *O'Banner v McDonald's Corp.*, 670 NE2d 632 (Ill 1996).

invoices, purchase orders, paychecks, and notices to employees should contain notice of the independent ownership and operation of the business. Finally, franchisors should require their franchisees to maintain appropriate comprehensive general liability insurance, workers' compensation insurance, and other appropriate insurance.

lawflix

Good Burger (1997)

This film is a story of the competition, mass marketing, and secret sauce issues in franchising. The movie provides a look at liability, product quality, and espionage.

For movie clips that illustrate business law concepts, see LawFlix at **www.cengage.com/blaw/dvl**.

MAKE THE CONNECTION

SUMMARY

The three principal forms of business organizations are sole proprietorships, partnerships, and corporations. A *sole proprietorship* is a form of business organization in which one person owns the business, controls all decisions, receives all profits, and has unlimited liability for all obligations and liabilities. A *partnership* involves the pooling of capital resources and talents of two or more persons whose goal is making a profit; the partners are subject to unlimited personal liability. However, newly created forms of business organizations—the *limited liability company* and the *limited liability partnership*—allow for tax treatment as a partnership with certain limited liability for the owners.

A business *corporation* exists to make a profit. It is created by government grant, and its shareholders elect a board of directors whose members are responsible for managing the business. A shareholder's liability is limited to the capital the shareholder invested in the business or paid for shares. Corporate existence continues without regard to the death of shareholders or the transfer of stock by them.

The selection of the form of organization is determined by the nature of the business, tax considerations, the financial risk involved, the importance of limited liability, and the extent of management control desired.

A *joint venture* exists when two or more persons combine their labor or property for a single business undertaking and share profits and losses as agreed. An unincorporated association is a combination of two or more persons for the pursuit of a common purpose.

A *cooperative* consists of two or more persons or enterprises, such as farmers, who cooperate to achieve a common objective, such as the distribution of farm products.

By a franchise, the owner of a trademark, trade name, or copyright licenses others to use the mark or copyright in selling goods or services. To protect against fraud, the FTC requires that franchisors provide prospective franchisees with a disclosure statement 10 days prior to any transaction. The Automobile Dealers' Day in Court Act and the Petroleum Marketing Practices Act are federal laws that provide covered franchisees with protection from bad-faith terminations. State laws also protect franchisees in a wide range of businesses. A franchisor is not liable to third persons dealing with its franchisees. Liability of the franchisor may, however, be imposed on the ground of the apparent authority of the franchisee or the latter's control by the franchisor. Liability of the franchisor may also arise in cases of product liability.

LEARNING OUTCOMES

After studying this chapter, you should be able to clearly explain:

A. PRINCIPAL FORMS OF BUSINESS ORGANIZATIONS

LO.1 Explain the advantages and disadvantages of the three principal forms of business organizations

> See the discussion on proprietorships, partnerships (LLPs and LLCs), and corporations beginning on p. 964.

B. SPECIALIZED FORMS OF ORGANIZATIONS

LO.2 Recognize that the rules of law governing the rights and liabilities of joint ventures are substantially the same as those that govern partnerships

> See the *PGI/Rathe* joint venture remedy on p. 966.

C. THE FRANCHISE BUSINESS FORMAT

LO.3 Evaluate whether a business arrangement is a franchise protected under state or federal law

> See the *Girl Scouts of Manitou* case applying a state's fair dealership law, p. 969.
> See the example where Mr. Arciniaga was allowed to proceed with his federal ADDCA lawsuit against General Motors on p. 970.

LO.4 Explain how the rights of the parties to a franchise agreement are determined by their contract

> See the *Burger King* example involving cancellation of franchises, p. 970.

LO.5 Explain why freedom from vicarious liability is a reason for franchisors to use the franchise format

> See the *McDonald's* case in which only the franchisee was liable for the torts to the minor emanating from the McDonald's restaurant, p. 972.

KEY TERMS

cooperative
corporations
franchise
franchise agreement
franchisee
franchisor
joint venture

limited liability
  company (LLC)
limited liability
  partnership (LLP)
partnership
sole or individual
  proprietorship

trade dress
trade name
trade secrets
trademarks
unincorporated
  association

QUESTIONS AND CASE PROBLEMS

1. When is a franchisor held liable to a third person dealing with or affected by the franchisee?

2. Jerome, Sheila, Gary, and Ella agreed to purchase a tract of land and make it available for use as a free playground for neighborhood children. They called the enterprise Meadowbrook Playground. Jerome and Gary improperly hung one of the playground swings, and a child was injured. Suit was brought against Meadowbrook Playground. Can damages be recovered?

3. Morris Friedman was president of Tiny Doubles International, Inc. He sold business opportunities for Tiny Doubles Studios, which made small photographic statues of people for customers. Friedman was the primary negotiator with prospective buyers of these studio business opportunities. He advised buyers up front that the opportunities were not franchises, and accordingly, he did not provide all of the information set forth in the disclosure rule on franchising, although he did provide full answers to all questions asked. Many businesses closed, however, because of lack of success. The FTC claims Friedman violated its disclosure rule. Friedman disagrees. Decide. [*FTC v Tiny Doubles Int'l, Inc.*, 1996 Bus. Franchise Guide (CCH) ¶ 10,831]

4. Wolf, King, and others sold business "opportunities" in vending machines by taking out ads in newspapers throughout the country. When individuals responded, telemarketers called "fronters" would tell them of false earnings estimates, and those who could afford $16,000 to $25,000 for vending machines were turned over to "closers" who promised wonderful results. References were provided who were "shills"—they did not own vending machines but were paid to tell "stories" that were monitored by Wolf, King, and other supervisors. None of the individuals was given franchise disclosure documents. King induced one investor to mortgage her house so that she could pay $70,000 for a number of vending machines. In three years Wolf, King, and others took in some $31.3 million. The FTC alleged that the defendants violated the FTC franchise disclosure rule.

    Is there a franchise disclosure rule violation if Wolf and King were merely selling vending machines? What if Wolf and King promised exclusive territories for the machines? Why would a franchise disclosure rule be necessary in this case? Decide. [*FTC v Wolf,* Bus. Franchise Guide ¶ 27,655 (CCH D Fla)]

5. Katherine Apostoleres owned the rights to Dunkin Donuts franchises in Brandon and Temple Terrace, Florida. The franchisor offered all its franchisees the right to renew their existing franchise agreements if they agreed to abide by advertising decisions favored by two-thirds of the local franchise owners in a given television market. Apostoleres refused the offer because she did not want to be bound by the two-thirds clause. Soon thereafter, Dunkin Donuts audited her two stores, and using a "yield and usage" analysis, it concluded that gross sales were being underreported. Based on these audits and a subsequent audit, Dunkin Donuts gave notice of immediate termination of Apostoleres's franchises, contending that the franchise agreement had been violated. Apostoleres stated that an implied obligation of good faith exists by operation of law in every contract, and she asserted that the audits were in retaliation for her refusal to accept the renewal agreement. The yield and usage test used in the audit was not specified in the franchise agreement as a measure to be used to enforce the franchisor's rights, and certain accounting experts testified as to the unreliability of this test. Was Dunkin Donuts liable for breach of its implied obligation of good faith in this case? [*Dunkin Donuts of America v Minerva, Inc.*, 956 F2d 1566 (11th Cir)]

6. To establish that a business is a "franchisee" qualifying for protection under the Illinois Franchise Disclosure Act, the business must demonstrate that it paid a franchise fee either directly or indirectly to the "franchisor" to enter the business. To-Am Equipment Company believed it had paid an implied fee in excess of $500 to enter the forklift business as a dealer for Mitsubishi-Caterpillar Forklift of America (MCFA) when it paid $1,658 for service manuals, which MCFA had commanded it to possess. MCFA denied that it had charged To-Am a franchise fee and asserted that it was not obligated to To-Am under the state Franchise Disclosure Act. Decide. [*To-Am Equipment co. v Mitsubishi-Caterpillar Forklift of America*, 853 Supp 987 (ND Ill)]

7. For a five-year period, Laurie Henry worked for James Doull, the owner of four Taco Bell franchises. During that time, she had an affair with Doull. He was the father of her two illegitimate children. Enraged over a domestic matter, Doull physically assaulted her at the Taco Bell Restaurant and then fired her and ordered her off the premises. Later, on Doull's recommendation, she was hired by a "company store" in an adjoining state. Henry brought suit against Doull, his corporate entity Taco Tia, Inc., and the Taco Bell Corporation (TBC). She did not characterize her suit as a case of sexual harassment. Rather, she contended that TBC was responsible for Doull's actions because he was TBC's agent. She sought damages for the loss of romantic and material satisfactions a person might expect from a traditional courtship and wedding. TBC denied that Doull was its employee or agent. The evidence showed that Henry knew that Doull's stores differed from TBC "company" stores. She insisted, having worked for four years for Doull at stores adorned with Taco-Bell signs, that Taco Bell was responsible for Doull's actions. Decide. [*Henry v Taco Tia, Inc.*, 606 So2d 1376 (La App)]

8. The Armory Committee was composed of officers from various National Guard units. It organized a New Year's Eve dance at a charge of $2 per person to defray costs. Perry, along with others, was a member of the Armory Committee. Libby was a paying guest at the dance who was injured by slipping on frozen ruts in the immediate approaches to the steps leading to the armory building where the dance was held. He sued Perry, Turner, and the other committee members. The evidence showed that every member of the committee had taken some part in planning or running the dance with the exception of Turner. Was the Armory Committee an unincorporated association or a joint venture? Decide. [*Libby v Perry*, 311 A2d 527 (Me)]

9. The Kawasaki Shop of Aurora, Illinois (dealer) advised Kawasaki Motors Corp. (manufacturer) that it intended to move its Kawasaki franchise from New York Street to Hill Avenue, which was in the same market area. The Hill Avenue location was also the site of a Honda franchise. The manufacturer's sales manager advised the dealer that he did not want the dealer to move in with Honda at the Hill Avenue site. In February, the dealer moved to the Hill Avenue location. Effective May 1, the manufacturer terminated the dealer's franchise. The dealer brought suit against the manufacturer under the state's Motor Vehicle Franchise Act, which made it unlawful to terminate franchises for site control (requiring that the dealer's site be used exclusively as a Kawasaki dealership). The manufacturer argued that it had a right to have its products sold by a dealer who was not affiliated with a competitor. Decide. [*Kawasaki Shop v Kawasaki Motors Corp.*, 544 NE2d 457 (Ill App)]

10. Goodward, a newly hired newspaper reporter for the *Cape Cod News*, learned that the local cranberry growers had made an agreement under which they pooled their cranberry crops each year and sold them at what they determined to be a fair price. Goodward believes that such an agreement is in restraint of trade and a violation of the antitrust laws. Is he correct?

11. Food Caterers of East Hartford, Connecticut, obtained a franchise from Chicken Delight to use that name at its store. Food Caterers agreed to the product standards and controls specified by the franchisor. The franchise contract required the franchisee to maintain a free delivery service to deliver hot, freshly prepared food to customers. The franchisee used a delivery truck that bore no sign or name. Its employee Carfiro was driving the truck in making a food delivery when he negligently struck and killed McLaughlin. The victim's estate sued Chicken Delight on the theory that Carfiro was its agent because he was doing work that Chicken Delight required and that benefited Chicken Delight. Was Carfiro the agent of Chicken Delight? [*McLaughlin's Estate v Chicken Delight, Inc.*, 321 A2d 456 (Conn)]

12. Groseth had the International Harvester (IH) truck franchise in Yankton, South Dakota. The franchise agreement Groseth signed required dealers to "cooperate with the Company by placing orders for goods in accordance with advance ordering programs announced by the Company." IH wanted to terminate Groseth's franchise because he refused to comply with IH's requirement that a computerized "dealer communication network" (DCN) be set up. Under the

DCN, each dealer was required to obtain a computer terminal, display screen, and software. The DCN was initially used for ordering parts and allowed IH to reduce the number of employees needed for manual processing of "parts" orders. Groseth refused to set up the DCN because of the expense. Moreover, he contended that the task of ordering parts was easily accomplished by telephone or written orders. Did IH have good cause to terminate Groseth's franchise? [*Groseth International Harvester, Inc. v International Harvester*, 442 NW2d 229 (SD)]

13. Brenner was in the scrap iron business. Almost daily, Plitt lent Brenner money with which to purchase scrap iron. The agreement of the parties was that when the scrap was sold, Plitt would be repaid and would receive an additional sum as compensation for making the loans. The loans were to be repaid in any case without regard to whether Brenner made a profit. A dispute arose over the nature of the relationship between the two men. Plitt claimed that it was a joint venture. Decide. [*Brenner v Plitt*, 34 A2d 853 (Md)]

14. Donald Salisbury, William Roberts, and others purchased property from Laurel Chapman, a partner of Chapman Realty, a franchisee of Realty World. The purchasers made payments directly to Laurel Chapman at the Realty World office, and Chapman was to make payments on the property's mortgage. However, Chapman did not make the payments and absconded with the funds. Salisbury and Roberts sued the franchisor, Realty World, claiming that Realty World was liable for the wrongful acts of the apparent agent, Chapman. Realty World and Chapman Realty were parties to a franchise agreement stating that the parties were franchisor and franchisee. The agreement contained a clause that required Chapman to prominently display a certificate in the office setting forth her status as an independent franchisee. Chapman displayed such a sign, but the plaintiffs did not recall seeing it. Chapman Realty hires, supervises, and sets the compensation for all of its employees. The plaintiffs pointed out that Chapman Realty used the service mark Realty World on its signs, both outside and inside its offices. They pointed out that a Realty World manual sets forth the general standards by which franchisees must run their businesses and that this represents clear control over the franchise. They contended that, all things considered, Realty World held out Chapman Realty as having authority to bind Realty World. Realty World disagreed, stating that both were independent businesses. Decide. [*Salisbury v Chapman and Realty World, Inc.*, 65 NE2d 127 (Ill App)]

15. H.C. Blackwell Co. held a franchise from Kenworth Truck Co. to sell its trucks. After 12 years, the franchise was nearing expiration. Kenworth notified Blackwell that the franchise would not be renewed unless Blackwell sold more trucks and improved its building and bookkeeping systems within the next 90 days. Blackwell spent $90,000 attempting to meet the demands of Kenworth but could not do so because a year was required to make the specified changes. Kenworth refused to renew the franchise. Blackwell sued Kenworth for damages under the federal Automobile Dealers' Day in Court Act. Blackwell claimed that Kenworth had refused to renew in bad faith. Decide. [*Blackwell v Kenworth Truck Co.*, 620 F2d 104 (5th Cir)]

CPA QUESTIONS

1. A joint venture is a(an):

   a. Association limited to no more than two persons in business for profit

   b. Enterprise of numerous co-owners in a nonprofit undertaking

   c. Corporate enterprise for a single undertaking of limited duration

   d. Association of persons engaged as co-owners in a single undertaking for profit

Chapter 42

PARTNERSHIPS

P artnerships may be created without the formality of even a written partnership agreement when two or more individuals simply operate a business for a profit as co-owners. In the 1970s, David Silvernail, Sr. operated a welding business out of a shop adjacent to his residence. Years later, his son Paul joined him in the business. In 1999, David withdrew from the business, and Paul continued to operate it. When the parties could not agree on a division of assets in 2002, a court reverted to partnership law to resolve the controversy.[1] Partnership relations are not narrowly governed by partnership law but are governed by the partners' partnership agreement. Only when the partnership agreement does not resolve an issue does partnership law apply. In many instances, individuals do not obtain legal advice in choosing the partnership form of business organization. Properly informed individuals today will probably not choose the partnership form of organization because partners are open to unlimited personal liability; they may choose a limited liability company to insulate the members from personal liability.

A. Nature and Creation

Partnerships are created by agreement. A codification of general partnership law is found in the Uniform Partnership Act, (UPA), which has been revised (Revised Uniform Partnership Act, or RUPA). Together, the UPA and the RUPA are in effect in 49 states.[2] Limited partnerships (LPs) and limited liability partnerships (LLPs) differ significantly from general partnerships and are discussed in the next chapter. The 1994 version of the Revised Uniform Partnership Act applies in 35 states.[3] Like the UPA, most of the provisions of the RUPA apply only when the partners do not have partnership agreement language that deals with the matter at issue.[4] Certain features of the RUPA that differ from those of the UPA are identified in the text.

1. Definition

A **partnership** (also called a **general partnership**) is a relationship created by the voluntary "association of two or more persons to carry on as co-owners a business for profit."[5] The persons so associated are called **partners** or **general partners**. A partner is the agent of the partnership and of each partner with respect to

partnership–pooling of capital resources and the business or professional talents of two or more individuals (partners) with the goal of making a profit.

general partnership– partnership in which the partners conduct as co-owners a business for profit, and each partner has a right to take part in the management of the business and has unlimited liability.

partner–one of two or more persons who jointly own and carry on a business for profit.

general partners–partners who publicly and actively engage in the transaction of firm business.

---

[1] *Silvernail v Silvernail*, 804 NYS2d 116 (App Div 2005).
[2] The UPA or the RUPA is in effect in all states except Louisiana.
[3] The RUPA or versions of it have been adopted by Alabama, Alaska, Arizona, Arkansas, California, Colorado, Connecticut, Delaware, District of Columbia, Florida, Hawaii, Idaho, Illinois, Iowa, Kansas, Maryland, Minnesota, Mississppi, Montana, Nebraska, Nevada, New Jersey, New Mexico, North Dakota, Ohio, Oklahoma, Oregon, Puerto Rico, South Dakota, Tennessee, Texas, Vermont, Virginia, Washington, West Virginia, and Wyoming. The RUPA was approved in 1992 and amended in 1993, 1994, and 1997. It provides for a transition period after passage, during which only newly created partnerships come under the new law, with all partnerships in the state eventually being governed by the RUPA (see RUPA § 1206(a)).
[4] *See Mission West v Republic*, 873 A2d 372 (Md App 2005).
[5] UPA § 6(1).

partnership matters. A partner is not an employee of the partnership even when doing work that would ordinarily be done by an employee.

C A S E   S U M M A R Y

A Partner Is Not an Employee

FACTS: Ford and Mitcham were partners engaged in construction. Ford was killed at work. His widow made a claim for workers' compensation against the partnership. Mitcham opposed the claim on the ground that Ford was a partner, not an employee.

DECISION: Workers' compensation denied. While a working partner does work, a partner is not an employee. The essential element of an employment relationship is the right of the employer to control the employee. Although a partner is required to act in a proper manner, a partner is not subject to the control of the partnership in the same sense as an employee and therefore is not an "employee" of the partnership for the purpose of workers' compensation. [**Ford v Mitcham 298 So2d 34 Ala Civ App 1974**]

---

2. Characteristics of a Partnership

A partnership has distinguishing characteristics:

1. A partnership is a voluntary, consensual relationship.

2. A partnership involves partners' contributions of capital, services, or a combination of these.

3. The partners are associated as co-owners to transact the business of the firm for profit.

unincorporated association–combination of two or more persons for the furtherance of a common nonprofit purpose.

If profit is not the object, the group will commonly be an **unincorporated association**.

The UPA does not make the partnership a separate entity, and, therefore, suit cannot be brought by the firm in its name in the absence of a special statute or procedural rule so providing. However, in RUPA states, partnerships are recognized as "entities."

3. Rights of Partners

The rights of partners are determined by the partnership agreement. If written, this agreement is interpreted by the same rules that govern the interpretation of any other written document. Any matter not covered by the partnership agreement may be covered by a provision of the applicable UPA or RUPA.

4. Partnership Agreement

Because of the complexity of the problems involved, *partnership agreements* are typically written. However, there is no requirement that they be in writing unless compliance with a statute of frauds is required. **For Example,** the world's highest-paid performers in the early 1990s, the New Kids on the Block, who grossed $74.1 million in one year, were a group started by promoter Maurice Starr. He obtained $60,000 from James Martorano, who was connected with organized crime, and $50,000 from businessman Jeffrey Furst to finance the initial recording and promotion of the group. Martorano and Furst testified that ultimately all three agreed with a handshake that 50 percent of the profits from the group would be shared between Martorano as a silent partner and Furst, who would also provide limousine service and security. They testified that Starr would keep half of the profits. Starr denied that a partnership existed because he believed that such an alleged business arrangement would have had to be reduced to writing with great detail. However, based on the evidence, which included damaging testimony that Starr tried to buy some witnesses' silence, a jury decided that a binding oral partnership agreement existed.[6]

To reduce or avoid disputes and litigation, partnership agreements should be in writing. Courts will enforce partnership agreements, under the standards of the law of contracts, according to the agreements' terms. **For Example,** dentist Steven Schwartz was terminated from a three-dentist practice "without cause" by vote of his two other partners. The partnership agreement allowed for termination of a partner as long as either party gave the other 90 days notice. The appeals court interpreted the partnership agreement as written, finding that the provision was entered into by sophisticated and highly educated professionals, and not in violation of public policy.[7]

The formal document that is prepared to evidence the contract of the parties is termed a **partnership agreement**, **articles of partnership**, or **articles of copartnership**. The partnership agreement governs the partnership during its existence and may contain provisions relating to dissolution. (See Figure 42.1.)

partnership agreement–
document prepared to evidence the contract of the parties. (Parties—partners or general partners)

articles of partnership–See *Partnership Agreement.*

articles of copartnership–
See *Partnership Agreement.*

CPA   ## 5. Determining the Existence of a Partnership

If the parties agree that the legal relationship between them shall be such that they in fact operate a business for profit as co-owners, a partnership is created even though the parties may not have labeled their new relationship as such.[8] The law is concerned with the substance of what is done rather than the name. Conversely, a partnership does not arise if the parties do not agree to the elements of a partnership even though they call it one.[9]

---

[6] *Boston Globe*, November 13, 1995, 13. For an example of a situation in which no oral partnership was found to exist, see *Prince v O'Brien*, 683 NYS2d 504 (App Div 1998). Marvin Prince and Darren O'Brien met and became friends while living in Toronto. Prince, a Jamaican native, helped O'Brien refine his reggae-singing ability and knowledge of Jamaican dialect, and participated in the coining of O'Brien's stage name "Snow." Before O'Brien became a success with his debut reggae album *12 Inches of Snow*, the friends may have casually discussed splitting their hypothetical profits equally but never agreed to share losses. Later, when Marvin Prince toured with O'Brien, he was designated and paid as an employee of O'Brien's corporation. The court found that Prince failed to prove the existence of an oral partnership agreement.

[7] *Schwartz v Family Dental Group*, PC, 943 A2d 1122 (Conn App 2008).

[8] *In re Estate of Bolinger*, 921 P2d 767 (Mont 1998).

[9] See *Cleland v Thirion*, 704 NYS2d 316 (App Div 2000).

CASE SUMMARY

The Case of the Absolutely Dumbfounded Investor (Partner)

FACTS: David Byker, an accountant, and Tom Mannes, a real estate professional, agreed to engage in an ongoing business enterprise to raise investment funds for separate real estate– related ventures and to share equally in the profits, losses, and expenses. Over the years, the parties pursued various individual limited partnerships, sharing equally in commissions, financing fees, and termination costs. Byker and Mannes then created a subsequent entity, Pier 1000, Ltd., to own and manage a marina. This venture was not successful, and they took profits from a prior entity and borrowed money to continue operations. The unsuccessful marina was later returned to its previous owners in exchange for assumption of Byker's and Mannes's direct obligations to that business. The nine-year business relationship between them ceased. Later, Byker approached Mannes and requested that he share in the payments resulting from losses that were incurred from their various entities. Mannes was, in his words, "absolutely dumbfounded" by the request, and he refused payment. Byker sued, contending that a general partnership was underlying all their business affairs. Mannes asserted that he merely invested in separate business ventures with Byker and that there were no other understandings between them.

DECISION: Judgment for David Byker. Partnership law does not require that individuals be aware of their status as "partners" to have a legal partnership. The intent to create a partnership is not required if the acts and the conduct of the parties otherwise evidence that the parties carried on as co-owners of a business for profit. No writing is needed to form a partnership. No name or tax ID number is necessary to attain legal status as a partnership, nor is it required that the parties must aggregate all entities under a general partnership tax return. Mannes filed his tax returns based on his share of the income and expense from the individual legal entities that existed with the legal status of each entity controlling his tax obligations. However, additional evidence indicated that a partnership existed, including the general agreement in principle from the beginning that they would share profits and losses together in their real estate investment business. While they should have created a legal entity to address the situation that precipitated the lawsuit, because they did not, partnership law applies. [**Byker v Mannes, 641 NW2d 210 Mich 2002**]

A partnership is shown to exist when it is established that the parties have agreed to the formation of a business organization that has the characteristics of a partnership. The burden of proving the existence of a partnership is on the person who claims that one exists.[10]

When the nature of the relationship is not clear, the following rules aid in determining whether the parties have created a partnership.

CPA   (A) CONTROL. The presence or absence of control of a business enterprise is significant in determining whether there is a partnership and whether a particular person is a partner.

---

[10] *MacArthur v Stein*, 934 P2d 214 (Mont 1997).

FIGURE 42-1 | *Partnership Agreement*

PARTNERSHIP AGREEMENT

THIS IS A PARTNERSHIP AGREEMENT EXECUTED AT CINCINNATI, OHIO, THIS 9TH DAY OF SEPTEMBER, 1998, BY AND AMONG LOUIS K. HALL, SHARON B. YOUNG, AND C. LYNN MUELLER, INDIVIDUALS RESIDING IN CINCINNATI, OHIO, HEREINAFTER SOMETIMES REFERRED TO INDIVIDUALLY AS "PARTNER" AND COLLECTIVELY AS "PARTNERS."

RECITALS

THE PARTNERS TO THIS AGREEMENT DESIRE TO ACQUIRE A CERTAIN PARCEL OF REAL ESTATE AND TO DEVELOP SUCH REAL ESTATE FOR LEASE OR SALE, ALL FOR INVESTMENT PURPOSES. THIS AGREEMENT IS BEING EXECUTED TO DELINEATE THE BASIS OF THEIR RELATIONSHIP.

PROVISIONS

1. NAME; AND PRINCIPAL OFFICES. THE NAME OF THE PARTNERSHIP SHALL BE: HALL, YOUNG AND MUELLER, ASSOCIATES. ITS PRINCIPAL PLACE OF BUSINESS SHALL BE AT: 201 RIVER ROAD, CINCINNATI, OHIO 45238.

2. PURPOSE. THE PURPOSE OF THE PARTNERSHIP SHALL BE TO PURCHASE AND OWN FOR INVESTMENT PURPOSES, A CERTAIN PARCEL OF REAL ESTATE LOCATED AT 602 SIXTH STREET, CINCINNATI, OHIO, AND TO ENGAGE IN ANY OTHER TYPE OF INVESTMENT ACTIVITIES THAT THE PARTNERSHIP MAY FROM TIME TO TIME HEREINAFTER UNANIMOUSLY AGREE UPON.

3. CAPITAL CONTRIBUTIONS. THE CAPITAL OF THE PARTNERSHIP SHALL BE THE AGGREGATE AMOUNT OF CASH AND PROPERTY CONTRIBUTED BY THE PARTNERS. A CAPITAL ACCOUNT SHALL BE MAINTAINED FOR EACH PARTNER.

A. CAPITAL CONTRIBUTIONS. ANY ADDITIONAL CAPITAL WHICH MAY BE REQUIRED BY THE PARTNERSHIP SHALL BE CONTRIBUTED TO THE PARTNERSHIP BY THE PARTNERS IN THE SAME RATIO AS THAT PARTNER'S ORIGINAL CONTRIBUTION TO CAPITAL AS TO THE TOTAL OF ALL ORIGINAL CAPITAL CONTRIBUTIONS TO THE PARTNERSHIP UNLESS OTHERWISE AGREED BY THE PARTNERS.

CPA (B) Sharing Profits and Losses. The fact that the parties share profits and losses is strong evidence of a partnership.[11]

CPA (C) Sharing Profits. An agreement that does not provide for sharing losses but does provide for sharing profits is evidence that the parties are partners. If the partners share profits, it is assumed that they will also share losses. Sharing profits is prima facie evidence of a partnership. However, a partnership is not to be inferred when profits are received in payment (1) of a debt, (2) of wages, (3) of an annuity to a deceased partner's surviving spouse or representative, (4) of interest, or (5) for the goodwill of the business.[12] **For Example,** the fact that one doctor receives one-half of the net income does not establish that doctor as a partner of another doctor when the former was guaranteed a minimum annual amount. Also, federal income tax and Social Security contributions were deducted from the payments to the doctor, thus indicating that the relationship was employer and employee. If there is no evidence of the reason for receiving the profits, a partnership of the parties involved exists.

CPA (D) Gross Returns. The sharing of gross returns is itself very slight, if any, evidence of partnership. **For Example,** in a case in which one party owned a show that was

---

[11] *Botsee Gates v Houston*, 897 NE2d 532 (Ind App 2008).
[12] UPA § 7(4).

exhibited on land owned by another under an agreement to divide the gross proceeds, no partnership was proven. There was no co-ownership or community of interest in the business.

CPA   (E) **Contribution of Skill or Labor.** The fact that all persons have not contributed capital to an enterprise does not establish that the enterprise is not a partnership. A partnership may be formed even though some of its members furnish only skill or labor.

C A S E   S U M M A R Y

Can You Fire Your Partner?

FACTS: On graduating from Vanderbilt University with a degree in economics, James Pettes began working for Video Magic, a video rental business. In 1987, Dr. Gordon Yukon, a pediatrician, wanted to invest in a two-store video business called Rent-a-Flick, with one store located on Quince Road and the other in Germantown. Pettes testified that Yukon paid $42,000 for the business. Pettes testified that they agreed they would be partners, with Pettes managing the two stores and earning the same amount he earned at Video Magic. Pettes testified that he worked 70 to 80 hours a week and his capital contribution was "sweat equity." He also testified that many times Yukon told him and others that Pettes and Yukon were partners. Pettes testified that in the middle of 1992, the parties agreed to divide the business so that the Germantown store would go to Yukon and the Quince Road store would go to Pettes. In December 1992, Pettes made a written demand for an accounting. On January 5, 1993, Dr. Yukon "fired" Pettes. Sutherland, an employee, testified that she questioned Yukon about this action because Pettes was a partner, and Yukon's reply was not a denial of the partnership but rather a claim that in the absence of written proof, Pettes could not prove such an arrangement. Pettes sued for breach of an oral partnership agreement and an accounting.

DECISION: Judgment for Pettes. From the totality of the proof in this case, the parties intended a partnership and co-ownership to the extent that a dissolution agreement would result in Yukon's acquiring the Germantown store and Pettes's acquiring the Quince Road store. The implied partnership and agreed dissolution of the partnership are binding on the parties, and Pettes is entitled to the value of the Quince Road store as of January 3, 1993. [**Pettes v Yukon, 912 SW2d 709 Tenn App 1995**]

CPA   (F) **Fixed Payment.** When a person who performs continuing services for another receives a fixed payment that does not depend on the existence of profit and is not affected by losses, that person is not a partner.

CPA   ## 6. Partners as to Third Persons

In some instances, persons who are in fact not partners may be held liable to third persons as though they were partners. This liability arises when they conduct themselves in such a manner that others are reasonably led to believe that they are partners and to act in reliance on that belief to their injury.[13] A person who is held liable as a partner under such circumstances is termed a *nominal partner*, a *partner by estoppel*, or an *ostensible partner*.

[13] UPA § 16(1); *Andrews v Elwell*, 367 F Supp 2d 35 (D Mass 2005).

Partnership liability may arise by estoppel when a person who in fact is not a partner is described as a partner in a document filed with the government provided the person so described has in some way participated in the filing of the document and the person claiming the benefit of the estoppel had knowledge of that document and relied on the statement. **For Example,** Jean Collins allowed the partnership of Holt and Schwark to use her name to help the partnership get started. A business name registration certificate filed at city hall and signed by all of the individuals specifies Holt, Schwark, and Collins as partners. If a creditor who sees this registration statement extends credit to the firm in reliance in part on the fact that Collins is a partner, Collins is estopped from denying that she is a partner. She has a partner's liability along with the other partners insofar as that creditor is concerned.

Under the RUPA, an apparent partnership or partnership by estoppel is called a *purported* partnership, and a third person who relies on the partnership's representations that the purported partner had authority to bind the partnership can hold it liable as if the purported partner were an actual partner with authority.[14] Under the RUPA, a partnership can limit potential liability with a publicly recorded statement of partnership authority or limitation on partner authority.[15]

CPA 7. Partnership Property

In general, partnership property consists of all property contributed by the partners or acquired for the firm or with its funds.

There is usually no limitation on the type and amount of property that a partnership may acquire. The firm may own real as well as personal property unless it is prohibited from doing so by statute or by the partnership agreement.

The parties may agree that real estate owned by one of the partners should become partnership property. When this intent exists, the particular property constitutes partnership property even if it is still in the name of the original owner.

Article 2 of the RUPA recognizes that partnerships are "entities" that can acquire and own property in the partnership's name. If a partner desires to retain an interest in property contributed to the partnership in RUPA states, the partner must condition the transfer of the property to the partnership to reflect this interest or set forth the condition in the partnership agreement. Otherwise, the property becomes partnership property under the entity theory, and the contributing partner has no right to get it back, even in liquidation.[16]

8. Tenancy in Partnership

tenancy in partnership– ownership relationship that exists between partners under the Uniform Partnership Act.

Under the UPA, partners hold title to firm property by **tenancy in partnership**.[17] The characteristics of such a tenancy are as follows:

1. Each partner has an equal right to use firm property for partnership purposes in the absence of a contrary agreement.

---

[14] RUPA § 308.
[15] RUPA § 303.
[16] RUPA § 204.
[17] UPA § 25(1); *Krause v Vollmar*, 614 NE2d 1136 (Ohio App 1992).

2. A partner possesses no divisible interest in any specific item of partnership property that can be voluntarily sold, assigned, or mortgaged by a partner.

3. A creditor of a partner cannot proceed against any specific items of partnership property. The creditor can proceed only against the partner's interest in the partnership. This is done by applying to a court for a **charging order**. By this procedure, the share of any profits that would be paid to the debtor-partner is paid to a receiver on behalf of the creditor, or the court may direct the sale of the interest of the debtor-partner in the partnership.

4. Upon the death of a partner, the partnership property vests in the surviving partners for partnership purposes and is not subject to the rights of the surviving spouse of the deceased partner.

charging order—order by a court, after a business partner's personal assets are exhausted, requiring that the partner's share of the profits be paid to a creditor until the debt is discharged.

CPA   ### 9. Assignment of a Partner's Interest

Although a partner cannot transfer specific items of partnership property in the absence of authority to so act on behalf of the partnership, a partner's interest in the partnership may be voluntarily assigned by the partner. The assignee does not become a partner without the consent of the other partners. Without this consent, the assignee is entitled to receive only the assignor's share of the profits during the continuance of the partnership and the assignor's interest upon the dissolution of the firm. The assignee has no right to participate in the management of the partnership or to inspect the books of the partnership.

B. Authority of Partners

The scope of a partner's authority is determined by the partnership agreement and by the nature of the partnership.

10. Authority of Majority of Partners

When there are more than two partners in a firm, the decision of the majority prevails in matters involving how the ordinary functions of the business will be conducted. To illustrate, a majority of the partners of a firm decide to increase the firm's advertising. They subsequently enter into a contract for that purpose. The transaction is valid and binds the firm and all of the partners.

Majority action is not binding if it contravenes the partnership agreement. For such matters, unanimous action is required.[18] Thus, the majority of the members cannot change the nature of the business against the protests of the minority.

When there are an even number of partners, an even division on a matter that requires majority approval is always a possibility. In such a case, the partnership is deadlocked. When the partners are evenly divided on any question, one partner has no authority to act.

[18] UPA § 18(h).

C A S E   S U M M A R Y

Strictly Business, or Trashing Your Partner?

FACTS: Summers and Dooley formed a partnership to collect trash. Summers became unable to work, and he hired a third man to do his work and paid him out of his personal funds. Summers suggested to Dooley that the third man be paid from the partnership funds, but Dooley refused to do so. Finally, Summers sued Dooley for reimbursement for the money he had spent to pay the third man.

DECISION: Judgment for Dooley. Summers had no authority to employ the third man at the expense of the firm. Because the partners were evenly divided on the question of such employment, Summers had no authority to act. [**Summers v Dooley, 481 P2d 318 (Idaho 1971)**]

If the division is over a basic issue and the partners persist in the deadlock so that it is impossible to continue the business, any one of the partners may petition the court to order the dissolution of the firm.

11. Express Authority of Individual Partners

express authority–
authority of an agent to
perform a certain act.

An individual partner may have **express authority** to perform certain acts either because the partnership agreement provides for this or because a sufficient number of partners have agreed to it.

A partner's authority to act for the firm is similar to that of an agent to act for a principal. Thus, in addition to express authority, a partner has the authority to do those acts that are customary for a member of a partnership conducting the particular business of that partnership.[19] As in the case of an agent, the acts of a partner in excess of authority do not ordinarily bind the partnership.

12. Customary Authority of Individual Partners

A partner, by virtue of being a comanager of the business, customarily has certain powers necessary and proper for carrying out that business. The scope of such powers varies with the nature of the partnership and with the business customs and usages of the area in which the partnership operates.

A partner may make any contract necessary to transact the firm's business.

C A S E   S U M M A R Y

"Jerry Should Have Run It by Me," Silvio Seethed

FACTS: Silvio Giannetti and his daughter and son-in-law, Anne Marie and Jerry Pruzinsky, are partners in a general partnership known as Giannetti Investment Company (GIC), which owns and operates Brougham Manor Apartments. Jerry entered into an access agreement with Omnicom, a provider of cable television services, giving Omnicom the right to enter Brougham Manor for purposes

---

[19] *Ball v Carlson*, 641 P2d 303 (Colo App 1981).

Continued

of installing, maintaining, and promoting cable service. Some time later, when he learned of the contract, Silvio denied Omnicom access to the property. Omnicom was unable to repair a signal leakage problem and was forced to discontinue cable service. Omnicom sued GIC for breach of contract. GIC contended that Jerry did not sign the agreement in the partnership name and thereby failed to bind GIC.

DECISION: Judgment for Omnicom. A contract executed in the name of a partner is binding on the partnership. Jerry executed the contract in the usual course of GIC's business, for it is a typical activity for an apartment complex to contract for cable television. [**Omnicom v Giannetti Investment Co., 561 NW2d 138 (Mich App 1997)**]

A partner can sell the firm's goods in the regular course of business, make purchases within the scope of the business, and borrow money for firm purposes. When borrowing money, a partner may execute commercial paper in the firm's name or give security such as a mortgage.[20] A partner may purchase insurance, hire employees, and adjust claims for or against the firm. Notice given to a partner is effective notice to the partnership.[21]

13. Limitations on Authority

The partners may agree to limit the powers of each partner. When a partner, contrary to such an agreement, executes a contract on behalf of the firm with a third person, the firm is bound if the third person was unaware of the limitation. In this case, the partner violating the agreement is liable to the other partners for any loss caused by the breach of the limitation. Under the UPA, if the third person knew of the limitation, the firm would not be bound.[22] Under the RUPA, the term *knew* is confined to actual knowledge,[23] which is cognitive awareness. Under the RUPA, a partnership may file a statement of partnership authority setting forth any restrictions on a general partner's authority.[24]

For Example, Bernard Roeger was general partner of RNR, with three limited partners. Restrictions were clearly set forth in the partnership agreement limiting Roeger's borrowing authority to no more than $650,000 for the construction of a building on partnership property. Roeger on behalf of RNR entered a construction loan agreement with People's Bank with a note and mortgage in the amount of $990,000, and over an 18-month period, the bank disbursed an aggregate sum of $952,699. The bank did not request a written consent from any of the other partners or review the partnership agreement. When the loan was not paid, the bank

---

[20] *U.S. Leather v H&W Partnership*, 60 F3d 222 (5th Cir 1995).
[21] *Cham, Hill, Inc., v Block & Veatch*, 557 NW2d 829 (Wis App 1996).
[22] UPA § 9(4).
[23] RUPA § 102(a).
[24] RUPA § 303.

| FIGURE 42-2 | *Limitations on Authority of Individual Partner to Bind Partnership* |

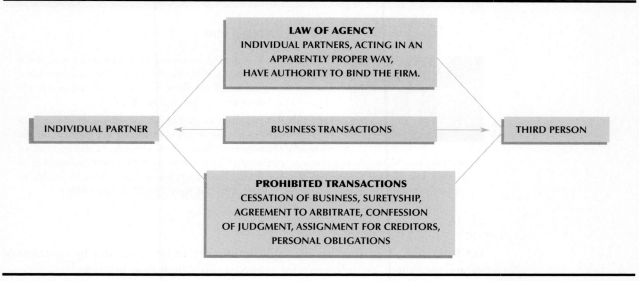

foreclosed on the property. RNR defended on behalf of the partnership that the bank negligently failed to investigate and discover the limitation on Roeger's authority to borrow. The case was decided for the bank because it had no actual knowledge or notice of the restriction on the general partner's authority. The court also pointed out that the partnership could have protected itself by filing a statement of partnership authority setting forth the restrictions on the general partner under RUPA section 303.[25]

A third person must not assume that a partner has all of the authority that the partner purports to have. If there is anything that would put a reasonable person on notice that the partner's powers are limited, the third person is bound by that limitation.

The third person must be on the alert for the following prohibited transactions because they warn that the partner with whom the third person deals has either restricted authority or no authority at all. (See Figure 42.2.)

14. Prohibited Transactions

A partner cannot enter into certain transactions on behalf of the partnership unless expressly authorized to do so. A third person entering into such a transaction does so at the risk that the partner has not been authorized. The following are prohibited transactions.

(A) CESSATION OF BUSINESS. A partner cannot bind the firm by a contract that would make it impossible for the firm to conduct its usual business.[26]

[25] *RNR Investments, Ltd. v People's First Community Bank*, 812 So2d 561 (Fla App 2002).
[26] *Wales v Roll*, 769 P2d 899 (Wyo 1989).

CASE SUMMARY

Family Feud

FACTS: The Patel family, consisting of parents and a son, was a partnership that owned and operated a motel. The parents made a contract to sell the motel, but thereafter the son refused to sell. He claimed that the contract of sale was not binding.

DECISION: Judgment for the son. The motel was not an asset held by the partnership for sale. It was an asset that was essential for the running of the partnership/business. Accordingly, neither one partner nor a majority had implied authority to sell the motel. To the contrary, the unanimous consent of all partners was required for the sale of the motel because such a sale would make it impossible to continue the partnership business. [**Patel v Patel, 260 Cal Rptr 255 (Cal App 1989)**]

(B) **SURETYSHIP.** A partner has no implied authority to bind the firm by contracts of surety, guarantee, or indemnity for purposes other than firm business.[27]

(C) **ARBITRATION.** A partner cannot submit controversies of the firm to arbitration "unless authorized by the other partners or unless they have abandoned the business."[28]

(D) **CONFESSION OF JUDGMENT.** All partners should have an opportunity to defend in court. Because of this, a partner cannot confess judgment against the firm on one of its obligations. Exceptions exist when the other partners consent or when they have abandoned the business.

(E) **ASSIGNMENT FOR CREDITORS.** A partner cannot make a general assignment of firm property for the benefit of creditors unless authorized by the other partners or unless they have abandoned the business.

(F) **PERSONAL OBLIGATIONS.** A partner cannot discharge personal obligations or claims of the firm by interchanging them in any way.

C. DUTIES, RIGHTS, AND LIABILITIES OF PARTNERS

The rights and duties of partners are based on their dual capacity of agent and co-owner.

15. Duties of partners

In many respects, the duties of a partner are the same as those of an agent.

(A) **LOYALTY AND GOOD FAITH.** Each partner must act in good faith toward the partnership. One partner must not take any advantage over the other(s) by the

[27] *First Interstate Bank of Oregon v Bergendahl*, 723 P2d 1005 (Or App 1986).
[28] UPA § 9(3)(e).

slightest misrepresentation or concealment.[29] Each partner owes a duty of loyalty to the firm. This duty requires a partner's devotion to the firm's business and bars making any secret profit at the expense of the firm.[30]

Moreover, the duty of loyalty bars the use of the firm's property for personal benefit or the exploitation of a business opportunity of the partnership for personal gain. **For Example,** when one partner renewed the lease of the building occupied by the firm but the lease was renewed in the name of that partner alone, that partner was compelled to hold the lease for the firm. The failure to renew the lease in the name of the firm was a breach of the duties of good faith and loyalty owed to the firm.

A partner cannot promote a competing business. A partner who does so is liable for damages sustained by the partnership.

Each partner also owes a fiduciary duty of good faith to all other partners. This duty extends to any transaction connected with the formation, conduct, or liquidation of the partnership.

A breach of fiduciary duty requires the complete forfeiture of all compensation during the period of the breach. **For Example,** general partners Michael Morton and Scott DeGraff breached their fiduciary duty to their partners when they did not disclose the parts of a deal they were keeping for themselves relating to a proposed relocation of the partnership's Las Vegas nightclub, Drink. Morton and DeGraff had been paid $833,190 in management fees during the period of time they were found to be in breach of their fiduciary duty to the partnership, and the court ordered them to return these funds to the partnership.[31]

(B) OBEDIENCE. Each partner is obligated to perform all duties and to obey all restrictions imposed by the partnership agreement or by the vote of the required number of partners.[32] **For Example,** when the partnership agreement required that each partner in an insurance sales firm give his "entire time" to the business and "not engage in any other business that would work to the disadvantage of the partnership," Richard Levatino's engaging in an insurance-related business outside the firm was a breach of the partnership agreement and was a proper basis for the assessment of punitive damages.[33]

(C) OTHER DUTIES. A partner must refrain from engaging in grossly negligent or intentional misconduct in transacting firm business under the RUPA.[34] Partners are accountable as a fiduciary and must hold as trustee for the firm any profits derived by a partner without the consent of the other partners.[35]

CPA 16. Rights of Partners as Owners

Each partner, in the absence of a contrary agreement, has the following rights. These rights stem from the fact that the partner is a co-owner of the partnership business.

---

[29] *Brosseau v Ranzau*, 81 SW3d 381 (Tex App 2002).
[30] Under RUPA 404(e), partners may pursue their own interests without automatically violating their fiduciary duties to the firm.
[31] *Caparos v Morton*, 845 NE2d 773 (Ill App 2006).
[32] *Cobin v Rice*, 823 F Supp 1419 (D Ind 1993).
[33] *Gates, Duncan, and VanCamp v Levatino*, 962 SW2d 21 (Tenn App 1997).
[34] RUPA § 404(c).
[35] UPA § 21; RUPA § 404(b)(1).

CPA (A) **MANAGEMENT.** Each partner has a right to take an equal part in transacting the business of the firm. It is immaterial that one partner contributed more than another or that one contributed only services.

Incidental to the right to manage the partnership, each partner has the right to possession of the partnership property for the purposes of the partnership.

CPA (B) **INSPECTION OF BOOKS.** All partners are equally entitled to inspect the books of the firm. "The partnership books shall be kept, subject to any agreement between the partners, at the principal place of business of the partnership, and every partner shall at all times have access to and may inspect and copy any of them."[36]

CPA (C) **SHARE OF PROFITS.** Each partner is entitled to a share of the profits. The partners may provide, if they so wish, that profits shall be shared in unequal proportions. In the absence of such a provision in the partnership agreement, each partner is entitled to an equal share of the profits without regard to the amount of capital contributed or services performed for the partnership.

CPA (D) **COMPENSATION.** In the absence of a contrary agreement, a partner is not entitled to compensation for services performed for the partnership. There is no right to compensation even if the services are unusual or more extensive than the services rendered by other partners. Consequently, when one partner becomes seriously ill and the other partners transact all of the firm's business, they are not entitled to compensation for those services. The sickness of a partner is considered a risk assumed in the relationship. No agreement can be inferred that the active partners are to be compensated even though the services rendered by them are such that they would ordinarily be rendered in the expectation of receiving compensation. As an exception, "a surviving partner is entitled to reasonable compensation for services performed in winding up the partnership affairs."[37]

Contrary to the preceding, the partners may agree that one of the partners will devote full time as manager of the business and receive for such services a salary in addition to the managing partner's share of the profits.

(E) **REPAYMENT OF LOANS.** A partner is entitled to the return of any money advanced to or for the firm. Such amounts must be separate and distinct from original or additional contributions to the capital of the firm.

CPA (F) **PAYMENT OF INTEREST.** In the absence of an agreement to the contrary, contributions to capital do not draw interest. The theory is that the profits constitute sufficient compensation. Advances by a partner in the form of loans are treated as if they were made by a stranger and bear interest from the date the advance is made. When the partnership business continues after dissolution, a retiring partner is entitled to interest on the value of her interest in the partnership.[38]

CPA (G) **CONTRIBUTION AND INDEMNITY.** A partner who pays more than a proportionate share of the debts of the firm has a right to contribution from the other partners. Under this principle, if an employee of a partnership negligently injures a third person while acting within the scope of employment and if the injured party collects

---

[36] UPA § 19. See *Smith v Brown & Jones*, 633 NYS2d 436 (Sup Ct 1995).
[37] UPA § 18(f).
[38] *Lewis v Edwards*, 554 SE2d 17 (NC App 2001).

damages from one partner, the latter may enforce contribution from the other partners to divide the loss proportionately among them.

The partnership must indemnify every partner for payments made and personal liabilities reasonably incurred in the ordinary and proper conduct of its business or for the preservation of its business or property. A partner has no right, however, to indemnity or reimbursement if the partner has (1) acted in bad faith, (2) negligently caused the necessity for payment, or (3) previously agreed to assume the expense alone.[39]

CPA (H) **DISTRIBUTION OF CAPITAL.** After the payment of all creditors and the repayment of loans made to the firm by partners, every partner is entitled to receive a share of the firm property upon dissolution. Unless otherwise stated in the partnership agreement, all partners are entitled to the return of their capital contributions.

After such distribution is made, each partner is the sole owner of the fractional part distributed to that partner rather than a co-owner of all the property as during the existence of the partnership.

CPA ## 17. Liability of Partners and Partnership

The liability of a partnership and of the partners for the acts of individual partners and of employees is governed by the same principles that apply to the liability of an employer or a principal for the acts of an employee or agent.

CPA (A) **NATURE AND EXTENT OF PARTNER'S LIABILITY.** Partners are jointly liable on all firm contracts. They are jointly and severally liable for all torts committed by an employee or one of the partners in the scope of the partnership business. When partners are liable for the wrongful injury caused a third person, the latter may sue all or any of the members of the firm.

C A S E   S U M M A R Y

"But the Jury Found Me Not Guilty of Malpractice," Dr. Antenucci Complained

FACTS: Daniel Zuckerman, a minor, and Elaine, his mother, brought a medical malpractice action against Dr. Joseph Antenucci and Dr. Jose Pena. Although the summons did not state that the two defendants were partners, the undisputed evidence at the trial established that this was their relationship and that the alleged acts of malpractice were done in the course of partnership business. The jury returned a verdict finding that Pena was guilty of malpractice but that Antenucci was not guilty of malpractice. The amount of the verdict was $4 million. Antenucci contended that he should not be held liable on a partnership theory for the act of his partner when the plaintiffs had not named the partnership entity on the summons and when the summons did not designate him as a partner.

[39] *Gramacy Equities Corp. v DuMont,* 531 NE2d 629 (NY App Div 1988).

C A S E   S U M M A R Y

Continued

DECISION: Judgment against Antenucci. When Antenucci was served with a summons that named him as a defendant, jurisdiction was acquired over him. This gave the court the right to decide his personal liability and any liability that he might have for the action of a partner. Antenucci, as a partner, was jointly and severally liable for the malpractice of the other partner. The court could enforce that liability by entering judgment against Antenucci. [**Zuckerman v Antenucci, 478 NYS2d 578 (App Div 1984)**]

Partners who have satisfied a claim against the partnership have the right to contribution from the other partners, whereby the liability is apportioned among all partners. Unlike the UPA, partners under the Revised Uniform Partnership Act (RUPA) are jointly and severally liable for both tort and contract obligations of the firm.[40] However, the RUPA alters the traditional applications of "joint and several" liability by requiring that the creditors and tort victims satisfy their claims against the partnership before pursuing the personal assets of a partner.

CPA

(b) LIABILITY OF NEW PARTNERS. A person admitted as a partner into an existing partnership has *limited liability* for all obligations of the partnership arising before such admission. This is a limited liability in that the preadmission claim may be satisfied only out of partnership property and does not extend to the individual property of the newly admitted partner.[41] **For Example,** Citizens Bank was unsuccessful in its attempt to satisfy part of a $1.2 million deficiency judgment against the Parkham-Woodman Medical partnership from the individual property of Dr. Hunley, who had joined the practice after the underlying obligation leading to the deficiency judgment was assumed.[42]

(c) EFFECT OF DISSOLUTION ON PARTNER'S LIABILITY. A partner remains liable after dissolution of the partnership unless expressly released by the creditors or unless all claims against the partnership have been satisfied. The dissolution of the partnership does not of itself discharge the existing liability of any partner. The individual property of a deceased partner is liable for the obligations of the partnership that were incurred while the deceased partner was alive. However, the individual creditors of the deceased partner have priority over the partnership creditors with respect to such property.[43]

18. Enforcement and Satisfaction of Creditors' Claims

The firm may have been sued in the name of all individual partners doing business as the partnership, as in the case of "*Plaintiff v A, B, C, doing business as the Ajax*

---

[40] RUPA § 307(d).
[41] UPA § 17; see also UPA § 41(1), (7).
[42] *Citizens Bank v Parkman Woodman Medical Associates*, 874 F Supp 705 (D Mass 1995).
[43] UPA § 36.

Warehouse." The partners named are bound by the judgment against the firm if they have been properly served in the suit.

If a debt is contractual in origin, common law requires that the partnership's assets be resorted to and exhausted before partnership creditors can reach a partner's individual assets.[44]

Personal creditors of a partner must first pursue the assets of that partner for satisfaction of their claims. After a partner's personal assets are exhausted, the creditor may enforce the unpaid portion of a judgment by obtaining a charging order against the partner's interest in the partnership. Under such an order, a court requires that the partner's share of the profits be paid to the creditor until the debt is discharged.

D. Dissolution and Termination

The end of a partnership's existence is marked by dissolution and termination.

CPA 19. Effect of Dissolution

Dissolution is the "change in the relationship of the partners caused by any partner ceasing to be associated in the carrying on as distinguished from the winding-up of the business."[45] Dissolution does not necessarily mean that the business has ended. If the partnership agreement provides that the business is to be continued by the remaining partner(s), it will continue without a winding up, and the former partner's interest will be bought out according to the partnership agreement. Also, when breach of the partnership agreement causes dissolution, innocent partners may continue the business, provided they pay the breaching partner the value of his or her interest.[46]

If no legal basis exists to continue the business, dissolution ends the right of the partnership to exist as a going concern, but it does not end the existence of the partnership.[47] Dissolution is followed by a winding-up period at the conclusion of which the partnership's legal existence terminates.

Dissolution reduces the authority of the partners. From the moment of dissolution, the partners lose authority to act for the firm "except so far as may be necessary to wind up partnership affairs or to complete transactions begun but not then finished."[48] The vested rights of the partners are not extinguished by dissolving the firm, and the existing liabilities remain.

20. Dissolution by Act of the Parties

A partnership may be dissolved by action of the parties. However, certain acts of the parties do not cause a dissolution.

---

[44] *McCune & McCune v Mountain Bell Tel. Co.*, 758 P2d 914 (Utah 1988).
[45] UPA § 29.
[46] UPA § 38 (2)(b).
[47] *Sheppard v Griffin*, 776 SW2d 119 (Tenn App 1989).
[48] UPA § 33.

(A) AGREEMENT. A partnership may be dissolved in accordance with the terms of the original agreement of the parties. This may be by the expiration of the period for which the relationship was to continue or by the performance of the object for which the partnership was organized.[49] The relationship may also be dissolved by subsequent agreement. The partners may agree to dissolve the firm before the lapse of the time specified in the articles of partnership or before the attainment of the object for which the firm was created.

(B) EXPULSION. A partnership is dissolved by the expulsion of any partner from the business, whether or not authorized by the partnership agreement.[50]

(C) ALIENATION OF INTEREST. Neither a voluntary sale of a partner's interest nor an involuntary sale for the benefit of creditors works a dissolution of the partnership.

(D) WITHDRAWAL. A partner has the power to withdraw from the partnership at any time. However, if the withdrawal violates the partnership agreement, the withdrawing partner becomes liable to the copartners for damages for breach of contract.[51] When the relationship is for no definite purpose or time, a partner may withdraw without liability at any time. **For Example,** a partner, Mary Harshman, was able to bring about the dissolution of a family partnership that held and managed 1,879 acres of land in New York state and force the distribution of the partnership assets because it was an at-will partnership with no definite term or particular objective to be achieved.[52] Restrictive provisions on later employment are commonly found in professional and marketing partnership agreements.

21. Dissolution by Operation of Law

A partnership is dissolved by **operation of law** in the following instances.

(A) DEATH. A partnership is dissolved immediately upon the death of any partner. Thus, when the executor of a deceased partner carries on the business with the remaining partner, there is legally a new firm.

(B) BANKRUPTCY. Bankruptcy of the firm or of one of the partners causes the dissolution of the firm; insolvency alone does not.

(C) ILLEGALITY. A partnership is dissolved by an event that makes it unlawful for the business of the partnership to be carried on or for the members to carry it on in partnership. To illustrate, when it is made unlawful by statute for judges to engage in the practice of law, a law firm is dissolved when one of its members becomes a judge.

22. Dissolution by Decree of Court

A court may decree the dissolution of a partnership for proper cause. A court will not order the dissolution for trifling causes or temporary grievances that do not involve a permanent harm or injury to the partnership.

The filing of a complaint seeking a judicial dissolution does not in itself cause a dissolution of the partnership; it is the decree of the court that has that effect.

operation of law–attaching of certain consequences to certain facts because of legal principles that operate automatically, as contrasted with consequences that arise because of the voluntary action of a party designed to create those consequences.

[49] UPA § 31(1)(a).
[50] *Susman v Cypress Venture,* 543 NE2d 184 (Ill App 1989).
[51] *BPR Group v Bendetson,* 906 NE2d 956 (Mass 2009).
[52] *Harshman v Pantaleoni,* 741 NYS2d 348 (App Div 2002).

A partner may obtain a decree of dissolution for any of the following reasons.

(A) INSANITY. A partner has been judicially declared insane or of unsound mind.

(B) INCAPACITY. One of the partners has become incapable of performing the terms of the partnership agreement.

(C) MISCONDUCT. One of the partners has been guilty of conduct that substantially prejudices the continuance of the business. The habitual drunkenness of a partner is a sufficient cause for judicial dissolution.

(D) IMPRACTICABILITY. One of the partners persistently or willfully acts in such a way that it is not reasonably practicable to carry on the partnership business. Dissolution will be granted when dissensions are so serious and persistent that continuance is impracticable or when all confidence and cooperation between the partners have been destroyed.

CASE SUMMARY

Strategy = Squeeze Out Dyas
Ethics (Trust, Fairness, Loyalty, Doing No Harm) = None
Law = Dissociation, Dissolution

FACTS: Edward Dyas and Joseph Della Ratta were equal owners of two hotels in Ocean City, Maryland. The "old" hotel was completed in 1988 and the "new" hotel was completed in 2006, with both properties owned under their Spa Motel General Partnership (Spa). They were also developers and equal owners of the Maresol Condominium project in Ocean City, which was completed in 2004 and held under Dyas's and Della Ratta's Bay View Limited Liability Company (Bay View). Della Ratta owned the construction company that built these projects, "DRI," and he also owned "CMC," the company that managed the two hotels. Dyas believed that Della Ratta was attempting to squeeze him out from ownership of Spa and Bay View. Under Dyas's analysis, Della Ratta's strategy in the general partnership, Spa, was to call for a very substantial capital contribution to pay claims asserted by CMC for alleged advances made by it to pay for operational expenses and to pay claims to DRI for the new hotel's construction costs. Dyas contended those calls were unauthorized because the underlying claims could not be substantiated and the partnership agreement required that the developers first seek a commercial loan.

With respect to Bay View, Dyas's theory of Della Ratta's squeeze-out strategy involved two ploys. First, that Della Ratta sought personally to purchase the loan from Severn Bank and obtain from it an assignment of the security instrument, on which Della Ratta then would foreclose, so that he could buy in at the foreclosure sale. Severn Bank, however, would not assign the loan to Della Ratta. Dyas further alleged that, as an alternate squeeze-out strategy, Della Ratta wrongfully refused to sell condominium units in Maresol. The resulting illiquidity would deprive Bay View of the cash needed to repay Severn Bank, so that Della Ratta could buy Maresol at a foreclosure sale conducted by Severn Bank. After a 10-day trial, the circuit court concluded that Dyas had proven these allegations. The ultimate findings of the trial court were that it was "no longer reasonably practicable to carry on the business" of Spa or of Bay View and that Dyas "had proved to the court's satisfaction facts sufficient for the court to grant a dissolution" of the entities. The court further ordered dissociation of Della Ratta as a partner in Spa. The court supervised the winding up of the general partnership. Della Ratta appealed.

Continued

DECISION: Judgment for Dyas. A review of Della Ratta's activities while a partner in Spa demonstrates satisfactory grounds for the dissociation and dissolution determinations of the trial court since his conduct was such that it was "not reasonably practicable to carry on the business in partnership with him." [**Della Ratta v Dyas, 961 A2d 629 (Md App 2008)**]

(E) **LACK OF SUCCESS.** The partnership cannot continue in business except at a loss.

(F) **EQUITABLE CIRCUMSTANCES.** A decree of dissolution will be granted under any other circumstances that equitably call for a dissolution. Such a situation exists when one partner was induced by fraud to enter into the partnership.

CPA   23. Dissociation Under the RUPA

Under the RUPA and its "entity" concept, a partner can leave the firm and not disrupt the partnership's legal existence. The RUPA uses the term *dissociation* for the departure of a partner[53] and reserves the term *dissolution* for those instances when a partner's departure results in the winding up and termination of the business.[54]

A partner has the absolute power to dissociate at will, just as a partner has the power to withdraw under the UPA, even if it is wrongful.[55] If wrongful, the partner is liable for damages for breach of contract.

A partner's dissociation from a firm ends the individual's right to participate in the management of the business. It also ends the duty of loyalty owed the firm, and the individual may compete with the firm once dissociated.[56] If the partnership business continues after a partner dissociates from a firm, the partnership must buy out the dissociated partner's interest based on his share of the higher of the liquidation value of the firm or the value of the firm's business as a going concern on the date of dissociation, with interest.[57]

The RUPA created "notices" to deal with lingering authority of a dissociated partner based on apparent authority. To avoid liability, notice of lack of authority or liability should be given to customers and creditors regarding the dissociation of a partner. A filing with the Secretary of State limits liability and authority to 90 days after filing.[58] If no notice is given or filed, the partnership may be bound by the acts of a dissociated partner for up to two years after dissociation based on apparent authority.[59]

CPA   24. Notice of Dissolution

Under some circumstances, one partner may continue to possess the power to make a contract that binds the partnership even though the partnership has been dissolved.

[53] RUPA § 601 cmt 1.
[54] RUPA § 801.
[55] RUPA § 601(1), 602(a).
[56] RUPA § 404(2).
[57] RUPA § 701(b).
[58] RUPA § 704.
[59] RUPA § 702.

(A) NOTICE TO PARTNERS. When the firm is dissolved by the act of a partner, notice must be given to the other partners unless that partner's act clearly shows an intent to withdraw from or to dissolve the firm. If the withdrawing partner acts without notice to the other partners, that partner is bound by contracts created for the firm.

When the dissolution is caused by the act, death, or bankruptcy of a partner, each partner is liable to the copartners for a share of any liability created by any other partner acting for the partnership without knowledge or notice of the act, death, or bankruptcy of the partner who caused the dissolution.

CPA

(B) NOTICE TO THIRD PERSONS. When dissolution is caused by the act of a partner or of the partners, notice must be given to third parties. A notice should expressly state that the partnership has been dissolved. Circumstances from which a termination may be inferred are generally not sufficient notice.

Thus, the fact that the partnership checks added the abbreviation *Inc.* after the partnership name was not sufficient notice that the partnership did not exist and that the business had been incorporated.

Actual notice of dissolution must be given to persons who have dealt with the firm.

CASE SUMMARY

Notice Necessary!

FACTS: Paul Babich ran a business under the name of House of Paul. The business became a partnership between Babich, Dyson, and Schnepp but continued under the same name. The partners arranged for printing advertising material with Philipp Lithographing Company, making contracts on three separate occasions for such printing. During the course of these dealings, the House of Paul became a corporation. When the printing bills were not paid in full, Philipp sued the partners as individuals. They claimed they were not liable because the corporation had made the contracts.

DECISION: Whether or not the House of Paul was a corporation with respect to a particular contract was not important because no notice had been given of its change from a partnership to a corporation. Having originally done business with the defendant as a partnership, Philipp could hold the individual persons liable as partners until notice to the contrary was given to Philipp. [**Philipp Lithographing Co. v Babich, 135 NW2d 343 (Wis 1965)**]

For persons who have had no dealings with the firm, a publication of the fact of dissolution is sufficient. Such notice may be by newspaper publication, by posting a placard in a public place, or by any similar method. Failure to give proper notice continues the power of each partner to bind the others with respect to third persons on contracts within the scope of the business.

When dissolution has been caused by operation of law, notice to third persons is not required. As between the partners, however, the UPA requires knowledge or notice of dissolution by death and bankruptcy.

25. Winding up Partnership Affairs

Most established partnerships deal with the question of how to proceed with the business upon the death of a partner in the written partnership agreement. The agreement may set forth a method for establishing the value of the deceased partner's interest as of the date of death or allow for the remaining partners to purchase the deceased partner's interest. The agreement may also allow for the continuation of the business as usual while the valuation process is completed. However, in the absence of an agreement, either express or implied, permitting the surviving partners to continue the business, the partners must wind up the business and account for the share of the deceased partner.[60]

When dissolution is obtained by court decree, the court may appoint a receiver to conduct the winding up of the partnership business. This may be done in the usual manner, or the receiver may sell the business as a going concern to those partners who wish to continue its operation.

With a few exceptions, all partners have the right to participate in the winding up of the business.[61]

CPA   ## 26. Distribution of Assets

Creditors of the firm have first claim on the assets of the partnership.[62] Difficulty arises when there is a contest between the creditors of the firm and the creditors of the individual partners. The general rule is that firm creditors have first claim on assets of the firm. The individual creditors share in the remaining assets, if any.

After the firm's liabilities to nonpartners have been paid, the assets of the partnership are distributed as follows: (1) each partner is entitled to a refund of advances made to or for the firm, (2) contributions to the capital of the firm are then returned, and (3) the remaining assets, if any, are divided equally as profits among the partners unless there is some other agreement. A partner who contributes only services to the partnership is not considered to have made a capital contribution, absent an agreement to the contrary.

C A S E   S U M M A R Y

Are Time and Labor Capital Contributions?
Fred Ott Says They Ought to Be

FACTS: Fred Ott and Charles Corley were partners doing business as "Lakewood Associates, a general partnership." Corley provided the capital to purchase the land to be sold by the partnership, called Lakewood Estates. Corley brought suit for the dissolution of the partnership, and Ott contended that his contributions of time and labor in improving Lakewood Estates should be credited to him as capital contributions in the distribution of assets.

---

[60] *Chaney v Burdett*, 560 SE2d 21 (Ga 2002); *King v Stoddard*, 104 Cal Rptr 903 (Cal App 1972).
[61] UPA § 37.
[62] *Holmes v Holmes*, 849 P2d 1140 (Or App 1993).

C A S E   S U M M A R Y

Continued

DECISION: Judgment for Corley. There was no evidence of any agreement between the partners that Ott's services should be credited as capital contributions. Therefore, the value of the services could not be credited as capital contributions in the distribution of assets. [**Corley v Ott, 485 SE2d 97 (SC 1997)**]

If the partnership has sustained a loss, the partners assume it equally in the absence of a contrary agreement. Distribution of partnership assets must be made on the basis of actual value when it is clear that the book values are merely nominal or arbitrary amounts.

A provision in a partnership agreement that upon the death of a partner the interest of the partner shall pass to that partner's surviving spouse is valid. Such a provision takes effect against the contention that it is not valid because it does not satisfy the requirements applicable to wills.

27. Continuation of Partnership Business

As a practical matter, the business of the partnership is commonly continued after dissolution and winding up. In all cases, however, there is a technical dissolution, winding up, and termination of the life of the original partnership.

If the business continues, either with the surviving partners or with them and additional partners, it is a new partnership. Again, as a practical matter, the liquidation of the old partnership may in effect be merely a matter of bookkeeping entries, with all partners contributing again or relending to the new business any payment to which they would be entitled from the liquidation of the original partnership.

MAKE THE CONNECTION

SUMMARY

A *partnership* is a relationship created by the voluntary association of two or more persons to carry on as co-owners a business for profit.

A partnership agreement governs the partnership during its existence and may also contain provisions relating to dissolution. The partnership agreement will generally be in writing, and this may be required by the statute of frauds. The existence of a partnership may be found from the existence of shared control in the running of the business and the fact that the parties share profits and losses. The sharing of gross returns, as opposed to profits, is slight evidence of a partnership.

Partners hold title to firm property by tenancy in partnership. A creditor of a partner cannot proceed against any specific item of partnership property but must obtain a charging order to seize the debtor-partner's share of the profits. An assignee of a partner's interest does not become a partner without the consent of the other partners and is entitled only to a share of the profits and the assignor's interest upon dissolution.

When there are more than two partners in a firm, the decisions of the majority prevail on ordinary matters relating to the firm's business unless the decisions are contrary to the partnership agreement. A partner's authority to act for the firm is similar to that of an agent to act for a principal. A partner may not bind the firm by a contract that makes it impossible for the firm to conduct its business.

A partner's duties are the same as those of an agent. If there is no contrary agreement, each partner has the right to take an equal part in the management of the business, to inspect the books, to share in the profits, and after payment of all of the firm's debts and the return of capital, to share in the firm's property or surplus upon dissolution.

Partners have unlimited personal liability for partnership liabilities. Partners are jointly liable on all firm contracts. They are jointly and severally liable for all torts committed by one of the partners or by a firm employee within the scope of the partnership's business. A partner remains liable after dissolution unless expressly released by creditors. An incoming partner is not liable for the existing debts of the partnership unless the new partner expressly assumes those debts.

Dissolution ends the right of the partnership to exist as a going concern. Dissolution is followed by a winding-up period and the distribution of assets. A partnership may be dissolved by the parties themselves in accordance with the terms of the partnership agreement, by the expulsion of a partner, by the withdrawal of a partner, or by the bankruptcy of the firm or one of the partners. A court may order dissolution of a partnership upon the petition of a partner because of the insanity, incapacity, or major misconduct of a partner. Dissolution may be decreed because of lack of success, impracticability, or other circumstances that equitably call for dissolution. Notice of dissolution, except dissolution by operation of law, must be given. Actual notice must be given to those who have dealt with the firm as a partnership.

All partners generally have a right to participate in the winding up of the business. After the firm's liabilities to nonpartners have been paid, the assets are distributed among the partners as follows: (1) refund of advances, (2) return of contributions to capital, and (3) division of remaining assets in accordance with the partnership agreement or, if no agreement is stated, division of net assets equally among the partners.

LEARNING OUTCOMES

After studying this chapter, you should be able to clearly explain:

A. NATURE AND CREATION

LO.1 Explain how partnerships are created by agreement, and understand that only when the partners' partnership agreement does not resolve an issue does partnership law apply

> See the example of the dentist who was terminated from the three-person dental partnership without cause by majority vote, where the partnership agreement allowed for such a termination, p. 985.

LO.2 Understand that no writing is needed to form a partnership, nor a tax ID number, nor a partnership name. All that is needed is clear evidence that the partners carried on as co-owners of a business for profit

> See the *Byker* case where one individual who carried on a business for a profit was dumbfounded to find out that he was, by law, a partner, p. 986.

B. AUTHORITY OF PARTNERS

LO.3 Distinguish between express authority and customary authority of a partner to act for a partnership

> See the discussion on the role of individual partners to act as expressly directed by a majority of partners (express authority) and to act on their own to make ordinary contracts necessary to transact the firm's business (customary authority) beginning on p. 991.

C. DUTIES, RIGHTS, AND LIABILITIES OF PARTNERS

LO.4 List the duties of partners to one another

> See the discussion and examples of partners' duties of loyalty, good faith, and obedience, beginning on p. 994.

D. DISSOLUTION AND TERMINATION

LO.5 Describe how a partnership may be dissolved by the acts of partners, by operation of law, and by order of the court

> See the example of withdrawal by a partner, Mary Harshman, without liability because the partnership was at-will, p. 1000.
> See the *Della Ratta* case involving partnership dissolution by decree of court because of impractability, p. 1001.

KEY TERMS

articles of copartnership	general partners	tenancy in partnership
articles of partnership	operation of law	unincorporated
charging order	partners	association
express authority	partnership	
general partnership	partnership agreement	

QUESTIONS AND CASE PROBLEMS

1. Ray, Linda, and Nancy form a partnership. Ray and Linda contribute property and cash. Nancy contributes only services. Linda dies, and the partnership is liquidated. After all debts are paid, the surplus is not sufficient to pay back Linda's estate and Ray for the property and cash originally contributed by Linda and Ray. Nancy claims that the balance should be divided equally among Ray, Linda's estate, and Nancy. Is she correct?

2. Baxter, Bigelow, Owens, and Dailey were partners in a New York City advertising agency. Owens, who was in poor health and wanted to retire, advised the partners that she had assigned her full and complete interest in the partnership to her son, Bartholomew, a highly qualified person with 10 years of experience in the advertising business. Baxter, Bigelow, and Dailey refused to allow Bartholomew to attend management meetings and refused his request to inspect the books. Bartholomew pointed out that his mother had invested as much in the firm as any other partner. He believed, as assignee of his mother's full and complete partnership interest, that he is entitled to (a) inspect the books as he sees fit and (b) participate fully in the management of the firm. Was Bartholomew correct?

3. Amy Gargulo and Paula Frisken operated as a partnership Kiddies Korner, an infants' and children's clothing store. They operated the business very successfully for three years, with both Paula and Amy doing the buying and Paula keeping the books and paying the bills. Amy and Paula decided to expand the business when an adjoining store became vacant. At the same time, they incorporated the business. Children's Apparel, Inc., was a major supplier to the business before the expansion. After the expansion, business did not increase as anticipated, and when a nationally known manufacturer of children's apparel opened a factory outlet nearby, the business could no longer pay its bills. Children's Apparel, which had supplied most of the store's stock after expansion, sued Amy and Paula as partners for bills due for expansion stock. Children's Apparel did not know that Amy and Paula had incorporated. Amy and Paula contended that the business was incorporated and that they therefore were not liable for business debts occurring after incorporation. Were Amy and Paula correct?

4. Calvin Johnson and Rudi Basecke did business as the Stockton Cheese Co., a partnership, which owned a building and equipment. The partners agreed to dissolve the partnership but never got around to completing the winding-up process. Calvin continued to use the building and to pay insurance on it but removed Rudi's name as an insured on the policy. When the building was later destroyed by fire, Calvin claimed the proceeds of the fire insurance policy because he and his wife were the named insureds on the policy and they had paid the premiums. Rudi claimed that although the partnership was dissolved before the fire, the winding up of the partnership was not completed at the time of the fire. He therefore claimed that he was entitled to half of the net proceeds of the policy. Decide. [*State Casualty v Johnson*, 766 SW2d 113 (Mo App)]

5. Samuel Shaw purchased a ticket through Delta Airlines to fly a "Delta Connection" flight on SkyWest Airlines to Elko, Nevada. He was seriously injured when the SkyWest plane crashed near Elko. SkyWest's relationship with Delta was a contractual business referral arrangement, whereby Delta benefits through its charges for issuing tickets to connecting passengers to and from smaller communities, and SkyWest benefits from revenue generated by passengers sent to it by Delta. Both firms make a profit from this arrangement. SkyWest and Delta are often mentioned together by Delta in national print advertisements. Shaw believed that regardless of how the airlines characterize themselves, these airlines are in fact partners because they share profits from their combined efforts. Delta contended that it had no control over SkyWest's airplane operations and that sharing profits as compensation for services does not create a partnership. Decide. [*Shaw v Delta Airlines, Inc.*, 798 F Supp 1453 (D Nev)]

6. Larson entered into a Special Manager Incentive Agreement (SMIA) with Tandy Corp. He agreed to manage a Radio Shack store for compensation equal to one-half of the adjusted gross profit of the store as computed by a specific formula and to provide the company with a $20,000 "security deposit" on equipment used to set up the store. The agreement was for a period of two years, automatically renewable annually until either party gave notice of termination 30 days prior to the end of a fiscal year. After some eight and one-half years of operating under renewed agreements, Tandy gave Larson notice of his termination. Larson sued Tandy, claiming that the SMIA was a partnership agreement because there were shared risks, expenses, profits, and losses. He sought an accounting for his reasonable share in the value of the store. Tandy argued that under the SMIA, Larson was an employee-manager, not a partner, and that the ultimate decision making on all matters was Tandy's. Decide. [*Larson v Tandy Corp*, 371 SE2d 663 (Ga App)]

7. Two brothers, Eugene and Marlowe Mehl, formed a partnership to operate the family farm. One year, Eugene Mehl withdrew $7,200 from the partnership account and bought the Dagmar Bar. The warranty deed and the liquor license to the bar were obtained in the names of Eugene Mehl and his wife, Bonnie. In a subsequent lawsuit, Marlowe claimed that the bar was a partnership asset. Decide. [*Mehl v Mehl*, 786 P2d 1173 (Mont)]

8. Chaiken and two others ran a barbershop. The Delaware Employment Security Commission claimed that the other two persons were employees of Chaiken and that Chaiken had failed to pay the unemployment compensation tax assessed against employers. His defense was on the ground that he had not "employed" the other two and that all three were partners. The evidence showed that Chaiken owned the barbershop; he continued to do business under the same trade name as he had before he was joined by the two additional barbers; and he had a separate contract with each of the two, which specified the days for work and the days off. It was also shown that Chaiken had registered the partnership name and the names of the three partners and that

federal tax returns used for partnerships had been filed. Decide. [*Chaiken v Employment Security Comm'n*, 274 A2d 707 (Del Sup Ct)]

9. Thomas Bartomeli decided to leave his employment to join his brother Raymond full-time in a small construction company. The brothers each contributed individual assets to the company and worked together to acquire equipment with both signing notes jointly to acquire certain equipment. Thomas considered himself a partner in the company; Raymond often referred to Thomas as his partner. It was the practice of the company to garage the equipment at Thomas's house. In 1983, the company was incorporated, but Thomas never held any shares in the company. On several occasions, Thomas's careless operation of equipment resulted in loss or damage to the company. Raymond became dissatisfied with Thomas's work performance, and on January 17, 1991, Thomas was removed as secretary of the corporation.

    On April 19, 1991, Thomas went to the company office and demanded a blank check from the secretary. Raymond found out about this demand and fired him. On April 20, 1991, Thomas demanded from Raymond either 50 percent of the company or certain equipment owned by the company. On April 22, 1991, Thomas was removed as vice president of the company. Raymond attempted to reach an agreement with Thomas on a division of company assets at that point but was not successful. Thereafter, Thomas sued his brother, alleging that Raymond had breached the brothers' contract of partnership. Because the company was a corporation, is it legally inconsistent for Thomas to contend that there was a contract for partnership in the company? How would you decide this case? [*Bartomeli v Bartomeli*, 783 A2d 1050 (Ct App)]

10. Friedman, the "O" Street Carpet Shop, Inc., and Langness formed a partnership known as NFL Associates. "O" Street Carpet's net contribution to capital was $5,004; Langness contributed $14,000 in cash; and Friedman contributed his legal services, on which no value was placed by the articles of partnership. The articles stated that Friedman was entitled to 10 percent of the profits and that Langness was to receive payments of $116.66 per month. The partnership's accountant treated the payments to Langness as a return of her capital. Years later, the partnership sold the rental property owned by the partnership, and the partnership was wound up. Friedman claimed that he was entitled to 10 percent of the partnership capital upon dissolution. Langness claimed that Friedman was not entitled to a capital distribution and that the monthly payments to her should not have been treated as a return of capital. Decide. [*Langness v "O" Street Carpet, Inc.*, 353 NW2d 709 (Neb)]

11. Ross, Marcos, and Albert are partners. Ross and Marcos each contributed $60,000 to the partnership; Albert contributed $30,000. At the end of the fiscal year, distributable profits total $150,000. Ross claims $60,000 as his share of the profits. Is he entitled to this sum?

12. Leland McElmurry was one of three partners of MHS Enterprises, a Michigan partnership. Commonwealth Capital Investment Corp. sued the partnership

and obtained a judgment of $1,137,285 against it, but the partnership could not pay the judgment. Commonwealth then sued McElmurry for the entire debt on the theory that, as a partner of MHS, he was liable for its debts. What, if any, is McElmurry's liability? [*Commonwealth Capital Investment Corp. v McElmurry*, 302 NW2d 222 (Mich App)]

13. Thomas Smith and Jackie Lea were partners in the logging business. In January 1981, they joined Gordon Redd and went into business running a sawmill, calling the business Industrial Hardwood Products (IHP). Smith and Lea used their logging equipment at the mill site. Smith hauled 400 loads of gravel, worth some $26,000, from his father's land for the mill yard in the process of getting the mill operational. Smith and Lea received $300 a week compensation for their work, which was reported on federal W-2 forms. They worked up to 65 hours per week and were not paid overtime. All three discussed business decisions. Smith and Lea had the authority to write checks and to hire and fire employees. Lea left the business in 1983 and was paid $20,000 by Redd. The testimony indicated that the three individuals agreed in January 1981 that as soon as the bank was paid off and Redd was paid his investment, Lea and Smith would be given an interest in the mill. No written agreement existed. Redd invested $410,452 in the business and withdrew $500,475 from it. As of December 31, 1986, IHP had sufficient retained earnings to retire the bank debt. In April 1987, Smith petitioned the Chancery Court for dissolution of the "partnership" and an accounting. Redd denied that any partnership agreement was formed and asserted that Smith was an employee because he was paid wages. He offered to pay Smith $50,000 for the gravel and use of his equipment. Decide. [*Smith v Redd*, 593 So2d 989 (Miss)]

14. Mason and Phyllis Ledbetter operated a business in Northbrook, Illinois, as a partnership called Ledbetters' Nurseries that specialized in the sale of garden lilies. The grounds of the nurseries were planted with numerous species of garden lilies, and hundreds of people toured the Ledbetters' gardens every day. After a tour, Sheila Clark offered to buy the facilities at a "top-notch price." Mason felt he could not refuse the high offer, and he signed a contract to sell all the facilities, including all flowers and the business name. When Phyllis refused to go along with the contract, Clark sued the Ledbetters' Nurseries partnership, seeking to obtain specific performance of the sales contract. Decide.

15. St. John Transportation Co., a corporation, made a contract with the partnership of Bilyeu and Herstel, contractors, by which the latter was to construct a ferryboat. Herstel, a member of the firm of contractors, executed a contract in the firm name with Benbow for certain materials and labor in connection with the construction of the ferryboat. In an action brought by Benbow to enforce a lien against the ferryboat, the *James Johns*, it was contended that all members of the firm were bound by the contract made by Herstel. Do you agree? [*Benbow v The Ferryboat James Johns*, 108 P 634 (Or)]

CPA QUESTIONS

1. Acorn and Bean were general partners in a farm machinery business. Acorn contracted, on behalf of the partnership, to purchase 10 tractors from Cobb Corp. Unknown to Cobb, Acorn was not authorized by the partnership to make such contracts. Bean refused to allow the partnership to accept delivery of the tractors, and Cobb sought to enforce the contract. Cobb will:

   a. Lose, because Acorn's action was beyond the scope of Acorn's implied authority

   b. Prevail, because Acorn had implied authority to bind the partnership

   c. Prevail, because Acorn had apparent authority to bind the partnership

   d. Lose, because Acorn's express authority was restricted, in writing, by the partnership agreement

2. Upon dissolution of a general partnership, distributions will be made on account of:

   I. Partners' capital accounts.

   II. Amounts owed partners with respect to profits.

   III. Amounts owed partners for loans to the partnership in the following order:

   a. III, I, II

   b. I, II, III

   c. II, III, I

   d. III, II, I

3. Which of the following statements is correct with respect to a limited partnership?

   a. A limited partner may *not* be an unsecured creditor of the limited partnership.

   b. A general partner may *not* also be a limited partner at the same time.

   c. A general partner may be a secured creditor of the limited partnership.

   d. A limited partnership can be formed with limited liability for all partners.

4. When a partner in a general partnership lacks actual or apparent authority to contract on behalf of the partnership, and the party contracted with is aware of this fact, the partnership will be bound by the contract if the other partners:

	Ratify the Contract	Amend the Partnership Agreement
a.	Yes	Yes
b.	Yes	No
c.	No	Yes
d.	No	No

Chapter 43

LPs, LLCs, and LLPs

A. THE ARRIVAL OF PARTNERSHIP LIMITED LIABILITY

Individuals owning businesses or professional firms are concerned about exposing their personal wealth to liability beyond that invested in their businesses or firms. As discussed previously, limited liability is not a feature of general partnership law. The concept of making limited liability available to general partnerships was considered by the RUPA Drafting Committee when it began its work to revise the Uniform Partnership Act in 1987, but the concept was rejected. A limited partnership form of business organization had existed since 1916 under the Uniform Limited Partnership Act with limited partners (investors) having limited liability, but the firms' general partners were exposed to personal liability for firm debts under this act. The concept of full limited liability for partnerships began to take hold in 1986 when businesses forming limited partnerships under the Revised Uniform Limited Partnership Act utilized corporate general partners, with the general partners avoiding limited liability by the simple expedient of incorporating.

An IRS ruling classifying a Wyoming limited liability company (LLC) as a partnership for tax purposes led to the rapid spread of LLC statutes to every state within six years of the IRS ruling.[1] As part of the limited liability trend established by the swift enactment of LLC laws throughout the country, most states have also enacted limited liability partnership (LLP) acts. Like LLCs, they provide businesses and those offering professional services the benefit of single taxation as a partnership as well as limited liability.

B. LIMITED PARTNERSHIP

limited partnership–
partnership that can be formed by "one or more general partners and one or more limited partners."

A limited partnership is a special kind of partnership.

1. Formation of Limited Partnerships

The Uniform Limited Partnership Act (ULPA) was approved by the National Conference of Commissioners on Uniform State Law in 1916. It was revised in 1976 (RULPA), and this RULPA was amended in 1985. All states except Louisiana have adopted a version of the RULPA.

limited partner–partner who neither takes part in the management of the partnership nor appears to the public to be a general partner.

general partner–
partnership in which the partners conduct as co-owners a business for profit, and each partner has a right to take part in the management of the business and has unlimited liability; general partners publicly and actively engage in the transaction of firm business.

CPA

(A) MEMBERS OF A LIMITED PARTNERSHIP. In a **limited partnership** certain members contribute capital but have limited liability for firm debts. The most these members can lose is their investment. These members are known as **limited partners.** The partners who manage the business and are personally liable for the firm debts are **general partners.**[2] A limited partnership can be formed by "one or more general partners and one or more limited partners."[3]

---

[1] Rev. Rul 88-76, 1988—2 CB 360.
[2] *Brooke v Mt. Hood Meadows, Ltd.*, 725 P2d 925 (Or App 1986).
[3] RULPA § 101(7).

CPA   (B) CERTIFICATE OF LIMITED PARTNERSHIP. Unlike a general partnership, a limited partnership can be created only by executing a certificate of limited partnership.

Under the 1985 amendments to the RULPA, the certificate requires the following information: (1) the limited partnership's name, (2) the address of the partnership's registered office and the name and business address of its agent for service of process, (3) the name and business address of each general partner, (4) the partnership's mailing address, and (5) the latest date on which the limited partnership is to dissolve. The names of the limited partners (the investors) are not required. This allows for the preservation of the confidentiality of the investors' names from competitors. Moreover, new investors may be admitted as limited partners without the significant administrative burden involved in amending the certificate, as was required under the ULPA. The RULPA provides for filing the certificate with the office of the secretary of state, as opposed to the local filing required under the ULPA.

When there is no filing of the limited partnership certificate, all participants have the status and liability of general partners in a general partnership. However, technical defects in the certificate do not prevent formation of a limited partnership if there has been substantial, good-faith compliance with the filing requirements.[4]

CPA   (c) LIMITED PARTNERSHIP AGREEMENT. The RULPA embodies the policy of freedom of contract and maximum flexibility regarding the limited partnership agreement.[5] Most limited partnership agreements are drafted almost exclusively by their founding general partners, and courts resolve ambiguities against the drafting general partners and in favor of the reasonable expectations of the limited partners. **For Example,** when the general partners of the Nantucket Island Associates Limited Partnership unilaterally amended the limited partnership agreement to add a new class of preferred limited partnership units with superior rights to existing unit holders, ambiguous agreement language was construed against the general partners by the court, and the general partners were found to be in breach of the agreement by adding the new class of units.[6]

2. Characteristics of Limited Partnerships

A limited partnership has the following characteristics.

CPA   (A) CAPITAL CONTRIBUTIONS. Under the ULPA, a limited partner contributed either cash or property but not services. Under the RULPA, however, a limited partner may contribute services.

CPA   (B) FIRM NAME. With certain exceptions, a limited partner's name cannot appear in the firm name. Under the RULPA, the words *limited partnership* must appear without abbreviation in the firm name.

CPA   (c) MANAGEMENT AND CONTROL OF THE FIRM. The general partners manage the business and are personally liable for firm debts. However, general partners may avoid personal liability by incorporating. Limited partners (the investors) have the right to

---

[4] RULPA § 201(b); *Fabry Partnership v Christensan*, 794 P2d 719 (Nev 1990).
[5] See *Gotham Partners, L.P. v Hallowood Realty Partners, L.P.*, 817 A2d 160 (Del 2002).
[6] *In re Nantucket Island Associates Limited Partnership Unit Holders Litigation*, 810 A2d 351 (Del Ch 2002).

a share of the profits and a return of capital upon dissolution and have limited liability. The limitation of liability is lost, however, if they participate in the control of the business, as seen in the *Gilroy, Sims & Associates Ltd.* case.

CASE SUMMARY

The Problem of Limited Partners in Control

FACTS: Gilroy, Sims & Associates, Ltd., was a limited partnership engaged in real estate development whose original general partners were Richard Gilroy and William Sims. Thomas Green and John Murphy, Jr., were listed as limited partners along with certain other individuals on the certificate of limited partnership. Green and Murphy took an active role in the day-to-day operations of the real estate developed by the limited partnership. Financing was obtained to construct the venture's building in St. Louis in 1968, and a mortgage was payable to American National Insurance Company over 27 years. In 1976, the partnership executed a Restated Agreement, and Green and Murphy became general partners of Gilroy, Sims, agreeing to "unlimited liability for the debts of the partnership." In the fall of 1990, the partnership stopped making mortgage payments. After foreclosure by American National, a deficiency of $1,437,840 was outstanding. Green and Murphy believed that as limited partners when the debt was incurred in 1968, they were absolved from any personal liability beyond the assets of the firm. American National disagreed.

DECISION: Judgment for American National Insurance Company. Green and Murphy expressly adopted the partnership obligation in the Restated Agreement executed in 1976. Moreover, although Green's and Murphy's limited partner status would ordinarily limit their personal liability to creditors to the amount of their investment, their active roles in taking part in the control of the business subjected them to potential general partner liability. [**American National Ins. Co. v Gilroy Associates, Ltd., 847 F Supp 971 (ED Mo 1995)**]

The RULPA lists a number of "safe harbor" activities in which limited partners may engage without losing their protection from liability. These activities include

1. Being a contractor for, or an agent or employee of, the limited partnership or of a general partner;

2. Consulting with and advising a general partner regarding the partnership business;

3. Acting as a surety for the limited partnership; and

4. Voting on partnership matters, such as dissolving and winding up the limited partnership or removing a general partner.

(D) **Right to Sue.** A limited partner may bring a derivative action on behalf of the limited partnership to enforce a claim that the limited partnership possesses against others but that the partnership refuses to enforce. This derivative suit is filed in the name of the limited partner, and the partnership is named as a defendant, with the limited partnership deriving the benefits of the action.

Limited partners may sue their partnership's general partner to protect the limited partners' interest. General partners today are commonly corporations with their own boards of directors and management teams, with the limited partnership format providing investment and tax incentives for investor–limited partners and the general partners reserving to themselves broad authority to act in the general partners' sole discretion and often in the general partners' own best interest. **For Example,** Donald Weedon and others formed a limited partnership under Delaware law to raise capital for the securities broker–dealer business. The partnership agreement, as allowed by Delaware law, gave the corporate general partners and its directors the right to restrict their fiduciary duties in managing the partnership and gave the general partner broad power to act, even in conflicted situations, subject only to very loose constraints of a subjective bad-faith standard. Nonemployee limited partners referred to by the court as the "outside investors" brought suit against the corporate general partners and members of the general partner's board of directors and top management for squeezing out all nonemployee limited partners and paying less than the fair value for their units in violation of fiduciary duties and the partnership agreement. The trial court decided in favor of the plaintiffs, stating in part:

> *… Even given the wide discretion the partnership agreement gives to the defendants to issue new units without fear of liability, the defendants managed to step out of bounds in one important respect. By deciding to permit the general partner's outside directors to acquire new units at a favorable price and by denying the same opportunity to Outside Investors, the defendants breached their contractual duties. This decision, I find, was not undertaken in good faith but instead as quid pro quo for the outside directors' willing assent to the issuance of a large number of new units to management and employees.…*

The plaintiffs received a make-whole remedy from the court with monetary damages tied to fair market values.[7]

(E) **DISSOLUTION.** The dissolution and winding up of limited partnerships is governed by the same principles applicable to general partnerships.

C. LIMITED LIABILITY COMPANIES

Limited liability company (LLC) acts were rapidly adopted by state legislatures throughout the country following a favorable tax ruling on this form of organization by the Internal Revenue Service.[8] This corporate-sounding entity is considered in this chapter because it is a form of limited partnership.

CPA   ## 3. Characteristics of LLCs

The IRS has determined that an LLC may qualify for partnership federal tax treatment. Unlike a corporation, an LLC pays no federal taxes on its income as an

---

[7] *Gelfman v Weeden Investors, L.P.*, 859 A2d 89 (Del Ch 2004).
[8] IRS Rev Rul 88-76. LLCs have been adopted by every state and the District of Columbia. A Uniform Limited Liability Company Act was approved by the National Conference of Commissioners on Uniform State Law.

entity. Instead, the income (or losses, deductions, and credits) flows through to the LLC's owners (called *members*) based on their proportionate interest in the company. The members report the income on their personal tax returns. The LLC combines this tax advantage with the limited liability feature of the corporate form of business organization. The owners and managers are not personally liable for the debts and obligations of the entity, provided that these individuals fulfill their common law duty to disclose that they are acting as agents for the limited liability company.

CPA (A) FORMATION. As set forth previously, general partnerships may be created without the formality of even a written partnership agreement when two individuals simply operate a business for profit as co-owners. LLCs, however, require a formal filing of articles of organization with the secretary of state in a manner similar to a filing of articles of incorporation by a corporation or a certificate of limited partnership for a limited partnership.

The articles for an LLC must contain the name, purpose, duration, registered agent, and principal office of the LLC. An LLC must use the words *limited liability company* or *LLC* in the company's name. The LLC is a legal entity with authority to conduct business in its own name.[9] LLC acts are characterized as "flexible statutes" because they generally permit owners to engage in the private ordering of relationships, with broad freedom of contract to govern these relationships as set forth in their operating agreements.[10]

CPA (B) CAPITAL CONTRIBUTIONS. An ownership interest in an LLC may be issued for cash, property, or services. The owners of the entity are known as *members*.

Capital contributions must comply with the "operating agreement" as discussed in the following paragraph. **For Example,** William Eichengrun claims his capital contribution to the LLC was in services not cash because he was the LLC's managing member. However, in proceedings to dissolve the LLC and distribute its assets, Eichengrun was not allowed to participate in the distribution because the operating agreement required that "initial capital contributions" of members be in cash or the fair market value of property.[11]

CPA (C) MANAGEMENT. Management of an LLC is vested in its members. An *operating agreement*, equivalent to the bylaws of a corporation or a partnership agreement, sets forth the specific management authority of members and managers.

The operating agreement need not be in writing. All amendments must be unanimous unless otherwise agreed to by the members. Oral amendments may modify written terms unless otherwise set forth in the operating agreement. To promote certainty in management, it is recommended that the operating agreement be in writing and that it be changed only by written amendments adopted by a specified percentage or number of members.

The management structure created in the operating agreement may provide for the company to be member managed. However, members commonly

---

[9] An individual has a right to appear before a court and represent himself or herself. However, a member of an LLC who as such is not personally liable for the LLC's actions cannot appear before a court on behalf of the LLC entity. The LLC may appear in court only through counsel. Thus, a nonattorney member of an LLC was not allowed to represent the LLC in a court case. *Collier v Cobalt, LLC,* 2002 WL 726640 (ED La 2002). *See also Gobe Media Group, LLC v Cisneros,* 959 A2d 892 (NJ Super 2008).

[10] *Elf Atochem N. America, Inc. v Jaffari,* 727 A2d 286 (Del Super Ct 1999).

[11] *KSI Rockville, LLC v Eichengrun,* 760 NYS2d 520 (App Div 2003).

delegate authority to run the entity to managers who may or may not be required to be members of the LLC. A member is not entitled to compensation for services performed by an LLC unless it is stipulated in the operating agreement. (Members receive profits and losses according to the terms of the operating agreement.)

In a member-managed company, each member has equal rights in management, with decisions made by a majority vote of the members.[12] In a manager-managed company, nonmanager members have no rights in management except for extraordinary matters, such as amending the operating agreement or consenting to merge with another entity.

Managers have the same fiduciary duties to the entity as corporate officers have to a corporation. In some states, members of manager-managed LLCs owe no fiduciary duty to the LCC unless a member exercises some or all of the authority of a manager pursuant to the operating agreement.[13]

CASE SUMMARY

Why You Need to Make Sure Business Relationship Obligations of Members Are Set Forth in the Operating Agreement!

FACTS: Stephen Doherty wrote Viper, a software program, for Lester Szlendak. Peter Katris and William Hamburg joined Szlendak and Doherty in forming an LLC to exploit the capabilities of the software. Katris and Hamburg were elected the "sole managers" of the LLC, and Szlendak and Doherty were members with marketing and technical responsibilities. Prior to and at the time of the LLC's formation, Doherty worked as an independent contractor for Patrick Carroll, an Ernst & Co. employee. Thereafter, Ernst & Co. hired Doherty to work for Carroll. As part of his duties, he developed a software program ultimately called WorldWideOptions Web (WWOW). Katris and the LLC sued Carroll, Ernst & Co., and Doherty, alleging that Doherty breached his fiduciary duty to the LLC and charging collusion by Carroll and Ernst in developing WWOW, which was functionally similar to Viper. From a judgment against the LLC, Katris appealed.

DECISION: Judgment against the LLC and Katris. Doherty was a member of a manager-managed LLC and exercised no managerial authority pursuant to the operating agreement. He owed no fiduciary duty to the LLC, and the collusion claim against Carroll and Ernst fails as a matter of law. [**Katris v Carroll, 842 NE2d 221 (Ill App 2005)**]

CPA   (D) **DISTRIBUTIONS.** Profits and losses are shared according to the terms of the operating agreement.

---

12 *IIC Holdings, LLC v HR Software Acquisition Group, Inc.*, 750 NYS2d 425 (Sup Ct 2002).

13 In *Remora Investments, LLC v Orr*, 673 SE2d 845 (Va 2009), the Virginia Supreme Court held that nothing in the statutory provisions relating to LLCs provides for fiduciary duties between members of an LLC or between a member and a manager of an LLC. The statutory standard of conduct for a manager of an LLC is to discharge duties in accordance with his or her good-faith business judgment of the best interests of the company, rather than by imposing fiduciary duties on members. In contrast, the Uniform Limited Liability Act of 2006, which has been adopted in Indiana and Idaho, states that members of an LLC owe each other the fiduciary duties of loyalty and care. See *Bush v Sage Health Care, LLC*, 203 P3d 694 (Idaho 2009). See also *Melcher v Apollo Medical Fund Management*, 208 NYS2d 207 (App Div 2006), referencing Delaware Code, Title 6 §18-110(c).

Liquidating distributions must first be applied to return all contributions not previously returned, and the remainder is distributed per capita to members unless members alter these rules in the operating agreement.

Any distribution made when the company is insolvent is unlawful. Each member or manager who votes to make an unlawful distribution is in violation of his or her fiduciary duty to the firm and is personally liable for the amount of distribution improperly paid. However, the individual may compel contribution from all other responsible members and managers.

(E) **LLC PROPERTY.** The LLC is an independent entity separate and distinct from the members. The LLC owns and holds property in its own name.[14]

CASE SUMMARY

"Another Person": The Unintended Consequences of an LLC Transaction

FACTS: In 1998, Shell and Texaco combined their retail marketing and refining activities into a limited liability company called Equilon Enterprises, LLC. They contributed all their western refining and marketing assets and assigned gas station leases and dealer agreements to the new LLC. Shell and Texaco, as the sole members of the LLC, received 100 percent of the ownership. The individual gas stations continued to sell Shell and Texaco products under their same leases and agreements. California law, identical in relevant part to the federal Petroleum Marketing Practices Act, states that a franchisor *"shall not sell, transfer, or assign to another person"* unless it first makes a bona fide offer to sell that interest to the franchisee. Forty-three independent Shell and Texaco dealers in southern California who leased from Shell and Texaco claimed that Shell and Texaco violated the California law by transferring the gas stations to the new LLC, Equilon, without offering them a chance to purchase the stations. Shell and Texaco contend that the law does not apply because they merely contributed their assets to an LLC that they controlled.

DECISION: Judgment for the independent dealers. What is the meaning of "another person" under the law in question? LLCs are distinct legal entities, separate from their members just as corporations are separate and distinct from their shareholders. Both corporations and LLCs are included within the definition of "person" under the state law. Because Equilon is an LLC, it is distinct from its members Shell and Texaco and is "another person" under the statute. The gas stations that were previously owned by the individual oil companies are now owned by "another person," Equilon.

Because Shell and Texaco relinquished title, possession, and control of the gas stations to Equilon, they "transferred" the properties to Equilon. Once members contribute assets to an LLC, those assets become capital of the LLC and the members lose any interest they had in the assets.

Under the plain language of the statute, the transaction at issue was a transfer to another person, Equilon, which triggered the duty to offer the gas stations to the franchisees first. [**Abrahim & Sons, Inc. v Equilon Enterprises, LLC, 252 F3d 958 (9th Cir 2002)**]

---

[14] *Northeast Realty, LLC v Misty Bayou, LLC*, 920 So2d 938 (La App 2006).

(F) ASSIGNMENT. An interest in an LLC is personal property and is generally assignable. However, LLC members cannot transfer the right to participate in management without the consent of the other members of the LLC. A creditor's right against a member's interest in an LLC is limited to a *charging order*. The creditor with such an order has only the rights of an assignee of an interest in an LLC.

(G) DISSOLUTION. Most LLC statutes provide that an LLC will dissolve by the consent of the members or upon the death, retirement, resignation, expulsion, or bankruptcy of a member. Statutes also provide, however, that the business of the LLC may be continued with the consent of all of the remaining members. With a change in IRS regulations away from its four-factor corporate characteristics test, discussed in the following section, some states have begun to amend LLC laws to give limited liability companies the option of perpetual existence.

Situations in which it is not reasonably practicable to carry on the business in conformity with the operating agreement may arise. The LLC statute commonly permits a court to decree dissolution of the LLC when such a situation occurs. **For Example,** Haley and Talcott each had a 50 percent interest in a real estate LLC. They had a falling out. The operating agreement contained an exit mechanism to buy out Haley's share, but the mechanism could not relieve Haley of his obligation as a personal guarantor for the LLC's mortgage. Because the LLC was deadlocked and the exit mechanism was not an adequate remedy, the court ordered the dissolution of the LLC and the sale of its property.[15]

Upon the winding up of an LLC, the assets are distributed according to the operating agreement. Should the agreement fail to provide for this event, the assets will be distributed according to the state's LLC statute.

(H) TAX CLASSIFICATION. The IRS applied a four-factor corporate characteristics test in determining whether an LLC would be taxed as a partnership or a corporation, allowing no more than two characteristics to exist to qualify for taxation as a partnership. The factors were continuity of life, centralized management, limited liability, and free transferability of interest. The four-factor test became obsolete on the implementation by the IRS of its so-called check-the-box entity classification election procedure available to unincorporated associations that are not publicly traded.[16] Now, if an LLC wants to be classified as a partnership, all it needs to do is make that election by checking the box on the appropriate IRS form.

(I) DISREGARDING THE LLC ENTITY. Some LLC statutes provide that courts may disregard the LLC entirely and hold the owners personally liable beyond their investments to the same extent as done in corporate law when exceptional circumstances demand.[17]

---

[15] *Haley v Talcott*, 864 A2d 86 (Del Ch 2004).
[16] Treas Reg 301.7701 *et seq.*
[17] *Net Jets Aviation, Inc. v LHC Communications, LLC*, 537 F3d 168 (2d Cir 2008).

FIGURE 43-1 | *Comparison of General Partnership, Limited Partnership, Limited Liability Company, and Limited Liability Partnership*

	General Partnership	Limited Partnership	Limited Liability Company (LLC)	Limited Liability Partnership (LLP)
Creation	No formality required.	Filing a certificate of limited partnership with appropriate state office.	Filing articles of organization with secretary of state.	Registration of LLP filed with state government.
Liability	Unlimited liability of each partner for firm debts.	General partners: unlimited liability for firm debts. Limited partners: no liability beyond loss of investment.	All members are liable for LLC debts to the extent of their capital contributions and equity in firm. No personal liability beyond this.	No liability for partners beyond their contributions and equity in firm, except unlimited personal liability for their own wrongful acts and those of persons whom they supervise.
Management	All partners according to their partnership agreement or the UPA or RUPA.	General partners according to their partnership agreement or the UPA or RUPA. Limited partners excluded.	By members of firm, who may delegate authority to managers.	All partners according to partnership agreement or the UPA.
Dissolution	As set forth in the partnership agreement or the UPA or RUPA.	As set forth in the partnership agreement or the ULPA or RULPA.	As set forth in LLC statute or articles of organization.	As set forth in partnership agreement or the UPA or RUPA.

CASE SUMMARY

Piercing the LLC Veil

FACTS: Kaycee Land and Livestock entered into a contract with Flahive Oil and Gas, LLC, allowing it to use the surface of its real property. Kaycee alleges that Flahive Oil and Gas caused environmental contamination of its real property. Because the LLC has no assets at this time, Kaycee seeks to pierce the limited liability company veil and disregard the LLC entity of Flahive Oil and Gas and hold Roger Flahive, the managing member of the LLC who directed all operations on the property, individually liable for the contamination. The question presented to the court is, "In the absence of fraud, is the remedy of piercing the veil available against a company formed under the Wyoming Limited Liability Company Act?"

DECISION: The equitable remedy of piercing the corporate veil is an available remedy under the Wyoming Limited Liability Company Act. When corporations fail to follow the statutorily mandated formalities, comingle funds, or ignore restrictions in their articles of incorporation regarding separate treatment of the corporate property, the courts deem it appropriate to disregard the separate identity and do not permit shareholders to be sheltered from liability to third parties for damages caused by the corporation's acts. No public policy exists to treat LLCs differently than corporations regarding veil piercing. [**Kaycee Land and Livestock v Flahive, 46 P3d 323 (Wyo 2002)**]

4. LLCs and Other Entities

LLCs are distinguishable from Subchapter S corporations and limited partnerships.

(A) LLC DISTINGUISHED FROM A SUBCHAPTER S CORPORATION. Under a Subchapter S corporation (so named from Subchapter S of the Internal Revenue Code), shareholders of a close corporation may be treated as partners for tax purposes and retain the benefit of limited liability under the corporate form. An S corporation is limited to 75 shareholders who must be U.S. citizens or resident aliens. Although partnerships and corporations may generally not be shareholders, employee stock ownership plans (ESOPs) and nonprofit entities may be. In contrast, an LLC has no limit on the number of owners, and there is no restriction on the types of entities or persons that may own an LLC. Thus, partnerships, corporations, and foreign investors may be owners of an LLC. Because substantial taxes on appreciated assets are payable on the liquidation of an S corporation, it is generally not feasible to convert an existing S corporation to an LLC.

CPA   **(B) LLC DISTINGUISHED FROM A LIMITED PARTNERSHIP.** Limited partners in a limited partnership have the advantage of limited liability. However, every limited partnership must have a general partner who manages the business, and this partner can be subject to unlimited liability. This structural feature is a major disadvantage of the limited partnership form that does not exist in a limited liability company (LLC). Also, individual limited partners may lose their limited liability if they participate in the control of the business. Under an LLC, the members may actively participate in the control of the business and still receive limited liability protection. As stated previously in this chapter, a general partner may avoid unlimited liability on a sizeable limited partnership project by incorporating.

(c) Usage. It is expected that the LLC will in many instances replace general and limited partnerships as well as close corporations and S corporations. The LLC will not replace the publicly traded corporation, however, because publicly traded partnerships and LLCs must be classified as corporations for tax purposes.[18]

D. Limited Liability Partnerships

As part of the limited liability trend established by the swift enactment of LLC laws throughout the country, most states have recently enacted limited liability partnership (LLP) acts. Like LLCs, they provide businesses and those offering professional services the benefit of single taxation as a partnership as well as limited liability.[19]

CPA   ## 5. Extent of Limited Liability

In a general partnership, partners are jointly liable for partnership debts and jointly and severally liable for partnership torts. LLP statutes were initially drafted to shield innocent partners from vicarious negligence or malpractice liability of their partners. Some states now provide "full shields" for innocent partners that eliminate the vicarious personal liability of these partners for the obligations of the partnership and free them from any obligation to contribute personal assets beyond their investments in the partnership. However, the "liability shield" of a registered limited liability partnership only applies to a partner's liability to third parties and does not shield against breaches of the partnership's or partners' obligations to each other. In every state, however, LLP partners remain fully liable for their own negligence and continue to have unlimited liability for the wrongful acts of those whom they directly supervise and control.

C A S E   S U M M A R Y

A Limited Shield

FACTS: Phillip Kuslansky sued his former law partners for breach of contract for failure to pay him the value of his interest in the registered limited liability partnership upon his withdrawal from the partnership. His former partners moved to dismiss the complaint, contending that they were shielded from liability with respect to the plaintiff partner who had withdrawn from the partnership. From a judgment for the defendant former partners, Kuslansky appealed.

DECISION: Judgment for Kuslansky. The state LLP law does not shield general partners in registered limited liability partnerships from personal liability for breaches of the partnership's or partners' obligations to each other. [**Kuslansky v Kuslansky, Robbins, Stechel and Cunningham, LLP, 858 NYS2d 213 (App Div 2008)**]

---

[18] See IRS Notice 88-75, 1988, 1988-2 CB 386. The traditional corporation retains many advantages, such as the low corporate income tax on corporate profits, which allows accumulation of capital for expansion or the distribution of all corporate earnings as compensation as well as providing fringe benefits for employee-owners with pretax dollars (IRC §§ 79, 119, 162).

[19] The 1994 Revised Uniform Partnership Act (RUPA) was amended in 1996 to include two new articles: Article 10, dealing with limited liability partnerships, and Article 11, dealing with foreign limited liability partnerships. Articles 1 through 11 constitute the Uniform Limited Liability Partnership Act.

Professional LLPs continue to be subject to professional regulations, and the appropriate regulating boards set the amount and type of malpractice insurance firms must carry to operate as an LLP.

For Example, to illustrate the effects of a change from a general partnership to an LLP, surgeons Jones, Smith, and Gray are partners. Jones inadvertently removed Miller's healthy kidney rather than his diseased kidney, and a jury returned a verdict of $2 million. Smith and Gray, although innocent partners, are jointly and severally liable along with Jones under general partnership law, and their personal assets can be reached to pay the judgment if necessary. Under an LLP, only partnership assets and the personal assets of Jones are available to pay the judgment. Smith's and Gray's personal assets cannot be reached.

CPA   ## 6. Registration and Usage

LLP statutes are designed to permit the conversion of existing general partnerships into limited liability partnerships. The statutes require registration with the secretary of state, and the name of the partnership must contain the term *limited liability partnership* or *LLP*.

Traditional partnership agreements, like those used by many accounting and law firms and other professional partnerships, can be converted into limited liability partnership agreements without major redrafting or renegotiating of the underlying agreements. It is thus expected that many of these professional firms will organize under this new form of partnership.

ethics & the law

When the Office of the Special Counsel concluded its work in both civil and criminal litigation against officers, directors, and consultants involved with failed savings and loan institutions in the late 1980s, it released a report on its work. On the civil side, the Office of the Special Counsel had obtained settlements from defendants in civil suits of $2.9 billion in restitution. Accounting firms, along with lawyers and consultants, comprised 71 percent of the defendants.

Because most accounting firms were organized as partnerships, the result was that many partners were required to dig into their personal assets to meet the restitution requirements imposed by the federal government. Since the creation of LLPs, all of the largest accounting firms in the United States have restructured, with most choosing the LLP for conducting business. All forms of restructuring will ensure limited personal liability for their principals.

Was the restructuring undertaken to avoid liability? Does limited liability insulate those who make decisions from liability for those decisions? Financiers attempt to determine what stake the officers in a corporation have in the corporation. Stock ownership and exposure to losses through the value of those shares are seen as a positive influence. Do liability limitations reduce the stake a principal has? Is it good to have decision makers separated from the costs of those decisions?

MAKE THE CONNECTION

SUMMARY

A limited partnership consists of one or more limited partners who contribute cash, property, or services without liability for losses beyond their investment, and one or more general partners, who manage the business and have unlimited personal liability. A limited partner's protection from unlimited liability may be lost if the partner participates in the control of the business. "Safe harbor" activities for limited partners are set forth in the RULPA. General partners may avoid personal liability by incorporating. A certificate of limited partnership must be filed when the partnership is formed for the law to apply. Otherwise, general partnership law applies.

A limited liability company is a hybrid form of business organization that combines the tax advantages of a partnership with the limited liability feature of the corporation. It must be formed in accordance with state law in order to have effect, and the designation LLC must appear with the company's name. Management of an LLC is vested in its members, and members can delegate authority to run the entity to managers, the terms of which are set forth in the company's operating agreement. Members receive profits and losses according to the operating agreement. A member's interest in an LLC is assignable, but consent of the other members is needed for the assignee to participate in the firm's management.

A limited liability partnership is a new form of business organization that allows existing partnerships to convert to this form without major renegotiation of the underlying partnership agreement. Innocent partners in a limited liability partnership are not personally liable for the torts of other partners beyond their investment in the firm.

LEARNING OUTCOMES

After studying this chapter, you should be able to clearly explain:

A. THE ARRIVAL OF PARTNERSHIP LIMITED LIABILITY

LO.1 Explain the history of making limited liability available to general partnerships

See the presentation of the developing law of partnership limited liability on p. 1014.

B. LIMITED PARTNERSHIP

LO.2 Explain the extent of a founding general partner's liability for the debts of the firm, and how unlimited liability can be avoided by utilization of a corporate general partner

See the discussion of general partners' avoidance of personal liability through incorporation, p. 1014.

LO.3 Explain the nature and extent of a limited partner's liability for the debts of the firm

See the *Gilroy* case in which limited partners (investors) lost their limitation of liability by participating in the control of the business, p. 1016.

C. LIMITED LIABILITY COMPANIES

LO.4 Explain the advantages of a limited liability company

> See the discussion of the advantages of an LLC, including the tax advantages of treatment as a partnership with the limited liability feature of a corporation, beginning on p. 1017.

D. LIMITED LIABILITY PARTNERSHIPS

LO.5 Explain how a limited liability partnership "shields" innocent partners from liability to third parties

> See the example involving Dr. Jones's removal of the wrong kidney, with innocent partners Smith's and Grey's personal assets being shielded from liability from a large judgment beyond partnership and Dr. Jones' assets, p. 1025.

KEY TERMS

general partners   limited partners   limited partnership

QUESTIONS AND CASE PROBLEMS

1. What is the principal advantage of an LLP over an LLC?

2. Alan Waung, a Hong Kong businessperson, purchased a golf course in Saginaw, Michigan, as an investment. As an avid golfer, Alan anticipates spending several weeks during the year at his "Northern Pines" course. He has been informed that a Subchapter S corporation would allow him and his family-member shareholders to be treated as partners for U.S. tax purposes while retaining the limited liability of the corporate form. Advise Mr. Waung on this matter. What form of business organization would you recommend?

3. Kate Haley, an experienced builder, formed a limited partnership in August 2009, along with two limited partners, Drs. Growbioski and Gailen, who each provided $100,000 to the partnership for initial capital for the construction of a medical office building near Stowe, Vermont. With the bustle of getting building and environmental permits and placating abutters to the property, as well as lining up suppliers and subcontractors and getting the job started, Kate simply did not find an opportunity to take the long drive to file the certificate of limited partnership with the secretary of state's office in Montpelier. A confluence of bad weather, an accident causing serious personal injury, financing disappointments, labor difficulties, design problems, and some personal problems resulted in the project being stopped before completion with some $550,000 in overdue bills. Dr. Growbioski has been approached by several suppliers and craftsmen seeking payment for supplies and work performed. As a limited partner, he believes that he is not liable for firm debts beyond his investment, which was $100,000. Explain to Dr. Growbioski his obligations at this point.

4. Alice Meyers, Monroe Moylan, and Bart Means practice medicine as Bay Area Anesthetics Associates (BAAA), a limited liability partnership. A newly certified nurse anesthesiologist, Mary Noyes, working with Dr. Means and not realizing a patient's allergy condition set forth on her chart, inadvertently administered the wrong anesthesia, which resulted in the patient's death. In a malpractice suit against Bay Area Anesthetics Associates, LLP, is the partnership liable for Mary Noyes's actions if she was employed by the hospital? What if she was employed by the partnership? Explain in detail.

5. Sabastian Hafner joined a start-up business with a business plan focused on making breads without common food allergens, such as wheat, yeast, dairy, and gluten, to be marketed in a major metropolitan area. The five founders of the business, including Sabastian, selected the limited liability company (LLC) as their form of business organization. The Articles of Organization for the limited liability company were duly filed with the secretary of state. The Operating Agreement simply provided that founding member Jillian Lopez would be the sole manager of the firm, and it set a salary for her at $40,000 per year. She hired employees to perform production, delivery, and sales work. Sebastian and the other three members spent time nights and early mornings "pitching in" at the bakery. After two months of diligent work, Sabastian, a second-year MBA student, sought back pay for the 40 hours each week he spent at the bakery during the previous eight weeks. He pointed out to the other members of the LLC that state law authorizes employees to sue for their wages. What are Sabastian's rights regarding pay for the service he performed for the LLC?

6. Hurwitz and Padden practiced law as equal partners for a short period of time before converting to an LLC. Some three years later, Padden informed Hurwitz that he intended to leave the firm. When they could not agree on how to divide $200,000 in fees relating to work acquired before the dissolution of the LLC, Hurwitz filed suit seeking an equal division of the fees under partnership principles. Padden contended that partnership principles should not apply to the dissolution of an LLC even though the state's LLC law incorporated the definition and use of the term *dissolution* from the UPA. Decide. [*Hurwitz v Padden*, 581 NW2d 359 (Minn App)]

7. Don Mason and Beth Daley were managers and members of Pacific Beach Developers, LLC (PBD), a start-up real estate development company focusing on rehabilitating older properties for increased rental values and possible resale. Daley made a contract with San Diego Architects Associates (SDAA) to provide plans for the rehabilitation of a 60-unit building on Ingraham Street for $97,000, signing the contract "Beth Daley, manager P.B.D. LLC." Financing for the Ingraham Street property fell through, and PBD's option on the property expired. Although Daley notified SDAA that the "Ingraham Street deal was off," SDAA had nearly completed its work, and SDAA brought suit for the contract price against both the LLC and Beth Daley. At the point the lawsuit was initiated, PBD had no working capital remaining, and Don and Beth had "moved on," having taken jobs as mutual fund salespersons. Advise Beth of her legal obligations to SDAA.

8. John and Amelia have general commitments from a number of individuals to invest in their Sproondrift Cove Club golf course and distinctive residential community in Duval County. John wants to form a limited partnership. He realizes that every limited partnership must have a general partner who manages the business and is subject to unlimited liability for all debts and liabilities of the limited partnership. But he says that is no problem because the general partner can be a corporation and can limit its liability exposure by simply creating a "shell" corporation. John stated to Amelia, "As officers of the corporate general partner, you and I can operate the business without the limited partners interfering … we run the show!" Amelia responded, "John, what you propose seems so very complicated, risky, and expensive. A number of our investors are relatives who may want to be listened to, and some of our investors are professionals who could give us some valuable advice. Maybe a limited liability company would be a better entity for us." Compare the advantages and disadvantages of an LLC with a limited partnership and recommend the most appropriate form of business organization for this venture.

9. Hacienda Farms, Ltd., was organized as a limited partnership with Ricardo de Escamilla as the general partner and James L. Russell and H. W. Andrews as limited partners. The partnership raised vegetables and truck crops that were marketed principally through a produce concern controlled by Andrews. All three individuals decided which crops were to be planted. The general partner had no power to withdraw money from the partnership's two bank accounts without the signature of one of the limited partners. After operating for some seven and one-half months under these procedures, the limited partners demanded that the general partner resign as farm manager, which he did. Six weeks later, the partnership went into bankruptcy. Laurance Holzman, as trustee in bankruptcy, brought an action against Russell and Andrews, claiming that they had become liable to the creditors of the partnership as general partners because they had taken part in the control of the partnership business. How would you decide the case under the ULPA? Would the outcome be different under the RULPA? [*Holzman v de Escamilla*, 195 P2d 833 (Cal App)]

10. Jerome Micco was a major shareholder and corporate officer of Micco and Co., Inc., which was a limited partner in Harbor Creek, Ltd., a limited partnership formed to build a condominium complex. Hommel, an electrical contractor, was the successful bidder on certain electrical work for the project. For several months, Hommel worked under the direction of the construction supervisor and was paid by the limited partnership for his work. Because of financial difficulties, the supervisor was released. Thereafter, Jerome Micco played a major role in the building of the project, directing what work was to be performed. Hommel submitted payment invoices directly to Micco. When Hommel was not paid, he sued Micco, contending that Micco was a limited partner who ran the operation personally and was personally responsible for the debt. Micco argued that he was an employee or agent of a corporation (Micco and Co., Inc.) and thus could not be held liable for the debt. The evidence reveals that Micco had no occasion to tell Hommel that he was acting as a corporate officer. Is it ethical for a corporate officer and shareholder to seek to

avoid individual liability in this case? How would you decide the case? [*Hommel v Micco*, 602 NE2d 1259 (Ohio App)]

11. Ralph and Maureen K. Hagan (collectively "Hagan") owned the Stuart Court Apartments in Richmond, Virginia. On April 30, 1994, Hagan executed an agreement with Adams Property Associates, Inc. (Adams), giving Adams the exclusive right to sell the property for $1,600,000. The agreement provided that if the property was "sold or exchanged" within one year, with or without Adams's assistance, Hagan would pay Adams a fee of 6 percent of the "gross sales amount." Seven days before the year expired, Hagan, Roy T. Tepper, and Lynn Parsons formed a limited liability company, Hagan, Parsons, & Tepper, LLC (HPT). By deed dated April 23, 1995, Hagan transferred the property to HPT. Adams contends it is entitled to a commission from Hagan pursuant to the April 1994 agreement. Hagan contends the transaction was just a contribution of capital to a new company, not a sale. Decide. [*Hagan v Adams Property Associates, Inc.*, 482 SE2d 805 (Va 1997)]

12. Peter Kertesz formed an LLC and operated it in South Florida under the business name "Mourning Flowers." The LLC specialized in the sale of flowers to funeral homes. Although Kertesz was initially the only member and manager, he ultimately granted ownership interests totaling 55 percent of the LLC to six individuals. In mid-2007, the members had a falling out that culminated in the majority removing Kertesz as managing member. Kertesz alleged that shortly after this, the LLC's distributors and clients "threatened to terminate their relationship with the LLC if Kertesz was not brought back into the operations of the LLC." These actions, Kertesz claimed, caused the LLC to suffer irreparable harm. Kertesz sought the judicial dissolution of the LLC on the basis of these circumstances and an alleged deadlock in management of the LLC, and sought the appointment of a receiver to protect the assets and goodwill of the LLC. What relief, if any, is Kertesz entitled to? [*Kertesz v The Spa Floral, LLC*, 994 So2d 473 (Fla App)]

CPA QUESTIONS

1. Which of the following statements is correct with respect to a limited partnership?

    a. A limited partner may *not* be an unsecured creditor of the limited partnership.

    b. A general partner may *not* also be a limited partner at the same time.

    c. A general partner may be a secured creditor of the limited partnership.

    d. A limited partnership can be formed with limited liability for all partners.

Chapter 44

CORPORATION FORMATION

T he corporation is one of the most important forms of business organization.

A. NATURE AND CLASSES

A *corporation* is an artificial person that is created by government action.

1. The Corporation as a Person

corporation—artificial being created by government grant, which for many purposes is treated as a natural person.

A **corporation** is an artificial person created by government action and granted certain powers. It exists in the eyes of the law as a person, separate and distinct from the persons who own the corporation.

The concept that the corporation is a distinct legal person means that the corporation's property is owned not by the persons who own shares in the corporation but by the corporation. Debts of the corporation are debts of this artificial person, not of the persons running the corporation or owning shares of stock in it.[1] The corporation can sue and be sued in its own name, but shareholders cannot be sued or held liable for corporate actions or obligations.[2]

CASE SUMMARY

Collins Claims Cardinal Rule

FACTS: Lisa Hayes sued Jennifer Collins seeking the repayment of a loan issued by her deceased husband to Collins's corporation. After her husband's death, Hayes learned that her husband had been having an affair with Collins and filed suit against Collins individually for the failure to repay the loan to the corporation. Collins filed an answer denying individual liability for the corporate debt.

DECISION: Judgment for Collins. The cardinal rule of corporate law is that a corporation possesses a legal existence separate and apart from its officers and shareholders; therefore, the mere operation of corporate business does not render one personally liable for corporate acts, including a corporate loan. [**Hayes v Collins 538 SE2d 785 (Ga App 2000)**]

certificate of incorporation—written approval from the state or national government for a corporation to be formed.

articles of incorporation—See certificate of incorporation.

charter—grant of authority from a government to exist as a corporation. Generally replaced today by a certificate of incorporation approving the articles of incorporation.

A corporation is formed by obtaining approval of a **certificate of incorporation**, **articles of incorporation**, or a **charter** from the state or national government.[3]

---

[1] *American Truck Lines, Inc. v Albino*, 424 SE2d 367 (Ga App 1992).

[2] Also, a corporation does not have standing to pursue a claim on behalf of its sole shareholders. See *Accurate Printers, Inc. v Stark*, 671 SE2d 228 (Ga App 2008).

[3] *Charter, certificate of incorporation*, and *articles of incorporation* are all terms used to refer to the documents that serve as evidence of a government's grant of corporate existence and powers. Most state incorporation statutes now provide for a certificate of incorporation issued by the secretary of state, but a Revised Model Business Corporation Act (RMBCA) has done away with the certificate of incorporation. Under the RMBCA, corporate existence begins when articles of incorporation are filed with the secretary of state. An endorsed copy of the articles together with a fee, receipt, or acknowledgment replaces the certificate of incorporation. See RMBCA §§ 1.25 and 2.03 and footnote 8 in this chapter.

2. Classifications of Corporations

Corporations may be classified in terms of their relationship to the public, the source of their authority, and the nature of their activities.

(A) PUBLIC, PRIVATE, AND QUASI-PUBLIC CORPORATIONS. A **public corporation** is one established for governmental purposes and for the administration of public affairs. A city is a public or municipal corporation acting under authority granted to it by the state.

A **private corporation** is one organized for charitable and benevolent purposes or for purposes of finance, industry, and commerce. Private corporations are often called *public* in business circles when their stock is sold to the public.

A **quasi-public corporation**, sometimes known as a public service corporation or a public utility, is a private corporation furnishing services on which the public is particularly dependent. An example of a quasi-public corporation is a gas and electric company.

(B) PUBLIC AUTHORITIES. The public increasingly demands that government perform services. Some of these are performed directly by government. Others are performed by separate corporations or **authorities** created by government. **For Example,** a city parking facility may be organized as a separate municipal parking authority, or a public housing project may be operated as an independent housing authority.

(C) DOMESTIC AND FOREIGN CORPORATIONS. A corporation is called a **domestic corporation** with respect to the state under whose law it has been incorporated. Any other corporation going into that state is called a **foreign corporation**. Thus, a corporation holding a Texas charter is a domestic corporation in Texas but a foreign corporation in all other states.[4]

(D) SPECIAL SERVICE CORPORATIONS. Corporations formed for transportation, banking, insurance, and savings and loan operations and similar specialized functions are subject to separate codes or statutes with regard to their organization. In addition, federal and state laws and administrative agencies regulate in detail the way these businesses are conducted.

(E) CLOSE CORPORATIONS. A corporation whose shares are held by a single shareholder or a small group of shareholders is known as a **close corporation**. Its shares are not traded publicly. Many such corporations are small firms that are incorporated to obtain either the advantage of limited liability or a tax benefit, or both.

Many states have statutes that have liberalized corporation law as it applies to close corporations. **For Example,** Nancy Davis Judson and Hall Davis IV are siblings who inherited their parents' stock in a domestic close corporation, Hall's Mortuary, Inc., a prominent and successful funeral home in Port Allen, Louisiana. Nancy was

---

public corporation—corporation that has been established for governmental purposes and for the administration of public affairs.

private corporation—corporation organized for charitable and benevolent purposes or for purposes of finance, industry, and commerce.

quasi-public corporation—private corporation furnishing services on which the public is particularly dependent, for example, a gas and electric company.

authorities—corporations formed by government that perform public service.

domestic corporation—corporation that has been incorporated by the state in question as opposed to incorporation by another state.

foreign corporation—corporation incorporated under the laws of another state.

close corporation—corporation whose shares are held by a single shareholder or a small group of shareholders.

---

[4] Failure of a foreign corporation to obtain a certificate of authority to do intrastate business in the state, under that state's door-closing statute, may mean that the foreign corporation cannot enforce a contract entered into in the state. **For Example,** TradeWinds Environmental Restoration, Inc., a New York–based company, entered into a contract with Alabama contractor BBC to do structural-drying services at a number of coastal condominiums after Hurricane Ivan in 2004. TradeWinds performed the work under the contract valued at $400,000. When TradeWinds sued for the money owed under the contract, the court determined that the "labor" performed is not an article of commerce, nor is the agreement to supply it an act of commerce. And the court determined that TradeWinds' business was intrastate, rather than interstate, and without a certificate of authority to perform the work, TradeWinds could not enforce the contract. *TradeWinds Environmental Restoration, Inc. v Brown Brothers Construction, LLC,* 999 So 2d 875 (Ala 2008).

the secretary-treasurer, a director, and shareholder of 50 percent of the corporation's stock. Hall was president, a director, and the shareholder of the other 50 percent of the corporation's stock. The siblings had a falling out. Nancy filed a court action to compel Hall to comply with the bylaws regarding her participation in the management of the business and to allow her access to all corporate records. Hall responded with accusations of his own. Thereafter, Hall alleged that he and Nancy were deadlocked in the management of corporate affairs and petitioned the court for involuntary dissolution and the appointment of a liquidator. Nancy objected and wanted a jury trial on a number of issues. The court applied a statute, nearly identical to a Delaware statute, "designed to obviate a deadlocked vote of two equal shareholders" of a close corporation and ordered the dissolution of the corporation.[5]

CPA

(F) Subchapter S Corporations. Subchapter S is a subdivision of the Internal Revenue Code. If corporate shareholders meet the requirements of this subdivision, they may elect Subchapter S status, which allows the shareholders to be treated as partners for tax purposes and retain the benefit of limited liability under the corporate form. A Subchapter S corporation is limited to 75 shareholders.

Under the Small Business Job Protection Act of 1996, employee stock ownership plans (ESOPs) and tax-exempt entities may be shareholders subject to certain special taxation rules.[6] Other reforms in this act make it easier for small businesses to comply with S corporation rules.

(G) Professional Corporations. A corporation may be organized for the purpose of conducting a profession. Each officer, director, and shareholder of a professional corporation must be licensed to practice the profession. Professional incorporation does not shield a practitioner from personal liability relating to the professional services rendered.

eleemosynary corporation–corporation organized for a charitable or benevolent purpose.

(H) Nonprofit Corporations. A *nonprofit corporation* (or an **eleemosynary corporation**), is one that is organized for charitable or benevolent purposes. Nonprofit corporations include hospitals, nursing homes, and universities.[7] Special procedures for incorporation are prescribed, and provision is made for a detailed examination of and hearing regarding the purpose, function, and methods of raising money for the enterprise.

3. Corporations and Governments

Problems arise about the power of governments to create and regulate corporations.

(A) Power to Create. Because by definition a corporation is created by government, the right to be a corporation must be obtained from the proper governmental agency. The federal government may create corporations whenever appropriate to carry out the powers granted to it.

police power–power to govern; the power to adopt laws for the protection of the public health, welfare, safety, and morals.

Generally, a state by virtue of its **police power** may create any kind of corporation for any purpose. Most states have a **general corporation code**, which

general corporation code–state's code listing certain requirements for creation of a corporation.

---

[5] *Judson v Davis*, 916 So2d 1106 (La App 2005).
[6] Pub L No 104-188 (August 20, 1996).
[7] The Committee on Corporate Laws of the American Bar Association has prepared a Model Nonprofit Corporation Act. A revised Model Nonprofit Corporation Act was approved in 1986.

lists certain requirements, and anyone who satisfies the requirements and files the necessary papers with the government may automatically become a corporation. In 1950, the American Bar Association (ABA) published a Model Business Corporation Act (MBCA) to assist legislative bodies in the modernization of state corporation laws. An updated version was published in 1969. Statutory language similar to that contained in the 1969 version of the MBCA has been adopted in whole or in part by 35 states. A complete revision of the model act was approved in 1984 (RMBCA).[8] Updates to the model act have been approved subsequent to the scandals involving public corporations in recent years.[9] Jurisdictions following the model act have made numerous modifications to reflect their differing views about balancing the interests of public corporations, shareholders, and management. Caution must therefore be exercised in making generalizations about model act jurisdictions. There is no *uniform* corporation act.

(B) POWER TO REGULATE. Subject to constitutional limitations, corporations may be regulated by statutes.

(1) Protection of the Corporation as a Person
The Constitution of the United States prohibits the national government and state governments from depriving any person of life, liberty, or property without due process of law. Many state constitutions contain a similar limitation on their respective state governments. A corporation is regarded as a "person" within the meaning of such provisions.

The federal Constitution prohibits a state from denying to any person within its jurisdiction the equal protection of the laws. No such express limitation is placed on the federal government, although the due process clause binding the federal government is liberally interpreted so that it prohibits substantial inequality of treatment.

(2) Protection of the Corporation as a Citizen
For certain purposes, such as determining the right to bring a lawsuit in a federal court, a corporation is a citizen of any state in which it has been incorporated and of the state where it has its principal place of business.

B. CORPORATE POWERS

Except for limitations in the federal Constitution or the state's own constitution, a state legislature may give corporations any lawful powers. The RMBCA contains

---

[8] The Revised Model Business Corporation Act (1984) was approved by the Committee on Corporate Laws Section of Business Law of the American Bar Association. The committee approved revisions to sections 6.40 and 8.33 on March 27, 1987, and to section 7.08 on June 16, 1996; changes to Subchapters B and D of Chapter 1 of the model act, which accommodate the use of electronic means for transmitting and filing required corporate documents with the secretary of state, were approved on September 20, 1997. Model act citations are to the 1984 Revised Model Business Corporation Act (RMBCA) unless designated otherwise.

[9] Revisions included in the 2005 edition of the act apply to directors' conflicting interest transactions, provisions relating to directors' involvement with corporate opportunities, and updates on the role and responsibilities of corporate directors and officers.

a general provision on corporate powers granting a corporation "the same powers as an individual to do all things necessary or convenient to carry out its business and affairs."[10]

4. Particular Powers

Modern corporation codes give corporations a wide range of powers.

(A) PERPETUAL LIFE. One of the distinctive features of a corporation is its perpetual or continuous life—the power to continue as an entity forever or for a stated period of time regardless of changes in stock ownership or the death of any shareholders.

(B) CORPORATE NAME. A corporation must have a name to identify it. As a general rule, it may select any name for this purpose. Most states require that the corporate name contain some word indicating the corporate character[11] and that the name not be the same as, or deceptively similar to, the name of any other corporation. Some statutes prohibit the use of a name that is likely to mislead the public.

(C) CORPORATE SEAL. A corporation may have a distinctive seal. However, a corporation need not use a seal in the transaction of business unless this is required by statute or a natural person in transacting that business would be required to use a seal.

CPA

bylaws–rules and regulations enacted by a corporation to govern the affairs of the corporation and its shareholders, directors, and officers.

(D) BYLAWS. Bylaws are the rules and regulations enacted by a corporation to govern the affairs of the corporation and its shareholders, directors, and officers.

Bylaws are adopted by shareholders, although in some states they may be adopted by the directors of the corporation. Approval by the state or an amendment of the corporate charter is not required to make the bylaws effective.

The bylaws are subordinate to the general law of the state, the statute under which the corporation is formed, and the charter of the corporation.[12] Bylaws that conflict with such superior authority or that are in themselves unreasonable are invalid. Bylaws that are valid are binding on all shareholders regardless of whether they know of the existence of those bylaws or were among the majority that consented to their adoption. Bylaws are not binding on third persons, however, unless they have notice or knowledge of them.

(E) STOCK. A corporation may issue certificates representing corporate stock. Under the RMBCA, authorized, but unissued, shares may be issued at the price set by the board of directors. Under UCC Article 8 (1978 and 1994 versions), securities may be "uncertificated," or not represented by an instrument.

(F) MAKING CONTRACTS. Corporation codes give corporations the power to make contracts.

(G) BORROWING MONEY. Corporations have the implied power to borrow money in carrying out their authorized business purposes.

---

[10] RMBCA § 3.02. State statutes generally contain similar broad catchall grants of powers.
[11] RMBCA § 4.01(a) declares that the corporate name must contain the word *corporation, company, incorporated,* or *limited* or an abbreviation of one of these words.
[12] *Roach v Bynum*, 403 So 2d 187 (Ala 1981).

(H) **EXECUTING NEGOTIABLE INSTRUMENTS.** Corporations have the power to issue or indorse negotiable instruments and to accept drafts.

(I) **ISSUING BONDS.** A corporation may exercise its power to borrow money by issuing bonds.

(J) **TRANSFERRING PROPERTY.** The corporate property may be leased, assigned for the benefit of creditors, or sold. In many states, however, a solvent corporation may not transfer all of its property without the consent of all or a substantial majority of its shareholders.

A corporation, having power to incur debts, may mortgage or pledge its property as security for those debts. This rule does not apply to public service companies, such as street transit systems and gas and electric companies.

(K) **ACQUIRING PROPERTY.** A corporation has the power to acquire and hold such property as is reasonably necessary for carrying out its express powers.

(L) **BUYING BACK STOCK.** Generally, a corporation may purchase its own stock if it is solvent at the time and the purchase does not impair capital. Stock that is reacquired by the corporation that issued it is commonly called **treasury stock**.

treasury stock–corporate stock that the corporation has reacquired.

Although treasury stock retains the character of outstanding stock, it has an inactive status while it is held by the corporation.[13] Thus, the treasury shares cannot be voted, nor can dividends be declared on them.

(M) **DOING BUSINESS IN ANOTHER STATE.** A corporation has the power to engage in business in other states. However, this does not exempt the corporation from satisfying valid restrictions imposed by the foreign state in which it seeks to do business.

(N) **PARTICIPATING IN AN ENTERPRISE.** Corporations may generally participate in an enterprise to the same extent as individuals. Not only may they enter into joint ventures, but also the modern statutory trend is to permit a corporation to be a member of a partnership, and a corporation may be a limited partner. The RMBCA authorizes a corporation "to be a promoter, partner, member, associate, or manager of any partnership, joint venture, trust, or other entity."[14]

(O) **PAYING EMPLOYEE BENEFITS.** The RMBCA empowers a corporation "to pay pensions and establish pension plans, pension trusts, profit-sharing plans, share bonus plans, share option plans, and benefit or incentive plans for any or all of its current or former directors, officers, employees, and agents."[15]

(P) **CHARITABLE CONTRIBUTIONS.** The RMBCA authorizes a corporation, without any limitation, "to make donations for the public welfare or for charitable, scientific, or

---

[13] When a corporation reacquires its own shares, it has the choice of retiring them and thus restoring them to the status of authorized, but unissued, shares or of treating them as still issued and available for transfer. The latter are described as treasury shares.

[14] RMBCA § 3.02(9).

[15] RMBCA § 3.02(12).

educational purposes."[16] In some states, a limitation is imposed on the amount that can be donated for charitable purposes.

5. *Ultra Vires* Acts

ultra vires—act or contract that the corporation does not have authority to do or make.

When a corporation acts in excess of or beyond the scope of its powers, the corporation's act is described as ***ultra vires***. Such an action is improper in the same way that it is improper for an agent to act beyond the scope of the authority given by the principal. It is also improper with respect to shareholders and creditors of the corporation because corporate funds have been diverted to unauthorized uses.

The modern corporation statute will state that every corporation formed under it will have certain powers unless the articles of incorporation expressly exclude some of the listed powers, and then the statute will list every possible power that is needed to run a business. In some states, the legislature makes a blanket grant of all power that a natural person running the business would possess.[17] The net result is that the modern corporation possesses such a broad scope of powers that it is difficult to find an action that is *ultra vires*. If a mining corporation should begin to manufacture television sets, that might be an *ultra vires* transaction, but such an extreme departure rarely happens.

Because nonprofit corporations have a more restricted range of powers than business corporations, actions not authorized by the charters of nonprofit corporations are more likely to be found *ultra vires*.[18]

C. CREATION AND TERMINATION OF THE CORPORATION

All states have general laws governing the creation of corporations.

CPA   ### 6. Promoters

promoters—persons who plan the formation of the corporation and sell or promote the idea to others.

Corporations come into existence as the result of the activities of one or more persons known as **promoters** who bring together persons interested in the enterprise, aid in obtaining subscriptions to stock, and set in motion the machinery that leads to the formation of the corporation itself.

A corporation is not liable on a contract made by its promoter for its benefit unless the corporation takes some affirmative action to adopt such a contract. This action may be express words of adoption, or it may be acceptance of the contract's benefits. A corporation may also become bound by such contracts through assignment or novation.

---

[16] RMBCA § 3.02(13).

[17] Note the broad powers granted under RMBCA § 3.02; see also Cal Corp Code §§ 202(b), 207, 208 for an all-purpose clause granting all of the powers of a natural person in carrying out business activities. See *MIC v Battle Mountain Corp.*, 70 P3d 1176 (Colo 2003), where Colorado's *ultra vires* statute prohibits claims that a corporation is acting beyond the scope of its powers.

[18] *Lovering v Seabrook Island Property Owners Ass'n*, 344 SE2d 862 (SC App 1986). But see *St. Louis v Institute of Med. Ed. & Res.*, 786 SW2d 885 (Mo App 1990).

The promoter is personally liable for all contracts made on behalf of the corporation before its existence unless the promoter is exempted by the terms of the agreement or by the circumstances surrounding it.[19]

C A S E   S U M M A R Y

The Promoter Is Personally Liable

FACTS: Clinton Investors Company, as landlord, entered into a three-year lease with the Clifton Park Learning Center as tenant. The lease was executed by Bernie Watkins, who represented himself to be the treasurer of the Learning Center. On May 31, 1984, the day before the lease term began, Watkins signed a rider to the lease. He again signed as treasurer of the tenant but identified the tenant as "the Clifton Park Learning Center, Inc." Watkins had not consulted an attorney regarding the formation of the corporation. He mistook the reservation of the business name with the secretary of state for the filing of a certificate of incorporation. On February 11, 1985, a certificate of incorporation was filed. By March 1986, the Learning Center had become delinquent in rental payments and other fees in the amount of $18,103. Clinton sued Watkins and the Learning Center for the amounts due. Watkins claimed that only the corporation was liable.

DECISION: Judgment against Watkins. Because no corporation existed when Watkins signed the lease with Clinton, his legal status was that of a promoter. The subsequent formation of a corporation and adoption of the lease did not relieve Watkins from liability in addition to his individual liability as a promoter. [**Clinton Investors Co. v Watkins, 536 NYS2d 270 (App Div 1989)**]

A promoter is liable for all torts committed in connection with the promoter's activities. The corporation is not ordinarily liable for the torts of the promoter, but it may become liable by its conduct after incorporation. If a promoter induces making a contract by fraud, the corporation is liable for the fraud if it assumes or ratifies the contract with knowledge or notice of such fraud.

A promoter stands in a fiduciary relation to the corporation and to stock subscribers and cannot make secret profits at their expense. Accordingly, if a promoter makes a secret profit on a sale of land to the corporation, the promoter must surrender the profit to the corporation.

The corporation is not liable in most states for the expenses and services of the promoter unless it subsequently promises to pay for them, or the corporation's charter or a statute imposes such liability on it.

7. Incorporation

incorporator—one or more natural persons or corporations who sign and file appropriate incorporation forms with a designated government official.

One or more natural persons or corporations may act as **incorporators** of a corporation by signing and filing appropriate forms with a designated

---

[19] See *GS Petroleum, Inc. v R and S Fuel, Inc.*, 2009 WL 1554680 (Del Super 2009), where the court found that the promoters were not liable on the preincorporation contract for the sale of a Shell gas station. The court reasoned that the terms of the contract did not intend promoter liability, and the business was incorporated by the buyer before taking possession of the business.

government official.[20] These papers are filed in duplicate, and a filing fee must be paid. The designated official (usually the secretary of state), after being satisfied that the forms conform to statutory requirements, stamps "Filed" and the date on each copy. The official then retains one copy and returns the other copy, along with a filing fee receipt, to the corporation.[21]

Statutes may require incorporators to give some form of public notice, such as by advertising in a newspaper, of their intention to form a corporation, stating its name, address, and general purpose.

8. Application for Incorporation

In most states, the process of forming a corporation is begun by filing an application for a certificate of incorporation. This application contains or is accompanied by articles of incorporation. The instrument is filed with the secretary of state and sets forth certain information about the new corporation. The articles of incorporation must contain (1) the name of the corporation, (2) the number of shares of stock the corporation is authorized to issue, (3) the street address of the corporation's initial registered office and the name of its initial registered agent, and (4) the name and address of each incorporator.[22] The articles of incorporation may also state the purpose or purposes for which the corporation is organized. If there is no "purpose clause," the corporation automatically has the purpose of engaging in any lawful business.[23] Also, if no reference is made to the duration of the corporation in the articles of incorporation, it will automatically have perpetual duration.[24]

9. The Certificate of Incorporation

Most state incorporation statutes now provide for a certificate of incorporation to be issued by the secretary of state after articles of incorporation that conform to state requirements have been filed. The Revised Model Business Corporation Act (RMBCA) has eliminated the certificate of incorporation in an effort to reduce the volume of paperwork handled by the secretary of state.

Under the RMBCA, corporate existence begins when the articles are filed with the secretary of state.[25] In some states, corporate existence begins when the proper government official issues a certificate of incorporation. In other states, it does not begin until an organizational meeting is held by the new corporation.

10. Proper and Defective Incorporation

corporation de jure—
corporation with a legal right to exist by virtue of law.

If the procedure for incorporation has been followed, the corporation has a legal right to exist. It is then called a **corporation de jure**, meaning that it is a corporation by virtue of law.

[20] RMBCA § 2.01.
[21] RMBCA § 1.25.
[22] RMBCA § 2.02.
[23] RMBCA § 3.01.
[24] RMBCA § 3.02.
[25] RMBCA § 2.03(a).

Assume that there is some defect in the corporation that is formed. If the defect is not a material one, the law usually overlooks the defect and holds that the corporation is a corporation de jure.

The RMBCA abolishes objections to irregularities and defects in incorporating. It provides that the

> *secretary of state's filing of the articles of incorporation is conclusive proof that the incorporators satisfied all conditions precedent to incorporation. ...*[26]

Many state statutes follow this pattern. Such an approach is based on the practical consideration that when countless persons are purchasing shares of stock and entering into business transactions with thousands of corporations, it becomes an absurdity to expect that anyone is going to make the detailed search that would be required to determine whether a given corporation is a corporation de jure.[27]

(A) DE FACTO CORPORATION. The defect in the incorporation may be so substantial that it cannot be ignored, and the corporation will not be accepted as a corporation de jure, yet compliance may be sufficient for recognizing that there is a corporation. When this occurs, the association is called a **de facto** corporation.

de facto–existing in fact as distinguished from as of right, as in the case of an officer or a corporation purporting to act as such without being elected to the office or having been properly incorporated.

Although conflict exists among authorities, the traditional elements of a de facto corporation are that (1) a valid law exists under which the corporation could have been properly incorporated, (2) an attempt to organize the corporation has been made in good faith, (3) a genuine attempt to organize in compliance with statutory requirements has been made, and (4) corporate powers have been used.

(B) CORPORATION BY ESTOPPEL. The defect in incorporation may be so great that by law the association cannot be accepted as a de facto corporation. In such a case then, there is no corporation. If the individuals involved proceed to run the business in spite of such irregularity, they may be held personally liable as partners for the business's debts.[28] This rule is sometimes not applied when a third person has dealt with the business as though it were a corporation.[29] In such instances, the third person is estopped from denying that the "corporation" had legal existence. In effect, there is **corporation by estoppel** with respect to that person.

corporation by estoppel–corporation that comes about when parties estop themselves from denying that the corporation exists.

Several jurisdictions that follow the 1969 MBCA have expressly retained the doctrines of corporation by estoppel and de facto corporations.[30] Numerous courts interpreting the language of the 1969 MBCA, however, have held that the doctrines of de facto corporation and corporation by estoppel no longer exist.

---

[26] RMBCA § 2.03(b).

[27] This trend and the reasons for it may be compared to those involved in the concept of the negotiability of commercial paper. Note the similar protection from defenses given to the person purchasing shares of stock for value and without notice. UCC § 8–202.

[28] In a minority of states, a court will not hold individuals liable as partners but will hold liable the person who committed the act on behalf of the business on the theory that that person was an agent who acted without authority and is therefore liable for breach of the implied warranties of the existence of a principal possessing capacity and of proper authorization.

[29] *Am South Bank v Holland,* 669 So 2d 151 (Ala Civ App 1994).

[30] See Ga Bus Corp Code § 22–5103; Minn Bus Corp Act § 301:08. See also *H. Rich Corp. v Feinberg,* 518 So 2d 377 (Fla App 1987).

CASE SUMMARY

No Estoppel Here

FACTS: Wayne and Diane Morse built a car wash in 1984 and operated it for approximately 11 months. Thereafter they entered into a contract with Douglas Durbano and Kevin Garn, both licensed attorneys acting as officers of American Vending Services, Inc. (AVSI), to purchase the car wash for $65,000 – $20,000 down and the remainder to be paid off monthly. Durbano and Garn claimed that they represented to the Morses that the corporate entity would purchase and operate the car wash. At the time the parties executed the contract on July 10, 1985, Durbano had not filed articles of incorporation for AVSI, although he had received permission from the Utah Division of Corporations to use the name American Vending Services, Inc. Durbano claimed a delay in filing the articles occurred because of a name conflict. The articles of incorporation for AVSI were finally executed on August 1, 1985, and subsequently filed on August 19, 1985. Durbano's explanation for not filing them before the parties executed the contract on July 10, 1985, was that he was "moving offices and was too busy and distracted to file the articles." AVSI operated the car wash for three years but never made any monthly payments to the Morses because of financial difficulties. The Morses sued AVSI as well as Durbano and Garn because the corporation did not legally exist when the parties executed the contract. The trial court dismissed the Morses' claims against Durbano and Garn, finding that Durbano's efforts to file articles of incorporation "constitute[d] a bona fide attempt to organize the corporation." A judgment was issued against AVSI for $76,832, but AVSI had no assets or income to satisfy the judgment. The court's decision was appealed by both parties.

DECISION: Judgment for the Morses. Section 146 of the MBCA imposes joint and several liability on Durbano and Garn for all of the debts and liabilities that arose as a result of their actions before the corporation legally existed. The corporation did not exist when Durbano and Garn executed the contract of July 10 to purchase the Morses' car wash. Their argument that the Morses dealt with a corporation, AVSI, and did not intend to bind them personally, and are therefore estopped to deny AVSI's corporate existence is rejected because the doctrine of corporation by estoppel does not exist in the state. Durbano and Garn are liable for the judgment amount of $76,832. [**American Vending Services, Inc. v Morse, 881 P2d 967 (Utah 1994)**]

With respect to preincorporation debts, the 1984 act imposes liability only on persons who act as, or on behalf of, a corporation while knowing that no corporation exists.[31]

11. Insolvency, Bankruptcy, and Reorganization

When a corporation has financial troubles so serious that it is insolvent, the best thing may be to go through bankruptcy or reorganization proceedings. The law with respect to bankruptcy and reorganizations is discussed in Chapter 35.

12. Forfeiture of Charter

In states that have adopted the RMBCA, the secretary of state may commence proceedings to administratively dissolve a corporation if (1) the corporation does

[31] RMBCA § 2.04.

not pay franchise taxes within 60 days after they are due, (2) the corporation does not file its annual report within 60 days after it is due, or (3) the corporation is without a registered agent or registered office for 60 days or more.[32] In other states, judicial proceedings may be brought to forfeit a corporate charter when the corporation repeatedly acts beyond the powers granted it or engages in illegal activity. After a corporate charter has been forfeited, the owners and officers of the dissolved corporation are not shielded from personal liability by using the corporate name when making contracts. **For Example,** Todd Crosland was president, director, and principal shareholder of Crosland Industries. Even though Crosland's corporate status was suspended and subsequently discontinued, Todd authorized a guarantee on a note in the name of the corporation. A default occurred and Crosland failed to honor its guarantee. Todd was personally liable on the guarantee.[33]

After a corporation is dissolved, a contract made by an officer of the dissolved corporation cannot be enforced against the other party to the contract. **For Example,** a lucrative contract with Florio Entertainment, Inc., was signed "Louis Lofredo, LL Associates as company president" using a letterhead "LL Associates, Inc." In fact, the corporation "LL Associates, Inc." had been dissolved years before the contract was negotiated and signed, and Lofredo had made no effort to reinstate the corporation. LL Associates, Inc., had no legal existence and thus could not be a party to the contract and could not enforce the contract.[34]

A corporation whose powers are suspended for nonpayment of taxes cannot sue or defend a lawsuit while its taxes remain unpaid.[35]

13. Judicial Dissolution

Judicial dissolution of a corporation may be decreed when its management is deadlocked and the deadlock cannot be broken by the shareholders.[36] In some states, a "custodian" may be appointed for a corporation when the shareholders are unable to break a deadlock in the board of directors and irreparable harm is threatened to, or sustained by, the corporation because of the deadlock.

D. CONSOLIDATIONS, MERGERS, AND CONGLOMERATES

Two or more corporations may be combined to form a new structure or enterprise.

CPA   ### 14. Definitions

Enterprises may be combined by a consolidation or merger of corporations or by the formation of a conglomerate.

---

[32] RMBCA § 14.20.

[33] *Murphy v Crosland*, 915 P2d 491 (Utah 1996). But see *L-Tec Electronics Corp. v Cougar Electronic Org. Inc.*, 198 F3d 85 (2d Cir 1999), where it was held that reinstatement of corporation relieved officers of any potential personal liability for actions taken in the corporation's name during a period when its corporate status had lapsed.

[34] *Animazing Entertainment, Inc. v Louis Lofredo Associates, Inc.*, 88 F Supp 2d 265 (SDNY 2000).

[35] *Kaufman, Inc. v Performance Plastering, Inc.*, 39 Cal Rptr 3d 33 (Cal App 2006).

[36] In re *212 East 52nd Street Corp.*, 712 NYS2d 777 (NY Sup 2000).

FIGURE 44-1 | *Consolidation*

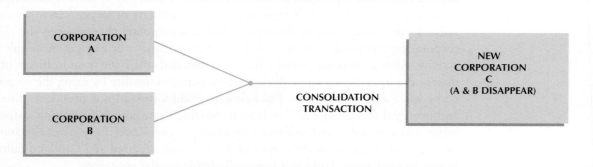

CPA

consolidation (of corporations)—combining of two or more corporations in which the corporate existence of each one ceases and a new corporation is created.

(A) CONSOLIDATION. In a **consolidation** of two or more corporations, their separate existences cease, and a new corporation with the property and assets of the old corporations comes into being (see Figure 44.1).

When a consolidation occurs, the new corporation ordinarily succeeds to the rights, powers, and immunities of its component parts. However, limitations may be imposed by constitution, statute, or certificate of incorporation.

CPA

merger (of corporations)—combining of corporations by which one absorbs the other and continues to exist, preserving its original charter and identity while the other corporation ceases to exist.

(B) MERGER. When two corporations **merge**, one absorbs the other. One corporation retains its original charter and identity and continues to exist; the other disappears, and its corporate existence terminates (see Figure 44.2).

A stockholder who objects to a proposed consolidation or merger or who fails to convert existing shares into stock of the new or continuing corporation may apply to a court to appraise the value of the stock that she holds.[37] Should either party act arbitrarily, vexatiously, or not in good faith in the appraisal process, the courts have the right to assess court costs and attorney fees. The new or continuing corporation is then required to pay the fair value of the stock to the stockholder.[38]

C A S E   S U M M A R Y

The Sound of Music: $63.44 per Share

FACTS: The Trapp Family Lodge, Inc. (TFL), was incorporated in 1962 as a holding company for certain assets of the Von Trapp family, including the Trapp Family Lodge, a resort hotel complex located in Stowe, Vermont, and other assets, including certain royalty rights related to the family's story as portrayed in a Broadway musical and a movie. A majority of TFL shareholders approved a merger with a new corporation in 1994, and the merger took place on January 28, 1995. The dissenting shareholders, holding 76,529 of the corporation's 198,000 outstanding shares, were paid $33.84 per share as fair value by the TFL board of directors. The dissenting shareholders brought suit seeking a higher price as fair value. After the trial court set the fair value of $63.44, TFL appealed.

---

[37] *Delaware Open MRI Radiology v Kessler*, 898 A2d 290 (Del Ch 2006).
[38] *Martin v Martin Brothers Container Corp.*, 241 F Supp 2d 815 (ND Ohio 2003).

C A S E   S U M M A R Y

Continued

DECISION: Judgment for the dissenting shareholders. Dissenters' rights statutes were enacted in response to the common law rule that required unanimous consent from shareholders to make fundamental changes in a corporation. Under this rule minority shareholders could block corporate change by refusing to cooperate in hope of establishing a nuisance value for their shares. In response, legislatures enacted statutes authorizing corporate changes by majority vote. To protect the interests of minority shareholders, statutes generally permit a dissenting minority to demand that the corporation buy back shares at fair value. The basic concept of fair value is that the stockholder is entitled to be paid for his or her "proportionate interest in a going concern." The trial court properly rejected the fact-specific appraisal made on behalf of the majority shareholders because it lacked thoroughness and credibility, unjustifiably reducing the value of the lodge operations and overstating income taxes to reduce after-tax cash flows. The court accepted the appraisal made on behalf of the minority shareholders that utilized the average of a net asset value method of evaluation and a discounted cash flow method of evaluation, and yielded a value of $63.44 per share. [**In re 75,629 Shares of Common Stock of Trapp Family Lodge, Inc., 725 A2d 927 (Vt 1999)**]

conglomerate–relationship of a parent corporation to subsidiary corporations engaged in diversified fields of activity unrelated to the field of activity of the parent corporation.

(C) CONGLOMERATE. **Conglomerate** describes the relationship of a parent corporation to subsidiary corporations engaged in diversified fields of activity unrelated to the parent corporation's field of activity. **For Example,** a wire-manufacturing corporation that owns all stock of a newspaper corporation and of a drug-manufacturing corporation would be described as a conglomerate. In contrast, if the wire-manufacturing company owned a mill that produced the metal used in making the wire and a mine that produced the ore that was used by the mill, the relationship would probably be described as an *integrated industry* rather than as a conglomerate. This term is merely a matter of usage rather than of legal definition. Likewise, when the parent company is not engaged in production or the rendering of services, it is customary to call it a *holding company*.

Without regard to whether the enterprise is a holding company or whether the group of corporations constitutes a conglomerate or an integrated industry, each part is a distinct corporation to which ordinary corporation law applies. In some

FIGURE 44-2 | *Merger*

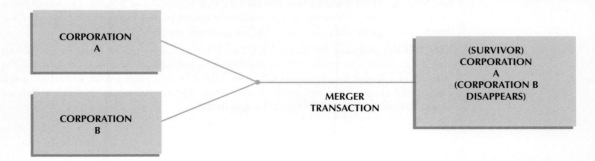

instances, additional principles apply because of the nature of the relationships existing among the several corporations involved.

15. Legality

Consolidations, mergers, and asset acquisitions between enterprises are prohibited by federal antitrust legislation when the effect is to lessen competition in interstate commerce. A business corporation may not merge with a charitable corporation because this combination would divert the assets of the respective corporations to purposes not intended by their shareholders.

16. Liability of Successor Corporations

When corporations are combined in any way, the question of who is liable for the debts and obligations of the predecessor corporation arises.

(A) MERGERS AND CONSOLIDATIONS. Generally, the enterprise engaging in or continuing the business after a merger or consolidation succeeds to all of the rights and property of the predecessor, or disappearing, corporation.[39]

CASE SUMMARY

A Marshmallow of a Case for the Plaintiff Marsh USA

FACTS: The Orleans Parish School Board ("School Board") in New Orleans, Louisiana, hired Johnson & Higgins, Inc. (J&H), in 1996, creating an ongoing insurance consulting agreement between them. The terms of the agreement provided that the School Board would pay J&H, Inc. for its consulting services and would later be reimbursed by the insurance carrier eventually selected by the School Board. Pursuant to their agreement, over the next few years, J&H's Mrs. Ippolito prepared several Requests for Proposals ("RFP") on behalf of the School Board. The School Board paid its fees for this consulting work without complaint. During this time, Johnson & Higgins merged with Marsh McLennan, a company that thereafter merged into Marsh USA, Inc. In 2001, Mrs. Ippolito prepared, at the request of the School Board, two more requests for proposals. Per the terms of the RFPs, Marsh was to receive $70,000 as its consulting fee under NO. 7656 and a $5,000 consulting fee under NO. 7657. Mrs. Ippolito and her staff spent several months working on the project for the School Board. The School Board never paid Marsh for the services and Marsh USA, Inc., sued the School Board for breach of contract, seeking payment of $75,000. The School Board asserted that Marsh USA was not a proper party to the lawsuit and that no contract had existed with it. From a judgment for Marsh USA, Inc., the School Board appealed.

DECISION: Judgment for Marsh USA, Inc. When two corporations merge or consolidate, the new successor corporation acquires all of the assets and rights of the former corporation. The minutes of a School Board meeting reflect the School Board's awareness of the merger in this case as well as its continuing contract with the firm. [**Marsh Advantage America v Orleans Parish School Board, 995 So2d 53 (La App 2008)**]

---

[39] *Corporate Express Office Products, Inc. v Phillips*, 847 So2d 406 (Fla 2003).

The enterprise continuing the business is also subject to all of the debts and liabilities of the predecessor corporation.[40]

Liabilities of predecessor corporations can be imposed on a successor corporation when the transaction is a de facto merger[41] or the successor is a mere continuation of the predecessor. **For Example,** Steven Stepp manufactured pleasure boats through Thoroughbred Power Boats, Inc., until August 1996 at which time Thoroughbred Power Boats, Inc., ceased manufacturing and selling boats. In August 1996, Velocity Power Boats, Inc., began manufacturing and selling pleasure boats at the same location. Stephen Stepp and his wife were the only officers and board members of both corporations. Finding that Velocity was merely a "new hat" for Thoroughbred Power Boats, Inc., with the same or similar management and ownership, Velocity Power Boats, Inc., was held liable as a successor corporation for damages for a May 6, 1995, boating accident caused by a defective Thoroughbred Power Boats, Inc., manufactured boat.[42]

(B) ASSET SALES. In contrast with a merger or consolidation, a corporation may merely purchase the assets of another business. In that case, the purchaser does not become liable for the obligations of the predecessor business. **For Example,** Hull Corporation sold one of its operating divisions to SP Industries, Inc. (SPI) for $6 million under an asset purchase agreement (APA) that stated that the buyer SPI assumed no liability for preclosing claims against Hull. In fact as Hull and SPI were negotiating the APA, Hull was having difficulties regarding engineering and installation work the division had performed in China for Berg Chilling Systems, Inc. Berg Chilling sued SPI under the doctrine of successor liability for the payment of a $1,650,000 arbitration award because of the defective work done by Hull in China. The court held that SPI did not assume Hull's contractual liability to Berg under any exception to the traditional corporate rule of successor nonliability.[43]

Corporations may seek to avoid liability for the obligations of a predecessor corporation by attempting to disguise a consolidation or merger as being merely a sale of assets. Courts will not recognize such a transaction and will impose a successor's liability on the successor corporation.[44] In addition, even when the old corporate entity is not formally dissolved, a finding of a de facto merger resulting in successor liability may occur. **For Example,** "old" Duro Industries, Inc., owed its supplier, Milliken & Co., $8,754,680 for raw materials and Milliken obtained a judgment for this amount from a New York court. Investors and related entities executed a plan acquiring the assets of old Duro, while shedding old Duro's debts to Milliken and establishing "new" Duro Textiles, LLC. New Duro had the same CEO

[40] *Beck v Roper Whitney, Inc.,* 190 F Supp 2d 524 (WDNY 2001).
[41] *Ulanet v D'Artagnan, Inc.,* 170 F Supp 2d 356 (EDNY 2001); see *Callahan & Sons, Inc. v Dykeman Electric Co. Inc.,* 2003 WL 21356450 (D Mass).
[42] *Paten v Thoroughbred Power Boats, Inc.,* 294 F3d 640 (5th Cir 2002).
[43] *Berg Chilling Systems Inc. v Hull Corp.,* 435 F3d 455 (3d Cir 2006).
[44] *State v Westwood Squibb Pharmaceutical Co., Inc.,* 981 F Supp 760 (WDNY 1997).

as old Duro, continued to sell the same product line, and employed all of old Duro's employees. The court found successor liability for the Milliken debt against new Duro.[45]

C A S E   S U M M A R Y

Corporate Shell Games Not Allowed

FACTS: Since 1976, McGhan/Cal. Inc., a manufacturer of prostheses used in breast augmentation surgery, and later McGhan/Del., received numerous complaints about its implants. It also received inquiries from the Food and Drug Administration. In April 1977, Mary Marks had surgery; two McGhan implants were used. Because of defects in the McGhan implants, Marks underwent three additional operations, eventually having the McGhan products replaced with implants manufactured by another company. In June 1977, McGhan/Cal. was acquired by a Delaware subsidiary of 3M, called McGhan/Del. Inc. McGhan/Del. removed the implants from the market in April 1979. On January 1, 1981, 3M's wholly owned subsidiary McGhan/Del. Inc. was reorganized as a division of 3M and dissolved. In January 1982, following her fourth surgery, Marks brought a product liability suit against 3M. 3M contended that it was not liable for the actions of the predecessor corporation.

DECISION: The transaction between the 3M subsidiary McGhan/Del. Inc. and McGhan/Cal. Inc. amounted to a de facto merger of the seller and the purchaser. McGhan/Cal. changed its name, distributed 3M stock to its shareholders, and dissolved, and all key employees signed employment contracts to work for the purchaser. No cash was paid for the business. The transaction was not an assets sale. The second reorganization amounted to a continuation of the de facto merger. Public policy requires that 3M, having accepted the benefits of a going concern, should also assume the costs that all other going concerns must bear. It should not be allowed to avoid liability to an injured person by merely shuffling paper and manipulating corporate entities. [**Marks v Minnesota Mining and Manufacturing Co., 232 Cal Rptr 594 (Cal App 1986)**]

lawflix

Barbarians at the Gate (1996) (R)

In this movie that focuses on the law and ethics of takeovers, you can see the manipulation that occurs and the impact greed has on the companies themselves.

For movie clips that illustrate business law concepts, see LawFlix at **www.cengage.com/blaw/dvl**.

---

[45] *Milliken & Co. v Duro Textiles, LLC*, 887 NE2d 244 (Mass 2008).

MAKE THE CONNECTION

SUMMARY

A *corporation* is an artificial person created by government action. It exists as a separate and distinct entity possessing certain powers. In most states, the corporation comes into existence when the secretary of state issues a certificate of incorporation. The most common forms of corporations are private business corporations whose stock is sold to the public (publicly held) and close corporations, which are business firms whose shares are not traded publicly. Corporations may be formed for purposes other than conducting a business. For example, there are nonprofit corporations, municipal corporations, and public authorities for governmental purposes.

An *ultra vires* act occurs when a corporation acts beyond the scope of the powers given it. Because states now grant broad powers to corporations, it is unlikely that a modern corporation would act beyond the scope of its powers.

A *promoter* is a person who brings together the persons interested in the enterprise and sets in motion all that must be done to form a corporation. A corporation is not liable on contracts made by its promoter for the corporation unless it adopts the contracts. The promoter is personally liable for contracts made for the corporation before its existence. A promoter stands in a fiduciary relation to the corporation and stockholders.

The procedures for incorporation are set forth in the statutes of each state. In most states, the corporation comes into existence on issuance of the certificate of incorporation. When all requirements have been satisfied, the corporation is a corporation de jure. When there has not been full compliance with all requirements for incorporation, a de facto corporation may be found to exist. Or when sufficient compliance for a de facto corporation does not exist, in some jurisdictions a third person may be estopped from denying the legal existence of the "corporation" with which it did business (corporation by estoppel).

A corporation has the power to continue as an entity forever or for a stated period of time regardless of changes in the ownership of the stock or the death of a shareholder. It may make contracts, issue stocks and bonds, borrow money, execute commercial paper, transfer and acquire property, acquire its own stock if it is solvent and the purchase does not impair capital, and make charitable contributions. Subject to limitations, a corporation has the power to do business in other states. A corporation may also participate in a business enterprise to the same extent as an individual; that is, it may be a partner in a partnership, or it may enter a joint venture or other enterprise. Special service corporations, such as banks, insurance companies, and railroads, are subject to separate statutes governing their organization and powers.

Two or more corporations may be combined to form a new enterprise. This combination may be a consolidation, with a new corporation coming into existence, or a merger, in which one corporation absorbs the other.

LEARNING OUTCOMES

After studying this chapter, you should be able to clearly explain:

A. NATURE AND CLASSES

LO.1 Recognize that a corporation is a separate legal entity, distinct and apart from its stockholders

> See the *Collins* case in which Ms. Collins was not personally liable for a loan to her corporation, p. 1032.

B. CORPORATE POWERS

LO.2 Explain the wide range of power given to corporations under modern corporate codes

> See the RMBCA general provision granting corporations "the same powers as an individual to do all things necessary or convenient to carry out its business and affairs," p. 1036.

C. CREATION AND TERMINATION OF THE CORPORATION

LO.3 Understand that the promoter is personally liable for preincorporation contracts

> See the *Clinton Investors Co.* case in which Watkins, a promoter, was held personally liable for a preincorporation lease, p. 1039.

D. CONSOLIDATIONS, MERGERS, AND CONGLOMERATES

LO.4 Explain a stockholder's option when he or she objects to a proposed consolidation or merger of the corporation

LO.5 Recognize that liabilities of predecessor corporations can be imposed on successor corporations when the transaction is a de facto merger or a continuation of the predecessor

> See the example of Velocity Power Boats, Inc., which became essentially a "new hat" for Thoroughbred Power Boats, Inc., with liability as a corporate successor for a defective Thoroughbred boat, p. 1047.

KEY TERMS

articles of incorporation	corporation	merge
authorities	corporation by estoppel	police power
bylaws	corporation de jure	private corporation
certificate of	de facto	promoters
incorporation	domestic corporation	public corporation
charter	eleemosynary corporation	quasi-public corporation
close corporation	foreign corporation	treasury stock
conglomerate	general corporation code	ultra vires
consolidation	incorporators	

QUESTIONS AND CASE PROBLEMS

1. Edwin Edwards and Karen Davis owned EEE, Inc., which owned three convenience stores, all of which sold gasoline. Reid Ellis delivered to the three

convenience stores $26,675.02 worth of gasoline for which he was not paid. Ellis proved that Edwards and Davis owned the business, ran it, and in fact personally ordered the gasoline. He claimed that they were personally liable for the debt owed him by EEE, Inc. Decide. [*Ellis v Edwards*, 348 SE2d 764 (Ga App)]

2. Graham and Black were each 50 percent shareholders of a building supply business. When Graham filed a petition to dissolve the corporation under RMBCA § 14.30, the court appointed a custodian with full powers to run the corporation's day-to-day operations. Subsequently, the court concluded that Black and Graham functioned as directors, they were deadlocked within the meaning of RMBCA § 14.30(2)(1), and adequate grounds existed to dissolve the corporation because of the lack of cooperation between Black and Graham and its probable irreparable harm to the business. The court entered an order directing that within one week of receiving an expected appraisal, each would submit a sealed bid in writing for the other's stock. The custodian was to accept the high bid, and the purchaser was to immediately tender the purchase price. In the event that neither stockholder made a bona fide offer, the custodian would be redesignated the receiver and proceed to dissolve the corporation (RMBCA § 14.32 [c]-[e]). The sale was unsuccessful, and by subsequent order, the court converted the custodianship into a receivership, directing that the receiver wind up and liquidate the business affairs of the corporation. Black did not believe that the successful business should be liquidated, and he directed his attorney to appeal. Decide. [*Black v Graham*, 464 SE2d 814 (Ga)]

3. Compare and contrast consolidations, mergers, and conglomerates.

4. On January 27, 1982, Joe Walker purchased a wheel-loader machine from Thompson & Green Machinery Co. (T&G). Walker signed a promissory note for $37,886.30 on behalf of "Music City Sawmill, Inc., by Joe Walker, President." When Sawmill was unable to make payments on the loader, the machine was returned to T&G. T&G brought suit against Sawmill and subsequently discovered that Sawmill had not been incorporated on January 27, 1982, when the machine was purchased but had been incorporated the next day. T&G then sued Walker individually. The lawsuit was Walker's first notice that Sawmill was not incorporated on the date of the sale. Walker's defense was that T&G dealt with Sawmill as a corporation and did not intend to bind him personally on the note and therefore was estopped to deny Sawmill's corporate existence. Decide based on the 1969 MBCA. What would be the result if the RMBCA applied? [*Thompson & Green Machinery Co. v Music City Lumber Co., Inc., Music City Sawmill Co., Inc.*, 683 SW2d 340 (Tenn App)]

5. North Pole, Inc., approved a plan to merge with its subsidiary, Santa's Workshop, Inc. The merger plan provided that certain of Workshop's shareholders would receive $3.50 per share. The highest independent appraisal of the stock was $4.04 per share. Hirschfeld, Inc., a shareholder, claimed the fair value was $16.80 per share. Workshop offered to make its corporate books and records available to Hirschfeld to assess the validity of the $16.80 demand. This offer was declined. Hirschfeld did not attempt to base the $16.80 demand on any recognizable method of stock valuation. Hirschfeld contended it had a

right to get the asking price. Refer to RMBCA §§ 13.02, 13.28, and 13.31. Could Hirschfeld have blocked the merger until Workshop paid the $16.80? Decide. [*Santa's Workshop v Hirschfeld, Inc.*, 851 P2d 264 (Colo App)]

6. Norman was organizing a new corporation: Collins Home Construction Co. Fairchild knew the corporation was not yet formed but made a contract by which he agreed to sell certain goods to Collins. The corporation was later organized and ratified the contract that Norman had made with Fairchild. Fairchild, however, did not perform the contract and was sued by Collins. Fairchild raised the defense that he had never made any contract with Collins and that a corporation that did not exist could not have made a contract. Were these defenses valid?

7. Morris Gray leased waterfront property on the Ross Barnett Reservoir to a restaurant, Edgewater Landing, Inc., for a 10-year term. After a year and a half, Edgewater's original shareholder, Billy Stegall, sold all of his shares in the corporation to Tom Bradley and Bradley's bookkeeper, Sandra Martin. Gray visited the property in the ninth year of the lease and found many problems with the condition of the property. He claimed that the lease required the tenant to make necessary repairs. Gray sued Edgewater Landing, Inc., and Tom Bradley and Sandra Martin individually for breach of the lease. Bradley and Martin replied that they were not liable for the debt of the corporation. Decide. [*Gray v Edgewater Landing, Inc.*, 541 So2d 1044 (Miss)]

8. Emmick was a director and shareholder of Colonial Manors, Inc. (CM). He organized another corporation named Oahe Enterprises, Inc. To obtain shares of the Oahe stock, Emmick transferred CM shares arbitrarily valued by him at $19 per share to Oahe. The CM shares had a book value of $.47 per share, but Emmick believed that the stock would increase to a value of $19. The directors of Oahe approved Emmick's payment with the valuation of $19 per share. Golden sued Emmick on the ground that he had fraudulently deceived Oahe Corp. about the value of the CM shares and thus had made a secret profit when he received the Oahe shares that had a much greater value than the CM shares he gave in exchange. Emmick contended that his firm opinion was that the future potential value of CM shares would surely reach $19 per share. Decide. [*Golden v Oahe Enterprises, Inc.*, 295 NW2d 160 (SD)]

9. Madison Associates purchased control of the majority of shares of 79 Realty Corp. from the Kimmelmans and the Zauders, who then resigned as directors. The Alpert group, which owned the remaining 26 percent of 79 Realty refused to sell their shares. Partners of Madison Associates replaced the Kimmelmans and Zauders as directors of 79 Realty Corp., and as controlling directors, they approved a plan to merge 79 Realty Corp. with the Williams Street Corp., which was owned by Madison Associates. A shareholders' meeting was called, and the merger was approved by two-thirds of the shareholders. The Alpert group's shares were then forcibly canceled, with the price paid for these shares determined at their fair market value. The Alpert group brought suit contending the merger was unlawful because the sole purpose was to benefit the Madison Associates. Decide. [*Alpert v 28 Williams Street Corp.*, 473 NE2d 19 (NY)]

10. The Seabrook Island Property Owners Association, Inc., is a nonprofit corporation organized under state law to maintain streets and open spaces owned by property owners of Seabrook Island. Seabrook Island Co. is the developer of Seabrook Island and has majority control of the board of directors of the association. The association's bylaws empower the board of directors to levy an annual maintenance charge. Neither the association's charter nor its bylaws authorize the board to assess any other charges. When the board levied, in addition to the annual maintenance charge, an emergency budget assessment on all members to rebuild certain bridges and to revitalize the beach, the Loverings and other property owners challenged in court the association's power to impose the assessment. Decide. [*Lovering v Seabrook Island Property Owners Ass'n,* 344 SE2d 862 (SC App)]

11. Adams and two other persons were promoters for a new corporation, Aldrehn Theaters Co. The promoters retained Kridelbaugh to perform legal services in connection with the incorporation of the new business and promised to pay him $1,500. Aldrehn was incorporated through Kridelbaugh's services, and the promoters became its only directors. Kridelbaugh attended a meeting of the board of directors at which he was told that he should obtain a permit for the corporation to sell stock because the directors wished to pay him for his previous services. The promoters failed to pay Kridelbaugh, and he sued the corporation. Was the corporation liable? [*Kridelbaugh v Aldrehn Theaters Co.,* 191 NW 803 (Iowa)]

12. On August 19, 1980, Joan Ioviero injured her hand when she slipped and fell while leaving the dining room at the Hotel Excelsior in Venice, Italy. This hotel was owned by an Italian corporation, Cigahotels, S.p.A. (The designation *S.p.A.* stands for *Societa per Azionean,* the Italian term for *corporation.*) In 1973, a firm called Ciga Hotels, Inc., was incorporated in New York. Its certificate of incorporation was amended in 1979, changing the name of the firm to Landia International Services, Inc. This New York corporation was employed by the Italian corporation Cigahotels, S.p.A., to provide sales and promotional services in the United States and Canada. Ioviero sought to hold the New York corporation liable for her hand injury at the Venice hotel. She pointed to the similarity of the first corporate name used by the New York firm to the name Cigahotels, S.p.A., and the fact that the New York firm represented the interests of the Italian firm in the United States as clear evidence that the two firms were the same single legal entity. She asked that the court disregard the separate corporate entities. The New York corporation moved that the case be dismissed because it was duly incorporated in New York and did not own the Excelsior Hotel in which Ioviero was injured. Decide. [*Ioviero v CigaHotel, Inc., aka Landia I.S., Inc.,* 475 NYS2d 880 (App Div)]

13. William Sullivan was ousted from the presidency of the New England Patriots Football Club, Inc. Later, he borrowed $5,348,000 to buy 100 percent control of the voting shares of the corporation. A condition of the loan was that he reorganize the Patriots so that the income from the corporation could be devoted to repayment of the personal loan and the team's assets could be used as collateral. Sullivan, therefore, arranged for a cash freeze-out merger of the

holders of the 120,000 shares of nonvoting stock. David Coggins, who owned 10 shares of nonvoting stock and took special pride in the fact that he was an owner of the team, refused the $15-a-share buyout and challenged the merger in court. He contended that the merger was not for a legitimate corporate purpose but to enable Sullivan to satisfy his personal loan. Sullivan contended that legitimate business purposes were given in the merger proxy statement, such as the National Football League's policy of discouraging public ownership of teams. Coggins responded that before the merger, Sullivan had 100 percent control of the voting stock and thus control of the franchise, and that no legal basis existed to eliminate public ownership. Decide. [*Coggins v New England Patriots Football Club*, 492 NE2d 1112 (Mass)]

CPA QUESTIONS

1. Which of the following statements is correct concerning the similarities between a limited partnership and a corporation?

    a. Each is created under a statute and must file a copy of its certificate with the proper state authorities.

    b. All corporate stockholders and all partners in a limited partnership have limited liability.

    c. Both are recognized for federal income tax purposes as taxable entities.

    d. Both are allowed statutorily to have perpetual existence.

2. Rice is a promoter of a corporation to be known as Dex Corp. On January 1, 1985, Rice signed a nine-month contract with Roe, a CPA, which provided that Roe would perform certain accounting services for Dex. Rice did not disclose to Roe that Dex had not been formed. Prior to the incorporation of Dex on February 1, 1985, Roe rendered accounting services pursuant to the contract. After rendering accounting services for an additional period of six months pursuant to the contract, Roe was discharged without cause by the board of directors of Dex. In the absence of any agreements to the contrary, who will be liable to Roe for breach of contract?

    a. Both Rice and Dex

    b. Rice only

    c. Dex only

    d. Neither Rice nor Dex

3. In general, which of the following must be contained in articles of incorporation?

    a. The names of the states in which the corporation will be doing business

    b. The name of the state in which the corporation will maintain its principal place of business

    c. The names of the initial officers and their terms of office

    d. The classes of stock authorized for issuance

Chapter 45

SHAREHOLDER RIGHTS IN CORPORATIONS

The two most common instruments used to provide funds for a corporation are stocks and bonds.

A. CORPORATE STOCKS AND BONDS

Ownership of a corporation is represented by stock. A *bond* is a corporate debt.

1. Nature of Stock

An interest in a corporation is based on ownership of one or more shares of stock of the corporation. Each share represents a fractional interest in the total property of the corporation. The shareholder does not own or have an interest in any specific property of the corporation; the corporation is the owner of all of its property. The terms *share, stock*, and *share of stock* mean the same thing.

(A) CAPITAL AND CAPITAL STOCK. *Capital* refers to the net assets of the corporation. Shares that have been issued to holders are said to be **outstanding**. **Capital stock** refers to the value received by the corporation for its outstanding stock.

outstanding–name for shares of a company that have been issued to stockholders.

capital stock–declared money value of the outstanding stock of the corporation.

(B) VALUATION OF STOCK. Corporate stock may have a specified **par value**. This means that the person subscribing to the stock and acquiring it from the corporation must pay that amount.

Shares may be issued with no par value. In that case, no amount is stated in the certificate, and the amount that the subscriber pays the corporation is determined by the board of directors. The Revised Model Business Corporation Act (RMBCA) eliminates the concept of par value, so stock issued by corporations in states following the RMBCA is always no par.

par value–specified monetary amount assigned by an issuing corporation for each share of its stock.

The value found by dividing the value of the net corporate assets by the number of shares outstanding is the **book value** of the shares. **For Example,** Roger Eggett entered a Shareholder Agreement in 1995 with Todd Cusick and Curtis Chisholm, forming the Wasatch Energy Corporation. The terms of the Shareholder Agreement provided that should a shareholder separate from the corporation, the remaining shareholders would have the option to purchase that shareholder's corporate stock. The remaining shareholders, as per the Shareholder Agreement, would either purchase the stock for book value, if the separating shareholder voluntarily left the corporation, or for par value if the shareholder was terminated for cause. The Shareholder Agreement defined *book value* as the shareholder's net equity in the corporation, which would be determined by Wasatch's certified year-end financial statements. The Shareholder Agreement defined *par value* as the original price the shareholder paid for the stock. Egget tendered his resignation two years later, and offered to sell his stock according to the Shareholder Agreement "for the audited book value of the corporation as of June 30, 1997 divided by the number of shares he owned." Wasatch Corp. responded by firing Egget, wrongly asserting the firing was for cause, and tendered him a check for the par value of his stock, $1,217, Eggett's original investment. Eggett sued and was awarded the book value of his

book value–value found by dividing the value of the corporate assets by the number of shares outstanding.

market value–price at which a share of stock can be voluntarily bought or sold in the open market.

shares, $135,671, plus $60,000 in attorney fees.[1] The **market value** of a share of stock is the price at which that stock can be voluntarily bought or sold in the open market.

2. Certificates of Stock and Uncertificated Shares

certificate of stock–document evidencing a shareholder's ownership of stock issued by a corporation.

A corporation ordinarily issues a **certificate of stock** or *share certificate* as evidence of the shareholder's ownership of stock. The issuance of such certificates is not essential either to the existence of a corporation or to the ownership of its stock.

In states that have adopted the 1978 and 1994 amendments to Article 8 of the UCC, uncertificated shares may be issued. Uncertificated shares are not represented by instruments. Their ownership and transfer are registered on the books maintained by, or on behalf of, the issuer corporation.[2]

common stock–stock that has no right or priority over any other stock of the corporation as to dividends or distribution of assets upon dissolution.

3. Kinds of Stock

The stock of a corporation may be divided into two or more classes.

CPA (A) CLASSIFICATION BY PREFERENCES. **Common stock** is ordinary stock that has no preferences. Each share usually entitles the holder to have one vote, to receive a share of the profits in the form of dividends when declared, and to participate in the distribution of capital upon dissolution of the corporation. **Preferred stock** has a priority over common stock. The priority may be with respect to either dividends or the distribution of capital upon dissolution of the corporation, or both. Preferred stock is ordinarily nonvoting.

preferred stock–stock that has a priority or preference as to payment of dividends or upon liquidation, or both.

CPA *(1) Cumulative Preferred Stock*
The right to receive dividends depends on the declaration of dividends by the board of directors for a particular period of time. If there is no fund from which the dividends may be declared or if the directors do not declare them from an available fund, the shareholder has no right to dividends. The fact that a shareholder has not received dividends for the current year does not in itself give the right to accumulate or carry over into the next year a claim for those dividends. However, in the absence of a statement that the right to dividends is noncumulative, courts frequently hold that preferred stock has the right to accumulate dividends for each year in which there was a surplus available for dividend payment but dividends were not declared.

CPA *(2) Participating Preferred Stock*
Sometimes the preferred stock is given the right of participation. If it is, then after the common shares receive dividends or a capital distribution is made equal to that first received by the preferred stock, both kinds participate or share equally in the balance.

[1] *Eggett v Wasatch Energy Corp.*, 29 P3d 668 (Utah App 2001).
[2] UCC § 8-102(1)(b). The 1978 and 1994 amendments to Article 8 of the UCC have been adopted in all of the states except Alabama.

(B) DURATION OF SHARES. Ordinarily, shares continue to exist for the life of the corporation. However, any kind of share, whether common or preferred, may be made terminable at an earlier date.

(C) FRACTIONAL SHARES. A corporation may issue fractional shares or scrip or certificates representing fractional shares. These can be sold or combined for the acquisition of whole shares.

4. Characteristics of Bonds

bond–obligation or promise in writing and sealed, generally of corporations, personal representatives, and trustees; fidelity bonds.

A **bond** is an instrument promising to repay a loan of money to a corporation. Typically, the loan is for a relatively long period of time, generally five years or longer. A bond obligates the corporation to pay the bondholder the amount of the loan, called the *principal*, at a stated time, called the **maturity date**, and to pay a fixed amount of *interest at* regular intervals, commonly every six months. The relationship between the bondholder and the issuing corporation is that of creditor and debtor. Unlike dividends, which are discretionary, bond interest must be paid. A bond may be secured by a mortgage or lien on corporate property. A **debenture** is an unsecured bond of the corporation with no specific corporate assets pledged as security for payment.

maturity date–date that a corporation is required to repay a loan to a bondholder.

debenture–unsecured bond of a corporation, with no specific corporate assets pledged as security for payment.

Bonds are negotiable securities.[3] Bonds held by owners whose names and addresses are registered on the books of the corporation are called **registered bonds.**

registered bonds–bonds held by owners whose names and addresses are registered on the books of the corporation.

5. Terms and Control

bond indenture–agreement setting forth the contractual terms of a particular bond issue.

The contractual terms of a particular bond issue are set forth in an agreement called a **bond indenture** or **deed**. An **indenture trustee**, usually a commercial banking institution, represents the interests of the bondholders in making sure that the corporation meets the terms and covenants of the bond issue.[4] For example, the terms of the bond indenture may require a **sinking fund**, by which the borrowing corporation is required to set aside a fixed amount of money each year toward the ultimate payment of the bonds. The indenture trustee makes certain that such terms are complied with in accordance with its responsibilities set forth in the bond indenture.

deed–instrument by which the grantor (owner of land) conveys or transfers the title to a grantee.

indenture trustee–usually a commercial banking institution, to represent the interests of the bondholders and ensure that the terms and covenants of the bond issue are met by the corporation.

Bondholders do not vote for directors or have the right to vote on matters on which shareholders vote. However, when the debt is risky, it is highly likely that significant restraints on the corporation's freedom of action will be imposed by the terms of the indenture.

sinking fund–fixed amount of money set aside each year by the borrowing corporation toward the ultimate payment of bonds.

B. ACQUISITION OF SHARES

Shares may be acquired from the corporation or from an existing shareholder.

[3] UCC § 8-105.
[4] *Lorenc v CSX Corp.*, CCH Sec L Rep 95298 (WD Pa 1990).

6. Nature of Acquisition

Shares of stock may be acquired (1) from the corporation by subscription, either before or after the corporation is organized, or (2) by transfer of existing shares from a shareholder or from the corporation. The transfer may be voluntary, as by a sale, gift, or bequest by will, or involuntary, as by an execution sale to pay the judgment of a creditor. The transfer may also take place by operation of law—as when the stock of a shareholder passes to the shareholder's trustee in bankruptcy.

7. Statute of Frauds

Under the 1978 version of Article 8, a contract for the sale of corporate shares must be evidenced by a writing, or it cannot be enforced.[5] The writing must show that there has been a contract for the sale of a stated quantity of described securities at a defined or stated price. The writing must be signed in the manner required by the statute of frauds for the sale of goods. The 1994 version of Article 8 renders the statute of frauds inapplicable to contracts for the sale or purchase of securities.[6] The commentary notes explain that the 1978 statute's potential for filtering out fraudulent claims is outweighed by the obstacles the statute presents to the development of modern commercial practices in the securities business.

No writing is required for a contract by which a broker agrees with a customer to buy or sell securities for the customer. That is an agency agreement, not a sale made between the customer and the broker.

8. Subscription

stock subscription— contract or agreement to buy a specific number and kind of shares when they are issued by the corporation.

A **stock subscription** is a contract or an agreement to buy a specific number and kind of shares when the corporation issues them. As in the case of any other contract, the agreement to subscribe to shares of a corporation may be avoided for fraud.

(A) SUBSCRIPTION BEFORE INCORPORATION. In many states, a preincorporation subscription of shares is an offer to the corporation. According to this view, it is necessary for the corporation to accept the subscription offer either expressly or by conduct. A few states hold that subscriptions automatically become binding contracts when the organization of the corporation has been completed. In some states, the preincorporation subscription is irrevocable for a stated period. The RMBCA provides that "a subscription for shares entered into before incorporation is irrevocable for six months unless the subscription agreement provides a longer or shorter period or all the subscribers agree to revocation."[7]

(B) SUBSCRIPTION AFTER INCORPORATION. Subscriptions may be made after incorporation. In that event, the transaction is like any other contract with the corporation. The offer of the subscription may come from the subscriber or from the corporation. In either case, there must be an **acceptance**. Upon acceptance, the

acceptance—unqualified assent to the act or proposal of another; as the acceptance of a draft (bill of exchange), of an offer to make a contract, of goods delivered by the seller, or of a gift or deed.

[5] UCC § 8-319(a); *Goldfinger v Brown*, 564 NYS2d 461 (App Div 1991).
[6] UCC § 8-113.
[7] RMBCA § 6.20(a).

subscriber immediately becomes a shareholder with all the rights, privileges, and liabilities of a shareholder even though she has not paid any of the purchase price. Moreover, the subscriber is a shareholder even though no share certificate has been issued. In contrast with a contract for immediate subscription to shares, the contract may be one for the future issue of shares. In that case, the contracting party has only a contract and is not a shareholder as of the formation of the contract.

9. Transfer of Shares

In the absence of a valid restriction, a shareholder may transfer shares to anyone.

(A) RESTRICTIONS ON TRANSFER. Restrictions on the transfer of stock are valid if they are not unreasonable. It is lawful to require that the corporation or other stockholders be given the first right to purchase stock before a shareholder may sell stock to an outsider.

C A S E   S U M M A R Y

Restrictions on Transfer of Stock Are Legal, Morris

FACTS: In 1974 Billy Fought, Brady Morris, Clayton Strong, and John Peyton organized Vicksburg Mold and Die, Inc., for the purpose of designing and manufacturing plastic and metal products. Each individual was issued 25 shares of stock. The shareholders entered into a stock redemption agreement requiring a stockholder wishing to sell his stock to offer proportionate shares to each stockholder. Morris was elected president and Fought vice president, and all four individuals worked at the plant. Strong retired in 1979 and sold his shares in accordance with the stock redemption plan. In 1983, Peyton decided to sell his shares and agreed to sell them all to Morris, thus giving Morris control of the corporation. Fought sued Morris for breach of his fiduciary duty to Fought and for the value of Fought's pro rata share of Peyton's stock.

DECISION: Judgment for Fought. Section 2 of the stock redemption agreement was designed to maintain a balance of power in the four-person close corporation. Before stock could be sold to others, it had to be offered to each shareholder on a pro rata basis. Each individual had an opportunity to maintain the initial balance of power. By purchasing all of Peyton's stock, Morris bought control of the corporation. In doing so, he violated the stock redemption agreement and thus breached his fiduciary duty as a director, officer, and shareholder. [**Fought v Morris, 543 So 2d 167 (Miss 1989)**]

A provision giving a corporation the right to purchase a shareholder's shares on the death of the shareholder is valid.

A restriction on the right of a certificate's purchaser to transfer his stock is not valid unless the restriction is conspicuously noted on the certificate or the transferee had actual knowledge of the restriction. A restriction on the transfer of stock is strictly interpreted.[8]

---

[8] *Capano v Wilmington Country Club, Inc.*, 2001 WL 1359254 (Del Ch 2001).

When no restrictions exist, the issuer has a duty to register the transfer. **For Example,** Richard Jones purchased 1,000 certificated shares of International Generic Corporation (IGC) from Madison Tucker on March 30, 2010, at fair market value. Tucker properly indorsed the certificates to Jones on that date, and her signatures were duly notarized. On September 15, 2010, Jones presented the securities to IGC to register the transfer of shares and to collect dividends for the second quarter (April 1 through June 30) and the third quarter (July 1 through September 30). IGC refused to register the shares in Jones's name, believing him to be a person of questionable integrity that it did not want as an "owner" of IGC. Under either the 1978 or 1994 version of Article 8 of the UCC, it was improper for IGC to fail to register the stock that had been transferred to a bona fide purchaser, Jones.[9] No restrictions existed on the certificate, and IGC had a duty to register the transfer and was liable for its failure to do so. Jones was entitled to the dividends from the date of presentation of the stock for transfer. Prior to that date, the issuer, IGC, was entitled to treat the registered owner, Madison Tucker, as exclusively entitled to exercise the rights of ownership, including the right to dividends.[10] Thus, IGC was not liable to Jones for the second-quarter dividends. However, dividends declared after the date of presentment, which included the third-quarter dividend declared in October 2010 with a record date in October, must be paid to Jones by IGC.

(B) **INTEREST TRANSFERRED.** The transfer of shares may be absolute; that is, it may divest all ownership and make the transferee the full owner. The transfer may be of only a partial interest in the stock, or the transfer may be for security, such as when stock is pledged to secure the repayment of a loan.

10. Mechanics of Transfer

When stock is represented by a certificate, the ownership of shares is transferred by the delivery of the certificate of stock, indorsed by its owner in blank or to a specified person. Ownership may also be transferred by the delivery of the certificate accompanied by a separate assignment or power of attorney executed by the owner.[11]

A delivery from the owner of the shares directly to the transferee is not required. It can be made to an intermediary. When there is no delivery of the share certificate to anyone, however, there is no transfer of ownership of the shares.

A physical transfer of the certificate without a necessary indorsement is effective as between the parties. Thus, a gift of shares is binding even though no indorsement has been made. An indorsement is required to make the transferee a bona fide purchaser.

---

[9] UCC § 8-401 (1978); UCC § 8-401 (1994).
[10] UCC § 8-207(1) (1978); UCC § 8-207(a) (1994).
[11] UCC § 8-309. The second alternative of a delivery of an unindorsed certificate is designed to keep the certificate clean— for example, when the transfer is for a temporary or special purpose, as in the case of a pledge of the certificate as security for a loan.

11. Effect of Transfer

The transfer of existing shares of stock may raise questions between the parties to the transfer and between them and the corporation.

(A) VALIDITY OF TRANSFER. Because a transfer of shares is a transfer of ownership, the transfer must satisfy the requirements governing any other transfer of property or agreement to transfer property.[12] As between the parties, a transfer may be set aside for any ground that would warrant similar relief under property law. If the transfer has been obtained by duress, the transferor may obtain a rescission of the transfer.

(B) NEGOTIABILITY. Under common law, the transferee of shares of stock had no greater right than the transferor because the certificate and the shares represented by the certificate were nonnegotiable. By statute, the common law rule has been changed by imparting negotiability to certificated stock. Just as various defenses cannot be asserted against the holder in due course of a commercial paper, statutory law provides that similar defenses cannot be raised against the person acquiring the certificate in good faith and for value. Against such a person, the defense cannot be raised that the transferor did not own the shares or did not have authority to deliver the certificate or that the transfer was made in violation of a restriction on transfer not known to the person and not noted conspicuously on the certificate.

Statements sent by the issuer identifying the ownership of uncertificated securities are neither certificated securities nor negotiable instruments. Although certificated securities have the quality of negotiability, they are not commercial paper within Article 3 of the UCC.

(C) SECURED TRANSACTION. Corporate stock is frequently delivered to a creditor as security for a debt owed by the shareholder. Thus, a debtor borrowing money from a bank may deliver shares of stock to the bank as collateral security for the repayment of the loan. A broker's customer purchasing stock on margin may leave the stock in the possession of the broker as security for the payment of any balance due. The delivery of the security to the creditor is a pledge. This gives rise to a perfected security interest without any filing by the creditor. In itself, the pledge does not make the pledgee of the corporate stock the owner of the stock.

(D) EFFECT OF TRANSFER ON CORPORATION. The corporation is entitled to treat as the owner of shares the person whose name is on the corporation's books as the owner. Therefore, until there is a transfer on its books, the corporation may still treat a transferor of shares as the owner. The corporation may properly refuse to recognize a transferee when the corporation is given notice or has knowledge that the transfer is void or in breach of trust. In such a case, the corporation properly refuses to register a transfer until the rights of the parties have been determined. The corporation may also refuse to register the transfer of shares when the outstanding certificate is not surrendered to it or there is a lack of satisfactory proof that the certificate has been lost, destroyed, or stolen.

---

[12] *Gallant v Kanterman*, 671 NYS2d 50 (App Div 1998).

CASE SUMMARY

UCC Rules!

FACTS: Equivest Associates, a partnership, owned 10,000 shares of Altec International Inc. Equivest pledged these shares to secure loans by Lloyds Bank. Sometime after pledging the stock, Equivest transferred beneficial ownership of 350 shares of Altec stock to Thorn Hoffman and 350 shares to John Erikson. Thereafter, in 1988, Altec elected to be treated as a Subchapter S corporation, which necessitated that shareholders return their old stock certificates and be issued new certificates. Neither Erikson nor Hoffman had certificates to return because their stock had been pledged by Equivest to Lloyds Bank. Altec had knowledge that Erikson and Hoffman were the beneficial owners of 700 shares of Altec stock. However, Altec distributed cash dividends to Equivest, the registered owner of the 10,000 shares during the period from 1988 until March 14, 1990, when Equivest defaulted on its loan to Lloyds Bank and Lloyds sold all of the pledged stock, including Hoffman's and Erikson's 700 shares, at public auction. Hoffman and Erikson contend that Altec should have made all cash distributions to them as shareholders, not Equivest. Altec contends it complied with the UCC by making distributions to the owner of record.

DECISION: Judgment for Altec. UCC § 8-207(1) permitted Altec to treat Equivest as the owner of the 700 shares because it was the registered owner according to Altec's corporate books and Hoffman and Erikson had not made the due presentment to Altec for registration of the transfer of the 700 shares. [**Hoffman v Altec Int'l Inc., 546 NW2d 162 (Wis App 1996)**]

12. Lost, Destroyed, and Stolen Share Certificates

The owner of a lost, destroyed, or stolen share certificate is entitled to a replacement if the owner files a sufficient indemnity bond and requests the new certificate within a reasonable time before the issuer has notice that the original certificate has been acquired by a bona fide purchaser. **For Example,** if established by clear and convincing evidence, Linda Rosso would be entitled to the replacement of damaged jointly held stock certificates that her late husband Richard disposed of and never replaced. The court pointed out that there is a distinction between certificates issued a shareholder and the "shares" issued the shareholder. A *share* is the actual property of the shareholder while the *certificate* is merely the authentic evidence of the stockholder's ownership of shares.[13] If, after the new security is issued, a bona fide purchaser appears with the original certificate, the corporation must register a transfer of the security to that person and accept that person as the owner of the shares.

`CPA` C. RIGHTS OF SHAREHOLDERS

The rights of shareholders stem from their status as owners.

---

[13] *Rosso v Rosso*, 701 NW2d 355 (Neb 2005).

CPA   13. Ownership Rights

Shareholder control over the corporation is indirect. Periodically (ordinarily once a year), the shareholders elect directors and by this means control the corporation. At other times, however, the shareholders have no right or power to control corporate activity so long as it is conducted within lawful channels.

CPA   (A) CERTIFICATES OF STOCK. A shareholder has the right to have a properly executed certificate as evidence of ownership of shares. An exception is made when the corporation is authorized to issue uncertificated securities.

CPA   (B) TRANSFER OF SHARES. Unless limited by a valid restriction, a shareholder has the right to transfer her shares. The shareholder may sell the shares at any price or transfer them as a gift. The fact that the seller sells at a price higher than the market price is not unlawful even if the seller is a director or an officer.

CASE SUMMARY

It's the Real Thing, Controlling Shares in Coke-Anderson, and You Have to Pay a Premium

FACTS: Paul Warlick, Jr., was the president and chief executive officer and a stockholder of Coca-Cola Bottling Company of Anderson, S.C. (Coke-Anderson). He controlled a majority of the shares of stock of the company. Warlick agreed to sell this controlling interest in Coke-Anderson to Coke-Asheville for a price greater than the market value of the shares. Wayne Shoaf, a minority shareholder, brought suit against Warlick, contending that Warlick had violated his fiduciary duty to the corporation by receiving an unlawful premium for the sale of the majority interest in Coke-Anderson.

DECISION: Judgment for Warlick. Paying or receiving a premium for the controlling shares of stock in a corporation is not unlawful. A majority shareholder who is also a director and an officer is generally under no duty to minority shareholders to refrain from receiving a premium on the sale of the controlling stock. [**Shoaf v Warlick, 380 SE2d 865 (SC App 1989)**]

CPA   14. Right to Vote

The right to vote means the right to vote at shareholders' meetings for the election of directors and on other special matters that shareholders must vote on.
For Example, a proposal to change the capital structure of the corporation or a proposal to sell all or substantially all assets of the corporation must be approved by the shareholders.

CPA   (A) WHO MAY VOTE. Ordinarily, only shareholders of record—those common shareholders in whose name the stock appears on the books of the corporation—are entitled to vote. The board of directors may fix a date for closing the corporate books for this purpose.

CPA

(B) NUMBER OF VOTES. Unless there is a provision to the contrary, for each share owned, each shareholder is entitled to one vote on each matter to be voted. This procedure is called *straight voting*, and it is the normal method for shareholder voting on corporate matters. However, in the case of voting to elect directors only, **cumulative voting** is mandatory in nearly half of the states. This requirement is imposed by either state constitution or state statute. Cumulative voting is permitted by law in other states when provided for in the articles of incorporation or bylaws.

Cumulative voting is a form of voting that is designed to give proportional representation on the board of directors to minority shareholders. Under a cumulative voting plan, each shareholder has as many votes as the number of shares owned multiplied by the number of directors to be elected. A shareholder may cast all of these votes for one candidate or may divide the votes between two or more candidates. This system enables minority shareholders to cast all of their votes for a candidate who will represent their interests on the board of directors.

Under straight voting, minority shareholders would always be outvoted. **For Example,** assume that minority shareholder Tyler Feldberg owned 400 shares of stock and majority shareholder C. J. Jones controlled the remaining 600 shares. Also assume that five directors are to be elected to the board. If straight voting were used for the election of directors, C. J., with 600 shares, would always outvote Tyler's 400 shares. However, under cumulative voting, Tyler would be allowed 2,000 votes (400 shares times five directors), and C. J. would be allowed 3,000 votes (600 shares times five directors). The five candidates with the highest number of votes will be elected. If Tyler casts 1,000 votes for each of two directors and C. J. casts 1,000 votes for each of three directors, Tyler, who owns 40 percent of the stock, is able to elect two-fifths of the board to represent his interests.

cumulative voting–system of voting for directors in which each shareholder has as many votes as the number of voting shares owned multiplied by the number of directors to be elected, and such votes can be distributed for the various candidates as desired.

(C) VOTING BY PROXY. A shareholder has the right to authorize another to vote the shares owned by the shareholder. This procedure is known as **voting by proxy**. In the absence of restrictions to the contrary, any person, even someone who is not a shareholder, may act as a proxy. The authorization from the shareholder may be made by any writing.[14] The authorization is also commonly called a **proxy**.

voting by proxy–authorizing someone else to vote the shares owned by the shareholder.

proxy–written authorization by a shareholder to another person to vote the stock owned by the shareholder; the person who is the holder of such a written authorization.

(D) VOTING AGREEMENTS AND TRUSTS. Shareholders, as a general rule, are allowed to enter into an agreement by which they concentrate their voting strength for the purpose of electing directors or voting on any other matter.

A **voting trust** is created when by agreement a group of shareholders or all of the shareholders transfer their shares in trust to one or more persons as trustees. The trustees are authorized to vote the stock during the life of the trust agreement.[15] In general, such agreements are upheld if their object is lawful. In some jurisdictions, such trusts cannot run beyond a stated number of years. There are some signs of a relaxation as to time. Several states have abandoned all time limitations, several have extended the time limitation, and many provide for an extension or renewal of the agreement.

voting trust–transfer by two or more persons of their shares of stock of a corporation to a trustee who is to vote the shares and act for such shareholders.

[14] RMBCA § 7.07.
[15] *Bettner Trust v Bettner*, 495 NE2d 194 (Ind App 1986).

CPA   ## 15. Preemptive Offer of Shares

preemptive right–
shareholder's right upon the increase of a corporation's capital stock to be allowed to subscribe to such a percentage of the new shares as the shareholder's old shares bore to the former total capital stock.

If the capital stock of a corporation is increased, shareholders ordinarily have the **preemptive right** to subscribe to the same percentage of the new shares that their old shares represented of the former total of capital stock. This right is given to enable shareholders to maintain their relative interests in the corporation.

The existence of a preemptive right may make it impossible to conclude a transaction in which the corporation is to transfer a block of stock as consideration. Moreover, practical difficulties arise as to how stock should be allocated among shareholders of different classes.

The RMBCA provides that shareholders do not have preemptive rights unless the articles of incorporation provide for them.

CPA   ## 16. Inspection of Books

A shareholder has the right to inspect the books of the shareholder's corporation. In some states, there are no limitations on this right. In most states, the inspection must be made in good faith, for proper motives, and at a reasonable time and place.[16] In many states, a shareholder must own a certain percentage of the outstanding stock of a corporation (commonly 5 percent) or must own at least one share of stock for a minimum amount of time (commonly six months) to have the right to inspect the books. A shareholder is not relegated to accepting opinions and numbers offered by a company's auditor and may employ an expert accountant of his own to review and analyze the books and records of the corporation.[17]

The purpose of inspection must be reasonably related to the shareholder's interest as a shareholder.[18] A shareholder is entitled to inspect the records to determine the financial condition of the corporation, the quality of its management, and any matters relating to rights or interests in the corporate business, such as the value of stock.[19]

C A S E   S U M M A R Y

... No Fury Like a Stockholder Scorned

FACTS: U.S. Die Casting, Inc., is a closely held Ohio corporation that owns 5 percent of Security First Corporation, a Delaware corporation, which owns an Ohio savings and loan bank. David Slyman is the president of U.S. Die and its sole stockholder. The defendant, Security First, entered into a merger agreement with Mid Am, Inc., a large regional bank holding company; and after the announcement of the merger, Security First's stock increased

---

[16] RMBCA § 16.02(c); *Leary v Foley*, 884 So2d 655 (La App 2004).
[17] *Missouri v III Investments, Inc.*, 80 SW3d 855 (Mo App 2002).
[18] *Hess v Reg-Ellen Machine Tool Corp.*, 423 F3d 653 (7th Cir 2005).
[19] *Ihrig v Frontier Equity Exchange*, 128 P3d 993 (Kan App 2006).

C A S E   S U M M A R Y

Continued

significantly. The merger agreement required Security First to pay a termination fee of $2 million plus third-party expenses not to exceed $250,000 contingent on the occurrence of certain events within one year after termination, should Security First pull out of the merger. The merger did not go through, and the market price for Security First stock dropped significantly. Security First gave as a reason for failing to go through with the merger "the realization that Mid Am's management philosophy and direction were fundamentally different from its own." Security First paid Mid Am $275,000 in expenses and agreed to pay an additional $2 million if a certain event occurred within one and one-half years after termination. U.S. Die submitted a written demand to Security First pursuant to section 220 to inspect all of its books and records related to the Mid Am merger and its termination. Security First refused to comply. The Court of Chancery granted U.S. Die's demand, and Security First appealed.

DECISION: Judgment for U.S. Die. Section 220 proceedings are an important part of the corporate governance landscape in Delaware. Stockholders have a right to at least a limited inquiry into books and records when they have established some credible basis to believe that there has been wrongdoing. Concerning the purpose for the inspection, Slyman testified:

> *I would like to make my own decision as to why the merger was not completed. Telling me that it was a difference of philosophies didn't get me to understand why it was not completed. The philosophy was there prior to it....*

Slyman's testimony does call into question the defendant's purported reason for abrogating the merger agreement—namely, "the realization that Mid Am's management philosophy and direction were fundamentally different from its own." The Court of Chancery found the defendant's reason suspect because management philosophies could have been researched before entering into the agreement. Expense payments made to Mid Am in excess of the stipulation in the merger agreement and payment of a termination fee for a period beyond the time period set forth in the agreement are a basis for U.S. Die to inspect books and records, subject to remand on the scope of the inspection. [**Security First v U.S. Die Casting, Inc., 687 A2d 563 (Del Super 1997)**]

A shareholder is entitled to inspect the books to obtain information needed for a lawsuit against the corporation or its directors or officers, to organize the other shareholders into an "opposition" party to remove the board of directors at the next election, or to buy the shares of other shareholders.[20]

Inspection has frequently been refused when it was sought merely from idle curiosity or for "speculative purposes." Inspection has sometimes been denied on the ground that it was sought merely to obtain a mailing list of persons who would be solicited to buy products of another enterprise. Inspection has also been refused when the object of the shareholder was to advance political or social beliefs without regard to the welfare of the corporation. Cases that deny the right of inspection do

---

[20] See *Kelley Manufacturing Co. v Martin*, 674 SE2d 92 (GA App 2009), where the court determined that two shareholders showed a proper purpose for seeking inspection of books: to enforce the company's bylaws; to ensure proper corporate governance and to determine if corporate waste, mismanagement, and other breaches of fiduciary duty were occurring; to inspect corporate records to protect the shareholders' substantial ownership interest; and to inspect records related to the shareholders' removal as trustees, directors, officers, and employees of the corporation.

so when it would be harmful to the corporation[21] or is sought only for the purpose of annoying, harassing, or causing vexation or of aiding competitors of the corporation.

(A) FORM OF BOOKS. There are generally no requirements regarding the form of corporate books and records. The RMBCA recognizes that corporate books and records may be stored in modern data storage systems. "A corporation shall maintain its records in written form or in any other form capable of conversion into written form within a reasonable time."[22]

(B) FINANCIAL STATEMENTS. The RMBCA requires a corporation to furnish annual financial statements. These statements include a balance sheet as of the end of the fiscal year, an income statement for that year, and a statement of changes in shareholders' equity for that year.[23] A number of state statutes contain similar provisions and set forth a statutory penalty for any officer responsible for providing the financial statements who fails to perform such duties after written request.

CPA   **17. Dividends**

A shareholder has the right to receive a proportion of dividends as they are declared, subject to the relative rights of other shareholders to preferences, accumulation of dividends, and participation. There is no absolute right that dividends be declared, but dividends, when declared, must be paid in the manner indicated.

CPA   **(A) FUNDS AVAILABLE FOR DECLARATION OF DIVIDENDS.** Statutes commonly provide that no dividends may be declared unless there is an "earned surplus" for their payment. Earned surplus, also known as *retained earnings*, consists of the accumulated profits earned by the corporation since its formation less prior dividend distributions. Dividend payments are prohibited if the corporation is insolvent or would be rendered insolvent by the payment of the dividend.

As an exception to these rules, a wasting assets corporation may pay dividends out of current net profits without regard to the preservation of the corporate assets. **Wasting assets corporations** are those designed to exhaust or use up the assets of the corporation (for example, by extracting oil, coal, iron, and other ores) as compared with manufacturing plants whose object is to preserve the plant as well as to continue to manufacture. A wasting assets corporation may also be formed for the purpose of buying and liquidating a stock of merchandise from a company that has received a discharge in bankruptcy court.

In some states, statutes provide that dividends may be declared from earned surplus or from current net profits without regard to the existence of a deficit from former years.

CPA   **(B) DISCRETION OF DIRECTORS.** Assuming that a fund is available for the declaration of dividends, it is then a matter primarily within the discretion of the board of directors whether a dividend shall be declared. The fact that there is an earned surplus that could be used for dividends does not mean that they must be declared.

wasting assets corporation–corporation designed to exhaust or use up the assets of the corporation, such as by extracting oil, coal, iron, and other ores.

---

[21] *Retail Property Investors, Inc., v Skeens*, 471 SE2d 181 (Va 1996).
[22] RMBCA § 16.01(d).
[23] RMBCA § 16.20. See *Troccoli v Lab Contract Industries, Inc.*, 687 NYS2d 400 (App Div 1999).

This rule is not affected by the nature of the shares. Thus, the fact that the shareholders hold cumulative preferred shares does not give them any right to demand a declaration of dividends or to interfere with an honest exercise of discretion by the directors.

Maintaining an adequate cash and working capital position is an important practical consideration in determining whether to declare a cash dividend. In general, courts refuse to substitute their judgment for the judgment of the directors of the corporation and interfere with their decision on dividend declaration only when it is shown that their conduct is harmful to the welfare of the corporation or its shareholders.[24]

(c) FORM OF DIVIDENDS. Customarily, a dividend is paid in money. However, it may be paid in property, such as a product manufactured by the corporation; in shares of other corporations held by the corporation; or in shares of the corporation itself.

(d) EFFECT OF TRANSFER OF SHARES. When a corporation declares a cash or property dividend, the usual practice is for the board of directors to declare a dividend as of a certain date—the *declaration date*—payable to shareholders of record on a stated future date—the *record date*—with a *payment date* following the record date, usually by some 30 days. The person who is the owner of the shares on the record date is entitled to the dividend even if the shares are transferred prior to the payment date.

If the dividend consists of shares in the corporation declaring the dividend, ownership of the dividend is determined by the date of distribution. Whoever is the owner of the shares when the stock dividend is distributed is entitled to the stock dividend. The reason for this variation from the cash dividend rule is that the declaration of a stock dividend has the effect of diluting the existing corporate assets among a larger number of shares. The value of the holding represented by each share is diminished as a result. Unless the person who owns the stock on the distribution date receives a proportionate share of the stock dividend, the net effect will be to lessen that person's holding.

18. Capital Distribution

Upon dissolution of the corporation, shareholders are entitled to receive any balance of the corporate assets that remains after the payment of all creditors. Certain classes of stock may have a preference or priority in this distribution.

CPA ## 19. Shareholders' Actions

When the corporation has the right to sue its directors, officers, or third persons for damages caused by them to the corporation or for breach of contract, one or more shareholders may bring such action if the corporation refuses to do so. This is a **derivative (secondary) action** in that the shareholder enforces only the cause of action of the corporation and any money recovery is paid into the corporate treasury.

In a derivative action, when a corporation has failed to enforce a right, a shareholder bringing such a suit must show that a demand was made on the

derivative action–
secondary action for damages or breach of contract brought by one or more corporate shareholders against directors, officers, or third persons.

[24] *Gabelli & Co. v Liggett Group, Inc.*, 479 A2d 276 (Del Super 1984).

directors to enforce the right in question. The shareholder must show (1) that the directors refused to enforce the right[25] or (2) that a demand that the directors enforce the right is excused because the directors are deemed incapable of making an impartial decision regarding the pursuit of the litigation. Additionally, where a special litigation committee (SLC) is formed by the board of directors with full authority to decide what position to take with regard to a derivative lawsuit, demand on the entire board may be excused on a case-by-case basis, as exemplified in the *AIG, Inc.*, case.

CASE SUMMARY

"Curb Your Enthusiasm," Defendants Greenberg and Smith Argue

FACTS: Plaintiff stockholders sued derivatively CEO Maurice Greenberg, CFO Howard Smith, and other former officers who had served on American Insurance Group's (AIG's) board of directors. The plaintiffs took this action on behalf of the corporation for damages the former officers had caused AIG by having the corporation engage in illegal acts. In one example, it was asserted by the plaintiffs that AIG had created a fictional reinsurance business transaction with General Reinsurance Corp. to inflate loss reserves, thus making AIG appear to be a healthier company than it actually was and inflating AIG's stock price. AIG's board of directors formed a special litigation committee (SLC) to look into the stockholder plaintiffs' allegations, giving full authority to the SLC to address the litigation. The SLC investigated all matters and decided to join this action as a direct plaintiff on behalf of the corporation, asserting breach of fiduciary duty and indemnification claims against former CEO Greenberg and former CFO Smith. The defendants, Greenberg and Smith, contended that the stockholder plaintiffs must make a demand on the full board. Moreover, they asserted that under procedural law, boards of directors should not be lightly bypassed by derivative plaintiffs.

DECISION: Judgment for the stockholder plaintiffs. Corporation law seeks to ensure that boards are not lightly bypassed by derivative plaintiffs and not allowed to usurp the board's right to manage the affairs of the corporation. AIG's board's primacy in decision making has been fully honored. The SLC chose to have AIG sue Greenberg and Smith itself, to seek dismissal of certain defendants and to otherwise take no position on the plaintiffs' claims. The board gave the SLC full authority to make this decision, and through the SLC the board asserted control over the lawsuit. Demand is thus excused and the plaintiffs are free to proceed against the defendants. [**AIG, Inc. v Greenberg, 965 A2d 763 (Del Ch 2009)**]

A special litigation committee is vested with enormous power to pursue a corporate claim or seek dismissal of a derivative suit. But courts will defer to the business judgment and conclusions of the SLC only if the directors involved possess a disinterested independence and do not have relationships that prevent an unprejudicial exercise of judgment. **For Example,** a *Wall Street Journal* article identified three corporate officers and directors of Comverse Technology as possibly backdating stock option grants. The board appointed a two-person SLC that did little more than remove the three who had planned and carried out the $51 million scheme. The court refused to dismiss the shareholders' derivative action because one

---

[25] *Marx v Akers*, 666 NE2d 1034 (NY 1996), But see *Potter v Hughes*, 546 F3d 1051 (9th Cir 2008).

of the two SLC members had been a member of the compensation committee that had failed to take any steps reasonably necessary to oversee the awarding of options. The court concluded that the SLC had not taken a vigorous approach to investigating the misconduct and resultant harm to the corporation and therefore allowed the shareholders' derivative action to proceed.[26]

Mere allegations that a director and other directors move in the same social circles or are characterized as close friends is not enough to negate a director's independence for presuit demand excusal purposes.

Shareholders may also intervene or join in an action brought against the corporation when the corporation refuses to defend the action against it or is not doing so in good faith. Otherwise, the shareholders may take no part in an action by or against the corporation.

Lawsuits may be brought by minority shareholders against majority shareholders who are oppressive toward minority shareholders. Oppressive conduct may include payment of grossly excessive salaries and fringe benefits to the majority stockholders who are also officers of the corporation. Shareholders may bring a derivative action to obtain a dissolution of the corporation by judicial decree.[27]

D. LIABILITY OF SHAREHOLDERS

A shareholder is ordinarily protected from the liabilities of the corporation. Some exceptions exist, however.

20. Limited Liability

The liability of a shareholder is generally limited. This means that the shareholder is not personally liable for the debts and liabilities of the corporation. The capital contributed by shareholders may be exhausted by the claims of creditors, but there is no personal liability for any unpaid balance.

21. Ignoring the Corporate Entity

Ordinarily a corporation is regarded and treated as a separate legal entity, and the law does not look behind a corporation to see who owns or controls it.

The fact that two corporations have identical shareholders does not justify a court's regarding the two corporations as one. Similarly, the fact that there is a close working relationship between two corporations does not in itself constitute any basis for ignoring their separate corporate entities when they in fact are separately run enterprises.

(A) **"PIERCING THE CORPORATE VEIL."** A court may disregard the corporate entity, or figuratively "pierce the corporate veil," when exceptional circumstances warrant. The decision whether to disregard the corporate entity is made on a case-by-case basis, weighing all factors before the court. Factors that may lead to piercing the corporate veil and imposing liability on its owners (the shareholders) are (1) the

---

[26] *In Re Comverse Technology, Inc.* 766 NYS2d 10 (App Div 2008).
[27] *Lasday v Weiner*, 652 NE2d 1198 (Ill App 1996). But see *Whithorn v Whithorn Farms, Inc.*, 195 P3d 836 (Mont 2008).

failure to maintain adequate corporate records and the commingling of corporate and other funds,[28] (2) grossly inadequate capitalization,[29] (3) the diversion by shareholders of corporate funds or assets,[30] (4) the formation of the corporation to evade an existing obligation, (5) the formation of the corporation to perpetrate a fraud or conceal illegality, and (6) a determination that injustice and inequitable consequences would result if the corporate entity were recognized.[31]

CASE SUMMARY

When the Lake Would Hold No Water, Could a Stream of Assets Be Diverted to "The Man" (C. Engle)?

FACTS: Gladys Boles and 28 other owners of property at Hidden Valley Lakes Development sued the corporate developer, National Development Co. Inc. (NDC), NDC's parent Sunstates Corporation, and the individual behind both corporations, Clyde Engle, for breach of contract and fraud. The centerpiece of this development, Crystal Lake, a 30-acre recreational lake, failed to hold water; and it was determined that it would never do so. Instead of having a 30-acre lake as the centerpiece, the plaintiffs had a 30-acre hole in the ground. While the controversy over NDC's breach of contract was pending, Engle made a "proposal" to the CEO of NDC to transfer $2.4 million in receivables to Sunstates in exchange for an unsecured promissory note. Evidence showed that all of Sunstates' assets were transferred to Engle, making the note NDC held from Sunstates worthless. Sunstates purchased approximately $1.9 million dollars of oriental art, antique jewelry, rare books, and other collectibles that were maintained in Engle's home in Illinois. Likewise, Sunstates purchased a Rolls Royce from Libco, a corporation in which Engle was the majority shareholder. This automobile also appeared to be in Engle's possession or control. The trial court awarded the plaintiffs $2,540,867 in compensatory damages and pierced the corporate veils of NDC and Sunstates and held Engle personally liable for the judgment. Engle appealed, contending that the corporations were separate legal entities with limited liability.

DECISION: The evidence supports the conclusion that NDC and Sunstates were instrumentalities of Engle and that he diverted their remaining assets. All of the corporations under Engle's control were insolvent, and it would be an injustice to allow him to use the corporate entity as a shield to thwart the satisfaction of the judgment in this case. The corporate entity was disregarded to accomplish justice in this case. [**Boles v National Development Co. Inc., 175 SW3d 226 (Tenn App 2005)**]

---

[28] *East Market v Tycorp Pizza IV, Inc.*, 625 SE2d 191, 198 (NC App 2006).

[29] In *Trevino v MERSCORP, Inc.*, 583 F Supp 2d 521 (D Del 2008), the court determined that a shortage of capital is not *per se* a reason to pierce the corporate veil; rather, a more relevant inquiry would be "was the entity established to defraud its creditors?" An example of grossly inadequate capitalization is found in *Klokke Corp. v Classic Exposition, Inc.*, 912 P2d 929 (Or App 1996), in which Classic's two shareholders invested $1,000 of capital to start a business and immediately took out a $200,000 loan. The business remained undercapitalized until part of it was sold. However, the two shareholders effectively withdrew all of the proceeds of the sale in October 1991, and the business was again without sufficient capital, leaving it unable to meet its financial obligations. The court held that the shareholders were personally liable up to the amount withdrawn in October 1991 after the partial sale of the business.

[30] See *Trustees of the National Elevator Industry Pension Fund v Lutyk*, 332 F3d 188 (3d Cir 2003), in which the Court of Appeals found the equitable remedy of piercing the corporate veil justified. The sole shareholder, Andrew Lutyk, siphoned funds over the final months of the corporation's operations while it was known to be deeply insolvent, used corporate funds to pay entertainment expenses without an identifiable business purpose, and commingled corporate assets with his own. Personal liability was imposed on Lutyk to make unpaid payments to a union's benefit plans.

[31] *Barton v Moore*, 558 NW2d 746 (Minn 1997).

(B) "Alter Ego" Theory. Some courts express their reasons for disregarding the corporate entity by stating that the corporation is the "*alter ego*" of the wrongdoer. A corporation is a separate and distinct person from the person or persons who own the corporation. However, when a corporation is so dominated and controlled by a shareholder(s), officer(s), or director(s) that the separate personalities of the individual and the corporation no longer exist and there is a wrongful use of that control, the courts will disregard the corporate entity so as not to sanction a fraud or injustice.[32] **For Example,** V&M Industries, Inc., owned land on which some 40,000 plus used tires caught fire. It took nearly a week to extinguish the fire and caused severe air pollution in the St. Louis area. Vernon Leirer originally owned 99 percent of V&M corporate stock; all corporate officers other than Leirer were nonfunctioning; the corporation was inadequately capitalized; no stock certificates were issued; and corporate records were generally not kept. At a time just before the fire, when Leirer was no longer a shareholder or officer, he exercised total direction and control over the corporation and "ran the show." The court held that to adhere to the fiction of separate corporate existence would sanction fraud. It concluded that V&M, Inc., was the *alter ego* for Leirer, and Leirer was personally responsible for civil penalties under the Environmental Protection Act.[33]

Limited liability is important to our economy because it encourages investors to make investments in high-risk ventures. It should be disregarded only in exceptional circumstances. When fraud or deceit is absent, other circumstances for piercing the corporate veil must be so strong as to clearly indicate that the corporation is the alter ego of the controlling person.

(C) Obtaining Advantages of Corporate Existence. Courts will not go behind the corporate identity merely because the corporation has been formed to obtain tax savings or to obtain limited liability for its shareholders. Similarly, the corporate entity will not be ignored merely because the corporation does not have sufficient assets to pay the claims against it.

One-person, family, and other closely held corporations are permissible and entitled to all of the advantages of corporate existence. The fact that the principal shareholder runs or oversees the day-to-day operations does not justify ignoring the corporate entity.

22. Other Exceptions to Limited Liability

Liability may be imposed on a shareholder as though there were no corporation when the court ignores the corporate entity either because of the particular circumstances of the case or because the corporation is so defectively organized that it is deemed not to exist.

(A) Wage Claims. Statutes sometimes provide that the shareholders shall have unlimited liability for the wage claims of corporate employees. This exception has been abandoned in some states in recent years or has been confined to corporate officers who are active in corporate decision making.[34]

---

[32] *Dishon v Ponthie*, 918 So 2d 1132 (La App 2005).
[33] *Illinois v V&M Industries*, 700 NE2d 746 (Ill App 1998).
[34] *Cusimano v Metro Auto, Inc.*, 860 P2d 532 (Colo App 1993).

(B) Unpaid Subscriptions. Most states prohibit the issuance of par value shares for less than par or except for "money, labor done, or property actually received." Whenever shares issued by a corporation are not fully paid for, the original subscriber receiving the shares, or any transferee who does not give value or who knows that the shares were not fully paid for, is liable for the unpaid balance if the corporation is insolvent and the money is required to pay its creditors.[35]

C A S E   S U M M A R Y

You've Got to Pay for Your Stock, Silly

FACTS: On July 19, 1984, Keith and Joan Bryan incorporated Bryan's Inc. The corporation was authorized to issue 100 shares of stock with a par value of $1,000 per share. The corporation issued 50 shares to Keith and 50 shares to Joan, although it did not receive any payment in labor, services, money, or property for the stock. On August 30, 1984, Bryan's Inc. bought Hanewald's dry goods store, giving Hanewald a promissory note for part of the purchase price. The business was not successful, and after four months, Keith and Joan Bryan decided to close the store. They disbursed all of the corporation's funds in payment of all bills except for the debt owed Hanewald. No corporate funds were available to pay this debt. Hanewald sued the Bryans individually for the amount owed. The Bryans contended that they were not personally liable for the corporation's debts.

DECISION: Judgment for Hanewald. Organizing a corporation to avoid personal liability is legitimate and a primary advantage to doing business in the corporate form. But proper capitalization is the principal prerequisite for this limited liability. Keith and Joan Bryan's failure to pay for their stock makes them liable to Hanewald, the corporate creditor, to the extent that the stock was not paid for. Because the debt to Hanewald, $36,000, was less than the par value of their stock, $100,000, the Bryans are personally liable for the entire corporate debt owed to Hanewald. [**Hanewald v Bryan's Inc., 429 NW2d 414 (ND 1988)**]

If the corporation has issued the shares as fully paid for, has given them as a bonus, or has agreed to release the subscriber for the unpaid balance, the corporation cannot recover that balance. The fact that the corporation is thus barred does not prevent creditors of the corporation from bringing an action to compel payment of the balance. The same rules are applied when stock is issued as fully paid for in return for property or services that were overvalued so that the stock is not actually paid for in full. A conflict of authority exists, however, as to whether the shareholder is liable from the mere fact that the property or service given for the shares was in fact overvalued by the directors or whether it must also be shown that the directors acted in bad faith in making the erroneous valuation. The trend of modern statutes is, in the absence of proof of fraud, to prohibit disputing the valuation placed by the corporation on services or property.

(C) Unauthorized Dividends. If dividends are improperly paid out of capital, shareholders are generally liable to creditors to the extent of such depletion of

---

[35] *Frasier v Trans-western Land Corp.*, 316 NW2d 612 (Neb 1982). But *see Brunfield v Horn*, 547 So 2d 415 (Ala 1989).

capital. In some states, the liability of a shareholder depends on whether the corporation was insolvent at the time and whether debts were existing at the time.

23. The Professional Corporation

The extent to which incorporation limits the liability of shareholders of a professional corporation depends on the interpretation of the statute under which the corporation was formed.

(A) ACT OF SHAREHOLDER IN CREATING LIABILITY. The statutes that authorize the formation of professional corporations usually require that share ownership be limited to duly licensed professionals. If a shareholder in a professional corporation, such as a corporation of physicians, negligently drives the professional corporation's automobile in going to attend a patient or is personally obligated on a contract made for the corporation or is guilty of malpractice, the physician-shareholder is liable without limit for the liability that has been created. This is the same rule of law that applies in the case of the ordinary business corporation.

Professional corporation statutes generally repeat the rule governing malpractice liability by stating that the liability of a shareholder for malpractice is not affected by the fact of incorporation.

(B) MALPRACTICE LIABILITY OF AN ASSOCIATE. The liability of a shareholder in a professional corporation for the malpractice of an associate varies from state to state depending on the language of the professional corporation statute in effect and on the court decisions under the statute.[36]

If the statute provides for limited liability, as in a business corporation, then where doctors *A, B*, and *C* are a professional corporation, *A* and *B* will not be liable for the malpractice of *C* beyond the extent of corporate assets. If the statute provides for vicarious personal liability, as in a partnership, and doctors *A, B*, and *C* are a professional corporation, each will have unlimited liability for any malpractice liability incurred by the others. Often the statutory reference to malpractice liability is not very clear, and the courts are called on to resolve the question of the liability of a professional shareholder for the malpractice of an associate.

lawflix

Meet Joe Black (1998) (PG-13)

A transfer of corporate control and the role of shareholder control is at the heart of this film about a corporation under takeover fire.

For movie clips that illustrate business law concepts, see LawFlix at **www.cengage.com/blaw/dvl.**

---

[36] ABA Model Professional Corporation Act Amendments (1984), § 34, offers three alternative positions regarding the liability of shareholders: (1) limited liability, as in a business corporation, (2) vicarious personal liability, as in a partnership, and (3) personal liability limited in amount and conditioned on financial responsibility in the form of insurance or a surety bond.

MAKE THE CONNECTION

SUMMARY

The ownership of a corporation is evidenced by a holder's shares of stock that have been issued by the corporation. Common stock is ordinary stock that has no preferences but entitles the holder to (1) participate in the control of the corporation by exercising one vote per share of record, (2) share in the profits in the form of dividends, and (3) participate, upon dissolution, in the distribution of net assets after the satisfaction of all creditors (including bondholders). Other classes of stock exist, such as preferred stock, that have priority over common stock with regard to distribution of dividends and/or assets upon liquidation. Shares may be acquired by subscription of an original issue or by transfer of existing shares.

Bonds are debt securities, and a bondholder is a creditor rather than an owner of the corporation. Bondholders' interests are represented by an indenture trustee who is responsible for ensuring that the corporation complies with the terms of the bond indenture.

Shareholders control the corporation, but this control is indirect. Through their voting rights, they elect directors, and by this means, they can control the corporation. *Preemptive rights*, if they exist, allow shareholders to maintain their voting percentages when the corporation issues additional shares of stock. Shareholders have the right to inspect the books of the corporation unless it would be harmful to the corporation. Shareholders also have the right to receive dividends when declared at the discretion of the directors. Shareholders may bring a derivative action on behalf of the corporation for damages to the corporation. Shareholders are ordinarily protected from liability for the acts of the corporation.

Ordinarily, each corporation is treated as a separate person, and the law does not look beyond the corporate identity merely because the corporation was formed to obtain tax savings or limited liability. The fact that two corporations have the same shareholders does not justify disregarding the separate corporate entities. However, when a corporation is formed to perpetrate a fraud, a court ignores the corporate form, or "pierces the corporate veil." The corporate form is also ignored to prevent injustice or because of the functional reality that the two corporations in question are one.

LEARNING OUTCOMES

After studying this chapter, you should be able to clearly explain:

A. CORPORATE STOCKS AND BONDS

LO.1 Explain how to calculate the book value of a share of stock

> See the example in which Roger Eggett was awarded the book value of his stock, p. 1056.

LO.2 Distinguish between stocks and bonds

> See the discussion of stocks as an ownership interest in a corporation and bonds as a corporate debt, beginning on p. 1056.

B. ACQUISITION OF SHARES

LO.3 Distinguish between subscriptions for and transfers of stock

See the discussion of stock subscriptions for new issues of stock on p. 1059.

See the discussion of transfers of shares and the impact of restrictions, beginning on p. 1060.

C. RIGHTS OF SHAREHOLDERS

LO.4 Explain the rights of shareholders

See the discussion of shareholder ownership rights, including the right to vote, inspect books and records, and receive dividends when declared, beginning on p. 1064.

LO.5 Explain the nature of a shareholder derivative lawsuit

See the *AIG* case, where stockholder plaintiffs were excused from making a demand on the full board, p. 1070.

D. LIABILITY OF SHAREHOLDERS

LO.6 Explain the exceptions to the limited liability of shareholders

See the *Boles* case where Engle diverted assets and, as a result, the corporate entity was disregarded to accomplish justice, p. 1072.

KEY TERMS

acceptance	deed	preferred stock
bond	derivative (secondary)	proxy
bond indenture	action	registered bonds
book value	indenture trustee	sinking fund
capital stock	market value	stock subscription
certificate of stock	maturity date	voting by proxy
common stock	outstanding	voting trust
cumulative voting	par value	wasting assets
debenture	preemptive right	corporations

QUESTIONS AND CASE PROBLEMS

1. Monica Beam, a shareholder of Martha Stewart Living Omnimedia, Inc. (MSO), filed a derivative action against Martha Stewart and the other MSO board of directors, alleging that Stewart breached her duties to MSO by illegally selling ImClone stock and mishandling media attention, thereby jeopardizing the financial future of MSO. Ms. Beam asserted that it would be a futile act to make a demand on the corporation because a majority of the outside directors were not independent of Stewart. Ms. Beam pleaded the particularized facts that director Darla Moore attended a wedding reception hosted by Stewart's personal lawyer for his daughter and was a longtime friend of Stewart; and that director Naomi Seligman made a phone call to publisher John Wiley, Inc., to

express concern over a planned book critical of Stewart. Should Ms. Beam be excused from making a demand on the board of directors to pursue the derivative action because the outside directors were not independent of Stewart? [*Beam v Stewart*, 845 A2d 1040 (Del 2004)]

2. Six members of the Weston family, who owned 6.8 percent of the stock of Weston Paper and Manufacturing Company, brought suit against three corporate directors and CFIS, a firm hired by the company to make the annual evaluation of the company's stock for allocating stock options to its employees. The Westons stated that their claims against the defendants were personal claims, alleging that they were injured by CFIS and the three directors who kept the price of the stock low to obtain more shares of stock through the stock option plan. From an adverse ruling on their right to maintain a direct action against the directors, the Westons appealed. How would you decide this case? [*Weston v Weston Paper and Manufacturing Co.*, 74 Ohio St 377]

3. Tomlinson and Hubbard were two of five shareholders in Multimedia Software Distributors, a corporation. The corporation was formed in 1992 and filed for bankruptcy in 1994. In 1996, Tomlinson filed a claim in his own name, alleging that Hubbard had breached his fiduciary duties to Tomlinson by diverting proceeds owned by Multimedia to another business owned by Hubbard. Hubbard contends that Tomlinson is an improper plaintiff. Decide. [*Hubbard v Tomlinson*, 747 NE2d 69 (Ind App)]

4. Russell Nugent was involved in the roofing business in Kansas City, incorporating his business as Russell Nugent Roofing, Inc. In 1985, the name was changed to On Top Roofing, Incorporated. On August 27, 1987, On Top, Inc., ceased to exist, and RNR, Inc., was incorporated. RNR, Inc., went out of business in 1988, and RLN Construction, Inc., was incorporated. In 1989, the business was organized as Russell Nugent, Inc. Nugent and his wife had been sole shareholders, officers, and directors of each corporation. When one roofing company was incorporated, the prior roofing company ceased doing business. All of the companies were located at the same business address and used the same telephone number. Nugent paid himself and his wife more than $100,000 in salaries in 1986. In 1986, the corporation paid $99,290 in rent for property that the Nugents owned. Nugent testified that he changed to a new corporation every time he needed to get a "fresh start." The evidence showed that he used the On Top Roofing logo on his trucks and Yellow Pages advertisements throughout the period of the successive corporations. Suppliers who were not paid for materials in 1986 and 1987 by the insolvent corporations sought to pierce the corporate veils and hold Nugent personally liable. Nugent defended that as a shareholder, he had no personal liability. Decide. [*K.C. Roofing Center v On Top Roofing, Inc.*, 807 SW2d 545 (Mo App)]

5. The stock of West End Development Co. was subject to a transfer restriction. This restriction required that any shareholder selling shares first offer every other shareholder the right to purchase a proportion of the shares being sold. The proportions were to be the same as the percentages of the outstanding

shares that the other shareholders already owned. This restriction was stated in the articles of incorporation but was not stated on the stock certificate of the corporation. The Taylors owned stock in the company and sold their stock to Vroom, an officer of the corporation, without first offering any stock to the other shareholders, as required by the restriction. The other shareholders brought an action against Vroom to recover from him the percentages of the shares they would have been entitled to if the Taylors had followed the transfer restriction. Decide. [*Irwin v West End Development Co.*, 481 F2d 34 (10th Cir)]

6. Siebrecht organized Siebrecht Realty Co., a corporation, and then transferred his building to the corporation in exchange for its stock. The corporation rented different parts of the building to different tenants. Elenkrieg, an employee of one of the tenants, fell and was injured because of the defective condition of a stairway. She sued Siebrecht individually on the ground that the corporation had been formed by him for the purpose of securing limited liability. Decide. [*Elenkrieg v Siebrecht*, 144 NE 519 (NY)]

7. William Carter, a former officer and employee of Wilson Construction Co., Inc., owned 317 shares of stock in Wilson. Carter left Wilson to become part owner and employee of C&L Contracting Co., which was a direct competitor of Wilson. Carter requested access to Wilson's corporate books to determine the value of his shares. Wilson refused, not wanting to divulge its business practices to a direct competitor. Decide. [*Carter v Wilson Construction Co., Inc.*, 348 SE2d 830 (NC App)]

8. Ken and Charlotte Maschmeier were the majority shareholders of Southside Press; each owned 1,300 shares. Marty and Larry Maschmeier, who each owned 1,200 shares of the corporation, had a falling out with Ken and Charlotte and were terminated as employees of the business. Ken and Charlotte started a new corporation, which employed most of the employees of the old corporation and which took most of its former customers. Gross receipts of Southside Press went from $613,258 down to $18,172 two years later. The $18,172 figure was from the lease of equipment. Ken and Charlotte continued to draw from Southside annual salaries of $20,000, which were in excess of the gross receipts of the business. Marty and Larry brought suit against Ken and Charlotte, alleging "oppressive" conduct. Ken and Charlotte stated that they had paid Marty and Larry excellent salaries when they were employed by the corporation. Ken and Charlotte contended they had a right to start a new corporation as they saw fit. Decide. [*Maschmeier v Southside Press, Inc.*, 435 NW2d 377 (Iowa App)]

9. Harper owned corporate stock, and telling O'Brien that he was going to give the stock to O'Brien, he handed the stock certificate to O'Brien. O'Brien requested Harper to indorse the certificate. Harper refused. Who was the owner of the stock? [*Smith v Augustine*, 368 NYS2d 675]

10. Ed Klein was the sole shareholder, director, and chief executive officer of The Gun Exchange, Inc., a retail firearms dealership. The inventory of The Gun

Exchange had been pledged as security for a $622,500 debt owed to InterFirst Bank. It also owed $231,484.60 to Sporting Goods, Inc.; this debt was unsecured. On May 20, InterFirst Bank notified Klein of its intention to foreclose on the inventory and sell it at public auction. InterFirst Bank further advised Klein that, pursuant to his personal guarantee, he would be responsible for any deficiency following the sale. Klein immediately incorporated The Gun Store, Inc., for the purpose of purchasing the assets of The Gun Exchange at the foreclosure sale. Before the foreclosure sale, Klein obtained a $650,000 line of credit from CharterBank on behalf of The Gun Store. At the sale, Klein purchased the assets of The Gun Exchange for $650,000 even though the highest prior bid was $175,000. (Had the $175,000 bid been accepted, Klein would have been personally liable for the deficiency to InterFirst Bank.)

After the foreclosure sale, no funds existed to pay the unsecured creditors of The Gun Exchange. Following the sale, The Gun Store began operating as a retail firearms dealer with the inventory purchased from the foreclosure sale. It operated in the same location and with the same personnel as The Gun Exchange. Sporting Goods, Inc., sued Klein individually for the $231,484.60. Klein contended that the corporate form under which he did business insulated him as a shareholder from liability for corporate obligations. Decide. Is it ethical to seek limited liability under the corporate form, as Klein did in this case? [*Klein v Sporting Goods, Inc.*, 772 SW2d 173 (Tex Civ App)]

11. Ibanez owned shares of stock in Farmers Underwriters. He left the stock certificate lying on top of his desk in his office. Many persons continually passed through the office, and one day Ibanez realized that someone had taken the certificate from the top of his desk. Ibanez applied to Farmers Underwriters for a duplicate stock certificate. The corporation refused to issue a duplicate on the ground that it was Ibanez's own fault that the original certificate had been stolen. Ibanez claimed that he was entitled to a new certificate even though he had been at fault. Was he correct? [*Ibanez v Farmers Underwriters Ass'n*, 534 P2d 1336 (Cal)]

12. On March 3, 2002, pursuant to a public offering, First All State Trucking Corp. (FAST) issued securities to investors in denominations of $1,000. The interest rate was 7 percent per year payable semiannually, and the maturity date was March 3, 2010. The rights and obligations of the issuer, FAST, and the holders of the securities were set forth in an indenture agreement. Because the securities were not secured by a mortgage or lien on corporate property, Alec believes they are shares of preferred stock. Is Alec correct? Fully explain the type of security involved, and discuss the extent of the holders' voting rights.

13. Linhart owned shares of stock in First National Bank. She borrowed money from the bank and pledged the stock as security. She later decided to transfer 70 head of cattle and the shares of stock to her son, but she could not deliver the share certificate to him because it was held by the bank. She therefore executed a bill of sale reciting the transfer of the cattle and the stock to the son. She gave him the bill of sale, and he had the bill recorded. After her death, the son

brought an action to determine the ownership of the stock. Was the son the owner of the shares?

14. Birt was a hospital patient. The doctor who treated him was a shareholder of a professional corporation organized under the Indiana Medical Professional Corporation Act. Birt claimed that the doctor who treated him was guilty of malpractice, and he sued the doctor. He also sued the professional corporation and all of its officers, directors, and shareholders. These other defendants asserted that they were not liable because the corporate entity shielded them. The plaintiff claimed that the corporation was not a shield because in fact all of the persons were rendering medical services and should be held liable as in a partnership. The statute did not expressly regulate the matter of limited liability beyond declaring that it did not change the law between a person supplying medical services and the patient. Decide. [*Birt v St. Mary Mercy Hospital*, 370 NE2d 379 (Ind App)]

15. Ronald Naquin, an employee of Air Engineered Systems & Services, Inc., owned one-third of its outstanding shares. After six years, he was fired and an offer was made to buy out his interest in Air Engineered at a price that Naquin thought inadequate. He then formed a competing business and made a written request to examine the corporate records of Air Engineered. This request was denied. Naquin filed suit to require Air Engineered to allow him to examine the books. Air Engineered raised the defense that he was a competitor seeking to gain unfair competitive advantage. Decide. [*Naquin v Air Engineered Systems & Services, Inc.*, 463 So2d 992 (La App)]

CPA QUESTIONS

1. A stockholder's right to inspect books and records of a corporation will be properly denied if the stockholder:

   a. Wants to use corporate stockholder records for a personal business

   b. Employs an agent to inspect the books and records

   c. Intends to commence a stockholder's derivative suit

   d. Is investigating management misconduct

2. The limited liability of a stockholder in a closely held corporation may be challenged successfully if the stockholder:

   a. Undercapitalized the corporation when it was formed

   b. Formed the corporation solely to have limited personal liability

   c. Sold property to the corporation

   d. Was a corporate officer, director, or employee

3. Price owns 2,000 shares of Universal Corp.'s $10 cumulative preferred stock. During its first year of operations, cash dividends of $5 per share were declared on the preferred stock but were never paid. In the second year, dividends on the

preferred stock were neither declared nor paid. If Universal is dissolved, which of the following statements is correct?

a. Universal will be liable to Price as an unsecured creditor for $10,000.

b. Universal will be liable to Price as a secured creditor for $20,000.

c. Price will have priority over the claims of Universal's bond owners.

d. Price will have priority over the claims of Universal's unsecured judgment creditors.

4. Under the Revised Model Business Corporation Act, a dissenting stockholder's appraisal right generally applies to which of the following corporate actions?

	Consolidations	Shares from mergers
a.	Yes	Yes
b.	Yes	No
c.	No	Yes
d.	No	No

Chapter 46

SECURITIES REGULATION

I s there anything that protects you when you buy corporate securities?

A. STATE REGULATION

To protect the public from the sale of fraudulent securities, many states have adopted statutes regulating the intrastate sale of securities.

CPA

1. State Blue Sky Laws

blue sky laws–state statutes designed to protect the public from the sale of worthless stocks and bonds.

State laws regulating securities are called **blue sky laws**. The term *blue sky* is derived from the purpose of such laws, which is to prevent the sale of speculative schemes that have no more value than the blue sky. The state statutes vary in detail. They commonly contain (1) an antifraud provision prohibiting fraudulent practices and imposing criminal penalties for violations, (2) broker-dealer licensing provisions regulating the persons engaged in the securities business, and (3) provisions for the registration of securities, including disclosure requirements, with a designated government official.

A Uniform Securities Act, covering the foregoing three categories of regulations, exists to provide guidance to states in updating their securities laws. This act also contains alternative regulations that can be adopted by states with different regulatory philosophies.

2. National Securities Markets Improvement Act

Congress reallocated responsibility between state and federal security regulators in the National Securities Markets Improvement Act (NSMIA) of 1996,[1] recognizing that the dual system of state and federal regulation of securities resulted in duplicative regulation and expenses. Title I of the act exempts from state review and registration securities offered by mutual funds and stocks listed on the New York Stock Exchange, the American Stock Exchange, the NASDAQ National Market system, and other stock exchanges identified by the Securities and Exchange Commission (SEC). The act preserves the states' authority to investigate and bring enforcement actions for fraud or deceit or for unlawful conduct by a broker or dealer in connection with securities transactions.[2] Also, the states may continue to collect filing fees for securities in effect as of October 25, 1996. The act also eliminates duplicative registration requirements for investment advisors by dividing regulatory authority between the SEC, which exclusively regulates investment advisors with assets under management of $25 million or more, and the states, which have the responsibility to regulate all investment advisors managing lower sums of money.[3]

---

[1] PL 104-290, 110 Stat 3416, 15 USC § 78a nt.
[2] The 1996 act amends § 18(c) of the 1933 Securities Act to accomplish this result.
[3] NSMIA § 303(a), which adds a new § 203A to the Investment Advisors Act of 1940.

B. Federal Regulation

The stock market crash of 1929 and the Great Depression that followed led to the enactment of federal legislation to regulate the securities industry.

3. Federal Laws Regulating the Securities Industry

Six federal securities regulation laws were passed between 1933 and 1940. The two principal laws that provide the basic framework for the federal regulation of the sale of securities in interstate commerce are the Securities Act of 1933 and the Securities Exchange Act of 1934.

The 1933 act deals with the original distribution of securities by the issuing corporations. It is a disclosure statute designed to secure essential facts for the investor. The 1934 act is concerned with the secondary distribution of securities in the national securities exchanges and in the over-the-counter markets. That is, the 1933 act regulates the issuance of securities by a corporation to the first owner. The 1934 act regulates the sale of securities from one owner to another. Four other federal laws deal with specific aspects of the securities industry.[4] These aspects include holding companies in utility businesses, trustees for debt securities, mutual funds, and investment advisors.

The Securities Enforcement Remedies and Penny Stock Reform Act of 1990[5] (Remedies Act) expands the enforcement remedies of the SEC to reduce fraudulent financial reporting and financial fraud. Under the Remedies Act, the SEC may start administrative proceedings against any person or entity, whether regulated by the SEC or not, and may issue a temporary cease-and-desist order prior to notice and a hearing. The SEC may also order an accounting and disgorgement of ill-gotten gains. In addition, the Remedies Act authorizes courts to bar individuals who have engaged in fraudulent activities from serving as officers and directors of public corporations.

The Securities Acts Amendments of 1990[6] authorize sanctions against SEC-regulated persons for violation of foreign laws. The amendments facilitate the ability of the SEC and foreign regulators to exchange information and cooperate in international securities law enforcement.

The Market Reform Act of 1990[7] was enacted to provide the SEC with powers to deal with market volatility. Under the law, the SEC has the power to suspend all trading when markets are excessively volatile. Also, the SEC may require "large traders" to identify themselves and provide information concerning their trading.

The Private Securities Litigation Reform Act (PSLRA) of 1995[8] was passed to alleviate abuses in private securities litigation. The intent of the act is to reduce the

---

[4] The Public Utility Holding Company Act of 1935 (15 USC § 79 *et seq.*) provides comprehensive regulation of holding companies and their subsidiaries in interstate gas and electric utilities businesses. The Trust Indenture Act of 1939 (15 USC §§ 77aaa to 77bbb) was enacted to protect the interests of the holders of bonds and other debt securities offered to the public in interstate commerce by requiring the appointment of independent institutional trustees. The Investment Company Act of 1940 (15 USC §§ 80a-1 to 80a-52) provides for the registration and comprehensive regulation of mutual funds and all other investment companies. The Investment Advisors Act of 1940 (15 USC §§ 80b-1 to 80b-21) requires registration with the Securities and Exchange Commission of all persons engaged in the business of providing investment advice in interstate commerce. In 1970, the Securities Investors Protection Act was enacted to protect investors from the business failures of brokers and dealers.

[5] PL 101-429, 104 Stat 931, 15 USC § 77g.

[6] PL 101-550, 104 Stat 2713, 15 USC § 78a.

[7] PL 101-432, 104 Stat 963, 15 USC § 78a.

[8] PL 104-67, 109 Stat 737, 15 USC § 78a nt.

e-commerce&cyberlaw

Facilitation of the Use of Electronic Record Keeping

Under the Electronic Signatures in Global and National Commerce Act of 2000 (E-Sign), brokerage firms and mutual funds may avoid the expense of paper mailings of legally required documents, such as monthly statements, trade confirmations, prospectuses, and financial reports, and deliver these documents or

"records" by electronic means. The consumer must, however, consent to receiving these electronic records, and the consumer must consent electronically or confirm the consent electronically. Moreover, firms must inform consumers of their right to receive hard copy documents.

number of lawsuits brought against issuers of securities and accounting firms. This law applies only to private securities litigation, and the SEC's enforcement activities are not affected by the act.

The NSMIA, previously referred to in regard to the allocation of responsibility for securities regulation between the states and the federal government, also provides for national standards allowing brokers and dealers to improve their ability to borrow funds to finance market-making and underwriting activities.[9] This act also provides new national standards regulating margin restriction.

The Sarbanes-Oxley Act of 2002[10] contains numerous reforms regarding corporate accountability, enhanced disclosure requirements, auditor- and accounting-related provisions, and enforcement and liability provisions, which will be discussed in this chapter and the subsequent chapter on accountants' liability.

CPA 4. Definition of Security

securities–stocks and bonds issued by a corporation. Under some investor protection laws, the term includes any interest in an enterprise that provides unearned income to its owner.

For the securities acts to apply, the transaction must involve a "security" within the meaning of the acts.[11] Congress adopted a definition of **security** sufficiently broad to encompass virtually any instrument that might be sold as an investment.

The definition of *security* includes not only investment instruments such as stocks and bonds but also "investment contracts." The definition of an *investment contract*, developed by the Supreme Court, is sufficiently broad to allow the securities acts to apply to a wide range of investment transactions or schemes, including the sale of bottled whiskey, cattle-breeding programs, and a limited liability partnership to operate local telephone companies.[12] Under the Supreme Court's definition, an investment contract exists if the following elements are present: (1) an investment of money, (2) a common enterprise, and (3) an expectation of future profits from the

---

[9] NSMIA § 104, PL 104-290, 110 Stat 3416, 15 USC § 776.

[10] PL 107-204, 116 Stat 745.

[11] The Supreme Court has consistently held that the definition of a security set forth in § 3(a)(10) of the 1934 act is identical to the definition set forth in § 2(1) of the 1933 act. The definition of security under these acts is not to be confused with the narrower definition in Article 8 of the Uniform Commercial Code. See *SEC v Infinity Group Co.,* 993 F Supp 321 (ED Pa 1998).

[12] *SEC v Shiner,* 268 F Supp 2d 1333 (SD Fla 2003).

efforts of others. **For Example,** the sale of citrus groves to investors, coupled with the execution of service contracts to plant, harvest, and sell the fruit and the distribution of the profits of the venture to the investors, is an investment contract. An instrument denominated as a "note" may in fact be a "security" subject to regulation under the 1934 act.[13]

CASE SUMMARY

10,000 Investors Wish They Had Missed This Opportunity

FACTS: "Opportunity doesn't always knock ... sometimes it rings" (ETS Payphones promotional brochure). And sometimes it hangs up. So it did for the 10,000 people who invested a total of $300 million in the payphone sale-and-leaseback arrangements touted by ETS under that slogan. Charles Edwards was the chairman, chief executive officer, and sole shareholder of ETS Payphones, Inc. Acting partly through a subsidiary, ETS sold payphones to the public via independent distributors. The payphones were offered packaged with a site lease, a five-year leaseback and management agreement, and a buyback agreement. The purchase price for the payphone packages was approximately $7,000. Under the leaseback and management agreement, purchasers received $82 per month, a 14 percent annual return. Purchasers were not involved in the day-to-day operation of the payphones they owned. ETS selected the site for the phones, installed the equipment, arranged for connection and long distance service, collected coin revenues, and maintained and repaired the phones. Under the buyback agreement, ETS promised to refund the full purchase price of the package at the end of the lease or within 180 days of the purchaser's request. The payphones did not generate enough revenue for ETS to make the payments required by the leaseback agreements, so the company depended on funds from new investors to meet its obligations. In September 2000, ETS filed for bankruptcy protection. The SEC brought this civil enforcement action alleging that Edwards and ETS had violated the registration requirements and antifraud provisions of the 1933 act. The district court concluded the arrangement was an "investment contract" subject to the securities laws. The Eleventh Circuit Court of Appeals reversed the lower court because the scheme offered a contractual entitlement to a fixed rather than a variable return.

DECISION: Judgment for the SEC. Congress's purpose in enacting the securities laws was to regulate investments in whatever form they are made and by whatever name they are called. To that end, it enacted a broad definition of "security" sufficient to encompass virtually any instrument that might be sold as an investment. The U.S. Supreme Court applied the *Hovey* test for an investment contract finding (1) an investment of money, (2) a common enterprise, and (3) an expectation of future "profits" from the efforts of others, including fixed returns based on contracts. The Court determined that the ETS investment scheme can be an "investment contract" and thus a "security" under the securities laws. It reversed and remanded the case to the Court of Appeals. [**SEC v Edwards, 540 US 389 (2004)**]

CPA   ## 5. Securities Act of 1933

The 1933 act deals with the original issue of securities. It prohibits the offer or sale of securities to the public in interstate commerce before a registration statement is

---

[13] *SEC v Wallenbrock*, 313 F3d 532 (9th Cir 2002).

registration statement—
document disclosing specific financial information regarding the security, the issuer, and the underwriter.

filed with the SEC. A **registration statement** is a document disclosing specific financial information regarding the security, the issuer, and the underwriter. The seller must also provide a prospectus to each potential purchaser of the securities.

thinking things through

Problem: Conflicts of Interest—Remedy: Commonsense Rules

Full-service brokerage firms serve both retail and corporate clients. On the retail side, brokers buy and sell stocks and bonds for retail clients from all walks of life. The firms' research analysts perform the very important function of studying the performance of companies listed on the major stock exchanges, and the analysts make recommendations on these companies' securities, such as "buy," "hold," or "sell," for the benefit of their brokers and clients. Brokerage firms also serve corporate clients by underwriting and distributing new issues of stocks and bonds. This is called the INVESTMENT BANKING function of the firm. When a manufacturing or service company issues securities for the first time, the transaction is called an INITIAL PUBLIC OFFERING or IPO. Lucrative fees are earned by brokerage firms from the successful placement of such issues. These securities are sold to retail clients and the public by the brokerage firms, with firm analysts' recommendations being an important element in the success of the placements and the overall profitability of the brokerage firms.

An investigation into Merrill Lynch by the New York Attorney General's Office revealed that while certain Merrill analysts were publicly recommending certain technology companies that were investment banking clients of the firm, internal e-mails indicated that these analysts believed the same companies were "crap" and "junk." One wrote to a colleague questioning his "positive" recommendation of a company whose numbers seemed weak to her, and his response to her was, he had written "pos," in place of [expletive deleted].

The public and retail clients believed that the firm's analysts were independent of the investment banking function of the firm and that the recommendations were made solely with retail clients' interests in mind. The New York Attorney General's Office concluded, however, that analysts and investment bankers were closely involved in each other's work and were not independent; that the analyst department's compensation was tied to the results of the investment banking department's results; and that analysts were negotiating with investment banking clients for ratings.

The SEC has promulgated rules to eliminate this type of blatant conflict of interest at full-service brokerage firms. These rules are based on management common sense. The rules include the following: (1) Investment banking divisions may not supervise firms' analysts, (2) compensation for analysts may not be linked to specific investment banking transactions, (3) analysts must disclose whether they own shares in a company they recommend and certify that their recommendations are their true opinions, (4) analysts appearing in public forums before the media must disclose whether they have an interest in the company being discussed, and (5) firms must make comprehensive disclosures about their rating systems and the firms they represent as investment banking clients.*

* Section 501(a) of the Sarbanes-Oxley Act requires the SEC to adopt rules that address potential conflicts of interest in securities research. Regulation Analyst Certification ("Regulation AC") requires certification of any research report by an analyst that the views expressed accurately reflect the analyst's personal views. Moreover, the written certification requires disclosure of any compensation received by the analyst that was either directly or indirectly paid in relation to the views or recommendations expressed in the report or the views expressed in any public appearance. The SEC has approved National Association of Securities Dealers (NASD) and New York Stock Exchange (NYSE) rule changes relating to research analyst conflicts of interest.

prospectus–information provided to each potential purchaser of securities setting forth the key information contained in the registration statement.

The **prospectus** sets forth the key information contained in the registration statement. The object is to provide the interested investor detailed information about the security and the enterprise. The SEC does not approve or disapprove the securities as being good or bad investments but only reviews the form and content of the registration statement and the prospectus to ensure full disclosure. The requirements of advance disclosure to the public through the filing of the registration statement with the SEC and the sending of a prospectus to each potential purchaser are commonly referred to as the **registration requirements** of the 1933 act.

CPA (A) APPLICABILITY. The 1933 act applies to (1) stocks, (2) corporate bonds, and (3) any conceivable type of corporate interest or instrument that has the characteristics of an investment security, including convertible securities and variable annuities. The act applies to all such instruments that have investment characteristics.

CPA (B) THE REGISTRATION PROCESS. Section 5 of the 1933 act provides for the division of the registration process into three time periods: (1) the prefiling period, (2) the waiting period, from the date of filing with the SEC to the date the registration statement becomes effective (a minimum of 20 days but commonly extended for additional 20-day periods after each amendment by the issuer in compliance with SEC requirements for additional information), and (3) the posteffective period. The time divisions allow the public an opportunity to study the information disclosed in the registration process before a sale can be made. Permissible, required, and prohibited activities during these time periods are set forth in Figure 46.1.

registration requirements– provisions of the Securities Act of 1933 requiring advance disclosure to the public of a new securities issue through filing a statement with the SEC and sending a prospectus to each potential purchaser.

CPA (C) REGULATION A OFFERINGS. Regulation A provides a simplified registration process for small issues of securities by small businesses. Although technically exempt from the 1933 act registration requirements, a Regulation A offering involves a "mini-registration" with the SEC. Under the SEC's Small Business Initiative, Regulation A applies to the offerings of securities up to $5 million in a 12-month period. Disclosure requirements are simplified by the use of the small corporate offerings registration (SCOR) form, with its question-and-answer, "fill-in-the-blank" format. Also, the financial statements required in a Regulation A offering are less extensive than those required for a registered public offering.

Issuers may broadly solicit indications of interest from prospective investors before filing an *offering statement* with the SEC. This allows the issuer to "test the waters" and explore investor interest before incurring the expenses associated with a Regulation A offering. Solicitation-of-interest documents must be factual and comply with the antifraud provisions of the securities acts. No sales may be made until the SEC qualifies the offering statement and the seller delivers the final-offering circular, including the offering price, to the investor.

CPA (D) REGISTRATION EXEMPTIONS. Certain private and limited offerings of securities are exempt from the registration requirements of the act under SEC Regulation D.

Offerings of securities restricted to residents of the state in which the issuing corporation is organized and doing business are exempt from federal regulation. This intrastate offering exemption is applied very narrowly by the SEC and the courts, and such offerings are subject to state laws.

FIGURE 46-1 | *Registration Periods*

	PROHIBITED OR REQUIRED ACTIVITIES	PERMITTED ACTIVITIES
PREFILING PERIOD	ISSUER MUST NOT SELL OR OFFER FOR SALE A SECURITY BEFORE REGISTRATION STATEMENT IS FILED.	ISSUER MAY PLAN WITH UNDERWRITERS THE DISTRIBUTION OF THE SECURITY.
WAITING PERIOD	NO FINAL SALE OF A SECURITY PERMITTED DURING THIS PERIOD.	PRELIMINARY PROSPECTUS* CONTAINING INFORMATION FROM THE REGISTRATION STATEMENT BEING REVIEWED BY THE SEC MAY BE DISTRIBUTED TO INVESTORS, WHO MAY MAKE OFFERS. ADVERTISEMENTS MAY BE PLACED IN FINANCIAL PUBLICATIONS, IDENTIFYING PARTICULARS OF THE SECURITY, FROM WHOM A PROSPECTUS CAN BE OBTAINED, AND BY WHOM ORDERS WILL BE EXECUTED.**
POSTEFFECTIVE PERIOD	MUST PROVIDE A COPY OF FINAL PROSPECTUS WITH EVERY WRITTEN OFFER, CONFIRMATION OF SALE, OR DELIVERY OF SECURITY. MUST UPDATE PROSPECTUS WHENEVER IMPORTANT NEW DEVELOPMENTS OCCUR OR AFTER NINE MONTHS.	SALES OF THE SECURITY MAY BE COMPLETED.

*The preliminary prospectus is commonly called the *red herring* prospectus because of the red ink caption required by the SEC, informing the public that a registration statement has been filed but is not yet effective and that no final sale can be made until after the effective date.

**These advertisements are sometimes called *tombstone ads* because they are commonly framed by a black ink border.

CPA *(1) Rule 506 Exemption*

The most important exemption under Regulation D is SEC Rule 506. This rule provides general permission to offer and sell to a potentially indefinite number of individuals who meet the definition of accredited investor.[14] It is commonly referred to as the *private placement exemption*. There is no limitation on the amount of money that can be raised by the offering.[15] Specific information must be provided to all buyers if any buyers are nonaccredited investors; the number of nonaccredited investors is limited to no more than 35.

CPA *(2) Rule 505 Exemption*

SEC Rule 505 of Regulation D exempts from registration offerings of less than $5 million to no more than 35 nonaccredited purchasers over a 12-month period.

---

[14] The term *accredited investor* is defined to include virtually every type of institution that participates in the private placement market such as banks, stock brokerage firms, insurance companies, mutual fund companies, retirement plans with assets in excess of $5 million, and so on as well as individual investors with substantial income or large net worth.

[15] *Kunz v SEC*, 2003 WL 1605865, 64 FedAppx 659 (10th Cir).

No limit exists on the number of accredited investors who may participate. No general solicitation or general advertising is permitted under Rule 505. If any prospective investors are nonaccredited, the issuer must furnish all investors specific information on the issuer, its business, and the securities offered for sale.

CPA   *(3) Rule 504 Exemption*

Under SEC Rule 504 of Regulation D, as amended in 1999, an issuer can offer and sell securities up to $1 million within a 12-month period without registration and without most of the restrictions contained in Rules 505 and 506.

CPA   *(4) Restrictions*

Securities acquired under Rules 506, 505, and 504 exemptions from registration are considered restricted securities. Their resale may require registration. Rules requiring registration of these Regulation D securities prior to resale ensure that investors purchase these securities as an investment rather than for public distribution. When there is no attempt to make public distributions, investors ordinarily fit within one of several exemptions to registration upon resale. Generally, all restrictions expire after two years.

CPA   (E) LIABILITY. Issuers, sellers, and "aiders and abettors" may be subject to civil and criminal liability under the 1933 act.

CPA   *(1) Issuer's Civil Liability for False or Misleading Statements*

The Securities Act of 1933 imposes civil liability under section 11 for making materially false or misleading statements in a registration statement and for omitting any required material fact. An issuing company has virtually no defense if there has been a false statement and a loss.

CPA   *(2) Civil Liability of Sellers of Securities*

Section 12 of the 1933 act applies to those who "offer or sell" securities and employ any device or scheme to defraud or obtain money by means of untrue statements of material facts. This section makes such persons or firms liable to purchasers for damages sustained.

CPA   *(3) Criminal Liability*

Section 24 of the 1933 act imposes criminal penalties on anyone who willfully makes untrue statements of material facts or omits required material facts from a registration statement. Section 17 of the act makes it unlawful for any person to employ any device, scheme, or artifice to defraud in the offer or sale of securities.

6. Securities Exchange Act of 1934

The 1934 act deals with the secondary distribution of securities. It was designed to prevent fraudulent and manipulative practices on the security exchanges and in over-the-counter markets. The act requires the disclosure of information to buyers and sellers of the securities. Furthermore, the act controls credit in these markets.

CPA   (A) **Registration and Reporting Requirements.** Exchanges, brokers, and dealers who deal in securities traded in interstate commerce or on any national security exchange must register with the SEC unless exempted by it.

Companies whose securities are listed on a national securities exchange and unlisted companies with assets in excess of $10 million and 500 or more shareholders are subject to the reporting requirements of the act.[16]

CPA   ### (1) Principal Reports

Form 10-K is the principal annual report form used by commercial and industrial companies required to file under the 1934 act. The reports require nonfinancial information about the registrant's activities during the year, such as the nature of the firm's business, the property or businesses it owns, and a statement concerning legal proceedings by or against the company. The report requires the submission of financial statements with management's analysis of the financial condition of the company as well as a report and analysis of the performance of corporate shares. It requires a listing of all directors and executive officers and disclosure of executive compensation information.

Registrants who are required to file 10-K reports must also file quarterly reports, called *10-Q reports*. The 10-Q reports are principally concerned with financial information relevant to the quarterly period.

The SEC requires that annual shareholder reports be submitted to shareholders in any proxy solicitation on behalf of management. These reports contain essentially the same information as the 10-K.

CPA   ### (2) Certifications and Disclosure Controls

The Sarbanes-Oxley Act of 2002 requires written certification of the 10-K and 10-Q reports by each company's CEO and CFO, as set forth in section 302(a) of the act and shown in the following excerpt. A "knowing" misrepresentation in connection with the certification process is punishable by fine up to $1 million and imprisonment of up to 10 years. A "willful" misrepresentation in connection with the certification process is punishable by fine up to $5 million and imprisonment of up to 20 years.[17]

Section 302(a) of the act requires CEOs and CFOs to certify that:

(1) *the signing officer has reviewed the report;*
(2) *based on the officer's knowledge, the report does not contain any untrue statement of a material fact or omit to state a material fact necessary in order to make the statements made, in light of the circumstances under which such statements were made, not misleading;*
(3) *based on such officer's knowledge, the financial statements, and other financial information included in the report, fairly present in all material respects the financial condition and results of operations of the issuer as of, and for, the periods presented in the report;*
(4) *the signing officers—*
    (A) are responsible for establishing and maintaining internal controls....

[16] 61 FR 21354, 21356 (May 9, 1996).
[17] 18 USC § 1350(c).

The SEC considers information "material" if there is a substantial likelihood that it would have been viewed by a reasonable investor as having significantly altered the total mix of information made available and if a reasonable investor would have considered the fact important in making an investment decision. The SEC has recommended that each company organize key employees into a "disclosure committee" responsible for considering the "materiality" of information and the company's disclosure obligations. For example, any transactions with insiders should be carefully considered for SEC filings.

Before Sarbanes-Oxley, many public companies published pro forma (provided in advance) financial results in press releases before filing their official quarterly reports with the SEC. This approach allowed these companies to cast their "financials" in a favorable light. The SEC financial statements are prepared under a set of accounting conventions called *generally accepted accounting principles*, or GAAP. Pro forma financial results are not prepared using GAAP, and they may not provide a true and accurate picture of a company's financial status. Section 401 of the Sarbanes-Oxley Act instructed the SEC to issue rules requiring the presentation of pro forma financial statements in a manner that does not contain material misstatements or omit material facts and can be reconciled with financial results using GAAP. SEC Regulation G imposes a broad range of limitations on the use of pro forma results. If a company issues a press release saying that its pro forma earnings will be $5 million for the quarter when its official GAAP earnings will be just $4 million, the company will have to disclose both figures and explain what expenses were excluded from the pro forma figures and why.

CPA (B) ANTIFRAUD PROVISION. Section 10(b) of the 1934 act makes it unlawful for any person to use any manipulative or deceptive device in contravention of SEC rules. Under the authority of Section 10(b) of the 1934 act, the SEC has promulgated *Rule 10b-5*. This rule is the principal antifraud rule relating to the secondary distribution of securities. The rule states:

> *It shall be unlawful for any person, directly or indirectly, by use of any means or instrumentality of interstate commerce, or of the mails or of any facility of any national securities exchange,*
>
> *(a) To employ any device, scheme, or artifice to defraud,*
> *(b) To make any untrue statement of a material fact or to omit to state a material fact necessary in order to make the statements made, in the light of the circumstances under which they were made, not misleading, or*
> *(c) To engage in any act, practice, or course of business that operates or would operate as a fraud or deceit upon any person, in connection with the purchase or sale of any security.*[18]

CPA *(1) Private Actions*

Rule 10b-5 applies to all securities, whether registered or not, as long as use is made of the mail, interstate commerce, or a national stock exchange. Subject to the safe harbor provisions of the Private Securities Litigation Reform Act as discussed in the

---

[18] 17 CFR § 240.10b-5.

following section, under Rule 10b-5, a civil action for damages may be brought by any private investor who purchased or sold a security and was injured because of false, misleading, or undisclosed information.[19]

CPA *(2) Liability for "Material Misstatements or Omissions of Fact."*
Rule 10b-5 prohibits the making of any untrue statement of a "material" fact or the omission of a material fact necessary to render statements made not misleading. In every Rule 10b-5 case, the plaintiff must show "reliance" on the misrepresentation and resulting injury. **For Example,** First Derivatives Traders were allowed to proceed against Janus Capital Management under Section 10(b) regarding prospectuses for a number of the individual Janus funds. The prospectuses stated that the funds had policies of discouraging market timing and that the funds engaged in measures to deter such behavior. The plaintiffs alleged that in fact fund managers explicitly permitted market timing and late trading to occur, and that the misleading statements were one substantial factor in the decline of the funds' investments.[20]

In a merger context, "materiality" depends on the probability that the transaction will be consummated and on the significance to the issuer of the securities.[21] That is, "materiality" depends on the facts and must be determined on a case-by-case basis. **For Example,** assume that Corporation *A* was involved in merger discussions with Corporation *B*. During this time, Corporation *A* made public statements denying that any merger negotiations were taking place or that it knew of any corporate developments that would account for heavy trading activity in its stock. Corporation *A* may be held liable for damages to its shareholders who sold their stock after the public denial of merger activity and before a later merger announcement.

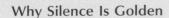

C A S E   S U M M A R Y

Why Silence Is Golden

FACTS: In December 1978, Combustion Engineering, Inc., and Basic Inc. agreed to merge. During the preceding two years, representatives of the two companies had meetings regarding the possibility of a merger. During this time, Basic made three public statements denying that any merger negotiations were taking place or that it knew of any corporate developments that would account for the heavy trading activity in its stock. Certain former shareholders who sold this stock between Basic's first public denial of merger activity and the public announcement of the merger brought a section 10(b) and Rule 10b-5 action against Basic and some of its directors. The former shareholders contended that Basic had made material misrepresentations in its public statements denying merger activity. Basic raised the defense that the alleged misrepresentations were not material and that there was no showing of reliance by the shareholders on Basic's statements.

[19] *Miller v Thane International, Inc.,* 519 F3d 879 (9th Cir 2008).
[20] *In re Mutual Funds Investment Litigation v Janus Capital Group,* 566 F3d 111 (4th Cir 2009). See also *SEC v Pentagon Capital Management, PLC,* 612 F Supp 2d 241 (SDNY 2009).
[21] See *Rizzo v The MacManus Group, Inc.,* 158 F Supp 2d 297 (SDNY 2001).

C A S E   S U M M A R Y

Continued

DECISION: The standard for materiality applicable to preliminary merger discussions is to be decided on a case-by-case basis depending on the probability that the transaction will be consummated and on its significance to the issuer. There is a presumption of reliance by the shareholders on the misstatements of the corporations. This presumption is supported by the policy of the 1934 act, which is to foster reliance on market integrity. However, the presumption may be rebutted by showing that the market price was not affected by the misrepresentation. The case is remanded for further proceedings consistent with this opinion. [**Basic Inc. v Levinson, 485 US 224 (1988)**]

CPA   (C) LITIGATION REFORM ACT. The Private Securities Litigation Reform Act (PSLRA, or the Litigation Reform Act) of 1995 was passed because of (1) congressional concern over an excess of frivolous private securities lawsuits, (2) the financial burdens placed on accountants and other professional advisors by such litigation, and (3) concern that the investors in a class-action lawsuit have their interests fairly represented. Important features of the act are as follows.

CPA   *(1) Safe Harbor Rules*
Issuers of securities frequently believed that lawsuits against them under Rule 10b-5 occurred simply because the corporation made a projection that failed to materialize. The Litigation Reform Act provides shelter for issuers from private liability for forward-looking statements that were not known to be false when made and that were accompanied by meaningful cautionary statements informing investors of contingencies that could cause results to differ from projected results.

To preserve the protections of the PSLRA, quarterly and annual reports to the SEC (Forms 10-Q and 10-K) and quarterly and annual reports to stockholders, as well as corporate press releases on financial matters, now commonly utilize the expression *forward-looking statements* regarding corporate statements that estimate or project the short-term and long-term outlook for a business. Moreover, these reports typically include a section entitled "Cautionary Statements" or "Risk Factors," and contain a statement such as:

> *Forward-looking statements as contained in this report involve a number of risks, including but not limited to product demand, pricing, market acceptance, supply problems, intellectual property rights and litigation, and risks in product and technology development.*

Corporations do not have to caution against every conceivable factor that may cause results to differ from the issuer's forward-looking statements. **For Example,** Ivax Corporation, a drug company, issued a press release including optimistic assumptions about future events. Attached to the release was an italicized warning that stated in specific detail the kinds of misfortunes that could befall Ivax and could cause results to differ from its forward-looking statements. This cautionary statement did not mention that a large goodwill writedown could occur; and when a writedown did occur, Ivax stock declined sharply. Harris, Wolpin, and others brought a Rule 10b-5 fraud suit against Ivax based on the omission of a warning about the writedown risk. The court held that the cautionary statements were sufficient to warn an investor of risks similar to that actually realized and the statements satisfied Ivax's burden to warn under the statute. Ivax was not required to list all risk factors, and the failure to mention one risk that in fact occurred did not "blow Ivax out of the safe harbor."[22]

CPA

(2) Litigation Reform

The Litigation Reform Act places a heightened pleading requirement on plaintiffs attempting to plead fraud in securities cases, and requires not only that the plaintiffs specify each statement alleged to have been false or misleading and the reason for the belief but also that the plaintiffs plead "scienter"—the mental state embracing intent to deceive, manipulate, or defraud.[23]

The Litigation Reform Act also provides for *proportionate liability*, as opposed to joint and several liability, for defendants who are found not to have knowingly committed a violation of the security laws. In addition, securities fraud is eliminated as a predicate for private RICO actions absent a prior criminal conviction. Under the act, frivolous private securities lawsuits require payment of the defendant's reasonable attorney fees.

CPA

(3) Class-Action Reforms

Reforms were necessary to protect against "lawyer-driven lawsuits" in which a class-action counsel would direct a "professional" plaintiff to buy a security to have standing to bring a class-action lawsuit. Thereafter, the class-action counsel would race to the courthouse to file before any other plaintiff and thus be able to claim enhanced standing to represent the class. The Litigation Reform Act provides that the status of lead plaintiff is offered to the person with the largest financial interest in the case, who then selects the lead counsel.

(4) Aiders and Abettors

In its *Central Bank of Denver*[24] decision, the U.S. Supreme Court ruled that a private investor may not bring an action under Section 10(b) of the 1934 act against "aiders and abettors" such as accountants, lawyers, and investment bankers who provide assistance to the primary violator. In enacting the Litigation Reform Act, Congress did not follow the then–SEC Chairman's recommendation that aiding and abetting liability in private claims be established in the act. Instead, Congress directed the SEC's prosecution of aiders and abettors. Courts, however, have

---

[22] *Harris v Ivax Corp.*, 182 F3d 799 (11th Cir 1999).

[23] In an October 26, 1999, Bloomberg Forum Conference Call, Lucent Technologies' CEO McGinn characterized Lucent as a market "leader" reaping "exceptionally strong growth in… optical networking" and described Lucent as growing at the same rate as the market (40 to 50 percent). After the conference call, Lucent stock moved from $59 per share to $80.62. The following year, however, the stock "tanked" to $2.19 a share, and investors who had purchased stock in 1999 and 2000 sued. In the fall of 1999, management e-mails acknowledged that the optical networking group was in "serious disrepair" and was up against a "revenue wall". The court determined that the plaintiffs were in compliance with the PSLRA and that McGinn's October 26, 1999, statement had not been "forward looking"—and that there were sufficient allegations to demonstrate that his statements had been misleading. Subsequently, the court approved a $610 million settlement of the case. *In Re Lucent Technologies Inc., Securities Litigation*, 307 F Supp 2d 633 (D NJ 2004).

[24] *Central Bank of Denver v First Interstate Bank of Denver*, 611 US 164 (1994).

affirmed a private cause of action under Section 10(b) with a rebuttable presumption of reliance on the defendant's deceptive acts (1) where there is an omission of a material fact by one who has a duty to disclose, or (2) under the **fraud-on-the-market** doctrine where reliance is presumed when the statements in question become public. The *Stoneridge Investments*[25] case is an example of "aiding and abetting" and the reluctance of the U.S. Supreme Court to expand the Section 10(b) private right of action where there was no duty to disclose and the deceptive acts were not communicated to the public.

fraud-on-the-market–a theory that in an open and developed securities market, the price of a stock is determined by the information on the company available to the public, and misleading statements will defraud purchasers of stock even if they do not directly rely on these statements.

C A S E   S U M M A R Y

The SEC Has an Exclusive on Aiders and Abettors!

FACTS: A class-action suit by investors (petitioners) was filed against Charter Communications, Inc. (Charter), a cable operator involved in a variety of fraudulent practices undertaken so that its quarterly reports would meet Wall Street expectations. The petitioners also named Scientific Atlanta and Motorola (respondents) as defendants, asserting a private right of action against these firms for damages under Section 10(b) of the 1934 act because their actions allowed Charter to mislead its auditor and issue misleading financial statements. Respondents Scientific Atlanta and Motorola were suppliers of cable converter boxes to Charter. In late 2000, Charter executives realized that the company would miss projected operating cash-flow numbers by $15 to $20 million. To help meet the shortfall, Charter arranged to overpay the respondents $20 for each set-top box it purchased—with the understanding that the respondents would return the overpayment by purchasing cable advertising from Charter. The transactions, it was alleged, had no economic substance; but, because Charter would then record the advertising purchases as revenue and capitalize its purchases of the set-top boxes—in violation of generally accepted accounting principles—the transactions would enable Charter to fool its auditor into approving a financial statement showing it met projected revenue and operating cash-flow numbers. The respondents agreed to the arrangement. Charter used the inflated number of $17 million on its financial statements that were filed with the SEC and reported to the public. The respondents had no role in preparing or disseminating Charter's financial statements, and their own statements booked the transactions as a wash. The Eighth Circuit ruled that the respondents were "aiders and abettors" and that the Section 10(b)–implied private right of action did not extend to them. The petitioners appealed to the U.S. Supreme Court.

DECISION: Judgment for Scientific Atlanta and Motorola. They had no role in preparing or disseminating the financial statements. Charter misled its auditor and filed the fraudulent financial statements. The respondents had no duty to disclose their transactions with Charter, and their deceptive acts were not communicated to the public. A court-created private cause of action could allow plaintiffs with weak cases to extort settlements from innocent companies through the disruption of extensive discovery and potential for uncertainty. Rather than a private right of action, Section 104 of the PSLRA allows the SEC to prosecute "aiders and abettors." [**Stoneridge Investment Partners, LLC v Scientific Atlanta, Inc., 552 U.S. 148 (2008)**]

---

25 *Stoneridge Investment Partners, LLC v Scientific Atlanta, Inc.,* 552 US 148 (2008).

CPA   *(5) Auditor Disclosure*

The Litigation Reform Act amends the 1934 act by requiring auditors who discover illegal acts to notify management and the board of directors and, in some cases, to notify the SEC if the issuer does not.[26] Auditors are relieved from liability for any such disclosure to the SEC.

CPA   *(6) Lawyer Reporting of Wrongdoing*

The ABA Model Rules of Professional Conduct, which serve as a basis for most states' ethics rules for lawyers, were revised in 2003 to free lawyers from their duty of confidentiality to those clients who use the lawyers' advice to commit a crime or fraud.[27] The ABA also revised its Model Rules to allow a lawyer who knows that an officer or employee of a corporation will likely harm the company to refer the matter to higher-up officials of the organization.[28]

7. Trading on Insider Information

Section 10(b) and Rule 10b-5 form a basis for imposing sanctions for trading on **insider information**. The Insider Trading and Securities Fraud Enforcement Act of 1988, which amended the 1934 act, gave the SEC authority to bring an action against an individual purchasing or selling a security while in possession of material inside information. The court may impose a civil penalty of up to three times the profit gained or loss avoided as a result of the unlawful sale. Persons who "aid or abet" in the violation may also be held liable under the act.

insider information– privileged information on company business only known to employees.

Under the 1988 insider trading act, "controlling persons," including employers whose lax supervision may allow employees to commit insider trading violations, are subject to civil penalties.[29] The SEC must prove "knowing" or "reckless" behavior by the controlling person. The 1988 law establishes bounty programs that allow the SEC to reward informants giving information on insider trading activity. The reward is up to 10 percent of any penalty imposed.

insider–full-time corporate employee or a director.

temporary insider– someone retained by a corporation for professional services on an as-needed basis, such as an attorney, accountant, or investment banker.

tippee–someone retained by a corporation for professional services on an as-needed basis, such as an attorney, accountant, or investment banker.

(A) TRADING BY INSIDERS AND TIPPEES. An **insider** may be a director or corporate employee. A **temporary insider** is someone retained by the corporation for professional services, such as an attorney, accountant, or investment banker. Insiders and temporary insiders are liable for inside trading when they fail to disclose material nonpublic information before trading on it and thus make a secret profit. A **tippee** is an individual who receives information from an insider or a temporary insider. A tippee is subject to the insider's fiduciary duty to shareholders when the insider has breached the fiduciary duty to shareholders by improperly disclosing the information to the tippee and when the tippee knows or should know there has been a breach.[30] Such a breach occurs when an insider benefits personally from her disclosure. When the insider does not breach a fiduciary duty, a tippee does not violate the securities laws.

---

[26] PL 104-671, 109 Stat 763, 15 USC § 78j-l nt.
[27] Model Rule 1.6, "Confidentiality of Information."
[28] Model Rule 1.13, "Organization as Client."
[29] PL 100-704, 102 Stat 4677, 15 USC § 78u-1(a)(2).
[30] *United States v Chestman, 974 F2d 564 (2d Cir 1991).*

CASE SUMMARY

No Secrets from Secrist!

FACTS: On March 6, 1973, Dirks, an investment analyst, received information from Secrist, a former officer of Equity Funding of America, alleging that the assets of Equity Funding were vastly overstated as the result of fraudulent corporate practices. On investigation by Dirks, certain corporation employees corroborated the charges of fraud. Neither Dirks nor his firm owned or traded any Equity Funding stock, but throughout his investigation, he openly discussed the information he had obtained with a number of clients and investors. The information from Dirks induced them to sell Equity Funding stock in excess of $16 million. On March 27, the New York Stock Exchange halted trading of Equity Funding stock, and a subsequent investigation revealed the vast fraud that had taken place. The SEC, investigating Dirks's role in the exposure of the fraud, claimed that Dirks had aided and abetted violations of the Securities Act of 1933, the Securities Exchange Act of 1934, and SEC Rule 10b-5 by repeating the allegations of fraud to members of the investment community who later sold their Equity Funding stock.

DECISION: Judgment for Dirks. Secrist, the insider, did not violate any fiduciary duty to shareholders when he disclosed information about the fraudulent practices to the tippee, Dirks. Secrist received no monetary or personal benefit for the information but was motivated by the desire to expose the fraud. Because the insider did not breach his fiduciary duty when he gave nonpublic information to Dirks, Dirks breached no duty when he passed the information on to investors. [**Dirks v SEC, 463 US 646 (1983)**]

(B) **MISAPPROPRIATORS.** Individuals who misappropriate or steal valuable non-public information in breach of a fiduciary duty to their employer and trade in securities on that information are guilty of insider trading as "misappropriators." **For Example,** an employee working for a financial printing firm was found guilty of insider trading under section 10(b) and Rule 10b-5.[31] While proofreading a financial document being prepared for a client firm, he figured out the identity of tender offer targets. Soon after that, he traded on this valuable nonpublic information to his advantage.

It is no defense to a section 10(b) and Rule 10b-5 criminal charge of participating in a "scheme to defraud" that the victim of the fraud (an employer) had no economic interest in the securities traded. The convictions of a stockbroker and a columnist for the *Wall Street Journal* were upheld under section 10(b) of the 1934 act. The columnist violated his fiduciary duty to his employer by revealing prepublication information about his column to the stockbroker. The stockbroker then used the information to trade in the securities identified in the column.[32]

Where an individual misappropriates confidential information for security trading purposes in breach of a fiduciary duty owed to the source of the information rather than to the shareholders who sold securities to the individual, that individual may be convicted of security fraud in violation of section 10(b) and Rule 10b-5.

[31] *SEC v Materia*, 745 F2d 197 (2d Cir 1984).
[32] *Carpenter v United States*, 484 US 19 (1987).

C A S E   S U M M A R Y

The Case of the Dastardly Misappropriator

FACTS: James O'Hagan was a partner in the law firm of Dorsey & Whitney in Minneapolis, Minnesota. In July 1988, Grand Metropolitan PLC, a company based in London, England, retained Dorsey & Whitney as local counsel to represent Grand Met regarding a potential tender offer for the common stock of the Pillsbury Company headquartered in Minneapolis. O'Hagan did no work on the Grand Met representation. Dorsey & Whitney withdrew from representing Grand Met on September 9, 1988. Less than a month later, on October 4, 1988, Grand Met publicly announced its tender offer for Pillsbury stock. Previously, on August 18, 1988, while Dorsey & Whitney was still representing Grand Met, O'Hagan began purchasing call options for Pillsbury stock. Each option gave him the right to purchase 100 shares of Pillsbury stock by a specified date in September 1988. Later in August and September, O'Hagan purchased additional Pillsbury call options. By the end of September, he owned 2,500 unexpired Pillsbury options, apparently more than any other individual investor. O'Hagan also purchased, in September 1988, some 5,000 shares of Pillsbury common stock at a price just under $39 per share. When Grand Met announced its tender offer in October, the price of Pillsbury stock rose to nearly $60 per share. O'Hagan then sold his Pillsbury call options and common stock, making a profit of more than $4.3 million. O'Hagan was charged and convicted of securities fraud in violation of section 10(b) and Rule 10b-5. On appeal, he claimed that he was not a "misappropriator," for he had no fiduciary duty to the Pillsbury shareholders from whom he purchased calls and stock; in fact, he had not even worked on the transaction at the law firm.

DECISION: Judgment against O'Hagan. "Misappropriation" requires that there be "deceptive" conduct "in connection with" a securities transaction. A fiduciary who pretends loyalty to the principal while secretly converting the principal's information for personal gain dupes or defrauds the principal. O'Hagan's failure to disclose his personal trading to his law firm and its client, Grand Met, was a breach of his fiduciary duty and was "deceptive" conduct "in connection with" a securities transaction. The misappropriation theory is designed to protect the integrity of the securities market against "outsiders" like O'Hagan, who have access to confidential information that will affect a company's stock price when revealed but have no fiduciary or other duty to the company's shareholders. [**United States v O'Hagan, 521 US 657 (1997)**]

(C) REGULATION **FD.** Effective October 23, 2000, the SEC adopted a new rule, Regulation FD (Fair Disclosure), to end the practice of selective disclosure by issuers of securities to security analysts and selected institutional investors of important nonpublic information, such as advance warnings of negative or positive earnings results, before disclosing the information to the general public. Those privy to the early release of the information had been able to make a profit or avoid a loss at the expense of the uniformed general public. For example, uninformed investors may have watched the price of XYZ Corporation fall from $47 a share to $32 a share over two days only to find out later in a subsequently disseminated general press release by the corporation that "earnings will not meet street estimates." Analysts with prior knowledge of the negative earnings reports were able to take action before the public was informed. Regulation FD requires that any disclosure be a public disclosure by filing Form 8-K or other disclosures to the public, including use of the Internet to broadly disseminate information.[33] **For Example,** when Kenneth Lewis, CEO of Bank of America, speaks to a group of investment analysts about his company at a Wall Street meeting, Bank of America may broadcast the talk over the Web and issue a press release summarizing Lewis' comments to comply with Regulation FD.

(D) **REMEDY FOR INVESTORS.** Investors who lack the inside information possessed by the insider and sell their stock during the relevant time period may recover damages from any insider who made use of undisclosed information. Recovery is by a civil action based on Rule 10b-5.

8. Disclosure of Ownership and Short-Swing Profits

Corporate directors and officers owning equity securities in their corporation and any shareholder owning more than 10 percent of any class of the corporation's equity securities are statutorily defined as insiders and must file with the SEC a disclosure statement regarding such ownership and all related transactions. This is required under section 16(a) of the 1934 act. Under section 403(a) of the Sarbanes-Oxley Act of 2002 and effective July 30, 2003, by SEC rule, these individuals must electronically report transactions in company stock to the SEC by the second business day after the transaction. Moreover, the transaction must be posted on the SEC's and the company's Web sites within one day after the filing date.

Section 16 is designed to prevent the unfair use of information available to these corporate insiders. This section prevents insiders from participating in short-term trading in their corporation's securities.

If such a person sells at a profit any of these securities less than six months after their purchase, the profit is called a **short-swing profit**. Under section 16(b), the corporation may sue a director, officer, or major stockholder for a short-swing profit.[34] The corporation may recover that profit even without a fraudulent intent in acquiring and selling the securities.

short-swing profit–profit realized by a corporate insider from selling securities less than six months after purchase.

9. Tender Offers

A corporation or group of investors may seek to acquire control of another corporation by making a general offer to all shareholders of the target corporation to purchase their shares for cash at a specified price. This is called a **cash tender offer**. The offer to purchase is usually contingent on the tender of a fixed number of shares sufficient to ensure takeover. The bid price is ordinarily higher than the prevailing market price. Should more shares be tendered than the offeror is willing to purchase, the tender offeror must purchase shares from each shareholder on a pro rata basis.

cash tender offer–general offer to all shareholders of a target corporation to purchase their shares for cash at a specified price.

The Williams Act, which amended the 1934 act,[35] was passed to ensure that public shareholders who are confronted with a cash tender offer will not be required to act without adequate information. Under section 14(d) of the Williams Act, a

---

[33] 17 CFR § 240.10b5-1.
[34] *Levy v Southbrook International Investments, Ltd.*, 263 F3d 10 (2d Cir 2001); *Donaghue v Natural Microsystems Corp.*, 198 F Supp 2d 487 (SDNY 2002).
[35] PL 90-439, 82 Stat 454, 15 USC § 78m(d), (e).

person making a tender offer must file appropriate SEC forms. These forms provide information about the background and identity of the person filing, the source of funds used to make stock purchases, the amount of stock beneficially owned, the purpose of the purchases, any plan the purchaser proposes to follow if it gains control over the target corporation, and any contracts or understandings that it has with other persons concerning the target corporation.[36]

Section 14(e) of the Williams Act is the antifraud section. It prohibits fraudulent, deceptive, or manipulative practices. SEC Rule 14e-1 requires any tender offer to remain open for a minimum of 20 business days from the date it is first published or given to security holders. Federal and state legislation, as well as administrative regulation, is aimed at requiring disclosure of information and allowance of a reasonable length of time for consideration of the facts. These requirements are designed to make agreement to takeovers the result of voluntary action based on full knowledge of material facts.

As far as the courts are concerned, takeovers must be regarded with a neutral eye. If there is misrepresentation or other misconduct, the law will interfere. Otherwise, freedom of contract requires that courts not interfere with the judgment of the contracting parties.

10. Regulation of Accountants and Attorneys by the SEC

Accountants play a vital role in financial reporting under the federal securities laws administered by the SEC. Sections 1, 12, 17, and 24 of the 1933 act and section 10 (b) of the 1934 act are the sections under which accountants may be subject to liability.

An accountant who prepares any statement, opinion, or other legal paper filed with the SEC with the preparer's consent is deemed to be practicing before the SEC. Because it relies so heavily on accountants, the SEC has promulgated Rule 2(e), which regulates and provides the basis for discipline of accountants, attorneys, and consultants who practice before the SEC.[37] Under Rule 2(e), the SEC may suspend or disbar from practice before it those who are unqualified or unethical or who have violated federal securities laws or SEC rules.[38]

Section 307 of the Sarbanes-Oxley Act explicitly requires the SEC to establish minimum standards of professional conduct for attorneys practicing before the SEC in the representation of publicly held companies. The act and SEC rules require that attorneys report evidence of material violations of securities laws, up the chain of command, to the companies' general counsel, CEO, audit committees, or the full board of directors.

---

[36] Section 14(d) requires a filing by any person making a tender offer that, if successful, would result in the acquisition of 5 percent of any class of an equity security required to be registered under the 1934 act. Section 13(d) of the act requires disclosure to the issuer, the SEC, and the appropriate stock exchange when a person acquires 5 percent of a class of equity security through stock purchases on exchanges or through private purchases. The person may have acquired the stock for investment purposes, not for control but must still file disclosure forms under §13(d). See *SEC v Bilzerian*, 814 F Supp 116 (DDC 1993). Section 14(d) applies only to shares to be acquired by tender offer.

[37] 17 CFR § 201.2e.

[38] Rule 2(e) provides: "Suspension and disbarment. (1) The Commission may deny, temporarily or permanently, the privilege of appearing or practicing before it in any way to any person who is found by the Commission after notice of an opportunity for hearing in the matter (i) not to possess the requisite qualifications to represent others, or (ii) to be lacking in character or integrity or to have engaged in unethical or improper professional conduct, or (iii) to have willfully violated, or willfully aided and abetted, the violation of any provision of the federal securities laws (15 USC §§ 77a to 80B-20), or the rules and regulations thereunder." 17 CFR § 201.2e.

e-commerce&cyberlaw

Douglas Colt was a second-year law student who developed a way to make money from the Internet. He set up a free Web site promising folks hot tips on stocks. However, Colt bought the stocks himself at low prices before pumping them up at his Web site. Once the shares were pumped up to a high enough price from the users of his Web site buying the shares, he would then sell all of his shares (i.e., dump them). Colt made more than $345,000 using the old tool of "pump-and-dump".

Colt had attracted 9,000 investors to his Web site (Fast-Trades.com). One of his shares, American Education Corporation, climbed 700 percent before he sold his holdings.

Those who participated in the pump-and-dump scam, including Colt's mother, a councilwoman from Colorado, agreed to a consent decree settlement. None will pay a fine and none will repay their profits. They have simply agreed not to violate federal securities laws in the future. Georgetown University, Colt's law school, said there will be no disciplinary action.

Did Colt violate insider trading laws or any federal securities laws?

Was Colt's conduct ethical?

Enforcement on insider trading has been on the increase. The SEC has created a new group, called its Cyberforce, to deal specifically with insider trading over the Internet.

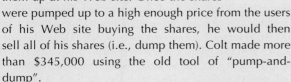 C. INDUSTRY SELF-REGULATION

The National Association of Securities Dealers (NASD) is a self-regulatory organization guided by procedural and conduct rules. It seeks to detect misconduct of regulated persons and firms, and may issue appropriate sanctions as a means of protecting investors. The sanctions are subject to SEC review and thereafter review by the U.S. Court of Appeals. **For Example,** PAZ Securities, Inc., and its president, Joseph Mizrachi, repeatedly failed to provide information requested by the NASD under its rules. The SEC affirmed the NASD's default judgment expelling PAZ and also barring Mizrachi from ever associating with an NASD member. The U.S. Court of Appeals ultimately upheld the SEC's sanctions since failure to respond is a significant harm to the self-regulatory system because it undermines the NASD's ability to detect misconduct.[39] Subsequently, the NASD and the New York Stock Exchange merged their member regulation functions into one self-regulatory organization, the Financial Industry Regulatory Authority (FINRA).

11. Arbitration of Securities Disputes

NASD member firms have adopted a code of arbitration that allows customers of NASD members to submit disputes to arbitration. The arbitration rights are contractual and are set forth in writing on opening an account with a dealer.

---

[39] *PAZ Securities, Inc. v SEC*, 566 F3d 1172 (DC Cir 2009).

Securities firms with seats on the New York Stock Exchange have a similar arbitration code. Parties who have agreed to arbitrate their securities disputes can be compelled to arbitrate rather than sue in courts.[40] Courts are very reluctant to vacate an arbitration award.

CASE SUMMARY

The Sting of Justice—Punitive Damages

FACTS: In 1985, petitioners Antonio Mastrobuono, then an assistant professor of medieval literature, and his wife, Diane Mastrobuono, an artist, opened a securities trading account with respondent Shearson Lehman Hutton, Inc. (SLH), by executing Shearson's standard client's agreement form. Respondent Nick DiMinico, a vice president of SLH, managed the Mastrobuonos' account until they closed it. The Mastrobuonos sued SLH for the fraudulent conduct of DiMinico, and the matter was referred to arbitration under NASD rules. A panel of three arbitrators convened hearings in Chicago, Illinois, where the Mastrobuonos lived, and the panel awarded them $115,274 for commissions and $44,053 for margin interest "as satisfaction for their claims." The panel also awarded them $400,000 as punitive damages. SLH refused to pay the punitive damages and was able to get this portion of the award vacated in a federal court action that was affirmed on appeal to the U.S. Court of Appeals for the Seventh Circuit. Under the terms of the customer agreement, the agreement was to be "governed by the laws of the State of New York," and disputes between the broker-dealer and the customer were to be "settled by arbitration" conducted under NASD rules. New York decisional law follows the "*Garrity* rule," which prohibits arbitrators from awarding punitive damages even in cases when courts may award such damages. By contrast, NASD arbitration rules anticipate that arbitrators will award a broad range of relief, including punitive damages. The Supreme Court decided to hear the case because of differing views held by the courts of appeals.

DECISION: Judgment for the Mastrobuonos. NASD's Code of Arbitration Procedure indicated that arbitrators may award "damages and other relief," and a manual provided to NASD arbitrators recognizes that "arbitrators may consider punitive damages as a remedy." The arbitration award should have been fully enforced, including the award for punitive damages. [**Mastrobuono v Shearson Lehman Hutton, 514 US 52 (1995)**]

lawflix

Wall Street (1987) (R)

This movie will walk you through not just the evolution of greed but the evolution of a young broker moving from gathering information to stealing it to obtaining it through insiders. The movie chronicles the market's regulations as well as an individual's loss of values.

For movie clips that illustrate business law concepts, see LawFlix at **www.cengage.com/blaw/dvl**.

---

[40] *99 Commercial Street, Inc. v Goldberg*, 811 F Supp 900 (SDNY 1992).

MAKE THE CONNECTION

SUMMARY

State blue sky laws, which apply only to intrastate transactions, protect the public from the sale of fraudulent securities. The term *security* is defined sufficiently broadly to encompass not only stocks and bonds but also any conceivable type of corporate interest that has investment characteristics.

Two principal laws provide the basic framework for federal regulation of the sale of securities in interstate commerce. The Securities Act of 1933 deals with the issue or original distribution of securities by issuing corporations. The Securities Exchange Act of 1934 regulates the secondary distribution or sale of securities on exchanges. These acts are administered by the Securities and Exchange Commission. Except for certain private and limited offerings, the 1933 act requires that a registration statement be filed with the SEC and that a prospectus be provided to each potential purchaser. Criminal and civil penalties exist for fraudulent statements made in this process. The 1934 act provides reporting requirements for companies whose securities are listed on a national exchange and unlisted companies that have assets in excess of $10 million and 500 or more shareholders.

Rule 10b-5 is the principal antifraud rule under the 1934 act. Trading on "inside information" is unlawful and may subject those involved to a civil penalty of three times the profit made on the improperly disclosed information. Cash tender offers are regulated by the SEC under authority of the Williams Act. The securities industry provides arbitration procedures to resolve disputes between customers and firms.

LEARNING OUTCOMES

After studying this chapter, you should be able to clearly explain:

A. STATE REGULATION

LO.1 Explain the meaning of state "blue sky laws"

> See the discussion of the common-content features of state securities laws such as antifraud provisions, licensing provisions, and regulation of securities on p. 1084.

B. FEDERAL REGULATION

LO.2 Define "security"

> See the *Edwards* case as an example of the broad definition of *security* sufficient to encompass virtually any instrument that might be sold as an investment, p. 1087.

LO.3 Compare and distinguish between the Securities Act of 1933 and the Securities Exchange Act of 1934

> See the discussion regarding the regulation of the original issue of securities, beginning on p. 1087.
>
> See the discussion regarding the secondary distribution of securities designed to prevent fraudulent and manipulative practices on the securities exchanges, beginning on p. 1091.

LO.4 ▶ Explain the factors that subject an individual to liability for insider trading
See the *Dirks* case that illustrates the rule that when the insider does not breach a fiduciary duty, a tippee does not violate securities laws, p. 1099. See the *O'Hagan* case regarding outsiders who have access to confidential information that will affect a company's stock price, p. 1100.

LO.5 ▶ Explain how securities firms regulate themselves and provide a process to resolve controversies relating to the sale of securities
See the discussion on the NASD and NYSE regulatory procedures and arbitration codes beginning on p. 1103.

KEY TERMS

blue sky laws	insider information	security
cash tender offer	prospectus	short-swing profit
fraud-on-the-market	registration requirements	temporary insider
insider	registration statement	tippee

QUESTIONS AND CASE PROBLEMS

1. What is the major distinction between the Securities Act of 1933 and the Securities Exchange Act of 1934?

2. On what rationale does the SEC allow the private placement of securities with accredited investors without any limitation on the amount that may be raised?

3. *Business Week* magazine is sent to a national distributor of magazines, Curtis Circulations Co., which sells the magazines to various wholesalers, including Hudson News. *Business Week* publishes a column entitled "Inside Wall Street," and the evidence shows that stocks discussed favorably in the column tend to increase in value after release to the public. *Business Week* has a strict confidentiality policy prior to release of the magazine to the public applicable to all employees involved in production and distribution. This policy also applies to Hudson News. Gregory Savage, an employee of Hudson News, and the "top person" in the delivery room area, arranged to have the "Inside Wall Street" column faxed to his neighbor, a stockbroker named Larry Strath, prior to the close of the market on Thursday and prior to release to the public that evening. Strath traded on the information and passed it on to Joseph Falcone, who likewise traded on the basis of this information. While Falcone paid Strath $200 for a copy of the column each week, he contends that the information he received was too remote from the *Business Week* confidentiality policy to be actionable by the SEC. What theory do you believe the SEC pursued against Falcone? What are the elements of the theory? How would you decide this case? [*United States v Falcone* 257 F3d 226 (2d Cir)]

4. Minnesota Prostate Research Labs, Inc. (MPRL), made an initial public offering of its shares in August 1998. It stated in its prospectus that research on laboratory animals indicated that the lab may have discovered a cure for prostate cancer in humans. MPRL pointed out as well that results in animal testing did not necessarily mean that the same positive result would occur in humans. MPRL shares initially traded at $10 per share in 1999 and rose to $18 in August 2001, when the MPRL prostate cancer drug was finally approved for sale to the public. Tuttle reviewed the initial prospectus and analysts' reports on the drug and purchased 10,000 shares at $18 per share on August 18, 2001. In September of 2002, an independent study of the four leading prostate medicines indicated that MPRL's product was as effective as sugar pills in curing prostate cancer and other prostate symptoms. The price of MPRL shares plummeted to $6 per share. Tuttle is contemplating a Rule 10b-5 securities fraud class-action lawsuit against MPRL. Advise him of his chances of success in this lawsuit and any expenses that he would be exposed to other than the cost of his attorney.

5. The following transactions in Heritage Cosmetics Co., Inc., stock took place: On January 21, Jones, the corporation's vice president of marketing, purchased 1,000 shares of stock at $25 per share. On January 24, Sylvan, a local banker and director of Heritage, purchased 500 shares of stock at $26 per share. On January 30, McCarthy, a secretary at Heritage, purchased 300 shares of stock at $26.50. On February 12, Winfried, a rich investor from New England, purchased 25,000 shares at an average price of $26 per share. At that time, Heritage had a total of 200,000 shares of stock outstanding. On June 14, Winfried sold his entire holding in Heritage at an average price of $35 per share. In a local newspaper interview, Winfried was quoted regarding his reasons for selling the stock: "I have not had the pleasure of meeting any person from Heritage, but I have the highest regard for the Heritage Company, ... I sold my stock simply because the market has gone too high and in my view is due for a correction." After independently reading Winfried's prediction on the stock market, Jones, Sylvan, and McCarthy sold their shares on June 15 for $33 per share. On June 20, Heritage Co. demanded that Jones, Sylvan, McCarthy, and Winfried pay the corporation the profits made on the sale of the stock. Was the corporation correct in making such a demand on each of these people?

6. Dorozhko hacked into the corporate network of Thomson Financial on October 17, 2007 at 2:15 P.M. and gained access to IMS Health's soon-to-be-released negative earnings announcement due out at 5:00 P.M. He purchased $41,670 worth of put options. IMS shares were trading at $29.56 at the close on October 17. On October 18, 2007, IMS Health's stock price plunged at the opening of trading to $21.20 per share, on the negative news issued at 5:00 P.M. on October 17. Within six minutes, Dorozhko sold the put options for a net profit of $286,456. Did Dorozhko's "hacking and trading" violate either the traditional or misappropriation theories of "insider trading"?

7. Mary Dale worked in the law office of Emory Stone, an attorney practicing securities law. While proofreading Mary's keying of a document relating to the

merger of two computer software companies, Emory joked to her, "If I weren't so ethical, I could make a few bucks on this info. Nomac Software stock prices are going to take off when this news hits 'The Street.'" That evening, Mary told her friend Rick Needleworth, a stockbroker, what her boss had said. Needleworth bought 500 shares of Nomac Software stock the next day and sold it three days later when the news of the merger was made public. He made a profit of $3,500. Did Dale, Stone, or Needleworth violate any securities law(s) or ethical principles with respect to the profit made by Needleworth?

8. International Advertising, Inc. (IA), would like to raise $10 million in new capital to open new offices in eastern Europe. It believes it could raise the capital by selling shares of stock to its directors and executive officers as well as to its bank and a large insurance company whose home office is located near IA's headquarters. Opposition to the financing plan exists because of the trouble, time, and cost involved with registering with the SEC. Advise IA how best to proceed with the registration of the new issue of stock.

9. Dubois sold Hocking a condominium that included an option to participate in a rental pool arrangement. Hocking elected to participate in the arrangement. Under it, the rental pool's agent rented condominiums, pooled the income, and after deducting a management fee, distributed the income to the owners on a pro rata basis. Hocking brought a Rule 10b-5 fraud action against Dubois. Dubois contended that the sale of the condominium was not a security under the securities acts, so Hocking could not bring a securities suit against her. Was Dubois correct? [*Hocking v Dubois*, 839 F2d 290 (9th Cir)]

10. William Rubin, president of Tri-State Mining Co., sought a loan from Bankers Trust Co. To secure the loan, he pledged worthless stock in six companies and represented that the stock was worth $1.7 million. He also arranged for fictitious quotations to appear in an investment reporting service used by the bank to value the pledged securities. The bank loaned Rubin $475,000 and took the securities as pledged collateral. In a criminal action against Rubin under section 17(a) of the 1933 act, Rubin's defense was that the pledging of securities did not constitute an offer or sale of securities under the act. Was Rubin correct? [*Rubin v United States*, 449 US 424]

11. J. C. Cowdin, a director of Curtis-Wright Co., phoned Robert Gintel, a partner of Cady, Roberts & Co., a stock brokerage house, and advised him that Curtis-Wright's quarterly dividend had been cut. Gintel immediately entered orders selling Curtis-Wright shares for his customers' accounts. The stock was selling at over $40 a share when the orders were executed but fell to $30 soon after the dividend cut was announced to the public. The SEC contended that the firm, Cady, Roberts & Co., and Gintel violated section 10(b) of the 1934 act, Rule 10b-5, and section 17(a) of the 1933 act. Gintel and Cady, Roberts & Co. disagreed. Decide. [*In re Cady, Roberts & Co.*, 40 SEC 907]

12. In a January 2000 prospectus for its initial public offering of shares, Apex Oil Discovery Co. (AODC) estimated a sizable volume of oil production based on the studies of two geologists and a test well at one of its Oklahoma properties.

A cautionary statement advised that the projections were only estimates based on the opinion of the two experts and a test well, and that actual production could vary significantly. Lutz bought 10,000 shares of Apex in May 2000 for $20 per share. By October 2000, 12 of its 15 drilling operations under way that year turned out to be dry holes. On October 18, 2000, AODC stock fell to $6 per share. Lutz brought a private securities civil action under SEC Rule 10b-5 against AODC, alleging that the AODC oil production estimates that induced him to buy the stock were fraudulent as evidenced by the 80 percent failure rate of its drilling operations. What defense, if any, does AODC have in this case? Decide.

13. Douglas Hansen, Leo Borrell, and Bobby Lawrence were three psychiatrists who recognized the need for an inpatient treatment facility for adolescents and children in their community. They became limited partners in building a for-profit psychiatric facility. Each had a 6.25 percent interest in the partnership. Healthcare International, Inc., the general partner with a 75 percent interest, had expertise in hospital construction, management, and operation. Hansen, Borrell, and Lawrence asserted that the managerial control of the partnership was undertaken and operated by the general partner to the exclusion of the limited partners. The doctors claimed that their interest was a security—"an investment contract"—that gave them status to file a securities suit against the general partner under the 1934 act. The general partner disagreed. Decide. [*L & B Hospital Ventures, Inc. v Health-care International, Inc.*, 894 F2d 150 (5th Cir)]

14. Texas International Speedway, Inc. (TIS), filed a registration statement and prospectus with the Securities and Exchange Commission offering a total of $4,398,900 in securities to the public. The proceeds of the sale were to be used to finance the construction of an automobile speedway. The entire issue was sold on the offering date. TIS did not meet with success, and the corporation filed a petition for bankruptcy. Huddleston and Bradley instituted a class-action suit in U.S. district court on behalf of themselves and other purchasers of TIS securities. Their complaint alleged violations of section 10 (b) of the 1934 act. The plaintiffs sued most of the participants in the offering, including the accounting firm of Herman & MacLean. Herman & MacLean had issued an opinion concerning certain financial statements and a pro forma balance sheet that were contained in the registration statement and prospectus. The plaintiffs claimed that the defendants had engaged in a fraudulent scheme to misrepresent or conceal material facts regarding the financial condition of TIS, including the costs incurred in building the speedway. Herman & MacLean contended that the case should be dismissed because section 11 of the 1933 act provides an express remedy for a misrepresentation in a registration statement, so an action under section 10(b) of the 1934 act is precluded. Decide. [*Herman & MacLean v Huddleston*, 459 US 375]

15. Melvin J. Ford, president of International Loan Network, Inc. (ILN), promoted ILN's financial enrichment programs to ILN members and prospective

members with evangelical fervor at revival-style "President's Night" gatherings. His basic philosophy was this:

The movement of money creates wealth. What we believe is that if you organize people and get money moving, it can actually create wealth.

One ILN program was the Maximum Consideration Program, which, somewhat like a chain letter, provided $5,000 awards to members who sold $3,000 worth of new memberships called PRAs and made a deposit on the purchases of nonresidential real estate. According to Ford, an individual purchasing $16,000 worth of PRAs could receive an award of up to $80,000 because "all of a sudden the velocity of money increases to such a point, the ability to create wealth expands to such a degree, that we could come back and give somebody an award for up to $80,000." The SEC contended that ILN was selling unregistered investment contracts in violation of the 1933 act. ILN disagreed, contending that the program never guaranteed a return and was thus not an investment contract. Decide. Could ILN have provided full disclosure to investors concerning the program in a prospectus if required by the 1933 act? [*SEC v ILN, Inc.*, 968 F2d 1304 (DC Cir)]

CPA QUESTIONS

1. Which of the following is least likely to be considered a security under the Securities Act of 1933?

   a. Stock options

   b. Warrants

   c. General partnership interests

   d. Limited partnership interests

2. Which of the following statements is correct regarding a common stock offering that requires registration under the Securities Act of 1933?

   a. The registration statement is automatically effective when filed with the SEC.

   b. The issuer would act unlawfully if it were to sell the common stock without providing the investor with a prospectus.

   c. The SEC will determine the investment value of the common stock before approving the offering.

   d. The issuer may make sales 10 days after filing the registration statement.

3. Hamilton Corp. is making a $4,500,000 securities offering under Rule 505 of Regulation D of the Securities Act of 1933. Under this regulation, Hamilton is:

   a. Required to provide full financial information to accredited investors only

   b. Allowed to make the offering through a general solicitation

   c. Limited to selling to no more than 35 nonaccredited investors

   d. Allowed to sell to an unlimited number of investors both accredited and nonaccredited

4. Under the liability provisions of Section 11 of the Securities Act of 1933, an auditor may help to establish the defense of due diligence if:

   I. The auditor performed an additional review of the audited statements to ensure that the statements were accurate as of the effective date of a registration statement

   II. The auditor complied with GAAS

   a. I only

   b. II only

   c. Both I and II

   d. Neither I nor II

5. Under the Securities Exchange Act of 1934, which of the following conditions generally will allow an issuer of securities to terminate the registration of a class of securities and suspend the duty to file periodic reports?

	The corporation has fewer than 300 shareholders	The securities are listed on a national securities exchange
a.	Yes	Yes
b.	Yes	No
c.	No	Yes
d.	No	No

Chapter 47

ACCOUNTANTS' LIABILITY AND MALPRACTICE

hen is a professional, such as an accountant, liable for harm caused by improper performance?

A. General Principles of Accountants' Liability

Whether an accountant can be held liable for malpractice requires a look at what constitutes malpractice, the effect of the others' conduct on liability, whether there are limitations on such liability, and whether there are damages that resulted from malpractice.

1. What Constitutes Malpractice?

An accountant who makes a contract to perform services has a duty to exercise the skill and care that are common for the accounting profession.[1] If the services are not rendered in accordance with those standards, the result is **malpractice**, as it is commonly called, which is a tort and a form of negligence.

Accountants are not insurers of the content of financial statements they prepare and, unless they agree to do so, are not normally liable for detecting fraud.[2] Changes made under Sarbanes-Oxley (covered later in the chapter), require accountants who perform audit work to undertake the role of certifying the internal controls of companies. This certification requirement was imposed with the hope that adequate internal controls can prevent fraud.[3] An accountant can, however, be held liable for turning a blind eye to suspicious issues and items.[4]

The standards for accountants' professional liability are found in state and federal statutes (See Chapter 46 for a discussion of federal securities issues, liabilities, and standards), court decisions, the actual contract with the client, generally accepted auditing standards (GAAS), and generally accepted accounting practices (GAAP).[5] Following GAAP and GAAS is persuasive but not conclusive evidence of meeting standards for the profession. Customs in any profession are persuasive but not conclusive evidence of professional performance.

Recovery from an accountant for malpractice requires proof of the elements of negligence (See Chapter 9 for more information). The duty and breach of duty elements are determined by the professional performance standards. The breach of professional standards must have caused the losses or damages, which must also be established.

Certified public accountants are liable for damages proximately caused by their negligence, or their failure to observe sound accounting practices. Accountants owe their clients a duty to exercise the degree of care, skill, and competence that

malpractice—practice that occurs when services are not properly rendered in accordance with commonly accepted standards; negligence by a professional in performing his or her skill.

---

[1] *AIG v Greenberg*, 965 A2d 763 (Del 2009).
[2] *In re Countrywide Litigation*, 588 F Supp 2d 1132 (CD Cal 2009).
[3] Section 404 of Sarbanes-Oxley has become a day-to-day term in business language as companies work to obtain their "404 certifications" from auditors. Securities and Exchange Commission, MANAGEMENT'S REPORTS ON INTERNAL CONTROLS OVER FINANCIAL REPORTING AND CERTIFICATION IN EXCHANGE ACT PERIODIC REPORTS, Securities Act Release No. 33-8283 (June 5, 2003).
[4] *In re MoneyGram Intern., Inc.* Securities Litigation, 626 F Supp 2d 947 (WD Minn 2009).
[5] *SEC v Chester Holdings, Ltd.*, 41 F Supp 2d 505 (DNJ 1999).

reasonably competent members of their profession would exercise under similar circumstances.[6] Accountants are also liable if they fail to call attention to a condition that causes losses if the client could have taken preventive steps following the accountant's warning.[7]

An accountant is liable to the client if the accountant negligently fails to detect or fraudulently conceals signs that an employee of the client is embezzling or the internal audit controls of the client's business are not being observed or are lax. An accountant who prepares tax returns and acts as tax manager for the client will be liable when additional taxes or penalties are assessed against the client as a result of the accountant's negligent advice. For example, a client may recover damages from the accountant when the accountant negligently fails to inform the client of the tax consequences of selling the business.[8]

CASE SUMMARY

This is Interesting—You Owe Me

FACTS: Bruce Ashland is a certified public accountant. He began providing services for Doug O'Bryan Contracting in 1987–1988. From 1979 through the first quarter of 1995, O'Bryan operated as a sole proprietorship. O'Bryan's well-drilling business prospered and grew during the early 1990s. On several occasions over the years, Ashland recommended to O'Bryan that he incorporate. O'Bryan ultimately followed Ashland's advice and incorporated effective April 1, 1995.

For taxation purposes, incorporating in April meant that O'Bryan remained a cash basis taxpayer for the first quarter of the year, January 1, 1995, through March 31, 1995. Then, on incorporation, the business changed to accrual basis accounting for the last three quarters, April 1, 1995, through December 31, 1995. When Ashland prepared O'Bryan's 1995 tax return in October 1996, he mistakenly calculated O'Bryan's income for the first quarter using accrual based figures. As a result, Ashland understated, and consequently underreported, O'Bryan's realized income for the first quarter.

Another accountant discovered Ashland's mistake during O'Bryan's divorce proceedings in 1997. O'Bryan's divorce attorney hired a different accountant to review and amend the mistaken return, and, as of June 28, 1998, O'Bryan had $239,933 in additional tax liability for 1995 plus interest. O'Bryan brought suit against Ashland for accountant malpractice seeking the interest the IRS charged on his unpaid tax liability. At trial, Ashland admitted negligence. The jury held Ashland liable for, among other things, the interest the IRS had assessed against O'Bryan, $39,038.83.

DECISION: The court, after looking at differing views around the country on awarding interest, concluded that damages for accountant's malpractice should put the client in the same position that he or she would have been in had the accountant not been negligent. Here, O'Bryan would not have owed the interest if Ashland had computed his taxes properly. O'Bryan was able to establish that he could have paid the taxes and while he had the use of the money that did not change the fact that he had to pay an additional sum that would not have been owed if his accountant had computed his taxes correctly. [**O'Bryan v Ashland**, 717 NW2d 632 (SD 2006)][9]

---

[6] *Greenstein, Logan & Co. v Burgess Marketing, Inc.* 744 SW2d 170 (Tex 1987).

[7] *Ronson v David S. Talesnick, CPA*, 33 F Supp 2d 347 (DNJ 1999).

[8] *Deloitte, Haskins, & Sells v Green*, 403 SE2d 818 (Ga 1991).

[9] Other courts have reached different results on the ability of the client to recover interest due the IRS. *Rosenbach v Diversified Group, Inc.*, 819 NYS 2d 851(NY Sup Ct. 2006). Some courts treat recovery as a jury issue. *Amato v KPMG LLP*, 2006 WL 2376245 (MD Pa).

2. Choice of Remedy

In addition to liability under tort law for malpractice, accountants may be held liable for breach of contract for their failure to meet professional standards.

(A) BREACH OF CONTRACT. A breach of an accountant's contract occurs if the audit work, for example, was not completed. In such a situation, the client need not pay the accountant's fee. If the work was complete, but there were minor errors, the damages caused by the error can be deducted from the fee.

Remedies for breach of contract are not available to third parties against accountants because they are not ordinarily considered third-party beneficiaries of contracts with accountants.

(B) TORT LIABILITY. A client or third party may be able to recover from an accountant on the basis of negligence, gross negligence, or fraud. These theories are covered in the remaining sections of the chapter.

Because malpractice is both a breach of contract and an independent tort, the client who is harmed has the choice of recovering for breach of contract or for the particular tort that is involved. Generally, the client will bring a tort action because there are higher damages under tort law than those afforded for a breach of contract. The statute of limitations on torts versus contracts may also influence the theory for liability. The statute of limitations begins to run on the tort of malpractice from the date the harm was discovered. The contract statute of limitations runs from the date the contract is breached. This time differential may be very important because in some cases, the client may not realize that there has been any harm until some time after a breach of the contract occurred.

3. The Environment of Accountants' Malpractice Liability

Accountants have moved from being primarily clerical business participants to being essential players in business strategies. In addition, accountants have moved from being employees of one employer to being independent contractors performing accounting services for many clients. Accountants are now employed to produce data that third parties use and rely on in making decisions about loans or investments. **For Example,** accountants prepare statements submitted to banks that will use those statements to determine whether to make a loan or extend a line of credit. Auditors' certifications of financial statements become part of the documents given to potential investors in companies. As these changes in the role of accountants took place, it became natural for courts to allow third parties relying on accountants' work and certifications to recover from the accountants when the accountants' and auditors' malpractice caused damages to them.

At the same time that these changes were taking place in the nature and role of accountants, changes were also taking place in other areas of the law. Manufacturers and parts suppliers were held liable to those who purchased the final products and were injured by defects in them. The rising tide of liability to third parties has naturally influenced the law regulating accountants.[10]

4. Limitation of Liability

Can accountants protect themselves from liability for malpractice claims of clients and third parties? Because the law generally permits any contracting party to limit or disclaim liability for negligence, an accountant may exclude liability for malpractice on a theory of negligence. Influenced by the consumer protection movement and by the law governing product liability, courts will require such disclaimers to be (1) clear and unambiguous and (2) conspicuous. If these requirements are not met, the disclaimers are not enforceable.

(A) SCOPE OF LIMITATION. Disclaimers are valid in certain limited circumstances.[11] **For Example,** when a client owns land in a foreign country, it is reasonable for the accountant to accept the valuation placed on the land by someone in that foreign country. The accountant should, however, include in the financial statement prepared for the client a statement that the valuation of that land was obtained from an identified person in the foreign country and that the accountant assumes no responsibility for the accuracy of that valuation. If the accountant's work has been so restricted, the accountant is protected from claims of third parties because there has been full disclosure about the accountant's limited information and ability to verify the work of others. **For Example,** when the accountant is restricted from examining accounts receivable and the accountant's certification states that no opinion was expressed as to accounts receivable, the accountant cannot be held liable if the accounts receivable turn out to be overstated.[12]

(B) LIMITATIONS ON EXCULPATORY PROVISIONS. A disclaimer based on lack of knowledge does not protect the accountant from liability if the accountant knew or had reason to know that the statements made were false. If the accountant states that he had no personal knowledge, he impliedly represents that he did not have any knowledge or reason to know that the statements were not correct. A disclaimer that is made when the accountant has reason to suspect that underlying information is false would be **misrepresentation** and would result in the accountant's liability.[13]

misrepresentation–false statement of fact made innocently without any intent to deceive.

---

[10] The interplay between the various areas of malpractice liability and those of accountants is seen further in the fact that the Restatement (Second) of Torts does not contain a separate provision applicable only to accountants but deals with the subject of malpractice liability of accountants to third parties in a general section (§ 552). Section 552 provides that

> [O]ne who in the course of his business, profession or employment, or in any other transaction in which he has a pecuniary interest, supplies false information for the guidance of others in their business transactions, is subject to liability for pecuniary loss caused to them by their justifiable reliance on the information, if he fails to exercise reasonable care or competence in obtaining or communicating the information.

The section then defines which parties can enforce this liability.

[11] The American Institute of Certified Public Accountants has a new ethics rule on liability limitations and indemnifications that took effect on July 1, 2009 and can be found at **www.aicpa.org/download/ethics/EDITED_Adopted_501_8_final.pdf**.

[12] *Stephans Industries, Inc. v Haskins & Sells,* 438 F2d 357 (10th Cir 1971).

[13] However, an accountant can provide financial information on an employee's severance package and disclaim liability by advising the employee to obtain independent tax advice. *Buehner v IBM Corp.,* 704 NYS2d 303 (2000).

limitation-of-liability clause–provision in a contract stating that one of the parties is not liable for damages in case of breach; also called exculpatory clause.

exculpatory clause– provision in a contract stating that one of the parties is not liable for damages in case of breach; also called *limitation-of-liability clause.*

In some states, a **limitation-of-liability** or **exculpatory clause** protects the accountant from a malpractice suit brought by a client only, not from a suit brought by a third party. In such cases, courts apply the general rule of contract law that only a party to a contract is bound by an exculpatory or limitation-of-liability clause.

B. ACCOUNTANTS' LIABILITY TO THIRD PARTIES: BEYOND PRIVITY

Most accountants' malpractice litigation involves the question of whether third parties may recover from the accountants, not on what standards of conduct accountants should observe. Various issues and factors, covered in both judicial decisions and statutes, determine whether accountants will be held liable to third parties.[14]

5. Status of the Accountant

An accountant may be a full-time employee of a company, an independent contractor doing regular work for a client, or an independent outside auditor. What constitutes negligence is the same for all three types of accountants. The liability of the accountant to the third party, when recognized, is based on the reliance of the third party on the work of the accountant.[15]

6. Conflicting Theories of Accountants' Third-Party Liability

There are a number of theories that have been developed to for third parties to recover for an accountant's negligence. These views may be identified as (1) the privity rule, (2) the contact rule, (3) the known user rule, (4) the foreseeable user rule, and (5) the intended user rule. In addition, some courts follow (6) a flexible rule, deciding each case as it arises. Each of these views is an attempt to draw a boundary line between the interloper and a "proper" plaintiff with sufficient connection to the accountant for recovery for the accountant's negligence. In some states, statutes define when nonprivity plaintiffs may recover for an accountant's negligence.[16]

privity rule–succession or chain of relationship to the same thing or right, such as privity of contract, privity of estate, privity of possession.

(A) THE PRIVITY RULE. The **privity rule** precludes a negligence malpractice suit by a third party. This rule holds that only the party in privity with the accountant— that is, the accountant's client—may recover from the accountant.[17] When the privity rule is applied, a bank lending money to the accountant's client cannot recover from the accountant for malpractice.

[14] *Chestnut Corp. v Pestine, Brinati, Gamer, Ltd.,* 667 NE2d 543 (Ill 1996).
[15] *Brown v KPMG Peat Marwick,* 756 SW2d 742 (Tex 1993).
[16] See, e.g., Ark Code Ann § 16-114-302; Ill Stat Ann § 225/450/30.1; Kan Stat Ann § 1-402; NJ Stat Ann § 2A:53A-25; Utah Code Ann § 58-26-12; and Wyo Stat § 33-3-201.
[17] This rule was originally known as the New York rule, *Ultramares Corp. v Touche,* 174 NE 441 (NY 1931). Although it has been replaced in New York by the contact rule, the privity rule is still the law in many jurisdictions. *Solow v Heard McElroy & Vestal, LLP,* 7 So3d 1269 La App (2009).

CASE SUMMARY

When the Company Goes Belly Up, Must the Accountant Ante Up?

FACTS: AUSA Life Insurance Company and others were institutional investors in the securities of JWP, Inc., a company that went belly up, resulting in nearly a 100 percent loss of their investments. Ernst & Young served as auditor for JWP from 1985 to 1992. During most of that period, JWP was in a period of rapid expansion financed by private placements of debt securities, and it became increasingly leveraged. By 1991, it was losing an average of $10 million per month. Ernst & Young knew of "accounting irregularities" from at least 1988 through 1991 but did not insist on their correction. Ernst & Young issued unqualified financial opinions for all of those years. One of the irregularities was recording anticipated future tax benefits of net operating loss in violation of GAAP.

AUSA and its fellow investors sued Ernst & Young for their losses. The federal district court dismissed the case, and AUSA appealed.

DECISION: Judgment for the investors. The court held that there was privity of contract between Ernst & Young and the investors because their purchase was a private placement, Ernst & Young knew who the investors were at the time it certified the financial statements for the sale of their interests, and it continued to provide certified financial information to them from 1985 to 1992. Because Ernst & Young had violated GAAP, there was negligence, and the investors were in a position to recover for breach of contract. However, upon retrial, while the court found the accounting firm could be held liable, it found that the firm could not have foreseen the disastrous acquisition that was the true cause of AUSA's note default and bankruptcy, precluding a finding of loss causation. [**AUSA Life Insurance Co. v Ernst & Young, 206 F3d 202 (2d Cir 2000), 119 F Supp 2d 394 (SDNY 2000), aff'd in unpublished opinion**]

(B) The Contact Rule. In relaxing the privity requirement, New York now allows a third party to recover from a negligent accountant if there was some contact between the third party and the accountant. **For Example,** an accountant may go to a bank to see what information the bank requires for the accountant's client to obtain a loan. In this case, there is a sufficient "link" or "contact" between the bank and the accountant to allow the bank to recover from the accountant if it sustains a loss because of the accountant's negligence.[18] The New York *contact rule* requires that the accountant meet or communicate with the nonprivity party to establish a relationship equivalent to privity. The accountant must also know the purpose of the accounting work and foresee the nonprivity party's reliance on that work.[19]

There must be enough contact with, or dealings between, the third party and the accountant to give the accountant reason to know that the third party was relying for a particular purpose on the financial statements prepared by the accountant.[20]

---

[18] *Credit Alliance Corp. v Arthur Andersen & Co.,* 483 NE2d 110 (NY 1985). Some courts are strict on the contact rule and describe the contact rule not as a different rule but as requiring "a relationship sufficiently intimate to be equated with privity." *Empire of American v Arthur Andersen & Co.,* 514 NYS2d 578 (NY 1987). The contact rule has been adopted by a minority of states. *Idaho Bank & Trust Co. v First Bankcorp of Idaho,* 772 P2d 720 (Idaho 1989), but see *ML-Lee Acquisition Fund, L.P. v. Deloitte & Touche,* 320 SC 143, 463 SE 2d 618 (SC App 1995), rehearing denied (Nov 17, 1995), certiorari granted (Aug 22, 1996)

[19] *Travelers Cas. and Sur. Co. of America v Ernst & Young LLP,* 542 F3d 475 (5th Cir 2008).

[20] The contact rule applies to malpractice defendants generally. It is not limited to suits against accountants. *Ossining Union Free School District v Anderson,* 539 NE2d 91 (NY 1989) but see *Indianapolis-Marion County Public Library v Charlier Clark & Linard, P.C.,* 900 NE2d 801 (Ind App 2009).

(C) THE KNOWN USER RULE. Under this rule for nonprivity parties, the accountant is liable to third parties who experience a loss as a result of the accountant's negligence when the accountant knew that the third party would be using the accountant's work product. **For Example,** a shareholder may recover from an accountant for negligently preparing and certifying an annual financial report that was prepared for distribution to shareholders.[21]

Under the known user rule, the fact that the nonprivity party's reliance on a financial statement was foreseeable does not entitle the third party to recover from the accountant for negligent preparation of the statement. The third party must show that the accountant knew the statement would be furnished to that plaintiff. Thus, under this rule, the plaintiff's reliance must thus be actually foreseen and not merely reasonably foreseeable.[22]

Under the known user rule, it is sufficient if the user or third party is a member of a known class even though the identity of the particular user is not known to the accountant. However, some states hold that when the identity of the intended user is known to the accountant, another party coming within the same class cannot recover from the accountant.[23] **For Example,** an accountant prepares a financial statement for a client with the knowledge that the client will take it to First National Bank to obtain a loan. First National Bank may recover from the accountant for negligent loss even though the bank never had any direct contact or dealings (that is, was never in privity) with the accountant. However, no one other than First National may seek recovery from the accountant for negligence.

The fact that the third party was a foreseeable user does not afford a basis for recovery in a "known user" state. When an accountant prepares a financial statement for the client and nothing is said about what further use of the statement will be made, creditors of the client cannot recover from the accountant for negligent preparation of the statement. The client would be the only known user.

If the court follows the privity rule or the contact rule described in the two preceding sections, the known user cannot seek recovery from the accountant for negligent malpractice. Moreover, some courts that follow the known user rule apply it so strictly that a substitute foreseeable user is not permitted to recover. To illustrate, assume that in the example just given, the client was refused the loan by First National Bank. The client might then make an application for a loan to Second National Bank. In known-user states, Second National Bank could not recover from the accountant because it was not a known user.

(D) THE FORESEEABLE USER RULE. The accountant may foresee that a particular class of unknown parties will rely on her work. **For Example,** when the accountant prepares a financial statement knowing that the client is going to use it to borrow money from some bank or finance company, the accountant foresees a class of lenders. Similarly, the accountant may know that the financial statement will be used to sell the stock

---

[21] *Boykin v Arthur Andersen & Co.,* 639 So 2d 504 (Ala 1994).

[22] *Lindner Fund v Abney,* 770 SW2d 437 (Mo App 1989). The rule that the nonprivity plaintiff may recover from the accountant for malpractice negligence only if the accountant's statement was furnished to that plaintiff, or the accountant knew that the client who was given the statement would in turn give the statement to the plaintiff, is often identified as "the Restatement rule." This rule is based on Restatement (Second) Torts § 522(2) (1977). There is, however, some uncertainty as to the exact boundaries of the Restatement rule. See *Selden v Burnett,* 754 P2d 256 (Alaska 1988); *Raritan River Steel Co. v Cherry, Bekaert & Holland,* 867 SE2d 609 (NC 1988).

[23] *Blue Bell, Inc. v Peat, Marwick, Mitchell & Co.,* 715 SW2d 408 (Tex App 1986).

of the client corporation. Here again, there is a foreseeable class consisting of unknown parties.

The *foreseeable user rule* imposes liability on the accountant for negligent malpractice when he can foresee the parties who will rely on his work in the financial statements. The foreseeable user rule allows these third parties to recover for their losses without regard to the lack of privity of contract between them and the accountant.[24]

CASE SUMMARY

Don't Count on Me; I'm Only the Auditor

FACTS: Audit firm Grant Thornton had prepared financial reports for use by the board of directors of First National Bank of Keystone (Keystone), in response to an investigation by the Office of the Comptroller of the Currency (OCC) that raised questions about the value of Keystone's loan portfolio. Stan Quay, a partner at Grant Thornton, was in charge of the 1998 audit. On March 24, 1999, Quay presented several members and prospective members of Keystone's board and Keystone's shareholders with draft copies of Keystone's 1998 financial statements and told them that Keystone was going to get an unqualified or "clean" audit opinion on its 1998 financial statements.

In April 1999, and despite the fact that Keystone was in fact insolvent at the end of 1998, Grant Thornton issued a clean audit report for Keystone. The audit report contained the following statement: "This report is intended for the information and use of the Board of Directors and Management of The First National Bank of Keystone and its regulatory agencies and should not be used by third parties for any other purpose."

Gary Ellis, a president of another bank, was being recruited in early 1999 by the Keystone board, to take the president's position at Keystone. Following the Keystone board meeting on March 24, 1999, Ellis met Quay and two other outside directors at a bar at the Fincastle Country Club. Quay spoke with Ellis and the two outside directors because Keystone did not have a chief financial officer, thus making Quay the only person capable of going over the financial statements with the others. At the country club, Quay told Ellis and the two outside directors that Keystone was going to receive a "clean [audit].." Ellis also attended the March 25, 1999 shareholders' meeting at which Quay informed the group that Grant Thornton was going to give Keystone a clean audit opinion for 1998. On March 30, 1999, Ellis visited Keystone. During this visit, Quay told Ellis once again that Keystone would receive a clean audit opinion for 1998.

Ellis signed a two-year contract at a base salary of $375,000 plus benefits, including the use of a corporate vehicle and a country club membership. He also purchased $49,500 in Keystone stock. By September 1999, Keystone Bank was closed. Ellis filed suit against Grant Thornton. The district court ruled in favor of Ellis on his negligent misrepresentation claim and found that he was entitled to $2,419,233 in damages. Grant Thornton appealed.

DECISION: The court held Grant Thornton was not liable because the executive's reliance on reports prepared for one purpose was misplaced. The report contained a specific disclaimer that indicated third parties—anyone beyond the board—were not permitted to rely on the report. The disclaimer protected Grant Thornton from liability to Ellis. [**Ellis v Grant Thornton LLP, 530 F3d 280 (4th Cir 2008)**]

---

[24] *Bily v Arthur Young & Co.,* 834 P2d 745 (Cal 1992). See also *Nycal Corp. v KPMG Peat Marwick LLP,* 688 NE2d 1368 (Mass 1998).

(E) **THE INTENDED USER RULE.** Fear that the foreseeability rule does not sufficiently restrict the number of potential claimants has led some courts to limit recovery to those nonprivity users who were not merely foreseeable but also expected or intended to rely on the work of the accountant in a particular transaction or another similar transaction.[25] In this view, the accountant must have furnished the information directly to the nonprivity user or to the client, knowing that the client would transmit the information to the nonprivity plaintiff.

(F) **THE FLEXIBLE RULE.** Some courts have rejected the requirement of privity for malpractice against accountants but have not adopted any of the rules discussed in the preceding sections. These courts prefer to keep the question open and to decide each case as it arises.

(G) **UNKNOWN USER.** When the accountant has no knowledge of, or reason to know of, any third party's use of the accountant's work, the third party is not able to come within any exception to the requirement of privity. Consequently, a nonprivity party cannot recover for the accountant's negligence when the accountant had no knowledge of any use that could affect the party.[26]

---

thinking things through

How Many Plaintiffs can there be in a Class-Action Securities Litigation? How Many Defendants?

With the collapse of companies such as Countrywide, New Century Financial, Lehman Brothers, and other firms affected by or involved in the subprime mortgage market, litigation against all of these firms' auditors is ongoing. The following is a list of all of the types of plaintiffs who have brought suit against auditors:

- Shareholders who purchased stock in the companies

- State pension funds with stock in their portfolios

- Banks and other institutions that lent money

- Banks and other institutions that accepted stock as collateral for loans

- Universities that received stock as endowment gifts

- Companies that contracted with the companies after having requested financial statements

Applying the various standards for accountant liability you have learned, discuss whether each of these groups will be able to recover from the auditors for these firms and why or why not.

---

7. Nonliability Parties

There are some third parties to whom accountants do not have liability.

(A) **INTERLOPERS.** No court imposes liability on the accountant to a total stranger who gets possession of the accountant's work and then sustains a loss because of a false

---

[25] *Bay Harbour Management LLC v Carothers*, 282 Fed Appx 71, 2008 WL 2566557 (CA 2 NY). Some courts regard this rule as representing the majority view. The foreseeable user rule brings the law with respect to accountants into harmony with the tort law relating to other parties and activities.

[26] *Sundamerican Bank & Trust Co. v Harrison*, 851 SW2d 563 (Mo App 1993).

statement in the work. This applies regardless of whether the statement was negligent or intentional. **For Example,** assume that a negligently prepared financial statement of a corporation is thrown in the wastepaper basket and is then retrieved by a security guard. If the guard thinks that the statement is a "hot tip" and invests in the stock of the corporation on the basis of the statement, the guard cannot recover from the accountant for negligence in preparing the statement. Accountants are not liable to interlopers, but courts continue to struggle with drawing the line between interlopers and rightful third parties.

(B) Parties Affected by the Decision of Accountant's Client. On the basis of information furnished by the accountant to a client, the client may make a decision that affects a third party. **For Example,** a report by an independent auditor may indicate that a fiscal officer of the client has not handled funds properly. The report may indicate that it is economically unsound to enter into a contract with a third party. Assume that the client relies on the accountant's report and fires the employee or refuses to make a contract with the third party. If the report of the accountant was negligently made and the true facts would not have justified the action taken by the client, most courts hold that third parties harmed in this indirect way have no cause of action.[27]

8. Defenses to Accountants' Liability: Contributory and Comparative Negligence of the Client or Third Party

(A) Contributory Negligence. When an accountant has been negligent, the client's comparative negligence may reduce the accountant's liability. To establish client **contributory negligence**, the accountant must show that the client contributed to the accountant's failure or that the client ignored the accountant's instructions. **For Example,** when the financial statement indicates that it is merely a working examination and is not certified by the accountant, the third party is negligent in relying on the statement and has been contributorily negligent.

contributory negligence— negligence of the plaintiff that contributes to injury and at common law bars recovery from the defendant although the defendant may have been more negligent than the plaintiff.

If those who are using a financial statement are highly sophisticated and have been warned by their advisers that the corporate assets have been overvalued, the users cannot hold the accountant who prepared the financial statement liable for negligence in overstating the value of the corporate assets. In such a case, the users ares contributorily negligent, something that reduces or eliminates the the accountant's liability.[28]

Some states ignore the contributory negligence of clients except in two circumstances. One is if the client interfered with the accountant's audit. Client interference with the accountant's work will excuse the accountant's liability. Another is if the client's negligence contributed to the accountant's negligence, but such contribution is not a bar to recovery by the client. For example. the negligence of the accountant's client in keeping records is not a bar to the accountants' liability to the client because the liability comes from the accountant's failure to discover the true facts.[29] The issue in these

---

[27] *Harper v Inkster Public Schools*, 404 NW2D 776 (Mich App 1987).
[28] *Scottish Heritable Trust v Peat Marwick Main & Co.*, 81 F3d 606 (5th Cir 1996).
[29] *World Radio Laboratories, Inc. v Coopers & Lybrand*, 538 NW2d 501 (Neb App 1995).

circumstances becomes not whether the accountant knew, but whether the accountant should have known.

comparative negligence—
defense to negligence that allows plaintiff to recover reduced damages based on his level of fault.

(B) **Comparative Negligence.** Some states apply the **comparative negligence** concept and permit proof of the client's negligence.[30] Under comparative negligence standards, the accountant and the client are assessed a percentage of blame for their respective levels of negligence in the use and preparation of the financial statements, and the client's recovery is reduced by its percentage of fault. **For Example,** if a jury finds that the client was responsible for 30 percent of the resulting loss, recovery from the accountant is reduced by 30 percent.

9. Accountants' Fraud Malpractice Liability to Third Parties

Society in general condemns fraud more strongly than it does negligence. There is greater liability of accountants for fraudulent malpractice.

(A) **What Constitutes Fraud by Accountants.** *Fraud* is defined as a false statement made with knowledge that it was false or with reckless indifference as to whether it was true[31] with the intent that the listener rely on it. A false statement in accounting typically occurs when the client's financial statements make it appear to be in a better financial position than is actually the case. **For Example,** in the case of Bernie Madoff Securities, the auditor signed off for years on financial statements that made the firm seem solvent when in fact, the company had lost $50 billion.

At times, falsified financial statements are used as a means to obtain a downgrade on the ratings for the financial condition of a corporation. Such undervaluation then induces shareholders to sell their stock to a dominant group of shareholders. The false financial statement purposely undervalues the corporation's assets to make the shareholders believe their stock has little value and that sale at the low price offered by the dominant group is a good buy.

(B) **Accountants' Fraud Liability to Intended Victims.** Fraud by an accountant typically misleads a third party or a class of parties, a group whose identity is known to the accountant. Any such victim, whether an identified party or member of a class of potential victims, may recover from the accountant for loss caused by fraud. Privity (relating to liability for negligence) is not required when the basis of the malpractice suit is fraud. The public policy of preventing fraud overrides the concern of holding accountants liable to third parties.

An accountant might certify a false financial statement for a corporate client with knowledge that it will be used to sell the corporation's securities to third parties.[32] If so, the third parties may recover from the accountant for the damages sustained. **For Example,** an accountant has been held liable for disguising the true character of a hoped-for profit from the sale and resale of real estate. The accountant described the sale and resale as "deferred income," although there was little reason to believe that the transaction could ever be completed because the buyer, who was obligated to pay $5 million for the property, had assets of only $100,000. The financial

[30] *American Nat'l Bank v Touche Ross & Co.*, 659 NE2d 1276 (Ohio 1996).
[31] In re *Dell Securities Litigation*, 591 F Supp 2d 877 (WD Tex 2009).
[32] In re *IMAX Securities Litigation*, 587 F Supp 2d 471 (SDNY 2008).

statement would have shown a loss instead of a substantial profit if the true character of this risky transaction had been disclosed.

C. SARBANES-OXLEY AUDITOR AND ACCOUNTING-RELATED PROVISIONS

Following the collapses of Enron and WorldCom during 2001–2002, Congress quickly passed sweeping legislation (see Chapter 8 and Chapter 46) designed to increase the liability for securities violations, financial fraud, and obstruction of justice and to impose new responsibility and accountability with regard to financial reporting by companies. Called the *Sarbanes-Oxley Act* (SOX or SarBox)), this legislation imposes substantial requirements on auditors and the standards and practices of the audit profession.

CASE SUMMARY

When the Auditor Just Duplicates What Management Wants

FACTS: Throughout the early and mid-1990s, Xerox had a significant market share in the digital copying products industry, a financially healthy company with revenues rising at a double-digit rate.

However, to get these earnings, Xerox had to reallocate revenues from service to the equipment portion of sales-type leases by assuming an artificial gross margin differential between the two lease components (or an assumed profit margin) that had no basis in economic reality. Xerox used this method to pull forward $617 million of equipment revenues from 1997–2000. Internally, KPMG referred to this method as "half-baked revenue recognition." Xerox's earnings were inflated $43 million as a result.

In 1996, KPMG objected to this practice as violating GAAP but, after arguments with Xerox senior management, approved its implementation in 1998, while continuing to criticize its use. In 1999, KPMG informed Xerox that this practice violated GAAP, but Xerox refused to follow this advice. Nevertheless, KPMG certified Xerox's 1999 and 2000 financial statements.

In 2001, Xerox began issuing a series of earnings restatements that would total $11 billion. In late 2001, Xerox announced that PriceWaterhouse Coopers, LLP ("PwC") was replacing KPMG as the company's new auditor for the 2001 fiscal year. Xerox paid a $10 million fine to the SEC to settle civil charges and also agreed to complete its restatement of earnings for 1997 through 2001.

Investors such as the Florida State pension plan and other individual investors (plaintiffs) brought suit against the executive officers of Xerox as well as Xerox's external auditor, KPMG, for fraud.

KPMG moved to have the complaint against it dismissed because it was not a party to the accounting fraud.

DECISION: The court found that the facts showed that KPMG was aware of accounting issues, that it raised these issues and problems to managers, and that each time, KPMG backed down on its concerns. It replaced the lead auditor on the Xerox account when Xerox requested that he be replaced. The court referred to the accounting firm as a "virtual pushover" for the client and that its complicity in the continuing misstatements was enough to have a case of fraud brought to trial. KPMG was aware of the accounting problems and allowed them to continue. Knowledge is the key element in fraud and the plaintiffs had included enough facts to show that knowledge. [**Carlson v Xerox Corp., 392 F Supp 2d 267 (D Conn 2005)**]

FIGURE 47-1 | *Theories of Accountants' Liability to Third Parties*

THEORY	TYPE OF LIABILITY	THIRD PARTY LIABILITY	CLIENT LIABILITY
STATUTORY	1933 SECURITIES ACT— OMISSION OR MISSTATEMENT IN REGISTRATION STATEMENT 1934 SECURITIES EXCHANGE ACT—10b (SEE CHAPTER 48)	PURCHASERS OF SHARES SHAREHOLDERS; PURCHASER OF SHARES	COMPANY
CONTRACT	BREACH OF CONTRACT	NO—NOT CONSIDERED THIRD PARTY BENEFICIARIES	MATERIAL BREACH; MINOR BREACH DAMAGES
TORT	PRIVITY REQUIRED	NO RECOVERY	RECOVERY ALLOWED UNLESS DEFENSES APPLY
	CONTACT RULE REQUIRED	CAN RECOVER IF ACTUAL CONTACT WITH ACCOUNTANT	
	KNOWN USER RULE	CAN RECOVER IF ACCOUNTANT KNOWS THIRD PARTY WILL USE FINANCIALS/WORK	
	FORESEEABLE USER RULE	CAN RECOVER IF ACCOUNTANT CAN FORESEE UNKNOWN PERSONS RELYING ON FINANCIALS	
	INTENDED USER RULE	CAN RECOVER IF ACCOUNTANT KNOWS CLIENT WILL GIVE IT TO ANOTHER	
	UNKNOWN USER	NO RECOVERY	
FRAUD	KNOWN AND UNKNOWN	RECOVERY	RECOVERY

10. Auditor Independence

One of the concerns reflected in SOX was that auditors were not exercising sufficient discretion and independence in conducting audits of their clients. The act takes several steps to increase the auditor's independence as it conducts its audits of company financial records.

(A) PUBLIC COMPANY ACCOUNTING OVERSIGHT BOARD. The first section of SOX created a new Public Company Accounting Oversight Board (PCAOB, often referred to

ethics&the law

The Accounting Firm that Said "No!"

Johns Manville, Inc., had been a producer of asbestos since the nineteenth century. Since 1936, health issues involving asbestos workers had been developing and included breathing difficulties as well as a cancer linked to asbestos fibers in the lungs. With each passing year, Manville and other producers experienced more litigation and liability.

Prior to 1982, the disclosures in Manville's financial statements had explained the pending and resolved liability suits but concluded that it was impossible, under Financial Accounting Standards Board Directive #5 (FASB-5), to quantify the potential liability: "The company is unable to predict at this time the outcome or liability in these cases." In 1982, Coopers & Lybrand, the auditors for Manville, were given a report from Manville's Litigation Analysis Group that the cost of disposition of all the asbestos suits would be $1.9 billion. Because of this expert opinion, Coopers & Lybrand told Manville that it was now possible to "reasonably estimate" the liability costs and refused to issue a clean audit report unless some form of financial disclosure regarding the asbestos liability was made.

Coopers & Lybrand felt that, based on its expert analysis, the liability was quantifiable. Manville fired Coopers & Lybrand and filed appropriate notices with the Securities and Exchange Commission that it was changing audit firms. Manville then hired Price Waterhouse as its new audit firm. After examining the records and the status of litigation as well as the expert opinions, Price Waterhouse also refused to issue a clean audit statement without the disclosure.

The effect of the refusals of both audit firms to issue clean financial opinions was that Manville declared bankruptcy on August 26, 1982, and was required to sign over $2.5 billion of its assets (mostly stock) and contribute 20 percent of its annual net income to a trust for asbestos workers. The result of the bankruptcy for Manville shareholders was the loss of their investment in the company.

Did the auditors do the right thing? Were their decisions ethical? Didn't their decisions in effect destroy the value of the shareholders' investment? Would you have done the same thing?

as *Peekaboo*) that is responsible for promoting high professional standards among auditors.[33] The board, which consists of five presidential appointees, is not a governmental body but a nonprofit organization with its own budgeting and staffing authority. No more than two members of the board can be CPAs, and members of the board operate on a full-time basis. The board has the following responsibilities:

- Operating a registration system for public accounting firms that prepare audit reports for companies that issue securities

- Enforcing and refining rules to ensure audit quality, ethics, and independence by auditors

- Conducting inspections of public accounting firms to determine their compliance with Sarbanes-Oxley requirements

---

[33] In the financial industry, professionals have translated the acronym for the new board, PCAOB, as *Peekaboo* because of the board's role in shedding light on financial systems and reporting.

- Investigating violations and imposing disciplinary sanctions where necessary for members of the profession
- Encouraging the highest professional standards among public accounting firms and auditors

(B) REGISTRATION WITH THE **PCAOB.** Any public accounting firm that conducts audits for companies that issue securities must file an annual registration statement with PCAOB. That registration requires the accounting firm to disclose all companies for which it has done audits and all the fees paid by those companies—both audit fees and nonaudit fees, commonly referred to as *consulting services.* The accounting firm is also required to disclose any sanctions and pending civil or criminal proceedings against it, along with its policies and procedures for quality control in audits. PCAOB then approves the accounting firm for continued work in the audit of issuers of securities. That approval or denial must be made within 45 days following the accounting firm's annual registration filing.

(C) MAINTAINING AUDITOR INDEPENDENCE. In many of the companies that experienced financial collapse prior to SOX, the companies' auditors had conflicts that may have tainted their independent judgment on accounting issues or even on whether the companies were viable entities. **For Example,** many of the audit firms received substantial fees from companies for management consulting services for which they were providing certified statements. Arthur Andersen received $21 million annually for its audit work with Enron and another $29 million for its consulting services. The consulting contract created a conflict that interfered with the audit firm's ability to make honest decisions in its audit work.

To help eliminate conflicts of interest, Sarbanes-Oxley prohibits certain activities by audit firms for their audit clients, including the following:

1. Bookkeeping and other services related to the accounting records or financial statements of the audit client
2. Design and implementation of financial information systems
3. Appraisal and valuation services, fairness opinions, and contribution-in-kind reports
4. Actuarial services
5. Internal audit outsourcing services
6. Management functions and human resources
7. Broker or dealer, investment adviser, and investment banking services
8. Legal services and expert services unrelated to the audit
9. Any other service that the board determines, by regulation, is impermissible[34]

All nonaudit services to be performed by the auditor for an audit client (except those listed above as expressly prohibited) require prior approval by the board.

---

[34] 15 USC § 78j-1.

In addition, to ensure that audit partners do not become entrenched, Sarbanes-Oxley requires audit firms to change audit partners at least once every five years.[35] The rotation of the audit partner in charge of a company account brings a new perspective to the issues in the financial systems and reports and helps to eliminate the bias of close, personal relationships that develop over longstanding working relationships.

SOX also requires accounting firms to set up internal systems for developing and monitoring professional ethics and for the discussion of ethical issues that arise during the course of the audits of clients.

11. Audit Committees

SOX also addresses issues on the corporate side of the interaction between auditors and companies—the audit committee of the company's board. Under the statute, audit committees must be composed of board members who are independent, defined in the statute as directors who do not accept consulting or other fees from the company and who are not affiliated with the company, certain of its employees, or any of its subsidiaries.[36]

Members of audit committees must also be allowed to interact with auditors without management being present and also be permitted to hire independent advisors. At least one member of the audit committee must be a financial expert or someone who understands financial reporting and audit work. The audit committee is now the central point for ensuring that SOX standards are being followed.

Audit committees are required to establish procedures whereby they can be notified of problems with the company's internal controls. Audit committees need to establish the means and mechanisms for monitoring the company's internal control systems so they can verify that financial reports are based on data generated by effective company reporting systems.

12. Records Retention

Accounting firm Arthur Andersen was convicted of one count of obstruction of justice for its destruction of Enron records while SEC investigations were pending. The conviction was later reversed because the court held that although there may have been sufficient evidence about individual Andersen employees' willful destruction of documents, the jury instructions were flawed in attributing that knowledge to the full Andersen firm automatically without proof of actual knowledge (an element required in all criminal cases; see Chapter 8).[37] The statute used for prosecution in that case was not specific enough to tie the firm to individual employee conduct. Furthermore, the penalties, even with such a conviction, were minimal. As discussed in Chapter 8, SOX substantially increased both the scope of and penalties for the obstruction of justice through

---

[35] *Id.*
[36] 15 USC § 1741.
[37] *Andersen, LLP v US,* 544 US 696 (2005). David Duncan, the partner in charge of the Enron account, withdrew his guilty plea on obstruction when the court reversed the firm's verdict.

e-commerce&cyberlaw

Destruction of Documents, Destruction of a Career, Destruction of a Firm

The congressional investigation into the Enron collapse uncovered the following e-mails:

- A May 28, 1999, e-mail to David Duncan from Benjamin Neuhausen, a member of Andersen's Professional Standards Group at its Chicago main office, evaluated the wisdom of having Enron's CFO Andrew Fastow as the principal in a company that was off the books and doing trades with Enron: "Setting aside the accounting, idea of a venture entity managed by CFO is terrible from a business point of view. Conflicts galore. Why would any director in his or her right mind ever approve such a scheme?"

- A June 1, 1999, e-mail from David Duncan responded: "[O]n your point 1 (i.e., the whole thing is a bad idea), I really couldn't agree more. Rest assured that I have already communicated and it has been agreed to by Andy that CEO, General [Counsel], and Board discussion and approval will be a requirement, on our part, for acceptance of a venture similar to what we have been discussing."

These e-mails are discoverable and admissible when litigation results from an auditor's work. The only protections are the privilege between lawyer and client, but these e-mails were between auditors who worked for the same audit firm.

accountants' and auditors' destruction of records. Under Sarbanes-Oxley, those who destroy, conceal, alter, or mutilate documents when either a civil or criminal investigation is pending are subject to up to 20 years' imprisonment as well as fines.[38]

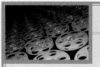

lawflix

Midnight Run (1988) (R)

Charles Grodin plays an accountant who embezzles from his mafia boss but gives the money to charity.

You can view a clip of this movie and others that illustrate business law concepts at the LawFlix site, located at **www.cengage.com/blaw/dvl**.

---

[38] 15 USC § 1512. Routine destruction of work papers is not considered obstruction. *Kerman v Martin Friedman, CPA,* 81 NYS 2d 387 (2005).

MAKE THE CONNECTION

SUMMARY

Professionals who agree to perform services for others must perform those services according to the standards of the profession. Accountants, as professionals, must perform their audit work at the levels and standards of competency and thoroughness established for their profession. If an accountant negligently fails to observe those standards, both a breach of contract and a tort occur. This tort of negligent breach of contract constitutes malpractice, and the other party to the contract can sue the wrongdoer either for breach of contract or for the negligence involved.

In some circumstances, not only is the accountant liable to its client, but it may also be liable for malpractice to certain categories of third parties who have used or relied on the financial statement. States and courts differ as to when an accountant is liable to third parties. Some courts do not recognize accountant liability to third parties; these courts require privity between the parties. Most courts hold accountants liable to some third parties but differ as to which third parties and how far to extend the accountant's liability. The various rules that determine accountant liability to third parties are the contact rule, which requires that the third party must have had some contact with the accountant before there can be liability; the known user rule in which the accountant is aware of the third party who will use the accountant's information; the foreseeability rule in which the accountant is held liable if it was possible to foresee that the third party would use the accountant's information; the intended user rule in which the client tells the accountant of the intended use of the audit work; the unknown user rule in which the accountant is not liable to third parties it could not have known would use the information or audit work; and the flexible rule that decides on a case-by-case basis.

Accountants guilty of fraud have liability to all third parties, even those not in privity of contract with the accountant.

To a limited degree, an accountant is protected from malpractice liability by a disclaimer of liability or by the contributory negligence of the plaintiff.

Sarbanes-Oxley(SOX) increases the penalties for accountants who destroy documents when civil or criminal investigations are pending. The act also prohibits conduct by accountants that creates a conflict of interest and requires audit firms to register for authorization to do audit work on public companies. Audit committees of boards are now required to work closely with auditors to make sure that the financial systems in the company and its reports are sound. A federal oversight board reviews the work of audit firms and is authorized to discipline audit firms and accountants for their failure to honor standards or comply with the law.

LEARNING OUTCOMES

After studying this chapter, you should be able to clearly explain:

A. GENERAL PRINCIPLES OF ACCOUNTANTS' LIABILITY

LO.1 Define *malpractice*
> See Section 1, on p. 1113.

LO.2 Distinguish malpractice liability from breach of contract liability
> See "Choice of Remedy" on p. 1115.
> See *Ellis v Grant Thornton LLP* on p. 1120.

B. ACCOUNTANTS' LIABILITY TO THIRD PARTIES: BEYOND PRIVITY

LO.3 List which third parties may recover for the malpractice liability of accountants and when they may do so
> See *AUSA Life Insurance Co. v Ernst & Young* on p. 1118.

LO.4 Discuss the difference between accounting malpractice and fraud
> See *Carlson v Xerox Corp* on p. 1124.

C. SARBANES-OXLEY AUDITOR AND ACCOUNTING-RELATED PROVISIONS

LO.5 Explain how Sarbanes-Oxley has affected the accounting profession and accountants' liability
> See E-Commerce & Cyberlaw on p. 1129.

KEY TERMS

comparative negligence   limitation-of-liability   privity rule
contributory negligence   malpractice
exculpatory clause   misrepresentation

QUESTIONS AND CASE PROBLEMS

1. The auditing firm of Timm, Schmidt & Co. prepared annual financial statements for Clintonville Fire Apparatus, Inc. (CFA). CFA showed these statements to Citizens State Bank and asked for loans. On the basis of the financial statements, Citizens loaned CFA approximately $380,000. Timm later discovered that the financial statements overvalued CFA by more than $400,000. Citizens demanded repayment of the loans. CFA could not pay the balance, and Citizens sued Timm and its malpractice liability insurer. They raised the defense that the suit was barred by lack of privity and the fact that no one in the Timm firm knew that CFA intended to use the financial statements to obtain loans from anyone. Is the lack of privity a defense? [*Citizens State Bank v Timm, Schmidt & Co.*, 335 NW2d 361 (Wis)]

2. Parente, Randolph, Orlando & Associates (Parente) is an accounting firm that had done auditing work for Sparkomatic for nearly 20 years. On June 14,

1993, Sparkomatic entered into a Memorandum of Intent with Williams Controls to sell Williams assets from Sparkomatic's Kenco division. The sale price was to be the "audited book value" of the assets, and the book value would be based on the June 30, 1993, balance sheet (which Parente did not prepare). Sparkomatic then engaged Parente to audit the financial statements for December 31, 1990, 1991, and 1992 and to prepare an interim balance sheet for 1993.

On August 1, 1993, Sparkomatic and Williams Controls entered into an asset purchase agreement, which required that Williams be furnished financials through June 1993 as prepared by "Sparkomatic's independent public accountant." Parente was not identified by name in the agreement. Parente did review the asset purchase agreement with Williams prior to commencing its work and knew that Williams would be using the information Parente prepared.

Following the closing, additional information came to light indicating that Williams had overpaid for the assets of Kenco, and Williams filed suit against Parente for negligence, negligent misrepresentation, and breach of contract. Parente moved for summary judgment. What should the decision be and why? Discuss several possible theories. [*Williams Controls v Parente, Randolph, Orlando, & Associates,* 39 F Supp 2d 517 (MD Pa)]

3. David S. Talesnick served as the accountant for Kenneth Ronson and his wife as well as for Ronson's company, performing accounting and tax services for all. From 1980 to 1983, Ronson, his wife, and his company invested in the White Rim Oil & Gas, Pine Coal, and Winchester Coal limited partnerships. During those years, the Ronsons and his company were able to report losses on their income tax returns because of these investments. However, the IRS determined that the limited partnerships were not qualified investments under the tax code and disallowed the loss deductions. The Ronsons and his company all owed back taxes, interest, and penalties as a result. The Ronsons disputed the finding and asked Talesnick how they might appeal the ruling and not have the interest clock ticking on what they owed. Talesnick wrote a letter and advised them to post a bond of $91,300, the amount then due. Talesnick was incorrect in his advice on payment and accrual of interest, and by the time the final determination was made against the Ronsons and Ronson's company, they owed $235,063 with interest. The Ronsons sued Talesnick for malpractice. Could they recover? How much? [*Ronson v Talesnick,* 33 F Supp 2d 347 (DNJ)]

4. The certified public accounting partnership of James, Guinn, and Head prepared a certified audit report of four corporations, known as the Paschal Enterprises, with knowledge that their report would be used to induce Shatterproof Glass Corp. to lend money to those corporations. The report showed the corporations to be solvent when in fact they were insolvent. Shatterproof relied on the audit report, loaned approximately $500,000 to the four corporations, and lost almost all of it because the liabilities of the companies were in excess of their assets. Shatterproof claimed that James and other accountants had been negligent in preparing the report and sued them to recover the loss on the loan. The accountants raised the

defense that they had been retained not by Shatterproof but by Paschal. Was this defense valid? [*Shatterproof Glass Corp. v James,* 466 SW2d 873 (Tex App)]

5. Landau made an audit and a financial report of Suits Galore, a clothing manufacturer. The statement prepared by Landau was not certified. It stated that it was a review report only and that no opinion was expressly stated by the accountant. On the basis of this report, William Iselin & Co. extended credit to Suits Galore. Shortly after, Suits Galore went into bankruptcy, and Iselin was not repaid the money it had loaned. Iselin sued Landau on the ground that the financial report had been negligently prepared and that Iselin could recover from Landau for the loss sustained. Was it correct? [*William Iselin & Co. v Landau,* 513 NYS2d 3]

6. For almost 13 years, Touche Ross had prepared the annual audit of Buttes Gas and Oil Co. Buttes wanted to obtain a loan from Dimensional Credit Corp. (DCC) and showed DCC its most recent annual audit. DCC made the loan on the basis of what it learned from the audit. The loan was not repaid, and DCC then realized that it had been misled by negligent statements about Buttes's financial condition that appeared in the annual statement prepared by Touche Ross. Would DCC be able to recover against Touche Ross for its negligence in preparing this report?

7. Henry Hatfield, CPA, was hired to prepare audited financial statements for Happy Campers, a nonprofit organization providing summer camp scholarships for inner-city, low-income children. The executive director of Happy Campers was embezzling but falsified records that Hatfield used in his audit. First Bank gave Happy Campers a $100,000 loan based on Hatfield's certified financials. The embezzlement was discovered, and Happy Campers defaulted on the loan. Can First Bank recover its loss from Hatfield?

8. What is the difference between the standards for auditor liability in a civil action by investors against the auditor vs. auditor liability for violation of securities laws?

9. Hicks, the president and manager of Intermountain Merchandising, wanted to sell the business to Montana Merchandising, Inc. To provide a basis for the transaction, he retained Bloomgren, an accountant, to make an audit of Intermountain. Bloomgren knew that Montana would use the audit report in making the purchase of the business from Intermountain. Bloomgren's audit report showed the Intermountain business as profitable. Thayer, Montana's president, relied on this report in agreeing to purchase the business of Inter-mountain and in agreeing to the terms of the purchase. Sometime later, it was discovered that the accountant had made a number of mistakes and that the business that was sold was actually insolvent. Thayer and Montana Merchandising sued Hicks and Bloomgren for damages. The suit claimed that the accountant had negligently misrepresented the facts. The accountant defended on the basis that Thayer was not in privity of contract with him and

therefore could not sue him. Was he right? [*Thayer v Hicks,* 793 P2d 784 (Mont)]

10. Seven shareholders of HM, a home furnishings retailer, filed suit for securities fraud and common law fraud arising from misrepresentations and omissions they alleged were made by HM's outside auditor, Deloitte & Touche, in connection with HM's annual report issued on May 30, 2000. Deloitte performed an audit of the financial statements of HM as of the fiscal year ending on February 29, 2000. The audit report was incorporated in full in HM's annual report (Form 10-K) for that fiscal year issued on May 30, 2000.

On March 22, 2000, Deloitte presented its unqualified audit report to the HM board of directors. On May 29, 2000, the HM board of directors approved the annual report, and it was filed with the Securities and Exchange Commission (SEC) on May 30, 2000.

Deloitte represented in the financial statement materials included in these reports that (1) Deloitte had audited the balance sheets, consolidated statements of operations, and stockholders' equity of HM, (2) HM's financial statements "present fairly, in all material respects, the financial position" of HM as of February 29, 2000, and (3) the audit was in conformity with accounting principles generally accepted in the United States. Deloitte's unqualified audit opinion also represented that, as of February 29, 2000, and May 30, 2000, HM was solvent; that it had almost $535 million in shareholder equity; and that its book value was $81 per share.

In fact, Deloitte was aware that the board of HM had instructed management to prepare for a bankruptcy filing and seek possible suitors for purchasing the company's assets. This information was not disclosed in the reports. By November 2003, HM issued a report with the following information:

- HM's assets had shrunk over $611,474,000.

- Total revenues for the quarter decreased 7.8 percent.

- Operating expenses exceeded revenue by more than $48 million.

- The net loss increased $536,835,000.

- Accounts payable increased by $27,313,000.

- The loss per share was $9.71.

- Total shareholder equity went from $534,748,000 in May 2000 to ($75,057), a decrease of $609,805,000.

That quarterly report also stated that more than $142.9 million in goodwill and all of the previously stated book value was gone. Can Deloitte & Touche be held liable? What would be the basis for such liability? [*Arnlund v Deloitte & Touche LLP,* 199 F Supp 2d 461 (ED Va)]

11. Equisure, Inc., was required to file audited financial statements when it applied for a listing on the American Stock Exchange (AMEX). Stirtz, Equisure's auditor,

issued a favorable audit opinion used for the AMEX application. Stirtz also issued "clean" opinions on Equisure's required SEC filings, such as its 10k.

Noram, a securities broker, loaned $900,000 in margin credit to purchasers of Equisure's stock based on the firm's audited financials. AMEX stopped trading on Equisure's stock because of allegations of insider trading and stock manipulation, and Noram was left without collateral for $2.5 million in loans. Stirtz resigned as Equisure's auditor, and Noram filed suit against Stirtz. The trial court granted Stirtz summary judgment. Noram appealed. Who is liable here? Was the court's decision correct? [*Noram Investment Services, Inc. v Stirtz Bernards Boyden*, 611 NW2d 372 (Minn App)]

CPA QUESTIONS

1. In general, the third-party (primary) beneficiary rule as applied to a CPA's legal liability in conducting an audit is relevant to which of the following causes of action against a CPA?

	Fraud	Constructive Fraud	Negligence
a.	Yes	Yes	No
b.	Yes	No	No
c.	No	Yes	Yes
d.	No	No	Yes

2. Beckler & Associates, CPAs, audited and gave an unqualified opinion on the financial statements of Queen Co. The financial statements contained misstatements that resulted in a material overstatement of Queen's net worth. Queen provided the audited financial statements to Mac Bank in connection with a loan made by Mac to Queen. Beckler knew that the financial statements would be provided to Mac. Queen defaulted on the loan. Mac sued Beckler to recover for its losses associated with Queen's default. Which of the following must Mac prove in order to recover?

   I. Beckler was negligent in conducting the audit.

   II. Mac relied on the financial statements.

   a. I only

   b. II only

   c. Both I and II

   d. Neither I nor II

3. In a common law action against an accountant, lack of privity is a viable defense if the plaintiff:

   a. Is the client's creditor who sues the accountant for negligence

   b. Can prove the presence of gross negligence that amounts to a reckless disregard for the truth

    c. Is the accountant's client

    d. Bases the action upon fraud

4. Cable Corp. orally engaged Drake & Co., CPAs, to audit its financial statements. Cable's management informed Drake that it suspected the accounts receivable were materially overstated. Though the financial statements Drake audited included a materially overstated accounts receivable balance, Drake issued an unqualified opinion. Cable used the financial statements to obtain a loan to expand its operations. Cable defaulted on the loan and incurred a substantial loss.

    If Cable sues Drake for negligence in failing to discover the overstatement, Drake's best defense would be that Drake did *not*

    a. Have privity of contract with Cable

    b. Sign an engagement letter

    c. Perform the audit recklessly or with an intent to deceive

    d. Violate generally accepted auditing standards in performing the audit

5. Which of the following services is a CPA generally required to perform when conducting a personal financial planning engagement?

    a. Assisting the client to identify tasks that are essential in order to take action on planning decisions

    b. Assisting the client to take action on planning decisions

    c. Monitoring progress in achieving goals

    d. Updating recommendations and revising planning decisions

6. Which of the following statements is (are) correct regarding the common law elements that must be proven to support a finding of constructive fraud against a CPA misrepresentation?

    I. The plaintiff has justifiably relied on the CPA's misrepresentation.

    II. The CPA has acted in a grossly negligent manner.

    a. I only

    b. II only

    c. Both I and II

    d. Neither I nor II

Chapter 48

MANAGEMENT OF CORPORATIONS

corporation is managed, directly or indirectly, by its shareholders, board of directors, and officers.

A. SHAREHOLDERS

As owners, the shareholders have the right to control the corporation.

1. Extent of Management Control by Shareholders

As a practical matter, control of the shareholders is generally limited to voting at shareholders' meetings to elect directors. In this sense, shareholders indirectly determine the management policies of the business. At shareholders' meetings, they may also vote to amend bylaws, approve shareholder resolutions, or vote on so-called extraordinary corporate matters. *Extraordinary matters* include the sale of corporate assets outside the regular course of the corporation's business or the merger or dissolution of the corporation.

2. Meetings of Shareholders

To have legal effect, action by the shareholders must ordinarily be taken at a regular or special meeting.

(A) REGULAR MEETINGS. The time and place of regular or stated meetings are usually prescribed by the articles of incorporation or the bylaws. Notice to shareholders of such meetings is ordinarily not required, but it is usually given as a matter of good business practice. Some statutes require that notice of all meetings be given.

(B) SPECIAL MEETINGS. Generally, notice must be given specifying the subject matter of special meetings. Unless otherwise prescribed, special meetings are called by the directors. It is sometimes provided that a special meeting may be called by a certain percentage of shareholders.[1] Notice of the day, hour, and place of a special meeting must be given to all shareholders. The notice must include a statement of the nature of the business to be transacted, and no other business may be transacted at this meeting.

(C) QUORUM. A valid meeting requires the presence of a quorum of the voting shareholders. A **quorum** is the minimum number of persons (shareholders or persons authorized to vote a stated proportion of the voting stock) required to transact business. If a quorum is present, a majority of those present may act on any matter unless there is an express requirement of a higher affirmative vote.

When a meeting opens with a quorum, the quorum is generally not broken if shareholders leave the meeting and those remaining are not sufficient to constitute a quorum.

quorum–minimum number of persons, shares represented, or directors who must be present at a meeting in order to lawfully transact business.

---

[1] NY Bus Corp Law § 603.

3. Action Without Meeting

A number of statutes provide for corporate action by shareholders without holding a meeting. The Revised Model Business Corporation Act (RMBCA) provides that "action required or permitted by this Act to be taken at a shareholders' meeting may be taken without a meeting if the action is taken by all shareholders entitled to vote on the action."[2] The action must be evidenced by a written consent describing the action taken, signed by all shareholders entitled to vote on the action, and delivered to the corporation for inclusion in the minutes.

B. DIRECTORS

The board of directors has oversight responsibility for a company's business affairs, including (1) approving strategic plans, (2) reviewing operating and financial results, (3) approving SEC filings, (4) approving the hiring of executives, (5) evaluating management's performance and approving executive compensation packages, (6) appointing and meeting with auditors, and (7) evaluating and acting on extraordinary matters, such as the merger, acquisition, or sale of the business.

Most states now permit the number of directors to be fixed by the bylaws. Many specify that the board of directors shall consist of not less than three directors; a few authorize one or more.[3] Professional corporation legislation often authorizes or is interpreted as authorizing a one- or two-person board of directors.

4. Qualifications

Eligibility for membership on a board of directors is determined by statute, articles of incorporation, or bylaws.[4] In the absence of a contrary provision, any person (including a nonresident, a minor, or a person who is not a shareholder) is eligible for membership. Bylaws may require that a director own stock in the corporation although this requirement is not ordinarily imposed.

CPA   5. Powers of Directors

The board of directors has authority to manage the corporation. Courts will not interfere with the board's discretion in the absence of (1) illegal conduct or (2) fraud harming the rights of creditors, shareholders, or the corporation.

The board of directors may enter into any contract or transaction necessary to carry out the business for which the corporation was formed. The board may appoint officers and other agents to act for the company, or it may appoint several of its own members as an executive committee to act for the board between board meetings. (See Figure 48.1.) Broad delegation of authority, however, may involve the risk of being treated as an unlawful abdication of the board's management power.

---

[2] RMBCA § 7.04(a).
[3] Del Code § 141(b). See also RMBCA § 8.03.
[4] In family-owned businesses, shareholder agreements are often utilized to impose restrictions on the voting of shares and eligibility standards for membership on the board of directors to maintain continuity of management, ownership, and control of a corporation. See *Miniat v EMI*, 315 F3d 712 (7th Cir 2002).

CASE SUMMARY

The Case of Medoff, the Marathon Man

FACTS: The Boston Athletic Association (BAA) is a nonprofit corporation created to sponsor the annual Boston Marathon. The BAA authorized its president, William Cloney, to negotiate contracts for it. Cloney executed a contract with attorney Marshall Medoff, giving Medoff exclusive power to promote the marathon. The BAA transferred to Medoff all rights to use the marathon name and logos. The contract's financial terms were extremely favorable to Medoff, who could renew the contract from year to year. When the BAA's board members learned of the contract, they declared that it was beyond the authorization vested in Cloney. The board brought an action to have the contract set aside. Medoff contended that Cloney had authority to make the contract and that therefore the contract bound the corporation.

DECISION: Judgment for the BAA. It is the obligation of the board to direct the corporation. Consistent with this obligation, a board may delegate general managerial functions to corporate officers, but certain powers cannot be delegated. The contract made with Medoff surrendered virtually complete control of the marathon to Medoff. The board in this case improperly delegated to Cloney the authority to make such a contract, which prevented accomplishment of the BAA's corporate purpose, that of sponsoring the marathon. Authority to make such a contract was beyond the power of the board to delegate. [**Boston Athletic Association v International Marathon, Inc., 467 NE2d 58 (Mass 1984)**]

CPA   ## 6. Conflict of Interest

A director is disqualified from taking part in corporate action involving a matter in which the director has an undisclosed conflicting interest. Because it cannot be known how the other directors would have acted if they had known of the conflict of interest, the corporation generally may avoid any transaction because of a director's secret disqualification.

A number of states provide by statute that a director's conflict of interest does not impair the transaction or contract entered into or authorized by the board of directors if the disqualified director disclosed the interest and if the contract or transaction is fair and reasonable with respect to the corporation. Thus, a director may lend money to a corporation if the board of directors is informed of the transaction and the terms approximate the market rate for businesses with similar credit ratings. Some states simply require notice of the conflicting interests and abstaining from all participation in the transaction. **For Example,** Delos Yancey, Jr., and Delos Yancey III were directors of State Mutual Insurance Co. Subsequently, they formed North American Services, Inc., and served as directors of both companies. State Mutual decided to sell one of its companies, Atlas Life Insurance, Inc. North American expressed an interest in purchasing Atlas, and thereafter the Yanceys recused themselves from State Mutual's decision-making process in selling the company. State Mutual sold Atlas to North American at a $5.2 million loss. Some two years later, North American resold Atlas for a $22.6 million gain, and a shareholder derivative suit was brought against the Yanceys. The court decided the

FIGURE 48-1 | *Powers of Directors*

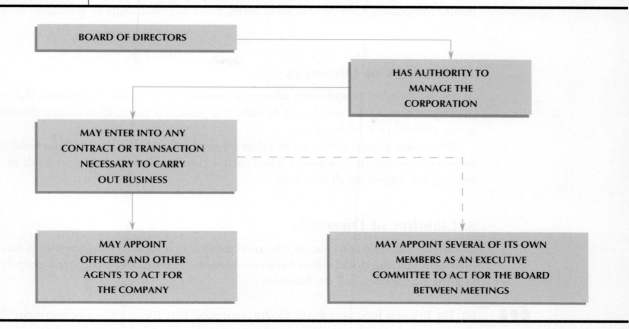

case in favor of the Yanceys, holding that they complied with the state's "safe harbor" law by giving notice of their conflicting interest to State Mutual and thereafter abstaining from all participation in the corporate transaction.[5]

To prevent conflicts of interest and covert compensation schemes, section 402(a) of the federal Sarbanes-Oxley Act[6] prohibits all loans either directly or indirectly to directors and executive officers by their corporations, with an exception for companies in the consumer credit business, who may make loans to directors and officers on terms no more favorable than those offered to the general public.

Prior to Sarbanes-Oxley, it was a common practice for publicly traded companies to provide low-interest loans to company officers. **For Example,** Bernard Ebbers, while CEO of WorldCom, Inc., used company stock as collateral for bank loans used to buy additional shares of WorldCom stock. When WorldCom's share prices weakened in late 2000 and Ebbers needed to put up additional collateral to cover his loans, WorldCom's board of directors decided to lend him more than $400 million dollars at just over 2 percent interest with no fixed due date. The company rate was far below the personal loan rate at banks near company headquarters of between 9.75 percent and 16.67 percent, and well below margin loan rates at 5 percent. Business conglomerate Tyco International Ltd. maintained a "key employee loan fund" that was used like a revolving line of credit by Tyco executives Dennis Kozlowski and Martin Swartz to fund their lavish lifestyles. The language of

---

[5] *Fisher v State Mutual Insurance Co.*, 290 F3d 1256 (11th Cir 2002).
[6] PL 107-204, 116 Stat 745.

Sarbanes-Oxley is broad and far reaching and prohibits all direct personal loans by public companies, such as relocation loans, tax loans, and loans to purchase securities.

7. Meetings of Directors

Action by directors is ordinarily taken at a meeting of the board of directors. Bylaws sometimes require the meeting to be held at a particular place. Generally, a director is not allowed to vote by proxy.

Most states permit action to be taken by the board of directors without holding an actual meeting. It is required when such action is taken that it be set forth in writing and signed by all directors.

8. Liability of Directors

In dealing with the corporation, the directors act in a fiduciary capacity. It is into their care that the stockholders have entrusted the control of the corporate property and the management of the business.

CPA   (A) The Business Judgment Rule. Courts recognize that the decisions of corporate directors often involve weighing and balancing legal, ethical, commercial, promotional, public relations, and other factors. Accordingly, courts will not sit in judgment on the wisdom of decisions made by directors. If the directors have acted in good faith on the basis of adequate information, courts will not enjoin the course of action taken by the directors.[7] Moreover, even though such action causes loss to the corporation, the directors will not be held personally liable for it. This principle is called the **business judgment rule (BJR)**.

business judgment rule (BJR)–rule that allows management immunity from liability for corporate acts where there is a reasonable indication that the acts were made in good faith with due care.

CPA   **(1) The Traditional Rule**
Courts apply the business judgment rule as a presumption that in making a business decision, the directors acted (1) on an informed basis, (2) in good faith, and (3) in the honest belief that the action taken was in the best interest of the corporation. The party challenging the directors' actions has the burden of proving that they did not act on an informed basis or in good faith or in the best interest of the corporation.[8] (See the *Disney* case.)

CPA   **(2) Application in Corporate Control Transactions**
When a corporation receives a takeover bid, the target board of directors may tend to take actions that are in their own interest and not in the interest of the shareholders. Courts have recognized the potential for director self-interest in this situation. (See the *Van Gorkom* case.)

---

[7] In discharging their duties, directors are not individually liable if, acting in good faith, they rely upon "the opinion of counsel for the corporation" or "written reports setting forth financial data concerning the corporation and prepared by an independent public accountant or certified public accountant or firm of such accountants"—which opinions or statements turn out to be flawed. *Casey v Brennan*, 344 NJ Super 83 (2002).

[8] *Huang Group v LTI*, 760 NE2d 14 (Ohio App 2002).

C A S E   S U M M A R Y

Problem: "A Mismatch of Cultures and Styles"
Solution: $140 Million Severance Payment
Shareholders: Not Happy !

FACTS: Michael Ovitz was a founder of Creative Artists Agency (CAA), an agency in 1995 with 1,400 of Hollywood's top actors, directors, writers, and musicians. Ovitz was considered one of the most powerful figures in Hollywood at that time. Because of the untimely death of Disney's prior president in a helicopter crash, Walt Disney Co. CEO Michael Eisner focused on hiring Ovitz as president. The chairman of Disney's compensation committee, Irwin Russell, in consultation with Eisner, negotiated the Ovitz employment agreement (OEA). As part of the OEA, if Disney fired Ovitz for any reason other than gross negligence or malfeasance, Ovitz would be entitled to a nonfault termination (NFT) package consisting of his remaining salary for the five-year period, bonuses, and the immediate vesting of stock options. Russell met with a compensation expert for advice on the contract and had telephone conversations with two compensation committee members, Sidney Poitier and Ignatio Lozano. CEO Eisner telephoned each member of the board of directors to inform them of his plan to hire Ovitz. On September 26, 1995, the Compensation Committee had a one-hour meeting to discuss several topics, including the OEA. Thereafter, the full board of directors met and elected Ovitz president of Disney. After he joined Disney, it soon became apparent that a "mismatch of cultures and styles" ensued and that Ovitz was not succeeding as president. The trial court gave an example as follows:

> *In January 1996, a corporate retreat was held at Walt Disney World in Orlando, Florida. At that retreat, Ovitz failed to integrate himself in the group of executives by declining to participate in group activities, insisting on a limousine, when the other executives, including Eisner, were taking a bus, and making inappropriate demands of the park employees. In short, Ovitz "was a little elitist for the egalitarian Walt Disney World cast members [employees]," and a poor fit with his fellow executives.*

When it became clear that Ovitz was not working out, Eisner considered his options. Sanford Litvak, Disney's general counsel, advised Eisner and other directors that Ovitz had not been shown to have been grossly negligent or malfeasant in his year at Disney, and no cause existed to avoid the NFT payments. Eisner decided it was necessary to terminate Ovitz on a nonfault basis and notified the board members. The board members supported this decision under the nonfault termination agreement. Ovitz was ultimately paid $140 million in severance pay. Stockholders brought a derivative suit, asserting that Eisner and the board of directors had breached their fiduciary duties in connection with Ovitz's hiring and termination. Years of litigation cumulated in a 37-day trial that ended on January 19, 2005.

DECISION: Judgment for the defendants. Eisner's actions should not serve as a model for directors and CEOs. By virtue of his imperial nature as CEO, he handicapped the board's decision-making abilities, stacking the board with his friends who, although not necessarily beholden to him in a legal sense, were more willing to support him unconditionally than truly independent directors. He failed to keep the board informed as he should have and failed to better involve the board in the process of hiring Ovitz, usurping the role for himself, although not a violation of law. Despite the legitimate criticisms leveled at Eisner, especially at having enthroned himself as the omnipotent and infallible monarch of his personal Magic Kingdom, Eisner's actions were taken in good faith and did not breach his fiduciary duty of care because he was not grossly negligent, nor was any other director in violation of a fiduciary duty. The redress for failures that arise from faithful management (not in violation of fiduciary duties) must come from the markets, not the courts. Corporate decisions are made, risks are taken, the results become apparent, capital flows accordingly, and shareholder value increases or decreases.
[In re Walt Disney Co. Derivative Litigation 907 A2d 693 (Del Ch 2005)]

CASE SUMMARY

Directors—Independent Evaluators, Not Pawns

FACTS: Jerome Van Gorkom was chairman and chief executive officer of Trans Union Inc. On September 13, Van Gorkom arranged a meeting with Jay Pritzker, a well-known takeover specialist and a social acquaintance, to determine his interest in acquiring Trans Union. On Thursday, September 18, Pritzker made an offer of $55 per share (a price suggested by Van Gorkom). Pritzker wanted a decision to be made by the board no later than Sunday, September 21. On Friday, Van Gorkom called a special meeting of the board of directors for noon the following day; no agenda was announced. At the directors' meeting, Van Gorkom made a 20-minute oral analysis of the merger transaction. He showed that the company was having difficulty generating sufficient income to offset its increasingly large investment tax credits. Van Gorkom discussed his meeting with Pritzker and the reasons for the meeting. Copies of the proposed merger agreement were delivered too late to be studied before or during the meeting. No consultants or investment advisors were called on to support the merger price of $55 per share. The merger was approved at the end of the two-hour meeting. Certain shareholders brought a class-action suit against the directors, contending that the board's decision was not the product of informed business judgment. The directors responded that their good-faith decision was shielded by the business judgment rule.

DECISION: Judgment for the shareholders. Directors cannot claim the protection of the business judgment rule if they have been grossly negligent in exercising their judgment. The directors approved the merger based on a 20-minute oral analysis by the president, Van Gorkom, at a hastily called board meeting with no prior notice of its purpose. No investment consultants or other experts were employed to assess the intrinsic value of the company, nor were the merger documents containing the terms of the merger available for study by the directors. Deciding to sell the company without any information and deliberation was gross negligence. The directors therefore could not claim the protection of the business judgment rule when they voted to "sell" the company for $55 per share. The directors are personally liable for damages. [**Smith v Van Gorkom, 488 A2d 858 (Del 1985)**]

(3) Protection of Directors

In the wake of court decisions holding directors personally liable for damages for gross negligence and in the wake of the resulting general reluctance of individuals to serve as directors, states have passed statutes to protect directors. The aim of the various state laws is essentially the same: to reduce the risk of personal liability for directors who act in good faith when their decisions are challenged. The laws permit a corporation, by a stockholder-approved amendment to its charter or certificate of incorporation, to protect its directors from monetary liability for duty-of-care violations (gross negligence) provided they have not acted in bad faith, breached their duty of loyalty, or gained an improper personal benefit.[9] The laws provide for indemnification and advancement of expenses.

---

[9] See Del Code § 102(b)(7); NY Bus Corp Law §§ 721–723; Ohio Gen Corp Law § 1701.59; Ind Bus Corp Law, ch 35, § 1(e); Mo Gen Bus Corp Law 351.355 §§ 2, 7.

For Example, to avoid supervision by the Office of Thrift Supervision (OTS), the directors of Oak Tree Savings Bank, a subsidiary of Landmark Land Company, Inc., which had loaned subsidiary land development companies $986 million, placed the bank in bankruptcy. Because of this, director Bernard Ille resigned. In civil proceedings brought against all of the bank directors, Ille successfully defended himself against the OTS charges. He thus would be entitled to mandatory indemnification from the bank. In addition, employees Trapani and Braun, who were subpoenaed and deposed under adversarial circumstances but were not charged, were deemed to have succeeded on the merits in their defense and were entitled to mandatory indemnification for legal expenses under state law. The other

thinking things through

Are the Days of the Imperial CEO Over?

Many changes clarifying the role of corporate directors have occurred since the Enron and WorldCom debacles that came to light in 2001. Federal regulations under the Sarbanes-Oxley Act now apply to directors and officers, and a Corporate Director's Guidebook* was revised and published in 2007 by the American Bar Association's Committee on Corporate Laws, explaining the general legal concepts that apply to directors of public companies. However, the core values associated with the corporate directors' role—good faith, general oversight, informed judgment, and dedication to the corporation's best interests—continue to be the touchstone for evaluating directors' conduct.

Michael Eisner, considered by many as the Imperial CEO, stacked the board with his friends and expected and received loyalty from them regarding all-important corporate decisions. Is it critical for a board's nominating/corporate governance committee to receive nominations from not only other directors but also institutional investors and shareholders rather than just the CEO—as was the case at Disney with CEO Eisner?**

The chairman of Disney's Compensation Committee hired a highly regarded consultant regarding Ovitz's employment contract and telephoned two members of the committee to inform them of progress. A vote was taken on September 26, after less than an hour of discussion by the committee, and thereafter Ovitz was elected president. As a best practice, should the entire compensation committee have been kept in the loop on this significant matter during negotiations by e-mail, executive summaries, and backup documentation? Should the Disney board have been given meaningful documentation on this appointment to study a week before the board meeting? Do you think it would have been good form for a Disney director back then to question Mr. Eisner regarding the Ovitz appointment: "I don't think we are ready to vote ... give us some more supporting documents"? Do you believe that members of a board of directors today feel much more entitled to have adequate and timely information and to ask the tough questions?

* *Corporate Director's Guidebook*, 5th ed. (American Bar Association, August 2007), **www.abanet.org/abastore**.

** See, for example, Boston Scientific's Corporate Governance Manual, Standing Committees and Code of Conduct available at **www.bostonscientifc.com** under Investor Relations. Boston Scientific's recent proxy statement reports that 10 of its 14 directors are "independent from management" under NYSE rules. Company bylaws invite shareholders to nominate individuals as directors along with nominations from the Nominating and Governance Committee and the CEO.

directors and employees charged were found not to have acted in good faith and were not entitled to indemnification.[10]

(b) ACTIONS AGAINST DIRECTORS. Actions against directors should be brought by the corporation. If the corporation fails to act, as is the case when the directors alleged to be liable control the corporation, shareholders may bring the action in a representative capacity for the corporation.[11]

(c) REMOVAL OF DIRECTOR. Ordinarily, directors are removed by vote of the shareholders. In some states, the board of directors may remove a director and elect a successor on the ground that the removed director (1) did not accept office, (2) failed to satisfy the qualifications for office, (3) was continually absent from the state without a leave of absence granted by the board, generally for a period of six months or more, (4) was discharged in bankruptcy, (5) was convicted of a felony, (6) was unable to perform the duties of director because of any illness or disability, generally for a period of six months or more, or (7) had been judicially declared of unsound mind.[12]

The RMBCA provides for removal of directors "with or without cause" by a majority vote of the shareholders unless the articles of incorporation provide that directors may be removed only for cause.[13] **For Example,** former Conseco, Inc., director Dennis Murray, Sr., was unsuccessful in his action against the board of directors challenging his removal from the board. The court held that the directors had unlimited authority to remove a fellow director without regard for the reasons why the other directors wished to remove him.[14] Directors may always be voted out of office at a regular meeting of shareholders held for the election of directors.

C. OFFICERS, AGENTS, AND EMPLOYEES

Corporations generally have a president, at least one vice president, a secretary, a treasurer, and frequently a chief executive officer (CEO). The duties of these officers are generally set forth in the corporation's bylaws. The duty of the secretary to keep minutes of the proceedings of shareholders and directors is commonly included. Corporation codes generally expressly permit the same person to be both secretary and treasurer. In large corporations, there is often a recording secretary and a corresponding secretary.

Sometimes the officers are elected by the shareholders, but usually they are appointed by the board of directors. The RMBCA follows the general pattern of providing for the appointment of officers by the board of directors.[15] Ordinarily, no particular formality is required to make such appointments. Unless prohibited, a director may hold an executive office.

Officers ordinarily hire the employees and agents of the corporation.

---

[10] *In re Landmark Land Co. of California,* 76 F3d 553 (4th Cir 1996).
[11] *In re Abbott Laboratories Derivative Shareholder Litigation,* 325 F3d 795 (7th Cir 2003).
[12] See California Corp Code § 807, recognizing grounds (1), (2), (5), and (7).
[13] RMBCA § 8.08(a).
[14] *Murray v Conseco, Inc.,* 766 NE2d 38 (Ind App 2002).
[15] RMBCA § 8.40(a).

9. Powers of Officers

The officers of a corporation are its agents. Consequently, their powers are controlled by the laws of agency.[16] As in the case of any other agency, a third person has the burden of proving that a particular officer had the authority he or she purported to have.

The fact that the officer or employee acting on behalf of the corporation is a major shareholder does not give either any greater agency powers. Moreover, the person dealing with the officer or employee is charged with knowledge of any limitation on authority contained in the recorded corporate charter or articles of incorporation.

When the nature of the transaction is unusual, that unusual nature should alert a third person to the necessity of specific authorization from the corporation.

(A) PRESIDENT. It is sometimes held that, in the absence of some limitation on authority, the president of a corporation has by virtue of that office the authority to act as agent on behalf of the corporation within the scope of the business in which the corporation is empowered to engage. It has also been held, however, that the president has such broad powers only when the president is the general manager of the corporation. In instances in which a corporation has a president and chief executive officer, the CEO has authority to exercise personal judgment and discretion in the administrative and executive functions of the corporation as endowed by its bylaws and the resolutions of the board of directors. When a corporation has both a CEO and a president, the CEO is ordinarily the officer entrusted with the broader decisional powers, whereas the president is the executing officer. The president does not have authority by virtue of that office to make a contract that, because of its unusual character, would require action by the board of directors or shareholders.[17]

The president cannot make a contract to fix long-term or unusual contracts of employment, release a claim of the corporation, promise that the corporation will later repurchase shares issued to a subscriber, or mortgage a corporate property.[18]

It is ordinarily held that the president of a business corporation is not authorized to execute commercial paper in the name of the corporation. However, the president may do so when authorized by the board of directors to borrow money for the corporation.

(B) OTHER OFFICERS AND EMPLOYEES. The authority of corporate employees and other officers, such as the secretary or treasurer, is generally limited to the duties of their office. However, the authority may be extended by the conduct of the corporation in accordance with the general principles governing apparent authority based on the conduct of the principal. An unauthorized act may, of course, be ratified. The authority of the general manager of the corporation is determined by principles of ordinary agency law.

---

[16] *IFC Credit Corp. v Nuova Pasta Co.*, 815 F Supp 268 (ND Ill 1993).
[17] *French v Chosin Few, Inc.*, 173 F Supp 2d (WDNY 2001).
[18] *Schmidt v Farm Credit Services*, 977 F2d 511 (10th Cir 1992).

10. Liability Relating to Fiduciary Duties

The relationship of officers to the corporation, like that of directors, is a fiduciary one. Officers, because of their access to corporate information developed in the pursuit of their daily duties on behalf of the corporation, have an obligation to inform the directors of material information relating to the business. Officers have an obligation not to make any secret financial gain at the expense of the corporation. Because of their level of knowledge of the business, officer-directors have a high fiduciary duty to the corporation.

(A) **CORPORATE OPPORTUNITIES.** If an officer diverts a corporate opportunity, the corporation may recover from the officer the profits of which the corporation has been deprived.

CASE SUMMARY

Ruling Wisely and Decently?

FACTS: Demoulas Super Markets, Inc. (DSM), was owned by brothers George and Telemachus Demoulas, each owning an equal number of shares of stock. From 1964 through May 1971, the company grew from 5 stores to a chain of 14 supermarkets, including 2 stores in New Hampshire. George died suddenly on June 27, 1971, and, at his death, Telemachus assumed control of DSM under the terms of a voting trust. In 1990, George's son Arthur, age 22 and a shareholder of DSM, brought a shareholder derivative action on behalf of DSM, contending that since George's death, Telemachus had diverted business opportunities away from DSM into other businesses that were solely owned by Telemachus's branch of the family. The evidence showed that in the 1970s two new corporations were formed and operated supermarkets in New Hampshire; DSM supplied the financing and management, but ownership was held in the name of Telemachus's sister and daughter. By 1986, these stores grew into a single supermarket chain operating under the Market Basket name and entirely owned by members of Telemachus's branch of the family. The trial court judge determined that Telemachus had diverted these corporate opportunities from DSM, and the court ordered the transfer of the assets and liabilities of the new corporations back to DSM. In her decision, the judge cited lines from *Ulysses*, by Alfred Lord Tennyson, in which Ulysses speaks lovingly of his son, Telemachus, expressing the belief that he would rule wisely and decently after his death. Telemachus denied that any acts were improper or gave rise to liability and charged that the judge was not impartial, as evidenced by her quotation from Tennyson's poem.

DECISION: Judgment against Telemachus. Judicial bias was not present, and the literary reference was simply the judge's stylistic way of stating the theme of her decision against Telemachus, based on the facts she had found. Telemachus had a fiduciary duty to DSM. A fiduciary violates his duty of loyalty by advancing the pecuniary interests of a child or a sibling in a manner that would constitute a breach if he had acted for himself. The record is clear that the New Hampshire companies were set up under Telemachus's direction and were independent in name only, with DSM managing and financing them. The return to DSM of the assets and liabilities of the diverted business was the proper remedy. [**Demoulas v Demoulas Super Markets, Inc., 677 NE2d 159 (Mass 1997); see also 787 NE2d 1059 (Mass 2003)**]

An opportunity that would be advantageous to the corporation must first be offered to the corporation before an officer or a director, who owes a fiduciary duty to the corporation, can take advantage of the opportunity. Full disclosure is required. Only if the opportunity is rejected by a majority of disinterested directors may the officer then take advantage of the opportunity. **For Example,** Nancy Harris was president of the Northeast Harbor Golf Club, Inc. In her capacity as club president, she learned of an opportunity to purchase the Gilpin property, which adjoined the golf club. Her private purchase of the property constituted the taking of a corporate opportunity and resulted in her liability to the club. Harris believed that her purchase, in a separate transaction, of the Smallidge land, which was adjacent to three of the golf club's holes and could be developed, was not usurpation of a corporate opportunity because she learned of the availability independently of the club. However, this also was a corporate opportunity because it was so closely related to the club's business. She was obligated to disclose the opportunity to the corporation and let it decide whether to pursue it.[19]

Officers may avail themselves of all opportunities lying outside the field of their duties as officers when business opportunities come to them in an individual capacity.[20]

(b) **Secret Profits.** Officers are liable to the corporation for secret profits made in connection with, or at the expense of, the business of the corporation.

(c) **Duty of Loyalty.** A corporate officer, while still employed by his or her firm, may be in breach of the officer's fiduciary duty of loyalty by recruiting key management employees to join a competing company by telling them about the competitor's beneficial compensation, signing bonuses, medical benefits, and superior computer systems. However, an officer may legally make arrangements before leaving the firm to compete in the future. The line separating mere preparation from active competition may be difficult to discern, and, if misjudged, may lead to significant liability for the officer and a competitor aider and abettor, as is evidenced by the *Security Title v Pope* case.

CASE SUMMARY

Walkin' with Linda Pope

FACTS: Linda Pope ran one of the largest and most successful title insurance branches in the title insurance industry for Security Title Insurance. First American Title Insurance sought to regain its top position in title insurance sales through its Talon division by recruiting key people from other companies who had relationships with key customers and other key employees. Talon recruited Pope.

---

[19] *Northeast Harbor Golf Club v Harris*, 725 A2d 1018 (Me 1999); see *Anderson v Bellino*, 658 NW2d 645 (Neb 2003).
[20] *Hill v Southeastern Floor Covering Co.*, 596 So2d 874 (Miss 1992).

CASE SUMMARY

Continued

While still employed by Security Title, Pope secretly solicited key management employees to join Talon–First American and planned to bring all 40 employees with her. She arranged for a Talon official, over drinks and dinners, to help with the recruiting by telling Security Title employees about Talon's beneficial compensation, signing bonuses, medical benefits, and superior computer system. Security Title asserted that Pope's actions, aided and abetted by Talon, resulted in $12,194,335 in lost profits after 35 employees walked out on October 20 which was when Security Title "walked her out"—fired Pope—having discovered her plans to leave. Security Title sued Pope for breach of fiduciary duty of loyalty and sued Talon–First American as an aider and abettor. Pope defended that she was merely making arrangements to compete in the future.

DECISION: Judgment for Security Title. Pope breached her fiduciary duty by improperly recruiting Security Title employees for Talon while she was still employed by Security Title. First American's argument that Pope had merely discussed her plans with the other employees and was only preparing to compete with Security Title flies in the face of a wealth of evidence presented to the jury. She secretly solicited key management employees to join a competitor and enticed employees to leave by telling them of bonuses and benefits. [**Security Title Agency, Inc. v Pope, 200 P3d 977 (Ariz App 2008)**]

11. Agents and Employees

The authority, rights, and liabilities of an agent or employee of a corporation are governed by the same rules as those applicable when the principal or employer is a natural person. The authority of corporate employees is also governed by general agency principles. **For Example,** when Juantai Li signed a promissory note in his own name and did not indicate that he was an agent of a corporation, he was held personally liable for $523,823 under the note he signed.[21]

The fact that a person is acting on behalf of a corporation does not serve as a shield from the liability that would be imposed for acts done on behalf of a natural person.

D. Liability

Limited liability is a major reason for incorporating. Management, however, is not free from all civil and criminal liability simply because the corporate form is used.

12. Liability of Management to Third Persons

Officers and managers of a corporation are not liable to third parties for the economic consequences of their advice so long as they acted in good faith to advance the interests of the corporation, even if they cause the corporation to refuse to deal with or break its contract with these third persons.

Ordinarily, the management of a corporation (its directors, officers, and executive employees) is not liable to third persons for the effect of its management or advice.

---

[21] *Wujin Nanxiashu v Ti-Well International*, 807 NYS2d 47 (App Div 2005).

The liability of a director or an officer for misconduct may usually be enforced only by the corporation or by shareholders bringing a derivative action on behalf of the corporation. Ordinarily, directors or officers are not liable to a third person for loss caused by the negligent performance of their duties as directors or officers even if, because of such negligence, the corporation is in turn liable to the third person to whom the corporation owed the duty to use care or was under a contract obligation to render a particular service.

However, in those rare cases when a director or an officer has in some way participated in or directed the tortious act, personal liability will attach. For example, a corporate officer and director may be held personally liable for the tort of fraud in the inducement regarding a false promise to grant an insurance agency an exclusive territory selling viatical settlements, by which life insurance policies of terminally ill people are purchased at a discount in exchange for an immediate cash settlement.[22]

ethics&the law

For the past five years, one of the concerns shareholders and others have raised about corporate officers is their level of compensation. Treasury Secretary Geithner identified executive compensation practices as a contributing factor to the financial crisis of 2008–2009, where incentives for short-term gains overwhelmed the checks and balances meant to mitigate the risk of excessive financial leverage. In addition, Kenneth Feinberg, the so-called "pay czar," has been empowered by Congress to decide the appropriate level of compensation for some of the United States' top financiers (Vikram Pandit of Citigroup and Kenneth Lewis of Bank of America) and industrialists (the new heads of GM and Chrysler), along with executives of other firms that, at the time of this writing, have yet to pay back money from the U.S. Treasury's Troubled Asset Relief Program (TARP). * The following

figures are some examples of CEO total annual compensation packages for 2009.

Company	CEO	Amount
Oracle	Lawrence J. Ellison	$ 556,980,000
Occidental Petroleum	Ray R. Irani	$ 222,640,000
Hess	John B. Hess	$ 154,580,000
Ultra Petroleum	Michael D. Watford	$ 116,930,000
EOG Resources	Mark G. Papa	$ 90,470,000
WR Berkley	William R. Berkley	$ 87,480,000
Burlington Santa Fe	Matthew K. Rose	$ 68,620,000
Allegheny Energy	Paul J. Evanson	$ 67,260,000
Monsanto	Hugh Grant	$ 64,600,000
Deere & Co.	Robert W. Lane	$ 61,300,000

Is it troubling to shareholders, and perhaps employees, that downsizing and cost cutting occur—but CEO salaries remain at the same levels or higher? If the board members approve the salaries, aren't they accountable to the shareholders?

** Stephen Labaton, "Treasury to Set Executives' Pay at 7 Ailing Firms," *New York Times*, June 11, 2009, **www.nytimes.com/2009/06/11/business/11pay.html**.

** Source: Forbes.com: CEO Compensation 2009

[22] *First Financial USA, Inc. v Steinger*, 760 So2d 996 (Fla App 2000).

13. Criminal Liability

Officers and directors, as well as the corporation itself, may be criminally accountable for business regulatory offenses.

(A) ACTIVE PARTICIPATION. Officers and directors, as in the case of agents, are personally responsible for any crimes committed by them even when they act on behalf of the corporation.[23] At the local level, they may be criminally responsible for violation of ordinances relating to sanitation, safety, and hours of closing.

At the state level, they may be criminally liable for conducting a business without obtaining necessary licenses or after the corporate certificate of incorporation has been forfeited.

At the federal level, officers and directors may be criminally liable for tax and securities law violations as well as egregious environmental protection law and worker safety law violations. International transactions may lead to potential criminal exposure. Under the Foreign Corrupt Practices Act, it is a crime for a U.S. firm to make payments or gifts to a foreign officer to obtain business. Not only is the U.S. corporation subject to a fine but also the officers and individuals involved are subject to fine and imprisonment.

(B) RESPONSIBLE CORPORATE OFFICER DOCTRINE. Officers and directors may be criminally liable under a number of federal and state statutes for failure to prevent the commission of a crime if they are found to be the "responsible corporate officers." These statutes include the Food, Drug and Cosmetic Act, the Federal Hazardous Substances Act, the Occupational Safety and Health Act, the Federal Water Pollution Act, and, at the state level, the California Corporate Criminal Liability Act. **For Example,** Gary Lundgren was a shareholder and officer of KIE, Inc., which owned and operated a sewage treatment plant on Ketron Island. He knew of the facility's discharge of pollutants into Puget Sound without a permit. As the "responsible corporate officer," he was held personally liable for a $250,000 penalty because he controlled the facility with knowledge of the violations.[24] The California Corporate Criminal Liability Act requires managers in control of corporate operations who have knowledge of "serious concealed dangers" to employees or customers to notify the appropriate regulatory authority or be subject to criminal liability.[25]

(C) LIABILITY OF THE CORPORATION ITSELF. A corporation itself may be convicted of a criminal offense if its agent committed the offense acting within the scope of the agent's authority. **For Example,** Steenberg Homes, Inc., was convicted of negligent criminal homicide in the deaths of two cyclists who were killed when the company's trailer truck, loaded with timber, disengaged from the tractor. If safety chains had been properly attached, the accident would not have happened, and the corporation's failure to establish and enforce safety procedures was a cause of the deaths of the cyclists.[26]

---

[23] *Joy Management Co. v City of Detroit*, 455 NW2d 55 (Mich App 1990).
[24] *State Department of Ecology v Lundgren*, 971 P2d 948 (Wash App 1999).
[25] Cal Penal Code § 387 (West 2006).
[26] *State v Steenberg Homes, Inc.*, 859 NW2d 668 (Wis App 1998).

(D) PUNISHMENT OF CORPORATIONS. Under the Organizational Federal Sentencing Guidelines, organizations, including corporations, trusts, pension funds, unions, and nonprofit organizations, are subject to greatly increased fines for criminal convictions. However, corporations and other covered organizations that implement an effective compliance program designed to prevent and detect corporate crimes and voluntarily disclose such crimes to the government will be subject to much lower fines under the guidelines.[27]

14. Indemnification of Officers, Directors, Employees, and Agents

While performing what they believe to be their duty, officers, directors, employees, and agents of corporations may commit acts for which they are later sued or criminally prosecuted. The RMBCA broadly authorizes the corporation to indemnify these persons if they acted in good faith and in a manner reasonably believed to be in, or not opposed to, the interests of the corporation and had no reason to believe that their conduct was unlawful.[28] In some states, statutory provision is made requiring the corporation to indemnify directors and officers for reasonable expenses incurred by them in defending unwarranted suits brought against them by shareholders.

15. Liability for Corporate Debts

Because the corporation is a separate legal person, debts that it owes are ordinarily the obligations of the corporation only. Consequently, neither directors nor officers are individually liable for corporate debts, even though it may have been their acts that gave rise to the debts.

In some states, liability for corporate debts is imposed on the corporation's officers and directors when the corporation improperly engages in business.

16. Protection of Shareholders

Shareholders may obtain protection from misconduct by management and by the majority of the shareholders. Shareholders may protect themselves by voting at the next annual election for new directors and for new officers if the latter are elected. Shareholders may take remedial action at a special meeting called for that purpose. Objecting shareholders may bring a legal action when the management misconduct complained of constitutes a legal wrong.[29]

17. Civil Liability of the Corporation

A corporation is liable to third persons for the acts of its officers, employees, and agents to the same extent that a natural person is liable for the acts of agents and

---

[27] U.S. Sentencing Commission Guidelines Manual §§ 8C2.5(f), 8C2.6. On April 8, 2004, the Commission adopted amendments to the Guidelines and requires a periodic assessment of the "risk of criminal conduct" by the corporation or organization.

[28] Subchapter 8E, added in 1980 and revised in 1994.

[29] *Christner v Anderson, Nietzke & Co.*, 444 NW2d 779 (Mich 1989).

employees. This means that the ordinary rules of agency law determine the extent to which the corporation is liable to a third person for a contract made or a tort committed by management personnel, employees, and agents.

lawflix

Smartest Guys in the Room (2005)(R)

The story of Enron executives and their ploys that duped creditors, analysts, shareholders, and employees. A look at what happens when a board is asleep at the wheel and the officers have unfettered authority.

Check out LawFlix at **www.cengage.com/blaw/dvl** to access movie clips that illustrate business law concepts.

MAKE THE CONNECTION

SUMMARY

Ordinarily, stockholder action is taken at a regular or special meeting of the stockholders. The presence of a quorum of the voting shareholders is required.

Management of a corporation is under the control of a board of directors elected by the shareholders. Courts will not interfere with the board's judgment in the absence of unusual conduct such as fraud. A director is disqualified from taking part in corporate action when the director has a conflict of interest. Action by directors is usually taken at a properly called meeting of the board. Directors act in a fiduciary capacity in dealing with the corporation. Directors who act in good faith and have exercised reasonable care are not liable for losses resulting from their management decisions. Ordinarily, directors are removed by shareholders.

Officers of a corporation, including a CEO, president, vice president, secretary, and treasurer, are usually selected and removed by the board of directors. Officers are agents of the corporation, and their powers are governed by the law of agency. Their relations with the corporation are fiduciary in nature, and they are liable for any secret profits and for diverting corporate opportunities to their own advantage.

Directors and officers, as in the case of agents generally, are personally responsible for any torts or crimes they commit even if they act on behalf of the corporation. The corporation itself may be prosecuted for crimes and is subject to fines if convicted. The ordinary rules of agency law determine the extent to which a corporation is liable for a contract made or tort committed by a director, officer, corporate agent, or employee.

LEARNING OUTCOMES

After studying this chapter, you should be able to clearly explain:

A. SHAREHOLDERS

LO.1 Explain how shareholders, as owners of the corporation, exercise limited control over management by voting at shareholders' meetings to elect directors

See the discussion of shareholder voting and meetings beginning on p. 1138.

B. DIRECTORS

LO.2 Explain the qualifications and powers of directors

See the discussion regarding the broad authority of directors to manage the corporation, beginning on p. 1139.

LO.3 Explain the liability of directors and the meaning of the business judgment rule (BJR)

See the *Walt Disney* case in which an unsuccessful action taken by directors was protected by the BJR, p. 1143.

See the *Van Gorkom* case in which directors were not protected by the BJR, because they were grossly negligent in their judgment, p. 1144.

C. OFFICERS, AGENTS, AND EMPLOYEES

LO.4 Explain the obligation of officers—who have access to corporate information and agency powers—to not violate their fiduciary duties to the corporation

See the *Demoulas Super Markets* case regarding diverting corporate opportunities, p. 1148.

See the *Security Title v Pope* case regarding a manager's duty of loyalty, p. 1149.

D. LIABILITY

LO.5 Explain how directors, officers, and the corporation itself may be criminally liable for regulatory offenses

See the Gary Lundgren example in which, as a "responsible corporate officer," Gary was held personally liable for environmental law violations, p. 1152.

KEY TERMS

business judgment rule (BJR)   quorum

QUESTIONS AND CASE PROBLEMS

1. Shareholders of Bear Stearns sued the directors of the corporation for damages for violation of the directors' fiduciary duties in effecting a stock-for-stock

merger with J. P. Morgan Chase for an implied value of $10 per share while the company's stock had previously reached a 15-month high of $160. On March 10, 2008, information began leaking into the market that Bear Stearns had a liquidity problem. On March 13, 2008, the company was forced to seek emergency financing from the Federal Reserve and J. P. Morgan Chase. By the weekend of March 14–16, the company could no longer operate without major financing. In an effort to preserve some shareholder value while averting the uncertainty of bankruptcy (where stockholders would likely receive nothing), and represented by teams of legal and financial experts and relying on their financial advisor Lazard Freres & Co.'s opinion that the "exchange ratio is fair, from a financial point of view, to the shareholders," the board of directors approved the initial merger agreement. The shareholder plaintiffs contended that the ultimate $10 share price paid was inadequate and they presented their experts who vigorously dissected the board's decisions. What defense, if any, would you raise on behalf of the Bear Stearns board of directors? [*In re Bear Stearns Litigation*, 870 NYS2d 709 (Sup 2008)]

2. In 1996, Congress offered national banks the opportunity to become Subchapter S entities. Amboy Bancorporation was a small, highly profitable New Jersey Bank that was overcapitalized. Amboy's president and CEO utilized Bank Advisory Group, Inc. (BAG), to calculate the fair value of individual shares of Amboy stock. The board of directors approved a merger cash buy-out program designed to reduce the shareholder base to below the 75 qualified shareholders necessary to obtain Subchapter S status. BAG incorrectly applied a minority and marketability discount to its evaluation of the fair value of the stock, bringing it down from $110 per share to $70.13 per share. Casey and other shareholders who cashed out under the plan at $73 per share sued the board of directors individually for damages for approving such a flawed plan. Are directors personally liable when they act in reliance on a report by an outside expert whose advice is flawed? If a public accounting firm or an attorney gave the flawed advice, would the directors be personally liable? [*Casey v Brennan*, 344 NJ Super 83]

3. The majority shareholder and president of Dunaway Drug Stores, Inc., William B. Dunaway, was structuring and executing the sale of virtually all of the corporation's assets to Eckerd Drug Co. While doing this, he negotiated a side noncompete agreement with Eckerd, giving Dunaway $300,000 plus a company car in exchange for a covenant not to compete for three years. He simultaneously amended two corporate leases with Eckerd, thereby decreasing the value of the corporation's leasehold estates. The board of directors approved the asset sale. Minority shareholders brought a derivative action against William Dunaway, claiming breach of his fiduciary duty in negotiating the undisclosed noncompete agreement, which did not require him to perform any service for buyer Eckerd Drug. Did William Dunaway make sufficient disclosure about all of the negotiations of the asset sale to Eckerd Drug? Did William Dunaway violate any fiduciary duty to the corporation? Decide. [*Dunaway v Parker*, 453 SE2d 43 (Ga App)]

4. Larry Phillips was hired for a two-year period as executive secretary of the Montana Education Association (MEA). Six months later, he was fired. He then sued MEA for breach of contract and sued the directors and some of the other employees of MEA on the theory that they had caused MEA to break the contract with him and were therefore guilty of the tort of maliciously interfering with his contract with MEA. The evidence showed that the individual defendants, without malice, had induced the corporation to break the contract with Phillips but that this had been done to further the welfare of the corporation. Was MEA liable for breach of contract? Were the individual defendants shielded from personal liability? [*Phillips v Montana Education Ass'n*, 610 P2d 154 (Mont)]

5. Christy Pontiac, a corporation, was indicted for theft by swindle and forgery involving a GM cash rebate program. Hesli, a middle-management employee of Christy Pontiac, had forged the cash rebate applications for two cars so that the rebate money was paid to Christy Pontiac instead of its customers. When confronted by a customer who should have received a rebate, the president of the dealership attempted to negotiate a settlement. The president did not contact GM headquarters until after an investigation was begun by the state attorney general. Christy Pontiac argued that it could not be held responsible for a crime involving specific intent because only natural persons, as opposed to corporations, can form such intent. Decide. [*State v Christy Pontiac-GMC, Inc.*, 354 NW2d 17 (Minn)]

6. Directors must always own stock of the corporation to ensure they will be attentive to their duties. Appraise this statement.

7. Discuss the power of a corporation president to employ a sales manager and to agree that the manager should be paid a stated amount per year plus a percentage of any increase in the dollar volume of sales that might take place.

8. Richard Grassgreen was executive vice president and then president and chief operating officer of Kinder-Care, Inc., the largest proprietary provider of child care in the country. The company was restructured in 1989 and changed its name to the Enstar Group, Inc. Between 1985 and 1990, while Grassgreen served as the corporation's investment manager, he invested millions of dollars of company money in junk bond deals with Michael Milken, and he secretly retained some $355,000 in commitment fees. When the corporation discovered this, Grassgreen repaid the corporation. It sued him to recover any compensation paid him over the five-year period during which the secret payments were made, some $5,197,663. Grassgreen defended that his conduct caused little, if any, damage to the corporation because the corporation did not lose any money on any of the investments for which he received personal fees. Decide. [*Enstar Group, Inc., v Grassgreen*, 812 F Supp 1562 (MD Ala)]

9. Danny Hill, the general manager of Southeastern Floor Covering Co., Inc. (SE), had full authority to run the business. His responsibilities included preparing and submitting bid proposals to general contractors for floor coverings and ceilings on construction projects. Hill prepared and submitted a

bid for a job for Chata Construction Co. for asbestos encapsulation, ceramic tile, ceilings, carpets, and vinyl tile flooring. However, because SE was not licensed by the EPA, the asbestos work was withdrawn. In the past, SE had used Larry Barnes's company, which was EPA licensed, to do asbestos work under a subcontract agreement. Hill did not pursue a subcontract with Barnes for the Chata job. Rather, Hill and Barnes worked up a bid together and submitted it to Chata for the asbestos work. The bid was accepted, and Hill made $90,000 from the Chata job. Two years later, SE found out about Hill's role in the asbestos work done for Chata, and the corporation sued him for the lost profits. Hill argued that SE was not licensed by the EPA to do asbestos work and thus could not claim a lost corporate opportunity when it was not qualified to do the work. Decide. Are any ethical principles applicable to this case? [*Hill v Southeastern Floor Covering Co.*, 596 So2d 874 (Miss)]

10. A director of a corporation cannot lend money to the corporation because that would create the danger of a conflict of interest between the director's status as a director and as a creditor. Appraise this statement.

11. Hamway and other minority shareholders brought an action against majority shareholders of Libbie Rehabilitation Center, Inc., including Frank Giannotti, CEO-director; Alex Grossman, president-director; Henry Miller, vice president–director; Ernest Dervishian, secretary and corporate attorney; and Lewis Cowardin, treasurer-director. The minority shareholders contended that the corporation paid excessive salaries to these director-officers and was wasting corporate assets. Prior to coming to Libbie, Giannotti had been a carpet and tile retailer, Grossman a pharmacist, Miller a real estate developer, Dervishian a lawyer, and Cowardin a jeweler. The evidence showed that the extent of their work for the corporation was very limited. For example, Cowardin, Libbie's finance officer, who was paid $78,121 in 1985, demonstrated no knowledge of the Medicare and Medicaid programs, the principal source of Libbie's income. Although he claimed to have spent 20 to 25 hours a week on corporate duties, he reported on the tax return for his jewelry business that he spent 75 percent of his working time in that business in 1984. One expert witness of the plaintiff testified that the five men were performing the management functions of one individual. The director-officers contended that the business was making a profit and that all salaries were approved by a board of directors that had extensive business experience. Were the directors within their rights to elect themselves officers and set pay for themselves as they saw fit? Did they violate any legal or ethical duty to their shareholders?

12. Anthony Yee was the president of Waipahu Auto Exchange, a corporation. As part of his corporate duties, he arranged financing for the company. Federal Services Finance Corp. drew 12 checks payable to the order of Waipahu Auto Exchange. These were then indorsed by its president, "Waipahu Auto Exchange, Limited, by Anthony Yee, President," and were cashed at two different banks. Bishop National Bank of Hawaii, on which the checks were drawn, charged its depositor, Federal Services, with the amount of the checks. Federal Services then sued Bishop National Bank to restore to its account the

amount of the 12 checks on the ground that Bishop National Bank had improperly made payment on the checks because Anthony Yee had no authority to cash them. Did Yee have authority to indorse and cash the checks? [*Federal Services Finance Corp. v Bishop Nat'l Bank of Hawaii*, 190 F2d 442 (9th Cir)]

13. Klinicki and Lundgren incorporated Berlinair, Inc., a closely held Oregon corporation. Lundgren was president and responsible for developing business. Klinicki served as vice president and director responsible for operations and maintenance. Klinicki owned one-third of the stock, and Lundgren controlled the rest. They both met with BFR, a consortium of Berlin travel agents, about contracting to operate some charter flights. After the initial meeting, all contracts with BFR were made by Lundgren, who learned that there was a good chance that the BFR contract would be available. He incorporated Air Berlin Charter Co. (ABC) and was its sole owner. He presented BFR with a contract proposal, and it awarded the contract to ABC. Although Lundgren was using Berlinair's working time and facilities, he managed to keep the negotiations a secret from Klinicki. When Klinicki discovered Lundgren's actions, he sued him for usurping a corporate opportunity for Berlinair. Lundgren contended that it was not a usurpation of corporate opportunity because Berlinair did not have the financial ability to undertake the contract with BFR. Decide. Are any ethical principles applicable to this case? Consider the applicability of Chief Justice Cardozo's statement in *Meinhard v Salmon*, 164 NE 545 (NY 1928), concerning the level of conduct for fiduciaries: "A trustee is held to something stricter than the morals of the marketplace. Not honesty alone, but the punctillo of an honor the most sensitive is then the standard of behavior... ." [*Klinicki v Lundgren*, 695 P2d 906 (Or)]

14. Rudolph Redmont, the president of Abbott Thinlite Corp., left Abbott to run Circle Corp. in competition with his former employer. It was claimed that he diverted contracts from his former employer to his new one, having gained the advantage of specific information about the deals in progress while employed by Abbott. Abbott sued Redmont and Circle Corp. to recover lost profits. Redmont contended that all of the contracts in question were made after he left Abbott, at which time his fiduciary duty to Abbott had ceased. Decide. [*Abbott Thinlite Corp. v Redmont*, 475 F2d 85 (2d Cir)]

15. William Gurtler was president and a board member of Unichem Corp., which produced and sold chemical laundry products. While president of Unichem, he encouraged his plant manager to leave to join a rival business, which Gurtler was going to join in the near future. Moreover, Gurtler sold Unichem products to his son, G. B. Gurtler, in January 1982 at a figure substantially below their normal price and on credit even though G. B. had no credit history. Gurtler made the sales with full knowledge that G. B. was going to start a rival business. Also at that time, Gurtler was aware that his wife was soliciting Unichem employees to join the new Gurtler Chemical Co., and he helped her design Gurtler's label so that it would look like Unichem's. On February 9, 1982, Gurtler guaranteed a $100,000 loan for Gurtler Chemical Co. with funds to be disbursed after he left Unichem, which occurred on March 12, 1982.

On March 15, 1982, he became president of Gurtler Chemical Co. Unichem sued Gurtler for breach of fiduciary duty and for the loss of profits that resulted. Gurtler contended that his sales to G. B. guaranteed needed revenue to Unichem and constituted a sound business decision that should be applauded and that was protected under the business judgment rule. Decide. Are any ethical principles applicable to this case? [*Unichem Corp. v Gurtler*, 498 NE2d 724 (Ill App)]

CPA QUESTIONS

1. Davis, a director of Active Corp., is entitled to:

   a. Serve on the board of a competing business

   b. Take sole advantage of a business opportunity that would benefit Active

   c. Rely on information provided by a corporate officer

   d. Unilaterally grant a corporate loan to one of Active's shareholders

2. Absent a specific provision in its articles of incorporation, a corporation's board of directors has the power to do all of the following *except*:

   a. Repeal the bylaws

   b. Declare dividends

   c. Fix compensation of directors

   d. Amend the articles of incorporation

3. Which of the following statements is correct regarding fiduciary duty?

   a. A director's fiduciary duty to the corporation may be discharged by merely disclosing his or her self-interest.

   b. A director owes a fiduciary duty to the shareholders but *not* to the corporation.

   c. A promoter of a corporation to be formed owes no fiduciary duty to anyone, unless the contract engaging the promoter so provides.

   d. A majority shareholder as such may owe a fiduciary duty to fellow shareholders.

Part 8

REAL PROPERTY AND ESTATES

Chapter 49

REAL PROPERTY

T he law of real property can be highly technical and still relies on vocabulary drawn from the days of feudal lords and castles. This chapter presents a simplified look at the law of real property.

A. NATURE OF REAL PROPERTY

real property—land and all rights in land.

Real property has special characteristics of permanence and uniqueness. These characteristics have strongly influenced the rules that society has developed to resolve disputes concerning real property.

1. Land

land—earth, including all things embedded in or attached thereto, whether naturally or by the act of humans.

Land means more than the surface of the earth. It is composed of the soil and all things of a permanent nature affixed to the ground, such as herbs, grass, trees, and other growing, natural products. The word also includes the waters on the ground and things that are embedded beneath the surface.

Technically, land extends downward to the earth's center and upward indefinitely. The general view is that the owner of the land owns the space above that land subject to the right of flying aircraft that do not interfere with the use of the land and are not dangerous to persons or property on the land.

CPA   2. Easements

easement—permanent right that one has in the land of another, as the right to cross another's land or an easement of way.

An **easement** is the right to use another's property, such as the right to cross another's land. Rights in another person's land also include profits. The easement belongs to the land that is benefited. The benefited land is called the **dominant tenement**, and the land that is subject to the easement is called the **servient tenement**.[1]

dominant tenement—land that is benefited by an easement.

(A) CREATION OF EASEMENT. Because an easement is an interest in land, an oral promise to create an easement is not binding because of the statute of frauds. An oral grant of an easement would be a license (see Section 4). An easement created by agreement is transferred by deed. However, an easement may also be created by implication. An **easement by implication** arises when one conveys part of the land that has been used as a dominant estate in relation to the part retained. **For Example,** if water pipes or drain pipes run from the part of the land conveyed through the part retained, there is an implied right to continue using the pipes. For an easement to be implied, the use, as in this case with the pipes, must be apparent, continuous, and reasonably necessary.

servient tenement—land that is subject to an easement.

easement by implication—easement not specifically created by deed that arises from the circumstances of the parties and the land location and access.

An easement by implication arises when one subdivides land and sells a portion to which no entry can be made except over the land retained or over the land of a stranger. The grantee's right to use the land retained by the grantor for the purpose of going to and from the land conveyed is known as a **way of necessity**.

way of necessity—grantee's right to use land retained by the grantor for going to and from the conveyed land.

[1] *City of Aurora v ACJ Partnership*, 209 P3d 1076 (Colo 2009).

CASE SUMMARY

Brick Walls Do Not Make for Good Neighbors

FACTS: The Friersons have a two-story building in Easley, South Carolina that shares a common wall with an adjacent two-story building owned by David and Patricia Watson. An outdoor stairway located on the Watsons' property provides access to the second floor of both buildings. A dispute arose when David Watson began to construct apartments on the second floor of his building and proposed to close off a connecting indoor hallway between the two properties at the top of the stairs located inside the building. The Friersons maintained that they had an easement to use both the outdoor stairway and the indoor hallway for access.

The Friersons' predecessors-in-interest, E. C., E. O., and D. M. Frierson, purchased the building in 1929 from the "Estate of R. F. Smith, Inc." The 1929 deed, dated January 14 and recorded on January 23, expressly conveyed "an easement in a certain four foot stairway in the back of the building, with right of ingress and egress on said stairway to the second story of said building." On January 21, 1929, two days before the deed was recorded, the parties to the sale executed a "Memorandum of Agreement" that granted an easement for the use of the hallway. The memo was not recorded.

The Friersons brought suit to stop Watson's construction. The Friersons claimed Watson's construction violated their easement by eliminating the hallway, which denied them access to the second floor of their building.

The circuit court determined that the Friersons had established an easement for use of the hallway by grant and by prescription and granted the Friersons' motion. David Watson appealed.

DECISION: The court held that the memo granted an easement that did not need to be recorded to be valid. Also, the ongoing use of the indoor easement by the parties indicated it had always existed. Recording would have helped, but it was not required to grant the easement. Affirmed. **[Frierson v Watson, 636 SE2d 872 (SC App 2006)]**

---

prescription–acquisition of a right to use the land of another, as an easement, by making hostile, visible, and notorious use of the land, continuing for the period specified by the local law.

An easement may be created by **prescription**. Under prescription, a person acquires an easement by adverse use, or use contrary to the landowner's use, for a statutory period. No easement is acquired by prescription if the use of the land is with the permission of the owner.

(B) TERMINATION OF EASEMENT. Once an easement has been granted, it cannot be destroyed by the act of the grantor. A "revocation" attempted without the easement owner's consent has no effect.

An easement may be lost by nonuse when surrounding circumstances show an intent to abandon the easement.[2] **For Example,** when a surface transit system had an easement to maintain trolley tracks but abandoned the easement when the tracks were removed and all surface transportation was discontinued, the easement was lost through abandonment. Likewise, when the owner of the easement planted a flower bed on the land across the end of the path of the easement, the intent to abandon the easement was evident.

---

[2] *Backman v Lawrence*, 210 P3d 75 (Idaho 2009).

CPA 3. Profits

profit–right to take a part of the soil or produce of another's land, such as timber or water.

Profits are rights to take part of the soil, subsurface materials, or resources or produce from land that belongs to another. **For Example,** profits could include the right to remove coal from the land of another and the right to use the water from another's land.

CPA 4. Licenses

license–personal privilege to do some act or series of acts upon the land of another, as the placing of a sign thereon, not amounting to an easement or a right of possession.

A **license** is a personal, revocable privilege to perform an act or series of acts on the land of another. Unlike an easement, a license is not an interest in land. **For Example,** the person allowed to come into the house to use the telephone has a license. The advertising company that has permission to paint a sign on the side of a building also has a license.

A license may be terminated at the will of the licensor. It continues only as long as the licensor is the owner of the land.

CPA 5. Liens

Real property may be subject to **liens** that arise by the voluntary act of the owner of the land. **For Example,** the lien of a mortgage is created when the owner borrows money and uses the land as security for repayment of the debt.

thinking things through

The Dryer Vent that Dumped on the Doc

Danetta Garfink owns a condominium unit at The Cloisters at Charles Condominiums. Garfink purchased her unit (one of the model units) in 1991 during the development and construction phase of the project. The original construction included installed household appliances in each unit, a clothes dryer among them. As originally installed, the clothes dryer was connected and vented into the furnace room, rather than to the outside of the building, contrary to the terms of the construction contract, and in violation of prevailing building codes and regulations.

In 2000, the clothes dryer malfunctioned and Garfink purchased a replacement from Sears, Roebuck & Co. After viewing the existing vent system, however, Sears refused to install the replacement because a "fire hazzard [sic] was identified."

Garfink took it upon herself to have the venting system rerouted. The new system was routed from the dryer through the wall of the laundry room into the adjoining garage, then through the garage and then the exterior wall. Garfink's immediate neighbor, Dr. Oscar Kantt, found that the new vent was within 17 feet of the front door of his residence, and Dr. Kantt complained about the discharge. Garfink says she has an easement for the dryer vent. Analyze whether she does have an easement. Be sure to think through the types of easements. [*Garfink v Cloisters at Charles, Inc.,* **897 A2d 206 (Md 2006)**]

Liens may also arise involuntarily, as in the case of **tax liens**, **judgment liens**, and **mechanic's liens**. In the case of taxes and judgments, the liens provide a means for enforcing the obligations of the owner of the land to pay the taxes or the judgment. Mechanic's liens give persons furnishing labor and materials in the improvement of real estate the right to proceed against the real estate for the collection of the amounts due them.

6. Fixtures

Under the laws relating to fixtures, personal property becomes real property.

CPA

(A) **DEFINITION.** A **fixture** is personal property that is attached to the earth or placed in a building in such a way or under such circumstances that it is considered part of the real property.

A person may buy a refrigerator, an air conditioner, a furnace, or some other item that is used in a building and then have the item installed. The question of whether such an item is a fixture, and therefore part of a building, can arise in a variety of situations: (1) The real estate tax assessor assesses the building and adds in the value of the item on the theory that it is part of the building, (2) the buyer of the item owns and then sells the building, and the new owner of the building claims that the item stays with the building, (3) the buyer places a mortgage on the building, and the mortgagee claims that the item is bound by the mortgage, (4) the buyer is a tenant in the building in which the item is installed, and the landlord claims that the item must stay in the building when the tenant leaves, and (5) the buyer does not pay in full for the item, and the seller of the item has a security interest that the seller wishes to enforce against the buyer or against the landlord of the building in which the buyer installs the item. The seller of the item may also assert a claim against the mortgagee of the building or against the buyer of the building. The determination of the rights of these parties depends on the common law of fixtures, as occasionally modified by statute.

lien–claim or right, against property, existing by virtue of the entry of a judgment against its owner or by the entry of a judgment and a levy thereunder on the property, or because of the relationship of the claimant to the particular property, such as an unpaid seller.

tax lien–lien on property by a government agency for nonpayment of taxes.

judgment lien–lien by a creditor who has won a verdict against the landowner in court.

mechanic's lien–protection afforded by statute to various kinds of laborers and persons supplying materials, by giving them a lien on the building and land that has been improved or added to by them.

fixture–personal property that has become so attached to or adapted to real estate that it has lost its character as personal property and is part of the real estate.

---

sports&entertainment law

Using a View as Easement or a License in Lieu of a Ticket

There are 13 rooftops on buildings that surround Wrigley Field. When the Chicago Cubs play at Wrigley, the rooftops are packed with folks who, with coolers full of drinks and plenty of food stacked on tables, are watching the games. Kayakers pack McCovey's Cove near San Francisco's SBC Park's right field to watch the Giants. Hot tubs and roofs overlook the Arizona Diamondback's games in Chase Ballpark (once BankOne Ballpark or BOB).

Do the folks using these areas need a license? An easement? If they own the property or are there with the owner's permission, are they permitted to watch the games?*

* Lee Jenkins, "The Best Seats in the House Are Just Outside Wrigley," *New York Times*, June 12, 2005, 8–1 (Sports 1).

CPA (B) Tests of a Fixture. In the absence of an agreement between the parties, the courts apply three tests to determine whether personal property has become a fixture.

(1) Annexation.

Generally, personal property becomes a fixture if it is so attached to the realty that it cannot be removed without materially damaging the real property or destroying the personal property itself. If the property is so affixed as to lose its specific identity, such as bricks in a wall, it becomes part of the realty. When cabinets are attached to kitchen walls so as to be immovable, they are fixtures.

(2) Adaptation.

Personal property especially adapted or suited to the use made of the building may constitute a fixture such as the pipes for a church organ.

(3) Intent.

One controlling test is the intention of the person affixing the property.[3] Intent is considered as of the time the property was affixed. In the absence of direct proof of such intent, courts resort to the nature of the property, the method of its attachment, and all the surrounding circumstances to determine intent.

The fact that machinery installed in a plant would be very difficult and expensive to move or is so delicate that the moving would cause damage is significant in reaching the conclusion that the owner installed the equipment as a permanent addition and intented to make the equipment fixtures. **For Example,** when the floors in a large apartment house are made of concrete and covered with a thin sheet of plywood to which wall-to-wall carpeting is stapled, the carpeting constitutes a fixture that cannot be removed from the building. Removal would probably destroy the carpeting because it was cut to size. In addition, the carpeting is necessary to make the building livable as an apartment.

CPA (C) Movable Machinery and Equipment. Machinery and equipment that are movable are ordinarily held not to be fixtures even though, in order to move them, it is necessary to unbolt them from the floor or to disconnect electrical wires or water pipes. **For Example,** refrigerators, freezers, and gas and electric ranges are not fixtures. They do not lose their character as personal property when they are readily removable after disconnecting pipes or unplugging wires. A portable window air conditioner that rests on a rack that is affixed to the windowsill by screws and is connected directly to the building only by an electric cord plug is not a fixture.

The mere fact that an item may be unplugged, however, does not establish that it is not a fixture. **For Example,** a computer and its related hardware constitute fixtures when there is such a mass of wires and cables under the floor that the installation gives the impression of permanence.

CPA (D) Trade Fixtures. Equipment that a tenant attaches to a rented building and uses in a trade or business is ordinarily removable by the tenant when the tenant permanently leaves the premises. Such equipment is commonly called a *trade fixture*.[4]

---

[3] *Englewood v Miami Valley Lighting, L.L.C.,* 911 NE2d 913 (Oh App 2009).
[4] *In re City of New York,* 899 NE 2d 933, 870 NYS 2d 827 (2008).

CASE SUMMARY

Falling Through the Cracks for the Home Team

FACTS: On September 29, 2000, Elaine Kohn and her then four-year-old daughter, Lori Kohn, attended the homecoming football game at Darlington High School. At about 2:30 P.M. on a glorious Wisconsin Saturday afternoon, young Lori fell through the space at the foot of her seat in the home bleachers to the ground 15 feet below and was injured. The home bleachers are a huge structure. They are 15 rows tall, over 100 feet long, and contain a 50-inch-wide walkway elevated 30 inches above the ground. They can seat nearly 1,500 individuals. They adjoin a rather large press box and incorporate a wheelchair access ramp. While it is unclear whether they are anchored to the ground, they clearly are not readily moveable. The Kohns brought suit in 2001 against Standard Steel Industries, Inc. (Standard was later purchased by Illinois Tool Works), a company that sold Darlington the bleachers for $16,167 in 1969. However, the suit was dismissed initially because Wisconsin has a 10-year statute of limitations (statute of repose) on recovery for injuries caused by improvements to real property.

The Wisconsin Court of Appeals reversed the lower court's dismissal, concluding that the bleachers were not an improvement to real property because there was no evidence that the bleachers were anchored to the ground. The Court of Appeals held that the Kohns' claims were governed by the three-year statute of limitations on personal injury and product liability actions rather than by the 10-year statute of repose. The Wisconsin Supreme Court then stepped, carefully, as it were, into the fray.

DECISION: The court held that the bleachers were fixtures and as improvements to real property could not be the basis for a lawsuit after 1979 (the 10-year limit). The bleachers had never been moved in the 30 years since their placement. Ramps and others structures were attached to them. The bleachers were an integral part of the facility and games could not take place without them being there. There was no evidence that the bleachers were annexed, but that test is not controlling in determining whether an item is a fixture. [**Kohn v Darlington Community School District, 686 NW2d 794 (Wis 2005)**]

CPA B. NATURE AND FORM OF REAL PROPERTY OWNERSHIP

fee simple estate – highest level of land ownership; full interest of unlimited duration.

life estate – an estate for the duration of a life.

leasehold estate – interest of a tenant in rented land.

estate in fee – largest estate possible, in which the owner has absolute and entire interest in the land.

A person's interest in real property may be defined in terms of the period of time for which the person will remain the owner as (1) a **fee simple estate** or (2) a **life estate**. These estates are termed *freehold estates*, which are interests of uncertain duration. At the time of creation of a freehold estate, a termination date is not known. When a person owns property for a specified period of time, this interest is not regarded as a freehold estate; it is a **leasehold estate**, subject to special rules of law.

CPA 7. Fee Simple Estate

An **estate in fee**, a fee simple, or a fee simple absolute lasts forever. The owner of such a land interest held in fee simple has the absolute and entire interest in the land. The important characteristics of this estate are that (1) it is alienable, or transferable, during life, (2) it is alienable by will, (3) it passes to heirs of the owner if it is not specifically devised (transferred by will), (4) it is subject to rights of the owner's surviving spouse, and (5) it can be attached or used to satisfy debts of the owner before or after death.

There are other forms of the fee simple estate generally used for control of land use. **Fee simple defeasibles** are interests that give the grantee all the rights of a fee simple holder provided that the grantee complies with certain restrictions. **For Example,** the grant "To Ralph Watkins so long as he uses the property for school purposes" is an example of a fee simple defeasible. Watkins will have all the rights of a fee simple holder provided that he uses the property for school purposes. If Watkins ever stops using the property for school purposes, the property reverts back to the grantor.

fee simple defeasibles—fee simple interest can be lost if restrictions on its use are violated.

CPA **8. Life Estate**

A *life estate* (or life tenancy), as its name indicates, lasts only during the life of a person (ordinarily its owner). Upon the death of the person by whose life the estate was measured, the owner of the life estate has no interest remaining to pass to heirs or by will. **For Example,** a grant of a life estate would be "To my husband, Nathan Jones, for life, and then to my children." Jones would hold title to the property only for the time he is alive. When Jones dies, he cannot give the property away by will. If Jones conveys the property while he is alive, the grantee for the property holds title to the land only until Jones's death.

CPA **9. Future Interests**

In several of the examples given to illustrate fee simple and life estates, interests were created in more than one person. **For Example,** in the preceding life estate example, the children of the grantor are given an interest in the land at the same time that Jones is. However, the interests of the children will not take effect until Jones dies. The children have a future interest in the land. Their interest is referred to as a **remainder interest** because they have the remaining interest in the land once the life estate ends.

In the Watkins fee simple defeasible example, the grantor has a future interest if Watkins violates the restriction. The grantor's interest is called a **possibility of reverter**. It is a future interest because it cannot exist unless Watkins violates the use restriction placed on his present interest.

remainder interest—land interest that follows a life estate.

possibility of reverter— nature of the interest held by the grantor after conveying land outright but subject to a condition or provision that may cause the grantee's interest to become forfeited and the interest to revert to the grantor or heirs.

C. LIABILITY TO THIRD PERSONS FOR CONDITION OF REAL PROPERTY

A person entering the land of another may be injured by the condition of the land. Who is liable for such harm?

CPA   ## 10. Common Law Rule

Under the common law, liability to a person entering onto land was controlled by the status of the injured person—that is, whether the person injured was a **trespasser**, a **licensee**, or an **invitee**. A different duty was owed by the owner (or occupier, as when a tenant is leasing property) of land to persons in each of these three categories.

trespass—an unauthorized action with respect to person or property.

licensee—someone on another's premises with the permission of the occupier, whose duty is to warn the licensee of nonobvious dangers.

invitee—person who enters another's land by invitation.

attractive nuisance doctrine—a rule imposing liability upon a landowner for injuries sustained by small children playing on the land when the landowner permits a condition to exist or maintains equipment that a reasonable person should realize would attract small children who could not realize the danger. The rule does not apply if an unreasonable burden would be imposed upon the landowner in taking steps to protect the children.

(A) TRESPASSERS. For a trespasser, the landowner ordinarily owes the duty of refraining from causing intentional harm only once the presence of the trespasser is known. The landowner is not under any duty to warn of dangers or to make the premises safe to protect the trespasser from harm. The most significant exception to this rule arises in the case of small children. Even when children are trespassers, they are generally afforded greater protection through the **attractive nuisance doctrine**. **For Example,** the owner of a tract of land was held liable for the death of a seven-year-old child who drowned in a creek on that land. Snow had covered the ice on the creek, and children running across the land did not know of the creek's location or the danger of the ice. The landowner had a duty to fence the creek, put up warnings, or control the children's access.[5]

(B) LICENSEES. *Licensees* are on the premises with the permission of the landowner, who owes the duty of warning of nonobvious dangers that are known to the owner. A host must warn a guest of such dangers. **For Example,** when a sliding glass door is "invisible" if the patio lights are on and the house lights are off, the owner must warn guests of the presence of the glass. The owner is liable if he has not warned guests of the danger and a guest is injured in shattering the glass. An owner, however, owes no duty to a licensee to take any steps to learn of the presence of dangers that are unknown to the owner.

(C) INVITEES. *Invitees* are persons who enter another's land by invitation. The entry is connected with the owner's business or with an activity the occupier conducts on the land. Business customers, for example, are invitees.

Owners have a duty to take reasonable steps to discover any danger and a duty to warn the invitee or to correct the danger. **For Example,** a store must make a reasonable inspection of the premises to determine that there is nothing on the floor that would be dangerous, such as a slippery substance that might cause a patron to fall. The store must correct the condition, appropriately rope off the danger area, or give suitable warning. If the owner of the premises fails to take the degree of care required and an invitee is harmed as a result, then the owner is liable for such harm.

In most states, the courts have expanded the concept of invitees beyond the category of customers, or those whose presence will economically benefit the occupier. Invitees now usually include members of the public who are invited onto the premises and who cannot be reasonably expected to make an inspection of the premises before using them and would not be able to make necessary repairs to dangerous conditions. Some courts have also made inroads into the prior law by treating a recurring licensee, such as a letter carrier, as an invitee. For more information on landowner liability, refer to Chapter 9 on torts.

[5] *Foss v. Kincade*, 766 NW 2d 317 (Minn 2009).

C A S E   S U M M A R Y

Taco Bell Drive-Thru Rage

FACTS: At approximately 3:00 A.M., on February 3, 2000, Sonya Winchell was driving two of her friends through a Fort Wayne Taco Bell drive-thru. When Winchell arrived in line, there was one car in front of her at the speaker. Winchell noticed that the occupants of the car, Remco Guy and Ariel Graham, were taking a long time placing their order and then got out of their car. At that point, Winchell yelled out her window, "Can we get moving, we are hungry!" Guy approached Winchell's car, stuck his head in the window, and "started cussing everybody out." Guy removed his head from the window, stuck it back in, and asked, "You got an F-ing problem?" Winchell responded by "drill[ing] him in the nose." Guy then pulled a gun out of his pants and shot Winchell. One of Winchell's passengers and others summoned police officers who were in a nearby parking lot.

Winchell survived the shooting, and Guy was convicted of attempted murder. Winchell filed a civil action against Guy and Graham, and against Taco Bell, alleging negligence. Taco Bell moved for summary judgment and the trial court granted it.

DECISION: Landowners have a duty to take reasonable precautions to protect their invitees from foreseeable criminal attacks. Taco Bell did owe a duty to its customers, including Winchell, to use reasonable care to protect them from injuries caused by other patrons and guests on their premises.

The line of sight between the employees of Taco Bell and the drive-thru was obstructed, that the video monitoring system was in a closet and not readily accessible to Taco Bell employees. No security guard was on duty that night. There had been previous calls to the police from the Taco Bell, including one in which there was also violence.

Taco Bell owed Winchell a duty as a matter of law and there were questions of fact regarding the elements of breach and causation. The trial court improperly granted Taco Bell's motion for summary judgment. Reversed. **[Winchell v Guy, 857 NE2d 1024 (Ind 2006)]**

D. Co-Ownership of Real Property

Real property may be owned by one or several persons, and the method of co-ownership determines the extent of the owners' rights.

11. Multiple Ownership

Several persons may have *concurrent interests* (or interests that exist at the same time) in the same real property. The forms of multiple ownership for real property are the same as those for personal property. Real property can be held by tenants in common, by joint tenants with right of survivorship, by tenants by the entirety, or under community property rights. When co-owners sell property, they hold the proceeds of sale by the same kind of tenancy as that in which they held the original property.

12. Condominiums

condominium –
combination of
co-ownership and
individual ownership.

A **condominium** is a combination of co-ownership and individual ownership. **For Example,** persons owning an office building or an apartment house by condominium are co-owners of the land and of the halls, lobby, elevators, stairways, exits, surrounding land, incinerator, laundry rooms, and other areas used in common. Each apartment or office in the building, however, is individually owned and is transferred in the same way as other forms of real property.

(A) CONTROL AND EXPENSE. In some states, owners of the various units in the condominium have equal voice in its management and share an equal part of its expenses. In others, control and liability for expenses are shared by a unit owner in the same ratio that the value of the unit bears to the value of the entire condominium project. In all states, unit owners have equal rights to use the common areas. An owners' association is created by the condominium owners to operate the common areas of the condominium property and resolve any disputes among owners.

The owner of each condominium unit makes the repairs required by the owner's deed or contract of ownership. The owner is prohibited from making any major change that would impair or damage the safety or value of an adjoining unit.

(B) COLLECTION OF EXPENSES FROM UNIT OWNER. When a unit owner fails to pay the owner's share of taxes, operating expenses, and repairs, the owners' association generally has the right to a lien against that owner's unit for the amount due.

(C) TORT LIABILITY. Most condominium projects fail to make provision for the liability of unit owners for a tort occurring in the common areas. A few states expressly provide that when a third person is injured in a common area, a suit may be brought only against the condominium association. Any judgment recovered is a charge against the association to be paid off as a common expense. When the condominium association is incorporated, the same result should be obtained by applying ordinary principles of corporation law. Under principles of corporation law, liability for torts occurring on the premises of the corporation would not be the liability of individual shareholders.

cooperative – group of two or more persons or enterprises that acts through a common agent with respect to a common objective, such as buying or selling.

(D) COOPERATIVES DISTINGUISHED. Ownership in a condominium is different from ownership in a **cooperative**. An apartment cooperative is typically a corporation that owns an apartment complex. The "ownership" interests of the apartment occupants are as stockholders of the corporation.

e-commerce&cyberlaw
Web Listings

The Internet has proven to be a help in selling real property. Real estate agents use the Web to post listings and provide potential buyers with virtual tours of properties that interest them. Visit the

National Association of Realtors Web site at **www.nar.com** and view its materials related to selling real property.

E. Transfer of Real Property by Deed

Although many of the technical limitations of the feudal system and earlier common law on transfer of land have disappeared, much of the law relating to the modern deed originated in those days.

deed–an instrument by which the grantor (owner of land) conveys or transfers the title to a grantee.

CPA   13. Definitions

A **deed** is an instrument or writing by which an owner or **grantor** transfers or conveys an interest in land to a new owner. The new owner is called a **grantee** or **transferee**. Real property may be either sold or given as a gift. A deed, however, is necessary to transfer title to land, even if it is a gift.

In contrast to the situation with a contract, no consideration is required to make a deed effective. Although consideration is not required to make a deed valid or to transfer title by deed, the absence of consideration may show that the owner makes the transfer to defraud creditors. The creditors may then be able to set aside the fraudulent transfer.

grantor–owner who transfers or conveys an interest in land to a new owner.

grantee–new owner of a land conveyance.

transferee–buyer or vendee.

CPA   14. Classification of Deeds

Deeds may be classified according to the interest conveyed as **quitclaim deeds** or **warranty deeds**. A quitclaim deed merely transfers whatever interest, if any, the grantor may have in the property without specifying that interest in any way. A warranty deed transfers a specified interest and warrants or guarantees that such interest is transferred. Figure 49.1 is a sample warranty deed.

quitclaim deed–deed by which the grantor purports to give up only whatever right or title the grantor may have in the property without specifying or warranting transfer of any particular interest.

CPA   15. Execution of Deeds

Ordinarily, the grantor must sign, by signature or mark, a deed. A deed must be executed and delivered by a person having capacity. A deed may be set aside by the grantor for fraud by the grantee if third persons have not acquired rights in the land in good faith.

warranty deed–deed by which the grantor conveys a specific estate or interest to the grantee and makes one or more of the covenants of title.

CPA   16. Delivery and Acceptance of Deeds

A deed has no effect and title does not pass until the deed has been delivered. Delivery is a matter of intent as shown by words and conduct; no particular form of ceremony is required. The essential intent in delivering a deed is not merely that the grantor intends to hand over physical control and possession of the paper on which the deed is written but also that the grantor intends thereby to transfer the ownership of the property described in the deed. That intent can be shown by handing it to the grantee or placing the deed, addressed to the grantee, in the mail or by giving it to a third person with directions to give it to the grantee.

An effective delivery of a deed may be made symbolically, or constructively, such as by delivering to the grantee the key to a locked box and informing the grantee that the deed to the property is in the box. **For Example,** the delivery of a safe deposit box key has been held to constitute delivery of a deed that was in the box.

FIGURE 49-1 | *Form of Warranty Deed*

THIS DEED, made the twentieth day of November, two thousand and . . . between James K. Damron, residing at 132 Spring Street in the Borough of Manhattan, City and State of New York, party of the first part, and Terrence S. Bloemker, residing at 14 Steinway Street in the Borough of Queens, City and State of New York, party of the second part,

WITNESSETH, that the party of the first part, in consideration of the sum of one dollar ($1), lawful money of the United States, and other good and valuable consideration paid by the party of the second part, does hereby grant and release unto the party of the second part, his heirs and assigns forever,

ALL that certain lot, piece, and parcel of land situated in the Borough of Manhattan, City and County of New York, and State of New York, and bounded and described as follows:

Beginning at a point on the northerly side of Spring Street, distant two hundred (200) feet westerly from the corner formed by the intersection of the northerly side of Spring Street with the westerly side of 6th Avenue, running thence northerly parallel with 6th Avenue one hundred (100) feet, thence westerly and parallel with said Spring Street one hundred (100) feet; thence southerly, again parallel with said 6th Avenue one hundred (100) feet to the northerly side of Spring Street, and thence easterly along the said northerly side of Spring Street one hundred (100) feet to the point or place of beginning.

Together with the appurtenances and all the estate and rights of the party of the first part in and to said premises.

TO HAVE AND TO HOLD the premises herein granted unto the party of the second part, his heirs and assigns forever.

AND the party of the first part covenants as follows:

First. That the party of the first part is seised of the said premises in fee simple, and has good right to convey the same;

Second. That the party of the second part shall quietly enjoy the said premises;

Third. That the said premises are free from encumbrances except as expressly stated;

Fourth. That the party of the first part will execute or procure any further necessary assurance of the title to said premises;

IN WITNESS WHEREOF, the party of the first part has hereunto set his hand and seal the day and year first above written.

JAMES K. DAMRON

(L.S.)

In presence of:

DIANA L. REILMAN

State of New York ⎫
County of New York ⎭ s.s.:*

On the twentieth day of November in the year two thousand and . . . , before me personally came James K. Damron, to me known and known to me to be the individual described in, and who executed, the foregoing instrument, and he acknowledged that he executed the same.

DIANA L. REILMAN
Notary Public, New York County

*Note: Acknowledgment before a notary public is not essential to the effectiveness of a deed, but it is typically required to qualify the deed for recording.

Generally, there must be an **acceptance** by the grantee. In all cases, an acceptance is presumed unless the grantee disclaims the transfer.

CPA ## 17. Recording of Deeds

acceptance–unqualified assent to the act or proposal of another, such as the acceptance of a draft (bill of exchange), of an offer to make a contract, of goods delivered by the seller, or of a gift or deed.

recorder–public official in charge of deeds.

The owner of land may record the deed in the office of a public official, sometimes called a **recorder** or *commissioner of deeds*. The recording is not required to make the deed effective to pass title, but it is done so that the public will know that the grantee is the present owner and thereby prevent the former owner from making any future transfer or transaction relating to the property.

When no document is recorded, states have statutes for determining who obtains title and who will be left to take action against the party that has conveyed the property to more than one person. **For Example,** suppose that Grant conveys a tract of land to Dee. Dee does not record her deed. Grant then conveys the same tract of land to Joe, who also does not record his deed, but Joe is unaware of Dee's acquisition. Then Grant conveys the same property to Larry who knows about Dee and Joe but records his deed. Who will hold title, and who will be left to pursue Grant for remedies? Under **race statutes**, the first party to record the deed holds title, so Larry holds title. Under **notice statutes**, the last good-faith or bona fide purchaser (BFP), someone who does not know about the previous conveyances, takes title. Under notice, Joe holds title because he is the last BFP. Larry knows about the prior transactions and that fact controls title, not the recording of his deed under notice statutes. Under **notice-race** or **race-notice statutes**, the first BFP to record the deed holds title. So, if Dee records first, she holds title. If Joe records first, he will. Larry has recorded but does not meet the second requirement of race-notice, which is that one must be the first BFP to record to take title in a race-notice statute. Suppose that Larry is a BFP, but Joe is not because he is aware of the conveyance to Dee. Under race, Larry holds title. Under notice, Larry holds title. Under race-notice, Larry wins again. If Dee records her deed, all of these issues are moot because recording the deed is complete notice for all subsequent purchasers.

race statute–statute under which the first party to record the deed holds the title.

notice statute–statute under which the last good faith or bona fide purchaser holds the title.

notice-race statute–statute under which the first bona fide purchaser to record the deed holds the title.

race-notice statute– see *notice-race statute*.

The fact that a deed is recorded provides notice to the world about who holds title. The recording of a deed, however, is only such notice if the deed was properly executed. Likewise, the grantee of land cannot claim any protection by virtue of the recording of a deed when (1) a claim is made by one whose title is superior to that of the owner of record, (2) the grantee had notice or knowledge of the adverse claim when title was acquired, (3) a person acting under a hostile claim was then in possession of the land, (4) the grantee received the land as a gift, or (5) the transfer to the grantee was fraudulent.

18. Additional Protection of Buyers

abstract of title–history of the transfers of title to a given piece of land, briefly stating the parties to and the effect of all deeds, wills, and judicial proceedings relating to the land.

In addition to the protection given to buyers and third persons by the recorded title to property, a buyer is generally protected by procuring title insurance or an abstract of title. An **abstract of title** is a summarized report of the title to the property as shown by the records, together with a report of all judgments, mortgages, and similar recorded claims against the property.

CASE SUMMARY

Selling the Same Property Twice and Then Disappearing

FACTS: Wallace Salls was the recorded owner of a 12.56-acre parcel of real property in Hunt County, Texas. In October 1984, Salls sold two adjoining tracts from the parcel. Tract I, consisting of 3.675 acres, was sold to Paula Malecek and her husband for $14,700. Tract II, consisting of 3.676 acres, was sold to David Minton and his wife for $14,704.

In September 1994, Salls sold the property again. This sale involved the entire 12.56-acre parcel, including the two tracts previously conveyed to Minton and Malecek. Shannon Cook, the purchaser of the entire parcel, did not record the deed until 1997. In 1999, Cook sold the 12.56-acre parcel to Fletcher.

An attorney named Robert Crouch handled all legal matters for both Malecek and Salls, including the drafting of the contract for deed for Tract I. Crouch also drafted the deeds when the property was conveyed to Cook and Fletcher. Crouch is now deceased. Salls filed bankruptcy sometime prior to 1989, and no one has been able to locate him for a number of years.

Fletcher filed a lawsuit against Minton seeking to quiet title to Tracts I and II. Minton denied Fletcher's allegations of ownership. Malecek intervened in the lawsuit and asserted that she was the owner of Tract I. The trial court held that Malecek was the owner of Tract I; Minton was the owner of Tract II; and Fletcher was entitled to reimbursement from Malecek for ad valorem taxes paid on Tract I. Fletcher appealed.

DECISION: An unrecorded conveyance is binding on those who have knowledge of the conveyance.. A person who acquires property in good faith, for value, and without notice of any third-party claim or interest is a bona fide purchaser. Status as a bona fide purchaser is an affirmative defense to a title dispute.

Fletcher, through her agent, had constructive, if not actual, notice of Minton's claims to both tracts at the time she purchased the property. Minton's use and occupation of the property was sufficiently open, visible, exclusive, and unequivocal to put Fletcher on notice of a competing claim. Fletcher is not entitled to the protection of a bona fide purchaser as to Tract I. Malecek is the owner of Tract I. Also, the trial court properly found that Minton is the owner of Tract II. Affirmed. [**Fletcher v Minton, 217 SW3d 755 (Tex App 2007)**]

---

19. Grantor's Warranties

The warranties of the grantor relate to the title transferred by the grantor and to the fitness of the property for use.

CPA

(A) **WARRANTIES OF TITLE.** In the common law deed, the grantor may expressly warrant or make certain *covenants* as to the title conveyed. The statutes authorizing a short form of deed provide that, unless otherwise stated in the deed, the grantor is presumed to have made certain **warranties of title**.

The more important of the **covenants (or warranties) of title** that the grantor may make are (1) **covenant of seisin**, or guarantee that the grantor owns the estate conveyed, (2) **covenant of right to convey**, or guarantee that the grantor, if not the owner as in the case of an agent, has the right or authority to make the conveyance, (3) **covenant against encumbrances**, or guarantee that the land is not subject to any right or interest of a third person, such as a lien or an easement, (4) **covenant of quiet enjoyment**, or

---

warranty of title–implied warranty that title to the goods is good and transfer is proper.

covenants of title–grantor's covenants of a deed that guarantee such matters as the right to make the conveyance, to ownership of the property, to freedom of the property from encumbrances, or that the grantee will not be disturbed in the quiet enjoyment of the land.

covenant of seisin– guarantee that the grantor of an interest in land owns the estate conveyed to a new owner.

covenant of right to convey–guarantee that the grantor of an interest in land, if not the owner, has the right or authority to make the conveyance to a new owner.

covenant against encumbrances–guarantee that conveyed land is not subject to any right or interest of a third person.

covenant of quiet enjoyment–covenant by the grantor of an interest in land that the grantee's possession of the land shall not be disturbed.

limited covenant–any covenant that does not provide the complete protection of a full covenant.

covenant of further assurances–promise that the grantor of an interest in land will execute any additional documents required to perfect the title of the grantee.

guarantee by the grantor that the grantee's possession of the land will not be disturbed either by the grantor, in the case of a **limited covenant**, or by the grantor or any person claiming title under the grantor, in the case of a general covenant, and (5) **covenant of further assurances**, or guarantee that the grantor will execute any additional documents that may be required to perfect the title of the grantee.

(B) Fitness for Use. Courts in most states hold that when a builder or real estate developer sells a new house to a home buyer, the buyer gets an implied warranty that the house and foundation are fit for occupancy or use. This warranty arises regardless of whether the house was purchased before, during, or after completion of construction.[6] This first buyer is not responsible for the builder warranty when the house is resold. However, there is authority that the second buyer may recover from the original contractor for breach of the implied warranty even though there is no privity of contract.[7]

20. Grantee's Covenants

In a deed, the grantee may agree to do or to refrain from doing certain acts. Such an agreement becomes a binding contract between the grantor and the grantee. The grantor may recover from the grantee for its breach.

run with the land–concept that certain covenants in a deed to land are deemed to run or pass with the land so that whoever owns the land is bound by or entitled to the benefit of the covenants.

    The right to enforce the covenant also **runs with the land** owned by the grantor to whom the promise was made. **For Example,** a promise not to use a tract of land for a parking lot between two adjoining landowners would be passed (conveyed) to any buyers who subsequently acquire these tracts. For more information on covenants, see Chapter 50, Environmental Law and Land Use Controls.

F. Other Methods of Transferring Real Property

Title to real property can also be acquired by eminent domain and by adverse possession.

eminent domain–power of government and certain kinds of corporations to take private property against the objection of the owner, provided the taking is for a public purpose and just compensation is made for it.

CPA | **21. Eminent Domain**

Under **eminent domain**, property is taken from its private owner for a public purpose. The title is then taken by a government or public authority. There are constitutionally protected rights of property owners under eminent domain. Known as the "takings clause," this portion of the Fifth Amendment to the U.S. Constitution requires compensation when private property is taken for public use. Two important issues arise under the takings clause: (1) whether there is a taking of property and (2) whether the property is taken for a public use. With respect to whether a taking has occurred, it is not necessary that the owner be physically

---

[6] *Richards v Powercraft Homes, Inc.*, 678 P2d 427 (Ariz 1984), but *see Long v Jeb Breithaupt Design Build Inc.*, 4 So 3d 930 (La App 2009).

[7] Many states have passed statutes that govern the extent of the implied warranty of habitability. Although the statutes vary, the types of defects covered include defects in construction, design, and appearance.

CASE SUMMARY

Little Pink Houses, for You, but Not for Me ... Anymore

FACTS: In 1978, the city of New London, Connecticut, undertook a redevelopment plan for purposes of creating a redeveloped area in and around the existing park at Fort Trumball. The plan had the goals of achieving all the related ambience a state park should have, including the absence of pink cottages and other architecturally eclectic homes. Part of the redevelopment plan was the city's deal with Pfizer Corporation for the location of its research facility in the area. The preface to the city's development plan stated that it would *"create jobs, increase tax and other revenues, encourage public access to and use of the city's waterfront, and eventually "build momentum" for the revitalization of the rest of the city, including its downtown area."*

Susette Kelo, and other property owners whose homes would be razed and whose land would be taken to allow for the park, Pfizer's facility, and other redevelopment (15 total owners including Kelo), asked to be permitted to stay in the area. The city refused their request.

Kelo and the other homeowners filed suit challenging New London's legal authority to take their homes. The trial court issued an injunction preventing New London from taking certain of the properties but allowing others to be taken. Those property owners who were held subject to eminent domain appealed.

The appellate court found for New London on all claims; the landowners appealed.

DECISION: In a 5-4 decision delivered by Justice Stevens, joined by Justices Kennedy, Souter, Ginsberg, and Breyer, the U.S. Supreme Court upheld the decision of the Connecticut Supreme Court. New London's taking of the homes of Kelo and others qualifies as a "public use." Local governments cannot take private land simply to give to a particular private party, but when the takings are part of a carefully considered economic development plan, then the takings are constitutional. Public purpose is a broad category for purposes of determining when takings are constitutional. Economic development is a legitimate and constitutionally protected public purpose. Local governments' determinations that areas are economically distressed is enough to justify a program of economic development and local authorities are entitled to make that determination. The courts will not second-guess local authorities. **[Kelo v City of New London, 545 US 469 (2005)]**

deprived of the property but that normal use of the property has been impaired or lost. Whether there is a public use for the taking is a question that continues to be challenged in court because the definition of public purpose is so broad. **For Example,** property can be taken to build a freeway as well as for the preservation of a historic site. In the eminent domain cases after 2000, much of the litigation centered on whether revitalization of areas with urban blight were permissible takings. Eminent domain has activated a concerned public as state and local governments take more and more houses and land for purposes of economic development.

22. Adverse Possession

adverse possession—hostile possession of real estate, which when actual, visible, notorious, exclusive, and continued for the required time, will vest the title to the land in the person in such adverse possession.

Title to land may be acquired by possessing it adversely for a statutorily prescribed period of time. A possessor who complies with the requirements for **adverse possession** can gain title. Those who adversely possess property gain title to property even though they had no right to use the property at the beginning of their use or possession.

To acquire title by adverse possession, the possession must be (1) actual, (2) visible and notorious, (3) exclusive, (4) hostile, and (5) continuous for a required period of time.

State statutes control the required time period, but the typical range is 10 to 20 years. Use or possession of land under a mistaken belief that one is the owner still qualifies for the "hostile" possession required under the fourth element listed.[8]

G. MORTGAGES

mortgage–interest in land given by the owner to a creditor as security for the payment of the creditor for a debt, the nature of the interest depending upon the law of the state where the land is located. (Parties—mortgagor, mortgagee)

An agreement that creates an interest in real property as security for an obligation until that obligation is repaid is a **mortgage**.

The property owner, whose interest in the property is given as security, is the *mortgagor*.

The person who receives the security is the *mortgagee*.

CPA   ### 23. Characteristics of a Mortgage

A mortgage has three characteristics: (1) the termination of the mortgagee's interest on the performance of the obligation secured by the mortgage, (2) the right of the mortgagee to enforce the mortgage by foreclosure on the mortgagor's failure to perform, and (3) the mortgagor's right to redeem or regain the property.

---

thinking things through

Putting the Brakes on Eminent Domain

Bailey's Brake Service, a bit of an eyesore at a main intersection near a failing downtown area of Mesa, Arizona, was a family-founded, owned, and operated business that had been open in its existing location since 1970. Lenhart's True Value Hardware store was also a longstanding Mesa business with a location south and east of Bailey's and a desire for a better location. The Lenharts had purchased the property abutting Bailey's but felt that the street facing Bailey's property was necessary for its location.

The city did a taking by eminent domain and then "reissued" the property to Lenhart's for its store. The Baileys challenged the city's taking in the Superior Court as unconstitutional, but the court held that the taking was constitutional as part of the city's plan for redevelopment and revitalization of the area. The Baileys appealed the trial court decision. Should the Baileys get their property back? Was this a proper eminent domain taking? [**Bailey v Myers, 76 P3d 398 (Az Ct App 2003)**]

---

[8] The state with the shortest period for adverse possession is Texas, whose adverse possession period can be as short as 3 years. The state with the longest adverse possession period is Wyoming, with 40 years.

ethics & the law

Hell Hath No Fury Like a NOWMP

The NIMBYs (Not In My Backyard) challenge the placement of everything from power plants to refineries to Wal-Marts. There are also the BANANAs (Build Absolutely Nothing Anywhere Near Anything). Finally, the NOWMPs (Not With My Property) are opposed to eminent domain, the taking of their property for a public use.

Think back to your readings on ethics in Chapter 3. What ethical principles could you apply in favor of the NIMBYs, the BANANAs, and the NOWMPs? What ethical principles could you apply that find that the NIMBYs, the BANANAs and the NOWMPs are acting unethically?

Source: For more information, see Marianne M. Jennings, "NIMBYs, BANANAs, LULUs, NOPEs, and NOWMPs: The Percolating World of Eminent Domain (The Par Boil Stage or Part I)," 33 *Real Estate Law Journal* (no. 4), 445–457 (2005).

24. Property Subject to Mortgage

In general, any form of property that may be sold or conveyed may be mortgaged. It is immaterial whether the right is a present right, a future interest, or merely a right in the land of another. It is not necessary that the mortgagor have complete or absolute ownership in the property. Mortgagors may mortgage any type of land interest they own.

CPA ## 25. Form of Mortgage

Because a mortgage of real property transfers an interest in the property, it must be in writing under the statute of frauds. As a general rule, no particular form of language is required if the language used expresses the intent of the parties to create a mortgage. Many state statutes provide a standardized form for mortgage language that may be used.

26. Creative Forms of Financing

In many situations in which a buyer seeks to purchase property, the conventional methods for obtaining a mortgage are not available because of affordability or qualifications required for a loan. Many creative forms of financing have been developed to help buyers purchase property. **For Example,** residential land buyers, particularly during the real estate boom in 2005–2006, obtain an **adjustable rate mortgage (ARM)**, in which the lower interest rates applied at the beginning of the mortgage help the buyer qualify for the loan. The ARM changes interest rates along with the market, going up and down, unless the ARM has a fixed minimum rate. Other buyers may have the seller finance their purchase through the use of a land or an installment contract. Some new forms of financing, such as the **reverse mortgage**, permit those who have paid off their mortgages on their property to get the value out of their property by having a mortgage company take a mortgage out on the property and pay them money over time. Many senior citizens are able to

adjustable rate mortgage (ARM) – mortgage with variable financing charges over the life of the loan.

reverse mortgage – mortgage in which the owners get their equity out of their home over a period of time and return the house to the lender upon their deaths.

obtain the additional monthly income they may need by this form of financing, which permits them to draw on their equity in their land. Because of the collapse of the subprime mortgage market in 2007–2008, these creative forms of financing are now under extensive state and federal regulation. In addition, state and federal reforms require additional disclosures about the full cost of financing a real property purchase through a mortgage, especially in the types of mortgages in which payments and interest rates fluctuate.

27. Recording or Filing of Mortgage

An unrecorded mortgage is still a valid and binding between and among the parties. A mortgage cannot be set aside on the ground that it has not been recorded. However, recording the mortgage does protect the mortgagee in terms of priority as against other creditors. The recording statutes discussed earlier also apply to mortgages.

28. Responsibilities of the Parties

The mortgagor and mortgagee have the following duties and liabilities when a mortgage is placed on real property.

CPA (A) TAXES, ASSESSMENTS, AND INSURANCE. The duty to pay taxes and assessments rests with the mortgagor. In the absence of an agreement, neither party is under a duty to insure the mortgaged property. Both parties, however, may insure their respective interests. It is common practice for the mortgagor to obtain a single policy of insurance on the property payable to the mortgagee and the mortgagor generally according to the standard mortgagee clause that pays the outstanding loan balance first.

(B) IMPAIRMENT OF SECURITY. The mortgagor is liable to the mortgagee for any damage to the property caused by the mortgagor that impairs the security of the mortgage by materially reducing the value of the property. Both the mortgagor and the mortgagee have a right of action against a third person who wrongfully injures the property.

29. Transfer of Interest

Questions arise as to transfers by the mortgagor and the mortgagee of their respective interests and of the liability of a transferee of the mortgagor.

CPA (A) TRANSFER BY MORTGAGOR. The mortgagor may ordinarily transfer the property without the consent of the mortgagee. Such a transfer passes only the interest of the mortgagor and does not divest or impair a properly recorded mortgage.

The transfer of the property by the mortgagor does not affect the liability of the mortgagor to the mortgagee. Unless the mortgagee has agreed to substitute the mortgagor's grantee for the mortgagor, the mortgagor remains liable for the mortgage debt as though no transfer had been made.[9]

CPA (B) LIABILITY OF THE PARTIES IN A TRANSFER BY A MORTGAGOR. There are two ways to transfer mortgaged property, and each way has different results in terms of personal liability for the transferee. In the assumption of a mortgage, the transferee agrees to

---

[9] *Williams v Countrywide Home Loans, Inc.,* 504 F Supp 2d 176 (WD Tex 2007).

assumption–mortgage transfers in which the transferee and mortgagor are liable and the property is subject to foreclosure by the mortgagee if payments are not made.

assume liability. In an **assumption**, the mortgagor remains liable, the transferee is liable, and the property is subject to foreclosure by the mortgagee in the event the payments are not made. **For Example,** if Bob sold his house with a $175,000 mortgage for $200,000 to Jane, Jane could pay Bob $25,000 cash and then agree to assume Bob's mortgage. Jane may get the benefit of a lower interest rate by assuming Bob's mortgage. Both Bob and Jane are personally liable, and the mortgagee may foreclose on the property if the payments are not made.

The second method of transfer is called a "subject to" transfer. In this type of transfer, the property is subject to foreclosure, but the transferee does not agree to assume the mortgage personally. The mortgagor remains liable in this type of transfer, too.

(c) Transfer by Mortgagee. In most states, a mortgage may be transferred or assigned by the mortgagee.

30. Rights of Mortgagee After Default

Upon the mortgagor's default, the mortgagee in some states is entitled to obtain possession of the property and collect the rents or to have a receiver appointed for that purpose. In all states, the mortgagee may enforce the mortgage by **foreclosure**, a judicial procedure resulting in sale of the mortgaged property.

foreclosure–procedure for enforcing a mortgage resulting in the public sale of the mortgaged property and, less commonly, in merely barring the right of the mortgagor to redeem the property from the mortgage.

Generally, upon any default under the terms of the mortgage agreement, the mortgagee has the right to accelerate the debt or declare that the entire mortgage debt is due. The mortgagee generally has this right even though the default related only to paying an installment or to doing some act, such as maintaining insurance on the property or producing receipts for taxes.

A sale resulting from the foreclosure of the mortgage ends the mortgage lien (subject to rights of redemption), and the property passes free of the mortgage to the buyer at the sale. However, the extinction of the mortgage by foreclosure does not destroy the debt that was secured by the mortgage. The mortgagor remains liable for any unpaid balance or deficiency. In many states, the mortgagor is generally given credit for the fair value of the property if it was purchased by the mortgagee.[10]

stay of foreclosure–delay of foreclosure obtained by the mortgagor to prevent undue hardship.

redemption–buying back of one's property, which has been sold because of a default, upon paying the amount that had been originally due together with interest and costs.

31. Rights of Mortgagor After Default

After default, the mortgagor may seek to stop or stay foreclosure or to redeem the mortgaged land.

(a) Stay of Foreclosure. In certain cases authorized by statute, a **stay (or delay) of foreclosure** may be obtained by the mortgagor to prevent undue hardship.

 (b) Redemption. The right of **redemption** is the right of the mortgagor to pay off the mortgage lien and all foreclosure expenses and, by so doing, acquire title to the property. State laws vary, but the right of redemption generally runs from the time of default through to six months after the foreclosure sale.

---

[10] *Carolina Bank v Chatham Station, Inc.,* 651 SE2d 386 (NC App 2007).

MAKE THE CONNECTION

SUMMARY

Real property includes land, buildings, fixtures, and rights in the land of another. Some land interests include the right to use the land, such as easements. Easements can be granted or arise by implication or prescription.

The interest held by a person in real property may be defined in terms of the period of time for which the person will remain the owner. The interest may be a fee simple estate, which lasts forever, or a life estate, which lasts for the life of a person. These estates are known as *freehold estates*. If the ownership interest exists for a specified number of days, months, or years, the interest is a leasehold estate.

Personal property may be attached to, or associated with, real property in such a way that it becomes real property. In such a case, it is called a *fixture*. To determine whether property has in fact become a fixture, the courts look to the method of attachment, to how the property is adapted to the realty, and to the intent of the person originally owning the personal property.

Under common law, the liability of a land owner for injury to third persons on the premises depends on the status of the third persons as trespassers, licensees, or invitees. Many jurisdictions, however, are ignoring these common law distinctions in favor of an ordinary negligence standard or are giving licensees the same protection as invitees.

Real property may be the subject of multiple ownership. The forms of multiple ownership are the same as those for personal property. In addition, there are special forms of co-ownership for real property, such as condominiums and cooperatives.

A *deed* is an instrument by which a grantor transfers an interest in land to a grantee. A deed can be a quitclaim deed or a warranty deed. To be effective, a deed must be signed or sealed by the grantor and delivered to the grantee. Recording the deed is not required to make the deed effective to pass title, but recording provides notice to the public that the grantee is the present owner. The warranties of the grantor relate to the title transferred by the grantor and to the fitness of the property for use. In the absence of any express warranty in the deed, no warranty of fitness arises under the common law in the sale or the conveyance of real estate. Most states today hold that when a builder or real estate developer sells a new home to a buyer, an implied warranty of habitability arises. Title to real estate may also be acquired by eminent domain and adverse possession.

An agreement that creates an interest in real property as security for an obligation and that ends upon the performance of the obligation is a mortgage. A mortgage must be in writing under the statute of frauds. If the mortgage is unrecorded, it is valid between the parties. The mortgage should be recorded to put good-faith purchasers on notice of the mortgage. A purchaser of the mortgaged property does not become liable for the mortgage debt unless the purchaser assumes the mortgage. The mortgagor still remains liable unless the mortgagee agrees to a substitution of parties. If the mortgagor defaults, the mortgagee may enforce the mortgage by foreclosure. Such foreclosure may be delayed because of undue hardship.

LEARNING OUTCOMES

After studying this chapter, you should be able to clearly explain:

A. NATURE OF REAL PROPERTY

LO.1 List the types of real property interests, the rights of the parties and their liabilities

> See *Kelo v City of New London* on p. 1179.
> See *Winchell v Guy* on p. 1172.

LO.2 Distinguish between liens, licenses, and easements

> See *Frierson v Watson* on p. 1165.
> See the Sports & Entertainment Law discussion of Wrigley Field on p. 1167.

B. NATURE AND FORM OF REAL PROPERTY OWNERSHIP

LO.3 Discuss the nature and form of real property ownership

> See **For Example,** on Ralph Watkins on p. 1170

C. LIABILITY TO THIRD PERSONS FOR CONDITION OF REAL PROPERTY

LO.4 Explain the liability of landowners for injury to others on their property.

> See the slip-and-fall example on p. 1171

D. CO-OWNERSHIP OF REAL PROPERTY

LO.5 Discuss the forms of co-ownership and parties' rights.

> See the example on p. 1172 of the rights of condominium owners.

E. TRANSFER OF REAL PROPERTY BY DEED

LO.6 Describe how deeds convey title to land

> See *Fletcher v Minton* on p. 1177.

F. OTHER METHODS OF TRANSFERRING REAL PROPERTY

G. MORTGAGES

LO.7 Describe the characteristics and effect of a mortgage

> See the **For Example,** discussion of Bob and Jane on p. 1183.

KEY TERMS

abstract of title
acceptance
adjustable rate mortgage (ARM)
adverse possession
assumption
attractive nuisance doctrine
condominium
cooperative
covenant against encumbrances
covenant of further assurances

covenant of quiet enjoyment
covenant of right to convey
covenant of seisin
covenants (or warranties) of title
deed
dominant tenement
easement
easement by implication
eminent domain
estate in fee
fee simple defeasibles

fee simple estate
fixture
foreclosure
grantee
grantor
invitee
judgment liens
land
leasehold estate
license
licensee
liens
life estate
limited covenant

mechanic's liens	race-notice statutes	stay (or delay) of
mortgage	real property	foreclosure
notice statutes	recorder	tax liens
notice-race	redemption	transferee
possibility of reverter	remainder interest	trespasser
prescription	reverse mortgage	warranties of title
profits	runs with the land	warranty deeds
quitclaim deeds	servient tenement	way of necessity
race statutes		

QUESTIONS AND CASE PROBLEMS

1. In 1972, Donald and Joyce Carnahan purchased a 1-acre lot located on a 22-acre lake. The purchase included a portion of the lake bed. The Carnahans used the lake for recreational activity in both winter and summer, and their activities included motorboats, jet skis, and wave runners. In 1991, the Moriah Property Owners Association, Inc., acquired title to the majority of the lots along the lake and imposed restrictive covenants on the use of the lake, including one that prohibited all motors on the lake except for those powered by 12-volt batteries. The Carnahans filed suit to establish a prescriptive easement in their right to use the lake for all their activities. Do you think the Carnahans acquired an easement by prescription? [*Carnahan v Moriah Property Owners Association, Inc.*, 716 NE2d 437 (Ind)]

2. Bunn and his wife claimed that they had an easement to enter and use the swimming pool on neighboring land. A contract between the former owners of the Bunns' property and the adjacent apartment complex contained a provision that the use of the apartment complex's swimming pool would be available to the purchaser and his family. No reference to the pool was made in the contract between the former owners and the Bunns, nor was there any reference to it in the deed conveying the property to the Bunns. Decide. [*Bunn v Offutt*, 222 SE2d 522 (Va)]

3. After executing the various deeds, J. M. Fernandez Jr. placed them in a closet (with other valuable papers) for safekeeping until they could be physically delivered to the various grantees, including Sylvia Sheppard, when she returned to Key West. This closet was in the home that Fernandez shared with Betty DeMerritt. They were not married but lived together the final 15 years of Fernandez's life. Shortly thereafter, Fernandez was debilitated by a stroke and became a total invalid. He never regained his health and died before Sylvia Sheppard could return to Key West to receive physical delivery of the deed personally from him. When Sylvia Sheppard did arrive in Key West, Betty DeMerritt gave her the deed. This took place two or three days after the death of Fernandez. When questioned as to why she turned the deed over to Sylvia, Betty DeMerritt stated, "I knew he wanted me to do it ... because he couldn't do it." She was speaking of Fernandez's physical disability. Does Sylvia have title to the property? Was there delivery? [*Kerr v Fernandez*, 792 So2d 685 (Fla)]

4. Kenneth Corson, 10, lived with his mother, Lynda Lontz, in an apartment building owned by Bruno and Carolyn Kosinski. While playing with other children who lived in the same building, Corson was drawn to a stairwell that provided access to the building's laundry room and roof. Corson and the other children climbed to the roof and discovered an area where they could jump from the roof of their building to that of the building next door. The children engaged in roof hopping for several days. On the last day, Corson misjudged his jump and fell the three stories to the ground below. Corson and his mother filed suit against the Kosinskis to collect damages for Corson's injuries. What theory might be used to hold the Kosinskis liable? [*Corson by Lontz v Kosinski*, 801 F Supp 75 (ND Ill)]

5. Determine whether the following would be fixtures or personal property.

   a. Refrigerator in a home

   b. Refrigerators in an apartment complex with furnished units

   c. Refrigerators in a restaurant kitchen

   d. Refrigeration/freezer units in a grocery store

   e. Mini-refrigerator in a student dorm

6. What is the relationship between trespass and adverse possession?

7. Bradham and other members and trustees of the Mount Olivet Church brought an action to cancel a mortgage on the church property. The mortgage had been executed previously by Davis and other former trustees of the church and given to Robinson as mortgagee. The court found that the church was not indebted to the mortgagee for any amount. Should the mortgage be canceled? [*Bradham v Robinson*, 73 SE2d 555 (NC)]

8. Miller executed a deed to real estate, naming Zieg as grantee. He placed the deed in an envelope on which was written "To be filed at my death" and put the envelope and deed in a safe deposit box in the National Bank that had been rented in the names of Miller and Zieg. After Miller's death, Zieg removed the deed from the safe deposit box. Moseley, as executor under Miller's will, brought an action against Zieg to declare the deed void. Decide. [*Moseley v Zieg*, 146 NW2d 72 (Neb)]

9. Henry Lile owned a house. When the land on which it was situated was condemned for a highway, he moved the house to the land of his daughter, Sarah Crick. In the course of construction work, blasting damaged the house. Sarah Crick sued the contractors, Terry & Wright, who claimed that Lile should be joined in the action as a plaintiff and that Sarah could not sue by herself because it was Lile's house. Were the defendants correct? [*Terry & Wright v Crick*, 418 SW2d 217 (Ky)]

10. Bradt believed his backyard ran all the way to a fence. Actually, a strip on Bradt's side of the fence belonged to his neighbor Giovannone, but Bradt never intended to take land away from anyone. Bradt later brought an action against

Giovannone to determine who owned the strip on Bradt's side of the fence. Who is the owner? Why? [*Bradt v Giovannone*, 315 NYS2d 96]

11. Robert E. Long owned land in the City of Hampton that he leased to Adams Outdoor Advertising Limited Partnership. Adams had an advertising billboard placed on the property. On October 6, 1993, Long notified Adams that he was terminating the lease. Adams accepted the termination and told Long that it would have the electrical service disconnected and would schedule demolition of the billboard for the first week in November. Long wanted to use the billboard to advertise his own business and filed suit to enjoin Adams from destroying the billboard. Long maintained the billboard was part of the land and belonged to him. Adams asserted that it owned the billboard as a lessee. The trial court found for Long, and Adams appealed. Decide. [*Adams Outdoor Adv., Ltd., Part. v Long*, 483 SE2d 224 (Va)]

12. Smikahl sold Hansen a tract of land on which were two houses and four trailer lots equipped with concrete patios and necessary connections for utility lines. The tract Hansen purchased was completely surrounded by the land owned by Smikahl and third persons. To get onto the highway, it was necessary to cross the Smikahl tract. Several years after the sale, Smikahl put a barbed wire fence around his land. Hansen sued to prevent obstruction to travel between his land and the highway over the Smikahl land. Smikahl's defense was that no such right of travel had been given to Hansen. Was he correct? [*Hansen v Smikahl*, 113 NW2d 210 (Neb)]

13. Martin Manufacturing decided to raise additional long-term capital by mortgaging an industrial park it owned. First National Loan Co. agreed to lend Martin $1 million and to take a note and first mortgage on the land and building. The mortgage was duly recorded. Martin sold the property to Marshall, who took the property and assumed the mortgage debt. Does Marshall have any personal liability on the mortgage debt? Is Martin still liable on the mortgage debt? Explain.

14. Christine and Steve Mallock buried their son in a burial plot purchased at Southern Memorial Park, Inc. Each year the Mallocks conducted a memorial service for their son at his burial plot. On the seventh anniversary of their son's death, the Mallocks went to their son's grave at 11:00 A.M. for the annual service, which generally took 30 minutes. When they arrived, they discovered that a tent and chairs set up for funeral services on the plot next to their son's grave were actually resting on his gravesite. The Mallocks asked Southern's management if the tent and chairs could be moved until they could conduct their service. The managers refused, and the Mallocks went ahead with their ceremony, cutting it to five minutes, after they moved the chairs and tents by themselves.

Southern's managers called the police and had the Mallocks evicted. Southern claimed the Mallocks had no rights on the property except for the grave and that their deed for the plot did not award an easement for access. Did the Mallocks have the right to access to the gravesite? [*Mallock v Southern Memorial Park, Inc.*, 561 So2d 330 (Fla Ct App)]

15. *O* conveys property to *A* on December 1, 2006. *O* conveys the same property to *B* who does not know about *A* and who records his deed on December 2, 2006. *O* then conveys the same property to *C*. Who has title to the property?

CPA QUESTIONS

The topic of insurance has been eliminated from the content outline for the CPA exam as of october 2009. However, the exam lags behind the content change, so this topic may continue to appear on the exam for six to 18 months.

1. Which of the following statements is correct with respect to a real estate mortgage?

   a. It must be signed only by the mortgagor (borrower).

   b. It must be recorded in order to be effective between the mortgagor and the mortgagee.

   c. It does *not* have to be recorded to be effective against third parties without notice if it is a purchase money mortgage.

   d. It is effective even if *not* delivered to the mortgagee.

2. To be enforceable against the mortgagor, a mortgage must meet all the following requirements *except:*

   a. Be delivered to the mortgagee

   b. Be in writing and signed by the mortgagor

   c. Be recorded by the mortgagee

   d. Include a description of the debt and land involved

3. Ritz owned a building in which there was a duly recorded first mortgage held by Lyn and a recorded second mortgage held by Jay. Ritz sold the building to Nunn. Nunn assumed the Jay mortgage and had no actual knowledge of the Lyn mortgage. Nunn defaulted on the payments to Jay. If both Lyn and Jay foreclosed and the proceeds of the sale were insufficient to pay both Lyn and Jay, then:

   a. Jay would be paid after Lyn was fully paid.

   b. Jay and Lyn would be paid proportionately.

   c. Nunn would be personally liable to Lyn but not to Jay.

   d. Nunn would be personally liable to Lyn and Jay.

4. Which of the following deeds will give a real property purchaser the greatest protection?

   a. Quitclaim

   b. Bargain and sale

   c. Special warranty

   d. General warranty

Chapter 50

ENVIRONMENTAL LAW AND LAND USE CONTROLS

A. STATUTORY ENVIRONMENTAL LAW

As the United States changed from a rural, agricultural society to an urban, industrial one, new laws were needed to prevent the pollution of the environment.

1. Air Pollution Regulation

Clean Air Act–federal legislation that establishes standards for air pollution levels and prevents further deterioration of air quality.

(A) **LEGISLATIVE HISTORY OF AIR POLLUTION REGULATION.** The first legislation that dealt with air pollution, passed in 1955, was the Air Pollution Control Act, which was simply a statutory recognition of a concern about air quality. Even the first statute regulating air pollution, the **Clean Air Act**, passed in 1963, produced no response from the states, which were charged with the responsibility of developing pollution standards and enforcement mechanisms. It was not until the 1970 amendments to the Clean Air Act that the federal law on air pollution got some teeth, for it was in those amendments that Congress established the federal agency responsible for enforcing the law, the Environmental Protection Agency (EPA). The EPA was authorized to establish national air quality standards and see that the states developed plans for the implementation of those standards.

nonattainment areas–"dirty" areas that do not meet federal standards under the Clean Air Act.

emissions offset policy–controls whether new factories can be built in a nonattainment area.

(B) **MODERN LEGISLATION AND REQUIREMENTS.** Under the 1970 Clean Air Act,[1] as well as the 1977 and 1990 amendments to it, states must measure their air content of sulfur dioxide, carbon monoxide, and hydrocarbons and then take appropriate steps to bring their air quality within the federal limits established for each of these. States that do not meet federal standards are called **nonattainment areas**, or *dirty areas,* and their plans for implementation are strictly reviewed by the EPA, which can halt federal highway funding in the event the implementation plan is not followed. Those states that do meet the federal standards must still have a plan to remain at that level.

For nonattainment areas, the EPA developed an **emissions offset policy**, which controls whether new factories can be built. For a new plant to obtain a permit to begin operations in a nonattainment area, the business proposing the new plant must be able to show that (1) the plant will have the greatest possible emissions controls, which means better than existing emissions standards, (2) the business has all of its other plants and operations in compliance with federal emissions standards, and (3) the new plant's emissions will be offset by reductions in emissions in other facilities in the area. This last requirement is often referred to as the **bubble concept**, which requires an examination of all emissions from all sources in an area. Before any new operations with emissions can be permitted, the business seeking approval must be able to show that overall emissions in the area will not increase.

bubble concept–method for determining total emissions in one area; all sources are considered in an area.

The 1990 amendments to the Clean Air Act increased the role of the bubble concept with the ability of businesses to transfer their emissions permits. Those businesses that can reduce their emissions below their allowable amounts or that can eliminate their emissions are free to transfer their permit rights to emit to someone else who can then use them without affecting total emissions in the bubble area. There is a market exchange for emissions permits because the EPA will not, under

[1] 42 USC § 1857 *et seq.*

the 1990 act, issue any additional permits beyond the rights to emission that already exist. Today, approximately 10 percent of all the emissions permit rights are owned by environmental groups.

(c) New Developments in Air Quality: The U.S. Supreme Court and the EPA. In *Environmental Defense v Duke Energy,* 549 US 561 (2007), the U.S. Supreme Court heard a case in which the EPA had brought suit against Duke Energy for implementing modifications to its coal-fired electricity plants without first filing for approval from the agency. Duke maintained that only major modifications to power plants required EPA approval, a standard the EPA had been following for years. However, the EPA based its expanded permit requirements for even minor modifications under the Prevention of Significant Deterioration (PSD) regulations. The EPA explained its shift because of the need for the prevention of carbon emissions and for addressing the problems stemming from global warming. New conditions, according to the EPA, required more intense and detailed intervention in plant modification in order to carry out its PSD mandate. The utilities challenged the agency's authority to act on greenhouse gases and global warming issues because there was no statutory provision that covered such an expansion. The court held that the EPA could step up its permit requirements and still be within its statutory authority in choosing which modifications to regulate via permit. The standard has now evolved to one that goes beyond best available technology (BAT) to maximum achievable control technology (MACT), a standard that is not controlled by cost alone.

In *Massachusetts v EPA,* 549 US 497 (2007), the Court held that the Clean Air Act mandated EPA action on greenhouse gases and global warming. Chief Justice Roberts and three other justices dissented because they maintained that redress of the EPA for inaction on global warming lies with Congress and the president, not the federal courts. The justices added that their position was one of jurisdiction and authority and "involves no judgment on whether global warming exists, what causes it, or the extent of the problem." With these decisions and the change of administration in 2009, the EPA has begun developing new regulations under the Clean Air Act. In addition, proposed legislation, known as "Cap-and-Trade," would create even more stringent bubble standards with fewer available permits.

2. Water Pollution Regulation

The first meaningful regulation in water pollution began at about the same time as effective air pollution regulation. The first legislation with enforcement power was passed in 1972 as the Federal Water Pollution Control Act and then amended and renamed in 1977 as the **Clean Water Act**.[2] Under the Clean Water Act, the EPA has developed **effluent guidelines**, which are ranges for discharges organized according to industrial groups and for specific plants in each of these groups. The guidelines establish the maximum amounts that can be discharged, and those maximums are coupled with a permit system that requires each plant to obtain a permit from the EPA before discharging anything into any type of pool, pond, river, lake, stream, or ocean. **For Example,** a plant that releases hot water from a steam

Clean Water Act–federal legislation that regulates water pollution through a control system.

effluent guidelines–EPA standards for maximum ranges of discharge into water.

---

[2] 33 USC § 1251 *et seq.* The pollution of navigable waters had been regulated by the Rivers and Harbors Act of 1899, which required a permit for discharging into navigable rivers, streams, and lakes.

generator must still have a permit just to release hot water into the stream near the plant. The EPA also has standards for the treatment of water that is used in a plant's production process before that water can be discharged.[3] **For Example,** a plant must still have a permit to discharge water even though that water is cleaner as it is discharged from the plant than it was when it was brought in to be used in production or manufacturing. However, the EPA is permitted to use cost-benefit analysis in setting the standards for the quality of the water that is released back into the river, lake, etc. Companies must use the **best available technology (BAT)**, but that does not mean the EPA cannot weigh costs and benefits.[4]

3. Solid Waste Disposal Regulation

The disposal of solid waste (garbage) has also been regulated since the 1960s, but the initial legislation simply provided money for research by state and local governments on how to dispose of solid waste.[5] In 1970, the **Resource Recovery Act** provided federal money for cities and states with recycling programs.

After several major open-dumping problems that produced community-wide illnesses, including those in the Love Canal area near Buffalo, New York, Congress passed the **Toxic Substances Control Act (TOSCA)**, which controls the manufacture, use, and disposal of toxic substances, a list of which the EPA developed. Along with TOSCA, Congress passed the **Resource Conservation and Recovery Act (RCRA)**, which regulates the disposal of potentially harmful substances through a permit system and uses federal grants to encourage the restoration of damaged resources.[6] **For Example,** many strip mine locations were restored due to the RCRA.

In 1980, Congress passed the **Comprehensive Environmental Response, Compensation, and Liability Act (CERCLA)**,[7] which authorizes the U.S. president to issue funds to be used for the cleanup of areas that were once disposal sites for hazardous wastes. The act set up a trust fund for cleanups, to be reimbursed by the company responsible for such hazardous wastes. The funds in the trust are available for government use but are not subject to attachment by private citizens who seek to get an area cleaned up by removing the hazardous waste. Under CERCLA, the EPA has the authority to designate **Superfund sites**, or parcels of land that are deemed to have, or potentially have, hazardous wastes that require cleanup.

The **Superfund Amendment and Reauthorization Act**, passed in 1986, authorizes the EPA to bring suit for the purpose of collecting the costs of cleanup from those who are responsible for the hazardous wastes on the site. The act and its judicial interpretations provide a very broad definition of who is responsible under CERCLA for the costs of cleanup. Four classes of parties can be held liable under CERCLA. "Owners and operators" of contaminated property are liable under the

---

best technology available– EPA standard to be met in order to release water used by a facility and then returned to its original source, such as river, lake, etc.

Resource Recovery Act– early federal solid waste disposal legislation that provided funding for states and local governments with recycling programs.

Toxic Substances Control Act (TOSCA)–first federal law to control the manufacture, use, and disposal of toxic substances.

Resource Conservation and Recovery Act (RCRA)– federal law that regulates the disposal of potentially harmful substances and encourages resource conservation and recovery.

Comprehensive Environmental Response, Compensation, and Liability Act (CERCLA)– federal law that authorizes the president to issue funds for the cleanup of areas that were once disposal sites for hazardous wastes.

Superfund sites–areas designated by the EPA for cleanup of hazardous waste.

Superfund Amendment and Reauthorization Act–federal law that authorizes the EPA to collect cleanup costs from those responsible for the ownership, leasing, dumping, or security of hazardous waste sites.

---

[3] In *Coeur Alaska v Southeast Alaska Conservation*, 129 SCt 2458 (2009) the court held that a project in an Alaskan lake under the supervision of the Army Corps of Engineers did not require an EPA permit process for the operator to obtain permission to dump fill dirt into the lake.

[4] *Entregy Corporation v Riverkeeper, Inc.*, 129 SCt 1498 (2009) (US), In the case, Entergy's cost of bringing cooling water intake structures to a higher level passed for new structures would be 9 times current costs. The court held the additional benefit achieved with new processes and equipment was too small to justify the cost.

[5] See the Solid Waste Disposal Act, 42 USC § 3251 *et seq.*, and the Resource Recovery and Policy Act of 1970, 42 USC § 3251 *et seq.*

[6] 42 USC § 6901 *et seq.*

[7] 42 USC § 9601 *et seq.*

statute. *Owners* include present owners as well as past owners, whether or not they are responsible for the hazardous wastes being dumped on the property. *Operators* include those who are leasing the property, again regardless of whether they are responsible for the hazardous waste being dumped. **For Example,** many gas stations have been designated as Superfund sites because the underground tanks have leaks, causing gas to seep into the soil. Current and past owners of such a station are responsible under CERCLA, as well as an owner who has converted the station into some other use.[8]

Other responsible parties under CERCLA include anyone who transported hazardous waste to a site and anyone who hired another or arranged to transport hazardous waste to the site. Lenders were, at one time, also held liable for cleanup costs in the event they took back property from a debtor. However, the Asset Conservation, Lender Liability, and Deposit Insurance Protection Act of 1996 provides an exclusion for lenders provided the lender does not actually participate in the management or operational affairs of the facility of the debtor.[9]

CASE SUMMARY

Don't Blame Me, I'm Only the Arranger

FACTS: In 1960, Brown & Bryant, Inc. (B & B), began operating an agricultural chemical distribution business. Using its own equipment, B & B applied its products to customers' farms. B & B opened its business on a 3.8 acre parcel of former farmland in Arvin, California, and in 1975, expanded operations onto an adjacent .9 acre parcel of land owned jointly by the Atchison, Topeka & Santa Fe Railway Company, and the Southern Pacific Transportation Company (Railroads). Waste water and chemical runoff from the facility was allowed to seep into the ground water below.

During its years of operation, B & B stored and distributed various hazardous chemicals on its property sold by Shell Oil Company (Shell). When B & B purchased chemicals from Shell Oil Company (Shell), and Shell would arrange for delivery by common carrier, f.o.b. destination. When the product arrived, it was transferred from tanker trucks to a bulk storage tank located on B & B's primary parcel. During each of these transfers leaks and spills could—and often did—occur. Although the common carrier and B & B used buckets to catch spills from hoses and gaskets connecting the tanker trucks to its bulk storage tank, the buckets sometimes overflowed or were knocked over, causing chemical spills onto the ground during the transfer process.

In the late 1970s Shell took several steps to encourage the safe handling of its products. Shell provided distributors with detailed safety manuals and instituted a voluntary discount program for distributors that made improvements in their bulk handling and safety facilities. Later, Shell required distributors to obtain an inspection by a qualified engineer and provide self-certification of compliance with applicable laws and regulations. B & B's Arvin facility was inspected twice and told Shell that it had made a number of recommended improvements to its facilities. Despite these improvements, B & B remained a " '[s]loppy' [o]perator." The EPA soon discovered significant contamination of soil and ground water.

---

[8] However, in *Acushnet Company v Mohasco*, 191 F3d 69 (1st Cir 1999), the court held that there must be some proof of causation between a company's conduct and the resulting toxic contamination.

[9] "Participating" does not include monitoring or enforcing the security agreement, monitoring or inspecting the premises, providing financial advice, mandating cleanup of hazardous materials, restructuring the loan, foreclosing, or selling or leasing the property. However, a parent corporation can be held liable for the conduct of a subsidiary if there is sufficient knowledge and control. *United States v Best Foods, Inc.*, 524 US 51 (1998).

CASE SUMMARY

Continued

By 1989, B & B was insolvent and ceased all operations. That same year, the Arvin facility was designated as a Superfund site. By 1998, the Governments had spent more than $8 million in cleanup costs.

In 1991, EPA (Governments) ordered the Railroads to conduct certain cleanup processes. The Railroads did so, incurring expenses of more than $3 million in the process. Seeking to recover at least a portion of these costs, the Railroads brought suit against B & B.

The District Court held that both the Railroads and Shell were potentially responsible parties (PRPs) under CERCLA—the Railroads because they were owners of a portion of the facility, and Shell because it had "arranged for" the disposal of hazardous substances through its sale and delivery of chemicals.

Although the court found the parties liable, it did not impose joint and several liability on Shell and the Railroads for the entire response cost incurred by the Governments. The court apportioned the Railroads' liability as 9% of the Governments' total response cost. Based on estimations of chemical spills of Shell products, the court held Shell liable for 6% of the total site response cost.

The state and local governments appealed the District Court's apportionment, and Shell cross-appealed the court's finding of liability. Applying a theory of arranger liability, the Ninth Circuit held that Shell arranged for the disposal of a hazardous substance.

The Court of Appeals held Shell and the Railroads jointly and severally liable for the Governments' cost of responding to the contamination of the Arvin facility.

The Railroads and Shell appealed.

DECISION: The primary pollution at the Arvin facility was contained in the southeastern portion of the facility most distant from the Railroads' parcel and the spills of hazardous chemicals that occurred on the Railroad parcel contributed to no more than 10% of the total site contamination, some of which did not require cleanup.

The court reversed the Court of Appeals' conclusion that the Railroads are subject to joint and several liability for all costs arising out of the contamination of the Arvin facility.

The court held that Shell should not be held liable as an arranger under CERCLA because it did not arrange for disposal and it ran responsible programs to get distributors to comply with its standards. However, there was not intent on the part of Shell to dump the chemicals by arranging for their delivery. The court also held that the Railroads' share of the site cleanup costs was reasonably apportioned at 9% and that the parties were not joint and severally liable. The judgment was reversed. [**Burlington Northern Railway/Shell Oil Co. v U.S., 129 S Ct 1870 (2009)**]

CERCLA liability has been extended to those who merge or buy corporations; these parties also buy into CERCLA liability, and liability under CERCLA cannot be avoided by a transfer of ownership. The U.S. Supreme Court has ruled in *United States v Bestfoods*, 525 US 51 (1998), that a parent corporation is not automatically liable under CERCLA for a subsidiary corporation's conduct but may be responsible if the subsidiary is simply a shell. In other words, CERCLA liability of parent corporations for the actions of their subsidiaries is governed by corporate law on piercing the corporate veil (see Chapter 44 for more information).

One of the new key areas for minimizing CERCLA liability is that of the self-audit, a company's internal investigation of its operations and lands to determine whether any environmental hazards are on its properties. Many companies wanted to know, for the sake of financial planning and minimizing harm, whether they had any Superfund issues. However, they did not want their voluntary investigations and cleanups to work against them. To encourage these types of internal investigations and self-reporting, the EPA developed its Incentives for Self-Policing, Disclosure, Correction, and Prevention of Violations. Under this EPA program, companies can have their penalties reduced and not waive any rights if they follow the procedures and meet the following requirements: (1) the violations were uncovered as part of a self-audit, (2) the violations were uncovered voluntarily, (3) the violations were reported to the EPA within 10 days, (4) the discovery was made independently and disclosed independently, and no one was threatening disclosure, (5) the violations are corrected within 60 days, (6) there is a written agreement that the conduct will not happen again, (7) there is no history of repeat violations, (8) no serious harm came to anyone as a result of the conduct, and (9) the company cooperates completely with the EPA. If these requirements are met, the company is eligible for reductions in fines and penalties of up to 75 percent.

CERCLA has perhaps been a too-effective environmental law. Because of the liability exposure on sites that were designated as Superfund sites, there were, as of 2002, over 450,000 sites around the country that were undeveloped and untouchable because of contamination. Called "**brownfields**," these sites are defined by the EPA as "real property, the expansion, redevelopment, or reuse of which may be complicated by the presence or potential presence of a hazardous substance, pollutant, or contaminant." Brownfields often contribute to urban blight and present a barrier to economic development and revitalization. As a result, the Small Business Liability Relief and Brownfields Revitalization Act was passed to allow 75 federal agencies to work together (as the *Federal Partnership Action Agenda*) to provide funding for proposals to clean up and enable the use of these brownfields. EPA rules now provide a process for application to become an "innocent landowner," or someone who seeks to develop the brownfield but wants an exemption from CERCLA exposure. That designation then allows the applicant to obtain federal funding for purposes of cleaning up and developing the brownfield.

brownfields – land that is a designated Superfund cleanup site but which lies fallow because no one is willing to risk liability by buying the property, even when the hazardous waste has been removed, or property no one is willing to spend the money to remove the hazardous waste.

4. Environmental Quality Regulation

The federal statutes on air, water, and solid waste pollution are directed at private parties in their use of land. However, the federal government also regulates itself in terms of its operations and impact on the environment. The **National Environmental Policy Act (NEPA)** requires federal agencies to consider the impact on the environment of their proposed projects.[10] An agency must prepare a report, called an **environmental impact statement (EIS)**, that documents the impact of the proposed federal project on the environment and covers consideration of practical and feasible alternatives with a lesser impact.[11] **For Example,** the federal government has been required to file an EIS for the Alaska oil pipeline, the extermination of wild horses, the construction of a post office, the implementation of a change in national park airport procedures that would permit jets to land, and highway construction.

National Environmental Policy Act (NEPA) – federal law that mandates study of a project's impact on the environment before it can be undertaken by any federal agency.

environmental impact statement (EIS) – formal report prepared under NEPA to document findings on the impact of a federal project on the environment.

[10] 42 USC § 4321 *et seq.*
[11] *Silveira v Las Gallina Valley Sanitary District*, 63 Cal Rptr 244 (1997).

5. Other Environmental Regulations

In addition to the major categories of environmental laws just covered, several other important statutes regulate specific areas of the environment. The **Noise Control Act** sets standards for noise from low-flying aircraft for the protection of landowners who are in flight paths.[12] The **Endangered Species Act (ESA)** gives the secretary of the interior the responsibility of identifying and protecting endangered terrestrial species, while the secretary of commerce is responsible for endangered marine species.[13] These cabinet-level federal officers have the authority to curtail any development, noise, or other act that threatens those species on their endangered lists.[14]

The **Safe Drinking Water Act** requires the EPA to establish national standards for contaminants in drinking water. The **Oil Pollution Act** is a federal law that came about following the oil spill from the *Exxon Valdez* off the coast of Alaska, which resulted in damage to the waters, fish, and birds in that area. Under this law, companies are financially responsible for the cleanup of their spills that occur in

Noise Control Act–federal law that controls noise emissions from low-flying aircraft.

Endangered Species Act (ESA)–federal law that identifies and protects species that are endangered from development or other acts that threaten their existence.

Safe Drinking Water Act–a federal law that establishes national standards for contaminants in drinking water.

Oil Pollution Act–federal law that assigns cleanup liability for oil spills in U.S. waters.

C A S E   S U M M A R Y

The Loggers and the Naturalists Can't Be Friends: The Spotted Owl

FACTS: Two U.S. agencies halted logging in the Pacific Northwest because it endangered the habitat of the northern spotted owl and the red-cockaded woodpecker, both endangered species. Sweet Home Chapter, a group of landowners, logging companies, and families dependent on the forest products industries in the Pacific Northwest, brought suit seeking clarification of the authority of the secretary of the interior and the director of the Fish and Wildlife Service to include habitation modification as a harm covered by the Endangered Species Act (ESA).

The federal district court found for the secretary and director and held that they had the authority to protect the northern spotted owl through a halt to logging. The Court of Appeals reversed. Babbitt, the secretary of the interior, appealed.

DECISION: The statutory word *harm* encompasses direct as well as indirect injuries. The broad purpose of the ESA supports the secretary's decision to extend protection against activities that cause the precise harms Congress enacted the statute to avoid—that is, to provide a means whereby the ecosystems upon which endangered species and threatened species depend may be conserved.

When it enacted the ESA, Congress delegated broad administrative and interpretive power to the secretary. The proper interpretation of a word such as *harm* involves a complex policy choice. When Congress has entrusted the secretary with broad discretion, courts should not substitute their views of wise policy. The judgment of the Court of Appeals was reversed.*
[**Babbitt v Sweet Home Chapter of Communities for a Great Oregon, 515 US 687 (1995)**]

* Congress passed legislation clarifying the meaning of ESA and allowed logging to continue for a limited time frame. During the time, the logging industry, paper manufacturers, and others using timber negotiated with environmental groups to achieve balance in logging. Known as the *sustainable forest initiative,* the cooperation among the parties who were once litigants achieved a compromise acceptable to both.

---

[12] 42 USC § 4901.
[13] 16 USC § 1530 *et seq.*
[14] The authority to bring suit rests with both landowners and environmentalists. *Bennett v Spear*, 520 US 154 (1997).

thinking things through

The Ranchers and the Suckers: Competing for Water

The Fish and Wildlife Service issued an opinion on the Klamath Irrigation Project in southern Oregon and northern California. The opinion concluded that the project must be halted because it could affect the Lost River Sucker and the Shortnose Sucker, two species of fish listed as endangered species as of 1988.

Halting the project meant that ranchers, such as Brad Bennett, would not be able to get the water they needed for their operations. Bennett and the other

ranchers filed suit alleging that the report had factual errors and was incorrect in its conclusion. They asked that the court intervene and prohibit Fish and Wildlife from halting the project. Environmental groups said that the ranchers could not bring suit under the Endangered Species Act (ESA) because they were not suing to obtain protection for the two species. Does the ESA permit the ranchers' suit? [**Bennett v Spear 520 US 154 (1997)**]

U.S. waters. The act also provides for substantial penalties for failure to take action to clean up a spill, and those penalties can be as high as $25,000 per day or $3,000 per barrel if the spill is the result of negligence or willful misconduct.[15] Failure to report a spill carries penalties of up to five years in prison and/or $250,000 per individual and $500,000 for corporations. In addition, civil penalties for the failure to clean up an oil spill can cost the company up to $50,000,000 in penalties.

6. State Environmental Regulation

All states have some form of environmental regulation, and their environmental agencies work closely with the EPA on enforcement and standards. All states have some form of hazardous waste controls that define hazardous waste differently and carry a range of penalties for violations. **For Example,** Oregon imposes a fine of $3,500 per animal killed as a result of hazardous waste dumping. Other states mandate disclosure of the history of property use before that property can be sold, transferred, or mortgaged.

B. Enforcement of Environmental Laws

Federal environmental laws can be enforced through criminal sanctions, penalties, injunctions, and suits by private citizens. In addition to federal enforcement rights,

---

[15] 33 USC § 2701 *et seq.* The act establishes a cleanup fund for those spills in which the party to blame is unknown or is financially unable to pay the cost of cleanup. The act also requires that boats be double-hulled. After three remands, the damages against awarded to those harmed by the spill totaled $4.5 billion. However, Exxon appealed the award of damages and the U.S. Supreme Court held that the punitive damages were limited to those upper limits in maritime law or about $500 million (an amount equal to the compensatory damages awarded in the case). Exxon Shipping Co. v. Baker, 128 S.Ct. 2605 (2008). Cites of all of the lower court decisions in the Exxon cases can be found referenced in the U.S. Supreme Court decision.

ethics & the law

Hitting a Jam on Logging

Asia Pacific Resources International Holdings, Ltd. (called April) entered an agreement with the World Wildlife Fund, an environmental activist group. The agreement curbs April's timber-cutting areas to preserve a natural rainforest with great diversity of species in Sumatra, Indonesia. Over the past 20 years, more than half of the forest has been cut down for lumber.

April's customers, such as Procter & Gamble (maker of Charmin and Bounty paper towels), were shunning the company because of its notorious reputation for damaging biodiverse areas in Indonesia. While April complied with Indonesian law (leaving 20 percent of the forest untouched), it did so in long ribbon strips that were insufficient to support the many species of wildlife located there.

Terms of the deal include the following:

- April will verify the source of all logs it purchases.

- April will plant tree plantations.

Local residents are not fond of the agreements because their livelihoods have been blocked as April closes its road and prohibits use by illegal loggers.

What advantages do you see in allowing nongovernmental groups to obtain private contract promises on environmental policy? What disadvantages do you see? What ethical issues exist for April?*

* Steve Stecklow, "Environmentalists, Loggers Near Deal on Asian Rainforest," *Wall Street Journal*, February 23, 2006, A1, A14.

---

certain common law remedies exist for the protection of property rights, such as the remedies for nuisance.

7. Parties Responsible for Enforcement

The EPA is the primary federal agency responsible for the enforcement of federal environmental laws, including those on air and water pollution, solid waste disposal, toxic substance control, and noise pollution. The EPA establishes emissions standards through regulation and then enforces them with a system of permits and sanctions for violations. The EPA works closely with state environmental agencies in enforcement.

Council on Environmental Quality (CEQ) – federal agency that establishes national policies on environmental quality and then recommends legislation to implement these policies.

The **Council on Environmental Quality (CEQ)** was established in 1966 as a part of the executive branch to establish national policy on environmental quality and then make recommendations for legislation for the implementation of that policy. Other federal agencies with responsibility for enforcement of federal environmental laws include the Department of Commerce, the Department of the Interior, the U.S. Forest Service, and the Bureau of Land Management.

Private citizens also have the right to enforce federal environmental laws through private litigation. **For Example,** a private citizen can bring a suit to halt the construction of a dam by the federal government if the agency responsible failed to conduct an environmental impact study or if the EIS is inadequate.

8. Criminal Penalties

Most of the federal environmental laws carry criminal penalties for violations. Figure 50.1 provides a summary of those penalties to which both companies and their employees are subject.

9. Civil Remedies

injunction–order of a court of equity to refrain from doing (negative injunction) or to do (affirmative or mandatory injunction) a specified act.

Although criminal remedies are costly to businesses, the EPA also has the authority to have the polluting activity halted through the use of **injunction**. The EPA simply brings suit against a business and shows that it is engaged in unauthorized dumping, the release of emissions in excess of a permit, or discharge without a permit. A court can then order the business to halt the activity that is resulting in the violation. In some cases, the effect of the injunction is to shut down the business. The business is then required to negotiate with the EPA to meet certain standards before the EPA will agree to have the injunction lifted.

FIGURE 50-1 | *Penalties for Violations of Federal Environmental Laws*

ACT	PENALTIES	PRIVATE SUIT
CLEAN AIR ACT	$25,000 PER DAY; UP TO 1 YEAR OF IMPRISONMENT; 15 YEARS AND/OR $1,000,000 FOR WILLFUL OR REPEAT VIOLATIONS; $10,000 REWARDS	CITIZEN SUITS; AUTHORIZED EPA SUIT FOR INJUNCTIVE RELIEF
CLEAN WATER ACT	$25,000 PER DAY, UP TO 1 YEAR; $50,000 AND/OR 3 YEARS FOR VIOLATIONS WITH KNOWLEDGE; $100,000 AND/OR 6 YEARS FOR SUBSEQUENT VIOLATIONS	CITIZEN SUITS; AUTHORIZED EPA SUIT FOR INJUNCTIVE RELIEF
RESOURCE CONSERVATION RECOVERY ACT (SOLID WASTE DISPOSAL ACT)	$250,000 AND/OR 15 YEARS' IMPRISONMENT FOR INTENTIONAL VIOLATIONS; $1,000,000 FOR CORPORATIONS, $50,000 AND/OR 5 YEARS FOR OTHERS	CITIZEN AND NEGLIGENCE SUITS (AFTER EPA REFUSES TO HANDLE)
HAZARDOUS SUBSTANCE/ RESPONSE TRUST	FUND FOR CLEANUP	EPA SUIT FOR INJUNCTIVE RELIEF AND REIMBURSEMENT OF TRUST FUNDS
OIL POLLUTION ACT	$25,000 PER DAY, OR $1,000 PER BARREL; $3,000 PER BARREL IF WILLFUL OR NEGLIGENT; $250,000 AND/OR 5 YEARS FOR FAILURE TO REPORT	PRIVATE SUITS

Private citizens can also bring suit for injunctions against companies that are in violation of federal law or not in compliance with statutory procedures. **For Example,** private citizens have filed suit against developers to stop construction when there is an issue of possible violation of the Endangered Species Act.

10. Private Remedies: Nuisance

nuisance – conduct that harms or prejudices another in the use of land or that harms or prejudices the public.

Conduct that unreasonably interferes with the enjoyment or use of land is a **nuisance**,[16] which may be smoke from a chemical plant that damages the paint on neighboring houses. It may be noise, dirt, or vibration from passing heavy trucks. Some conduct is clearly so great an interference that it is easy to conclude that it constitutes a nuisance, but not every interference is a nuisance. Furthermore, determining whether the interference is sufficiently great to be halted as unreasonable is frequently difficult. The fact that the activity or business is lawful and is conducted in a lawful manner does not mean that it is not a nuisance. The effect on others determines whether there is a nuisance.[17] A landfill may be a nuisance even though it is operated by a city in a non-negligent manner and in accordance with the state's solid waste disposal statutes.[18]

The courts attempt to balance the social utility of the activity with the resulting harm. The mere fact that there is harm does not establish that there is a nuisance. When community welfare outweighs the harm to land and owners, the activity is not a nuisance.[19] **For Example,** courts have held that smoke, fumes, and noise from public utilities and power plants were not nuisances, although they did create harm. The interests of the community in the activity of the public utilities outweighed the interests of those affected.

Those affected by a nuisance are entitled to damages for the loss of the use of the land or for harm that is caused by the nuisance. Sometimes, an injunction that stops the conduct is necessary. If the nuisance is permanent, the damages are the loss in value of the land. If the nuisance can be stopped, the measure of damages is the reduction in value of the property during the time of the nuisance.[20]

private nuisance – nuisance that affects only one or a few individuals.

public nuisance – nuisance that affects the community or public at large.

(A) PRIVATE AND PUBLIC NUISANCES. When a nuisance affects only one or a few persons, it is called a **private nuisance**. When it affects the community or public at large, it is called a **public nuisance**. Planting trees or erecting a fence, although otherwise lawful, constitutes a public nuisance when it creates a traffic hazard by obscuring an intersection. However, a landowner did not create a public nuisance by allowing trees to grow tall even though the height of the trees required the neighboring county airport to alter its approach patterns, which, in turn, triggered the Federal Aviation Administration to order the airport to shorten the usable portion of its

---

[16] *Mills v Kimbley*, 909 NE2d 1068 (Ind App 2009).
[17] *North Carolina ex rel. Cooper v Tennessee Valley Authority*, 593 FSupp2d 812 (WD NC 2009).
[18] *Williams v Great Falls*, 732 P2d 1315 (Mont 1987).
[19] *Boyne v Town of Glastonbury*, 955 A2d 645 (Conn App 2008).
[20] *Myers v Wild Wilderness Raceway, L.L.C.*, 908 NE2d 950 (Oh App 2009).

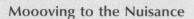

CASE SUMMARY

Moooving to the Nuisance

FACTS: Spur Industries operated a cattle feedlot near Youngtown and Sun City, Arizona (communities 14 to 15 miles west of Phoenix). Spur had been operating the feedlot since 1956, and the area had been agricultural since 1911.

In 1959 Del E. Webb began development of the Sun City area, a retirement community. Webb purchased the 20,000 acres of land for about $750 per acre.

In 1960 Spur began an expansion program in which its operating area grew from 5 acres to 115 acres.

At the time of the suit, Spur was feeding between 20,000 and 30,000 head of cattle, which produced 35 to 40 pounds of wet manure per head per day, or over one million pounds per day. And despite the admittedly good feedlot management and good housekeeping practices of Spur, the resulting odor and flies produced an annoying if not unhealthy situation as far as the senior citizens of southern Sun City were concerned. There is no doubt that some of the citizens of Sun City were unable to enjoy the outdoor living which Del Webb had advertised. Del Webb was faced with sales resistance from prospective purchasers as well as strong and persistent complaints from the people who had purchased homes in that area. Nearly 1,300 lots could not be sold. Webb then filed suit alleging Spur's operation was a nuisance because of the flies and odors constantly drifting over Sun City. The trial court enjoined Spur's operations and Spur appealed.

DECISION: The court held that because Del Webb had "moved to the nuisance" that Spur could not be required to shut down its operations. Rather, Spur would have to relocate because of the court's actions of balancing the interests of the important cattle industry in Arizona with the equally important housing/retirement industry. However, Del Webb would have to compensate Spur for the costs of the move—$11 million. [**Spur Industries, Inc. v Del E. Webb Development Co., 494 P2d 700 Az (1972)**]

runways.[21] The existence of a statutory environmental protection procedure may bar or supersede the common law of nuisance.

(B) REMEDY FOR NUISANCE. A criminal nuisance may be terminated by abatement or closure by government authority. A civil nuisance may be stopped by an injunction, and the injured person may sue for money damages for the harm caused.

When an injunction is issued, the court must exercise great care to halt the nuisance while avoiding going too far by enjoining conduct that is otherwise lawful.[22]

(C) THE TECHNOLOGICAL ENVIRONMENT OF THE LAW OF NUISANCE. As technology changes, new ways of manufacturing, new methods of transportation, and new ways of living develop. As the environment changes, corresponding changes are reflected in the law. **For Example,** the presence of overhead wires and the possibility of electromagnetic field exposure has resulted in courts balancing the interests of utilities and the delivery of power with the safety of homeowners.

---

[21] *County of Westchester v Town of Greenwich, Connecticut*, 76 F3d 42 (2d Cir 1996).
[22] *Hill v Lindner*, 769 NW2d 427 (ND 2009).

e-commerce&cyberlaw

Because any electrical current sets up a magnetic field, computers and wire transmissions to and from computers set up magnetic fields that might affect electrical equipment in buildings on neighboring land. The stronger the current, the greater the magnetic field.

For example, Meridian Data Processing Center is an independent contractor that performed all of the data processing for many banks and stockbrokers. Because of the large number of computers and direct wire lines to its customers, the Center's operation set up a substantial magnetic field that interfered with some of the electronic display equipment in several neighboring stores. The stores sued to obtain an injunction against the Center for creating a nuisance. However, unless the stores can show some negligence in the maintenance of the Center's equipment that produced unnecessary sparking or a similar cause of electrical disturbance, they have not established a nuisance. Because of the social utility of the Center's business, a court would not condemn this necessary activity as a nuisance. If, however, the stores could suggest a reasonable method of shielding the equipment, it is possible that the court would order the Center to take such protective measures.

11. Private Remedies: Due Diligence

due diligence–process of checking the environmental history and nature of land prior to purchase.

Another method by which problems with land are remedied is through sales transactions in which the buyer demands that a situation or problem on the land be fixed before signing a contract for purchase. **Due diligence** is the process by which the buyer conducts a thorough investigation of the property and its current and former uses to determine whether any problems with respect to environmental law or nuisance exist. Due diligence is conducted through a search of public records, an inspection of the land, and often, when problems appear in these first two steps, some soil testing. This advance determination of problems is a civil means for land cleanup because sellers will be unable to transfer their properties until they meet the buyers' standards, determined by a close examination of the property for violations.

C. Land Use Controls

In addition to environmental laws, other restrictions, both private and public, place controls and limits on how land can be used.

12. Restrictive Covenants in Private Contracts

restrictive covenants– covenants in a deed by which the grantee agrees to refrain from doing specified acts.

Real estate developers find that when there are consistent patterns in the appearance of a neighborhood's homes and buildings (for example, similarity of design instead of a hodge-podge look), the property values are enhanced. To make sure this consistency is maintained, developers place **restrictive covenants** on the land that obligate the buyers to honor limitations in their use of their property, the nature of buildings that will be maintained or constructed on the land, and so on. If a restrictive covenant is valid, it binds buyers who had actual notice or knowledge of the restrictions. The notice comes from a notation in the deed about the covenants; the covenants then are said to "run with the land." That is, all owners are subject to them and all owners in that development have the right to stop another owner from violating the covenant.

A restrictive covenant must be clearly stated to be effective. Contract rules apply in interpreting covenants. If any uncertainty exists, the covenant will be construed strictly in favor of the free use of the land. When there is no uncertainty and no reason to depart from the meaning of the words of the covenant, a court will enforce those words.

Because of property rights, courts interpret restrictive covenants narrowly to permit the greatest possible use of the land. However, courts often disagree as to what is permitted by a restrictive covenant. **For Example,** courts have decided differently the issue of the use of a single-family residence for providing day care services when the covenants for that neighborhood prohibit the operation of a business out of a home. [23]

Restrictive covenants that violate laws or constitutional rights are not valid. For example, a restrictive covenant that discriminates against persons with disabilities is void because it violates the Fair Housing Act. [24]

A restrictive covenant that has not been enforced or observed is no longer valid. For example, if houses in a neighborhood have had their roofs replaced with materials that did not comply with the restrictive covenants but no one objects, those new materials become the standard for the neighborhood, not the covenant materials. [25]

13. Public Zoning

zoning–restrictions imposed by government on the use of designated land to ensure an orderly physical development of the regulated area.

By **zoning**, a governmental unit such as a city adopts an ordinance imposing restrictions on the use of the land. The object of zoning is to ensure an orderly physical development of the regulated area. In effect, zoning is the same as restrictive covenants; the difference is in the source of authority. In most cases, zoning is based on an ordinance of a local political subdivision, such as a municipality or a county. Restrictive covenants, on the other hand, are created by agreement of the parties.

The zoning power permits any regulation that is conducive to advancing public health, welfare, and safety. The object of a particular zoning regulation may be to prevent high-density population.

Some zoning ordinances may be conservation inspired. An ordinance may prohibit or regulate the extraction of natural resources from any land within the zoned area. The fact that a zoning restriction limits the owner in the use of a property does not amount to a "taking" of property for which compensation must be made. [26] If, however, the zoning law deprived the owner of use of the land in any fashion, that would be a "taking" that required compensation.

---

[23] *Martellini v Little Angels Day Care, Inc.*, 847 A2d 838 (RI 2004).
[24] *Villas West II of Willowridge Homeowners Ass'n, Inc. v McGlothin*, 885 NE2d 1274 (Ind 2008).
[25] *Stuart v Chawney*, 560 NW2d 336 (Mich App 1997).
[26] *Cablevision Systems Corp. v F.C.C.*, 570 F3d 83 (CA 9 2009).

sports&entertainment law

Hell Hath No Fury Like a Star Who Loses Garden Space

Ralph Horowitz owned land located in the Los Angeles area that had been zoned for manufacturing and warehousing. When he acquired the land, it had not been used for those purposes since 1992 when about 350 local residents had begun a communal garden there. The garden included trees and had even been praised by the Los Angeles mayor as a lovely respite among the industrial plants and warehouses. Mr. Horowitz had difficulty getting the gardeners to leave the property. He agreed to allow them to harvest their gardens and then leave, but they refused to leave. Among the gardeners and their supporters were Danny Glover, Laura Dern, Joan Baez, and Daryl Hannah. After several days of lofty

protest, Ms. Hannah had to be removed from a tree by police who were using a fire truck ladder. She stated, "I'm very confident this is the morally right thing to do, to take a principled stand in solidarity with the farmers." Some violence broke out as police removed other protestors who had chained themselves to a walnut tree in the garden. The gardeners said they wanted Mr. Horowitz to commit the land to an urban garden.*

What are their rights? What are Mr. Horowitz's rights?

* **www.bbc.com**, accessed June 14, 2006.

(A) Nonconforming Use. When the use of land is in conflict with a zoning ordinance at the time the ordinance goes into effect, such use is described as a **nonconforming use**. **For Example,** when a zoning ordinance that requires a setback of 25 feet from the boundary line is adopted, an existing building that has a 10-foot setback is a nonconforming use.

A nonconforming use has a constitutionally protected right to continue, but if the nonconforming use is discontinued, it cannot be resumed.[27] The right to a nonconforming use may be lost by abandonment. If a garage is a nonconforming use and its owner stops using it as a garage and uses it for storing goods, a return to the use of the property as a garage will be barred by abandonment.

At times, a real estate development or building construction is only partly completed when a zoning ordinance that would prohibit such development or building is adopted. To avoid hardship for the persons involved, it is customary to exempt partly finished projects from the zoning ordinance just as though they were existing nonconforming uses.[28]

nonconforming use—use of land that conflicts with a zoning ordinance at the time the ordinance goes into effect.

(B) Variance. The administrative agency charged with the enforcement of a zoning ordinance may grant a **variance**. This permits the owner of the land to use it in a specified manner that is inconsistent with the zoning ordinance.

Agencies ordinarily are reluctant to permit a variance when neighboring property owners object because, to the extent that variation is permitted, the basic plan of the zoning ordinance is defeated. Likewise, the allowance of an individual variation,

variance—permission of a landowner to use the land in a specified manner that is inconsistent with the zoning ordinance.

[27] *Gorgone v District of Columbia Bd. of Zoning Adjustment*, 973 A2d 692 (DC 2009).
[28] See, for example, *Vial v Provo City*, 210 P3d 947 (UT App 2009).

CASE SUMMARY

No Tattoos in My Neighborhood

FACTS: Hold Fast Tattoo (Plaintiff) wished to open a tattoo studio on North Sheridan Road in the City of North Chicago and obtained a prospective lessor at its desired location. In accordance with North Chicago's zoning ordinance, Hold Fast Tattoo applied for a special use permit to operate a tattoo studio at that location. On June 21, 2007, the Zoning Board of Appeals of North Chicago recommended approval of the permit to its city council. The proposal was discussed at two council meetings, on July 9, 2007 and July 16, 2007, and Hold Fast Tattoo's request for a special use permit was ultimately denied. The city council informed Hold Fast that its special use permit was denied because it was "not the kind of business" the council wanted in North Chicago. Hold Fast filed suit.

DECISION: The court held that there were no First Amendment violations in prohibiting the tattoo parlor because the tattoo parlor was not speaking; its clients were the ones speaking and they were not prohibited from having tattoos. This control only related to where they could obtain tattoos. The court also held that cities are permitted to have zoning plans and regulations that restrict certain types of businesses as long as there is a public purpose. The city was worried about the level of traffic and congestion from the business and the court found that there was a legitimate public purpose in excluding tattoo parlors from the area. [**Hold Fast Tattoo, LLC v City of North Chicago, 580 F Supp 2d 656 (ND Ill 2008)**]

spot zoning–allowing individual variation in zoning.

or **spot zoning**, may result in such inequality as to be condemned by the courts.[29] In addition, there is a consideration of practical expediency. If variances are readily granted, every property owner will request a variance and flood the agency with these requests.

When the desired use of land is in harmony with the general nature of surrounding areas, a zoning variance is usually granted. A zoning variance is not granted on the ground of hardship, however, when the landowner created the hardship by purchasing land that was subject to a zoning ordinance.

lawflix

Erin Brockovich (2000) (R)

The movie is the story of ground water pollution and private litigation for recovery.

For movie clips that illustrate business law concepts, see LawFlix at **www.cengage.com/blaw/dvl**.

[29] *Wilson v Brick Tp. Zoning Bd. of Adjustment*, 963 A2d 1208 (NJ Super 2009).

MAKE THE CONNECTION

SUMMARY

Public and private regulations apply to land use. The public regulations consist of environmental laws and zoning. Environmental laws exist at both the state and the federal levels. At the federal level, regulations govern air pollution through limits on emissions and permits for discharges; water pollution with permit requirements, discharge prohibitions, and treatment standards; solid waste disposal with limitations on dumping and liability for cleanup when hazardous materials are found on property; and environmental quality through the use of advance studies on projects and their impact on the environment. Other federal regulations on the environment protect endangered species, set standards for drinking water, and impose liability for oil spills as well as safety standards for oil tankers.

Environmental laws are primarily enforced at the federal level by the Environmental Protection Agency (EPA), but other federal agencies as well as state agencies work together to enforce these laws, using criminal and civil penalties and injunctions to halt pollution. Private citizens also have the right to bring suit under federal statutes to enforce the requirements imposed.

A *nuisance* is a public or private interference with the use and enjoyment of land, and individuals can bring suit to halt nuisances. Courts perform a balancing test in deciding how to handle concerns about nuisances. They seek to balance the use and enjoyment of land with the economic interests of all involved parties.

Restrictive covenants in deeds are valid land use restrictions that pass from owner to owner and are enforceable as long as they do not violate any constitutional rights. *Zoning* is a public means of regulating land use. Zoning laws are part of an overall plan for development adopted by a governmental entity. Some landowners can obtain variances from zoning laws, and some preexisting uses are permitted to continue with the protection of a nonconforming use.

LEARNING OUTCOMES

After studying this chapter, you should be able to clearly explain:

A. STATUTORY ENVIRONMENTAL LAW

LO.1 List and describe the federal statutes that regulate various aspects of the environment
>   See *Massachusetts v EPA* on p. 1192.
>   See the discussion of the air, water, and waste statutes beginning on p. 1191.

B. ENFORCEMENT OF ENVIRONMENTAL LAWS

LO.2 Explain how environmental laws are enforced and describe the criminal penalties for violation of environmental laws
>   See the list of penalties in Figure 50.1

LO.3 Define *nuisance* and list the remedies available
See *Spur Industries v Del Webb* on p.1202.

C. LAND USE CONTROLS

LO.4 Explain the role and application of covenants and zoning laws
See *Hold Fast Tattoo, LLC v City of North Chicago* on p. 1206.

KEY TERMS

best technology available
brownfields
bubble concept
Clean Air Act
Clean Water Act
Comprehensive
   Environmental
   Response,
   Compensation, and
   Liability Act (CERCLA)
Council on
   Environmental Quality
   (CEQ)
due diligence
effluent guidelines

emissions offset policy
Endangered Species Act
   (ESA)
environmental impact
   statement (EIS)
injunction
National Environmental
   Policy Act (NEPA)
Noise Control Act
nonattainment areas
nonconforming use
nuisance
Oil Pollution Act
private nuisance
public nuisance

Resource Conservation
   and Recovery Act
   (RCRA)
Resource Recovery Act
restrictive covenants
Safe Drinking Water Act
spot zoning
Superfund Amendment
   and Reauthorization Act
Superfund sites
Toxic Substances Control
   Act (TOSCA)
variance
zoning

QUESTIONS AND CASE PROBLEMS

1. Union Electric wishes to construct a new coal-fired plant in the northeastern corner of Arizona. Union plans to use the maximum achievement technology for the scrubbers on the plant to reduce emissions. Will Union be able to obtain a permit from the EPA to build and operate the new power plant? Discuss the issues that Union faces.

2. Federal Oil Co. was loading a tanker with fuel oil when the loading hose snapped for some unknown reason and about 1,000 gallons of oil poured into the ocean. Federal Oil was prosecuted for this water pollution. It raised the defense that it had exercised due care, was not at fault in any way, and had not intended to pollute the water. What statutes could be used to prosecute Federal Oil? What are the potential penalties?

3. Philip Carey Co. owned a tract of land in Plymouth Township, Pennsylvania, on which it deposited a large pile of manufacturing waste containing asbestos. Carey sold the land to Celotex, and Celotex sold the land to Smith Land & Improvement Corp. The EPA notified Smith that unless it took steps to eliminate the asbestos hazard, the EPA would do the work and pursue reimbursement. Smith cleaned up the land to the EPA's satisfaction at a cost of $218,945.44. Smith asked Celotex and Carey for reimbursement. Which firms

have liability for the cleanup costs? [*Smith Land & Improvement Corp. v Celotex*, 851 F2d 86 (3d Cir)]

4. The McConnells bought a home in Sherwood Estates. The land was subject to a restrictive covenant that "no building, fence, or other structure" could be built on the land without the approval of the developer of the property. The McConnells built a dog pen in their yard that consisted of a cement base with fencing surrounding the base. They claimed that approval was not required on the theory that the restrictive covenant did not apply because it showed an intent to restrict only major construction, not minor additions to the landscape. A lawsuit was brought to compel the McConnells to remove the dog pen because prior approval had not been obtained. Are restrictive covenants applied this expansively to homeowners? Must the McConnells have prior approval? [*Sherwood Estates Homes Ass'n, Inc. v McConnell*, 714 SW2d 848 (Mo App)]

5. General Automotive operates Grand Auto Parts Stores, which receive used automotive batteries from customers as trade-ins. General's policy in disposing of these batteries had been to drive a screwdriver through each spent battery and then sell them to a battery-cracking plant operated by Morris P. Kirk & Sons, Inc., which extracted and smelted the lead. After the lead was extracted from the batteries, Kirk washed and crushed the battery casings, loaded them into a dump truck, and then dumped them. Tons of pieces of crushed batteries were dumped onto Catellus Development Corp.'s property. Under CERCLA, Catellus sought to recover from General the costs of cleaning up the hazardous battery parts from its property. General maintained that it was not liable because it sold the batteries to Kirk, and Kirk did the dumping. Was General correct? [*Catellus Development Corp. v United States*, 34 F3d 748 (9th Cir)]

6. A zoning ordinance of the city of Dallas, Texas, prohibited the use of property in a residential district for gasoline filling stations. Lombardo brought an action against the city to test the validity of the ordinance. He contended that the ordinance violated the rights of the owners of property in such districts. Do you agree with this contention? [*Lombardo v City of Dallas*, 73 SW2d 475 (Tex)]

7. Taback began building a vacation home on a parcel of wooded land. It was to be a three-story house, 31 feet high. This height violated the local zoning ordinance that limited residential homes to two and one-half stories, not exceeding 35 feet. When Taback learned of this violation, he applied for a zoning variance. Because of the delay of the zoning board and because winter was approaching, Taback finished the construction of the building as a three-story house. At a later hearing before the zoning board, he showed that it would be necessary for him to rebuild the third floor to convert the house into a two and one-half story house. The zoning board recognized that Taback's violation could not be seen from neighboring properties. Was Taback entitled to a zoning variance? [*Taback v Town of Woodstock Zoning Board of Appeals*, 521 NYS2d 838 (App Div)]

8. Bermuda Run Country Club, Inc., developed a tract of land, formed a country club, and sold some of the lots to individual buyers. Following various sales and

litigation, an agreement was executed giving the board of governors power to veto club members' assessments. The agreement declared that this was a restrictive covenant that would run with the land and bind subsequent owners. The corporation that later purchased the country club claimed it did not have that effect. Was the provision in question a restrictive covenant that ran with the land? [*Bermuda Run Country Club, Inc. v Atwell*, 465 SE2d 9 (NC App)]

9. The Stallcups lived in a rural section of the state. In front of their house ran a relatively unused, unimproved public county road. Wales Trucking Co. transported concrete pipe from the plant where it was made to a lake where the pipe was used to construct a water line to bring water to a nearby city. In the course of four months, Wales made 825 trips over the road, carrying from 58,000 to 72,000 pounds of pipe per trip and making the same number of empty return trips. Because the heavy use of the road by Wales cut up the dirt and made it like ashes, the Stallcups sued Wales for damages caused by the deposit of dust on their house and for the physical annoyance and discomfort it caused. Wales defended its position on the ground that it had not been negligent and that its use of the road was not unlawful. Decide. [*Wales Trucking Co. v Stallcup*, 465 SE2d 44 (Tex Civ App)]

10. Some sections of the city of Manitou Springs have hills of varying degrees of slope. To protect against water drainage and erosion, the city adopted a hillside zoning ordinance that required homes on hillsides to be surrounded by more open land than in the balance of the city. Sellon owned land on a hillside and claimed that the hillside ordinance was unconstitutional because it did not treat all homeowners equally. Was the ordinance valid? [*Sellon v City of Manitou Springs*, 745 P2d 229 (Colo)]

11. Patrick Bossenberry owned a house in a planned community area. Each lot in the area was limited by a restrictive covenant to use for a single-family dwelling. The covenant defined *family* as a blood or marital relationship between most of the occupants. Bossenberry rented his building to Kay-Jan, Inc., which wanted to use the building as a care home for not more than six adult mentally retarded persons. The neighbors sought to enjoin this use as a breach of the covenant. A number of Michigan statutes had been adopted that advanced the public policy of providing care for mentally retarded persons. Could the neighbors prevent the use of the property as a care home for mentally retarded adults? [*Craig v Bossenberry*, 351 NW2d 596 (Mich App)]

12. Kenneth and Mary Norpel purchased a house, and Kenneth attached a 35-foot flagpole to it. He did not obtain the permission of the architectural committee of the Stone Hill Community Association. This consent was required by a restrictive covenant to which the Norpel house was subject. The association objected to the flagpole from which Norpel then flew the American flag. The association brought an action to compel the removal of the pole. Norpel claimed that as a combat veteran of World War II, he had a constitutionally protected right to fly the American flag. Can he be compelled to remove the flagpole?

13. In 1997, Isbell purchased a building in San Diego with the intent to open an adult entertainment establishment there. Because this building was located within 1,000 feet of a residential area, however, a San Diego zoning ordinance precluded him from operating there. Isbell applied for a variance but was unsuccessful. He then filed suit, arguing that the city's ordinance violates the First Amendment, and that its standards for variances violate the equal protection clause. Can the city restrict the operation of this business? What must the city be able to establish? [*Isbell v City of San Diego*, 258 F3d 1108 (9th Cir)]

14. Explain why a company would want to perform a self-audit to determine whether it has any environmental violations.

15. Manufacturer's National Bank of Detroit had extended credit to Z&Z Leasing and had taken a mortgage on Z&Z's property as security for the line of credit. Z&Z defaulted on its payments, and Manufacturer's took possession of the property. The EPA then notified the bank that underground storage tanks on the property were leaking hazardous materials and that the cleanup would be in the $10,000,000 range. Is Manufacturer's liable for the cleanup costs? Are there other parties the EPA could pursue for the costs? [*Z&Z Leasing, Inc. v Graying Reel, Inc.*, 873 F Supp 51 (DC)]

CPA QUESTIONS

1. Which of the following remedies is available against a real property owner to enforce the provisions of federal acts regulating air and water pollution?

	Citizen Suits Against the Environmental Protection Agency to Enforce Compliance	State Suits to Enforce the Laws Against Violators	Citizen Suits Against Violators to Enforce the Laws
a.	Yes	Yes	Yes
b.	Yes	Yes	No
c.	No	Yes	Yes
d.	Yes	No	Yes

2. Under the Comprehensive Environmental Response, Compensation, and Liability Act (CERCLA), commonly known as Superfund, which of the following parties would be liable to the Environmental Protection Agency (EPA) for the expense of cleaning up a hazardous waste disposal site?

    I. The current owner or operator of the site

    II. The person who transported the wastes to the site

    III. The person who owned or operated the site at the time of the disposal

a. I and II

b. I and III

    c. II and III

    d. I, II, and III

3. The National Environment Policy Act was passed to enhance and preserve the environment. Which of the following is not true?

    a. The act applies to all federal agencies.

    b. The act requires that an environmental impact statement be provided if any proposed federal legislation may significantly affect the environment.

    c. Enforcement of the act is primarily accomplished by litigation of persons who decide to challenge federal government decisions.

    d. The act provides generous tax breaks to those companies that help accomplish national environmental policy.

4. Which of the following actions should a business take to qualify for leniency if an environmental violation has been committed?

	Conduct Environmental Audits	Report Environmental Violations to the Government
a.	Yes	Yes
b.	Yes	No
c.	No	Yes
d.	No	No

Chapter 51

LEASES

I f you cannot buy a house or piece of business property, leasing such a property from someone who does own it may be the answer.

A. CREATION AND TERMINATION

Leases are governed by the common law of property as modified by **judicial** decisions and statutes.[1]

1. Definition and Nature

lease–agreement between the owner of property and a tenant by which the former agrees to give possession of the property to the latter in consideration of the payment of rent. (Parties—landlord or lessor, tenant or lessee)

lessor–one who conveys real or personal property by a lease; a landlord.

landlord–one who leases real property to another.

lessee–one who has a possessory interest in real or personal property under a lease; a tenant.

tenant–one who holds or possesses real property by any kind of right or title; one who pays rent for the temporary use and occupation of another's real property under a lease.

A **lease** is the relationship in which one person is in lawful possession of real property owned by another. In common usage, *lease* also refers to the agreement that creates that relationship.

The person who owns the real property and permits the occupation of the premises is known as the **lessor**, or **landlord**. The **lessee**, or **tenant**, is the one who occupies the property. A lease establishes the relationship of landlord and tenant.

2. Creation of the Lease Relationship

The relationship of landlord and tenant is created by an express or implied contract. An oral lease is valid at common law, but statutes in most states require written leases for certain tenancies. Many states provide that a lease for a term exceeding one year must be in writing.

(A) ANTIDISCRIMINATION. Statutes in many states prohibit an owner who rents property for profit from discriminating against prospective tenants on the basis of race, color, religion, or national origin. Also, the federal *Fair Housing Act* prohibits such discrimination. In addition, landlords are subject to the Americans with Disabilities Act (ADA) and must make reasonable accommodations for tenants with disabilities.[2]

(B) UNCONSCIONABILITY. At common law, the parties to a lease had freedom to include such terms as they chose. However, that freedom has been curbed in some states that require that leases follow the pattern of UCC section 2-302 and not include terms and conditions that are unconscionable.[3] **For Example,** a provision in a residential lease stating that the landlord cutting off heat or water will not constitute an eviction is unconscionable. Such a clause does not prevent the tenant from recovering on the grounds of unconscionability or for breach of the implied warranty of habitability when there has been no heat or water.

---

[1] A uniform act, the Uniform Residential Landlord and Tenant Act (URLTA), has been adopted in some form in 20 states. The 20 states are: Alaska, Arizona, Connecticut, Florida, Hawaii, Iowa, Kansas, Kentucky, Michigan, Mississippi, Montana, Nebraska, New Mexico, Oklahoma, Oregon, Rhode Island, South Carolina, Tennessee, Virginia, and Washington. URLTA does not apply to dorm rooms, fraternities, or halfway houses. *Burke v Oxford House of Oregon Chapter V*, 103 P3d 1184 (Or App 2004).

[2] *Salute v Stratford Green Apartments*, 136 F3d 293 (2d Cir 1998) and see *Giebeler v M & B Associates*, 343 F3d 1143 (9th Cir 2003) for an even broader interpretation of the protections of ADA.

[3] *35 Park Ave. Corp. v Campagna*, 48 NY2d 813, 399 NE2d 1144, 424 NYS2d 123 (1979); URLTA § 1.303.

3. Classification of Tenancies

Tenancies are classified by duration as tenancies for years, from year to year, at will, and by sufferance.

CPA

tenancy for years–tenancy for a fixed period of time, even though the time is less than a year.

(A) TENANCY FOR YEARS. A **tenancy for years** is one under which the tenant has a lease that runs for a definite duration. The expression "for years" is used to describe such a tenancy whether the duration of the tenancy is for only six months or as long as 10 years.

periodic tenancy–tenancy that continues indefinitely for a specified rental period until terminated; often called a month-to-month tenancy.

(B) PERIODIC TENANCY. A **periodic tenancy** is one under which a tenant has a lease that has an indefinite duration and under which the tenant pays annual, monthly, or weekly rent. This tenancy does not terminate at the end of a year, month, or week except with proper notice. Proper notice, in most states, means giving notice for at least one period before ending the lease. **For Example,** on a month-to-month tenancy, the notice must be at least one month prior to ending the lease.

In almost all states, a periodic tenancy is implied if the tenant, with the consent of the landlord, stays in possession of property after a tenancy for years. Consent exists when there is an express statement or by conduct, such as when a landlord continues to accept rent.[4]

CPA

tenancy at will–holding of land for an indefinite period that may be terminated at any time by the landlord or by the landlord and tenant acting together.

(C) TENANCY AT WILL. When a lease runs for an indefinite period, which may be terminated at any time by the landlord or the tenant, a **tenancy at will** exists. A person who enters into possession of land for an indefinite period with the owner's permission but without any agreement as to rent is a tenant at will. Statutes in some states and decisions in others require advance notice of termination of this kind of tenancy.

CPA

tenancy at sufferance–lease arrangement in which the tenant occupies the property at the discretion of the landlord.

(D) TENANCY AT SUFFERANCE. When a tenant remains in possession after the termination of the lease without permission of the landlord, the landlord may treat the tenant as either a trespasser or a tenant. Until the landlord elects to do one or the other, a **tenancy at sufferance** exists. **For Example,** if John's one-year lease expired on January 31, 2010, and John remained in the apartment for a week, he would be a tenant at sufferance during that week. If John's landlord accepted a rental payment at the end of the first week, John would be a *periodic* or *month-to-month tenant*. In this situation, John was a tenant for years, a tenant at sufferance, and then a periodic tenant.

4. Termination of Lease

A lease is generally not terminated by the death, insanity, or bankruptcy of either party except in the case of a tenancy at will. Leases may be terminated in the following ways.

(A) TERMINATION BY NOTICE. Unless prohibited by statute, a lease may give the landlord the power to terminate it by giving notice to the tenant. In states that follow the common law on termination by notice, it is immaterial why the landlord

---

[4] *Bayne v Smith*, 965A2d 265 (Pa Super 2009).

terminates. A provision in a lease giving the landlord the right to terminate the lease by notice is strictly construed against the landlord.

(B) EXPIRATION OF TERM IN A TENANCY FOR YEARS. A tenancy for years ends upon the expiration of the term. There is no requirement that one party give the other any notice of termination. However, a lease may require express notice in this type of lease with a specified term except when a statute prohibits the landlord from imposing such a requirement.

(C) NOTICE IN A PERIODIC TENANCY. In the absence of an agreement of the parties, notice for termination of a periodic tenancy is now usually governed by statute. It is common practice for the parties to require 30 or 60 days' notice to end a tenancy from year to year.

(D) DESTRUCTION OF PROPERTY. By either an express provision in a lease or under a statutory provision, tenants are released from their liability to pay rent if the leased premises are destroyed. Alternatively, the amount of rent may be reduced in proportion to the loss. For example, a tenant may only be able to use one-half of the property, so the rent would be cut in half. Such statutes do not require the landlord to repair or restore the property to its former condition.

When the lease covers rooms or an apartment in a building, a destruction of the leased premises terminates the lease.

(E) FRAUD. Because a lease is based on a contract, a lease agreement is subject to the contract defense of fraud. (See Chapter 14.)

(F) TRANSFER OF THE TENANT. Residential leases may contain a provision for termination if there is a change in the tenant's circumstances, such as the tenant's being transferred by an employer to another city or on the tenant's being called into active military service. Such provisions are strictly construed against the tenant. Tenants should be certain to request personal circumstances provisions in their leases that are broad enough to cover these types of job events and military duty.

5. Notice of Termination

When notice of termination is required, no particular words are necessary to constitute a sufficient notice so long as the words used clearly indicate the intention of the party. The notice, whether given by the landlord or the tenant, must be definite. Statutes sometimes require that the notice be in writing. In the absence of such a provision, however, oral notice is generally sufficient.

6. Renewal of Lease

When a lease terminates for any reason, the landlord and the tenant ordinarily enter into a new agreement if they wish to extend or renew the lease. The power to renew the lease may be stated in the original lease by declaring that the lease runs indefinitely, as from year to year, subject to being terminated by either party's giving written notice of a specified number of days or months before the termination date. Renewal provisions are strictly construed against the tenant.

The lease may require the tenant to give written notice of intention to renew the lease. In such a case, there is no renewal if the tenant does not give the required notice but merely remains on the premises after the expiration of the original term.[5]

B. Rights and Duties of Parties

The rights and duties of the landlord and tenant are based on principles of real estate law and contract law. There is an increasing tendency to treat the residential lease like any other type of consumer contract and to govern the rights and duties of the parties by general principles of contract law.

7. Possession

possession–exclusive dominion and control of property.

The tenant has the right to acquire **possession** of the property and to remain in possession of that property until the term of the lease has expired or he or she is removed according to legal proceedings provided to landlords for removal of tenants in breach of the lease.

(A) **Right of Possession.** By making a lease, the lessor or landlord agrees to give possession of the premises to the tenant at the time specified in the lease. If the landlord rents a building that is being constructed, there is an implied promise in the contract that the leased premises will be ready for occupancy on the date specified in the lease for the beginning of the lease term.

If the landlord interferes with the tenant's possession, the landlord has breached the lease agreement, and legal remedies are available to the tenant. *Interference* is generally defined to be an eviction that occurs by judicial proceedings or when the landlord prevents access by the tenant, as when the locks are changed and the tenant does not have a key. If the landlord wrongfully deprives the tenant of the use of one room when the tenant is entitled to use an entire apartment or building, there is a partial eviction. An eviction in violation of the lease or law entitles the tenant to collect damages from the landlord for interference with possession of the leased premises.

covenant of quiet enjoyment–covenant by the grantor of an interest in land to not disturb the grantee's possession of the land.

(B) **Covenant of Quiet Enjoyment.** Most written leases today contain an express promise by the landlord called a **covenant of quiet enjoyment**. Such a provision protects the tenant from interference with possession by the landlord or the landlord's agent, but it does not impose liability on the landlord for the unlawful acts of third persons.[6]

constructive eviction–act or omission of the landlord that substantially deprives the tenant of the use and enjoyment of the premises.

(C) **Constructive Eviction.** A **constructive eviction** occurs when some act or omission of the landlord substantially deprives the tenant of the use and enjoyment of the premises.

To establish a constructive eviction, the tenant must show that the condition of the property is such that it is impossible for the tenant to remain in possession. In addition, constructive eviction is not established unless the tenant actually leaves the premises. If the tenant continues to occupy the premises for more than a reasonable time after what is claimed to be a constructive eviction, the tenant waives or loses the right to object to the landlord's conduct. The definition of *constructive*

[5] *Garrido v Empty Nester Homes, Ltd.*, not reported in NE2d, 2004 WL 51791 (Ohio App 2004).
[6] *Hinton v Sealander Brokerage Co.*, 917 A2d 95 (DC 2007).

eviction requires the establishment of conditions so awful that a tenant is forced to leave. The tenant's remaining behind in the leased premises contradicts one of the elements required for establishing constructive eviction.[7] **For Example,** a condition of constructive eviction would be sewage backing up through the bathtub. The tenant could claim the sewage in the apartment constituted constructive eviction, but the tenant would also need to move out of the apartment.

8. Use of Premises

The lease generally specifies those uses authorized for the tenant. In the absence of express or implied restrictions, a tenant is entitled to use the premises for any lawful purpose for which they are adapted or for which they are ordinarily employed or in a manner contemplated by the parties in executing the lease. A provision specifying the use to be made of the property is strictly construed against the tenant.

(A) CHANGE OF USE. If the tenant uses the property for any purpose other than the one specified, the landlord has the option to declare the lease terminated.

(B) CONTINUED USE OF PROPERTY. A tenant is ordinarily required to give the landlord notice of nonuse or vacancy of the premises. This notice is a practical issue; landlords need to be aware when premises are vacant because there is an increased danger of damage to the premises by vandalism or fire. Also, there is commonly a provision in the landlord's fire insurance policy making it void if a vacancy continues for a specified time.

(C) RULES. The modern lease generally contains a blanket agreement by the tenant to abide by the provisions of rules and regulations adopted by the landlord. These rules are generally binding on the tenant whether they exist at the time the lease was made or are adopted afterward.

(D) PROHIBITION OF PETS. A lease restriction prohibiting pet ownership is valid, as are cleaning fees for violations of the restriction.

9. Rent

The tenant is under a duty to pay rent as compensation to the landlord. The amount of rent agreed to by the parties may be subject to government regulation, as when a city or county has enacted rent control laws.[8]

(A) TIME OF PAYMENT. The time of payment of rent is ordinarily fixed by the lease. When the lease does not specify the time of payment, rent generally is not due until the end of the term. However, statutes or custom may require rent to be paid monthly or may require a substantial deposit before the lease begins.

CPA   (B) ASSIGNMENT. If the lease is assigned (the tenant's entire interest is transferred to a third person), the assignee is liable to the landlord for the rent. However, the

---

[7] Some states prohibit a landlord of residential property from willfully turning off the utilities of a tenant for the purpose of evicting the tenant. *City and County of San Francisco v Sainez*, 77 Cal App 4th 1302, 92 Cal Rptr 2d 418, (Cal App 2000) (imposing civil penalty of $663,000 for shutting off utilities for 530 days). Such conduct is also a violation of ULTRA §§ 2.104 and 4.105.

[8] *Fisher v City of Berkeley, California*, 475 US 260 (1986).

assignment does not in itself discharge the tenant from the duty to pay the rent. If the assignee of the lease does not make the lease payments, the landlord may bring an action for the rent against either the original tenant or the assignee, or both, but is entitled to payment of only what is due under the lease, not a double amount as collected from each party. A **sublessee** (a person to whom part of a tenant's interest is transferred) ordinarily is not liable to the original lessor for rent unless that liability has been expressly assumed or is imposed by statute.

sublessee–person with lease rights for a period of less than the term of the original lease (also *subtenant*).

(C) **RENT ESCALATION.** When property is rented for a long term, it is common to include some provision for the automatic increase of the rent at periodic intervals. Such a provision is often tied to increases in the cost of living or in the landlord's operating costs and is called an **escalation clause**. There may, however, also be rent controls that would prohibit such rent increases.[9]

escalation clause– provision for the automatic increase of the rent at periodic intervals.

10. Repairs and Condition of Premises

In the absence of an agreement to the contrary, the tenant has no duty to make repairs. When the landlord makes repairs, reasonable care must be exercised to make them in a proper manner. The tenant is liable for any damage to the premises caused by his or her willful or negligent acts.

(A) **INSPECTION OF PREMISES.** Under the URLTA, the landlord has the right to enter the leased premises for emergency purposes or with notice to the tenant for repairs, evaluations, and estimates.

(B) **HOUSING LAWS.** Various laws protect tenants by requiring landlords to observe specified safety, health, and fire prevention standards. Some statutes require a landlord who leases a building for dwelling purposes to keep it in a condition fit for habitation. Leases commonly require the tenant to obey local ordinances and laws relating to the care and use of the premises.

Landlords must comply with the ADA. Compliance means that landlords cannot discriminate on the basis of disability in deciding whether to rent to a particular tenant. Also, landlords are required to make reasonable modifications to accommodate tenants with disabilities, which can include everything from making sure that sidewalks on the property are smooth enough for operation of wheelchairs to permitting guide dogs to live with their sight-impaired owners.[10]

One of the developing areas of landlord-tenant law involves landlords' rights with regard to leasing to convicts and those who are registered as sex offenders. About 600,000 inmates are released from prisons each year, and their housing choices generally involve leasing.[11] The federal government requires public housing authorities to screen and evict tenants for drug-related or "safety-threatening" behavior. Public housing authorities that receive federal funds must include a lease clause that requires automatic lease termination for any drug or violent criminal activity, even if the activity does not occur on the landlord's property.

[9] *Id.*
[10] *Crowder v Kitagawa*, 81 F3d 1480 (9th Cir 1996); *Kinney v Yerusalim*, 9 F3d 1067 (3d Cir 1993); *cert. denied*, 511 US 1033 (1996).
[11] Heidi Lee Cain, "Housing Our Criminals: Finding Housing for the Ex-Offender in the Twenty-First Century," 33 *Golden Gate U. L. Rev.* 131 (2003).

CASE SUMMARY

But I'm Innocent!!!

FACTS: Several young men, grandsons of William Lee and Barbara Hill, both of whom were residents on leases of the Oakland Housing Authority (OHA), were caught in the apartment complex parking lot smoking marijuana. The daughter of Pearlie Rucker, who resided with her and was listed on the OHA lease as a resident, was found with cocaine and a crack cocaine pipe three blocks from Rucker's apartment. On three instances within a two-month period, the caregiver of Herman Walker (another OHA resident) and two others were found with cocaine in Walker's apartment.

After OHA initiated the eviction proceedings in state court against the Hills, Rucker, and Walker, they commenced actions against OHA in federal district court, challenging the Department of Housing and Urban Development's (HUD's) interpretation of the federal statute requiring eviction of tenants for criminal activity or the failure to control criminal activity in their apartments. The tenants of OHA argued that the federal statute and HUD regulations result in the eviction of "innocent" tenants and are unconstitutional.

The district court issued a preliminary injunction, enjoining OHA from terminating the leases of the tenants. A panel of the Court of Appeals reversed, and the full Court of Appeals reversed the panel and reinstated the district court's injunction. HUD appealed to the U.S. Supreme Court.

DECISION: Congress, wanting to ensure the safety of public housing, allowed the eviction for criminal activity in leased property even when the tenants were not involved. There are no constitutional issues as long as the proper processes under state law for eviction are followed. **[Department of Housing and Urban Development v Rucker, 535 US 125 (2002)]**

thinking things through

With Friends and Relatives Like These ...

Apply the *Rucker* case and determine if eviction is proper in the following circumstances.

Santosha Scarborough was a resident of a public housing. The lease prohibited the possession of guns and any criminal activity by the tenant or tenants' guests. Her cousin, Delante Simmons, entered her apartment after he had been drinking and began an altercation with her. Scarborough's boyfriend, Desmond Barr, who was also present, withdrew a shotgun and fatally shot Simmons. Executing a search warrant for the apartment the next day, the police found a loaded 12-gauge semiautomatic shotgun next to the water heater in the furnace room, a loaded semiautomatic pistol under the seat cushion of a

couch, a box of Remington shotgun ammunition containing 23 shotgun shells, and a box of cartridges for the semiautomatic pistol. Barr was later acquitted of second-degree murder (the jury accepted his claim of self-defense) but convicted of possession of an unregistered firearm and ammunition.

Santosha was evicted from her apartment the day after the shotgun was found. Ms. Scarborough objected because she had not been involved in any criminal activity. Could she still be evicted?

[Scarborough v Winn Residential LLP/Atlantic Terrace Apartments, 890 A2d 249 (DC 2006)]

CPA

warranty of habitability –
implied warranty that the
leased property is fit for
dwelling by tenants.

(C) WARRANTY OF HABITABILITY. At common law, a landlord was not bound by any obligation that the premises be fit for use unless the lease contained an express warranty to that effect. Most jurisdictions now reject this view and have created a **warranty of habitability** to protect tenants. The warranty of habitability requires, in most states, that the premises have running water, have heat in winter, and be free from structural defects and infestation. If the landlord breaches a warranty of habitability, the tenant is entitled to damages. These damages may be offset against the rent that is due, or if no rent is due, the tenant may bring an independent lawsuit to recover damages from the landlord.[12]

CASE SUMMARY

Don't Let the Bedbugs Bite

FACTS: Geoffrey Green lived in a rent-control apartment in New York City. Bedbugs in his apartment forced him and his partner, Dana Shapiro, to sleep with the lights on, and rotate between sleeping in the bedroom, the kitchen, and the living room. They did not use the bedroom between May and August in 2005 and 2006.

Mr. Green testified that from April 2005 through July 2008, he did not have a single full night's sleep during the summer months. Lack of sleep affected Mr. Green's relationship with Ms. Shapiro and his ability to get to work on time.

Mr. Green withheld rent from October 2005 through January 2007, but only for the prime bedbugs months, i.e., non-winter months, during this period for a total amount of $5,665.84. His landlord (Petitioner) brought a forcible detainer action to have him evicted. Mr. Green counterclaimed for his damages from the bedbugs. Mr. Green offered into evidence two zip-loc bags containing dead bedbugs.

The exterminator for the complex had come to spray the building but said he never saw any live or dead bedbugs in the Green/Shapiro apartment except the specimens that Mr. Green had shown him, in a Ziploc bag. The exterminator believed Green and Shapiro (Respondents) may have brought the bedbugs with them from their previous apartment. Theresa Lonng, a neighbor, testified that she had bedbugs in her apartment, but that she also had had them in her apartment in the building next door, where she had lived until moving next to Mr. Green and Ms. Shapiro.

DECISION: The presence of bedbugs was a breach of the warranty of habitability, regardless of where the bugs came from. As the court noted, those who travel run the risk of bedbugs and landlords must be prepared to eliminate the bugs, wherever and however they land.

The court did question the credibility of tenants who would stay in a bug-infested place for three years without some more diligent form of action. However, the court awarded the tenants a rent abatement to cover September 2005 through December 2006. The first documented notification to the landlord regarding the alleged condition was in September 2005. That was the first documented phone call to the exterminator, and the tenants withheld their rent in September and October of 2005. Based on the log of bites that was kept by the tenants for January 2007 forward, the court found that the tenants had failed to establish the presence of bedbugs from January 2007 forward, and that the bites documented were in all likelihood other insect bites.

The tenants received a 12 percent abatement in rent, for the period of September 2005 through December 2006, totaling $2724.21. [**Bender v Green, 874 NYS2d 786 (NY Civ Ct 2009)**]

[12] *In re Cassell*, 13 Fed Appx 298 (6th Cir 2001).

(D) **ABATEMENT AND ESCROW PAYMENT OF RENT.** To protect tenants from unsound living conditions, statutes sometimes provide that a tenant is not required to pay rent as long as the premises are not fit to live in. As a compromise, some statutes require the tenant to continue to pay the rent but require that it be paid into an escrow or agency account. The money in the escrow account is paid to the landlord only upon proof that the necessary repairs have been made to the premises.

11. Improvements

In the absence of a special agreement, neither the tenant nor the landlord is under a duty to make improvements, as contrasted with repairs.[13] Either party may, as a term of the original lease, agree to make improvements, in which case a failure to perform will result in liability in an action for damages for breach of contract brought by the other party. In the absence of an agreement to the contrary, improvements become part of the realty and belong to the landlord.

12. Taxes and Assessments

In the absence of an agreement to the contrary, the landlord, not the tenant, is usually under a duty to pay taxes and/or assessments. The lease may provide for an increase in rent if taxes on the rented property are increased.[14]

If taxes or assessments are increased because of improvements made by the tenant, the landlord is liable for such increases if the improvements remain with the property. If the improvements can be removed by the tenant, the amount of the increase must be paid by the tenant.

13. Tenant's Deposit

A landlord may require a tenant to make a deposit to protect the landlord from any default on the part of the tenant.[15] There may be statutory limits on the amount of the deposit. Some states provide tenants with protections on these deposits. For example, the landlord may have to hold the deposits in a trust fund or be responsible for paying interest for the period the deposit is held. The landlord may be subject to a penalty if the money is used before the lease would allow for its use.

14. Protection from Retaliation

The URLTA and most state laws protect tenants from retaliation by the landlord for the tenants' exercise of their lawful rights or reporting the landlord for violations of housing and sanitation codes. The types of retaliation from which reporting tenants are protected include refusing to renew a lease and evicting the tenant.

---

[13] The Americans with Disabilities Act requires commercial landlords and tenants to comply with legal requirements for access by the disabled. Shopping centers, medical offices, banks, and professional buildings must be in compliance. See *Pinnock v International House of Pancakes*, 844 F Supp 574 (SD Cal 1993); *Anderson v Little League Baseball, Inc.*, 794 F Supp 342 (D Ariz 1992).

[14] *Brown v Johnston*, 85 P3d 422 (Wyo 2004).

[15] URLTA § 2.101(a).

15. Remedies of Landlord

If a tenant fails to pay rent, the landlord may bring an ordinary lawsuit to collect the amount due and in some states may seize and hold the property of the tenant.

(A) **LANDLORD'S LIEN.** In the absence of an agreement or a statute, the landlord does not have a lien on the personal property or crops of the tenant for money due for rent. The parties may create, by express or implied contract, a lien in favor of the landlord for rent and also for advances, taxes, or damages for failure to make repairs. In the absence of a statutory provision, the lien of the landlord is superior to the claims of all other persons except prior lienors and good-faith purchasers.

(B) **SUIT FOR RENT.** Whether or not the landlord has a lien for unpaid rent, the landlord may collect rent from the tenant as specified in the lease. In some states, the landlord is permitted to bring a combined action against the tenant to recover the possession of the premises and the overdue rent at the same time.

(C) **RECOVERY OF POSSESSION.** A lease commonly provides that on the breach of any of its provisions by the tenant, such as the failure to pay rent, the lease terminates or the landlord may exercise the option to declare the lease terminated. When the lease is terminated for any reason, the landlord then has the right to evict the tenant and retake possession of the property.

Modern cases hold that a landlord cannot lock out a tenant for overdue rent. The landlord must employ legal process to regain possession even if the lease expressly gives the landlord the right to self-help.

The landlord may resort to legal process to evict the tenant to enforce the right to possession of the premises. Statutes in many states provide a summary remedy to recover possession that is much more efficient than the slow common law remedies. Often referred to as a **forcible entry and detainer**, this action restores the property to the landlord's possession unless the tenant complies with payment requirements.

forcible entry and detainer– action by the landlord to have the tenant removed for nonpayment of rent.

(D) **LANDLORD'S DUTY TO MITIGATE DAMAGES.** If the tenant leaves the premises before the expiration of the lease, is the landlord under any duty to rent the premises again to reduce the rent or damages for which the departing tenant will be liable? By common law and majority rule, a tenant owns an estate in land, and if the tenant abandons it, there is no duty on the landlord to find a new tenant for the premises. But a growing minority view places greater emphasis on the contractual aspects of a lease. Under this view, when the tenant abandons the property, thereby defaulting on the contract, the landlord has a duty to seek to mitigate the damages caused by the tenant's breach and make a reasonable effort to rent the abandoned property.

C. LIABILITY FOR INJURY ON PREMISES

When the tenant, a member of the tenant's family, or a third person is injured because of the condition of the premises, the question of who is liable for the damages sustained by the injured person arises.

16. Landlord's Liability to Tenant

At common law, in the absence of a covenant to keep the premises in repair, the landlord was not liable for the tenant's personal injuries caused by the defective condition of the premises that, by the lease, are placed under the control of the tenant. Likewise, the landlord was not liable for the harm caused by an obvious condition that was known to the tenant at the time the lease was made.[16] However, recent cases have imposed liability on landlords for their failure to keep leased premises in repair, even when there is no covenant of repair.

(A) CRIMES OF THIRD PERSONS. Ordinarily, the landlord is not liable to the tenant for crimes committed on the premises by third persons, such as when a third person enters the premises and commits larceny or murder. The landlord is not required to establish a security system to protect the tenant from crimes of third persons.

In contrast, when the criminal acts of third persons are reasonably foreseeable, the landlord may be held liable for the harm caused a tenant. **For Example,** when a tenant has repeatedly reported that the deadbolt on the apartment door is broken, the landlord is liable for the tenant's loss when a thief enters through the door because such criminal conduct was foreseeable. Likewise, when the landlord of a large apartment complex does not take reasonable steps to prevent repeated criminal

sports&entertainment law

The Quarter Pipe 360 Liability Issue

Timothy Lucier, two days shy of his thirteenth birthday, went with his father and several of his friends to Impact (a commercial skate park located in East Providence, Rhode Island) to skateboard to celebrate his birthday. At the skate park, Timothy's father signed the waiver that was required of all who used the park. Timothy donned a helmet, kneepads, and elbow pads, and then he and his friends used the skate park half pipes and quarter pipes. At one point, Timothy climbed on top of the quarter pipe, and as he pushed forward to go down the ramp, the front wheel of his skateboard caught inside a "nub" or "little tiny hole" in the ramp, causing the tail of his skateboard to swing around in a clockwise direction. Timothy twisted off the skateboard and fell on his right leg causing a spiral fracture in his right

leg. Timothy said that after he fell, he looked back at the ramp and saw that there was a split in the wood covering the ramp.

Timothy's parents filed suit against Impact Recreation, Ltd., the operator of the skateboard facility, and Eugene Voll, Impact's landlord. They alleged that there had been a failure by the landlord to ensure that the commercial tenant was not engaging in an activity that was inherently dangerous to the public at large.

Voll required Impact to have insurance, obtain signed waivers from all participants, and obtain his approval prior to the installation of any equipment. Do you believe the landlord is liable to the Luciers? Why or why not? **[Lucier v Impact Recreation, LTD., 864 A2d 635 (RI 2005)]**

[16] *O'Neill v Dunham*, 203 P3d 68 (Kan App 2009).

acts, the landlord is liable to the tenant for the harm caused by the foreseeable criminal act of a third person.[17]

(B) LIMITATION OF LIABILITY. A number of courts, however, have restricted the landlord's power to limit liability in the case of residential, as distinguished from commercial, leasing. A provision in a residential lease excusing a landlord from liability for damage caused by water, snow, or ice is void.

Third persons on the premises, even with the consent of the tenant, are generally not bound by a clause exonerating the landlord. Such third persons may generally recover from the landlord when they sustain injuries.

CASE SUMMARY

Parking Outside the Gate and Living in a Gated Community: High Risk

FACTS: Arnel Management Company manages the Pheasant Ridge Apartments. Pheasant Ridge is a 620-unit, multibuilding apartment complex with over 1,000 residents, situated on 20.59 acres in Rowland Heights, California. Before the gated entrance to the complex are two parking lots; one is a visitor lot, and the other is the parking lot for the leasing office, located on the other side of the road. There are two security gates just past the parking lot. The gates are remote-control operated. Most of the property's parking spaces lie behind these gates by the apartments.

Yu Fang Tan and his wife, Chun Kuei Chang, and their child moved into Pheasant Ridge in July 2002 and received one assigned parking space. Tenants could pay an additional fee for a garage, but Tan chose not to rent one. Tenants with a second car could park in unassigned parking spaces located throughout the complex, or in one of the two lots—as long as the car was removed from the leasing office lot before 7:00 a.m.

At around 11:30 p.m. on December 28, 2002, Tan returned home and tried to find an unassigned open parking space because his wife had parked the family's other car in their assigned space. Unable to locate an available space, he parked in the leasing office parking lot outside the gated area.

As Tan was parking his car, an unidentified man approached him and asked for help. When Tan opened his window, the man pointed a gun and told him to get out of the car because the man wanted it. Tan responded, "Okay. Let me park my car first." But then the car rolled a little, and at that point, the assailant shot Tang in the neck. The incident rendered Tan a quadriplegic. Tan and Chang filed suit against Arnel for their negligent management of the complex as well as its policy of not providing sufficient parking inside the gated area and of charging more for such additional spaces. The trial court granted judgment on the pleadings for Arnel, and Tan and Chang appealed.

DECISION: There had been a chain of events at the apartment complex and, particularly, in the parking lots that put the landlord on notice that there was a need for additional precautions. An expert had recommended various solutions that did not require a great deal of expense such as (1) moving the existing security gates from the back of the access road, and (2) installing "very similar" gates before the visitor and leasing office parking lots. The expert also noted that you don't get much more foreseeability in a property situation than was present in this situation. Reversed. [**Yu Fang Tan v Arnel Management Co., 170 Cal App 4th 1087, 88 Cal Rptr 3d 754 (Cal App 2009)**]

---

[17] *Saylor v Villcar Realty, L.L.C.*, 999 So2d 61 (La. App. 2008).

(c) Indemnification of Landlord. The modern lease commonly contains a provision declaring that the tenant will indemnify the landlord for any liability of the landlord to a third person that arises from the tenant's use of the rented premises.

17. Landlord's Liability to Third Persons

A landlord is ordinarily not liable to third persons injured because of the condition of any part of the rented premises that is in the possession of a tenant by virtue of a lease. If the landlord retains control over a portion of the premises, such as hallways or stairways, however, a landlord's liability exists for injuries to third persons caused by failure to exercise proper care in connection with that part of the premises. Most courts impose liability on the landlord for harm caused to a third person when the landlord was obligated, under a contract with the tenant, to correct the condition that caused the harm or to keep the premises in repair.

CPA ## 18. Tenant's Liability to Third Persons

A tenant in possession has control of the property and is liable when his or her failure to use due care under the circumstances causes harm to (1) licensees, such as a person allowed to use a telephone, and (2) invitees, such as customers entering a store. For both classes, the liability is the same as that of an owner in possession of property. It is likewise immaterial whether the property is used for residential or business purposes.

The liability of the tenant to third persons is not affected by the fact that the landlord may have contracted in the lease to make repairs that, if made, would have avoided the injury. The tenant can be protected, however, in the same manner that the landlord can be protected: by procuring liability insurance for indemnity against loss from claims of third persons.

reversionary interest— interest that a lessor has in property that is subject to an outstanding lease.

D. Transfer of Rights

Both the landlord and the tenant have property and contract rights with respect to the lease. Can they be transferred or assigned? A landlord who sells his property transfers the **reversionary interest** in the leased premises to the buyer. The tenant also has transfer rights.

assignment—transfer of a right. Generally used in connection with personal property rights, as rights under a contract, commercial paper, an insurance policy, a mortgage, or a lease. (Parties—assignor, assignee)

CPA ## 19. Tenant's Assignment of Lease and Sublease

An **assignment** of a lease is a transfer by the tenant of the tenant's entire interest in the premises to a third person. A tenancy for years may be assigned by the tenant unless the tenant is restricted from making such an assignment by the terms of the lease or by a statute. A **sublease** is a transfer to a third person, the *sublessee*, of less than the tenant's entire interest, or full lease term.

sublease—a transfer of the premises by the lessee to a third person, the sublessee or subtenant, for a period of less than the term of the original lease.

(a) Limitations on Rights. The lease may contain provisions denying or limiting the right to assign or sublet. Such restrictions protect the landlord from new tenants who might damage the property or be financially irresponsible.

Restrictions in the lease are construed liberally in favor of the tenant. No violation of a provision prohibiting assignment or subleasing occurs when the tenant merely permits someone else to use the premises.

(B) Effect of Assignment or Sublease. An assignee or a sublessee has no greater rights than the original lessee.[18] An assignee becomes bound by the obligations of the lease by the act of taking possession of the premises.

Neither the act of subletting nor the landlord's agreement to it releases the original tenant from liability under the terms of the original lease. When a lease is assigned, the original tenant remains liable for the rent that becomes due thereafter.

The tenant should require the sublessee to perform all obligations under the original lease and to indemnify the tenant for any loss caused if the sublessee defaults. Such liability on the part of the sublessee requires an express covenant. The fact that the sublease is made "subject to" the terms of the original lease merely recognizes the superiority of the original lease but does not impose any duty on the sublessee to perform the tenant's obligation under the original lease. If the sublessee promises to assume the obligations of the original lease, the landlord, as a third-party beneficiary, may recover from the sublessee for breach of the provisions of the original lease.

lawflix

Barefoot in the Park (1967) (PG)

The movie is a study about Manhattan newlyweds in which you can see many issues about habitability and constructive eviction. Discuss the options the couple has for remedies.

For movie clips that illustrate business law concepts, see LawFlix at **www.cengage.com/blaw/dvl.**

MAKE THE CONNECTION

SUMMARY

The agreement between a lessor and a lessee by which the latter holds possession of real property owned by the former is a lease. Statutes in many states prohibit discrimination by an owner who rents property. Statutes in some states require that the lease not be unconscionable. Tenancies are classified according to duration as tenancies for years, from year to year, at will, and at sufferance.

A lease is generally not terminated by the death, insanity, or bankruptcy of either party except for a tenancy at will. Leases are usually terminated by the expiration of the specified term, notice, surrender, forfeiture, or destruction of the property or because of fraud. A tenant has the right to acquire possession at the beginning of the lease and has the right to retain possession until the lease is ended. Evictions may be either actual or constructive. The tenant is under a duty to pay rent as compensation to the landlord.

An assignment of a lease by the tenant is a transfer of the tenant's entire interest in the property to a third person; a sublease is a transfer of less than an entire interest—in either space or time. A lease may prohibit both an assignment and a sublease. If the lease is assigned, the assignee is liable to the landlord for the rent. Such an assignment, however, does not discharge the tenant from the duty to pay rent. In a sublease, the sublessee is not liable to the original lessor for rent unless that liability has been assumed or is imposed by statute.

The tenant need not make repairs to the premises, absent an agreement to the contrary. A warranty of habitability was not implied at common law, but most states now reject this view and imply in residential leases a warranty that the premises are fit for habitation.

A landlord is usually liable to the tenant only for injuries caused by latent defects or by defects that are not apparent but of which the landlord had knowledge. The landlord is not liable to the tenant for crimes of third persons unless they are reasonably foreseeable.

LEARNING OUTCOMES

After studying this chapter, you should be able to clearly explain:

A. CREATION AND TERMINATION

LO.1 List the ways in which a lease may be terminated
See the discussion of the types of tenancies on p. 1215.

B. RIGHTS AND DUTIES OF PARTIES

LO.2 List and explain the rights and duties of the parties to a lease
See *Bender v Green* on p. 1221.

C. LIABILITY FOR INJURY ON PREMISES

LO.3 Describe a landlord's liability for a tenant's and a third person's injuries sustained on the premises
See *Yu Fang Tan v Arnel Management Co.* on p. 1225.
See the Sports & Entertainment Law discussion of the quarter pipe on p. 1224.

D. TRANSFER OF RIGHTS

LO.4 Define *sublease* and *assignment of a lease* and distinguish between them
See the discussion of transfer of rights on p. 1226.

KEY TERMS

assignment	escalation clause	lease
constructive eviction	forcible entry and	lessee
covenant of quiet	detainer	lessor
enjoyment	landlord	periodic tenancy

possession   sublessee   tenant
reversionary interest   tenancy at sufferance   warranty of habitability
sublease   tenancy at will

QUESTIONS AND CASE PROBLEMS

1. Johnny C. Carpenter and Harvey E. Hill died of asphyxiation when a fire broke
   out in their Hattiesburg, Mississippi, apartment on the morning of February 20,
   1983. There were no smoke detectors in the apartment at the time of the fire, as
   required under Hattiesburg City Ordinance 2021. The administrators of the
   estates of Carpenter and Hill filed suit against London, Stetelman, and
   Kirkwood, the owners and managers of the apartment complex. Who is liable?
   [*Hill v London, Stetelman, and Kirkwood, Inc.*, 906 F2d 204 (5th Cir)]

2. King leased a single dwelling to Moorehead. King brought an action against
   Moorehead to recover the premises because of nonpayment of rent and to
   collect the unpaid rent. Moorehead raised the defense that the house was not
   habitable and that it violated the housing code. Is this defense valid? Explain.
   [*King v Moorehead*, 495 SW2d 65 (Mo App)]

3. Rod had a five-year lease in a building owned by Darwood and had agreed to
   pay $800 a month rent. After two years, Rod assigned his rights under the lease
   to Kelly. Kelly moved in and paid the rent for a year and then, owing two months'
   rent, moved out without Darwood's knowledge or consent. Darwood demanded
   that Rod pay him the past-due rent. Must Rod do so? Why or why not?

4. Sue A. Merrill injured her right shoulder when she fell as she was ascending the
   front steps leading to the porch and front door of the mobile home that her
   daughter, Sherri Pritchard, rented from Alvina Jansma. The step became loose
   during the time Ms. Pritchard rented the home. Prior to the fall, Ms. Pritchard
   had attempted to repair the step by securing it with nails. When that failed, she
   informed the manager of the property that the step was loose. The manager
   suggested Ms. Pritchard try using screws to secure the step. Ms. Pritchard told
   the manager she did not have a screw gun. The manager had one and said she
   would screw the step into place. Subsequently, and without Ms. Pritchard's
   knowledge, the manager attempted to repair the step. Apparently, that effort
   was unsuccessful and Ms. Merrill fell when the step separated from the porch as
   she stepped on it. Ms. Merrill filed a negligence claim against Ms. Jansma to
   recover for her medical expenses, lost wages, and damages for emotional distress
   and pain and suffering. Could Ms. Merrill recover? [*Merrill v Jansma*, 86 P3d
   270 (Wyo)]

5. Alexis Gale was shot and killed while working in the rented business offices of
   her employer, Mon Ami International. Gale's husband sued the property
   owners and managers of the office complex where Mon Ami's rented offices
   were located, claiming the landlord had breached a duty to provide adequate
   security at the complex. The lease provided that the landlord would provide
   security services in the common areas of the complex and that the lessee was

given exclusive control of the portion of the premises rented as office space. Gale was shot and killed by a coworker, not in a common area over which the landlord had control but in the Mon Ami office space over which the lessee had exclusive control and in which the landlord had no duty to provide security. Gale's husband also alleged that the landlord knew an attack was about to take place because of some strange happenings that had taken place earlier that day. That morning, a maintenance worker noticed a man opening the back door of the Mon Ami office from the inside. This man appeared to be acting strangely: He took a handkerchief out of his suit pocket and picked up a briefcase sitting outside the door. He was wearing what the worker described as a costume-type wig on his head but looked vaguely familiar. Later that day, Gale's body was discovered. The maintenance worker reported what he had seen to the landlord and to the police. It was eventually determined that this was the coworker who had shot Gale, and it was also determined that the landlord knew of numerous arguments between Gale and the coworker. Gale's spouse alleged that the landlord had a duty to prevent the shooting. Did such a duty exist? [*Gale v North Meadow Associates*, 466 SE2d 648 (Ga App)]

6. On June 21, 1997, Julio Ramos was helping his cousin move out of a second-floor apartment. He positioned himself on the outer side of the second-floor balcony railing, his feet between its spindles, to pass furniture to a friend on the ground below. While perched in this precarious position, Ramos held onto the railing with one hand and used his other hand to move the furniture. The reason for this method of removing the furniture was that many pieces were too large to be taken down the stairs. After approximately an hour of moving furniture in this manner, Ramos heard some cracking and felt the railing giving way. He released the furniture and attempted to grab onto the railing with both hands, but the spindles broke, and Ramos fell to the ground.

   Ramos brought suit against the landlord to recover for his injuries. How does this case compare to the *Tan* case? Should the landlord in this case be held liable? [*Ramos v Granajo*, 822 A2d 936 (RI)]

7. A tenant leased an apartment in which so much noise emanated from surrounding apartments late at night and in the wee hours of the morning that he could not get much sleep. The tenant brought suit against the landlord, alleging that the landlord had breached the implied warranty of habitability. Is the tenant correct? Can noise be a breach of the warranty of habitability? [*Nostrand Gardens Co-op v Howard*, 634 NYS2d 505]

8. Morgan, who rented an apartment in the Melrose Apartments, wanted Melrose to hire additional security guards to protect the lessees from possible crimes. Was Melrose required to do so when crimes by third persons were not reasonably foreseeable?

9. During the remodeling of an apartment building, tenants had so much dust from the construction settle in their apartment that they experienced damage to their expensive sound and recording equipment. They had rented the very specialized and large apartment because it was suitable to use as a recording studio. Would the presence of the dust be grounds for constructive eviction?

Would it be a breach of the warranty of habitability? The construction workers wore masks during the time they were working on the building. [*Minjak Co. v Rudolph*, 528 NYS2d 554]

10. Cantanese leased a building for the operation of his drugstore from Saputa. He moved his drugstore from Saputa's building to another location but continued to pay rent to Saputa. Saputa, fearing that he was losing his tenant, entered the premises without Cantanese's permission and made extensive alterations to the premises to suit two physicians who had agreed to rent the premises from Saputa. Cantanese informed Saputa that he regarded the making of the unauthorized repairs as grounds for canceling the lease. Saputa then claimed that Cantanese was liable for the difference between the rent that Cantanese had agreed to pay and the rent that the doctors would pay for the remainder of the term of the Cantanese lease. Was Cantanese liable for such rent? [*Saputa v Cantanese*, 182 So2d 826 (La App)]

11. Sargent rented a second-floor apartment in a building owned by Ross. Anna, Sargent's four-year-old daughter, fell from an outdoor stairway and was killed. Suit was brought against Ross for her death. Ross contended that she did not have control over the stairway and therefore was not liable for its condition. Was this defense valid? [*Sargent v Ross*, 308 A2d 528 (NH)]

12. Charles leased a house from Donald for four years. The rent agreed on was $850 per month. After two years, Charles assigned his rights under the lease to Smith, who moved in and paid rent regularly for a year. Owing rent, Smith moved out sometime later without Donald's knowledge or consent. Donald demanded that Charles pay the rent. Is Charles liable?

13. Green rented an apartment from Stockton Realty. The three-story building had a washroom and clothesline on the roof for use by the tenants. The clothesline ran very near the skylight, and there was no guard rail between the clothesline and the skylight. Green's friend, who was 14 years old, was helping Green remove clothes from the line when she tripped on an object and fell against the skylight. The glass was too weak to support her weight, and she fell to the floor below, sustaining serious injuries. Is the landlord responsible for damages for the injury sustained? Decide. [*Reiman v Moore*, 180 P2d 452 (Cal)]

14. Suzanne Andres was injured when she fell from the balcony of her second-floor apartment in the Roswell-Windsor Village Apartments. Andres was leaning against the railing on the balcony when it gave out, and she and the railing fell to the ground. Andres filed suit against Roswell-Windsor for its failure to maintain the railing. Roswell-Windsor maintains that the railing was not in a common area and was in Andres's exclusive possession and that she was responsible for its maintenance or at least letting the manager know the railing needed repairs. Should Andres recover from the landlord for her injuries? [*Andres v Roswell-Windsor Village Apartments*, 777 F2d 671 (11th Cir)]

15. Williams, an elderly man who was sensitive to heat, rented an apartment in the Parker House. His apartment was fully air-conditioned, which enabled him to stand the otherwise unbearable heat of the summer. The landlord was

dissatisfied with the current rent, and although the lease had a year to run, insisted that Williams agree to an increase. Williams refused. The landlord attempted to force Williams to pay the increase by turning off the electricity and thereby stopping the apartment's air conditioners. He also sent up heat on the hot days. After one week of such treatment, Williams, claiming that he had been evicted, moved out. Has there been an eviction? Explain.

CPA QUESTIONS

1. Which of the following provisions must be included to have an enforceable written residential lease?

	A Description of the Leased Premises	A Due Date for the Payment of Rent
a.	Yes	Yes
b.	Yes	No
c.	No	Yes
d.	No	No

2. Bronson is a residential tenant with a 10-year written lease. In the absence of specific provisions in the lease to the contrary, which of the following statements is correct?

   a. The premises may not be sublet for less than the full remaining term.

   b. Bronson may not assign the lease.

   c. The landlord's death will automatically terminate the lease.

   d. Bronson's purchase of the property will terminate the lease.

3. Which of the following provisions must be included in a residential lease agreement?

   a. A description of the leased premises.

   b. The due date for payment of rent.

   c. A requirement that the tenant have public liability insurance.

   d. A requirement that the landlord will perform all structural repairs to the property.

Chapter 52

DECEDENTS' ESTATES AND TRUSTS

What happens to your property after you die? Public policy dictates that your debts be settled, that property owned at the time of your death be applied to the payment of estate administration expenses and your debts, and that any remainder be distributed among those entitled to receive it.

The law of decedents' estates is governed by state statutes and court decisions. There is wide variation in state law and only 16 states have adopted the **Uniform Probate Code (UPC)**.[1]

A. Wills

When a **decedent** has died with a valid will, he or she is said to have died **testate**, and the will determines who is entitled to receive the estate property after creditors have been paid. If the decedent did not make a valid will, laws for **intestate** distribution determine the distribution.

1. Definitions

Testate distribution describes the distribution that is made when the decedent leaves a valid will. A **will** is ordinarily a writing that provides for a distribution of property upon death but that confers no rights prior to that time. A man who makes a will is called a **testator**; a woman, a **testatrix**.

A gift of personal property by will is a **legacy** or **bequest**, in which case the beneficiary may also be called a **legatee**. A gift of real property by will is a **devise**, and the beneficiary may be called a **devisee**.

2. Parties to Will

Each state has variations on the qualifications of persons who wish to make a will. The following requirements are typical.

(A) **Testator.** Generally, the right to make a will is limited to persons 18 or older. The testator must have **testamentary capacity**,[2] which means that a person must have sufficient mental capacity to understand that the writing that is being executed is a will—that is, that it disposes of the person's property after death. The testator must also have a reasonable appreciation of who the beneficiaries of his will are as well as a grasp of the identity of relatives and friends and the nature and extent of the property that will be given and to whom upon death.

Testamentary capacity is challenged by surviving relatives quite often. Eccentric behavior does not mean that the individual lacks capacity. The excessive and

---

Uniform Probate Code (UPC)–uniform statute on wills and administration of estates.

decedent–person whose estate is being administered.

testate–condition of leaving a will upon death.

intestate–condition of dying without a will as to any property.

testate distribution– distribution of an estate in accordance with the will of the decedent.

will–instrument executed with the formality required by law, by which a person makes a disposition of his or her property to take effect upon death.

testator, testatrix–man, woman who makes a will.

legacy–gift of money made by will.

bequest–gift of personal property by will.

legatee–beneficiary who receives a gift of personal property by will.

devise–gift of real estate made by will.

devisee–beneficiary of a devise.

testamentary capacity– sufficient mental capacity to understand that a writing being executed is a will and what that entails.

---

[1] The Uniform Probate Code has been adopted in Alaska, Arizona, Colorado, Florida, Hawaii, Idaho, Maine, Michigan, Minnesota, Montana, Nebraska, New Mexico, North Dakota, South Carolina, South Dakota, and Utah. Twenty other states have adopted portions of the UPC: Arkansas, California, Georgia, Illinois, Indiana, Kansas, Kentucky, Maryland, Missouri, New Jersey, Ohio, Oklahoma, Oregon, Pennsylvania, Texas, Virginia, Washington, West Virginia, Wisconsin, and Wyoming. The predominant form of the UPC continues to be the 1969 version, but the 1990 and 2003 versions have been integrated into existing UPC states' statutes.
[2] *In re Estate of Minor*, 939 So 2d 861 (Miss App 2006).

CASE SUMMARY

Just Because You Don't Understand Contracts Doesn't Mean You Lack Capacity

FACTS: After an 11-month struggle with esophageal cancer, Leonard R. Brener died on December 8, 2001, at age 85. He had never married. He had no children. He had a long and successful career as a stockbroker. The value of his estate approximated $8 million. Several nieces and nephews survived him. He had originally left nearly all of his estate to the Carroll Center for the Blind, the Perkins School for the Blind, and Beth Israel Deaconess Medical Center, Inc. The gifts to these nonprofit organizations during Brener's life and through his will were made through detailed living, testamentary, and pour-over trusts. Brener said he did not understand all aspects of the trusts. During the last five weeks of his life he was hospitalized and drafted and executed the final version of his will, which made one niece and her husband the primary beneficiaries of his estate. The nonprofit organizations sought to have the will set aside for lack of testamentary capacity.

During those five weeks of terminal illness, Brener spoke of committing suicide by jumping out of the window, complained of depression, and often complained to his lawyer that he did not understand all the estate planning tools that were being used in his will. The staff at the hospital testified that Brener did not seem confused and was aware that he was dying and wanted to be sure his affairs were in order.

The lower court held that there is a presumption of mental capacity that the nonprofits were not able to overcome with testimony from either a doctor or those who had daily contact with Brener. The nonprofit organizations appealed.

DECISION: The court held that there is a presumption of capacity. The fact that a testator is depressed during the final stages of a terminal illness and expresses a desire to pass away did not mean that he lacked capacity. Also, where a doctor's testimony is contradictory, the presumption of capacity rests with the doctor who testified to sufficient capacity. The fact that Brener constantly complained that he did not understand the language in the wills and trusts did not mean that he lacked testamentary capacity. Contractual capacity is different from testamentary capacity and the latter only requires an understanding that property is to be transferred, how much will be transferred, and to whom. Brener's niece was a loyal visitor during his final illness and helped take care of his needs with the health-care workers. She was a logical beneficiary as well as a relative. The will executed during the final five weeks was valid because the testator had sufficient capacity to make it. [**Maimonides School v Coles, 881 NE2d 778 (Mass App 2008)**]

continued use of alcohol or multiple medications, producing mental deterioration, may be sufficient to justify the conclusion that the decedent lacked testamentary capacity. However, there can be lucid periods even among those who suffer from addictions. Expert testimony, the observations of friends and relatives, and the conduct of the decedent prior to death are all relevant factors in determining whether there was testamentary capacity.

beneficiary–person to whom the proceeds of a life insurance policy are payable, a person for whose benefit property is held in trust, or a person given property by a will; the ultimate recipient of the benefit of a funds transfer.

(B) **BENEFICIARY.** Generally, the capacity of the **beneficiary** is not an issue. However, when part of a decedent's estate passes to a minor, a guardian may be appointed to administer that interest for the minor. If a will directs that any share payable to a minor be held by a particular person as trustee for the minor, the minor's interest will be so held, and a guardian is not required. Statutes often provide that if the estate or interest of the minor is not large, it may be paid directly to the minor or to the parent or person by whom the minor is maintained.

3. Testamentary Intent

testamentary intent– designed to take effect at death, as by disposing of property or appointing a personal representative.

To execute a valid, testators must demonstrate an intent to transfer property upon their deaths. This is called **testamentary intent**.[3] Ordinarily, this is an intention that certain persons become the owners of certain property upon the death of the testator. However, a writing also manifests a testamentary intent when the testator designates an executor only and does not make any disposition of property.

4. Form

Because the privilege of disposing of property by will is purely statutory, the will must be executed in the manner required by state statutes. Unless statutory requirements are met, the will is invalid, and the testator is considered to have died intestate. In such a case, the decedent's property will be distributed according to the laws of intestacy of the particular state.

attestation clause– clause that indicates a witness has observed either the execution of the will or the testator's acknowledgment of the writing as the testator's will.

(A) WRITING. Ordinarily, a will must be in writing. Some state statutes, however, permit oral wills in limited circumstances, and the use of videotaped wills is gaining some legal ground.

self-proved wills– wills that eliminate some formalities of proof by being executed according to statutory requirements.

(B) SIGNATURE. A written will must be signed by the testator. In case of physical incapacity, the testator may be assisted in signing the will. Witnesses to the will can then verify that simple marks were indeed made by the testator while experiencing a physically debilitating condition.

Generally, a will must be signed at the bottom or end. The purpose of this requirement is to prevent unscrupulous persons from taking a will that has been validly signed and writing or typing additional provisions in the space below the signature.

acknowledgment– admission or confirmation, generally of an instrument and usually made before a person authorized to administer oaths, such as a notary public; used to establish that the instrument was executed by the person making the instrument, that it was a voluntary act, or that the instrument is recorded.

(C) ATTESTATION. Attestation is the act of witnessing the execution of a will. Generally, attestation consists of a witness signing the will following a clause that declares that the witness either saw the testator sign the will or that the testator told the witness that he or she did indeed sign the will. The clause that describes what the witness saw or knows is called an **attestation clause**. Statutes often require that attestation be made by the witnesses in the presence of the testator and in the presence of each other. Most states and the Uniform Probate Code (UPC) require two witnesses; a few states require three.

Self-proved wills are wills that carry a presumption that they are valid if executed according to the requirements set forth by statute. The UPC recognizes self-proved wills. A will may be simultaneously executed, attested, and made self-proving by acknowledgment by the testator and by affidavits of the witnesses.

affidavit– statement of facts set forth in written form and supported by the oath or affirmation of the person making the statement setting forth that such facts are true on the basis of actual knowledge or on information and belief. The affidavit is executed before a notary public or other person authorized to administer oaths.

The **acknowledgment** and **affidavits** must each be made before an officer authorized to administer oaths under state law, such as a notary. They acknowledgement and affidavits must carry an official seal, such as a notary's seal must be evidenced by the officer's certificate under official seal.

[3] *Hampton Roads Seventh-Day Adventist Church v Stevens*, 657 SE2d 80 (Va 2008).

e–commerce&cyberlaw

WHERE THERE'S A VIDEO, IS THERE A WILL?

With technology, wills are no longer always just written but may be supplemented with electronic verification. The American Bar Association's Web site (**www.abanet.org**) offers the following thoughts on the new trend in video wills:

More and more people are preparing a video in which they read the will and explain why certain gifts were made and others not made. The video recording might also show the execution of the will.

Should a disgruntled relative decide to challenge the will, the video can provide compelling proof that the person making the will was mentally competent and observed the formalities of execution.

Keep in mind that videos do not last forever and are subject to damage. You should consult a lawyer before making such a video to find out about your state's laws on video wills. Generally, such a video would supplement.

The self-proving provisions attached to the will are not a part of the will. Self-proving provisions allow a will to be admitted to probate without requiring the testimony of the witnesses to the will. The will itself must still meet the requirements of the law. The execution of a valid will is a condition precedent to use of the self-proving provisions.

In some states, a witness cannot be a beneficiary under the will. In those states, use of a beneficiary as a witness will not affect the will, but the witness's share is limited to whatever his or her intestate share would have been if there had been no will. Under the UPC, a will can be validly witnessed by an interested person.

(D) DATE. There is generally no requirement that a testator date a will, but a dated will does reduce confusion. When there are several wills, the most recent one will control when there are conflicting provisions between and among the wills.

5. Modification of Will

A will may be modified by executing a *codicil*, a separate writing that amends a will. The will, except as changed by the codicil, remains the same. The effect is that the provisions of the codicil are substituted for those provisions of the will that are inconsistent with the codicil. A codicil must be executed with all the formality of a will and is treated in all other respects the same as a will.

A will cannot be modified merely by crossing out a clause and writing in what the testator wishes. Such an **interlineation** is not operative unless it is executed with the same formality required of a will or, in some states, unless the will is republished in its interlineated form.

interlineation—writing between the lines or adding to the provisions of a document, the effect thereof depending upon the nature of the document.

revoke—testator's act of taking back his or her will and its provisions.

6. Revocation of Will

At any time during the testator's life, the testator may **revoke** the will made or make changes in its terms. It may be revoked by act of the testator or by operation of law.

CASE SUMMARY

When Wife #2 Finds Wife #1's Will with a Lot of Lines Through It

FACTS: On June 15, 1982, Shirley Joyce Speers signed a "Last Will and Testament." It named her husband, Ralph Speers, as her executor. It also gave her daughter, Sherry Arlene Ross, her household furnishings and appliances, and her son, Daniel Eugene Speers, her livestock. Her husband was named the beneficiary of the rest of the estate, provided he paid the estate's expenses. If he failed to do so, his share went to their children and grandsons. The will was probably witnessed and signed, but not notarized. The witnesses did not see any lines or strikeouts in the will when they signed it. Shirley died on April 20, 1997, and the will was not probated at the time of her death.

After his wife's death, Ralph married Ann Speers. Ralph died some time before June of 2005, and Ann then discovered a copy of Shirley's will with lines through it and cross-outs. She filed a petition seeking to admit the will to probate. The will she submitted contained several handwritten strikeouts and interlineations. Shirley's children objected to the admission of the will, arguing that it was invalid because the original will was destroyed. The court found for Ann and the children appealed. The Court of Appeals reversed and Ann appealed.

DECISION: The court affirmed, holding that the original will was not self-proving because of the lack of a notary seal and because its strike-outs indicated that Shirley had revoked its provisions. The result was a completely different distribution of property under state intestacy law for Shirley's estate and, as a result, for Ralph's. Whether the will was admitted determined whether Ann or the children inherited Ralph's property. A dissent in the case concluded that the will should be admitted and that the witnesses' testimony had been clouded by the cross-outs and lines in the copy of the will. [**In re Estate of Speers, 179 P3d 1265 (Okl 2008)**]

A testator must have the same degree of mental capacity to revoke a will as is required to make one.

(A) REVOCATION BY ACT OF TESTATOR. A will or a codicil is revoked when the testator destroys, burns, or tears it or crosses out the provisions of the will or codicil with the intention to revoke them. The revocation may be in whole or in part.[4]

(B) REVOCATION BY OPERATION OF LAW. In certain instances, statutes provide that a change of circumstances has the effect of a revocation. **For Example,** when a person marries after executing a will, the will is revoked or is presumed revoked unless it was made in contemplation of marriage or unless it provided for the future spouse. In some states, the revocation is not total but is effective only to the extent of allowing the spouse to take such share of the estate as that to which the spouse would have been entitled had there been no will.

The birth or adoption of a child after the execution of a will commonly works a revocation or partial revocation of the will as to that child. In the case of a partial revocation, the child is entitled to receive the same share as if the testator had died intestate.

The divorce of the testator does not in itself work a revocation. However, the majority of courts hold that if a property settlement is carried out on the basis of the

---

[4] A change in will terms still requires capacity. *In re Klingman*, 60 AD3d 949, 875 NYS2d 554 (2009).

divorce, a prior will of the testator is revoked, at least to the extent of the legacy given to the divorced spouse.

7. Election to Take Against the Will

To protect the husband or wife of a testator, the surviving spouse may generally ignore the provisions of a will and elect to take against the will. In such a case, the surviving spouse receives the share of the estate he or she would have received had the testator died without leaving a will or receives a fractional share specified by statute.

The right to take against the will is generally barred by certain kinds of misconduct by the surviving spouse. If a spouse is guilty of desertion or nonsupport that would have justified the decedent's obtaining a divorce, the surviving spouse usually cannot elect to take against the will.

8. Disinheritance

disinherited – excluded from sharing in the estate of a decedent.

With some exceptions, any person may be **disinherited** or excluded from sharing in the estate of a decedent.[5] A person who would inherit if there were no will is excluded from receiving any part of a decedent's estate if the decedent has left a will giving everything to other persons.

9. Special Types of Wills

In certain situations, special types of wills are used.

---

sports&entertainment law

Heath Ledger's Probate: Uncertain, Complex, and International

Actor Heath Ledger, who died of an overdose, has one of the most complicated probates the U.S. courts have seen. Here are some issues that create the complexity:

1. Mr. Ledger never revised his will after his daughter was born. There are no provisions in his will for her.

2. Mr. Ledger was never married to Michelle Williams, the mother of his daughter.

3. Mr. Ledger's father is named as the executor of the estate, but he is a resident of Australia.

4. Most of Mr. Ledger's property is in the United States.

5. Several relatives have questioned whether Mr. Ledger's father is suited for the job of executor because of alleged "mismanagement" of his own father's estate.

6. Several individuals have come forward seeking paternity determination on another child alleged to be Mr. Ledger's.

Think through all the probate processes this estate will require.*

** Brenda Rodriguez, Melanie Ambrose, Helen Martin, Marianne Bilkey, Louise Talbot, Lesley Messer, Alyssa Shelasky, and Mary Green, "Family Secrets," *People*, April 14, 2008, pp. 48–51.*

---

[5] One exception, for example, is a surviving spouse. A surviving spouse has marital property rights and cannot be disinherited completely.

holographic will – unwitnessed will written by hand.

(A) HOLOGRAPHIC WILLS. A **holographic will** is an unwitnessed will that is written by the testator entirely by hand. Some states make no distinction between holographic and other wills. Other states apply the general law of wills to holographic wills, with certain variations. Some states require that a holographic will be dated. Under the UPC, a holographic will is valid, whether witnessed or not, if the signatures and the material provisions are in the handwriting of the testator.[6]

living will – document by which individuals may indicate that if they become unable to express their wishes and are in an irreversible, incurable condition, they do not want life-sustaining medical treatments.

(B) LIVING WILLS. **Living wills** are documents individuals use to decide in advance what level of life-sustaining medical treatments that want if they become unable to express their wishes and are in an irreversible, incurable condition. (see Figure 52.1). Living wills are legal in most states. Such personal wishes are entitled to constitutional protection as long as they are expressed clearly.

B. ADMINISTRATION OF DECEDENTS' ESTATES

A decedent's estate consists of the assets the decedent owned at death, and the administration of the estate requires a determination of who is entitled to receive that property. If the decedent owed debts, those debts must be paid first. After those payments, any balance must be distributed according to the terms of the will or by the intestate law if the decedent did not leave a valid will.

10. Definitions

executor, executrix – man, woman named in a will to administer the estate of the decedent.

administrator, administratrix – man, woman appointed to wind up and settle the estate of a person who has died without a will.

personal representatives – administrators and executors who represent decedents under the UPC.

probate – procedure for formally establishing or proving that a given writing is the last will and testament of the person who purportedly signed it.

The decedent has the privilege of naming the person who will administer the estate. A man named in a will to administer the estate of the decedent is an **executor**; a woman, an **executrix**. If the decedent failed to name an executor or executrix or did not leave a will, the law permits another person, usually a close relative, to be appointed to wind up the estate. This person is an **administrator** or **administratrix**. Administrators and executors are referred to generally under the UPC as **personal representatives** of the decedents because they represent the decedents or stand in their place.

11. Probate of Will

Probate is the act by which the proper court or official accepts a will and declares that the instrument satisfies the statutory requirements as the will of the testator. Until a will is probated, it has no legal effect.

When witnesses have signed a will, generally they must appear and state that they saw the testator sign the will (unless the will is self-proving). If those witnesses cannot be found, have died, or are outside the jurisdiction, the will may be probated nevertheless. When no witnesses are required, it is customary to require two or more persons to identify the signature of the testator at the time of probate.

After the probate witnesses have made their statements under oath, the official or court will ordinarily admit the will to probate in the absence of any circumstances indicating that the writing should not be probated. A certificate or decree that

---

[6] Determination of the validity of a holographic will requires the court to examine the nature of the document submitted for probate. *Succession of Gourgis*, 1 So3d 528 (La App 2008).

FIGURE 52-1 | *Living Will*

Living Will

INSTRUCTIONS

This is an important legal document It sets forth your directions regarding medical treatment. You have the right to refuse treatment you do not want. You may make changes in any of these directions, or add to them, to conform them to your personal wishes.

I, _John Jones_____ , being of sound mind, make this statement as a directive to be followed if I become permanently unable to participate in decisions regarding my medical care. These instructions reflect my firm and settled commitment to decline medical treatment under the circumstances indicated below:

I direct my attending physician to withhold or withdraw treatment that serves only to prolong the process of my dying, if I should be in an incurable or irreversible mental or physical condition with no reasonable expectation of recovery.

These instructions apply if I am (a) in a terminal condition; (b) permanently unconscious; or (c) if I am conscious but have irreversible brain damage and will never regain the ability to make decisions and express my wishes.

I direct that treatment be limited to measures to keep me comfortable and to relieve pain, including any pain that might occur by withholding or withdrawing treatment.

While I understand that I am not legally required to be specific about future treatments, if I am in the condition(s) described above I feel especially strongly about the following forms of treatment:

I do not want cardiac resuscitation.
I do not want mechanical respiration.
I do not want tube feeding.
I do not want antibiotics.
I do want maximum pain relief.

Other directions (insert personal instructions): _NONE_____

_____

Sign and date here in the presence of two adult witnesses, who should also sign.

These directions express my legal right to refuse treatment, under the law of [name of state]. I intend my instructions to be carried out, unless I have rescinded them in a new writing or by clearly indicating that I have changed my mind.

Signed: _____*John Jones*_____

Witness: _____*Earl Hummel*_____

       Address: _*7852 Bailey Avenue*_____

                  *Buffalo, New York*_____

Witness: _____*Ramona Yaley*_____

       Address: _*8921 Clinton Street*_____

                  *Buffalo, New York*_____

Keep the signed original with your personal papers at home. Give copies of the signed original to your doctor, family, lawyer, and others who might be involved in your care.

officially declares that the will is the will of the testator and has been admitted to probate is then issued.

Any qualified person who wishes to object to the probate of the will on the ground that it is not a proper will may appear before the official or court prior to the entry of the decree of probate. A person may petition after probate to have the probate of the will set aside.

12. Will Contest

The probate of a will may be refused or set aside on the ground that the will is not the free expression of the intention of the testator. It may be attacked on the ground of (1) a lack of mental capacity to execute a will, (2) undue influence, duress, fraud, or mistake existing at the time of the execution of the will that induced or led to its execution, or (3) forgery.[7] With the exception of mental capacity, these terms consist of the same elements they do in contract law.

If any one of these problems exists, the probate court can refuse to admit the will for probate. The decedent's estate is then distributed as if there had been no will unless an earlier will can be probated.

13. When Administration is Not Necessary

No administration is required when the decedent did not own any property at the time of death. In some states, special statutes provide for a simplified administration

---

C A S E   S U M M A R Y

There's a Melody in the Heirs

FACTS: John C. Ramsey Sr. (Senior) executed a will in the last months of his life that left the bulk of his estate to Melody Taylor, his paramour. Senior's relationships with his son and grandsons were strained, and his will included the following clause:

> *I have intentionally provided significant, yet smaller amounts for my son and grandsons because they have for several years alienated my affections by being irresponsible, contentious, and constantly seeking financial support from me rather than providing for themselves.*
>
> *I have made provisions for MELODY J. TAYLOR because MELODY J. TAYLOR provides me care and support.*

Senior was suffering from cancer and renal failure, and his pain was extraordinary. His doctors prescribed high doses of morphine that Melody administered. Senior died from an overdose of morphine.

John Ramsey Jr. (Junior), Senior's son, challenged the validity of the will on the grounds of undue influence as well as felonious killing of a testator by a beneficiary. The trial court found there was undue influence and refused to admit the will to probate. Melody appealed.

DECISION: Judgment for Melody. There was a long history of bad blood between Junior and Senior. Further, Senior had disinherited Junior long before Melody came into the picture. The clear statement in the will that he knew he was leaving out Junior and why was indicative of clear thinking and lack of duress from Melody. Senior also had independent advice on his will and took his time in executing it. Melody's administration of the fatal drug dose was pursuant to physician's instructions, and she was still entitled to inherit under the valid will that was admitted to probate. **Ramsey v Taylor, 999 P2d 1178 (Or App 2000)**

---

[7] *Pope v McWilliams*, 632 SE2d 640 (Ga 2006).

ethics&the law
Brooke Astor and the Promise to the Servants

In 2007, New York socialite and philanthropist Brooke Astor died at age 105. Her will was admitted to probate in August 2007 and as of May 2009 was still being challenged. The challenge to the will was filed by Chase Bank, her trust administrator, and a friend, Mrs. Annette de la Renta. Under her 1997 will, her grandsons were to receive a substantial portion of her estate. But under a 2002 will, she left more of her estate to her son, who has been accused by one of her grandsons of neglecting Mrs. Astor's care and pilfering from her in the final years of her life. Barbara Walters and Henry Kissinger, both of whom were friends of Mrs. Astor, have testified that she did not know them or her party guests during 2001. Ms. Walters cried in court when she was shown a photograph of them together, the last one, a meeting at which Mrs. Astor did not recognize Ms. Walters.

Under her 1997 will, Mrs. Astor provided for her secretaries, housekeepers, and gardeners. The provisions in the 1997 will matched the promises she had made to them. "I will take care of you," was an oral promise Mrs. Astor made to many who worked for her. The 2002 will eliminates those devises and bequests.

The employees were loyal and their relationship with Mrs. Astor was good. Mrs. Astor had promised her gardener in Maine the greenhouse on her property so that he could start his own business when she died. In addition, during her life, Mrs. Astor always provided for her retired servants, sending them monthly pension checks, checks that stopped with the will contest.

Chase Bank says that its hands are tied and it cannot send the checks. Explain the legal issues in this situation, then discuss the ethical obligations of the bank, Mrs. Astor's relatives, and those who do inherit under either will.

when the decedent leaves only a small estate. Likewise, when all property owned by the decedent was owned with another person as joints tenants with right of survivorship, no administration is required.

14. Appointment of Personal Representative

Both executors and administrators must be appointed to their roles by a court or an officer designated by law. The appointment is made by granting to the personal representative **letters testamentary**, in the case of an executor, or **letters of administration**, in the case of an administrator.

letters testamentary– written authorization given to an executor of an estate as evidence of appointment and authority.

letters of administration– written authorization given to an administrator of an estate as evidence of appointment and authority.

claims– right to payment.

15. Proof of Claims Against the Estate

State statutes vary widely on how **claims** against a decedent's estate are presented. In very general terms, statutes provide for some form of public notice of the grant of letters testamentary or letters of administration. Creditors are then required to give notice of their claims within a period specified by either statute or a court order (for example, within six months). In most states, failure to present a claim within the specified time bars the claim.

thinking things through
Not Quite "Layed" to Rest

Ken Lay, the former CEO of Enron, a company that collapsed because of accounting fraud, died shortly after being found guilty on all counts of bank and securities fraud. Legal experts noted that his criminal conviction no longer has any effect because he did not have a chance to appeal the verdict before his death. However, civil suits by shareholders and pension plans were pending against Mr. Lay. Will the assets of his estate still be subject to claims in the event these plaintiffs win their suits? Will the suits continue?

16. Construction of a Will

The will of a decedent is interpreted according to the ordinary or plain meaning evidenced by its words. The court will strive to give effect to every provision of the will to avoid concluding that any part of the decedent's estate was not disposed of by the will.[8]

17. Testate Distribution of an Estate

general legacies–certain sums of money bequeathed to named persons by the testator; to be paid out of the decedent's assets generally without specifying any particular fund or source from which the payment is to be made.

specific legacies–identified property bequeathed by a testator; also called *specific devises.*

abate–put a stop to a nuisance; reduce or cancel a legacy because the estate of the decedent is insufficient to make payment in full.

adeemed–canceled; as in a specifically bequeathed property being sold or given away by the testator prior to death, thus canceling the bequest.

The last phase of the administration of the estate by the decedent's personal representative is the distribution of property remaining after the payment of all debts and taxes in accordance with the provisions of the will or by intestacy rules if there was no valid will.

There are various types of gifts under a will. A testator can bequeath to named persons certain sums of money called **general legacies**, or gifts in which no particular money is specified. The testator may also bequeath identified property called **specific legacies** or *specific devises.* **For Example,** a testator may give "$1,000 to *A;* $1,000 to *B;* my automobile to *C.*" The first two bequests are general; the third is specific. After such specific bequests, the testator may make a bequest of everything remaining, called a *residuary bequest,* such as "the balance of my estate to *D.*"

(A) ABATEMENT OF LEGACIES. Assume in the preceding example that after all debts are paid, only $1,500 and the automobile remain. What disposition is to be made? Legacies **abate** or bear loss in the following order: (1) residuary, (2) general, (3) specific. The law also holds that legacies of the same class abate proportionately. **For Example,** in the hypothetical case, *C,* the specific legatee, would receive the automobile; *A* and *B,* the general legatees, would each receive $750; and *D,* the residuary legatee, would receive nothing.

(B) ADEMPTION OF PROPERTY. When specifically bequeathed property is sold or given away by the testator prior to death, the bequest is considered **adeemed,** or canceled. The specific legatee in this instance is not entitled to receive any property or money.

---

[8] *In re Estate of Sharek,* 930 A2d 388 (NH 2007).

Ademption has the same consequence as though the testator had formally canceled the bequest. **For Example,** if Aunt Claire left her 2003 Honda Accord to her niece, Helen, but Aunt Claire sold the Honda Accord in 2005 and died in 2007, Helen receives nothing from Aunt Claire's estate because the bequest of the Honda is adeemed or canceled.

antilapse statutes—statutes providing that the children or heirs of a deceased beneficiary may take the legacy in the place of the deceased beneficiary.

(C) ANTILAPSE STATUTES. If the beneficiary named in the testator's will died before the testator and the testator did not make any alternate provision applicable in such a case, the gift ordinarily does not lapse. **Antilapse statutes** commonly provide that the gift to the deceased beneficiary shall not lapse but that the children or heirs of that beneficiary may take the legacy in the place of the deceased beneficiary. An antilapse statute does not apply if the testator specified a disposition that should be made of the gift if the original legatee had died.

18. Intestate Distribution of an Estate

If the decedent does not effectively dispose of all property by will or does not have a will, the decedent's property is distributed to certain relatives. Because such persons acquire or succeed to the rights of the decedent and because the circumstances under which they do so is the absence of an effective will, it is said that they acquire title by **intestate succession**.

intestate succession—distribution, made as directed by statute, of a decedent's property not effectively disposed of by will.

The right of intestate succession or inheritance is not a basic right of the citizen or an inalienable right. It exists only because the state legislature so provides. It is within the power of the state legislature to modify or destroy the right to inherit property.

Although wide variations exist among the statutory provisions of the states, a common pattern of intestate distribution exists.

(A) SPOUSES. The surviving spouse of the decedent, whether husband or wife, shares in the estate. Generally, the amount received is a fraction that varies with the number of children. If no children survive, the spouse is generally entitled to take the entire estate. Otherwise, the surviving spouse ordinarily receives a one-half or one-third share of the estate.

lineals—relationship that exists when one person is a direct descendant of the other; also *called lineal descendants.*

(B) LINEALS. **Lineals**, or lineal descendants, are blood descendants of the decedent. Lineal descendants include children and grandchildren. That portion of the estate that is not distributed to the surviving spouse is generally distributed to lineals.

(C) PARENTS. If the estate has not been fully distributed by this time, the remainder is commonly distributed to the decedent's parents.

(D) COLLATERAL HEIRS. These are persons who are not descendants of the decedent but are related through a common ancestor. Generally, brothers and sisters and their descendants share any part of the estate that has not already been distributed. Statutes vary as to how far distribution will be made to the descendants of brothers and sisters. Under some statutes, a degree of relationship is specified, such as first cousins, and no person more remotely related to the decedent is permitted to share in the estate.

If the entire estate is not distributed within the permitted degree of relationship, the property that has not been distributed is given to the state government. This

FIGURE 52-2 | *Distribution per Capita and per Stirpes*

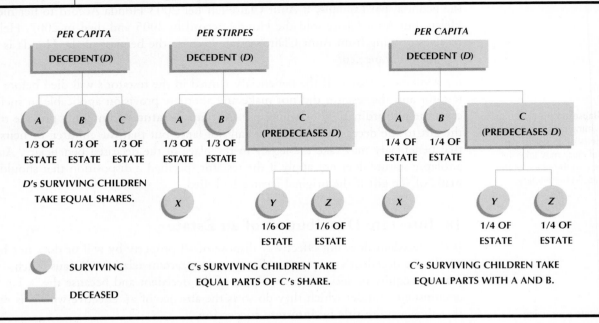

right of the state to take the property is the **right of escheat**. Under some statutes, the right of escheat arises only when there is no relative of the decedent, however remotely related.

(E) **DISTRIBUTION PER CAPITA AND PER STIRPES.** The fact that different generations of distributees may be entitled to receive the estate creates a problem of determining the proportions in which distribution is to be made (see Figure 52.2). When all the distributees stand in the same degree of relationship to the decedent, distribution is made **per capita**, each receiving the same share. **For Example,** if the decedent is survived by three children—*A, B,* and *C*—each of them is entitled to receive one-third of the estate.

If the distributees stand in different degrees of relationship, distribution is made in as many equal parts as there are family lines, or **stirpes**, represented in the nearest generation. Parents take to the exclusion of their children or subsequent descendants, and when members of the nearest generation have died, their descendants take by way of representation. This is called **distribution per stirpes**, or *stirpital distribution.* **For Example,** Thomas dies leaving two living children, *A* and *B*, and one child, *C*, who predeceased him but left two children (Thomas's grandchildren, *D* and *E*). *A* and *B* would each take one-third of Thomas's estate, and *D* and *E* would, under a **per stirpes** distribution, split a one-third interest, each receiving one-sixth of the estate.

(F) **MURDER OF DECEDENT.** Statutes generally provide that a person who murders the decedent cannot inherit from the victim by intestacy. In the absence of such a statute, courts are divided over whether the heir may inherit.

CASE SUMMARY

Guilty Father, Innocent Child: Does the Child Inherit as a Grandchild?

FACTS: On April 30, 1993, Kent Van Der Veen murdered his parents, Morris and Deanne Van Der Veen. Kent was 19 years old at the time and two years earlier had fathered a child who had been legally adopted by persons not identified in the court proceedings. Morris and Deanne were not aware of the existence of Kent's child prior to their deaths.

The 1989 joint will of Morris and Deanne Van Der Veen provided for the following distribution of their estate after debts and obligations were paid:

Upon the death of the survivor of us, each of us hereby gives, devises, and bequeaths all of the rest, residue, and remainder of our property of every kind, character, and description, and wherever located, unto our children, Laura Ann Van Der Veen and Kent Phillip Van Der Veen, equally and per stirpes.

Kent Van Der Veen was disqualified from inheriting any portion of his parents' estate under Kansas's slayer statute. Kent's child, the biological grandchild of Morris and Deanne, petitioned to inherit one-half of her biological grandparents' estate. The grandchild is identified in the case only as D.B.B. The trial court denied the grandchild any interest in the estate, and the grandchild appealed.

DECISION: Judgment for the grandchild. Just treatment of the other beneficiaries does not demand that the slayer's heirs be disqualified or penalized. The Van Der Veens intended for their daughter to take one-half of their estate. Their knowledge of Kent's troubled nature is reflected in a provision of the Van Der Veens' will that nominates Laura to serve as Kent's guardian and conservator. Nonetheless, they bequeathed one-half of their estate to him. There is nothing that indicates the Van Der Veens intended for Laura to receive the entire estate in the event of Kent's incapacity or disqualification. They would not have intended for Kent's innocent child to be disqualified in order for Laura to receive the entire estate. **In re Estate of Morris P. Van Der Veen, 935 P2d 1042 (Kan 1997)**[9]

(G) DEATH OF DISTRIBUTEE AFTER DECEDENT. The persons entitled to distribution of a decedent's estate are determined as of the date of death. If a distributee dies after that, the rights of the distributee are not lost but pass from the original decedent's estate to the deceased distributee's estate.

(H) SIMULTANEOUS DEATH. The **Uniform Simultaneous Death Act**[10] provides that when survivorship cannot be established, the property of each person shall be disposed of as if he or she had survived the other.

C. TRUSTS

A **trust** is a legal device by which property, real or personal, is held by one person for the benefit of another. Legal problems in the area of trusts invariably require a

---

Uniform Simultaneous Death Act—law providing that when survivorship cannot be established, the property of each person shall be disposed of as though he or she had survived the other.

trust—transfer of property by one person to another with the understanding or declaration that such property be held for the benefit of another; the holding of property by the owner in trust for another, upon a declaration of trust, without a transfer to another person. (Parties— settlor, trustee, beneficiary)

---

[9] For more information on slayer statutes see Karen J. Sneddon, "Should Cain's Children Inherit Abel's Property? Wading Into the Extended Slayer Rule Quagmire," 76 *Univ. Mo. K.C. Law Rev.* 101(2007).

[10] The 1940 version of this act has been adopted in all states except Louisiana and Ohio. The newest version of the act (1993) has been adopted in Arizona, Colorado, Hawaii, Kansas, Montana, New Mexico, North Dakota, South Dakota, and Virginia.

determination of the nature of the relationship created by the trust and the rights and obligations of the parties with respect to that relationship.

19. Definitions

The property owner who creates the trust is the **settlor**. (The word *settlor* is taken from the old legal language of "settling the property in trust.") The settlor is sometimes called the **donor** or **trustor**. The person to whom the property is transferred in trust is the **trustee**. The person for whose benefit the trustee holds the property is the beneficiary (or ***cestui que trust***).

Property held in trust is sometimes called the **trust corpus**, *trust fund, trust estate,* or *trust res.* A distinction is made between the **principal**, or the property in trust, and the **income** that is earned by the principal and distributed by the trustee.

If the trust is created to take effect within the lifetime of the settlor, it is a **living trust**, or an *inter vivos trust.* If the trust is provided for in the settlor's will and is to become effective only when the will takes effect after death, the trust is called a **testamentary trust**.

20. Creation of Trusts

The requirements for creating a trust are not uniform, but there are certain typical requirements.

(A) CAPACITY OF BENEFICIARY. The capacity of the beneficiary of the trust to hold property or to contract is immaterial. Many trusts are created because the beneficiary lacks legal or actual capacity to manage the property. The trustee, as the holder of legal title, must have capacity.

(B) FORMALITY. In creating a trust, it is common practice to execute a writing, called a **trust agreement** or *deed of trust.* No particular form of language is necessary to create a trust as long as the property, the trust purpose, and the beneficiaries are designated. If an *inter vivos* trust relates to an interest in land, the statute of frauds requires that the trust be in writing with the details of the trust included. A writing signed by the trustee and referring to a deed from the trustor can satisfy this requirement. When the trust depends on a transfer of title to land, there must be a valid transfer of the title to the trustee. If a trust is created by the will of the settlor, there must be a writing that meets the requirements of a will.

(C) INTENTION. The settler must express some intention to place property in trust. It is not necessary, however, that the word *trust* or *trustee* be used. The settlor will ordinarily name a trustee, but failure to do so is not fatal to the trust because a trustee will be appointed by the court.

(D) IDENTITY OF BENEFICIARY. Every trust must have a beneficiary. In a private trust, the beneficiaries must be identified by name, description, or designation of the class to which the beneficiaries belong. In a charitable trust, it is sufficient that the beneficiaries be members of the public at large or a general class of the public.

---

settlor—one who settles property in trust or creates a trust estate.

donor—person making a gift.

trustor—donor or settlor who is the owner of property and creates a trust in the property.

trustee—party who has legal title to estate and manages it.

cestui que trust—beneficiary or person for whose benefit the property is held in trust.

trust corpus—fund or property that is transferred to the trustee or held by the settlor as the body or subject matter of the trust; also called *trust fund, trust estate,* and *trust res.*

principal—person or firm who employs an agent; the person who, with respect to a surety, is primarily liable to the third person or creditor; property held in trust.

income—money earned by the principal, or property in trust, and distributed by the trustee.

living trust—trust created to take effect within the lifetime of the settlor; also called *inter vivos* trust.

testamentary trust—trust that becomes effective only when the settlor's will takes effect after death.

trust agreement—instrument creating a trust; also called *deed of trust.*

21. Nature of Beneficiary's Interest

legal title–title held by the trustee in a trust situation.

equitable title–beneficial interest in a trust.

spendthrift trust–a trust that, to varying degrees, provides that creditors of the beneficiary shall not be able to reach the principal or income held by the trustee and that the beneficiary shall not be able to assign any interest in the trust.

When property is transferred to a trust, the trustee has **legal title** and the beneficiary has **equitable title**. The beneficiary may transfer or assign such interest in the trust. The beneficiary's creditors may reach that interest in satisfaction of their claims. However, the trustor can protect beneficiaries from creditors by creating a **spendthrift trust**, which does not allow creditors of the beneficiary to attach the beneficial interest, nor is the beneficiary permitted to assign or pledge that interest.[11]

22. Powers of Trustee

A trustee can exercise only those powers that are given by law or the trust instrument or those that the court will construe as being given by implication. Modern trusts commonly give the trustee discretion to make decisions on matters that could not be foreseen by the settlor. **For Example,** the trustee may be authorized to expend principal as well as income when, in the trustee's opinion, it is necessary for the education or medical care of a beneficiary.

23. Duties of Trustee

The duty of a trustee is to administer the trust. The trustee who accepts the appointment must take all necessary steps to carry out the trust in a proper manner.

(A) PERFORMANCE. A trustee is under a duty to carry out the trust according to its terms and is personally liable for any loss sustained from an unjustified failure to perform such duties. A trustee cannot delegate the performance of personal duties.

(B) DUE CARE. The trustee is under a duty to use reasonable skill, prudence, and diligence in the performance of trust duties. More simply stated, the trustee must use the care that would be exercised by a reasonable person under the circumstances.

(C) LOYALTY. A trustee is entitled to compensation but it not permitted to profit personally from the position of trustee.[12]

(D) POSSESSION AND PRESERVATION OF TRUST PROPERTY. The trustee has a duty to take possession of trust property and to preserve it from loss or damage. If the property includes accounts receivable or outstanding debts, the trustee is responsible for collecting them.

(E) PRODUCTION OF INCOME. By either express or implied direction, the trustee is required to invest the money or property in enterprises or transactions that will yield an income to the estate. A trustee must invest the trust property as a reasonable and prudent investor would.

(F) ACCOUNTING AND INFORMATION. A trustee must keep accurate records so that it can be determined whether the trust has been properly administered. On request by a beneficiary, the trustee must furnish information about the trust. Periodically or at

---

[11] However, in *In re Marriage of Sharp*, 860 NE2d 539 (Ill App 2006), the court held that once payments have been made from the trust that they are subject to attachment for back child support.
[12] *Moretz v Miller*, 486 SE2d 85 (NC App 1997).

FIGURE 52-3 | *Trust Principal/Income Allocation*

PRINCIPAL	PAYABLE FROM PRINCIPAL
ORIGINAL TRUST PROPERTY	LOANS (PRINCIPAL)
PROCEEDS AND GAINS	LITIGATION EXPENSES
FROM SALE	PERMANENT IMPROVEMENTS
INSURANCE PAYMENTS	COSTS OF PURCHASE
NEW PROPERTY PURCHASED	
WITH PRINCIPAL	
STOCK DIVIDENDS	
STOCK SPLITS	

INCOME	PAYABLE FROM INCOME
RENT	LOANS (INTEREST)
INTEREST	TAXES
CASH	INSURANCE PREMIUMS
DIVIDENDS	REPAIRS
ROYALTIES	

certain times, as determined by the law in each state, a trustee must file an account in court. At such time, the court examines the stewardship of the trust.

In some trusts, the trustee must balance the interests of the life beneficiary (the party entitled to the income from the trust while he or she is alive) with those of the eventual recipients of the trust res. **For Example,** a testator might put this provision in her will: "To my husband in trust for his life, and upon his death in fee simple to my children." How does the trustee account for rental income? What if the rental properties need repairs? Do the repairs come from the income, or are they taken from principal? There are clear rules for the allocation of income and principal and the expenses of operation of the trust and the trust properties. These rules are summarized in Figure 52.3.

24. Remedies for Breach of Trust

A breach of trust may occur in a variety of ways. The manner in which a trust is breached affects the remedies available. These remedies include the following: (1) A money judgment against the trustee for losses, (2) an injunction, (3) criminal prosecution for misconduct, (4) recovery of trust property, (5) removal of the trustee for misconduct, and (6) recovery from any third parties who participated in a breach of trust

25. Termination of Trust

A trust may be terminated (1) by its own terms—for example, the trust is an education fund that has a termination date of college graduation, (2) because of the impossibility of attaining the object of the trust—for example, the trust is for the trustor's grandchild and his only child has died before having any children, (3) via revocation by the settlor when allowed by the terms of the trust, but trusts are presumed irrevocable unless the trust document permits revocation, (4) by merger of all interests in the same person (as when there is only one trustee and one beneficiary and they are the same person), or (5) upon the request of all the beneficiaries, as approved by a court, when there is no express purpose that requires continuation of the trust.

lawflix

Melvin and Howard (1980) (PG)

An interesting look at the difficulty of establishing the validity of an eccentric's will, particularly when the provisions of that will defy conventional notions of proper distribution of one's largesse upon death.

For movie clips that illustrate business law concepts, see LawFlix at **www.cengage.com/blaw/dvl**.

MAKE THE CONNECTION

SUMMARY

A *will* is a writing that provides for a disposition of property to take effect upon death. A man who makes a will is called a *testator;* a woman, a *testatrix*. The person to whom property is left by will is a *beneficiary*. A *legacy* is a gift of personal property by will; a gift of real property by will is a *devise*. A testator must have testamentary capacity to make a will and must manifest some intention that the will is to be effective only upon death. The will must be signed by the testator and be witnessed.

A will may be modified by a codicil or revoked either by the act of the testator or by operation of law.

Probate is the process by which a proper court official accepts a will. Probate may be refused or set aside on grounds that the will is not the free expression of the testator.

A *holographic* will is an unwitnessed will written entirely in the handwriting of the testator. A *self-proved will* may be admitted to probate without the testimony of subscribing witnesses. A *living will* allows a person to make wishes known regarding life-sustaining medical treatment.

If there is a valid will, the last phase of administration of the estate is the distribution of property after the payment of all debts and taxes. *General legacies* are bequests of money, whereas *specific legacies* or *specific devises* are gifts of identified personal or real property. Legacies abate in the following order: residuary, general, and specific. If a beneficiary named in the will has died before the testator and no alternate provision has been made for that beneficiary, antilapse statutes provide that the gift will not lapse. In that event, the children or heirs of the beneficiary may take the legacy in the place of the deceased beneficiary.

If the decedent does not dispose of all property by will or does not have a will, the property will be distributed according to state intestacy statutes. A surviving spouse may generally elect to take the statutory allocation instead of that provided in the will.

The estate of the testator will be administered by the person appointed in the will (the *executor*) or, if there is no will, by a person appointed by the court (an *administrator*). Creditors who have claims against the estate are required to give notice of their claims to the personal representative; otherwise, the claims will be barred.

A *trust* is a legal device by which property is held by one person for the benefit of another. The settlor creates the trust, and the person for whose benefit the trustee holds the property is the beneficiary. Property held in trust is called the *trust corpus, trust fund, trust estate,* or *trust res.*

A trust is usually created by a trust agreement or deed of trust. No particular form or language is required. A trust is not created unless an active duty is placed on the trustee to manage the property in some manner. A trustee's acceptance of duties is presumed.

Legal title to trust property is given to the trustee, and the beneficiary holds equitable title. A beneficiary may transfer an interest in the trust except in the case of a spendthrift trust.

The trustee can exercise only those powers that are given by law or the trust instrument. The trustee must administer the trust and carry out the trust in a proper manner. A trustee is liable for breach of the terms of the trust agreement. A trust comes to an end when its terms so provide or when it becomes impossible to attain the object of the trust.

LEARNING OUTCOMES

After studying this chapter, you should be able to clearly explain:

A. WILLS

LO.1 Define *testamentary capacity* and *testamentary intent*
See *Maimonides School v Coles* on p. 1235.

LO.2 Discuss how a valid will is created
See *Ramsey v Taylor* on p. 1242.

LO.3 Explain how a will may be modified or revoked
See *In re Estate of Speers* on p. 1238.

B. ADMINISTRATION OF DECEDENTS' ESTATES

LO.4 Describe briefly the probate and contest of a will
See the Ethics & the Law discussion of Brooke Astor on p. 1243

LO.5 Describe the ordinary pattern of distribution by intestacy
See Figure 52.2 on p. 1246.
See *In re Estate of Morris P. Van Der Veen* on p. 1247.

C. TRUSTS

LO.6 Explain the nature of a trust
See Sections 20–22 on trust terminology and creation.

KEY TERMS

abate	administrator	antilapse statutes
acknowledgment	administratrix	attestation clause
adeemed	affidavits	beneficiary

bequest
cestui que trust
claims
decedent
devise
devisee
disinherited
distribution per stirpes
donor
equitable title
executor
executrix
general legacies
holographic will
income
interlineation
intestate
intestate succession
legacy

legal title
legatee
letters of administration
letters testamentary
lineals
living trust
living wills
per capita
per stirpes
personal representatives
principal
probate
revoke
right of escheat
self-proved wills
settlor
specific legacies
spendthrift trust
stirpes

testamentary capacity
testamentary intent
testamentary trust
testate
testate distribution
testator
testatrix
trust
trust agreement
trust corpus
trustee
trustor
Uniform Probate Code
  (UPC)
Uniform Simultaneous
  Death Act
will

QUESTIONS AND CASE PROBLEMS

1. Joseph McKinley Bryan was an elderly, wealthy, and eccentric man. Before his death, he had made provisions for a testamentary trust for his grandchildren and great-grandchildren. Under the terms of the trust, each grandchild who survived him was to receive $500,000, and each great-grandchild who survived him was to receive $100,000. By the time of Bryan's death on April 26, 1995, there had been at least five versions of the trust's provisions. His will was originally dated June 29, 1990, but the trust agreement was originally made in 1985, with two changes in 1988, one in 1990, and another in 1992. In May 1995, NationsBank Corp., the trustee, notified Bryan's grandchildren by letter that they would be receiving only $100,000. Because the grandchildren had understood that they were to receive $500,000, they asked to see the trust agreements. The trustee refused, contending that there was no duty to share the agreement with the trust beneficiaries. Was the trustee right? [*Taylor v NationsBank Corp.*, 481 SE2d 358 (NC App)]

2. Irene Bracewell was married to W. T. Bracewell and they had a son, Charles. Although Irene loved both her husband and her son, it was clear to everyone that her husband and her son did not get along. Often, Irene did not get along with W. T., and she spent a great deal of time living on Charles's ranch. Charles had named a lake on his property Lake Irene and paid considerable attention to his mother when she lived with him. Irene suffered from Parkinson's disease, hypertension, hyperthyroidism, anxiety, and degenerative bone disease. She had a long list of medications including tranquilizers. Irene and W. T. executed wills in 1975 that left their property to each other. In 1989, while living with Charles, Irene was taking so much medication that doctors

said she suffered from dementia, delusions, hallucinations, paranoia, and incoherence. Charles took her to have a new will executed that left all of her property to him. When she died in 1995, W. T. wanted the 1975 will probated because he said Irene lacked capacity to make the 1989 will valid. The probate court refused to admit the 1989 will, and Charles appealed. Did she have testamentary capacity? What factors should the court consider? [*Bracewell v Bracewell*, 20 SW2d 14 (Tex App)]

3. Iona wrote her will. The following year, she wrote another will that expressly revoked the earlier will. Later, while cleaning house, she came across the second will. She mistakenly thought that it was the first will and tore it up because the first will had been revoked. Iona died shortly thereafter. The beneficiaries named in the second will claimed that the second will should be probated. The beneficiaries named in the first will claimed that the second will had been revoked when it was torn up. Had the second will been revoked?

4. Logsdon, who had three children, disliked one of them without any reason. In his will, he left only a small amount to the child he disliked and gave the bulk of his estate to the remaining two. On his death, the disliked child claimed that the will was void and had been obtained by undue influence. Do you agree? [*Logsdon v Logsdon*, 104 NE2d 622 (Ill)]

5. Field executed a will. On her death, the will was found in her safe deposit box, but the part of it containing the fifth bequest had been torn from the will. This torn fragment was also found in the box. There was no evidence that anyone other than Field had ever opened the box. A proceeding was brought to determine whether the will was entitled to be probated. Had the will been revoked? Was the will still valid with a portion torn from it? [*Flora v Hughes*, 228 SW2d 27 (Ky)]

6. Miller wrote a will that was 11 pages long and enclosed it in an envelope, which she sealed. She then wrote on the envelope "My last will & testament" and signed her name below this statement. This was the only place where she signed her name on any of the papers. Was this signature sufficient to allow this writing to be admitted to probate as her will? [*Miller's Executor v Shannon*, 299 SW2d 103 (Ky)]

7. Lingenfelter's will was offered for probate and was opposed. The testatrix was sick, highly nervous, and extremely jealous, and she committed suicide a week after executing the will. She had, however, seemed to understand the will when she discussed it with an attorney. The will disinherited her husband because she feared he was not faithful to her despite the fact that he was seriously ill when she wrote the will. He died the day after she executed the will, and she grieved his death terribly for one week before committing suicide. Did she have the capacity to make a will? Should it be admitted to probate? [*In re Lingenfelter's Estate*, 241 P2d 990 (Cal)]

8. Copenhaver wrote a will in ink, which was found with her other papers in her bedroom at her death. Pencil lines had been drawn through every provision of the will and the signature. There was no evidence as to the circumstances under

which this had been done. Was the will revoked? Why or why not? [*Franklin v Maclean*, 66 SE2d 504 (Va)]

9. George Baxter executed a will that left the bulk of his estate to the Church of Christ in New Boston, Texas. Two members of the church served as the witnesses for the will. Is the will valid? [*In re Estate of Gordon*, 519 SW2d 902 (Tex)]

10. Jeanette Wall worked for D. J. Sharron for many years. Sharron executed a will leaving his entire estate to Jeanette. He reexecuted the same will sometime thereafter with the same provisions. Sharron's children contested the will, offering evidence that Sharron was a very sick man, physically as well as mentally, and that Wall was active in Sharron's business as well as his personal life. They offered no evidence that Wall had any involvement in the procurement of the original or the reexecuted will. Who is entitled to the estate? Why? [*Wall v Hodges*, 465 So 2d 359 (Ala App)]

11. In 1984, Alexander Tolin executed a will under which the residue of his estate was to be devised to his friend Adair Creaig. The will was prepared by Steven Fine, Tolin's attorney, and executed in Fine's office. Fine retained the original will, and gave a blue-backed photocopy to Tolin. In 1989, Tolin executed a codicil to the will that changed the residuary beneficiary from Creaig to Broward Art Guild, Inc. Fine prepared the codicil, and retained the original, giving Tolin a blue-backed photocopy of the original executed codicil.

    Tolin died in 1990. Six months before his death, he told his neighbor Ed Weinstein, who was a retired attorney, that he made a mistake and wished to revoke the codicil and reinstate Creaig as the residuary beneficiary. Weinstein told Tolin he could do this by tearing up the original codicil. Tolin handed Weinstein a blue-backed document that Tolin said was the original codicil. Weinstein looked at the document; it appeared to him to be the original, and gave it back to Tolin. Tolin then tore up and destroyed the document with the intent and for the purpose of revocation.

    Some time after Tolin's death, Weinstein spoke with Fine and found out for the first time that Fine had the original will and codicil. Creaig filed a petition to determine if there had been a revocation of the codicil. From a judgment that Tolin's destruction of a copy of the codicil was not an effective revocation of the codicil, Creaig appealed. Who is correct about the revocation and why? [*In re Estate of Tolin*, 622 So2d 988 (Fla)]

12. Valerie and Flora are the beneficiaries of a trust left to them by their mother upon her death. Their mother named Art Casanelli, a family friend, as the trustee. Flora has seen Art driving a new car and has learned that he just purchased a new and rather large home. She is concerned about the trust funds and Art's unfettered access to them. How can she determine whether Art is using trust funds? What happens if she finds that he is?

13. Can a murderer inherit property from his victim? Why or why not?

14. James Horne's will provides that his estate is to be distributed to his heirs per capita. Upon his death, two of his three children are surviving and his deceased child left two children (James's grandchildren). His will provides that all his

property is to be distributed per capita to these children and grandchildren. How will the property be distributed? How would it be distributed if he had provided for a per stirpes distribution?

15. Craig delivers bonds in the amount of $100,000 to White in trust to hold and to pay over the income in quarterly payments to Craig's niece, Helen, during her minority. Who is the settlor or creator of the trust? Who is the trustee? Who is the beneficiary?

CPA QUESTIONS

The topic of insurance has been eliminated from the content outline for the CPA exam as of october 2009. However, the exam lags behind the content change, so this topic may continue to appear on the exam for six to 18 months.

1. On July 1, Sutter created a living trust by transferring the legal title to 500 shares of Pine Corporation common stock to Ellis as trustee and named Clay as the sole beneficiary. The trust granted Ellis broad powers to sell and repurchase stock as she saw fit. On June 25, a few days before the trust was created, Pine Corporation distributed cash dividends of $1 per share on its common stock. On July 15, Ellis sold the common stock for $105 per share, which was $5 more than the purchase price that Sutter had paid. Ignoring taxes, how much is in the principal of this trust on July 16?

   A. $ 2,500

   B. $50,000

   C. $52,500

   D. $53,000

2. Match the letter in list A-D with the appropriate numbered item.

   A. Principal includes this.

   B. Income includes this.

   C. This is payable from principal.

   D. This is payable from income.

   1. Shares of stock purchased before the trust was formed and placed in the trust.

   2. Cash dividends received on the stock up to the formation of the trust.

   3. Cash dividends received on the stock after formation of the trust.

   4. Stock dividends after the trust is formed.

   5. Stock splits after the trust is formed.

   6. Rental property placed in the trust.

3. Which of the following expenditures resulting from a trust's ownership of commercial real estate should be allocated to the trust's principal?

   a. Building management fees.

   b. Insurance premiums.

   c. Sidewalk assessments.

   d. Depreciation.

4. On June 16, 1992, Eble placed 800 shares of Singh Corp.'s common stock in a trust for the benefit of Eble's child. On June 1, 1992, Singh's board of directors had declared a cash dividend of $2 per share on Singh's common stock. Payment was made on July 30, 1993 to shareholders of record on June 30, 1992. What amount of the dividend should be allocated to trust income?

   a. $0

   b. $800

   c. $1,200

   d. $1,600

5. Cox transferred assets into a trust under which Smart is entitled to receive the income for life. After Smart's death, the remaining assets are to be given to Mix. In 1998, the trust received rent of $1,000, stock dividends of $6,000, interest on certificates of deposit of $3,000, municipal bond interest of $4,000, and proceeds of $7,000 from the sale of bonds. Both Smart and Mix are still alive. What amount of the 1998 receipts should be allocated to trust principal?

   A. $ 7,000

   B. $ 8,000

   C. $13,000

   D. $15,000

HOW TO FIND THE LAW

In order to determine what the law on a particular question or issue is, it may be necessary to examine (1) compilations of constitutions, treaties, statutes, executive orders, proclamations, and administrative regulations; (2) reports of state and federal court decisions; (3) digests of opinions; (4) treatises on the law; and (5) loose-leaf services. These sources can be either researched traditionally or using fee-and/or non-fee-based computerized legal research accessed through the World Wide Web.

A. COMPILATIONS

In the consideration of a legal problem in business it is necessary to determine whether the matter is affected or controlled by a constitution, national or state; by a national treaty; by an Act of Congress or a state legislature, or by a city ordinance; by a decree or proclamation of the President of the United States, a governor, or a mayor; or by a regulation of a federal, state, or local administrative agency.

Each body or person that makes laws, regulations, or ordinances usually compiles and publishes at the end of each year or session all of the matter that it has adopted. In addition to the periodical or annual volumes, it is common to compile all the treaties, statutes, regulations, or ordinances in separate volumes. To illustrate, the federal Anti-Injunction Act may be cited as the Act of March 23, 1932, 47 Stat 70, 29 USC Sections 101 et seq. This means that this law was enacted on March 23, 1932, and that it can be found at page 70 in Volume 47 of the reports that contain all of the statutes adopted by the Congress.

The second part of the citation, 29 USC Sections 101 et seq., means that in the collection of all of the federal statutes, which is known as the United States Code, the full text of the statute can be found in the sections of the 29th title beginning with Section 101.

B. COURT DECISIONS

For complicated or important legal cases or when an appeal is to be taken, a court will generally write an opinion, which explains why the court made the decision. Appellate courts as a rule write opinions. The great majority of these decisions, particularly in the case of the appellate courts, are collected and printed. In order to avoid confusion, the opinions of each court are ordinarily printed in a separate set of reports, either by official reporters or private publishers.

In the reference "Pennoyer v Neff, 95 US 714, 24 LEd 565," the first part states the names of the parties. It does not necessarily tell who was the plaintiff and who was the defendant. When an action is begun in a lower court, the first name is that of the plaintiff and the second name that of the defendant. When the case is appealed, generally the name of the person taking the appeal appears on the records of the higher court as the first one and that of the adverse party as the second. Sometimes, therefore, the original order of the names of the parties is reversed.

The balance of the reference consists of two citations. The first citation, 95 US 714, means that the opinion which the court filed in the case of Pennoyer v Neff may be found on page 714 of the 95th volume of a series of books in which are printed officially the opinions of the United States Supreme Court. Sometimes the same opinion is printed in two different sets of volumes. In the example, 24 LEd 565 means that in the 24th volume of another set of books, called Lawyer's Edition, of the United States Supreme Court Reports, the same opinion begins on page 565.

In opinions by a state court there may also be two citations, as in the case of "Morrow v Corbin, 122 Tex 553, 62 SW2d 641." This means that the opinion in the lawsuit between Morrow and Corbin may be found in the 122d volume of the reports of the highest court of Texas, beginning on page 553; and also in Volume 62 of the Southwestern Reporter, Second Series, at page 641.

The West Publishing Company publishes a set of sectional reporters covering the entire United States. They are called "sectional" because each reporter, instead of being limited to a particular court or a particular state, covers the decisions of the courts of a particular section of the country. Thus the decisions of the courts of Arkansas, Kentucky, Missouri, Tennessee, and Texas are printed by the West Publishing company as a group in a sectional reporter called the Southwestern Reporter.[1] Because of the large number of decisions involved, generally only the opinions of the state appellate courts are printed. A number of states[2] have discontinued publication of the opinions of their courts, and those opinions are now found only in the West reporters.

The reason for the "Second Series" in the Southwestern citation is that when there were 300 volumes in the original series, instead of calling the next volume 301, the publisher called it Volume 1, Second Series. Thus 62 SW2d Series really means the 362d volume of the Southwestern Reporter. Six to eight volumes appear in a year for each geographic section.

In addition to these state reporters, the West Publishing Company publishes a Federal Supplement, which primarily reports the opinions of the Federal District Courts; the Federal Reporter, which primarily reports the decisions of the United States Courts of Appeals; and the Supreme Court Reporter, which reports the decisions of the United States Supreme Court. The Supreme Court decisions are also reported in a separate set called the Lawyers' Edition, published by the Lawyers Cooperative Publishing Company.

The reports published by the West Publishing Company and Lawyers Cooperative Publishing Company are unofficial reports, while those bearing the name or abbreviation of the United States or of a state, such as "95 US 714" or "122 Tex 553" are official reports. This means that in the case of the latter, the particular court, such as the United States Supreme Court, has officially authorized that its decisions be printed and that by federal statute such official printing is made. In the case of the unofficial reporters, the publisher prints the decisions of a court on its own initiative. Such opinions are part of the public domain and not subject to any copyright or similar restriction.

C. Digests of Opinions

The reports of court decisions are useful only if one has the citation, that is, the name and volume number of the book and the page number of the opinion one is seeking. For this reason, digests of the decisions have been prepared. These digests organize the entire field of law under major headings, which are then arranged in alphabetical order. Under each heading, such as "Contracts," the subject is divided into the different questions that can arise with respect to that field. A master outline is thus created on the subject. This outline includes short paragraphs describing what each case holds and giving its citation.

D. Treatises and Restatements

Very helpful in finding a case or a statute are the treatises on the law. These may be special books, each written by an author on a particular subject, such as Williston on Contracts, Bogert on Trusts, Fletcher on Corporations, or they may be general encyclopedias, as in the case of American Jurisprudence, American Jurisprudence, Second, and Corpus Juris Secundum.

Another type of treatise is found in the restatements of the law prepared by the American Law Institute. Each restatement consists of one or more volumes devoted to a particular phase of the law, such as the Restatement of the Law of Contracts, Restatement of the Law of Agency, and Restatement of the Law of Property. In each restatement, the American Law Institute, acting through special committees of judges, lawyers, and professors of law, has set forth what the law is; and in many areas where there is no law or the present rule is regarded as unsatisfactory, the restatement specifies what the Institute deems to be the desirable rule.

E. Loose-Leaf Services

A number of private publishers, notably Commerce Clearing House and Prentice-Hall, publish loose-leaf books devoted to particular branches of the law. Periodically, the publisher sends to the purchaser a number of pages that set forth any decision, regulation, or statute made or adopted since the prior set of pages was prepared. Such services are unofficial.

F. Computerized Legal Research

National and local computer services are providing constantly widening assistance for legal research. The database in such a system may be opinions, statutes, or administrative regulations stored word for word; or the later history of a particular case giving its full citation and

---

[1] The sectional reporters are: Atlantic—A. (Connecticut, Delaware, District of Columbia, Maine, Maryland, New Hampshire, New Jersey, Pennsylvania, Rhode Island, Vermont); Northeastern—N.E. (Illinois, Indiana, Massachusetts, New York, Ohio); N.W. (Iowa, Michigan, Minnesota, Nebraska, North Dakota, South Dakota, Wisconsin); Pacific—P. (Alaska, Arizona, California, Colorado, Hawaii, Idaho, Kansas, Montana, Nevada, New Mexico, Oklahoma, Oregon, Utah, Washington, Wyoming); Southeastern—S.E. (Georgia, North Carolina, South Carolina, Virginia, West Virginia); Southwestern—S.W. (Arkansas, Kentucky, Missouri, Tennessee, Texas); and Southern—So. (Alabama, Florida, Louisiana, Mississippi). There is also a special New York State reporter known as the New York Supplement and a special California State reporter known as the California Reporter.

[2] See, for example, Alaska, Florida, Iowa, Kentucky, Louisiana, Maine, Mississippi, Missouri, North Dakota, Oklahoma, Texas, and Wyoming.

showing whether the case has been followed by other courts; or the text of forms and documents. By means of a terminal connected to the system, the user can retrieve the above information at a great saving of time and with the assurance that it is up-to-date.

There are two leading, fee-based systems for computer-aided research. Listed alphabetically, they are LEXIS and WESTLAW.

A specialized service of legal forms for business is provided by Shepard's BUSINESS LAW CASE MANAGEMENT SYSTEM. A monthly fee is required for usage.

Numerous free, private sites offer a lot of legal resources. The federal government offers a variety of case law, regulations, and code enactments, either pending or newly promulgated. To find the most comprehensive source of government-maintained legal information, go to **http://www.house.gov**.

Increasingly, some states offer their regulations and codes online. As an example, go to the State of California's site, **www.leginfo.ca.gov**, as an example of a government-based legal information provider. For a complete listing of state homepages, go to **http://www.house.gov/house/govsites.shtml**.

For sources of all types of law, and legal resources, the internet site, Hieros Gamos, **www.hg.org** claims that "virtually all online and offline (published) legal information is accessible within three levels." It is important to note, however, that non-fee-based services do not guarantee the integrity of the information provided. Therefore, when accessing free information over the Internet, one should be careful to double-check the authority of the provider and the accuracy of the data obtained. This caution extends to sites maintained by federal and state governments as well.

The computer field has expanded to such an extent that there is now a Legal Software Review of over 500 pages prepared by Lawyers Library, 12761 New Hall Ferry, Florissant, MO 63033.

We the people of the United States of America, in order to form a more perfect union, establish justice, insure domestic tranquility, provide for the common defense, promote the general welfare, and secure the blessings of liberty to ourselves and our posterity, do ordain and establish this Constitution for the United States of America.

Article I

SECTION 1

All legislative powers herein granted shall be vested in a Congress of the United States, which shall consist of a Senate and House of Representatives.

SECTION 2

1. The House of Representatives shall be composed of members chosen every second year by the people of the several States, and the electors in each State shall have the qualifications requisite for electors of the most numerous branch of the State legislature.

2. No person shall be a representative who shall not have attained to the age of twenty-five years, and been seven years a citizen of the United States, and who shall not, when elected, be an inhabitant of that State in which he shall be chosen.

3. Representatives and direct taxes shall be apportioned among the several States which may be included within this Union, according to their respective numbers, which shall be determined by adding to the whole number of free persons, including those bound to service for a term of years, and excluding Indians not taxed, three fifths of all other persons.[1] The actual enumeration shall be made within three years after the first meeting of the Congress of the United States, and within every subsequent term of ten years, in such manner as they shall by law direct. The number of representatives shall not exceed one for every thirty thousand, but each State shall have at least one representative; and until such enumeration shall be made, the State of New Hampshire shall be entitled to choose three, Massachusetts eight, Rhode Island and Providence Plantations one, Connecticut five, New York six, New Jersey four, Pennsylvania eight, Delaware one, Maryland six, Virginia ten, North Carolina five, South Carolina five, and Georgia three.

4. When vacancies happen in the representation from any State, the executive authority thereof shall issue writs of election to fill such vacancies.

5. The House of Representatives shall choose their speaker and other officers; and shall have the sole power of impeachment.

SECTION 3

1. The Senate of the United States shall be composed of two senators from each State, chosen by the legislature thereof, for six years; and each senator shall have one vote.

2. Immediately after they shall be assembled in consequence of the first election, they shall be divided as equally as may be into three classes. The seats of the senators of the first class shall be vacated at the expiration of the second year, of the second class at the expiration of the fourth year, and of the third class at the expiration of the sixth year, so that one third may be chosen every second year; and if vacancies happen by resignation, or otherwise, during the recess of the legislature of any State, the executive thereof may make temporary appointments until the next meeting of the legislature, which shall then fill such vacancies.[2]

3. No person shall be a senator who shall not have attained to the age of thirty years, and been nine years a citizen of the United States, and who shall not, when elected, be an inhabitant of that State for which he shall be chosen.

4. The Vice President of the United States shall be President of the Senate, but shall have no vote, unless they be equally divided.

[1] See the 14th Amendment.

[2] See the 17th Amendment.

5. The Senate shall choose their other officers, and also a president pro tempore, in the absence of the Vice President, or when he shall exercise the office of the President of the United States.

6. The Senate shall have the sole power to try all impeachments. When sitting for that purpose, they shall be on oath or affirmation. When the President of the United States is tried, the chief justice shall preside: and no person shall be convicted without the concurrence of two thirds of the members present.

7. Judgment in cases of impeachment shall not extend further than to removal from office, and disqualification to hold and enjoy any office of honor, trust or profit under the United States: but the party convicted shall nevertheless be liable and subject to indictment, trial, judgment and punishment, according to law.

SECTION 4

1. The times, places, and manner of holding elections for senators and representatives, shall be prescribed in each State by the legislature thereof; but the Congress may at any time by law make or alter such regulations, except as to the places of choosing senators.

2. The Congress shall assemble at least once in every year, and such meeting shall be on the first Monday in December, unless they shall by law appoint a different day.

SECTION 5

1. Each House shall be the judge of the elections, returns and qualifications of its own members, and a majority of each shall constitute a quorum to do business; but a smaller number may adjourn from day to day, and may be authorized to compel the attendance of absent members, in such manner, and under such penalties as each House may provide.

2. Each House may determine the rules of its proceedings, punish its members for disorderly behavior, and, with the concurrence of two thirds, expel a member.

3. Each House shall keep a journal of its proceedings, and from time to time publish the same, excepting such parts as may in their judgment require secrecy; and the yeas and nays of the members of either House on any question shall, at the desire of one fifth of those present, be entered on the journal.

4. Neither House, during the session of Congress, shall, without the consent of the other, adjourn for more than three days, nor to any other place than that in which the two Houses shall be sitting.

SECTION 6

1. The senators and representatives shall receive a compensation for their services, to be ascertained by law, and paid out of the Treasury of the United States. They shall in all cases, except treason, felony, and breach of the peace, be privileged from arrest during their attendance at the session of their respective Houses, and in going to and returning from the same; and for any speech or debate in either House, they shall not be questioned in any other place.

2. No senator or representative shall, during the time for which he was elected, be appointed to any civil office under the authority of the United States, which shall have been created, or the emoluments whereof shall have been increased during such time; and no person holding any office under the United States shall be a member of either House during his continuance in office.

SECTION 7

1. All bills for raising revenue shall originate in the House of Representatives; but the Senate may propose or concur with amendments as on other bills.

2. Every bill which shall have passed the House of Representatives and the Senate, shall, before it becomes a law, be presented to the President of the United States; if he approves he shall sign it, but if not he shall return it, with his objections to that House in which it shall have originated, who shall enter the objections at large on their journal, and proceed to reconsider it. If after such reconsideration two thirds of that House shall agree to pass the bill, it shall be sent, together with the objections, to the other House, by which it shall likewise be reconsidered, and if approved by two thirds of that House, it shall become a law. But in all such cases the votes of both Houses shall be determined by yeas and nays, and the names of the persons voting for and against the bill shall be entered on the journal of each House respectively. If any bill shall not be returned by the President within ten days (Sundays excepted) after it shall have been presented to him, the same shall be a law, in like manner as if he had signed it, unless the Congress by their adjournment prevent its return, in which case it shall not be a law.

3. Every order, resolution, or vote to which the concurrence of the Senate and the House of Representatives may be necessary (except on a question of adjournment) shall be presented to the President of the United States; and before the same shall take effect, shall be approved by him, or being disapproved by him, shall be repassed by two thirds of the Senate and House of Representatives, according to the rules and limitations prescribed in the case of a bill.

SECTION 8

The Congress shall have the power

1. To lay and collect taxes, duties, imposts, and excises, to pay the debts and provide for the common defense and general welfare of the United States; but all duties, imposts, and excises shall be uniform throughout the United States;

2. To borrow money on the credit of the United States;

3. To regulate commerce with foreign nations, and among the several States, and with the Indian tribes;

4. To establish a uniform rule of naturalization, and uniform laws on the subject of bankruptcies throughout the United States;

5. To coin money, regulate the value thereof, and of foreign coin, and fix the standard of weights and measures;

6. To provide for the punishment of counterfeiting the securities and current coin of the United States;

7. To establish post offices and post roads;

8. To promote the progress of science and useful arts, by securing for limited times to authors and inventors the exclusive rights to their respective writings and discoveries;

9. To constitute tribunals inferior to the Supreme Court;

10. To define and punish piracies and felonies committed on the high seas, and offenses against the law of nations;

11. To declare war, grant letters of marque and reprisal, and make rules concerning captures on land and water;

12. To raise and support armies, but no appropriation of money to that use shall be for a longer term than two years;

13. To provide and maintain a navy;

14. To make rules for the government and regulation of the land and naval forces;

15. To provide for calling forth the militia to execute the laws of the Union, suppress insurrections and repel invasions;

16. To provide for organizing, arming, and disciplining the militia, and for governing such part of them as may be employed in the service of the United States, reserving to the States respectively, the appointment of the officers, and the authority of training the militia according to the discipline prescribed by Congress;

17. To exercise exclusive legislation in all cases whatsoever, over such district (not exceeding ten miles square) as may, by cession of particular States, and the acceptance of Congress, become the seat of the government of the United States, and to exercise like authority over all places purchased by the consent of the legislature of the State in which the same shall be, for the erection of forts, magazines, arsenals, dockyards, and other needful buildings; and

18. To make all laws which shall be necessary and proper for carrying into execution the foregoing powers, and all other powers vested by this Constitution in the government of the United States, or in any department or officer thereof.

SECTION 9

1. The migration or importation of such persons as any of the States now existing shall think proper to admit, shall not be prohibited by the Congress prior to the year one thousand eight hundred and eight, but a tax or duty may be imposed on such importation, not exceeding ten dollars for each person.

2. The privilege of the writ of habeas corpus shall not be suspended, unless when in cases of rebellion or invasion the public safety may require it.

3. No bill of attainder or ex post facto law shall be passed.

4. No capitation, or other direct, tax shall be laid, unless in proportion to the census or enumeration hereinbefore directed to be taken.[3]

5. No tax or duty shall be laid on articles exported from any State.

6. No preference shall be given by any regulation of commerce or revenue to the ports of one State over those of another: nor shall vessels bound to, or from, one State be obliged to enter, clear, or pay duties in another.

7. No money shall be drawn from the treasury, but in consequence of appropriations made by law; and a regular statement and account of the receipts and expenditures of all public money shall be published from time to time.

8. No title of nobility shall be granted by the United States: and no person holding any office of profit or trust under them, shall, without the consent of the Congress, accept of any present, emolument, office, or title, of any kind whatever, from any king, prince, or foreign State.

SECTION 10

1. No State shall enter into any treaty, alliance, or confederation; grant letters of marque and reprisal; coin money; emit bills of credit; make anything but gold and silver coin a tender in payment of debts; pass any bill of attainder, ex post facto law, or law impairing the obligation of contracts, or grant any title of nobility.

2. No State shall, without the consent of the Congress, lay any imposts or duties on imports or exports, except what may be absolutely necessary for executing its inspection laws: and the net produce of all duties and imposts laid by any State on imports or exports, shall be for the use of the treasury of the United States; and all such laws shall be subject to the revision and control of the Congress.

3. No State shall, without the consent of the Congress, lay any duty of tonnage, keep troops, or ships of war in time of peace, enter into any agreement or compact with another State, or with a foreign power, or engage in war, unless actually invaded, or in such imminent danger as will not admit of delay.

Article II

SECTION 1

1. The executive power shall be vested in a President of the United States of America. He shall hold his office during the term of four years, and, together with the Vice President, chosen for the same term, be elected as follows:

2. Each State shall appoint, in such manner as the legislature thereof may direct, a number of electors, equal to the whole number of senators and representatives to which the State may be entitled in the Congress: but no senator or representative, or person holding an office of trust or profit under the United States, shall be appointed an elector.

[3] See the 16th Amendment.

The electors shall meet in their respective States, and vote by ballot for two persons, of whom one at least shall not be an inhabitant of the same State with themselves. And they shall make a list of all the persons voted for, and of the number of votes for each; which list they shall sign and certify, and transmit sealed to the seat of the government of the United States, directed to the president of the Senate. The president of the Senate shall, in the presence of the Senate and House of Representatives, open all the certificates, and the votes shall then be counted. The person having the greatest number of votes shall be the President, if such number be a majority of the whole number of electors appointed; and if there be more than one who have such majority, and have an equal number of votes, then the House of Representatives shall immediately choose by ballot one of them for President; and if no person have a majority, then from the five highest on the list the said House shall in like manner choose the President. But in choosing the President, the votes shall be taken by States, the representation from each State having one vote; a quorum for this purpose shall consist of a member or members from two thirds of the States, and a majority of all the States shall be necessary to a choice. In every case, after the choice of the President, the person having the greatest number of votes of the electors shall be the Vice President. But if there should remain two or more who have equal votes, the Senate shall choose from them by ballot the Vice President.[4]

3. The Congress may determine the time of choosing the electors, and the day on which they shall give their votes; which day shall be the same throughout the United States.

4. No person except a natural born citizen, or a citizen of the United States, at the time of the adoption of this Constitution, shall be eligible to the office of President; neither shall any person be eligible to that office who shall not have attained to the age of thirty-five years, and been fourteen years a resident within the United States.

5. In the case of removal of the President from office, or of his death, resignation, or inability to discharge the powers and duties of the said office, the same shall devolve on the Vice President, and the Congress may by law provide for the case of removal, death, resignation, or inability, both of the President and Vice President, declaring what officer shall then act as President, and such officer shall act accordingly, until the disability be removed, or a President shall be elected.

6. The President shall, at stated times, receive for his services a compensation, which shall neither be increased nor diminished during the period for which he shall have been elected, and he shall not receive within that period any other emolument from the United States, or any of them.

7. Before he enter on the execution of his office, he shall take the following oath or affirmation:—"I do solemnly swear (or affirm) that I will faithfully execute the office of President of the United States, and will to the best of my ability, preserve, protect and defend the Constitution of the United States."

SECTION 2

1. The President shall be commander in chief of the army and navy of the United States, and of the militia of the several States, when called into the actual service of the United States; he may require the opinion, in writing, of the principal officer in each of the executive departments, upon any subject relating to the duties of their respective office, and he shall have power to grant reprieves and pardons for offenses against the United States, except in cases of impeachment.

2. He shall have power, by and with the advice and consent of the Senate, to make treaties, provided two thirds of the senators present concur; and he shall nominate, and by and with the advice and consent of the Senate, shall appoint ambassadors, other public ministers and consuls, judges of the Supreme Court, and all other officers of the United States, whose appointments are not herein otherwise provided for, and which shall be established by law: but the Congress may by law vest the appointment of such inferior officers, as they think proper, in the President alone, in the courts of law, or in the heads of departments.

3. The President shall have power to fill up all vacancies that may happen during the recess of the Senate, by granting commissions which shall expire at the end of their next session.

SECTION 3

He shall from time to time give to the Congress information of the state of the Union, and recommend to their consideration such measures as he shall judge necessary and expedient; he may, on extraordinary occasions, convene both Houses, or either of them, and in case of disagreement between them with respect to the time of adjournment, he may adjourn them to such time as he shall think proper; he shall receive ambassadors and other public ministers; he shall take care that the laws be faithfully executed, and shall commission all the officers of the United States.

SECTION 4

The President, Vice President, and all civil officers of the United States, shall be removed from office on impeachment for, and conviction of, treason, bribery, or other high crimes and misdemeanors.

Article III

SECTION 1

The judicial power of the United States shall be vested in one Supreme Court, and in such inferior courts as the Congress may from time to time ordain and establish. The judges, both of the Supreme and inferior courts, shall hold their offices during good behavior, and shall, at stated

---

[4] Superseded by the 12th Amendment.

times, receive for their services, a compensation, which shall not be diminished during their continuance in office.

SECTION 2

1. The judicial power shall extend to all cases, in law and equity, arising under this Constitution, the laws of the United States, and treaties made, or which shall be made, under their authority;—to all cases affecting ambassadors, other public ministers and consuls;—to all cases of admiralty and maritime jurisdiction;—to controversies to which the United States shall be a party;—to controversies between two or more States; between a State and citizens of another State;[5]—between citizens of different States;—between citizens of the same State claiming lands under grants of different States, and between a State, or the citizens thereof, and foreign States, citizens or subjects.

2. In all cases affecting ambassadors, other public ministers and consuls, and those in which a State shall be party, the Supreme Court shall have original jurisdiction. In all the other cases before mentioned, the Supreme Court shall have appellate jurisdiction, both as to law and to fact, with such exceptions, and under such regulations as the Congress shall make.

3. The trial of all crimes, except in cases of impeachment, shall be by jury; and such trial shall be held in the State where the said crimes shall have been committed; but when not committed within any State, the trial shall be at such place or places as the Congress may by law have directed.

SECTION 3

1. Treason against the United States shall consist only in levying war against them, or in adhering to their enemies, giving them aid and comfort. No person shall be convicted of treason unless on the testimony of two witnesses to the same overt act, or on confession in open court.

2. The Congress shall have power to declare the punishment of treason, but no attainder of treason shall work corruption of blood, or forfeiture except during the life of the person attainted.

Article IV

SECTION 1

Full faith and credit shall be given in each State to the public acts, records, and judicial proceedings of every other State. And the Congress may by general laws prescribe the manner in which such acts, records and proceedings shall be proved, and the effect thereof.

SECTION 2

1. The citizens of each State shall be entitled to all privileges and immunities of citizens in the several States.[6]

2. A person charged in any State with treason, felony, or other crime, who shall flee from justice, and be found in another State, shall on demand of the executive authority of the State from which he fled, be delivered up to be removed to the State having jurisdiction of the crime.

3. No person held to service or labor in one State under the laws thereof, escaping into another, shall in consequence of any law or regulation therein, be discharged from such service or labor, but shall be delivered up on claim of the party to whom such service or labor may be due.[7]

SECTION 3

1. New States may be admitted by the Congress into this Union; but no new State shall be formed or erected within the jurisdiction of any other State, nor any State be formed by the junction of two or more States, or parts of States, without the consent of the legislatures of the States concerned as well as of the Congress.

2. The Congress shall have power to dispose of and make all needful rules and regulations respecting the territory or other property belonging to the United States; and nothing in this Constitution shall be so construed as to prejudice any claims of the United States, or of any particular State.

SECTION 4

The United States shall guarantee to every State in this Union a republican form of government, and shall protect each of them against invasion; and on application of the legislature, or of the executive (when the legislature cannot be convened) against domestic violence.

Article V

The Congress, whenever two thirds of both Houses shall deem it necessary, shall propose amendments to this Constitution, or, on the application of the legislature of two thirds of the several States, shall call a convention for proposing amendments, which in either case, shall be valid to all intents and purposes, as part of this Constitution when ratified by the legislatures of three fourths of the several States, or by conventions in three fourths thereof, as the one or the other mode of ratification may be proposed by the Congress; provided that no amendment which may be made prior to the year one thousand eight hundred and eight shall in any manner affect the first and fourth clauses in the ninth section of the first article; and that no State, without its consent, shall be deprived of its equal suffrage in the Senate.

Article VI

1. All debts contracted and engagements entered into, before the adoption of this Constitution, shall be as valid

---

[5] See the 11th Amendment.
[6] See the 14th Amendment, Sec. 1.

[7] See the 13th Amendment.

against the United States under this Constitution, as under the Confederation.[8]

2. This Constitution, and the laws of the United States which shall be made in pursuance thereof; and all treaties made, or which shall be made, under the authority of the United States, shall be the supreme law of the land; and the judges in every State shall be bound thereby, anything in the Constitution or laws of any State to the contrary notwithstanding.

3. The senators and representatives before mentioned, and the members of the several State legislatures, and all executive and judicial officers, both of the United States and of the several States, shall be bound by oath or affirmation to support this Constitution; but no religious test shall ever be required as a qualification to any office or public trust under the United States.

Article VII

The ratification of the conventions of nine States shall be sufficient for the establishment of this Constitution between the States so ratifying the same.

Done in Convention by the unanimous consent of the States present the seventeenth day of September in the year of our Lord one thousand seven hundred and eighty-seven, and of the independence of the United States of America the twelfth. In witness whereof we have hereunto subscribed our names.

A. AMENDMENTS

First Ten Amendments passed by Congress Sept. 25, 1789.

Ratified by three-fourths of the States December 15, 1791.

Amendment I

Congress shall make no law respecting an establishment of religion, or prohibiting the free exercise thereof; or abridging the freedom of speech, or of the press; or the right of the people peaceably to assemble, and to petition the government for a redress of grievances.

Amendment II

A well regulated militia, being necessary to the security of a free State, the right of the people to keep and bear arms, shall not be infringed.

Amendment III

No soldier shall, in time of peace be quartered in any house, without the consent of the owner, nor in time of war, but in a manner to be prescribed by law.

Amendment IV

The right of the people to be secure in their persons, houses, papers, and effects, against unreasonable searches and seizures, shall not be violated, and no warrants shall issue, but upon probable cause, supported by oath or affirmation, and particularly describing the place to be searched, and the person or things to be seized.

Amendment V

No person shall be held to answer for a capital, or otherwise infamous crime, unless on a presentment or indictment of a grand jury, except in cases arising in the land or naval forces, or in the militia, when in actual service in time of war or public danger; nor shall any person be subject for the same offense to be twice put in jeopardy of life or limb; nor shall be compelled in any criminal case to be a witness against himself, nor be deprived of life, liberty, or property, without due process of law; nor shall private property be taken for public use without just compensation.

Amendment VI

In all criminal prosecutions, the accused shall enjoy the right to a speedy and public trial, by an impartial jury of the State and district wherein the crime shall have been committed, which district shall have been previously ascertained by law, and to be informed of the nature and cause of the accusation; to be confronted with the witnesses against him; to have compulsory process for obtaining witnesses in his favor, and to have the assistance of counsel for his defense.

Amendment VII

In suits at common law, where the value in controversy shall exceed twenty dollars, the right of trial by jury shall be preserved, and no fact tried by a jury shall be otherwise reexamined in any court of the United States, then according to the rules of the common law.

Amendment VIII

Excessive bail shall not be required, nor excessive fines imposed, nor cruel and unusual punishments inflicted.

[8] See the 14th Amendment, Sec. 4.

Amendment IX

The enumeration in the Constitution of certain rights shall not be construed to deny or disparage others retained by the people.

Amendment X

The powers not delegated to the United States by the Constitution, nor prohibited by it to the States, are reserved to the States respectively, or to the people.

Amendment XI

Passed by Congress March 5, 1794. Ratified January 8, 1798.

The judicial power of the United States shall not be construed to extend to any suit in law or equity, commenced or prosecuted against one of the United States by citizens of another State, or by citizens or subjects of any foreign State.

Amendment XII

Passed by Congress December 12, 1803. Ratified September 25, 1804.

The electors shall meet in their respective States, and vote by ballot for President and Vice President, one of whom, at least, shall not be an inhabitant of the same State with themselves; they shall name in their ballots the person voted for as President, and in distinct ballots the person voted for as Vice President, and they shall make distinct lists of all persons voted for as President and of all persons voted for as Vice President, and of the number of votes for each, which lists they shall sign and certify, and transmit sealed to the seat of the government of the United States, directed to the President of the Senate;—The President of the Senate shall, in the presence of the Senate and House of Representatives, open all the certificates and the votes shall then be counted;—The person having the greatest number of votes for President, shall be the President, if such number be a majority of the whole number of electors appointed; and if no person have such majority, then from the persons having the highest numbers not exceeding three on the list of those voted for as President, the House of Representatives shall choose immediately, by ballot, the President. But in choosing the President, the votes shall be taken by States, the representation from each State having one vote; a quorum for this purpose shall consist of a member or members from two thirds of the States, and a majority of all the States shall be necessary to a choice. And if the House of Representatives shall not choose a President whenever the right of choice shall devolve upon them, before the fourth day of March next following, then the Vice President shall act as President, as in the case of the death or other constitutional disability of the President. The person having the greatest number of votes as Vice President shall be the Vice President, if such number be a majority of the whole number of electors appointed, and if no person have a majority, then from the two highest numbers on the list, the Senate shall choose the Vice President; a quorum for the purpose shall consist of two thirds of the whole number of Senators, and a majority of the whole number shall be necessary to a choice. But no person constitutionally ineligible to the office of President shall be eligible to that of Vice President of the United States.

Amendment XIII

Passed by Congress February 1, 1865. Ratified December 18, 1865.

SECTION 1

Neither slavery nor involuntary servitude, except as punishment for crime whereof the party shall have been duly convicted, shall exist within the United States, or any place subject to their jurisdiction.

SECTION 2

Congress shall have power to enforce this article by appropriate legislation.

Amendment XIV

Passed by Congress June 16, 1866. Ratified July 23, 1868.

SECTION 1

All persons born or naturalized in the United States, and subject to the jurisdiction thereof, are citizens of the United States and of the State wherein they reside. No State shall make or enforce any law which shall abridge the privileges or immunities of citizens of the United States; nor shall any State deprive any person of life, liberty, or property, without due process of law; nor deny to any person within its jurisdiction the equal protection of the laws.

SECTION 2

Representatives shall be apportioned among the several States according to their respective numbers, counting the whole number of persons in each State, excluding Indians not taxed. But when the right to vote at any election for the choice of electors for President and Vice President of the United States, representatives in Congress, the executive and judicial officers of a State, or the members of the legislature thereof, is denied to any of the male inhabitants of such State, being twenty-one years of age, and citizens of the United States, or in any way abridged, except for participation in rebellion, or other crime, the basis of representation therein shall be reduced in the proportion which the number of such male citizens shall bear to the whole number of male citizens twenty-one years of age in such State.

SECTION 3

No person shall be a senator or representative in Congress, or elector of President and Vice President, or hold any office, civil or military, under the United States, or under any State, who having previously taken an oath, as a member of Congress, or as an officer of the United States, or as a member of any State legislature, or as an executive or judicial officer of any State, to support the Constitution of the United States, shall have engaged in insurrection or rebellion against the same, or given aid or comfort to the enemies thereof. But Congress may by a vote of two thirds of each House, remove such disability.

SECTION 4

The validity of the public debt of the United States, authorized by law, including debts incurred for payment of pensions and bounties for services in suppressing insurrection or rebellion, shall not be questioned. But neither the United States nor any State shall assume or pay any debt or obligation incurred in aid of insurrection or rebellion against the United States, or any claim for the loss or emancipation of any slave; but all such debts, obligations, and claims shall be held illegal and void.

SECTION 5

The Congress shall have power to enforce, by appropriate legislation, the provisions of this article.

Amendment XV

Passed by Congress February 27, 1869. Ratified March 30, 1870.

SECTION 1

The right of citizens of the United States to vote shall not be denied or abridged by the United States or by any State on account of race, color, or previous condition of servitude.

SECTION 2

The Congress shall have power to enforce this article by appropriate legislation.

Amendment XVI

Passed by Congress July 12, 1909. Ratified February 25, 1913.

The Congress shall have power to lay and collect taxes on incomes, from whatever source derived, without apportionment among the several States, and without regard to any census or enumeration.

Amendment XVII

Passed by Congress May 16, 1912. Ratified May 31, 1913.

The Senate of the United States shall be composed of two senators from each State, elected by the people thereof, for six years; and each senator shall have one vote. The electors in each State shall have the qualifications requisite for electors of the most numerous branch of the State legislature.

When vacancies happen in the representation of any State in the Senate, the executive authority of such State shall issue writs of election to fill such vacancies: Provided, That the legislature of any State may empower the executive thereof to make temporary appointments until the people fill the vacancies by election as the legislature may direct.

This amendment shall not be so construed as to affect the election or term of any senator chosen before it becomes valid as part of the Constitution.

Amendment XVIII

Passed by Congress December 17, 1917. Ratified January 29, 1919.

After one year from the ratification of this article, the manufacture, sale, or transportation of intoxicating liquors within, the importation thereof into, or the exportation thereof from the United States and all territory subject to the jurisdiction thereof for beverage purposes is hereby prohibited.

The Congress and the several States shall have concurrent power to enforce this article by appropriate legislation.

This article shall be inoperative unless it shall have been ratified as an amendment to the Constitution by the legislatures of the several States, as provided in the Constitution, within seven years from the date of the submission hereof to the States by Congress.

Amendment XIX

Passed by Congress June 5, 1919. Ratified August 26, 1920.

The right of citizens of the United States to vote shall not be denied or abridged by the United States or by any State on account of sex.

The Congress shall have power by appropriate legislation to enforce the provisions of this article.

Amendment XX

Passed by Congress March 3, 1932. Ratified January 23, 1933.

SECTION 1

The terms of the President and Vice President shall end at noon on the 20th day of January, and the terms of Senators and Representatives at noon on the 3d day of January, of the years in which such terms would have ended if this article had not been ratified; and the terms of their successors shall then begin.

SECTION 2

The Congress shall assemble at least once in every year, and such meeting shall begin at noon on the 3d day of January, unless they shall by law appoint a different day.

SECTION 3

If, at the time fixed for the beginning of the term of the President, the President-elect shall have died, the Vice President-elect shall become President. If a President shall not have been chosen before the time fixed for the beginning of his term, or if the President-elect shall have failed to qualify, then the Vice President-elect shall act as President until a President shall have qualified; and the Congress may by law provide for the case wherein neither a President-elect nor a Vice President-elect shall have qualified, declaring who shall then act as President, or the manner in which one who is to act shall be selected, and such person shall act accordingly until a President or Vice President shall have qualified.

SECTION 4

The Congress may by law provide for the case of the death of any of the persons from whom the House of Representatives may choose a President whenever the right of choice shall have devolved upon them, and for the case of the death of any of the persons from whom the Senate may choose a Vice President whenever the right of choice shall have devolved upon them.

SECTION 5

Sections 1 and 2 shall take effect on the 15th day of October following the ratification of this article.

SECTION 6

This article shall be inoperative unless it shall have been ratified as an amendment to the Constitution by the legislatures of three-fourths of the several States within seven years from the date of its submission.

Amendment XXI

Passed by Congress February 20, 1933. Ratified December 5, 1933.

SECTION 1

The eighteenth article of amendment to the Constitution of the United States is hereby repealed.

SECTION 2

The transportation or importation into any State, Territory, or possession of the United States for delivery or use therein of intoxicating liquors in violation of the laws thereof, is hereby prohibited.

SECTION 3

This article shall be inoperative unless it shall have been ratified as an amendment to the Constitution by conventions in the several States, as provided in the Constitution, within seven years from the date of the submission thereof to the States by the Congress.

Amendment XXII

Passed by Congress March 24, 1947. Ratified February 26, 1951.

SECTION 1

No person shall be elected to the office of the President more than twice, and no person who has held the office of President, or acted as President, for more than two years of a term to which some other person was elected President shall be elected to the office of the President more than once. But this article shall not apply to any person holding the office of President when this article was proposed by the Congress, and shall not prevent any person who may be holding the office of President, or acting as President, during the term within which this article becomes operative from holding the office of President or acting as President during the remainder of such term.

SECTION 2

This article shall be inoperative unless it shall have been ratified as an amendment to the Constitution by the legislatures of three-fourths of the several States within seven years from the date of its submission to the States by the Congress.

Amendment XXIII

Passed by Congress June 16, 1960. Ratified April 3, 1961.

SECTION 1

The District constituting the seat of Government of the United States shall appoint in such manner as the Congress may direct:

A number of electors of President and Vice President equal to the whole number of Senators and Representatives in Congress to which the District would be entitled if it were a State, but in no event more than the least populous State; they shall be in addition to those appointed by the States, but they shall be considered, for the purposes of the election of President and Vice President, to be electors appointed by a State; and they shall meet in the District and perform such duties as provided by the twelfth article of amendment.

SECTION 2

The Congress shall have power to enforce this article by appropriate legislation.

Amendment XXIV

Passed by Congress August 27, 1962. Ratified February 4, 1964.

SECTION 1

The right of citizens of the United States to vote in any primary or other election for President or Vice President, for electors for President or Vice President, or for Senator or Representative in Congress, shall not be denied or abridged by the United States or any State by reason of failure to pay any poll tax or other tax.

SECTION 2

The Congress shall have power to enforce this article by appropriate legislation.

Amendment XXV

Passed by Congress July 6, 1965. Ratified February 23, 1967.

SECTION 1

In case of the removal of the President from office or of his death or resignation, the Vice President shall become President.

SECTION 2

Whenever there is a vacancy in the office of the Vice President, the President shall nominate a Vice President who shall take office upon confirmation by a majority vote of both Houses of Congress.

SECTION 3

Whenever the President transmits to the President pro tempore of the Senate and the Speaker of the House of Representatives his written declaration that he is unable to discharge the powers and duties of his office, and until he transmits to them a written declaration to the contrary, such powers and duties shall be discharged by the Vice President as Acting President.

SECTION 4

Whenever the Vice President and a majority of either the principal officers of the executive departments or of such other body as Congress may by law provide, transmit to the President pro tempore of the Senate and the Speaker of the House of Representatives their written declaration that the President is unable to discharge the powers and duties of his office, the Vice President shall immediately assume the powers and duties of the office as Acting President.

Thereafter, when the President transmits to the President pro tempore of the Senate and the Speaker of the House of Representatives his written declaration that no inability exists, he shall resume the powers and duties of his office unless the Vice President and a majority of either the principal officers of the executive department or of such other body as Congress may by law provide, transmit within four days to the President pro tempore of the Senate and the Speaker of the House of Representatives their written declaration that the President is unable to discharge the powers and duties of his office. Thereupon Congress shall decide the issue, assembling within forty-eight hours for that purpose if not in session. If the Congress, within twenty-one days after receipt of the latter written declaration, or, if Congress is not in session, within twenty-one days after Congress is required to assemble, determines by two-thirds vote of both Houses that the President is unable to discharge the powers and duties of his office, the Vice President shall continue to discharge the same as Acting President; otherwise, the President shall resume the powers and duties of his office.

Amendment XXVI

Passed by Congress March 23, 1971. Ratified July 5, 1971.

SECTION 1

The right of citizens of the United States, who are eighteen years of age or older, to vote shall not be denied or abridged by the United States or by any State on account of age.

Amendment XXVII

Passed by Congress September 25, 1789. Ratified May 18, 1992.

No law, varying the compensation for the services of the Senators and Representatives, shall take effect, until an election of Representatives shall have intervened.

UNIFORM COMMERCIAL CODE

(Adopted in fifty-two jurisdictions; all fifty States, although Louisiana has adopted only Articles 1, 3, 4, 7, 8, and 9; the District of Columbia; and the Virgin Islands.)
The Code consists of the following articles:

ARTICLE 1 GENERAL PROVISIONS

Part 1 Short Title, Construction, Application and Subject Matter of the Act

§1—101. SHORT TITLE
This Act shall be known and may be cited as Uniform Commercial Code.

§1—102. PURPOSES; RULES OF CONSTRUCTION; VARIATION BY AGREEMENT
(1) This Act shall be liberally construed and applied to promote its underlying purposes and policies.

(2) Underlying purposes and policies of this Act are
(a) to simplify, clarify and modernize the law governing commercial transactions;
(b) to permit the continued expansion of commercial practices through custom, usage and agreement of the parties;
(c) to make uniform the law among the various jurisdictions.

(3) The effect of provisions of this Act may be varied by agreement, except as otherwise provided in this Act and except that the obligations of good faith, diligence, reasonableness and care prescribed by this Act may not be disclaimed by agreement but the parties may by agreement determine the standards by which the performance of such obligations is to be measured if such standards are not manifestly unreasonable.

(4) The presence in certain provisions of this Act of the words "unless otherwise agreed" or words of similar import does not imply that the effect of other provisions may not be varied by agreement under subsection (3).

(5) In this Act unless the context otherwise requires
(a) words in the singular number include the plural, and in the plural include the singular;
(b) words of the masculine gender include the feminine and the neuter, and when the sense so indicates words of the neuter gender may refer to any gender.

§1—103. SUPPLEMENTARY GENERAL PRINCIPLES OF LAW APPLICABLE
Unless displaced by the particular provisions of this Act, the principles of law and equity, including the law merchant and the law relative to capacity to contract, principal and agent, estoppel, fraud, misrepresentation, duress, coercion, mistake, bankruptcy, or other validating or invalidating cause shall supplement its provisions.

§1—104. CONSTRUCTION AGAINST IMPLICIT REPEAL

This Act being a general act intended as a unified coverage of its subject matter, no part of it shall be deemed to be impliedly repealed by subsequent legislation if such construction can reasonably be avoided.

§1—105. TERRITORIAL APPLICATION OF THE ACT; PARTIES' POWER TO CHOOSE APPLICABLE LAW

(1) Except as provided hereafter in this section, when a transaction bears a reasonable relation to this state and also to another state or nation the parties may agree that the law either of this state or of such other state or nation shall govern their rights and duties. Failing such agreement this Act applies to transactions bearing an appropriate relation to this state.

(2) Where one of the following provisions of this Act specifies the applicable law, that provision governs and a contrary agreement is effective only to the extent permitted by the law (including the conflict of laws rules) so specified:

Rights of creditors against sold goods. Section 2—402.

> Applicability of the Article on Leases. Sections 2A—105 and 2A—106.
> Applicability of the Article on Bank Deposits and Collections. Section 4—102.
> Governing law in the Article on Funds Transfers. Section 4A—507.
> Letters of Credit, Section 5—116.
> Bulk sales subject to the Article on Bulk Sales. Section 6—103.
> Applicability of the Article on Investment Securities. Section 8—106.
> Law governing perfection, the effect of perfection or nonperfection, and the priority of security interests and agricultural liens. Sections 9—301 through 9—307.
> As amended in 1972, 1987, 1988, 1989, 1994, 1995, and 1999.

§1—106. REMEDIES TO BE LIBERALLY ADMINISTERED

(1) The remedies provided by this Act shall be liberally administered to the end that the aggrieved party may be put in as good a position as if the other party had fully performed but neither consequential or special nor penal damages may be had except as specifically provided in this Act or by other rule of law.

(2) Any right or obligation declared by this Act is enforceable by action unless the provision declaring it specifies a different and limited effect.

§1—107. WAIVER OR RENUNCIATION OF CLAIM OR RIGHT AFTER BREACH

Any claim or right arising out of an alleged breach can be discharged in whole or in part without consideration by a written waiver or renunciation signed and delivered by the aggrieved party.

§1—108. SEVERABILITY

If any provision or clause of this Act or application thereof to any person or circumstances is held invalid, such invalidity shall not affect other provisions or applications of the Act which can be given effect without the invalid provision or application, and to this end the provisions of this Act are declared to be severable.

§1—109. SECTION CAPTIONS

Section captions are parts of this Act.

Part 2 General Definitions and Principles of Interpretation

§1—201. GENERAL DEFINITIONS

Subject to additional definitions contained in the subsequent Articles of this Act which are applicable to specific Articles or Parts thereof, and unless the context otherwise requires, in this Act:

(1) "Action" in the sense of a judicial proceeding includes recoupment, counterclaim, set-off, suit in equity and any other proceedings in which rights are determined.

(2) "Aggrieved party" means a party entitled to resort to a remedy.

(3) "Agreement" means the bargain of the parties in fact as found in their language or by implication from other circumstances including course of dealing or usage of trade or course of performance as provided in this Act (Sections 1—205 and 2—208). Whether an agreement has legal consequences is determined by the provisions of this Act, if applicable; otherwise by the law of contracts (Section 1—103). (Compare "Contract".)

(4) "Bank" means any person engaged in the business of banking.

(5) "Bearer" means the person in possession of an instrument, document of title, or certificated security payable to bearer or indorsed in blank.

(6) "Bill of lading" means a document evidencing the receipt of goods for shipment issued by a person engaged in the business of transporting or forwarding goods, and includes an airbill. "Airbill" means a document serving for air transportation as a bill of lading does for marine or rail transportation, and includes an air consignment note or air waybill.

(7) "Branch" includes a separately incorporated foreign branch of a bank.

(8) "Burden of establishing" a fact means the burden of persuading the triers of fact that the existence of the fact is more probable than its non-existence.

(9) "Buyer in ordinary course of business" means a person that buys goods in good faith, without knowledge that the sale violates the rights of another person in the goods, and in the ordinary course from a person, other than a pawnbroker, in the business of selling goods of that kind. A person buys goods in the ordinary course if the sale to the person comports with the usual or customary practices in the kind of business in which the seller is engaged or with the seller's own usual or customary practices. A person that sells oil, gas, or other minerals at the wellhead or minehead is a person in the business of selling goods of that kind. A buyer in ordinary course of business may buy for cash, by exchange of other property, or on secured or unsecured credit, and may acquire goods or documents of title under a pre-existing contract for sale. Only a buyer that takes possession of the goods or has a right to recover the goods from the seller under Article 2 may be a buyer in ordinary course of business. A person that acquires goods in a transfer in bulk or as security for or in total or partial satisfaction of a money debt is not a buyer in ordinary course of business.

(10) "Conspicuous": A term or clause is conspicuous when it is so written that a reasonable person against whom it is to operate ought to have noticed it. A printed heading in capitals (as: NON-NEGOTIABLE BILL OF LADING) is conspicuous. Language in the body of a form is "conspicuous" if it is in larger or other contrasting type or color. But in a telegram any stated term is "conspicuous". Whether a term or clause is "conspicuous" or not is for decision by the court.

(11) "Contract" means the total legal obligation which results from the parties' agreement as affected by this Act and any other applicable rules of law. (Compare "Agreement".)

(12) "Creditor" includes a general creditor, a secured creditor, a lien creditor and any representative of creditors, including an assignee for the benefit of creditors, a trustee in bankruptcy, a receiver in equity and an executor or administrator of an insolvent debtor's or assignor's estate.

(13) "Defendant" includes a person in the position of defendant in a cross-action or counterclaim.

(14) "Delivery" with respect to instruments, documents of title, chattel paper, or certificated securities means voluntary transfer of possession.

(15) "Document of title" includes bill of lading, dock warrant, dock receipt, warehouse receipt or order for the delivery of goods, and also any other document which in the regular course of business or financing is treated as adequately evidencing that the person in possession of it is entitled to receive, hold and dispose of the document and the goods it covers. To be a document of title a document must purport to be issued by or addressed to a bailee and purport to cover goods in the bailee's possession which are either identified or are fungible portions of an identified mass.

(16) "Fault" means wrongful act, omission or breach.

(17) "Fungible" with respect to goods or securities means goods or securities of which any unit is, by nature or usage of trade, the equivalent of any other like unit. Goods which are not fungible shall be deemed fungible for the purposes of this Act to the extent that under a particular agreement or document unlike units are treated as equivalents.

(18) "Genuine" means free of forgery or counterfeiting.

(19) "Good faith" means honesty in fact in the conduct or transaction concerned.

(20) "Holder" with respect to a negotiable instrument, means the person in possession if the instrument is payable to bearer or, in the cases of an instrument payable to an identified person, if the identified person is in possession. "Holder" with respect to a document of title means the person in possession if the goods are deliverable to bearer or to the order of the person in possession.

(21) To "honor" is to pay or to accept and pay, or where a credit so engages to purchase or discount a draft complying with the terms of the credit.

(22) "Insolvency proceedings" includes any assignment for the benefit of creditors or other proceedings intended to liquidate or rehabilitate the estate of the person involved.

(23) A person is "insolvent" who either has ceased to pay his debts in the ordinary course of business or cannot pay his debts as they become due or is insolvent within the meaning of the federal bankruptcy law.

(24) "Money" means a medium of exchange authorized or adopted by a domestic or foreign government and includes a monetary unit of account established by an intergovernmental organization or by agreement between two or more nations.

(25) A person has "notice" of a fact when
   (a) he has actual knowledge of it; or
   (b) he has received a notice or notification of it; or
   (c) from all the facts and circumstances known to him at the time in question he has reason to know that it exists.

A person "knows" or has "knowledge" of a fact when he has actual knowledge of it. "Discover" or "learn" or a word or phrase of similar import refers to knowledge rather than to reason to know. The time and circumstances under which a notice or notification may cease to be effective are not determined by this Act.

(26) A person "notifies" or "gives" a notice or notification to another by taking such steps as may be reasonably required to inform the other in ordinary course whether or not such other actually comes to know of it. A person "receives" a notice or notification when

(a) it comes to his attention; or

(b) it is duly delivered at the place of business through which the contract was made or at any other place held out by him as the place for receipt of such communications.

(27) Notice, knowledge or a notice or notification received by an organization is effective for a particular transaction from the time when it is brought to the attention of the individual conducting that transaction, and in any event from the time when it would have been brought to his attention if the organization had exercised due diligence. An organization exercises due diligence if it maintains reasonable routines for communicating significant information to the person conducting the transaction and there is reasonable compliance with the routines. Due diligence does not require an individual acting for the organization to communicate information unless such communication is part of his regular duties or unless he has reason to know of the transaction and that the transaction would be materially affected by the information.

(28) "Organization" includes a corporation, government or governmental subdivision or agency, business trust, estate, trust, partnership or association, two or more persons having a joint or common interest, or any other legal or commercial entity.

(29) "Party", as distinct from "third party", means a person who has engaged in a transaction or made an agreement within this Act.

(30) "Person" includes an individual or an organization (See Section 1—102).

(31) "Presumption" or "presumed" means that the trier of fact must find the existence of the fact presumed unless and until evidence is introduced which would support a finding of its non-existence.

(32) Purchase" includes taking by sale, discount, negotiation, mortgage, pledge, lien, issue or re-issue, gift or any other voluntary transaction creating an interest in property.

(33) "Purchaser" means a person who takes by purchase.

(34) "Remedy" means any remedial right to which an aggrieved party is entitled with or without resort to a tribunal.

(35) "Representative" includes an agent, an officer of a corporation or association, and a trustee, executor or administrator of an estate, or any other person empowered to act for another.

(36) "Rights" includes remedies.

(37) "Security interest" means an interest in personal property or fixtures which secures payment or performance of an obligation. The term also includes any interest of a consignor and a buyer of accounts, chattel paper, a payment intangible, or a promissory note in a transaction that is subject to Article 9. The special property interest of a buyer of goods on identification of those goods to a contract for sale under Section 2—401 is not a "security interest", but a buyer may also acquire a "security interest" by complying with Article 9. Except as otherwise provided in Section 2—505, the right of a seller or lessor of goods under Article 2 or 2A to retain or acquire possession of the goods is not a "security interest", but a seller or lessor may also acquire a "security interest" by complying with Article 9. The retention or reservation of title by a seller of goods notwithstanding shipment or delivery to the buyer (Section 2—401) is limited in effect to a reservation of a "security interest".

Whether a transaction creates a lease or security interest is determined by the facts of each case; however, a transaction creates a security interest if the consideration the lessee is to pay the lessor for the right to possession and use of the goods is an obligation for the term of the lease not subject to termination by the lessee, and

(a) the original term of the lease is equal to or greater than the remaining economic life of the goods,

(b) the lessee is bound to renew the lease for the remaining economic life of the goods or is bound to become the owner of the goods,

(c) the lessee has an option to renew the lease for the remaining economic life of the goods for no additional consideration or nominal additional consideration upon compliance with the lease agreement, or

(d) the lessee has an option to become the owner of the goods for no additional consideration or nominal additional consideration upon compliance with the lease agreement.

A transaction does not create a security interest merely because it provides that

(a) the present value of the consideration the lessee is obligated to pay the lessor for the right to possession and use of the goods is substantially equal to or is greater than the fair market value of the goods at the time the lease is entered into,

(b) the lessee assumes risk of loss of the goods, or agrees to pay taxes, insurance, filing, recording, or registration fees, or service or maintenance costs with respect to the goods,

(c) the lessee has an option to renew the lease or to become the owner of the goods,

(d) the lessee has an option to renew the lease for a fixed rent that is equal to or greater than the reasonably predictable fair market rent for the use of the goods for the term of the renewal at the time the option is to be performed, or

(e) the lessee has an option to become the owner of the goods for a fixed price that is equal to or greater than the reasonably predictable fair market value of the goods at the time the option is to be performed.

For purposes of this subsection (37):

(x) Additional consideration is not nominal if (i) when the option to renew the lease is granted to the lessee the rent is stated to be the fair market rent for the use of the goods for the term of the renewal determined at the time the option is to be performed, or (ii) when the option to become the owner of the goods is granted to the lessee the price is stated to be the fair market value of the goods determined at the time the option is to be performed. Additional consideration is nominal if it is less than the lessee's reasonably predictable cost of performing under the lease agreement if the option is not exercised;

(y) "Reasonably predictable" and "remaining economic life of the goods" are to be determined with reference to the facts and circumstances at the time the transaction is entered into; and

(z) "Present value" means the amount as of a date certain of one or more sums payable in the future, discounted to the date certain. The discount is determined by the interest rate specified by the parties if the rate is not manifestly unreasonable at the time the transaction is entered into; otherwise, the discount is determined by a commercially reasonable rate that takes into account the facts and circumstances of each case at the time the transaction was entered into.

(38) "Send" in connection with any writing or notice means to deposit in the mail or deliver for transmission by any other usual means of communication with postage or cost of transmission provided for and properly addressed and in the case of an instrument to an address specified thereon or otherwise agreed, or if there be none to any address reasonable under the circumstances. The receipt of any writing or notice within the time at which it would have arrived if properly sent has the effect of a proper sending.

(39) "Signed" includes any symbol executed or adopted by a party with present intention to authenticate a writing.

(40) "Surety" includes guarantor.

(41) "Telegram" includes a message transmitted by radio, teletype, cable, any mechanical method of transmission, or the like.

(42) "Term" means that portion of an agreement which relates to a particular matter.

(43) "Unauthorized" signature means one made without actual, implied or apparent authority and includes a forgery.

(44) "Value". Except as otherwise provided with respect to negotiable instruments and bank collections (Sections 3—303, 4—210 and 4—211) a person gives "value" for rights if he acquires them

(a) in return for a binding commitment to extend credit or for the extension of immediately available credit whether or not drawn upon and whether or not a chargeback is provided for in the event of difficulties in collection; or

(b) as security for or in total or partial satisfaction of a pre-existing claim; or

(c) by accepting delivery pursuant to a preexisting contract for purchase; or

(d) generally, in return for any consideration sufficient to support a simple contract.

(45) "Warehouse receipt" means a receipt issued by a person engaged in the business of storing goods for hire.

(46) "Written" or "writing" includes printing, typewriting or any other intentional reduction to tangible form.

§1—202. PRIMA FACIE EVIDENCE BY THIRD PARTY DOCUMENTS

A document in due form purporting to be a bill of lading, policy or certificate of insurance, official weigher's or inspector's certificate, consular invoice, or any other document authorized or required by the contract to be issued by a third party shall be prima facie evidence of its own authenticity and genuineness and of the facts stated in the document by the third party.

§1—203. OBLIGATION OF GOOD FAITH

Every contract or duty within this Act imposes an obligation of good faith in its performance or enforcement.

§1—204. TIME; REASONABLE TIME; "SEASONABLY"

(1) Whenever this Act requires any action to be taken within a reasonable time, any time which is not manifestly unreasonable may be fixed by agreement.

(2) What is a reasonable time for taking any action depends on the nature, purpose and circumstances of such action.

(3) An action is taken "seasonably" when it is taken at or within the time agreed or if no time is agreed at or within a reasonable time.

§1—205. COURSE OF DEALING AND USAGE OF TRADE

(1) A course of dealing is a sequence of previous conduct between the parties to a particular transaction which is fairly to be regarded as establishing a common basis of understanding for interpreting their expressions and other conduct.

(2) A usage of trade is any practice or method of dealing having such regularity of observance in a place, vocation or trade as to justify an expectation that it will be

observed with respect to the transaction in question. The existence and scope of such a usage are to be proved as facts. If it is established that such a usage is embodied in a written trade code or similar writing the interpretation of the writing is for the court.

(3) A course of dealing between parties and any usage of trade in the vocation or trade in which they are engaged or of which they are or should be aware give particular meaning to and supplement or qualify terms of an agreement.

(4) The express terms of an agreement and an applicable course of dealing or usage of trade shall be construed wherever reasonable as consistent with each other; but when such construction is unreasonable express terms control both course of dealing and usage of trade and course of dealing controls usage trade.

(5) An applicable usage of trade in the place where any part of performance is to occur shall be used in interpreting the agreement as to that part of the performance.

(6) Evidence of a relevant usage of trade offered by one party is not admissible unless and until he has given the other party such notice as the court finds sufficient to prevent unfair surprise to the latter.

§1—206. STATUTE OF FRAUDS FOR KINDS OF PERSONAL PROPERTY NOT OTHERWISE COVERED

(1) Except in the cases described in subsection (2) of this section a contract for the sale of personal property is not enforceable by way of action or defense beyond five thousand dollars in amount or value of remedy unless there is some writing which indicates that a contract for sale has been made between the parties at a defined or stated price, reasonably identifies the subject matter, and is signed by the party against whom enforcement is sought or by his authorized agent.

(2) Subsection (1) of this section does not apply to contracts for the sale of goods (Section 2—201) nor of securities (Section 8—113) nor to security agreements (Section 9—203).

As amended in 1994.

§1—207. PERFORMANCE OR ACCEPTANCE UNDER RESERVATION OF RIGHTS

(1) A party who with explicit reservation of rights performs or promises performance or assents to performance in a manner demanded or offered by the other party does not thereby prejudice the rights reserved. Such words as "without prejudice", "under protest" or the like are sufficient.

(2) Subsection (1) does not apply to an accord and satisfaction.

As amended in 1990.

§1—208. OPTION TO ACCELERATE AT WILL

A term providing that one party or his successor in interest may accelerate payment or performance or require collateral or additional collateral "at will" or "when he deems himself insecure" or in words of similar import shall be construed to mean that he shall have power to do so only if he in good faith believes that the prospect of payment or performance is impaired. The burden of establishing lack of good faith is on the party against whom the power has been exercised.

§1—209. SUBORDINATED OBLIGATIONS

An obligation may be issued as subordinated to payment of another obligation of the person obligated, or a creditor may subordinate his right to payment of an obligation by agreement with either the person obligated or another creditor of the person obligated. Such a subordination does not create a security interest as against either the common debtor or a subordinated creditor. This section shall be construed as declaring the law as it existed prior to the enactment of this section and not as modifying it.

Added 1966.

Note: *This new section is proposed as an optional provision to make it clear that a subordination agreement does not create a security interest unless so intended.*

ARTICLE 2 SALES

Part 1 Short Title, General Construction and Subject Matter

§2—101. SHORT TITLE

This Article shall be known and may be cited as Uniform Commercial Code—Sales.

§2—102. SCOPE; CERTAIN SECURITY AND OTHER TRANSACTIONS EXCLUDED FROM THIS ARTICLE

Unless the context otherwise requires, this Article applies to transactions in goods; it does not apply to any transaction which although in the form of an unconditional contract to sell or present sale is intended to operate only as a security transaction nor does this Article impair or repeal any statute regulating sales to consumers, farmers or other specified classes of buyers.

§2—103. DEFINITIONS AND INDEX OF DEFINITIONS

(1) In this Article unless the context otherwise requires
    (a) "Buyer" means a person who buys or contracts to buy goods.
    (b) "Good faith" in the case of a merchant means honesty in fact and the observance of reasonable commercial standards of fair dealing in the trade.

(c) "Receipt" of goods means taking physical possession of them.

(d) "Seller" means a person who sells or contracts to sell goods.

(2) Other definitions applying to this Article or to specified Parts thereof, and the sections in which they appear are:

"Acceptance". Section 2—606.
"Banker's credit". Section 2—325.
"Between merchants". Section 2—104.
"Cancellation". Section 2—106(4).
"Commercial unit". Section 2—105.
"Confirmed credit". Section 2—325.
"Conforming to contract". Section 2—106.
"Contract for sale". Section 2—106.
"Cover". Section 2—712.
"Entrusting". Section 2—403.
"Financing agency". Section 2—104.
"Future goods". Section 2—105.
"Goods". Section 2—105.
"Identification". Section 2—501.
"Installment contract". Section 2—612.
"Letter of Credit". Section 2—325.
"Lot". Section 2—105.
"Merchant". Section 2—104.
"Overseas". Section 2—323.
"Person in position of seller". Section 2—707.
"Present sale". Section 2—106.
"Sale". Section 2—106.
"Sale on approval". Section 2—326.
"Sale or return". Section 2—326.
"Termination". Section 2—106.

(3) The following definitions in other Articles apply to this Article:

"Check". Section 3—104.
"Consignee". Section 7—102.
"Consignor". Section 7—102.
"Consumer goods". Section 9—109.
"Dishonor". Section 3—507.
"Draft". Section 3—104.

(4) In addition Article 1 contains general definitions and principles of construction and interpretation applicable throughout this Article.

As amended in 1994 and 1999.

§2—104. DEFINITIONS: "MERCHANT"; "BETWEEN MERCHANTS"; "FINANCING AGENCY"

(1) "Merchant" means a person who deals in goods of the kind or otherwise by his occupation holds himself out as having knowledge or skill peculiar to the practices or goods involved in the transaction or to whom such knowledge or skill may be attributed by his employment of an agent or broker or other intermediary who by his occupation holds himself out as having such knowledge or skill.

(2) "Financing agency" means a bank, finance company or other person who in the ordinary course of business makes advances against goods or documents of title or who by arrangement with either the seller or the buyer intervenes in ordinary course to make or collect payment due or claimed under the contract for sale, as by purchasing or paying the seller's draft or making advances against it or by merely taking it for collection whether or not documents of title accompany the draft. "Financing agency" includes also a bank or other person who similarly intervenes between persons who are in the position of seller and buyer in respect to the goods (Section 2—707).

(3) "Between merchants" means in any transaction with respect to which both parties are chargeable with the knowledge or skill of merchants.

§2—105. DEFINITIONS: TRANSFERABILITY; "GOODS"; "FUTURE" GOODS; "LOT"; "COMMERCIAL UNIT"

(1) "Goods" means all things (including specially manufactured goods) which are movable at the time of identification to the contract for sale other than the money in which the price is to be paid, investment securities (Article 8) and things in action. "Goods" also includes the unborn young of animals and growing crops and other identified things attached to realty as described in the section on goods to be severed from realty (Section 2—107).

(2) Goods must be both existing and identified before any interest in them can pass. Goods which are not both existing and identified are "future" goods. A purported present sale of future goods or of any interest therein operates as a contract to sell.

(3) There may be a sale of a part interest in existing identified goods.

(4) An undivided share in an identified bulk of fungible goods is sufficiently identified to be sold although the quantity of the bulk is not determined. Any agreed proportion of such a bulk or any quantity thereof agreed upon by number, weight or other measure may to the extent of the seller's interest in the bulk be sold to the buyer who then becomes an owner in common.

(5) "Lot" means a parcel or a single article which is the subject matter of a separate sale or delivery, whether or not it is sufficient to perform the contract.

(6) "Commercial unit" means such a unit of goods as by commercial usage is a single whole for purposes of sale and division of which materially impairs its character or value on the market or in use. A commercial unit may be a single article (as a machine) or a set of articles (as a suite of furniture or an assortment of sizes) or a quantity (as a bale, gross, or carload) or any other unit treated in use or in the relevant market as a single whole.

§2—106. DEFINITIONS: "CONTRACT"; "AGREEMENT"; "CONTRACT FOR SALE"; "SALE"; "PRESENT SALE"; "CONFORMING TO CONTRACT; "TERMINATION"; "CANCELLATION"

(1) In this Article unless the context otherwise requires "contract" and "agreement" are limited to those relating to the present or future sale of goods. "Contract for sale" includes both a present sale of goods and a contract to sell goods at a future time. A "sale" consists in the passing of title from the seller to the buyer for a price (Section 2—401). A "present sale" means a sale which is accomplished by the making of the contract.

(2) Goods or conduct including any part of a performance are "conforming" or conform to the contract when they are in accordance with the obligations under the contract.

(3) "Termination" occurs when either party pursuant to a power created by agreement or law puts an end to the contract otherwise than for its breach. On "termination" all obligations which are still executory on both sides are discharged but any right based on prior breach or performance survives.

(4) "Cancellation" occurs when either party puts an end to the contract for breach by the other and its effect is the same as that of "termination" except that the cancelling party also retains any remedy for breach of the whole contract or any unperformed balance.

§2—107. GOODS TO BE SEVERED FROM REALTY: RECORDING

(1) A contract for the sale of minerals or the like (including oil and gas) or a structure or its materials to be removed from realty is a contract for the sale of goods within this Article if they are to be severed by the seller but until severance a purported present sale thereof which is not effective as a transfer of an interest in land is effective only as a contract to sell.

(2) A contract for the sale apart from the land of growing crops or other things attached to realty and capable of severance without material harm thereto but not described in subsection (1) or of timber to be cut is a contract for the sale of goods within this Article whether the subject matter is to be severed by the buyer or by the seller even though it forms part of the realty at the time of contracting, and the parties can by identification effect a present sale before severance.

(3) The provisions of this section are subject to any third party rights provided by the law relating to realty records, and the contract for sale may be executed and recorded as a document transferring an interest in land and shall then constitute notice to third parties of the buyer's rights under the contract for sale.

As amended in 1972.

Part 2 Form, Formation and Readjustment of Contract

§2—201. FORMAL REQUIREMENTS; STATUTE OF FRAUDS

(1) Except as otherwise provided in this section a contract for the sale of goods for the price of $500 or more is not enforceable by way of action or defense unless there is some writing sufficient to indicate that a contract for sale has been made between the parties and signed by the party against whom enforcement is sought or by his authorized agent or broker. A writing is not insufficient because it omits or incorrectly states a term agreed upon but the contract is not enforceable under this paragraph beyond the quantity of goods shown in such writing.

(2) Between merchants if within a reasonable time a writing in confirmation of the contract and sufficient against the sender is received and the party receiving it has reason to know its contents, its satisfies the requirements of subsection (1) against such party unless written notice of objection to its contents is given within ten days after it is received.

(3) A contract which does not satisfy the requirements of subsection (1) but which is valid in other respects is enforceable

(a) if the goods are to be specially manufactured for the buyer and are not suitable for sale to others in the ordinary course of the seller's business and the seller, before notice of repudiation is received and under circumstances which reasonably indicate that the goods are for the buyer, has made either a substantial beginning of their manufacture or commitments for their procurement; or

(b) if the party against whom enforcement is sought admits in his pleading, testimony or otherwise in court that a contract for sale was made, but the contract is not enforceable under this provision beyond the quantity of goods admitted; or

(c) with respect to goods for which payment has been made and accepted or which have been received and accepted (Sec. 2—606).

§2—202. FINAL WRITTEN EXPRESSION: PAROL OR EXTRINSIC EVIDENCE

Terms with respect to which the confirmatory memoranda of the parties agree or which are otherwise set forth in a writing intended by the parties as a final expression of their agreement with respect to such terms as are included therein may not be contradicted by evidence of any prior agreement or of a contemporaneous oral agreement but may be explained or supplemented

(a) by course of dealing or usage of trade (Section 1—205) or by course of performance (Section 2—208); and

(b) by evidence of consistent additional terms unless the court finds the writing to have been intended also as a complete and exclusive statement of the terms of the agreement.

§2—203. SEALS INOPERATIVE

The affixing of a seal to a writing evidencing a contract for sale or an offer to buy or sell goods does not constitute the writing a sealed instrument and the law with respect to sealed instruments does not apply to such a contract or offer.

§2—204. FORMATION IN GENERAL

(1) A contract for sale of goods may be made in any manner sufficient to show agreement, including conduct by both parties which recognizes the existence of such a contract.

(2) An agreement sufficient to constitute a contract for sale may be found even though the moment of its making is undetermined.

(3) Even though one or more terms are left open a contract for sale does not fail for indefiniteness if the parties have intended to make a contract and there is a reasonably certain basis for giving an appropriate remedy.

§2—205. FIRM OFFERS

An offer by a merchant to buy or sell goods in a signed writing which by its terms gives assurance that it will be held open is not revocable, for lack of consideration, during the time stated or if no time is stated for a reasonable time, but in no event may such period of irrevocability exceed three months; but any such term of assurance on a form supplied by the offeree must be separately signed by the offeror.

§2—206. OFFER AND ACCEPTANCE IN FORMATION OF CONTRACT

(1) Unless other unambiguously indicated by the language or circumstances

(a) an offer to make a contract shall be construed as inviting acceptance in any manner and by any medium reasonable in the circumstances;

(b) an order or other offer to buy goods for prompt or current shipment shall be construed as inviting acceptance either by a prompt promise to ship or by the prompt or current shipment of conforming or nonconforming goods, but such a shipment of non-conforming goods does not constitute an acceptance if the seller seasonably notifies the buyer that the shipment is offered only as an accommodation to the buyer.

(2) Where the beginning of a requested performance is a reasonable mode of acceptance an offeror who is not notified of acceptance within a reasonable time may treat the offer as having lapsed before acceptance.

§2—207. ADDITIONAL TERMS IN ACCEPTANCE OR CONFIRMATION

(1) A definite and seasonable expression of acceptance or a written confirmation which is sent within a reasonable time operates as an acceptance even though it states terms additional to or different from those offered or agreed upon, unless acceptance is expressly made conditional on assent to the additional or different terms.

(2) The additional terms are to be construed as proposals for addition to the contract. Between merchants such terms become part of the contract unless:

(a) the offer expressly limits acceptance to the terms of the offer;

(b) they materially alter it; or

(c) notification of objection to them has already been given or is given within a reasonable time after notice of them is received.

(3) Conduct by both parties which recognizes the existence of a contract is sufficient to establish a contract for sale although the writings of the parties do not otherwise establish a contract. In such case the terms of the particular contract consist of those terms on which the writings of the parties agree, together with any supplementary terms incorporated under any other provisions of this Act.

§2—208. COURSE OF PERFORMANCE OR PRACTICAL CONSTRUCTION

(1) Where the contract for sale involves repeated occasions for performance by either party with knowledge of the nature of the performance and opportunity for objection to it by the other, any course of performance accepted or acquiesced in without objection shall be relevant to determine the meaning of the agreement.

(2) The express terms of the agreement and any such course of performance, as well as any course of dealing and usage of trade, shall be construed whenever reasonable as consistent with each other; but when such construction is unreasonable, express terms shall control course of performance and course of performance shall control both course of dealing and usage of trade (Section 1—205).

(3) Subject to the provisions of the next section on modification and waiver, such course of performance shall be relevant to show a waiver or modification of any term inconsistent with such course of performance.

§2—209. MODIFICATION, RESCISSION AND WAIVER

(1) An agreement modifying a contract within this Article needs no consideration to be binding.

(2) A signed agreement which excludes modification or rescission except by a signed writing cannot be otherwise modified or rescinded, but except as between merchants such a requirement on a form supplied by the merchant must be separately signed by the other party.

(3) The requirements of the statute of frauds section of this Article (Section 2—201) must be satisfied if the contract as modified is within its provisions.

(4) Although an attempt at modification or rescission does not satisfy the requirements of subsection (2) or (3) it can operate as a waiver.

(5) A party who has made a waiver affecting an executory portion of the contract may retract the waiver by reasonable notification received by the other party that strict performance will be required of any term waived, unless the retraction would be unjust in view of a material change of position in reliance on the waiver.

§2—210. DELEGATION OF PERFORMANCE; ASSIGNMENT OF RIGHTS

(1) A party may perform his duty through a delegate unless otherwise agreed or unless the other party has a substantial interest in having his original promisor perform or control the acts required by the contract. No delegation of performance relieves the party delegating of any duty to perform or any liability for breach.

(2) Except as otherwise provided in Section 9—406, unless otherwise agreed, all rights of either seller or buyer can be assigned except where the assignment would materially change the duty of the other party, or increase materially the burden or risk imposed on him by his contract, or impair materially his chance of obtaining return performance. A right to damages for breach of the whole contract or a right arising out of the assignor's due performance of his entire obligation can be assigned despite agreement otherwise.

(3) The creation, attachment, perfection, or enforcement of a security interest in the seller's interest under a contract is not a transfer that materially changes the duty of or increases materially the burden or risk imposed on the buyer or impairs materially the buyer's chance of obtaining return performance within the purview of subsection (2) unless, and then only to the extent that, enforcement actually results in a delegation of material performance of the seller. Even in that event, the creation, attachment, perfection, and enforcement of the security interest remain effective, but (i) the seller is liable to the buyer for damages caused by the delegation to the extent that the damages could not reasonably by prevented by the buyer, and (ii) a court having jurisdiction may grant other appropriate relief, including cancellation of the contract for sale or an injunction against enforcement of the security interest or consummation of the enforcement.

(4) Unless the circumstnaces indicate the contrary a prohibition of assignment of "the contract" is to be construed as barring only the delegation to the assignees of the assignor's performance.

(5) An assignment of "the contract" or of "all my rights under the contract" or an assignment in similar general terms is an assignment of rights and unless the language or the circumstances (as in an assignment for security) indicate the contrary, it is a delegation of performance of the duties of the assignor and its acceptance by the assignee constitutes a promise by him to perform those duties. This promise is enforceable by either the assignor or the other party to the original contract.

(6) The other party may treat any assignment which delegates performance as creating reasonable grounds for insecurity and may without prejudice to his rights against the assignor demand assurances from the assignee (Section 2—609).

As amended in 1999.

Part 3 General Obligation and Construction of Contract

§2—301. GENERAL OBLIGATIONS OF PARTIES

The obligation of the seller is to transfer and deliver and that of the buyer is to accept and pay in accordance with the contract.

§2—302. UNCONSCIONABLE CONTRACT OR CLAUSE

(1) If the court as a matter of law finds the contract or any clause of the contract to have been unconscionable at the time it was made the court may refuse to enforce the contract, or it may enforce the remainder of the contract without the unconscionable clause, or it may so limit the application of any unconscionable clause as to avoid any unconscionable result.

(2) When it is claimed or appears to the court that the contract or any clause thereof may be unconscionable the parties shall be afforded a reasonable opportunity to present evidence as to its commercial setting, purpose and effect to aid the court in making the determination.

§2—303. ALLOCATIONS OR DIVISION OF RISKS

Where this Article allocates a risk or a burden as between the parties "unless otherwise agreed", the agreement may not only shift the allocation but may also divide the risk or burden.

§2—304. PRICE PAYABLE IN MONEY, GOODS, REALTY, OR OTHERWISE

(1) The price can be made payable in money or otherwise. If it is payable in whole or in part in goods each party is a seller of the goods which he is to transfer.

(2) Even though all or part of the price is payable in an interest in realty the transfer of the goods and the seller's obligations with reference to them are subject to this Article, but not the transfer of the interest in realty or the transferor's obligations in connection therewith.

§2—305. OPEN PRICE TERM

(1) The parties if they so intend can conclude a contract for sale even though the price is not settled. In such a case the price is a reasonable price at the time for delivery if

(a) nothing is said as to price; or

(b) the price is left to be agreed by the parties and they fail to agree; or

(c) the price is to be fixed in terms of some agreed market or other standard as set or recorded by a third person or agency and it is not so set or recorded.

(2) A price to be fixed by the seller or by the buyer means a price for him to fix in good faith.

(3) When a price left to be fixed otherwise than by agreement of the parties fails to be fixed through fault of one party the other may at his option treat the contract as cancelled or himself fix a reasonable price.

(4) Where, however, the parties intend not to be bound unless the price be fixed or agreed and it is not fixed or agreed there is no contract. In such a case the buyer must return any goods already received or if unable so to do must pay their reasonable value at the time of delivery and the seller must return any portion of the price paid on account.

§2—306. OUTPUT, REQUIREMENTS AND EXCLUSIVE DEALINGS

(1) A term which measures the quantity by the output of the seller or the requirements of the buyer means such actual output or requirements as may occur in good faith, except that no quantity unreasonably disproportionate to any stated estimate or in the absence of a stated estimate to any normal or otherwise comparable prior output or requirements may be tendered or demanded.

(2) A lawful agreement by either the seller or the buyer for exclusive dealing in the kind of goods concerned imposes unless otherwise agreed an obligation by the seller to use best efforts to supply the goods and by the buyer to use best efforts to promote their sale.

§2—307. DELIVERY IN SINGLE LOT OR SEVERAL LOTS

Unless otherwise agreed all goods called for by a contract for sale must be tendered in a single delivery and payment is due only on such tender but where the circumstances give either party the right to make or demand delivery in lots the price if it can be apportioned may be demanded for each lot.

§2—308. ABSENCE OF SPECIFIED PLACE FOR DELIVERY

Unless otherwise agreed

(a) the place for delivery of goods is the seller's place of business or if he has none his residence; but

(b) in a contract for sale of identified goods which to the knowledge of the parties at the time of contracting are in some other place, that place is the place for their delivery; and

(c) documents of title may be delivered through customary banking channels.

§2—309. ABSENCE OF SPECIFIC TIME PROVISIONS; NOTICE OF TERMINATION

(1) The time for shipment or delivery or any other action under a contract if not provided in this Article or agreed upon shall be a reasonable time.

(2) Where the contract provides for successive performances but is indefinite in duration it is valid for a reasonable time but unless otherwise agreed may be terminated at any time by either party.

(3) Termination of a contract by one party except on the happening of an agreed event requires that reasonable notification be received by the other party and an agreement dispensing with notification is invalid if its operation would be unconscionable.

§2—310. OPEN TIME FOR PAYMENT OR RUNNING OF CREDIT; AUTHORITY TO SHIP UNDER RESERVATION

Unless otherwise agreed

(a) payment is due at the time and place at which the buyer is to receive the goods even though the place of shipment is the place of delivery; and

(b) if the seller is authorized to send the goods he may ship them under reservation, and may tender the documents of title, but the buyer may inspect the goods after their arrival before payment is due unless such inspection is inconsistent with the terms of the contract (Section 2—513); and

(c) if delivery is authorized and made by way of documents of title otherwise than by subsection (b) then payment is due at the time and place at which the buyer is to receive the documents regardless of where the goods are to be received; and

(d) where the seller is required or authorized to ship the goods on credit the credit period runs from the time of shipment but post-dating the invoice or delaying its dispatch will correspondingly delay the starting of the credit period.

§2—311. OPTIONS AND COOPERATION RESPECTING PERFORMANCE

(1) An agreement for sale which is otherwise sufficiently definite (subsection (3) of Section 2—204) to be a contract is not made invalid by the fact that it leaves particulars of performance to be specified by one of the parties. Any such specification must be made in good faith and within limits set by commercial reasonableness.

(2) Unless otherwise agreed specifications relating to assortment of the goods are at the buyer's option and except as otherwise provided in subsections (1)(c) and (3) of Section 2—319 specifications or arrangements relating to shipment are at the seller's option.

(3) Where such specification would materially affect the other party's performance but is not seasonably made or where one party's cooperation is necessary to the agreed performance of the other but is not seasonably forthcoming, the other party in addition to all other remedies

    (a) is excused for any resulting delay in his own performance; and

    (b) may also either proceed to perform in any reasonable manner or after the time for a material part of his own performance treat the failure to specify or to cooperate as a breach by failure to deliver or accept the goods.

§2—312. WARRANTY OF TITLE AND AGAINST INFRINGEMENT; BUYER'S OBLIGATION AGAINST INFRINGEMENT

(1) Subject to subsection (2) there is in a contract for sale a warranty by the seller that

    (a) the title conveyed shall be good, and its transfer rightful; and

    (b) the goods shall be delivered free from any security interest or other lien or encumbrance of which the buyer at the time of contracting has no knowledge.

(2) A warranty under subsection (1) will be excluded or modified only by specific language or by circumstances which give the buyer reason to know that the person selling does not claim title in himself or that he is purporting to sell only such right or title as he or a third person may have.

(3) Unless otherwise agreed a seller who is a merchant regularly dealing in goods of the kind warrants that the goods shall be delivered free of the rightful claim of any third person by way of infringement or the like but a buyer who furnishes specifications to the seller must hold the seller harmless against any such claim which arises out of compliance with the specifications.

§2—313. EXPRESS WARRANTIES BY AFFIRMATION, PROMISE, DESCRIPTION, SAMPLE

(1) Express warranties by the seller are created as follows:

    (a) Any affirmation of fact or promise made by the seller to the buyer which relates to the goods and becomes part of the basis of the bargain creates an express warranty that the goods shall conform to the affirmation or promise.

    (b) Any description of the goods which is made part of the basis of the bargain creates an express warranty that the goods shall conform to the description.

    (c) Any sample or model which is made part of the basis of the bargain creates an express warranty that the whole of the goods shall conform to the sample or model.

(2) It is not necessary to the creation of an express warranty that the seller use formal words such as "warrant" or "guarantee" or that he have a specific intention to make a warranty, but an affirmation merely of the value of the goods or a statement purporting to be merely the seller's opinion or commendation of the goods does not create a warranty.

§2—314. IMPLIED WARRANTY: MERCHANTABILITY; USAGE OF TRADE

(1) Unless excluded or modified (Section 2—316), a warranty that the goods shall be merchantable is implied in a contract for their sale if the seller is a merchant with respect to goods of that kind. Under this section the serving for value of food or drink to be consumed either on the premises or elsewhere is a sale.

(2) Goods to be merchantable must be at least such as

    (a) pass without objection in the trade under the contract description; and

    (b) in the case of fungible goods, are of fair average quality within the description; and

    (c) are fit for the ordinary purposes for which such goods are used; and

    (d) run, within the variations permitted by the agreement, of even kind, quality and quantity within each unit and among all units involved; and

    (e) are adequately contained, packaged, and labeled as the agreement may require; and

    (f) conform to the promises or affirmations of fact made on the container or label if any.

(3) Unless excluded or modified (Section 2—316) other implied warranties may arise from course of dealing or usage of trade.

§2—315. IMPLIED WARRANTY: FITNESS FOR PARTICULAR PURPOSE

Where the seller at the time of contracting has reason to know any particular purpose for which the goods are required and that the buyer is relying on the seller's skill or judgment to select or furnish suitable goods, there is unless excluded or modified under the next section an implied warranty that the goods shall be fit for such purpose.

§2—316. EXCLUSION OR MODIFICATION OF WARRANTIES

(1) Words or conduct relevant to the creation of an express warranty and words or conduct tending to negate or limit warranty shall be construed wherever reasonable as consistent with each other; but subject to the provisions of this Article on parol or extrinsic evidence (Section 2—202) negation or limitation is inoperative to the extent that such construction is unreasonable.

(2) Subject to subsection (3), to exclude or modify the implied warranty of merchantability or any part of it the language must mention merchantability and in case of a writing must be conspicuous, and to exclude or modify any implied warranty of fitness the exclusion must be by a writing and conspicuous. Language to exclude all implied warranties of fitness is sufficient if it states, for example, that "There are no warranties which extend beyond the description on the face hereof."

(3) Notwithstanding subsection (2)

(a) unless the circumstances indicate otherwise, all implied warranties are excluded by expressions like "as is", "with all faults" or other language which in common understanding calls the buyer's attention to the exclusion of warranties and makes plain that there is no implied warranty; and

(b) when the buyer before entering into the contract has examined the goods or the sample or model as fully as he desired or has refused to examine the goods there is no implied warranty with regard to defects which an examination ought in the circumstances to have revealed to him; and

(c) an implied warranty can also be excluded or modified by course of dealing or course of performance or usage of trade.

(4) Remedies for breach of warranty can be limited in accordance with the provisions of this Article on liquidation or limitation of damages and on contractual modification of remedy (Sections 2—718 and 2—719).

§2—317. CUMULATION AND CONFLICT OF WARRANTIES EXPRESS OR IMPLIED

Warranties whether express or implied shall be construed as consistent with each other and as cumulative, but if such construction is unreasonable the intention of the parties shall determine which warranty is dominant. In ascertaining that intention the following rules apply:

(a) Exact or technical specifications displace an inconsistent sample or model or general language of description.

(b) A sample from an existing bulk displaces inconsistent general language of description.

(c) Express warranties displace inconsistent implied warranties other than an implied warranty of fitness for a particular purpose.

§2—318. THIRD PARTY BENEFICIARIES OF WARRANTIES EXPRESS OR IMPLIED

Note: If this Act is introduced in the Congress of the United States this section should be omitted. (States to select one alternative.)

Alternative A

A seller's warranty whether express or implied extends to any natural person who is in the family or household of his buyer or who is a guest in his home if it is reasonable to expect that such person may use, consume or be affected by the goods and who is injured in person by breach of the warranty. A seller may not exclude or limit the operation of this section.

Alternative B

A seller's warranty whether express or implied extends to any natural person who may reasonably be expected to use, consume or be affected by the goods and who is injured in person by breach of the warranty. A seller may not exclude or limit the operation of this section.

Alternative C

A seller's warranty whether express or implied extends to any person who may reasonably be expected to use, consume or be affected by the goods and who is injured by breach of the warranty. A seller may not exclude or limit the operation of this section with respect to injury to the person of an individual to whom the warranty extends.

As amended 1966.

§2—319. F.O.B. AND F.A.S. TERMS

(1) Unless otherwise agreed the term F.O.B. (which means "free on board") at a named place, even though used only in connection with the stated price, is a delivery term under which

(a) when the term is F.O.B. the place of shipment, the seller must at that place ship the goods in the manner provided in this Article (Section 2—504) and bear the expense and risk of putting them into the possession of the carrier; or

(b) when the term is F.O.B. the place of destination, the seller must at his own expense and risk transport the goods to that place and there tender delivery of them in the manner provided in this Article (Section 2—503);

    (c) when under either (a) or (b) the term is also F.O.B. vessel, car or other vehicle, the seller must in addition at his own expense and risk load the goods on board. If the term is F.O.B. vessel the buyer must name the vessel and in an appropriate case the seller must comply with the provisions of this Article on the form of bill of lading (Section 2—323).

(2) Unless otherwise agreed the term F.A.S. vessel (which means "free alongside") at a named port, even though used only in connection with the stated price, is a delivery term under which the seller must

    (a) at his own expense and risk deliver the goods alongside the vessel in the manner usual in that port or on a dock designated and provided by the buyer; and

    (b) obtain and tender a receipt for the goods in exchange for which the carrier is under a duty to issue a bill of lading.

(3) Unless otherwise agreed in any case falling within subsection (1)(a) or (c) or subsection (2) the buyer must seasonably give any needed instructions for making delivery, including when the term is F.A.S. or F.O.B. the loading berth of the vessel and in an appropriate case its name and sailing date. The seller may treat the failure of needed instructions as a failure of cooperation under this Article (Section 2—311). He may also at his option move the goods in any reasonable manner preparatory to delivery or shipment.

(4) Under the term F.O.B. vessel or F.A.S. unless otherwise agreed the buyer must make payment against tender of the required documents and the seller may not tender nor the buyer demand delivery of the goods in substitution for the documents.

§2—320. C.I.F. AND C. & F. TERMS

(1) The term C.I.F. means that the price includes in a lump sum the cost of the goods and the insurance and freight to the named destination. The term C. & F. or C.F. means that the price so includes cost and freight to the named destination.

(2) Unless otherwise agreed and even though used only in connection with the stated price and destination, the term C.I.F. destination or its equivalent requires the seller at his own expense and risk to

    (a) put the goods into the possession of a carrier at the port for shipment and obtain a negotiable bill or bills of lading covering the entire transportation to the named destination; and

    (b) load the goods and obtain a receipt from the carrier (which may be contained in the bill of lading) showing that the freight has been paid or provided for; and

    (c) obtain a policy or certificate of insurance, including any war risk insurance, of a kind and on terms then current at the port of shipment in the usual amount, in the currency of the contract, shown to cover the same goods covered by the bill of lading and providing for payment of loss to the order of the buyer or for the account of whom it may concern; but the seller may add to the price the amount of the premium for any such war risk insurance; and

    (d) prepare an invoice of the goods and procure any other documents required to effect shipment or to comply with the contract; and

    (e) forward and tender with commercial promptness all the documents in due form and with any indorsement necessary to perfect the buyer's rights.

(3) Unless otherwise agreed the term C. & F. or its equivalent has the same effect and imposes upon the seller the same obligations and risks as a C.I.F. term except the obligation as to insurance.

(4) Under the term C.I.F. or C. & F. unless otherwise agreed the buyer must make payment against tender of the required documents and the seller may not tender nor the buyer demand delivery of the goods in substitution for the documents.

§2—321. C.I.F. OR C. & F.: "NET LANDED WEIGHTS"; "PAYMENT ON ARRIVAL"; WARRANTY OF CONDITION ON ARRIVAL

Under a contract containing a term C.I.F. or C.& F.

(1) Where the price is based on or is to be adjusted according to "net landed weights", "delivered weights", "out turn" quantity or quality or the like, unless otherwise agreed the seller must reasonably estimate the price. The payment due on tender of the documents called for by the contract is the amount so estimated, but after final adjustment of the price a settlement must be made with commercial promptness.

(2) An agreement described in subsection (1) or any warranty of quality or condition of the goods on arrival places upon the seller the risk of ordinary deterioration, shrinkage and the like in transportation but has no effect on the place or time of identification to the contract for sale or delivery or on the passing of the risk of loss.

(3) Unless otherwise agreed where the contract provides for payment on or after arrival of the goods the seller must before payment allow such preliminary inspection as is feasible; but if the goods are lost delivery of the documents and payment are due when the goods should have arrived.

§2—322. DELIVERY "EX-SHIP"

(1) Unless otherwise agreed a term for delivery of goods "ex-ship" (which means from the carrying vessel) or in equivalent language is not restricted to a particular ship and requires delivery from a ship which has reached a place at the named port of destination where goods of the kind are usually discharged.

    (2) Under such a term unless otherwise agreed
        (a) the seller must discharge all liens arising out of the carriage and furnish the buyer with a direction which puts the carrier under a duty to deliver the goods; and
        (b) the risk of loss does not pass to the buyer until the goods leave the ship's tackle or are otherwise properly unloaded.

§2—323. FORM OF BILL OF LADING REQUIRED IN OVERSEAS SHIPMENT; "OVERSEAS"

(1) Where the contract contemplates overseas shipment and contains a term C.I.F. or C. & F. or F.O.B. vessel, the seller unless otherwise agreed must obtain a negotiable bill of lading stating that the goods have been loaded on board or, in the case of a term C.I.F. or C. & F., received for shipment.

    (2) Where in a case within subsection (1) a bill of lading has been issued in a set of parts, unless otherwise agreed if the documents are not to be sent from abroad the buyer may demand tender of the full set; otherwise only one part of the bill of lading need be tendered. Even if the agreement expressly requires a full set
        (a) due tender of a single part is acceptable within the provisions of this Article on cure of improper delivery (subsection (1) of Section 2—508); and
        (b) even though the full set is demanded, if the documents are sent from abroad the person tendering an incomplete set may nevertheless require payment upon furnishing an indemnity which the buyer in good faith deems adequate.

    (3) A shipment by water or by air or a contract contemplating such shipment is "overseas" insofar as by usage of trade or agreement it is subject to the commercial, financing or shipping practices characteristic of international deep water commerce.

§2—324. "NO ARRIVAL, NO SALE" TERM

Under a term "no arrival, no sale" or terms of like meaning, unless otherwise agreed,

(a) the seller must properly ship conforming goods and if they arrive by any means he must tender them on arrival but he assumes no obligation that the goods will arrive unless he has caused the non-arrival; and

(b) where without fault of the seller the goods are in part lost or have so deteriorated as no longer to conform to the contract or arrive after the contract time, the buyer may proceed as if there had been casualty to identified goods (Section 2—613).

§2—325. "LETTER OF CREDIT" TERM; "CONFIRMED CREDIT"

(1) Failure of the buyer seasonably to furnish an agreed letter of credit is a breach of the contract for sale.

    (2) The delivery to seller of a proper letter of credit suspends the buyer's obligation to pay. If the letter of credit is dishonored, the seller may on seasonable notification to the buyer require payment directly from him.

    (3) Unless otherwise agreed the term "letter of credit" or "banker's credit" in a contract for sale means an irrevocable credit issued by a financing agency of good repute and, where the shipment is overseas, of good international repute. The term "confirmed credit" means that the credit must also carry the direct obligation of such an agency which does business in the seller's financial market.

§2—326. SALE ON APPROVAL AND SALE OR RETURN; RIGHTS OF CREDITORS

(1) Unless otherwise agreed, if delivered goods may be returned by the buyer even though they conform to the contract, the transaction is
        (a) a "sale on approval" if the goods are delivered primarily for use, and
        (b) a "sale or return" if the goods are delivered primarily for resale.

    (2) Goods held on approval are not subject to the claims of the buyer's creditors until acceptance; goods held on sale or return are subject to such claims while in the buyer's possession.

    (3) Any "or return" term of a contract for sale is to be treated as a separate contract for sale within the statute of frauds section of this Article (Section 2—201) and as contradicting the sale aspect of the contract within the provisions of this Article or on parol or extrinsic evidence (Section 2—202).

    As amended in 1999.

§2—327. SPECIAL INCIDENTS OF SALE ON APPROVAL AND SALE OR RETURN

(1) Under a sale on approval unless otherwise agreed
        (a) although the goods are identified to the contract the risk of loss and the title do not pass to the buyer until acceptance; and
        (b) use of the goods consistent with the purpose of trial is not acceptance but failure seasonably to notify the seller of election to return the goods is acceptance, and if the goods conform to the contract acceptance of any part is acceptance of the whole; and

(c) after due notification of election to return, the return is at the seller's risk and expense but a merchant buyer must follow any reasonable instructions.

(2) Under a sale or return unless otherwise agreed

(a) the option to return extends to the whole or any commercial unit of the goods while in substantially their original condition, but must be exercised seasonally; and

(b) the return is at the buyer's risk and expense.

§2—328. SALE BY AUCTION

(1) In a sale by auction if goods are put up in lots each lot is the subject of a separate sale.

(2) A sale by auction is complete when the auctioneer so announces by the fall of the hammer or in other customary manner. Where a bid is made while the hammer is falling in acceptance of a prior bid the auctioneer may in his discretion reopen the bidding or declare the goods sold under the bid on which the hammer was falling.

(3) Such a sale is with reserve unless the goods are in explicit terms put up without reserve. In an auction with reserve the auctioneer may withdraw the goods at any time until he announces completion of the sale. In an auction without reserve, after the auctioneer calls for bids on an article or lot, that article or lot cannot be withdrawn unless no bid is made within a reasonable time. In either case a bidder may retract his bid until the auctioneer's announcement of completion of the sale, but a bidder's retraction does not revive any previous bid.

(4) If the auctioneer knowingly receives a bid on the seller's behalf or the seller makes or procures such as bid, and notice has not been given that liberty for such bidding is reserved, the buyer may at his option avoid the sale or take the goods at the price of the last good faith bid prior to the completion of the sale. This subsection shall not apply to any bid at a forced sale.

Part 4 Title, Creditors and Good Faith Purchasers

§2—401. PASSING OF TITLE; RESERVATION FOR SECURITY; LIMITED APPLICATION OF THIS SECTION

Each provision of this Article with regard to the rights, obligations and remedies of the seller, the buyer, purchasers or other third parties applies irrespective of title to the goods except where the provision refers to such title. Insofar as situations are not covered by the other provisions of this Article and matters concerning title became material the following rules apply:

(1) Title to goods cannot pass under a contract for sale prior to their identification to the contract (Section 2—501), and unless otherwise explicitly agreed the buyer acquires by their identification a special property as limited by this Act. Any retention or reservation by the seller of the title (property) in goods shipped or delivered to the buyer is limited in effect to a reservation of a security interest. Subject to these provisions and to the provisions of the Article on Secured Transactions (Article 9), title to goods passes from the seller to the buyer in any manner and on any conditions explicitly agreed on by the parties.

(2) Unless otherwise explicitly agreed title passes to the buyer at the time and place at which the seller completes his performance with reference to the physical delivery of the goods, despite any reservation of a security interest and even though a document of title is to be delivered at a different time or place; and in particular and despite any reservation of a security interest by the bill of lading

(a) if the contract requires or authorizes the seller to send the goods to the buyer but does not require him to deliver them at destination, title passes to the buyer at the time and place of shipment; but

(b) if the contract requires delivery at destination, title passes on tender there.

(3) Unless otherwise explicitly agreed where delivery is to be made without moving the goods,

(a) if the seller is to deliver a document of title, title passes at the time when and the place where he delivers such documents; or

(b) if the goods are at the time of contracting already identified and no documents are to be delivered, title passes at the time and place of contracting.

(4) A rejection or other refusal by the buyer to receive or retain the goods, whether or not justified, or a justified revocation of acceptance revests title to the goods in the seller. Such revesting occurs by operation of law and is not a "sale".

§2—402. RIGHTS OF SELLER'S CREDITORS AGAINST SOLD GOODS

(1) Except as provided in subsections (2) and (3), rights of unsecured creditors of the seller with respect to goods which have been identified to a contract for sale are subject to the buyer's rights to recover the goods under this Article (Sections 2—502 and 2—716).

(2) A creditor of the seller may treat a sale or an identification of goods to a contract for sale as void if as against him a retention of possession by the seller is fraudulent under any rule of law of the state where the goods are situated, except that retention of possession in good faith and current course of trade by a merchant-seller for a commercially reasonable time after a sale or identification is not fraudulent.

(3) Nothing in this Article shall be deemed to impair the rights of creditors of the seller

(a) under the provisions of the Article on Secured Transactions (Article 9); or

(b) where identification to the contract or delivery is made not in current course of trade but in satisfaction of or as security for a pre-existing claim for money, security or the like and is made under circumstances which under any rule of law of the state where the goods are situated would apart from this Article constitute the transaction a fraudulent transfer or voidable preference.

§2—403. POWER TO TRANSFER; GOOD FAITH PURCHASE OF GOODS; "ENTRUSTING"

(1) A purchaser of goods acquires all title which his transferor had or had power to transfer except that a purchaser of a limited interest acquires rights only to the extent of the interest purchased. A person with voidable title has power to transfer a good title to a good faith purchaser for value. When goods have been delivered under a transaction of purchase the purchaser has such power even though

(a) the transferor was deceived as to the identity of the purchaser, or

(b) the delivery was in exchange for a check which is later dishonored, or

(c) it was agreed that the transaction was to be a "cash sale", or

(d) the delivery was procured through fraud punishable as larcenous under the criminal law.

(2) Any entrusting of possession of goods to a merchant who deals in goods of that kind gives him power to transfer all rights of the entruster to a buyer in ordinary course of business.

(3) "Entrusting" includes any delivery and any acquiescence in retention of possession regardless of any condition expressed between the parties to the delivery or acquiescence and regardless of whether the procurement of the entrusting or the possessor's disposition of the goods have been such as to be larcenous under the criminal law.

(4) The rights of other purchasers of goods and of lien creditors are governed by the Articles on Secured Transactions (Article 9), Bulk Transfers (Article 6) and Documents of Title (Article 7).

As amended in 1988.

Part 5 Performance

§2—501. INSURABLE INTEREST IN GOODS; MANNER OF IDENTIFICATION OF GOODS

(1) The buyer obtains a special property and an insurable interest in goods by identification of existing goods as goods to which the contract refers even though the goods so identified are non-conforming and he has an option to return or reject them. Such identification can be made at any time and in any manner explicitly agreed to by the parties. In the absence of explicit agreement identification occurs

(a) when the contract is made if it is for the sale of goods already existing and identified;

(b) if the contract is for the sale of future goods other than those described in paragraph (c), when goods are shipped, marked or otherwise designated by the seller as goods to which the contract refers;

(c) when the crops are planted or otherwise become growing crops or the young are conceived if the contract is for the sale of unborn young to be born within twelve months after contracting or for the sale of crops to be harvested within twelve months or the next normal harvest season after contracting whichever is longer.

(2) The seller retains an insurable interest in goods so long as title to or any security interest in the goods remains in him and where the identification is by the seller alone he may until default or insolvency or notification to the buyer that the identification is final substitute other goods for those identified.

(3) Nothing in this section impairs any insurable interest recognized under any other statute or rule of law.

§2—502. BUYER'S RIGHT TO GOODS ON SELLER'S INSOLVENCY

(1) Subject to subsections (2) and (3) and even though the goods have not been shipped a buyer who has paid a part or all of the price of goods in which he has a special property under the provisions of the immediately preceding section may on making and keeping good a tender of any unpaid portion of their price recover them from the seller if:

(a) in the case of goods bought for personal, family, or household purposes, the seller repudiates or fails to deliver as required by the contract; or

(b) in all cases, the seller becomes insolvent within ten days after receipt of the first installment on their price.

(2) The buyer's right to recover the goods under subsection (1)(a) vests upon acquisition of a special property, even if the seller had not then repudiated or failed to deliver.

(3) If the identification creating his special property has been made by the buyer he acquires the right to recover the goods only if they conform to the contract for sale.

As amended in 1999.

§2—503. MANNER OF SELLER'S TENDER OF DELIVERY

(1) Tender of delivery requires that the seller put and hold conforming goods at the buyer's disposition and give the

buyer any notification reasonably necessary to enable him to take delivery. The manner, time and place for tender are determined by the agreement and this Article, and in particular

(a) tender must be at a reasonable hour, and if it is of goods they must be kept available for the period reasonably necessary to enable the buyer to take possession; but

(b) unless otherwise agreed the buyer must furnish facilities reasonably suited to the receipt of the goods.

(2) Where the case is within the next section respecting shipment tender requires that the seller comply with its provisions.

(3) Where the seller is required to deliver at a particular destination tender requires that he comply with subsection (1)and also in any appropriate case tender documents as described in subsections (4) and (5) of this section.

(4) Where goods are in the possession of a bailee and are to be delivered without being moved

(a) tender requires that the seller either tender a negotiable document of title covering such goods or procure acknowledgment by the bailee of the buyer's right to possession of the goods; but

(b) tender to the buyer of a non-negotiable document of title or of a written direction to the bailee to deliver is sufficient tender unless the buyer seasonably objects, and receipt by the bailee of notification of the buyer's rights fixes those rights as against the bailee and all third persons; but risk of loss of the goods and of any failure by the bailee to honor the non-negotiable document of title or to obey the direction remains on the seller until the buyer has had a reasonable time to present the document or direction, and a refusal by the bailee to honor the document or to obey the direction defeats the tender.

(5) Where the contract requires the seller to deliver documents

(a) he must tender all such documents in correct form, except as provided in this Article with respect to bills of lading in a set (subsection (2) of Section 2—323); and

(b) tender through customary banking channels is sufficient and dishonor of a draft accompanying the documents constitutes non-acceptance or rejection.

§2—504. SHIPMENT BY SELLER

Where the seller is required or authorized to send the goods to the buyer and the contract does not require him to deliver them at a particular destination, then unless otherwise agreed he must

(a) put the goods in the possession of such a carrier and make such a contract for their transportation as may be reasonable having regard to the nature of the goods and other circumstances of the case; and

(b) obtain and promptly deliver or tender in due form any document necessary to enable the buyer to obtain possession of the goods or otherwise required by the agreement or by usage of trade; and

(c) promptly notify the buyer of the shipment.

Failure to notify the buyer under paragraph (c) or to make a proper contract under paragraph (a) is a ground for rejection only if material delay or loss ensues.

§2—505. SELLER'S SHIPMENT UNDER RESERVATION

(1) Where the seller has identified goods to the contract by or before shipment:

(a) his procurement of a negotiable bill of lading to his own order or otherwise reserves in him a security interest in the goods. His procurement of the bill to the order of a financing agency or of the buyer indicates in addition only the seller's expectation of transferring that interest to the person named.

(b) a non-negotiable bill of lading to himself or his nominee reserves possession of the goods as security but except in a case of conditional delivery (subsection (2)of Section 2—507) a non-negotiable bill of lading naming the buyer as consignee reserves no security interest even though the seller retains possession of the bill of lading.

(2) When shipment by the seller with reservation of a security interest is in violation of the contract for sale it constitutes an improper contract for transportation within the preceding section but impairs neither the rights given to the buyer by shipment and identification of the goods to the contract nor the seller's powers as a holder of a negotiable document.

§2—506. RIGHTS OF FINANCING AGENCY

(1) A financing agency by paying or purchasing for value a draft which relates to a shipment of goods acquires to the extent of the payment or purchase and in addition to its own rights under the draft and any document of title securing it any rights of the shipper in the goods including the right to stop delivery and the shipper's right to have the draft honored by the buyer.

(2) The right to reimbursement of a financing agency which has in good faith honored or purchased the draft under commitment to or authority from the buyer is not impaired by subsequent discovery of defects with reference to any relevant document which was apparently regular on its face.

§2—507. EFFECT OF SELLER'S TENDER; DELIVERY ON CONDITION

(1) Tender of delivery is a condition to the buyer's duty to accept the goods and, unless otherwise agreed, to his duty to pay for them. Tender entitles the seller to acceptance of the goods and to payment according to the contract.

(2) Where payment is due and demanded on the delivery to the buyer of goods or documents of title, his right as against the seller to retain or dispose of them is conditional upon his making the payment due.

§2—508. CURE BY SELLER OF IMPROPER TENDER OR DELIVERY; REPLACEMENT

(1) Where any tender or delivery by the seller is rejected because non-conforming and the time for performance has not yet expired, the seller may seasonably notify the buyer of his intention to cure and may then within the contract time make a conforming delivery.

(2) Where the buyer rejects a non-conforming tender which the seller had reasonable grounds to believe would be acceptable with or without money allowance the seller may if he seasonably notifies the buyer have a further reasonable time to substitute a conforming tender.

§2—509. RISK OF LOSS IN THE ABSENCE OF BREACH

(1) Where the contract requires or authorizes the seller to ship the goods by carrier

      (a) if it does not require him to deliver them at a particular destination, the risk of loss passes to the buyer when the goods are duly delivered to the carrier even though the shipment is under reservation (Section 2—505); but

      (b) if it does require him to deliver them at a particular destination and the goods are there duly tendered while in the possession of the carrier, the risk of loss passes to the buyer when the goods are there duly so tendered as to enable the buyer to take delivery.

(2) Where the goods are held by a bailee to be delivered without being moved, the risk of loss passes to the buyer

      (a) on his receipt of a negotiable document of title covering the goods; or

      (b) on acknowledgment by the bailee of the buyer's right to possession of the goods; or

      (c) after his receipt of a non-negotiable document of title or other written direction to deliver, as provided in subsection (4)(b) of Section 2—503.

(3) In any case not within subsection (1) or (2), the risk of loss passes to the buyer on his receipt of the goods if the seller is a merchant; otherwise the risk passes to the buyer on tender of delivery.

(4) The provisions of this section are subject to contrary agreement of the parties and to the provisions of this Article on sale on approval (Section 2—327) and on effect of breach on risk of loss (Section 2—510).

§2—510. EFFECT OF BREACH ON RISK OF LOSS

(1) Where a tender or delivery of goods so fails to conform to the contract as to give a right of rejection the risk of their loss remains on the seller until cure or acceptance.

(2) Where the buyer rightfully revokes acceptance he may to the extent of any deficiency in his effective insurance coverage treat the risk of loss as having rested on the seller from the beginning.

(3) Where the buyer as to conforming goods already identified to the contract for sale repudiates or is otherwise in breach before risk of their loss has passed to him, the seller may to the extent of any deficiency in his effective insurance coverage treat the risk of loss as resting on the buyer for a commercially reasonable time.

§2—511. TENDER OF PAYMENT BY BUYER; PAYMENT BY CHECK

(1) Unless otherwise agreed tender of payment is a condition to the seller's duty to tender and complete any delivery.

(2) Tender of payment is sufficient when made by any means or in any manner current in the ordinary course of business unless the seller demands payment in legal tender and gives any extension of time reasonably necessary to procure it.

(3) Subject to the provisions of this Act on the effect of an instrument on an obligation (Section 3—310), payment by check is conditional and is defeated as between the parties by dishonor of the check on due presentment.

As amended in 1994.

§2—512. PAYMENT BY BUYER BEFORE INSPECTION

(1) Where the contract requires payment before inspection non-conformity of the goods does not excuse the buyer from so making payment unless

      (a) the non-conformity appears without inspection; or

      (b) despite tender of the required documents the circumstances would justify injunction against honor under this Act (Section 5—109(b)).

(2) Payment pursuant to subsection (1) does not constitute an acceptance of goods or impair the buyer's right to inspect or any of his remedies.

As amended in 1995.

§2—513. BUYER'S RIGHT TO INSPECTION OF GOODS

(1) Unless otherwise agreed and subject to subsection (3), where goods are tendered or delivered or identified to the contract for sale, the buyer has a right before payment or acceptance to inspect them at any reasonable place and time and in any reasonable manner. When the seller is required or authorized to send the goods to the buyer, the inspection may be after their arrival.

(2) Expenses of inspection must be borne by the buyer but may be recovered from the seller if the goods do not conform and are rejected.

(3) Unless otherwise agreed and subject to the provisions of this Article on C.I.F. contracts (subsection (3) of Section 2—321), the buyer is not entitled to inspect the goods before payment of the price when the contract provides

    (a) for delivery "C.O.D." or on other like terms; or

    (b) for payment against documents of title, except where such payment is due only after the goods are to become available for inspection.

(4) A place or method of inspection fixed by the parties is presumed to be exclusive but unless otherwise expressly agreed it does not postpone identification or shift the place for delivery or for passing the risk of loss. If compliance becomes impossible, inspection shall be as provided in this section unless the place or method fixed was clearly intended as an indispensable condition failure of which avoids the contract.

§2—514. WHEN DOCUMENTS DELIVERABLE ON ACCEPTANCE; WHEN ON PAYMENT

Unless otherwise agreed documents against which a draft is drawn are to be delivered to the drawee on acceptance of the draft if it is payable more than three days after presentment; otherwise, only on payment.

§2—515. PRESERVING EVIDENCE OF GOODS IN DISPUTE

In furtherance of the adjustment of any claim or dispute

(a) either party on reasonable notification to the other and for the purpose of ascertaining the facts and preserving evidence has the right to inspect, test and sample the goods including such of them as may be in the possession or control of the other; and

(b) the parties may agree to a third party inspection or survey to determine the conformity or condition of the goods and may agree that the findings shall be binding upon them in any subsequent litigation or adjustment.

Part 6 Breach, Repudiation and Excuse

§2—601. BUYER'S RIGHTS ON IMPROPER DELIVERY

Subject to the provisions of this Article on breach in installment contracts (Section 2—612) and unless otherwise agreed under the sections on contractual limitations of remedy (Sections 2—718 and 2—719), if the goods or the tender of delivery fail in any respect to conform to the contract, the buyer may

(a) reject the whole; or

    (b) accept the whole; or

    (c) accept any commercial unit or units and reject the rest.

§2—602. MANNER AND EFFECT OF RIGHTFUL REJECTION

(1) Rejection of goods must be within a reasonable time after their delivery or tender. It is ineffective unless the buyer seasonably notifies the seller.

(2) Subject to the provisions of the two following sections on rejected goods (Sections 2—603 and 2—604),

    (a) after rejection any exercise of ownership by the buyer with respect to any commercial unit is wrongful as against the seller; and

    (b) if the buyer has before rejection taken physical possession of goods in which he does not have a security interest under the provisions of this Article (subsection (3) of Section 2—711), he is under a duty after rejection to hold them with reasonable care at the seller's disposition for a time sufficient to permit the seller to remove them; but

    (c) the buyer has no further obligations with regard to goods rightfully rejected.

(3) The seller's rights with respect to goods wrongfully rejected are governed by the provisions of this Article on Seller's remedies in general (Section 2—703).

§2—603. MERCHANT BUYER'S DUTIES AS TO RIGHTFULLY REJECTED GOODS

(1) Subject to any security interest in the buyer (subsection (3) of Section 2—711), when the seller has no agent or place of business at the market of rejection a merchant buyer is under a duty after rejection of goods in his possession or control to follow any reasonable instructions received from the seller with respect to the goods and in the absence of such instructions to make reasonable efforts to sell them for the seller's account if they are perishable or threaten to decline in value speedily. Instructions are not reasonable if on demand indemnity for expenses is not forthcoming.

(2) When the buyer sells goods under subsection (1), he is entitled to reimbursement from the seller or out of the

proceeds for reasonable expenses of caring for and selling them, and if the expenses include no selling commission then to such commission as is usual in the trade or if there is none to a reasonable sum not exceeding ten per cent on the gross proceeds.

(3) In complying with this section the buyer is held only to good faith and good faith conduct hereunder is neither acceptance nor conversion nor the basis of an action for damages.

§2—604. BUYER'S OPTIONS AS TO SALVAGE OF RIGHTFULLY REJECTED GOODS

Subject to the provisions of the immediately preceding section on perishables if the seller gives no instructions within a reasonable time after notification of rejection the buyer may store the rejected goods for the seller's account or reship them to him or resell them for the seller's account with reimbursement as provided in the preceding section. Such action is not acceptance or conversion.

§2—605. WAIVER OF BUYER'S OBJECTIONS BY FAILURE TO PARTICULARIZE

(1) The buyer's failure to state in connection with rejection a particular defect which is ascertainable by reasonable inspection precludes him from relying on the unstated defect to justify rejection or to establish breach

(a) where the seller could have cured it if stated seasonably; or

(b) between merchants when the seller has after rejection made a request in writing for a full and final written statement of all defects on which the buyer proposes to rely.

(2) Payment against documents made without reservation of rights precludes recovery of the payment for defects apparent on the face of the documents.

§2—606. WHAT CONSTITUTES ACCEPTANCE OF GOODS

(1) Acceptance of goods occurs when the buyer

(a) after a reasonable opportunity to inspect the goods signifies to the seller that the goods are conforming or that he will take or retain them in spite of their nonconformity; or

(b) fails to make an effective rejection (subsection (1) of Section 2—602), but such acceptance does not occur until the buyer has had a reasonable opportunity to inspect them; or

(c) does any act inconsistent with the seller's ownership; but if such act is wrongful as against the seller it is an acceptance only if ratified by him.

(2) Acceptance of a part of any commercial unit is acceptance of that entire unit.

§2—607. EFFECT OF ACCEPTANCE; NOTICE OF BREACH; BURDEN OF ESTABLISHING BREACH AFTER ACCEPTANCE; NOTICE OF CLAIM OR LITIGATION TO PERSON ANSWERABLE OVER

(1) The buyer must pay at the contract rate for any goods accepted.

(2) Acceptance of goods by the buyer precludes rejection of the goods accepted and if made with knowledge of a non-conformity cannot be revoked because of it unless the acceptance was on the reasonable assumption that the non-conformity would be seasonably cured but acceptance does not of itself impair any other remedy provided by this Article for non-conformity.

(3) Where a tender has been accepted

(a) the buyer must within a reasonable time after he discovers or should have discovered any breach notify the seller of breach or be barred from any remedy; and

(b) if the claim is one for infringement or the like (subsection (3) of Section 2—312) and the buyer is sued as a result of such a breach he must so notify the seller within a reasonable time after he receives notice of the litigation or be barred from any remedy over for liability established by the litigation.

(4) The burden is on the buyer to establish any breach with respect to the goods accepted.

(5) Where the buyer is sued for breach of a warranty or other obligation for which his seller is answerable over

(a) he may give his seller written notice of the litigation. If the notice states that the seller may come in and defend and that if the seller does not do so he will be bound in any action against him by his buyer by any determination of fact common to the two litigations, then unless the seller after seasonable receipt of the notice does come in and defend he is so bound.

(b) if the claim is one for infringement or the like (subsection (3) of Section 2—312) the original seller may demand in writing that his buyer turn over to him control of the litigation including settlement or else be barred from any remedy over and if he also agrees to bear all expense and to satisfy any adverse judgment, then unless the buyer after seasonable receipt of the demand does turn over control the buyer is so barred.

(6) The provisions of subsections (3), (4) and (5) apply to any obligation of a buyer to hold the seller harmless against infringement or the like (subsection (3) of Section 2—312).

§2—608. REVOCATION OF ACCEPTANCE IN WHOLE OR IN PART

(1) The buyer may revoke his acceptance of a lot or commercial unit whose non-conformity substantially impairs its value to him if he has accepted it

(a) on the reasonable assumption that its non-conformity would be cured and it has not been seasonably cured; or

(b) without discovery of such non-conformity if his acceptance was reasonably induced either by the difficulty of discovery before acceptance or by the seller's assurances.

(2) Revocation of acceptance must occur within a reasonable time after the buyer discovers or should have discovered the ground for it and before any substantial change in condition of the goods which is not caused by their own defects. It is not effective until the buyer notifies the seller of it.

(3) A buyer who so revokes has the same rights and duties with regard to the goods involved as if he had rejected them.

§2—609. RIGHT TO ADEQUATE ASSURANCE OF PERFORMANCE

(1) A contract for sale imposes an obligation on each party that the other's expectation of receiving due performance will not be impaired. When reasonable grounds for insecurity arise with respect to the performance of either party the other may in writing demand adequate assurance of due performance and until he receives such assurance may if commercially reasonable suspend any performance for which he has not already received the agreed return.

(2) Between merchants the reasonableness of grounds for insecurity and the adequacy of any assurance offered shall be determined according to commercial standards.

(3) Acceptance of any improper delivery or payment does not prejudice the party's right to demand adequate assurance of future performance.

(4) After receipt of a justified demand failure to provide within a reasonable time not exceeding thirty days such assurance of due performance as is adequate under the circumstances of the particular case is a repudiation of the contract.

§2—610. ANTICIPATORY REPUDIATION

When either party repudiates the contract with respect to a performance not yet due the loss of which will substantially impair the value of the contract to the other, the aggrieved party may

(a) for a commercially reasonable time await performance by the repudiating party; or

(b) resort to any remedy for breach (Section 2—703 or Section 2—711), even though he has notified the repudiating party that he would await the latter's performance and has urged retraction; and

(c) in either case suspend his own performance or proceed in accordance with the provisions of this Article on the seller's right to identify goods to the contract notwithstanding breach or to salvage unfinished goods (Section 2—704).

§2—611. RETRACTION OF ANTICIPATORY REPUDIATION

(1) Until the repudiating party's next performance is due he can retract his repudiation unless the aggrieved party has since the repudiation cancelled or materially changed his position or otherwise indicated that he considers the repudiation final.

(2) Retraction may be by any method which clearly indicates to the aggrieved party that the repudiating party intends to perform, but must include any assurance justifiably demanded under the provisions of this Article (Section 2—609).

(3) Retraction reinstates the repudiating party's rights under the contract with due excuse and allowance to the aggrieved party for any delay occasioned by the repudiation.

§2—612. "INSTALLMENT CONTRACT"; BREACH

(1) An "installment contract" is one which requires or authorizes the delivery of goods in separate lots to be separately accepted, even though the contract contains a clause "each delivery is a separate contract" or its equivalent.

(2) The buyer may reject any installment which is non-conforming if the non-conformity substantially impairs the value of that installment and cannot be cured or if the non-conformity is a defect in the required documents; but if the non-conformity does not fall within subsection (3) and the seller gives adequate assurance of its cure the buyer must accept that installment.

(3) Whenever non-conformity or default with respect to one or more installments substantially impairs the value of the whole contract there is a breach of the whole. But the aggrieved party reinstates the contract if he accepts a non-conforming installment without seasonably notifying of cancellation or if he brings an action with respect only to past installments or demands performance as to future installments.

§2—613. CASUALTY TO IDENTIFIED GOODS

Where the contract requires for its performance goods identified when the contract is made, and the goods suffer casualty without fault of either party before the risk of loss passes to the buyer, or in a proper case under a "no arrival, no sale" term (Section 2—324) then

(a) if the loss is total the contract is avoided; and

(b) if the loss is partial or the goods have so deteriorated as no longer to conform to the contract the buyer may nevertheless demand inspection and at his option either treat the contract as voided or accept the goods with due allowance from the contract price for the deterioration or the deficiency in quantity but without further right against the seller.

§2—614. SUBSTITUTED PERFORMANCE

(1) Where without fault of either party the agreed berthing, loading, or unloading facilities fail or an agreed type of carrier becomes unavailable or the agreed manner of delivery otherwise becomes commercially impracticable but a commercially reasonable substitute is available, such substitute performance must be tendered and accepted.

(2) If the agreed means or manner of payment fails because of domestic or foreign governmental regulation, the seller may withhold or stop delivery unless the buyer provides a means or manner of payment which is commercially a substantial equivalent. If delivery has already been taken, payment by the means or in the manner provided by the regulation discharges the buyer's obligation unless the regulation is discriminatory, oppressive or predatory.

§2—615. EXCUSE BY FAILURE OF PRESUPPOSED CONDITIONS

Except so far as a seller may have assumed a greater obligation and subject to the preceding section on substituted performance:

(a) Delay in delivery or non-delivery in whole or in part by a seller who complies with paragraphs (b) and (c) is not a breach of his duty under a contract for sale if performance as agreed has been made impracticable by the occurrence of a contingency the nonoccurrence of which was a basic assumption on which the contract was made or by compliance in good faith with any applicable foreign or domestic governmental regulation or order whether or not it later proves to be invalid.

(b) Where the causes mentioned in paragraph (a) affect only a part of the seller's capacity to perform, he must allocate production and deliveries among his customers but may at his option include regular customers not then under contract as well as his own requirements for further manufacture. He may so allocate in any manner which is fair and reasonable.

(c) The seller must notify the buyer seasonably that there will be delay or non-delivery and, when allocation is

required under paragraph (b), of the estimated quota thus made available for the buyer.

§2—616. PROCEDURE ON NOTICE CLAIMING EXCUSE

(1) Where the buyer receives notification of a material or indefinite delay or an allocation justified under the preceding section he may by written notification to the seller as to any delivery concerned, and where the prospective deficiency substantially impairs the value of the whole contract under the provisions of this Article relating to breach of installment contracts (Section 2—612), then also as to the whole,

(a) terminate and thereby discharge any unexecuted portion of the contract; or

(b) modify the contract by agreeing to take his available quota in substitution.

(2) If after receipt of such notification from the seller the buyer fails so to modify the contract within a reasonable time not exceeding thirty days the contract lapses with respect to any deliveries affected.

(3) The provisions of this section may not be negated by agreement except in so far as the seller has assumed a greater obligation under the preceding section.

Part 7 Remedies

§2—701. REMEDIES FOR BREACH OF COLLATERAL CONTRACTS NOT IMPAIRED

Remedies for breach of any obligation or promise collateral or ancillary to a contract for sale are not impaired by the provisions of this Article.

§2—702. SELLER'S REMEDIES ON DISCOVERY OF BUYER'S INSOLVENCY

(1) Where the seller discovers the buyer to be insolvent he may refuse delivery except for cash including payment for all goods theretofore delivered under the contract, and stop delivery under this Article (Section 2—705).

(2) Where the seller discovers that the buyer has received goods on credit while insolvent he may reclaim the goods upon demand made within ten days after the receipt, but if misrepresentation of solvency has been made to the particular seller in writing within three months before delivery the ten day limitation does not apply. Except as provided in this subsection the seller may not base a right to reclaim goods on the buyer's fraudulent or innocent misrepresentation of solvency or of intent to pay.

(3) The seller's right to reclaim under subsection (2) is subject to the rights of a buyer in ordinary course or other good faith purchaser under this Article (Section 2—403). Successful reclamation of goods excludes all other remedies with respect to them.

§2—703. SELLER'S REMEDIES IN GENERAL

Where the buyer wrongfully rejects or revokes acceptance of goods or fails to make a payment due on or before delivery or repudiates with respect to a part or the whole, then with respect to any goods directly affected and, if the breach is of the whole contract (Section 2—612), then also with respect to the whole undelivered balance, the aggrieved seller may

(a) withhold delivery of such goods;

(b) stop delivery by any bailee as hereafter provided (Section 2—705);

(c) proceed under the next section respecting goods still unidentified to the contract;

(d) resell and recover damages as hereafter provided (Section 2—706);

(e) recover damages for non-acceptance (Section 2—708) or in a proper case the price (Section 2—709);

(f) cancel.

§2—704. SELLER'S RIGHT TO IDENTIFY GOODS TO THE CONTRACT NOTWITHSTANDING BREACH OR TO SALVAGE UNFINISHED GOODS

(1) An aggrieved seller under the preceding section may

(a) identify to the contract conforming goods not already identified if at the time he learned of the breach they are in his possession or control;

(b) treat as the subject of resale goods which have demonstrably been intended for the particular contract even though those goods are unfinished.

(2) Where the goods are unfinished an aggrieved seller may in the exercise of reasonable commercial judgment for the purposes of avoiding loss and of effective realization either complete the manufacture and wholly identify the goods to the contract or cease manufacture and resell for scrap or salvage value or proceed in any other reasonable manner.

§2—705. SELLER'S STOPPAGE OF DELIVERY IN TRANSIT OR OTHERWISE

(1) The seller may stop delivery of goods in the possession of a carrier or other bailee when he discovers the buyer to be insolvent (Section 2—702) and may stop delivery of carload, truckload, planeload or larger shipments of express or freight when the buyer repudiates or fails to make a payment due before delivery or if for any other reason the seller has a right to withhold or reclaim the goods.

(2) As against such buyer the seller may stop delivery until

(a) receipt of the goods by the buyer; or

(b) acknowledgment to the buyer by any bailee of the goods except a carrier that the bailee holds the goods for the buyer; or

(c) such acknowledgment to the buyer by a carrier by reshipment or as warehouseman; or

(d) negotiation to the buyer of any negotiable document of title covering the goods.

(3) (a) To stop delivery the seller must so notify as to enable the bailee by reasonable diligence to prevent delivery of the goods.

(b) After such notification the bailee must hold and deliver the goods according to the directions of the seller but the seller is liable to the bailee for any ensuing charges or damages.

(c) If a negotiable document of title has been issued for goods the bailee is not obliged to obey a notification to stop until surrender of the document.

(d) A carrier who has issued a non-negotiable bill of lading is not obliged to obey a notification to stop received from a person other than the consignor.

§2—706. SELLER'S RESALE INCLUDING CONTRACT FOR RESALE

(1) Under the conditions stated in Section 2—703 on seller's remedies, the seller may resell the goods concerned or the undelivered balance thereof. Where the resale is made in good faith and in a commercially reasonable manner the seller may recover the difference between the resale price and the contract price together with any incidental damages allowed under the provisions of this Article (Section 2—710), but less expenses saved in consequence of the buyer's breach.

(2) Except as otherwise provided in subsection (3) or unless otherwise agreed resale may be at public or private sale including sale by way of one or more contracts to sell or of identification to an existing contract of the seller. Sale may be as a unit or in parcels and at any time and place and on any terms but every aspect of the sale including the method, manner, time, place and terms must be commercially reasonable. The resale must be reasonably identified as referring to the broken contract, but it is not necessary that the goods be in existence or that any or all of them have been identified to the contract before the breach.

(3) Where the resale is at private sale the seller must give the buyer reasonable notification of his intention to resell.

(4) Where the resale is at public sale

(a) only identified goods can be sold except where there is a recognized market for a public sale of futures in goods of the kind; and

(b) it must be made at a usual place or market for public sale if one is reasonably available and except in the case of goods which are perishable or threaten to decline in value speedily the seller

must give the buyer reasonable notice of the time
and place of the resale; and

(c) if the goods are not to be within the view of
those attending the sale the notification of sale
must state the place where the goods are located
and provide for their reasonable inspection by
prospective bidders; and

(d) the seller may buy.

(5) A purchaser who buys in good faith at a resale
takes the goods free of any rights of the original buyer even
though the seller fails to comply with one or more of the
requirements of this section.

(6) The seller is not accountable to the buyer for
any profit made on any resale. A person in the position
of a seller (Section 2—707) or a buyer who has
rightfully rejected or justifiably revoked acceptance
must account for any excess over the amount of his
security interest, as hereinafter defined (subsection (3) of
Section 2—711).

§2—707. "PERSON IN THE POSITION OF A SELLER"

(1) A "person in the position of a seller" includes as
against a principal an agent who has paid or become
responsible for the price of goods on behalf of his principal
or anyone who otherwise holds a security interest or other
right in goods similar to that of a seller.

(2) A person in the position of a seller may as
provided in this Article withhold or stop delivery (Section
2—705) and resell (Section 2—706) and recover incidental
damages (Section 2—710).

§2—708. SELLER'S DAMAGES FOR NON-ACCEPTANCE OR REPUDIATION

(1) Subject to subsection (2) and to the provisions of
this Article with respect to proof of market price
(Section 2—723), the measure of damages for non-
acceptance or repudiation by the buyer is the difference
between the market price at the time and place for
tender and the unpaid contract price together with
any incidental damages provided in this Article
(Section 2—710), but less expenses saved in consequence
of the buyer's breach.

(2) If the measure of damages provided in subsection
(1) is inadequate to put the seller in as good a position as
performance would have done then the measure of
damages is the profit (including reasonable overhead)
which the seller would have made from full performance by
the buyer, together with any incidental damages provided
in this Article (Section 2—710), due allowance for costs
reasonably incurred and due credit for payments or
proceeds of resale.

§2—709. ACTION FOR THE PRICE

(1) When the buyer fails to pay the price as it becomes
due the seller may recover, together with any incidental
damages under the next section, the price

(a) of goods accepted or of conforming goods
lost or damaged within a commercially reasonable
time after risk of their loss has passed to the
buyer; and

(b) of goods identified to the contract if the seller
is unable after reasonable effort to resell them at a
reasonable price or the circumstances reasonably
indicate that such effort will be unavailing.

(2) Where the seller sues for the price he must hold
for the buyer any goods which have been identified to the
contract and are still in his control except that if resale
becomes possible he may resell them at any time prior to
the collection of the judgment. The net proceeds of any
such resale must be credited to the buyer and payment of
the judgment entitles him to any goods not resold.

(3) After the buyer has wrongfully rejected or revoked
acceptance of the goods or has failed to make a payment
due or has repudiated (Section 2—610), a seller who is
held not entitled to the price under this section shall
nevertheless be awarded damages for non-acceptance under
the preceding section.

§2—710. SELLER'S INCIDENTAL DAMAGES

Incidental damages to an aggrieved seller include any
commercially reasonable charges, expenses or commissions
incurred in stopping delivery, in the transportation, care
and custody of goods after the buyer's breach, in connection with return or resale of the goods or otherwise
resulting from the breach.

§2—711. BUYER'S REMEDIES IN GENERAL; BUYER'S SECURITY INTEREST IN REJECTED GOODS

(1) Where the seller fails to make delivery or repudiates or
the buyer rightfully rejects or justifiably revokes acceptance
then with respect to any goods involved, and with respect
to the whole if the breach goes to the whole contract
(Section 2—612), the buyer may cancel and whether or
not he has done so may in addition to recovering so much
of the price as has been paid

(a) "cover" and have damages under the next
section as to all the goods affected whether or not
they have been identified to the contract; or

(b) recover damages for non-delivery as provided
in this Article (Section 2—713).

(2) Where the seller fails to deliver or repudiates
buyer may also

(a) if the goods have been identified recover
them as provided in this Article (Section 2—
502); or

(b) in a proper case obtain specific performance or replevy the goods as provided in this Article (Section 2—716).

(3) On rightful rejection or justifiable revocation of acceptance a buyer has a security interest in goods in his possession or control for any payments made on their price and any expenses reasonably incurred in their inspection, receipt, transportation, care and custody and may hold such goods and resell them in like manner as an aggrieved seller (Section 2—706).

§2—712. "COVER"; BUYER'S PROCUREMENT OF SUBSTITUTE GOODS

(1) After a breach within the preceding section the buyer may "cover" by making in good faith and without unreasonable delay any reasonable purchase of or contract to purchase goods in substitution for those due from the seller.

(2) The buyer may recover from the seller as damages the difference between the cost of cover and the contract price together with any incidental or consequential damages as hereinafter defined (Section 2—715), but less expenses saved in consequence of the seller's breach.

(3) Failure of the buyer to effect cover within this section does not bar him from any other remedy.

§2—713. BUYER'S DAMAGES FOR NON-DELIVERY OR REPUDIATION

(1) Subject to the provisions of this Article with respect to proof of market price (Section 2—723), the measure of damages for non-delivery or repudiation by the seller is the difference between the market price at the time when the buyer learned of the breach and the contract price together with any incidental and consequential damages provided in this Article (Section 2—715), but less expenses saved in consequence of the seller's breach.

(2) Market price is to be determined as of the place for tender or, in cases of rejection after arrival or revocation of acceptance, as of the place of arrival.

§2—714. BUYER'S DAMAGES FOR BREACH IN REGARD TO ACCEPTED GOODS

(1) Where the buyer has accepted goods and given notification (subsection (3) of Section 2—607) he may recover as damages for any non-conformity of tender the loss resulting in the ordinary course of events from the seller's breach as determined in any manner which is reasonable.

(2) The measure of damages for breach of warranty is the difference at the time and place of acceptance between the value of the goods accepted and the value they would have had if they had been as warranted, unless special circumstances show proximate damages of a different amount.

(3) In a proper case any incidental and consequential damages under the next section may also be recovered.

§2—715. BUYER'S INCIDENTAL AND CONSEQUENTIAL DAMAGES

(1) Incidental damages resulting from the seller's breach include expenses reasonably incurred in inspection, receipt, transportation and care and custody of goods rightfully rejected, any commercially reasonable charges, expenses or commissions in connection with effecting cover and any other reasonable expense incident to the delay or other breach.

(2) Consequential damages resulting from the seller's breach include

(a) any loss resulting from general or particular requirements and needs of which the seller at the time of contracting had reason to know and which could not reasonably be prevented by cover or otherwise; and

(b) injury to person or property proximately resulting from any breach of warranty.

§2—716. BUYER'S RIGHT TO SPECIFIC PERFORMANCE OR REPLEVIN

(1) Specific performance may be decreed where the goods are unique or in other proper circumstances.

(2) The decree for specific performance may include such terms and conditions as to payment of the price, damages, or other relief as the court may deem just.

(3) The buyer has a right of replevin for goods identified to the contract if after reasonable effort he is unable to effect cover for such goods or the circumstances reasonably indicate that such effort will be unavailing or if the goods have been shipped under reservation and satisfaction of the security interest in them has been made or tendered. In the case of goods bought for personal, family, or household purposes, the buyer's right of replevin vests upon acquisition of a special property, even if the seller had not then repudiated or failed to deliver.

As amended in 1999.

§2—717. DEDUCTION OF DAMAGES FROM THE PRICE

The buyer on notifying the seller of his intention to do so may deduct all or any part of the damages resulting from any breach of the contract from any part of the price still due under the same contract.

§2—718. LIQUIDATION OR LIMITATION OF DAMAGES; DEPOSITS

(1) Damages for breach by either party may be liquidated in the agreement but only at an amount which is

reasonable in the light of the anticipated or actual harm caused by the breach, the difficulties of proof of loss, and the inconvenience or nonfeasibility of otherwise obtaining an adequate remedy. A term fixing unreasonably large liquidated damages is void as a penalty.

(2) Where the seller justifiably withholds delivery of goods because of the buyer's breach, the buyer is entitled to restitution of any amount by which the sum of his payments exceeds

(a) the amount to which the seller is entitled by virtue of terms liquidating the seller's damages in accordance with subsection (1), or

(b) in the absence of such terms, twenty per cent of the value of the total performance for which the buyer is obligated under the contract or $500, whichever is smaller.

(3) The buyer's right to restitution under subsection (2) is subject to offset to the extent that the seller establishes

(a) a right to recover damages under the provisions of this Article other than subsection (1), and

(b) the amount or value of any benefits received by the buyer directly or indirectly by reason of the contract.

(4) Where a seller has received payment in goods their reasonable value or the proceeds of their resale shall be treated as payments for the purposes of subsection (2); but if the seller has notice of the buyer's breach before reselling goods received in part performance, his resale is subject to the conditions laid down in this Article on resale by an aggrieved seller (Section 2—706).

§2—719. CONTRACTUAL MODIFICATION OR LIMITATION OF REMEDY

(1) Subject to the provisions of subsections (2) and (3) of this section and of the preceding section on liquidation and limitation of damages,

(a) the agreement may provide for remedies in addition to or in substitution for those provided in this Article and may limit or alter the measure of damages recoverable under this Article, as by limiting the buyer's remedies to return of the goods and repayment of the price or to repair and replacement of nonconforming goods or parts; and

(b) resort to a remedy as provided is optional unless the remedy is expressly agreed to be exclusive, in which case it is the sole remedy.

(2) Where circumstances cause an exclusive or limited remedy to fail of its essential purpose, remedy may be had as provided in this Act.

(3) Consequential damages may be limited or excluded unless the limitation or exclusion is unconscionable. Limitation of consequential damages for injury to the

person in the case of consumer goods is prima facie unconscionable but limitation of damages where the loss is commercial is not.

§2—720. EFFECT OF "CANCELLATION" OR "RESCISSION" ON CLAIMS FOR ANTECEDENT BREACH

Unless the contrary intention clearly appears, expressions of "cancellation" or "rescission" of the contract or the like shall not be construed as a renunciation or discharge of any claim in damages for an antecedent breach.

§2—721. REMEDIES FOR FRAUD

Remedies for material misrepresentation or fraud include all remedies available under this Article for non-fraudulent breach. Neither rescission or a claim for rescission of the contract for sale nor rejection or return of the goods shall bar or be deemed inconsistent with a claim for damages or other remedy.

§2—722. WHO CAN SUE THIRD PARTIES FOR INJURY TO GOODS

Where a third party so deals with goods which have been identified to a contract for sale as to cause actionable injury to a party to that contract

(a) a right of action against the third party is in either party to the contract for sale who has title to or a security interest or a special property or an insurable interest in the goods; and if the goods have been destroyed or converted a right of action is also in the party who either bore the risk of loss under the contract for sale or has since the injury assumed that risk as against the other;

(b) if at the time of the injury the party plaintiff did not bear the risk of loss as against the other party to the contract for sale and there is no arrangement between them for disposition of the recovery, his suit or settlement is, subject to his own interest, as a fiduciary for the other party to the contract;

(c) either party may with the consent of the other sue for the benefit of whom it may concern.

§2—723. PROOF OF MARKET PRICE: TIME AND PLACE

(1) If an action based on anticipatory repudiation comes to trial before the time for performance with respect to some or all of the goods, any damages based on market price (Section 2—708 or Section 2—713) shall be determined according to the price of such goods prevailing at the time when the aggrieved party learned of the repudiation.

(2) If evidence of a price prevailing at the times or places described in this Article is not readily available the price prevailing within any reasonable time before or after the time described or at any other place which in commercial judgment or under usage of trade would serve as a reasonable substitute for the one described may be used, making any proper allowance for the cost of transporting the goods to or from such other place.

(3) Evidence of a relevant price prevailing at a time or place other than the one described in this Article offered by one party is not admissible unless and until he has given the other party such notice as the court finds sufficient to prevent unfair surprise.

§2—724. ADMISSIBILITY OF MARKET QUOTATIONS

Whenever the prevailing price or value of any goods regularly bought and sold in any established commodity market is in issue, reports in official publications or trade journals or in newspapers or periodicals of general circulation published as the reports of such market shall be admissible in evidence. The circumstances of the preparation of such a report may be shown to affect its weight but not its admissibility.

§2—725. STATUTE OF LIMITATIONS IN CONTRACTS FOR SALE

(1) An action for breach of any contract for sale must be commenced within four years after the cause of action has accrued. By the original agreement the parties may reduce the period of limitation to not less than one year but may not extend it.

(2) A cause of action accrues when the breach occurs, regardless of the aggrieved party's lack of knowledge of the breach. A breach of warranty occurs when tender of delivery is made, except that where a warranty explicitly extends to future performance of the goods and discovery of the breach must await the time of such performance the cause of action accrues when the breach is or should have been discovered.

(3) Where an action commenced within the time limited by subsection (1) is so terminated as to leave available a remedy by another action for the same breach such other action may be commenced after the expiration of the time limited and within six months after the termination of the first action unless the termination resulted from voluntary discontinuance or from dismissal for failure or neglect to prosecute.

(4) This section does not alter the law on tolling of the statute of limitations nor does it apply to causes of action which have accrued before this Act becomes effective.

ARTICLE 2 AMENDMENTS (EXCERPTS)

Part 1 Short Title, General Construction and Subject Matter
* * * *

§2—103. DEFINITIONS AND INDEX OF DEFINITIONS

(1) In this article unless the context otherwise requires
* * * *

(b) "Conspicuous", with reference to a term, means so written, displayed, or presented that a reasonable person against which it is to operate ought to have noticed it. A term in an electronic record intended to evoke a response by an electronic agent is conspicuous if it is presented in a form that would enable a reasonably configured electronic agent to take it into account or react to it without review of the record by an individual. Whether a term is "conspicuous" or not is a decision for the court. Conspicuous terms include the following:

    (i) for a person:

      (A) a heading in capitals equal to or greater in size than the surrounding text, or in contrasting type, font, or color to the surrounding text of the same or lesser size;

      (B) language in the body of a record or display in larger type than the surrounding text, or in contrasting type, font, or color to the surrounding text of the same size, or set off from surrounding text of the same size by symbols or other marks that call attention to the language; and

    (ii) for a person or an electronic agent, a term that is so placed in a record or display that the person or electronic agent cannot proceed without taking action with respect to the particular term.

(c) "Consumer" means an individual who buys or contracts to buy goods that, at the time of contracting, are intended by the individual to be used primarily for personal, family, or household purposes.

(d) "Consumer contract" means a contract between a merchant seller and a consumer.
* * * *

(j) "Good faith" means honesty in fact and the observance of reasonable commercial standards of fair dealing.

(k) "Goods" means all things that are movable at the time of identification to a contract for sale. The term includes future goods, specially manufactured goods, the unborn young of animals, growing crops, and other identified things attached to realty as described in Section 2—107. The term does not include information, the money in which the price is to be paid, investment securities under Article 8, the subject matter of foreign exchange transactions, and choses in action.

* * * *

(m) "Record" means information that is inscribed on a tangible medium or that is stored in an electronic or other medium and is retrievable in perceivable form.

(n) "Remedial promise" means a promise by the seller to repair or replace the goods or to refund all or part of the price upon the happening of a specified event.

* * * *

(p) "Sign" means, with present intent to authenticate or adopt a record,
　(i) to execute or adopt a tangible symbol; or
　(ii) to attach to or logically associate with the record an electronic sound, symbol, or process.

* * * *

Part 2 Form, Formation, Terms and Readjustment of Contract; Electronic Contracting

§2—201. FORMAL REQUIREMENTS; STATUTE OF FRAUDS

(1) A contract for the sale of goods for the price of $5,000 or more is not enforceable by way of action or defense unless there is some record sufficient to indicate that a contract for sale has been made between the parties and signed by the party against whom which enforcement is sought or by the party's authorized agent or broker. A record is not insufficient because it omits or incorrectly states a term agreed upon but the contract is not enforceable under this subsection beyond the quantity of goods shown in the record.

(2) Between merchants if within a reasonable time a record in confirmation of the contract and sufficient against the sender is received and the party receiving it has reason to know its contents, it satisfies the requirements of subsection (1) against such party the recipient unless notice of objection to its contents is given in a record within 10 days after it is received.

(3) A contract which does not satisfy the requirements of subsection (1) but which is valid in other respects is enforceable

(a) if the goods are to be specially manufactured for the buyer and are not suitable for sale to others in the ordinary course of the seller's business and the seller, before notice of repudiation is received and under circumstances which reasonably indicate that the goods are for the buyer, has made either a substantial beginning of their manufacture or commitments for their procurement; or

(b) if the party against whom which enforcement is sought admits in the party's pleading, or in the party's testimony or otherwise under oath that a contract for sale was made, but the contract is not enforceable under this paragraph beyond the quantity of goods admitted; or

(c) with respect to goods for which payment has been made and accepted or which have been received and accepted (Sec. 2—606).

(4) A contract that is enforceable under this section is not rendered unenforceable merely because it is not capable of being performed within one year or any other applicable period after its making.

* * * *

§2—207. TERMS OF CONTRACT; EFFECT OF CONFIRMATION

If (i) conduct by both parties recognizes the existence of a contract although their records do not otherwise establish a contract, (ii) a contract is formed by an offer and acceptance, or (iii) a contract formed in any manner is confirmed by a record that contains terms additional to or different from those in the contract being confirmed, the terms of the contract, subject to Section 2—202, are:

(a) terms that appear in the records of both parties;

(b) terms, whether in a record or not, to which both parties agree; and

(c) terms supplied or incorporated under any provision of this Act.

* * * *

Part 3 General Obligation and Construction of Contract

* * * *

§2—312. WARRANTY OF TITLE AND AGAINST INFRINGEMENT; BUYER'S OBLIGATION AGAINST INFRINGEMENT

(1) Subject to subsection (2) there is in a contract for sale a warranty by the seller that

(a) the title conveyed shall be good, good and its transfer rightful and shall not, because of any colorable claim to or interest in the goods, unreasonably expose the buyer to litigation; and

(b) the goods shall be delivered free from any security interest or other lien or encumbrance of which the buyer at the time of contracting has no knowledge.

(2) Unless otherwise agreed a seller that is a merchant regularly dealing in goods of the kind warrants that the goods shall be delivered free of the rightful claim of any third person by way of infringement or the like but a buyer that furnishes specifications to the seller must hold the seller harmless against any such claim that arises out of compliance with the specifications.

(3) A warranty under this section may be disclaimed or modified only by specific language or by circumstances that give the buyer reason to know that the seller does not claim title, that the seller is purporting to sell only the right or title as the seller or a third person may have, or that the seller is selling subject to any claims of infringement or the like.

§2—313. EXPRESS WARRANTIES BY AFFIRMATION, PROMISE, DESCRIPTION, SAMPLE; REMEDIAL PROMISE

(1) In this section, "immediate buyer" means a buyer that enters into a contract with the seller.
* * * *

(4) Any remedial promise made by the seller to the immediate buyer creates an obligation that the promise will be performed upon the happening of the specified event.

§2—313A. OBLIGATION TO REMOTE PURCHASER CREATED BY RECORD PACKAGED WITH OR ACCOMPANYING GOODS

(1) This section applies only to new goods and goods sold or leased as new goods in a transaction of purchase in the normal chain of distribution. In this section:

(a) "Immediate buyer" means a buyer that enters into a contract with the seller.

(b) "Remote purchaser" means a person that buys or leases goods from an immediate buyer or other person in the normal chain of distribution.

(2) If a seller in a record packaged with or accompanying the goods makes an affirmation of fact or promise that relates to the goods, provides a description that relates to the goods, or makes a remedial promise, and the seller reasonably expects the record to be, and the record is, furnished to the remote purchaser, the seller has an obligation to the remote purchaser that:

(a) the goods will conform to the affirmation of fact, promise or description unless a reasonable person in the position of the remote purchaser would not believe that the affirmation of fact, promise or description created an obligation; and

(b) the seller will perform the remedial promise.

(3) It is not necessary to the creation of an obligation under this section that the seller use formal words such as "warrant" or "guarantee" or that the seller have a specific intention to undertake an obligation, but an affirmation merely of the value of the goods or a statement purporting to be merely the seller's opinion or commendation of the goods does not create an obligation.

(4) The following rules apply to the remedies for breach of an obligation created under this section:

(a) The seller may modify or limit the remedies available to the remote purchaser if the modification or limitation is furnished to the remote purchaser no later than the time of purchase or if the modification or limitation is contained in the record that contains the affirmation of fact, promise or description.

(b) Subject to a modification or limitation of remedy, a seller in breach is liable for incidental or consequential damages under Section 2—715, but the seller is not liable for lost profits.

(c) The remote purchaser may recover as damages for breach of a seller's obligation arising under subsection (2) the loss resulting in the ordinary course of events as determined in any manner that is reasonable.

(5) An obligation that is not a remedial promise is breached if the goods did not conform to the affirmation of fact, promise or description creating the obligation when the goods left the seller's control.

§2—313B. OBLIGATION TO REMOTE PURCHASER CREATED BY COMMUNICATION TO THE PUBLIC

(1) This section applies only to new goods and goods sold or leased as new goods in a transaction of purchase in the normal chain of distribution. In this section:

(a) "Immediate buyer" means a buyer that enters into a contract with the seller.

(b) "Remote purchaser" means a person that buys or leases goods from an immediate buyer or other person in the normal chain of distribution.

(2) If a seller in advertising or a similar communication to the public makes an affirmation of fact or promise that relates to the goods, provides a description that relates to the goods, or makes a remedial promise, and the remote purchaser enters into a transaction of purchase with knowledge of and with the expectation that the goods will conform to the affirmation of fact, promise, or description, or that the seller will perform the remedial promise, the seller has an obligation to the remote purchaser that:

(a) the goods will conform to the affirmation of fact, promise or description unless a reasonable person in the position of the remote purchaser would not believe that the affirmation of fact, promise or description created an obligation; and

    (b) the seller will perform the remedial promise.

(3) It is not necessary to the creation of an obligation under this section that the seller use formal words such as "warrant" or "guarantee" or that the seller have a specific intention to undertake an obligation, but an affirmation merely of the value of the goods or a statement purporting to be merely the seller's opinion or commendation of the goods does not create an obligation.

(4) The following rules apply to the remedies for breach of an obligation created under this section:

    (a) The seller may modify or limit the remedies available to the remote purchaser if the modification or limitation is furnished to the remote purchaser no later than the time of purchase. The modification or limitation may be furnished as part of the communication that contains the affirmation of fact, promise or description.

    (b) Subject to a modification or limitation of remedy, a seller in breach is liable for incidental or consequential damages under Section 2—715, but the seller is not liable for lost profits.

    (c) The remote purchaser may recover as damages for breach of a seller's obligation arising under subsection (2) the loss resulting in the ordinary course of events as determined in any manner that is reasonable.

(5) An obligation that is not a remedial promise is breached if the goods did not conform to the affirmation of fact, promise or description creating the obligation when the goods left the seller's control.

* * * *

§2—316. EXCLUSION OR MODIFICATION OF WARRANTIES.

* * * *

(2) Subject to subsection (3), to exclude or modify the implied warranty of merchantability or any part of it in a consumer contract the language must be in a record, be conspicuous and state "The seller undertakes no responsibility for the quality of the goods except as otherwise provided in this contract," and in any other contract the language must mention merchantability and in case of a record must be conspicuous. Subject to subsection (3), to exclude or modify the implied warranty of fitness the exclusion must be in a record and be conspicuous. Language to exclude all implied warranties of fitness in a consumer contract must state "The seller assumes no responsibility that the goods will be fit for any particular purpose for which you may be buying these goods, except as otherwise provided in the contract," and in any other contract the language is sufficient if it states, for example, that "There are no warranties which extend beyond the description on the face hereof." Language that satisfies the requirements of this subsection for the exclusion and modification of a warranty in a consumer contract also satisfies the requirements for any other contract.

(3) Notwithstanding subsection (2):

    (a) unless the circumstances indicate otherwise, all implied warranties are excluded by expressions like "as is", "with all faults" or other language which in common understanding calls the buyer's attention to the exclusion of warranties, makes plain that there is no implied warranty, and in a consumer contract evidenced by a record is set forth conspicuously in the record; and

    (b) when the buyer before entering into the contract has examined the goods or the sample or model as fully as desired or has refused to examine the goods after a demand by the seller there is no implied warranty with regard to defects which an examination ought in the circumstances to have revealed to the buyer; and

    (c) an implied warranty can also be excluded or modified by course of dealing or course of performance or usage of trade.

* * * *

§2—318. THIRD PARTY BENEFICIARIES OF WARRANTIES EXPRESS OR IMPLIED

(1) In this section:

    (a) "Immediate buyer" means a buyer that enters into a contract with the seller.

    (b) "Remote purchaser" means a person that buys or leases goods from an immediate buyer or other person in the normal chain of distribution.

Alternative A to subsection (2)

(2) A seller's warranty whether express or implied to an immediate buyer, a seller's remedial promise to an immediate buyer, or a seller's obligation to a remote purchaser under Section 2—313A or 2—313B extends to any natural person who is in the family or household of the immediate buyer or the remote purchaser or who is a guest in the home of either if it is reasonable to expect that the person may use, consume or be affected by the goods and who is injured in person by breach of the warranty, remedial promise or obligation. A seller may not exclude or limit the operation of this section.

Alternative B to subsection (2)

(2) A seller's warranty whether express or implied to an immediate buyer, a seller's remedial promise to an immediate buyer, or a seller's obligation to a remote purchaser under Section 2—313A or 2—313B extends to any natural

person who may reasonably be expected to use, consume or be affected by the goods and who is injured in person by breach of the warranty, remedial promise or obligation. A seller may not exclude or limit the operation of this section.

Alternative C to subsection (2)

(2)   A seller's warranty whether express or implied to an immediate buyer, a seller's remedial promise to an immediate buyer, or a seller's obligation to a remote purchaser under Section 2—313A or 2—313B extends to any person that may reasonably be expected to use, consume or be affected by the goods and that is injured by breach of the warranty, remedial promise or obligation. A seller may not exclude or limit the operation of this section with respect to injury to the person of an individual to whom the warranty, remedial promise or obligation extends.
* * * *

Part 5 Performance
* * * *

§2—502. BUYER'S RIGHT TO GOODS ON SELLER'S INSOLVENCY

(1)   Subject to subsections (2) and (3) and even though the goods have not been shipped a buyer who that has paid a part or all of the price of goods in which the buyer has a special property under the provisions of the immediately preceding section may on making and keeping good a tender of any unpaid portion of their price recover them from the seller if:

    (a)   in the case of goods bought by a consumer, the seller repudiates or fails to deliver as required by the contract; or

    (b)   in all cases, the seller becomes insolvent within ten days after receipt of the first installment on their price.

(2)   The buyer's right to recover the goods under subsection (1) vests upon acquisition of a special property, even if the seller had not then repudiated or failed to deliver.

(3)   If the identification creating the special property has been made by the buyer, the buyer acquires the right to recover the goods only if they conform to the contract for sale.
* * * *

§2—508. CURE BY SELLER OF IMPROPER TENDER OR DELIVERY; REPLACEMENT

(1)   Where the buyer rejects goods or a tender of delivery under Section 2—601 or 2—612 or except in a consumer contract justifiably revokes acceptance under Section 2—608(1)(b) and the agreed time for performance has not expired, a seller that has performed in good faith, upon seasonable notice to the buyer and at the seller's own expense, may cure the breach of contract by making a conforming tender of delivery within the agreed time. The seller shall compensate the buyer for all of the buyer's reasonable expenses caused by the seller's breach of contract and subsequent cure.

(2)   Where the buyer rejects goods or a tender of delivery under Section 2—601 or 2—612 or except in a consumer contract justifiably revokes acceptance under Section 2—608(1)(b) and the agreed time for performance has expired, a seller that has performed in good faith, upon seasonable notice to the buyer and at the seller's own expense, may cure the breach of contract, if the cure is appropriate and timely under the circumstances, by making a tender of conforming goods. The seller shall compensate the buyer for all of the buyer's reasonable expenses caused by the seller's breach of contract and subsequent cure.

§2—509. RISK OF LOSS IN THE ABSENCE OF BREACH

(1)   Where the contract requires or authorizes the seller to ship the goods by carrier

    (a)   if it does not require the seller to deliver them at a particular destination, the risk of loss passes to the buyer when the goods are delivered to the carrier even though the shipment is under reservation (Section 2—505); but

    (b)   if it does require the seller to deliver them at a particular destination and the goods are there tendered while in the possession of the carrier, the risk of loss passes to the buyer when the goods are there so tendered as to enable the buyer to take delivery.

(2)   Where the goods are held by a bailee to be delivered without being moved, the risk of loss passes to the buyer

    (a)   on the buyer's receipt of a negotiable document of title covering the goods; or

    (b)   on acknowledgment by the bailee to the buyer of the buyer's right to possession of the goods; or

    (c)   after the buyer's receipt of a non-negotiable document of title or other direction to deliver in a record, as provided in subsection (4)(b) of Section 2—503.

(3)   In any case not within subsection (1) or (2), the risk of loss passes to the buyer on the buyer's receipt of the goods.
* * * *

§2—513. BUYER'S RIGHT TO INSPECTION OF GOODS
* * * *

(3)   Unless otherwise agreed, the buyer is not entitled to inspect the goods before payment of the price when the contract provides

    (a)   for delivery on terms that under applicable course of performance, course of dealing, or usage of trade are interpreted to preclude inspection before payment; or

(b) for payment against documents of title, except where such payment is due only after the goods are to become available for inspection.

* * * *

Part 6 Breach, Repudiation and Excuse
* * * *

§2—605. WAIVER OF BUYER'S OBJECTIONS BY FAILURE TO PARTICULARIZE

(1) The buyer's failure to state in connection with rejection a particular defect or in connection with revocation of acceptance a defect that justifies revocation precludes the buyer from relying on the unstated defect to justify rejection or revocation of acceptance if the defect is ascertainable by reasonable inspection

(a) where the seller had a right to cure the defect and could have cured it if stated seasonably; or

(b) between merchants when the seller has after rejection made a request in a record for a full and final statement in record form of all defects on which the buyer proposes to rely.

(2) A buyer's payment against documents tendered to the buyer made without reservation of rights precludes recovery of the payment for defects apparent on the face of the documents.
* * * *

§2—607. EFFECT OF ACCEPTANCE; NOTICE OF BREACH; BURDEN OF ESTABLISHING BREACH AFTER ACCEPTANCE; NOTICE OF CLAIM OR LITIGATION TO PERSON ANSWERABLE OVER
* * * *

(3) Where a tender has been accepted

(a) the buyer must within a reasonable time after the buyer discovers or should have discovered any breach notify the seller; however, failure to give timely notice bars the buyer from a remedy only to the extent that the seller is prejudiced by the failure and

(b) if the claim is one for infringement or the like (subsection (3) of Section 2—312) and the buyer is sued as a result of such a breach the buyer must so notify the seller within a reasonable time after the buyer receives notice of the litigation or be barred from any remedy over for liability established by the litigation.
* * * *

§2—608. REVOCATION OF ACCEPTANCE IN WHOLE OR IN PART
* * * *

(4) If a buyer uses the goods after a rightful rejection or justifiable revocation of acceptance, the following rules apply:

(a) Any use by the buyer that is unreasonable under the circumstances is wrongful as against the seller and is an acceptance only if ratified by the seller.

(b) Any use of the goods that is reasonable under the circumstances is not wrongful as against the seller and is not an acceptance, but in an appropriate case the buyer shall be obligated to the seller for the value of the use to the buyer.
* * * *

§2—612. "INSTALLMENT CONTRACT"; BREACH
* * * *

(2) The buyer may reject any installment which is non-conforming if the non-conformity substantially impairs the value of that installment to the buyer or if the non-conformity is a defect in the required documents; but if the non-conformity does not fall within subsection (3) and the seller gives adequate assurance of its cure the buyer must accept that installment.

(3) Whenever non-conformity or default with respect to one or more installments substantially impairs the value of the whole contract there is a breach of the whole. But the aggrieved party reinstates the contract if the party accepts a non-conforming installment without seasonably notifying of cancellation or if the party brings an action with respect only to past installments or demands performance as to future installments.
* * * *

Part 7 Remedies

§2—702. SELLER'S REMEDIES ON DISCOVERY OF BUYER'S INSOLVENCY
* * * *

(2) Where the seller discovers that the buyer has received goods on credit while insolvent the seller may reclaim the goods upon demand made within a reasonable time after the buyer's receipt of the goods. Except as provided in this subsection the seller may not base a right to reclaim goods on the buyer's fraudulent or innocent misrepresentation of solvency or of intent to pay.
* * * *

§2—705. SELLER'S STOPPAGE OF DELIVERY IN TRANSIT OR OTHERWISE

(1) The seller may stop delivery of goods in the possession of a carrier or other bailee when the seller discovers the buyer to be insolvent (Section 2—702) or when the buyer repudiates or fails to make a payment due before delivery or if for any other reason the seller has a right to withhold or reclaim the goods.
* * * *

§2—706. SELLER'S RESALE INCLUDING CONTRACT FOR RESALE

(1) In an appropriate case involving breach by the buyer, the seller may resell the goods concerned or the undelivered

balance thereof. Where the resale is made in good faith and in a commercially reasonable manner the seller may recover the difference between the contract price and the resale price together with any incidental or consequential damages allowed under the provisions of this Article (Section 2—710), but less expenses saved in consequence of the buyer's breach.

* * * *

§2—708. SELLER'S DAMAGES FOR NON-ACCEPTANCE OR REPUDIATION

(1) Subject to subsection (2) and to the provisions of this Article with respect to proof of market price (Section 2—723)

   (a) the measure of damages for non-acceptance by the buyer is the difference between the contract price and the market price at the time and place for tender together with any incidental or consequential damages provided in this Article (Section 2—710), but less expenses saved in consequence of the buyer's breach; and

   (b) the measure of damages for repudiation by the buyer is the difference between the contract price and the market price at the place for tender at the expiration of a commercially reasonable time after the seller learned of the repudiation, but no later than the time stated in paragraph (a), together with any incidental or consequential damages provided in this Article (Section 2—710), but less expenses saved in consequence of the buyer's breach.

(2) If the measure of damages provided in subsection (1) or in Section 2—706 is inadequate to put the seller in as good a position as performance would have done then the measure of damages is the profit (including reasonable overhead) which the seller would have made from full performance by the buyer, together with any incidental or consequential damages provided in this Article (Section 2—710).

§2—709. ACTION FOR THE PRICE

(1) When the buyer fails to pay the price as it becomes due the seller may recover, together with any incidental or consequential damages under the next section, the price

   (a) of goods accepted or of conforming goods lost or damaged within a commercially reasonable time after risk of their loss has passed to the buyer; and

   (b) of goods identified to the contract if the seller is unable after reasonable effort to resell them at a reasonable price or the circumstances reasonably indicate that such effort will be unavailing.

* * * *

§2—710. SELLER'S INCIDENTAL AND CONSEQUENTIAL DAMAGES

(1) Incidental damages to an aggrieved seller include any commercially reasonable charges, expenses or commissions incurred in stopping delivery, in the transportation, care and custody of goods after the buyer's breach, in connection with return or resale of the goods or otherwise resulting from the breach.

(2) Consequential damages resulting from the buyer's breach include any loss resulting from general or particular requirements and needs of which the buyer at the time of contracting had reason to know and which could not reasonably be prevented by resale or otherwise.

(3) In a consumer contract, a seller may not recover consequential damages from a consumer.

* * * *

§2—713. BUYER'S DAMAGES FOR NON-DELIVERY OR REPUDIATION

(1) Subject to the provisions of this Article with respect to proof of market price (Section 2—723), if the seller wrongfully fails to deliver or repudiates or the buyer rightfully rejects or justifiably revokes acceptance

   (a) the measure of damages in the case of wrongful failure to deliver by the seller or rightful rejection or justifiable revocation of acceptance by the buyer is the difference between the market price at the time for tender under the contract and the contract price together with any incidental or consequential damages provided in this Article (Section 2—715), but less expenses saved in consequence of the seller's breach; and

   (b) the measure of damages for repudiation by the seller is the difference between the market price at the expiration of a commercially reasonable time after the buyer learned of the repudiation, but no later than the time stated in paragraph (a), and the contract price together with any incidental or consequential damages provided in this Article (Section 2—715), but less expenses saved in consequence of the seller's breach.

* * * *

§2—725. STATUTE OF LIMITATIONS IN CONTRACTS FOR SALE

(1) Except as otherwise provided in this section, an action for breach of any contract for sale must be commenced within the later of four years after the right of action has accrued under subsection (2) or (3) or one year after the breach was or should have been discovered, but no longer than five years after the right of action accrued. By the original agreement the parties may reduce the period of limitation to not less than one year but may not extend it; however, in a consumer contract, the period of limitation may not be reduced.

(2) Except as otherwise provided in subsection (3), the following rules apply:

(a) Except as otherwise provided in this subsection, a right of action for breach of a contract accrues when the breach occurs, even if the aggrieved party did not have knowledge of the breach.

(b) For breach of a contract by repudiation, a right of action accrues at the earlier of when the aggrieved party elects to treat the repudiation as a breach or when a commercially reasonable time for awaiting performance has expired.

(c) For breach of a remedial promise, a right of action accrues when the remedial promise is not performed when due.

(d) In an action by a buyer against a person that is answerable over to the buyer for a claim asserted against the buyer, the buyer's right of action against the person answerable over accrues at the time the claim was originally asserted against the buyer.

(3) If a breach of a warranty arising under Section 2—312, 2—313(2), 2—314, or 2—315, or a breach of an obligation other than a remedial promise arising under Section 2—313A or 2—313B, is claimed the following rules apply:

(a) Except as otherwise provided in paragraph (c), a right of action for breach of a warranty arising under Section 2—313(2), 2—314 or 2—315 accrues when the seller has tendered delivery to the immediate buyer, as defined in Section 2—313, and has completed performance of any agreed installation or assembly of the goods.

(b) Except as otherwise provided in paragraph (c), a right of action for breach of an obligation other than a remedial promise arising under Section 2—313A or 2—313B accrues when the remote purchaser, as defined in sections 2—313A and 2—313B, receives the goods.

(c) Where a warranty arising under Section 2—313(2) or an obligation other than a remedial promise arising under 2—313A or 2—313B explicitly extends to future performance of the goods and discovery of the breach must await the time for performance the right of action accrues when the immediate buyer as defined in Section2—313 or the remote purchaser as defined in Sections 2—313A and 2—313B discovers or should have discovered the breach.

(d) A right of action for breach of warranty arising under Section 2—312 accrues when the aggrieved party discovers or should have discovered the breach. However, an action for breach of the warranty of non-infringement may not be commenced more than six years after tender of delivery of the goods to the aggrieved party.

* * * *

ARTICLE 2A LEASES

Part 1 General Provisions

§2A—101. SHORT TITLE

This Article shall be known and may be cited as the Uniform Commercial Code—Leases.

§2A—102. SCOPE

This Article applies to any transaction, regardless of form, that creates a lease.

§2A—103. DEFINITIONS AND INDEX OF DEFINITIONS

(1) In this Article unless the context otherwise requires:

(a) "Buyer in ordinary course of business" means a person who in good faith and without knowledge that the sale to him [or her] is in violation of the ownership rights or security interest or leasehold interest of a third party in the goods buys in ordinary course from a person in the business of selling goods of that kind but does not include a pawnbroker. "Buying" may be for cash or by exchange of other property or on secured or unsecured credit and includes receiving goods or documents of title under a pre-existing contract for sale but does not include a transfer in bulk or as security for or in total or partial satisfaction of a money debt.

(b) "Cancellation" occurs when either party puts an end to the lease contract for default by the other party.

(c) "Commercial unit" means such a unit of goods as by commercial usage is a single whole for purposes of lease and division of which materially impairs its character or value on the market or in use. A commercial unit may be a single article, as a machine, or a set of articles, as a suite of furniture or a line of machinery, or a quantity, as a gross or carload, or any other unit treated in use or in the relevant market as a single whole.

(d) "Conforming" goods or performance under a lease contract means goods or performance that are in accordance with the obligations under the lease contract.

(e) "Consumer lease" means a lease that a lessor regularly engaged in the business of leasing or selling makes to a lessee who is an individual and who takes under the lease primarily for a personal, family, or household purpose [, if the total payments to be made under the lease contract, excluding payments for options to renew or buy, do not exceed $____].

(f) "Fault" means wrongful act, omission, breach, or default.

(g) "Finance lease" means a lease with respect to which:

(i) the lessor does not select, manufacture or supply the goods;

(ii) the lessor acquires the goods or the right to possession and use of the goods in connection with the lease; and

(iii) one of the following occurs:

(A) the lessee receives a copy of the contract by which the lessor acquired the goods or the right to possession and use of the goods before signing the lease contract;

(B) the lessee's approval of the contract by which the lessor acquired the goods or the right to possession and use of the goods is a condition to effectiveness of the lease contract;

(C) the lessee, before signing the lease contract, receives an accurate and complete statement designating the promises and warranties, and any disclaimers of warranties, limitations or modifications of remedies, or liquidated damages, including those of a third party, such as the manufacturer of the goods, provided to the lessor by the person supplying the goods in connection with or as part of the contract by which the lessor acquired the goods or the right to possession and use of the goods; or

(D) if the lease is not a consumer lease, the lessor, before the lessee signs the lease contract, informs the lessee in writing (a) of the identity of the person supplying the goods to the lessor, unless the lessee has selected that person and directed the lessor to acquire the goods or the right to possession and use of the goods from that person, (b) that the lessee is entitled under this Article to any promises and warranties, including those of any third party, provided to the lessor by the person supplying the goods in connection with or as part of the contract by which the lessor acquired the goods or the right to possession and use of the goods, and (c) that the lessee may communicate with the person supplying the goods to the lessor and receive an accurate and complete statement of those promises and warranties, including any disclaimers and limitations of them or of remedies.

(h) "Goods" means all things that are movable at the time of identification to the lease contract, or are fixtures (Section 2A—309), but the term does not include money, documents, instruments, accounts, chattel paper, general intangibles, or minerals or the like, including oil and gas, before extraction. The term also includes the unborn young of animals.

(i) "Installment lease contract" means a lease contract that authorizes or requires the delivery of goods in separate lots to be separately accepted, even though the lease contract contains a clause "each delivery is a separate lease" or its equivalent.

(j) "Lease" means a transfer of the right to possession and use of goods for a term in return for consideration, but a sale, including a sale on approval or a sale or return, or retention or creation of a security interest is not a lease. Unless the context clearly indicates otherwise, the term includes a sublease.

(k) "Lease agreement" means the bargain, with respect to the lease, of the lessor and the lessee in fact as found in their language or by implication from other circumstances including course of dealing or usage of trade or course of performance as provided in this Article. Unless the context clearly indicates otherwise, the term includes a sublease agreement.

(l) "Lease contract" means the total legal obligation that results from the lease agreement as affected by this Article and any other applicable rules of law. Unless the context clearly indicates otherwise, the term includes a sublease contract.

(m) "Leasehold interest" means the interest of the lessor or the lessee under a lease contract.

(n) "Lessee" means a person who acquires the right to possession and use of goods under a lease. Unless the context clearly indicates otherwise, the term includes a sublessee.

(o) "Lessee in ordinary course of business" means a person who in good faith and without knowledge that the lease to him [or her] is in violation of the ownership rights or security interest or leasehold interest of a third party in the goods, leases in ordinary course from a person in the business of selling or leasing goods of that kind but does not include a pawnbroker. "Leasing" may be for cash or by exchange of other property or on secured or unsecured credit and includes receiving goods or documents of title under a pre-existing lease contract but does not include a transfer in bulk or as security for or in total or partial satisfaction of a money debt.

(p) "Lessor" means a person who transfers the right to possession and use of goods under a lease.

Unless the context clearly indicates otherwise, the term includes a sublessor.

(q) "Lessor's residual interest" means the lessor's interest in the goods after expiration, termination, or cancellation of the lease contract.

(r) "Lien" means a charge against or interest in goods to secure payment of a debt or performance of an obligation, but the term does not include a security interest.

(s) "Lot" means a parcel or a single article that is the subject matter of a separate lease or delivery, whether or not it is sufficient to perform the lease contract.

(t) "Merchant lessee" means a lessee that is a merchant with respect to goods of the kind subject to the lease.

(u) "Present value" means the amount as of a date certain of one or more sums payable in the future, discounted to the date certain. The discount is determined by the interest rate specified by the parties if the rate was not manifestly unreasonable at the time the transaction was entered into; otherwise, the discount is determined by a commercially reasonable rate that takes into account the facts and circumstances of each case at the time the transaction was entered into.

(v) "Purchase" includes taking by sale, lease, mortgage, security interest, pledge, gift, or any other voluntary transaction creating an interest in goods.

(w) "Sublease" means a lease of goods the right to possession and use of which was acquired by the lessor as a lessee under an existing lease.

(x) "Supplier" means a person from whom a lessor buys or leases goods to be leased under a finance lease.

(y) "Supply contract" means a contract under which a lessor buys or leases goods to be leased.

(z) "Termination" occurs when either party pursuant to a power created by agreement or law puts an end to the lease contract otherwise than for default.

(2) Other definitions applying to this Article and the sections in which they appear are:

"Accessions". Section 2A—310(1).
"Construction mortgage". Section 2A—309(1)(d).
"Encumbrance". Section 2A—309(1)(e).
"Fixtures". Section 2A—309(1)(a).
"Fixture filing". Section 2A—309(1)(b).
"Purchase money lease". Section 2A—309(1)(c).

(3) The following definitions in other Articles apply to this Article:

"Accounts". Section 9—106.

"Between merchants". Section 2—104(3).
"Buyer". Section 2—103(1)(a).
"Chattel paper". Section 9—105(1)(b).
"Consumer goods". Section 9—109(1).
"Document". Section 9—105(1)(f).
"Entrusting". Section 2—403(3).
"General intangibles". Section 9—106.
"Good faith". Section 2—103(1)(b).
"Instrument". Section 9—105(1)(i).
"Merchant". Section 2—104(1).
"Mortgage". Section 9—105(1)(j).
"Pursuant to commitment". Section 9—105(1)(k).
"Receipt". Section 2—103(1)(c).
"Sale". Section 2—106(1).
"Sale on approval". Section 2—326.
"Sale or return". Section 2—326.
"Seller". Section 2—103(1)(d).

(4) In addition Article 1 contains general definitions and principles of construction and interpretation applicable throughout this Article.

As amended in 1990 and 1999.

§2A—104. LEASES SUBJECT TO OTHER LAW

(1) A lease, although subject to this Article, is also subject to any applicable:

(a) certificate of title statute of this State: (list any certificate of title statutes covering automobiles, trailers, mobile homes, boats, farm tractors, and the like);

(b) certificate of title statute of another jurisdiction (Section 2A—105); or

(c) consumer protection statute of this State, or final consumer protection decision of a court of this State existing on the effective date of this Article.

(2) In case of conflict between this Article, other than Sections 2A—105, 2A—304(3), and 2A—305(3), and a statute or decision referred to in subsection (1), the statute or decision controls.

(3) Failure to comply with an applicable law has only the effect specified therein.

As amended in 1990.

§2A—105. TERRITORIAL APPLICATION OF ARTICLE TO GOODS COVERED BY CERTIFICATE OF TITLE

Subject to the provisions of Sections 2A—304(3) and 2A—305(3), with respect to goods covered by a certificate of title issued under a statute of this State or of another jurisdiction, compliance and the effect of compliance or noncompliance with a certificate of title statute are governed by the law (including the conflict of laws rules) of the jurisdiction issuing the certificate until the earlier of (a) surrender of the certificate, or (b) four months after the goods are removed from that jurisdiction and thereafter until a new certificate of title is issued by another jurisdiction.

§2A—106. LIMITATION ON POWER OF PARTIES TO CONSUMER LEASE TO CHOOSE APPLICABLE LAW AND JUDICIAL FORUM

(1) If the law chosen by the parties to a consumer lease is that of a jurisdiction other than a jurisdiction in which the lessee resides at the time the lease agreement becomes enforceable or within 30 days thereafter or in which the goods are to be used, the choice is not enforceable.

(2) If the judicial forum chosen by the parties to a consumer lease is a forum that would not otherwise have jurisdiction over the lessee, the choice is not enforceable.

§2A—107. WAIVER OR RENUNCIATION OF CLAIM OR RIGHT AFTER DEFAULT

Any claim or right arising out of an alleged default or breach of warranty may be discharged in whole or in part without consideration by a written waiver or renunciation signed and delivered by the aggrieved party.

§2A—108. UNCONSCIONABILITY

(1) If the court as a matter of law finds a lease contract or any clause of a lease contract to have been unconscionable at the time it was made the court may refuse to enforce the lease contract, or it may enforce the remainder of the lease contract without the unconscionable clause, or it may so limit the application of any unconscionable clause as to avoid any unconscionable result.

(2) With respect to a consumer lease, if the court as a matter of law finds that a lease contract or any clause of a lease contract has been induced by unconscionable conduct or that unconscionable conduct has occurred in the collection of a claim arising from a lease contract, the court may grant appropriate relief.

(3) Before making a finding of unconscionability under subsection (1) or (2), the court, on its own motion or that of a party, shall afford the parties a reasonable opportunity to present evidence as to the setting, purpose, and effect of the lease contract or clause thereof, or of the conduct.

(4) In an action in which the lessee claims unconscionability with respect to a consumer lease:

(a) If the court finds unconscionability under subsection (1) or (2), the court shall award reasonable attorney's fees to the lessee.

(b) If the court does not find unconscionability and the lessee claiming unconscionability has brought or maintained an action he [or she] knew to be groundless, the court shall award reasonable

attorney's fees to the party against whom the claim is made.

(c) In determining attorney's fees, the amount of the recovery on behalf of the claimant under subsections (1) and (2) is not controlling.

§2A—109. OPTION TO ACCELERATE AT WILL

(1) A term providing that one party or his [or her] successor in interest may accelerate payment or performance or require collateral or additional collateral "at will" or "when he [or she] deems himself [or herself] insecure" or in words of similar import must be construed to mean that he [or she] has power to do so only if he [or she] in good faith believes that the prospect of payment or performance is impaired.

(2) With respect to a consumer lease, the burden of establishing good faith under subsection (1) is on the party who exercised the power; otherwise the burden of establishing lack of good faith is on the party against whom the power has been exercised.

Part 2 Formation and Construction of Lease Contract

§2A—201. STATUTE OF FRAUDS

(1) A lease contract is not enforceable by way of action or defense unless:

(a) the total payments to be made under the lease contract, excluding payments for options to renew or buy, are less than $1,000; or

(b) there is a writing, signed by the party against whom enforcement is sought or by that party's authorized agent, sufficient to indicate that a lease contract has been made between the parties and to describe the goods leased and the lease term.

(2) Any description of leased goods or of the lease term is sufficient and satisfies subsection (1)(b), whether or not it is specific, if it reasonably identifies what is described.

(3) A writing is not insufficient because it omits or incorrectly states a term agreed upon, but the lease contract is not enforceable under subsection (1)(b) beyond the lease term and the quantity of goods shown in the writing.

(4) A lease contract that does not satisfy the requirements of subsection (1), but which is valid in other respects, is enforceable:

(a) if the goods are to be specially manufactured or obtained for the lessee and are not suitable for lease or sale to others in the ordinary course of the lessor's business, and the lessor, before notice of repudiation is received and under circumstances that reasonably indicate that the goods are for the lessee, has made either a substantial beginning of their manufacture or commitments for their procurement;

(b) if the party against whom enforcement is sought admits in that party's pleading, testimony or otherwise in court that a lease contract was made, but the lease contract is not enforceable under this provision beyond the quantity of goods admitted; or

(c) with respect to goods that have been received and accepted by the lessee.

(5) The lease term under a lease contract referred to in subsection (4) is:

(a) if there is a writing signed by the party against whom enforcement is sought or by that party's authorized agent specifying the lease term, the term so specified;

(b) if the party against whom enforcement is sought admits in that party's pleading, testimony, or otherwise in court a lease term, the term so admitted; or

(c) a reasonable lease term.

§2A—202. FINAL WRITTEN EXPRESSION: PAROL OR EXTRINSIC EVIDENCE

Terms with respect to which the confirmatory memoranda of the parties agree or which are otherwise set forth in a writing intended by the parties as a final expression of their agreement with respect to such terms as are included therein may not be contradicted by evidence of any prior agreement or of a contemporaneous oral agreement but may be explained or supplemented:

(a) by course of dealing or usage of trade or by course of performance; and

(b) by evidence of consistent additional terms unless the court finds the writing to have been intended also as a complete and exclusive statement of the terms of the agreement.

§2A—203. SEALS INOPERATIVE

The affixing of a seal to a writing evidencing a lease contract or an offer to enter into a lease contract does not render the writing a sealed instrument and the law with respect to sealed instruments does not apply to the lease contract or offer.

§2A—204. FORMATION IN GENERAL

(1) A lease contract may be made in any manner sufficient to show agreement, including conduct by both parties which recognizes the existence of a lease contract.

(2) An agreement sufficient to constitute a lease contract may be found although the moment of its making is undetermined.

(3) Although one or more terms are left open, a lease contract does not fail for indefiniteness if the parties have

intended to make a lease contract and there is a reasonably certain basis for giving an appropriate remedy.

§2A—205. FIRM OFFERS

An offer by a merchant to lease goods to or from another person in a signed writing that by its terms gives assurance it will be held open is not revocable, for lack of consideration, during the time stated or, if no time is stated, for a reasonable time, but in no event may the period of irrevocability exceed 3 months. Any such term of assurance on a form supplied by the offeree must be separately signed by the offeror.

§2A—206. OFFER AND ACCEPTANCE IN FORMATION OF LEASE CONTRACT

(1) Unless otherwise unambiguously indicated by the language or circumstances, an offer to make a lease contract must be construed as inviting acceptance in any manner and by any medium reasonable in the circumstances.

(2) If the beginning of a requested performance is a reasonable mode of acceptance, an offeror who is not notified of acceptance within a reasonable time may treat the offer as having lapsed before acceptance.

§2A—207. COURSE OF PERFORMANCE OR PRACTICAL CONSTRUCTION

(1) If a lease contract involves repeated occasions for performance by either party with knowledge of the nature of the performance and opportunity for objection to it by the other, any course of performance accepted or acquiesced in without objection is relevant to determine the meaning of the lease agreement.

(2) The express terms of a lease agreement and any course of performance, as well as any course of dealing and usage of trade, must be construed whenever reasonable as consistent with each other; but if that construction is unreasonable, express terms control course of performance, course of performance controls both course of dealing and usage of trade, and course of dealing controls usage of trade.

(3) Subject to the provisions of Section 2A—208 on modification and waiver, course of performance is relevant to show a waiver or modification of any term inconsistent with the course of performance.

§2A—208. MODIFICATION, RESCISSION AND WAIVER

(1) An agreement modifying a lease contract needs no consideration to be binding.

(2) A signed lease agreement that excludes modification or rescission except by a signed writing may not be otherwise modified or rescinded, but, except as between merchants, such a requirement on a form supplied by a merchant must be separately signed by the other party.

(3) Although an attempt at modification or rescission does not satisfy the requirements of subsection (2), it may operate as a waiver.

(4) A party who has made a waiver affecting an executory portion of a lease contract may retract the waiver by reasonable notification received by the other party that strict performance will be required of any term waived, unless the retraction would be unjust in view of a material change of position in reliance on the waiver.

§2A—209. LESSEE UNDER FINANCE LEASE AS BENEFICIARY OF SUPPLY CONTRACT

(1) The benefit of the supplier's promises to the lessor under the supply contract and of all warranties, whether express or implied, including those of any third party provided in connection with or as part of the supply contract, extends to the lessee to the extent of the lessee's leasehold interest under a finance lease related to the supply contract, but is subject to the terms warranty and of the supply contract and all defenses or claims arising therefrom.

(2) The extension of the benefit of supplier's promises and of warranties to the lessee (Section 2A—209(1)) does not: (i) modify the rights and obligations of the parties to the supply contract, whether arising therefrom or otherwise, or (ii) impose any duty or liability under the supply contract on the lessee.

(3) Any modification or rescission of the supply contract by the supplier and the lessor is effective between the supplier and the lessee unless, before the modification or rescission, the supplier has received notice that the lessee has entered into a finance lease related to the supply contract. If the modification or rescission is effective between the supplier and the lessee, the lessor is deemed to have assumed, in addition to the obligations of the lessor to the lessee under the lease contract, promises of the supplier to the lessor and warranties that were so modified or rescinded as they existed and were available to the lessee before modification or rescission.

(4) In addition to the extension of the benefit of the supplier's promises and of warranties to the lessee under subsection (1), the lessee retains all rights that the lessee may have against the supplier which arise from an agreement between the lessee and the supplier or under other law.

As amended in 1990.

§2A—210. EXPRESS WARRANTIES

(1) Express warranties by the lessor are created as follows:
(a) Any affirmation of fact or promise made by the lessor to the lessee which relates to the goods and becomes part of the basis of the bargain creates an express warranty that the goods will conform to the affirmation or promise.

(b) Any description of the goods which is made part of the basis of the bargain creates an express warranty that the goods will conform to the description.

(c) Any sample or model that is made part of the basis of the bargain creates an express warranty that the whole of the goods will conform to the sample or model.

(2) It is not necessary to the creation of an express warranty that the lessor use formal words, such as "warrant" or "guarantee," or that the lessor have a specific intention to make a warranty, but an affirmation merely of the value of the goods or a statement purporting to be merely the lessor's opinion or commendation of the goods does not create a warranty.

§2A—211. WARRANTIES AGAINST INTERFERENCE AND AGAINST INFRINGEMENT; LESSEE'S OBLIGATION AGAINST INFRINGEMENT

(1) There is in a lease contract a warranty that for the lease term no person holds a claim to or interest in the goods that arose from an act or omission of the lessor, other than a claim by way of infringement or the like, which will interfere with the lessee's enjoyment of its leasehold interest.

(2) Except in a finance lease there is in a lease contract by a lessor who is a merchant regularly dealing in goods of the kind a warranty that the goods are delivered free of the rightful claim of any person by way of infringement or the like.

(3) A lessee who furnishes specifications to a lessor or a supplier shall hold the lessor and the supplier harmless against any claim by way of infringement or the like that arises out of compliance with the specifications.

§2A—212. IMPLIED WARRANTY OF MERCHANTABILITY

(1) Except in a finance lease, a warranty that the goods will be merchantable is implied in a lease contract if the lessor is a merchant with respect to goods of that kind.

(2) Goods to be merchantable must be at least such as
(a) pass without objection in the trade under the description in the lease agreement;
(b) in the case of fungible goods, are of fair average quality within the description;
(c) are fit for the ordinary purposes for which goods of that type are used;
(d) run, within the variation permitted by the lease agreement, of even kind, quality, and quantity within each unit and among all units involved;
(e) are adequately contained, packaged, and labeled as the lease agreement may require; and

(f) conform to any promises or affirmations of fact made on the container or label.

(3) Other implied warranties may arise from course of dealing or usage of trade.

§2A—213. IMPLIED WARRANTY OF FITNESS FOR PARTICULAR PURPOSE

Except in a finance of lease, if the lessor at the time the lease contract is made has reason to know of any particular purpose for which the goods are required and that the lessee is relying on the lessor's skill or judgment to select or furnish suitable goods, there is in the lease contract an implied warranty that the goods will be fit for that purpose.

§2A—214. EXCLUSION OR MODIFICATION OF WARRANTIES

(1) Words or conduct relevant to the creation of an express warranty and words or conduct tending to negate or limit a warranty must be construed wherever reasonable as consistent with each other; but, subject to the provisions of Section 2A—202 on parol or extrinsic evidence, negation or limitation is inoperative to the extent that the construction is unreasonable.

(2) Subject to subsection (3), to exclude or modify the implied warranty of merchantability or any part of it the language must mention "merchantability", be by a writing, and be conspicuous. Subject to subsection (3), to exclude or modify any implied warranty of fitness the exclusion must be by a writing and be conspicuous. Language to exclude all implied warranties of fitness is sufficient if it is in writing, is conspicuous and states, for example, "There is no warranty that the goods will be fit for a particular purpose".

(3) Notwithstanding subsection (2), but subject to subsection (4),

    (a) unless the circumstances indicate otherwise, all implied warranties are excluded by expressions like "as is" or "with all faults" or by other language that in common understanding calls the lessee's attention to the exclusion of warranties and makes plain that there is no implied warranty, if in writing and conspicuous;

    (b) if the lessee before entering into the lease contract has examined the goods or the sample or model as fully as desired or has refused to examine the goods, there is no implied warranty with regard to defects that an examination ought in the circumstances to have revealed; and

    (c) an implied warranty may also be excluded or modified by course of dealing, course of performance, or usage of trade.

(4) To exclude or modify a warranty against interference or against infringement (Section 2A—211) or any part of it, the language must be specific, be by a writing, and be conspicuous, unless the circumstances, including course of performance, course of dealing, or usage of trade, give the lessee reason to know that the goods are being leased subject to a claim or interest of any person.

§2A—215. CUMULATION AND CONFLICT OF WARRANTIES EXPRESS OR IMPLIED

Warranties, whether express or implied, must be construed as consistent with each other and as cumulative, but if that construction is unreasonable, the intention of the parties determines which warranty is dominant. In ascertaining that intention the following rules apply:

(a) Exact or technical specifications displace an inconsistent sample or model or general language of description.

    (b) A sample from an existing bulk displaces inconsistent general language of description.

    (c) Express warranties displace inconsistent implied warranties other than an implied warranty of fitness for a particular purpose.

§2A—216. THIRD-PARTY BENEFICIARIES OF EXPRESS AND IMPLIED WARRANTIES

Alternative A

A warranty to or for the benefit of a lessee under this Article, whether express or implied, extends to any natural person who is in the family or household of the lessee or who is a guest in the lessee's home if it is reasonable to expect that such person may use, consume, or be affected by the goods and who is injured in person by breach of the warranty. This section does not displace principles of law and equity that extend a warranty to or for the benefit of a lessee to other persons. The operation of this section may not be excluded, modified, or limited, but an exclusion, modification, or limitation of the warranty, including any with respect to rights and remedies, effective against the lessee is also effective against any beneficiary designated under this section.

Alternative B

A warranty to or for the benefit of a lessee under this Article, whether express or implied, extends to any natural person who may reasonably be expected to use, consume, or be affected by the goods and who is injured in person by breach of the warranty. This section does not displace principles of law and equity that extend a warranty to or for the benefit of a lessee to other persons. The operation of this section may not be excluded, modified, or limited, but an exclusion, modification, or limitation of the warranty, including any with respect to rights and remedies, effective against the lessee is also effective against the beneficiary designated under this section.

Alternative C

A warranty to or for the benefit of a lessee under this Article, whether express or implied, extends to any person who may reasonably be expected to use, consume, or be affected by the goods and who is injured by breach of the warranty. The operation of this section may not be excluded, modified, or limited with respect to injury to the person of an individual to whom the warranty extends, but an exclusion, modification, or limitation of the warranty, including any with respect to rights and remedies, effective against the lessee is also effective against the beneficiary designated under this section.

§2A—217. IDENTIFICATION

Identification of goods as goods to which a lease contract refers may be made at any time and in any manner explicitly agreed to by the parties. In the absence of explicit agreement, identification occurs:

(a) when the lease contract is made if the lease contract is for a lease of goods that are existing and identified;

(b) when the goods are shipped, marked, or otherwise designated by the lessor as goods to which the lease contract refers, if the lease contract is for a lease of goods that are not existing and identified; or

(c) when the young are conceived, if the lease contract is for a lease of unborn young of animals.

§2A—218. INSURANCE AND PROCEEDS

(1) A lessee obtains an insurable interest when existing goods are identified to the lease contract even though the goods identified are nonconforming and the lessee has an option to reject them.

(2) If a lessee has an insurable interest only by reason of the lessor's identification of the goods, the lessor, until default or insolvency or notification to the lessee that identification is final, may substitute other goods for those identified.

(3) Notwithstanding a lessee's insurable interest under subsections (1) and (2), the lessor retains an insurable interest until an option to buy has been exercised by the lessee and risk of loss has passed to the lessee.

(4) Nothing in this section impairs any insurable interest recognized under any other statute or rule of law.

(5) The parties by agreement may determine that one or more parties have an obligation to obtain and pay for insurance covering the goods and by agreement may determine the beneficiary of the proceeds of the insurance.

§2A—219. RISK OF LOSS

(1) Except in the case of a finance lease, risk of loss is retained by the lessor and does not pass to the lessee. In the case of a finance lease, risk of loss passes to the lessee.

(2) Subject to the provisions of this Article on the effect of default on risk of loss (Section 2A—220), if risk of loss is to pass to the lessee and the time of passage is not stated, the following rules apply:

(a) If the lease contract requires or authorizes the goods to be shipped by carrier

  (i) and it does not require delivery at a particular destination, the risk of loss passes to the lessee when the goods are duly delivered to the carrier; but

  (ii) if it does require delivery at a particular destination and the goods are there duly tendered while in the possession of the carrier, the risk of loss passes to the lessee when the goods are there duly so tendered as to enable the lessee to take delivery.

(b) If the goods are held by a bailee to be delivered without being moved, the risk of loss passes to the lessee on acknowledgment by the bailee of the lessee's right to possession of the goods.

(c) In any case not within subsection (a) or (b), the risk of loss passes to the lessee on the lessee's receipt of the goods if the lessor, or, in the case of a finance lease, the supplier, is a merchant; otherwise the risk passes to the lessee on tender of delivery.

§2A—220. EFFECT OF DEFAULT ON RISK OF LOSS

(1) Where risk of loss is to pass to the lessee and the time of passage is not stated:

(a) If a tender or delivery of goods so fails to conform to the lease contract as to give a right of rejection, the risk of their loss remains with the lessor, or, in the case of a finance lease, the supplier, until cure or acceptance.

(b) If the lessee rightfully revokes acceptance, he [or she], to the extent of any deficiency in his [or her] effective insurance coverage, may treat the risk of loss as having remained with the lessor from the beginning.

(2) Whether or not risk of loss is to pass to the lessee, if the lessee as to conforming goods already identified to a lease contract repudiates or is otherwise in default under the lease contract, the lessor, or, in the case of a finance lease, the supplier, to the extent of any deficiency in his [or her] effective insurance coverage may treat the risk of loss as resting on the lessee for a commercially reasonable time.

§2A—221. CASUALTY TO IDENTIFIED GOODS

If a lease contract requires goods identified when the lease contract is made, and the goods suffer casualty without fault of the lessee, the lessor or the supplier before delivery, or the goods suffer casualty before risk of loss passes to the lessee pursuant to the lease agreement or Section 2A—219, then:

(a) if the loss is total, the lease contract is avoided; and

(b) if the loss is partial or the goods have so deteriorated as to no longer conform to the lease contract, the lessee may nevertheless demand inspection and at his [or her] option either treat the lease contract as avoided or, except in a finance lease that is not a consumer lease, accept the goods with due allowance from the rent payable for the balance of the lease term for the deterioration or the deficiency in quantity but without further right against the lessor.

Part 3 Effect of Lease Contract

§2A—301. ENFORCEABILITY OF LEASE CONTRACT

Except as otherwise provided in this Article, a lease contract is effective and enforceable according to its terms between the parties, against purchasers of the goods and against creditors of the parties.

§2A—302. TITLE TO AND POSSESSION OF GOODS

Except as otherwise provided in this Article, each provision of this Article applies whether the lessor or a third party has title to the goods, and whether the lessor, the lessee, or a third party has possession of the goods, notwithstanding any statute or rule of law that possession or the absence of possession is fraudulent.

§2A—303. ALIENABILITY OF PARTY'S INTEREST UNDER LEASE CONTRACT OR OF LESSOR'S RESIDUAL INTEREST IN GOODS; DELEGATION OF PERFORMANCE; TRANSFER OF RIGHTS

(1) As used in this section, "creation of a security interest" includes the sale of a lease contract that is subject to Article9, Secured Transactions, by reason of Section 9—109(a)(3).

(2) Except as provided in subsections (3) and Section 9—407, a provision in a lease agreement which (i) prohibits the voluntary or involuntary transfer, including a transfer by sale, sublease, creation or enforcement of a security interest, or attachment, levy, or other judicial process, of an interest of a party under the lease contract or of the lessor's residual interest in the goods, or (ii) makes such a transfer an event of default, gives rise to the rights and remedies provided in subsection (4), but a transfer that is prohibited or is an event of default under the lease agreement is otherwise effective.

(3) A provision in a lease agreement which (i) prohibits a transfer of a right to damages for default with respect to the whole lease contract or of a right to payment arising out of the transferor's due performance of the transferor's entire obligation, or (ii) makes such a transfer an event of default, is not enforceable, and such a transfer is not a transfer that materially impairs the propsect of

obtaining return performance by, materially changes the duty of, or materially increases the burden or risk imposed on, the other party to the lease contract within the purview of subsection (4).

(4) Subject to subsection (3) and Section 9—407:
(a) if a transfer is made which is made an event of default under a lease agreement, the party to the lease contract not making the transfer, unless that party waives the default or otherwise agrees, has the rights and remedies described in Section 2A—501(2);
(b) if paragraph (a) is not applicable and if a transfer is made that (i) is prohibited under a lease agreement or (ii) materially impairs the prospect of obtaining return performance by, materially changes the duty of, or materially increases the burden or risk imposed on, the other party to the lease contract, unless the party not making the transfer agrees at any time to the transfer in the lease contract or otherwise, then, except as limited by contract, (i) the transferor is liable to the party not making the transfer for damages caused by the transfer to the extent that the damages could not reasonably be prevented by the party not making the transfer and (ii) a court having jurisdiction may grant other appropriate relief, including cancellation of the lease contract or an injunction against the transfer.

(5) A transfer of "the lease" or of "all my rights under the lease", or a transfer in similar general terms, is a transfer of rights and, unless the language or the circumstances, as in a transfer for security, indicate the contrary, the transfer is a delegation of duties by the transferor to the transferee. Acceptance by the transferee constitutes a promise by the transferee to perform those duties. The promise is enforceable by either the transferor or the other party to the lease contract.

(6) Unless otherwise agreed by the lessor and the lessee, a delegation of performance does not relieve the transferor as against the other party of any duty to perform or of any liability for default.

(7) In a consumer lease, to prohibit the transfer of an interest of a party under the lease contract or to make a transfer an event of default, the language must be specific, by a writing, and conspicuous.

As amended in 1990 and 1999.

§2A—304. SUBSEQUENT LEASE OF GOODS BY LESSOR

(1) Subject to Section 2A—303, a subsequent lessee from a lessor of goods under an existing lease contract obtains, to the extent of the leasehold interest transferred, the leasehold interest in the goods that the lessor had or had power to transfer, and except as provided in subsection (2)

and Section 2A—527(4), takes subject to the existing lease contract. A lessor with voidable title has power to transfer a good leasehold interest to a good faith subsequent lessee for value, but only to the extent set forth in the preceding sentence. If goods have been delivered under a transaction of purchase the lessor has that power even though:

    (a) the lessor's transferor was deceived as to the identity of the lessor;

    (b) the delivery was in exchange for a check which is later dishonored;

    (c) it was agreed that the transaction was to be a "cash sale"; or

    (d) the delivery was procured through fraud punishable as larcenous under the criminal law.

(2) A subsequent lessee in the ordinary course of business from a lessor who is a merchant dealing in goods of that kind to whom the goods were entrusted by the existing lessee of that lessor before the interest of the subsequent lessee became enforceable against that lessor obtains, to the extent of the leasehold interest transferred, all of that lessor's and the existing lessee's rights to the goods, and takes free of the existing lease contract.

(3) A subsequent lessee from the lessor of goods that are subject to an existing lease contract and are covered by a certificate of title issued under a statute of this State or of another jurisdiction takes no greater rights than those provided both by this section and by the certificate of title statute.

As amended in 1990.

§2A—305. SALE OR SUBLEASE OF GOODS BY LESSEE

(1) Subject to the provisions of Section 2A—303, a buyer or sublessee from the lessee of goods under an existing lease contract obtains, to the extent of the interest transferred, the leasehold interest in the goods that the lessee had or had power to transfer, and except as provided in subsection (2) and Section 2A—511(4), takes subject to the existing lease contract. A lessee with a voidable leasehold interest has power to transfer a good leasehold interest to a good faith buyer for value or a good faith sublessee for value, but only to the extent set forth in the preceding sentence. When goods have been delivered under a transaction of lease the lessee has that power even though:

    (a) the lessor was deceived as to the identity of the lessee;

    (b) the delivery was in exchange for a check which is later dishonored; or

    (c) the delivery was procured through fraud punishable as larcenous under the criminal law.

(2) A buyer in the ordinary course of business or a sublessee in the ordinary course of business from a lessee who is a merchant dealing in goods of that kind to whom the goods were entrusted by the lessor obtains, to the extent

of the interest transferred, all of the lessor's and lessee's rights to the goods, and takes free of the existing lease contract.

(3) A buyer or sublessee from the lessee of goods that are subject to an existing lease contract and are covered by a certificate of title issued under a statute of this State or of another jurisdiction takes no greater rights than those provided both by this section and by the certificate of title statute.

§2A—306. PRIORITY OF CERTAIN LIENS ARISING BY OPERATION OF LAW

If a person in the ordinary course of his [or her] business furnishes services or materials with respect to goods subject to a lease contract, a lien upon those goods in the possession of that person given by statute or rule of law for those materials or services takes priority over any interest of the lessor or lessee under the lease contract or this Article unless the lien is created by statute and the statute provides otherwise or unless the lien is created by rule of law and the rule of law provides otherwise.

§2A—307. PRIORITY OF LIENS ARISING BY ATTACHMENT OR LEVY ON, SECURITY INTERESTS IN, AND OTHER CLAIMS TO GOODS

(1) Except as otherwise provided in Section 2A—306, a creditor of a lessee takes subject to the lease contract.

(2) Except as otherwise provided in subsection (3) and in Sections 2A—306 and 2A—308, a creditor of a lessor takes subject to the lease contract unless the creditor holds a lien that attached to the goods before the lease contract became enforceable.

(3) Except as otherwise provided in Sections 9—317, 9—321, and 9—323, a lessee takes a leasehold interest subject to a security interest held by a creditor of the lessor.

As amended in 1990 and 1999.

§2A—308. SPECIAL RIGHTS OF CREDITORS

(1) A creditor of a lessor in possession of goods subject to a lease contract may treat the lease contract as void if as against the creditor retention of possession by the lessor is fraudulent under any statute or rule of law, but retention of possession in good faith and current course of trade by the lessor for a commercially reasonable time after the lease contract becomes enforceable is not fraudulent.

(2) Nothing in this Article impairs the rights of creditors of a lessor if the lease contract (a) becomes enforceable, not in current course of trade but in satisfaction of or as security for a pre-existing claim for money, security, or the like, and (b) is made under circumstances which under any statute or rule of law apart from this Article would constitute the transaction a fraudulent transfer or voidable preference.

(3) A creditor of a seller may treat a sale or an identification of goods to a contract for sale as void if as against the creditor retention of possession by the seller is fraudulent under any statute or rule of law, but retention of possession of the goods pursuant to a lease contract entered into by the seller as lessee and the buyer as lessor in connection with the sale or identification of the goods is not fraudulent if the buyer bought for value and in good faith.

§2A—309. LESSOR'S AND LESSEE'S RIGHTS WHEN GOODS BECOME FIXTURES

(1) In this section:

    (a) goods are "fixtures" when they become so related to particular real estate that an interest in them arises under real estate law;

    (b) a "fixture filing" is the filing, in the office where a mortgage on the real estate would be filed or recorded, of a financing statement covering goods that are or are to become fixtures and conforming to the requirements of Section 9—502(a) and (b);

    (c) a lease is a "purchase money lease" unless the lessee has possession or use of the goods or the right to possession or use of the goods before the lease agreement is enforceable;

    (d) a mortgage is a "construction mortgage" to the extent it secures an obligation incurred for the construction of an improvement on land including the acquisition cost of the land, if the recorded writing so indicates; and

    (e) "encumbrance" includes real estate mortgages and other liens on real estate and all other rights in real estate that are not ownership interests.

(2) Under this Article a lease may be of goods that are fixtures or may continue in goods that become fixtures, but no lease exists under this Article of ordinary building materials incorporated into an improvement on land.

(3) This Article does not prevent creation of a lease of fixtures pursuant to real estate law.

(4) The perfected interest of a lessor of fixtures has priority over a conflicting interest of an encumbrancer or owner of the real estate if:

    (a) the lease is a purchase money lease, the conflicting interest of the encumbrancer or owner arises before the goods become fixtures, the interest of the lessor is perfected by a fixture filing before the goods become fixtures or within ten days thereafter, and the lessee has an interest of record in the real estate or is in possession of the real estate; or

    (b) the interest of the lessor is perfected by a fixture filing before the interest of the encumbrancer or owner is of record, the lessor's interest has priority over any conflicting interest of a predecessor in title of the encumbrancer or owner, and the lessee has an interest of record in the real estate or is in possession of the real estate.

(5) The interest of a lessor of fixtures, whether or not perfected, has priority over the conflicting interest of an encumbrancer or owner of the real estate if:

    (a) the fixtures are readily removable factory or office machines, readily removable equipment that is not primarily used or leased for use in the operation of the real estate, or readily removable replacements of domestic appliances that are goods subject to a consumer lease, and before the goods become fixtures the lease contract is enforceable; or

    (b) the conflicting interest is a lien on the real estate obtained by legal or equitable proceedings after the lease contract is enforceable; or

    (c) the encumbrancer or owner has consented in writing to the lease or has disclaimed an interest in the goods as fixtures; or

    (d) the lessee has a right to remove the goods as against the encumbrancer or owner. If the lessee's right to remove terminates, the priority of the interest of the lessor continues for a reasonable time.

(6) Notwithstanding paragraph (4)(a) but otherwise subject to subsections (4) and (5), the interest of a lessor of fixtures, including the lessor's residual interest, is subordinate to the conflicting interest of an encumbrancer of the real estate under a construction mortgage recorded before the goods become fixtures if the goods become fixtures before the completion of the construction. To the extent given to refinance a construction mortgage, the conflicting interest of an encumbrancer of the real estate under a mortgage has this priority to the same extent as the encumbrancer of the real estate under the construction mortgage.

(7) In cases not within the preceding subsections, priority between the interest of a lessor of fixtures, including the lessor's residual interest, and the conflicting interest of an encumbrancer or owner of the real estate who is not the lessee is determined by the priority rules governing conflicting interests in real estate.

(8) If the interest of a lessor of fixtures, including the lessor's residual interest, has priority over all conflicting interests of all owners and encumbrancers of the real estate, the lessor or the lessee may (i) on default, expiration, termination, or cancellation of the lease agreement but subject to the agreement and this Article, or (ii) if necessary to enforce other rights and remedies of the lessor or lessee under this Article, remove the goods from the real estate, free and clear of all conflicting interests of all owners and encumbrancers of the real estate, but the lessor or lessee must reimburse any encumbrancer or owner of the real estate who is not the lessee and who has not otherwise

agreed for the cost of repair of any physical injury, but not for any diminution in value of the real estate caused by the absence of the goods removed or by any necessity of replacing them. A person entitled to reimbursement may refuse permission to remove until the party seeking removal gives adequate security for the performance of this obligation.

(9) Even though the lease agreement does not create a security interest, the interest of a lessor of fixtures, including the lessor's residual interest, is perfected by filing a financing statement as a fixture filing for leased goods that are or are to become fixtures in accordance with the relevant provisions of the Article on Secured Transactions (Article 9).

As amended in 1990 and 1999.

§2A—310. LESSOR'S AND LESSEE'S RIGHTS WHEN GOODS BECOME ACCESSIONS

(1) Goods are "accessions" when they are installed in or affixed to other goods.

(2) The interest of a lessor or a lessee under a lease contract entered into before the goods became accessions is superior to all interests in the whole except as stated in subsection (4).

(3) The interest of a lessor or a lessee under a lease contract entered into at the time or after the goods became accessions is superior to all subsequently acquired interests in the whole except as stated in subsection (4) but is subordinate to interests in the whole existing at the time the lease contract was made unless the holders of such interests in the whole have in writing consented to the lease or disclaimed an interest in the goods as part of the whole.

(4) The interest of a lessor or a lessee under a lease contract described in subsection (2) or (3) is subordinate to the interest of

(a) a buyer in the ordinary course of business or a lessee in the ordinary course of business of any interest in the whole acquired after the goods became accessions; or

(b) a creditor with a security interest in the whole perfected before the lease contract was made to the extent that the creditor makes subsequent advances without knowledge of the lease contract.

(5) When under subsections (2) or (3) and (4) a lessor or a lessee of accessions holds an interest that is superior to all interests in the whole, the lessor or the lessee may (a) on default, expiration, termination, or cancellation of the lease contract by the other party but subject to the provisions of the lease contract and this Article, or (b) if necessary to enforce his [or her] other rights and remedies under this Article, remove the goods from the whole, free and clear of all interests in the whole, but he [or she] must reimburse any holder of an interest in the whole who is not the lessee and who has not otherwise agreed for the cost of repair of any physical injury but not for any diminution in

value of the whole caused by the absence of the goods removed or by any necessity for replacing them. A person entitled to reimbursement may refuse permission to remove until the party seeking removal gives adequate security for the performance of this obligation.

§2A—311. PRIORITY SUBJECT TO SUBORDINATION

Nothing in this Article prevents subordination by agreement by any person entitled to priority.

As added in 1990.

Part 4 Performance of Lease Contract: Repudiated, Substituted and Excused

§2A—401. INSECURITY: ADEQUATE ASSURANCE OF PERFORMANCE

(1) A lease contract imposes an obligation on each party that the other's expectation of receiving due performance will not be impaired.

(2) If reasonable grounds for insecurity arise with respect to the performance of either party, the insecure party may demand in writing adequate assurance of due performance. Until the insecure party receives that assurance, if commercially reasonable the insecure party may suspend any performance for which he [or she] has not already received the agreed return.

(3) A repudiation of the lease contract occurs if assurance of due performance adequate under the circumstances of the particular case is not provided to the insecure party within a reasonable time, not to exceed 30 days after receipt of a demand by the other party.

(4) Between merchants, the reasonableness of grounds for insecurity and the adequacy of any assurance offered must be determined according to commercial standards.

(5) Acceptance of any nonconforming delivery or payment does not prejudice the aggrieved party's right to demand adequate assurance of future performance.

§2A—402. ANTICIPATORY REPUDIATION

If either party repudiates a lease contract with respect to a performance not yet due under the lease contract, the loss of which performance will substantially impair the value of the lease contract to the other, the aggrieved party may:

(a) for a commercially reasonable time, await retraction of repudiation and performance by the repudiating party;

(b) make demand pursuant to Section 2A—401 and await assurance of future performance adequate under the circumstances of the particular case; or

(c) resort to any right or remedy upon default under the lease contract or this Article, even though the aggrieved party has notified the repudiating party that the aggrieved party would await the repudiating party's performance and assurance and has urged retraction. In addition, whether or not the aggrieved party is pursuing one of the foregoing remedies, the aggrieved party may suspend performance or, if the aggrieved party is the lessor, proceed in accordance with the provisions of this Article on the lessor's right to identify goods to the lease contract notwithstanding default or to salvage unfinished goods (Section 2A—524).

§2A—403. RETRACTION OF ANTICIPATORY REPUDIATION

(1) Until the repudiating party's next performance is due, the repudiating party can retract the repudiation unless, since the repudiation, the aggrieved party has cancelled the lease contract or materially changed the aggrieved party's position or otherwise indicated that the aggrieved party considers the repudiation final.

(2) Retraction may be by any method that clearly indicates to the aggrieved party that the repudiating party intends to perform under the lease contract and includes any assurance demanded under Section 2A—401.

(3) Retraction reinstates a repudiating party's rights under a lease contract with due excuse and allowance to the aggrieved party for any delay occasioned by the repudiation.

§2A—404. SUBSTITUTED PERFORMANCE

(1) If without fault of the lessee, the lessor and the supplier, the agreed berthing, loading, or unloading facilities fail or the agreed type of carrier becomes unavailable or the agreed manner of delivery otherwise becomes commercially impracticable, but a commercially reasonable substitute is available, the substitute performance must be tendered and accepted.

(2) If the agreed means or manner of payment fails because of domestic or foreign governmental regulation:
> (a) the lessor may withhold or stop delivery or cause the supplier to withhold or stop delivery unless the lessee provides a means or manner of payment that is commercially a substantial equivalent; and
> (b) if delivery has already been taken, payment by the means or in the manner provided by the regulation discharges the lessee's obligation unless the regulation is discriminatory, oppressive, or predatory.

§2A—405. EXCUSED PERFORMANCE

Subject to Section 2A—404 on substituted performance, the following rules apply:

(a) Delay in delivery or nondelivery in whole or in part by a lessor or a supplier who complies with paragraphs (b) and (c) is not a default under the lease contract if performance as agreed has been made impracticable by the occurrence of a contingency the nonoccurrence of which was a basic assumption on which the lease contract was made or by compliance in good faith with any applicable foreign or domestic governmental regulation or order, whether or not the regulation or order later proves to be invalid.

(b) If the causes mentioned in paragraph (a) affect only part of the lessor's or the supplier's capacity to perform, he [or she] shall allocate production and deliveries among his [or her] customers but at his [or her] option may include regular customers not then under contract for sale or lease as well as his [or her] own requirements for further manufacture. He [or she] may so allocate in any manner that is fair and reasonable.

(c) The lessor seasonably shall notify the lessee and in the case of a finance lease the supplier seasonably shall notify the lessor and the lessee, if known, that there will be delay or nondelivery and, if allocation is required under paragraph (b), of the estimated quota thus made available for the lessee.

§2A—406. PROCEDURE ON EXCUSED PERFORMANCE

(1) If the lessee receives notification of a material or indefinite delay or an allocation justified under Section 2A—405, the lessee may by written notification to the lessor as to any goods involved, and with respect to all of the goods if under an installment lease contract the value of the whole lease contract is substantially impaired (Section 2A—510):
> (a) terminate the lease contract (Section 2A—505(2)); or
> (b) except in a finance lease that is not a consumer lease, modify the lease contract by accepting the available quota in substitution, with due allowance from the rent payable for the balance of the lease term for the deficiency but without further right against the lessor.

(2) If, after receipt of a notification from the lessor under Section 2A—405, the lessee fails so to modify the lease agreement within a reasonable time not exceeding 30 days, the lease contract lapses with respect to any deliveries affected.

§2A—407. IRREVOCABLE PROMISES: FINANCE LEASES

(1) In the case of a finance lease that is not a consumer lease the lessee's promises under the lease contract become irrevocable and independent upon the lessee's acceptance of the goods.

(2) A promise that has become irrevocable and independent under subsection (1):

(a) is effective and enforceable between the parties, and by or against third parties including assignees of the parties, and

(b) is not subject to cancellation, termination, modification, repudiation, excuse, or substitution without the consent of the party to whom the promise runs.

(3) This section does not affect the validity under any other law of a covenant in any lease contract making the lessee's promises irrevocable and independent upon the lessee's acceptance of the goods.

As amended in 1990.

Part 5 Default A. In General

§2A—501. DEFAULT: PROCEDURE

(1) Whether the lessor or the lessee is in default under a lease contract is determined by the lease agreement and this Article.

(2) If the lessor or the lessee is in default under the lease contract, the party seeking enforcement has rights and remedies as provided in this Article and, except as limited by this Article, as provided in the lease agreement.

(3) If the lessor or the lessee is in default under the lease contract, the party seeking enforcement may reduce the party's claim to judgment, or otherwise enforce the lease contract by self-help or any available judicial procedure or nonjudicial procedure, including administrative proceeding, arbitration, or the like, in accordance with this Article.

(4) Except as otherwise provided in Section 1—106 (1) or this Article or the lease agreement, the rights and remedies referred to in subsections (2) and (3) are cumulative.

(5) If the lease agreement covers both real property and goods, the party seeking enforcement may proceed under this Part as to the goods, or under other applicable law as to both the real property and the goods in accordance with that party's rights and remedies in respect of the real property, in which case this Part does not apply.

As amended in 1990.

§2A—502. NOTICE AFTER DEFAULT

Except as otherwise provided in this Article or the lease agreement, the lessor or lessee in default under the lease contract is not entitled to notice of default or notice of enforcement from the other party to the lease agreement.

§2A—503. MODIFICATION OR IMPAIRMENT OF RIGHTS AND REMEDIES

(1) Except as otherwise provided in this Article, the lease agreement may include rights and remedies for default in addition to or in substitution for those provided in this Article and may limit or alter the measure of damages recoverable under this Article.

(2) Resort to a remedy provided under this Article or in the lease agreement is optional unless the remedy is expressly agreed to be exclusive. If circumstances cause an exclusive or limited remedy to fail of its essential purpose, or provision for an exclusive remedy is unconscionable, remedy may be had as provided in this Article.

(3) Consequential damages may be liquidated under Section 2A—504, or may otherwise be limited, altered, or excluded unless the limitation, alteration, or exclusion is unconscionable. Limitation, alteration, or exclusion of consequential damages for injury to the person in the case of consumer goods is prima facie unconscionable but limitation, alteration, or exclusion of damages where the loss is commercial is not prima facie unconscionable.

(4) Rights and remedies on default by the lessor or the lessee with respect to any obligation or promise collateral or ancillary to the lease contract are not impaired by this Article.

As amended in 1990.

§2A—504. LIQUIDATION OF DAMAGES

(1) Damages payable by either party for default, or any other act or omission, including indemnity for loss or diminution of anticipated tax benefits or loss or damage to lessor's residual interest, may be liquidated in the lease agreement but only at an amount or by a formula that is reasonable in light of the then anticipated harm caused by the default or other act or omission.

(2) If the lease agreement provides for liquidation of damages, and such provision does not comply with subsection (1), or such provision is an exclusive or limited remedy that circumstances cause to fail of its essential purpose, remedy may be had as provided in this Article.

(3) If the lessor justifiably withholds or stops delivery of goods because of the lessee's default or insolvency (Section2A—525 or 2A—526), the lessee is entitled to restitution of any amount by which the sum of his [or her] payments exceeds:

(a) the amount to which the lessor is entitled by virtue of terms liquidating the lessor's damages in accordance with subsection (1); or

(b) in the absence of those terms, 20 percent of the then present value of the total rent the lessee was obligated to pay for the balance of the lease term, or, in the case of a consumer lease, the lesser of such amount or$500.

(4) A lessee's right to restitution under subsection (3) is subject to offset to the extent the lessor establishes:

(a) a right to recover damages under the provisions of this Article other than subsection (1); and

(b) the amount or value of any benefits received by the lessee directly or indirectly by reason of the lease contract.

§2A—505. CANCELLATION AND TERMINATION AND EFFECT OF CANCELLATION, TERMINATION, RESCISSION, OR FRAUD ON RIGHTS AND REMEDIES

(1) On cancellation of the lease contract, all obligations that are still executory on both sides are discharged, but any right based on prior default or performance survives, and the cancelling party also retains any remedy for default of the whole lease contract or any unperformed balance.

(2) On termination of the lease contract, all obligations that are still executory on both sides are discharged but any right based on prior default or performance survives.

(3) Unless the contrary intention clearly appears, expressions of "cancellation," "rescission," or the like of the lease contract may not be construed as a renunciation or discharge of any claim in damages for an antecedent default.

(4) Rights and remedies for material misrepresentation or fraud include all rights and remedies available under this Article for default.

(5) Neither rescission nor a claim for rescission of the lease contract nor rejection or return of the goods may bar or be deemed inconsistent with a claim for damages or other right or remedy.

§2A—506. STATUTE OF LIMITATIONS

(1) An action for default under a lease contract, including breach of warranty or indemnity, must be commenced within 4 years after the cause of action accrued. By the original lease contract the parties may reduce the period of limitation to not less than one year.

(2) A cause of action for default accrues when the act or omission on which the default or breach of warranty is based is or should have been discovered by the aggrieved party, or when the default occurs, whichever is later. A cause of action for indemnity accrues when the act or omission on which the claim for indemnity is based is or should have been discovered by the indemnified party, whichever is later.

(3) If an action commenced within the time limited by subsection (1) is so terminated as to leave available a remedy by another action for the same default or breach of warranty or indemnity, the other action may be commenced after the expiration of the time limited and within 6 months after the termination of the first action unless the termination resulted from voluntary discontinuance or from dismissal for failure or neglect to prosecute.

(4) This section does not alter the law on tolling of the statute of limitations nor does it apply to causes of action that have accrued before this Article becomes effective.

§2A—507. PROOF OF MARKET RENT: TIME AND PLACE

(1) Damages based on market rent (Section 2A—519 or 2A—528) are determined according to the rent for the use of the goods concerned for a lease term identical to the remaining lease term of the original lease agreement and prevailing at the times specified in Sections 2A—519 and 2A—528.

(2) If evidence of rent for the use of the goods concerned for a lease term identical to the remaining lease term of the original lease agreement and prevailing at the times or places described in this Article is not readily available, the rent prevailing within any reasonable time before or after the time described or at any other place or for a different lease term which in commercial judgment or under usage of trade would serve as a reasonable substitute for the one described may be used, making any proper allowance for the difference, including the cost of transporting the goods to or from the other place.

(3) Evidence of a relevant rent prevailing at a time or place or for a lease term other than the one described in this Article offered by one party is not admissible unless and until he [or she] has given the other party notice the court finds sufficient to prevent unfair surprise.

(4) If the prevailing rent or value of any goods regularly leased in any established market is in issue, reports in official publications or trade journals or in newspapers or periodicals of general circulation published as the reports of that market are admissible in evidence. The circumstances of the preparation of the report may be shown to affect its weight but not its admissibility.

As amended in 1990.

B. Default by Lessor

§2A—508. LESSEE'S REMEDIES

(1) If a lessor fails to deliver the goods in conformity to the lease contract (Section 2A—509) or repudiates the lease contract (Section 2A—402), or a lessee rightfully rejects the goods (Section 2A—509) or justifiably revokes acceptance of the goods (Section 2A—517), then with respect to any goods involved, and with respect to all of the goods if under an installment lease contract the value of the whole lease contract is substantially impaired (Section 2A—510), the lessor is in default under the lease contract and the lessee may:

(a) cancel the lease contract (Section 2A—505(1));

(b) recover so much of the rent and security as has been paid and is just under the circumstances;

(c) cover and recover damages as to all goods affected whether or not they have been identified to the lease contract (Sections 2A—518 and 2A—520), or recover damages for nondelivery (Sections 2A—519 and 2A—520);

(d) exercise any other rights or pursue any other remedies provided in the lease contract.

(2) If a lessor fails to deliver the goods in conformity to the lease contract or repudiates the lease contract, the lessee may also:

(a) if the goods have been identified, recover them (Section 2A—522); or

(b) in a proper case, obtain specific performance or replevy the goods (Section 2A—521).

(3) If a lessor is otherwise in default under a lease contract, the lessee may exercise the rights and pursue the remedies provided in the lease contract, which may include a right to cancel the lease, and in Section 2A—519(3).

(4) If a lessor has breached a warranty, whether express or implied, the lessee may recover damages (Section 2A—519(4)).

(5) On rightful rejection or justifiable revocation of acceptance, a lessee has a security interest in goods in the lessee's possession or control for any rent and security that has been paid and any expenses reasonably incurred in their inspection, receipt, transportation, and care and custody and may hold those goods and dispose of them in good faith and in a commercially reasonable manner, subject to Section 2A—527(5).

(6) Subject to the provisions of Section 2A—407, a lessee, on notifying the lessor of the lessee's intention to do so, may deduct all or any part of the damages resulting from any default under the lease contract from any part of the rent still due under the same lease contract.

As amended in 1990.

§2A—509. LESSEE'S RIGHTS ON IMPROPER DELIVERY; RIGHTFUL REJECTION

(1) Subject to the provisions of Section 2A—510 on default in installment lease contracts, if the goods or the tender or delivery fail in any respect to conform to the lease contract, the lessee may reject or accept the goods or accept any commercial unit or units and reject the rest of the goods.

(2) Rejection of goods is ineffective unless it is within a reasonable time after tender or delivery of the goods and the lessee seasonably notifies the lessor.

§2A—510. INSTALLMENT LEASE CONTRACTS: REJECTION AND DEFAULT

(1) Under an installment lease contract a lessee may reject any delivery that is nonconforming if the nonconformity substantially impairs the value of that delivery and cannot be cured or the nonconformity is a defect in the required documents; but if the nonconformity does not fall within subsection (2) and the lessor or the supplier gives adequate assurance of its cure, the lessee must accept that delivery.

(2) Whenever nonconformity or default with respect to one or more deliveries substantially impairs the value of

the installment lease contract as a whole there is a default with respect to the whole. But, the aggrieved party reinstates the installment lease contract as a whole if the aggrieved party accepts a nonconforming delivery without seasonably notifying of cancellation or brings an action with respect only to past deliveries or demands performance as to future deliveries.

§2A—511. MERCHANT LESSEE'S DUTIES AS TO RIGHTFULLY REJECTED GOODS

(1) Subject to any security interest of a lessee (Section 2A—508(5)), if a lessor or a supplier has no agent or place of business at the market of rejection, a merchant lessee, after rejection of goods in his [or her] possession or control, shall follow any reasonable instructions received from the lessor or the supplier with respect to the goods. In the absence of those instructions, a merchant lessee shall make reasonable efforts to sell, lease, or otherwise dispose of the goods for the lessor's account if they threaten to decline in value speedily. Instructions are not reasonable if on demand indemnity for expenses is not forthcoming.

(2) If a merchant lessee (subsection (1)) or any other lessee (Section 2A—512) disposes of goods, he [or she] is entitled to reimbursement either from the lessor or the supplier or out of the proceeds for reasonable expenses of caring for and disposing of the goods and, if the expenses include no disposition commission, to such commission as is usual in the trade, or if there is none, to a reasonable sum not exceeding 10 percent of the gross proceeds.

(3) In complying with this section or Section 2A—512, the lessee is held only to good faith. Good faith conduct hereunder is neither acceptance or conversion nor the basis of an action for damages.

(4) A purchaser who purchases in good faith from a lessee pursuant to this section or Section 2A—512 takes the goods free of any rights of the lessor and the supplier even though the lessee fails to comply with one or more of the requirements of this Article.

§2A—512. LESSEE'S DUTIES AS TO RIGHTFULLY REJECTED GOODS

(1) Except as otherwise provided with respect to goods that threaten to decline in value speedily (Section 2A—511) and subject to any security interest of a lessee (Section 2A—508(5)):

(a) the lessee, after rejection of goods in the lessee's possession, shall hold them with reasonable care at the lessor's or the supplier's disposition for a reasonable time after the lessee's seasonable notification of rejection;

(b) if the lessor or the supplier gives no instructions within a reasonable time after notification of rejection, the lessee may store the rejected goods for the lessor's or the supplier's account or ship them to the lessor or the supplier or dispose of them for the lessor's or the supplier's account with reimbursement in the manner provided in Section 2A—511; but

(c) the lessee has no further obligations with regard to goods rightfully rejected.

(2) Action by the lessee pursuant to subsection (1) is not acceptance or conversion.

§2A—513. CURE BY LESSOR OF IMPROPER TENDER OR DELIVERY; REPLACEMENT

(1) If any tender or delivery by the lessor or the supplier is rejected because nonconforming and the time for performance has not yet expired, the lessor or the supplier may seasonably notify the lessee of the lessor's or the supplier's intention to cure and may then make a conforming delivery within the time provided in the lease contract.

(2) If the lessee rejects a nonconforming tender that the lessor or the supplier had reasonable grounds to believe would be acceptable with or without money allowance, the lessor or the supplier may have a further reasonable time to substitute a conforming tender if he [or she] seasonably notifies the lessee.

§2A—514. WAIVER OF LESSEE'S OBJECTIONS

(1) In rejecting goods, a lessee's failure to state a particular defect that is ascertainable by reasonable inspection precludes the lessee from relying on the defect to justify rejection or to establish default:

(a) if, stated seasonably, the lessor or the supplier could have cured it (Section 2A—513); or

(b) between merchants if the lessor or the supplier after rejection has made a request in writing for a full and final written statement of all defects on which the lessee proposes to rely.

(2) A lessee's failure to reserve rights when paying rent or other consideration against documents precludes recovery of the payment for defects apparent on the face of the documents.

§2A—515. ACCEPTANCE OF GOODS

(1) Acceptance of goods occurs after the lessee has had a reasonable opportunity to inspect the goods and

(a) the lessee signifies or acts with respect to the goods in a manner that signifies to the lessor or the supplier that the goods are conforming or that the lessee will take or retain them in spite of their nonconformity; or

(b) the lessee fails to make an effective rejection of the goods (Section 2A—509(2)).

(2) Acceptance of a part of any commercial unit is acceptance of that entire unit.

§2A—516. EFFECT OF ACCEPTANCE OF GOODS; NOTICE OF DEFAULT; BURDEN OF ESTABLISHING DEFAULT AFTER ACCEPTANCE; NOTICE OF CLAIM OR LITIGATION TO PERSON ANSWERABLE OVER

(1) A lessee must pay rent for any goods accepted in accordance with the lease contract, with due allowance for goods rightfully rejected or not delivered.

(2) A lessee's acceptance of goods precludes rejection of the goods accepted. In the case of a finance lease, if made with knowledge of a nonconformity, acceptance cannot be revoked because of it. In any other case, if made with knowledge of a nonconformity, acceptance cannot be revoked because of it unless the acceptance was on the reasonable assumption that the nonconformity would be seasonably cured. Acceptance does not of itself impair any other remedy provided by this Article or the lease agreement for nonconformity.

(3) If a tender has been accepted:

(a) within a reasonable time after the lessee discovers or should have discovered any default, the lessee shall notify the lessor and the supplier, if any, or be barred from any remedy against the party notified;

(b) except in the case of a consumer lease, within a reasonable time after the lessee receives notice of litigation for infringement or the like (Section 2A—211) the lessee shall notify the lessor or be barred from any remedy over for liability established by the litigation; and

(c) the burden is on the lessee to establish any default.

(4) If a lessee is sued for breach of a warranty or other obligation for which a lessor or a supplier is answerable over the following apply:

(a) The lessee may give the lessor or the supplier, or both, written notice of the litigation. If the notice states that the person notified may come in and defend and that if the person notified does not do so that person will be bound in any action against that person by the lessee by any determination of fact common to the two litigations, then unless the person notified after seasonable receipt of the notice does come in and defend that person is so bound.

(b) The lessor or the supplier may demand in writing that the lessee turn over control of the litigation including settlement if the claim is one for infringement or the like (Section 2A—211) or else be barred from any remedy over. If the demand states that the lessor or the supplier agrees to bear all expense and to satisfy any adverse judgment, then unless the lessee after seasonable receipt of the demand does turn over control the lessee is so barred.

(5) Subsections (3) and (4) apply to any obligation of a lessee to hold the lessor or the supplier harmless against infringement or the like (Section 2A—211).

As amended in 1990.

§2A—517. REVOCATION OF ACCEPTANCE OF GOODS

(1) A lessee may revoke acceptance of a lot or commercial unit whose nonconformity substantially impairs its value to the lessee if the lessee has accepted it:

    (a) except in the case of a finance lease, on the reasonable assumption that its nonconformity would be cured and it has not been seasonably cured; or

    (b) without discovery of the nonconformity if the lessee's acceptance was reasonably induced either by the lessor's assurances or, except in the case of a finance lease, by the difficulty of discovery before acceptance.

(2) Except in the case of a finance lease that is not a consumer lease, a lessee may revoke acceptance of a lot or commercial unit if the lessor defaults under the lease contract and the default substantially impairs the value of that lot or commercial unit to the lessee.

(3) If the lease agreement so provides, the lessee may revoke acceptance of a lot or commercial unit because of other defaults by the lessor.

(4) Revocation of acceptance must occur within a reasonable time after the lessee discovers or should have discovered the ground for it and before any substantial change in condition of the goods which is not caused by the nonconformity. Revocation is not effective until the lessee notifies the lessor.

(5) A lessee who so revokes has the same rights and duties with regard to the goods involved as if the lessee had rejected them.

As amended in 1990.

§2A—518. COVER; SUBSTITUTE GOODS

(1) After a default by a lessor under the lease contract of the type described in Section 2A—508(1), or, if agreed, after other default by the lessor, the lessee may cover by making any purchase or lease of or contract to purchase or lease goods in substitution for those due from the lessor.

(2) Except as otherwise provided with respect to damages liquidated in the lease agreement (Section 2A—504) or otherwise determined pursuant to agreement of the parties (Sections 1—102(3) and 2A—503), if a lessee's cover is by lease agreement substantially similar to the original lease agreement and the new lease agreement is made in good faith and in a commercially reasonable manner, the lessee may recover from the lessor as damages (i) the present value, as of the date of the commencement of the term of the new lease agreement, of the rent under the new lease agreement applicable to that period of the new lease term which is comparable to the then remaining term of the original lease agreement minus the present value as of the same date of the total rent for the then remaining lease term of the original lease agreement, and (ii) any incidental or consequential damages, less expenses saved in consequence of the lessor's default.

(3) If a lessee's cover is by lease agreement that for any reason does not qualify for treatment under subsection (2), or is by purchase or otherwise, the lessee may recover from the lessor as if the lessee had elected not to cover and Section 2A—519 governs.

As amended in 1990.

§2A—519. LESSEE'S DAMAGES FOR NON-DELIVERY, REPUDIATION, DEFAULT, AND BREACH OF WARRANTY IN REGARD TO ACCEPTED GOODS

(1) Except as otherwise provided with respect to damages liquidated in the lease agreement (Section 2A—504) or otherwise determined pursuant to agreement of the parties (Sections 1—102(3) and 2A—503), if a lessee elects not to cover or a lessee elects to cover and the cover is by lease agreement that for any reason does not qualify for treatment under Section 2A—518(2), or is by purchase or otherwise, the measure of damages for non-delivery or repudiation by the lessor or for rejection or revocation of acceptance by the lessee is the present value, as of the date of the default, of the then market rent minus the present value as of the same date of the original rent, computed for the remaining lease term of the original lease agreement, together with incidental and consequential damages, less expenses saved in consequence of the lessor's default.

(2) Market rent is to be determined as of the place for tender or, in cases of rejection after arrival or revocation of acceptance, as of the place of arrival.

(3) Except as otherwise agreed, if the lessee has accepted goods and given notification (Section 2A—516 (3)), the measure of damages for non-conforming tender or delivery or other default by a lessor is the loss resulting in the ordinary course of events from the lessor's default as determined in any manner that is reasonable together with incidental and consequential damages, less expenses saved in consequence of the lessor's default.

(4) Except as otherwise agreed, the measure of damages for breach of warranty is the present value at the time and place of acceptance of the difference between the value of the use of the goods accepted and the value if they had been as warranted for the lease term, unless special circumstances show proximate damages of a different amount, together with incidental and consequential damages, less expenses saved in consequence of the lessor's default or breach of warranty.

As amended in 1990.

§2A—520. LESSEE'S INCIDENTAL AND CONSEQUENTIAL DAMAGES

(1) Incidental damages resulting from a lessor's default include expenses reasonably incurred in inspection, receipt, transportation, and care and custody of goods rightfully rejected or goods the acceptance of which is justifiably revoked, any commercially reasonable charges, expenses or commissions in connection with effecting cover, and any other reasonable expense incident to the default.

(2) Consequential damages resulting from a lessor's default include:

(a) any loss resulting from general or particular requirements and needs of which the lessor at the time of contracting had reason to know and which could not reasonably be prevented by cover or otherwise; and

(b) injury to person or property proximately resulting from any breach of warranty.

§2A—521. LESSEE'S RIGHT TO SPECIFIC PERFORMANCE OR REPLEVIN

(1) Specific performance may be decreed if the goods are unique or in other proper circumstances.

(2) A decree for specific performance may include any terms and conditions as to payment of the rent, damages, or other relief that the court deems just.

(3) A lessee has a right of replevin, detinue, sequestration, claim and delivery, or the like for goods identified to the lease contract if after reasonable effort the lessee is unable to effect cover for those goods or the circumstances reasonably indicate that the effort will be unavailing.

§2A—522. LESSEE'S RIGHT TO GOODS ON LESSOR'S INSOLVENCY

(1) Subject to subsection (2) and even though the goods have not been shipped, a lessee who has paid a part or all of the rent and security for goods identified to a lease contract (Section 2A—217) on making and keeping good a tender of any unpaid portion of the rent and security due under the lease contract may recover the goods identified from the lessor if the lessor becomes insolvent within 10 days after receipt of the first installment of rent and security.

(2) A lessee acquires the right to recover goods identified to a lease contract only if they conform to the lease contract.

C. Default by Lessee

§2A—523. LESSOR'S REMEDIES

(1) If a lessee wrongfully rejects or revokes acceptance of goods or fails to make a payment when due or repudiates with respect to a part or the whole, then, with respect to any goods involved, and with respect to all of the goods if under an installment lease contract the value of the whole lease contract is substantially impaired (Section 2A—510), the lessee is in default under the lease contract and the lessor may:

(a) cancel the lease contract (Section 2A—505 (1));

(b) proceed respecting goods not identified to the lease contract (Section 2A—524);

(c) withhold delivery of the goods and take possession of goods previously delivered (Section 2A—525);

(d) stop delivery of the goods by any bailee (Section 2A—526);

(e) dispose of the goods and recover damages (Section 2A—527), or retain the goods and recover damages (Section 2A—528), or in a proper case recover rent (Section 2A—529)

(f) exercise any other rights or pursue any other remedies provided in the lease contract.

(2) If a lessor does not fully exercise a right or obtain a remedy to which the lessor is entitled under subsection (1), the lessor may recover the loss resulting in the ordinary course of events from the lessee's default as determined in any reasonable manner, together with incidental damages, less expenses saved in consequence of the lessee's default.

(3) If a lessee is otherwise in default under a lease contract, the lessor may exercise the rights and pursue the remedies provided in the lease contract, which may include a right to cancel the lease. In addition, unless otherwise provided in the lease contract:

(a) if the default substantially impairs the value of the lease contract to the lessor, the lessor may exercise the rights and pursue the remedies provided in subsections (1) or (2); or

(b) if the default does not substantially impair the value of the lease contract to the lessor, the lessor may recover as provided in subsection (2).

As amended in 1990.

§2A—524. LESSOR'S RIGHT TO IDENTIFY GOODS TO LEASE CONTRACT

(1) After default by the lessee under the lease contract of the type described in Section 2A—523(1) or 2A—523(3) (a) or, if agreed, after other default by the lessee, the lessor may:

(a) identify to the lease contract conforming goods not already identified if at the time the lessor learned of the default they were in the lessor's or the supplier's possession or control; and

(b) dispose of goods (Section 2A—527(1)) that demonstrably have been intended for the particular lease contract even though those goods are unfinished.

(2) If the goods are unfinished, in the exercise of reasonable commercial judgment for the purposes of avoiding loss and of effective realization, an aggrieved lessor or the supplier may either complete manufacture and wholly identify the goods to the lease contract or cease manufacture and lease, sell, or otherwise dispose of the goods for scrap or salvage value or proceed in any other reasonable manner.

As amended in 1990.

§2A—525. LESSOR'S RIGHT TO POSSESSION OF GOODS

(1) If a lessor discovers the lessee to be insolvent, the lessor may refuse to deliver the goods.

(2) After a default by the lessee under the lease contract of the type described in Section 2A—523(1) or 2A—523(3)(a) or, if agreed, after other default by the lessee, the lessor has the right to take possession of the goods. If the lease contract so provides, the lessor may require the lessee to assemble the goods and make them available to the lessor at a place to be designated by the lessor which is reasonably convenient to both parties. Without removal, the lessor may render unusable any goods employed in trade or business, and may dispose of goods on the lessee's premises (Section 2A—527).

(3) The lessor may proceed under subsection (2) without judicial process if that can be done without breach of the peace or the lessor may proceed by action.

As amended in 1990.

§2A—526. LESSOR'S STOPPAGE OF DELIVERY IN TRANSIT OR OTHERWISE

(1) A lessor may stop delivery of goods in the possession of a carrier or other bailee if the lessor discovers the lessee to be insolvent and may stop delivery of carload, truckload, planeload, or larger shipments of express or freight if the lessee repudiates or fails to make a payment due before delivery, whether for rent, security or otherwise under the lease contract, or for any other reason the lessor has a right to withhold or take possession of the goods.

(2) In pursuing its remedies under subsection (1), the lessor may stop delivery until

    (a) receipt of the goods by the lessee;

    (b) acknowledgment to the lessee by any bailee of the goods, except a carrier, that the bailee holds the goods for the lessee; or

    (c) such an acknowledgment to the lessee by a carrier via reshipment or as warehouseman.

(3) (a) To stop delivery, a lessor shall so notify as to enable the bailee by reasonable diligence to prevent delivery of the goods.

    (b) After notification, the bailee shall hold and deliver the goods according to the directions of the lessor, but the lessor is liable to the bailee for any ensuing charges or damages.

    (c) A carrier who has issued a nonnegotiable bill of lading is not obliged to obey a notification to stop received from a person other than the consignor.

§2A—527. LESSOR'S RIGHTS TO DISPOSE OF GOODS

(1) After a default by a lessee under the lease contract of the type described in Section 2A—523(1) or 2A—523(3)(a) or after the lessor refuses to deliver or takes possession of goods (Section 2A—525 or 2A—526), or, if agreed, after other default by a lessee, the lessor may dispose of the goods concerned or the undelivered balance thereof by lease, sale, or otherwise.

(2) Except as otherwise provided with respect to damages liquidated in the lease agreement (Section 2A—504) or otherwise determined pursuant to agreement of the parties (Sections 1—102(3) and 2A—503), if the disposition is by lease agreement substantially similar to the original lease agreement and the new lease agreement is made in good faith and in a commercially reasonable manner, the lessor may recover from the lessee as damages (i) accrued and unpaid rent as of the date of the commencement of the term of the new lease agreement, (ii) the present value, as of the same date, of the total rent for the then remaining lease term of the original lease agreement minus the present value, as of the same date, of the rent under the new lease agreement applicable to that period of the new lease term which is comparable to the then remaining term of the original lease agreement, and (iii) any incidental damages allowed under Section 2A—530, less expenses saved in consequence of the lessee's default.

(3) If the lessor's disposition is by lease agreement that for any reason does not qualify for treatment under subsection (2), or is by sale or otherwise, the lessor may recover from the lessee as if the lessor had elected not to dispose of the goods and Section 2A—528 governs.

(4) A subsequent buyer or lessee who buys or leases from the lessor in good faith for value as a result of a disposition under this section takes the goods free of the original lease contract and any rights of the original lessee even though the lessor fails to comply with one or more of the requirements of this Article.

(5) The lessor is not accountable to the lessee for any profit made on any disposition. A lessee who has rightfully rejected or justifiably revoked acceptance shall account to the lessor for any excess over the amount of the lessee's security interest (Section 2A—508(5)).

As amended in 1990.

§2A—528. LESSOR'S DAMAGES FOR NON-ACCEPTANCE, FAILURE TO PAY, REPUDIATION, OR OTHER DEFAULT

(1) Except as otherwise provided with respect to damages liquidated in the lease agreement (Section 2A—504) or otherwise determined pursuant to agreement of the parties (Section 1—102(3) and 2A—503), if a lessor elects to retain the goods or a lessor elects to dispose of the goods and the disposition is by lease agreement that for any reason does not qualify for treatment under Section 2A—527(2), or is by sale or otherwise, the lessor may recover from the lessee as damages for a default of the type described in Section 2A—523(1) or 2A—523(3)(a), or if agreed, for other default of the lessee, (i) accrued and unpaid rent as of the date of the default if the lessee has never taken possession of the goods, or, if the lessee has taken possession of the goods, as of the date the lessor repossesses the goods or an earlier date on which the lessee makes a tender of the goods to the lessor, (ii) the present value as of the date determined under clause (i) of the total rent for the then remaining lease term of the original lease agreement minus the present value as of the same date of the market rent as the place where the goods are located computed for the same lease term, and (iii) any incidental damages allowed under Section 2A—530, less expenses saved in consequence of the lessee's default.

(2) If the measure of damages provided in subsection (1) is inadequate to put a lessor in as good a position as performance would have, the measure of damages is the present value of the profit, including reasonable overhead, the lessor would have made from full performance by the lessee, together with any incidental damages allowed under Section 2A—530, due allowance for costs reasonably incurred and due credit for payments or proceeds of disposition.

As amended in 1990.

§2A—529. LESSOR'S ACTION FOR THE RENT

(1) After default by the lessee under the lease contract of the type described in Section 2A—523(1) or 2A—523(3)(a) or, if agreed, after other default by the lessee, if the lessor complies with subsection (2), the lessor may recover from the lessee as damages:

    (a) for goods accepted by the lessee and not repossessed by or tendered to the lessor, and for conforming goods lost or damaged within a commercially reasonable time after risk of loss passes to the lessee (Section 2A—219), (i) accrued and unpaid rent as of the date of entry of judgment in favor of the lessor (ii) the present value as of the same date of the rent for the then remaining lease term of the lease agreement, and (iii) any incidental damages allowed under

Section 2A—530, less expenses saved in consequence of the lessee's default; and

    (b) for goods identified to the lease contract if the lessor is unable after reasonable effort to dispose of them at a reasonable price or the circumstances reasonably indicate that effort will be unavailing, (i) accrued and unpaid rent as of the date of entry of judgment in favor of the lessor, (ii) the present value as of the same date of the rent for the then remaining lease term of the lease agreement, and (iii) any incidental damages allowed under Section 2A—530, less expenses saved in consequence of the lessee's default.

(2) Except as provided in subsection (3), the lessor shall hold for the lessee for the remaining lease term of the lease agreement any goods that have been identified to the lease contract and are in the lessor's control.

(3) The lessor may dispose of the goods at any time before collection of the judgment for damages obtained pursuant to subsection (1). If the disposition is before the end of the remaining lease term of the lease agreement, the lessor's recovery against the lessee for damages is governed by Section 2A—527 or Section 2A—528, and the lessor will cause an appropriate credit to be provided against a judgment for damages to the extent that the amount of the judgment exceeds the recovery available pursuant to Section 2A—527 or 2A—528.

(4) Payment of the judgment for damages obtained pursuant to subsection (1) entitles the lessee to the use and possession of the goods not then disposed of for the remaining lease term of and in accordance with the lease agreement.

(5) After default by the lessee under the lease contract of the type described in Section 2A—523(1) or Section 2A—523(3)(a) or, if agreed, after other default by the lessee, a lessor who is held not entitled to rent under this section must nevertheless be awarded damages for non-acceptance under Sections 2A—527 and 2A—528.

As amended in 1990.

§2A—530. LESSOR'S INCIDENTAL DAMAGES

Incidental damages to an aggrieved lessor include any commercially reasonable charges, expenses, or commissions incurred in stopping delivery, in the transportation, care and custody of goods after the lessee's default, in connection with return or disposition of the goods, or otherwise resulting from the default.

§2A—531. STANDING TO SUE THIRD PARTIES FOR INJURY TO GOODS

(1) If a third party so deals with goods that have been identified to a lease contract as to cause actionable injury to a party to the lease contract (a) the lessor has a right of

action against the third party, and (b) the lessee also has a right of action against the third party if the lessee:

> (i)   has a security interest in the goods;
>
> (ii) has an insurable interest in the goods; or
>
> (iii) bears the risk of loss under the lease contract or has since the injury assumed that risk as against the lessor and the goods have been converted or destroyed.

(2) If at the time of the injury the party plaintiff did not bear the risk of loss as against the other party to the lease contract and there is no arrangement between them for disposition of the recovery, his [or her] suit or settlement, subject to his [or her] own interest, is as a fiduciary for the other party to the lease contract.

(3) Either party with the consent of the other may sue for the benefit of whom it may concern.

§2A—532. LESSOR'S RIGHTS TO RESIDUAL INTEREST

In addition to any other recovery permitted by this Article or other law, the lessor may recover from the lessee an amount that will fully compensate the lessor for any loss of or damage to the lessor's residual interest in the goods caused by the default of the lessee.

As added in 1990.

REVISED ARTICLE 3
NEGOTIABLE INSTRUMENTS

Part 1 General Provisions and Definitions

§3—101. SHORT TITLE

This Article may be cited as Uniform Commercial Code—Negotiable Instruments.

§3—102. SUBJECT MATTER

(a) This Article applies to negotiable instruments. It does not apply to money, to payment orders governed by Article 4A, or to securities governed by Article 8.

(b) If there is conflict between this Article and Article 4 or 9, Articles 4 and 9 govern.

(c) Regulations of the Board of Governors of the Federal Reserve System and operating circulars of the Federal Reserve Banks supersede any inconsistent provision of this Article to the extent of the inconsistency.

§3—103. DEFINITIONS

(a) In this Article:

> (1) "Acceptor" means a drawee who has accepted a draft.
>
> (2) "Drawee" means a person ordered in a draft to make payment.
>
> (3) "Drawer" means a person who signs or is identified in a draft as a person ordering payment.
>
> (4) "Good faith" means honesty in fact and the observance of reasonable commercial standards of fair dealing.
>
> (5) "Maker" means a person who signs or is identified in a note as a person undertaking to pay.
>
> (6) "Order" means a written instruction to pay money signed by the person giving the instruction. The instruction may be addressed to any person, including the person giving the instruction, or to one or more persons jointly or in the alternative but not in succession. An authorization to pay is not an order unless the person authorized to pay is also instructed to pay.
>
> (7) "Ordinary care" in the case of a person engaged in business means observance of reasonable commercial standards, prevailing in the area in which the person is located, with respect to the business in which the person is engaged. In the case of a bank that takes an instrument for processing for collection or payment by automated means, reasonable commercial standards do not require the bank to examine the instrument if the failure to examine does not violate the bank's prescribed procedures and the bank's procedures do not vary unreasonably from general banking usage not disapproved by this Article or Article 4.
>
> (8) "Party" means a party to an instrument.
>
> (9) "Promise" means a written undertaking to pay money signed by the person undertaking to pay. An acknowledgment of an obligation by the obligor is not a promise unless the obligor also undertakes to pay the obligation.
>
> (10) "Prove" with respect to a fact means to meet the burden of establishing the fact (Section 1—201(8)).
>
> (11) "Remitter" means a person who purchases an instrument from its issuer if the instrument is payable to an identified person other than the purchaser.

(b) [Other definitions' section references deleted.]

(c) [Other definitions' section references deleted.]

(d) In addition, Article 1 contains general definitions and principles of construction and interpretation applicable throughout this Article.

§3—104. NEGOTIABLE INSTRUMENT

(a) Except as provided in subsections (c) and (d), "negotiable instrument" means an unconditional promise or order to pay a fixed amount of money, with or without interest or other charges described in the promise or order, if it:

(1)   is payable to bearer or to order at the time it is issued or first comes into possession of a holder;

(2)   is payable on demand or at a definite time; and

(3)   does not state any other undertaking or instruction by the person promising or ordering payment to do any act in addition to the payment of money, but the promise or order may contain (i) an undertaking or power to give, maintain, or protect collateral to secure payment, (ii) an authorization or power to the holder to confess judgment or realize on or dispose of collateral, or (iii) a waiver of the benefit of any law intended for the advantage or protection of an obligor.

(b)   "Instrument" means a negotiable instrument.

(c)   An order that meets all of the requirements of subsection (a), except paragraph (1), and otherwise falls within the definition of "check" in subsection (f) is a negotiable instrument and a check.

(d)   A promise or order other than a check is not an instrument if, at the time it is issued or first comes into possession of a holder, it contains a conspicuous statement, however expressed, to the effect that the promise or order is not negotiable or is not an instrument governed by this Article.

(e)   An instrument is a "note" if it is a promise and is a "draft" if it is an order. If an instrument falls within the definition of both "note" and "draft," a person entitled to enforce the instrument may treat it as either.

(f)   "Check" means (i) a draft, other than a documentary draft, payable on demand and drawn on a bank or (ii) a cashier's check or teller's check. An instrument may be a check even though it is described on its face by another term, such as "money order."

(g)   "Cashier's check" means a draft with respect to which the drawer and drawee are the same bank or branches of the same bank.

(h)   "Teller's check" means a draft drawn by a bank (i) on another bank, or (ii) payable at or through a bank.

(i)   "Traveler's check" means an instrument that (i) is payable on demand, (ii) is drawn on or payable at or through a bank, (iii) is designated by the term "traveler's check" or by a substantially similar term, and (iv) requires, as a condition to payment, a countersignature by a person whose specimen signature appears on the instrument.

(j)   "Certificate of deposit" means an instrument containing an acknowledgment by a bank that a sum of money has been received by the bank and a promise by the bank to repay the sum of money. A certificate of deposit is a note of the bank.

§3—105. ISSUE OF INSTRUMENT

(a)   "Issue" means the first delivery of an instrument by the maker or drawer, whether to a holder or nonholder, for the purpose of giving rights on the instrument to any person.

(b)   An unissued instrument, or an unissued incomplete instrument that is completed, is binding on the maker or drawer, but nonissuance is a defense. An instrument that is conditionally issued or is issued for a special purpose is binding on the maker or drawer, but failure of the condition or special purpose to be fulfilled is a defense.

(c)   "Issuer" applies to issued and unissued instruments and means a maker or drawer of an instrument.

§3—106. UNCONDITIONAL PROMISE OR ORDER

(a)   Except as provided in this section, for the purposes of Section 3—104(a), a promise or order is unconditional unless it states (i) an express condition to payment, (ii) that the promise or order is subject to or governed by another writing, or (iii) that rights or obligations with respect to the promise or order are stated in another writing. A reference to another writing does not of itself make the promise or order conditional.

(b)   A promise or order is not made conditional (i) by a reference to another writing for a statement of rights with respect to collateral, prepayment, or acceleration, or (ii) because payment is limited to resort to a particular fund or source.

(c)   If a promise or order requires, as a condition to payment, a countersignature by a person whose specimen signature appears on the promise or order, the condition does not make the promise or order conditional for the purposes of Section 3—104(a). If the person whose specimen signature appears on an instrument fails to countersign the instrument, the failure to countersign is a defense to the obligation of the issuer, but the failure does not prevent a transferee of the instrument from becoming a holder of the instrument.

(d)   If a promise or order at the time it is issued or first comes into possession of a holder contains a statement, required by applicable statutory or administrative law, to the effect that the rights of a holder or transferee are subject to claims or defenses that the issuer could assert against the original payee, the promise or order is not thereby made conditional for the purposes of Section 3—104(a); but if the promise or order is an instrument, there cannot be a holder in due course of the instrument.

§3—107. INSTRUMENT PAYABLE IN FOREIGN MONEY

Unless the instrument otherwise provides, an instrument that states the amount payable in foreign money may be paid in the foreign money or in an equivalent amount in dollars calculated by using the current bank-offered spot rate at the place of payment for the purchase of dollars on the day on which the instrument is paid.

§3—108. PAYABLE ON DEMAND OR AT DEFINITE TIME

(a) A promise or order is "payable on demand" if it (i) states that it is payable on demand or at sight, or otherwise indicates that it is payable at the will of the holder, or (ii) does not state any time of payment.

(b) A promise or order is "payable at a definite time" if it is payable on elapse of a definite period of time after sight or acceptance or at a fixed date or dates or at a time or times readily ascertainable at the time the promise or order is issued, subject to rights of (i) prepayment, (ii) acceleration, (iii) extension at the option of the holder, or (iv) extension to a further definite time at the option of the maker or acceptor or automatically upon or after a specified act or event.

(c) If an instrument, payable at a fixed date, is also payable upon demand made before the fixed date, the instrument is payable on demand until the fixed date and, if demand for payment is not made before that date, becomes payable at a definite time on the fixed date.

§3—109. PAYABLE TO BEARER OR TO ORDER

(a) A promise or order is payable to bearer if it:
> (1) states that it is payable to bearer or to the order of bearer or otherwise indicates that the person in possession of the promise or order is entitled to payment;
> (2) does not state a payee; or
> (3) states that it is payable to or to the order of cash or otherwise indicates that it is not payable to an identified person.

(b) A promise or order that is not payable to bearer is payable to order if it is payable (i) to the order of an identified person or (ii) to an identified person or order. A promise or order that is payable to order is payable to the identified person.

(c) An instrument payable to bearer may become payable to an identified person if it is specially indorsed pursuant to Section 3—205(a). An instrument payable to an identified person may become payable to bearer if it is indorsed in blank pursuant to Section 3—205(b).

§3—110. IDENTIFICATION OF PERSON TO WHOM INSTRUMENT IS PAYABLE

(a) The person to whom an instrument is initially payable is determined by the intent of the person, whether or not authorized, signing as, or in the name or behalf of, the issuer of the instrument. The instrument is payable to the person intended by the signer even if that person is identified in the instrument by a name or other identification that is not that of the intended person. If more than one person signs in the name or behalf of the issuer of an instrument and all the signers do not intend the same person as payee, the instrument is payable to any person intended by one or more of the signers.

(b) If the signature of the issuer of an instrument is made by automated means, such as a check-writing machine, the payee of the instrument is determined by the intent of the person who supplied the name or identification of the payee, whether or not authorized to do so.

(c) A person to whom an instrument is payable may be identified in any way, including by name, identifying number, office, or account number. For the purpose of determining the holder of an instrument, the following rules apply:
> (1) If an instrument is payable to an account and the account is identified only by number, the instrument is payable to the person to whom the account is payable. If an instrument is payable to an account identified by number and by the name of a person, the instrument is payable to the named person, whether or not that person is the owner of the account identified by number.
> (2) If an instrument is payable to:
>> (i) a trust, an estate, or a person described as trustee or representative of a trust or estate, the instrument is payable to the trustee, the representative, or a successor of either, whether or not the beneficiary or estate is also named;
>> (ii) a person described as agent or similar representative of a named or identified person, the instrument is payable to the represented person, the representative, or a successor of the representative;
>> (iii) a fund or organization that is not a legal entity, the instrument is payable to a representative of the members of the fund or organization; or
>> (iv) an office or to a person described as holding an office, the instrument is payable to the named person, the incumbent of the office, or a successor to the incumbent.

(d) If an instrument is payable to two or more persons alternatively, it is payable to any of them and may be negotiated, discharged, or enforced by any or all of them in possession of the instrument. If an instrument is payable to two or more persons not alternatively, it is payable to all of them and may be negotiated, discharged, or enforced only by all of them. If an instrument payable to two or more persons is ambiguous as to whether it is payable to the persons alternatively, the instrument is payable to the persons alternatively.

§3—111. PLACE OF PAYMENT

Except as otherwise provided for items in Article 4, an instrument is payable at the place of payment stated in the instrument. If no place of payment is stated, an instrument is payable at the address of the drawee or maker stated in the instrument. If no address is stated, the place of payment is the place of business of the drawee or maker. If a drawee or maker has more than one place of business, the place of payment is any place of business of the drawee or maker chosen by the person entitled to enforce the instrument. If the drawee or maker has no place of business, the place of payment is the residence of the drawee or maker.

§3—112. INTEREST

(a) Unless otherwise provided in the instrument, (i) an instrument is not payable with interest, and (ii) interest on an interest-bearing instrument is payable from the date of the instrument.

(b) Interest may be stated in an instrument as a fixed or variable amount of money or it may be expressed as a fixed or variable rate or rates. The amount or rate of interest may be stated or described in the instrument in any manner and may require reference to information not contained in the instrument. If an instrument provides for interest, but the amount of interest payable cannot be ascertained from the description, interest is payable at the judgment rate in effect at the place of payment of the instrument and at the time interest first accrues.

§3—113. DATE OF INSTRUMENT

(a) An instrument may be antedated or postdated. The date stated determines the time of payment if the instrument is payable at a fixed period after date. Except as provided in Section 4—401(c), an instrument payable on demand is not payable before the date of the instrument.

(b) If an instrument is undated, its date is the date of its issue or, in the case of an unissued instrument, the date it first comes into possession of a holder.

§3—114. CONTRADICTORY TERMS OF INSTRUMENT

If an instrument contains contradictory terms, typewritten terms prevail over printed terms, handwritten terms prevail over both, and words prevail over numbers.

§3—115. INCOMPLETE INSTRUMENT

(a) "Incomplete instrument" means a signed writing, whether or not issued by the signer, the contents of which show at the time of signing that it is incomplete but that the signer intended it to be completed by the addition of words or numbers.

(b) Subject to subsection (c), if an incomplete instrument is an instrument under Section 3—104, it may be enforced according to its terms if it is not completed, or according to its terms as augmented by completion. If an incomplete instrument is not an instrument under Section 3—104, but, after completion, the requirements of Section 3—104 are met, the instrument may be enforced according to its terms as augmented by completion.

(c) If words or numbers are added to an incomplete instrument without authority of the signer, there is an alteration of the incomplete instrument under Section 3—407.

(d) The burden of establishing that words or numbers were added to an incomplete instrument without authority of the signer is on the person asserting the lack of authority.

§3—116. JOINT AND SEVERAL LIABILITY; CONTRIBUTION

(a) Except as otherwise provided in the instrument, two or more persons who have the same liability on an instrument as makers, drawers, acceptors, indorsers who indorse as joint payees, or anomalous indorsers are jointly and severally liable in the capacity in which they sign.

(b) Except as provided in Section 3—419(e) or by agreement of the affected parties, a party having joint and several liability who pays the instrument is entitled to receive from any party having the same joint and several liability contribution in accordance with applicable law.

(c) Discharge of one party having joint and several liability by a person entitled to enforce the instrument does not affect the right under subsection (b) of a party having the same joint and several liability to receive contribution from the party discharged.

§3—117. OTHER AGREEMENTS AFFECTING INSTRUMENT

Subject to applicable law regarding exclusion of proof of contemporaneous or previous agreements, the obligation of a party to an instrument to pay the instrument may be modified, supplemented, or nullified by a separate agreement of the obligor and a person entitled to enforce the instrument, if the instrument is issued or the obligation is incurred in reliance on the agreement or as part of the same transaction giving rise to the agreement. To the extent an obligation is modified, supplemented, or nullified by an agreement under this section, the agreement is a defense to the obligation.

§3—118. STATUTE OF LIMITATIONS

(a) Except as provided in subsection (e), an action to enforce the obligation of a party to pay a note payable at a definite time must be commenced within six years after the due date or dates stated in the note or, if a due date is accelerated, within six years after the accelerated due date.

(b) Except as provided in subsection (d) or (e), if demand for payment is made to the maker of a note payable on demand, an action to enforce the obligation of a party to pay the note must be commenced within six years after the demand. If no demand for payment is made to the maker, an action to enforce the note is barred if neither principal nor interest on the note has been paid for a continuous period of 10 years.

(c) Except as provided in subsection (d), an action to enforce the obligation of a party to an unaccepted draft to pay the draft must be commenced within three years after dishonor of the draft or 10 years after the date of the draft, whichever period expires first.

(d) An action to enforce the obligation of the acceptor of a certified check or the issuer of a teller's check, cashier's check, or traveler's check must be commenced within three years after demand for payment is made to the acceptor or issuer, as the case may be.

(e) An action to enforce the obligation of a party to a certificate of deposit to pay the instrument must be commenced within six years after demand for payment is made to the maker, but if the instrument states a due date and the maker is not required to pay before that date, the six-year period begins when a demand for payment is in effect and the due date has passed.

(f) An action to enforce the obligation of a party to pay an accepted draft, other than a certified check, must be commenced (i) within six years after the due date or dates stated in the draft or acceptance if the obligation of the acceptor is payable at a definite time, or (ii) within six years after the date of the acceptance if the obligation of the acceptor is payable on demand.

(g) Unless governed by other law regarding claims for indemnity or contribution, an action (i) for conversion of an instrument, for money had and received, or like action based on conversion, (ii) for breach of warranty, or (iii) to enforce an obligation, duty, or right arising under this Article and not governed by this section must be commenced within three years after the [cause of action] accrues.

§3—119. NOTICE OF RIGHT TO DEFEND ACTION

In an action for breach of an obligation for which a third person is answerable over pursuant to this Article or Article 4, the defendant may give the third person written notice of the litigation, and the person notified may then give similar notice to any other person who is answerable over. If the notice states (i) that the person notified may come in and defend and (ii) that failure to do so will bind the person notified in an action later brought by the person giving the notice as to any determination of fact common to the two litigations, the person notified is so bound unless after seasonable receipt of the notice the person notified does come in and defend.

Part 2 Negotiation, Transfer, and Indorsement

§3—201. NEGOTIATION

(a) "Negotiation" means a transfer of possession, whether voluntary or involuntary, of an instrument by a person other than the issuer to a person who thereby becomes its holder.

(b) Except for negotiation by a remitter, if an instrument is payable to an identified person, negotiation requires transfer of possession of the instrument and its indorsement by the holder. If an instrument is payable to bearer, it may be negotiated by transfer of possession alone.

§3—202. NEGOTIATION SUBJECT TO RESCISSION

(a) Negotiation is effective even if obtained (i) from an infant, a corporation exceeding its powers, or a person without capacity, (ii) by fraud, duress, or mistake, or (iii) in breach of duty or as part of an illegal transaction.

(b) To the extent permitted by other law, negotiation may be rescinded or may be subject to other remedies, but those remedies may not be asserted against a subsequent holder in due course or a person paying the instrument in good faith and without knowledge of facts that are a basis for rescission or other remedy.

§3—203. TRANSFER OF INSTRUMENT; RIGHTS ACQUIRED BY TRANSFER

(a) An instrument is transferred when it is delivered by a person other than its issuer for the purpose of giving to the person receiving delivery the right to enforce the instrument.

(b) Transfer of an instrument, whether or not the transfer is a negotiation, vests in the transferee any right of the transferor to enforce the instrument, including any right as a holder in due course, but the transferee cannot acquire rights of a holder in due course by a transfer, directly or indirectly, from a holder in due course if the transferee engaged in fraud or illegality affecting the instrument.

(c) Unless otherwise agreed, if an instrument is transferred for value and the transferee does not become a holder because of lack of indorsement by the transferor, the transferee has a specifically enforceable right to the unqualified indorsement of the transferor, but negotiation of the instrument does not occur until the indorsement is made.

(d) If a transferor purports to transfer less than the entire instrument, negotiation of the instrument does not occur. The transferee obtains no rights under this Article and has only the rights of a partial assignee.

§3—204. INDORSEMENT

(a) "Indorsement" means a signature, other than that of a signer as maker, drawer, or acceptor, that alone or accompanied by other words is made on an instrument for the purpose of (i) negotiating the instrument, (ii) restricting payment of the instrument, or (iii) incurring indorser's liability on the instrument, but regardless of the intent of the signer, a signature and its accompanying words is an indorsement unless the accompanying words, terms of the instrument, place of the signature, or other circumstances unambiguously indicate that the signature was made for a purpose other than indorsement. For the purpose of determining whether a signature is made on an instrument, a paper affixed to the instrument is a part of the instrument.

(b) "Indorser" means a person who makes an indorsement.

(c) For the purpose of determining whether the transferee of an instrument is a holder, an indorsement that transfers a security interest in the instrument is effective as an unqualified indorsement of the instrument.

(d) If an instrument is payable to a holder under a name that is not the name of the holder, indorsement may be made by the holder in the name stated in the instrument or in the holder's name or both, but signature in both names may be required by a person paying or taking the instrument for value or collection.

§3—205. SPECIAL INDORSEMENT; BLANK INDORSEMENT; ANOMALOUS INDORSEMENT

(a) If an indorsement is made by the holder of an instrument, whether payable to an identified person or payable to bearer, and the indorsement identifies a person to whom it makes the instrument payable, it is a "special indorsement." When specially indorsed, an instrument becomes payable to the identified person and may be negotiated only by the indorsement of that person. The principles stated in Section 3—110 apply to special indorsements.

(b) If an indorsement is made by the holder of an instrument and it is not a special indorsement, it is a "blank indorsement." When indorsed in blank, an instrument becomes payable to bearer and may be negotiated by transfer of possession alone until specially indorsed.

(c) The holder may convert a blank indorsement that consists only of a signature into a special indorsement by writing, above the signature of the indorser, words identifying the person to whom the instrument is made payable.

(d) "Anomalous indorsement" means an indorsement made by a person who is not the holder of the instrument. An anomalous indorsement does not affect the manner in which the instrument may be negotiated.

§3—206. RESTRICTIVE INDORSEMENT

(a) An indorsement limiting payment to a particular person or otherwise prohibiting further transfer or negotiation of the instrument is not effective to prevent further transfer or negotiation of the instrument.

(b) An indorsement stating a condition to the right of the indorsee to receive payment does not affect the right of the indorsee to enforce the instrument. A person paying the instrument or taking it for value or collection may disregard the condition, and the rights and liabilities of that person are not affected by whether the condition has been fulfilled.

(c) If an instrument bears an indorsement (i) described in Section 4—201(b), or (ii) in blank or to a particular bank using the words "for deposit," "for collection," or other words indicating a purpose of having the instrument collected by a bank for the indorser or for a particular account, the following rules apply:

(1) A person, other than a bank, who purchases the instrument when so indorsed converts the instrument unless the amount paid for the instrument is received by the indorser or applied consistently with the indorsement.

(2) A depositary bank that purchases the instrument or takes it for collection when so indorsed converts the instrument unless the amount paid by the bank with respect to the instrument is received by the indorser or applied consistently with the indorsement.

(3) A payor bank that is also the depositary bank or that takes the instrument for immediate payment over the counter from a person other than a collecting bank converts the instrument unless the proceeds of the instrument are received by the indorser or applied consistently with the indorsement.

(4) Except as otherwise provided in paragraph (3), a payor bank or intermediary bank may disregard the indorsement and is not liable if the proceeds of the instrument are not received by the indorser or applied consistently with the indorsement.

(d) Except for an indorsement covered by subsection (c), if an instrument bears an indorsement using words to the effect that payment is to be made to the indorsee as agent, trustee, or other fiduciary for the benefit of the indorser or another person, the following rules apply:

(1) Unless there is notice of breach of fiduciary duty as provided in Section 3—307, a person who purchases the instrument from the indorsee or takes the instrument from the indorsee for collection or payment may pay the proceeds of payment or the value given for the instrument to the indorsee without regard to whether the indorsee violates a fiduciary duty to the indorser.

(2) A subsequent transferee of the instrument or person who pays the instrument is neither given notice nor otherwise affected by the restriction in the indorsement unless the transferee or payor knows that the fiduciary dealt with the instrument or its proceeds in breach of fiduciary duty.

(e) The presence on an instrument of an indorsement to which this section applies does not prevent a purchaser of the instrument from becoming a holder in due course of the instrument unless the purchaser is a converter under subsection (c) or has notice or knowledge of breach of fiduciary duty as stated in subsection (d).

(f) In an action to enforce the obligation of a party to pay the instrument, the obligor has a defense if payment would violate an indorsement to which this section applies and the payment is not permitted by this section.

§3—207. REACQUISITION

Reacquisition of an instrument occurs if it is transferred to a former holder, by negotiation or otherwise. A former holder who reacquires the instrument may cancel indorsements made after the reacquirer first became a holder of the instrument. If the cancellation causes the instrument to be payable to the reacquirer or to bearer, the reacquirer may negotiate the instrument. An indorser whose indorsement is canceled is discharged, and the discharge is effective against any subsequent holder.

Part 3 Enforcement of Instruments

§3—301. PERSON ENTITLED TO ENFORCE INSTRUMENT

"Person entitled to enforce" an instrument means (i) the holder of the instrument, (ii) a nonholder in possession of the instrument who has the rights of a holder, or (iii) a person not in possession of the instrument who is entitled to enforce the instrument pursuant to Section 3—309 or 3—418(d). A person may be a person entitled to enforce the instrument even though the person is not the owner of the instrument or is in wrongful possession of the instrument.

§3—302. HOLDER IN DUE COURSE

(a) Subject to subsection (c) and Section 3—106(d), "holder in due course" means the holder of an instrument if:

(1) the instrument when issued or negotiated to the holder does not bear such apparent evidence of forgery or alteration or is not otherwise so irregular or incomplete as to call into question its authenticity; and

(2) the holder took the instrument (i) for value, (ii) in good faith, (iii) without notice that the instrument is overdue or has been dishonored or that there is an uncured default with respect to payment of another instrument issued as part of the same series, (iv) without notice that the instrument contains an unauthorized signature or has been altered, (v) without notice of any claim to the instrument described in Section 3—306, and (vi) without notice that any party has a defense or claim in recoupment described in Section 3—305(a).

(b) Notice of discharge of a party, other than discharge in an insolvency proceeding, is not notice of a defense under subsection (a), but discharge is effective against a person who became a holder in due course with notice of the discharge. Public filing or recording of a document does not of itself constitute notice of a defense, claim in recoupment, or claim to the instrument.

(c) Except to the extent a transferor or predecessor in interest has rights as a holder in due course, a person does not acquire rights of a holder in due course of an instrument taken (i) by legal process or by purchase in an execution, bankruptcy, or creditor's sale or similar proceeding, (ii) by purchase as part of a bulk transaction not in ordinary course of business of the transferor, or (iii) as the successor in interest to an estate or other organization.

(d) If, under Section 3—303(a)(1), the promise of performance that is the consideration for an instrument has been partially performed, the holder may assert rights as a holder in due course of the instrument only to the fraction of the amount payable under the instrument equal to the value of the partial performance divided by the value of the promised performance.

(e) If (i) the person entitled to enforce an instrument has only a security interest in the instrument and (ii) the person obliged to pay the instrument has a defense, claim in recoupment, or claim to the instrument that may be asserted against the person who granted the security interest, the person entitled to enforce the instrument may assert rights as a holder in due course only to an amount payable under the instrument which, at the time of enforcement of the instrument, does not exceed the amount of the unpaid obligation secured.

(f) To be effective, notice must be received at a time and in a manner that gives a reasonable opportunity to act on it.

(g) This section is subject to any law limiting status as a holder in due course in particular classes of transactions.

§3—303. VALUE AND CONSIDERATION

(a) An instrument is issued or transferred for value if:

(1) the instrument is issued or transferred for a promise of performance, to the extent the promise has been performed;

(2) the transferee acquires a security interest or other lien in the instrument other than a lien obtained by judicial proceeding;

(3) the instrument is issued or transferred as payment of, or as security for, an antecedent claim against any person, whether or not the claim is due;

(4) the instrument is issued or transferred in exchange for a negotiable instrument; or

(5) the instrument is issued or transferred in exchange for the incurring of an irrevocable obligation to a third party by the person taking the instrument.

(b) "Consideration" means any consideration sufficient to support a simple contract. The drawer or maker of an instrument has a defense if the instrument is issued without consideration. If an instrument is issued for a promise of performance, the issuer has a defense to the extent performance of the promise is due and the promise has not been performed. If an instrument is issued for value as stated in subsection (a), the instrument is also issued for consideration.

§3—304. OVERDUE INSTRUMENT

(a) An instrument payable on demand becomes overdue at the earliest of the following times:

(1) on the day after the day demand for payment is duly made;

(2) if the instrument is a check, 90 days after its date; or

(3) if the instrument is not a check, when the instrument has been outstanding for a period of time after its date which is unreasonably long under the circumstances of the particular case in light of the nature of the instrument and usage of the trade.

(b) With respect to an instrument payable at a definite time the following rules apply:

(1) If the principal is payable in installments and a due date has not been accelerated, the instrument becomes overdue upon default under the instrument for nonpayment of an installment, and the instrument remains overdue until the default is cured.

(2) If the principal is not payable in installments and the due date has not been accelerated, the instrument becomes overdue on the day after the due date.

(3) If a due date with respect to principal has been accelerated, the instrument becomes overdue on the day after the accelerated due date.

(c) Unless the due date of principal has been accelerated, an instrument does not become overdue if there is default in payment of interest but no default in payment of principal.

§3—305. DEFENSES AND CLAIMS IN RECOUPMENT

(a) Except as stated in subsection (b), the right to enforce the obligation of a party to pay an instrument is subject to the following:

(1) a defense of the obligor based on (i) infancy of the obligor to the extent it is a defense to a simple contract, (ii) duress, lack of legal capacity, or illegality of the transaction which, under other law, nullifies the obligation of the obligor, (iii) fraud that induced the obligor to sign the instrument with neither knowledge nor reasonable opportunity to learn of its character or its essential terms, or (iv) discharge of the obligor in insolvency proceedings;

(2) a defense of the obligor stated in another section of this Article or a defense of the obligor that would be available if the person entitled to enforce the instrument were enforcing a right to payment under a simple contract; and

(3) a claim in recoupment of the obligor against the original payee of the instrument if the claim arose from the transaction that gave rise to the instrument; but the claim of the obligor may be asserted against a transferee of the instrument only to reduce the amount owing on the instrument at the time the action is brought.

(b) The right of a holder in due course to enforce the obligation of a party to pay the instrument is subject to defenses of the obligor stated in subsection (a)(1), but is not subject to defenses of the obligor stated in subsection (a)(2) or claims in recoupment stated in subsection (a)(3) against a person other than the holder.

(c) Except as stated in subsection (d), in an action to enforce the obligation of a party to pay the instrument, the obligor may not assert against the person entitled to enforce the instrument a defense, claim in recoupment, or claim to the instrument (Section 3—306) of another person, but the other person's claim to the instrument may be asserted by the obligor if the other person is joined in the action and personally asserts the claim against the person entitled to enforce the instrument. An obligor is not obliged to pay the instrument if the person seeking enforcement of the instrument does not have rights of a holder in due course and the obligor proves that the instrument is a lost or stolen instrument.

(d) In an action to enforce the obligation of an accommodation party to pay an instrument, the accommodation party may assert against the person entitled to enforce the instrument any defense or claim in recoupment under subsection (a) that the accommodated party could assert against the person entitled to enforce the instrument, except the defenses of discharge in insolvency proceedings, infancy, and lack of legal capacity.

§3—306. CLAIMS TO AN INSTRUMENT

A person taking an instrument, other than a person having rights of a holder in due course, is subject to a claim of a property or possessory right in the instrument or its proceeds, including a claim to rescind a negotiation and to recover the instrument or its proceeds. A person having rights of a holder in due course takes free of the claim to the instrument.

§3—307. NOTICE OF BREACH OF FIDUCIARY DUTY

(a)   In this section:

(1)   "Fiduciary" means an agent, trustee, partner, corporate officer or director, or other representative owing a fiduciary duty with respect to an instrument.

(2)   "Represented person" means the principal, beneficiary, partnership, corporation, or other person to whom the duty stated in paragraph (1) is owed.

(b)   If (i) an instrument is taken from a fiduciary for payment or collection or for value, (ii) the taker has knowledge of the fiduciary status of the fiduciary, and (iii) the represented person makes a claim to the instrument or its proceeds on the basis that the transaction of the fiduciary is a breach of fiduciary duty, the following rules apply:

(1)   Notice of breach of fiduciary duty by the fiduciary is notice of the claim of the represented person.

(2)   In the case of an instrument payable to the represented person or the fiduciary as such, the taker has notice of the breach of fiduciary duty if the instrument is (i) taken in payment of or as security for a debt known by the taker to be the personal debt of the fiduciary, (ii) taken in a transaction known by the taker to be for the personal benefit of the fiduciary, or (iii) deposited to an account other than an account of the fiduciary, as such, or an account of the represented person.

(3)   If an instrument is issued by the represented person or the fiduciary as such, and made payable to the fiduciary personally, the taker does not have notice of the breach of fiduciary duty unless the taker knows of the breach of fiduciary duty.

(4)   If an instrument is issued by the represented person or the fiduciary as such, to the taker as payee, the taker has notice of the breach of fiduciary duty if the instrument is (i) taken in payment of or as security for a debt known by the taker to be the personal debt of the fiduciary, (ii) taken in a transaction known by the taker to be for the personal benefit of the fiduciary, or

(iii) deposited to an account other than an account of the fiduciary, as such, or an account of the represented person.

§3—308. PROOF OF SIGNATURES AND STATUS AS HOLDER IN DUE COURSE

(a)   In an action with respect to an instrument, the authenticity of, and authority to make, each signature on the instrument is admitted unless specifically denied in the pleadings. If the validity of a signature is denied in the pleadings, the burden of establishing validity is on the person claiming validity, but the signature is presumed to be authentic and authorized unless the action is to enforce the liability of the purported signer and the signer is dead or incompetent at the time of trial of the issue of validity of the signature. If an action to enforce the instrument is brought against a person as the undisclosed principal of a person who signed the instrument as a party to the instrument, the plaintiff has the burden of establishing that the defendant is liable on the instrument as a represented person under Section 3—402(a).

(b)   If the validity of signatures is admitted or proved and there is compliance with subsection (a), a plaintiff producing the instrument is entitled to payment if the plaintiff proves entitlement to enforce the instrument under Section 3—301, unless the defendant proves a defense or claim in recoupment. If a defense or claim in recoupment is proved, the right to payment of the plaintiff is subject to the defense or claim, except to the extent the plaintiff proves that the plaintiff has rights of a holder in due course which are not subject to the defense or claim.

§3—309. ENFORCEMENT OF LOST, DESTROYED, OR STOLEN INSTRUMENT

(a)   A person not in possession of an instrument is entitled to enforce the instrument if (i) the person was in possession of the instrument and entitled to enforce it when loss of possession occurred, (ii) the loss of possession was not the result of a transfer by the person or a lawful seizure, and (iii) the person cannot reasonably obtain possession of the instrument because the instrument was destroyed, its whereabouts cannot be determined, or it is in the wrongful possession of an unknown person or a person that cannot be found or is not amenable to service of process.

(b)   A person seeking enforcement of an instrument under subsection (a) must prove the terms of the instrument and the person's right to enforce the instrument. If that proof is made, Section 3—308 applies to the case as if the person seeking enforcement had produced the instrument. The court may not enter judgment in favor of the person seeking enforcement unless it finds that the person required to pay the instrument is adequately protected against loss that might occur by reason of a claim by another person to enforce the instrument. Adequate protection may be provided by any reasonable means.

§3—310. EFFECT OF INSTRUMENT ON OBLIGATION FOR WHICH TAKEN

(a) Unless otherwise agreed, if a certified check, cashier's check, or teller's check is taken for an obligation, the obligation is discharged to the same extent discharge would result if an amount of money equal to the amount of the instrument were taken in payment of the obligation. Discharge of the obligation does not affect any liability that the obligor may have as an indorser of the instrument.

(b) Unless otherwise agreed and except as provided in subsection (a), if a note or an uncertified check is taken for an obligation, the obligation is suspended to the same extent the obligation would be discharged if an amount of money equal to the amount of the instrument were taken, and the following rules apply:

(1) In the case of an uncertified check, suspension of the obligation continues until dishonor of the check or until it is paid or certified. Payment or certification of the check results in discharge of the obligation to the extent of the amount of the check.

(2) In the case of a note, suspension of the obligation continues until dishonor of the note or until it is paid. Payment of the note results in discharge of the obligation to the extent of the payment.

(3) Except as provided in paragraph (4), if the check or note is dishonored and the obligee of the obligation for which the instrument was taken is the person entitled to enforce the instrument, the obligee may enforce either the instrument or the obligation. In the case of an instrument of a third person which is negotiated to the obligee by the obligor, discharge of the obligor on the instrument also discharges the obligation.

(4) If the person entitled to enforce the instrument taken for an obligation is a person other than the obligee, the obligee may not enforce the obligation to the extent the obligation is suspended. If the obligee is the person entitled to enforce the instrument but no longer has possession of it because it was lost, stolen, or destroyed, the obligation may not be enforced to the extent of the amount payable on the instrument, and to that extent the obligee's rights against the obligor are limited to enforcement of the instrument.

(c) If an instrument other than one described in subsection (a) or (b) is taken for an obligation, the effect is (i) that stated in subsection (a) if the instrument is one on which a bank is liable as maker or acceptor, or (ii) that stated in subsection (b) in any other case.

§3—311. ACCORD AND SATISFACTION BY USE OF INSTRUMENT

(a) If a person against whom a claim is asserted proves that (i) that person in good faith tendered an instrument to the claimant as full satisfaction of the claim, (ii) the amount of the claim was unliquidated or subject to a bona fide dispute, and (iii) the claimant obtained payment of the instrument, the following subsections apply.

(b) Unless subsection (c) applies, the claim is discharged if the person against whom the claim is asserted proves that the instrument or an accompanying written communication contained a conspicuous statement to the effect that the instrument was tendered as full satisfaction of the claim.

(c) Subject to subsection (d), a claim is not discharged under subsection (b) if either of the following applies:

(1) The claimant, if an organization, proves that (i) within a reasonable time before the tender, the claimant sent a conspicuous statement to the person against whom the claim is asserted that communications concerning disputed debts, including an instrument tendered as full satisfaction of a debt, are to be sent to a designated person, office, or place, and (ii) the instrument or accompanying communication was not received by that designated person, office, or place.

(2) The claimant, whether or not an organization, proves that within 90 days after payment of the instrument, the claimant tendered repayment of the amount of the instrument to the person against whom the claim is asserted. This paragraph does not apply if the claimant is an organization that sent a statement complying with paragraph (1)(i).

(d) A claim is discharged if the person against whom the claim is asserted proves that within a reasonable time before collection of the instrument was initiated, the claimant, or an agent of the claimant having direct responsibility with respect to the disputed obligation, knew that the instrument was tendered in full satisfaction of the claim.

§3—312. LOST, DESTROYED, OR STOLEN CASHIER'S CHECK, TELLER'S CHECK, OR CERTIFIED CHECK.*

(a) In this section:

(1) "Check" means a cashier's check, teller's check, or certified check.

*[Section 3—312 was not adopted as part of the 1990 Official Text of Revised Article 3. It was officially approved and recommended for enactment in all states in August 1991 by the National Conference of Commissioners on Uniform State Laws.]

(2) "Claimant" means a person who claims the right to receive the amount of a cashier's check, teller's check, or certified check that was lost, destroyed, or stolen.

(3) "Declaration of loss" means a written statement, made under penalty of perjury, to the effect that (i) the declarer lost possession of a check, (ii) the declarer is the drawer or payee of the check, in the case of a certified check, or the remitter or payee of the check, in the case of a cashier's check or teller's check, (iii) the loss of possession was not the result of a transfer by the declarer or a lawful seizure, and (iv) the declarer cannot reasonably obtain possession of the check because the check was destroyed, its whereabouts cannot be determined, or it is in the wrongful possession of an unknown person or a person that cannot be found or is not amenable to service of process.

(4) "Obligated bank" means the issuer of a cashier's check or teller's check or the acceptor of a certified check.

(b) A claimant may assert a claim to the amount of a check by a communication to the obligated bank describing the check with reasonable certainty and requesting payment of the amount of the check, if (i) the claimant is the drawer or payee of a certified check or the remitter or payee of a cashier's check or teller's check, (ii) the communication contains or is accompanied by a declaration of loss of the claimant with respect to the check, (iii) the communication is received at a time and in a manner affording the bank a reasonable time to act on it before the check is paid, and (iv) the claimant provides reasonable identification if requested by the obligated bank. Delivery of a declaration of loss is a warranty of the truth of the statements made in the declaration. If a claim is asserted in compliance with this subsection, the following rules apply:

(1) The claim becomes enforceable at the later of (i) the time the claim is asserted, or (ii) the 90th day following the date of the check, in the case of a cashier's check or teller's check, or the 90th day following the date of the acceptance, in the case of a certified check.

(2) Until the claim becomes enforceable, it has no legal effect and the obligated bank may pay the check or, in the case of a teller's check, may permit the drawee to pay the check. Payment to a person entitled to enforce the check discharges all liability of the obligated bank with respect to the check.

(3) If the claim becomes enforceable before the check is presented for payment, the obligated bank is not obliged to pay the check.

(4) When the claim becomes enforceable, the obligated bank becomes obliged to pay the amount of the check to the claimant if payment of the check has not been made to a person entitled to enforce the check. Subject to Section 4—302(a)(1), payment to the claimant discharges all liability of the obligated bank with respect to the check.

(c) If the obligated bank pays the amount of a check to a claimant under subsection (b)(4) and the check is presented for payment by a person having rights of a holder in due course, the claimant is obliged to (i) refund the payment to the obligated bank if the check is paid, or (ii) pay the amount of the check to the person having rights of a holder in due course if the check is dishonored.

(d) If a claimant has the right to assert a claim under subsection (b) and is also a person entitled to enforce a cashier's check, teller's check, or certified check which is lost, destroyed, or stolen, the claimant may assert rights with respect to the check either under this section or Section 3—309.

Added in 1991.

Part 4 Liability of Parties

§3—401. SIGNATURE

(a) A person is not liable on an instrument unless (i) the person signed the instrument, or (ii) the person is represented by an agent or representative who signed the instrument and the signature is binding on the represented person under Section 3—402.

(b) A signature may be made (i) manually or by means of a device or machine, and (ii) by the use of any name, including a trade or assumed name, or by a word, mark, or symbol executed or adopted by a person with present intention to authenticate a writing.

§3—402. SIGNATURE BY REPRESENTATIVE

(a) If a person acting, or purporting to act, as a representative signs an instrument by signing either the name of the represented person or the name of the signer, the represented person is bound by the signature to the same extent the represented person would be bound if the signature were on a simple contract. If the represented person is bound, the signature of the representative is the "authorized signature of the represented person" and the represented person is liable on the instrument, whether or not identified in the instrument.

(b) If a representative signs the name of the representative to an instrument and the signature is an authorized signature of the represented person, the following rules apply:

(1) If the form of the signature shows unambiguously that the signature is made on behalf of the represented person who is identified in the instrument, the representative is not liable on the instrument.

(2) Subject to subsection (c), if (i) the form of the signature does not show unambiguously that the signature is made in a representative capacity or (ii) the represented person is not identified in the instrument, the representative is liable on the instrument to a holder in due course that took the instrument without notice that the representative was not intended to be liable on the instrument. With respect to any other person, the representative is liable on the instrument unless the representative proves that the original parties did not intend the representative to be liable on the instrument.

(c) If a representative signs the name of the representative as drawer of a check without indication of the representative status and the check is payable from an account of the represented person who is identified on the check, the signer is not liable on the check if the signature is an authorized signature of the represented person.

§3—403. UNAUTHORIZED SIGNATURE

(a) Unless otherwise provided in this Article or Article 4, an unauthorized signature is ineffective except as the signature of the unauthorized signer in favor of a person who in good faith pays the instrument or takes it for value. An unauthorized signature may be ratified for all purposes of this Article.

(b) If the signature of more than one person is required to constitute the authorized signature of an organization, the signature of the organization is unauthorized if one of the required signatures is lacking.

(c) The civil or criminal liability of a person who makes an unauthorized signature is not affected by any provision of this Article which makes the unauthorized signature effective for the purposes of this Article.

§3—404. IMPOSTORS; FICTITIOUS PAYEES

(a) If an impostor, by use of the mails or otherwise, induces the issuer of an instrument to issue the instrument to the impostor, or to a person acting in concert with the impostor, by impersonating the payee of the instrument or a person authorized to act for the payee, an indorsement of the instrument by any person in the name of the payee is effective as the indorsement of the payee in favor of a person who, in good faith, pays the instrument or takes it for value or for collection.

(b) If (i) a person whose intent determines to whom an instrument is payable (Section 3—110(a) or (b)) does not intend the person identified as payee to have any interest in the instrument, or (ii) the person identified as payee of an instrument is a fictitious person, the following rules apply until the instrument is negotiated by special indorsement:

(1) Any person in possession of the instrument is its holder.

(2) An indorsement by any person in the name of the payee stated in the instrument is effective as the indorsement of the payee in favor of a person who, in good faith, pays the instrument or takes it for value or for collection.

(c) Under subsection (a) or (b), an indorsement is made in the name of a payee if (i) it is made in a name substantially similar to that of the payee or (ii) the instrument, whether or not indorsed, is deposited in a depositary bank to an account in a name substantially similar to that of the payee.

(d) With respect to an instrument to which subsection (a) or (b) applies, if a person paying the instrument or taking it for value or for collection fails to exercise ordinary care in paying or taking the instrument and that failure substantially contributes to loss resulting from payment of the instrument, the person bearing the loss may recover from the person failing to exercise ordinary care to the extent the failure to exercise ordinary care contributed to the loss.

§3—405. EMPLOYER'S RESPONSIBILITY FOR FRAUDULENT INDORSEMENT BY EMPLOYEE

(a) In this section:

(1) "Employee" includes an independent contractor and employee of an independent contractor retained by the employer.

(2) "Fraudulent indorsement" means (i) in the case of an instrument payable to the employer, a forged indorsement purporting to be that of the employer, or (ii) in the case of an instrument with respect to which the employer is the issuer, a forged indorsement purporting to be that of the person identified as payee.

(3) "Responsibility" with respect to instruments means authority (i) to sign or indorse instruments on behalf of the employer, (ii) to process instruments received by the employer for bookkeeping purposes, for deposit to an account, or for other disposition, (iii) to prepare or process instruments for issue in the name of the employer, (iv) to supply information determining the names or addresses of payees of instruments to be issued in the name of the employer, (v) to control the disposition of instruments to be issued in the name of the employer, or (vi) to act otherwise with respect to instruments in a responsible capacity. "Responsibility" does not include authority that merely allows an employee to have access to instruments or blank or incomplete instrument forms that are being stored or transported or are part of incoming or outgoing mail, or similar access.

(b) For the purpose of determining the rights and liabilities of a person who, in good faith, pays an instrument or takes it for value or for collection, if an employer entrusted an employee with responsibility with respect to the instrument and the employee or a person acting in concert with the employee makes a fraudulent indorsement of the instrument, the indorsement is effective as the indorsement of the person to whom the instrument is payable if it is made in the name of that person. If the person paying the instrument or taking it for value or for collection fails to exercise ordinary care in paying or taking the instrument and that failure substantially contributes to loss resulting from the fraud, the person bearing the loss may recover from the person failing to exercise ordinary care to the extent the failure to exercise ordinary care contributed to the loss.

(c) Under subsection (b), an indorsement is made in the name of the person to whom an instrument is payable if (i) it is made in a name substantially similar to the name of that person or (ii) the instrument, whether or not indorsed, is deposited in a depositary bank to an account in a name substantially similar to the name of that person.

§3—406. NEGLIGENCE CONTRIBUTING TO FORGED SIGNATURE OR ALTERATION OF INSTRUMENT

(a) A person whose failure to exercise ordinary care substantially contributes to an alteration of an instrument or to the making of a forged signature on an instrument is precluded from asserting the alteration or the forgery against a person who, in good faith, pays the instrument or takes it for value or for collection.

(b) Under subsection (a), if the person asserting the preclusion fails to exercise ordinary care in paying or taking the instrument and that failure substantially contributes to loss, the loss is allocated between the person precluded and the person asserting the preclusion according to the extent to which the failure of each to exercise ordinary care contributed to the loss.

(c) Under subsection (a), the burden of proving failure to exercise ordinary care is on the person asserting the preclusion. Under subsection (b), the burden of proving failure to exercise ordinary care is on the person precluded.

§3—407. ALTERATION

(a) "Alteration" means (i) an unauthorized change in an instrument that purports to modify in any respect the obligation of a party, or (ii) an unauthorized addition of words or numbers or other change to an incomplete instrument relating to the obligation of a party.

(b) Except as provided in subsection (c), an alteration fraudulently made discharges a party whose obligation is affected by the alteration unless that party assents or is precluded from asserting the alteration. No other alteration

discharges a party, and the instrument may be enforced according to its original terms.

(c) A payor bank or drawee paying a fraudulently altered instrument or a person taking it for value, in good faith and without notice of the alteration, may enforce rights with respect to the instrument (i) according to its original terms, or (ii) in the case of an incomplete instrument altered by unauthorized completion, according to its terms as completed.

§3—408. DRAWEE NOT LIABLE ON UNACCEPTED DRAFT

A check or other draft does not of itself operate as an assignment of funds in the hands of the drawee available for its payment, and the drawee is not liable on the instrument until the drawee accepts it.

§3—409. ACCEPTANCE OF DRAFT; CERTIFIED CHECK

(a) "Acceptance" means the drawee's signed agreement to pay a draft as presented. It must be written on the draft and may consist of the drawee's signature alone. Acceptance may be made at any time and becomes effective when notification pursuant to instructions is given or the accepted draft is delivered for the purpose of giving rights on the acceptance to any person.

(b) A draft may be accepted although it has not been signed by the drawer, is otherwise incomplete, is overdue, or has been dishonored.

(c) If a draft is payable at a fixed period after sight and the acceptor fails to date the acceptance, the holder may complete the acceptance by supplying a date in good faith.

(d) "Certified check" means a check accepted by the bank on which it is drawn. Acceptance may be made as stated in subsection (a) or by a writing on the check which indicates that the check is certified. The drawee of a check has no obligation to certify the check, and refusal to certify is not dishonor of the check.

§3—410. ACCEPTANCE VARYING DRAFT

(a) If the terms of a drawee's acceptance vary from the terms of the draft as presented, the holder may refuse the acceptance and treat the draft as dishonored. In that case, the drawee may cancel the acceptance.

(b) The terms of a draft are not varied by an acceptance to pay at a particular bank or place in the United States, unless the acceptance states that the draft is to be paid only at that bank or place.

(c) If the holder assents to an acceptance varying the terms of a draft, the obligation of each drawer and indorser that does not expressly assent to the acceptance is discharged.

§3—411. REFUSAL TO PAY CASHIER'S CHECKS, TELLER'S CHECKS, AND CERTIFIED CHECKS

(a) In this section, "obligated bank" means the acceptor of a certified check or the issuer of a cashier's check or teller's check bought from the issuer.

(b) If the obligated bank wrongfully (i) refuses to pay a cashier's check or certified check, (ii) stops payment of a teller's check, or (iii) refuses to pay a dishonored teller's check, the person asserting the right to enforce the check is entitled to compensation for expenses and loss of interest resulting from the nonpayment and may recover consequential damages if the obligated bank refuses to pay after receiving notice of particular circumstances giving rise to the damages.

(c) Expenses or consequential damages under subsection (b) are not recoverable if the refusal of the obligated bank to pay occurs because (i) the bank suspends payments, (ii) the obligated bank asserts a claim or defense of the bank that it has reasonable grounds to believe is available against the person entitled to enforce the instrument, (iii) the obligated bank has a reasonable doubt whether the person demanding payment is the person entitled to enforce the instrument, or (iv) payment is prohibited by law.

§3—412. OBLIGATION OF ISSUER OF NOTE OR CASHIER'S CHECK

The issuer of a note or cashier's check or other draft drawn on the drawer is obliged to pay the instrument (i) according to its terms at the time it was issued or, if not issued, at the time it first came into possession of a holder, or (ii) if the issuer signed an incomplete instrument, according to its terms when completed, to the extent stated in Sections 3—115 and 3—407. The obligation is owed to a person entitled to enforce the instrument or to an indorser who paid the instrument under Section 3—415.

§3—413. OBLIGATION OF ACCEPTOR

(a) The acceptor of a draft is obliged to pay the draft (i) according to its terms at the time it was accepted, even though the acceptance states that the draft is payable "as originally drawn" or equivalent terms, (ii) if the acceptance varies the terms of the draft, according to the terms of the draft as varied, or (iii) if the acceptance is of a draft that is an incomplete instrument, according to its terms when completed, to the extent stated in Sections 3—115 and 3—407. The obligation is owed to a person entitled to enforce the draft or to the drawer or an indorser who paid the draft under Section 3—414 or 3—415.

(b) If the certification of a check or other acceptance of a draft states the amount certified or accepted, the obligation of the acceptor is that amount. If (i) the certification or acceptance does not state an amount, (ii) the amount of the instrument is subsequently raised, and (iii) the instrument is then negotiated to a holder in due course, the obligation of the acceptor is the amount of the instrument at the time it was taken by the holder in due course.

§3—414. OBLIGATION OF DRAWER

(a) This section does not apply to cashier's checks or other drafts drawn on the drawer.

(b) If an unaccepted draft is dishonored, the drawer is obliged to pay the draft (i) according to its terms at the time it was issued or, if not issued, at the time it first came into possession of a holder, or (ii) if the drawer signed an incomplete instrument, according to its terms when completed, to the extent stated in Sections 3—115 and 3—407. The obligation is owed to a person entitled to enforce the draft or to an indorser who paid the draft under Section 3—415.

(c) If a draft is accepted by a bank, the drawer is discharged, regardless of when or by whom acceptance was obtained.

(d) If a draft is accepted and the acceptor is not a bank, the obligation of the drawer to pay the draft if the draft is dishonored by the acceptor is the same as the obligation of an indorser under Section 3—415(a) and (c).

(e) If a draft states that it is drawn "without recourse" or otherwise disclaims liability of the drawer to pay the draft, the drawer is not liable under subsection (b) to pay the draft if the draft is not a check. A disclaimer of the liability stated in subsection (b) is not effective if the draft is a check.

(f) If (i) a check is not presented for payment or given to a depositary bank for collection within 30 days after its date, (ii) the drawee suspends payments after expiration of the 30-day period without paying the check, and (iii) because of the suspension of payments, the drawer is deprived of funds maintained with the drawee to cover payment of the check, the drawer to the extent deprived of funds may discharge its obligation to pay the check by assigning to the person entitled to enforce the check the rights of the drawer against the drawee with respect to the funds.

§3—415. OBLIGATION OF INDORSER

(a) Subject to subsections (b), (c), and (d) and to Section 3—419(d), if an instrument is dishonored, an indorser is obliged to pay the amount due on the instrument (i) according to the terms of the instrument at the time it was indorsed, or (ii) if the indorser indorsed an incomplete instrument, according to its terms when completed, to the extent stated in Sections 3—115 and 3—407. The obligation of the indorser is owed to a person entitled to enforce the instrument or to a subsequent indorser who paid the instrument under this section.

(b) If an indorsement states that it is made "without recourse" or otherwise disclaims liability of the indorser, the indorser is not liable under subsection (a) to pay the instrument.

(c) If notice of dishonor of an instrument is required by Section 3—503 and notice of dishonor complying with that section is not given to an indorser, the liability of the indorser under subsection (a) is discharged.

(d) If a draft is accepted by a bank after an indorsement is made, the liability of the indorser under subsection (a) is discharged.

(e) If an indorser of a check is liable under subsection (a) and the check is not presented for payment, or given to a depositary bank for collection, within 30 days after the day the indorsement was made, the liability of the indorser under subsection (a) is discharged.

As amended in 1993.

§3—416. TRANSFER WARRANTIES

(a) A person who transfers an instrument for consideration warrants to the transferee and, if the transfer is by indorsement, to any subsequent transferee that:

(1) the warrantor is a person entitled to enforce the instrument;

(2) all signatures on the instrument are authentic and authorized;

(3) the instrument has not been altered;

(4) the instrument is not subject to a defense or claim in recoupment of any party which can be asserted against the warrantor; and

(5) the warrantor has no knowledge of any insolvency proceeding commenced with respect to the maker or acceptor or, in the case of an unaccepted draft, the drawer.

(b) A person to whom the warranties under subsection (a) are made and who took the instrument in good faith may recover from the warrantor as damages for breach of warranty an amount equal to the loss suffered as a result of the breach, but not more than the amount of the instrument plus expenses and loss of interest incurred as a result of the breach.

(c) The warranties stated in subsection (a) cannot be disclaimed with respect to checks. Unless notice of a claim for breach of warranty is given to the warrantor within 30 days after the claimant has reason to know of the breach and the identity of the warrantor, the liability of the warrantor under subsection (b) is discharged to the extent of any loss caused by the delay in giving notice of the claim.

(d) A [cause of action] for breach of warranty under this section accrues when the claimant has reason to know of the breach.

§3—417. PRESENTMENT WARRANTIES

(a) If an unaccepted draft is presented to the drawee for payment or acceptance and the drawee pays or accepts the draft, (i) the person obtaining payment or acceptance, at the time of presentment, and (ii) a previous transferor of the draft, at the time of transfer, warrant to the drawee making payment or accepting the draft in good faith that:

(1) the warrantor is, or was, at the time the warrantor transferred the draft, a person entitled to enforce the draft or authorized to obtain payment or acceptance of the draft on behalf of a person entitled to enforce the draft;

(2) the draft has not been altered; and

(3) the warrantor has no knowledge that the signature of the drawer of the draft is unauthorized.

(b) A drawee making payment may recover from any warrantor damages for breach of warranty equal to the amount paid by the drawee less the amount the drawee received or is entitled to receive from the drawer because of the payment. In addition, the drawee is entitled to compensation for expenses and loss of interest resulting from the breach. The right of the drawee to recover damages under this subsection is not affected by any failure of the drawee to exercise ordinary care in making payment. If the drawee accepts the draft, breach of warranty is a defense to the obligation of the acceptor. If the acceptor makes payment with respect to the draft, the acceptor is entitled to recover from any warrantor for breach of warranty the amounts stated in this subsection.

(c) If a drawee asserts a claim for breach of warranty under subsection (a) based on an unauthorized indorsement of the draft or an alteration of the draft, the warrantor may defend by proving that the indorsement is effective under Section 3—404 or 3—405 or the drawer is precluded under Section 3—406 or 4—406 from asserting against the drawee the unauthorized indorsement or alteration.

(d) If (i) a dishonored draft is presented for payment to the drawer or an indorser or (ii) any other instrument is presented for payment to a party obliged to pay the instrument, and (iii) payment is received, the following rules apply:

(1) The person obtaining payment and a prior transferor of the instrument warrant to the person making payment in good faith that the warrantor is, or was, at the time the warrantor transferred the instrument, a person entitled to enforce the instrument or authorized to obtain payment on behalf of a person entitled to enforce the instrument.

(2) The person making payment may recover from any warrantor for breach of warranty an amount equal to the amount paid plus expenses and loss of interest resulting from the breach.

(e) The warranties stated in subsections (a) and (d) cannot be disclaimed with respect to checks. Unless notice of a claim for breach of warranty is given to the warrantor within 30 days after the claimant has reason to know of the breach and the identity of the warrantor, the liability of the warrantor under subsection (b) or (d) is discharged to the extent of any loss caused by the delay in giving notice of the claim.

(f) A [cause of action] for breach of warranty under this section accrues when the claimant has reason to know of the breach.

§3—418. PAYMENT OR ACCEPTANCE BY MISTAKE

(a) Except as provided in subsection (c), if the drawee of a draft pays or accepts the draft and the drawee acted on the mistaken belief that (i) payment of the draft had not been stopped pursuant to Section 4—403 or (ii) the signature of the drawer of the draft was authorized, the drawee may recover the amount of the draft from the person to whom or for whose benefit payment was made or, in the case of acceptance, may revoke the acceptance. Rights of the drawee under this subsection are not affected by failure of the drawee to exercise ordinary care in paying or accepting the draft.

(b) Except as provided in subsection (c), if an instrument has been paid or accepted by mistake and the case is not covered by subsection (a), the person paying or accepting may, to the extent permitted by the law governing mistake and restitution, (i) recover the payment from the person to whom or for whose benefit payment was made or (ii) in the case of acceptance, may revoke the acceptance.

(c) The remedies provided by subsection (a) or (b) may not be asserted against a person who took the instrument in good faith and for value or who in good faith changed position in reliance on the payment or acceptance. This subsection does not limit remedies provided by Section 3—417 or 4—407.

(d) Notwithstanding Section 4—215, if an instrument is paid or accepted by mistake and the payor or acceptor recovers payment or revokes acceptance under subsection (a) or (b), the instrument is deemed not to have been paid or accepted and is treated as dishonored, and the person from whom payment is recovered has rights as a person entitled to enforce the dishonored instrument.

§3—419. INSTRUMENTS SIGNED FOR ACCOMMODATION

(a) If an instrument is issued for value given for the benefit of a party to the instrument ("accommodated party") and another party to the instrument ("accommodation party") signs the instrument for the purpose of incurring liability on the instrument without being a direct beneficiary of the value given for the instrument, the instrument is signed by the accommodation party "for accommodation."

(b) An accommodation party may sign the instrument as maker, drawer, acceptor, or indorser and, subject to subsection (d), is obliged to pay the instrument in the capacity in which the accommodation party signs. The obligation of an accommodation party may be enforced notwithstanding any statute of frauds and whether or not the accommodation party receives consideration for the accommodation.

(c) A person signing an instrument is presumed to be an accommodation party and there is notice that the instrument is signed for accommodation if the signature is an anomalous indorsement or is accompanied by words indicating that the signer is acting as surety or guarantor with respect to the obligation of another party to the instrument. Except as provided in Section 3—605, the obligation of an accommodation party to pay the instrument is not affected by the fact that the person enforcing the obligation had notice when the instrument was taken by that person that the accommodation party signed the instrument for accommodation.

(d) If the signature of a party to an instrument is accompanied by words indicating unambiguously that the party is guaranteeing collection rather than payment of the obligation of another party to the instrument, the signer is obliged to pay the amount due on the instrument to a person entitled to enforce the instrument only if (i) execution of judgment against the other party has been returned unsatisfied, (ii) the other party is insolvent or in an insolvency proceeding, (iii) the other party cannot be served with process, or (iv) it is otherwise apparent that payment cannot be obtained from the other party.

(e) An accommodation party who pays the instrument is entitled to reimbursement from the accommodated party and is entitled to enforce the instrument against the accommodated party. An accommodated party who pays the instrument has no right of recourse against, and is not entitled to contribution from, an accommodation party.

§3—420. CONVERSION OF INSTRUMENT

(a) The law applicable to conversion of personal property applies to instruments. An instrument is also converted if it is taken by transfer, other than a negotiation, from a person not entitled to enforce the instrument or a bank makes or obtains payment with respect to the instrument for a person not entitled to enforce the instrument or receive payment. An action for conversion of an instrument may not be brought by (i) the issuer or acceptor of the instrument or (ii) a payee or indorsee who did not receive delivery of the instrument either directly or through delivery to an agent or a co-payee.

(b) In an action under subsection (a), the measure of liability is presumed to be the amount payable on the instrument, but recovery may not exceed the amount of the plaintiff's interest in the instrument.

(c) A representative, other than a depositary bank, who has in good faith dealt with an instrument or its proceeds on behalf of one who was not the person entitled to enforce the instrument is not liable in conversion to that person beyond the amount of any proceeds that it has not paid out.

Part 5 Dishonor

§3—501. PRESENTMENT

(a) "Presentment" means a demand made by or on behalf of a person entitled to enforce an instrument (i) to pay the instrument made to the drawee or a party obliged to pay the instrument or, in the case of a note or accepted draft payable at a bank, to the bank, or (ii) to accept a draft made to the drawee.

(b) The following rules are subject to Article 4, agreement of the parties, and clearing-house rules and the like:

(1) Presentment may be made at the place of payment of the instrument and must be made at the place of payment if the instrument is payable at a bank in the United States; may be made by any commercially reasonable means, including an oral, written, or electronic communication; is effective when the demand for payment or acceptance is received by the person to whom presentment is made; and is effective if made to any one of two or more makers, acceptors, drawees, or other payors.

(2) Upon demand of the person to whom presentment is made, the person making presentment must (i) exhibit the instrument, (ii) give reasonable identification and, if presentment is made on behalf of another person, reasonable evidence of authority to do so, and (…) sign a receipt on the instrument for any payment made or surrender the instrument if full payment is made.

(3) Without dishonoring the instrument, the party to whom presentment is made may (i) return the instrument for lack of a necessary indorsement, or (ii) refuse payment or acceptance for failure of the presentment to comply with the terms of the instrument, an agreement of the parties, or other applicable law or rule.

(4) The party to whom presentment is made may treat presentment as occurring on the next business day after the day of presentment if the party to whom presentment is made has established a cut-off hour not earlier than 2 P.M. for the receipt and processing of instruments presented for payment or acceptance and presentment is made after the cut-off hour.

§3—502. DISHONOR

(a) Dishonor of a note is governed by the following rules:

(1) If the note is payable on demand, the note is dishonored if presentment is duly made to the maker and the note is not paid on the day of presentment.

(2) If the note is not payable on demand and is payable at or through a bank or the terms of the note require presentment, the note is dishonored if presentment is duly made and the note is not paid on the day it becomes payable or the day of presentment, whichever is later.

(3) If the note is not payable on demand and paragraph (2) does not apply, the note is dishonored if it is not paid on the day it becomes payable.

(b) Dishonor of an unaccepted draft other than a documentary draft is governed by the following rules:

(1) If a check is duly presented for payment to the payor bank otherwise than for immediate payment over the counter, the check is dishonored if the payor bank makes timely return of the check or sends timely notice of dishonor or nonpayment under Section 4—301 or 4—302, or becomes accountable for the amount of the check under Section 4—302.

(2) If a draft is payable on demand and paragraph (1) does not apply, the draft is dishonored if presentment for payment is duly made to the drawee and the draft is not paid on the day of presentment.

(3) If a draft is payable on a date stated in the draft, the draft is dishonored if (i) presentment for payment is duly made to the drawee and payment is not made on the day the draft becomes payable or the day of presentment, whichever is later, or (ii) presentment for acceptance is duly made before the day the draft becomes payable and the draft is not accepted on the day of presentment.

(4) If a draft is payable on elapse of a period of time after sight or acceptance, the draft is dishonored if presentment for acceptance is duly made and the draft is not accepted on the day of presentment.

(c) Dishonor of an unaccepted documentary draft occurs according to the rules stated in subsection (b)(2), (3), and (4), except that payment or acceptance may be delayed without dishonor until no later than the close of the third business day of the drawee following the day on which payment or acceptance is required by those paragraphs.

(d) Dishonor of an accepted draft is governed by the following rules:

(1) If the draft is payable on demand, the draft is dishonored if presentment for payment is duly

made to the acceptor and the draft is not paid on the day of presentment.

(2) If the draft is not payable on demand, the draft is dishonored if presentment for payment is duly made to the acceptor and payment is not made on the day it becomes payable or the day of presentment, whichever is later.

(e) In any case in which presentment is otherwise required for dishonor under this section and presentment is excused under Section 3—504, dishonor occurs without presentment if the instrument is not duly accepted or paid.

(f) If a draft is dishonored because timely acceptance of the draft was not made and the person entitled to demand acceptance consents to a late acceptance, from the time of acceptance the draft is treated as never having been dishonored.

§3—503. NOTICE OF DISHONOR

(a) The obligation of an indorser stated in Section 3—415 (a) and the obligation of a drawer stated in Section 3—414 (d) may not be enforced unless (i) the indorser or drawer is given notice of dishonor of the instrument complying with this section or (ii) notice of dishonor is excused under Section 3—504(b).

(b) Notice of dishonor may be given by any person; may be given by any commercially reasonable means, including an oral, written, or electronic communication; and is sufficient if it reasonably identifies the instrument and indicates that the instrument has been dishonored or has not been paid or accepted. Return of an instrument given to a bank for collection is sufficient notice of dishonor.

(c) Subject to Section 3—504(c), with respect to an instrument taken for collection by a collecting bank, notice of dishonor must be given (i) by the bank before midnight of the next banking day following the banking day on which the bank receives notice of dishonor of the instrument, or (ii) by any other person within 30 days following the day on which the person receives notice of dishonor. With respect to any other instrument, notice of dishonor must be given within 30 days following the day on which dishonor occurs.

§3—504. EXCUSED PRESENTMENT AND NOTICE OF DISHONOR

(a) Presentment for payment or acceptance of an instrument is excused if (i) the person entitled to present the instrument cannot with reasonable diligence make presentment, (ii) the maker or acceptor has repudiated an obligation to pay the instrument or is dead or in insolvency proceedings, (iii) by the terms of the instrument presentment is not necessary to enforce the obligation of indorsers or the drawer, (iv) the drawer or indorser whose obligation is being enforced has waived presentment or otherwise has no reason to expect or right to require that the instrument

be paid or accepted, or (v) the drawer instructed the drawee not to pay or accept the draft or the drawee was not obligated to the drawer to pay the draft.

(b) Notice of dishonor is excused if (i) by the terms of the instrument notice of dishonor is not necessary to enforce the obligation of a party to pay the instrument, or (ii) the party whose obligation is being enforced waived notice of dishonor. A waiver of presentment is also a waiver of notice of dishonor.

(c) Delay in giving notice of dishonor is excused if the delay was caused by circumstances beyond the control of the person giving the notice and the person giving the notice exercised reasonable diligence after the cause of the delay ceased to operate.

§3—505. EVIDENCE OF DISHONOR

(a) The following are admissible as evidence and create a presumption of dishonor and of any notice of dishonor stated:

> (1) a document regular in form as provided in subsection (b) which purports to be a protest;
> (2) a purported stamp or writing of the drawee, payor bank, or presenting bank on or accompanying the instrument stating that acceptance or payment has been refused unless reasons for the refusal are stated and the reasons are not consistent with dishonor;
> (3) a book or record of the drawee, payor bank, or collecting bank, kept in the usual course of business which shows dishonor, even if there is no evidence of who made the entry.

(b) A protest is a certificate of dishonor made by a United States consul or vice consul, or a notary public or other person authorized to administer oaths by the law of the place where dishonor occurs. It may be made upon information satisfactory to that person. The protest must identify the instrument and certify either that presentment has been made or, if not made, the reason why it was not made, and that the instrument has been dishonored by nonacceptance or nonpayment. The protest may also certify that notice of dishonor has been given to some or all parties.

Part 6 Discharge and Payment

§3—601. DISCHARGE AND EFFECT OF DISCHARGE

(a) The obligation of a party to pay the instrument is discharged as stated in this Article or by an act or agreement with the party which would discharge an obligation to pay money under a simple contract.

(b) Discharge of the obligation of a party is not effective against a person acquiring rights of a holder in due course of the instrument without notice of the discharge.

§3—602. PAYMENT

(a)   Subject to subsection (b), an instrument is paid to the extent payment is made (i) by or on behalf of a party obliged to pay the instrument, and (ii) to a person entitled to enforce the instrument. To the extent of the payment, the obligation of the party obliged to pay the instrument is discharged even though payment is made with knowledge of a claim to the instrument under Section 3—306 by another person.

(b)   The obligation of a party to pay the instrument is not discharged under subsection (a) if:

(1)   a claim to the instrument under Section 3—306 is enforceable against the party receiving payment and (i) payment is made with knowledge by the payor that payment is prohibited by injunction or similar process of a court of competent jurisdiction, or (ii) in the case of an instrument other than a cashier's check, teller's check, or certified check, the party making payment accepted, from the person having a claim to the instrument, indemnity against loss resulting from refusal to pay the person entitled to enforce the instrument; or

(2)   the person making payment knows that the instrument is a stolen instrument and pays a person it knows is in wrongful possession of the instrument.

§3—603. TENDER OF PAYMENT

(a)   If tender of payment of an obligation to pay an instrument is made to a person entitled to enforce the instrument, the effect of tender is governed by principles of law applicable to tender of payment under a simple contract.

(b)   If tender of payment of an obligation to pay an instrument is made to a person entitled to enforce the instrument and the tender is refused, there is discharge, to the extent of the amount of the tender, of the obligation of an indorser or accommodation party having a right of recourse with respect to the obligation to which the tender relates.

(c)   If tender of payment of an amount due on an instrument is made to a person entitled to enforce the instrument, the obligation of the obligor to pay interest after the due date on the amount tendered is discharged. If presentment is required with respect to an instrument and the obligor is able and ready to pay on the due date at every place of payment stated in the instrument, the obligor is deemed to have made tender of payment on the due date to the person entitled to enforce the instrument.

§3—604. DISCHARGE BY CANCELLATION OR RENUNCIATION

(a)   A person entitled to enforce an instrument, with or without consideration, may discharge the obligation of a party to pay the instrument (i) by an intentional voluntary act, such as surrender of the instrument to the party, destruction, mutilation, or cancellation of the instrument, cancellation or striking out of the party's signature, or the addition of words to the instrument indicating discharge, or (ii) by agreeing not to sue or otherwise renouncing rights against the party by a signed writing.

(b)   Cancellation or striking out of an indorsement pursuant to subsection (a) does not affect the status and rights of a party derived from the indorsement.

§3—605. DISCHARGE OF INDORSERS AND ACCOMMODATION PARTIES

(a)   In this section, the term "indorser" includes a drawer having the obligation described in Section 3—414(d).

(b)   Discharge, under Section 3—604, of the obligation of a party to pay an instrument does not discharge the obligation of an indorser or accommodation party having a right of recourse against the discharged party.

(c)   If a person entitled to enforce an instrument agrees, with or without consideration, to an extension of the due date of the obligation of a party to pay the instrument, the extension discharges an indorser or accommodation party having a right of recourse against the party whose obligation is extended to the extent the indorser or accommodation party proves that the extension caused loss to the indorser or accommodation party with respect to the right of recourse.

(d)   If a person entitled to enforce an instrument agrees, with or without consideration, to a material modification of the obligation of a party other than an extension of the due date, the modification discharges the obligation of an indorser or accommodation party having a right of recourse against the person whose obligation is modified to the extent the modification causes loss to the indorser or accommodation party with respect to the right of recourse. The loss suffered by the indorser or accommodation party as a result of the modification is equal to the amount of the right of recourse unless the person enforcing the instrument proves that no loss was caused by the modification or that the loss caused by the modification was an amount less than the amount of the right of recourse.

(e)   If the obligation of a party to pay an instrument is secured by an interest in collateral and a person entitled to enforce the instrument impairs the value of the interest in collateral, the obligation of an indorser or accommodation party having a right of recourse against the obligor is discharged to the extent of the impairment. The value of an interest in collateral is impaired to the extent (i) the value of the interest is reduced to an amount less than the amount of the right of recourse of the party asserting discharge, or (ii) the reduction in value of the interest causes an increase in the amount by which the amount of the right of recourse exceeds the value of the interest.

The burden of proving impairment is on the party asserting discharge.

(f) If the obligation of a party is secured by an interest in collateral not provided by an accommodation party and a person entitled to enforce the instrument impairs the value of the interest in collateral, the obligation of any party who is jointly and severally liable with respect to the secured obligation is discharged to the extent the impairment causes the party asserting discharge to pay more than that party would have been obliged to pay, taking into account rights of contribution, if impairment had not occurred. If the party asserting discharge is an accommodation party not entitled to discharge under subsection (e), the party is deemed to have a right to contribution based on joint and several liability rather than a right to reimbursement. The burden of proving impairment is on the party asserting discharge.

(g) Under subsection (e) or (f), impairing value of an interest in collateral includes (i) failure to obtain or maintain perfection or recordation of the interest in collateral, (ii) release of collateral without substitution of collateral of equal value, (iii) failure to perform a duty to preserve the value of collateral owed, under Article 9 or other law, to a debtor or surety or other person secondarily liable, or (iv) failure to comply with applicable law in disposing of collateral.

(h) An accommodation party is not discharged under subsection (c), (d), or (e) unless the person entitled to enforce the instrument knows of the accommodation or has notice under Section 3—419(c) that the instrument was signed for accommodation.

(i) A party is not discharged under this section if (i) the party asserting discharge consents to the event or conduct that is the basis of the discharge, or (ii) the instrument or a separate agreement of the party provides for waiver of discharge under this section either specifically or by general language indicating that parties waive defenses based on suretyship or impairment of collateral.

ADDENDUM TO REVISED ARTICLE 3 NOTES TO LEGISLATIVE COUNSEL

(1) If revised Article 3 is adopted in your state, the reference in Section 2—511 to Section 3—802 should be changed to Section 3—310.

(2) If revised Article 3 is adopted in your state and the Uniform Fiduciaries Act is also in effect in your state, you may want to consider amending Uniform Fiduciaries Act @3:§9 to conform to Section 3—307(b)(2)(iii) and (4)(iii). See Official Comment 3 to Section 3—307.

REVISED ARTICLE 4 BANK DEPOSITS AND COLLECTIONS

Part 1 General Provisions and Definitions

§4—101. SHORT TITLE

This Article may be cited as Uniform Commercial Code— Bank Deposits and Collections.

As amended in 1990.

§4—102. APPLICABILITY

(a) To the extent that items within this Article are also within Articles 3 and 8, they are subject to those Articles. If there is conflict, this Article governs Article 3, but Article 8 governs this Article.

(b) The liability of a bank for action or non-action with respect to an item handled by it for purposes of presentment, payment, or collection is governed by the law of the place where the bank is located. In the case of action or non-action by or at a branch or separate office of a bank, its liability is governed by the law of the place where the branch or separate office is located.

§4—103. VARIATION BY AGREEMENT; MEASURE OF DAMAGES; ACTION CONSTITUTING ORDINARY CARE

(a) The effect of the provisions of this Article may be varied by agreement, but the parties to the agreement cannot disclaim a bank's responsibility for its lack of good faith or failure to exercise ordinary care or limit the measure of damages for the lack or failure. However, the parties may determine by agreement the standards by which the bank's responsibility is to be measured if those standards are not manifestly unreasonable.

(b) Federal Reserve regulations and operating circulars, clearing-house rules, and the like have the effect of agreements under subsection (a), whether or not specifically assented to by all parties interested in items handled.

(c) Action or non-action approved by this Article or pursuant to Federal Reserve regulations or operating circulars is the exercise of ordinary care and, in the absence of special instructions, action or non-action consistent with clearing-house rules and the like or with a general banking usage not disapproved by this Article, is prima facie the exercise of ordinary care.

(d) The specification or approval of certain procedures by this Article is not disapproval of other procedures that may be reasonable under the circumstances.

(e) The measure of damages for failure to exercise ordinary care in handling an item is the amount of the item reduced by an amount that could not have been realized by the exercise of ordinary care. If there is also bad faith it includes any other damages the party suffered as a proximate consequence.

As amended in 1990.

§4—104. DEFINITIONS AND INDEX OF DEFINITIONS

(a) In this Article, unless the context otherwise requires:

(1) "Account" means any deposit or credit account with a bank, including a demand, time, savings, passbook, share draft, or like account, other than an account evidenced by a certificate of deposit;

(2) "Afternoon" means the period of a day between noon and midnight;

(3) "Banking day" means the part of a day on which a bank is open to the public for carrying on substantially all of its banking functions;

(4) "Clearing house" means an association of banks or other payors regularly clearing items;

(5) "Customer" means a person having an account with a bank or for whom a bank has agreed to collect items, including a bank that maintains an account at another bank;

(6) "Documentary draft" means a draft to be presented for acceptance or payment if specified documents, certificated securities (Section 8—102) or instructions for uncertificated securities (Section 8—102), or other certificates, statements, or the like are to be received by the drawee or other payor before acceptance or payment of the draft;

(7) "Draft" means a draft as defined in Section 3—104 or an item, other than an instrument, that is an order;

(8) "Drawee" means a person ordered in a draft to make payment;

(9) "Item" means an instrument or a promise or order to pay money handled by a bank for collection or payment. The term does not include a payment order governed by Article 4A or a credit or debit card slip;

(10) "Midnight deadline" with respect to a bank is midnight on its next banking day following the banking day on which it receives the relevant item or notice or from which the time for taking action commences to run, whichever is later;

(11) "Settle" means to pay in cash, by clearing-house settlement, in a charge or credit or by remittance, or otherwise as agreed. A settlement may be either provisional or final;

(12) "Suspends payments" with respect to a bank means that it has been closed by order of the supervisory authorities, that a public officer has been appointed to take it over, or that it ceases or refuses to make payments in the ordinary course of business.

(b) [Other definitions' section references deleted.]

(c) [Other definitions' section references deleted.]

(d) In addition, Article 1 contains general definitions and principles of construction and interpretation applicable throughout this Article.

§4—105. "BANK"; "DEPOSITARY BANK"; "PAYOR BANK"; "INTERMEDIARY BANK"; "COLLECTING BANK"; "PRESENTING BANK"

In this Article:

(1) "Bank" means a person engaged in the business of banking, including a savings bank, savings and loan association, credit union, or trust company;

(2) "Depositary bank" means the first bank to take an item even though it is also the payor bank, unless the item is presented for immediate payment over the counter;

(3) "Payor bank" means a bank that is the drawee of a draft;

(4) "Intermediary bank" means a bank to which an item is transferred in course of collection except the depositary or payor bank;

(5) "Collecting bank" means a bank handling an item for collection except the payor bank;

(6) "Presenting bank" means a bank presenting an item except a payor bank.

§4—106. PAYABLE THROUGH OR PAYABLE AT BANK: COLLECTING BANK

(a) If an item states that it is "payable through" a bank identified in the item, (i) the item designates the bank as a collecting bank and does not by itself authorize the bank to pay the item, and (ii) the item may be presented for payment only by or through the bank.

Alternative A

(b) If an item states that it is "payable at" a bank identified in the item, the item is equivalent to a draft drawn on the bank.

Alternative B

(b) If an item states that it is "payable at" a bank identified in the item, (i) the item designates the bank as a collecting bank and does not by itself authorize the bank to pay the item, and (ii) the item may be presented for payment only by or through the bank.

(c) If a draft names a nonbank drawee and it is unclear whether a bank named in the draft is a co-drawee or a collecting bank, the bank is a collecting bank.

As added in 1990.

§4—107. SEPARATE OFFICE OF BANK

A branch or separate office of a bank is a separate bank for the purpose of computing the time within which and determining the place at or to which action may be taken or notices or orders shall be given under this Article and under Article 3.

As amended in 1962 and 1990.

§4—108. TIME OF RECEIPT OF ITEMS

(a) For the purpose of allowing time to process items, prove balances, and make the necessary entries on its books to determine its position for the day, a bank may fix an afternoon hour of 2 P.M. or later as a cutoff hour for the handling of money and items and the making of entries on its books.

(b) An item or deposit of money received on any day after a cutoff hour so fixed or after the close of the banking day may be treated as being received at the opening of the next banking day.

As amended in 1990.

§4—109. DELAYS

(a) Unless otherwise instructed, a collecting bank in a good faith effort to secure payment of a specific item drawn on a payor other than a bank, and with or without the approval of any person involved, may waive, modify, or extend time limits imposed or permitted by this [act] for a period not exceeding two additional banking days without discharge of drawers or indorsers or liability to its transferor or a prior party.

(b) Delay by a collecting bank or payor bank beyond time limits prescribed or permitted by this [act] or by instructions is excused if (i) the delay is caused by interruption of communication or computer facilities, suspension of payments by another bank, war, emergency conditions, failure of equipment, or other circumstances beyond the control of the bank, and (ii) the bank exercises such diligence as the circumstances require.

§4—110. ELECTRONIC PRESENTMENT

(a) "Agreement for electronic presentment" means an agreement, clearing-house rule, or Federal Reserve regulation or operating circular, providing that presentment of an item may be made by transmission of an image of an item or information describing the item ("presentment notice") rather than delivery of the item itself. The agreement may provide for procedures governing retention, presentment, payment, dishonor, and other matters concerning items subject to the agreement.

(b) Presentment of an item pursuant to an agreement for presentment is made when the presentment notice is received.

(c) If presentment is made by presentment notice, a reference to "item" or "check" in this Article means the presentment notice unless the context otherwise indicates.

As added in 1990.

§4—111. STATUTE OF LIMITATIONS

An action to enforce an obligation, duty, or right arising under this Article must be commenced within three years after the [cause of action] accrues.

As added in 1990.

Part 2 Collection of Items: Depositary and Collecting Banks

§4—201. STATUS OF COLLECTING BANK AS AGENT AND PROVISIONAL STATUS OF CREDITS; APPLICABILITY OF ARTICLE; ITEM INDORSED "PAY ANY BANK"

(a) Unless a contrary intent clearly appears and before the time that a settlement given by a collecting bank for an item is or becomes final, the bank, with respect to an item, is an agent or sub-agent of the owner of the item and any settlement given for the item is provisional. This provision applies regardless of the form of indorsement or lack of indorsement and even though credit given for the item is subject to immediate withdrawal as of right or is in fact withdrawn; but the continuance of ownership of an item by its owner and any rights of the owner to proceeds of the item are subject to rights of a collecting bank, such as those resulting from outstanding advances on the item and rights of recoupment or setoff. If an item is handled by banks for purposes of presentment, payment, collection, or return, the relevant provisions of this Article apply even though action of the parties clearly establishes that a particular bank has purchased the item and is the owner of it.

(b) After an item has been indorsed with the words "pay any bank" or the like, only a bank may acquire the rights of a holder until the item has been:

(1) returned to the customer initiating collection; or
(2) specially indorsed by a bank to a person who is not a bank.

As amended in 1990.

§4—202. RESPONSIBILITY FOR COLLECTION OR RETURN; WHEN ACTION TIMELY

(a) A collecting bank must exercise ordinary care in:

(1) presenting an item or sending it for presentment;
(2) sending notice of dishonor or nonpayment or returning an item other than a documentary draft to the bank's transferor after learning that the item has not been paid or accepted, as the case may be;

(3) settling for an item when the bank receives final settlement; and

(4) notifying its transferor of any loss or delay in transit within a reasonable time after discovery thereof.

(b) A collecting bank exercises ordinary care under subsection (a) by taking proper action before its midnight deadline following receipt of an item, notice, or settlement. Taking proper action within a reasonably longer time may constitute the exercise of ordinary care, but the bank has the burden of establishing timeliness.

(c) Subject to subsection (a)(1), a bank is not liable for the insolvency, neglect, misconduct, mistake, or default of another bank or person or for loss or destruction of an item in the possession of others or in transit.

As amended in 1990.

§4—203. EFFECT OF INSTRUCTIONS

Subject to Article 3 concerning conversion of instruments (Section 3—420) and restrictive indorsements (Section 3—206), only a collecting bank's transferor can give instructions that affect the bank or constitute notice to it, and a collecting bank is not liable to prior parties for any action taken pursuant to the instructions or in accordance with any agreement with its transferor.

§4—204. METHODS OF SENDING AND PRESENTING; SENDING DIRECTLY TO PAYOR BANK

(a) A collecting bank shall send items by a reasonably prompt method, taking into consideration relevant instructions, the nature of the item, the number of those items on hand, the cost of collection involved, and the method generally used by it or others to present those items.

(b) A collecting bank may send:

(1) an item directly to the payor bank;

(2) an item to a nonbank payor if authorized by its transferor; and

(3) an item other than documentary drafts to a nonbank payor, if authorized by Federal Reserve regulation or operating circular, clearing-house rule, or the like.

(c) Presentment may be made by a presenting bank at a place where the payor bank or other payor has requested that presentment be made.

As amended in 1990.

§4—205. DEPOSITARY BANK HOLDER OF UNINDORSED ITEM

If a customer delivers an item to a depositary bank for collection:

(1) the depositary bank becomes a holder of the item at the time it receives the item for collection if the customer at the time of delivery was a holder of the item, whether or not the customer indorses the item, and, if the bank satisfies the other requirements of Section 3—302, it is a holder in due course; and

(2) the depositary bank warrants to collecting banks, the payor bank or other payor, and the drawer that the amount of the item was paid to the customer or deposited to the customer's account.

As amended in 1990.

§4—206. TRANSFER BETWEEN BANKS

Any agreed method that identifies the transferor bank is sufficient for the item's further transfer to another bank.

As amended in 1990.

§4—207. TRANSFER WARRANTIES

(a) A customer or collecting bank that transfers an item and receives a settlement or other consideration warrants to the transferee and to any subsequent collecting bank that:

(1) the warrantor is a person entitled to enforce the item;

(2) all signatures on the item are authentic andauthorized;

(3) the item has not been altered;

(4) the item is not subject to a defense or claim in recoupment (Section 3—305(a)) of any party that can be asserted against the warrantor; and

(5) the warrantor has no knowledge of any insolvency proceeding commenced with respect to the maker or acceptor or, in the case of an unaccepted draft, the drawer.

(b) If an item is dishonored, a customer or collecting bank transferring the item and receiving settlement or other consideration is obliged to pay the amount due on the item (i) according to the terms of the item at the time it was transferred, or (ii) if the transfer was of an incomplete item, according to its terms when completed as stated in Sections 3—115 and 3—407. The obligation of a transferor is owed to the transferee and to any subsequent collecting bank that takes the item in good faith. A transferor cannot disclaim its obligation under this subsection by an indorsement stating that it is made "without recourse" or otherwise disclaiming liability.

(c) A person to whom the warranties under subsection (a) are made and who took the item in good faith may recover from the warrantor as damages for breach of warranty an amount equal to the loss suffered as a result of the breach, but not more than the amount of the item plus expenses and loss of interest incurred as a result of the breach.

(d) The warranties stated in subsection (a) cannot be disclaimed with respect to checks. Unless notice of a claim for breach of warranty is given to the warrantor within 30 days after the claimant has reason to know of the breach and the identity of the warrantor, the warrantor is discharged to the extent of any loss caused by the delay in giving notice of the claim.

(e) A cause of action for breach of warranty under this section accrues when the claimant has reason to know of the breach.

As amended in 1990.

§4—208. PRESENTMENT WARRANTIES

(a) If an unaccepted draft is presented to the drawee for payment or acceptance and the drawee pays or accepts the draft, (i) the person obtaining payment or acceptance, at the time of presentment, and (ii) a previous transferor of the draft, at the time of transfer, warrant to the drawee that pays or accepts the draft in good faith that:

> (1) the warrantor is, or was, at the time the warrantor transferred the draft, a person entitled to enforce the draft or authorized to obtain payment or acceptance of the draft on behalf of a person entitled to enforce the draft;
>
> (2) the draft has not been altered; and
>
> (3) the warrantor has no knowledge that the signature of the purported drawer of the draft is unauthorized.

(b) A drawee making payment may recover from a warrantor damages for breach of warranty equal to the amount paid by the drawee less the amount the drawee received or is entitled to receive from the drawer because of the payment. In addition, the drawee is entitled to compensation for expenses and loss of interest resulting from the breach. The right of the drawee to recover damages under this subsection is not affected by any failure of the drawee to exercise ordinary care in making payment. If the drawee accepts the draft (i) breach of warranty is a defense to the obligation of the acceptor, and (ii) if the acceptor makes payment with respect to the draft, the acceptor is entitled to recover from a warrantor for breach of warranty the amounts stated in this subsection.

(c) If a drawee asserts a claim for breach of warranty under subsection (a) based on an unauthorized indorsement of the draft or an alteration of the draft, the warrantor may defend by proving that the indorsement is effective under Section 3—404 or 3—405 or the drawer is precluded under Section 3—406 or 4—406 from asserting against the drawee the unauthorized indorsement or alteration.

(d) If (i) a dishonored draft is presented for payment to the drawer or an indorser or (ii) any other item is presented for payment to a party obliged to pay the item, and the item is paid, the person obtaining payment and a prior transferor of the item warrant to the person making payment in good faith that the warrantor is, or was, at the time the warrantor transferred the item, a person entitled to enforce the item or authorized to obtain payment on behalf of a person entitled to enforce the item. The person making payment may recover from any warrantor for breach of warranty an amount equal to the amount paid plus expenses and loss of interest resulting from the breach.

(e) The warranties stated in subsections (a) and (d) cannot be disclaimed with respect to checks. Unless notice of a claim for breach of warranty is given to the warrantor within 30 days after the claimant has reason to know of the breach and the identity of the warrantor, the warrantor is discharged to the extent of any loss caused by the delay in giving notice of the claim.

(f) A cause of action for breach of warranty under this section accrues when the claimant has reason to know of the breach.

As amended in 1990.

§4—209. ENCODING AND RETENTION WARRANTIES

(a) A person who encodes information on or with respect to an item after issue warrants to any subsequent collecting bank and to the payor bank or other payor that the information is correctly encoded. If the customer of a depositary bank encodes, that bank also makes the warranty.

(b) A person who undertakes to retain an item pursuant to an agreement for electronic presentment warrants to any subsequent collecting bank and to the payor bank or other payor that retention and presentment of the item comply with the agreement. If a customer of a depositary bank undertakes to retain an item, that bank also makes this warranty.

(c) A person to whom warranties are made under this section and who took the item in good faith may recover from the warrantor as damages for breach of warranty an amount equal to the loss suffered as a result of the breach, plus expenses and loss of interest incurred as a result of the breach.

As added in 1990.

§4—210. SECURITY INTEREST OF COLLECTING BANK IN ITEMS, ACCOMPANYING DOCUMENTS AND PROCEEDS

(a) A collecting bank has a security interest in an item and any accompanying documents or the proceeds of either:

> (1) in case of an item deposited in an account, to the extent to which credit given for the item has been withdrawn or applied;
>
> (2) in case of an item for which it has given credit available for withdrawal as of right, to the extent of the credit given, whether or not the credit is drawn upon or there is a right of charge-back; or
>
> (3) if it makes an advance on or against the item.

(b) If credit given for several items received at one time or pursuant to a single agreement is withdrawn or applied in part, the security interest remains upon all the items, any accompanying documents or the proceeds of either. For the purpose of this section, credits first given are first withdrawn.

(c) Receipt by a collecting bank of a final settlement for an item is a realization on its security interest in the item, accompanying documents, and proceeds. So long as the bank does not receive final settlement for the item or give up possession of the item or accompanying documents for purposes other than collection, the security interest continues to that extent and is subject to Article 9, but:

(1) no security agreement is necessary to make the security interest enforceable (Section 9—203 (1)(a));

(2) no filing is required to perfect the security interest; and

(3) the security interest has priority over con-flicting perfected security interests in the item, accompanying documents, or proceeds.

As amended in 1990 and 1999.

§4—211. WHEN BANK GIVES VALUE FOR PURPOSES OF HOLDER IN DUE COURSE

For purposes of determining its status as a holder in due course, a bank has given value to the extent it has a security interest in an item, if the bank otherwise complies with the requirements of Section 3—302 on what constitutes a holder in due course.

As amended in 1990.

§4—212. PRESENTMENT BY NOTICE OF ITEM NOT PAYABLE BY, THROUGH, OR AT BANK; LIABILITY OF DRAWER OR INDORSER

(a) Unless otherwise instructed, a collecting bank may present an item not payable by, through, or at a bank by sending to the party to accept or pay a written notice that the bank holds the item for acceptance or payment. The notice must be sent in time to be received on or before the day when presentment is due and the bank must meet any requirement of the party to accept or pay under Section 3—501 by the close of the bank's next banking day after it knows of the requirement.

(b) If presentment is made by notice and payment, acceptance, or request for compliance with a requirement under Section 3—501 is not received by the close of business on the day after maturity or, in the case of demand items, by the close of business on the third banking day after notice was sent, the presenting bank may treat the item as dishonored and charge any drawer or indorser by sending it notice of the facts.

As amended in 1990.

§4—213. MEDIUM AND TIME OF SETTLEMENT BY BANK

(a) With respect to settlement by a bank, the medium and time of settlement may be prescribed by Federal Reserve regulations or circulars, clearing-house rules, and the like, or agreement. In the absence of such prescription:

(1) the medium of settlement is cash or credit to an account in a Federal Reserve bank of or specified by the person to receive settlement; and

(2) the time of settlement is:

(i) with respect to tender of settlement by cash, a cashier's check, or teller's check, when the cash or check is sent or delivered;

(ii) with respect to tender of settlement by credit in an account in a Federal Reserve Bank, when the credit is made;

(iii) with respect to tender of settlement by a credit or debit to an account in a bank, when the credit or debit is made or, in the case of tender of settlement by authority to charge an account, when the authority is sent or delivered; or

(iv) with respect to tender of settlement by a funds transfer, when payment is made pursuant to Section 4A—406(a) to the person receiving settlement.

(b) If the tender of settlement is not by a medium authorized by subsection (a) or the time of settlement is not fixed by subsection (a), no settlement occurs until the tender of settlement is accepted by the person receiving settlement.

(c) If settlement for an item is made by cashier's check or teller's check and the person receiving settlement, before its midnight deadline:

(1) presents or forwards the check for collection, settlement is final when the check is finally paid; or

(2) fails to present or forward the check for collection, settlement is final at the midnight deadline of the person receiving settlement.

(d) If settlement for an item is made by giving authority to charge the account of the bank giving settlement in the bank receiving settlement, settlement is final when the charge is made by the bank receiving settlement if there are funds available in the account for the amount of the item.

As amended in 1990.

§4—214. RIGHT OF CHARGE-BACK OR REFUND; LIABILITY OF COLLECTING BANK: RETURN OF ITEM

(a) If a collecting bank has made provisional settlement with its customer for an item and fails by reason of dishonor, suspension of payments by a bank, or otherwise to receive settlement for the item which is or becomes final, the bank may revoke the settlement given by it, charge back the amount of any credit given for the item to its customer's account, or obtain refund from its customer, whether or not it is able to return the item, if by its midnight deadline or within a longer reasonable time after it learns the facts it returns the item or sends notification of the facts. If the return or notice is delayed beyond the bank's midnight deadline or a longer reasonable time after it learns the facts, the bank may revoke the settlement, charge back the credit, or obtain refund from its customer, but it is liable for any loss resulting from the delay. These rights to revoke, charge back, and obtain refund terminate if and when a settlement for the item received by the bank is or becomes final.

(b) A collecting bank returns an item when it is sent or delivered to the bank's customer or transferor or pursuant to its instructions.

(c) A depositary bank that is also the payor may charge back the amount of an item to its customer's account or obtain refund in accordance with the section governing return of an item received by a payor bank for credit on its books (Section 4—301).

(d) The right to charge back is not affected by:
    (1) previous use of a credit given for the item; or
    (2) failure by any bank to exercise ordinary care with respect to the item, but a bank so failing remains liable.

(e) A failure to charge back or claim refund does not affect other rights of the bank against the customer or any other party.

(f) If credit is given in dollars as the equivalent of the value of an item payable in foreign money, the dollar amount of any charge-back or refund must be calculated on the basis of the bank-offered spot rate for the foreign money prevailing on the day when the person entitled to the charge-back or refund learns that it will not receive payment in ordinary course.

As amended in 1990.

§4—215. FINAL PAYMENT OF ITEM BY PAYOR BANK; WHEN PROVISIONAL DEBITS AND CREDITS BECOME FINAL; WHEN CERTAIN CREDITS BECOME AVAILABLE FOR WITHDRAWAL

(a) An item is finally paid by a payor bank when the bank has first done any of the following:
    (1) paid the item in cash;
    (2) settled for the item without having a right to revoke the settlement under statute, clearing-house rule, or agreement; or

    (3) made a provisional settlement for the item and failed to revoke the settlement in the time and manner permitted by statute, clearing-house rule, or agreement.

(b) If provisional settlement for an item does not become final, the item is not finally paid.

(c) If provisional settlement for an item between the presenting and payor banks is made through a clearing house or by debits or credits in an account between them, then to the extent that provisional debits or credits for the item are entered in accounts between the presenting and payor banks or between the presenting and successive prior collecting banks seriatim, they become final upon final payment of the item by the payor bank.

(d) If a collecting bank receives a settlement for an item which is or becomes final, the bank is accountable to its customer for the amount of the item and any provisional credit given for the item in an account with its customer becomes final.

(e) Subject to (i) applicable law stating a time for availability of funds and (ii) any right of the bank to apply the credit to an obligation of the customer, credit given by a bank for an item in a customer's account becomes available for withdrawal as of right:
    (1) if the bank has received a provisional settlement for the item, when the settlement becomes final and the bank has had a reasonable time to receive return of the item and the item has not been received within that time;
    (2) if the bank is both the depositary bank and the payor bank, and the item is finally paid, at the opening of the bank's second banking day following receipt of the item.

(f) Subject to applicable law stating a time for availability of funds and any right of a bank to apply a deposit to an obligation of the depositor, a deposit of money becomes available for withdrawal as of right at the opening of the bank's next banking day after receipt of the deposit.

As amended in 1990.

§4—216. INSOLVENCY AND PREFERENCE

(a) If an item is in or comes into the possession of a payor or collecting bank that suspends payment and the item has not been finally paid, the item must be returned by the receiver, trustee, or agent in charge of the closed bank to the presenting bank or the closed bank's customer.

(b) If a payor bank finally pays an item and suspends payments without making a settlement for the item with its customer or the presenting bank which settlement is or becomes final, the owner of the item has a preferred claim against the payor bank.

(c) If a payor bank gives or a collecting bank gives or receives a provisional settlement for an item and thereafter suspends payments, the suspension does not prevent or interfere with the settlement's becoming final if the finality occurs automatically upon the lapse of certain time or the happening of certain events.

(d) If a collecting bank receives from subsequent parties settlement for an item, which settlement is or becomes final and the bank suspends payments without making a settlement for the item with its customer which settlement is or becomes final, the owner of the item has a preferred claim against the collecting bank.

As amended in 1990.

Part 3 Collection of Items: Payor Banks

§4—301. DEFERRED POSTING; RECOVERY OF PAYMENT BY RETURN OF ITEMS; TIME OF DISHONOR; RETURN OF ITEMS BY PAYOR BANK

(a) If a payor bank settles for a demand item other than a documentary draft presented otherwise than for immediate payment over the counter before midnight of the banking day of receipt, the payor bank may revoke the settlement and recover the settlement if, before it has made final payment and before its midnight deadline, it

    (1) returns the item; or

    (2) sends written notice of dishonor or nonpayment if the item is unavailable for return.

(b) If a demand item is received by a payor bank for credit on its books, it may return the item or send notice of dishonor and may revoke any credit given or recover the amount thereof withdrawn by its customer, if it acts within the time limit and in the manner specified in subsection (a).

(c) Unless previous notice of dishonor has been sent, an item is dishonored at the time when for purposes of dishonor it is returned or notice sent in accordance with this section.

(d) An item is returned:

    (1) as to an item presented through a clearing house, when it is delivered to the presenting or last collecting bank or to the clearing house or is sent or delivered in accordance with clearing-house rules; or

    (2) in all other cases, when it is sent or delivered to the bank's customer or transferor or pursuant to instructions.

As amended in 1990.

§4—302. PAYOR BANK'S RESPONSIBILITY FOR LATE RETURN OF ITEM

(a) If an item is presented to and received by a payor bank, the bank is accountable for the amount of:

    (1) a demand item, other than a documentary draft, whether properly payable or not, if the bank, in any case in which it is not also the depositary bank, retains the item beyond midnight of the banking day of receipt without settling for it or, whether or not it is also the depositary bank, does not pay or return the item or send notice of dishonor until after its midnight deadline; or

    (2) any other properly payable item unless, within the time allowed for acceptance or payment of that item, the bank either accepts or pays the item or returns it and accompanying documents.

(b) The liability of a payor bank to pay an item pursuant to subsection (a) is subject to defenses based on breach of a presentment warranty (Section 4—208) or proof that the person seeking enforcement of the liability presented or transferred the item for the purpose of defrauding the payor bank.

As amended in 1990.

§4—303. WHEN ITEMS SUBJECT TO NOTICE, STOP-PAYMENT ORDER, LEGAL PROCESS, OR SETOFF; ORDER IN WHICH ITEMS MAY BE CHARGED OR CERTIFIED

(a) Any knowledge, notice, or stop-payment order received by, legal process served upon, or setoff exercised by a payor bank comes too late to terminate, suspend, or modify the bank's right or duty to pay an item or to charge its customer's account for the item if the knowledge, notice, stop-payment order, or legal process is received or served and a reasonable time for the bank to act thereon expires or the setoff is exercised after the earliest of the following:

    (1) the bank accepts or certifies the item;

    (2) the bank pays the item in cash;

    (3) the bank settles for the item without having a right to revoke the settlement under statute, clearing-house rule, or agreement;

    (4) the bank becomes accountable for the amount of the item under Section 4—302 dealing with the payor bank's responsibility for late return of items; or

    (5) with respect to checks, a cutoff hour no earlier than one hour after the opening of the next banking day after the banking day on which the bank received the check and no later than the close of that next banking day or, if no cutoff hour is fixed, the close of the next banking day after the banking day on which the bank received the check.

(b) Subject to subsection (a), items may be accepted, paid, certified, or charged to the indicated account of its customer in any order.

As amended in 1990.

Part 4 Relationship Between Payor Bank and Its Customer

§4—401. WHEN BANK MAY CHARGE CUSTOMER'S ACCOUNT

(a) A bank may charge against the account of a customer an item that is properly payable from the account even though the charge creates an overdraft. An item is properly payable if it is authorized by the customer and is in accordance with any agreement between the customer and bank.

(b) A customer is not liable for the amount of an overdraft if the customer neither signed the item nor benefited from the proceeds of the item.

(c) A bank may charge against the account of a customer a check that is otherwise properly payable from the account, even though payment was made before the date of the check, unless the customer has given notice to the bank of the postdating describing the check with reasonable certainty. The notice is effective for the period stated in Section 4—403(b) for stop-payment orders, and must be received at such time and in such manner as to afford the bank a reasonable opportunity to act on it before the bank takes any action with respect to the check described in Section 4—303. If a bank charges against the account of a customer a check before the date stated in the notice of postdating, the bank is liable for damages for the loss resulting from its act. The loss may include damages for dishonor of subsequent items under Section 4—402.

(d) A bank that in good faith makes payment to a holder may charge the indicated account of its customer according to:

(1) the original terms of the altered item; or

(2) the terms of the completed item, even though the bank knows the item has been completed unless the bank has notice that the completion was improper.

As amended in 1990.

§4—402. BANK'S LIABILITY TO CUSTOMER FOR WRONGFUL DISHONOR; TIME OF DETERMINING INSUFFICIENCY OF ACCOUNT

(a) Except as otherwise provided in this Article, a payor bank wrongfully dishonors an item if it dishonors an item that is properly payable, but a bank may dishonor an item that would create an overdraft unless it has agreed to pay the overdraft.

(b) A payor bank is liable to its customer for damages proximately caused by the wrongful dishonor of an item. Liability is limited to actual damages proved and may include damages for an arrest or prosecution of the customer or other consequential damages. Whether any consequential damages are proximately caused by the wrongful dishonor is a question of fact to be determined in each case.

(c) A payor bank's determination of the customer's account balance on which a decision to dishonor for insufficiency of available funds is based may be made at any time between the time the item is received by the payor bank and the time that the payor bank returns the item or gives notice in lieu of return, and no more than one determination need be made. If, at the election of the payor bank, a subsequent balance determination is made for the purpose of reevaluating the bank's decision to dishonor the item, the account balance at that time is determinative of whether a dishonor for insufficiency of available funds is wrongful.

As amended in 1990.

§4—403. CUSTOMER'S RIGHT TO STOP PAYMENT; BURDEN OF PROOF OF LOSS

(a) A customer or any person authorized to draw on the account if there is more than one person may stop payment of any item drawn on the customer's account or close the account by an order to the bank describing the item or account with reasonable certainty received at a time and in a manner that affords the bank a reasonable opportunity to act on it before any action by the bank with respect to the item described in Section 4—303. If the signature of more than one person is required to draw on an account, any of these persons may stop payment or close the account.

(b) A stop-payment order is effective for six months, but it lapses after 14 calendar days if the original order was oral and was not confirmed in writing within that period. A stop-payment order may be renewed for additional six-month periods by a writing given to the bank within a period during which the stop-payment order is effective.

(c) The burden of establishing the fact and amount of loss resulting from the payment of an item contrary to a stop-payment order or order to close an account is on the customer. The loss from payment of an item contrary to a stop-payment order may include damages for dishonor of subsequent items under Section 4—402.

As amended in 1990.

§4—404. BANK NOT OBLIGED TO PAY CHECK MORE THAN SIX MONTHS OLD

A bank is under no obligation to a customer having a checking account to pay a check, other than a certified check, which is presented more than six months after its date, but it may charge its customer's account for a payment made thereafter in good faith.

§4—405. DEATH OR INCOMPETENCE OF CUSTOMER

(a) A payor or collecting bank's authority to accept, pay, or collect an item or to account for proceeds of its collection, if otherwise effective, is not rendered ineffective by incompetence of a customer of either bank existing at the time the item is issued or its collection is undertaken if the bank does not know of an adjudication of incompetence. Neither death nor incompetence of a customer revokes the authority to accept, pay, collect, or account until the bank knows of the fact of death or of an adjudication of incompetence and has reasonable opportunity to act on it.

(b) Even with knowledge, a bank may for 10 days after the date of death pay or certify checks drawn on or before the date unless ordered to stop payment by a person claiming an interest in the account.

As amended in 1990.

§4—406. CUSTOMER'S DUTY TO DISCOVER AND REPORT UNAUTHORIZED SIGNATURE OR ALTERATION

(a) A bank that sends or makes available to a customer a statement of account showing payment of items for the account shall either return or make available to the customer the items paid or provide information in the statement of account sufficient to allow the customer reasonably to identify the items paid. The statement of account provides sufficient information if the item is described by item number, amount, and date of payment.

(b) If the items are not returned to the customer, the person retaining the items shall either retain the items or, if the items are destroyed, maintain the capacity to furnish legible copies of the items until the expiration of seven years after receipt of the items. A customer may request an item from the bank that paid the item, and that bank must provide in a reasonable time either the item or, if the item has been destroyed or is not otherwise obtainable, a legible copy of the item.

(c) If a bank sends or makes available a statement of account or items pursuant to subsection (a), the customer must exercise reasonable promptness in examining the statement or the items to determine whether any payment was not authorized because of an alteration of an item or because a purported signature by or on behalf of the customer was not authorized. If, based on the statement or items provided, the customer should reasonably have discovered the unauthorized payment, the customer must promptly notify the bank of the relevant facts.

(d) If the bank proves that the customer failed, with respect to an item, to comply with the duties imposed on the customer by subsection (c), the customer is precluded from asserting against the bank:

(1) the customer's unauthorized signature or any alteration on the item, if the bank also proves that it suffered a loss by reason of the failure; and

(2) the customer's unauthorized signature or alteration by the same wrongdoer on any other item paid in good faith by the bank if the payment was made before the bank received notice from the customer of the unauthorized signature or alteration and after the customer had been afforded a reasonable period of time, not exceeding 30 days, in which to examine the item or statement of account and notify the bank.

(e) If subsection (d) applies and the customer proves that the bank failed to exercise ordinary care in paying the item and that the failure substantially contributed to loss, the loss is allocated between the customer precluded and the bank asserting the preclusion according to the extent to which the failure of the customer to comply with subsection (c) and the failure of the bank to exercise ordinary care contributed to the loss. If the customer proves that the bank did not pay the item in good faith, the preclusion under subsection (d) does not apply.

(f) Without regard to care or lack of care of either the customer or the bank, a customer who does not within one year after the statement or items are made available to the customer (subsection (a)) discover and report the customer's unauthorized signature on or any alteration on the item is precluded from asserting against the bank the unauthorized signature or alteration. If there is a preclusion under this subsection, the payor bank may not recover for breach or warranty under Section 4—208 with respect to the unauthorized signature or alteration to which the preclusion applies.

As amended in 1990.

§4—407. PAYOR BANK'S RIGHT TO SUBROGATION ON IMPROPER PAYMENT

If a payor has paid an item over the order of the drawer or maker to stop payment, or after an account has been closed, or otherwise under circumstances giving a basis for objection by the drawer or maker, to prevent unjust enrichment and only to the extent necessary to prevent loss to the bank by reason of its payment of the item, the payor bank is subrogated to the rights

(1) of any holder in due course on the item against the drawer or maker;

(2) of the payee or any other holder of the item against the drawer or maker either on the item or under the transaction out of which the item arose; and

(3) of the drawer or maker against the payee or any other holder of the item with respect to the transaction out of which the item arose.

As amended in 1990.

Part 5 Collection of Documentary Drafts

§4—501. HANDLING OF DOCUMENTARY DRAFTS; DUTY TO SEND FOR PRESENTMENT AND TO NOTIFY CUSTOMER OF DISHONOR

A bank that takes a documentary draft for collection shall present or send the draft and accompanying documents for presentment and, upon learning that the draft has not been paid or accepted in due course, shall seasonably notify its customer of the fact even though it may have discounted or bought the draft or extended credit available for withdrawal as of right.

As amended in 1990.

§4—502. PRESENTMENT OF "ON ARRIVAL" DRAFTS

If a draft or the relevant instructions require presentment "on arrival", "when goods arrive" or the like, the collecting bank need not present until in its judgment a reasonable time for arrival of the goods has expired. Refusal to pay or accept because the goods have not arrived is not dishonor; the bank must notify its transferor of the refusal but need not present the draft again until it is instructed to do so or learns of the arrival of the goods.

§4—503. RESPONSIBILITY OF PRESENTING BANK FOR DOCUMENTS AND GOODS; REPORT OF REASONS FOR DISHONOR; REFEREE IN CASE OF NEED

Unless otherwise instructed and except as provided in Article 5, a bank presenting a documentary draft:

(1) must deliver the documents to the drawee on acceptance of the draft if it is payable more than three days after presentment, otherwise, only on payment; and

(2) upon dishonor, either in the case of presentment for acceptance or presentment for payment, may seek and follow instructions from any referee in case of need designated in the draft or, if the presenting bank does not choose to utilize the referee's services, it must use diligence and good faith to ascertain the reason for dishonor, must notify its transferor of the dishonor and of the results of its effort to ascertain the reasons therefor, and must request instructions.

However, the presenting bank is under no obligation with respect to goods represented by the documents except to follow any reasonable instructions seasonably received; it has a right to reimbursement for any expense incurred in following instructions and to prepayment of or indemnity for those expenses.

As amended in 1990.

§4—504. PRIVILEGE OF PRESENTING BANK TO DEAL WITH GOODS; SECURITY INTEREST FOR EXPENSES

(a) A presenting bank that, following the dishonor of a documentary draft, has seasonably requested instructions but does not receive them within a reasonable time may store, sell, or otherwise deal with the goods in any reasonable manner.

(b) For its reasonable expenses incurred by action under subsection (a) the presenting bank has a lien upon the goods or their proceeds, which may be foreclosed in the same manner as an unpaid seller's lien.

As amended in 1990.

ARTICLE 4A FUNDS TRANSFERS

Part 1 Subject Matter and Definitions

§4A—101. SHORT TITLE

This Article may be cited as Uniform Commercial Code-Funds Transfers.

§4A—102. SUBJECT MATTER

Except as otherwise provided in Section 4A—108, this Article applies to funds transfers defined in Section 4A—104.

§4A—103. PAYMENT ORDER—DEFINITIONS

(a) In this Article:

(1) "Payment order" means an instruction of a sender to a receiving bank, transmitted orally, electronically, or in writing, to pay, or to cause another bank to pay, a fixed or determinable amount of money to a beneficiary if:

(i) the instruction does not state a condition to payment to the beneficiary other than time of payment,

(ii) the receiving bank is to be reimbursed by debiting an account of, or otherwise receiving payment from, the sender, and

(iii) the instruction is transmitted by the sender directly to the receiving bank or to an agent, funds-transfer system, or communication system for transmittal to the receiving bank.

(2) "Beneficiary" means the person to be paid by the beneficiary's bank.

(3) "Beneficiary's bank" means the bank identified in a payment order in which an account of the beneficiary is to be credited pursuant to the order or which otherwise is to make payment to

the beneficiary if the order does not provide for payment to an account.

(4) "Receiving bank" means the bank to which the sender's instruction is addressed.

(5) "Sender" means the person giving the instruction to the receiving bank.

(b) If an instruction complying with subsection (a)(1) is to make more than one payment to a beneficiary, the instruction is a separate payment order with respect to each payment.

(c) A payment order is issued when it is sent to the receiving bank.

§4A—104. FUNDS TRANSFER—DEFINITIONS

In this Article:

(a) "Funds transfer" means the series of transactions, beginning with the originator's payment order, made for the purpose of making payment to the beneficiary of the order. The term includes any payment order issued by the originator's bank or an intermediary bank intended to carry out the originator's payment order. A funds transfer is completed by acceptance by the beneficiary's bank of a payment order for the benefit of the beneficiary of the originator's payment order.

(b) "Intermediary bank" means a receiving bank other than the originator's bank or the beneficiary's bank.

(c) "Originator" means the sender of the first payment order in a funds transfer.

(d) "Originator's bank" means (i) the receiving bank to which the payment order of the originator is issued if the originator is not a bank, or (ii) the originator if the originator is a bank.

§4A—105. OTHER DEFINITIONS

(a) In this Article:

(1) "Authorized account" means a deposit account of a customer in a bank designated by the customer as a source of payment of payment orders issued by the customer to the bank. If a customer does not so designate an account, any account of the customer is an authorized account if payment of a payment order from that account is not inconsistent with a restriction on the use of that account.

(2) "Bank" means a person engaged in the business of banking and includes a savings bank, savings and loan association, credit union, and trust company. A branch or separate office of a bank is a separate bank for purposes of this Article.

(3) "Customer" means a person, including a bank, having an account with a bank or from whom a bank has agreed to receive payment orders.

(4) "Funds-transfer business day" of a receiving bank means the part of a day during which the receiving bank is open for the receipt, processing, and transmittal of payment orders and cancellations and amendments of payment orders.

(5) "Funds-transfer system" means a wire transfer network, automated clearing house, or other communication system of a clearing house or other association of banks through which a payment order by a bank may be transmitted to the bank to which the order is addressed.

(6) "Good faith" means honesty in fact and the observance of reasonable commercial standards of fair dealing.

(7) "Prove" with respect to a fact means to meet the burden of establishing the fact (Section 1—201(8)).

(b) Other definitions applying to this Article and the sections in which they appear are:

"Acceptance"	Section 4A—209
"Beneficiary"	Section 4A—103
"Beneficiary's bank"	Section 4A—103
"Executed"	Section 4A—301
"Execution date"	Section 4A—301
"Funds transfer"	Section 4A—104
"Funds-transfer system rule"	Section 4A—501
"Intermediary bank"	Section 4A—104
"Originator"	Section 4A—104
"Originator's bank"	Section 4A—104
"Payment by beneficiary's bank to beneficiary"	Section 4A—405
"Payment by originator to beneficiary"	Section 4A—406
"Payment by sender to receiving bank"	Section 4A—403
"Payment date"	Section 4A—401
"Payment order"	Section 4A—103
"Receiving bank"	Section 4A—103
"Security procedure"	Section 4A—201
"Sender"	Section 4A—103

(c) The following definitions in Article 4 apply to this Article:

"Clearing house"	Section 4—104
"Item"	Section 4—104
"Suspends payments"	Section 4—104

(d) In addition, Article 1 contains general definitions and principles of construction and interpretation applicable throughout this Article.

§4A—106. TIME PAYMENT ORDER IS RECEIVED

(a) The time of receipt of a payment order or communication cancelling or amending a payment order is determined by the rules applicable to receipt of a notice stated in Section 1—201(27). A receiving bank may fix a cut-off time or times on a funds-transfer business day for the receipt and processing of payment orders and communications cancelling or amending payment orders. Different cut-off times may apply to payment orders, cancellations, or amendments, or to different categories of payment orders, cancellations, or amendments. A cut-off time may apply to senders generally or different cut-off times may apply to different senders or categories of payment orders. If a payment order or communication cancelling or amending a payment order is received after the close of a funds-transfer business day or after the appropriate cut-off time on a funds-transfer business day, the receiving bank may treat the payment order or communication as received at the opening of the next funds-transfer business day.

(b) If this Article refers to an execution date or payment date or states a day on which a receiving bank is required to take action, and the date or day does not fall on a funds-transfer business day, the next day that is a funds-transfer business day is treated as the date or day stated, unless the contrary is stated in this Article.

§4A—107. FEDERAL RESERVE REGULATIONS AND OPERATING CIRCULARS

Regulations of the Board of Governors of the Federal Reserve System and operating circulars of the Federal Reserve Banks supersede any inconsistent provision of this Article to the extent of the inconsistency.

§4A—108. EXCLUSION OF CONSUMER TRANSACTIONS GOVERNED BY FEDERAL LAW

This Article does not apply to a funds transfer any part of which is governed by the Electronic Fund Transfer Act of 1978 (Title XX, Public Law 95—630, 92 Stat. 3728, 15 U.S.C. §1693 et seq.) as amended from time to time.

Part 2 Issue and Acceptance of Payment Order

§4A—201. SECURITY PROCEDURE

"Security procedure" means a procedure established by agreement of a customer and a receiving bank for the purpose of (i) verifying that a payment order or communication amending or cancelling a payment order is that of the customer, or (ii) detecting error in the transmission or the content of the payment order or communication. A security procedure may require the use of algorithms or other codes, identifying words or numbers, encryption, callback procedures, or similar security devices. Comparison of a signature on a payment order or communication with an authorized specimen signature of the customer is not by itself a security procedure.

§4A—202. AUTHORIZED AND VERIFIED PAYMENT ORDERS

(a) A payment order received by the receiving bank is the authorized order of the person identified as sender if that person authorized the order or is otherwise bound by it under the law of agency.

(b) If a bank and its customer have agreed that the authenticity of payment orders issued to the bank in the name of the customer as sender will be verified pursuant to a security procedure, a payment order received by the receiving bank is effective as the order of the customer, whether or not authorized, if (i) the security procedure is a commercially reasonable method of providing security against unauthorized payment orders, and (ii) the bank proves that it accepted the payment order in good faith and in compliance with the security procedure and any written agreement or instruction of the customer restricting acceptance of payment orders issued in the name of the customer. The bank is not required to follow an instruction that violates a written agreement with the customer or notice of which is not received at a time and in a manner affording the bank a reasonable opportunity to act on it before the payment order is accepted.

(c) Commercial reasonableness of a security procedure is a question of law to be determined by considering the wishes of the customer expressed to the bank, the circumstances of the customer known to the bank, including the size, type, and frequency of payment orders normally issued by the customer to the bank, alternative security procedures offered to the customer, and security procedures in general use by customers and receiving banks similarly situated. A security procedure is deemed to be commercially reasonable if (i) the security procedure was chosen by the customer after the bank offered, and the customer refused, a security procedure that was commercially reasonable for that customer, and (ii) the customer expressly agreed in writing to be bound by any payment order, whether or not authorized, issued in its name and accepted by the bank in compliance with the security procedure chosen by the customer.

(d) The term "sender" in this Article includes the customer in whose name a payment order is issued if the order is the authorized order of the customer under subsection (a), or it is effective as the order of the customer under subsection (b).

(e) This section applies to amendments and cancellations of payment orders to the same extent it applies to payment orders.

(f) Except as provided in this section and in Section 4A—203(a)(1), rights and obligations arising under this section or Section 4A—203 may not be varied by agreement.

§4A—203. UNENFORCEABILITY OF CERTAIN VERIFIED PAYMENT ORDERS

(a) If an accepted payment order is not, under Section 4A—202(a), an authorized order of a customer identified as sender, but is effective as an order of the customer pursuant to Section 4A—202(b), the following rules apply:

> (1) By express written agreement, the receiving bank may limit the extent to which it is entitled to enforce or retain payment of the payment order.
> (2) The receiving bank is not entitled to enforce or retain payment of the payment order if the customer proves that the order was not caused, directly or indirectly, by a person (i) entrusted at any time with duties to act for the customer with respect to payment orders or the security procedure, or (ii) who obtained access to transmitting facilities of the customer or who obtained, from a source controlled by the customer and without authority of the receiving bank, information facilitating breach of the security procedure, regardless of how the information was obtained or whether the customer was at fault. Information includes any access device, computer software, or the like.

(b) This section applies to amendments of payment orders to the same extent it applies to payment orders.

§4A—204. REFUND OF PAYMENT AND DUTY OF CUSTOMER TO REPORT WITH RESPECT TO UNAUTHORIZED PAYMENT ORDER

(a) If a receiving bank accepts a payment order issued in the name of its customer as sender which is (i) not authorized and not effective as the order of the customer under Section 4A—202, or (ii) not enforceable, in whole or in part, against the customer under Section 4A—203, the bank shall refund any payment of the payment order received from the customer to the extent the bank is not entitled to enforce payment and shall pay interest on the refundable amount calculated from the date the bank received payment to the date of the refund. However, the customer is not entitled to interest from the bank on the amount to be refunded if the customer fails to exercise ordinary care to determine that the order was not authorized by the customer and to notify the bank of the relevant facts within a reasonable time not exceeding 90 days after the date the customer received notification from the bank that the order was accepted or that the customer's account was debited with respect to the order. The bank is

not entitled to any recovery from the customer on account of a failure by the customer to give notification as stated in this section.

(b) Reasonable time under subsection (a) may be fixed by agreement as stated in Section 1—204(1), but the obligation of a receiving bank to refund payment as stated in subsection (a) may not otherwise be varied by agreement.

§4A—205. ERRONEOUS PAYMENT ORDERS

(a) If an accepted payment order was transmitted pursuant to a security procedure for the detection of error and the payment order (i) erroneously instructed payment to a beneficiary not intended by the sender, (ii) erroneously instructed payment in an amount greater than the amount intended by the sender, or (iii) was an erroneously transmitted duplicate of a payment order previously sent by the sender, the following rules apply:

> (1) If the sender proves that the sender or a person acting on behalf of the sender pursuant to Section 4A—206 complied with the security procedure and that the error would have been detected if the receiving bank had also complied, the sender is not obliged to pay the order to the extent stated in paragraphs (2) and (3).
> (2) If the funds transfer is completed on the basis of an erroneous payment order described in clause (i) or (iii) of subsection (a), the sender is not obliged to pay the order and the receiving bank is entitled to recover from the beneficiary any amount paid to the beneficiary to the extent allowed by the law governing mistake and restitution.
> (3) If the funds transfer is completed on the basis of a payment order described in clause (ii) of subsection (a), the sender is not obliged to pay the order to the extent the amount received by the beneficiary is greater than the amount intended by the sender. In that case, the receiving bank is entitled to recover from the beneficiary the excess amount received to the extent allowed by the law governing mistake and restitution.

(b) If (i) the sender of an erroneous payment order described in subsection (a) is not obliged to pay all or part of the order, and (ii) the sender receives notification from the receiving bank that the order was accepted by the bank or that the sender's account was debited with respect to the order, the sender has a duty to exercise ordinary care, on the basis of information available to the sender, to discover the error with respect to the order and to advise the bank of the relevant facts within a reasonable time, not exceeding 90 days, after the bank's notification was received by the sender. If the bank proves that the sender failed to perform that duty, the sender is liable to the bank for the loss the bank proves it incurred as a result of the failure, but the liability of the sender may not exceed the amount of the sender's order.

(c) This section applies to amendments to payment orders to the same extent it applies to payment orders.

§4A—206. TRANSMISSION OF PAYMENT ORDER THROUGH FUNDS-TRANSFER OR OTHER COMMUNICATION SYSTEM

(a) If a payment order addressed to a receiving bank is transmitted to a funds-transfer system or other third party communication system for transmittal to the bank, the system is deemed to be an agent of the sender for the purpose of transmitting the payment order to the bank. If there is a discrepancy between the terms of the payment order transmitted to the system and the terms of the payment order transmitted by the system to the bank, the terms of the payment order of the sender are those transmitted by the system. This section does not apply to a funds-transfer system of the Federal Reserve Banks.

(b) This section applies to cancellations and amendments to payment orders to the same extent it applies to payment orders.

§4A—207. MISDESCRIPTION OF BENEFICIARY

(a) Subject to subsection (b), if, in a payment order received by the beneficiary's bank, the name, bank account number, or other identification of the beneficiary refers to a nonexistent or unidentifiable person or account, no person has rights as a beneficiary of the order and acceptance of the order cannot occur.

(b) If a payment order received by the beneficiary's bank identifies the beneficiary both by name and by an identifying or bank account number and the name and number identify different persons, the following rules apply:

(1) Except as otherwise provided in subsection (c), if the beneficiary's bank does not know that the name and number refer to different persons, it may rely on the number as the proper identification of the beneficiary of the order. The beneficiary's bank need not determine whether the name and number refer to the same person.

(2) If the beneficiary's bank pays the person identified by name or knows that the name and number identify different persons, no person has rights as beneficiary except the person paid by the beneficiary's bank if that person was entitled to receive payment from the originator of the funds transfer. If no person has rights as beneficiary, acceptance of the order cannot occur.

(c) If (i) a payment order described in subsection (b) is accepted, (ii) the originator's payment order described the beneficiary inconsistently by name and number, and (iii) the beneficiary's bank pays the person identified by

number as permitted by subsection (b)(1), the following rules apply:

(1) If the originator is a bank, the originator is obliged to pay its order.

(2) If the originator is not a bank and proves that the person identified by number was not entitled to receive payment from the originator, the originator is not obliged to pay its order unless the originator's bank proves that the originator, before acceptance of the originator's order, had notice that payment of a payment order issued by the originator might be made by the beneficiary's bank on the basis of an identifying or bank account number even if it identifies a person different from the named beneficiary. Proof of notice may be made by any admissible evidence. The originator's bank satisfies the burden of proof if it proves that the originator, before the payment order was accepted, signed a writing stating the information to which the notice relates.

(d) In a case governed by subsection (b)(1), if the beneficiary's bank rightfully pays the person identified by number and that person was not entitled to receive payment from the originator, the amount paid may be recovered from that person to the extent allowed by the law governing mistake and restitution as follows:

(1) If the originator is obliged to pay its payment order as stated in subsection (c), the originator has the right to recover.

(2) If the originator is not a bank and is not obliged to pay its payment order, the originator's bank has the right to recover.

§4A—208. MISDESCRIPTION OF INTERMEDIARY BANK OR BENEFICIARY'S BANK

(a) This subsection applies to a payment order identifying an intermediary bank or the beneficiary's bank only by an identifying number.

(1) The receiving bank may rely on the number as the proper identification of the intermediary or beneficiary's bank and need not determine whether the number identifies a bank.

(2) The sender is obliged to compensate the receiving bank for any loss and expenses incurred by the receiving bank as a result of its reliance on the number in executing or attempting to execute the order.

(b) This subsection applies to a payment order identifying an intermediary bank or the beneficiary's bank both by name and an identifying number if the name and number identify different persons.

(1) If the sender is a bank, the receiving bank may rely on the number as the proper identification of the intermediary or beneficiary's bank if

the receiving bank, when it executes the sender's order, does not know that the name and number identify different persons. The receiving bank need not determine whether the name and number refer to the same person or whether the number refers to a bank. The sender is obliged to compensate the receiving bank for any loss and expenses incurred by the receiving bank as a result of its reliance on the number in executing or attempting to execute the order.

(2) If the sender is not a bank and the receiving bank proves that the sender, before the payment order was accepted, had notice that the receiving bank might rely on the number as the proper identification of the intermediary or beneficiary's bank even if it identifies a person different from the bank identified by name, the rights and obligations of the sender and the receiving bank are governed by subsection (b)(1), as though the sender were a bank. Proof of notice may be made by any admissible evidence. The receiving bank satisfies the burden of proof if it proves that the sender, before the payment order was accepted, signed a writing stating the information to which the notice relates.

(3) Regardless of whether the sender is a bank, the receiving bank may rely on the name as the proper identification of the intermediary or beneficiary's bank if the receiving bank, at the time it executes the sender's order, does not know that the name and number identify different persons. The receiving bank need not determine whether the name and number refer to the same person.

(4) If the receiving bank knows that the name and number identify different persons, reliance on either the name or the number in executing the sender's payment order is a breach of the obligation stated in Section 4A—302(a)(1).

§4A—209. ACCEPTANCE OF PAYMENT ORDER

(a) Subject to subsection (d), a receiving bank other than the beneficiary's bank accepts a payment order when it executes the order.

(b) Subject to subsections (c) and (d), a beneficiary's bank accepts a payment order at the earliest of the following times:

(1) When the bank (i) pays the beneficiary as stated in Section 4A—405(a) or 4A—405(b), or (ii) notifies the beneficiary of receipt of the order or that the account of the beneficiary has been credited with respect to the order unless the notice indicates that the bank is rejecting the order or that funds with respect to the order may

not be withdrawn or used until receipt of payment from the sender of the order;

(2) When the bank receives payment of the entire amount of the sender's order pursuant to Section 4A—403(a)(1) or 4A—403(a)(2); or

(3) The opening of the next funds-transfer business day of the bank following the payment date of the order if, at that time, the amount of the sender's order is fully covered by a withdrawable credit balance in an authorized account of the sender or the bank has otherwise received full payment from the sender, unless the order was rejected before that time or is rejected within (i) one hour after that time, or (ii) one hour after the opening of the next business day of the sender following the payment date if that time is later. If notice of rejection is received by the sender after the payment date and the authorized account of the sender does not bear interest, the bank is obliged to pay interest to the sender on the amount of the order for the number of days elapsing after the payment date to the day the sender receives notice or learns that the order was not accepted, counting that day as an elapsed day. If the withdrawable credit balance during that period falls below the amount of the order, the amount of interest payable is reduced accordingly.

(c) Acceptance of a payment order cannot occur before the order is received by the receiving bank. Acceptance does not occur under subsection (b)(2) or (b)(3) if the beneficiary of the payment order does not have an account with the receiving bank, the account has been closed, or the receiving bank is not permitted by law to receive credits for the beneficiary's account.

(d) A payment order issued to the originator's bank cannot be accepted until the payment date if the bank is the beneficiary's bank, or the execution date if the bank is not the beneficiary's bank. If the originator's bank executes the originator's payment order before the execution date or pays the beneficiary of the originator's payment order before the payment date and the payment order is subsequently cancelled pursuant to Section 4A—211(b), the bank may recover from the beneficiary any payment received to the extent allowed by the law governing mistake and restitution.

§4A—210. REJECTION OF PAYMENT ORDER

(a) A payment order is rejected by the receiving bank by a notice of rejection transmitted to the sender orally, electronically, or in writing. A notice of rejection need not use any particular words and is sufficient if it indicates that the receiving bank is rejecting the order or will not execute or pay the order. Rejection is effective when the notice is given if transmission is by a means that is reasonable in the circumstances. If notice of rejection is given by a means that is not reasonable, rejection is effective when the notice is received. If an agreement of the sender and receiving bank establishes the means to be used to reject a payment order, (i) any means complying with the agreement is reasonable and (ii) any means not complying is not reasonable unless no significant delay in receipt of the notice resulted from the use of the noncomplying means.

(b) This subsection applies if a receiving bank other than the beneficiary's bank fails to execute a payment order despite the existence on the execution date of a withdrawable credit balance in an authorized account of the sender sufficient to cover the order. If the sender does not receive notice of rejection of the order on the execution date and the authorized account of the sender does not bear interest, the bank is obliged to pay interest to the sender on the amount of the order for the number of days elapsing after the execution date to the earlier of the day the order is cancelled pursuant to Section 4A—211(d) or the day the sender receives notice or learns that the order was not executed, counting the final day of the period as an elapsed day. If the withdrawable credit balance during that period falls below the amount of the order, the amount of interest is reduced accordingly.

(c) If a receiving bank suspends payments, all unaccepted payment orders issued to it are are deemed rejected at the time the bank suspends payments.

(d) Acceptance of a payment order precludes a later rejection of the order. Rejection of a payment order precludes a later acceptance of the order.

§4A—211. CANCELLATION AND AMENDMENT OF PAYMENT ORDER

(a) A communication of the sender of a payment order cancelling or amending the order may be transmitted to the receiving bank orally, electronically, or in writing. If a security procedure is in effect between the sender and the receiving bank, the communication is not effective to cancel or amend the order unless the communication is verified pursuant to the security procedure or the bank agrees to the cancellation or amendment.

(b) Subject to subsection (a), a communication by the sender cancelling or amending a payment order is effective to cancel or amend the order if notice of the communication is received at a time and in a manner affording the receiving bank a reasonable opportunity to act on the communication before the bank accepts the payment order.

(c) After a payment order has been accepted, cancellation or amendment of the order is not effective unless the receiving bank agrees or a funds-transfer system rule allows cancellation or amendment without agreement of the bank.

(1) With respect to a payment order accepted by a receiving bank other than the beneficiary's bank, cancellation or amendment is not effective unless a conforming cancellation or amendment of the payment order issued by the receiving bank is also made.

(2) With respect to a payment order accepted by the beneficiary's bank, cancellation or amendment is not effective unless the order was issued in execution of an unauthorized payment order, or because of a mistake by a sender in the funds transfer which resulted in the issuance of a payment order (i) that is a duplicate of a payment order previously issued by the sender, (ii) that orders payment to a beneficiary not entitled to receive payment from the originator, or (iii) that orders payment in an amount greater than the amount the beneficiary was entitled to receive from the originator. If the payment order is cancelled or amended, the beneficiary's bank is entitled to recover from the beneficiary any amount paid to the beneficiary to the extent allowed by the law governing mistake and restitution.

(d) An unaccepted payment order is cancelled by operation of law at the close of the fifth funds-transfer business day of the receiving bank after the execution date or payment date of the order.

(e) A cancelled payment order cannot be accepted. If an accepted payment order is cancelled, the acceptance is nullified and no person has any right or obligation based on the acceptance. Amendment of a payment order is deemed to be cancellation of the original order at the time of amendment and issue of a new payment order in the amended form at the same time.

(f) Unless otherwise provided in an agreement of the parties or in a funds-transfer system rule, if the receiving bank, after accepting a payment order, agrees to cancellation or amendment of the order by the sender or is bound by a funds-transfer system rule allowing cancellation or amendment without the bank's agreement, the sender, whether or not cancellation or amendment is effective, is liable to the bank for any loss and expenses, including reasonable attorney's fees, incurred by the bank as a result of the cancellation or amendment or attempted cancellation or amendment.

(g) A payment order is not revoked by the death or legal incapacity of the sender unless the receiving bank knows of the death or of an adjudication of incapacity by a court of competent jurisdiction and has reasonable opportunity to act before acceptance of the order.

(h) A funds-transfer system rule is not effective to the extent it conflicts with subsection (c)(2).

§4A—212. LIABILITY AND DUTY OF RECEIVING BANK REGARDING UNACCEPTED PAYMENT ORDER

If a receiving bank fails to accept a payment order that it is obliged by express agreement to accept, the bank is liable for breach of the agreement to the extent provided in the agreement or in this Article, but does not otherwise have any duty to accept a payment order or, before acceptance, to take any action, or refrain from taking action, with respect to the order except as provided in this Article or by express agreement. Liability based on acceptance arises only when acceptance occurs as stated in Section 4A—209, and liability is limited to that provided in this Article. A receiving bank is not the agent of the sender or beneficiary of the payment order it accepts, or of any other party to the funds transfer, and the bank owes no duty to any party to the funds transfer except as provided in this Article or by express agreement.

Part 3 Execution of Sender's Payment Order by Receiving Bank

§4A—301. EXECUTION AND EXECUTION DATE

(a) A payment order is "executed" by the receiving bank when it issues a payment order intended to carry out the payment order received by the bank. A payment order received by the beneficiary's bank can be accepted but cannot be executed.

(b) "Execution date" of a payment order means the day on which the receiving bank may properly issue a payment order in execution of the sender's order. The execution date may be determined by instruction of the sender but cannot be earlier than the day the order is received and, unless otherwise determined, is the day the order is received. If the sender's instruction states a payment date, the execution date is the payment date or an earlier date on which execution is reasonably necessary to allow payment to the beneficiary on the payment date.

§4A—302. OBLIGATIONS OF RECEIVING BANK IN EXECUTION OF PAYMENT ORDER

(a) Except as provided in subsections (b) through (d), if the receiving bank accepts a payment order pursuant to Section 4A—209(a), the bank has the following obligations in executing the order:

(1) The receiving bank is obliged to issue, on the execution date, a payment order complying with the sender's order and to follow the sender's instructions concerning (i) any intermediary bank or funds-transfer system to be used in carrying out the funds transfer, or (ii) the means by which payment orders are to be transmitted in the funds transfer. If the originator's bank issues a payment order to an intermediary bank, the originator's bank is obliged to instruct the intermediary bank according to the instruction of the originator. An intermediary bank in the funds transfer is

similarly bound by an instruction given to it by the sender of the payment order it accepts.

(2) If the sender's instruction states that the funds transfer is to be carried out telephonically or by wire transfer or otherwise indicates that the funds transfer is to be carried out by the most expeditious means, the receiving bank is obliged to transmit its payment order by the most expeditious available means, and to instruct any intermediary bank accordingly. If a sender's instruction states a payment date, the receiving bank is obliged to transmit its payment order at a time and by means reasonably necessary to allow payment to the beneficiary on the payment date or as soon thereafter as is feasible.

(b) Unless otherwise instructed, a receiving bank executing a payment order may (i) use any funds-transfer system if use of that system is reasonable in the circumstances, and (ii) issue a payment order to the beneficiary's bank or to an intermediary bank through which a payment order conforming to the sender's order can expeditiously be issued to the beneficiary's bank if the receiving bank exercises ordinary care in the selection of the intermediary bank. A receiving bank is not required to follow an instruction of the sender designating a funds-transfer system to be used in carrying out the funds transfer if the receiving bank, in good faith, determines that it is not feasible to follow the instruction or that following the instruction would unduly delay completion of the funds transfer.

(c) Unless subsection (a)(2) applies or the receiving bank is otherwise instructed, the bank may execute a payment order by transmitting its payment order by first class mail or by any means reasonable in the circumstances. If the receiving bank is instructed to execute the sender's order by transmitting its payment order by a particular means, the receiving bank may issue its payment order by the means stated or by any means as expeditious as the means stated.

(d) Unless instructed by the sender, (i) the receiving bank may not obtain payment of its charges for services and expenses in connection with the execution of the sender's order by issuing a payment order in an amount equal to the amount of the sender's order less the amount of the charges, and (ii) may not instruct a subsequent receiving bank to obtain payment of its charges in the same manner.

§4A—303. ERRONEOUS EXECUTION OF PAYMENT ORDER

(a) A receiving bank that (i) executes the payment order of the sender by issuing a payment order in an amount greater than the amount of the sender's order, or (ii) issues a payment order in execution of the sender's order and then issues a duplicate order, is entitled to payment of the amount of the sender's order under Section 4A—402(c) if that subsection is otherwise satisfied. The bank is entitled to recover from the beneficiary of the erroneous order the excess payment received to the extent allowed by the law governing mistake and restitution.

(b) A receiving bank that executes the payment order of the sender by issuing a payment order in an amount less than the amount of the sender's order is entitled to payment of the amount of the sender's order under Section 4A—402(c) if (i) that subsection is otherwise satisfied and (ii) the bank corrects its mistake by issuing an additional payment order for the benefit of the beneficiary of the sender's order. If the error is not corrected, the issuer of the erroneous order is entitled to receive or retain payment from the sender of the order it accepted only to the extent of the amount of the erroneous order. This subsection does not apply if the receiving bank executes the sender's payment order by issuing a payment order in an amount less than the amount of the sender's order for the purpose of obtaining payment of its charges for services and expenses pursuant to instruction of the sender.

(c) If a receiving bank executes the payment order of the sender by issuing a payment order to a beneficiary different from the beneficiary of the sender's order and the funds transfer is completed on the basis of that error, the sender of the payment order that was erroneously executed and all previous senders in the funds transfer are not obliged to pay the payment orders they issued. The issuer of the erroneous order is entitled to recover from the beneficiary of the order the payment received to the extent allowed by the law governing mistake and restitution.

§4A—304. DUTY OF SENDER TO REPORT ERRONEOUSLY EXECUTED PAYMENT ORDER

If the sender of a payment order that is erroneously executed as stated in Section 4A—303 receives notification from the receiving bank that the order was executed or that the sender's account was debited with respect to the order, the sender has a duty to exercise ordinary care to determine, on the basis of information available to the sender, that the order was erroneously executed and to notify the bank of the relevant facts within a reasonable time not exceeding 90 days after the notification from the bank was received by the sender. If the sender fails to perform that duty, the bank is not obliged to pay interest on any amount refundable to the sender under Section 4A—402(d) for the period before the bank learns of the execution error. The bank is not entitled to any recovery from the sender on account of a failure by the sender to perform the duty stated in this section.

§4A—305. LIABILITY FOR LATE OR IMPROPER EXECUTION OR FAILURE TO EXECUTE PAYMENT ORDER

(a) If a funds transfer is completed but execution of a payment order by the receiving bank in breach of Section 4A—302 results in delay in payment to the beneficiary, the bank is obliged to pay interest to either the originator or the beneficiary of the funds transfer for the period of delay caused by the improper execution. Except as provided in subsection (c), additional damages are not recoverable.

(b) If execution of a payment order by a receiving bank in breach of Section 4A—302 results in (i) noncompletion of the funds transfer, (ii) failure to use an intermediary bank designated by the originator, or (iii) issuance of a payment order that does not comply with the terms of the payment order of the originator, the bank is liable to the originator for its expenses in the funds transfer and for incidental expenses and interest losses, to the extent not covered by subsection (a), resulting from the improper execution. Except as provided in subsection (c), additional damages are not recoverable.

(c) In addition to the amounts payable under subsections (a) and (b), damages, including consequential damages, are recoverable to the extent provided in an express written agreement of the receiving bank.

(d) If a receiving bank fails to execute a payment order it was obliged by express agreement to execute, the receiving bank is liable to the sender for its expenses in the transaction and for incidental expenses and interest losses resulting from the failure to execute. Additional damages, including consequential damages, are recoverable to the extent provided in an express written agreement of the receiving bank, but are not otherwise recoverable.

(e) Reasonable attorney's fees are recoverable if demand for compensation under subsection (a) or (b) is made and refused before an action is brought on the claim. If a claim is made for breach of an agreement under subsection (d) and the agreement does not provide for damages, reasonable attorney's fees are recoverable if demand for compensation under subsection (d) is made and refused before an action is brought on the claim.

(f) Except as stated in this section, the liability of a receiving bank under subsections (a) and (b) may not be varied by agreement.

Part 4 Payment

§4A—401. PAYMENT DATE

"Payment date" of a payment order means the day on which the amount of the order is payable to the beneficiary by the beneficiary's bank. The payment date may be determined by instruction of the sender but cannot be earlier than the day the order is received by the beneficiary's bank and, unless otherwise determined, is the day the order is received by the beneficiary's bank.

§4A—402. OBLIGATION OF SENDER TO PAY RECEIVING BANK

(a) This section is subject to Sections 4A—205 and 4A—207.

(b) With respect to a payment order issued to the beneficiary's bank, acceptance of the order by the bank obliges the sender to pay the bank the amount of the order, but payment is not due until the payment date of the order.

(c) This subsection is subject to subsection (e) and to Section 4A—303. With respect to a payment order issued to a receiving bank other than the beneficiary's bank, acceptance of the order by the receiving bank obliges the sender to pay the bank the amount of the sender's order. Payment by the sender is not due until the execution date of the sender's order. The obligation of that sender to pay its payment order is excused if the funds transfer is not completed by acceptance by the beneficiary's bank of a payment order instructing payment to the beneficiary of that sender's payment order.

(d) If the sender of a payment order pays the order and was not obliged to pay all or part of the amount paid, the bank receiving payment is obliged to refund payment to the extent the sender was not obliged to pay. Except as provided in Sections 4A—204 and 4A—304, interest is payable on the refundable amount from the date of payment.

(e) If a funds transfer is not completed as stated in subsection (c) and an intermediary bank is obliged to refund payment as stated in subsection (d) but is unable to do so because not permitted by applicable law or because the bank suspends payments, a sender in the funds transfer that executed a payment order in compliance with an instruction, as stated in Section 4A—302(a)(1), to route the funds transfer through that intermediary bank is entitled to receive or retain payment from the sender of the payment order that it accepted. The first sender in the funds transfer that issued an instruction requiring routing through that intermediary bank is subrogated to the right of the bank that paid the intermediary bank to refund as stated in subsection (d).

(f) The right of the sender of a payment order to be excused from the obligation to pay the order as stated in subsection (c) or to receive refund under subsection (d) may not be varied by agreement.

§4A—403. PAYMENT BY SENDER TO RECEIVING BANK

(a) Payment of the sender's obligation under Section 4A—402 to pay the receiving bank occurs as follows:

(1) If the sender is a bank, payment occurs when the receiving bank receives final settlement of the obligation through a Federal Reserve Bank or through a funds-transfer system.

(2) If the sender is a bank and the sender (i) credited an account of the receiving bank with the sender, or (ii) caused an account of the receiving bank in another bank to be credited, payment occurs when the credit is withdrawn or, if not withdrawn, at midnight of the day on which the credit is withdrawable and the receiving bank learns of that fact.

(3) If the receiving bank debits an account of the sender with the receiving bank, payment occurs when the debit is made to the extent the debit is covered by a withdrawable credit balance in the account.

(b) If the sender and receiving bank are members of a funds-transfer system that nets obligations multilaterally among participants, the receiving bank receives final settlement when settlement is complete in accordance with the rules of the system. The obligation of the sender to pay the amount of a payment order transmitted through the funds-transfer system may be satisfied, to the extent permitted by the rules of the system, by setting off and applying against the sender's obligation the right of the sender to receive payment from the receiving bank of the amount of any other payment order transmitted to the sender by the receiving bank through the funds-transfer system. The aggregate balance of obligations owed by each sender to each receiving bank in the funds-transfer system may be satisfied, to the extent permitted by the rules of the system, by setting off and applying against that balance the aggregate balance of obligations owed to the sender by other members of the system. The aggregate balance is determined after the right of setoff stated in the second sentence of this subsection has been exercised.

(c) If two banks transmit payment orders to each other under an agreement that settlement of the obligations of each bank to the other under Section 4A—402 will be made at the end of the day or other period, the total amount owed with respect to all orders transmitted by one bank shall be set off against the total amount owed with respect to all orders transmitted by the other bank. To the extent of the setoff, each bank has made payment to the other.

(d) In a case not covered by subsection (a), the time when payment of the sender's obligation under Section 4A—402(b) or 4A—402(c) occurs is governed by applicable principles of law that determine when an obligation is satisfied.

§4A—404. OBLIGATION OF BENEFICIARY'S BANK TO PAY AND GIVE NOTICE TO BENEFICIARY

(a) Subject to Sections 4A—211(e), 4A—405(d), and 4A—405(e), if a beneficiary's bank accepts a payment order, the bank is obliged to pay the amount of the order to the beneficiary of the order. Payment is due on the payment date of the order, but if acceptance occurs on the payment date after the close of the funds-transfer business day of the bank, payment is due on the next funds-transfer business day. If the bank refuses to pay after demand by the beneficiary and receipt of notice of particular circumstances that will give rise to consequential damages as a result of nonpayment, the beneficiary may recover damages resulting from the refusal to pay to the extent the bank had notice of the damages, unless the bank proves that it did not pay because of a reasonable doubt concerning the right of the beneficiary to payment.

(b) If a payment order accepted by the beneficiary's bank instructs payment to an account of the beneficiary, the bank is obliged to notify the beneficiary of receipt of the order before midnight of the next funds-transfer business day following the payment date. If the payment order does not instruct payment to an account of the beneficiary, the bank is required to notify the beneficiary only if notice is required by the order. Notice may be given by first class mail or any other means reasonable in the circumstances. If the bank fails to give the required notice, the bank is obliged to pay interest to the beneficiary on the amount of the payment order from the day notice should have been given until the day the beneficiary learned of receipt of the payment order by the bank. No other damages are recoverable. Reasonable attorney's fees are also recoverable if demand for interest is made and refused before an action is brought on the claim.

(c) The right of a beneficiary to receive payment and damages as stated in subsection (a) may not be varied by agreement or a funds-transfer system rule. The right of a beneficiary to be notified as stated in subsection (b) may be varied by agreement of the beneficiary or by a funds-transfer system rule if the beneficiary is notified of the rule before initiation of the funds transfer.

§4A—405. PAYMENT BY BENEFICIARY'S BANK TO BENEFICIARY

(a) If the beneficiary's bank credits an account of the beneficiary of a payment order, payment of the bank's obligation under Section 4A—404(a) occurs when and to the extent (i) the beneficiary is notified of the right to withdraw the credit, (ii) the bank lawfully applies the credit to a debt of the beneficiary, or (iii) funds with respect to the order are otherwise made available to the beneficiary by the bank.

(b) If the beneficiary's bank does not credit an account of the beneficiary of a payment order, the time when payment of the bank's obligation under Section 4A—404(a) occurs is governed by principles of law that determine when an obligation is satisfied.

(c) Except as stated in subsections (d) and (e), if the beneficiary's bank pays the beneficiary of a payment order under a condition to payment or agreement of the

beneficiary giving the bank the right to recover payment from the beneficiary if the bank does not receive payment of the order, the condition to payment or agreement is not enforceable.

(d) A funds-transfer system rule may provide that payments made to beneficiaries of funds transfers made through the system are provisional until receipt of payment by the beneficiary's bank of the payment order it accepted. A beneficiary's bank that makes a payment that is provisional under the rule is entitled to refund from the beneficiary if (i) the rule requires that both the beneficiary and the originator be given notice of the provisional nature of the payment before the funds transfer is initiated, (ii) the beneficiary, the beneficiary's bank, and the originator's bank agreed to be bound by the rule, and (iii) the beneficiary's bank did not receive payment of the payment order that it accepted. If the beneficiary is obliged to refund payment to the beneficiary's bank, acceptance of the payment order by the beneficiary's bank is nullified and no payment by the originator of the funds transfer to the beneficiary occurs under Section 4A—406.

(e) This subsection applies to a funds transfer that includes a payment order transmitted over a funds-transfer system that (i) nets obligations multilaterally among participants, and (ii) has in effect a loss-sharing agreement among participants for the purpose of providing funds necessary to complete settlement of the obligations of one or more participants that do not meet their settlement obligations. If the beneficiary's bank in the funds transfer accepts a payment order and the system fails to complete settlement pursuant to its rules with respect to any payment order in the funds transfer, (i) the acceptance by the beneficiary's bank is nullified and no person has any right or obligation based on the acceptance, (ii) the beneficiary's bank is entitled to recover payment from the beneficiary, (iii) no payment by the originator to the beneficiary occurs under Section 4A—406, and (iv) subject to Section 4A—402(e), each sender in the funds transfer is excused from its obligation to pay its payment order under Section 4A—402 (c) because the funds transfer has not been completed.

§4A—406. PAYMENT BY ORIGINATOR TO BENEFICIARY; DISCHARGE OF UNDERLYING OBLIGATION

(a) Subject to Sections 4A—211(e), 4A—405(d), and 4A—405(e), the originator of a funds transfer pays the beneficiary of the originator's payment order (i) at the time a payment order for the benefit of the beneficiary is accepted by the beneficiary's bank in the funds transfer and (ii) in an amount equal to the amount of the order accepted by the beneficiary's bank, but not more than the amount of the originator's order.

(b) If payment under subsection (a) is made to satisfy an obligation, the obligation is discharged to the same extent discharge would result from payment to the beneficiary of the same amount in money, unless (i) the payment under subsection (a) was made by a means prohibited by the contract of the beneficiary with respect to the obligation, (ii) the beneficiary, within a reasonable time after receiving notice of receipt of the order by the beneficiary's bank, notified the originator of the beneficiary's refusal of the payment, (iii) funds with respect to the order were not withdrawn by the beneficiary or applied to a debt of the beneficiary, and (iv) the beneficiary would suffer a loss that could reasonably have been avoided if payment had been made by a means complying with the contract. If payment by the originator does not result in discharge under this section, the originator is subrogated to the rights of the beneficiary to receive payment from the beneficiary's bank under Section 4A—404(a).

(c) For the purpose of determining whether discharge of an obligation occurs under subsection (b), if the beneficiary's bank accepts a payment order in an amount equal to the amount of the originator's payment order less charges of one or more receiving banks in the funds transfer, payment to the beneficiary is deemed to be in the amount of the originator's order unless upon demand by the beneficiary the originator does not pay the beneficiary the amount of the deducted charges.

(d) Rights of the originator or of the beneficiary of a funds transfer under this section may be varied only by agreement of the originator and the beneficiary.

Part 5 Miscellaneous Provisions

§4A—501. VARIATION BY AGREEMENT AND EFFECT OF FUNDS-TRANSFER SYSTEM RULE

(a) Except as otherwise provided in this Article, the rights and obligations of a party to a funds transfer may be varied by agreement of the affected party.

(b) "Funds-transfer system rule" means a rule of an association of banks (i) governing transmission of payment orders by means of a funds-transfer system of the association or rights and obligations with respect to those orders, or (ii) to the extent the rule governs rights and obligations between banks that are parties to a funds transfer in which a Federal Reserve Bank, acting as an intermediary bank, sends a payment order to the beneficiary's bank. Except as otherwise provided in this Article, a funds-transfer system rule governing rights and obligations between participating banks using the system may be effective even if the rule conflicts with this Article and indirectly affects another party to the funds transfer who does not consent to the rule. A funds-transfer system rule may also govern rights and obligations of parties other than participating banks using the system to the extent stated in Sections 4A—404(c), 4A—405(d), and 4A—507(c).

§4A—502. CREDITOR PROCESS SERVED ON RECEIVING BANK; SETOFF BY BENEFICIARY'S BANK

(a) As used in this section, "creditor process" means levy, attachment, garnishment, notice of lien, sequestration, or similar process issued by or on behalf of a creditor or other claimant with respect to an account.

(b) This subsection applies to creditor process with respect to an authorized account of the sender of a payment order if the creditor process is served on the receiving bank. For the purpose of determining rights with respect to the creditor process, if the receiving bank accepts the payment order the balance in the authorized account is deemed to be reduced by the amount of the payment order to the extent the bank did not otherwise receive payment of the order, unless the creditor process is served at a time and in a manner affording the bank a reasonable opportunity to act on it before the bank accepts the payment order.

(c) If a beneficiary's bank has received a payment order for payment to the beneficiary's account in the bank, the following rules apply:

(1) The bank may credit the beneficiary's account. The amount credited may be set off against an obligation owed by the beneficiary to the bank or may be applied to satisfy creditor process served on the bank with respect to the account.

(2) The bank may credit the beneficiary's account and allow withdrawal of the amount credited unless creditor process with respect to the account is served at a time and in a manner affording the bank a reasonable opportunity to act to prevent withdrawal.

(3) If creditor process with respect to the beneficiary's account has been served and the bank has had a reasonable opportunity to act on it, the bank may not reject the payment order except for a reason unrelated to the service of process.

(d) Creditor process with respect to a payment by the originator to the beneficiary pursuant to a funds transfer may be served only on the beneficiary's bank with respect to the debt owed by that bank to the beneficiary. Any other bank served with the creditor process is not obliged to act with respect to the process.

§4A—503. INJUNCTION OR RESTRAINING ORDER WITH RESPECT TO FUNDS TRANSFER

For proper cause and in compliance with applicable law, a court may restrain (i) a person from issuing a payment order to initiate a funds transfer, (ii) an originator's bank from executing the payment order of the originator, or (iii) the beneficiary's bank from releasing funds to the beneficiary or the beneficiary from withdrawing the funds. A court may not otherwise restrain a person from issuing a payment order, paying or receiving payment of a payment order, or otherwise acting with respect to a funds transfer.

§4A—504. ORDER IN WHICH ITEMS AND PAYMENT ORDERS MAY BE CHARGED TO ACCOUNT; ORDER OF WITHDRAWALS FROM ACCOUNT

(a) If a receiving bank has received more than one payment order of the sender or one or more payment orders and other items that are payable from the sender's account, the bank may charge the sender's account with respect to the various orders and items in any sequence.

(b) In determining whether a credit to an account has been withdrawn by the holder of the account or applied to a debt of the holder of the account, credits first made to the account are first withdrawn or applied.

§4A—505. PRECLUSION OF OBJECTION TO DEBIT OF CUSTOMER'S ACCOUNT

If a receiving bank has received payment from its customer with respect to a payment order issued in the name of the customer as sender and accepted by the bank, and the customer received notification reasonably identifying the order, the customer is precluded from asserting that the bank is not entitled to retain the payment unless the customer notifies the bank of the customer's objection to the payment within one year after the notification was received by the customer.

§4A—506. RATE OF INTEREST

(a) If, under this Article, a receiving bank is obliged to pay interest with respect to a payment order issued to the bank, the amount payable may be determined (i) by agreement of the sender and receiving bank, or (ii) by a funds-transfer system rule if the payment order is transmitted through a funds-transfer system.

(b) If the amount of interest is not determined by an agreement or rule as stated in subsection (a), the amount is calculated by multiplying the applicable Federal Funds rate by the amount on which interest is payable, and then multiplying the product by the number of days for which interest is payable. The applicable Federal Funds rate is the average of the Federal Funds rates published by the Federal Reserve Bank of New York for each of the days for which interest is payable divided by 360. The Federal Funds rate for any day on which a published rate is not available is the same as the published rate for the next preceding day for which there is a published rate. If a receiving bank that accepted a payment order is required to refund payment to the sender of the order because the funds transfer was not completed, but the failure to complete was not due to any fault by the bank, the interest payable is reduced by a percentage equal to the reserve requirement on deposits of the receiving bank.

§4A—507. CHOICE OF LAW

(a) The following rules apply unless the affected parties otherwise agree or subsection (c) applies:

(1) The rights and obligations between the sender of a payment order and the receiving bank are governed by the law of the jurisdiction in which the receiving bank is located.

(2) The rights and obligations between the beneficiary's bank and the beneficiary are governed by the law of the jurisdiction in which the beneficiary's bank is located.

(3) The issue of when payment is made pursuant to a funds transfer by the originator to the beneficiary is governed by the law of the jurisdiction in which the beneficiary's bank is located.

(b) If the parties described in each paragraph of subsection (a) have made an agreement selecting the law of a particular jurisdiction to govern rights and obligations between each other, the law of that jurisdiction governs those rights and obligations, whether or not the payment order or the funds transfer bears a reasonable relation to that jurisdiction.

(c) A funds-transfer system rule may select the law of a particular jurisdiction to govern (i) rights and obligations between participating banks with respect to payment orders transmitted or processed through the system, or (ii) the rights and obligations of some or all parties to a funds transfer any part of which is carried out by means of the system. A choice of law made pursuant to clause (i) is binding on participating banks. A choice of law made pursuant to clause (ii) is binding on the originator, other sender, or a receiving bank having notice that the funds-transfer system might be used in the funds transfer and of the choice of law by the system when the originator, other sender, or receiving bank issued or accepted a payment order. The beneficiary of a funds transfer is bound by the choice of law if, when the funds transfer is initiated, the beneficiary has notice that the funds-transfer system might be used in the funds transfer and of the choice of law by the system. The law of a jurisdiction selected pursuant to this subsection may govern, whether or not that law bears a reasonable relation to the matter in issue.

(d) In the event of inconsistency between an agreement under subsection (b) and a choice-of-law rule under subsection (c), the agreement under subsection (b) prevails.

(e) If a funds transfer is made by use of more than one funds-transfer system and there is inconsistency between choice-of-law rules of the systems, the matter in issue is governed by the law of the selected jurisdiction that has the most significant relationship to the matter in issue.

* * * *

Revised Article 9 Secured Transactions

Part 1 General Provisions [Subpart 1. Short Title, Definitions, and General Concepts]

§9—101. SHORT TITLE

This article may be cited as Uniform Commercial Code—Secured Transactions.

§9—102. DEFINITIONS AND INDEX OF DEFINITIONS

(a) In this article:

(1) "Accession" means goods that are physically united with other goods in such a manner that the identity of the original goods is not lost.

(2) "Account", except as used in "account for", means a right to payment of a monetary obligation, whether or not earned by performance, (i) for property that has been or is to be sold, leased, licensed, assigned, or otherwise disposed of, (ii) for services rendered or to be rendered, (iii) for a policy of insurance issued or to be issued, (iv) for a secondary obligation incurred or to be incurred, (v) for energy provided or to be provided, (vi) for the use or hire of a vessel under a charter or other contract, (vii) arising out of the use of a credit or charge card or information contained on or for use with the card, or (viii) as winnings in a lottery or other game of chance operated or sponsored by a State, governmental unit of a State, or person licensed or authorized to operate the game by a State or governmental unit of a State. The term includes health-care insurance receivables. The term does not include (i) rights to payment evidenced by chattel paper or an instrument, (ii) commercial tort claims, (iii) deposit accounts, (iv) investment property, (v) letter-of-credit rights or letters of credit, or (vi) rights to payment for money or funds advanced or sold, other than rights arising out of the use of a credit or charge card or information contained on or for use with the card.

(3) "Account debtor" means a person obligated on an account, chattel paper, or general intangible. The term does not include persons obligated to pay a negotiable instrument, even if the instrument constitutes part of chattel paper.

(4) "Accounting", except as used in "accounting for", means a record:

(A) authenticated by a secured party;

(B) indicating the aggregate unpaid secured obligations as of a date not more than 35 days earlier or 35 days later than the date of the record; and

(C) identifying the components of the obligations in reasonable detail.

(5) "Agricultural lien" means an interest, other than a security interest, in farm products:

(A) which secures payment or performance of an obligation for:

(i) goods or services furnished in connection with a debtor's farming operation; or

(ii) rent on real property leased by a debtor in connection with its farming operation;

(B) which is created by statute in favor of a person that:

(i) in the ordinary course of its business furnished goods or services to a debtor in connection with a debtor's farming operation; or

(ii) leased real property to a debtor in connection with the debtor's farming operation; and

(C) whose effectiveness does not depend on the person's possession of the personal property.

(6) "As-extracted collateral" means:

(A) oil, gas, or other minerals that are subject to a security interest that:

(i) is created by a debtor having an interest in the minerals before extraction; and

(ii) attaches to the minerals as extracted; or

(B) accounts arising out of the sale at the wellhead or minehead of oil, gas, or other minerals in which the debtor had an interest before extraction.

(7) "Authenticate" means:

(A) to sign; or

(B) to execute or otherwise adopt a symbol, or encrypt or similarly process a record in whole or in part, with the present intent of the authenticating person to identify the person and adopt or accept a record.

(8) "Bank" means an organization that is engaged in the business of banking. The term includes savings banks, savings and loan associations, credit unions, and trust companies.

(9) "Cash proceeds" means proceeds that are money, checks, deposit accounts, or the like.

(10) "Certificate of title" means a certificate of title with respect to which a statute provides for

the security interest in question to be indicated on the certificate as a condition or result of the security interest's obtaining priority over the rights of a lien creditor with respect to the collateral.

(11) "Chattel paper" means a record or records that evidence both a monetary obligation and a security interest in specific goods, a security interest in specific goods and software used in the goods, a security interest in specific goods and license of software used in the goods, a lease of specific goods, or a lease of specific goods and license of software used in the goods. In this paragraph, "monetary obligation" means a monetary obligation secured by the goods or owed under a lease of the goods and includes a monetary obligation with respect to software used in the goods. The term does not include (i) charters or other contracts involving the use or hire of a vessel or (ii) records that evidence a right to payment arising out of the use of a credit or charge card or information contained on or for use with the card. If a transaction is evidenced by records that include an instrument or series of instruments, the group of records taken together constitutes chattel paper.

(12) "Collateral" means the property subject to a security interest or agricultural lien. The term includes:

(A) proceeds to which a security interest attaches;

(B) accounts, chattel paper, payment intangibles,and promissory notes that have been sold; and

(C) goods that are the subject of a consignment.

(13) "Commercial tort claim" means a claim arising in tort with respect to which:

(A) the claimant is an organization; or

(B) the claimant is an individual and the claim:

(i) arose in the course of the claimant's business or profession; and

(ii) does not include damages arising out of personal injury to or the death of an individual.

(14) "Commodity account" means an account maintained by a commodity intermediary in which a commodity contract is carried for a commodity customer.

(15) "Commodity contract" means a commodity futures contract, an option on a commodity futures contract, a commodity option, or another contract if the contract or option is:

(A) traded on or subject to the rules of a board of trade that has been designated as a contract market for such a contract pursuant to federal commodities laws; or

(B) traded on a foreign commodity board of trade,exchange, or market, and is carried on the books of a commodity intermediary for a commodity customer.

(16) "Commodity customer" means a person for which a commodity intermediary carries a commodity contract on its books.

(17) "Commodity intermediary" means a person that:

(A) is registered as a futures commission merchant under federal commodities law; or

(B) in the ordinary course of its business provides clearance or settlement services for a board of trade that has been designated as a contract market pursuant to federal commodities law.

(18) "Communicate" means:

(A) to send a written or other tangible record;

(B) to transmit a record by any means agreed upon by the persons sending and receiving the record; or

(C) in the case of transmission of a record to or by a filing office, to transmit a record by any means prescribed by filing-office rule.

(19) "Consignee" means a merchant to which goods are delivered in a consignment.

(20) "Consignment" means a transaction, regardless of its form, in which a person delivers goods to a merchant for the purpose of sale and:

(A) the merchant:

(i) deals in goods of that kind under a name other than the name of the person making delivery;

(ii) is not an auctioneer; and

(iii) is not generally known by its creditors to be substantially engaged in selling the goods of others;

(B) with respect to each delivery, the aggregate value of the goods is $1,000 or more at the time of delivery;

(C) the goods are not consumer goods immediately before delivery; and

(D) the transaction does not create a security interest that secures an obligation.

(21) "Consignor" means a person that delivers goods to a consignee in a consignment.

(22) "Consumer debtor" means a debtor in a consumer transaction.

(23) "Consumer goods" means goods that are used or bought for use primarily for personal, family, or household purposes.

(24) "Consumer-goods transaction" means a consumer transaction in which:

(A) an individual incurs an obligation primarily for personal, family, or household purposes; and

(B) a security interest in consumer goods secures the obligation.

(25) "Consumer obligor" means an obligor who is an individual and who incurred the obligation as part of a transaction entered into primarily for personal, family, or household purposes.

(26) "Consumer transaction" means a transaction in which (i) an individual incurs an obligation primarily for personal, family, or household purposes, (ii) a security interest secures the obligation, and (iii) the collateral is held or acquired primarily for personal, family, or household purposes. The term includes consumer-goods transactions.

(27) "Continuation statement" means an amendment of a financing statement which:

(A) identifies, by its file number, the initial financing statement to which it relates; and

(B) indicates that it is a continuation statement for, or that it is filed to continue the effectiveness of, the identified financing statement.

(28) "Debtor" means:

(A) a person having an interest, other than a security interest or other lien, in the collateral, whether or not the person is an obligor;

(B) a seller of accounts, chattel paper, payment intangibles, or promissory notes; or

(C) a consignee.

(29) "Deposit account" means a demand, time, savings, passbook, or similar account maintained with a bank. The term does not include investment property or accounts evidenced by an instrument.

(30) "Document" means a document of title or a receipt of the type described in Section 7—201(2).

(31) "Electronic chattel paper" means chattel paper evidenced by a record or records consisting of information stored in an electronic medium.

(32) "Encumbrance" means a right, other than an ownership interest, in real property. The term includes mortgages and other liens on real property.

(33) "Equipment" means goods other than inventory, farm products, or consumer goods.

(34) "Farm products" means goods, other than standing timber, with respect to which the debtor is engaged in a farming operation and which are:

(A) crops grown, growing, or to be grown, including:

(i) crops produced on trees, vines, and bushes; and

(ii) aquatic goods produced in aquacultural operations;

(B) livestock, born or unborn, including aquatic goods produced in aquacultural operations;

(C) supplies used or produced in a farming operation; or

(D) products of crops or livestock in their unmanufactured states.

(35) "Farming operation" means raising, cultivating, propagating, fattening, grazing, or any other farming, livestock, or aquacultural operation.

(36) "File number" means the number assigned to an initial financing statement pursuant to Section 9—519(a).

(37) "Filing office" means an office designated in Section 9—501 as the place to file a financing statement.

(38) "Filing-office rule" means a rule adopted pursuant to Section 9—526.

(39) "Financing statement" means a record or records composed of an initial financing statement and any filed record relating to the initial financing statement.

(40) "Fixture filing" means the filing of a financing statement covering goods that are or are to become fixtures and satisfying Section 9—502(a) and (b). The term includes the filing of a financing statement covering goods of a transmitting utility which are or are to become fixtures.

(41) "Fixtures" means goods that have become so related to particular real property that an interest in them arises under real property law.

(42) "General intangible" means any personal property, including things in action, other than accounts, chattel paper, commercial tort claims, deposit accounts, documents, goods, instruments, investment property, letter-of-credit rights, letters of credit, money, and oil, gas, or other minerals before extraction. The term includes payment intangibles and software.

(43) "Good faith" means honesty in fact and the observance of reasonable commercial standards of fair dealing.

(44) "Goods" means all things that are movable when a security interest attaches. The term includes (i) fixtures, (ii) standing timber that is to be cut and removed under a conveyance or contract for sale, (iii) the unborn young of animals, (iv) crops grown, growing, or to be grown, even if the crops are produced on trees, vines, or bushes, and (v) manufactured homes.

The term also includes a computer program embedded in goods and any supporting information provided in connection with a transaction relating to the program if (i) the program is associated with the goods in such a manner that it customarily is considered part of the goods, or (ii) by becoming the owner of the goods, a person acquires a right to use the program in connection with the goods. The term does not include a computer program embedded in goods that consist solely of the medium in which the program is embedded. The term also does not include accounts, chattel paper, commercial tort claims, deposit accounts, documents, general intangibles, instruments, investment property, letter-of-credit rights, letters of credit, money, or oil, gas, or other minerals before extraction.

(45) "Governmental unit" means a subdivision, agency, department, county, parish, municipality, or other unit of the government of the United States, a State, or a foreign country. The term includes an organization having a separate corporate existence if the organization is eligible to issue debt on which interest is exempt from income taxation under the laws of the United States.

(46) "Health-care-insurance receivable" means an interest in or claim under a policy of insurance which is a right to payment of a monetary obligation for health-care goods or services provided.

(47) "Instrument" means a negotiable instrument or any other writing that evidences a right to the payment of a monetary obligation, is not itself a security agreement or lease, and is of a type that in ordinary course of business is transferred by delivery with any necessary indorsement or assignment. The term does not include (i) investment property, (ii) letters of credit, or (iii) writings that evidence a right to payment arising out of the use of a credit or charge card or information contained on or for use with the card.

(48) "Inventory" means goods, other than farm products, which:

    (A) are leased by a person as lessor;

    (B) are held by a person for sale or lease or to be furnished under a contract of service;

    (C) are furnished by a person under a contract of service; or

    (D) consist of raw materials, work in process, or materials used or consumed in a business.

(49) "Investment property" means a security, whether certificated or uncertificated, security entitlement, securities account, commodity contract, or commodity account.

(50) "Jurisdiction of organization", with respect to a registered organization, means the jurisdiction under whose law the organization is organized.

(51) "Letter-of-credit right" means a right to payment or performance under a letter of credit, whether or not the beneficiary has demanded or is at the time entitled to demand payment or performance. The term does not include the right of a beneficiary to demand payment or performance under a letter of credit.

(52) "Lien creditor" means:

    (A) a creditor that has acquired a lien on the property involved by attachment, levy, or the like;

    (B) an assignee for benefit of creditors from the time of assignment;

    (C) a trustee in bankruptcy from the date of the filing of the petition; or

    (D) a receiver in equity from the time of appointment.

(53) "Manufactured home" means a structure, transportable in one or more sections, which, in the traveling mode, is eight body feet or more in width or 40 body feet or more in length, or, when erected on site, is 320 or more square feet, and which is built on a permanent chassis and designed to be used as a dwelling with or without a permanent foundation when connected to the required utilities, and includes the plumbing, heating, air-conditioning, and electrical systems contained therein. The term includes any structure that meets all of the requirements of this paragraph except the size requirements and with respect to which the manufacturer voluntarily files a certification required by the United States Secretary of Housing and Urban Development and complies with the standards established under Title 42 of the United States Code.

(54) "Manufactured-home transaction" means a secured transaction:

    (A) that creates a purchase-money security interest in a manufactured home, other than a manufactured home held as inventory; or

    (B) in which a manufactured home, other than a manufactured home held as inventory, is the primary collateral.

(55) "Mortgage" means a consensual interest in real property, including fixtures, which secures payment or performance of an obligation.

(56) "New debtor" means a person that becomes bound as debtor under Section 9—203(d) by a security agreement previously entered into by another person.

(57) "New value" means (i) money, (ii) money's worth in property, services, or new credit, or (iii) release by a transferee of an interest in property previously transferred to the transferee. The term does not include an obligation substituted for another obligation.

(58) "Noncash proceeds" means proceeds other than cash proceeds.

(59) "Obligor" means a person that, with respect to an obligation secured by a security interest in or an agricultural lien on the collateral, (i) owes payment or other performance of the obligation, (ii) has provided property other than the collateral to secure payment or other performance of the obligation, or (iii) is otherwise accountable in whole or in part for payment or other performance of the obligation. The term does not include issuers or nominated persons under a letter of credit.

(60) "Original debtor", except as used in Section 9—310(c), means a person that, as debtor, entered into a security agreement to which a new debtor has become bound under Section 9—203(d).

(61) "Payment intangible" means a general intangible under which the account debtor's principal obligation is a monetary obligation.

(62) "Person related to", with respect to an individual, means:
  (A) the spouse of the individual;
  (B) a brother, brother-in-law, sister, or sister-in-law of the individual;
  (C) an ancestor or lineal descendant of the individual or the individual's spouse; or
  (D) any other relative, by blood or marriage, of the individual or the individual's spouse who shares the same home with the individual.

(63) "Person related to", with respect to an organization, means:
  (A) a person directly or indirectly controlling, controlled by, or under common control with the organization;
  (B) an officer or director of, or a person performing similar functions with respect to, the organization;
  (C) an officer or director of, or a person performing similar functions with respect to, a person described in subparagraph (A);
  (D) the spouse of an individual described in subparagraph (A), (B), or (C); or
  (E) an individual who is related by blood or marriage to an individual described in subparagraph (A), (B), (C), or (D) and shares the same home with the individual.

(64) "Proceeds", except as used in Section 9—609 (b), means the following property:
  (A) whatever is acquired upon the sale, lease, license, exchange, or other disposition of collateral;
  (B) whatever is collected on, or distributed on account of, collateral;
  (C) rights arising out of collateral;
  (D) to the extent of the value of collateral, claims arising out of the loss, nonconformity, or interference with the use of, defects or infringement of rights in, or damage to, the collateral; or
  (E) to the extent of the value of collateral and to the extent payable to the debtor or the secured party, insurance payable by reason of the loss or nonconformity of, defects or infringement of rights in, or damage to, the collateral.

(65) "Promissory note" means an instrument that evidences a promise to pay a monetary obligation, does not evidence an order to pay, and does not contain an acknowledgment by a bank that the bank has received for deposit a sum of money or funds.

(66) "Proposal" means a record authenticated by a secured party which includes the terms on which the secured party is willing to accept collateral in full or partial satisfaction of the obligation it secures pursuant to Sections 9—620, 9—621, and 9—622.

(67) "Public-finance transaction" means a secured transaction in connection with which:
  (A) debt securities are issued;
  (B) all or a portion of the securities issued have an initial stated maturity of at least 20 years; and
  (C) the debtor, obligor, secured party, account debtor or other person obligated on collateral, assignor or assignee of a secured obligation, or assignor or assignee of a security interest is a State or a governmental unit of a State.

(68) "Pursuant to commitment", with respect to an advance made or other value given by a secured party, means pursuant to the secured party's obligation, whether or not a subsequent event of default or other event not within the secured party's control has relieved or may relieve the secured party from its obligation.

(69) "Record", except as used in "for record", "of record", "record or legal title", and "record owner", means information that is inscribed on a tangible medium or which is stored in an electronic or other medium and is retrievable in perceivable form.

(70) "Registered organization" means an organization organized solely under the law of a single State or the United States and as to which the State or the United States must maintain a public record showing the organization to have been organized.

(71) "Secondary obligor" means an obligor to the extent that:

    (A) the obligor's obligation is secondary; or

    (B) the obligor has a right of recourse with respect to an obligation secured by collateral against the debtor, another obligor, or property of either.

(72) "Secured party" means:

    (A) a person in whose favor a security interest is created or provided for under a security agreement, whether or not any obligation to be secured is outstanding;

    (B) a person that holds an agricultural lien;

    (C) a consignor;

    (D) a person to which accounts, chattel paper, payment intangibles, or promissory notes have been sold;

    (E) a trustee, indenture trustee, agent, collateral agent, or other representative in whose favor a security interest or agricultural lien is created or provided for; or

    (F) a person that holds a security interest arising under Section 2—401, 2—505, 2—711(3), 2A—508(5), 4—210, or 5—118.

(73) "Security agreement" means an agreement that creates or provides for a security interest.

(74) "Send", in connection with a record or notification, means:

    (A) to deposit in the mail, deliver for transmission, or transmit by any other usual means of communication, with postage or cost of transmission provided for, addressed to any address reasonable under the circumstances; or

    (B) to cause the record or notification to be received within the time that it would have been received if properly sent under subparagraph (A).

(75) "Software" means a computer program and any supporting information provided in connection with a transaction relating to the program. The term does not include a computer program that is included in the definition of goods.

(76) "State" means a State of the United States, the District of Columbia, Puerto Rico, the United States Virgin Islands, or any territory or insular possession subject to the jurisdiction of the United States.

(77) "Supporting obligation" means a letter-of-credit right or secondary obligation that supports the payment or performance of an account, chattel paper, a document, a general intangible, an instrument, or investment property.

(78) "Tangible chattel paper" means chattel paper evidenced by a record or records consisting of information that is inscribed on a tangible medium.

(79) "Termination statement" means an amendment of a financing statement which:

    (A) identifies, by its file number, the initial financing statement to which it relates; and

    (B) indicates either that it is a termination statement or that the identified financing statement is no longer effective.

(80) "Transmitting utility" means a person primarily engaged in the business of:

    (A) operating a railroad, subway, street railway, or trolley bus;

    (B) transmitting communications electrically, electromagnetically, or by light;

    (C) transmitting goods by pipeline or sewer; or

    (D) transmitting or producing and transmitting electricity, steam, gas, or water.

(b) The following definitions in other articles apply to this article:

"Applicant."	Section 5—102
"Beneficiary."	Section 5—102
"Broker."	Section 8—102
"Certificated security."	Section 8—102
"Check."	Section 3—104
"Clearing corporation."	Section 8—102
"Contract for sale."	Section 2—106
"Customer."	Section 4—104
"Entitlement holder."	Section 8—102
"Financial asset."	Section 8—102
"Holder in due course."	Section 3—302
"Issuer" (with respect to a letter of credit or letter-of-credit right).	Section 5—102
"Issuer" (with respect to a security).	Section 8—201
"Lease."	Section 2A—103
"Lease agreement."	Section 2A—103
"Lease contract."	Section 2A—103
"Leasehold interest."	Section 2A—103
"Lessee."	Section 2A—103
"Lessee in ordinary course of business."	Section 2A—103
"Lessor."	Section 2A—103

"Lessor's residual interest."	Section 2A—103
"Letter of credit."	Section 5—102
"Merchant."	Section 2—104
"Negotiable instrument."	Section 3—104
"Nominated person."	Section 5—102
"Note."	Section 3—104
"Proceeds of a letter of credit."	Section 5—114
"Prove."	Section 3—103
"Sale."	Section 2—106
"Securities account."	Section 8—501
"Securities intermediary."	Section 8—102
"Security."	Section 8—102
"Security certificate."	Section 8—102
"Security entitlement."	Section 8—102
"Uncertificated security."	Section 8—102

(c) Article 1 contains general definitions and principles of construction and interpretation applicable throughout this article.

Amended in 1999 and 2000.

§9—103. PURCHASE-MONEY SECURITY INTEREST; APPLICATION OF PAYMENTS; BURDEN OF ESTABLISHING

(a) In this section:

(1) "purchase-money collateral" means goods or software that secures a purchase-money obligation incurred with respect to that collateral; and

(2) "purchase-money obligation" means an obligation of an obligor incurred as all or part of the price of the collateral or for value given to enable the debtor to acquire rights in or the use of the collateral if the value is in fact so used.

(b) A security interest in goods is a purchase-money security interest:

(1) to the extent that the goods are purchase-money collateral with respect to that security interest;

(2) if the security interest is in inventory that is or was purchase-money collateral, also to the extent that the security interest secures a purchase-money obligation incurred with respect to other inventory in which the secured party holds or held a purchase-money security interest; and

(3) also to the extent that the security interest secures a purchase-money obligation incurred with respect to software in which the secured party holds or held a purchase-money security interest.

(c) A security interest in software is a purchase-money security interest to the extent that the security interest also secures a purchase-money obligation incurred with respect to goods in which the secured party holds or held a purchase-money security interest if:

(1) the debtor acquired its interest in the software in an integrated transaction in which it acquired an interest in the goods; and

(2) the debtor acquired its interest in the software for the principal purpose of using the software in the goods.

(d) The security interest of a consignor in goods that are the subject of a consignment is a purchase-money security interest in inventory.

(e) In a transaction other than a consumer-goods transaction, if the extent to which a security interest is a purchase-money security interest depends on the application of a payment to a particular obligation, the payment must be applied:

(1) in accordance with any reasonable method of application to which the parties agree;

(2) in the absence of the parties' agreement to a reasonable method, in accordance with any intention of the obligor manifested at or before the time of payment; or

(3) in the absence of an agreement to a reasonable method and a timely manifestation of the obligor's intention, in the following order:

(A) to obligations that are not secured; and

(B) if more than one obligation is secured, to obligations secured by purchase-money security interests in the order in which those obligations were incurred.

(f) In a transaction other than a consumer-goods transaction, a purchase-money security interest does not lose its status as such, even if:

(1) the purchase-money collateral also secures an obligation that is not a purchase-money obligation;

(2) collateral that is not purchase-money collateral also secures the purchase-money obligation; or

(3) the purchase-money obligation has been renewed, refinanced, consolidated, or restructured.

(g) In a transaction other than a consumer-goods transaction, a secured party claiming a purchase-money security interest has the burden of establishing the extent to which the security interest is a purchase-money security interest.

(h) The limitation of the rules in subsections (e), (f), and (g) to transactions other than consumer-goods transactions is intended to leave to the court the determination of the proper rules in consumer-goods transactions. The court may not infer from that limitation the nature of the proper rule in consumer-goods transactions and may continue to apply established approaches.

§9—104. CONTROL OF DEPOSIT ACCOUNT

(a) A secured party has control of a deposit account if:

(1) the secured party is the bank with which the deposit account is maintained;

(2) the debtor, secured party, and bank have agreed in an authenticated record that the bank will comply with instructions originated by the secured party directing disposition of the funds in the deposit account without further consent by the debtor; or

(3) the secured party becomes the bank's customer with respect to the deposit account.

(b) A secured party that has satisfied subsection (a) has control, even if the debtor retains the right to direct the disposition of funds from the deposit account.

§9—105. CONTROL OF ELECTRONIC CHATTEL PAPER

A secured party has control of electronic chattel paper if the record or records comprising the chattel paper are created, stored, and assigned in such a manner that:

(1) a single authoritative copy of the record or records exists which is unique, identifiable and, except as otherwise provided in paragraphs (4), (5), and (6), unalterable;

(2) the authoritative copy identifies the secured party as the assignee of the record or records;

(3) the authoritative copy is communicated to and maintained by the secured party or its designated custodian;

(4) copies or revisions that add or change an identified assignee of the authoritative copy can be made only with the participation of the secured party;

(5) each copy of the authoritative copy and any copy of a copy is readily identifiable as a copy that is not the authoritative copy; and

(6) any revision of the authoritative copy is readily identifiable as an authorized or unauthorized revision.

§9—106. CONTROL OF INVESTMENT PROPERTY

(a) A person has control of a certificated security, uncertificated security, or security entitlement as provided in Section 8—106.

(b) A secured party has control of a commodity contract if:

(1) the secured party is the commodity intermediary with which the commodity contract is carried; or

(2) the commodity customer, secured party, and commodity intermediary have agreed that the commodity intermediary will apply any value distributed on account of the commodity contract as directed by the secured party without further consent by the commodity customer.

(c) A secured party having control of all security entitlements or commodity contracts carried in a securities account or commodity account has control over the securities account or commodity account.

§9—107. CONTROL OF LETTER-OF-CREDIT RIGHT

A secured party has control of a letter-of-credit right to the extent of any right to payment or performance by the issuer or any nominated person if the issuer or nominated person has consented to an assignment of proceeds of the letter of credit under Section 5—114(c) or otherwise applicable law or practice.

§9—108. SUFFICIENCY OF DESCRIPTION

(a) Except as otherwise provided in subsections (c), (d), and (e), a description of personal or real property is sufficient, whether or not it is specific, if it reasonably identifies what is described.

(b) Except as otherwise provided in subsection (d), a description of collateral reasonably identifies the collateral if it identifies the collateral by:

(1) specific listing;

(2) category;

(3) except as otherwise provided in subsection (e), a type of collateral defined in [the Uniform Commercial Code];

(4) quantity;

(5) computational or allocational formula or procedure; or

(6) except as otherwise provided in subsection (c), any other method, if the identity of the collateral is objectively determinable.

(c) A description of collateral as "all the debtor's assets" or "all the debtor's personal property" or using words of similar import does not reasonably identify the collateral.

(d) Except as otherwise provided in subsection (e), a description of a security entitlement, securities account, or commodity account is sufficient if it describes:

(1) the collateral by those terms or as investment property; or

(2) the underlying financial asset or commodity contract.

(e) A description only by type of collateral defined in [the Uniform Commercial Code] is an insufficient description of:

(1) a commercial tort claim; or

(2) in a consumer transaction, consumer goods, a security entitlement, a securities account, or a commodity account.

[Subpart 2. Applicability of Article]

§9—109. SCOPE

(a) Except as otherwise provided in subsections (c) and (d), this article applies to:

(1) a transaction, regardless of its form, that creates a security interest in personal property or fixtures by contract;

(2) an agricultural lien;

(3) a sale of accounts, chattel paper, payment intangibles, or promissory notes;

(4) a consignment;

(5) a security interest arising under Section 2—401, 2—505, 2—711(3), or 2A—508(5), as provided in Section 9—110; and

(6) a security interest arising under Section 4—210 or 5—118.

(b) The application of this article to a security interest in a secured obligation is not affected by the fact that the obligation is itself secured by a transaction or interest to which this article does not apply.

(c) This article does not apply to the extent that:

(1) a statute, regulation, or treaty of the United States preempts this article;

(2) another statute of this State expressly governs the creation, perfection, priority, or enforcement of a security interest created by this State or a governmental unit of this State;

(3) a statute of another State, a foreign country, or a governmental unit of another State or a foreign country, other than a statute generally applicable to security interests, expressly governs creation, perfection, priority, or enforcement of a security interest created by the State, country, or governmental unit; or

(4) the rights of a transferee beneficiary or nominated person under a letter of credit are independent and superior under Section 5—114.

(d) This article does not apply to:

(1) a landlord's lien, other than an agricultural lien;

(2) a lien, other than an agricultural lien, given by statute or other rule of law for services or materials, but Section 9—333 applies with respect to priority of the lien;

(3) an assignment of a claim for wages, salary, or other compensation of an employee;

(4) a sale of accounts, chattel paper, payment intangibles, or promissory notes as part of a sale of the business out of which they arose;

(5) an assignment of accounts, chattel paper, payment intangibles, or promissory notes which is for the purpose of collection only;

(6) an assignment of a right to payment under a contract to an assignee that is also obligated to perform under the contract;

(7) an assignment of a single account, payment intangible, or promissory note to an assignee in full or partial satisfaction of a preexisting indebtedness;

(8) a transfer of an interest in or an assignment of a claim under a policy of insurance, other than an assignment by or to a health-care provider of a health-care-insurance receivable and any subsequent assignment of the right to payment, but Sections 9—315 and 9—322 apply with respect to proceeds and priorities in proceeds;

(9) an assignment of a right represented by a judgment, other than a judgment taken on a right to payment that was collateral;

(10) a right of recoupment or set-off, but:

(A) Section 9—340 applies with respect to the effectiveness of rights of recoupment or set-off against deposit accounts; and

(B) Section 9—404 applies with respect to defenses or claims of an account debtor;

(11) the creation or transfer of an interest in or lien on real property, including a lease or rents thereunder, except to the extent that provision is made for:

(A) liens on real property in Sections 9—203 and 9—308;

(B) fixtures in Section 9—334;

(C) fixture filings in Sections 9—501, 9—502, 9—512, 9—516, and 9—519; and

(D) security agreements covering personal and real property in Section 9—604;

(12) an assignment of a claim arising in tort, other than a commercial tort claim, but Sections 9—315 and 9—322 apply with respect to proceeds and priorities in proceeds; or

(13) an assignment of a deposit account in a consumer transaction, but Sections 9—315 and 9—322 apply with respect to proceeds and priorities in proceeds.

§9—110. SECURITY INTERESTS ARISING UNDER ARTICLE 2 OR 2A

A security interest arising under Section 2—401, 2—505, 2—711(3), or 2A—508(5) is subject to this article. However, until the debtor obtains possession of the goods:

(1) the security interest is enforceable, even if Section 9—203(b)(3) has not been satisfied;

(2) filing is not required to perfect the security interest;

(3) the rights of the secured party after default by the debtor are governed by Article 2 or 2A; and

(4) the security interest has priority over a conflicting security interest created by the debtor.

Part 2 Effectiveness of Security Agreement; Attachment of Security Interest; Rights of Parties to Security Agreement [Subpart 1. Effectiveness and Attachment]

§9—201. GENERAL EFFECTIVENESS OF SECURITY AGREEMENT

(a) Except as otherwise provided in [the Uniform Commercial Code], a security agreement is effective according to its terms between the parties, against purchasers of the collateral, and against creditors.

(b) A transaction subject to this article is subject to any applicable rule of law which establishes a different rule for consumers and [insert reference to (i) any other statute or regulation that regulates the rates, charges, agreements, and practices for loans, credit sales, or other extensions of credit and (ii) any consumer-protection statute or regulation].

(c) In case of conflict between this article and a rule of law, statute, or regulation described in subsection (b), the rule of law, statute, or regulation controls. Failure to comply with a statute or regulation described in subsection (b) has only the effect the statute or regulation specifies.

(d) This article does not:

(1) validate any rate, charge, agreement, or practice that violates a rule of law, statute, or regulation described in subsection (b); or

(2) extend the application of the rule of law, statute, or regulation to a transaction not otherwise subject to it.

§9—202. TITLE TO COLLATERAL IMMATERIAL

Except as otherwise provided with respect to consignments or sales of accounts, chattel paper, payment intangibles, or promissory notes, the provisions of this article with regard to rights and obligations apply whether title to collateral is in the secured party or the debtor.

§9—203. ATTACHMENT AND ENFORCEABILITY OF SECURITY INTEREST; PROCEEDS; SUPPORTING OBLIGATIONS; FORMAL REQUISITES

(a) A security interest attaches to collateral when it becomes enforceable against the debtor with respect to the collateral, unless an agreement expressly postpones the time of attachment.

(b) Except as otherwise provided in subsections (c) through (i), a security interest is enforceable against the debtor and third parties with respect to the collateral only if:

(1) value has been given;

(2) the debtor has rights in the collateral or the power to transfer rights in the collateral to a secured party; and

(3) one of the following conditions is met:

(A) the debtor has authenticated a security agreement that provides a description of the collateral and, if the security interest covers timber to be cut, a description of the land concerned;

(B) the collateral is not a certificated security and is in the possession of the secured party under Section 9—313 pursuant to the debtor's security agreement;

(C) the collateral is a certificated security in registered form and the security certificate has been delivered to the secured party under Section 8—301 pursuant to the debtor's security agreement; or

(D) the collateral is deposit accounts, electronic chattel paper, investment property, or letter-of-credit rights, and the secured party has control under Section 9—104, 9—105, 9—106, or 9—107 pursuant to the debtor's security agreement.

(c) Subsection (b) is subject to Section 4—210 on the security interest of a collecting bank, Section 5—118 on the security interest of a letter-of-credit issuer or nominated person, Section 9—110 on a security interest arising under Article 2 or 2A, and Section 9—206 on security interests in investment property.

(d) A person becomes bound as debtor by a security agreement entered into by another person if, by operation of law other than this article or by contract:

(1) the security agreement becomes effective to create a security interest in the person's property; or

(2) the person becomes generally obligated for the obligations of the other person, including the obligation secured under the security agreement, and acquires or succeeds to all or substantially all of the assets of the other person.

(e) If a new debtor becomes bound as debtor by a security agreement entered into by another person:

(1) the agreement satisfies subsection (b)(3) with respect to existing or after-acquired property of the new debtor to the extent the property is described in the agreement; and

(2) another agreement is not necessary to make a security interest in the property enforceable.

(f) The attachment of a security interest in collateral gives the secured party the rights to proceeds provided by Section 9—315 and is also attachment of a security interest in a supporting obligation for the collateral.

(g) The attachment of a security interest in a right to payment or performance secured by a security interest or other lien on personal or real property is also attachment of a security interest in the security interest, mortgage, or other lien.

(h) The attachment of a security interest in a securities account is also attachment of a security interest in the security entitlements carried in the securities account.

(i) The attachment of a security interest in a commodity account is also attachment of a security interest in the commodity contracts carried in the commodity account.

§9—204. AFTER-ACQUIRED PROPERTY; FUTURE ADVANCES

(a) Except as otherwise provided in subsection (b), a security agreement may create or provide for a security interest in after-acquired collateral.

(b) A security interest does not attach under a term constituting an after-acquired property clause to:

(1) consumer goods, other than an accession when given as additional security, unless the debtor acquires rights in them within 10 days after the secured party gives value; or

(2) a commercial tort claim.

(c) A security agreement may provide that collateral secures, or that accounts, chattel paper, payment intangibles, or promissory notes are sold in connection with, future advances or other value, whether or not the advances or value are given pursuant to commitment.

§9—205. USE OR DISPOSITION OF COLLATERAL PERMISSIBLE

(a) A security interest is not invalid or fraudulent against creditors solely because:

(1) the debtor has the right or ability to:

(A) use, commingle, or dispose of all or part of the collateral, including returned or repossessed goods;

(B) collect, compromise, enforce, or otherwise deal with collateral;

(C) accept the return of collateral or make repossessions; or

(D) use, commingle, or dispose of proceeds; or

(2) the secured party fails to require the debtor to account for proceeds or replace collateral.

(b) This section does not relax the requirements of possession if attachment, perfection, or enforcement of a security interest depends upon possession of the collateral by the secured party.

§9—206. SECURITY INTEREST ARISING IN PURCHASE OR DELIVERY OF FINANCIAL ASSET

(a) A security interest in favor of a securities intermediary attaches to a person's security entitlement if:

(1) the person buys a financial asset through the securities intermediary in a transaction in which the person is obligated to pay the purchase price

to the securities intermediary at the time of the purchase; and

(2) the securities intermediary credits the financial asset to the buyer's securities account before the buyer pays the securities intermediary.

(b) The security interest described in subsection (a) secures the person's obligation to pay for the financial asset.

(c) A security interest in favor of a person that delivers a certificated security or other financial asset represented by a writing attaches to the security or other financial asset if:

(1) the security or other financial asset:

(A) in the ordinary course of business is transferred by delivery with any necessary indorsement or assignment; and

(B) is delivered under an agreement between persons in the business of dealing with such securities or financial assets; and

(2) the agreement calls for delivery against payment.

(d) The security interest described in subsection (c) secures the obligation to make payment for the delivery.

[Subpart 2. Rights and Duties]

§9—207. RIGHTS AND DUTIES OF SECURED PARTY HAVING POSSESSION OR CONTROL OF COLLATERAL

(a) Except as otherwise provided in subsection (d), a secured party shall use reasonable care in the custody and preservation of collateral in the secured party's possession. In the case of chattel paper or an instrument, reasonable care includes taking necessary steps to preserve rights against prior parties unless otherwise agreed.

(b) Except as otherwise provided in subsection (d), if a secured party has possession of collateral:

(1) reasonable expenses, including the cost of insurance and payment of taxes or other charges, incurred in the custody, preservation, use, or operation of the collateral are chargeable to the debtor and are secured by the collateral;

(2) the risk of accidental loss or damage is on the debtor to the extent of a deficiency in any effective insurance coverage;

(3) the secured party shall keep the collateral identifiable, but fungible collateral may be commingled; and

(4) the secured party may use or operate the collateral:

(A) for the purpose of preserving the collateral or its value;

(B) as permitted by an order of a court having competent jurisdiction; or

(C) except in the case of consumer goods, in the manner and to the extent agreed by the debtor.

(c) Except as otherwise provided in subsection (d), a secured party having possession of collateral or control of collateral under Section 9—104, 9—105, 9—106, or 9—107:

(1) may hold as additional security any proceeds, except money or funds, received from the collateral;

(2) shall apply money or funds received from the collateral to reduce the secured obligation, unless remitted to the debtor; and

(3) may create a security interest in the collateral.

(d) If the secured party is a buyer of accounts, chattel paper, payment intangibles, or promissory notes or a consignor:

(1) subsection (a) does not apply unless the secured party is entitled under an agreement:

(A) to charge back uncollected collateral; or

(B) otherwise to full or limited recourse against the debtor or a secondary obligor based on the nonpayment or other default of an account debtor or other obligor on the collateral; and

(2) subsections (b) and (c) do not apply.

§9—208. ADDITIONAL DUTIES OF SECURED PARTY HAVING CONTROL OF COLLATERAL

(a) This section applies to cases in which there is no outstanding secured obligation and the secured party is not committed to make advances, incur obligations, or otherwise give value.

(b) Within 10 days after receiving an authenticated demand by the debtor:

(1) a secured party having control of a deposit account under Section 9—104(a)(2) shall send to the bank with which the deposit account is maintained an authenticated statement that releases the bank from any further obligation to comply with instructions originated by the secured party;

(2) a secured party having control of a deposit account under Section 9—104(a)(3) shall:

(A) pay the debtor the balance on deposit in the deposit account; or

(B) transfer the balance on deposit into a deposit account in the debtor's name;

(3) a secured party, other than a buyer, having control of electronic chattel paper under Section 9—105 shall:

(A) communicate the authoritative copy of the electronic chattel paper to the debtor or its designated custodian;

(B) if the debtor designates a custodian that is the designated custodian with which the authoritative copy of the electronic chattel paper is maintained for the secured party, communicate to the custodian an authenticated record releasing the designated custodian from any further obligation to comply with instructions originated by the secured party and instructing the custodian to comply with instructions originated by the debtor; and

(C) take appropriate action to enable the debtor or its designated custodian to make copies of or revisions to the authoritative copy which add or change an identified assignee of the authoritative copy without the consent of the secured party;

(4) a secured party having control of investment property under Section 8—106(d)(2) or 9—106 (b) shall send to the securities intermediary or commodity intermediary with which the security entitlement or commodity contract is maintained an authenticated record that releases the securities intermediary or commodity intermediary from any further obligation to comply with entitlement orders or directions originated by the secured party; and

(5) a secured party having control of a letter-of-credit right under Section 9—107 shall send to each person having an unfulfilled obligation to pay or deliver proceeds of the letter of credit to the secured party an authenticated release from any further obligation to pay or deliver proceeds of the letter of credit to the secured party.

§9—209. DUTIES OF SECURED PARTY IF ACCOUNT DEBTOR HAS BEEN NOTIFIED OF ASSIGNMENT

(a) Except as otherwise provided in subsection (c), this section applies if:

(1) there is no outstanding secured obligation; and

(2) the secured party is not committed to make advances, incur obligations, or otherwise give value.

(b) Within 10 days after receiving an authenticated demand by the debtor, a secured party shall send to an account debtor that has received notification of an assignment to the secured party as assignee under Section 9—406(a) an authenticated record that releases the account debtor from any further obligation to the secured party.

(c) This section does not apply to an assignment constituting the sale of an account, chattel paper, or payment intangible.

§9—210. REQUEST FOR ACCOUNTING; REQUEST REGARDING LIST OF COLLATERAL OR STATEMENT OF ACCOUNT

(a) In this section:

(1) "Request" means a record of a type described in paragraph (2), (3), or (4).

(2) "Request for an accounting" means a record authenticated by a debtor requesting that the recipient provide an accounting of the unpaid obligations secured by collateral and reasonably identifying the transaction or relationship that is the subject of the request.

(3) "Request regarding a list of collateral" means a record authenticated by a debtor requesting that the recipient approve or correct a list of what the debtor believes to be the collateral securing an obligation and reasonably identifying the transaction or relationship that is the subject of the request.

(4) "Request regarding a statement of account" means a record authenticated by a debtor requesting that the recipient approve or correct a statement indicating what the debtor believes to be the aggregate amount of unpaid obligations secured by collateral as of a specified date and reasonably identifying the transaction or relationship that is the subject of the request.

(b) Subject to subsections (c), (d), (e), and (f), a secured party, other than a buyer of accounts, chattel paper, payment intangibles, or promissory notes or a consignor, shall comply with a request within 14 days after receipt:

(1) in the case of a request for an accounting, by authenticating and sending to the debtor an accounting; and

(2) in the case of a request regarding a list of collateral or a request regarding a statement of account, by authenticating and sending to the debtor an approval or correction.

(c) A secured party that claims a security interest in all of a particular type of collateral owned by the debtor may comply with a request regarding a list of collateral by sending to the debtor an authenticated record including a statement to that effect within 14 days after receipt.

(d) A person that receives a request regarding a list of collateral, claims no interest in the collateral when it receives the request, and claimed an interest in the collateral at an earlier time shall comply with the request within 14 days after receipt by sending to the debtor an authenticated record:

(1) disclaiming any interest in the collateral; and

(2) if known to the recipient, providing the name and mailing address of any assignee of or successor to the recipient's interest in the collateral.

(e) A person that receives a request for an accounting or a request regarding a statement of account, claims no interest in the obligations when it receives the request, and claimed an interest in the obligations at an earlier time shall comply with the request within 14 days after receipt by sending to the debtor an authenticated record:

(1) disclaiming any interest in the obligations; and

(2) if known to the recipient, providing the name and mailing address of any assignee of or successor to the recipient's interest in the obligations.

(f) A debtor is entitled without charge to one response to a request under this section during any six-month period. The secured party may require payment of a charge not exceeding $25 for each additional response.

As amended in 1999.

Part 3 Perfection and Priority [Subpart 1. Law Governing Perfection and Priority]

§9—301. LAW GOVERNING PERFECTION AND PRIORITY OF SECURITY INTERESTS

Except as otherwise provided in Sections 9—303 through 9—306, the following rules determine the law governing perfection, the effect of perfection or nonperfection, and the priority of a security interest in collateral:

(1) Except as otherwise provided in this section, while a debtor is located in a jurisdiction, the local law of that jurisdiction governs perfection, the effect of perfection or nonperfection, and the priority of a security interest in collateral.

(2) While collateral is located in a jurisdiction, the local law of that jurisdiction governs perfection, the effect of perfection or nonperfection, and the priority of a possessory security interest in that collateral.

(3) Except as otherwise provided in paragraph (4), while negotiable documents, goods, instruments, money, or tangible chattel paper is located in a jurisdiction, the local law of that jurisdiction governs:

(A) perfection of a security interest in the goods by filing a fixture filing;

(B) perfection of a security interest in timber to be cut; and

(C) the effect of perfection or nonperfection and the priority of a nonpossessory security interest in the collateral.

(4) The local law of the jurisdiction in which the wellhead or minehead is located governs perfection, the effect of perfection or nonperfection, and the priority of a security interest in as-extracted collateral.

§9—302. LAW GOVERNING PERFECTION AND PRIORITY OF AGRICULTURAL LIENS

While farm products are located in a jurisdiction, the local law of that jurisdiction governs perfection, the effect of perfection or nonperfection, and the priority of an agricultural lien on the farm products.

§9—303. LAW GOVERNING PERFECTION AND PRIORITY OF SECURITY INTERESTS IN GOODS COVERED BY A CERTIFICATE OF TITLE

(a) This section applies to goods covered by a certificate of title, even if there is no other relationship between the jurisdiction under whose certificate of title the goods are covered and the goods or the debtor.

(b) Goods become covered by a certificate of title when a valid application for the certificate of title and the applicable fee are delivered to the appropriate authority. Goods cease to be covered by a certificate of title at the earlier of the time the certificate of title ceases to be effective under the law of the issuing jurisdiction or the time the goods become covered subsequently by a certificate of title issued by another jurisdiction.

(c) The local law of the jurisdiction under whose certificate of title the goods are covered governs perfection, the effect of perfection or nonperfection, and the priority of a security interest in goods covered by a certificate of title from the time the goods become covered by the certificate of title until the goods cease to be covered by the certificate of title.

§9—304. LAW GOVERNING PERFECTION AND PRIORITY OF SECURITY INTERESTS IN DEPOSIT ACCOUNTS

(a) The local law of a bank's jurisdiction governs perfection, the effect of perfection or nonperfection, and the priority of a security interest in a deposit account maintained with that bank.

(b) The following rules determine a bank's jurisdiction for purposes of this part:

(1) If an agreement between the bank and the debtor governing the deposit account expressly provides that a particular jurisdiction is the bank's jurisdiction for purposes of this part, this article, or [the Uniform Commercial Code], that jurisdiction is the bank's jurisdiction.

(2) If paragraph (1) does not apply and an agreement between the bank and its customer governing the deposit account expressly provides that the agreement is governed by the law of a particular jurisdiction, that jurisdiction is the bank's jurisdiction.

(3) If neither paragraph (1) nor paragraph (2) applies and an agreement between the bank and

its customer governing the deposit account expressly provides that the deposit account is maintained at an office in a particular jurisdiction, that jurisdiction is the bank's jurisdiction.

(4) If none of the preceding paragraphs applies, the bank's jurisdiction is the jurisdiction in which the office identified in an account statement as the office serving the customer's account is located.

(5) If none of the preceding paragraphs applies, the bank's jurisdiction is the jurisdiction in which the chief executive office of the bank is located.

§9—305. LAW GOVERNING PERFECTION AND PRIORITY OF SECURITY INTERESTS IN INVESTMENT PROPERTY

(a) Except as otherwise provided in subsection (c), the following rules apply:

(1) While a security certificate is located in a jurisdiction, the local law of that jurisdiction governs perfection, the effect of perfection or nonperfection, and the priority of a security interest in the certificated security represented thereby.

(2) The local law of the issuer's jurisdiction as specified in Section 8—110(d) governs perfection, the effect of perfection or nonperfection, and the priority of a security interest in an uncertificated security.

(3) The local law of the securities intermediary's jurisdiction as specified in Section 8—110(e) governs perfection, the effect of perfection or nonperfection, and the priority of a security interest in a security entitlement or securities account.

(4) The local law of the commodity intermediary's jurisdiction governs perfection, the effect of perfection or nonperfection, and the priority of a security interest in a commodity contract or commodity account.

(b) The following rules determine a commodity intermediary's jurisdiction for purposes of this part:

(1) If an agreement between the commodity intermediary and commodity customer governing the commodity account expressly provides that a particular jurisdiction is the commodity intermediary's jurisdiction for purposes of this part, this article, or [the Uniform Commercial Code], that jurisdiction is the commodity intermediary's jurisdiction.

(2) If paragraph (1) does not apply and an agreement between the commodity intermediary and commodity customer governing the commodity account expressly provides that the

agreement is governed by the law of a particular jurisdiction, that jurisdiction is the commodity intermediary's jurisdiction.

(3) If neither paragraph (1) nor paragraph (2) applies and an agreement between the commodity intermediary and commodity customer governing the commodity account expressly provides that the commodity account is maintained at an office in a particular jurisdiction, that jurisdiction is the commodity intermediary's jurisdiction.

(4) If none of the preceding paragraphs applies, the commodity intermediary's jurisdiction is the jurisdiction in which the office identified in an account statement as the office serving the commodity customer's account is located.

(5) If none of the preceding paragraphs applies, the commodity intermediary's jurisdiction is the jurisdiction in which the chief executive office of the commodity intermediary is located.

(c) The local law of the jurisdiction in which the debtor is located governs:

(1) perfection of a security interest in investment property by filing;

(2) automatic perfection of a security interest in investment property created by a broker or securities intermediary; and

(3) automatic perfection of a security interest in a commodity contract or commodity account created by a commodity intermediary.

§9—306. LAW GOVERNING PERFECTION AND PRIORITY OF SECURITY INTERESTS IN LETTER-OF-CREDIT RIGHTS

(a) Subject to subsection (c), the local law of the issuer's jurisdiction or a nominated person's jurisdiction governs perfection, the effect of perfection or nonperfection, and the priority of a security interest in a letter-of-credit right if the issuer's jurisdiction or nominated person's jurisdiction is a State.

(b) For purposes of this part, an issuer's jurisdiction or nominated person's jurisdiction is the jurisdiction whose law governs the liability of the issuer or nominated person with respect to the letter-of-credit right as provided in Section 5—116.

(c) This section does not apply to a security interest that is perfected only under Section 9—308(d).

§9—307. LOCATION OF DEBTOR

(a) In this section, "place of business" means a place where a debtor conducts its affairs.

(b) Except as otherwise provided in this section, the following rules determine a debtor's location:

(1) A debtor who is an individual is located at the individual's principal residence.

(2) A debtor that is an organization and has only one place of business is located at its place of business.

(3) A debtor that is an organization and has more than one place of business is located at its chief executive office.

(c) Subsection (b) applies only if a debtor's residence, place of business, or chief executive office, as applicable, is located in a jurisdiction whose law generally requires information concerning the existence of a nonpossessory security interest to be made generally available in a filing, recording, or registration system as a condition or result of the security interest's obtaining priority over the rights of a lien creditor with respect to the collateral. If subsection (b) does not apply, the debtor is located in the District of Columbia.

(d) A person that ceases to exist, have a residence, or have a place of business continues to be located in the jurisdiction specified by subsections (b) and (c).

(e) A registered organization that is organized under the law of a State is located in that State.

(f) Except as otherwise provided in subsection (i), a registered organization that is organized under the law of the United States and a branch or agency of a bank that is not organized under the law of the United States or a State are located:

(1) in the State that the law of the United States designates, if the law designates a State of location;

(2) in the State that the registered organization, branch, or agency designates, if the law of the United States authorizes the registered organization, branch, or agency to designate its State of location; or

(3) in the District of Columbia, if neither paragraph (1) nor paragraph (2) applies.

(g) A registered organization continues to be located in the jurisdiction specified by subsection (e) or (f) notwithstanding:

(1) the suspension, revocation, forfeiture, or lapse of the registered organization's status as such in its jurisdiction of organization; or

(2) the dissolution, winding up, or cancellation of the existence of the registered organization.

(h) The United States is located in the District of Columbia.

(i) A branch or agency of a bank that is not organized under the law of the United States or a State is located in the State in which the branch or agency is licensed, if all branches and agencies of the bank are licensed in only one State.

(j) A foreign air carrier under the Federal Aviation Act of 1958, as amended, is located at the designated office of the agent upon which service of process may be made on behalf of the carrier.

(k) This section applies only for purposes of this part.

[Subpart 2. Perfection]

§9—308. WHEN SECURITY INTEREST OR AGRICULTURAL LIEN IS PERFECTED; CONTINUITY OF PERFECTION

(a) Except as otherwise provided in this section and Section 9—309, a security interest is perfected if it has attached and all of the applicable requirements for perfection in Sections 9—310 through 9—316 have been satisfied. A security interest is perfected when it attaches if the applicable requirements are satisfied before the security interest attaches.

(b) An agricultural lien is perfected if it has become effective and all of the applicable requirements for perfection in Section 9—310 have been satisfied. An agricultural lien is perfected when it becomes effective if the applicable requirements are satisfied before the agricultural lien becomes effective.

(c) A security interest or agricultural lien is perfected continuously if it is originally perfected by one method under this article and is later perfected by another method under this article, without an intermediate period when it was unperfected.

(d) Perfection of a security interest in collateral also perfects a security interest in a supporting obligation for the collateral.

(e) Perfection of a security interest in a right to payment or performance also perfects a security interest in a security interest, mortgage, or other lien on personal or real property securing the right.

(f) Perfection of a security interest in a securities account also perfects a security interest in the security entitlements carried in the securities account.

(g) Perfection of a security interest in a commodity account also perfects a security interest in the commodity contracts carried in the commodity account.

Legislative Note: Any statute conflicting with subsection (e) must be made expressly subject to that subsection.

§9—309. SECURITY INTEREST PERFECTED UPON ATTACHMENT

The following security interests are perfected when they attach:

(1) a purchase-money security interest in consumer goods, except as otherwise provided in Section 9—311(b) with respect to consumer goods that are subject to a statute or treaty described in Section 9—311(a);

(2) an assignment of accounts or payment intangibles which does not by itself or in conjunction with other assignments to the same assignee transfer a significant part of the assignor's outstanding accounts or payment intangibles;

(3) a sale of a payment intangible;

(4) a sale of a promissory note;

(5) a security interest created by the assignment of a health-care-insurance receivable to the provider of the health-care goods or services;

(6) a security interest arising under Section 2—401, 2—505, 2—711(3), or 2A—508(5), until the debtor obtains possession of the collateral;

(7) a security interest of a collecting bank arising under Section 4—210;

(8) a security interest of an issuer or nominated person arising under Section 5—118;

(9) a security interest arising in the delivery of a financial asset under Section 9—206(c);

(10) a security interest in investment property created by a broker or securities intermediary;

(11) a security interest in a commodity contract or a commodity account created by a commodity intermediary;

(12) an assignment for the benefit of all creditors of the transferor and subsequent transfers by the assignee thereunder; and

(13) a security interest created by an assignment of a beneficial interest in a decedent's estate; and

(14) a sale by an individual of an account that is a right to payment of winnings in a lottery or other game of chance.

§9—310. WHEN FILING REQUIRED TO PERFECT SECURITY INTEREST OR AGRICULTURAL LIEN; SECURITY INTERESTS AND AGRICULTURAL LIENS TO WHICH FILING PROVISIONS DO NOT APPLY

(a) Except as otherwise provided in subsection (b) and Section 9—312(b), a financing statement must be filed to perfect all security interests and agricultural liens.

(b) The filing of a financing statement is not necessary to perfect a security interest:

(1) that is perfected under Section 9—308(d), (e), (f), or (g);

(2) that is perfected under Section 9—309 when it attaches;

(3) in property subject to a statute, regulation, or treaty described in Section 9—311(a);

(4) in goods in possession of a bailee which is perfected under Section 9—312(d)(1) or (2);

(5) in certificated securities, documents, goods, or instruments which is perfected without filing or possession under Section 9—312(e), (f), or (g);

(6) in collateral in the secured party's possession under Section 9—313;

(7) in a certificated security which is perfected by delivery of the security certificate to the secured party under Section 9—313;

(8) in deposit accounts, electronic chattel paper, investment property, or letter-of-credit rights

which is perfected by control under Section 9—314;

(9) in proceeds which is perfected under Section 9—315; or

(10) that is perfected under Section 9—316.

(c) If a secured party assigns a perfected security interest or agricultural lien, a filing under this article is not required to continue the perfected status of the security interest against creditors of and transferees from the original debtor.

§9—311. PERFECTION OF SECURITY INTERESTS IN PROPERTY SUBJECT TO CERTAIN STATUTES, REGULATIONS, AND TREATIES

(a) Except as otherwise provided in subsection (d), the filing of a financing statement is not necessary or effective to perfect a security interest in property subject to:

(1) a statute, regulation, or treaty of the United States whose requirements for a security interest's obtaining priority over the rights of a lien creditor with respect to the property preempt Section 9—310(a);

(2) [list any certificate-of-title statute covering automobiles, trailers, mobile homes, boats, farm tractors, or the like, which provides for a security interest to be indicated on the certificate as a condition or result of perfection, and any non-Uniform Commercial Code central filing statute]; or

(3) a certificate-of-title statute of another jurisdiction which provides for a security interest to be indicated on the certificate as a condition or result of the security interest's obtaining priority over the rights of a lien creditor with respect to the property.

(b) Compliance with the requirements of a statute, regulation, or treaty described in subsection (a) for obtaining priority over the rights of a lien creditor is equivalent to the filing of a financing statement under this article. Except as otherwise provided in subsection (d) and Sections 9—313 and 9—316(d) and (e) for goods covered by a certificate of title, a security interest in property subject to a statute, regulation, or treaty described in subsection (a) may be perfected only by compliance with those requirements, and a security interest so perfected remains perfected notwithstanding a change in the use or transfer of possession of the collateral.

(c) Except as otherwise provided in subsection (d) and Section 9—316(d) and (e), duration and renewal of perfection of a security interest perfected by compliance with the requirements prescribed by a statute, regulation, or treaty described in subsection (a) are governed by the statute, regulation, or treaty. In other respects, the security interest is subject to this article.

(d) During any period in which collateral subject to a statute specified in subsection (a)(2) is inventory held for sale or lease by a person or leased by that person as lessor and that person is in the business of selling goods of that kind, this section does not apply to a security interest in that collateral created by that person.

Legislative Note: This Article contemplates that perfection of a security interest in goods covered by a certificate of title occurs upon receipt by appropriate State officials of a properly tendered application for a certificate of title on which the security interest is to be indicated, without a relation back to an earlier time. States whose certificate-of-title statutes provide for perfection at a different time or contain a relation-back provision should amend the statutes accordingly.

§9—312. PERFECTION OF SECURITY INTERESTS IN CHATTEL PAPER, DEPOSIT ACCOUNTS, DOCUMENTS, GOODS COVERED BY DOCUMENTS, INSTRUMENTS, INVESTMENT PROPERTY, LETTER-OF-CREDIT RIGHTS, AND MONEY; PERFECTION BY PERMISSIVE FILING; TEMPORARY PERFECTION WITHOUT FILING OR TRANSFER OF POSSESSION

(a) A security interest in chattel paper, negotiable documents, instruments, or investment property may be perfected by filing.

(b) Except as otherwise provided in Section 9—315 (c) and (d) for proceeds:

(1) a security interest in a deposit account may be perfected only by control under Section 9—314;

(2) and except as otherwise provided in Section 9—308(d), a security interest in a letter-of-credit right may be perfected only by control under Section 9—314; and

(3) a security interest in money may be perfected only by the secured party's taking possession under Section 9—313.

(c) While goods are in the possession of a bailee that has issued a negotiable document covering the goods:

(1) a security interest in the goods may be perfected by perfecting a security interest in the document; and

(2) a security interest perfected in the document has priority over any security interest that becomes perfected in the goods by another method during that time.

(d) While goods are in the possession of a bailee that has issued a nonnegotiable document covering the goods, a security interest in the goods may be perfected by:

   (1) issuance of a document in the name of the secured party;

   (2) the bailee's receipt of notification of the secured party's interest; or

   (3) filing as to the goods.

(e) A security interest in certificated securities, negotiable documents, or instruments is perfected without filing or the taking of possession for a period of 20 days from the time it attaches to the extent that it arises for new value given under an authenticated security agreement.

(f) A perfected security interest in a negotiable document or goods in possession of a bailee, other than one that has issued a negotiable document for the goods, remains perfected for 20 days without filing if the secured party makes available to the debtor the goods or documents representing the goods for the purpose of:

   (1) ultimate sale or exchange; or

   (2) loading, unloading, storing, shipping, transshipping, manufacturing, processing, or otherwise dealing with them in a manner preliminary to their sale or exchange.

(g) A perfected security interest in a certificated security or instrument remains perfected for 20 days without filing if the secured party delivers the security certificate or instrument to the debtor for the purpose of:

   (1) ultimate sale or exchange; or

   (2) presentation, collection, enforcement, renewal, or registration of transfer.

(h) After the 20-day period specified in subsection (e), (f), or (g) expires, perfection depends upon compliance with this article.

§9—313. WHEN POSSESSION BY OR DELIVERY TO SECURED PARTY PERFECTS SECURITY INTEREST WITHOUT FILING

(a) Except as otherwise provided in subsection (b), a secured party may perfect a security interest in negotiable documents, goods, instruments, money, or tangible chattel paper by taking possession of the collateral. A secured party may perfect a security interest in certificated securities by taking delivery of the certificated securities under Section 8—301.

(b) With respect to goods covered by a certificate of title issued by this State, a secured party may perfect a security interest in the goods by taking possession of the goods only in the circumstances described in Section 9—316(d).

(c) With respect to collateral other than certificated securities and goods covered by a document, a secured party takes possession of collateral in the possession of a person other than the debtor, the secured party, or a lessee of the collateral from the debtor in the ordinary course of the debtor's business, when:

   (1) the person in possession authenticates a record acknowledging that it holds possession of the collateral for the secured party's benefit; or

   (2) the person takes possession of the collateral after having authenticated a record acknowledging that it will hold possession of collateral for the secured party's benefit.

(d) If perfection of a security interest depends upon possession of the collateral by a secured party, perfection occurs no earlier than the time the secured party takes possession and continues only while the secured party retains possession.

(e) A security interest in a certificated security in registered form is perfected by delivery when delivery of the certificated security occurs under Section 8—301 and remains perfected by delivery until the debtor obtains possession of the security certificate.

(f) A person in possession of collateral is not required to acknowledge that it holds possession for a secured party's benefit.

(g) If a person acknowledges that it holds possession for the secured party's benefit:

   (1) the acknowledgment is effective under subsection (c) or Section 8—301(a), even if the acknowledgment violates the rights of a debtor; and

   (2) unless the person otherwise agrees or law other than this article otherwise provides, the person does not owe any duty to the secured party and is not required to confirm the acknowledgment to another person.

(h) A secured party having possession of collateral does not relinquish possession by delivering the collateral to a person other than the debtor or a lessee of the collateral from the debtor in the ordinary course of the debtor's business if the person was instructed before the delivery or is instructed contemporaneously with the delivery:

   (1) to hold possession of the collateral for the secured party's benefit; or

   (2) to redeliver the collateral to the secured party.

(i) A secured party does not relinquish possession, even if a delivery under subsection (h) violates the rights of a debtor. A person to which collateral is delivered under subsection (h) does not owe any duty to the secured party and is not required to confirm the delivery to another person unless the person otherwise agrees or law other than this article otherwise provides.

§9—314. PERFECTION BY CONTROL

(a) A security interest in investment property, deposit accounts, letter-of-credit rights, or electronic chattel paper may be perfected by control of the collateral under Section 9—104, 9—105, 9—106, or 9—107.

(b) A security interest in deposit accounts, electronic chattel paper, or letter-of-credit rights is perfected by control under Section 9—104, 9—105, or 9—107 when the secured party obtains control and remains perfected by control only while the secured party retains control.

(c) A security interest in investment property is perfected by control under Section 9—106 from the time the secured party obtains control and remains perfected by control until:

(1) the secured party does not have control; and

(2) one of the following occurs:

(A) if the collateral is a certificated security, the debtor has or acquires possession of the security certificate;

(B) if the collateral is an uncertificated security, the issuer has registered or registers the debtor as the registered owner; or

(C) if the collateral is a security entitlement, the debtor is or becomes the entitlement holder.

§9—315. SECURED PARTY'S RIGHTS ON DISPOSITION OF COLLATERAL AND IN PROCEEDS

(a) Except as otherwise provided in this article and in Section 2—403(2):

(1) a security interest or agricultural lien continues in collateral notwithstanding sale, lease, license, exchange, or other disposition thereof unless the secured party authorized the disposition free of the security interest or agricultural lien; and

(2) a security interest attaches to any identifiable proceeds of collateral.

(b) Proceeds that are commingled with other property are identifiable proceeds:

(1) if the proceeds are goods, to the extent provided by Section 9—336; and

(2) if the proceeds are not goods, to the extent that the secured party identifies the proceeds by a method of tracing, including application of equitable principles, that is permitted under law other than this article with respect to commingled property of the type involved.

(c) A security interest in proceeds is a perfected security interest if the security interest in the original collateral was perfected.

(d) A perfected security interest in proceeds becomes unperfected on the 21st day after the security interest attaches to the proceeds unless:

(1) the following conditions are satisfied:

(A) a filed financing statement covers the original collateral;

(B) the proceeds are collateral in which a security interest may be perfected by filing in the office in which the financing statement has been filed; and

(C) the proceeds are not acquired with cash proceeds;

(2) the proceeds are identifiable cash proceeds; or

(3) the security interest in the proceeds is perfected other than under subsection (c) when the security interest attaches to the proceeds or within 20 days thereafter.

(e) If a filed financing statement covers the original collateral, a security interest in proceeds which remains perfected under subsection (d)(1) becomes unperfected at the later of:

(1) when the effectiveness of the filed financing statement lapses under Section 9—515 or is terminated under Section 9—513; or

(2) the 21st day after the security interest attaches to the proceeds.

§9—316. CONTINUED PERFECTION OF SECURITY INTEREST FOLLOWING CHANGE IN GOVERNING LAW

(a) A security interest perfected pursuant to the law of the jurisdiction designated in Section 9—301(1) or 9—305(c) remains perfected until the earliest of:

(1) the time perfection would have ceased under the law of that jurisdiction;

(2) the expiration of four months after a change of the debtor's location to another jurisdiction; or

(3) the expiration of one year after a transfer of collateral to a person that thereby becomes a debtor and is located in another jurisdiction.

(b) If a security interest described in subsection (a) becomes perfected under the law of the other jurisdiction before the earliest time or event described in that subsection, it remains perfected thereafter. If the security interest does not become perfected under the law of the other jurisdiction before the earliest time or event, it becomes unperfected and is deemed never to have been perfected as against a purchaser of the collateral for value.

(c) A possessory security interest in collateral, other than goods covered by a certificate of title and as-extracted collateral consisting of goods, remains continuously perfected if:

(1) the collateral is located in one jurisdiction and subject to a security interest perfected under the law of that jurisdiction;

(2) thereafter the collateral is brought into another jurisdiction; and

(3) upon entry into the other jurisdiction, the security interest is perfected under the law of the other jurisdiction.

(d) Except as otherwise provided in subsection (e), a security interest in goods covered by a certificate of title which is perfected by any method under the law of another jurisdiction when the goods become covered by a certificate of title from this State remains perfected until the security interest would have become unperfected under the law of the other jurisdiction had the goods not become so covered.

(e) A security interest described in subsection (d) becomes unperfected as against a purchaser of the goods for value and is deemed never to have been perfected as against a purchaser of the goods for value if the applicable requirements for perfection under Section 9—311(b) or 9—313 are not satisfied before the earlier of:

(1) the time the security interest would have become unperfected under the law of the other jurisdiction had the goods not become covered by a certificate of title from this State; or

(2) the expiration of four months after the goods had become so covered.

(f) A security interest in deposit accounts, letter-of-credit rights, or investment property which is perfected under the law of the bank's jurisdiction, the issuer's jurisdiction, a nominated person's jurisdiction, the securities intermediary's jurisdiction, or the commodity intermediary's jurisdiction, as applicable, remains perfected until the earlier of:

(1) the time the security interest would have become unperfected under the law of that jurisdiction; or

(2) the expiration of four months after a change of the applicable jurisdiction to another jurisdiction.

(g) If a security interest described in subsection (f) becomes perfected under the law of the other jurisdiction before the earlier of the time or the end of the period described in that subsection, it remains perfected thereafter. If the security interest does not become perfected under the law of the other jurisdiction before the earlier of that time or the end of that period, it becomes unperfected and is deemed never to have been perfected as against a purchaser of the collateral for value.

[Subpart 3. Priority]

§9—317. INTERESTS THAT TAKE PRIORITY OVER OR TAKE FREE OF SECURITY INTEREST OR AGRICULTURAL LIEN

(a) A security interest or agricultural lien is subordinate to the rights of:

(1) a person entitled to priority under Section 9—322; and

(2) except as otherwise provided in subsection (e), a person that becomes a lien creditor before the earlier of the time:

(A) the security interest or agricultural lien is perfected; or

(B) one of the conditions specified in Section 9—203(b)(3) is met and a financing statement covering the collateral is filed.

(b) Except as otherwise provided in subsection (e), a buyer, other than a secured party, of tangible chattel paper, documents, goods, instruments, or a security certificate takes free of a security interest or agricultural lien if the buyer gives value and receives delivery of the collateral without knowledge of the security interest or agricultural lien and before it is perfected.

(c) Except as otherwise provided in subsection (e), a lessee of goods takes free of a security interest or agricultural lien if the lessee gives value and receives delivery of the collateral without knowledge of the security interest or agricultural lien and before it is perfected.

(d) A licensee of a general intangible or a buyer, other than a secured party, of accounts, electronic chattel paper, general intangibles, or investment property other than a certificated security takes free of a security interest if the licensee or buyer gives value without knowledge of the security interest and before it is perfected.

(e) Except as otherwise provided in Sections 9—320 and 9—321, if a person files a financing statement with respect to a purchase-money security interest before or within 20 days after the debtor receives delivery of the collateral, the security interest takes priority over the rights of a buyer, lessee, or lien creditor which arise between the time the security interest attaches and the time of filing.

As amended in 2000.

§9—318. NO INTEREST RETAINED IN RIGHT TO PAYMENT THAT IS SOLD; RIGHTS AND TITLE OF SELLER OF ACCOUNT OR CHATTEL PAPER WITH RESPECT TO CREDITORS AND PURCHASERS

(a) A debtor that has sold an account, chattel paper, payment intangible, or promissory note does not retain a legal or equitable interest in the collateral sold.

(b) For purposes of determining the rights of creditors of, and purchasers for value of an account or chattel paper from, a debtor that has sold an account or chattel paper, while the buyer's security interest is unperfected, the debtor is deemed to have rights and title to the account or chattel paper identical to those the debtor sold.

§9—319. RIGHTS AND TITLE OF CONSIGNEE WITH RESPECT TO CREDITORS AND PURCHASERS

(a) Except as otherwise provided in subsection (b), for purposes of determining the rights of creditors of, and purchasers for value of goods from, a consignee, while the goods are in the possession of the consignee, the consignee is deemed to have rights and title to the goods identical to those the consignor had or had power to transfer.

(b) For purposes of determining the rights of a creditor of a consignee, law other than this article determines the rights and title of a consignee while goods are in the consignee's possession if, under this part, a perfected security interest held by the consignor would have priority over the rights of the creditor.

§9—320. BUYER OF GOODS

(a) Except as otherwise provided in subsection (e), a buyer in ordinary course of business, other than a person buying farm products from a person engaged in farming operations, takes free of a security interest created by the buyer's seller, even if the security interest is perfected and the buyer knows of its existence.

(b) Except as otherwise provided in subsection (e), a buyer of goods from a person who used or bought the goods for use primarily for personal, family, or household purposes takes free of a security interest, even if perfected, if the buyer buys:

(1) without knowledge of the security interest;
(2) for value;
(3) primarily for the buyer's personal, family, or household purposes; and
(4) before the filing of a financing statement covering the goods.

(c) To the extent that it affects the priority of a security interest over a buyer of goods under subsection (b), the period of effectiveness of a filing made in the jurisdiction in which the seller is located is governed by Section 9—316(a) and (b).

(d) A buyer in ordinary course of business buying oil, gas, or other minerals at the wellhead or minehead or after extraction takes free of an interest arising out of an encumbrance.

(e) Subsections (a) and (b) do not affect a security interest in goods in the possession of the secured party under Section 9—313.

§9—321. LICENSEE OF GENERAL INTANGIBLE AND LESSEE OF GOODS IN ORDINARY COURSE OF BUSINESS

(a) In this section, "licensee in ordinary course of business" means a person that becomes a licensee of a general intangible in good faith, without knowledge that the license violates the rights of another person in the general intangible, and in the ordinary course from a person in the business of licensing general intangibles of that kind. A person becomes a licensee in the ordinary course if the license to the person comports with the usual or customary practices in the kind of business in which the licensor is engaged or with the licensor's own usual or customary practices.

(b) A licensee in ordinary course of business takes its rights under a nonexclusive license free of a security interest in the general intangible created by the licensor, even if the security interest is perfected and the licensee knows of its existence.

(c) A lessee in ordinary course of business takes its leasehold interest free of a security interest in the goods created by the lessor, even if the security interest is perfected and the lessee knows of its existence.

§9—322. PRIORITIES AMONG CONFLICTING SECURITY INTERESTS IN AND AGRICULTURAL LIENS ON SAME COLLATERAL

(a) Except as otherwise provided in this section, priority among conflicting security interests and agricultural liens in the same collateral is determined according to the following rules:

(1) Conflicting perfected security interests and agricultural liens rank according to priority in time of filing or perfection. Priority dates from the earlier of the time a filing covering the collateral is first made or the security interest or agricultural lien is first perfected, if there is no period thereafter when there is neither filing nor perfection.
(2) A perfected security interest or agricultural lien has priority over a conflicting unperfected security interest or agricultural lien.
(3) The first security interest or agricultural lien to attach or become effective has priority if conflicting security interests and agricultural liens are unperfected.

(b) For the purposes of subsection (a)(1):

(1) the time of filing or perfection as to a security interest in collateral is also the time of filing or perfection as to a security interest in proceeds; and
(2) the time of filing or perfection as to a security interest in collateral supported by a supporting obligation is also the time of filing or perfection as to a security interest in the supporting obligation.

(c) Except as otherwise provided in subsection (f), a security interest in collateral which qualifies for priority over a conflicting security interest under Section 9—327, 9—328, 9—329, 9—330, or 9—331 also has priority over a conflicting security interest in:

(1) any supporting obligation for the collateral; and
(2) proceeds of the collateral if:
(A) the security interest in proceeds is perfected;

(B) the proceeds are cash proceeds or of the same type as the collateral; and

(C) in the case of proceeds that are proceeds of proceeds, all intervening proceeds are cash proceeds, proceeds of the same type as the collateral, or an account relating to the collateral.

(d) Subject to subsection (e) and except as otherwise provided in subsection (f), if a security interest in chattel paper, deposit accounts, negotiable documents, instruments, investment property, or letter-of-credit rights is perfected by a method other than filing, conflicting perfected security interests in proceeds of the collateral rank according to priority in time of filing.

(e) Subsection (d) applies only if the proceeds of the collateral are not cash proceeds, chattel paper, negotiable documents, instruments, investment property, or letter-of-credit rights.

(f) Subsections (a) through (e) are subject to:

(1) subsection (g) and the other provisions of this part;

(2) Section 4—210 with respect to a security interest of a collecting bank;

(3) Section 5—118 with respect to a security interest of an issuer or nominated person; and

(4) Section 9—110 with respect to a security interest arising under Article 2 or 2A.

(g) A perfected agricultural lien on collateral has priority over a conflicting security interest in or agricultural lien on the same collateral if the statute creating the agricultural lien so provides.

§9—323. FUTURE ADVANCES

(a) Except as otherwise provided in subsection (c), for purposes of determining the priority of a perfected security interest under Section 9—322(a)(1), perfection of the security interest dates from the time an advance is made to the extent that the security interest secures an advance that:

(1) is made while the security interest is perfected only:

(A) under Section 9—309 when it attaches; or

(B) temporarily under Section 9—312(e), (f), or (g); and

(2) is not made pursuant to a commitment entered into before or while the security interest is perfected by a method other than under Section 9—309 or 9—312(e), (f), or (g).

(b) Except as otherwise provided in subsection (c), a security interest is subordinate to the rights of a person that becomes a lien creditor to the extent that the security interest secures an advance made more than 45 days after the person becomes a lien creditor unless the advance is made:

(1) without knowledge of the lien; or

(2) pursuant to a commitment entered into without knowledge of the lien.

(c) Subsections (a) and (b) do not apply to a security interest held by a secured party that is a buyer of accounts, chattel paper, payment intangibles, or promissory notes or a consignor.

(d) Except as otherwise provided in subsection (e), a buyer of goods other than a buyer in ordinary course of business takes free of a security interest to the extent that it secures advances made after the earlier of:

(1) the time the secured party acquires knowledge of the buyer's purchase; or

(2) 45 days after the purchase.

(e) Subsection (d) does not apply if the advance is made pursuant to a commitment entered into without knowledge of the buyer's purchase and before the expiration of the 45-day period.

(f) Except as otherwise provided in subsection (g), a lessee of goods, other than a lessee in ordinary course of business, takes the leasehold interest free of a security interest to the extent that it secures advances made after the earlier of:

(1) the time the secured party acquires knowledge of the lease; or

(2) 45 days after the lease contract becomes enforceable.

(g) Subsection (f) does not apply if the advance is made pursuant to a commitment entered into without knowledge of the lease and before the expiration of the 45-day period.

As amended in 1999.

§9—324. PRIORITY OF PURCHASE-MONEY SECURITY INTERESTS

(a) Except as otherwise provided in subsection (g), a perfected purchase-money security interest in goods other than inventory or livestock has priority over a conflicting security interest in the same goods, and, except as otherwise provided in Section 9—327, a perfected security interest in its identifiable proceeds also has priority, if the purchase-money security interest is perfected when the debtor receives possession of the collateral or within 20 days thereafter.

(b) Subject to subsection (c) and except as otherwise provided in subsection (g), a perfected purchase-money security interest in inventory has priority over a conflicting security interest in the same inventory, has priority over a conflicting security interest in chattel paper or an instrument constituting proceeds of the inventory and in proceeds of the chattel paper, if so provided in Section 9—330, and, except as otherwise provided in Section 9—327, also has priority in identifiable cash proceeds of the inventory to the extent the identifiable cash proceeds are received on or before the delivery of the inventory to a buyer, if:

>   (1) the purchase-money security interest is perfected when the debtor receives possession of the inventory;
>
>   (2) the purchase-money secured party sends an authenticated notification to the holder of the conflicting security interest;
>
>   (3) the holder of the conflicting security interest receives the notification within five years before the debtor receives possession of the inventory; and
>
>   (4) the notification states that the person sending the notification has or expects to acquire a purchase-money security interest in inventory of the debtor and describes the inventory.

(c) Subsections (b)(2) through (4) apply only if the holder of the conflicting security interest had filed a financing statement covering the same types of inventory:

>   (1) if the purchase-money security interest is perfected by filing, before the date of the filing; or
>
>   (2) if the purchase-money security interest is temporarily perfected without filing or possession under Section 9—312(f), before the beginning of the 20-day period thereunder.

(d) Subject to subsection (e) and except as otherwise provided in subsection (g), a perfected purchase-money security interest in livestock that are farm products has priority over a conflicting security interest in the same livestock, and, except as otherwise provided in Section 9—327, a perfected security interest in their identifiable proceeds and identifiable products in their unmanufactured states also has priority, if:

>   (1) the purchase-money security interest is perfected when the debtor receives possession of the livestock;
>
>   (2) the purchase-money secured party sends an authenticated notification to the holder of the conflicting security interest;
>
>   (3) the holder of the conflicting security interest receives the notification within six months before the debtor receives possession of the livestock; and
>
>   (4) the notification states that the person sending the notification has or expects to acquire a purchase-money security interest in livestock of the debtor and describes the livestock.

(e) Subsections (d)(2) through (4) apply only if the holder of the conflicting security interest had filed a financing statement covering the same types of livestock:

>   (1) if the purchase-money security interest is perfected by filing, before the date of the filing; or
>
>   (2) if the purchase-money security interest is temporarily perfected without filing or possession under Section 9—312(f), before the beginning of the 20-day period thereunder.

(f) Except as otherwise provided in subsection (g), a perfected purchase-money security interest in software has priority over a conflicting security interest in the same collateral, and, except as otherwise provided in Section 9—327, a perfected security interest in its identifiable proceeds also has priority, to the extent that the purchase-money security interest in the goods in which the software was acquired for use has priority in the goods and proceeds of the goods under this section.

(g) If more than one security interest qualifies for priority in the same collateral under subsection (a), (b), (d), or (f):

>   (1) a security interest securing an obligation incurred as all or part of the price of the collateral has priority over a security interest securing an obligation incurred for value given to enable the debtor to acquire rights in or the use of collateral; and
>
>   (2) in all other cases, Section 9—322(a) applies to the qualifying security interests.

§9—325. PRIORITY OF SECURITY INTERESTS IN TRANSFERRED COLLATERAL

(a) Except as otherwise provided in subsection (b), a security interest created by a debtor is subordinate to a security interest in the same collateral created by another person if:

>   (1) the debtor acquired the collateral subject to the security interest created by the other person;
>
>   (2) the security interest created by the other person was perfected when the debtor acquired the collateral; and
>
>   (3) there is no period thereafter when the security interest is unperfected.

(b) Subsection (a) subordinates a security interest only if the security interest:

>   (1) otherwise would have priority solely under Section 9—322(a) or 9—324; or
>
>   (2) arose solely under Section 2—711(3) or 2A—508(5).

§9—326. PRIORITY OF SECURITY INTERESTS CREATED BY NEW DEBTOR

(a) Subject to subsection (b), a security interest created by a new debtor which is perfected by a filed financing statement that is effective solely under Section 9—508 in collateral in which a new debtor has or acquires rights is subordinate to a security interest in the same collateral which is perfected other than by a filed financing statement that is effective solely under Section 9—508.

(b) The other provisions of this part determine the priority among conflicting security interests in the same collateral perfected by filed financing statements that are effective solely under Section 9—508. However, if the security agreements to which a new debtor became bound as debtor were not entered into by the same original debtor, the conflicting security interests rank according to priority in time of the new debtor's having become bound.

§9—327. PRIORITY OF SECURITY INTERESTS IN DEPOSIT ACCOUNT

The following rules govern priority among conflicting security interests in the same deposit account:

(1) A security interest held by a secured party having control of the deposit account under Section 9—104 has priority over a conflicting security interest held by a secured party that does not have control.

(2) Except as otherwise provided in paragraphs (3) and (4), security interests perfected by control under Section 9—314 rank according to priority in time of obtaining control.

(3) Except as otherwise provided in paragraph (4), a security interest held by the bank with which the deposit account is maintained has priority over a conflicting security interest held by another secured party.

(4) A security interest perfected by control under Section 9—104(a)(3) has priority over a security interest held by the bank with which the deposit account is maintained.

§9—328. PRIORITY OF SECURITY INTERESTS IN INVESTMENT PROPERTY

The following rules govern priority among conflicting security interests in the same investment property:

(1) A security interest held by a secured party having control of investment property under Section 9—106 has priority over a security interest held by a secured party that does not have control of the investment property.

(2) Except as otherwise provided in paragraphs (3) and (4), conflicting security interests held by secured parties each of which has control under Section 9—106 rank according to priority in time of:

    (A) if the collateral is a security, obtaining control;

    (B) if the collateral is a security entitlement carried in a securities account and:

      (i) if the secured party obtained control under Section 8—106(d)(1), the secured party's becoming the person for which the securities account is maintained;

      (ii) if the secured party obtained control under Section 8—106(d)(2), the securities intermediary's agreement to comply with the secured party's entitlement orders with respect to security entitlements carried or to be carried in the securities account; or

      (iii) if the secured party obtained control through another person under Section 8—106(d)(3), the time on which priority would be based under this paragraph if the other person were the secured party; or

    (C) if the collateral is a commodity contract carried with a commodity intermediary, the satisfaction of the requirement for control specified in Section 9—106(b)(2) with respect to commodity contracts carried or to be carried with the commodity intermediary.

(3) A security interest held by a securities intermediary in a security entitlement or a securities account maintained with the securities intermediary has priority over a conflicting security interest held by another secured party.

(4) A security interest held by a commodity intermediary in a commodity contract or a commodity account maintained with the commodity intermediary has priority over a conflicting security interest held by another secured party.

(5) A security interest in a certificated security in registered form which is perfected by taking delivery under Section 9—313(a) and not by control under Section 9—314 has priority over a conflicting security interest perfected by a method other than control.

(6) Conflicting security interests created by a broker, securities intermediary, or commodity intermediary which are perfected without control under Section 9—106 rank equally.

(7) In all other cases, priority among conflicting security interests in investment property is governed by Sections 9—322 and 9—323.

§9—329. PRIORITY OF SECURITY INTERESTS IN LETTER-OF-CREDIT RIGHT

The following rules govern priority among conflicting security interests in the same letter-of-credit right:

(1) A security interest held by a secured party having control of the letter-of-credit right under Section 9—107 has priority to the extent of its control over a conflicting security interest held by a secured party that does not have control.

(2) Security interests perfected by control under Section 9—314 rank according to priority in time of obtaining control.

§9—330. PRIORITY OF PURCHASER OF CHATTEL PAPER OR INSTRUMENT

(a) A purchaser of chattel paper has priority over a security interest in the chattel paper which is claimed merely as proceeds of inventory subject to a security interest if:

    (1) in good faith and in the ordinary course of the purchaser's business, the purchaser gives new

value and takes possession of the chattel paper or obtains control of the chattel paper under Section 9—105; and

(2) the chattel paper does not indicate that it has been assigned to an identified assignee other than the purchaser.

(b) A purchaser of chattel paper has priority over a security interest in the chattel paper which is claimed other than merely as proceeds of inventory subject to a security interest if the purchaser gives new value and takes possession of the chattel paper or obtains control of the chattel paper under Section 9—105 in good faith, in the ordinary course of the purchaser's business, and without knowledge that the purchase violates the rights of the secured party.

(c) Except as otherwise provided in Section 9—327, a purchaser having priority in chattel paper under subsection (a) or (b) also has priority in proceeds of the chattel paper to the extent that:

(1) Section 9—322 provides for priority in the proceeds; or

(2) the proceeds consist of the specific goods covered by the chattel paper or cash proceeds of the specific goods, even if the purchaser's security interest in the proceeds is unperfected.

(d) Except as otherwise provided in Section 9—331 (a), a purchaser of an instrument has priority over a security interest in the instrument perfected by a method other than possession if the purchaser gives value and takes possession of the instrument in good faith and without knowledge that the purchase violates the rights of the secured party.

(e) For purposes of subsections (a) and (b), the holder of a purchase-money security interest in inventory gives new value for chattel paper constituting proceeds of the inventory.

(f) For purposes of subsections (b) and (d), if chattel paper or an instrument indicates that it has been assigned to an identified secured party other than the purchaser, a purchaser of the chattel paper or instrument has knowledge that the purchase violates the rights of the secured party.

§9—331. PRIORITY OF RIGHTS OF PURCHASERS OF INSTRUMENTS, DOCUMENTS, AND SECURITIES UNDER OTHER ARTICLES; PRIORITY OF INTERESTS IN FINANCIAL ASSETS AND SECURITY ENTITLEMENTS UNDER ARTICLE 8

(a) This article does not limit the rights of a holder in due course of a negotiable instrument, a holder to which a negotiable document of title has been duly negotiated, or a protected purchaser of a security. These holders or

purchasers take priority over an earlier security interest, even if perfected, to the extent provided in Articles 3, 7, and 8.

(b) This article does not limit the rights of or impose liability on a person to the extent that the person is protected against the assertion of a claim under Article 8.

(c) Filing under this article does not constitute notice of a claim or defense to the holders, or purchasers, or persons described in subsections (a) and (b).

§9—332. TRANSFER OF MONEY; TRANSFER OF FUNDS FROM DEPOSIT ACCOUNT

(a) A transferee of money takes the money free of a security interest unless the transferee acts in collusion with the debtor in violating the rights of the secured party.

(b) A transferee of funds from a deposit account takes the funds free of a security interest in the deposit account unless the transferee acts in collusion with the debtor in violating the rights of the secured party.

§9—333. PRIORITY OF CERTAIN LIENS ARISING BY OPERATION OF LAW

(a) In this section, "possessory lien" means an interest, other than a security interest or an agricultural lien:

(1) which secures payment or performance of an obligation for services or materials furnished with respect to goods by a person in the ordinary course of the person's business;

(2) which is created by statute or rule of law in favor of the person; and

(3) whose effectiveness depends on the person's possession of the goods.

(b) A possessory lien on goods has priority over a security interest in the goods unless the lien is created by a statute that expressly provides otherwise.

§9—334. PRIORITY OF SECURITY INTERESTS IN FIXTURES AND CROPS

(a) A security interest under this article may be created in goods that are fixtures or may continue in goods that become fixtures. A security interest does not exist under this article in ordinary building materials incorporated into an improvement on land.

(b) This article does not prevent creation of an encumbrance upon fixtures under real property law.

(c) In cases not governed by subsections (d) through (h), a security interest in fixtures is subordinate to a conflicting interest of an encumbrancer or owner of the related real property other than the debtor.

(d) Except as otherwise provided in subsection (h), a perfected security interest in fixtures has priority over a conflicting interest of an encumbrancer or owner of the real property if the debtor has an interest of record in or is in possession of the real property and:

    (1) the security interest is a purchase-money security interest;

    (2) the interest of the encumbrancer or owner arises before the goods become fixtures; and

    (3) the security interest is perfected by a fixture filing before the goods become fixtures or within 20 days thereafter.

  (e) A perfected security interest in fixtures has priority over a conflicting interest of an encumbrancer or owner of the real property if:

    (1) the debtor has an interest of record in the real property or is in possession of the real property and the security interest:

        (A) is perfected by a fixture filing before the interest of the encumbrancer or owner is of record; and

        (B) has priority over any conflicting interest of a predecessor in title of the encumbrancer or owner;

    (2) before the goods become fixtures, the security interest is perfected by any method permitted by this article and the fixtures are readily removable:

        (A) factory or office machines;

        (B) equipment that is not primarily used or leased for use in the operation of the real property; or

        (C) replacements of domestic appliances that are consumer goods;

    (3) the conflicting interest is a lien on the real property obtained by legal or equitable proceedings after the security interest was perfected by any method permitted by this article; or

    (4) the security interest is:

        (A) created in a manufactured home in a manufactured-home transaction; and

        (B) perfected pursuant to a statute described in Section 9—311(a)(2).

  (f) A security interest in fixtures, whether or not perfected, has priority over a conflicting interest of an encumbrancer or owner of the real property if:

    (1) the encumbrancer or owner has, in an authenticated record, consented to the security interest or disclaimed an interest in the goods as fixtures; or

    (2) the debtor has a right to remove the goods as against the encumbrancer or owner.

  (g) The priority of the security interest under paragraph (f)(2) continues for a reasonable time if the debtor's right to remove the goods as against the encumbrancer or owner terminates.

  (h) A mortgage is a construction mortgage to the extent that it secures an obligation incurred for the construction of an improvement on land, including the acquisition cost of the land, if a recorded record of the mortgage so indicates. Except as otherwise provided in subsections (e) and (f), a security interest in fixtures is subordinate to a construction mortgage if a record of the mortgage is recorded before the goods become fixtures and the goods become fixtures before the completion of the construction. A mortgage has this priority to the same extent as a construction mortgage to the extent that it is given to refinance a construction mortgage.

  (i) A perfected security interest in crops growing on real property has priority over a conflicting interest of an encumbrancer or owner of the real property if the debtor has an interest of record in or is in possession of the real property.

  (j) Subsection (i) prevails over any inconsistent provisions of the following statutes:

    [List here any statutes containing provisions inconsistent with subsection (i).]

    Legislative Note: States that amend statutes to remove provisions inconsistent with subsection (i) need not enact subsection (j).

§9—335. ACCESSIONS

(a) A security interest may be created in an accession and continues in collateral that becomes an accession.

  (b) If a security interest is perfected when the collateral becomes an accession, the security interest remains perfected in the collateral.

  (c) Except as otherwise provided in subsection (d), the other provisions of this part determine the priority of a security interest in an accession.

  (d) A security interest in an accession is subordinate to a security interest in the whole which is perfected by compliance with the requirements of a certificate-of-title statute under Section 9—311(b).

  (e) After default, subject to Part 6, a secured party may remove an accession from other goods if the security interest in the accession has priority over the claims of every person having an interest in the whole.

  (f) A secured party that removes an accession from other goods under subsection (e) shall promptly reimburse any holder of a security interest or other lien on, or owner of, the whole or of the other goods, other than the debtor, for the cost of repair of any physical injury to the whole or the other goods. The secured party need not reimburse the holder or owner for any diminution in value of the whole or the other goods caused by the absence of the accession removed or by any necessity for replacing it. A person entitled to reimbursement may refuse permission to remove until the secured party gives adequate assurance for the performance of the obligation to reimburse.

§9—336. COMMINGLED GOODS

(a) In this section, "commingled goods" means goods that are physically united with other goods in such a manner that their identity is lost in a product or mass.

(b) A security interest does not exist in commingled goods as such. However, a security interest may attach to a product or mass that results when goods become commingled goods.

(c) If collateral becomes commingled goods, a security interest attaches to the product or mass.

(d) If a security interest in collateral is perfected before the collateral becomes commingled goods, the security interest that attaches to the product or mass under subsection (c) is perfected.

(e) Except as otherwise provided in subsection (f), the other provisions of this part determine the priority of a security interest that attaches to the product or mass under subsection (c).

(f) If more than one security interest attaches to the product or mass under subsection (c), the following rules determine priority:

(1) A security interest that is perfected under subsection (d) has priority over a security interest that is unperfected at the time the collateral becomes commingled goods.

(2) If more than one security interest is perfected under subsection (d), the security interests rank equally in proportion to the value of the collateral at the time it became commingled goods.

§9—337. PRIORITY OF SECURITY INTERESTS IN GOODS COVERED BY CERTIFICATE OF TITLE

If, while a security interest in goods is perfected by any method under the law of another jurisdiction, this State issues a certificate of title that does not show that the goods are subject to the security interest or contain a statement that they may be subject to security interests not shown on the certificate:

(1) a buyer of the goods, other than a person in the business of selling goods of that kind, takes free of the security interest if the buyer gives value and receives delivery of the goods after issuance of the certificate and without knowledge of the security interest; and

(2) the security interest is subordinate to a conflicting security interest in the goods that attaches, and is perfected under Section 9—311(b), after issuance of the certificate and without the conflicting secured party's knowledge of the security interest.

§9—338. PRIORITY OF SECURITY INTEREST OR AGRICULTURAL LIEN PERFECTED BY FILED FINANCING STATEMENT PROVIDING CERTAIN INCORRECT INFORMATION

If a security interest or agricultural lien is perfected by a filed financing statement providing information described in Section 9—516(b)(5) which is incorrect at the time the financing statement is filed:

(1) the security interest or agricultural lien is subordinate to a conflicting perfected security interest in the collateral to the extent that the holder of the conflicting security interest gives value in reasonable reliance upon the incorrect information; and

(2) a purchaser, other than a secured party, of the collateral takes free of the security interest or agricultural lien to the extent that, in reasonable reliance upon the incorrect information, the purchaser gives value and, in the case of chattel paper, documents, goods, instruments, or a security certificate, receives delivery of the collateral.

§9—339. PRIORITY SUBJECT TO SUBORDINATION

This article does not preclude subordination by agreement by a person entitled to priority.

[Subpart 4. Rights of Bank]

§9—340. EFFECTIVENESS OF RIGHT OF RECOUPMENT OR SET-OFF AGAINST DEPOSIT ACCOUNT

(a) Except as otherwise provided in subsection (c), a bank with which a deposit account is maintained may exercise any right of recoupment or set-off against a secured party that holds a security interest in the deposit account.

(b) Except as otherwise provided in subsection (c), the application of this article to a security interest in a deposit account does not affect a right of recoupment or set-off of the secured party as to a deposit account maintained with the secured party.

(c) The exercise by a bank of a set-off against a deposit account is ineffective against a secured party that holds a security interest in the deposit account which is perfected by control under Section 9—104(a)(3), if the set-off is based on a claim against the debtor.

§9—341. BANK'S RIGHTS AND DUTIES WITH RESPECT TO DEPOSIT ACCOUNT

Except as otherwise provided in Section 9—340(c), and unless the bank otherwise agrees in an authenticated record, a bank's rights and duties with respect to a deposit account maintained with the bank are not terminated, suspended, or modified by:

(1) the creation, attachment, or perfection of a security interest in the deposit account;

(2) the bank's knowledge of the security interest; or

(3) the bank's receipt of instructions from the secured party.

§9—342. BANK'S RIGHT TO REFUSE TO ENTER INTO OR DISCLOSE EXISTENCE OF CONTROL AGREEMENT

This article does not require a bank to enter into an agreement of the kind described in Section 9—104(a)(2), even if its customer so requests or directs. A bank that has entered into such an agreement is not required to confirm the existence of the agreement to another person unless requested to do so by its customer.

Part 4 Rights of Third Parties

§9—401. ALIENABILITY OF DEBTOR'S RIGHTS

(a) Except as otherwise provided in subsection (b) and Sections 9—406, 9—407, 9—408, and 9—409, whether a debtor's rights in collateral may be voluntarily or involuntarily transferred is governed by law other than this article.

(b) An agreement between the debtor and secured party which prohibits a transfer of the debtor's rights in collateral or makes the transfer a default does not prevent the transfer from taking effect.

§9—402. SECURED PARTY NOT OBLIGATED ON CONTRACT OF DEBTOR OR IN TORT

The existence of a security interest, agricultural lien, or authority given to a debtor to dispose of or use collateral, without more, does not subject a secured party to liability in contract or tort for the debtor's acts or omissions.

§9—403. AGREEMENT NOT TO ASSERT DEFENSES AGAINST ASSIGNEE

(a) In this section, "value" has the meaning provided in Section 3—303(a).

(b) Except as otherwise provided in this section, an agreement between an account debtor and an assignor not to assert against an assignee any claim or defense that the account debtor may have against the assignor is enforceable by an assignee that takes an assignment:

(1) for value;

(2) in good faith;

(3) without notice of a claim of a property or possessory right to the property assigned; and

(4) without notice of a defense or claim in recoupment of the type that may be asserted against a person entitled to enforce a negotiable instrument under Section 3—305(a).

(c) Subsection (b) does not apply to defenses of a type that may be asserted against a holder in due course of a negotiable instrument under Section 3—305(b).

(d) In a consumer transaction, if a record evidences the account debtor's obligation, law other than this article requires that the record include a statement to the effect that the rights of an assignee are subject to claims or defenses that the account debtor could assert against the original obligee, and the record does not include such a statement:

(1) the record has the same effect as if the record included such a statement; and

(2) the account debtor may assert against an assignee those claims and defenses that would have been available if the record included such a statement.

(e) This section is subject to law other than this article which establishes a different rule for an account debtor who is an individual and who incurred the obligation primarily for personal, family, or household purposes.

(f) Except as otherwise provided in subsection (d), this section does not displace law other than this article which gives effect to an agreement by an account debtor not to assert a claim or defense against an assignee.

§9—404. RIGHTS ACQUIRED BY ASSIGNEE; CLAIMS AND DEFENSES AGAINST ASSIGNEE

(a) Unless an account debtor has made an enforceable agreement not to assert defenses or claims, and subject to subsections (b) through (e), the rights of an assignee are subject to:

(1) all terms of the agreement between the account debtor and assignor and any defense or claim in recoupment arising from the transaction that gave rise to the contract; and

(2) any other defense or claim of the account debtor against the assignor which accrues before the account debtor receives a notification of the assignment authenticated by the assignor or the assignee.

(b) Subject to subsection (c) and except as otherwise provided in subsection (d), the claim of an account debtor against an assignor may be asserted against an assignee under subsection (a) only to reduce the amount the account debtor owes.

(c) This section is subject to law other than this article which establishes a different rule for an account debtor who is an individual and who incurred the obligation primarily for personal, family, or household purposes.

(d) In a consumer transaction, if a record evidences the account debtor's obligation, law other than this article requires that the record include a statement to the effect that the account debtor's recovery against an assignee with respect to claims and defenses against the assignor may not exceed amounts paid by the account debtor under the record, and the record does not include such a statement, the extent to which a claim of an account debtor against the assignor may be asserted against an assignee is determined as if the record included such a statement.

(e) This section does not apply to an assignment of a health-care-insurance receivable.

§9—405. MODIFICATION OF ASSIGNED CONTRACT

(a) A modification of or substitution for an assigned contract is effective against an assignee if made in good faith. The assignee acquires corresponding rights under the modified or substituted contract. The assignment may provide that the modification or substitution is a breach of contract by the assignor. This subsection is subject to subsections (b) through (d).

(b) Subsection (a) applies to the extent that:

(1) the right to payment or a part thereof under an assigned contract has not been fully earned by performance; or

(2) the right to payment or a part thereof has been fully earned by performance and the account debtor has not received notification of the assignment under Section 9—406(a).

(c) This section is subject to law other than this article which establishes a different rule for an account debtor who is an individual and who incurred the obligation primarily for personal, family, or household purposes.

(d) This section does not apply to an assignment of a health-care-insurance receivable.

§9—406. DISCHARGE OF ACCOUNT DEBTOR; NOTIFICATION OF ASSIGNMENT; IDENTIFICATION AND PROOF OF ASSIGNMENT; RESTRICTIONS ON ASSIGNMENT OF ACCOUNTS, CHATTEL PAPER, PAYMENT INTANGIBLES, AND PROMISSORY NOTES INEFFECTIVE

(a) Subject to subsections (b) through (i), an account debtor on an account, chattel paper, or a payment intangible may discharge its obligation by paying the assignor until, but not after, the account debtor receives a notification, authenticated by the assignor or the assignee, that the amount due or to become due has been assigned and that payment is to be made to the assignee. After receipt of the notification, the account debtor may discharge its obligation by paying the assignee and may not discharge the obligation by paying the assignor.

(b) Subject to subsection (h), notification is ineffective under subsection (a):

(1) if it does not reasonably identify the rights assigned;

(2) to the extent that an agreement between an account debtor and a seller of a payment intangible limits the account debtor's duty to pay a person other than the seller and the limitation is effective under law other than this article; or

(3) at the option of an account debtor, if the notification notifies the account debtor to make

less than the full amount of any installment or other periodic payment to the assignee, even if:

(A) only a portion of the account, chattel paper, or payment intangible has been assigned to that assignee;

(B) a portion has been assigned to another assignee; or

(C) the account debtor knows that the assignment to that assignee is limited.

(c) Subject to subsection (h), if requested by the account debtor, an assignee shall seasonably furnish reasonable proof that the assignment has been made. Unless the assignee complies, the account debtor may discharge its obligation by paying the assignor, even if the account debtor has received a notification under subsection (a).

(d) Except as otherwise provided in subsection (e) and Sections 2A—303 and 9—407, and subject to subsection (h), a term in an agreement between an account debtor and an assignor or in a promissory note is ineffective to the extent that it:

(1) prohibits, restricts, or requires the consent of the account debtor or person obligated on the promissory note to the assignment or transfer of, or the creation, attachment, perfection, or enforcement of a security interest in, the account, chattel paper, payment intangible, or promissory note; or

(2) provides that the assignment or transfer or the creation, attachment, perfection, or enforcement of the security interest may give rise to a default, breach, right of recoupment, claim, defense, termination, right of termination, or remedy under the account, chattel paper, payment intangible, or promissory note.

(e) Subsection (d) does not apply to the sale of a payment intangible or promissory note.

(f) Except as otherwise provided in Sections 2A—303 and 9—407 and subject to subsections (h) and (i), a rule of law, statute, or regulation that prohibits, restricts, or requires the consent of a government, governmental body or official, or account debtor to the assignment or transfer of, or creation of a security interest in, an account or chattel paper is ineffective to the extent that the rule of law, statute, or regulation:

(1) prohibits, restricts, or requires the consent of the government, governmental body or official, or account debtor to the assignment or transfer of, or the creation, attachment, perfection, or enforcement of a security interest in the account or chattel paper; or

(2) provides that the assignment or transfer or the creation, attachment, perfection, or enforcement of the security interest may give rise to a default, breach, right of recoupment, claim,

defense, termination, right of termination, or remedy under the account or chattel paper.

(g) Subject to subsection (h), an account debtor may not waive or vary its option under subsection (b)(3).

(h) This section is subject to law other than this article which establishes a different rule for an account debtor who is an individual and who incurred the obligation primarily for personal, family, or household purposes.

(i) This section does not apply to an assignment of a health-care-insurance receivable.

(j) This section prevails over any inconsistent provisions of the following statutes, rules, and regulations: [List here any statutes, rules, and regulations containing provisions inconsistent with this section.] *Legislative Note: States that amend statutes, rules, and regulations to remove provisions inconsistent with this section need not enact subsection (j).*

As amended in 1999 and 2000.

§9—407. RESTRICTIONS ON CREATION OR ENFORCEMENT OF SECURITY INTEREST IN LEASEHOLD INTEREST OR IN LESSOR'S RESIDUAL INTEREST

(a) Except as otherwise provided in subsection (b), a term in a lease agreement is ineffective to the extent that it:

(1) prohibits, restricts, or requires the consent of a party to the lease to the assignment or transfer of, or the creation, attachment, perfection, or enforcement of a security interest in an interest of a party under the lease contract or in the lessor's residual interest in the goods; or

(2) provides that the assignment or transfer or the creation, attachment, perfection, or enforcement of the security interest may give rise to a default, breach, right of recoupment, claim, defense, termination, right of termination, or remedy under the lease.

(b) Except as otherwise provided in Section 2A—303 (7), a term described in subsection (a)(2) is effective to the extent that there is:

(1) a transfer by the lessee of the lessee's right of possession or use of the goods in violation of the term; or

(2) a delegation of a material performance of either party to the lease contract in violation of the term.

(c) The creation, attachment, perfection, or enforcement of a security interest in the lessor's interest under the lease contract or the lessor's residual interest in the goods is not a transfer that materially impairs the lessee's prospect of obtaining return performance or materially changes the duty of or materially increases the burden or risk imposed on the lessee within the purview of Section 2A—303(4)

unless, and then only to the extent that, enforcement actually results in a delegation of material performance of the lessor.

As amended in 1999.

§9—408. RESTRICTIONS ON ASSIGNMENT OF PROMISSORY NOTES, HEALTH-CARE-INSURANCE RECEIVABLES, AND CERTAIN GENERAL INTANGIBLES INEFFECTIVE

(a) Except as otherwise provided in subsection (b), a term in a promissory note or in an agreement between an account debtor and a debtor which relates to a health-care-insurance receivable or a general intangible, including a contract, permit, license, or franchise, and which term prohibits, restricts, or requires the consent of the person obligated on the promissory note or the account debtor to, the assignment or transfer of, or creation, attachment, or perfection of a security interest in, the promissory note, health-care-insurance receivable, or general intangible, is ineffective to the extent that the term:

(1) would impair the creation, attachment, or perfection of a security interest; or

(2) provides that the assignment or transfer or the creation, attachment, or perfection of the security interest may give rise to a default, breach, right of recoupment, claim, defense, termination, right of termination, or remedy under the promissory note, health-care-insurance receivable, or general intangible.

(b) Subsection (a) applies to a security interest in a payment intangible or promissory note only if the security interest arises out of a sale of the payment intangible or promissory note.

(c) A rule of law, statute, or regulation that prohibits, restricts, or requires the consent of a government, governmental body or official, person obligated on a promissory note, or account debtor to the assignment or transfer of, or creation of a security interest in, a promissory note, health-care-insurance receivable, or general intangible, including a contract, permit, license, or franchise between an account debtor and a debtor, is ineffective to the extent that the rule of law, statute, or regulation:

(1) would impair the creation, attachment, or perfection of a security interest; or

(2) provides that the assignment or transfer or the creation, attachment, or perfection of the security interest may give rise to a default, breach, right of recoupment, claim, defense, termination, right of termination, or remedy under the promissory note, health-care-insurance receivable, or general intangible.

(d) To the extent that a term in a promissory note or in an agreement between an account debtor and a debtor which relates to a health-care-insurance receivable or general intangible or a rule of law, statute, or regulation described in subsection (c) would be effective under law other than this article but is ineffective under subsection (a) or (c), the creation, attachment, or perfection of a security interest in the promissory note, health-care-insurance receivable, or general intangible:

    (1) is not enforceable against the person obligated on the promissory note or the account debtor;

    (2) does not impose a duty or obligation on the person obligated on the promissory note or the account debtor;

    (3) does not require the person obligated on the promissory note or the account debtor to recognize the security interest, pay or render performance to the secured party, or accept payment or performance from the secured party;

    (4) does not entitle the secured party to use or assign the debtor's rights under the promissory note, health-care-insurance receivable, or general intangible, including any related information or materials furnished to the debtor in the transaction giving rise to the promissory note, health-care-insurance receivable, or general intangible;

    (5) does not entitle the secured party to use, assign, possess, or have access to any trade secrets or confidential information of the person obligated on the promissory note or the account debtor; and

    (6) does not entitle the secured party to enforce the security interest in the promissory note, health-care-insurance receivable, or general intangible.

(e) This section prevails over any inconsistent provisions of the following statutes, rules, and regulations:

    [List here any statutes, rules, and regulations containing provisions inconsistent with this section.]

    Legislative Note: States that amend statutes, rules, and regulations to remove provisions inconsistent with this section need not enact subsection (e).

As amended in 1999.

§9—409. RESTRICTIONS ON ASSIGNMENT OF LETTER-OF-CREDIT RIGHTS INEFFECTIVE

(a) A term in a letter of credit or a rule of law, statute, regulation, custom, or practice applicable to the letter of credit which prohibits, restricts, or requires the consent of an applicant, issuer, or nominated person to a beneficiary's assignment of or creation of a security interest in a letter-of-credit right is ineffective to the extent that the term or rule of law, statute, regulation, custom, or practice:

    (1) would impair the creation, attachment, or perfection of a security interest in the letter-of-credit right; or

    (2) provides that the assignment or the creation, attachment, or perfection of the security interest may give rise to a default, breach, right of recoupment, claim, defense, termination, right of termination, or remedy under the letter-of-credit right.

(b) To the extent that a term in a letter of credit is ineffective under subsection (a) but would be effective under law other than this article or a custom or practice applicable to the letter of credit, to the transfer of a right to draw or otherwise demand performance under the letter of credit, or to the assignment of a right to proceeds of the letter of credit, the creation, attachment, or perfection of a security interest in the letter-of-credit right:

    (1) is not enforceable against the applicant, issuer, nominated person, or transferee beneficiary;

    (2) imposes no duties or obligations on the applicant, issuer, nominated person, or transferee beneficiary; and

    (3) does not require the applicant, issuer, nominated person, or transferee beneficiary to recognize the security interest, pay or render performance to the secured party, or accept payment or other performance from the secured party.

As amended in 1999.

Part 5 Filing [Subpart 1. Filing Office; Contents and Effectiveness of Financing Statement]

§9—501. FILING OFFICE

(a) Except as otherwise provided in subsection (b), if the local law of this State governs perfection of a security interest or agricultural lien, the office in which to file a financing statement to perfect the security interest or agricultural lien is:

    (1) the office designated for the filing or recording of a record of a mortgage on the related real property, if:

        (A) the collateral is as-extracted collateral or timber to be cut; or

        (B) the financing statement is filed as a fixture filing and the collateral is goods that are or are to become fixtures; or

    (2) the office of [ ] [or any office duly authorized by [ ]], in all other cases, including a case in which the collateral is goods that are or are to become fixtures and the financing statement is not filed as a fixture filing.

(b) The office in which to file a financing statement to perfect a security interest in collateral, including fixtures, of a transmitting utility is the office of [ ]. The financing statement also constitutes a fixture filing as to the collateral indicated in the financing statement which is or is to become fixtures.

Legislative Note: The State should designate the filing office where the brackets appear. The filing office may be that of a governmental official (e.g., the Secretary of State) or a private party that maintains the State's filing system.

§9—502. CONTENTS OF FINANCING STATEMENT; RECORD OF MORTGAGE AS FINANCING STATEMENT; TIME OF FILING FINANCING STATEMENT

(a)   Subject to subsection (b), a financing statement is sufficient only if it:

(1)   provides the name of the debtor;

(2)   provides the name of the secured party or a representative of the secured party; and

(3)   indicates the collateral covered by the financing statement.

(b)   Except as otherwise provided in Section 9—501 (b), to be sufficient, a financing statement that covers as-extracted collateral or timber to be cut, or which is filed as a fixture filing and covers goods that are or are to become fixtures, must satisfy subsection (a) and also:

(1)   indicate that it covers this type of collateral;

(2)   indicate that it is to be filed [for record] in the real property records;

(3)   provide a description of the real property to which the collateral is related [sufficient to give constructive notice of a mortgage under the law of this State if the description were contained in a record of the mortgage of the real property]; and

(4)   if the debtor does not have an interest of record in the real property, provide the name of a record owner.

(c)   A record of a mortgage is effective, from the date of recording, as a financing statement filed as a fixture filing or as a financing statement covering as-extracted collateral or timber to be cut only if:

(1)   the record indicates the goods or accounts that it covers;

(2)   the goods are or are to become fixtures related to the real property described in the record or the collateral is related to the real property described in the record and is as-extracted collateral or timber to be cut;

(3)   the record satisfies the requirements for a financing statement in this section other than an indication that it is to be filed in the real property records; and

(4)   the record is [duly] recorded.

(d)   A financing statement may be filed before a security agreement is made or a security interest otherwise attaches.

Legislative Note: Language in brackets is optional. Where the State has any special recording system for real property other than the usual grantor-grantee index (as, for instance, a tract system or a title registration or Torrens system) local adaptations of subsection (b) and Section 9—519(d) and (e) may be necessary. See, e.g., Mass. Gen. Laws Chapter 106, Section 9—410.

§9—503. NAME OF DEBTOR AND SECURED PARTY

(a)   A financing statement sufficiently provides the name of the debtor:

(1)   if the debtor is a registered organization, only if the financing statement provides the name of the debtor indicated on the public record of the debtor's jurisdiction of organization which shows the debtor to have been organized;

(2)   if the debtor is a decedent's estate, only if the financing statement provides the name of the decedent and indicates that the debtor is an estate;

(3)   if the debtor is a trust or a trustee acting with respect to property held in trust, only if the financing statement:

(A)   provides the name specified for the trust in its organic documents or, if no name is specified, provides the name of the settlor and additional information sufficient to distinguish the debtor from other trusts having one or more of the same settlors; and

(B)   indicates, in the debtor's name or otherwise, that the debtor is a trust or is a trustee acting with respect to property held in trust; and

(4)   in other cases:

(A)   if the debtor has a name, only if it provides the individual or organizational name of the debtor; and

(B)   if the debtor does not have a name, only if it provides the names of the partners, members, associates, or other persons comprising the debtor.

(b)   A financing statement that provides the name of the debtor in accordance with subsection (a) is not rendered ineffective by the absence of:

(1)   a trade name or other name of the debtor; or

(2)   unless required under subsection (a)(4)(B), names of partners, members, associates, or other persons comprising the debtor.

(c)   A financing statement that provides only the debtor's trade name does not sufficiently provide the name of the debtor.

(d)   Failure to indicate the representative capacity of a secured party or representative of a secured party does not affect the sufficiency of a financing statement.

(e) A financing statement may provide the name of more than one debtor and the name of more than one secured party.

§9—504. INDICATION OF COLLATERAL

A financing statement sufficiently indicates the collateral that it covers if the financing statement provides:

(1) a description of the collateral pursuant to Section 9—108; or

(2) an indication that the financing statement covers all assets or all personal property.

As amended in 1999.

§9—505. FILING AND COMPLIANCE WITH OTHER STATUTES AND TREATIES FOR CONSIGNMENTS, LEASES, OTHER BAILMENTS, AND OTHER TRANSACTIONS

(a) A consignor, lessor, or other bailor of goods, a licensor, or a buyer of a payment intangible or promissory note may file a financing statement, or may comply with a statute or treaty described in Section 9—311(a), using the terms "consignor", "consignee", "lessor", "lessee", "bailor", "bailee", "licensor", "licensee", "owner", "registered owner", "buyer", "seller", or words of similar import, instead of the terms "secured party" and "debtor".

(b) This part applies to the filing of a financing statement under subsection (a) and, as appropriate, to compliance that is equivalent to filing a financing statement under Section 9—311(b), but the filing or compliance is not of itself a factor in determining whether the collateral secures an obligation. If it is determined for another reason that the collateral secures an obligation, a security interest held by the consignor, lessor, bailor, licensor, owner, or buyer which attaches to the collateral is perfected by the filing or compliance.

§9—506. EFFECT OF ERRORS OR OMISSIONS

(a) A financing statement substantially satisfying the requirements of this part is effective, even if it has minor errors or omissions, unless the errors or omissions make the financing statement seriously misleading.

(b) Except as otherwise provided in subsection (c), a financing statement that fails sufficiently to provide the name of the debtor in accordance with Section 9—503(a) is seriously misleading.

(c) If a search of the records of the filing office under the debtor's correct name, using the filing office's standard search logic, if any, would disclose a financing statement that fails sufficiently to provide the name of the debtor in accordance with Section 9—503(a), the name provided does not make the financing statement seriously misleading.

(d) For purposes of Section 9—508(b), the "debtor's correct name" in subsection (c) means the correct name of the new debtor.

§9—507. EFFECT OF CERTAIN EVENTS ON EFFECTIVENESS OF FINANCING STATEMENT

(a) A filed financing statement remains effective with respect to collateral that is sold, exchanged, leased, licensed, or otherwise disposed of and in which a security interest or agricultural lien continues, even if the secured party knows of or consents to the disposition.

(b) Except as otherwise provided in subsection (c) and Section 9—508, a financing statement is not rendered ineffective if, after the financing statement is filed, the information provided in the financing statement becomes seriously misleading under Section 9—506.

(c) If a debtor so changes its name that a filed financing statement becomes seriously misleading under Section 9—506:

(1) the financing statement is effective to perfect a security interest in collateral acquired by the debtor before, or within four months after, the change; and

(2) the financing statement is not effective to perfect a security interest in collateral acquired by the debtor more than four months after the change, unless an amendment to the financing statement which renders the financing statement not seriously misleading is filed within four months after the change.

§9—508. EFFECTIVENESS OF FINANCING STATEMENT IF NEW DEBTOR BECOMES BOUND BY SECURITY AGREEMENT

(a) Except as otherwise provided in this section, a filed financing statement naming an original debtor is effective to perfect a security interest in collateral in which a new debtor has or acquires rights to the extent that the financing statement would have been effective had the original debtor acquired rights in the collateral.

(b) If the difference between the name of the original debtor and that of the new debtor causes a filed financing statement that is effective under subsection (a) to be seriously misleading under Section 9—506:

(1) the financing statement is effective to perfect a security interest in collateral acquired by the new debtor before, and within four months after, the new debtor becomes bound under Section 9B—203(d); and

(2) the financing statement is not effective to perfect a security interest in collateral acquired by the new debtor more than four months after the new debtor becomes bound under Section 9—203(d) unless an initial financing statement providing the name of the new debtor is filed before the expiration of that time.

(c) This section does not apply to collateral as to which a filed financing statement remains effective against the new debtor under Section 9—507(a).

§9—509. PERSONS ENTITLED TO FILE A RECORD

(a) A person may file an initial financing statement, amendment that adds collateral covered by a financing statement, or amendment that adds a debtor to a financing statement only if:

    (1) the debtor authorizes the filing in an authenticated record or pursuant to subsection (b) or (c); or

    (2) the person holds an agricultural lien that has become effective at the time of filing and the financing statement covers only collateral in which the person holds an agricultural lien.

(b) By authenticating or becoming bound as debtor by a security agreement, a debtor or new debtor authorizes the filing of an initial financing statement, and an amendment, covering:

    (1) the collateral described in the security agreement; and

    (2) property that becomes collateral under Section 9—315(a)(2), whether or not the security agreement expressly covers proceeds.

(c) By acquiring collateral in which a security interest or agricultural lien continues under Section 9—315(a)(1), a debtor authorizes the filing of an initial financing statement, and an amendment, covering the collateral and property that becomes collateral under Section 9—315(a)(2).

(d) A person may file an amendment other than an amendment that adds collateral covered by a financing statement or an amendment that adds a debtor to a financing statement only if:

    (1) the secured party of record authorizes the filing; or

    (2) the amendment is a termination statement for a financing statement as to which the secured party of record has failed to file or send a termination statement as required by Section 9—513(a) or (c), the debtor authorizes the filing, and the termination statement indicates that the debtor authorized it to be filed.

(e) If there is more than one secured party of record for a financing statement, each secured party of record may authorize the filing of an amendment under subsection (d).

As amended in 2000.

§9—510. EFFECTIVENESS OF FILED RECORD

(a) A filed record is effective only to the extent that it was filed by a person that may file it under Section 9—509.

(b) A record authorized by one secured party of record does not affect the financing statement with respect to another secured party of record.

(c) A continuation statement that is not filed within the six-month period prescribed by Section 9—515(d) is ineffective.

§9—511. SECURED PARTY OF RECORD

(a) A secured party of record with respect to a financing statement is a person whose name is provided as the name of the secured party or a representative of the secured party in an initial financing statement that has been filed. If an initial financing statement is filed under Section 9—514 (a), the assignee named in the initial financing statement is the secured party of record with respect to the financing statement.

(b) If an amendment of a financing statement which provides the name of a person as a secured party or a representative of a secured party is filed, the person named in the amendment is a secured party of record. If an amendment is filed under Section 9—514(b), the assignee named in the amendment is a secured party of record.

(c) A person remains a secured party of record until the filing of an amendment of the financing statement which deletes the person.

§9—512. AMENDMENT OF FINANCING STATEMENT

[Alternative A]

(a) Subject to Section 9—509, a person may add or delete collateral covered by, continue or terminate the effectiveness of, or, subject to subsection (e), otherwise amend the information provided in, a financing statement by filing an amendment that:

    (1) identifies, by its file number, the initial financing statement to which the amendment relates; and

    (2) if the amendment relates to an initial financing statement filed [or recorded] in a filing office described in Section 9—501(a)(1), provides the information specified in Section 9—502(b).

[Alternative B]

(a) Subject to Section 9—509, a person may add or delete collateral covered by, continue or terminate the effectiveness of, or, subject to subsection (e), otherwise amend the information provided in, a financing statement by filing an amendment that:

    (1) identifies, by its file number, the initial financing statement to which the amendment relates; and

(2) if the amendment relates to an initial financing statement filed [or recorded] in a filing office described in Section 9—501(a)(1), provides the date [and time] that the initial financing statement was filed [or recorded] and the information specified in Section 9—502(b).

[End of Alternatives]

(b) Except as otherwise provided in Section 9—515, the filing of an amendment does not extend the period of effectiveness of the financing statement.

(c) A financing statement that is amended by an amendment that adds collateral is effective as to the added collateral only from the date of the filing of the amendment.

(d) A financing statement that is amended by an amendment that adds a debtor is effective as to the added debtor only from the date of the filing of the amendment.

(e) An amendment is ineffective to the extent it:
(1) purports to delete all debtors and fails to provide the name of a debtor to be covered by the financing statement; or
(2) purports to delete all secured parties of record and fails to provide the name of a new secured party of record.

Legislative Note: States whose real-estate filing offices require additional information in amendments and cannot search their records by both the name of the debtor and the file number should enact Alternative B to Sections 9—512(a), 9—518(b), 9—519(f), and 9—522(a).

§9—513. TERMINATION STATEMENT

(a) A secured party shall cause the secured party of record for a financing statement to file a termination statement for the financing statement if the financing statement covers consumer goods and:
(1) there is no obligation secured by the collateral covered by the financing statement and no commitment to make an advance, incur an obligation, or otherwise give value; or
(2) the debtor did not authorize the filing of the initial financing statement.

(b) To comply with subsection (a), a secured party shall cause the secured party of record to file the termination statement:
(1) within one month after there is no obligation secured by the collateral covered by the financing statement and no commitment to make an advance, incur an obligation, or otherwise give value; or
(2) if earlier, within 20 days after the secured party receives an authenticated demand from a debtor.

(c) In cases not governed by subsection (a), within 20 days after a secured party receives an authenticated demand from a debtor, the secured party shall cause the secured party of record for a financing statement to send to the debtor a termination statement for the financing statement or file the termination statement in the filing office if:
(1) except in the case of a financing statement covering accounts or chattel paper that has been sold or goods that are the subject of a consignment, there is no obligation secured by the collateral covered by the financing statement and no commitment to make an advance, incur an obligation, or otherwise give value;
(2) the financing statement covers accounts or chattel paper that has been sold but as to which the account debtor or other person obligated has discharged its obligation;
(3) the financing statement covers goods that were the subject of a consignment to the debtor but are not in the debtor's possession; or
(4) the debtor did not authorize the filing of the initial financing statement.

(d) Except as otherwise provided in Section 9—510, upon the filing of a termination statement with the filing office, the financing statement to which the termination statement relates ceases to be effective. Except as otherwise provided in Section 9—510, for purposes of Sections 9—519(g), 9—522(a), and 9—523(c), the filing with the filing office of a termination statement relating to a financing statement that indicates that the debtor is a transmitting utility also causes the effectiveness of the financing statement to lapse.

As amended in 2000.

§9—514. ASSIGNMENT OF POWERS OF SECURED PARTY OF RECORD

(a) Except as otherwise provided in subsection (c), an initial financing statement may reflect an assignment of all of the secured party's power to authorize an amendment to the financing statement by providing the name and mailing address of the assignee as the name and address of the secured party.

(b) Except as otherwise provided in subsection (c), a secured party of record may assign of record all or part of its power to authorize an amendment to a financing statement by filing in the filing office an amendment of the financing statement which:
(1) identifies, by its file number, the initial financing statement to which it relates;
(2) provides the name of the assignor; and
(3) provides the name and mailing address of the assignee.

(c) An assignment of record of a security interest in a fixture covered by a record of a mortgage which is effective as a financing statement filed as a fixture filing under

Section 9—502(c) may be made only by an assignment of record of the mortgage in the manner provided by law of this State other than [the Uniform Commercial Code].

§9—515. DURATION AND EFFECTIVENESS OF FINANCING STATEMENT; EFFECT OF LAPSED FINANCING STATEMENT

(a) Except as otherwise provided in subsections (b), (e), (f), and (g), a filed financing statement is effective for a period of five years after the date of filing.

(b) Except as otherwise provided in subsections (e), (f), and (g), an initial financing statement filed in connection with a public-finance transaction or manufactured-home transaction is effective for a period of 30 years after the date of filing if it indicates that it is filed in connection with a public-finance transaction or manufactured-home transaction.

(c) The effectiveness of a filed financing statement lapses on the expiration of the period of its effectiveness unless before the lapse a continuation statement is filed pursuant to subsection (d). Upon lapse, a financing statement ceases to be effective and any security interest or agricultural lien that was perfected by the financing statement becomes unperfected, unless the security interest is perfected otherwise. If the security interest or agricultural lien becomes unperfected upon lapse, it is deemed never to have been perfected as against a purchaser of the collateral for value.

(d) A continuation statement may be filed only within six months before the expiration of the five-year period specified in subsection (a) or the 30-year period specified in subsection (b), whichever is applicable.

(e) Except as otherwise provided in Section 9—510, upon timely filing of a continuation statement, the effectiveness of the initial financing statement continues for a period of five years commencing on the day on which the financing statement would have become ineffective in the absence of the filing. Upon the expiration of the five-year period, the financing statement lapses in the same manner as provided in subsection (c), unless, before the lapse, another continuation statement is filed pursuant to subsection (d). Succeeding continuation statements may be filed in the same manner to continue the effectiveness of the initial financing statement.

(f) If a debtor is a transmitting utility and a filed financing statement so indicates, the financing statement is effective until a termination statement is filed.

(g) A record of a mortgage that is effective as a financing statement filed as a fixture filing under Section 9—502(c) remains effective as a financing statement filed as a fixture filing until the mortgage is released or satisfied of record or its effectiveness otherwise terminates as to the real property.

§9—516. WHAT CONSTITUTES FILING; EFFECTIVENESS OF FILING

(a) Except as otherwise provided in subsection (b), communication of a record to a filing office and tender of the filing fee or acceptance of the record by the filing office constitutes filing.

(b) Filing does not occur with respect to a record that a filing office refuses to accept because:

(1) the record is not communicated by a method or medium of communication authorized by the filing office;

(2) an amount equal to or greater than the applicable filing fee is not tendered;

(3) the filing office is unable to index the record because:

(A) in the case of an initial financing statement, the record does not provide a name for the debtor;

(B) in the case of an amendment or correction statement, the record:

(i) does not identify the initial financing statement as required by Section 9—512 or 9—518, as applicable; or

(ii) identifies an initial financing statement whose effectiveness has lapsed under Section 9—515;

(C) in the case of an initial financing statement that provides the name of a debtor identified as an individual or an amendment that provides a name of a debtor identified as an individual which was not previously provided in the financing statement to which the record relates, the record does not identify the debtor's last name; or

(D) in the case of a record filed [or recorded] in the filing office described in Section 9—501(a)(1), the record does not provide a sufficient description of the real property to which it relates;

(4) in the case of an initial financing statement or an amendment that adds a secured party of record, the record does not provide a name and mailing address for the secured party of record;

(5) in the case of an initial financing statement or an amendment that provides a name of a debtor which was not previously provided in the financing statement to which the amendment relates, the record does not:

(A) provide a mailing address for the debtor;

(B) indicate whether the debtor is an individual or an organization; or

(C) if the financing statement indicates that the debtor is an organization, provide:

(i) a type of organization for the debtor;

(ii) a jurisdiction of organization for the debtor; or

(iii) an organizational identification number for the debtor or indicate that the debtor has none;

(6) in the case of an assignment reflected in an initial financing statement under Section 9—514 (a) or an amendment filed under Section 9—514 (b), the record does not provide a name and mailing address for the assignee; or

(7) in the case of a continuation statement, the record is not filed within the six-month period prescribed by Section 9—515(d).

(c) For purposes of subsection (b):

(1) a record does not provide information if the filing office is unable to read or decipher the information; and

(2) a record that does not indicate that it is an amendment or identify an initial financing statement to which it relates, as required by Section 9—512, 9—514, or 9—518, is an initial financing statement.

(d) A record that is communicated to the filing office with tender of the filing fee, but which the filing office refuses to accept for a reason other than one set forth in subsection (b), is effective as a filed record except as against a purchaser of the collateral which gives value in reasonable reliance upon the absence of the record from the files.

§9—517. EFFECT OF INDEXING ERRORS

The failure of the filing office to index a record correctly does not affect the effectiveness of the filed record.

§9—518. CLAIM CONCERNING INACCURATE OR WRONGFULLY FILED RECORD

(a) A person may file in the filing office a correction statement with respect to a record indexed there under the person's name if the person believes that the record is inaccurate or was wrongfully filed.

[Alternative A]

(b) A correction statement must:

(1) identify the record to which it relates by the file number assigned to the initial financing statement to which the record relates;

(2) indicate that it is a correction statement; and

(3) provide the basis for the person's belief that the record is inaccurate and indicate the manner in which the person believes the record should be amended to cure any inaccuracy or provide the basis for the person's belief that the record was wrongfully filed.

[Alternative B]

(b) A correction statement must:

(1) identify the record to which it relates by:

(A) the file number assigned to the initial financing statement to which the record relates; and

(B) if the correction statement relates to a record filed [or recorded] in a filing office described in Section 9—501(a)(1), the date [and time] that the initial financing statement was filed [or recorded] and the information specified in Section 9—502(b);

(2) indicate that it is a correction statement; and

(3) provide the basis for the person's belief that the record is inaccurate and indicate the manner in which the person believes the record should be amended to cure any inaccuracy or provide the basis for the person's belief that the record was wrongfully filed.

[End of Alternatives]

(c) The filing of a correction statement does not affect the effectiveness of an initial financing statement or other filed record.

Legislative Note: States whose real-estate filing offices require additional information in amendments and cannot search their records by both the name of the debtor and the file number should enact Alternative B to Sections 9—512(a), 9—518(b), 9—519(f), and 9—522(a).

[Subpart 2. Duties and Operation of Filing Office]

§9—519. NUMBERING, MAINTAINING, AND INDEXING RECORDS; COMMUNICATING INFORMATION PROVIDED IN RECORDS

(a) For each record filed in a filing office, the filing office shall:

(1) assign a unique number to the filed record;

(2) create a record that bears the number assigned to the filed record and the date and time of filing;

(3) maintain the filed record for public inspection; and

(4) index the filed record in accordance with subsections (c), (d), and (e).

(b) A file number [assigned after January 1, 2002,] must include a digit that:

(1) is mathematically derived from or related to the other digits of the file number; and

(2) aids the filing office in determining whether a number communicated as the file number includes a single-digit or transpositional error.

(c) Except as otherwise provided in subsections (d) and (e), the filing office shall:

(1) index an initial financing statement according to the name of the debtor and index all filed records relating to the initial financing statement in a manner that associates with one another an initial financing statement and all filed records relating to the initial financing statement; and

(2) index a record that provides a name of a debtor which was not previously provided in the financing statement to which the record relates also according to the name that was not previously provided.

(d) If a financing statement is filed as a fixture filing or covers as-extracted collateral or timber to be cut, [it must be filed for record and] the filing office shall index it:

(1) under the names of the debtor and of each owner of record shown on the financing statement as if they were the mortgagors under a mortgage of the real property described; and

(2) to the extent that the law of this State provides for indexing of records of mortgages under the name of the mortgagee, under the name of the secured party as if the secured party were the mortgagee thereunder, or, if indexing is by description, as if the financing statement were a record of a mortgage of the real property described.

(e) If a financing statement is filed as a fixture filing or covers as-extracted collateral or timber to be cut, the filing office shall index an assignment filed under Section 9—514(a) or an amendment filed under Section 9—514(b):

(1) under the name of the assignor as grantor; and

(2) to the extent that the law of this State provides for indexing a record of the assignment of a mortgage under the name of the assignee, under the name of the assignee.

[Alternative A]

(f) The filing office shall maintain a capability:

(1) to retrieve a record by the name of the debtor and by the file number assigned to the initial financing statement to which the record relates; and

(2) to associate and retrieve with one another an initial financing statement and each filed record relating to the initial financing statement.

[Alternative B]

(f) The filing office shall maintain a capability:

(1) to retrieve a record by the name of the debtor and:

(A) if the filing office is described in Section 9—501(a)(1), by the file number assigned to the initial financing statement to which the

record relates and the date [and time] that the record was filed [or recorded]; or

(B) if the filing office is described in Section 9—501(a)(2), by the file number assigned to the initial financing statement to which the record relates; and

(2) to associate and retrieve with one another an initial financing statement and each filed record relating to the initial financing statement.

[End of Alternatives]

(g) The filing office may not remove a debtor's name from the index until one year after the effectiveness of a financing statement naming the debtor lapses under Section 9—515 with respect to all secured parties of record.

(h) The filing office shall perform the acts required by subsections (a) through (e) at the time and in the manner prescribed by filing-office rule, but not later than two business days after the filing office receives the record in question.

[(i) Subsection[s] [(b)] [and] [(h)] do[es] not apply to a filing office described in Section 9—501(a)(1).]

Legislative Notes:

1. *States whose filing offices currently assign file numbers that include a verification number, commonly known as a "check digit," or can implement this requirement before the effective date of this Article should omit the bracketed language in subsection (b).*

2. *In States in which writings will not appear in the real property records and indices unless actually recorded the bracketed language in subsection (d) should be used.*

3. *States whose real-estate filing offices require additional information in amendments and cannot search their records by both the name of the debtor and the file number should enact Alternative B to Sections 9—512(a), 9—518(b), 9—519(f), and 9—522(a).*

4. *A State that elects not to require real-estate filing offices to comply with either or both of subsections (b) and (h) may adopt an applicable variation of subsection (i) and add "Except as otherwise provided in subsection (i)," to the appropriate subsection or subsections.*

§9—520. ACCEPTANCE AND REFUSAL TO ACCEPT RECORD

(a) A filing office shall refuse to accept a record for filing for a reason set forth in Section 9—516(b) and may refuse to accept a record for filing only for a reason set forth in Section 9—516(b).

(b) If a filing office refuses to accept a record for filing, it shall communicate to the person that presented the record the fact of and reason for the refusal and the date and time the record would have been filed had the filing office accepted it. The communication must be made at the time and in the manner prescribed by filing-office rule but [, in the case of a filing office described in Section 9—501(a)(2),] in no event more than two business days after the filing office receives the record.

(c) A filed financing statement satisfying Section 9—502(a) and (b) is effective, even if the filing office is required to refuse to accept it for filing under subsection (a). However, Section 9—338 applies to a filed financing statement providing information described in Section 9—516(b)(5) which is incorrect at the time the financing statement is filed.

(d) If a record communicated to a filing office provides information that relates to more than one debtor, this part applies as to each debtor separately.

Legislative Note: A State that elects not to require real-property filing offices to comply with subsection (b) should include the bracketed language.

§9—521. UNIFORM FORM OF WRITTEN FINANCING STATEMENT AND AMENDMENT

(a) A filing office that accepts written records may not refuse to accept a written initial financing statement in the following form and format except for a reason set forth in Section 9—516(b):

[NATIONAL UCC FINANCING STATEMENT (FORM UCC1)(REV. 7/29/98)]
[NATIONAL UCC FINANCING STATEMENT ADDENDUM (FORM UCC1Ad)(REV. 07/29/98)]

(b) A filing office that accepts written records may not refuse to accept a written record in the following form and format except for a reason set forth in Section 9—516(b):

[NATIONAL UCC FINANCING STATEMENT AMENDMENT (FORM UCC3)(REV. 07/29/98)]
[NATIONAL UCC FINANCING STATEMENT AMENDMENT ADDENDUM (FORM UCC3Ad) (REV. 07/29/98)]

§9—522. MAINTENANCE AND DESTRUCTION OF RECORDS

[Alternative A]

(a) The filing office shall maintain a record of the information provided in a filed financing statement for at least one year after the effectiveness of the financing statement has lapsed under Section 9—515 with respect to all secured parties of record. The record must be retrievable by using the name of the debtor and by using the file number assigned to the initial financing statement to which the record relates.

[Alternative B]

(a) The filing office shall maintain a record of the information provided in a filed financing statement for at least one year after the effectiveness of the financing statement has lapsed under Section 9—515 with respect to all secured parties of record. The record must be retrievable by using the name of the debtor and:

(1) if the record was filed [or recorded] in the filing office described in Section 9—501(a)(1), by using the file number assigned to the initial financing statement to which the record relates and the date [and time] that the record was filed [or recorded]; or

(2) if the record was filed in the filing office described in Section 9—501(a)(2), by using the file number assigned to the initial financing statement to which the record relates.

[End of Alternatives]

(b) Except to the extent that a statute governing disposition of public records provides otherwise, the filing office immediately may destroy any written record evidencing a financing statement. However, if the filing office destroys a written record, it shall maintain another record of the financing statement which complies with subsection (a).

Legislative Note: States whose real-estate filing offices require additional information in amendments and cannot search their records by both the name of the debtor and the file number should enact Alternative B to Sections 9—512(a), 9—518(b), 9—519(f), and 9—522(a).

§9—523. INFORMATION FROM FILING OFFICE; SALE OR LICENSE OF RECORDS

(a) If a person that files a written record requests an acknowledgment of the filing, the filing office shall send to the person an image of the record showing the number assigned to the record pursuant to Section 9—519(a)(1) and the date and time of the filing of the record. However, if the person furnishes a copy of the record to the filing office, the filing office may instead:

(1) note upon the copy the number assigned to the record pursuant to Section 9—519(a)(1) and the date and time of the filing of the record; and

(2) send the copy to the person.

(b) If a person files a record other than a written record, the filing office shall communicate to the person an acknowledgment that provides:

(1) the information in the record;

(2) the number assigned to the record pursuant to Section 9—519(a)(1); and

(3) the date and time of the filing of the record.

(c) The filing office shall communicate or otherwise make available in a record the following information to any person that requests it:

(1) whether there is on file on a date and time specified by the filing office, but not a date earlier than three business days before the filing office receives the request, any financing statement that:

(A) designates a particular debtor [or, if the request so states, designates a particular debtor at the address specified in the request];

(B) has not lapsed under Section 9—515 with respect to all secured parties of record; and

(C) if the request so states, has lapsed under Section 9—515 and a record of which is maintained by the filing office under Section 9—522(a);

(2) the date and time of filing of each financing statement; and

(3) the information provided in each financing statement.

(d) In complying with its duty under subsection (c), the filing office may communicate information in any medium. However, if requested, the filing office shall communicate information by issuing [its written certificate] [a record that can be admitted into evidence in the courts of this State without extrinsic evidence of its authenticity].

(e) The filing office shall perform the acts required by subsections (a) through (d) at the time and in the manner prescribed by filing-office rule, but not later than two business days after the filing office receives the request.

(f) At least weekly, the [insert appropriate official or governmental agency] [filing office] shall offer to sell or license to the public on a nonexclusive basis, in bulk, copies of all records filed in it under this part, in every medium from time to time available to the filing office.

Legislative Notes:

1. States whose filing office does not offer the additional service of responding to search requests limited to a particular address should omit the bracketed language in subsection (c)(1)(A).

2. A State that elects not to require real-estate filing offices to comply with either or both of subsections (e) and (f) should specify in the appropriate subsection(s) only the filing office described in Section 9—501(a)(2).

§9—524. DELAY BY FILING OFFICE

Delay by the filing office beyond a time limit prescribed by this part is excused if:

(1) the delay is caused by interruption of communication or computer facilities, war, emergency conditions, failure of equipment, or other circumstances beyond control of the filing office; and

(2) the filing office exercises reasonable diligence under the circumstances.

§9—525. FEES

(a) Except as otherwise provided in subsection (e), the fee for filing and indexing a record under this part, other than an initial financing statement of the kind described in subsection (b), is [the amount specified in subsection (c), if applicable, plus]:

(1) $[X] if the record is communicated in writing and consists of one or two pages;

(2) $[2X] if the record is communicated in writing and consists of more than two pages; and

(3) $[1/2X] if the record is communicated by another medium authorized by filing-office rule.

(b) Except as otherwise provided in subsection (e), the fee for filing and indexing an initial financing statement of the following kind is [the amount specified in subsection (c), if applicable, plus]:

(1) $_____ if the financing statement indicates that it is filed in connection with a public-finance transaction;

(2) $_____ if the financing statement indicates that it is filed in connection with a manufactured-home transaction.

[Alternative A]

(c) The number of names required to be indexed does not affect the amount of the fee in subsections (a) and (b).

[Alternative B]

(c) Except as otherwise provided in subsection (e), if a record is communicated in writing, the fee for each name more than two required to be indexed is $_____.

[End of Alternatives]

(d) The fee for responding to a request for information from the filing office, including for [issuing a certificate showing] [communicating] whether there is on file any financing statement naming a particular debtor, is:

(1) $_____ if the request is communicated in writing; and

(2) $_____ if the request is communicated by another medium authorized by filing-office rule.

(e) This section does not require a fee with respect to a record of a mortgage which is effective as a financing statement filed as a fixture filing or as a financing statement covering as-extracted collateral or timber to be cut under Section 9—502(c). However, the recording and satisfaction fees that otherwise would be applicable to the record of the mortgage apply.

Legislative Notes:

1. *To preserve uniformity, a State that places the provisions of this section together with statutes setting fees for other services should do so without modification.*

2. *A State should enact subsection (c), Alternative A, and omit the bracketed language in subsections (a) and (b) unless its indexing system entails a substantial additional cost when indexing additional names.*

As amended in 2000.

§9—526. FILING-OFFICE RULES

(a) The [insert appropriate governmental official or agency] shall adopt and publish rules to implement this article. The filing-office rules must be[:

  (1)] consistent with this article[; and

  (2) adopted and published in accordance with the [insert any applicable state administrative procedure act]].

  (b) To keep the filing-office rules and practices of the filing office in harmony with the rules and practices of filing offices in other jurisdictions that enact substantially this part, and to keep the technology used by the filing office compatible with the technology used by filing offices in other jurisdictions that enact substantially this part, the [insert appropriate governmental official or agency], so far as is consistent with the purposes, policies, and provisions of this article, in adopting, amending, and repealing filing-office rules, shall:

  (1) consult with filing offices in other jurisdictions that enact substantially this part; and

  (2) consult the most recent version of the Model Rules promulgated by the International Association of Corporate Administrators or any successor organization; and

  (3) take into consideration the rules and practices of, and the technology used by, filing offices in other jurisdictions that enact substantially this part.

§9—527. DUTY TO REPORT

The [insert appropriate governmental official or agency] shall report [annually on or before _____] to the [Governor and Legislature] on the operation of the filing office. The report must contain a statement of the extent to which:

(1) the filing-office rules are not in harmony with the rules of filing offices in other jurisdictions that enact substantially this part and the reasons for these variations; and

  (2) the filing-office rules are not in harmony with the most recent version of the Model Rules promulgated by the International Association of Corporate Administrators, or any successor organization, and the reasons for these variations.

Part 6 Default [Subpart 1. Default and Enforcement of Security Interest]

§9—601. RIGHTS AFTER DEFAULT; JUDICIAL ENFORCEMENT; CONSIGNOR OR BUYER OF ACCOUNTS, CHATTEL PAPER, PAYMENT INTANGIBLES, OR PROMISSORY NOTES

(a) After default, a secured party has the rights provided in this part and, except as otherwise provided in Section 9—602, those provided by agreement of the parties. A secured party:

  (1) may reduce a claim to judgment, foreclose, or otherwise enforce the claim, security interest, or agricultural lien by any available judicial procedure; and

  (2) if the collateral is documents, may proceed either as to the documents or as to the goods they cover.

  (b) A secured party in possession of collateral or control of collateral under Section 9—104, 9—105, 9—106, or 9—107 has the rights and duties provided in Section 9—207.

  (c) The rights under subsections (a) and (b) are cumulative and may be exercised simultaneously.

  (d) Except as otherwise provided in subsection (g) and Section 9—605, after default, a debtor and an obligor have the rights provided in this part and by agreement of the parties.

  (e) If a secured party has reduced its claim to judgment, the lien of any levy that may be made upon the collateral by virtue of an execution based upon the judgment relates back to the earliest of:

  (1) the date of perfection of the security interest or agricultural lien in the collateral;

  (2) the date of filing a financing statement covering the collateral; or

  (3) any date specified in a statute under which the agricultural lien was created.

  (f) A sale pursuant to an execution is a foreclosure of the security interest or agricultural lien by judicial procedure within the meaning of this section. A secured party may purchase at the sale and thereafter hold the collateral free of any other requirements of this article.

  (g) Except as otherwise provided in Section 9—607 (c), this part imposes no duties upon a secured party that is a consignor or is a buyer of accounts, chattel paper, payment intangibles, or promissory notes.

§9—602. WAIVER AND VARIANCE OF RIGHTS AND DUTIES

Except as otherwise provided in Section 9—624, to the extent that they give rights to a debtor or obligor and impose duties on a secured party, the debtor or obligor may not waive or vary the rules stated in the following listed sections:

(1) Section 9—207(b)(4)(C), which deals with use and operation of the collateral by the secured party;

(2) Section 9—210, which deals with requests for an accounting and requests concerning a list of collateral and statement of account;

(3) Section 9—607(c), which deals with collection and enforcement of collateral;

(4) Sections 9—608(a) and 9—615(c) to the extent that they deal with application or payment of noncash proceeds of collection, enforcement, or disposition;

(5) Sections 9—608(a) and 9—615(d) to the extent that they require accounting for or payment of surplus proceeds of collateral;

(6) Section 9—609 to the extent that it imposes upon a secured party that takes possession of collateral without judicial process the duty to do so without breach of the peace;

(7) Sections 9—610(b), 9—611, 9—613, and 9—614, which deal with disposition of collateral;

(8) Section 9—615(f), which deals with calculation of a deficiency or surplus when a disposition is made to the secured party, a person related to the secured party, or a secondary obligor;

(9) Section 9—616, which deals with explanation of the calculation of a surplus or deficiency;

(10) Sections 9—620, 9—621, and 9—622, which deal with acceptance of collateral in satisfaction of obligation;

(11) Section 9—623, which deals with redemption of collateral;

(12) Section 9—624, which deals with permissible waivers; and

(13) Sections 9—625 and 9—626, which deal with the secured party's liability for failure to comply with this article.

§9—603. AGREEMENT ON STANDARDS CONCERNING RIGHTS AND DUTIES

(a) The parties may determine by agreement the standards measuring the fulfillment of the rights of a debtor or obligor and the duties of a secured party under a rule stated in Section 9—602 if the standards are not manifestly unreasonable.

(b) Subsection (a) does not apply to the duty under Section 9—609 to refrain from breaching the peace.

§9—604. PROCEDURE IF SECURITY AGREEMENT COVERS REAL PROPERTY OR FIXTURES

(a) If a security agreement covers both personal and real property, a secured party may proceed:

(1) under this part as to the personal property without prejudicing any rights with respect to the real property; or

(2) as to both the personal property and the real property in accordance with the rights with respect to the real property, in which case the other provisions of this part do not apply.

(b) Subject to subsection (c), if a security agreement covers goods that are or become fixtures, a secured party may proceed:

(1) under this part; or

(2) in accordance with the rights with respect to real property, in which case the other provisions of this part do not apply.

(c) Subject to the other provisions of this part, if a secured party holding a security interest in fixtures has priority over all owners and encumbrancers of the real property, the secured party, after default, may remove the collateral from the real property.

(d) A secured party that removes collateral shall promptly reimburse any encumbrancer or owner of the real property, other than the debtor, for the cost of repair of any physical injury caused by the removal. The secured party need not reimburse the encumbrancer or owner for any diminution in value of the real property caused by the absence of the goods removed or by any necessity of replacing them. A person entitled to reimbursement may refuse permission to remove until the secured party gives adequate assurance for the performance of the obligation to reimburse.

§9—605. UNKNOWN DEBTOR OR SECONDARY OBLIGOR

A secured party does not owe a duty based on its status as secured party:

(1) to a person that is a debtor or obligor, unless the secured party knows:

(A) that the person is a debtor or obligor;

(B) the identity of the person; and

(C) how to communicate with the person; or

(2) to a secured party or lienholder that has filed a financing statement against a person, unless the secured party knows:

(A) that the person is a debtor; and

(B) the identity of the person.

§9—606. TIME OF DEFAULT FOR AGRICULTURAL LIEN

For purposes of this part, a default occurs in connection with an agricultural lien at the time the secured party becomes entitled to enforce the lien in accordance with the statute under which it was created.

§9—607. COLLECTION AND ENFORCEMENT BY SECURED PARTY

(a) If so agreed, and in any event after default, a secured party:

(1) may notify an account debtor or other person obligated on collateral to make payment or otherwise render performance to or for the benefit of the secured party;

(2) may take any proceeds to which the secured party is entitled under Section 9—315;

(3) may enforce the obligations of an account debtor or other person obligated on collateral and exercise the rights of the debtor with respect to the obligation of the account debtor or other person obligated on collateral to make payment or otherwise render performance to the debtor, and with respect to any property that secures the obligations of the account debtor or other person obligated on the collateral;

(4) if it holds a security interest in a deposit account perfected by control under Section 9—104(a)(1), may apply the balance of the deposit account to the obligation secured by the deposit account; and

(5) if it holds a security interest in a deposit account perfected by control under Section 9—104(a)(2) or (3), may instruct the bank to pay the balance of the deposit account to or for the benefit of the secured party.

(b) If necessary to enable a secured party to exercise under subsection (a)(3) the right of a debtor to enforce a mortgage nonjudicially, the secured party may record in the office in which a record of the mortgage is recorded:

(1) a copy of the security agreement that creates or provides for a security interest in the obligation secured by the mortgage; and

(2) the secured party's sworn affidavit in record-able form stating that:

(A) a default has occurred; and

(B) the secured party is entitled to enforce the mortgage nonjudicially.

(c) A secured party shall proceed in a commercially reasonable manner if the secured party:

(1) undertakes to collect from or enforce an obligation of an account debtor or other person obligated on collateral; and

(2) is entitled to charge back uncollected collateral or otherwise to full or limited recourse against the debtor or a secondary obligor.

(d) A secured party may deduct from the collections made pursuant to subsection (c) reasonable expenses of collection and enforcement, including reasonable attorney's fees and legal expenses incurred by the secured party.

(e) This section does not determine whether an account debtor, bank, or other person obligated on collateral owes a duty to a secured party.

As amended in 2000.

§9—608. APPLICATION OF PROCEEDS OF COLLECTION OR ENFORCEMENT; LIABILITY FOR DEFICIENCY AND RIGHT TO SURPLUS

(a) If a security interest or agricultural lien secures payment or performance of an obligation, the following rules apply:

(1) A secured party shall apply or pay over for application the cash proceeds of collection or enforcement under Section 9—607 in the following order to:

(A) the reasonable expenses of collection and enforcement and, to the extent provided for by agreement and not prohibited by law, reasonable attorney's fees and legal expenses incurred by the secured party;

(B) the satisfaction of obligations secured by the security interest or agricultural lien under which the collection or enforcement is made; and

(C) the satisfaction of obligations secured by any subordinate security interest in or other lien on the collateral subject to the security interest or agricultural lien under which the collection or enforcement is made if the secured party receives an authenticated demand for proceeds before distribution of the proceeds is completed.

(2) If requested by a secured party, a holder of a subordinate security interest or other lien shall furnish reasonable proof of the interest or lien within a reasonable time. Unless the holder complies, the secured party need not comply with the holder's demand under paragraph (1)(C).

(3) A secured party need not apply or pay over for application noncash proceeds of collection and enforcement under Section 9—607 unless the failure to do so would be commercially unreasonable. A secured party that applies or pays over for application noncash proceeds shall do so in a commercially reasonable manner.

(4) A secured party shall account to and pay a debtor for any surplus, and the obligor is liable for any deficiency.

(b) If the underlying transaction is a sale of accounts, chattel paper, payment intangibles, or promissory notes, the debtor is not entitled to any surplus, and the obligor is not liable for any deficiency.

As amended in 2000.

§9—609. SECURED PARTY'S RIGHT TO TAKE POSSESSION AFTER DEFAULT

(a) After default, a secured party:

    (1) may take possession of the collateral; and

    (2) without removal, may render equipment unusable and dispose of collateral on a debtor's premises under Section 9—610.

(b) A secured party may proceed under subsection (a):

    (1) pursuant to judicial process; or

    (2) without judicial process, if it proceeds without breach of the peace.

(c) If so agreed, and in any event after default, a secured party may require the debtor to assemble the collateral and make it available to the secured party at a place to be designated by the secured party which is reasonably convenient to both parties.

§9—610. DISPOSITION OF COLLATERAL AFTER DEFAULT

(a) After default, a secured party may sell, lease, license, or otherwise dispose of any or all of the collateral in its present condition or following any commercially reasonable preparation or processing.

(b) Every aspect of a disposition of collateral, including the method, manner, time, place, and other terms, must be commercially reasonable. If commercially reasonable, a secured party may dispose of collateral by public or private proceedings, by one or more contracts, as a unit or in parcels, and at any time and place and on any terms.

(c) A secured party may purchase collateral:

    (1) at a public disposition; or

    (2) at a private disposition only if the collateral is of a kind that is customarily sold on a recognized market or the subject of widely distributed standard price quotations.

(d) A contract for sale, lease, license, or other disposition includes the warranties relating to title, possession, quiet enjoyment, and the like which by operation of law accompany a voluntary disposition of property of the kind subject to the contract.

(e) A secured party may disclaim or modify warranties under subsection (d):

    (1) in a manner that would be effective to disclaim or modify the warranties in a voluntary disposition of property of the kind subject to the contract of disposition; or

    (2) by communicating to the purchaser a record evidencing the contract for disposition and including an express disclaimer or modification of the warranties.

(f) A record is sufficient to disclaim warranties under subsection (e) if it indicates "There is no warranty relating to title, possession, quiet enjoyment, or the like in this disposition" or uses words of similar import.

§9—611. NOTIFICATION BEFORE DISPOSITION OF COLLATERAL

(a) In this section, "notification date" means the earlier of the date on which:

    (1) a secured party sends to the debtor and any secondary obligor an authenticated notification of disposition; or

    (2) the debtor and any secondary obligor waive the right to notification.

(b) Except as otherwise provided in subsection (d), a secured party that disposes of collateral under Section 9—610 shall send to the persons specified in subsection (c) a reasonable authenticated notification of disposition.

(c) To comply with subsection (b), the secured party shall send an authenticated notification of disposition to:

    (1) the debtor;

    (2) any secondary obligor; and

    (3) if the collateral is other than consumer goods:

        (A) any other person from which the secured party has received, before the notification date, an authenticated notification of a claim of an interest in the collateral;

        (B) any other secured party or lienholder that, 10 days before the notification date, held a security interest in or other lien on the collateral perfected by the filing of a financing statement that:

            (i) identified the collateral;

            (ii) was indexed under the debtor's name as of that date; and

            (iii) was filed in the office in which to file a financing statement against the debtor covering the collateral as of that date; and

        (C) any other secured party that, 10 days before the notification date, held a security interest in the collateral perfected by compliance with a statute, regulation, or treaty described in Section 9—311(a).

(d) Subsection (b) does not apply if the collateral is perishable or threatens to decline speedily in value or is of a type customarily sold on a recognized market.

(e) A secured party complies with the requirement for notification prescribed by subsection (c)(3)(B) if:

    (1) not later than 20 days or earlier than 30 days before the notification date, the secured party requests, in a commercially reasonable manner, information concerning financing statements indexed under the debtor's name in the office indicated in subsection (c)(3)(B); and

    (2) before the notification date, the secured party:

        (A) did not receive a response to the request for information; or

        (B) received a response to the request for information and sent an authenticated notification of disposition to each secured party or other lienholder named in that response whose financing statement covered the collateral.

§9—612. TIMELINESS OF NOTIFICATION BEFORE DISPOSITION OF COLLATERAL

(a) Except as otherwise provided in subsection (b), whether a notification is sent within a reasonable time is a question of fact.

(b) In a transaction other than a consumer transaction, a notification of disposition sent after default and 10 days or more before the earliest time of disposition set forth in the notification is sent within a reasonable time before the disposition.

§9—613. CONTENTS AND FORM OF NOTIFICATION BEFORE DISPOSITION OF COLLATERAL: GENERAL

Except in a consumer-goods transaction, the following rules apply:

(1) The contents of a notification of disposition are sufficient if the notification:

(A) describes the debtor and the secured party;

(B) describes the collateral that is the subject of the intended disposition;

(C) states the method of intended disposition;

(D) states that the debtor is entitled to an accounting of the unpaid indebtedness and states the charge, if any, for an accounting; and

(E) states the time and place of a public disposition or the time after which any other disposition is to be made.

(2) Whether the contents of a notification that lacks any of the information specified in paragraph (1) are nevertheless sufficient is a question of fact.

(3) The contents of a notification providing substantially the information specified in paragraph (1) are sufficient, even if the notification includes:

(A) information not specified by that paragraph; or

(B) minor errors that are not seriously misleading.

(4) A particular phrasing of the notification is not required.

(5) The following form of notification and the form appearing in Section 9—614(3), when completed, each provides sufficient information:

NOTIFICATION OF DISPOSITION OF COLLATERAL

To: *[Name of debtor, obligor, or other person to which the notification is sent]*

From: *[Name, address, and telephone number of secured party]*

Name of Debtor(s): *[Include only if debtor(s) are not an addressee]*

[For a public disposition:]

We will sell [or lease or license, *as applicable*] the *[describe collateral]* [to the highest qualified bidder] in public as follows:

Day and Date: _____
Time: _____
Place: _____

[For a private disposition:]

We will sell [or lease or license, *as applicable*] the *[describe collateral]* privately sometime after *[day and date]*.

You are entitled to an accounting of the unpaid indebtedness secured by the property that we intend to sell [or lease or license, *as applicable*] [for a charge of $_____]. You may request an accounting by calling us at *[telephone number]*.

[End of Form]

As amended in 2000.

§9—614. CONTENTS AND FORM OF NOTIFICATION BEFORE DISPOSITION OF COLLATERAL: CONSUMER-GOODS TRANSACTION

In a consumer-goods transaction, the following rules apply:

(1) A notification of disposition must provide the following information:

(A) the information specified in Section 9—613(1);

(B) a description of any liability for a deficiency of the person to which the notification is sent;

(C) a telephone number from which the amount that must be paid to the secured party to redeem the collateral under Section 9—623 is available; and

(D) a telephone number or mailing address from which additional information concerning the disposition and the obligation secured is available.

(2) A particular phrasing of the notification is not required.

(3) The following form of notification, when completed, provides sufficient information:

[Name and address of secured party]
[Date]

NOTICE OF OUR PLAN TO SELL PROPERTY

[Name and address of any obligor who is also a debtor]

Subject: *[Identification of Transaction]*
We have your [describe collateral], because you broke promises in our agreement.
[For a public disposition:]
We will sell *[describe collateral]* at public sale. A sale could include a lease or license. The sale will be held as follows:

Date: _____
Time: _____
Place: _____

You may attend the sale and bring bidders if you want.

[For a private disposition:]

We will sell *[describe collateral]* at private sale sometime after *[date]*. A sale could include a lease or license.
The money that we get from the sale (after paying our costs) will reduce the amount you owe. If we get less money than you owe, you *[will or will not, as applicable]* still owe us the difference. If we get more money than you owe, you will get the extra money, unless we must pay it to someone else.
You can get the property back at any time before we sell it by paying us the full amount you owe (not just the past due payments), including our expenses. To learn the exact amount you must pay, call us at *[telephone number]*.

If you want us to explain to you in writing how we have figured the amount that you owe us, you may call us at *[telephone number]* [or write us at *[secured party's address]*] and request a written explanation. [We will charge you $_____ for the explanation if we sent you another written explanation of the amount you owe us within the last six months.]

If you need more information about the sale call us at *[telephone number]* [or write us at *[secured party's address]*].
We are sending this notice to the following other people who have an interest in [describe collateral] or who owe money under your agreement:
[Names of all other debtors and obligors, if any]

[End of Form]

(4) A notification in the form of paragraph (3) is sufficient, even if additional information appears at the end of the form.

(5) A notification in the form of paragraph (3) is sufficient, even if it includes errors in information not required by paragraph (1), unless the error is misleading with respect to rights arising under this article.

(6) If a notification under this section is not in the form of paragraph (3), law other than this article determines the effect of including information not required by paragraph (1).

§9—615. APPLICATION OF PROCEEDS OF DISPOSITION; LIABILITY FOR DEFICIENCY AND RIGHT TO SURPLUS

(a) A secured party shall apply or pay over for application the cash proceeds of disposition under Section 9—610 in the following order to:

(1) the reasonable expenses of retaking, holding, preparing for disposition, processing, and disposing, and, to the extent provided for by agreement and not prohibited by law, reasonable attorney's fees and legal expenses incurred by the secured party;

(2) the satisfaction of obligations secured by the security interest or agricultural lien under which the disposition is made;

(3) the satisfaction of obligations secured by any subordinate security interest in or other subordinate lien on the collateral if:

(A) the secured party receives from the holder of the subordinate security interest or other lien an authenticated demand for proceeds before distribution of the proceeds is completed; and

(B) in a case in which a consignor has an interest in the collateral, the subordinate security interest or other lien is senior to the interest of the consignor; and

(4) a secured party that is a consignor of the collateral if the secured party receives from the consignor an authenticated demand for proceeds before distribution of the proceeds is completed.

(b) If requested by a secured party, a holder of a subordinate security interest or other lien shall furnish reasonable proof of the interest or lien within a reasonable time. Unless the holder does so, the secured party need not comply with the holder's demand under subsection (a)(3).

(c) A secured party need not apply or pay over for application noncash proceeds of disposition under Section 9—610 unless the failure to do so would be commercially unreasonable. A secured party that applies or pays over for application noncash proceeds shall do so in a commercially reasonable manner.

(d) If the security interest under which a disposition is made secures payment or performance of an obligation, after making the payments and applications required by subsection (a) and permitted by subsection (c):

(1) unless subsection (a)(4) requires the secured party to apply or pay over cash proceeds to a consignor, the secured party shall account to and pay a debtor for any surplus; and

(2) the obligor is liable for any deficiency.

(e) If the underlying transaction is a sale of accounts, chattel paper, payment intangibles, or promissory notes:

(1) the debtor is not entitled to any surplus; and

(2) the obligor is not liable for any deficiency.

(f) The surplus or deficiency following a disposition is calculated based on the amount of proceeds that would have been realized in a disposition complying with this part to a transferee other than the secured party, a person related to the secured party, or a secondary obligor if:

(1) the transferee in the disposition is the secured party, a person related to the secured party, or a secondary obligor; and

(2) the amount of proceeds of the disposition is significantly below the range of proceeds that a complying disposition to a person other than the secured party, a person related to the secured party, or a secondary obligor would have brought.

(g) A secured party that receives cash proceeds of a disposition in good faith and without knowledge that the receipt violates the rights of the holder of a security interest or other lien that is not subordinate to the security interest or agricultural lien under which the disposition is made:

(1) takes the cash proceeds free of the security interest or other lien;

(2) is not obligated to apply the proceeds of the disposition to the satisfaction of obligations secured by the security interest or other lien; and

(3) is not obligated to account to or pay the holder of the security interest or other lien for any surplus.

As amended in 2000.

§9—616. EXPLANATION OF CALCULATION OF SURPLUS OR DEFICIENCY

(a) In this section:

(1) "Explanation" means a writing that:

(A) states the amount of the surplus or deficiency;

(B) provides an explanation in accordance with subsection (c) of how the secured party calculated the surplus or deficiency;

(C) states, if applicable, that future debits, credits, charges, including additional credit service charges or interest, rebates, and expenses may affect the amount of the surplus or deficiency; and

(D) provides a telephone number or mailing address from which additional information concerning the transaction is available.

(2) "Request" means a record:

(A) authenticated by a debtor or consumer obligor;

(B) requesting that the recipient provide an explanation; and

(C) sent after disposition of the collateral under Section 9—610.

(b) In a consumer-goods transaction in which the debtor is entitled to a surplus or a consumer obligor is liable for a deficiency under Section 9—615, the secured party shall:

(1) send an explanation to the debtor or consumer obligor, as applicable, after the disposition and:

(A) before or when the secured party accounts to the debtor and pays any surplus or first makes written demand on the consumer obligor after the disposition for payment of the deficiency; and

(B) within 14 days after receipt of a request; or

(2) in the case of a consumer obligor who is liable for a deficiency, within 14 days after receipt of a request, send to the consumer obligor a record waiving the secured party's right to a deficiency.

(c) To comply with subsection (a)(1)(B), a writing must provide the following information in the following order:

(1) the aggregate amount of obligations secured by the security interest under which the disposition was made, and, if the amount reflects a rebate of unearned interest or credit service charge, an indication of that fact, calculated as of a specified date:

(A) if the secured party takes or receives possession of the collateral after default, not more than 35 days before the secured party takes or receives possession; or

(B) if the secured party takes or receives possession of the collateral before default or does not take possession of the collateral, not more than 35 days before the disposition;

(2) the amount of proceeds of the disposition;

(3) the aggregate amount of the obligations after deducting the amount of proceeds;

(4) the amount, in the aggregate or by type, and types of expenses, including expenses of retaking, holding, preparing for disposition, processing, and disposing of the collateral, and attorney's fees secured by the collateral which are known to the secured party and relate to the current disposition;

(5) the amount, in the aggregate or by type, and types of credits, including rebates of interest or credit service charges, to which the obligor is known to be entitled and which are not reflected in the amount in paragraph (1); and

(6) the amount of the surplus or deficiency.

(d) A particular phrasing of the explanation is not required. An explanation complying substantially with the requirements of subsection (a) is sufficient, even if it includes minor errors that are not seriously misleading.

(e) A debtor or consumer obligor is entitled without charge to one response to a request under this section during any six-month period in which the secured party did not send to the debtor or consumer obligor an explanation pursuant to subsection (b)(1). The secured party may require payment of a charge not exceeding $25 for each additional response.

§9—617. RIGHTS OF TRANSFEREE OF COLLATERAL

(a) A secured party's disposition of collateral after default:

(1) transfers to a transferee for value all of the debtor's rights in the collateral;

(2) discharges the security interest under which the disposition is made; and

(3) discharges any subordinate security interest or other subordinate lien [other than liens created under [cite acts or statutes providing for liens, if any, that are not to be discharged]].

(b) A transferee that acts in good faith takes free of the rights and interests described in subsection (a), even if the secured party fails to comply with this article or the requirements of any judicial proceeding.

(c) If a transferee does not take free of the rights and interests described in subsection (a), the transferee takes the collateral subject to:

(1) the debtor's rights in the collateral;

(2) the security interest or agricultural lien under which the disposition is made; and

(3) any other security interest or other lien.

§9—618. RIGHTS AND DUTIES OF CERTAIN SECONDARY OBLIGORS

(a) A secondary obligor acquires the rights and becomes obligated to perform the duties of the secured party after the secondary obligor:

(1) receives an assignment of a secured obligation from the secured party;

(2) receives a transfer of collateral from the secured party and agrees to accept the rights and assume the duties of the secured party; or

(3) is subrogated to the rights of a secured party with respect to collateral.

(b) An assignment, transfer, or subrogation described in subsection (a):

(1) is not a disposition of collateral under Section 9—610; and

(2) relieves the secured party of further duties under this article.

§9—619. TRANSFER OF RECORD OR LEGAL TITLE

(a) In this section, "transfer statement" means a record authenticated by a secured party stating:

(1) that the debtor has defaulted in connection with an obligation secured by specified collateral;

(2) that the secured party has exercised its post-default remedies with respect to the collateral;

(3) that, by reason of the exercise, a transferee has acquired the rights of the debtor in the collateral; and

(4) the name and mailing address of the secured party, debtor, and transferee.

(b) A transfer statement entitles the transferee to the transfer of record of all rights of the debtor in the collateral specified in the statement in any official filing, recording, registration, or certificate-of-title system covering the collateral. If a transfer statement is presented with the applicable fee and request form to the official or office responsible for maintaining the system, the official or office shall:

(1) accept the transfer statement;

(2) promptly amend its records to reflect the transfer; and

(3) if applicable, issue a new appropriate certificate of title in the name of the transferee.

(c) A transfer of the record or legal title to collateral to a secured party under subsection (b) or otherwise is not of itself a disposition of collateral under this article and does not of itself relieve the secured party of its duties under this article.

§9—620. ACCEPTANCE OF COLLATERAL IN FULL OR PARTIAL SATISFACTION OF OBLIGATION; COMPULSORY DISPOSITION OF COLLATERAL

(a) Except as otherwise provided in subsection (g), a secured party may accept collateral in full or partial satisfaction of the obligation it secures only if:

(1) the debtor consents to the acceptance under subsection (c);

(2) the secured party does not receive, within the time set forth in subsection (d), a notification of objection to the proposal authenticated by:

(A) a person to which the secured party was required to send a proposal under Section 9—621; or

(B) any other person, other than the debtor, holding an interest in the collateral subordinate to the security interest that is the subject of the proposal;

(3) if the collateral is consumer goods, the collateral is not in the possession of the debtor when the debtor consents to the acceptance; and

(4) subsection (e) does not require the secured party to dispose of the collateral or the debtor waives the requirement pursuant to Section 9—624.

(b) A purported or apparent acceptance of collateral under this section is ineffective unless:

(1) the secured party consents to the acceptance in an authenticated record or sends a proposal to the debtor; and

(2) the conditions of subsection (a) are met.

(c) For purposes of this section:

(1) a debtor consents to an acceptance of collateral in partial satisfaction of the obligation it secures only if the debtor agrees to the terms of the acceptance in a record authenticated after default; and

(2) a debtor consents to an acceptance of collateral in full satisfaction of the obligation it secures only if the debtor agrees to the terms of the acceptance in a record authenticated after default or the secured party:

(A) sends to the debtor after default a proposal that is unconditional or subject only to a condition that collateral not in the possession of the secured party be preserved or maintained;

(B) in the proposal, proposes to accept collateral in full satisfaction of the obligation it secures; and

(C) does not receive a notification of objection authenticated by the debtor within 20 days after the proposal is sent.

(d) To be effective under subsection (a)(2), a notification of objection must be received by the secured party:

(1) in the case of a person to which the proposal was sent pursuant to Section 9—621, within 20 days after notification was sent to that person; and

(2) in other cases:

(A) within 20 days after the last notification was sent pursuant to Section 9—621; or

(B) if a notification was not sent, before the debtor consents to the acceptance under subsection (c).

(e) A secured party that has taken possession of collateral shall dispose of the collateral pursuant to Section 9—610 within the time specified in subsection (f) if:

(1) 60 percent of the cash price has been paid in the case of a purchase-money security interest in consumer goods; or

(2) 60 percent of the principal amount of the obligation secured has been paid in the case of a non-purchase-money security interest in consumer goods.

(f) To comply with subsection (e), the secured party shall dispose of the collateral:

(1) within 90 days after taking possession; or

(2) within any longer period to which the debtor and all secondary obligors have agreed in an agreement to that effect entered into and authenticated after default.

(g) In a consumer transaction, a secured party may not accept collateral in partial satisfaction of the obligation it secures.

§9—621. NOTIFICATION OF PROPOSAL TO ACCEPT COLLATERAL

(a) A secured party that desires to accept collateral in full or partial satisfaction of the obligation it secures shall send its proposal to:

(1) any person from which the secured party has received, before the debtor consented to the acceptance, an authenticated notification of a claim of an interest in the collateral;

(2) any other secured party or lienholder that, 10 days before the debtor consented to the acceptance, held a security interest in or other lien on the collateral perfected by the filing of a financing statement that:

(A) identified the collateral;

(B) was indexed under the debtor's name as of that date; and

(C) was filed in the office or offices in which to file a financing statement against the debtor covering the collateral as of that date; and

(3) any other secured party that, 10 days before the debtor consented to the acceptance, held a security interest in the collateral perfected by compliance with a statute, regulation, or treaty described in Section 9—311(a).

(b) A secured party that desires to accept collateral in partial satisfaction of the obligation it secures shall send its proposal to any secondary obligor in addition to the persons described in subsection (a).

§9—622. EFFECT OF ACCEPTANCE OF COLLATERAL

(a) A secured party's acceptance of collateral in full or partial satisfaction of the obligation it secures:

(1) discharges the obligation to the extent consented to by the debtor;

(2) transfers to the secured party all of a debtor's rights in the collateral;

(3) discharges the security interest or agricultural lien that is the subject of the debtor's consent and any subordinate security interest or other subordinate lien; and

(4) terminates any other subordinate interest.

(b) A subordinate interest is discharged or terminated under subsection (a), even if the secured party fails to comply with this article.

§9—623. RIGHT TO REDEEM COLLATERAL

(a) A debtor, any secondary obligor, or any other secured party or lienholder may redeem collateral.

(b) To redeem collateral, a person shall tender:
(1) fulfillment of all obligations secured by the collateral; and
(2) the reasonable expenses and attorney's fees described in Section 9—615(a)(1).

(c) A redemption may occur at any time before a secured party:
(1) has collected collateral under Section 9—607;
(2) has disposed of collateral or entered into a contract for its disposition under Section 9—610; or
(3) has accepted collateral in full or partial satisfaction of the obligation it secures under Section 9—622.

§9—624. WAIVER

(a) A debtor or secondary obligor may waive the right to notification of disposition of collateral under Section 9—611 only by an agreement to that effect entered into and authenticated after default.

(b) A debtor may waive the right to require disposition of collateral under Section 9—620(e) only by an agreement to that effect entered into and authenticated after default.

(c) Except in a consumer-goods transaction, a debtor or secondary obligor may waive the right to redeem collateral under Section 9—623 only by an agreement to that effect entered into and authenticated after default.

[Subpart 2. Noncompliance with Article]

§9—625. REMEDIES FOR SECURED PARTY'S FAILURE TO COMPLY WITH ARTICLE

(a) If it is established that a secured party is not proceeding in accordance with this article, a court may order or restrain collection, enforcement, or disposition of collateral on appropriate terms and conditions.

(b) Subject to subsections (c), (d), and (f), a person is liable for damages in the amount of any loss caused by a failure to comply with this article. Loss caused by a failure to comply may include loss resulting from the debtor's inability to obtain, or increased costs of, alternative financing.

(c) Except as otherwise provided in Section 9—628:
(1) a person that, at the time of the failure, was a debtor, was an obligor, or held a security interest in or other lien on the collateral may recover damages under subsection (b) for its loss; and
(2) if the collateral is consumer goods, a person that was a debtor or a secondary obligor at the time a secured party failed to comply with this part may recover for that failure in any event an amount not less than the credit service charge plus 10 percent of the principal amount of the obligation or the time-price differential plus 10 percent of the cash price.

(d) A debtor whose deficiency is eliminated under Section 9—626 may recover damages for the loss of any surplus. However, a debtor or secondary obligor whose deficiency is eliminated or reduced under Section 9—626 may not otherwise recover under subsection (b) for noncompliance with the provisions of this part relating to collection, enforcement, disposition, or acceptance.

(e) In addition to any damages recoverable under subsection (b), the debtor, consumer obligor, or person named as a debtor in a filed record, as applicable, may recover $500 in each case from a person that:
(1) fails to comply with Section 9—208;
(2) fails to comply with Section 9—209;
(3) files a record that the person is not entitled to file under Section 9—509(a);
(4) fails to cause the secured party of record to file or send a termination statement as required by Section 9—513(a) or (c);
(5) fails to comply with Section 9—616(b)(1) and whose failure is part of a pattern, or consistent with a practice, of noncompliance; or
(6) fails to comply with Section 9—616(b)(2).

(f) A debtor or consumer obligor may recover damages under subsection (b) and, in addition, $500 in each case from a person that, without reasonable cause, fails to comply with a request under Section 9—210. A recipient of a request under Section 9—210 which never claimed an interest in the collateral or obligations that are the subject of a request under that section has a reasonable excuse for failure to comply with the request within the meaning of this subsection.

(g) If a secured party fails to comply with a request regarding a list of collateral or a statement of account under Section 9—210, the secured party may claim a security interest only as shown in the list or statement included in the request as against a person that is reasonably misled by the failure.

As amended in 2000.

§9—626. ACTION IN WHICH DEFICIENCY OR SURPLUS IS IN ISSUE

(a) In an action arising from a transaction, other than a consumer transaction, in which the amount of a deficiency or surplus is in issue, the following rules apply:
(1) A secured party need not prove compliance with the provisions of this part relating to collection, enforcement, disposition, or acceptance unless the debtor or a secondary obligor places the secured party's compliance in issue.
(2) If the secured party's compliance is placed in issue, the secured party has the burden of

establishing that the collection, enforcement, disposition, or acceptance was conducted in accordance with this part.

(3) Except as otherwise provided in Section 9—628, if a secured party fails to prove that the collection, enforcement, disposition, or acceptance was conducted in accordance with the provisions of this part relating to collection, enforcement, disposition, or acceptance, the liability of a debtor or a secondary obligor for a deficiency is limited to an amount by which the sum of the secured obligation, expenses, and attorney's fees exceeds the greater of:

(A) the proceeds of the collection, enforcement, disposition, or acceptance; or

(B) the amount of proceeds that would have been realized had the noncomplying secured party proceeded in accordance with the provisions of this part relating to collection, enforcement, disposition, or acceptance.

(4) For purposes of paragraph (3)(B), the amount of proceeds that would have been realized is equal to the sum of the secured obligation, expenses, and attorney's fees unless the secured party proves that the amount is less than that sum.

(5) If a deficiency or surplus is calculated under Section 9—615(f), the debtor or obligor has the burden of establishing that the amount of proceeds of the disposition is significantly below the range of prices that a complying disposition to a person other than the secured party, a person related to the secured party, or a secondary obligor would have brought.

(b) The limitation of the rules in subsection (a) to transactions other than consumer transactions is intended to leave to the court the determination of the proper rules in consumer transactions. The court may not infer from that limitation the nature of the proper rule in consumer transactions and may continue to apply established approaches.

§9—627. DETERMINATION OF WHETHER CONDUCT WAS COMMERCIALLY REASONABLE

(a) The fact that a greater amount could have been obtained by a collection, enforcement, disposition, or acceptance at a different time or in a different method from that selected by the secured party is not of itself sufficient to preclude the secured party from establishing that the collection, enforcement, disposition, or acceptance was made in a commercially reasonable manner.

(b) A disposition of collateral is made in a commercially reasonable manner if the disposition is made:

(1) in the usual manner on any recognized market;

(2) at the price current in any recognized market at the time of the disposition; or

(3) otherwise in conformity with reasonable commercial practices among dealers in the type of property that was the subject of the disposition.

(c) A collection, enforcement, disposition, or acceptance is commercially reasonable if it has been approved:

(1) in a judicial proceeding;

(2) by a bona fide creditors' committee;

(3) by a representative of creditors; or

(4) by an assignee for the benefit of creditors.

(d) Approval under subsection (c) need not be obtained, and lack of approval does not mean that the collection, enforcement, disposition, or acceptance is not commercially reasonable.

§9—628. NONLIABILITY AND LIMITATION ON LIABILITY OF SECURED PARTY; LIABILITY OF SECONDARY OBLIGOR

(a) Unless a secured party knows that a person is a debtor or obligor, knows the identity of the person, and knows how to communicate with the person:

(1) the secured party is not liable to the person, or to a secured party or lienholder that has filed a financing statement against the person, for failure to comply with this article; and

(2) the secured party's failure to comply with this article does not affect the liability of the person for a deficiency.

(b) A secured party is not liable because of its status as secured party:

(1) to a person that is a debtor or obligor, unless the secured party knows:

(A) that the person is a debtor or obligor;

(B) the identity of the person; and

(C) how to communicate with the person; or

(2) to a secured party or lienholder that has filed a financing statement against a person, unless the secured party knows:

(A) that the person is a debtor; and

(B) the identity of the person.

(c) A secured party is not liable to any person, and a person's liability for a deficiency is not affected, because of any act or omission arising out of the secured party's reasonable belief that a transaction is not a consumer-goods transaction or a consumer transaction or that goods are not consumer goods, if the secured party's belief is based on its reasonable reliance on:

(1) a debtor's representation concerning the purpose for which collateral was to be used, acquired, or held; or

(2) an obligor's representation concerning the purpose for which a secured obligation was incurred.

(d)   A secured party is not liable to any person under Section 9—625(c)(2) for its failure to comply with Section 9—616.

(e)   A secured party is not liable under Section 9—625(c)(2) more than once with respect to any one secured obligation.

Part 7 Transition

§9—701. EFFECTIVE DATE

This [Act] takes effect on July 1, 2001.

§9—702. SAVINGS CLAUSE

(a)   Except as otherwise provided in this part, this [Act] applies to a transaction or lien within its scope, even if the transaction or lien was entered into or created before this [Act] takes effect.

(b)   Except as otherwise provided in subsection (c) and Sections 9—703 through 9—709:

(1)   transactions and liens that were not governed by [former Article 9], were validly entered into or created before this [Act] takes effect, and would be subject to this [Act] if they had been entered into or created after this [Act] takes effect, and the rights, duties, and interests flowing from those transactions and liens remain valid after this [Act] takes effect; and

(2)   the transactions and liens may be terminated, completed, consummated, and enforced as required or permitted by this [Act] or by the law that otherwise would apply if this [Act] had not taken effect.

(c)   This [Act] does not affect an action, case, or proceeding commenced before this [Act] takes effect.

As amended in 2000.

§9—703. SECURITY INTEREST PERFECTED BEFORE EFFECTIVE DATE

(a)   A security interest that is enforceable immediately before this [Act] takes effect and would have priority over the rights of a person that becomes a lien creditor at that time is a perfected security interest under this [Act] if, when this [Act] takes effect, the applicable requirements for enforceability and perfection under this [Act] are satisfied without further action.

(b)   Except as otherwise provided in Section 9—705, if, immediately before this [Act] takes effect, a security interest is enforceable and would have priority over the rights of a person that becomes a lien creditor at that time, but the applicable requirements for enforceability or perfection under this [Act] are not satisfied when this [Act] takes effect, the security interest:

(1)   is a perfected security interest for one year after this [Act] takes effect;

(2)   remains enforceable thereafter only if the security interest becomes enforceable under Section 9—203 before the year expires; and

(3)   remains perfected thereafter only if the applicable requirements for perfection under this [Act] are satisfied before the year expires.

§9—704. SECURITY INTEREST UNPERFECTED BEFORE EFFECTIVE DATE

A security interest that is enforceable immediately before this [Act] takes effect but which would be subordinate to the rights of a person that becomes a lien creditor at that time:

(1)   remains an enforceable security interest for one year after this [Act] takes effect;

(2)   remains enforceable thereafter if the security interest becomes enforceable under Section 9—203 when this [Act] takes effect or within one year thereafter; and

(3)   becomes perfected:

(A)   without further action, when this [Act] takes effect if the applicable requirements for perfection under this [Act] are satisfied before or at that time; or

(B)   when the applicable requirements for perfection are satisfied if the requirements are satisfied after that time.

§9—705. EFFECTIVENESS OF ACTION TAKEN BEFORE EFFECTIVE DATE

(a)   If action, other than the filing of a financing statement, is taken before this [Act] takes effect and the action would have resulted in priority of a security interest over the rights of a person that becomes a lien creditor had the security interest become enforceable before this [Act] takes effect, the action is effective to perfect a security interest that attaches under this [Act] within one year after this [Act] takes effect. An attached security interest becomes unperfected one year after this [Act] takes effect unless the security interest becomes a perfected security interest under this [Act] before the expiration of that period.

(b)   The filing of a financing statement before this [Act] takes effect is effective to perfect a security interest to the extent the filing would satisfy the applicable requirements for perfection under this [Act].

(c)   This [Act] does not render ineffective an effective financing statement that, before this [Act] takes effect, is filed and satisfies the applicable requirements for perfection under the law of the jurisdiction governing perfection as provided in [former Section 9—103]. However, except as otherwise provided in subsections (d) and (e) and

Section 9—706, the financing statement ceases to be effective at the earlier of:

>> (1) the time the financing statement would have ceased to be effective under the law of the jurisdiction in which it is filed; or
>> (2) June 30, 2006.

(d) The filing of a continuation statement after this [Act] takes effect does not continue the effectiveness of the financing statement filed before this [Act] takes effect. However, upon the timely filing of a continuation statement after this [Act] takes effect and in accordance with the law of the jurisdiction governing perfection as provided in Part 3, the effectiveness of a financing statement filed in the same office in that jurisdiction before this [Act] takes effect continues for the period provided by the law of that jurisdiction.

(e) Subsection (c)(2) applies to a financing statement that, before this [Act] takes effect, is filed against a transmitting utility and satisfies the applicable requirements for perfection under the law of the jurisdiction governing perfection as provided in [former Section 9—103] only to the extent that Part 3 provides that the law of a jurisdiction other than the jurisdiction in which the financing statement is filed governs perfection of a security interest in collateral covered by the financing statement.

(f) A financing statement that includes a financing statement filed before this [Act] takes effect and a continuation statement filed after this [Act] takes effect is effective only to the extent that it satisfies the requirements of Part 5 for an initial financing statement.

§9—706. WHEN INITIAL FINANCING STATEMENT SUFFICES TO CONTINUE EFFECTIVENESS OF FINANCING STATEMENT

(a) The filing of an initial financing statement in the office specified in Section 9—501 continues the effectiveness of a financing statement filed before this [Act] takes effect if:

>> (1) the filing of an initial financing statement in that office would be effective to perfect a security interest under this [Act];
>> (2) the pre-effective-date financing statement was filed in an office in another State or another office in this State; and
>> (3) the initial financing statement satisfies subsection (c).

(b) The filing of an initial financing statement under subsection (a) continues the effectiveness of the pre-effective-date financing statement:

>> (1) if the initial financing statement is filed before this [Act] takes effect, for the period provided in [former Section 9—403] with respect to a financing statement; and

>> (2) if the initial financing statement is filed after this [Act] takes effect, for the period provided in Section 9—515 with respect to an initial financing statement.

(c) To be effective for purposes of subsection (a), an initial financing statement must:

>> (1) satisfy the requirements of Part 5 for an initial financing statement;
>> (2) identify the pre-effective-date financing statement by indicating the office in which the financing statement was filed and providing the dates of filing and file numbers, if any, of the financing statement and of the most recent continuation statement filed with respect to the financing statement; and
>> (3) indicate that the pre-effective-date financing statement remains effective.

§9—707. AMENDMENT OF PRE-EFFECTIVE-DATE FINANCING STATEMENT

(a) In this section, "Pre-effective-date financing statement" means a financing statement filed before this [Act] takes effect.

(b) After this [Act] takes effect, a person may add or delete collateral covered by, continue or terminate the effectiveness of, or otherwise amend the information provided in, a pre-effective-date financing statement only in accordance with the law of the jurisdiction governing perfection as provided in Part 3. However, the effectiveness of a pre-effective-date financing statement also may be terminated in accordance with the law of the jurisdiction in which the financing statement is filed.

(c) Except as otherwise provided in subsection (d), if the law of this State governs perfection of a security interest, the information in a pre-effective-date financing statement may be amended after this [Act] takes effect only if:

>> (1) the pre-effective-date financing statement and an amendment are filed in the office specified in Section 9—501;
>> (2) an amendment is filed in the office specified in Section 9—501 concurrently with, or after the filing in that office of, an initial financing statement that satisfies Section 9—706(c); or
>> (3) an initial financing statement that provides the information as amended and satisfies Section 9—706(c) is filed in the office specified in Section 9—501.

(d) If the law of this State governs perfection of a security interest, the effectiveness of a pre-effective-date financing statement may be continued only under Section 9—705(d) and (f) or 9—706.

(e) Whether or not the law of this State governs perfection of a security interest, the effectiveness of a pre-effective-date financing statement filed in this State may be terminated after this [Act] takes effect by filing a termination statement in the office in which the pre-effective-date financing statement is filed, unless an initial financing statement that satisfies Section 9—706(c) has been filed in the office specified by the law of the jurisdiction governing perfection as provided in Part 3 as the office in which to file a financing statement.

As amended in 2000.

§9—708. PERSONS ENTITLED TO FILE INITIAL FINANCING STATEMENT OR CONTINUATION STATEMENT

A person may file an initial financing statement or a continuation statement under this part if:

(1)   the secured party of record authorizes the filing; and
    (2)   the filing is necessary under this part:
        (A)   to continue the effectiveness of a financing statement filed before this [Act] takes effect; or
        (B)   to perfect or continue the perfection of a security interest.
As amended in 2000.

§9—709. PRIORITY

(a)   This [Act] determines the priority of conflicting claims to collateral. However, if the relative priorities of the claims were established before this [Act] takes effect, [former Article 9] determines priority.

(b)   For purposes of Section 9—322(a), the priority of a security interest that becomes enforceable under Section 9—203 of this [Act] dates from the time this [Act] takes effect if the security interest is perfected under this [Act] by the filing of a financing statement before this [Act] takes effect which would not have been effective to perfect the security interest under [former Article 9]. This subsection does not apply to conflicting security interests each of which is perfected by the filing of such a financing statement.

As amended in 2000.

A

abate—put a stop to a nuisance; reduce or cancel a legacy because the estate of the decedent is insufficient to make payment in full.

absolute guaranty—agreement that creates the same obligation for the guarantor as a suretyship does for the surety; a guaranty of payment creates an absolute guaranty.

absolute privilege—complete defense against the tort of defamation, as in the speeches of members of Congress on the floor and witnesses in a trial.

abstract of title—history of the transfers of title to a given piece of land, briefly stating the parties to and the effect of all deeds, wills, and judicial proceedings relating to the land.

acceptance—unqualified assent to the act or proposal of another; as the acceptance of a draft (bill of exchange), of an offer to make a contract, of goods delivered by the seller, or of a gift or deed.

acceptor—drawee who has accepted the liability of paying the amount of money specified in a draft.

accommodation party—person who signs an instrument to lend credit to another party to the paper.

accord and satisfaction—agreement to substitute for an existing debt some alternative form of discharging that debt, coupled with the actual discharge of the debt by the substituted performance.

acknowledgment—admission or confirmation, generally of an instrument and usually made before a person authorized to administer oaths, such as a notary public; used to establish that the instrument was executed by the person making the instrument, that it was a voluntary act, or that the instrument is recorded.

acquired distinctiveness—through advertising, use and association, over time, an ordinary descriptive word or phase has taken on a new source-identifying meaning and functions as a mark in the eyes of the public

act-of-state doctrine—doctrine whereby every sovereign state is bound to respect the independence of every other sovereign state, and the courts of one country will not sit in judgment of another government's acts done within its own territory.

adeemed—canceled; as in a specifically bequeathed property being sold or given away by the testator prior to death, thus canceling the bequest.

adjustable rate mortgage (ARM)—mortgage with variable financing charges over the life of the loan.

administrative agency—government body charged with administering and implementing legislation.

administrative law—law governing administrative agencies.

Administrative Procedure Act—federal law that establishes the operating rules for administrative agencies.

administrative regulations—rules made by state and federal administrative agencies.

administrator, administratrix—person (man, woman) appointed to wind up and settle the estate of a person who has died without a will.

admissibility—the quality of the evidence in a case that allows it to be presented to the jury.

adverse possession—hostile possession of real estate, which when actual, visible, notorious, exclusive, and continued for the required time, will vest the title to the land in the person in such adverse possession.

advising bank—bank that tells beneficiary that letter of credit has been issued.

affidavit—statement of facts set forth in written form and supported by the oath or affirmation of the person making the statement setting forth that such facts are true on the basis of actual knowledge or on information and belief. The affidavit is executed before a notary public or other person authorized to administer oaths.

affirm—action taken by an appellate court that approves the decision of the court below.

affirmative action plan (AAP)—plan to have a diverse and representative workforce.

after-acquired goods—goods acquired after a security interest has attached.

agency—the relationship that exists between a person identified as a principal and another by virtue of which the latter may make contracts with third persons on behalf of the principal. (Parties—principal, agent, third person)

agent—person or firm who is authorized by the principal or by operation of law to make contracts with third persons on behalf of the principal.

airbill—document of title issued to a shipper whose goods are being sent via air.

alteration—unauthorized change or completion of a negotiable instrument designed to modify the obligation of a party to the instrument.

alternative payees—those persons to whom a negotiable instrument is made payable, any one of whom may indorse and take delivery of it.

ambiguous—having more than one reasonable interpretation.

answer—what a defendant must file to admit or deny facts asserted by the plaintiff.

anticipatory breach—promisor's repudiation of the contract prior to the time that performance is required when such repudiation is accepted by the promisee as a breach of the contract.

anticipatory repudiation—repudiation made in advance of the time for performance of the contract obligations.

antilapse statutes—statutes providing that the children or heirs of a deceased beneficiary may take the legacy in the place of the deceased beneficiary.

apparent authority—appearance of authority created by the principal's words or conduct.

appeal—taking a case to a reviewing court to determine whether the judgment of the lower court or administrative agency was correct. (Parties—appellant, appellee)

appellate jurisdiction—the power of a court to hear and decide a given class of cases on appeal from another court or administrative agency.

appropriation—taking of an image, likeness, or name for commercial advantage.

arbitration—the settlement of disputed questions, whether of law or fact, by one or more arbitrators by whose decision the parties agree to be bound.

Article 2—section of the Uniform Commercial Code that governs contracts for the sale of goods.

articles of copartnership—See *Partnership Agreement.*

articles of incorporation—document filed to create a corporation; the basic structure of a company and the rights of its owners.

articles of partnership—See *Partnership Agreement.*

assignee—third party to whom contract benefits are transferred.

assignment—transfer of a right. Generally used in connection with personal property rights, as rights under a contract, commercial paper, an insurance policy, a mortgage, or a lease. (Parties—assignor, assignee)

assignor—party who assigns contract rights to a third party.

association tribunal—a court created by a trade association or group for the resolution of disputes among its members.

assumption—mortgage transfers in which the transferee and mortgagor are liable and the property is subject to foreclosure by the mortgagee if payments are not made.

attestation clause—clause that indicates a witness has observed either the execution of the will or the testator's acknowledgment of the writing as the testator's will.

attorney in fact—agent authorized to act for another under a power of attorney.

attorney-client privilege—right of individual to have discussions with his/her attorney kept private and confidential

attractive nuisance doctrine—a rule imposing liability upon a landowner for injuries sustained by small children playing on the land when the landowner permits a condition to exist or maintains equipment that a reasonable person should realize would attract small children who could not realize the danger. The rule does not apply if an unreasonable burden would be imposed upon the landowner in taking steps to protect the children.

authorities—corporations formed by government that perform public service.

automatic perfection—perfection given by statute without specific filing or possession requirements on the part of the creditor.

automatic stay—order to prevent creditors from taking action such as filing suits or seeking foreclosure against the debtor.

B

bad check laws—laws making it a criminal offense to issue a bad check with intent to defraud.

bailee—person who accepts possession of a property.

bailee's lien—specific, possessory lien of the bailee upon the goods for work done to them. Commonly extended by statute to any bailee's claim for compensation, eliminating the necessity of retention of possession.

bailment—relationship that exists when personal property is delivered into the possession of another under an agreement, express or implied, that the identical property will be returned or will be delivered in accordance with the agreement. (Parties—bailor, bailee)

bailment for mutual benefit—bailment in which the bailor and bailee derive a benefit from the bailment.

bailor—person who turns over the possession of a property.

balance sheet test—comparison of assets to liabilities made to determine solvency.

bankruptcy—procedure by which one unable to pay debts may surrender all assets in excess of any exemption claim to the court for administration and distribution to creditors, and the debtor is given a discharge that releases him from the unpaid balance due on most debts.

bankruptcy courts—court of special jurisdiction to determine bankruptcy issues.

battle of the forms—merchants' exchanges of invoices and purchase orders with differing boilerplate terms.

bearer—person in physical possession of commercial paper payable to bearer, a document of title directing delivery to bearer, or an investment security in bearer form.

bearer paper—instrument with no payee, payable to cash or payable to bearer.

bedrock view—a strict constructionist interpretation of a constitution.

beneficiary—person to whom the proceeds of a life insurance policy are payable, a person for whose benefit property is held in trust, or a person given property by a will; the ultimate recipient of the benefit of a funds transfer.

beneficiary's bank—the final bank, which carries out the payment order, in the chain of a transfer of funds.

bequest—gift of personal property by will.

bicameral—a two-house form of the legislative branch of government.

bilateral contract—agreement under which one promise is given in exchange for another.

bill of lading—document issued by a carrier acknowledging the receipt of goods and the terms of the contract of transportation.

bill of sale—writing signed by the seller reciting that the personal

property therein described has been sold to the buyer.

blackmail—extortion demands made by a nonpublic official.

blank indorsement—an indorsement that does not name the person to whom the paper, document of title, or investment security is negotiated.

blocking laws—laws that prohibit the disclosure, copying, inspection, or removal of documents located in the enacting country in compliance with orders from foreign authorities.

blue sky laws—state statutes designed to protect the public from the sale of worthless stocks and bonds.

bona fide—in good faith; without any fraud or deceit.

bond—obligation or promise in writing and sealed, generally of corporations, personal representatives, and trustees; fidelity bonds.

bond indenture—agreement setting forth the contractual terms of a particular bond issue.

book value—value found by dividing the value of the corporate assets by the number of shares outstanding.

breach—failure to act or perform in the manner called for in a contract.

breach of the peace—violation of the law in the repossession of the collateral.

brownfields—land that is a designated Superfund cleanup site but which lies fallow because no one is willing to risk liability by buying the property, even when the hazardous waste has been removed or property no one is willing to spend the money to remove the hazardous waste.

bubble concept—method for determining total emissions in one area; all sources are considered in an area.

business ethics—balancing the goal of profits with values of individuals and society.

business judgment rule (BJR)—rule that allows management immunity from liability for corporate acts where there is a reasonable indication that the acts were made in good faith with due care.

bylaws—rules and regulations enacted by a corporation to govern the affairs of the corporation and its shareholders, directors, and officers.

C

cancellation provision—crossing out of a part of an instrument or a destruction of all legal effect of the instrument, whether by act of party, upon breach by the other party, or pursuant to agreement or decree of court.

capital stock—declared money value of the outstanding stock of the corporation.

cargo insurance—insurance that protects a cargo owner against financial loss if goods being shipped are lost or damaged at sea.

carrier—individual or organization undertaking the transportation of goods.

case law—law that includes principles that are expressed for the first time in court decisions.

cash surrender value—sum paid the insured upon the surrender of a policy to the insurer.

cash tender offer—general offer to all shareholders of a target corporation to purchase their shares for cash at a specified price.

cashier's check—draft drawn by a bank on itself.

cause of action—right to damages or other judicial relief when a legally protected right of the plaintiff is violated by an unlawful act of the defendant.

cease-and-desist order—order issued by a court or administrative agency to stop a practice that it decides is improper.

certificate of deposit (CD)—promise-to- pay instrument issued by a bank.

certificate of incorporation—written approval from the state or national government for a corporation to be formed.

certificate of stock—document evidencing a shareholder's ownership of stock issued by a corporation.

certified check—check for which the bank has set aside in a special account sufficient funds to pay it; payment is made when check is presented regardless of amount in drawer's account at that time; discharges all parties except certifying bank when holder requests certification.

cestui que trust—beneficiary or person for whose benefit the property is held in trust.

CF—cost and freight.

Chapter 11 bankruptcy—reorganization form of bankruptcy under federal law.

Chapter 7 bankruptcy—liquidation form of bankruptcy under federal law.

Chapter 13 bankruptcy—proceeding of consumer debt readjustment plan bankruptcy.

charging order—order by a court, after a business partner's personal assets are exhausted, requiring that the partner's share of the profits be paid to a creditor until the debt is discharged.

charter—grant of authority from a government to exist as a corporation. Generally replaced today by a certificate of incorporation approving the articles of incorporation.

check—order by a depositor on a bank to pay a sum of money to a payee; a bill of exchange drawn on a bank and payable on demand.

choice-of-law clause—clause in an agreement that specifies which law will govern should a dispute arise.

chose in action—intangible personal property in the nature of claims

against another, such as a claim for accounts receivable or wages.

CIF—cost, insurance, and freight.

civil disobedience—the term used when natural law proponents violate positive law.

claim—right to payment.

Clayton Act—a federal law that prohibits price discrimination.

Clean Air Act—federal legislation that establishes standards for air pollution levels and prevents further deterioration of air quality.

Clean Water Act—federal legislation that regulates water pollution through a control system.

close corporation—corporation whose shares are held by a single shareholder or a small group of shareholders.

close-connection doctrine—circumstantial evidence, such as an ongoing or a close relationship, that can serve as notice of a problem with an instrument.

COD—cash on delivery.

coinsurance clause—clause requiring the insured to maintain insurance on property up to a stated amount and providing that to the extent that this is not done, the insured is to be deemed a coinsurer with the insurer, so that the latter is liable only for its proportionate share of the amount of insurance required to be carried.

collateral—property pledged by a borrower as security for a debt.

comity—principle of international and national law that the laws of all nations and states deserve the respect legitimately demanded by equal participants.

commerce clause—that section of the U.S. Constitution allocating business regulation.

commercial impracticability—situation that occurs when costs of performance rise suddenly and performance of a contract will result in a substantial loss.

commercial lease—any nonconsumer lease.

commercial paper—written, transferable, signed promise or order to pay a specified sum of money; a negotiable instrument.

commercial unit—standard of the trade for shipment or packaging of a good.

commission merchant—bailee to whom goods are consigned for sale.

commission or factorage—consignee's compensation.

common carrier—carrier that holds out its facilities to serve the general public for compensation without discrimination.

common law—the body of unwritten principles originally based upon the usages and customs of the community that were recognized and enforced by the courts.

common stock—stock that has no right or priority over any other stock of the corporation as to dividends or distribution of assets upon dissolution.

community property—cotenancy held by husband and wife in property acquired during their marriage under the law of some of the states, principally in the southwestern United States.

comparative negligence—defense to negligence that allows plaintiff to recover reduced damages based on his level of fault.

compensatory damages—sum of money that will compensate an injured plaintiff for actual loss.

complaint—the initial pleading filed by the plaintiff in many actions, which in many states may be served as original process to acquire jurisdiction over the defendant.

composition of creditors—agreement among creditors that each shall accept a partial payment as full payment in consideration of the other creditors doing the same.

Comprehensive Environmental Response, Compensation, and Liability Act (CERCLA)—federal law that authorizes the president to issue funds for the cleanup of areas that were once disposal sites for hazardous wastes.

computer crimes—wrongs committed using a computer or with knowledge of computers.

concealment—failure to volunteer information not requested.

condition—stipulation or prerequisite in a contract, will, or other instrument.

condition precedent—event that if unsatisfied would mean that no rights would arise under a contract.

condition subsequent—event whose occurrence or lack thereof terminates a contract.

condominium—combination of co-ownership and individual ownership.

confidential relationship—relationship in which, because of the legal status of the parties or their respective physical or mental conditions or knowledge, one party places full confidence and trust in the other.

conflict of interest—conduct that compromises an employee's allegiance to that company.

conglomerate—relationship of a parent corporation to subsidiary corporations engaged in diversified fields of activity unrelated to the field of activity of the parent corporation.

consent decrees—informal settlements of enforcement actions brought by agencies.

consequential damages—damages the buyer experiences as a result of the seller's breach with respect to a third party; also called *special damages*.

consideration—promise or performance that the promisor demands as the price of the promise.

consignee—(1) person to whom goods are shipped, (2) dealer who sells goods for others.

consignment—bailment made for the purpose of sale by the bailee. (Parties—consignor, consignee)

consignor—(1) person who delivers goods to the carrier for shipment, (2) party with title who turns goods over to another for sale.

consolidation (of corporations)—combining of two or more corporations in which the corporate existence of each one ceases and a new corporation is created.

conspiracy—agreement between two or more persons to commit an unlawful act.

constitution—a body of principles that establishes the structure of a government and the relationship of the government to the people who are governed.

constructive bailment—bailment imposed by law as opposed to one created by contract, whereby the bailee must preserve the property and redeliver it to the owner.

constructive delivery—See *Symbolic Delivery*.

constructive eviction—act or omission of the landlord that substantially deprives the tenant of the use and enjoyment of the premises.

consumer—any buyer afforded special protections by statute or regulation.

consumer credit—credit for personal, family, and household use.

consumer goods—goods used or bought primarily for personal, family, or household use.

consumer lease—lease of goods by a natural person for personal, family, or household use.

Consumer Product Safety Improvement Act—federal law that sets standards for the types of paints used in toys; a response to the lead paint found in toys made in China; requires tracking for international production; increases penalties

contract—a binding agreement based on the genuine assent of the parties, made for a lawful object, between competent parties, in the form required by law, and generally supported by consideration.

contract carrier—carrier that transports on the basis of individual contracts that it makes with each shipper.

contract interference—tort in which a third party interferes with others' freedom to contract.

contract of adhesion—contract offered by a dominant party to a party with inferior bargaining power on a take-it-or-leave-it basis.

contract under seal—contract executed by affixing a seal or making an impression on the paper or on some adhering substance such as wax attached to the document.

contracting agent—agent with authority to make contracts; person with whom the buyer deals.

Contracts for the International Sale of Goods (CISG)—uniform international contract code contracts for international sale of goods.

contractual capacity—ability to understand that a contract is being made and to understand its general meaning.

contribution—right of a co-obligor who has paid more than a proportionate share to demand that the other obligor pay the amount of the excess payment made.

contributory negligence—negligence of the plaintiff that contributes to injury and at common law bars recovery from the defendant although the defendant may have been more negligent than the plaintiff.

conversion—act of taking personal property by a person not entitled to it and keeping it from its true owner or prior possessor without consent.

cooperative—group of two or more persons or enterprises that acts through a common agent with respect to a common objective, such as buying or selling.

copyright—exclusive right given by federal statute to the creator of a literary or an artistic work to use, reproduce, and display the work.

corporation—artificial being created by government grant, which for many purposes is treated as a natural person.

corporation by estoppel—corporation that comes about when parties estop themselves from denying that the corporation exists.

corporation de jure—corporation with a legal right to exist by virtue of law.

correspondent bank—will honor the letter of credit from the domestic bank of the buyer.

cost plus—method of determining the purchase price or contract price equal to the seller's or contractor's costs plus a stated percentage as the profit.

co-sureties—sureties for the same debtor and obligor.

cotenancy—when two or more persons hold concurrent rights and interests in the same property.

Council on Environmental Quality (CEQ)—federal agency that establishes national policies on environmental quality and then recommends legislation to implement these policies.

counterclaim—a claim that the defendant in an action may make against the plaintiff.

counteroffer—proposal by an offeree to the offeror that changes the terms of, and thus rejects, the original offer.

course of dealing—pattern of performance between two parties to a contract.

court—a tribunal established by government to hear and decide matters properly brought to it.

covenant against encumbrances—guarantee that conveyed land is not subject to any right or interest of a third person.

covenant of further assurances—promise that the grantor of an interest in land will execute any additional documents required to perfect the title of the grantee.

covenant of quiet enjoyment—covenant by the grantor of an interest in land to not disturb the grantee's possession of the land.

covenant of right to convey—guarantee that the grantor of an interest in land, if not the owner, has the right or authority to make the conveyance to a new owner.

covenant of seisin—guarantee that the grantor of an interest in land owns the estate conveyed to a new owner.

covenants of title—grantor's covenants of a deed that guarantee such matters as the right to make the conveyance, to ownership of the property, to freedom of the property from encumbrances, or that the grantee will not be disturbed in the quiet enjoyment of the land.

credit transfer—transaction in which a person making payment, such as a buyer, requests payment be made to the beneficiary's bank.

creditor—person (seller or lender) who is owed money; also may be a secured party.

crime—violation of the law that is punished as an offense against the state or government.

cross-examination—the examination made of a witness by the attorney for the adverse party.

cumulative voting—system of voting for directors in which each shareholder has as many votes as the number of voting shares owned multiplied by the number of directors to be elected, and such votes can be distributed for the various candidates as desired.

customary authority—authority of an agent to do any act that, according to the custom of the community, usually accompanies the transaction for which the agent is authorized to act.

cybercrime—crimes committed via the Internet.

cyberlaw—laws and precedent applicable to Internet transactions and communications.

cyberspace—World Wide Web and Internet communication.

cybersquatters—term for those who register and set up domain names on the Internet for resale to the famous users of the names in question.

D

de facto—existing in fact as distinguished from as of right, as in the case of an officer or a corporation purporting to act as such without being elected to the office or having been properly incorporated.

debenture—unsecured bond of a corporation, with no specific corporate assets pledged as security for payment.

debit transfer—transaction in which a beneficiary entitled to money requests payment from a bank according to a prior agreement.

debtor—buyer on credit (i.e., a borrower).

decedent—person whose estate is being administered.

deed—instrument by which the grantor (owner of land) conveys or transfers the title to a grantee.

defamation—untrue statement by one party about another to a third party.

defendant—party charged with a violation of civil or criminal law in a proceeding.

definite time—time of payment computable from the face of the instrument.

delegated powers—powers expressly granted the national government by the Constitution.

delegation—transfer to another of the right and power to do an act.

delegation of duties—transfer of duties by a contracting party to another person who is to perform them.

delivery—constructive or actual possession.

demand draft—draft that is payable upon presentment.

demurrer—a pleading to dismiss the adverse party's pleading for not stating a cause of action or a defense.

deposition—the testimony of a witness taken out of court before a person authorized to administer oaths.

depositor—person, or bailor, who gives property for storage.

derivative action—secondary action for damages or breach of contract brought by one or more corporate shareholders against directors, officers, or third persons.

development statement—statement that sets forth significant details of a real estate or property development as required by the federal Land Sales Act.

devise—gift of real estate made by will.

devisee—beneficiary of a devise.

direct damages—losses that are caused by breach of a contract.

direct examination—examination of a witness by his or her attorney.

directed verdict—a direction by the trial judge to the jury to return a verdict in favor of a specified party to the action.

disability—any incapacity resulting from bodily injury or disease to engage in any occupation for remuneration or profit.

discharge in bankruptcy—order of the bankruptcy court relieving the debtor from obligation to pay the unpaid balance of most claims.

disclosed principal—principal whose identity is made known by the agent as well as the fact that the agent is acting on the principal's behalf.

discovery—procedures for ascertaining facts prior to the time of trial in order to eliminate the element of surprise in litigation.

dishonor—status when the primary party refuses to pay the instrument according to its terms.

disinherited—excluded from sharing in the estate of a decedent.

Dispute Settlement Body—means, provided by the World Trade Organization, for member countries to resolve trade disputes rather than engage in unilateral trade sanctions or a trade war.

distinctiveness—capable of serving the source-identifying function of a mark.

distribution per stirpes—distribution of an estate made in as many equal parts as there are family lines represented in the nearest generation; also known as stirpital distribution.

distributor—entity that takes title to goods and bears the financial and commercial risks for the subsequent sale of the goods.

divestiture order—a court order to dispose of interests that could lead to a monopoly.

divisible contract—agreement consisting of two or more parts, each calling for corresponding performances of each part by the parties.

document of title—document treated as evidence that a person is entitled to receive, hold, and dispose of the document and the goods it covers.

domestic corporation—corporation that has been incorporated by the state in question as opposed to incorporation by another state.

dominant tenement—land that is benefited by an easement.

donee—recipient of a gift.

donor—person making a gift.

double indemnity—provision for payment of double the amount specified by the insurance contract if death is caused by an accident and occurs under specified circumstances.

draft or bill of exchange—an unconditional order in writing by one person upon another, signed by the person giving it, and ordering the person to whom it is directed to pay upon demand or at a definite time a sum certain in money to order or to bearer.

drawee—person to whom the draft is addressed and who is ordered to pay the amount of money specified in the draft.

drawer—person who writes out and creates a draft or bill of exchange, including a check.

due diligence—process of checking the environmental history and nature of land prior to purchase.

due process—the constitutional right to be heard, question witnesses, and present evidence.

due process clause—in the Fifth and Fourteenth Amendments, a guarantee of protection from unreasonable procedures and unreasonable laws.

dumping—selling goods in another country at less than their fair value.

duress—conduct that deprives the victim of free will and that generally gives the victim the right to set aside any transaction entered into under such circumstances.

duty—an obligation of law imposed on a person to perform or refrain from performing a certain act.

E

easement—permanent right that one has in the land of another, as the right to cross another's land or an easement of way.

easement by implication—easement not specifically created by deed that arises from the circumstances of the parties and the land location and access.

economic duress—threat of financial loss.

Economic Espionage Act (EEA)—federal law that makes it a felony to copy, download, transmit, or in any way transfer proprietary files, documents, and information from a computer to an unauthorized person.

economic strikers—union strikers trying to enforce bargaining demands when an impasse has been reached in the negotiation process for a collective bargaining agreement.

effects doctrine—doctrine that states that U.S. courts will assume jurisdiction and will apply antitrust laws to conduct outside of the United States when the activity of business firms has direct and substantial effect on U.S. commerce; the rule has been modified to require that the effect on U.S. commerce also be foreseeable.

effluent guidelines—EPA standards for maximum ranges of discharge into water.

electronic funds transfer (EFT)—any transfer of funds (other than a transaction originated by a check, draft, or similar paper instrument) that is initiated through an electronic terminal, telephone, computer, or magnetic tape so as to authorize a financial institution to debit or credit an account.

Electronic Funds Transfer Act (EFTA)—federal law that provides consumers with rights and protections in electronic funds transfers.

eleemosynary corporation—corporation organized for a charitable or benevolent purpose.

embezzlement—statutory offense consisting of the unlawful conversion of property entrusted to the wrongdoer.

eminent domain—power of government and certain kinds of corporations to take private property against the objection of the owner, provided the taking is for a public purpose and just compensation is made for it.

emissions offset policy—controls whether new factories can be built in a nonattainment area.

employment-at-will doctrine—doctrine in which the employer has historically been allowed to terminate the employment contract at any time for any reason or for no reason.

en banc—the term used when the full panel of judges on the appellate court hears a case.

encoding warranty—warranty made by any party who encodes electronic information on an instrument; a warranty of accuracy.

Endangered Species Act (ESA)—federal law that identifies and protects species that are endangered from development or other acts that threaten their existence.

endowment insurance—insurance that pays the face amount of the policy if the insured dies within the policy period.

environmental impact statement (EIS)—formal report prepared under NEPA to document findings on the impact of a federal project on the environment.

equitable title—beneficial interest in a trust.

equity—the body of principles that originally developed because of the inadequacy of the rules then applied by the common law courts of England.

escalation clause—provision for the automatic increase of the rent at periodic intervals.

escheat—transfer to the state of the title to a decedent's property when the owner of the property dies intestate and is not survived by anyone capable of taking the property as heir.

E-sign—signature over the Internet.

estate in fee—largest estate possible, in which the owner has absolute and entire interest in the land.

estoppel—principle by which a person is barred from pursuing a certain course of action or of disputing the truth of certain matters.

ethics—a branch of philosophy dealing with values that relate to the nature of human conduct and values associated with that conduct.

ex post facto law—a law making criminal an act that was lawful when done or that increases the penalty when done. Such laws are generally prohibited by constitutional provisions.

exculpatory clause—provision in a contract stating that one of the parties is not liable for damages in case of breach; also called *limitation-of-liability clause*.

executed contract—agreement that has been completely performed.

execution—the carrying out of a judgment of a court, generally directing that property owned by the defendant be sold and the proceeds first be used to pay the execution or judgment creditor.

executive branch—the branch of government (e.g., the president) formed to execute the laws.

executor, executrix—person (man, woman) named in a will to administer the estate of the decedent.

executory contract—agreement by which something remains to be done by one or both parties.

exhaustion of administrative remedies—requirement that an agency make its final decision before the parties can go to court.

existing goods—goods that physically exist and are owned by the seller at the time of a transaction.

exoneration—agreement or provision in an agreement that one party shall not be held liable for loss; the right of the surety to demand that those primarily liable pay the claim for which the surety is secondarily liable.

expert witness—one who has acquired special knowledge in a particular field as through practical experience or study, or both, whose opinion is admissible as an aid to the trier of fact.

export sale—direct sale to customers in a foreign country.

express authorization—authorization of an agent to perform a certain act.

express contract—agreement of the parties manifested by their words, whether spoken or written.

express warranty—statement by the defendant relating to the goods, which statement is part of the basis of the bargain.

extortion—illegal demand by a public officer acting with apparent authority.

F

facilitation payments—(or grease payments) legal payments to speed up or ensure performance of normal government duties.

factor—bailee to whom goods are consigned for sale.

fair use—principle that allows the limited use of copyrighted material for teaching, research, and news reporting.

false imprisonment—intentional detention of a person without that person's consent; called the shopkeeper's tort when shoplifters are unlawfully detained.

FAS—free alongside the named vessel.

federal district court—a general trial court of the federal system.

Federal Register—government publication issued five days a week that lists all administrative regulations, all presidential proclamations and executive orders, and other documents and classes of documents that the president or Congress direct to be published.

Federal Register Act—federal law requiring agencies to make public disclosure of proposed rules, passed rules, and activities.

Federal Sentencing Guidelines—federal standards used by judges in determining mandatory sentence terms for those convicted of federal crimes.

federal system—the system of government in which a central government is given power to administer to national concerns while individual states retain the power to administer to local concerns.

fee simple defeasibles—fee simple interest can be lost if restrictions on its use are violated.

fee simple estate—highest level of land ownership; full interest of unlimited duration.

felony—criminal offense that is punishable by confinement in prison for more than one year or by death, or that is expressly stated by statute to be a felony.

field warehousing—stored goods under the exclusive control of a warehouse but kept on the owner's premises rather than in a warehouse.

Fifth Amendment—constitutional protection against self-incrimination; also guarantees due process.

finance lease—three-party lease agreement in which there is a lessor, a lessee, and a financier.

financing statement—brief statement (record) that gives sufficient information to alert third persons that a particular creditor may have a security interest in the collateral described.

fire insurance policy—a contract that indemnifies the insured for property destruction or damage caused by fire.

firm offer—offer stated to be held open for a specified time, which must be so held in some states even in the absence of an option contract, or under the UCC, with respect to merchants.

first-in-time provision—creditor whose interest attached first has priority in the collateral when two creditors have a secured interest.

first-to-perfect basis—rule of priorities that holds that first in time in perfecting a security interest, mortgage, judgment, lien, or other property attachment right should have priority.

fixture—personal property that has become so attached to or adapted to real estate that it has lost its character as personal property and is part of the real estate.

floating lien—claim in a changing or shifting stock of goods of the buyer.

FOB place of destination—general commercial language for delivery to the buyer.

FOB place of shipment—"ship to" contract.

forbearance—refraining from doing an act.

forcible entry and detainer—action by the landlord to have the tenant removed for nonpayment of rent.

foreclosure—procedure for enforcing a mortgage resulting in the public sale of the mortgaged property and, less commonly, in merely barring the right of the mortgagor to redeem the property from the mortgage.

foreign corporation—corporation incorporated under the laws of another state.

Foreign Corrupt Practices Act (FCPA)—federal law that makes it a felony to influence decision makers in other countries for the purpose of obtaining business, such as contracts for sales and services; also imposes financial reporting requirements on certain U.S. corporations.

forged or unauthorized indorsement—instrument indorsed by an agent for a principal without authorization or authority.

forgery—fraudulently making or altering an instrument that apparently creates or alters a legal liability of another.

formal contracts—written contracts or agreements whose formality signifies the parties' intention to abide by the terms.

Fourth Amendment—privacy protection in the U.S. Constitution; prohibits unauthorized searches and seizures.

franchise—(1) privilege or authorization, generally exclusive, to engage in a particular activity within a particular geographic area, such as a government franchise to operate a taxi company within a specified city, or a private franchise as the grant by a manufacturer of a right to sell products within a particular territory or for a particular number of years; (2) right to vote.

franchise agreement—sets forth rights of franchisee to use trademarks, etc., of franchisor.

franchisee—person to whom franchise is granted.

franchising—granting of permission to use a trademark, trade name, or copyright under specified conditions; a form of licensing.

franchisor—party granting the franchise.

fraud—making of a false statement of a past or existing fact, with knowledge of its falsity or with reckless indifference as to its truth, with the intent to cause another to rely thereon, and such person does rely thereon and is harmed thereby.

fraud in factum—fraud committed through deception on documents or the nature of the transaction as opposed to the subject matter or parties in the transaction (fraud in the inducement).

fraud in the inducement—fraud that occurs when a person is persuaded or induced to execute an instrument because of fraudulent statements.

fraud-on-the-market—a theory that in an open and developed securities market, the price of a stock is determined by the information on the company available to the public, and misleading statements will defraud purchasers of stock even if they do not directly rely on these statements.

Freedom of Information Act—federal law permitting citizens to request documents and records from administrative agencies.

freight forwarder—one who contracts to have goods transported and, in turn, contracts with carriers for such transportation.

freight insurance—insures that ship-owner will receive payment for transportation charges.

full warranty—obligation of a seller to fix or replace a defective product within a reasonable time without cost to the buyer.

funds transfer—communication of instructions or requests to pay a specific sum of money to the credit of a specified account or person without an actual physical passing of money.

fungible goods—homogeneous goods of which any unit is the equivalent of any other unit.

future goods—goods that exist physically but are not owned by the seller and goods that have not yet been produced.

G

garnishment—the name given in some states to attachment proceedings.

general agent—agent authorized by the principal to transact all affairs in connection with a particular type of business or trade or to transact all business at a certain place.

general corporation code—state's code listing certain requirements for creation of a corporation.

general jurisdiction—the power to hear and decide most controversies involving legal rights and duties.

general legacies—certain sums of money bequeathed to named persons by the testator; to be paid out of the decedent's assets generally without specifying any particular fund or source from which the payment is to be made.

general partnership—partnership in which the partners conduct as co-owners a business for profit, and each partner has a right to take part in the management of the business and has unlimited liability.

general partners—partners who publicly and actively engage in the transaction of firm business.

gift—title to an owner's personal property voluntarily transferred by a party not receiving anything in exchange.

gift causa mortis—gift, made by the donor in the belief that death was immediate and impending, that is revoked or is revocable under certain circumstances.

good faith—absence of knowledge of any defects in or problems; "pure heart and an empty head."

goods—anything movable at the time it is identified as the subject of a transaction.

grantee—new owner of a land conveyance.

grantor—owner who transfers or conveys an interest in land to a new owner.

gratuitous bailment—bailment in which the bailee does not receive any compensation or advantage.

gray market goods—foreign-made goods with U.S. trademarks brought into the United States by a third party without the consent of the trademark owners to compete with these owners.

grease payments—(or facilitation payments) legal payments to speed up or ensure performance of normal government duties.

guarantor—one who undertakes the obligation of guaranty.

guaranty—agreement or promise to answer for a debt; an undertaking to pay the debt of another if the creditor first sues the debtor.

guaranty of collection—form of guaranty in which creditor cannot proceed against guarantor until after proceeding against debtor.

guaranty of payment—absolute promise to pay when a debtor defaults.

guest—transient who contracts for a room or site at a hotel.

H

hearsay evidence—statements made out of court that are offered in court as proof of the information contained in the statements and that, subject to many exceptions, are not admissible in evidence.

holder—someone in possession of an instrument that runs to that person (i.e., is made payable to that person, is indorsed to that person, or is bearer paper).

holder in due course—a holder who has given value, taken in good faith without notice of dishonor, defenses, or that instrument is overdue, and who is afforded special rights or status.

holder through a holder in due course—holder of an instrument who attains holder-in-due-course status because a holder in due course has held it previous to him or her.

holographic will—unwitnessed will written by hand.

homeowners insurance policy—combination of standard fire insurance and comprehensive personal liability insurance.

hotelkeeper—one regularly engaged in the business of offering living accommodations to all transient persons.

hull insurance—insurance that covers physical damage on a freight-moving vessel.

I

identification—point in the transaction when the buyer acquires an interest in the goods subject to the contract.

identified—term applied to particular goods selected by either the buyer or the seller as the goods called for by the sales contract.

identity theft—use of another's credit tools, social security number, or other IDs to obtain cash, goods, or credit without permission.

illusory promise—promise that in fact does not impose any obligation on the promisor.

impeach—using prior inconsistent evidence to challenge the credibility of a witness.

implied contract—contract expressed by conduct or implied or deduced from the facts.

implied warranty—warranty that was not made but is implied by law.

implied warranty of merchantability—group of promises made by the seller, the most important of which is that the goods are fit for the ordinary purposes for which they are sold.

impostor rule—an exception to the rules on liability for forgery that covers situations such as the embezzling payroll clerk.

in pari delicto—equally guilty; used in reference to a transaction as to which relief will not be granted to either party because both are equally guilty of wrongdoing.

incidental authority—authority of an agent that is reasonably necessary to execute express authority.

incidental damages—incurred by the nonbreaching party as part of the process of trying to cover (buy substitute goods) or sell (selling subject matter of contract to another); includes storage fees, commissions, and the like.

income—money earned by the principal, or property in trust, and distributed by the trustee.

incontestability clause—provision that after the lapse of a specified time the insurer cannot dispute the policy on the ground of misrepresentation or fraud of the insured or similar wrongful conduct.

incorporation by reference—contract consisting of both the original or skeleton document and the detailed statement that is incorporated in it.

incorporator—one or more natural persons or corporations who sign and file appropriate incorporation forms with a designated government official.

indemnity—right of a person secondarily liable to require that a person primarily liable pay for loss sustained when the secondary party discharges the obligation that the primary party should have discharged; the right of an agent to be paid the amount of any loss or damage sustained without fault because of obedience to the principal's instructions; an undertaking by one person for a consideration to pay another person a sum of money to indemnify that person when a specified loss is incurred.

indemnity contract—agreement by one person, for consideration, to pay another person a sum of money in the event that the other person sustains a specified loss.

indenture trustee—usually a commercial banking institution, to represent the interests of the bondholders and ensure that the terms and covenants of the bond issue are met by the corporation.

independent contractor—contractor who undertakes to perform a specified task according to the terms of a contract but over whom the other contracting party has no control except as provided for by the contract.

indorsee—party to whom special indorsement is made.

indorsement—signature of the payee on an instrument.

indorser—secondary party (or obligor) on a note.

informal contract—simple oral or written contract.

informal settlements—negotiated disposition of a matter before an administrative agency, generally without public sanctions.

infringement—violation of trademarks, patents, or copyrights by copying or using material without permission.

injunction—order of a court of equity to refrain from doing (negative injunction) or to do (affirmative or mandatory injunction) a specified act.

inland marine—insurance that covers domestic shipments of goods over land and inland waterways.

insider—full-time corporate employee or a director or their relatives.

insider information—privileged information on company business only known to employees.

insolvency—excess of debts and liabilities over assets, or inability to pay debts as they mature.

instruction—summary of the law given to jurors by the judge before deliberation begins.

insurable interest—the right to hold a valid insurance policy on a person or property.

insurance—a plan of security against risks by charging the loss against a fund created by the payments made by policyholders.

insurance agent—agent of an insurance company.

insurance broker—independent contractor who is not employed by any one insurance company.

insured—person to whom the promise in an insurance contract is made.

insurer—promisor in an insurance contract.

integrity—the adherence to one's values and principles despite the costs and consequences.

intellectual property rights—trademark, copyright, and patent rights protected by law.

intended beneficiary—third person of a contract whom the contract is intended to benefit.

intentional infliction of emotional distress—tort that produces mental anguish caused by conduct that exceeds all bounds of decency.

intentional tort—civil wrong that results from intentional conduct.

inter vivos gift—any transaction that takes place between living persons and creates rights prior to the death of any of them.

interest in the authority—form of agency in which an agent has been given or paid for the right to exercise authority.

interest in the subject matter—form of agency in which an agent is given an interest in the property with which that agent is dealing.

interlineation—writing between the lines or adding to the provisions of a document, the effect thereof depending upon the nature of the document.

intermediary bank—bank between the originator and the beneficiary bank in the transfer of funds.

interrogatories—written questions used as a discovery tool that must be answered under oath.

intestate—condition of dying without a will as to any property.

intestate succession—distribution, made as directed by statute, of a decedent's property not effectively disposed of by will.

invasion of privacy—tort of intentional intrusion into the private affairs of another.

investigative consumer report—report on a person based on personal investigation and interviews.

invitee—person who enters another's land by invitation.

involuntary bankruptcy—proceeding in which a creditor or creditors file the petition for relief with the bankruptcy court.

issuer—party who issues a document such as a letter of credit or a document of title such as a warehouse receipt or bill of lading.

J

joint tenancy—estate held jointly by two or more with the right of survivorship as between them, unless modified by statute.

joint venture—relationship in which two or more persons or firms combine their labor or property for a single undertaking and share profits and losses equally unless otherwise agreed.

judge—primary officer of the court.

judgment lien—lien by a creditor who has won a verdict against the landowner in court.

judgment n.o.v. (or *non obstante veredicto,* "notwithstanding the verdict") — a judgment entered after verdict upon the motion of the losing party on the ground that the verdict is so wrong that a judgment should be entered the opposite of the verdict.

judicial branch—the branch of government (courts) formed to interpret the laws.

judicial or execution sale—sale made under order of court by an officer appointed to make the sale or by an officer having such authority as incident to the office. The sale may have the effect of divesting liens on the property.

judicial triage—court management tool used by judges to expedite certain cases in which time is of the essence, such as asbestos cases in which the plaintiffs are gravely ill.

jurisdiction—the power of a court to hear and determine a given class of cases; the power to act over a particular defendant.

jurisdictional rule of reason—rule that balances the vital interests, including laws and policies, of the United States with those of a foreign country.

jury—a body of citizens sworn by a court to determine by verdict the issues of fact submitted to them.

L

land—earth, including all things embedded in or attached thereto, whether naturally or by the act of humans.

landlord—one who leases real property to another.

law—the order or pattern of rules that society establishes to govern the conduct of individuals and the relationships among them.

lease—agreement between the owner of property and a tenant by which the former agrees to give possession of the property to the latter in consideration of the payment of rent. (Parties—landlord or lessor, tenant or lessee)

leasehold estate—interest of a tenant in rented land.

legacy—gift of money made by will.

legal title—title held by the trustee in a trust situation.

legatee—beneficiary who receives a gift of personal property by will.

legislative branch—the branch of government (e.g., Congress) formed to make the laws.

lessee—one who has a possessory interest in real or personal property under a lease; a tenant.

lessor—one who conveys real or personal property by a lease; a landlord.

letter of credit—commercial device used to guarantee payment to a seller, primarily in an international business transaction.

letters of administration—written authorization given to an administrator of an estate as evidence of appointment and authority.

letters testamentary—written authorization given to an executor of an estate as evidence of appointment and authority.

liability insurance—covers the shipowner's liability if the ship causes damage to another ship or its cargo.

libel—written or visual defamation without legal justification.

license—personal privilege to do some act or series of acts upon the land of another, as the placing of a sign thereon, not amounting to an easement or a right of possession.

licensee—someone on another's premises with the permission of the occupier, whose duty is to warn the licensee of nonobvious dangers.

licensing—transfer of technology rights to a product so that it may be produced by a different business organization in a foreign country in exchange for royalties and other payments as agreed.

lien—claim or right, against property, existing by virtue of the entry of a judgment against its owner or by the entry of a judgment and a levy thereunder on the property, or because of the relationship of the claimant to the particular property, such as an unpaid seller.

life estate—an estate for the duration of a life.

limitation-of-liability clause—provision in a contract stating that one of the parties shall not be liable for damages in case of breach; also called an exculpatory clause.

limited covenant—any covenant that does not provide the complete protection of a full covenant.

limited defenses—defenses available to secondary parties if the presenting party is a holder in due course.

limited liability partnership (LLP)—partnership in which at least one partner has a liability limited to the loss of the capital contribution made to the partnership.

limited partner—partner who neither takes part in the management of the partnership nor appears to the public to be a general partner.

limited partnership—partnership that can be formed by "one or more general partners and one or more limited partners."

limited (special) jurisdiction—the authority to hear only particular kinds of cases.

limited warranty—any warranty that does not provide the complete protection of a full warranty.

lineals—relationship that exists when one person is a direct descendant of the other; also called lineal descendants.

liquidated damages—damages established in advance of breach as an alternative to establishing compensatory damages at the time of the breach.

liquidated damages clause—specification of exact compensation in case of a breach of contract.

liquidation—process of converting property into money whether of particular items of property or of all the assets of a business or an estate.

living trust—trust created to take effect within the lifetime of the settlor; also called inter vivos trust.

living will—document by which individuals may indicate that if they become unable to express their wishes and are in an irreversible, incurable condition, they do not want life-sustaining medical treatments.

living-document view—the term when a constitution is interpreted according to changes in conditions.

lottery—any plan by which a consideration is given for a chance to win a prize; it consists of three elements: (1) there must be a payment of money or something of value for an opportunity to win, (2) a prize must be available,

and (3) the prize must be offered by lot or chance.

M

mailbox rule—timing for acceptance tied to proper acceptance.

maker—party who writes or creates a promissory note.

malpractice—when services are not properly rendered in accordance with commonly accepted standards; negligence by a professional in performing his or her skill.

marine insurance—policies that cover perils relating to the transportation of goods.

market power—the ability to control price and exclude competitors.

market value—price at which a share of stock can be voluntarily bought or sold in the open market.

mask work—specific form of expression embodied in a chip design, including the stencils used in manufacturing semiconductor chip products.

mass picketing—illegal tactic of employees massing together in great numbers to effectively shut down entrances of the employer's facility.

maturity date—date that a corporation is required to repay a loan to a bondholder.

means test—new standard under the Reform Act that requires the court to find that the debtor does not have the means to repay creditors; goes beyond the past requirement of petitions being granted on the simple assertion of the debtor saying, "I have debts."

mechanic's lien—protection afforded by statute to various kinds of laborers and persons supplying materials, by giving them a lien on the building and land that has been improved or added to by them.

mediation—the settlement of a dispute through the use of a messenger who carries to each side of the dispute the issues and offers in the case.

merchant—seller who deals in specific goods classified by the UCC.

merger (of corporations)—combining of corporations by which one absorbs the other and continues to exist, preserving its original charter and identity while the other corporation ceases to exist.

minitrial—a trial held on portions of the case or certain issues in the case.

Miranda *warnings*—warnings required to prevent self-incrimination in a criminal matter.

mirror image rule—common law contract rule on acceptance that requires language to be absolutely the same as the offer, unequivocal and unconditional.

misdemeanor—criminal offense with a sentence of less than one year that is neither treason nor a felony.

misrepresentation—false statement of fact made innocently without any intent to deceive.

mistrial—a court's declaration that terminates a trial and postpones it to a later date; commonly entered when evidence has been of a highly prejudicial character or when a juror has been guilty of misconduct.

money—medium of exchange.

money order—draft issued by a bank or a nonbank.

moral relativism—takes into account motivation and circumstance to determine whether an act was ethical.

mortgage—interest in land given by the owner to a creditor as security for the payment of the creditor for a debt, the nature of the interest depending upon the law of the state where the land is located. (Parties—mortgagor, mortgagee) *most-favored-nation clause*—clause in treaties between countries whereby any privilege subsequently granted to a third country in relation to a given treaty subject is extended to the other party to the treaty.

motion for summary judgment—request that the court decide a case on basis of law only because there are no material issues disputed by the parties.

motion to dismiss—a pleading that may be filed to attack the adverse party's pleading as not stating a cause of action or a defense.

N

National Environmental Policy Act (NEPA)—federal law that mandates study of a project's impact on the environment before it can be undertaken by any federal agency.

natural law—a system of principles to guide human conduct independent of, and sometimes contrary to, enacted law and discovered by man's rational intelligence.

necessaries—things indispensable or absolutely necessary for the sustenance of human life.

negligence—failure to exercise due care under the circumstances in consequence of which harm is proximately caused to one to whom the defendant owed a duty to exercise due care.

negotiability—quality of an instrument that affords special rights and standing.

negotiable bill of lading—document of title that by its terms calls for goods to be delivered ''to the bearer'' or ''to the order of'' a named person.

negotiable instruments—drafts, promissory notes, checks, and certificates of deposit that, in proper form, give special rights as ''negotiable commercial paper.''

negotiable warehouse receipt—receipt that states the covered goods will be delivered ''to the bearer'' or ''to the order of.''

negotiation—the transfer of commercial paper by indorsement and delivery by the person to whom it is then payable in the case of order paper and by physical transfer in the case of bearer paper.

Noise Control Act—federal law that controls noise emissions from low-flying aircraft.

nominal damages—nominal sum awarded the plaintiff in order to establish that legal rights have been violated although the plaintiff in fact has not sustained any actual loss or damages.

nonattainment areas—"dirty" areas that do not meet federal standards under the Clean Air Act.

nonconforming use—use of land that conflicts with a zoning ordinance at the time the ordinance goes into effect.

nonconsumer lease—lease that does not satisfy the definition of a consumer lease; also known as a commercial lease.

nonnegotiable bill of lading—See *Straight Bill of Lading.*

nonnegotiable instrument—contract, note, or draft that does not meet negotiability requirements of Article 3.

nonnegotiable warehouse receipt—receipt that states the covered goods received will be delivered to a specific person.

notice of dishonor—notice that an instrument has been dishonored; such notice can be oral, written, or electronic but is subject to time limitations.

notice statute—statute under which the last good faith or bona fide purchaser holds the title.

notice-race statute—statute under which the first bona fide purchaser to record the deed holds the title.

novation—substitution for an old contract with a new one that either replaces an existing obligation with a new obligation or replaces an original party with a new party.

nuisance—conduct that harms or prejudices another in the use of land or that harms or prejudices the public.

O

obligee—promisee who can claim the benefit of the obligation.

obligor—promisor.

ocean marine—policies that cover transportation of goods in vessels in international and coastal trade.

offer—expression of an offeror's willingness to enter into a contractual agreement.

offeree—person to whom an offer is made.

offeror—person who makes an offer.

Oil Pollution Act—federal law that assigns cleanup liability for oil spills in U.S. waters.

ombudsman—a government official or organization employee designated by statute or the organization/company to examine citizen and/or employee complaints.

open meeting law—law that requires advance notice of agency meeting and public access.

opening statements—statements by opposing attorneys that tell the jury what their cases will prove.

operation of law—attaching of certain consequences to certain facts because of legal principles that operate automatically as contrasted with consequences that arise because of the voluntary action of a party designed to create those consequences.

option contract—contract to hold an offer to make a contract open for a fixed period of time.

order of relief—the order from the bankruptcy judge that starts the protection for the debtor; when the order of relief is entered by the court, the debtor's creditors must stop all proceedings and work through the bankruptcy court to recover debts (if possible). Court finding that creditors have met the standards for bankruptcy petitions.

order paper—instrument payable to the order of a party.

original jurisdiction—the authority to hear a controversy when it is first brought to court.

originator—party who originates the funds transfer.

output contract—contract of a producer to sell its entire production or output to a buyer.

outstanding—name for shares of a company that have been issued to stockholders.

overdraft—negative balance in a drawer's account.

P

par value—specified monetary amount assigned by an issuing corporation for each share of its stock.

parol evidence rule—rule that prohibits the introduction into evidence of oral or written statements made prior to or contemporaneously with the execution of a complete written contract, deed, or instrument, in the absence of clear proof of fraud, accident, or mistake causing the omission of the statement in question.

partially disclosed principal—principal whose existence is made known but whose identity is not.

partner—one of two or more persons who jointly own and carry on a business for profit.

partnership—pooling of capital resources and the business or professional talents of two or more individuals (partners) with the goal of making a profit.

partnership agreement—document prepared to evidence the contract of the parties. (Parties—partners or general partners)

party—person involved in a legal transaction; may be a natural person, an artificial person (e.g., a corporation), or an unincorporated enterprise (e.g., a government agency).

past consideration—something that has been performed in the past and which, therefore, cannot be consideration for a promise made in the present.

payable to order—term stating that a negotiable instrument is payable to the order of any person described in it or to a person or order.

payee—party to whom payment is to be made.

payment order—direction given by an originator to his or her bank or by any bank to a subsequent bank to make a specified funds transfer.

per capita—method of distributing estate assets on an equal-per-person basis.

per stirpes—method for distribution of an estate that divides property equally down family lines.

perfected security interest—security interest with priority because of filing, possession, automatic or temporary priority status.

periodic tenancy—tenancy that continues indefinitely for a specified rental period until terminated; often called a month-to- month tenancy.

personal property—property that is movable or intangible, or rights in such things.

personal representative—administrator or executor who represents decedents under UPC.

physical duress—threat of physical harm to person or property.

plaintiff—the party who initiates a lawsuit.

pleadings—the papers filed by the parties in an action in order to set forth the facts and frame the issues to be tried, although, under some systems, the pleadings merely give notice or a general indication of the nature of the issues.

pledge—bailment given as security for the payment of a debt or the performance of an obligation owed to the pledgee. (Parties—pledgor, pledgee)

police power—the power to govern; the power to adopt laws for the protection of the public health, welfare, safety, and morals.

policy—paper evidencing the contract of insurance.

positive law—law enacted and codified by governmental authority.

possession—exclusive dominion and control of property.

possibility of reverter—nature of the interest held by the grantor after conveying land outright but subject to a condition or provision that may cause the grantee's interest to become forfeited and the interest to revert to the grantor or heirs.

postdate—to insert or place on an instrument a later date than the actual date on which it was executed.

power of attorney—written authorization to an agent by the principal.

precedent—a decision of a court that stands as the law for a particular problem in the future.

predatory lending—a practice on the part of the subprime lending market whereby lenders take advantage of less sophisticated consumers or those who are desperate for funds by using the lenders' superior bargaining positions to obtain credit terms that go well beyond compensating them for their risk.

predicate act—qualifying underlying offense for RICO liability.

preemption—the federal government's superior regulatory position over state laws on the same subject area.

preemptive right—shareholder's right upon the increase of a corporation's capital stock to be allowed to subscribe to such a percentage of the new shares as the shareholder's old shares bore to the former total capital stock.

preferences—transfers of property by a debtor to one or more specific creditors to enable these creditors to obtain payment for debts owed.

preferential transfers—certain transfers of money or security interests in the time frame just prior to bankruptcy that can be set aside if voidable.

preferred stock—stock that has a priority or preference as to payment of dividends or upon liquidation, or both.

prescription—acquisition of a right to use the land of another, as an easement, by making hostile, visible, and notorious use of the land, continuing for the period specified by the local law.

presentment—formal request for payment on an instrument.

price discrimination—the charging practice by a seller of different prices to different buyers for commodities of similar grade and quality, resulting in reduced competition or a tendency to create a monopoly.

prima facie—evidence that, if believed, is sufficient by itself to lead to a particular conclusion.

primary party—party to whom the holder or holder in due course must turn first to obtain payment.

primary picketing—legal presentations in front of a business notifying the public of a labor dispute.

primum non nocere—"above all do no harm."

principal—person or firm who employs an agent; person who, with

respect to a surety, is primarily liable to the third person or creditor; property held in trust.

principal debtor—original borrower or debtor.

prior art—a showing that an invention as a whole would have been obvious to a person of ordinary skill in the art when the invention was patented

private carrier—carrier owned by the shipper, such as a company's own fleet of trucks.

private corporation—corporation organized for charitable and benevolent purposes or for purposes of finance, industry, and commerce.

private law—the rules and regulations parties agree to as part of their contractual relationships.

private nuisance—nuisance that affects only one or a few individuals.

privileges and immunities clause—a clause that entitles a person going into another state to make contracts, own property, and engage in business to the same extent as citizens of that state.

privity—succession or chain of relationship to the same thing or right, such as privity of contract, privity of estate, privity of possession.

privity of contract—relationship between a promisor and the promisee.

privity rule—succession or chain of relationship to the same thing or right, such as privity of contract, privity of estate, privity of possession.

pro rata—proportionately, or divided according to a rate or standard.

probate—procedure for formally establishing or proving that a given writing is the last will and testament of the person who purportedly signed it.

procedural law—the law that must be followed in enforcing rights and liabilities.

process—paperwork served personally on a defendant in a civil case.

product disparagement—false statements made about a product or business.

profit—right to take a part of the soil or produce of another's land, such as timber or water.

promisee—person to whom a promise is made.

promisor—person who makes a promise.

promissory estoppel—doctrine that a promise will be enforced although it is not supported by consideration when the promisor should have reasonably expected that the promise would induce action or forbearance of a definite and substantial character on the part of the promised and injustice can be avoided only by enforcement of the promise.

promissory note—unconditional promise in writing made by one person to another, signed by the maker engaging to pay on demand, or at a definite time, a sum certain in money to order or to bearer. (Parties—maker, payee)

promoters—persons who plan the formation of the corporation and sell or promote the idea to others.

proof of claim—written statement, signed by the creditor or an authorized representative, setting forth any claim made against the debtor and the basis for it.

property report—condensed version of a property development statement filed with the secretary of HUD and given to a prospective customer at least 48 hours before signing a contract to buy or lease property.

prosecutor—party who originates a criminal proceeding.

prospectus—information provided to each potential purchaser of securities setting forth the key information contained in the registration statement.

proxy—written authorization by a shareholder to another person to vote the stock owned by the shareholder; the person who is the holder of such a written authorization.

public corporation—corporation that has been established for governmental purposes and for the administration of public affairs.

public nuisance—nuisance that affects the community or public at large.

public policy—certain objectives relating to health, morals, and integrity of government that the law seeks to advance by declaring invalid any contract that conflicts with those objectives even though there is no statute expressly declaring such a contract illegal.

public warehouses—entities that serve the public generally without discrimination.

pump-and-dump—self-touting a stock to drive its price up and then selling it.

punitive damages—damages, in excess of those required to compensate the plaintiff for the wrong done, that are imposed in order to punish the defendant because of the particularly wanton or willful character of wrongdoing; also called exemplary damages.

purchase money security interest (PMSI)—the security interest in the goods a seller sells on credit that become the collateral for the creditor/seller.

Q

qualified indorsement—an indorsement that includes words such as "without recourse" that disclaims certain liability of the indorser to a maker or a drawee.

qualified privilege—media privilege to print inaccurate information without liability for defamation, so long as a retraction is printed and there was no malice.

quantum meruit—"as much as deserved;" an action brought for the value of the services rendered the defendant when there was no express contract as to the purchase price.

quasi contract—court-imposed obligation to prevent unjust enrichment in the absence of a contract.

quasi-judicial proceedings—forms of hearings in which the rules of evidence and procedure are more relaxed but each side still has a chance to be heard.

quasi-public corporation—private corporation furnishing services on which the public is particularly dependent, for example, a gas and electric company.

quitclaim deed—deed by which the grantor purports to give up only whatever right or title the grantor may have in the property without specifying or warranting transfer of any particular interest.

quorum—minimum number of persons, shares represented, or directors who must be present at a meeting in order to lawfully transact business.

R

race statute—statute under which the first party to record the deed holds the title.

race-notice statute—See *Notice-Race Statute.*

Racketeer Influenced and Corrupt Organizations (RICO) Act—federal law, initially targeting organized crime, that has expanded in scope and provides penalties and civil recovery for multiple criminal offenses, or a pattern of racketeering.

real property—land and all rights in land.

recognizance—obligation entered into before a court to do some act, such as to appear at a later date for a hearing. Also called a *contract of record.*

recorder—public official in charge of deeds.

recross-examination—an examination by the other side's attorney that follows the redirect examination.

redemption—buying back of one's property, which has been sold because of a default, upon paying the amount that had been originally due together with interest and costs.

redirect examination—questioning after cross-examination, in which the attorney for the witness testifying may ask the same witness other questions to overcome effects of the cross-examination.

reference to a third person—settlement that allows a nonparty to resolve the dispute.

reformation—remedy by which a written instrument is corrected when it fails to express the actual intent of both parties because of fraud, accident, or mistake.

registered bonds—bonds held by owners whose names and addresses are registered on the books of the corporation.

registration requirements—provisions of the Securities Act of 1933 requiring advance disclosure to the public of a new securities issue through filing a statement with the SEC and sending a prospectus to each potential purchaser.

registration statement—document disclosing specific financial information regarding the security, the issuer, and the underwriter.

remainder interest—land interest that follows a life estate.

remand—term used when an appellate court sends a case back to trial court for additional hearings or a new trial.

remedy—action or procedure that is followed in order to enforce a right or to obtain damages for injury to a right.

rent-a-judge plan—dispute resolution through private courts with judges paid to be referees for the cases.

representative capacity—action taken by one on behalf of another, as the act of a personal representative on behalf of a decedent's estate, or action taken both on one's behalf and on behalf of others, as a shareholder bringing a representative action.

repudiation—result of a buyer or seller refusing to perform the contract as stated.

request for production of documents—discovery tool for uncovering paper evidence in a case.

requirements contract—contract in which the buyer buys its needs (requirements) from the seller.

rescission—action of one party to a contract to set the contract aside when the other party is guilty of a breach of the contract.

reservation of rights—assertion by a party to a contract that even though a tendered performance (e.g., a defective product) is accepted, the right to damages for nonconformity to the contract is reserved.

Resource Conservation and Recovery Act (RCRA)—federal law that regulates the disposal of potentially harmful substances and encourages resource conservation and recovery.

Resource Recovery Act—early federal solid waste disposal legislation that provided funding for states and local governments with recycling programs.

respondeat superior—doctrine that the principal or employer is vicariously liable for the unauthorized torts committed by an agent or employee while acting within the scope of the agency or the course of the employment, respectively.

restrictive covenants—covenants in a deed by which the grantee agrees to refrain from doing specified acts.

restrictive indorsement—an indorsement that restricts further transfer, such as in trust for or to the use of some other person, is conditional, or for collection or deposit.

reverse—the term used when the appellate court sets aside the verdict or judgment of a lower court.

reverse mortgage—mortgage in which the owners get their equity out of their home over a period of time and return the house to the lender upon their deaths.

reversible error—an error or defect in court proceedings of so serious a nature that on appeal the appellate court will set aside the proceedings of the lower court.

reversionary interest—interest that a lessor has in property that is subject to an outstanding lease.

revoke—testator's act of taking back his or her will and its provisions.

right—legal capacity to require another person to perform or refrain from an action.

right of escheat—right of the state to take the property of a decedent that has not been distributed.

right of first refusal—right of a party to meet the terms of a proposed contract before it is executed, such as a real estate purchase agreement.

right of privacy—the right to be free from unreasonable intrusion by others.

right to cure—second chance for a seller to make a proper tender of conforming goods.

right-to-work laws—laws restricting unions and employees from negotiating clauses in their collective bargaining agreements that make union membership compulsory.

risk—peril or contingency against which the insured is protected by the contract of insurance.

risk of loss—in contract performance, the cost of damage or injury to the goods contracted for.

Robinson-Patman Act—a federal statute designed to eliminate price discrimination in interstate commerce.

run with the land—concept that certain covenants in a deed to land are deemed to run or pass with the land so that whoever owns the land is bound by or entitled to the benefit of the covenants.

S

Safe Drinking Water Act—a federal law that establishes national standards for contaminants in drinking water.

sale on approval—term indicating that no sale takes place until the buyer approves or accepts the goods.

sale or return—sale in which the title to the property passes to the buyer at the time of the transaction but the buyer is given the option of returning the property and restoring the title to the seller.

search engine—Internet service used to locate Web sites.

search warrant—judicial authorization for a search of property where there is the expectation of privacy.

seasonable—timely.

secondary meaning—a legal term signifying the words in question have taken on a new meaning with the public, capable of serving a source-identifying function of a mark.

secondary parties—called secondary obligors under Revised Article 3; parties to an instrument to whom holders turn when the primary party, for whatever reason, fails to pay the instrument.

secondary picketing—picketing an employer with which a union has no dispute to persuade the employer to stop doing business with a party to the dispute; generally illegal under the NLRA.

secrecy laws—confidentiality laws applied to home-country banks.

secured party—person owed the money, whether as a seller or a lender, in a secured transaction in personal property.

secured transaction—credit sale of goods or a secured loan that provides special protection for the creditor.

securities—stocks and bonds issued by a corporation. Under some investor protection laws, the term includes any interest in an enterprise that provides unearned income to its owner.

security agreement—agreement of the creditor and the debtor that the creditor will have a security interest.

security interest—property right that enables the creditor to take possession of the property if the debtor does not pay the amount owed.

self-help repossession—creditor's right to repossess the collateral without judicial proceedings.

self-proved wills—wills that eliminate some formalities of proof by being executed according to statutory requirements.

selling on consignment—entrusting a person with possession of property for the purpose of sale.

semiconductor chip product—product placed on a piece of semiconductor material in accordance with a predetermined pattern that is intended to perform electronic circuitry functions.

service mark—mark that identifies a service.

servient tenement—land that is subject to an easement.

settlor—one who settles property in trust or creates a trust estate.

severalty—ownership of property by one person.

shared powers—powers that are held by both state and national governments.

Sherman Antitrust Act—a federal statute prohibiting combinations and contracts in restraint of interstate trade, now generally inapplicable to labor union activity.

shop right—right of an employer to use in business without charge an invention discovered by an employee during working hours and with the employer's material and equipment.

shopkeeper's privilege—right of a store owner to detain a suspected shoplifter based on reasonable cause and for a reasonable time without resulting liability for false imprisonment.

short-swing profit—profit realized by a corporate insider from selling securities less than six months after purchase.

sinking fund—fixed amount of money set aside each year by the borrowing corporation toward the ultimate payment of bonds.

situational ethics—a flexible standard of ethics that permits an examination of circumstances and motivation before attaching the label of right or wrong to conduct.

Sixth Amendment—the U.S. constitutional amendment that guarantees a speedy trial.

slander—defamation of character by spoken words or gestures.

slander of title—malicious making of false statements as to a seller's title.

small claims courts—courts that resolve disputes between parties when those disputes do not exceed a minimal

level; no lawyers are permitted; the parties represent themselves.

sole or individual proprietorship—form of business ownership in which one individual owns the business.

soliciting agent—salesperson.

sovereign compliance doctrine—doctrine that allows a defendant to raise as an affirmative defense to an antitrust action the fact that the defendant's actions were compelled by a foreign state.

sovereign immunity doctrine—doctrine that states that a foreign sovereign generally cannot be sued unless an exception to the Foreign Sovereign Immunities Act of 1976 applies.

special agent—agent authorized to transact a specific transaction or to do a specific act.

special drawing rights (SDRs)—rights that allow a country to borrow enough money from other International Money Fund (IMF) members to permit that country to maintain the stability of its currency's relationship to other world currencies.

special indorsement—an indorsement that specifies the person to whom the instrument is indorsed.

specific legacies—identified property bequeathed by a testator; also called specific devises.

specific lien—right of a creditor to hold particular property or assert a lien on particular property of the debtor because of the creditor's having done work on or having some other association with the property, as distinguished from having a lien generally against the assets of the debtor merely because the debtor is indebted to the lien holder.

specific performance—action brought to compel the adverse party to perform a contract on the theory that merely suing for damages for its breach will not be an adequate remedy.

spendthrift trust—a trust that, to varying degrees, provides that creditors of the beneficiary shall not be able to reach the principal or income held by the trustee and that the beneficiary shall not be able to assign any interest in the trust.

spot zoning—allowing individual variation in zoning.

stakeholder analysis—the term used when a decision maker views a problem from different perspectives and measures the impact of a decision on various groups.

stakeholders—those who have a stake, or interest, in the activities of a corporation; stakeholders include employees, members of the community in which the corporation operates, vendors, customers, and any others who are affected by the actions and decisions of the corporation.

stale check—a check whose date is longer than six months ago.

standby letter—letter of credit for a contractor ensuring he will complete the project as contracted.

stare decisis—"let the decision stand"; the principle that the decision of a court should serve as a guide or precedent and control the decision of a similar case in the future.

status quo ante—original positions of the parties.

statute of frauds—statute that, in order to prevent fraud through the use of perjured testimony, requires that certain kinds of transactions be evidenced in writing in order to be binding or enforceable.

statute of limitations—statute that restricts the period of time within which an action may be brought.

statutory law—legislative acts declaring, commanding, or prohibiting something.

stay of foreclosure—delay of foreclosure obtained by the mortgagor to prevent undue hardship.

stirpes—family lines; distribution per stirpes refers to the manner in which descendants take property by right of representation.

stock subscription—contract or agreement to buy a specific number and kind of shares when they are issued by the corporation.

stop payment order—order by a depositor to the bank to refuse to make payment of a check when presented for payment.

straight (or nonnegotiable) bill of lading —document of title that consigns transported goods to a named person.

strict liability—civil wrong for which there is absolute liability because of the inherent danger in the underlying activity, for example, the use of explosives.

strict tort liability—product liability theory that imposes liability upon the manufacturer, seller, or distributor of goods for harm caused by defective goods.

subject matter jurisdiction—judicial authority to hear a particular type of case.

sublease—a transfer of the premises by the lessee to a third person, the sublessee or subtenant, for a period of less than the term of the original lease.

sublessee—person with lease rights for a period of less than the term of the original lease; also known as subtenant.

subprime lending market—a credit market that makes loans to high-risk consumers (those who have bankruptcies, no credit history, or a poor credit history), often loaning money to pay off other debts the consumer has due.

subrogation—right of a party secondarily liable to stand in the place of the creditor after making payment to the creditor and to enforce the creditor's

right against the party primarily liable in order to obtain indemnity from such primary party.

substantial impairment—material defect in a good.

substantial performance—equitable rule that if a good-faith attempt to perform does not precisely meet the terms of the agreement, the agreement will still be considered complete if the essential purpose of the contract is accomplished.

substantive law—the law that defines rights and liabilities.

substitute check—electronic image of a paper check that a bank can create and that has the same legal effect as the original instrument.

substitution—substitution of a new contract between the same parties.

sum certain—amount due under an instrument that can be computed from its face with only reference to interest rates.

summary jury trial—a mock or dry-run trial for parties to get a feel for how their cases will play to a jury.

summation—the attorney address that follows all the evidence presented in court and sums up a case and recommends a particular verdict be returned by the jury.

Superfund Amendment and Reauthorization Act—federal law that authorizes the EPA to collect cleanup costs from those responsible for the ownership, leasing, dumping, or security of hazardous waste sites.

Superfund sites—areas designated by the EPA for cleanup of hazardous waste.

surety—obligor of a suretyship; primarily liable for the debt or obligation of the principal debtor.

suretyship—undertaking to pay the debt or be liable for the default of another.

symbolic delivery—delivery of goods by delivery of the means of control, such as a key or a relevant document of title, such as a negotiable bill of lading; also called constructive delivery.

T

takeover laws—laws that guard against unfairness in corporate takeover situations.

tariff—(1) domestically—government-approved schedule of charges that may be made by a regulated business, such as a common carrier or warehouser; (2) internationally—tax imposed by a country on goods crossing its borders, without regard to whether the purpose is to raise revenue or to discourage the traffic in the taxed goods.

tax lien—lien on property by a government agency for nonpayment of taxes.

teller's check—draft drawn by a bank on another bank in which it has an account.

temporary insider—someone retained by a corporation for professional services on an as-needed basis, such as an attorney, accountant, or investment banker.

temporary perfection—perfection given for a limited period of time to creditors.

tenancy at sufferance—lease arrangement in which the tenant occupies the property at the discretion of the landlord.

tenancy at will—holding of land for an indefinite period that may be terminated at any time by the landlord or by the landlord and tenant acting together.

tenancy by entirety or tenancy by entireties—transfer of property to both husband and wife.

tenancy for years—tenancy for a fixed period of time, even though the time is less than a year.

tenancy in common—relationship that exists when two or more persons own undivided interests in property.

tenancy in partnership—ownership relationship that exists between partners under the Uniform Partnership Act.

tenant—one who holds or possesses real property by any kind of right or title; one who pays rent for the temporary use and occupation of another's real property under a lease.

tender—goods have arrived, are available for pickup, and buyer is notified.

term insurance—policy written for a specified number of years that terminates at the end of that period.

termination statement—document (record), which may be requested by a paid-up debtor, stating that a security interest is no longer claimed under the specified financing statement.

testamentary capacity—sufficient mental capacity to understand that a writing being executed is a will and what that entails.

testamentary intent—designed to take effect at death, as by disposing of property or appointing a personal representative.

testamentary trust—trust that becomes effective only when the settlor's will takes effect after death.

testate—condition of leaving a will upon death.

testate distribution—distribution of an estate in accordance with the will of the decedent.

testator, testatrix—man, woman who makes a will.

third-party beneficiary—third person whom the parties to a contract intend to benefit by the making of the contract and to confer upon such person the right to sue for breach of contract.

time draft—bill of exchange payable at a stated time after sight or at a definite time.

tippee—individual who receives information about a corporation from an insider or temporary insider.

tort—civil wrong that interferes with one's property or person.

Toxic Substances Control Act (TOSCA)—first federal law to control the manufacture, use, and disposal of toxic substances.

trade dress—product's total image including its overall packaging look.

trade libel—written defamation about a product or service.

trade name—name under which a business is carried on and, if fictitious, must be registered.

trade secret—any formula, device, or compilation of information that is used in one's business and is of such a nature that it provides an advantage over competitors who do not have the information.

trademark—mark that identifies a product.

transferee—buyer or vendee.

traveler's check—check that is payable on demand provided it is countersigned by the person whose specimen signature appears on the check.

treasury stock—corporate stock that the corporation has reacquired.

treble damages—three times the damages actually sustained.

trespass—an unauthorized action with respect to person or property.

trial de novo—a trial required to preserve the constitutional right to a jury trial by allowing an appeal to proceed as though there never had been any prior hearing or decision.

tripartite—three-part division (of government).

trust—transfer of property by one person to another with the understanding or declaration that such property be held for the benefit of another; the holding of property by the owner in trust for another, upon a declaration of trust, without a transfer to another person. (Parties—settlor, trustee, beneficiary)

trust agreement—instrument creating a trust; also called deed of trust.

trust corpus—fund or property that is transferred to the trustee or held by the settlor as the body or subject matter of the trust; also called *trust fund, trust estate,* and *trust res.*

trustee—party who has legal title to estate and manages it.

trustee in bankruptcy—impartial person elected to administer the debtor's estate.

trustor—donor or settlor who is the owner of property and creates a trust in the property.

tying—the anticompetitive practice of requiring buyers to purchase one product in order to get another.

U

ultra vires—act or contract that the corporation does not have authority to do or make.

unconscionable—unreasonable, not guided or restrained by conscience and often referring to a contract grossly unfair to one party because of the superior bargaining powers of the other party.

underwriter—insurer.

undisclosed principal—principal on whose behalf an agent acts without disclosing to the third person the fact of agency or the identity of the principal.

undue influence—influence that is asserted upon another person by one who dominates that person.

Uniform Probate Code (UPC)—uniform statute on wills and administration of estates.

Uniform Simultaneous Death Act—law providing that when survivorship

cannot be established, the property of each person shall be disposed of as though he or she had survived the other.

unilateral contract—contract under which only one party makes a promise.

unincorporated association—combination of two or more persons for the furtherance of a common nonprofit purpose.

universal agent—agent authorized by the principal to do all acts that can lawfully be delegated to a representative.

universal defenses—defenses that are regarded as so basic that the social interest in preserving them outweighs the social interest of giving negotiable instruments the freely transferable qualities of money; accordingly, such defenses are given universal effect and may be raised against all holders.

USA Patriot Act—federal law that, among other things, imposes reporting requirements on banks.

usage of trade—language and customs of an industry.

usury—lending money at an interest rate that is higher than the maximum rate allowed by law.

uttering—crime of issuing or delivering a forged instrument to another person.

V

valid—legal.

valid contract—agreement that is binding and enforceable.

value—consideration or antecedent debt or security given in exchange for the transfer of a negotiable instrument or creation of a security interest.

variance—permission of a landowner to use the land in a specified manner that is inconsistent with the zoning ordinance.

vicarious liability—imposing liability for the fault of another.

void agreement—agreement that cannot be enforced.

voidable contract—agreement that is otherwise binding and enforceable but may be rejected at the option of one of the parties as the result of specific circumstances.

voidable title—title of goods that carries with it the contingency of an underlying problem.

voir dire examination—the preliminary examination of a juror or a witness to ascertain fitness to act as such.

voluntary bankruptcy—proceeding in which the debtor files the petition for relief.

voting by proxy—authorizing someone else to vote the shares owned by the shareholder.

voting trust—transfer by two or more persons of their shares of stock of a corporation to a trustee who is to vote the shares and act for such shareholders.

W

waiver—release or relinquishment of a known right or objection.

warehouse—entity engaged in the business of storing the goods of others for compensation.

warehouse receipt—receipt issued by the warehouse for stored goods. Regulated by the UCC, which clothes the receipt with some degree of negotiability.

warrant—authorization via court order to search private property for tools or evidence of a crime.

warranty—promise either express or implied about the nature, quality, or performance of the goods.

warranty against encumbrances—warranty that there are no liens or other encumbrances to goods except those noted by seller.

warranty deed—deed by which the grantor conveys a specific estate or interest to the grantee and makes one or more of the covenants of title.

warranty of habitability—implied warranty that the leased property is fit for dwelling by tenants.

warranty of title—implied warranty that title to the goods is good and transfer is proper.

wasting assets corporation—corporation designed to exhaust or use up the assets of the corporation, such as by extracting oil, coal, iron, and other ores.

way of necessity—grantee's right to use land retained by the grantor for going to and from the conveyed land.

White-Collar Crime Penalty Enhancement Act of 2002—federal reforms passed as a result of the collapses of companies such as Enron; provides for longer sentences and higher fines for both executives and companies.

white-collar crimes—crimes that do not use nor threaten to use force or violence or do not cause injury to persons or property.

whole life insurance—ordinary life insurance providing lifetime insurance protection.

will—instrument executed with the formality required by law by which a person makes a disposition of his or her property to take effect upon death.

writ of certiorari—order by the U.S. Supreme Court granting a right of review by the court of a lower court decision.

wrongfully dishonored—error by a bank in refusing to pay a check.

Z

zoning—restrictions imposed by government on the use of designated land to ensure an orderly physical development of the regulated area.

case index

Opinion cases are in italic type for the case summary; cited cases are in roman type. Cases new to this edition are in red.